TENTH EDITION

AUDITING

A RISK-BASED APPROACH TO CONDUCTING A QUALITY AUDIT

KARLA M. JOHNSTONE ▪ **AUDREY A. GRAMLING** ▪ **LARRY E. RITTENBERG**

University of Wisconsin—Madison   *Colorado State University*   *University of Wisconsin—Madison*

CENGAGE
Learning·

Australia • Brazil • Mexico • Singapore • United Kingdom • United States

Auditing: A Risk-Based Approach to Conducting a Quality Audit, Tenth Edition
Karla M. Johnstone, Audrey A. Gramling, and Larry E. Rittenberg

Vice President, General Manager, Social Science & Qualitative Business: Erin Joyner

Product Director: Mike Schenk

Senior Product Manager: Sharon Oblinger

Senior Content Developer: Maggie Kubale

Product Assistant: Adele Scholtz

Brand Manager: Courtney Doyle Chambers

Marketing Coordinator: Eileen Corcoran

Art and Cover Direction, Production Management, and Composition: Lumina Datamatics, Inc.

Senior Content Developer: Sally Nieman

Senior Manufacturing Planner: Doug Wilke

Cover Image(s): © leungchopan/Shutterstock, © photo.ua/Shutterstock, © olavs/Shutterstock, © SeanPavonePhoto/Shutterstock

Intellectual Property:
  Analyst: Christina Ciaramella

For product information and technology assistance, contact us at
Cengage Learning Customer & Sales Support, 1-800-354-9706

For permission to use material from this text or product, submit all requests online at **www.cengage.com/permissions**
Further permissions questions can be emailed to **permissionrequest@cengage.com**

Unless otherwise noted, all items © Cengage Learning

Library of Congress Control Number: 2014955989

Student Edition ISBN: 978-1-305-08058-4

Student Edition with CD ISBN: 978-1-305-08057-7

Cengage Learning
20 Channel Center Street
Boston, MA 02210
USA

Cengage Learning is a leading provider of customized learning solutions with office locations around the globe, including Singapore, the United Kingdom, Australia, Mexico, Brazil, and Japan. Locate your local office at: **www.cengage.com/global**

Cengage Learning products are represented in Canada by Nelson Education, Ltd.

To learn more about Cengage Learning Solutions, visit **www.cengage.com**

Purchase any of our products at your local college store or at our preferred online store **www.cengagebrain.com**

Printed in the United States of America
Print Number: 01   Print Year: 2015

Dedication

We dedicate this book to our families who encourage and support us through many hours of development, to our students who inspire us to always improve, to our mentors who guide us, to our professional friends who continue to educate us, and to our colleagues who challenge us.

KARLA M. JOHNSTONE
AUDREY A. GRAMLING
LARRY E. RITTENBERG

BRIEF CONTENTS

CONTENTS

CHAPTER **2**

The Auditor's Responsibilities Regarding Fraud and Mechanisms to Address Fraud: Regulation and Corporate Governance   40

CHAPTER **5**

Professional Auditing Standards and the Audit Opinion Formulation Process   180

Professional Auditing Standards   182

CHAPTER **8**

Specialized Audit Tools: Sampling and Generalized Audit Software 340

CHAPTER **9**

Auditing the Revenue Cycle 390

CHAPTER 14

Activities Required in Completing a Quality Audit 662

CHAPTER **15**

Audit Reports on Financial Statements   720

Principles Underlying Audit Reporting   722

Standard Unqualified Audit Reports on Financial Statements   723

Unqualified Audit Reports with Explanatory Language   729

Qualified Reports, Adverse Reports, and Disclaimers   738

Comparisons of Modifications to the Standard Unqualified Audit Report   745

Audit Reports on Internal Control Over Financial Reporting   746

CHAPTER 16

Advanced Topics Concerning Complex Auditing Judgments   770

CHAPTER **17**

Other Services Provided by Audit Firms   826

Nonaudit Attestation Services Provided by Audit Firms   827

Reviews and Compilations   830

Reviews of Interim Financial Information for Audit Clients   837

Special Considerations for Reporting   839

Attestation on Agreed-Upon Procedures, Financial Forecasts and Projections, and Pro Forma Financial Information   847

PREFACE

The auditing environment continues to change in dramatic ways, and university graduates entering the profession must be prepared for a high standard of responsibility. Examples of recent and emerging changes include:

- The American Institute of Certified Public Accountants (AICPA) completed its project to clarify its auditing standards with the issuance of Statement on Auditing Standards No. 128, *Using the Work of Internal Auditors,* in 2014.
- The International Auditing and Assurance Standards Board (IAASB) completed its project to clarify its auditing standards and revised some of its clarity standards in 2013.
- The Public Company Accounting Oversight Board (PCAOB) has now issued eighteen Auditing Standards, with the adoption of Auditing Standard No. 18 – *Related Parties,* in 2014.
- The AICPA has a current project to clarify its attestation standards, with approval of the final standards expected in 2015. As part the attestation clarity project, the ASB will continue its general strategy of converging its standards with the standards of the IAASB.
- The AICPA's Professional Ethics Executive Committee (PEEC) adopted a revised *Code of Professional Conduct* in January 2014, with an effective date of December 15, 2014. Additionally, the *Code* includes two conceptual frameworks with a delayed effective date of December 15, 2015.
- The PCAOB and the IAASB are each considering substantial revisions to the content of the standard audit report.
- The Committee of Sponsoring Organizations (COSO) of the Treadway Commission issued an updated *Internal Control–Integrated Framework* in 2013.

The tenth edition of *Auditing: A Risk-Based Approach to Conducting a Quality Audit* represents the most up-to-date professional guidance available, and reflects the clarified auditing standards of the IAASB and the AICPA and the newest PCAOB standards. It discusses COSO's updated *Internal Control–Integrated Framework* and integrates discussions of fraud risk throughout the textbook. In short, the tenth edition helps students understand the full range of auditing issues in the evolving global environment.

Just as significantly, the tenth edition features updated end-of-chapter materials and associated online content with grading guidance that have been developed to help students prepare for exams and understand real-life auditing scenarios. This material is updated, streamlined, and user friendly, with each problem linked to a specific learning objective. In addition, students will gain valuable experience by using the professional ACL auditing software that is packaged with each new textbook. New end-of-chapter features include a *Fraud Focus: Contemporary and Historical Cases* section that highlights contemporary and historical fraud-related cases, a multi-chapter analytical procedures case problem whereby students will gain experience performing analytical procedures, and auditing standards application problems that provide students with practice at completing task-based simulations similar to what they will see on the CPA exam.

Revision Themes and Enhancements of the Tenth Edition

1. *Extended coverage of analytical procedures.* The textbook now contains updated and extended coverage of planning, substantive, and review-related analytical procedures. Updated *Chapter 6* and *Chapter 7* contain discussion of analytical procedures, processes, and best practices, and an end-of-chapter case in the pharmaceutical industry (*Chapters 9, 11,* and *13*) is now included, with online excel files containing underlying data.

2. *Online student materials.* Select end-of-chapter materials now contain online student-led problems that enable student interaction and self-grading. This feature will enable integration with a "flipped classroom" approach to instruction and learning.

3. *Student Access to CPA Exam Questions.* With the purchase of this textbook, students receive exclusive access to Roger's CPA Review (rogerCPAreview.com). Roger's CPA review questions are also available in the Instructor's Resource Center, as well as assignable content in CengageNOW.

4. *Auditing Standards Application Problems.* The textbook contains a *Standards Appendix*, and new end-of-chapter homework problems requiring students to review and apply the material in the *Standards Appendix*. These problems provide students with practice at completing task-based simulations similar to what they will see on the CPA exam; they are highlighted with an identifying icon.

5. *Emerging Issues.* A new feature, *Emerging Issues*, is included throughout most chapters and contains up-to-date discussion of contemporary issues to keep students and instructors focused on new trends.

6. *Enhanced Focus on Fraud.* A new feature, *Focus on Fraud*, is included throughout most chapters to highlight fraud-related implications for the audit. End-of-chapter materials include a "Fraud Focus: Contemporary and Historical Cases" section that highlights contemporary and historical fraud-related cases

7. *Audit Practice Case.* New online content that features very extensive audit working papers and data analysis task requirements is included in the online materials for the textbook. Look for this case at the textbook web site, where the case is located. See "Brony's Bikes."

8. *Improved Test Bank.* Tagging for all questions in the Test Bank has been updated to include: Learning Objective, AICPA, Level of Difficulty, accreditation body tagging, and Bloom's Taxonomy.

9. *Two PowerPoint slide decks for each chapter.* Each chapter now contains a detailed PowerPoint slide deck for instructor use, and a less detailed PowerPoint slide deck for student use. This feature will enable integration with a "flipped classroom" approach to instruction and learning.

Hallmark Pedagogical Features

Continued emphasis on professional skepticism. This emphasis provides students with the tools to learn how to apply the concept of professional skepticism. This edition contains an introduction to this topic in *Chapter 1* as well as in end-of-chapter materials throughout the text, which are highlighted with an identifying icon. This emphasis helps students see the practical application of this concept.

Continued emphasis on professional judgment. In addition to the focus on professional judgment in this textbook, numerous exercises emphasize this key auditing skill, including analyses of Ford's and Toyota's SEC filings and proxy statements. Further, the end-of-chapter materials help ensure that students understand the link between mandatory financial reporting and auditing, risk assessment, transaction cycles, and analytical procedures.

Professional Judgment in Context feature. Each chapter opens with a real-life example from practice that illustrates the judgments involved in auditing. The examples tie to the learning objectives in the chapter and address important topics such as fraud, regulation, audit quality, auditing standards, and professional skepticism. The following provides an example of this feature that is included in *Chapter 5*.

PROFESSIONAL JUDGMENT IN CONTEXT

The Importance of Adhering to Professional Auditing Standards as Illustrated in the Audits Performed by Sherb & Co. LLP

Auditors who adhere to the professional auditing standards are viewed as conducting a quality audit. A lack of adherence to the professional auditing standards heightens the risk that the auditor will provide an unqualified audit opinion on financial statements that are materially misstated. This lesson is highlighted in audits provided by Sherb & Co. LLP. In November 2013, the Securities and Exchange Commission (SEC) announced sanctions against the New York-based audit firm, its founder, two other partners, and an audit manager for their roles in the failed audits of three China-based companies publicly traded in the United States. One of the companies they audited—China Sky One Medical, Inc.—has since been charged by the SEC with financial fraud.

An SEC investigation found that Sherb & Co. LLP, and its auditors, falsely represented in audit reports that they had conducted their audits in accordance with U.S. auditing standards. However, Sherb failed to properly plan and execute audits; failed to obtain sufficient audit evidence on sales, revenue, and bank balances; and ignored factors suggesting the presence of fraud. Further, the auditors failed to exercise professional skepticism and due care. They also failed to maintain complete documentation of their audit work.

To settle the SEC's charges, the firm and the four auditors agreed to be barred from practicing as accountants for any publicly traded company regulated by the SEC. The firm also agreed to pay a $75,000 penalty.

The co-director of the SEC's Division of Enforcement indicated that the firm and its auditors failed to live up to their professional obligations in multiple audits during a five-year period.

As you read through this chapter, consider the following questions:

- What is the role of auditing standards and their underlying principles in promoting a quality audit? (LO 1, 2)
- How does the fundamental concept of professional skepticism relate to audit quality? (LO 2)
- What audit evidence is necessary for opining on a client's financial statements? (LO 6)
- How does audit documentation provide evidence related to audit quality? (LO 7)
- What audit activities are conducted during the audit opinion formulation process to provide reasonable assurance about a client's financial statements? (LO 8, 9, 10, 11, 12)
- How does professional judgment and ethical decision making contribute to audit quality? (LO 13)

For further details on this case, see Securities and Exchange Commission Accounting and Auditing Enforcement Release No. 3512 (November 2013).

Professional decision-making and ethical decision-making frameworks. Decision-making frameworks, complete with a chapter-opening *Professional Judgment in Context* feature, require students to think about real-life professional and ethical decisions associated with that chapter. End-of-chapter materials continue the use of these professional and ethical decision-making frameworks to help students address contemporary issues. These problems are marked with identifying icons.

Continued emphasis on the audit opinion formulation process to help organize study. A chapter-opening *Audit Opinion Formulation Process* figure helps students identify the major phases in the audit process and see how those steps within that process relate to specific chapters.

This textbook describes how auditors go through a structured judgment process to issue an audit opinion. This process is referred to as the *Audit Opinion Formulation Process*, and it serves as the foundation for this textbook. The process consists of five phases. Phase I concerns client acceptance and continuance. Once a client is accepted (or the audit firm decides to continue to provide services to a client), the auditor needs to perform risk assessment procedures to thoroughly understand the client's business (or update prior knowledge in the case of a continuing client), its industry, its competition, and its management and governance processes (including internal controls) to determine the likelihood that financial accounts might be materially misstated (Phase II). In some audits, the auditor also obtains evidence about internal control operating effectiveness through testing those controls (Phase III). Much of what most people think of as auditing, the obtaining of substantive evidence about accounts, disclosures, and assertions occurs in Phase IV. The information gathered in Phases I through III greatly influences the amount of testing to be performed in Phase IV. Finally, in Phase V, the auditor completes the audit and makes a decision about what type of audit report to issue.

Also fundamental to students' understanding is the framework's inclusion of the auditing profession, fraud, regulation, corporate governance, and audit quality. Further fundamentals highlighted in the *Audit Opinion Formulation Process* include discussion of professional liability and the need for quality audit judgments and ethical decisions, as depicted below.

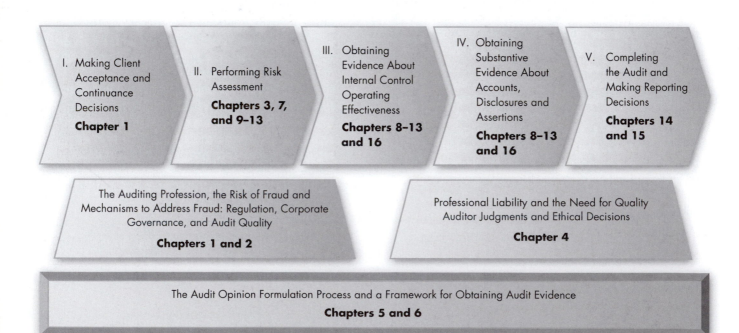

Auditing in Practice features, *Focus on Fraud* features, *Emerging Issues* features, and chapter exhibits. Chapters contain multiple *Auditing in Practice* features, *Focus on Fraud* features, *Emerging Issues* features, and exhibits that highlight important, relevant, and practical examples and information related to chapter topics. Selected end-of-chapter materials require students to review these features and exhibits to answer related questions. Below is an example of an *Auditing in Practice* feature from *Chapter 1*.

Why Is Owning Stock in an Audit Client Unacceptable?

AUDITING IN PRACTICE

In 2005, Susan Birkert was an audit senior working for KPMG on the audit engagement of Comtech Corporation. One of Susan's friends asked her whether she thought that Comtech stock was a good investment. She responded that, indeed, it was a good investment. At that point, her friend asked if she would like him to purchase Comtech stock on her behalf. She agreed and gave her friend $5,000 to make the purchase under his name rather than hers. She did so because she was aware that owning stock in one's audit client is not allowed because of independence concerns. If auditors own stock in their audit clients, they are not independent of their clients because they are part owners. Therefore, rather than acting in an unbiased manner during the conduct of the audit, they might make judgments that favor the client company rather than

external users of the financial statements. Even if the auditor does not actually behave in a biased manner and is independent in fact, external users may *perceive* an independence conflict—the auditor would not be independent in appearance.

Susan continued working on the Comtech engagement well into 2006, and she lied when she responded to KPMG's yearly written requirements to comply with the firm's independence policies. Prompted by an anonymous tip later in 2006, KPMG launched an internal investigation into the matter and terminated her employment. The PCAOB barred her from serving as an external auditor for a period of at least one year.

For further details on this case, see PCAOB Release No. 105-2007-003.

Following is an example of an *Emerging Issues* feature from *Chapter 6*.

PCAOB Considers Change in Auditing Standard for Auditing Estimates

EMERGING ISSUE

In response to issues identified during the inspection of accounting firms, comments received from members of the PCAOB Standing Advisory Group (SAG), and the Financial Accounting Standards Board's (FASB) proposed accounting standard on financial instruments, the PCAOB staff began drafting a proposal for a standard on auditing

accounting estimates, including fair value measurements and related disclosures. The Board anticipates proposing a standard for public comment during 2014. Timing of standard-setting projects is subject to change. Be sure to check the PCAOB web site for updates on this emerging issue.

Following is an example of a *Focus on Fraud* feature from *Chapter 9*.

Channel Stuffing at ArthroCare—The Importance of Professional Skepticism

Auditors need to be professionally skeptical and make judgments on whether and when sales should be recognized as revenue. The ArthroCare case highlights the material misstatements that can occur if a client chooses to improperly record revenue and the auditor fails to detect the misstatement.

ArthroCare is a manufacturer of medical devices, based in Austin, Texas, whose shares are traded on NASDAQ. From 2006 through the first quarter of 2008, two company sales executives, John Raffle and David Applegate, were alleged to have engaged in a channel stuffing scheme that improperly inflated company revenue and earnings. Specifically, the two salesmen shipped certain products to distributors even though the distributors often did not need them or have the ability to pay for them. Chief executive officer (CEO) Michael Baker and chief financial officer (CFO) Michael Gluk were also implicated in the scheme. As a result, for 2006,

2007, and the first quarter of 2008, revenues were overstated by, respectively, 7.9%, 14.1%, and 17.4%, totaling almost $72.3 million. For the same period, net income was overstated by 14.5% in 2006, 8,694% for 2007, and 315% for the first quarter of 2008, totaling about $53.7 million. The company eventually restated its financial statements.

In 2014, former executives John Raffle and David Applegate pled guilty to conspiracy to commit securities and wire fraud. ArthroCare agreed to pay a $30 million fine to resolve the investigation.

The charges against Baker and Gluk were maintained. In 2013, they were charged with leading a $400 million scheme to defraud investors and a trial date was set for 2014.

For further information on the progression of this case, refer to ArthroCare Corp. Securities Litigation, case number 1:08-cv-00574 in the U.S. District Court for the Western District of Texas.

Real-life corporate disclosures to provide practical applications. The Ford and Toyota end-of-chapter case uses the actual SEC filings and proxy materials from Ford Motor Company and Toyota Motor Corporation. These exercises use real-life corporate disclosures to help students extract the practical applications from the chapter concepts. Starting in *Chapter 2*, the authors introduce the case and discuss how they have conducted this case in their own classes. Using this case enables students to see the practical application of theoretical concepts using companies that are familiar, are high profile (in the news), and vary in terms of their financial condition and U.S. versus international domicile.

Practice-oriented audit case. On the CengageNOW web site, you will find a tool that will help your students engage in a practice-oriented audit case. Brony's Bikes is an auditing case that is as close to the "real world" as students can get until they enter the profession. This case encompasses a complete auditing scenario spanning from Performing Risk Assessment (Phase II of the Audit Opinion Formulation Process) to making reporting decisions (Phase V of the Audit Opinion Formulation Process). The case includes 13 modules that address specific activities included in the Audit Opinion Formulation Process. The authors have structured these 13 modules so that each can be undertaken independently of the other modules. For example, Module I, *Assessment of Inherent Risk*, takes the students through the audit planning process based on AU-C 200 *Overall Objectives of the Independent Auditor and the Conduct of an Audit in Accordance With Generally Accepted Auditing Standards*, AU-C 300 *Planning an Audit*, and AU 315-C *Understanding the Entity and Its Environment and Assessing the Risks* *of Material Misstatement.* Module I can be assigned on a stand-alone basis or along with any or all of the other modules at the instructor's discretion.

Students gain experience with auditing documentation including many working papers. Analytical procedures are performed in Excel worksheets requiring conclusions and recommendations. Each module includes authoritative references from the AICPA's Clarified AU Sections (AU-C). This combination of practice vis-à-vis auditing standards can be of significant benefit to students in preparing for the AUD Section of the CPA exam. CengageNOW is an online teaching and learning resource that gives you more control in less time and delivers better outcomes—NOW!

CengageNOW features:

- End-of-chapter homework from the textbook written by the authors
- Interactive eBook
- Personalized Study Plan
- Course Management Tools, including an online gradebook

With its engaging learning and assessment tools, CengageNOW supports the entire student workflow, from motivation to mastery. For instructors, CengageNOW provides control and customization with the opportunity to tailor the learning experience to improve outcomes.

CengageNOW also includes all of the Brony's Bikes modules, the requirements, the draft working papers and online assessments to assure that student have mastered the case objectives. The instructor may choose to assign any or all of the modules to the students with solutions to be prepared in physical documents for submission to the instructor. The assessment process is significantly streamlined within CengageNOW. Once the students have completed a module they simply go to the CengageNOW textbook site and answer the module questions. CengageNOW does all the evaluation work for the instructor and reports each student's level of mastery of the module.

ACL generalized audit software with updated cases. Version 9 of the ACL Desktop Education Edition, the most popular generalized audit software, comes with each new copy of this textbook. The tenth edition integrates ACL software into end-of-chapter materials. An *ACL Appendix* and tutorial is located at the end of the text. The *ACL Appendix* contains an overview of the basic functions of ACL followed by a brief, illustrated tutorial to help students learn how to use the basic features of Version 9 of the ACL Desktop Education Edition.

ACL cases include the following:

1. *Pell Grants*, a fraud investigation case related to this student grant program. (*Chapter 6*)
2. *Husky Accounts Receivable*, which includes exercises in which students identify unpaid invoices and sales made over credit limits, perform cut-off analyses, conduct aging analyses, and identify procedures to be performed based upon their results. (*Chapter 9*)
3. *FloorMart Sales and Inventory*, which requires students to identify store locations in which data appear to indicate potential inaccuracies, and to identify procedures to gather additional evidence. (*Chapter 9*)
4. *Husky Inventory*, which includes exercises in which students identify potentially obsolete inventory, calculate inventory turnover, consider possible write-downs, and prepare a report based on their results. (*Chapter 11*)
5. *Benford's Law Case*, a fraud case dealing with employee expense reimbursements and the application of Benford's Law of numbers. (*Chapter 16*)

Organization of the Tenth Edition

The tenth edition is organized as follows:

Chapter 1 and *Chapter 2*: **Auditing: Integral to the Economy; The Auditor's Responsibilities Regarding Fraud and Mechanisms to Address Fraud: Regulation and Corporate Governance**. These chapters provide the foundation for students to understand the economic context in which external auditing exists. *Chapter 1* defines the objective of external auditing and describes its role in meeting society's demands for reliable financial and internal control information. *Chapter 1* identifies parties involved in preparing and auditing financial statements, lists the types of audit service providers, identifies organizations that affect the external auditing profession, defines audit quality and introduces the Financial Reporting Council's *Audit Quality Framework*, and identifies professional requirements that help to achieve high quality and minimize auditor exposure to lawsuits. *Chapter 1* also describes the process by which audit firms make client acceptance and continuance decisions. *Chapter 2* defines the types of fraud and the fraud triangle, describes examples of recent financial reporting frauds, explains the findings of the third COSO report on fraud, discusses users' expectations of auditors' fraud-related responsibilities, explains how the requirements of the Sarbanes-Oxley Act of 2002 reflect frauds perpetrated in the late 1990s and early 2000s, and defines corporate governance and identifies parties involved in corporate governance.

Chapter 3: **Internal Control over Financial Reporting: Responsibilities of Management and External Auditors**. *Chapter 3* articulates the importance of internal control over financial reporting, defines management's responsibility related to internal control, defines internal control as presented in COSO's updated *Internal Control–Integrated Framework*, identifies and describes the components and principles of internal control as presented in that framework, identifies management's responsibilities related to documenting internal control over financial reporting, and describes management's responsibility to evaluate and report on internal controls. *Chapter 3* explains how to distinguish between material weaknesses, significant deficiencies, and control deficiencies in internal control over financial reporting.

Chapter 4. **Professional Liability, Auditor Judgment Frameworks, and Professional Responsibilities**. *Chapter 4* discusses the liability environment in which auditors operate and explores the effects of lawsuits on audit firms; lists laws from which auditor liability is derived; and describes possible causes of action, remedies or sanctions, and auditor defenses under both common and statutory law. *Chapter 4* also articulates frameworks for making quality professional and ethical decisions and illustrates how to apply these frameworks in selected audit settings. Finally, *Chapter 4* describes and applies the IESBA's *Code of Ethics* and the AICPA's *Code of Professional Conduct*.

Chapter 5. **Professional Auditing Standards and the Audit Opinion Formulation Process**. *Chapter 5* identifies and compares the various auditing standards, discusses the foundational principles underlying the auditing standards, lists the phases and related activities in the audit opinion formulation process, explains the concept of accounting cycles, describes the assertions that are inherent to financial statements, defines audit evidence and the purpose and types of audit procedures used to obtain audit evidence, and discusses the importance of audit documentation.

Chapter 6. **A Framework for Audit Evidence**. *Chapter 6* discusses the importance of the evidence concepts of sufficiency and appropriateness, identifies factors affecting the sufficiency and appropriateness of audit evidence, illustrates professional judgments about the type and timing of audit procedures, discusses the use and application of substantive analytical procedures, identifies issues relating to audit evidence needed for accounts involving management estimates, and discusses issues involving specialists and related-party transactions. *Chapter 6* also describes the characteristics of quality audit documentation and explains the nature, design, and purposes of audit programs.

Chapter 7. **Planning the Audit: Identifying and Responding to the Risks of Material Misstatement.** *Chapter 7* defines the concept of *material misstatement* and discusses the importance of materiality judgments in the audit context. *Chapter 7* also identifies the risks of material misstatement and describes how they relate to audit risk and detection risk. *Chapter 7* illustrates the use of planning analytical procedures and brainstorming to identify areas of heightened risk of material misstatement, along with describing how auditors respond to assessed risks of material misstatement.

Chapter 8. **Specialized Audit Tools: Sampling and Generalized Audit Software.** *Chapter 8* conveys the terminology and approaches recommended in the AICPA's 2012 sampling guidance. *Chapter 8* describes how auditors use sampling and generalized audit software, explains the objectives of sampling for testing controls and account balances, compares and contrasts nonstatistical and statistical sampling, describes attribute sampling, describes the sampling process used to gather evidence about misstatements in account balances and assertions, describes monetary unit sampling, and explains how to use generalized audit software to automate the audit process.

Chapters 9–13. **Performing Audits Using the Transaction Cycle Approach:** *Chapter 9* – **Auditing the Revenue Cycle;** *Chapter 10* – **Auditing Cash and Marketable Securities;** *Chapter 11* – **Auditing Inventory, Goods and Services, and Accounts Payable: The Acquisition and Payment Cycle;** *Chapter 12* – **Auditing Long-Lived Assets: Acquisition, Use, Impairment, and Disposal;** and *Chapter 13* – **Auditing Debt Obligations and Stockholders' Equity Transactions.** These five chapters focus on the application of concepts developed earlier for assessing risk, identifying and testing controls designed to address those risks, and using substantive approaches to testing account balances. Each chapter contains topic-relevant discussion of identifying significant accounts, disclosures, and relevant assertions; identifying and assessing inherent risks, fraud risks, and control risks; using planning analytical procedures to identify possible material misstatement; determining appropriate responses to identified risks of material misstatement; determining appropriate tests of controls and considering results of tests of controls; and determining and applying sufficient appropriate substantive audit procedures.

Chapters 14–15. **Activities Required in Completing a Quality Audit** *and* **Audit Reports on Financial Statements.** *Chapter 14* discusses numerous tasks that are conducted as part of completing the audit. These include reviewing activities relating to detected misstatements, loss contingencies, accounting estimates, disclosure adequacy, noncompliance with laws or regulations, going-concern considerations, review analytical procedures, management representations, subsequent events, omitted audit procedures, and engagement quality review; and audit committee and management communications. Once these activities are completed, the auditor makes a reporting decision, which is described in *Chapter 15*. This chapter identifies the principles underlying audit reporting on financial statements, describes the information that is included in a standard unqualified audit report, and describes financial statements requiring the following report modifications: unqualified audit report with explanatory language, qualified report, adverse report, and a disclaimer of opinion. *Chapter 15* also describes the information that is included in a standard unqualified audit report on internal control over financial reporting and identifies the appropriate audit report modifications for situations requiring other than an unqualified report on internal control over financial reporting. *Chapter 15* also contains discussion of the PCAOB and IAASB proposals regarding revisions to the content of the standard audit report.

Chapter 16. **Advanced Topics Concerning Complex Auditing Judgments**. *Chapter 16* discusses the nature and types of complex judgments that permeate audit engagements and identifies complex audit judgments based on a review of a company's financial statements. *Chapter 16* describes a process for assessing whether misstatements are material. It also describes audit considerations for long-term liabilities involving subjectivity, merger and acquisition activities, and assessing management's fair value estimates and related impairment judgments. The Chapter also describes audit considerations for financial instruments, and understanding and evaluating the client's internal audit function.

Chapter 17. **Other Services Provided by Audit Firms**. *Chapter 17* describes other services provided by audit firms. This chapter explains review and compilation engagements, procedures and reporting requirements for providing assurance on interim financial information, special considerations for unique financial statement audit situations, and attestation engagements. An important component of this chapter is a discussion of the proposed changes to the AICPA's *Statements on Standards for Accounting and Review Services* (SSARSs) and its *Attestation Standards*. *Chapter 17* also discusses forensic accounting and distinguishes between forensic accounting and auditing. Finally, *Chapter 17* describes sustainability reporting and articulates the auditor's role in providing assurance on management sustainability reports.

Supplements

CengageBrain: Instructors and students can find most of the textbook's support materials online at CengageBrain (www.cengagebrain.com), including the solutions manual, PowerPoint slides, ACL data spreadsheet files, and other resources.

Solutions Manual: The Solutions Manual contains the solutions to all end-of-chapter assignments. It is available on the instructor's page at www.cengagebrain.com.

PowerPoint Slides: Instructors can bring their lectures to life with engaging PowerPoint slides that are interesting, visually stimulating, and paced for student comprehension. These slides are ideal as lecture tools and provide a clear guide for student study and note-taking. PowerPoint slides are downloadable by chapter on the instructor's page at www.cengagebrain.com. Each chapter contains both an instructor version of the slides as well as a condensed version intended for student use as they prepare for class.

Test Bank: Cengage Learning Testing Powered by Cognero is a flexible, online system that allows you to:

- author, edit, and manage test bank content from multiple Cengage Learning solutions,
- create multiple test versions in an instant,
- deliver tests from your LMS, your classroom, or wherever you want. The Test Bank is also available in Microsoft Word.

ACL Desktop Education Edition, Version 9: Each new copy of the tenth edition comes with ACL's Desktop Education Edition, Version 9, at no additional cost. ACL is the most popular professional audit analytics software used in public accounting today. The software enhances the analysis of cases that are couched in significant account balances, such as inventory and accounts receivable.

Analytical Procedures: A Case in the Context of the Pharmaceutical Industry (*Chapters 9, 11,* and *13*): The case contains online excel files that students download and analyze. The case enables students to practice developing and conducting planning and substantive analytical procedures. The case was developed using the published financial statements of three prominent companies in this industry, with adaptations to make the case suitable for classroom use. Students will access an Excel file on the text's web site at www.cengagebrain.com. The Excel file contains financial data and information from footnote disclosures.

Ford and Toyota Case Solution: To ensure that users have access to the most recent version of the Ford and Toyota case solutions as of the most recent fiscal year end, the authors will post an updated solution to all Ford and Toyota cases to the instructor's page at www.cengagebrain.com. This updated solution will appear on the instructor's page of the textbook's web site approximately two months after the SEC filings become available.

Example Syllabi: The authors' syllabi for this edition of the textbook are available at the instructor's page at www.cengagebrain.com. These may be helpful to instructors as they consider alternative ways to use the textbook and alternative presentation formats for the syllabi. Instructors should feel free to update these to individual uses.

Acknowledgments

We are grateful to members of the staff at Cengage Learning for their help in developing the tenth edition: Sharon Oblinger, senior product manager; Maggie Kubale, senior content developer; Adam Goetz, associate content developer; Kristen Hurd, senior brand manager; Joseph Malcolm, content project manager; and Charisse Darin, marketing manager.

We appreciate Lawrence Chui (University of St. Thomas) for his work on the end of chapter material and Joe Kastantin (University of Wisconsin–LaCrosse) for his further development of the Brony's Bicycle case and for converting end of chapter problems for CNOW.

The following instructors have provided invaluable feedback to the publisher and the authors, and we wish to thank them for their insights:

George R. Aldhizer, III, Wake Forest University
Erick O. Bell, University of San Francisco
Katherine Boswell, University of Louisiana at Monroe
Barry Bryan, Southern Methodist University
Susan R. Cockrell, Austin Peay State University
Eric Condie, University of Wisconsin–Madison
Frank Daroca, Loyola Marymount University
Roger S. Debreceny, University of Hawai'i at Manoa
Sean Dennis, University of Wisconsin–Madison
Todd DeZoort, The University of Alabama
Magdy Farag, California State Polytechnic University, Pomona Bill
Fowler, Abilene Christian University
Marvin Gordon, Northwestern University
Carl W. Hollingsworth, Clemson University
Mary Jepperson, College of Saint Benedict/Saint John's University
Mary Lewis Haley, Cumberland University
Steve Kachelmeier, University of Texas at Austin
Joe Kastantin, University of Wisconsin–LaCrosse
Ralph D. Licastro, The Pennsylvania State University
Jason MacGregor, Baylor University
Brian W. Mayhew, University of Wisconsin
Paul H. Mihalek, Central Connecticut State University
Michael J. Miller, Sullivan University
Andreas Nicolaou, Bowling Green State University

D. Robert Okopny, Eastern Michigan University
Denise M. Patterson, California State University, Fresno
Marshall K. Pitman, University of Texas at San Antonio
Lydia Radnik, University of North Texas
Michael A. Ridenour Jr., Pennsylvania State University–Fayette
Cindy Seipel, New Mexico State University
Amy Sexton, Morehead State University
Mike Shapeero, Bloomsburg University of Pennsylvania
Joel M. Strong, St. Cloud State University
Judy A. Thomas, Columbia College of Missouri
Jerry L. Turner, Texas Christian University
Michael Ulinski, Pace University
Kelly Ann Ulto, Fordham University
Donna L. Whitten, Purdue University North Central
Jeffrey Wong, University of Nevada, Reno
Laura M. Zellers, Wichita State University

We are very grateful to ACL Services, Ltd., for permission to distribute its software and tutorials and for permission to reprint related images.

Karla M. Johnstone
Audrey A. Gramling
Larry E. Rittenberg

ABOUT THE AUTHORS

KARLA M. JOHNSTONE

Karla M. Johnstone, PhD, CPA, is the Ernst & Young (EY) Professor of Accounting and Information Systems at the University of Wisconsin–Madison, School of Business. She teaches auditing, and her research investigates auditor decision making, including auditors' client acceptance and continuance decisions, how fraud risk and fraud brainstorming affect audit planning and audit fees, client–auditor negotiation, and audit budget-setting processes. She has also published various articles on accounting curriculum effectiveness. Professor Johnstone serves on the editorial boards of several academic journals and is active in the Auditing Section of the American Accounting Association (AAA), currently serving as an Editor at *Auditing: A Journal of Practice & Theory*. She has worked as a corporate accountant and as a staff auditor, and she was a doctoral fellow in residence at Coopers & Lybrand.

AUDREY A. GRAMLING

Audrey A. Gramling, PhD, CPA, CIA is the Accounting Department Chair and Professor at Colorado State University. Previously, she held the Treece Endowed Chair and was Accounting Department Professor and Chair at Bellarmine University. She has been on the accounting faculty at Kennesaw State University, Georgia State University, Wake Forest University, and University of Illinois at Urbana-Champaign. Professor Gramling's research investigates both internal and external auditing issues, with a focus on decision behavior of auditors, external auditor independence, internal control reporting, and other factors affecting the market for audit and assurance services. Prior to earning her Ph.D. at the University of Arizona, Professor Gramling worked as an external auditor at a predecessor firm of Deloitte and as an internal auditor at Georgia Institute of Technology. She has also served a one-year appointment as an Academic Accounting Fellow in the Office of the Chief Accountant at the U.S. Securities and Exchange Commission. She is the past-President of the Auditing Section of the American Accounting Association and has served in an advisory role to the Committee of Sponsoring Organizations (COSO).

LARRY E. RITTENBERG

Larry E. Rittenberg, PhD, CPA, CIA, is Professor Emeritus, Department of Accounting and Information Systems, at the University of Wisconsin–Madison, where he taught courses in auditing, risk management, and corporate governance. He is also Chair Emeritus of the COSO of the Treadway Commission, where he has provided oversight of the development of the COSO Enterprise Risk Management Framework as well as the COSO Guidance for Smaller Businesses. He has served as Vice-Chair of Professional Practices for the Institute of Internal Auditors (IIA) and President of the IIA Research Foundation; and has been a member of the Auditing Standards Committee of the AAA Auditing Section, the AICPA's Computer Audit Subcommittee, the Information Technology Committee, and the NACD Blue Ribbon Commission on Audit Committees; and Vice-President and Treasurer of the AAA. He is a member of an audit committee, the board, and the governance committee of Woodward Governor, a publicly traded company, and has consulted on audit committee, risk, and control issues with the largest public company in China. More recently, he has been named as one of the seven members of the International Oversight Council for Professional Practice of the IIA. Professor Rittenberg served as Staff Auditor for Ernst & Young and has coauthored five books and monographs and numerous articles.

Recommendations from Instructors
Who Have Used Our Textbook Previously

"I selected this textbook because I believe that it presents a realistic approach to the integrated audit. Having worked with several of the Global Seven firms, it is evident to me that the authors have been diligent in writing a book that mirrors the risk-based approach to the audit. In addition, my students have enjoyed outstanding success on the AUD Exam having used this text as their primary study resource."

Professor Barry J. Bryan
Southern Methodist University

"I have used [this] text for five years now and it has been an outstanding resource for teaching my students the fundamentals of contemporary auditing. Text discussions and end-of-chapter applications help me to develop students' critical analysis and judgment skills, sensitivity and responses to ethical dilemmas, and understanding and appreciation of the essential role of professional skepticism in auditing…. My impression based on use of successive editions of the text is that the authors have worked very hard to ensure it is up-to-date as auditing standards and related guidance evolve and audit-relevant events occur in the rapidly-changing business environment. Without reservation, I highly recommend this text."

Professor Tim Bell
University of North Florida

"As a former auditor and current audit professor, I find the book very easy to follow and well written. The content is organized in a similar fashion to the audit process itself, which I think is essential for students' understanding. The authors also include topics that I have not found in any other auditing textbook (e.g., an entire chapter on corporate governance, sections on upcoming changes or changes soon to be integrated into the profession). This textbook simply *feels* more up to date about current events in auditing."

Professor Kim Westermann
Florida International University

"This textbook hits the sweet spot of the bat! As far as I am concerned it hits a home run! Not too complex yet not too simple, the right amount of standards presentation/explanation then a great example to illustrate the standard in the real world. This textbook is well organized and presents the materials and issues as an auditor would confront them in an actual audit. I like the inclusion of ACL on the disc that accompanies the book. The ACL materials are presented in such a manner that tech savvy students can do the assignments with a minimum of instruction."

Professor Douglas E. Ziegenfuss
Old Dominion University

AUDITING

A RISK-BASED APPROACH TO CONDUCTING A QUALITY AUDIT

1 Auditing: Integral to the Economy

CHAPTER OVERVIEW AND LEARNING OBJECTIVES

Capital markets depend on reliable information about organizations. This information provides a basis for making many types of decisions, including investing and lending decisions. If the capital markets do not receive reliable information, investors and others lose confidence in the system, make poor decisions, and may lose a great deal of money. The external auditing profession helps enhance the reliability of information used throughout the capital markets. Individual external auditors make professional and ethical judgments about the information provided by organizations. Professional judgment and the processes used to make such judgments are critical to the usefulness of the external auditing profession and to individual auditors as they conduct quality audits.

Through studying this chapter, you will be able to achieve these learning objectives:

1. Define the objective of external auditing and describe its role in meeting society's demands for reliable financial and internal control information.

2. Identify parties involved in preparing and auditing financial statements and briefly describe their roles.

3. List the types of audit service providers and the skills and knowledge needed by professionals entering the external auditing profession.

4. Identify organizations that affect the external auditing profession and the nature of their effects.

5. Define audit quality and identify drivers of audit quality as specified by the Financial Reporting Council's *Audit Quality Framework*.

6. Identify professional requirements that help to achieve audit quality and minimize auditor exposure to lawsuits.

7. Describe the process by which audit firms make client acceptance and continuance decisions.

On December 20, 2011, the Public Company Accounting Oversight Board (PCAOB) revoked the ability of Bentleys Brisbane Partnership (an external audit firm) to perform public company audits, and the Board imposed a monetary penalty of $10,000 on Robert Forbes, the audit partner in charge of the audit of Alloy Steel International. These penalties were imposed because the PCAOB concluded that Bentleys and Forbes failed to exercise **due professional care** (a standard of care expected to be demonstrated by a competent auditing professional), failed to exercise **professional skepticism** (an attitude that includes a questioning mind and critical assessment of audit evidence), and failed to obtain sufficient evidence necessary to issue an audit opinion on the financial statements of Alloy Steel's 2006 fiscal year-end financial statements. The PCAOB also concluded that Bentleys violated PCAOB quality-control standards because the firm did not develop policies to ensure that the work performed by its personnel met PCAOB auditing standards, and the Board said that the firm did not undertake audits that the firm could reasonably expect to be completed with professional competence.

Alloy Steel International is an American company headquartered in Malaga, Australia. Alloy's stock was traded on the Over-the-Counter Bulletin Board, and as such was subject to the Securities and Exchange Commission's (SEC) rules and requirements. Its auditors were subject to the PCAOB's rules and requirements. On the audit of Alloy, Bentleys and Forbes made a number of critical mistakes. Bentleys and Forbes used an unregistered audit firm in Australia to actually perform the audit work, rather than performing the audit work themselves. Bentleys' and Forbes' involvement on the engagement was limited to reviewing the unregistered audit firm's workpapers. The unregistered audit firm's personnel had no training or experience in conducting audits that complied with PCAOB standards. Despite these factors, Bentleys and Forbes issued and signed an unqualified audit report on Alloy's 2006 financial statements.

For further details on this case, see PCAOB disciplinary proceedings in Release No. 105-2011-007.

As you read through this chapter, consider the following questions:

- What is the objective of auditing, and what process should auditors follow to accomplish this objective? (LO 1)
- Why do companies obtain audited financial statements? (LO 1)
- Who are the users of audited financial statements? (LO 1)
- What skills and knowledge are needed to be a competent audit professional? (LO 3)
- Why is it vital to perform an audit in a quality manner? (LO 5)
- Why are low-quality audits, like those performed in this case, harmful? (LO 5)
- Should Bentleys and Forbes have agreed to conduct this audit in the first place? (LO 6, 7)

Overview of the External Auditing Profession

 LO 1 Define the objective of external auditing and describe its role in meeting society's demands for reliable financial and internal control information.

Introduction to the External Auditing Profession

A **financial statement audit** is a:

> systematic process of objectively obtaining and evaluating evidence regarding assertions about economic actions and events to ascertain the degree of correspondence between those assertions and established criteria; and communicating the results to interested users.[1]

The external auditing profession performs a unique task. While managers create the financial statements and design internal control systems, the objective of external auditing is to provide opinions on the reliability of the financial statements and, as part of an **integrated audit**, provide opinions on internal control effectiveness. For external auditing to have value, the

---

[1] Auditing Concepts Committee 1972. Report of the Committee on Basic Auditing Concepts. *The Accounting Review*, 47, Supp. 18.

public needs to have confidence in the objectivity and accuracy of the opinions provided by external auditors.

A free-market economy can exist only if there is sharing of reliable information among interested parties. The market is further strengthened if the information is transparent and unbiased—that is, the data are not presented in such a way that it favors one party over another. An organization's reported information must reflect the economics of its transactions and the current economic condition of both its assets and liabilities. The external audit is intended to enhance the confidence that users can place on management-prepared financial statements. When the auditor has no reservations about management's financial statements or internal controls, the report is referred to as an **unqualified audit report**. Such a report is shown in *Exhibit 1.1*. You will note in *Exhibit 1.1* that the audit firm PricewaterhouseCoopers has provided two opinions. One opinion states that the audit firm believes that the financial statements of Ford are fairly stated. The other opinion states that PricewaterhouseCoopers believes that Ford's internal control over financial reporting was effective as of Ford's year-end, December 31, 2013.

PricewaterhouseCoopers was able to provide these opinions after going through a systematic process of objectively obtaining and evaluating sufficient appropriate evidence. If the auditor had reservations about the fair presentation of the financial statements, the audit report would be modified to explain the nature of the auditor's reservations (covered in *Chapter 15*). And if the auditor had reservations about the effectiveness of the client's internal controls, the auditor would issue an **adverse opinion** on internal controls.

External Auditing: A Special Function

External auditing is a "special function" as described by Chief Justice Warren Burger in a 1984 Supreme Court decision:

> By certifying the public reports that collectively depict a corporation's financial status, the independent auditor assumes a public responsibility transcending any employment relationship with the client. The independent public accountant performing this special function owes ultimate allegiance to the corporation's creditors and stockholders, as well as to the investing public. This "public watchdog" function demands … complete fidelity to the public trust.[2]

Chief Justice Burger's statement captures the essence of the external auditing profession. Auditors serve a number of parties, but the most important is the public, as represented by investors, lenders, workers, and others who make decisions based on financial information about an organization. Auditing requires the highest level of technical competence, freedom from bias, and concern for the integrity of the financial reporting process. In essence, auditors should view themselves as guardians of the capital markets.

The public expects auditors to (a) find fraud, (b) require accounting principles that best portray the spirit of the concepts adopted by accounting standard setters, and (c) be independent of management. When it comes to being independent, auditors must not only be independent *in fact*, but they must act in a manner that ensures that they are independent *in appearance*. For example, if an audit partner's uncle was the CEO at the partner's client company, users could reasonably worry about a conflict of interest. It is entirely possible that the audit partner has, in fact, an independent mental attitude. However, the audit partner would not be independent in appearance in this scenario. Further complicating matters, consider that management and the audit committee

---

[2] *United States v. Arthur Young & Co. et al*, U.S. Supreme Court, No. 82–687 [52 U.S.L.W.4355 (U.S., Mar. 21, 1984)].

| EXHIBIT 1.1 | Integrated Audit Report |

REPORT OF INDEPENDENT REGISTERED AUDIT FIRM

To the Board of Directors and Stockholders of Ford Motor Company

In our opinion, the accompanying consolidated balance sheets and the related consolidated statements of income, comprehensive income, equity and cash flows, including pages 66 through 144, present fairly, in all material respects, the financial position of Ford Motor Company and its subsidiaries at December 31, 2013 and December 31, 2012, and the results of their operations and their cash flows for each of the three years in the period ended December 31, 2013 in conformity with accounting principles generally accepted in the United States of America. Also in our opinion, the Company maintained, in all material respects, effective internal control over financial reporting as of December 31, 2013, based on criteria established in *Internal Control - Integrated Framework (1992)* issued by the Committee of Sponsoring Organizations of the Treadway Commission (COSO). The Company's management is responsible for these financial statements, for maintaining effective internal control over financial reporting and for its assessment of the effectiveness of internal control over financial reporting, included in Management's Report on Internal Control over Financial Reporting in this Annual Report. Our responsibility is to express opinions on these financial statements and on the Company's internal control over financial reporting based on our integrated audits. We conducted our audits in accordance with the standards of the Public Company Accounting Oversight Board (United States). Those standards require that we plan and perform the audits to obtain reasonable assurance about whether the financial statements are free of material misstatement and whether effective internal control over financial reporting was maintained in all material respects. Our audits of the financial statements included examining, on a test basis, evidence supporting the amounts and disclosures in the financial statements, assessing the accounting principles used and significant estimates made by management, and evaluating the overall financial statement presentation. Our audit of internal control over financial reporting included obtaining an understanding of internal control over financial reporting, assessing the risk that a material weakness exists, and testing and evaluating the design and operating effectiveness of internal control based on the assessed risk. Our audits also included performing such other procedures as we considered necessary in the circumstances. We believe that our audits provide a reasonable basis for our opinions.

Our audits were conducted for the purpose of forming an opinion on the basic financial statements taken as a whole. The accompanying sector balance sheets and the related sector statements of income and of cash flows are presented for purposes of additional analysis and are not a required part of the basic financial statements. Such information has been subjected to the auditing procedures applied in the audit of the basic financial statements and, in our opinion, is fairly stated in all material respects in relation to the basic financial statements taken as a whole.

A company's internal control over financial reporting is a process designed to provide reasonable assurance regarding the reliability of financial reporting and the preparation of financial statements for external purposes in accordance with generally accepted accounting principles. A company's internal control over financial reporting includes those policies and procedures that (i) pertain to the maintenance of records that, in reasonable detail, accurately and fairly reflect the transactions and dispositions of the assets of the company; (ii) provide reasonable assurance that transactions are recorded as necessary to permit preparation of financial statements in accordance with generally accepted accounting principles, and that receipts and expenditures of the company are being made only in accordance with authorizations of management and directors of the company; and (iii) provide reasonable assurance regarding prevention or timely detection of unauthorized acquisition, use, or disposition of the company's assets that could have a material effect on the financial statements.

Because of its inherent limitations, internal control over financial reporting may not prevent or detect misstatements. Also, projections of any evaluation of effectiveness to future periods are subject to the risk that controls may become inadequate because of changes in conditions, or that the degree of compliance with the policies or procedures may deteriorate.

/s/ PricewaterhouseCoopers LLP

PricewaterhouseCoopers LLP
Detroit, Michigan
February 18, 2014

Source: *http://corporate.ford.com/doc/ar2013-report_of_independent_registered_public_accounting_firm.pdf*

Why Is Owning Stock in an Audit Client Unacceptable?

In 2005, Susan Birkert was an audit senior working for KPMG on the audit engagement of Comtech Corporation. One of Susan's friends asked her whether she thought that Comtech stock was a good investment. She responded that, indeed, it was a good investment. At that point, her friend asked if she would like him to purchase Comtech stock on her behalf. She agreed and gave her friend $5,000 to make the purchase under his name rather than hers. She did so because she was aware that owning stock in one's audit client is not allowed because of independence concerns. If auditors own stock in their audit clients, they are not independent of their clients because they are part owners. Therefore, rather than acting in an unbiased manner during the conduct of the audit, they might make judgments that favor the client company rather than

external users of the financial statements. Even if the auditor does not actually behave in a biased manner and is independent in fact, external users may *perceive* an independence conflict—the auditor would not be independent in appearance.

Susan continued working on the Comtech engagement well into 2006, and she lied when she responded to KPMG's yearly written requirements to comply with the firm's independence policies. Prompted by an anonymous tip later in 2006, KPMG launched an internal investigation into the matter and terminated her employment. The PCAOB barred her from serving as an external auditor for a period of at least one year.

For further details on this case, see PCAOB Release No. 105-2007-003.

expect cost-effective audits. Thus, the auditing profession faces many pressures—keeping fees low, making careful decisions regarding independence, and conducting a quality audit. The *Auditing in Practice* feature "Why Is Owning Stock in an Audit Client Unacceptable?" is an example of a situation in which a young auditor violated independence rules, leading to her being sanctioned by the PCAOB and being fired by her audit firm employer.

The Need for Unbiased Reporting and Independent Assurance

Effective capital markets require quality financial reporting. An organization's financial statements should reflect a true and fair view of the organization's financial results. The statements should not favor one user over another. However, the interests of the various users can conflict. Current shareholders might want management to use accounting principles that result in higher levels of reported income, while lending institutions might prefer a conservative approach to valuation and income recognition. *Exhibit 1.2* presents an overview of potential financial statement users and the decisions they make based on the financial reports.

Why do financial statement users need independent assurance about information provided by management? Shouldn't the information provided by management be reliable? The need for independent assurance arises from several factors:

- *Potential bias*—Management has incentives to bias financial information in order to convey a better impression of the financial data than real circumstances might merit. For example, management's compensation may be tied to profitability or stock price, so managers may be tempted to "bend" generally accepted accounting principles (GAAP) to make the organization's performance look better.
- *Remoteness*—An organization and the users of its financial information are often remote from each other, both in terms of geographic distance and the extent of information available to the both parties. Most users

EXHIBIT 1.2   Users of Audited Financial Statements

User	Types of Decisions
Management	Review performance, make operational decisions, report results to capital markets
Stockholders	Buy or sell stock
Bondholders	Buy or sell bonds
Financial institutions	Evaluate loan decisions, considering interest rates, terms, and risk
Taxing authorities	Determine taxable income and tax due
Regulatory agencies	Develop regulations and monitor compliance
Labor unions	Make collective bargaining decisions
Court system	Assess the financial position of a company in litigation
Vendors	Assess credit risk
Retired employees	Protect employees from surprises concerning pensions and other post-retirement benefits

cannot interview management, tour a company's plant, or review its financial records firsthand; instead, they must rely on financial statements to communicate the results of management's performance. These factors can tempt management to keep information from users or bend GAAP so the organization looks better.

- *Complexity*—Transactions, information, and processing systems are often very complex, so it can be difficult to determine their proper presentation. This factor provides an opportunity for management to deceive users.
- *Consequences*—When financial information is not reliable, investors and other users lose a significant source of information that they need to make decisions that have important consequences. Without reliable financial information, users may invest in securities or may lend money to a company that is committing a fraud, and once the fraud is revealed users are in a position of losing significant amounts of money.

These factors suggest a role for external auditors who are independent. Independence requires objectivity and freedom from bias and is often referred to as the *cornerstone* of the auditing profession. Without independence, audits would lack value.

Overall Objectives in Conducting an Audit

The overall objective of an audit is to obtain reasonable assurance about whether the financial statements are free from material misstatement and to report on the financial statements based on the auditor's findings. In completing these objectives, the auditor:

- Complies with relevant ethical requirements
- Plans and performs an audit with professional skepticism
- Exercises professional judgment
- Obtains sufficient appropriate evidence on which to base the auditor's opinion
- Conducts the audit in accordance with professional auditing standards

Overview of the Audit Opinion Formulation Process

To be able to provide reasonable assurance, auditors go through a structured process, which we refer to as the *audit opinion formulation process*. *Exhibit 1.3* presents that process.

EXHIBIT 1.3   The Audit Opinion Formulation Process

I. Making Client Acceptance and Continuance Decisions
Chapter 1

II. Performing Risk Assessment
Chapters 3, 7, and 9–13

III. Obtaining Evidence About Internal Control Operating Effectiveness
Chapters 8–13 and 16

IV. Obtaining Substantive Evidence About Accounts, Disclosures and Assertions
Chapters 8–13 and 16

V. Completing the Audit and Making Reporting Decisions
Chapters 14 and 15

The Auditing Profession, the Risk of Fraud and Mechanisms to Address Fraud: Regulation, Corporate Governance, and Audit Quality
Chapters 1 and 2

Professional Liability and the Need for Quality Auditor Judgments and Ethical Decisions
Chapter 4

The Audit Opinion Formulation Process and a Framework for Obtaining Audit Evidence
Chapters 5 and 6

Phase I of the audit opinion formulation process concerns client acceptance and continuance. Auditors are not required to perform audits for any organization that asks; auditors choose whether to perform each individual audit. Audit firms have procedures to help them ensure that they are not associated with clients where management integrity is in question or where a company might otherwise present the audit firm with unnecessarily high risk (such as client financial failure or regulatory action against the client). Once a client is accepted (or the audit firm decides to continue to provide services to a client), the auditor needs to perform risk assessment procedures to thoroughly understand the client's business (or update prior knowledge in the case of a continuing client), its industry, its competition, and its management and governance processes (including internal controls) to determine the likelihood that financial accounts might be in error (Phase II). In some audits, the auditor will also obtain evidence about internal control operating effectiveness through testing those controls (Phase III). Much of what most people think of as auditing, the obtaining of substantive evidence about accounts, disclosures, and assertions, occurs in Phase IV. The information gathered in Phases I through III will greatly influence the amount of testing to be performed in Phase IV. Finally, in Phase V, the auditor will complete the audit and make a decision about what type of audit report to issue.

Parties Involved in Preparing and Auditing Financial Statements

LO 2 Identify parties involved in preparing and auditing financial statements and briefly describe their roles.

Various parties are involved in preparing and auditing financial statements and related disclosures; *Exhibit 1.4* depicts these parties. Management has responsibilities for (a) preparing and presenting financial statements in accordance with the applicable financial reporting framework; (b) designing, implementing, and maintaining internal control over financial reporting; and (c) providing the auditors with information relevant to the financial statements and internal controls. The internal audit function

EXHIBIT 1.4 Parties Involved in Preparing and Auditing Financial Statements

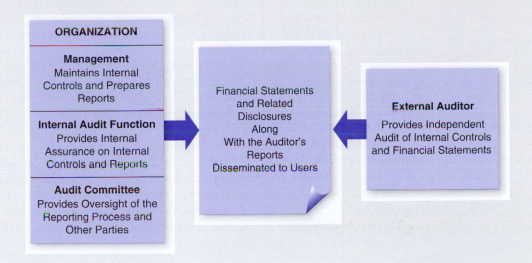

provides management and the audit committee with assurance on internal controls and reports. The audit committee, a subcommittee of the organization's board of directors, oversees both management and the internal auditors; they also hire the external auditor. The external auditor's job is to obtain reasonable assurance about whether management's statements are materially accurate and to provide a publicly available report. External auditors conduct their procedures and make judgments in accordance with professional standards (described in *Chapter 5*). The audited financial statements are provided to users who have an interest in the organization.

Providers of External Auditing Services

The external auditing profession includes sole-practitioner firms, local and regional firms, and large multinational professional services firms such as the Big 4. The Big 4 firms are KPMG, Deloitte Touche Tohmatsu (Deloitte in the United States), PricewaterhouseCoopers (pwc), and EY. The organizational structure of these firms is quite complex. For example, each of the Big 4 firms is actually a network of member firms. Each of the member firms enters into agreements to share a common name, brand, and quality standards. In most cases, member firms are organized as a partnership or limited liability corporation within each country. Some smaller firms also practice internationally through an affiliation with a network of firms. For example, a number of regional or local firms belong to an affiliation of such firms under the name of Moore Stephens, and another group operates under the name of Baker Tilly. Many public accounting firms have also organized their practices along industry lines to better serve clients in those industries. These often include categories such as financial services, retailing, not-for-profit, manufacturing, and government.

The organizational hierarchy of audit firms is structured with partners (or owners) at the top level; these individuals are responsible for the overall conduct of each audit. Next in the hierarchy are managers, who review the audit work performed by seniors and staff personnel. Seniors are responsible for overseeing the day-to-day activities on a specific audit, and they oversee entry-level personnel who perform many of the basic auditing procedures. Partners and managers are responsible for many audit engagements that are being conducted simultaneously, whereas seniors and staff are usually assigned to fewer audits at one time.

LO 3 List the types of audit service providers and the skills and knowledge needed by professionals entering the external auditing profession.

Skills and Knowledge Needed to Enter the External Auditing Profession

The requirements of those entering the auditing profession are demanding. Audits are performed in teams where each auditor is expected to complete tasks requiring considerable technical knowledge and expertise. Auditors also need well-developed skills in leadership, teamwork, communication, decision making, and general professionalism. In terms of technical knowledge and expertise, auditors must understand accounting and auditing authoritative literature, develop industry and client-specific knowledge, develop and apply computer skills, evaluate internal controls, and assess and respond to fraud risk. Furthermore, a strong ethical foundation is critical for each auditor.

In terms of professionalism, auditors make presentations to management and audit committee members, exercise logical reasoning, communicate decisions to users, manage and supervise others by providing meaningful feedback, act with integrity and ethics, interact in a team environment, collaborate with others, and maintain a professional presence. While external auditors at all types of audit firms need these skills, the work environment differs across audit firms. *The Auditing in Practic*e feature "Should I Work for a Large or a Small Audit Firm?" explores differences in the workplace at some of these firms.

Organizations Affecting the External Auditing Profession

External auditing is a profession with many organizations shaping and regulating the services provided by those in the profession.

LO 4 Identify organizations that affect the external auditing profession and the nature of their effects.

Congress

During the early 2000s, various shocks affected the future of the auditing profession. Some of the major shocks included (a) the failure of one of the largest audit firms in the world (Arthur Andersen & Co.); (b) four of the largest bankruptcies in history—and each of the bankruptcies occurred in companies

---

Should I Work for a Large or a Small Audit Firm?

AUDITING IN PRACTICE

The workplace environment at large audit firms differs significantly from small audit firms. Some differences are described here. Of course, these are broad generalities, and people will perceive these differences as relatively more or less appealing depending on their personalities and long-term career goals.

	Larger Audit Firms	Smaller Audit Firms
Working in a team environment	• Multiple teams that typically disband after each audit engagement	• Teams that overlap across engagements
Work specialization	• Specialized by function, i.e., audit or tax, but usually not both • May also be specialized by industry	• Less specialized by function; an individual may work across functions and industries
Organizational culture	• Relatively formal	• Relatively less formal
Staff turnover	• Relatively higher	• Relatively lower

where fraud had taken place—that led to billions of dollars in investment and retirement fund losses by investors; (c) a sense that auditors were not independent of management; and (d) a question as to whether the auditing profession could sufficiently govern itself to ensure that it would always act in the public interest. In response to these shocks, Congress passed the **Sarbanes-Oxley Act of 2002**.[3] This legislation, which we expand upon in *Chapter 2*, has had a significant impact on audit firms through:

- Increasing auditor independence requirements
- Enhancing the role and importance of the audit committee
- Requiring reporting on internal control over financial reporting
- Providing oversight of the external auditing profession by the PCAOB

Public Company Accounting Oversight Board

The PCAOB (*www.pcaobus.org*) is a private sector, nonprofit organization that oversees auditors of public companies. The overall goal of the PCAOB is to protect the interests of investors and further the public interest in the preparation of informative, fair, and independent audit reports. The PCAOB has four primary responsibilities related to auditors of public companies: (1) registering audit firms that audit public companies; (2) periodically inspecting registered audit firms; (3) establishing auditing and related standards for registered audit firms; and (4) investigating and disciplining registered audit firms for violations of relevant laws or professional standards.

Who Are the Leaders of the PCAOB?

AUDITING IN **PRACTICE**

As of 2014, the five board members of the PCAOB include the following individuals:

Board Member Name	Prior Work Experience and Professional Qualifications
James Doty, Chairman served since 2011	Attorney; general counsel of the SEC; partner in a law firm specializing in securities and corporate law
Lewis Ferguson, served since 2011	Attorney; general counsel of the PCAOB; partner in a law firm specializing in securities regulation, disclosure issues, and corporate governance; senior vice president, general counsel and director of Wright Medical Technology; adjunct law professor
Jay Hanson, served since 2011	CPA; partner at McGladrey & Pullen LLP and national director of accounting for that firm; served as chairman of Financial Reporting Executive Committee of the AICPA
Jeanette Franzel, served since 2012	CPA; managing director of the Government Accountability Office
Steven Harris, served since 2008	Attorney; senior vice president and special counsel at APCO Worldwide, which specializes in advising clients on financial transactions, corporate governance, crisis management, and government affairs

Board members are replaced on a planned, rotational basis in order to provide a fresh perspective periodically. Each term of service is five years, and no board member may serve more than two terms.

---

[3] Sarbanes-Oxley Act of 2002, H.R. Bill 3762.

The *Auditing in Practice* feature "Who Are the Leaders of the PCAOB?" describes the professional qualifications of the five board members of the PCAOB. It is interesting to note that not all are external auditors. In fact, the rules for the PCAOB state that no more than two board members may be Certified Public Accountants (CPAs). This design choice was made deliberately to ensure that the Board was not unduly dominated by members of the external auditing profession, thereby helping assure users of financial statements that this important regulator is representing the broad interests of users, not just serving the preferences of the external auditing profession.

The Securities and Exchange Commission

The **Securities and Exchange Commission** (SEC, *www.sec.gov*) was established by Congress in 1934 to regulate the capital market system. The SEC has oversight responsibilities for the PCAOB and for all public companies that are traded on U.S. stock exchanges. The SEC has the authority to establish GAAP for companies whose stock is publicly traded, although it has generally delegated this authority to the Financial Accounting Standards Board (FASB).

Actions by the SEC have important implications for public company auditors. In response to the independence requirements of Sarbanes-Oxley, the SEC made its auditor independence rules more stringent. The SEC also has a responsibility to prosecute public companies and their auditors for violating SEC laws, including fraudulent accounting. For example, in recent years, the SEC has brought actions against companies and auditors including (a) Dell for failing to disclose material information and for improper accounting related to the use of "cookie jar" reserves, (b) Lucent for inappropriate revenue recognition, (c) a former Deloitte & Touche partner for a lack of independence, (d) Ernst & Young for allowing premature revenue recognition and improper deferral of costs in its audits of Bally Total Fitness Holding Corporation, and (e) a former KPMG partner for insider trading, among many others. The *Focus on Fraud* feature "Locating Enforcement Actions on the SEC Web Site" provides instructions on how to locate enforcement actions that the SEC has released and illustrates the ongoing efforts by the SEC to ensure both quality financial reporting and quality auditing.

American Institute of Certified Public Accountants

The **American Institute of Certified Public Accountants** (AICPA, *www.aicpa.org*) has long served as the primary governing organization of

---

Locating Enforcement Actions on the SEC Web Site

FOCUS on FRAUD

The SEC issues enforcement actions to penalize individuals and firms in the accounting and auditing professions for wrongdoings; these public disclosures are also intended to have a deterrence effect. Enforcement releases make for very interesting reading! Take these steps to see recent enforcement releases:

- Go to *www.sec.gov*.
- Click "Enforcement."
- Click "Accounting and Auditing."
- Click the appropriate year.
- Click the enforcement release that you wish to read.

the public accounting profession. That role changed with the establishment of the PCAOB as the body for setting auditing standards for the audits of public companies. However, the AICPA continues to develop standards for audits of nonpublic companies. The ACIPA is responsible for a peer review program in which registered firms are subject to periodic peer review of their nonpublic audits. The AICPA also provides continuing education programs, and through its Board of Examiners, prepares and administers the Uniform CPA Examination.

The Center for Audit Quality

The **Center for Audit Quality** (CAQ, *www.thecaq.org*), an organization affiliated with the AICPA, is dedicated to enhancing investor confidence and trust in the financial markets. The CAQ is a thought leader in fostering audit quality, collaborating with auditors and financial statement users about emerging issues and advocating for accounting and auditing standards that promote auditors' effectiveness.

International Auditing and Assurance Standards Board

The **International Auditing and Assurance Standards Board** (IAASB, *www.ifac.org/iaasb*) is a part of the International Federation of Accountants (IFAC), a global organization for the accounting profession. The IAASB sets International Standards on Auditing (ISAs) and facilitates the convergence of national and international auditing standards.[4]

Committee of Sponsoring Organizations

The **Committee of Sponsoring Organizations of the Treadway Commission** (COSO, *www.coso.org*) is a recognized provider of guidance on internal control, enterprise risk management, and fraud deterrence. COSO is sponsored by five organizations, including the Financial Executives International, the American Institute of Certified Public Accountants, the American Accounting Association, the Institute of Internal Auditors, and the Association of Accountants and Financial Professionals in Business (IMA). COSO provides the internal control framework that serves as the benchmark for auditors who assess the effectiveness of their client's internal controls.

Accounting Standard Setters

Generally Accepted Accounting Principles (GAAP) in the United States have traditionally been set by the FASB, with approval by the SEC. International accounting standards (IFRS—International Financial Reporting Standards) are set by the International Financial Reporting Standards Foundation of the **International Accounting Standards Board** (IASB).[5] During the past several years, the U.S. and international standard setters have worked toward global harmonization of U.S. and international accounting standards.

---

[4] When referring to external auditing standards, we will use the term *generally accepted auditing standards* (GAAS). We recognize that multiple organizations set GAAS, including the AICPA, the IAASB, and the PCAOB.

[5] When referring to financial reporting requirements, we will use the term *generally accepted accounting principles* (GAAP) for financial reporting, recognizing that the criteria may be developed by either the FASB or the IASB. In some instances, we will use the term *applicable financial reporting framework*. The auditor will determine which of the financial reporting frameworks is applicable to the audit and then apply that framework to determine whether the principles underlying that framework are properly applied.

State Boards of Accountancy

CPAs are licensed by state boards of accountancy, which are charged with regulating the profession at the state level. All state boards require passage of the Uniform CPA Examination as one criterion for licensure. However, education and experience requirements vary by state. In terms of education, most states require 150 college semester hours for CPA licensure, although in some states a candidate may be able to sit for the CPA exam with only 120 hours. Some states require candidates to have external auditing experience before issuing them a license to practice; other states give credit for audit experience related to private or governmental accounting. The work experience requirement can also vary with the level of education. Most states have reciprocal agreements for recognizing public accountants from other states; in some instances, however, a state may require either additional experience or coursework before issuing a license.

The Court System

The court system acts as a quality-control mechanism for the auditing profession. Third parties may sue CPAs under federal securities laws, various state statutes, and common law for substandard audit work. Although the profession often becomes alarmed when large damages are awarded to plaintiffs in suits against audit firms, the courts help ensure that the profession meets its responsibilities to third parties.

Audit Quality

LO 5 Define audit quality and identify drivers of audit quality as specified by the Financial Reporting Council's *Audit Quality Framework.*

Assuring that the audit is conducted in a quality manner is paramount to fulfilling users' expectations about the auditor's role in the capital markets. Throughout this book, we discuss approaches that auditors use to achieve audit quality. But before proceeding, it is worthwhile to take a moment to reflect on a very fundamental question: What is **audit quality**?

A definition published by the GAO (2003) states that a quality audit is one performed "in accordance with generally accepted auditing standards (GAAS) to provide reasonable assurance that the audited financial statements and related disclosures are (1) presented in accordance with GAAP and (2) are not materially misstated whether due to errors or fraud."[6]

The Financial Reporting Council (FRC) developed the *Audit Quality Framework* to provide guidance on specific drivers of audit quality. The FRC is the United Kingdom's independent regulator responsible for promoting investment in securities through good corporate governance and financial reporting.

The FRC's *Audit Quality Framework* states that there are five primary drivers of audit quality, including (1) audit firm culture, (2) the skills and personal qualities of audit partners and staff, (3) the effectiveness of the audit process, (4) the reliability and usefulness of audit reporting, and (5) factors outside the control of auditors that affect audit quality. *Exhibit 1.5* contains an overview of the FRC's *Audit Quality Framework.* The *Framework* recognizes that effective audit processes, by themselves, are not sufficient to achieve audit quality. Rather, it is a package of factors that includes a culture that influences auditors who in turn influence audit procedures. However, there are other factors, outside of the control of the audit firm, that affect audit quality and thereby the overall quality of the audited

---

[6] Government Accountability Office (GAO). 2003. Public Accounting Firms: Required Study on the Potential Effects of Mandatory Audit Firm Rotation. GAO Report 04–216 (November).

EXHIBIT **1.5**   Drivers of Audit Quality

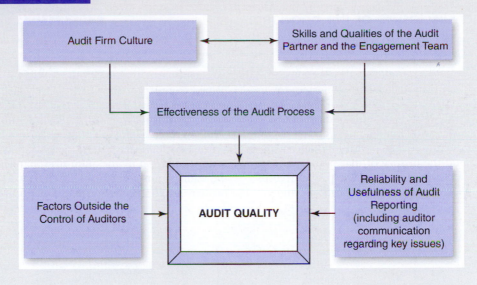

financial statements. These factors include the robustness of the accounting framework as well as the regulatory and legal environments.

Audit Firm Culture

According to the FRC, audit firm culture contributes positively to audit quality when the leadership of the firm completes the following types of activities:

- Creating a work culture where audit quality is valued and rewarded
- Emphasizing that "doing the right thing" is appropriate from a public interest perspective and that doing the right thing helps develop and maintain both individual and audit firm reputation
- Ensuring that audit firm employees have enough time and resources to address difficult issues that may arise
- Ensuring that monetary considerations do not adversely affect audit quality
- Promoting the benefits of having audit partners seek guidance on difficult issues and supporting their professional judgment
- Ensuring that the audit firm has quality systems in place for making client acceptance and continuation decisions
- Fostering evaluation and compensation practices that promote personal characteristics important to quality auditing
- Ensuring that audit quality is monitored within the audit firm and that appropriate consequences are taken when audit quality is found to be lacking

Skills and Qualities of the Engagement Team

The FRC notes that audit firm employees positively contribute to audit quality when they engage in the following types of activities:

- Understanding the client's business and adhering to auditing and ethical standards
- Exhibiting professional skepticism and addressing issues identified during the audit

Requiring Disclosure of the Engagement Partner and Certain Participants in the Audit

On December 4, 2013, the PCAOB re-proposed an earlier proposed amendment that would require disclosure of the name of the audit partner. The PCAOB would like to identify the audit partner because it believes that doing so would increase the usefulness of the auditor's report and would help users understand the history of that partner's involvement in the engagement. The proposal also calls for disclosure of the names, locations, and extent of participation of other audit firms that helped conduct the audit. Many audit engagements are conducted with the assistance of other audit firms, yet this information is generally not revealed publicly in the United States. The proposal would help users understand the extent of audit work that is not conducted by the audit firm that actually signs the audit report. Watch the PCAOB web site for further development regarding this proposal.

- Ensuring that staff performing audit work have appropriate levels of experience and that they are properly supervised by their superiors
- Ensuring that partners and managers provide lower level staff with mentoring and on-the-job training opportunities
- Attending to and learning during training intended to aid in understanding audit, accounting, and industry specialist issues

The skills and qualities of the engagement team are important to audit quality, yet the identity of key members of the engagement team is currently requiring not publicly disclosed in the United States. The *Emerging Issues* feature "Requiring Disclosure of the Engagement Partner and Certain Participants in the Audit" describes an amendment to PCAOB standards that would require disclosure of the name of the audit partner and involvement of other audit firms that participated in conducting the audit.

Effectiveness of the Audit Process

The FRC recognizes that the audit process itself contributes in a positive way to audit quality when the following activities and processes are in place:

- The audit methodology is well structured and:
  - Encourages partners and managers to be work diligently in planning the audit
  - Provides a framework and the procedures to obtain sufficient appropriate audit evidence in an effective and efficient manner
  - Requires appropriate audit documentation
  - Provides for complying with auditing standards but does not inhibit professional judgment
  - Ensures that audit work is effectively reviewed
  - Includes audit quality-control procedures that are effective, understood, and applied
- Quality technical support is available when auditors encounter unfamiliar situations requiring assistance or guidance.
- Ethical standards are communicated and achieved, thereby aiding auditors' integrity, objectivity, and independence.
- Auditors' evidence collection is not constrained by financial pressures.

Reliability and Usefulness of Audit Reporting

According to the FRC, audit reports contribute to audit quality when they have the following attributes:

- Audit reports are written in a way that clearly and unambiguously conveys the auditor's opinion on the financial statements and addresses the needs of users of financial statements.
- Auditors appropriately conclude as to the truth and fairness of the financial statements (e.g., in the United States, concluding that the financial statements are fairly presented in accordance with GAAP).
- The auditor communicates with the audit committee about the following:
  - Audit scope (in other words, what the auditor is engaged to accomplish)
  - Threats to auditor objectivity
  - Important risks identified and judgments that were made in reaching the audit opinion
  - Qualitative aspects of the client's accounting and reporting and possible ways of improving financial reporting

Factors Outside the Control of Auditors That Affect Audit Quality

The FRC is realistic, and it explicitly recognizes that some factors that affect audit quality are outside of the direct control of the external auditor, such as client corporate governance and the regulatory environment. The FRC recognizes that good corporate governance includes audit committees that are robust in dealing with issues and a greater emphasis by the client on getting things right as opposed to getting done by a particular date. Further, a regulatory environment that emphasizes audit quality over all else is critical.

The profession worldwide is, of course, committed to providing quality audits. The *Emerging Issues* feature "IAASB's Framework for Audit Quality" describes a framework for audit quality that has been released by the IAASB. The *Emerging Issues* feature "Audit Quality Indicators" highlights the PCAOB's efforts related to measuring and monitoring audit quality.

Achieving Audit Quality and Minimizing Lawsuits

LO 6 Identify professional requirements that help achieve audit quality and minimize auditor exposure to lawsuits.

If an audit is not conducted in a quality manner, the auditor and audit firm are susceptible to lawsuits. While we expand on legal implications for the external auditing profession in *Chapter 4*, we discuss here how certain professional requirements help achieve audit quality, and thus how they can minimize the exposure of external auditors to lawsuits.

These requirements include (1) maintaining auditor independence, (2) participating in review programs, (3) issuing engagement letters, (4) evaluating the audit firm's limitations, and (5) maintaining quality audit documentation.

Auditor Independence Requirements

The SEC, PCAOB, and AICPA all have requirements related to auditor independence that are intended to assist auditors in conducting a quality audit.

SEC and PCAOB Independence Requirements

The SEC and PCAOB's independence requirements are applicable to auditors of public companies. These two organizations have set complementary independence requirements. The PCAOB's independence requirements are designed to address specific requirements in the Sarbanes-Oxley Act of 2002 (see *Chapter 2* for specific details).

IAASB's Framework for Audit Quality

EMERGING ISSUE

In 2014, the IAASB released a framework for audit quality containing the following key elements:

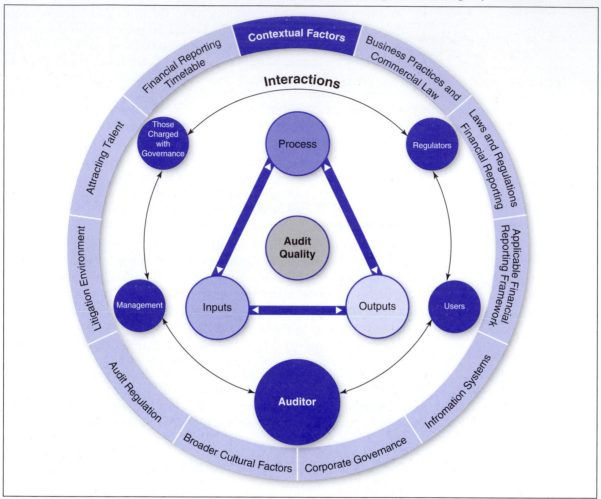

The framework:

- Describes the input, process, and output factors that affect audit quality at the engagement, firm, and national levels
- Describes the importance of appropriate interactions between parties in the audit process and how these interactions can improve audit quality and the perception of audit quality

- Shows how audit quality can be affected by factors such as laws and regulations, litigation environment, corporate governance, and financial reporting framework

See IAASB's web site for a copy of the complete framework.

The following two paragraph summarize the SEC's commitment to independence:

The independence requirement serves two related, but distinct, public policy goals. One goal is to foster high quality audits by minimizing the possibility that any external factors will influence an auditor's judgments. The auditor must approach each audit with professional skepticism and must have the capacity and the willingness to decide issues in an unbiased and objective manner, even

Audit Quality Indicators

EMERGING ISSUE

The PCAOB has undertaken an audit quality indicator project, or AQI project. The AQI project is directed at: (1) developing a portfolio of quantitative measures that provide new insights into audit quality, and (2) deploying those measures in a manner that best promotes audit quality. The PCAOB has speculated that a portfolio of about 15 indicators may be sufficient to present a balanced scorecard of audit quality, with no single indicator likely to be determinative of audit quality. This project, which begins with a PCAOB Concept Release in 2014, will likely take a number of years for completion. Be sure to watch the PCAOB's web site for updates on this project.

when the auditor's decisions may be against the interests of management of the audit client or against the interests of the auditor's own accounting firm.

The other related goal is to promote investor confidence in the financial statements of public companies. Investor confidence in the integrity of publicly available financial information is the cornerstone of our securities market … . Investors are more likely to invest, and pricing is more likely to be efficient, where there is greater assurance that the financial information disclosed by issuers is reliable … [that] assurance will flow from knowledge that the financial information has been subjected to rigorous examination by competent and objective auditors.[7]

The SEC has taken a principles-based approach in dealing with independence issues. All of the SEC statements on independence follow from four basic principles that define when an auditor is in a position that impairs independence. Those principles dictate that auditor independence is impaired when the auditor has a relationship that:

- Creates a mutual or conflicting interest between the accountant and the audit client
- Places the accountant in the position of auditing his or her own work
- Results in the accountant acting as management or an employee of the audit client
- Places the accountant in a position of being an advocate for the audit client[8]

AICPA Requirements: A Conceptual Framework on Independence

The AICPA has articulated a conceptual framework on independence. That framework describes seven categories of threats to independence, which are circumstances that could lead to an auditor lacking independence in fact or in appearance. These various threats to independence include:

1. *Self-review threat*—occurs when the audit firm also provides nonaudit work for the client, such as preparing source documents used to generate the client's financial statements. Independence is threatened because it may appear that the auditor is reviewing his or her own work.
2. *Advocacy threat*—occurs when the auditor acts to promote the client's interests, such as representing the client in tax court. Independence is threatened because it may appear that the auditor cares more about the client than external users of the financial statements.

---

[7] U.S. Securities and Exchange Commission, Final Rule: Revision of the Commission's Auditor Independence Requirements, February 5, 2001.
[8] Op. cit.

3. *Adverse interest threat*—occurs when the auditor and the client are in opposition to one another, such as when either party has initiated litigation against the other. Independence is threatened because the auditor may take actions that are intended to weaken the client's chances in the litigation and may appear to care more about the audit firm and its interests rather than those of the company or external users of the financial statements.

4. *Familiarity threat*—occurs when the auditor has some longstanding relationship with an important person associated with the client. Examples include:
   - The audit partner's close relative is employed in a key position at the client.
   - The audit partner has been assigned to the client for a long period of time and has developed very close personal relationships with top management.
   - A member of the audit team has a close personal friend who is employed in a key position at the client.
   - A member of the audit team was recently a director or officer at the client.

   In each of these examples, independence is threatened because the auditor may act in a way that favors the client or individual employed at the client rather than external users of the financial statements.

5. *Undue influence threat*—occurs when client management attempts to coerce or provide excessive influence over the auditor. Examples include:
   - Top management threatens to replace the auditor or the audit firm because of a disagreement over an accounting issue.
   - Top management pressures the auditor to reduce the amount of work they do on the audit in order to achieve lower audit fees.
   - An employee of the client gives the auditor a gift that is clearly significant or economically important to the auditor.

   In each of these examples, independence is threatened because the auditor may act in a way that favors the client or individual employed at the client rather than external users of the financial statements.

6. *Financial self-interest threat*—occurs when the auditor has a direct financial relationship with the client, such as owning stock in the client company, owing money to the client company, or when the audit client makes up the vast majority of the audit firm's total revenue. Independence is threatened because the auditor's judgment may be unduly influenced by their own financial interests rather than acting in the best interests of external users of the financial statements.

7. *Management participation threat*—occurs when the auditor takes on the role of management or completes functions that management should reasonably complete, such as establishing internal controls or hiring/firing client employees. Independence is threatened because the auditor is acting as management, and so would in essence be reviewing his or her own work.

The AICPA also articulates safeguards to avoid the independence problems associated with these threats. These safeguards include:

1. Safeguards created by the profession or regulation. Examples include:
   - Education, continuing education, and training requirements
   - Professional standards and disciplinary punishments
   - External review of audit firms' quality-control systems
   - Legislation concerning independence requirements
   - Audit partner rotation requirements for publicly traded companies, which include mandatory partner rotation after five years of service
   - Nonaudit (e.g., consulting) work not allowed for companies for which the auditor provides external audit work

2. Safeguards created by the audit client. Examples include:
   - Client personnel with expertise to adequately complete necessary management and accounting tasks without the involvement or advice of the auditor
   - Appropriate tone at the top of the client
   - Policies and procedures to ensure accurate financial reporting
   - Policies and procedures to ensure appropriate relationships with the audit firm
3. Safeguards created by the audit firm. Examples include:
   - Audit firm leadership that stresses the importance of independence
   - Audit firm quality-control policies and procedures
   - Audit firm monitoring processes to detect instances of possible independence violations
   - Disciplinary mechanisms to promote compliance with independence policies and procedures
   - Rotation of senior engagement personnel

Review Programs

Three types of review programs exist:

- External inspections/peer reviews
- Engagement quality reviews
- Interoffice reviews

External Inspections/Peer Reviews

The PCAOB performs inspections of registered audit firms every year for audit firms that have over 100 public company audits and every three years for the other registered audit firms. You can access inspection reports on the PCAOB's web site. Many of these reports identify audit performance deficiencies found by the inspectors.

The AICPA has a peer review program that reviews and evaluates those portions of an audit firm's accounting and auditing practice that are not inspected by the PCAOB; the focus of the peer reviews is for nonpublic audit clients. The reviews are conducted by auditors from another external audit firm and provide an objective assessment of the appropriateness of the firm's quality-control policies and procedures as well as of the degree of compliance with them. Peer review reports are issued to the audit firm and are available from the AICPA.

Engagement Quality Reviews

An audit partner not otherwise involved in the audit performs an **engagement quality review** (also referred to as **concurring partner review**) near the end of each audit to make sure that documented evidence supports the audit opinion. Such reviews are required for audits of public companies, and it is desirable for firms to conduct these reviews on all audits. The concurring partner should be familiar with the nature of the business being audited. Some single-partner audit firms arrange with other small firms to perform concurring reviews for each other before issuing audit reports.

AICPA The AICPA has no formal requirement for engagement quality review on individual audit engagements. However, the AICPA does require that firms establish specific criteria by which they decide on a systematic basis the clients that should have such a review. The AICPA still requires the firms to undergo a quality review process at the overall audit firm level on a periodic basis, and (a) the absence of specific criteria for engagement quality reviews or (b) the absence of adherence to those criteria would be considered a deficiency when overall audit firm reviews are performed.

Recall that the AICPA standards concern nonpublicly traded entities, and many of the firm's clients may be very small and have only one or two people assigned to the total audit. Thus, in the view of the AICPA (and many smaller firms), it would not make economic sense to have an engagement quality review for clients that are both uncomplicated and small. Some of the criteria that the firms use to decide that an engagement quality review is needed include riskiness of client, size of client, and the extent of outside distribution of audit report (and thus, potentially the legal liability for the auditor).

PCAOB   PCAOB guidance requires an engagement quality review, and the engagement quality reviewer must evaluate all significant judgments made by the engagement team and consider the team's evaluation of the client's risks. The guidance specifically states that the engagement quality reviewer must have competence, independence, integrity, and objectivity, and the standard requires that all phases of the review be carefully documented.

IAASB   Similar to the PCAOB, the IAASB requires that the engagement quality reviewer evaluate significant risks and the engagement team's responses to those risks, judgments made (particularly relating to addressing risks and materiality), the disposition of misstatements identified during the engagement (whether corrected or not), and matters communicated to management and others charged with governance over the organization.

Interoffice Reviews

An **interoffice review** is a review of one office of an audit firm by professionals from another office of the same firm to assure that the policies and procedures established by the firm are being followed. Like external inspections/peer reviews, interoffice reviews include selecting and reviewing a sample of audits to help assure that quality work was performed.

Engagement Letters

The **engagement letter** states the scope of the work to be done on the audit so that there should be no doubt in the mind of the client, external auditor, or the court system as to the expectations agreed to by the external auditor and the client. The engagement letter, which includes the audit fee, also includes a description of the timing of the external auditor's work and a description of documentation that the client is expected to provide to the external auditor. In writing an engagement letter, care should be taken when describing the degree of responsibility the auditor takes with respect to discovering fraud and misstatements. If the client wants its auditors to go beyond the requirements of the auditing standards, the auditors should have their attorneys review the wording to make sure that it says not only what is intended but also what is possible.

Items in the engagement letter typically include:

- The objective and scope of the audit of the financial statements
- The responsibilities of the auditor
- The responsibilities of management
- A statement that because of the inherent limitations of an audit, together with the inherent limitations of internal control, an unavoidable risk exists that some material misstatements may not be detected, even though the audit is properly planned and performed in accordance with relevant auditing standards
- The identification of the applicable financial reporting framework for the preparation of the financial statements

- A reference to the expected form and content of any reports to be issued by the auditor and a statement about circumstances that may arise in which a report may differ from its expected form and content

Audit Firm Limitations

An external audit firm should not undertake an engagement that it is not qualified to handle. Doing so is especially important for smaller, growing firms that may be tempted to agree to conduct an audit for which they are not qualified or not large enough to perform. Statistics show that firms covered by an AICPA professional liability insurance plan that are most susceptible to litigation are those with staffs of eleven to twenty-five auditors. They appear to become overzealous, leading to low audit quality and exposure to subsequent litigation.

Audit Documentation

The audit team should document everything done on the audit. It is difficult to persuade a jury or a regulator such as the PCAOB that something was done that is not documented. Audit documentation should clearly show evidence of supervisory review, particularly in those areas with the greatest potential for improprieties, such as inventories, revenue recognition, and accounting estimates. The documentation should indicate what tests were performed, who performed them, and any significant judgments made (along with the rationale for those judgments). We further address audit documentation in *Chapter 5* and *Chapter 6*.

Client Acceptance and Continuance Decisions

LO 7 Describe the process by which audit firms make client acceptance and continuance decisions.

An important element of quality control deals with accepting and retaining audit clients. Audit firms and individual engagement partners make client acceptance and continuance decisions (sometimes called client retention decisions), either immediately before agreeing to conduct an audit or immediately after completing the audit. These decisions are just a part of an audit firm's overall portfolio management activities. In essence, one can view an individual audit client as an individual stock in an investment portfolio. That is, some stocks (clients) are more risky, but yield better returns; some stocks (clients) are less risky, but yield weaker returns. Still other stocks (clients) do not present a clear picture of their risk-return profile. In the context of auditing, better returns does not just mean higher audit fees, but instead may also include the upside potential of a client that may become publicly traded, the reputational visibility that an audit firm gains when they audit a superior and well-known company, and so forth. Accomplishing portfolio management, of which client acceptance and continuance decisions are just one part, is the key to an audit firm's long-run survival and its ability to offer quality audit services to its clients. Audit firm culture plays a role in audit firm portfolio management, in that some audit firms are more willing to provide service to risky clients than are other audit firms.

As depicted in *Exhibit 1.6*, an audit firm begins each period with a given number of clients in its portfolio. Some clients voluntarily depart from the audit firm, such as in the case of a company going bankrupt or merging with another company; other reasons include fee issues, service issues, changes in location, poor working relationships, and so on. Other clients are newly accepted into the audit firm's portfolio based on the **client acceptance decision**. These clients are evaluated based upon their relative risk and audit fee profile. The audit firm makes a proposal (and in some cases a formal bid) to the client if the audit firm decides the client is acceptable; if the client accepts, the audit firm adds the client to its portfolio.

EXHIBIT **1.6** Audit Firm Portfolio Management

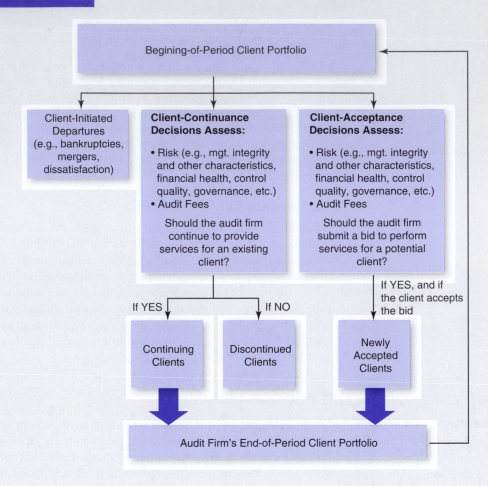

Existing clients for which the audit firm provided services in the preceding period are evaluated by the audit firm and the individual engagement partner at the completion of the audit to determine whether the audit firm should continue to provide services in the next period. The process by which this decision is made is called the **client continuance decision**. In short, the engagement partner and the audit firm must decide, based on what they know about the client, whether it is worthwhile to retain the client in the firm's portfolio. Like the client acceptance decision, the client continuance decision is made based on a consideration of the client's relative risk and audit fee profile. Discontinued clients are those the audit firm eliminates from its portfolio based on the client continuance decision; the clients will be informed that the firm will no longer be associated with them after the current period audit report is issued. Continuing clients are those the audit firm will continue its ongoing relationship with; the firm will continue to be associated with them once the current period audit report is issued.

Auditors are not required to perform audits for any organization that asks. The auditor wants to accept audit engagements (whether for new or existing clients) only when the preconditions for an audit are present. Generally, these preconditions include:

* *Management's use of an acceptable financial reporting framework*. Without an acceptable financial reporting framework (e.g., GAAP or

IFRS), management does not have an appropriate basis for the preparation of the financial statements, and the auditor does not have suitable criteria for auditing the financial statements.

- *The agreement of management that it acknowledges and understands its responsibilities.* These responsibilities include the preparation and fair presentation of the financial statements, along with the design, implementation, and maintenance of internal control over financial reporting. Further, management needs to agree to provide the auditor with access to all relevant information, such as records, documentation, and so on, and unrestricted access to persons within the organization.

As highlighted in the *Auditing in Practice* feature "Accepting a New Audit Engagement," an additional procedure for new clients typically includes communication with the predecessor audit firm.

Client Acceptance and Continuance-Related Risks

The following are some of the key types of risk that audit firms consider when they make client acceptance and client continuance decisions:

- *Client entity characteristics.* For example, a history of earnings management or of making unrealistic promises to analysts; failing to meet market expectations or consistently just meeting those expectations; difficulties in relationships with prior professional service providers, such as attorneys; and high-risk business models, such as Internet gaming.
- *Independence risk factors.* For example, the engagement partner has a business or family relationship with the client; client management was a former employee of the audit firm; the client purchases consulting services from the audit firm; or the audit firm has some other independence-related conflict with the client.
- *Third party/due diligence risk factors.* For example, the reason for the client to change auditors is unknown or is due to negative relationship factors, the predecessor audit firm is unwilling to discuss the reasons for the client's departure, there have been significant changes in the

---

AUDITING IN **PRACTICE**

Accepting a New Audit Engagement

Before accepting a new audit client, the auditor should request that management authorizes the predecessor auditor to respond to the auditor's inquiries on issues that will assist the auditor in determining whether to accept the new client. If management refuses to authorize the predecessor auditor to respond or limits the response, the auditor should inquire about the reasons and consider the implications in deciding whether to accept the engagement.

The communication with the predecessor auditor may be either written or oral, although obtaining the communication in writing is better. Matters addressed include:

- Information that might bear on the integrity of management

- Disagreements with management about accounting policies, auditing procedures, or other similarly significant matters
- Communications to those charged with governance regarding fraud and noncompliance with laws or regulations by the entity
- Communications to management and those charged with governance regarding significant deficiencies and material weaknesses in internal control
- The predecessor auditor's understanding about the reasons for the change of auditors

While U.S. auditing standards require the auditor's communications with the predecessor auditors for an initial audit, international auditing standards do not include this requirement.

ownership structure of the entity or evidence that key members of management have prior histories of financial fraud or other types of legal difficulties.

- *Quantitative risk factors.* For example, the client is in significant financial stress, is having difficulty raising capital or paying its existing debts, or is experiencing significant cash flow problems.
- *Qualitative risk factors.* For example, the industry in which the client operates is either in the early development stage or late in its product life cycle; there are minimal barriers to entry to the client's business model; the business model is weak or untested; there are low profit margins; the client's products have multiple viable substitutes; there are significant supply chain risks; there is significant production or operational complexity; or there are risks related to strong union presence.
- *Entity organizational or governance risks.* For example, the organizational structure is inappropriate for the business operations of the entity, there are weak internal controls, there is weak governance, management is unqualified or lacks integrity, and the internal audit function is weak or nonexistent.
- *Financial reporting risks.* For example, the client uses inappropriate estimates in its financial reporting judgments, management has a history of misrepresentations or unwillingness to correct detected misstatements, the financial statement line items involve a significant amount of judgment or complexity, there are large or unusual transactions that management records at quarter or year-end, or the prior audit report is other than an unqualified report.

In addition to these risk factors, an important consideration in client continuance decisions involves the audit firm's growth strategy. Audit firms may discontinue serving a client because the client does not fit the profile the firm is hoping to achieve. For example, a Big 4 firm may discontinue serving a smaller client because it is not sufficiently profitable, or the client may not be in an industry the firm wants to emphasize. On the other hand, some smaller audit firms may discontinue serving a larger client because they do not have the size or expertise to serve the client as the client grows larger, becomes more geographically dispersed, or increases in complexity. See the *Focus on Fraud* feature "Why Might an Audit Firm Refuse to Continue Providing Services to a Client? The Case of Longtop Financial Technologies and Deloitte" for an example of auditor resignation due to suspicions of fraud.

Audit firm portfolio management decisions, which include client acceptance and continuance decisions, are critical to achieve audit quality. If an audit firm accepts or continues to provide service to a potentially problematic client such as a client that is in very weak financial condition, a client that has very poor internal controls, a client that is perpetrating a fraud, or a client with poor management integrity, it may be difficult for the audit firm to provide a quality audit. For example, a client in weak financial condition may be unable to pay a reasonable audit fee, and so the audit firm may find itself in a position of not having enough budgeted audit hours to do a quality audit. Or a client with weak internal controls may be difficult to audit because of unreliable financial data. Similarly, a client perpetrating a fraud, or one with weak management integrity, may present financial information that is intentionally unreliable, and so again the audit may be difficult to conduct in a way that results in an accurate audit opinion. Given the importance of client acceptance and continuance decisions to audit quality, audit firms with strong cultures of quality place great emphasis on developing, maintaining, and monitoring systems of quality control that yield good decisions in this regard.

Why Might an Audit Firm Refuse to Continue Providing Services to a Client? The Case of Longtop Financial Technologies and Deloitte

Deloitte audited the financial statements of Longtop Financial Technologies (Longtop) both before and after the company's 2007 initial public offering. In May 2011, Deloitte resigned from the Longtop engagement, citing concerns about management fraud. The allegations are that Longtop's top management, including the chief operating officer, interfered with the audit confirmation process. In fact, there is currently widespread concern that significant collusion has been taking place between Chinese companies and their banks, including evidence that banks are signing false confirmations of their clients' cash accounts. The reason for the false confirmations is that the Chinese companies, including Longtop, had been recording fictitious revenues and fictitious inflows of cash to agree with the revenues. When Deloitte personnel confronted Longtop management, the auditors were subject to seizure of their audit workpapers and were faced with physical threats to try to prevent the auditors from leaving the property. Here is the resignation letter from Deloitte Shanghai to the Longtop Audit Committee on May 22, 2011:

BY EMAIL & BY REGISTERED MAIL
The Audit Committee
Longtop Financial Technologies Limited
No. 61 Wanghai Road, Xiamen Software Park
Xiamen, Fujian Province
People's Republic of China
Attention: Mr. Thomas Gurnee, Chairman of the Audit Committee

Dear Sirs,

Longtop Financial Technologies Limited (the "Company") and together with its subsidiaries (the "Group") Audit for the Year Ended 31 March 2011

We hereby give you formal notice of our resignation as auditor of the Company.

Background and significant issues encountered by Deloitte Touche Tohmatsu CPA Ltd. (China) ("Deloitte")

As part of the process for auditing the Company's financial statements for the year ended 31 March 2011, we determined that, in regard to bank confirmations, it was appropriate to perform follow up visits to certain banks. These audit steps were recently performed and identified a number of very serious defects including: statements by bank staff that their bank had no record of certain transactions; confirmation replies previously received were said to be false; significant differences in deposit balances reported by the bank staff compared with the amounts

identified in previously received confirmations (and in the books and records of the Group); and significant bank borrowings reported by bank staff not identified in previously received confirmations (and not recorded in the books and records of the Group).

In the light of this, a formal second round of bank confirmation was initiated on 17 May. Within hours however, as a result of intervention by the Company's officials including the Chief Operating Officer, the confirmation process was stopped amid serious and troubling new developments including: calls to banks by the Company asserting that Deloitte was not their auditor; seizure by the Company's staff of second round bank confirmation documentation on bank premises; threats to stop our staff leaving the Company premises unless they allowed the Company to retain our audit files then on the premises; and then seizure by the Company of certain of our working papers.

In that connection, we must insist that you promptly return our documents.

Then on 20 May the Chairman of the Company, Mr. Jia Xiao Gong called our Eastern Region Managing Partner, Mr. Paul Sin, and informed him in the course of their conversation that "there were fake revenue in the past so there were fake cash recorded on the books". Mr. Jia did not answer when questioned as to the extent and duration of the discrepancies. When asked who was involved, Mr. Jia answered: "senior management".

We bring these significant issues to your attention in the context of our responsibilities under Statement on Auditing Standards No. 99 "Consideration of Fraud in a Financial Statement Audit" issued by the American Institute of Certified Public Accountants.

Reasons for our resignation

The reasons for our resignation include: 1) the recently identified falsity of the Group's financial records in relation to cash at bank and loan balances (and also now seemingly in the sales revenue); 2) the deliberate interference by the management in our audit process; and 3) the unlawful detention of our audit files. These recent developments undermine our ability to rely on the representations of the management which is an essential element of the audit process; hence our resignation.

Prior periods' financial reports and our reports thereon

We have reached the conclusion that we are no longer able to place reliance on management

(Continued)

representations in relation to prior period financial reports. Accordingly, we request that the Company take immediate steps to make the necessary 8-K filing to state that continuing reliance should no longer be placed on our audit reports on the previous financial statements and moreover that we decline to be associated with any of the Company's financial communications during 2010 and 2011.

Our consent

We hereby consent to a copy of this letter being supplied to the SEC and the succeeding auditor to be appointed.

Section 10A of the Securities Exchange Act of 1934 (U.S.)

In our view, without providing any legal conclusion, the circumstances mentioned above could constitute illegal acts for purposes of Section 10A of the Securities Exchange Act of 1934. Accordingly, we remind the Board of its obligations under Section 10A of the Securities Exchange Act, including the notice requirements to the U.S. Securities and Exchange Commission. You may consider taking legal advice on this.

Yours faithfully,

/s/ Deloitte Touche Tohmatsu CPA Ltd.

c.c.: The Board of Directors

Postscript: Ultimately, the SEC delisted Longtop because the company failed to file its annual report for FYE March 31, 2011. Similar delistings occurred at other Chinese companies with stock traded in U.S. markets, including Advanced Battery Technologies, China MediaExpress Holdings, and Shengda Tech. These examples serve as a serious warning to audit firms as they enter high-risk international markets and as they make their client continuance decisions.

Source: Deloitte Shanghai, May 22, 2011.

SUMMARY AND NEXT STEPS

By now, you can appreciate the role that external auditing plays in providing independent assurance on financial and internal control information. You should have a basic understanding of the audit opinion formulation process and of the skills and knowledge needed by auditing professionals. Most notably, we hope that you recognize the importance of audit quality, understand the drivers of audit quality, and recognize the professional requirements that help achieve audit quality and minimize auditor exposure to lawsuits.

One of the big concerns for auditors in conducting a quality audit is the existence of fraud. In the next chapter, we provide examples of fraud and describe auditors' responsibilities for detecting fraud. We also discuss the many mechanisms that are in place to help prevent fraud and to help ensure that financial information is accurate and reliable.

SIGNIFICANT TERMS

Adverse opinion An adverse opinion should be expressed when the auditor believes that the financial statements taken as a whole are *not presented fairly* in conformity with GAAP or when the auditor believes that the client's internal control over financial reporting is not effective.

American Institute of Certified Public Accountants (AICPA) As the primary professional organization for CPAs, it has a number of committees to develop professional standards for the conduct of nonpublic company audits and other services performed by its members and to self-regulate the profession.

Audit quality Performing an audit in accordance with generally accepted auditing standards (GAAS) to provide reasonable assurance that the audited financial statements and related disclosures are presented in accordance with GAAP and providing assurance that those financial statements are not materially misstated whether due to errors or fraud.

Center for Audit Quality (CAQ) An organization affiliated with the AICPA that is dedicated to enhancing investor confidence and trust in the financial markets.

Client acceptance decision The process by which a new client is evaluated by the audit firm and individual engagement partner prior to being accepted into the audit firm's portfolio of clients.

Client continuance decision The process by which existing clients for which the audit firm provided services in the preceding period are evaluated by the audit firm and the individual engagement partner at the completion of the audit to determine whether the audit firm should continue to provide services again in the next period.

Committee of Sponsoring Organizations of the Treadway Commission (COSO) An organization that provides thought leadership and guidance on enterprise risk management, internal control, and fraud deterrence.

Concurring partner review Occurs when an audit partner not otherwise involved in the audit independently reviews each audit to make sure that documented evidence supports the audit opinion. Otherwise known as an engagement quality review.

Due professional care A standard of care expected to be demonstrated by a competent professional in his or her field of expertise, set by GAAS but supplemented in specific implementation instances by the standard of care expected by a reasonably prudent auditor.

Engagement letter A communication between the audit firm and the audit committee that states the scope of the work to be done on the audit so that there can be no doubt in the mind of the client, external auditor, or the court system as to the expectations agreed to by the external auditor and the client.

Engagement quality review Occurs when an audit partner not otherwise involved in the audit independently reviews each audit to make sure that documented evidence supports the audit opinion. Otherwise known as a concurring partner review.

Financial statement audit A systematic process of objectively obtaining evidence regarding assertions about economic actions and events to ascertain the degree of correspondence between those assertions and established criteria and communicating the results to interested users.

Generally accepted accounting principles (GAAP) GAAP refers to generally accepted accounting principles for financial reporting. Throughout the book we recognize that the criteria may be developed by either the FASB or the IASB. GAAP has general acceptance and provides criteria by which to assess the fairness of a financial statement presentation.

Generally accepted auditing standards (GAAS) GAAS refers to professional external auditing standards that are followed by auditors when conducting a financial statement audit. Throughout the book, when we refer to professional external auditing standards, we will use the term GAAS (generally accepted auditing standards). We recognize that GAAS are set by several bodies, including the AICPA, the IAASB, and the PCAOB.

Integrated audit   Type of audit provided when an external auditor is engaged to perform an audit of the effectiveness of internal control over financial reporting (the audit of internal control over financial reporting) that is integrated with an audit of the financial statements.

International Accounting Standards Board (IASB)   This organization issues International Financial Reporting Standards (IFRS) and is working to be the one provider of accounting standards around the world.

International Auditing and Assurance Standards Board (IAASB)   A part of the International Federation of Accountants that is responsible for issuing auditing and assurance standards. Its goal is to harmonize auditing standards on a global basis.

International Standards for Auditing (ISAs)   Standards issued by the IAASB for all auditors who are following international auditing standards.

Interoffice review   A review of one office of the audit firm by professionals from another office to assure that the policies and procedures established by the firm are being followed.

Professional skepticism   An attitude that includes a questioning mind and critical assessment of audit evidence.

Public Company Accounting Oversight Board (PCAOB)   A quasi-public board, appointed by the SEC, to provide oversight of the firms that audit public companies registered with the SEC. It has the authority to set auditing standards for the audits of public companies.

Sarbanes-Oxley Act of 2002   Broad legislation mandating new standard setting for audits of public companies and new standards for corporate governance.

Securities and Exchange Commission (SEC)   The governmental body with the oversight responsibility to ensure the proper and efficient operation of capital markets in the United States.

Unqualified audit report   The standard audit report that describes the auditor's work and communicates the auditor's opinion that the financial statements are fairly presented in accordance with GAAP.

TRUE/FALSE QUESTIONS

1-1   `LO 1`   When the auditor has no reservations about management's financial statements or internal controls, the audit opinion is said to be unqualified.

1-2   `LO 1`   Independence is referred to as the cornerstone of the auditing profession.

1-3   `LO 2`   The sole responsibility of management with regard to financial reporting involves preparing and presenting financial statements in accordance with the applicable financial reporting framework.

1-4   `LO 2`   The internal audit function is designed primarily to assist the external auditor in providing assurance to third-party users of the financial statements.

1-5   `LO 3`   The Big 4 audit firms are the only types of firms that conduct financial statement audits.

1-6 `LO 3` With regard to working in a team environment, larger audit firms typically have teams with more continuity and overlap across engagements, whereas smaller audit firms typically have multiple teams that typically disband after each engagement.

1-7 `LO 4` Congress passed the Sarbanes-Oxley Act of 2002 in response to a variety of major economic shocks during the early 2000s.

1-8 `LO 4` The AICPA sets auditing standards for auditors of non-public companies in the United States.

1-9 `LO 5` Audit quality is achieved when the audit is performed in accordance with GAAS and when it provides reasonable assurance that the financial statements have been presented in accordance with GAAP and are not materially misstated due to errors or fraud.

1-10 `LO 5` One of the key drivers of audit quality is the gross margin achieved by the audit firm and the ability of the engagement partner to maintain those margins over the duration of the audit engagement.

1-11 `LO 6` The three primary types of review programs include: (1) external inspections/peer reviews, (2) engagement quality reviews, and (3) interoffice reviews.

1-12 `LO 6` The engagement letter states the scope of the work to be done on the audit so that there should be no doubt in the mind of the client, external auditor, or the court system as to the expectations agreed to by the external auditor and the client.

1-13 `LO 7` Existing clients for which the audit firm provided services in the preceding period are evaluated by the audit firm and by the individual engagement partner at the completion of the audit to determine whether the audit firm should continue to provide services again in the next period; the process by which this evaluation occurs is called the client continuance decision.

1-14 `LO 7` Audit firms may discontinue serving a client because the client does not fit the profile or growth strategy of the audit firm.

MULTIPLE-CHOICE QUESTIONS

1-15 `LO 1` Which of the following factors does not create a demand for external audit services?
a. Potential bias by management in providing information.
b. Requirements of the Center for Audit Quality (CAQ).
c. Complexity of the accounting processing systems.
d. Remoteness between a user and the organization.

1-16 `LO 1` Which of the following expectations can users of the audit report reasonably expect with regard to the audited financial statements?
a. The financial statements include all financial disclosures desired by users.
b. The financial statements are presented fairly in accordance with GAAP.
c. The financial statements are free from all errors.
d. All of the above are reasonable expectations.
e. None of the above are reasonable expectations.

1-17 `LO 2` Which of the following parties are involved in preparing and auditing financial statements?
a. Management.
b. Audit committee.
c. Internal audit function.

    d. External auditor.

    e. All of the above.

1-18 **LO 2** Which of the following are the responsibilities of the external auditor in auditing financial statements?

    a. Maintaining internal controls and preparing financial reports.

    b. Providing internal assurance on internal control and financial reports.

    c. Providing internal oversight of the reporting process.

    d. All of the above.

    e. None of the above.

1-19 **LO 3** In which of the following categories do Big 4 audit firms operate?

    a. Sole-practitioner firms.

    b. Local firms.

    c. Regional firms.

    d. Multinational firms.

1-20 **LO 3** In terms of technical knowledge and expertise, which of the following should external auditors be able to do?

    a. Understand accounting and auditing authoritative literature.

    b. Develop industry and client-specific knowledge.

    c. Develop and apply computer skills.

    d. All of the above.

    e. None of the above.

1-21 **LO 4** The AICPA remains a valuable organization to the external auditing profession because of its continuing involvement in which of the following activities?

    a. The audit standard setting process for audits of publicly traded companies.

    b. Regulation and enforcement of the internal auditing profession.

    c. Education and administration of the CPA exam.

    d. Promulgation of financial accounting standards.

1-22 **LO 4** Which of the following organizations is the primary organization that performs inspections of registered external audit firms that audit public companies?

    a. PCAOB

    b. CAQ

    c. AICPA

    d. FASB

1-23 **LO 5** Audit quality involves which of the following?

    a. Performing an audit in accordance with GAAS to provide reasonable assurance that the audited financial statements and related disclosures are presented in accordance with GAAP and providing assurance that those financial statements are not materially misstated whether due to errors or fraud.

    b. Performing an audit in accordance with GAAP to provide reasonable assurance that the audited financial statements and related disclosures are presented in accordance with GAAS and providing assurance that those financial statements are not materially misstated whether due to errors or fraud.

    c. Performing an audit in accordance with GAAS to provide absolute assurance that the audited financial statements and related disclosures are presented in accordance with GAAP and providing assurance that those financial statements are not materially misstated whether due to errors or fraud.

d. Performing an audit in accordance with GAAS to provide reasonable assurance that the audited financial statements and related disclosures are presented in accordance with GAAP and providing assurance that those financial statements contain no misstatements due to errors or fraud.

1-24 `LO 5`   Which of the following factors is not a driver of audit quality as discussed by the FRC?
a. Audit firm culture.
b. Skills and personal qualities of client management.
c. Reliability and usefulness of audit reporting.
d. Factors outside the control of auditors.

1-25 `LO 6`   Which of the following is not a threat to auditor independence?
a. Self-review threat.
b. Advocacy threat.
c. Adverse interest threat.
d. Regulatory interest threat.

1-26 `LO 6`   The PCAOB performs external inspections of external audit firms registered to audit publicly traded companies. Which of the following statements is accurate regarding the timing of those inspections?
a. Inspections occur once a year for audit firms that conduct over 50 public clients in a given year.
b. Inspections occur once every three years for audit firms that conduct over 100 public clients in a given year.
c. Inspections occur once a year for audit firms that conduct over 100 public clients in a given year.
d. Inspections occur once every five years for audit firms that conduct over 50 public clients in a given year.

1-27 `LO 7`   With regard to client acceptance/continuance decisions, which of the following is false?
a. Client acceptance/continuance decisions are one part of the audit firm's overall portfolio management activities.
b. The primary driver of the client acceptance/continuance decision is the level of audit fees that can be charged to the client.
c. One can view an individual audit client as analogous to an individual stock in an investment portfolio.
d. Existing clients for which the audit firm provided services in the preceding period are evaluated by the audit firm and individual engagement partner at the completion of the audit to determine whether the audit firm should continue to provide services in the next period.

1-28 `LO 7`   Which of the following factors is an example of a risk relevant to the client continuance decision?
a. Client entity characteristics.
b. Independence risk factors.
c. Third party/due diligence risk factors.
d. All of the above.

REVIEW AND SHORT CASE QUESTIONS

NOTE: Completing Review and Short Case Questions does not require the student to reference additional resources and materials.

1-29 `LO 1`   What is the objective of external auditing? Describe the role of external auditing in meeting society's demands for unbiased financial and internal control information.

1-30 `LO 1`   What is the special function that auditors perform? Whom does the external auditing profession serve in performing this special function?

NOTE: For the remaining problems, we make special note of those addressing fraud, international issues, professional skepticism, and ethics.

1-31 LO 1 What factors create a demand for an independent external audit?

1-32 LO 1 How does an audit enhance the quality of financial statements and management's reports on internal control? Does an audit guarantee a fair presentation of a company's financial statements?

1-33 LO 1 Why is it important that users perceive auditors to be independent? What is the difference between *being independent in fact* and *being independent in appearance*?

1-34 LO 1 It has been stated that auditors must be independent because audited financial statements must serve the needs of a wide variety of users. If the auditor were to favor one group, such as existing shareholders, there might be a bias against another group, such as prospective investors.
a. What steps has the external auditing profession taken to minimize potential bias toward important users and thereby encourage auditor independence?
b. Refer to *Exhibit 1.2* and describe the users of audited financial statements and the decisions that they need to make based on reliable information.

ETHICS

1-35 LO 1 Refer to the *Auditing in Practice* feature "Why Is Owning Stock in an Audit Client Unacceptable?" and answer the following:
a. Describe the unethical actions of Susan Birkert.
b. Compare and contrast the ideas of *independence in fact* and *independence in appearance* in the context of this case.
c. Do you think that Susan's punishments were appropriate? Defend your answer.

1-36 LO 1, 3 McIver's Swimwear Distributors is a relatively small, privately held swimwear distribution company that operates in the Midwest and handles several product lines, including footwear, clothing, and swimteam supplies. It sells directly to swimwear shops and does not sell to the big retailers. It has approximately $8 million in sales and wants to grow at about 20% per year for the next five years. It is also considering a takeover or a merger with another swimwear distributorship that operates in the same region.
a. Explain why management might want an independent audit of its financial statements.
b. What are the factors that McIver's might consider in deciding whether to seek an audit from a large national audit firm, a regional audit firm, or a local firm?
c. What types of users might be interested in McIver's financial results?

1-37 LO 2 Refer to *Exhibit 1.4* and identify the primary parties involved in preparing and auditing financial statements, and briefly describe their roles.

1-38 LO 3 List the various types of audit service providers. What types of audit firms are best suited for auditing large multinational companies versus small, regional companies that are not publicly traded?

1-39 LO 3 What types of skills and knowledge are needed by professionals entering the external auditing profession?

1-40 LO 3 Refer to the *Auditing in Practice* feature "Should I Work for a Large or a Small Audit Firm?". Compare and contrast the workplace environments at larger versus smaller audit firms. Explain which type of environment you think would best fit your preferences.

INTERNATIONAL

1-41 **LO 4** Briefly describe the various roles of the following organizations that affect the external auditing profession and the nature of those effects:
a. Congress
b. Public Company Accounting Oversight Board (PCAOB)
c. Securities and Exchange Commission (SEC)
d. American Institute of Certified Public Accountants (AICPA)
e. Center for Audit Quality (CAQ)
f. International Auditing and Assurance Standards Board (IAASB)
g. Committee of Sponsoring Organizations of the Treadway Commission (COSO)

1-42 **LO 4** Distinguish between the roles of the PCAOB and the AICPA in (a) setting audit standards, (b) performing quality-control reviews of member firms, and (c) setting accounting standards.

1-43 **LO 4** The PCAOB has the authority to set auditing standards for all audits of public companies registered in the United States. The AICPA continues to set auditing standards for nonpublic companies through its Auditing Standards Board (ASB).
a. What are the pros and cons of having potentially different auditing standards for both public and nonpublic companies?
b. In what ways might you expect auditing standards for audits of nonpublic companies to differ from the standards for public companies?

1-44 **LO 4** Refer to the *Auditing in Practice* feature "Who Are the Leaders of the PCAOB?". Why is there a requirement that no more than two of the board members are CPAs?

INTERNATIONAL

1-45 **LO 5** Define audit quality. What are the five primary drivers of audit quality as articulated by the Financial Reporting Council's *Audit Quality Framework*?

INTERNATIONAL

1-46 **LO 5** Refer to *Exhibit 1.5*, the *Audit Quality Framework*.
a. How does positive audit firm culture, along with expert skills and qualities of both the audit partner and the engagement team, affect audit quality?
b. What factors outside the control of the external auditor affect audit quality?
c. Why do users care about audit quality? Are there certain users who might care more about audit quality than others? Explain.

1-47 **LO 6** Auditing standards emphasize the importance of independence. Explain why independence is often considered the cornerstone of the auditing profession. Explain why independence issues were a primary concern of Congress when it developed the Sarbanes-Oxley Act.

1-48 **LO 6** Describe the following requirements that help achieve audit quality and thereby help minimize the exposure of external auditors to lawsuits:
a. Maintaining auditor independence
b. Participating in review programs
c. Issuing engagement letters
d. Evaluating the audit firm's limitations
e. Maintaining high-quality audit documentation

1-49 **LO 6**   Describe the seven threats to independence articulated in the AICPA's independence conceptual framework.

1-50 **LO 6**   Describe the safeguards to independence articulated in the AICPA's independence conceptual framework, and provide examples of each.

1-51 **LO 7**   Describe how individual audit clients are both similar to and different from individual stocks in an investment portfolio. What is the difference between a client acceptance decision and a client continuance decision? In which decision-making setting does the auditor have the benefit of deeper knowledge of the client?

1-52 **LO 7**   Refer to *Exhibit 1.6*. What are the three possibilities that may happen to the clients in the audit firm's beginning-of-period client portfolio? What are the two main factors that auditors consider in making client acceptance and continuance decisions?

1-53 **LO 7**   The following are the key types of risk that audit firms consider when they make client acceptance and continuance decisions. Provide examples of each of these types of risk.
- Client entity characteristics
- Independence risk factors
- Third-party/due diligence risk factors
- Quantitative risk factors
- Qualitative risk factors
- Entity organizational or governance risks
- Financial reporting risks

FRAUD FOCUS: CONTEMPORARY AND HISTORICAL CASES

FRAUD

INTERNATIONAL

Longtop Financial Technologies and Deloitte
1-54 **(LO 7)**   Refer to the *Focus on Fraud* feature "Why Might an Audit Firm Refuse to Continue Providing Services to a Client? The Case of Longtop Financial Technologies and Deloitte". Read the e-mail that Deloitte sent to Longtop management describing their reasons for resigning from the engagement. Briefly describe Deloitte's main complaints. Deloitte and other large audit firms would like very much to operate in the China market. What risks do you think might be unique to accepting and retaining clients in a foreign country that is not necessarily supportive of U.S. interests?

INTERNATIONAL

PROFESSIONAL SKEPTICISM

FRAUD

PCAOB
1-55 **(LO 1, 3, 5, 6, 7)**   Refer to the *Professional Judgment in Context* feature at the outset of the chapter, which discusses the PCAOB enforcement action related to the audit of Alloy Steel International. As you will recall, Robert Forbes was the audit partner in charge of the Alloy Steel engagement, and he made several critical mistakes that adversely affected audit quality.
a. What is the objective of external auditing, and how did Forbes' and Bentley's actions fail to achieve that objective?
b. Why did Alloy Steel require an independent audit on its financial statements?
c. Which parties are likely users of Alloy Steel's financial statements? How might they have been adversely affected by Forbes' actions?
d. In most situations, we would worry about fraud in terms of the client, not the audit firm. In this case, Robert Forbes essentially committed fraud in that he signed the audit report

knowing that he did not do the work required of him. What skills and knowledge were required to do a quality audit of Alloy Steel's financial statements? How did the individuals who actually performed the audit work on the Alloy Steel engagement fail in this regard?

e. Refer to *Exhibit 1.5*. Explain how the facts in this case relate to each of the drivers of audit quality identified in *Exhibit 1.5*. If a particular driver is not applicable to this case, state why.

f. Should Bentleys and Forbes have agreed to conduct this audit in the first place?

FRAUD

PROFESSIONAL SKEPTICISM

1-56

Enron and Arthur Andersen LLP
(LO 1, 2, 5)

Enron was an energy company based in Houston, Texas, that made energy trades. It was formed in 1985 with the merger of Houston Natural Gas and InterNorth. After an aggressive expansion plan that involved risky financing transactions outside the original, fundamental business model of the company, Enron was billions of dollars in debt. Enron concealed this debt through hidden transactions with related-party partnerships, fraudulent accounting, and illegal loans. Enron is considered to be one of the largest and most important financial reporting frauds in history. The company ultimately filed for bankruptcy in 2001.

One of the reasons that Enron was able to get away with the fraud for some time was because of a low-quality audit by its external audit firm, Arthur Andersen. Prior to the failure of Enron in 2001, Arthur Andersen had been involved in two other major audit failures. These failed audits, related to frauds at Waste Management (1996) and Sunbeam (1997), should have raised red flags for management and any outside observers that some of the audit firm's internal quality assurance processes were not working. When the federal government uncovered Enron's fraud along with the string of poor quality audits at Arthur Andersen, the government forced the audit firm out of business.

Internal documentation at Arthur Andersen showed that there were conflicts between the auditors and the audit committee of Enron, and that even though there were many individuals concerned about the accounting and disclosure practices at Enron, nothing was done by Andersen to report these problems. In fact, the leading partner on the audit, David Duncan, actively worked to ensure that Enron's fraudulent financial reporting went uncovered. It appears that Duncan was motivated by the fact that Arthur Andersen was earning enormous consulting fees on the Enron engagement; Enron was a hugely important client for him personally and for the Houston office of Arthur Andersen. Together, these conflicts of interest clouded his independent judgment and professional skepticism.

Around the time that Enron declared bankruptcy in late 2001, Arthur Andersen personnel in the Houston office began aggressively destroying documentation relating to the Enron engagement. This action enabled the federal government to file charges against Arthur Andersen that ultimately led to the downfall of the audit firm. The Sarbanes-Oxley Act of 2002 was enacted partially in response to the Enron fraud and the revelation of the poor audit conducted by Arthur Andersen, which is why this case is of particular historical relevance. Considering these facts, answer the following questions:

a. Members of Enron management were the individuals who perpetrated the financial statement fraud. Given this, why do you think the auditors were held responsible when they are not the ones actually making the fraudulent journal entries?

b. Explain why the consulting fees and importance of Enron to David Duncan and the Houston office of Arthur Andersen might have affected Duncan's independence, and thus the quality of the audits he supervised.

c. Describe the likely users of Enron's audited financial statements. How were these various user groups likely affected by the fraud?

d. How might the sequential list of frauds perpetrated by Arthur Andersen clients (Waste Management, Sunbeam, and finally Enron) have affected the decision by the SEC and federal prosecutors to aggressively seek Arthur Andersen's legal demise?

APPLICATION ACTIVITIES

NOTE: Completing Application Activities requires students to reference additional resources and materials.

PCAOB

1-57 **(LO 4)**   Access the PCAOB web site at *www.pcaobus.org*.

a. List the members of the Board and describe their backgrounds. What are their professional qualifications?

b. Identify the most recent auditing standard issued by the PCAOB. Describe the nature of the standard and discuss the reason that the Board issued the standard.

AICPA

1-58 **(LO 4)**   Access information about the Auditing Standards Board on the AICPA web site at *www.aicpa.org*.

a. Identify the members of the Board and describe their backgrounds. What are their professional qualifications?

b. Identify the most recent auditing standard issued by the AICPA. Describe the nature of the standard and discuss the reason(s) that the Board issued the standard.

IAASB

INTERNATIONAL   **1-59** **(LO 4)**   Access the IAASB web site at *www.ifac.org/auditing-assurance*.

a. List the members of the Board and describe their backgrounds. What are their professional qualifications?

b. Identify the most recent auditing standard issued by the IAASB. Describe the nature of the standard and discuss the reason(s) that the Board issued the standard.

SEC

FRAUD   **1-60** **(LO 4)**   Access the SEC web site at *http://www.sec.gov*.

a. Refer to the *Focus on Fraud* feature "Locating Enforcement Actions on the SEC Web Site." Follow the directions and locate an enforcement action taken against an audit firm or an external auditor in the recent past.

b. Identify the most recent Staff Accounting Bulletin that provides guidance to the profession, and describe the guidance given.

PCAOB

PROFESSIONAL SKEPTICISM   **1-61** **(LO 1, 4, 5)**   In April 2010, the PCAOB issued a disciplinary order instituting disciplinary proceedings, making findings, and imposing sanctions in the case of Robert T. Taylor, CPA (both the firm and the individual auditor). The order can be found in

PCAOB Release No. 105–2010–006 at *www.pcaobus.org*. (*Hint*: Search in the "Enforcement" section of the web site, then go to "settled disciplinary orders," then scroll down to see the disciplinary order against Taylor.) Review the PCAOB web site, access this release, and answer the following questions.

a. What is the PCAOB and what authority does it have to issue disciplinary orders and impose sanctions?
b. What is the PCAOB's source of potential violations of law or PCAOB rules?
c. The order in the case of Robert T. Taylor recognizes that PCAOB standards require that an auditor exercise due professional care, exercise professional skepticism, and obtain sufficient evidence on which to base an opinion on the financial statements. Describe instances in which the respondents in the order did not adhere to these requirements, resulting in low audit quality.
d. What sanctions were imposed in this case? Do the sanctions seem appropriate?

ACADEMIC RESEARCH CASES

NOTE: Completing Academic Research Cases requires students to reference additional resources and materials.

SEARCH HINT

It is easy to locate academic research articles! Use a search engine such as Google Scholar or an electronic research platform such as ABI Inform, and search using the author names and part of the article title.

1-62 **LO 3** Locate and read the article listed below and answer the following questions:

Almer, E. D., M. Lightbody, L. E. Single, and B. Vigilante. 2011. New leadership tracks in accounting firms: an alternative to the partnership. *Current Issues in Auditing* 5 (1): A39–A53.

a. What is the issue being addressed in the paper?
b. What are the findings of the paper?
c. Why is this paper important to auditors, and what are the implications of this paper for the auditing profession?
d. Describe the research methodology used as a basis for the conclusions.
e. Describe any limitations of the research.

1-63 **LO 5, 6** Locate and read the article listed below and answer the following questions:

Lo´pez, D. M. and G. F. Peters. 2012. The effect of workload compression on audit quality. *Auditing: A Journal of Practice & Theory* (31) 4: 139–165.

a. What is the issue being addressed in the paper?
b. What are the findings of the paper?
c. Why is this paper important to auditors, and what are the implications of this paper for the auditing profession?
d. Describe the research methodology used as a basis for the conclusions.
e. Describe any limitations of the research.

2

The Auditor's Responsibilities Regarding Fraud and Mechanisms to Address Fraud: Regulation and Corporate Governance

CHAPTER OVERVIEW AND LEARNING OBJECTIVES

When conducting a quality audit, auditors are particularly concerned about the potential occurrence of fraud. There are various types of fraud and many motivations, opportunities, and rationalizations explaining why people perpetrate fraud. In this chapter, we provide examples of both historical and more recent fraud schemes, and we discuss implications for auditors of recent regulations designed to prevent and detect fraud. We then describe corporate governance, a process by which the owners and creditors of an organization exert control through requiring accountability for the resources entrusted to the organization. We also explain how effective corporate governance can reduce fraud risk.

Through studying this chapter, you will be able to achieve these learning objectives:

1. Define the various types of fraud that affect organizations.

2. Define the fraud triangle and describe its three elements.

3. Describe implications for auditors of recent fraudulent financial reporting cases and the 2010 COSO report on fraud.

4. Discuss auditors' fraud-related responsibilities and users' related expectations.

5. Explain how various requirements in the Sarbanes-Oxley Act of 2002 are designed to help prevent the types of frauds perpetrated in the late 1990s and early 2000s.

6. Define corporate governance, identify the parties involved, and describe their respective activities.

THE AUDIT OPINION FORMULATION PROCESS

I. Making Client Acceptance and Continuance Decisions

Chapter 1

II. Performing Risk Assessment

Chapters 3, 7, and 9–13

III. Obtaining Evidence About Internal Control Operating Effectiveness

Chapters 8–13 and 16

IV. Obtaining Substantive Evidence About Accounts, Disclosures and Assertions

Chapters 8–13 and 16

V. Completing the Audit and Making Reporting Decisions

Chapters 14 and 15

The Auditing Profession, the Risk of Fraud and Mechanisms to Address Fraud: Regulation, Corporate Governance, and Audit Quality

Chapters 1 and 2

Professional Liability and the Need for Quality Auditor Judgments and Ethical Decisions

Chapter 4

The Audit Opinion Formulation Process and a Framework for Obtaining Audit Evidence

Chapters 5 and 6

PROFESSIONAL JUDGMENT IN CONTEXT
Examples of Fraud in Organizations

Milwaukee-based Koss Corporation reported an embezzlement of funds of approximately $31 million orchestrated by its chief financial officer (CFO) over a five-year period when the company's reported earnings were only $26 million. The CFO used the funds for personal goods, such as expensive coats, jewelry, and other personal items, which were mostly kept in storage facilities. Interestingly, the CFO was neither an accountant nor a certified public accountant (CPA); the chief executive officer (CEO) had a college degree in anthropology; most of the board members had served on the board for 20–30 years; and the company made highly technical products that were in very competitive markets.

In another fraud, a senior benefits executive at Hitachi America, Inc. diverted approximately $8 million from Hitachi by creating a separate bank account that included the Hitachi name, but that was controlled by him. The funds that were diverted included payments from health providers and insurance companies intended for the Hitachi's employee benefit plans. The executive used the

$8 million in the new account to purchase an expensive vacation home and a new Lexus automobile, among other items.

In addition to outright thefts, fraud can also involve fraudulent financial reporting. For example, WorldCom orchestrated its fraud, in part, by capitalizing items that should have been recorded as expenses, thereby increasing current-period income. Charter Communications inflated revenue by selling control boxes back to its supplier and then repurchasing them later. Dell, Inc. admitted to manipulating its reported income by not accurately disclosing payments that it received from computer-chip maker Intel. The payments were in exchange for Dell's agreement not to use chips from Intel's rival, Advanced Micro Devices. These payments accounted for 76% of Dell's operating income in early 2007. Dell also covered earnings shortages by dipping into reserves and claimed that the seemingly strong financial results were due to high quality management and efficient operations. In 2014, the Securities and Exchange Commission

(SEC) alleged that Diamond Foods engaged in financial reporting fraud to overstate the company's income by delaying the recording of costs paid to the company's walnut growers. Diamond Foods was facing significant gross margin declines because of steep price increases for the company's main raw material, and by delaying the recording of costs the company was able to exceed analysts' earnings expectations. In an international setting, Sino-Forest fraudulently asserted that it owned vast amounts of timberlands in China, when in fact the company did not have sufficient proof of ownership. The Ontario Securities Commission began investigating allegations of the fraud in 2012, and the company ultimately was delisted and entered bankruptcy shortly thereafter.

As you read through this chapter, consider the following questions:

- What are the major types of fraud? What are the major characteristics of fraud that auditors should consider? (LO 1, 2)
- To what extent should the auditor be responsible for identifying the risk of fraud, and then determining whether material fraud actually exists? (LO 4)
- How can a quality audit prevent or detect various types of frauds? (LO 4)
- How can society as a whole, and the external auditing profession in particular, act to prevent and detect fraud? (LO 4, 5, 6)
- What is corporate governance, and how can effective corporate governance prevent these types of frauds? (LO 6)

Fraud Defined

LO 1 Define the various types of fraud that affect organizations.

Fraud is an intentional act involving the use of deception that results in a misstatement of the financial statements. Two types of misstatements are relevant to auditors' consideration of fraud: (a) misstatements arising from misappropriation of assets and (b) misstatements arising from fraudulent financial reporting. Intent to deceive is what distinguishes fraud from errors. Auditors routinely find financial errors in their clients' books, but errors are *not* intentional.

Misstatements Arising from Misappropriation of Assets

Asset misappropriation occurs when a perpetrator steals or misuses an organization's assets. Asset misappropriations are the dominant fraud scheme perpetrated against small businesses, and the perpetrators are usually employees. Asset misappropriations include embezzling cash receipts, stealing assets, or causing the organization to pay for goods or services that the organization did not receive. Asset misappropriation commonly occurs when employees:

- Gain access to cash and manipulate accounts to cover up cash thefts
- Manipulate cash disbursements through fake organizations
- Steal inventory or other assets and manipulate the financial records to cover up the fraud

An important contemporary example of asset misappropriation is the famous Madoff Ponzi scheme, which *Exhibit 2.1* describes.

Misstatements Arising from Fraudulent Financial Reporting

The intentional manipulation of reported financial results to misstate the economic condition of the organization is called **fraudulent financial reporting**. The *Focus on Fraud* feature "The Great Salad Oil Swindle of 1963" is a classic example of fraudulent financial reporting. The perpetrator of such a fraud generally seeks gain through the rise in stock price and the commensurate increase in personal wealth. Sometimes the perpetrator does not seek direct personal gain, but instead uses the fraudulent financial reporting to "help" the organization avoid bankruptcy or to avoid some

| EXHIBIT **2.1** | The Bernie Madoff Ponzi Scheme |

A **Ponzi scheme** occurs when the deposits of current investors are used to pay returns on the deposits of previous investors; no real investment is happening. A Ponzi scheme will collapse if new investors do not join, or their deposits are too small to pay an adequate return to previous investors. Ponzi schemes are based on two fundamentals: trust and greed. The trust comes from building a relationship with the potential victims. Usually, in Ponzi schemes, the person perpetrating the fraud has gained trust through (a) direct, observable actions by others, (b) professional or other affiliations, or (c) through personal references by others. The greed comes from the investors who see an opportunity to obtain higher than usual returns, and because the trust is there, they do not perform their normal due diligence. Both trust and greed were prevalent in the Madoff scheme.

In March 2009, Madoff pleaded guilty to eleven federal crimes and admitted to turning his wealth management business into a massive Ponzi scheme that defrauded thousands of investors of billions of dollars. Madoff said he began the Ponzi scheme in the early 1990s. However, federal investigators believe the fraud began as early as the 1980s and that the investment operation may never have been legitimate. The amount missing from client accounts, including fabricated gains, was almost $65 billion. On June 29, 2009, Madoff was sentenced to 150 years in prison, the maximum allowed.

Madoff built a veil of trust by running a legitimate brokerage firm, and at one time was the chair of NASDAQ. He often appeared on CNBC talking about the securities industry. Madoff took advantage of his unique ties to the investment community to encourage further investment, and he always sold the idea of an investment into his company as one of "special privilege." He conducted the scheme by hiring individuals who were paid commissions to bring in more investors. Obviously, the scheme can only work as long as the funds brought into the scheme in future years are sufficient to continue to pay all the previous investors. Ponzi schemes eventually become too big and collapse. However, until the collapse, Madoff led an extremely lavish lifestyle.

Madoff conducted the scheme by keeping all of the transactions off his formal books. He employed a CPA firm to audit the books, but the firm consisted of only one employee and there is no indication that the CPA firm ever visited Madoff's offices or that any real audit was actually performed. However, note that the investors never asked for such audit reports. This is where the importance of greed plays a part. The investors felt they were part of something special, and they enjoyed earning high investment returns. They trusted Madoff, so they let down their guard by not asking for typical due diligence information of which an external audit is an important part.

Although not verified, a rumor (as reported on a CNBC Primetime Special) alleges that Madoff chose to surrender and plead guilty because one of the investors was with the Russian mob and Madoff feared for both his life and that of his sons. Madoff is currently serving his life sentence in federal prison, and one of his sons committed suicide two years after the fraud was revealed. During the time of this fraud, the Public Company Accounting Oversight Board (PCAOB) did not require that hedge funds like Madoff's be audited by audit firms registered with the PCAOB. Following the Madoff fraud, in July 2010 Congress gave the PCAOB oversight of the audits of SEC-registered brokers and dealers. Auditors of broker-dealers must now be registered with and inspected by the PCAOB, and the PCAOB sets standards for audits of broker-dealers.

other negative financial outcome. Three common ways in which fraudulent financial reporting can take place include:

1. Manipulation, falsification, or alteration of accounting records or supporting documents
2. Misrepresentation or omission of events, transactions, or other significant information
3. Intentional misapplication of accounting principles

Common types of fraudulent financial reporting include:

- Improper revenue recognition
- Improper deferral of costs and expenses
- Improper asset valuation

The Great Salad Oil Swindle of 1963

FOCUS on **FRAUD**

The Great Salad Oil Swindle was one of the first modern large-scale frauds involving financial reporting. It was perpetrated by Allied Crude Vegetable Oil in New Jersey. The concept was simple: The company could overstate its financial position by claiming that it had more inventory than it actually had. Overstated assets provide the company the opportunity to understate expenses and to overstate income. The fraud ultimately cost creditors and suppliers about $150 million (over 1 billion in current dollars).

The fraud was fairly simple. The company stored salad oil in large tanks. It issued numerous receipts all showing that it owned a large amount of salad oil inventory. The auditor did observe part of the inventory, but did so by checking the various tanks one after another. The company accomplished the fraud by doing the following:

- First, it filled the tanks with a large inside container of water.
- Second, it created an outer layer with salad oil, so if the auditor checked the oil from an opening on top, the auditor would find oil.
- Third, the company pumped the oil underground from one tank to another in anticipation of the auditor's planned inspection route.

This is a historically relevant fraud and has practical application today, because fraud perpetrators continue to use similar types of inventory manipulation to commit fraud.

- Concealed liabilities
- Misrepresentations or omissions in financial statement footnotes of Management Discussion and Analysis (MD&A)

The Fraud Triangle

LO 2 Define the fraud triangle and describe its three elements.

The term **fraud triangle** was introduced by career criminologist Don Cressey in the 1950s. Cressey identified three factors that are generally present when fraud occurs. Research has reinforced the validity of the fraud triangle.

The three elements of the fraud triangle, as shown in *Exhibit 2.2*, include:

- Incentive to commit fraud
- Opportunity to commit and conceal the fraud
- Rationalization—the mind-set of the fraudster to justify committing the fraud

Factors associated with these elements are referred to as fraud risk factors or **red flags**.

EXHIBIT **2.2**   The Fraud Triangle

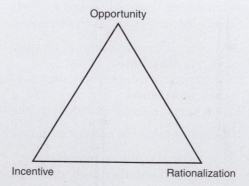

We illustrate the fraud triangle with a simple example from a fraud that took place in a construction company. The company did paving, sewer, and gutter work. It started small but grew to about $30 million in annual revenue. The construction work was performed at various locations throughout Michigan and Colorado. The company often purchased supplies at the job location, which were signed for by a construction employee and forwarded to the accountant for payment. The company had one accountant, but the president of the company approved all payments and formally signed off on them. When the president retired, his son replaced him, and the son spent more time growing the paving business than on accounting. He trusted the accountant because of the work the accountant had done for his father; therefore, he spent considerably less time in reviewing and signing off on payments than his father had done.

Now consider how the fraud triangle worked in this case. The essence of the fraud was that the accountant prepared bogus invoices for a bogus vendor, set the account up in his name, and prepared receiving slips and purchase orders to gain approval for the payments. First, what were the *incentives* for the fraud? Like many similar situations, the accountant faced considerable personal financial problems, mostly associated with taking care of his elderly parents, who had unpaid medical bills. Second, because the new president no longer reviewed items for payment, the *opportunity* (deficiencies in controls) presented itself. Third, the *rationalization* was a little more complex. Like most frauds, the fraudster thought that it would be a one-time extra payment to get him over the difficult times, and like most frauds, when the fraud was not detected, there was a further opportunity to grow it. The other part of the rationalization was more subtle. When the new president furnished all of the vice-presidents and job supervisors with new pickup trucks, the accountant did not receive one, nor did he receive a very substantial bonus, as compared to the job superintendents. The accountant felt that the amount of money he was taking was no different than what the job superintendents and vice-presidents were getting. In other words, he rationalized his actions to himself by believing that he "deserved" the payments.

When the auditor starts to consider the likelihood of fraud—either through misappropriation of assets or through fraudulent financial reporting—the auditor should start with consideration of the three elements of the triangle.

Incentives or Pressures to Commit Fraud

The audit team should consider the incentives or pressures to commit fraud on each engagement, including the most likely areas in which fraud might take place. These incentives include the following for fraudulent financial reporting:

- Management compensation schemes
- Other financial pressures for either improved earnings or an improved balance sheet
- Debt covenants
- Pending retirement or stock option expirations
- Personal wealth tied to either financial results or survival of the company
- Greed—for example, the backdating of stock options was performed by individuals who already had millions of dollars of wealth through stock

Incentives relating to asset misappropriation include:

- Personal factors, such as severe financial difficulties
- Pressure from family, friends, or the culture to live a more lavish lifestyle than one's personal earnings enable
- Addictions to gambling or drugs

Opportunities to Commit Fraud

One of the most fundamental and consistent findings in fraud research is that there must be some opportunity for fraud to be committed. Although this may sound obvious—that is, "everyone has an opportunity to commit fraud"—it really conveys much more. It means that not only an opportunity exists but either there is a lack of controls or the complexities associated with a transaction are such that the perpetrator assesses the risk of being caught as low. Some of the opportunities to commit fraud that the auditor should consider include the following:

- Significant related-party transactions
- A company's industry position, such as the ability to dictate terms or conditions to suppliers or customers that might allow individuals to structure fraudulent transactions
- Management's inconsistency involving subjective judgments regarding assets or accounting estimates
- Simple transactions that are made complex through an unusual recording process
- Complex or difficult-to-understand transactions, such as financial derivatives or special-purpose entities
- Ineffective monitoring of management by the board, either because the board of directors is not independent or effective, or because there is a domineering manager
- Complex or unstable organizational structure
- Weak or nonexistent internal controls, especially a lack of segregation of duties

Rationalizing the Fraud

Rationalization is a crucial component in most frauds. Rationalization involves a person reconciling unlawful or unethical behavior, such as stealing, with the commonly accepted notions of decency and trust. For fraudulent financial reporting, the rationalization can range from "saving the company" to personal greed and includes thoughts such as:

- This is a one-time thing to get us through the current crisis and survive until things get better.
- Everybody cheats on the financial statements a little; we are just playing the same game.
- We will be in violation of all of our debt covenants unless we find a way to get this debt off the financial statements.
- We need a higher stock price to acquire company XYZ, or to keep our employees through stock options, and so forth.

For asset misappropriation, personal rationalizations often revolve around mistreatment by the organization or a sense of entitlement (such as, "the company owes me!") by the individual perpetrating the fraud. Following are some common rationalizations for asset misappropriation:

- Fraud is justified to save a family member or loved one from financial crisis.
- I will lose everything (family, home, car, and so on) if I don't take the money.
- No help is available from outside.
- This is "borrowing," and I intend to pay the stolen money back at some point.
- Something is owed by the organization because others are treated better.
- I simply do not care about the consequences of my actions or of accepted notions of decency and trust; I have to look out for myself.

Recent History of Fraudulent Financial Reporting

LO 3 Describe implications for auditors of recent fraudulent financial reporting cases and the 2010 COSO report on fraud.

We now turn to a discussion of recent frauds, their implications for external auditors, a report by the Committee of Sponsoring Organizations of the Treadway Commission (COSO) on the general characteristics of major financial reporting frauds, and a detailed discussion of the Enron fraud.

Examples of Recent Frauds and Implications for External Auditors

Exhibit 2.3 contains examples of fraudulent financial reporting in the recent past. Of course, there are many more frauds that were discovered during this time; this is a glimpse of a few notable instances.

EXHIBIT 2.3	Examples of Recent Fraudulent Financial Reporting

Company	Nature of the Fraud
Enron (2001)	Considered by many to be one of the most significant frauds of the early 2000s, Enron was initially a utility company that management converted into an energy trading company. When energy trades went bad, management covered up financial problems by: • Shifting debt to off–balance sheet special entities • Recognizing revenue on impaired assets by selling them to special-purpose entities that they controlled • Engaging in round-tripping trades, which are trades that eventually found the assets returning to Enron after initially recognizing sales and profits • Numerous other related-party transactions
WorldCom (2002)	In what would end in one of the largest bankruptcies of all time, WorldCom was the second-largest U.S. long-distance phone company (after AT&T). The company pursued an aggressive growth strategy of acquiring other telecommunications companies. When the financial results of these acquisitions faltered, management decreased expenses and increased revenues through the following: • Recording bartered transactions as sales; for example, trading the right to use lines in one part of the world to similar rights to another part of the world • Using restructuring reserves established through acquisitions to decrease expenses; for example, over-accruing reserves upon acquiring a company and later "releasing" those reserves to decrease expenses of future periods • Capitalizing line costs (rentals paid to other phone companies) rather than expensing them as would have been appropriate
Parmalat (2003)	Parmalat is an Italian multinational company specializing in milk, fruit juice, and other food products. In the late 1990s, the company acquired various international subsidiaries and funded the acquisitions with debt. Ultimately, the fraud led to the largest bankruptcy in Europe. The company siphoned cash from subsidiaries through a complex scheme that: • Overstated cash and included the false recording of cash ostensibly held at major banks • Understated debt by entering into complex transactions with off-shore subsidiaries in tax-haven places such as countries in the Caribbean
HealthSouth (2003)	HealthSouth runs the largest group of inpatient rehabilitation hospitals in the United States. Top management directed company employees to grossly exaggerate earnings in order to meet shareholder and analyst expectations. A wide variety of schemes were used, including: • Billing group psychiatric sessions as individual sessions; for example, with ten people in a group session, billing for ten individual sessions instead of one group session • Using adjusted journal entries to both reduce expenses and enhance revenues

(continued)

EXHIBIT **2.3**   Examples of Recent Fraudulent Financial Reporting (*continued*)

Company	Nature of the Fraud
Dell (2005)	Dell is a U.S. computer maker that ultimately was forced to pay the SEC $100 million to settle fraud charges against the company. The fraud included various disclosure inaccuracies, including: • Misleading investors by miscategorizing large payments from Intel, which were essentially bribes to ensure that Dell would not use central processing units manufactured by Intel's main rival • Misrepresenting the Intel payments as involving operations, enabling the company to meet its earnings targets • Failing to disclose the true reason for the company's profitability declines that occurred after Intel refused to continue making the payments
Koss Corp. (2009)	Koss Corporation is a U.S. headphone manufacturer. The CFO misappropriated approximately $31 million of funds for her personal use during a period of time in which reported earnings was $26 million. Ultimately, she had to pay $34 million in restitution and was given an eleven-year prison sentence. She perpetrated the fraud through a process consisting of: • Intimidation of lower-level employees • Sole approval for large expenditures made through American Express and other corporate credit cards • Lack of supervisory review and approval by the CEO • Lack of audit committee oversight • Lack of an effective internal audit function
Olympus (2011)	Olympus is a large multinational manufacturer involved in the medical, life science, industrial, and imaging industries. Its top-level executives and boards: • Concealed large losses related to securities investments for over two decades • Switched audit firms during the period because company management clashed with their external auditor over accounting issues • Committed fraud, which was eventually revealed when the company's president was fired after discovering and objecting to accounting irregularities
Longtop Financial Technologies (2011)	Longtop was the first Chinese software company to be listed on the New York Stock Exchange (NYSE) and was the leading software development provider in the financial services industry in that country. This fraud highlighted the risks that investors face when investing their money in Chinese companies with weak corporate governance. The company: • Exaggerated profit margins by shifting staffing expenses to another entity • Recorded fake cash to cover up fake revenue that had been previously recognized • Threatened the audit firm personnel and tried to physically retain the audit firm's workpapers when the auditors uncovered the fraud
Peregrine Financial Group (2012)	Peregrine Financial Group was a financial futures firm whose founder and sole shareholder, Russell Wasendorf, embezzled over $200 million during a 20-year period. Wasendorf concealed the fraud by: • Assuming complete and sole control over the bank statements • Forging the bank statements when they were reviewed by the firm's auditor Just before the fraud was discovered, the futures industry transitioned to an electronic confirmation system for bank statements that enabled the auditor to view the true bank statements. Knowing that the fraud would be uncovered in a few days, Wasendorf unsuccessfully attempted suicide and was ultimately sent to prison.

(*continued*)

| EXHIBIT **2.3** | Examples of Recent Fraudulent Financial Reporting (*continued*) |

Company	Nature of the Fraud
Sino-Forest Corporation (2012)	Sino-Forest is a China-based company in the timber production and wood fiber industry. The company's top-level management orchestrated a financial reporting fraud and personally benefited by engaging in lucrative transactions between Sino-Forest and other companies that were secretly controlled by top-level management of Sino-Forest. The fraudulent actions perpetrated by management included: • Significantly overstating the valuation of timber assets • Making false public statements about the company's performance in order to manipulate stock price • Convincing suppliers and intermediaries in timber products transactions to hinder the investigation into the fraud
Diamond Foods, Inc. (2014)	Diamond Foods is a large producer of snack food and culinary nut products. Walnuts are one of the company's primary raw materials. During 2010, the price of walnuts rose dramatically, which threatened to reduce the company's net income. The company's CFO, Steven Neil, orchestrated a fraudulent financial reporting scheme that involved the following activities and outcomes: • He instructed accounting personnel to delay recording the cost of walnuts acquired during 2010, thereby overstating earnings by $10.5 million. • He again instructed accounting personnel to delay recording the cost of walnuts acquired during 2011, this time overstating earnings by $23.6 million. • As a result, the company exceeded analyst earnings targets, leading to increases in the company's stock price to over $90 per share. • The company raised $181 million in a stock offering when the share price was artificially high. • Once the fraud was revealed, the stock price fell to just $17 per share, representing a market capitalization loss of about $1.7 billion.

The patterns evident across the frauds presented in *Exhibit 2.3* imply the following regarding the conduct of the audit:

- The auditor should be aware of the pressure that analyst following and earnings expectations create for top management.
- If there are potential problems with revenue, the audit cannot be completed until there is sufficient time to examine major year-end transactions.
- The auditor must understand complex transactions to determine their economic substance and the parties that have economic obligations.
- The auditor must clearly understand and analyze weaknesses in an organization's internal controls in order to determine where and how a fraud may take place.
- Audit procedures must be developed to address specific opportunities for fraud to take place.

These examples also illustrate that auditors must exercise professional skepticism in analyzing the possibility of fraud and must be especially alert to trends in performance, or results that are not consistent with other companies, in determining whether extended audit procedures should be performed. Further, those procedures cannot simply be an

The Crucial Role of Professional Skepticism

FOCUS on **FRAUD**

What is *professional skepticism*, and how does an auditor maintain proper professional skepticism in an environment in which the auditor's personal experiences might consist only of audits in which no fraud was ever found? After all, we are all products of our experiences, and many times our audit experience will tell us that we spent extra time investigating something that showed nothing was wrong, resulting in increased audit time, but no discovery of wrongdoing. How do we approach each situation as something unique, and not the total culmination of our past experiences?

The Center for Audit Quality (CAQ), in its 2010 report on fraud, describes professional skepticism as follows:

> Skepticism involves the validation of information through probing questions, the critical assessment of evidence, and attention to inconsistencies. Skepticism is not an end in itself and is not meant to encourage a hostile atmosphere or micromanagement; it is an essential element of the professional objectivity required of all participants in the financial reporting supply chain. Skepticism throughout the supply chain increases not only the likelihood that fraud will be detected, but also the perception that fraud will be detected, which reduces the risk that fraud will be attempted.

Similar to the CAQ report, International Standards on Auditing define professional skepticism as follows:

> Professional skepticism is an attitude that includes a questioning mind and a critical assessment of audit evidence. Professional skepticism requires an ongoing questioning of whether the information and audit evidence obtained suggests that a material misstatement due to fraud may exist. (ISA 240, para. 23)

The Standard goes on to state:

> The auditor's previous experience with the entity contributes to an understanding of the entity. However, although the auditor cannot be expected to fully disregard past experience with the entity about the honesty and integrity of management and those charged with governance, the maintenance of an attitude of professional skepticism is important because there may have been changes in circumstances. When making inquiries and performing other audit procedures, the auditor exercises professional skepticism and is not satisfied with less-than-persuasive audit evidence based on a belief that management and those charged with governance are honest and have integrity. With respect to those charged with governance, maintaining an attitude of professional skepticism means that the auditor carefully considers the reasonableness of responses to inquiries of those charged with governance, and other information obtained from them, in light of all other evidence obtained during the audit. (ISA 240, para. 25)

The report by the Global Public Policy Committee, "Enhancing Auditor Professional Skepticism" (November 2013), articulates a variety of definitions of professional skepticism and introduces a professional skepticism continuum. The skepticism continuum is founded on the belief that professional skepticism is related to a questioning mind, and that an individual may range from a neutral mind-set, to a presumptive doubt mind-set, to complete doubt. Complete trust would be outside the range on the continuum of professional skepticism. The continuum then relates to evidence collection, whereby lower skepticism is associated with less audit evidence and documentation and higher skepticism is associated with more audit evidence and documentation.

Taken together, these definitions highlight that the key elements to successfully exercising professional skepticism include obtaining strong evidence and analyzing that evidence through critical assessment, attention to inconsistencies, and asking probing (often open-ended) questions. The essence of auditing is to bring professional skepticism to the audit and to be alert to all of the possibilities that may cause the auditor to be misled.

expansion of normal procedures. Rather, the procedures must be targeted at discovering potential fraud when there are red flags, suggesting a heightened risk of fraud. The *Focus on Fraud* feature "The Crucial Role of Professional Skepticism" provides definitions and further explanation of this important concept.

The 2010 COSO Report

COSO has conducted three major studies on fraudulent financial reporting. The most recent study, published in 2010, was of companies that were cited by the SEC during the time period of 1998–2007 for fraudulent financial reporting. The analysis identified the major characteristics of companies that had perpetrated fraud. The analysis also focused on comparing fraud and nonfraud companies of similar sizes and in similar industries to determine which factors were the best in discriminating between the fraud and the nonfraud companies. Some of the major findings were:

- The amount and incidence of fraud remains high. The total amount of fraud was more than $120 billion spread across just 300 companies.
- The median size of the company perpetrating the fraud rose tenfold to $100 million during the 1998–2007 period (as compared to the previous ten years).
- There was heavy involvement in the fraud by the CEO and/or CFO, with at least one of them named in 89% of the cases.
- The most common fraud involved revenue recognition—60% of the cases during the latest period compared to 50% in previous periods.
- One-third of the companies changed auditors during the latter part of the fraud (with the full knowledge of the audit committee) compared to less than half that amount of auditor changes taking place with the non-fraud companies.
- Consistent with previous COSO studies, the majority of the frauds took place at companies that were listed on the over-the-counter (OTC) market, rather than those listed on the NYSE or NASDAQ.

Overall, the 2010 COSO report shows that fraudulent financial reporting remains a very significant problem. Commonly cited motivations for fraud included the need to meet internal or external earnings expectations, an attempt to conceal the company's deteriorating financial condition, the need to increase the stock price, the need to bolster financial performance for pending equity or debt financing, or the desire to increase management compensation based on financial results.[1]

The Enron Fraud: A Key Driver of Regulatory Change

Enron is perhaps the most famous fraud of the early 2000s, representing almost everything that was wrong at the time with corporate governance, accounting, financial analysts, banking, and the external auditing profession. How did it happen? Enron was a utility company that developed a new concept and rode the new concept to unbelievable stock market highs. Just prior to its collapse, it had a stock value of $90 per share, which eventually became worthless. The concept: It would increase market efficiency by developing the most sophisticated system in the world to trade electricity, natural gas, and related resources. It would separate the production of energy—a capital-intensive process—from the trading and use of the resources. It would improve market efficiency by increasing the scope of energy production and expanding the output of the local utility to the nation and the world. Energy would flow where the highest market bid for it, which is a fundamental concept of economics. Enron hired MBA traders who were provided lucrative bonuses for meeting profit objectives. Competition among the traders was encouraged, and risks were encouraged; but most of all, reported profits were rewarded. However, much of the company, at its

---

[1] COSO, Fraudulent Financial Reporting: 1998–2007, An Analysis of U.S. Public Companies, 2010, available at *www.coso.org*.

heart, remained a utility. It needed heavy amounts of cash to support its trading positions, and it needed to continually report higher profits to sustain stock market valuations. Most of the top executives of the company were compensated primarily through stock.

The nature of fraud that took place was widespread. Much of the fraud involved special-purpose entities (SPEs), partnerships that often involved substantial loans from banks to be secured by assets transferred to the SPE, partners dominated by Enron executives, and a small outside interest (exceeding 3% per the accounting rule). The company transferred devalued assets to the SPEs and recognized gains on the books. It kept borrowing off the books by having the SPEs borrow from banks and purchase Enron assets. It even recognized over $100 million in anticipated sales that it hoped would occur with a joint venture with Blockbuster on rental movies over the Internet. The SPEs were used such that Enron's balance sheet looked healthy because it minimized the debt on the balance sheet; the SPEs also increased reported income by hiding all losses.

What were the failures that allowed the Enron fraud to occur? Unfortunately, the answer is that the failures were widespread and include problems in the following areas:

- *Management Accountability.* Management was virtually not accountable to anyone as long as the company showed dramatic stock increases justified by earnings growth. Company management had a "good story," and anyone who questioned them was viewed as being stupid. Compensation was based on stock price. Apparently stock valuation was based on a good story and fictitious numbers.
- *Corporate Governance.* Although the board appeared to be independent, most of the board members had close ties to management of the company through philanthropic organizations. Some board members hardly ever attended a meeting, and they certainly did not ask hard questions. Finally, the board waived a conflict-of-interest provision in their code of ethics that allowed Andy Fastow, the treasurer of the company, to profit handsomely from related-party transactions.
- *Accounting Rules.* Accounting became more rule-oriented and complex. Accountants used obscure pronouncements, such as those dealing with SPEs that were designed for leasing transactions, and applied them to other entities for which such accounting was never intended. Accounting was looked at as a tool to earn more money and not as a mechanism to portray economic reality.
- *The Financial Analyst Community.* Financial analysts who were riding the bubble of the dot-com economy concluded that they did not have tools to appropriately value many of the emerging companies. Rather than analyze the underlying fundamentals, the analysts relied too much on earnings guidance provided by management. Managers who achieved the projected guidance were rewarded; those who did not were severely punished. Analysts came to accept pro forma accounting statements, more aptly described as what would occur as long as nothing bad happened.
- *Banking and Investment Banking.* Many large financial institutions were willing participants in the process because they were rewarded with large underwriting fees for other Enron work. Enron management was smart enough to know that the investment bankers were also rewarded on the amount of fees they generated.
- *The External Auditing Profession and Arthur Andersen.* At the time of Enron, the largest five external audit firms referred to themselves as professional service firms with diverse lines of business. All of the firms had large consulting practices. Arthur Andersen performed internal audit

work for Enron, in addition to performing the external audit. The consulting fees of many clients dramatically exceeded the audit fees. Partners were compensated on revenue and profitability. Worse yet, auditors were hired by management that sometimes succeeded in pressuring auditors to acquiesce to aggressive financial reporting preferences. In short, there is a perception that audit quality was low during this period of time. The final straw for Arthur Andersen was that when federal authorities began investigating the bankruptcy of Enron, the Houston office auditors on the Enron engagement began aggressively destroying documentation and evidence related to their failed audit. Ultimately, this action was what enabled federal authorities to force the downfall of Arthur Andersen.

An Overview of the Auditor's Fraud-Related Responsibilities and Users' Expectations

LO 4 Discuss auditors' fraud-related responsibilities and users' related expectations.

Given the prevalence of fraud, it is important to consider the auditor's role related to fraud detection. In October 2010, the CAQ issued a paper titled "Deterring and Detecting Financial Reporting Fraud—A Platform for Action."[2] The CAQ views fraud-related responsibilities as the key means to improve the external auditor's contribution to society and to gain respect for the auditing profession. However, the CAQ also recognizes that preventing and detecting fraud cannot be the job of the external auditor alone; all the parties involved in preparing and opining on audited financial statements need to play a role in preventing and detecting fraud. The CAQ report identifies three ways in which individuals involved in the financial reporting process (management, audit committee, internal audit, external audit, and regulatory authorities) can mitigate the risk of fraudulent financial reporting. These individuals need to:

- Acknowledge that there needs to exist a strong, highly ethical tone at the top of an organization that permeates the corporate culture, including an effective fraud risk management program
- Exercise professional skepticism, a questioning mind-set that strengthens professional objectivity, in evaluating and/or preparing financial reports
- Remember that strong communication among those involved in the financial reporting process is critical.

Fraud-Related Requirements in Professional Auditing Standards

Auditing standards historically have reflected a belief that it is not reasonable to expect auditors to detect cleverly implemented frauds. However, it is increasingly clear that the general public, as reflected in the orientation of the PCAOB, expects that auditors have a responsibility to detect and report on material frauds, as noted here:

The mission of the PCAOB is to restore the confidence of investors, and society generally, in the independent auditors of companies. There is no doubt that repeated revelations of accounting scandals and audit failures have seriously

---

[2] Center for Audit Quality, *Deterring and Detecting Financial Reporting Fraud—A Platform for Action*, available at *www.thecaq.org/Anti-FraudInitiative/CFraudReport.pdf*.

damaged public confidence. The detection of material fraud is a reasonable expectation of users of audited financial statements. Society needs and expects assurance that financial information has not been materially misstated because of fraud. *Unless an independent audit can provide this assurance, it has little if any value to society.*[3] [emphasis added]

Professional auditing standards require the auditor to plan and perform an audit that will detect material misstatements resulting from fraud. As part of that requirement, auditors should begin an audit with a brainstorming session that focuses on how and where fraud could occur within the organization. Auditors also need to communicate with the audit committee and management about the risks of fraud and how they are addressed. The auditor should then plan the audit to be responsive to an organization's susceptibility to fraud. *Exhibit 2.4* provides details on the PCAOB, the American Institute of Certified Public Accountants (AICPA), and the International Auditing and Assurance Standards Board (IAASB) standards on audit considerations regarding fraud. The guidance from the AICPA and IAASB is essentially identical, with just minor wording differences in the standards. The PCAOB standard differs in terms of wording, but the substance of the guidance is the same.

EXHIBIT 2.4 **Professional Standards on Audit Considerations Regarding Fraud**

Considerations Regarding Fraud	PCAOB AU 316	AICPA AU-C 240	IAASB ISA 240
Management's responsibilities	Management is responsible for designing and implementing programs and controls to prevent, deter, and detect fraud.	The primary responsibility for the prevention and detection of fraud rests with both those charged with governance of the entity and management.	The primary responsibility for the prevention and detection of fraud rests with both those charged with governance of the entity and management.
The auditor's responsibilities	The auditor is responsible for planning and performing the audit to obtain reasonable assurance about whether the financial statements are free of material misstatement, whether caused by error or fraud. The standard acknowledges that there is an unavoidable risk that some material misstatements may be undetected, even if the audit is properly planned and performed.	The auditor is responsible for obtaining reasonable assurance that the financial statements as a whole are free of material misstatement, whether caused by error or fraud. The standard acknowledges that there is an unavoidable risk that some material misstatements may be undetected, even if the audit is properly planned and performed.	The auditor is responsible for obtaining reasonable assurance that the financial statements as a whole are free of material misstatement, whether caused by error or fraud. The standard acknowledges that there is an unavoidable risk that some material misstatements may be undetected, even if the audit is properly planned and performed.

(continued)

---

[3] Douglas R. Carmichael, *The PCAOB and the Social Responsibility of the Independent Auditor*, Chief Auditor, Public Accounting Oversight Board, speech given to Midyear Auditing Section meeting of the American Accounting Association, January 16, 2004.

EXHIBIT 2.4 Professional Standards on Audit Considerations Regarding Fraud (*continued*)

Considerations Regarding Fraud	PCAOB AU 316	AICPA AU-C 240	IAASB ISA 240
Professional skepticism	Furthermore, professional skepticism requires an ongoing questioning of whether the information and evidence obtained suggests that a material misstatement due to fraud has occurred. In exercising professional skepticism in gathering and evaluating evidence, the auditor should not be satisfied with less-than-persuasive evidence because of a belief that management is honest.	The auditor should maintain professional skepticism, regardless of the auditor's past experience with honesty and integrity of management and those charged with governance. The auditor should investigate when management or those charged with governance provide unsatisfactory responses (e.g., inconsistent, vague, or implausible) to questions. The auditor may accept records and documents as genuine but should investigate if the auditor believes that such an assumption is not appropriate.	The auditor should maintain professional skepticism, regardless of the auditor's past experience with honesty and integrity of management and those charged with governance. The auditor should investigate when management or those charged with governance provide unsatisfactory responses (e.g., inconsistent, vague, or implausible) to questions. The auditor may accept records and documents as genuine but should investigate if the auditor believes that such an assumption is not appropriate.
Risk assessment	The auditor should formally assess fraud risk through a discussion among the engagement team members (commonly referred to as a **fraud brainstorming**). The auditor should identify unusual or unexpected relationships in performing analytical procedures that might indicate fraud.	The auditor should formally assess fraud risk through a discussion among the engagement team members (commonly referred to as a *fraud brainstorming*). The auditor should identify unusual or unexpected relationships in performing analytical procedures that might indicate fraud.	The auditor should formally assess fraud risk through a discussion among the engagement team members (commonly referred to as a *fraud brainstorming*). The auditor should identify unusual or unexpected relationships in performing analytical procedures that might indicate fraud.
Risk response	The auditor must respond to identified fraud risks. Responses should include ensuring that audit personnel are adequately trained and supervised, evaluating whether subjective or complex transactions may indicate fraud, and incorporating an element of unpredictability in the nature, timing, and extent of audit procedures.	The auditor must respond to identified fraud risks. Responses should include ensuring that audit personnel are adequately trained and supervised, evaluating whether subjective or complex transactions may indicate fraud, and incorporating an element of unpredictability in the nature, timing, and extent of audit procedures.	The auditor must respond to identified fraud risks. Responses should include ensuring that audit personnel are adequately trained and supervised, evaluating whether subjective or complex transactions may indicate fraud, and incorporating an element of unpredictability in the nature, timing, and extent of audit procedures.

The *Emerging Issues* feature "The SEC's Focus on Detecting and Prosecuting Fraud" describes the SEC's recently expanded fraud detection and prosecution agenda. In subsequent chapters, we discuss specific ways in which auditors can respond to fraud in various phases of the audit.

The SEC's Focus on Detecting and Prosecuting Fraud

EMERGING ISSUE

Under the leadership of the new chair of the SEC, Mary Jo White, the SEC has increased its focus on detecting and prosecuting financial reporting fraud. The SEC's Division of Enforcement is on the front lines of this enforcement agenda. The SEC has set up a Fraud and Audit Task Force to assist with resulting enforcement actions. In addition, the SEC has organized a unit, the Center for Risk and Quantitative Analytics, that is using sophisticated data analytic tools to analyze financial statements for the possibility of fraud.

The Sarbanes-Oxley Act of 2002 as a Regulatory Response to Fraud

LO 5 Explain how various requirements in the Sarbanes-Oxley Act of 2002 are designed to help prevent the types of frauds perpetrated in the late 1990s and early 2000s.

The financial scandals and associated stock market declines in the late 1990s and early 2000s dramatically illustrated the costs of inappropriate ethical decisions by various parties, of weak corporate governance, of low audit quality, and of insufficient auditor independence. The bankruptcy of Enron and the subsequent collapse of Arthur Andersen were such dramatic events that Congress was compelled to respond, and it did so in the form of the **Sarbanes-Oxley Act of 2002**. *Exhibit 2.5* summarizes the major provisions of the Sarbanes-Oxley Act. The Sarbanes-Oxley Act applies to publicly traded companies, not privately held organizations. However, since the Sarbanes-Oxley Act was enacted, privately held organizations often view the requirements of the Act as best practice and sometimes adhere to the requirements even though they are not legally required to do so.

As is clear from reading *Exhibit 2.5*, many sections of the Sarbanes-Oxley Act were written to respond to various abuses of the financial reporting process in the late 1990s and early 2000s, and many provisions affect auditors and the auditing profession directly through requirements intended to increase audit quality. For example, Title I and its relevant sections effectively remove self-regulation of the auditing profession and replace it with independent oversight by the PCAOB. Section 201 prevents audit firms from providing many consulting services to audit clients, which was an issue cited as a significant driver of the failed audits of Enron. Sections 204, 301, and 407 significantly expand the power, responsibilities, and disclosures of corporate audit committees, thereby addressing concerns over weak corporate governance. Audit committees are directly responsible for the oversight of the company's external auditors and have the power to hire and fire the auditors. Section 404 requires management assessment and external audit firm attestation regarding the effectiveness of internal control over financial reporting—a key structural problem in many organizations experiencing fraud. Finally, many sections of the Sarbanes-Oxley Act significantly enhance the penalties for criminal wrongdoing that affects the securities markets, individual shareholders, and the general public.

| EXHIBIT **2.5** | Significant Provisions of the Sarbanes-Oxley Act of 2002 |

Section	Requirements

TITLE 1: Public Company Accounting Oversight Board

101 — *Establishment and administrative provisions.* The Board:
- Is a nonprofit corporation, not an agency of the U.S. government
- Will have five financially literate members who are prominent individuals of integrity and reputation with a commitment to the interests of investors and the public
- Has authority to set standards related to audit reports and to conduct inspections of registered public accounting firms

102 — *Registration with the Board.* Accounting firms auditing public companies must register with the PCAOB.

103 — *Auditing, quality control, and independence standards and rules.* The Board will:
- Establish or adopt rules regarding the conduct of audits and regarding audit firm quality-control standards
- Require audit firms to describe the scope of testing of issuers' internal control structure

104 — *Inspections of registered public accounting firms.* The Board will:
- Inspect annually registered accounting firms that audit 100 or more issuers
- Inspect at least every three years registered accounting firms that audit fewer than 100 issuers
- Publicly report results of its inspections

105 — *Investigations and disciplinary proceedings.* The Board will:
- Adopt procedures for disciplining registered accounting firms
- Require registered accounting firms to provide documentation and testimony that the Board deems necessary to conduct investigations
- Be able to sanction registered accounting firms for noncooperation with investigations

106 — *Foreign public accounting firms.* Foreign accounting firms must comply with the same rules related to the PCAOB as domestic accounting firms.

107 — *Commission oversight of the Board.* The SEC has oversight and enforcement authority over the Board, including in processes involving standards setting, enforcement, and disciplinary procedures.

108 — *Accounting standards.* The SEC will recognize as "generally accepted" accounting principles that are established by a standard setter that meets the Act's criteria.

109 — *Funding.* Registered accounting firms and issuers will pay for the operations of the Board.

TITLE II: Auditor Independence

201 — *Services outside the scope of practice of auditors.* There exist a variety of services that registered accounting firms may not perform for issuers, such as bookkeeping, systems design, appraisal services, and internal auditing, among others. Tax services may be performed, but only with pre-approval by the audit committee.

202 — *Preapproval requirements.* All audit and nonaudit services (with certain exceptions based on size and practicality) must be approved by the audit committee of the issuer.

203 — *Audit partner rotation.* The lead partner and reviewing partner must rotate off the issuer engagement at least every five years.

204 — *Auditor reports to audit committees.* Registered accounting firms must report to the audit committee issues concerning:
- Critical accounting policies and practices
- Alternative treatments of financial information within generally accepted accounting principles that have been considered by management, as well as the preferred treatment of the accounting firm
- Significant written communications between the accounting firm and management

(continued)

EXHIBIT **2.5**	Significant Provisions of the Sarbanes-Oxley Act of 2002 (*continued*)

Section	Requirements
205	*Conforming amendments.* This section details minor wording changes between the Sarbanes-Oxley Act and the Securities Act of 1934.
206	*Conflicts of interest.* Registered accounting firms may not perform audits for an issuer whose CEO, CFO, controller, chief accounting officer, or other equivalent position was employed by the accounting firm during the one-year period preceding the audit. This is known as a *cooling-off period.*
207	*Study of mandatory rotation of registered public accounting firms.* The Comptroller General of the United States shall conduct a study addressing this issue.

TITLE III: Corporate Responsibility

301	*Public company audit committees.*

- Audit committees are to be directly responsible for the appointment, compensation, and oversight of the work of registered accounting firms.
- Each audit committee member shall be independent.
- Audit committees must establish whistle-blowing mechanisms within issuers.
- Audit committees have the authority to engage their own independent counsel.
- Issuers must provide adequate funding for audit committees.

302	*Corporate responsibility for financial reports.* The signing officers (usually the CEO and CFO):

- Will certify in quarterly and annual reports filed with the SEC that the report does not contain untrue statements of material facts and that the financial statements and disclosures present fairly (in all material respects) the financial condition and results of operations of the issuer
- Must establish and maintain effective internal controls to ensure reliable financial statements and disclosures
- Are responsible for designing internal controls, assessing their effectiveness, and disclosing material deficiencies in controls to the audit committee and to the registered accounting firm

303	*Improper influence on conduct of audits.* Officers of issuers may not take action to fraudulently influence, coerce, manipulate, or mislead the registered accounting firm or its employees.

TITLE IV: Enhanced Financial Disclosures

401	*Disclosures in periodic reports.*

- Financial reports must be in accordance with generally accepted accounting principles and must reflect material correcting adjustments proposed by the registered accounting firm.
- Material off–balance sheet transactions and other relationships with unconsolidated entities or persons must be disclosed.
- The SEC must issue new rules on pro forma figures and must study the issues of off–balance sheet transactions and the use of SPEs.

402	*Enhanced conflict of interest provisions.* Issuers may not extend credit to directors or executive offers.
403	*Disclosures of transactions involving management and principal stockholders.* Requires that any director, officer, or shareholder who owns more than 10%of the company's equity securities publicly disclose that fact.
404	*Management assessment of internal controls.*

- Annual reports must state the responsibility of management for establishing and maintaining an adequate internal control structure and procedures for financial reporting.
- Annual reports must contain an assessment of the effectiveness of the internal control structure and procedures of the issuer for financial reporting.
- Each registered accounting firm must attest to and report on the assessment made by the management of the issuer, and such attestation must not be the subject of a separate engagement (in other words, requires an integrated audit).

(continued)

| EXHIBIT **2.5** | Significant Provisions of the Sarbanes-Oxley Act of 2002 (*continued*) |

Section	Requirements
406	*Code of ethics for senior financial officers.* The SEC must issue rules requiring issuers to disclose whether or not the issuer has adopted a code of ethics for senior financial officers (and if not, the issuer must explain the rationale).
407	*Disclosure of audit committee financial expert.* The SEC must issue rules to require issuers to disclose whether or not the audit committee of the issuer includes at least one member who is a financial expert (and if not, the issuer must explain the rationale).

SECTION V: Analyst Conflicts of Interest

| 501 | *Treatment of securities analysts.* Registered securities associations and national securities exchanges must adopt rules to address concerns about conflicts of interest for analysts that recommend equity securities. |

SECTION VI: Commission Resources and Authority

| 601 | *Enhanced funding for the SEC.* The SEC's budget is increased to enable stronger enforcement and regulation of parties involved in the securities markets. |
| 602 | *Appearance and practice before the Commission.* The SEC may censure any person, or deny, temporarily or permanently, the privilege of appearing or practicing before the SEC if that person is found:
• Not to possess the requisite qualifications to represent others
• To be lacking in character or integrity, or to have engaged in unethical or improper professional conduct
• To have willfully violated or willfully aided and abetted the violation of any provision of the securities laws |

SECTION VII: Studies and Reports

701	*U.S. Government Accountability Office (GAO) study and report regarding consolidation of public accounting firms.* The comptroller general of the United States shall conduct a study addressing factors leading to consolidation of public accounting firms since 1989 and the reduction in the number of firms capable of providing audit services to large national and multinational businesses subject to the securities laws.
702	*Commission study and report regarding credit-rating agencies.* The SEC shall conduct a study on the role and function of credit-rating agencies in the operation of the securities market.
703	*Study and report on violators and violations.* The SEC shall conduct a study to determine the number of securities professionals (public accountants, public accounting firms, investment bankers, brokers, dealers, attorneys, etc.) who have aided and abetted a violation of the federal securities laws but have not been sanctioned, disciplined, or otherwise penalized.
704	*Study of enforcement actions.* The comptroller general of the United States shall review and analyze all enforcement actions by the SEC involving violations of reporting requirements imposed under the securities laws and restatements over the five-year period preceding the Sarbanes-Oxley Act.
705	*Study of investment banks.* The comptroller general of the United States shall conduct a study on whether investment banks and financial advisers assisted public companies in manipulating their earnings and obfuscating their true financial condition.

SECTION VIII: Corporate and Criminal Fraud Accountability

| 802 | *Criminal penalties for altering documents.* Stronger penalties are now imposed for crimes involving the destruction, alteration, falsification, or destruction of financial records or corporate audit records. |
| 805 | *Review of federal sentencing guidelines for obstruction of justice and extensive criminal fraud.* Sentencing guidelines are enhanced for fraud and obstruction of justice sentences. |

(*continued*)

EXHIBIT 2.5 Significant Provisions of the Sarbanes-Oxley Act of 2002 (*continued*)

Section	Requirements
806	*Protection for employees of publicly traded companies who provide evidence of fraud.* This section provides whistle-blower protection to protect against retaliation in fraud cases.
807	*Criminal penalties for defrauding shareholders of publicly traded companies.* Stronger penalties are now imposed for crimes involving securities fraud.

TITLE IX: White–Collar Crime Penalty Enhancements

903	*Criminal penalties for mail and wire fraud.* This section increases penalties for these violations.
904	Criminal penalties for violations of the Employee Retirement Income Security Act of 1974. This section increases penalties for violations of this Act.
905	*Amendment to sentencing guidelines relating to certain white-collar offenses.* The United States Sentencing Commission shall review and amend Federal Sentencing Guidelines related to provisions of the Sarbanes-Oxley Act.
906	*Corporate responsibility for financial reports.* This section provides penalties for corporate directors who knowingly provide incorrect certifications of financial statements and reports.

TITLE X: Corporate Tax Returns

1001	*Sense of the Senate regarding the signing of corporate tax returns by CEOs.* The CEO must sign the corporate tax return.

TITLE XI: Corporate Fraud and Accountability

1102	*Tampering with a record or otherwise impeding an official proceeding.* This section provides penalties for whoever corruptly alters, destroys, mutilates, or conceals a record, document, or other object (or attempts to do so) with the intent to impair the object's integrity and availability for use in an official proceeding. It also provides penalties for whoever otherwise obstructs, influences, or impedes any official proceeding, or attempts to do so.
1105	*Authority of the Commission to prohibit persons from serving as officers or directors.* The SEC may prohibit from serving before it as an officer or director any individual who has violated Section 10(b) of the Securities Act of 1934 or Section 8A of the Securities Act of 1933.
1106	*Increased criminal penalties under Securities Act of 1934.* This section provides increased penalties for violations of the Securities Act of 1934.

The Post Sarbanes-Oxley World: A Time of Improved Corporate Governance

LO 6 Define corporate governance, identify the parties involved, and describe their respective activities.

With the requirements of the Sarbanes-Oxley Act and the realization that many of the frauds of the late 1990s and early 2000s might have been prevented or detected earlier, the overall environment for doing business changed toward enhanced accountability and governance. Most notably, the business environment now includes a greater focus on corporate governance, the role of corporate governance in preventing fraud, and the important role that audit committees play in ensuring reliable financial reporting.

What Is Corporate Governance?

Corporate governance is a process by which the owners (stockholders) and creditors of an organization exert control and require accountability for the resources entrusted to the organization. The owners elect a board of

EXHIBIT 2.6   Overview of Corporate Governance Responsibilities and Accountabilities

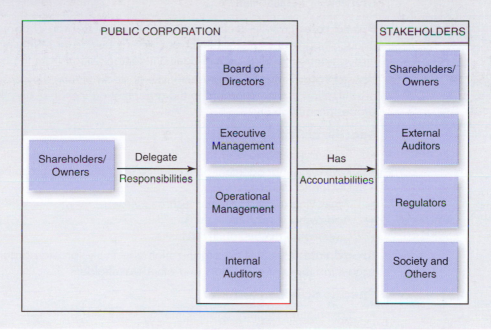

directors to provide oversight of the organization's activities and accountability to stakeholders.

Exhibit 2.6 portrays the various parties involved in corporate governance. Governance starts with the owners delegating responsibilities to management through an elected **board of directors**—including a subcommittee of the board that serves as an **audit committee**. In turn, responsibilities are handed to operating units with oversight and assistance from internal auditors. The board of directors and its audit committee oversee management, and, in that role, are expected to protect the stockholders' rights and ensure that controls exist to prevent and detect fraud. However, it is important to recognize that management is part of the governance framework; management can influence who sits on the board and the audit committee, as well as other governance controls that might be put into place.

In return for the responsibilities (and power) given to management and the board, governance demands accountability back through the system to the owners and other stakeholders. **Stakeholders** include anyone who is influenced, either directly or indirectly, by the actions of a company. Management and the board have responsibilities to act within the laws of society and to meet various requirements of creditors and employees and other stakeholders.

Exhibit 2.7 describes the responsibilities of major parties involved in corporate governance. Importantly, note that these parties each have unique responsibilities, but they rely on the other parties to do their share to help ensure quality financial reporting through effective corporate governance.

Principles of Effective Corporate Governance

What characteristics and actions on the part of organizations are important to quality corporate governance? In 2010, a commission sponsored by the

EXHIBIT **2.7**	Corporate Governance Responsibilities

Party	Overview of Responsibilities
Stockholders	**Broad role:** Provide effective oversight through election of board members, through approval of major initiatives (such as buying or selling stock), and through annual reports on management compensation from the board
Board of Directors	**Broad role:** The major representatives of stockholders; they ensure that the organization is run according to the organization's charter and that there is proper accountability.
	Specific activities include: • Selecting management • Reviewing management performance and determining compensation • Declaring dividends • Approving major changes, such as mergers • Approving corporate strategy • Overseeing accountability activities
Management	**Broad role:** Manage the organization effectively; provide accurate and timely accountability to shareholders and other stakeholders
	Specific activities include: • Formulating strategy and risk management • Implementing effective internal controls • Developing financial and other reports to meet public, stakeholder, and regulatory requirements • Managing and reviewing operations • Implementing an effective ethical environment
Audit Committees of the Board of Directors	**Broad role:** Provide oversight of the internal and external audit function and over the process of preparing the annual financial statements and public reports on internal control
	Specific activities include: • Selecting the external audit firm • Approving any nonaudit work performed by the audit firm • Selecting and/or approving the appointment of the chief audit executive (internal auditor) • Reviewing and approving the scope and budget of the internal audit function • Discussing audit findings with internal and external auditors, and advising the board (and management) on specific actions that should be taken
Regulators and Standards Setters SEC, AICPA, FASB, PCAOB, IAASB	**Broad role:** Set accounting and auditing standards dictating underlying financial reporting and auditing concepts; set the expectations of audit quality and accounting quality
	Specific activities include: • Establishing accounting principles • Establishing auditing standards • Interpreting previously issued standards • Enforcing adherence to relevant standards and rules for public companies and their auditors

NYSE issued a report identifying key core governance principles. The principles related to boards and management include:

• The board's fundamental objective should be to build long-term sustainable growth in shareholder value for the corporation.

- Successful corporate governance depends upon successful management of the company, as management has the primary responsibility for creating a culture of performance with integrity and ethical behavior.
- Effective corporate governance should be integrated with the company's business strategy and not viewed as simply a compliance obligation.
- Transparency is a critical element of effective corporate governance, and companies should make regular efforts to ensure that they have sound disclosure policies and practices.
- Independence and objectivity are necessary attributes of board members; however, companies must also strike the right balance in the appointment of independent and nonindependent directors to ensure an appropriate range and mix of expertise, diversity, and knowledge on the board.

In addition to these types of broad principles, the NYSE has mandated certain corporate governance guidelines that registrants must follow, including:

- Boards need to consist of a majority of independent directors.
- Boards need to hold regular executive sessions of independent directors without management present.
- Boards must have a nominating/corporate governance committee composed entirely of independent directors.
- The nominating/corporate governance committee must have a written charter that addresses the committee's purpose and responsibilities, and there must be an annual performance evaluation of the committee.
- Boards must have a compensation committee composed entirely of independent directors.
- The compensation committee must have a written charter that addresses the committee's purpose and responsibilities, which must include (at a minimum) the responsibility to review and approve corporate goals relevant to CEO compensation, to make recommendations to the board about non-CEO compensation and incentive-based compensation plans, and to produce a report on executive compensation; there must also be an annual performance evaluation of the committee.
- Boards must have an audit committee with a minimum of three independent members.
- The audit committee must have a written charter that addresses the committee's purpose and responsibilities, and the committee must produce an audit committee report; there must also be an annual performance evaluation of the committee.
- Companies must adopt and disclose corporate governance guidelines addressing director qualification standards, director responsibilities, director access to management and independent advisors, director compensation, director continuing education, management succession, and an annual performance evaluation of the board.
- Companies must adopt and disclose a code of business conduct and ethics for directors, officers, and employees.
- Foreign companies must disclose how their corporate governance practices differ from those followed by domestic companies.
- CEOs must provide an annual certification of compliance with corporate governance standards.
- Companies must have an internal audit function, whether housed internally or outsourced.

Effective governance is important to the conduct of an audit for one very simple reason: Organizations with effective corporate governance are less likely to experience fraud and are therefore less risky to audit. For that reason, most audit firms are not willing to accept potential audit clients unless the clients demonstrate a strong commitment to effective corporate governance. The auditor is in a much better position to provide a quality audit when governance mechanisms, such as the board and the audit committee, adhere to and embrace fundamental principles of effective governance. At those types of organizations, the auditor can serve as an independent party working with other governance parties, such as the management, the board, and the audit committee, to help assure reliable financial reporting. However, in organizations where governance is not well developed or is heavily influenced by management, the auditor may decide that the risk of fraud is unduly high and that the audit firm is going to have to bear too much responsibility for assuring reliable financial reporting. In essence, ineffective corporate governance increases fraud risk to an extent that at some point the client is not auditable from a risk-mitigation standpoint.

Responsibilities of Audit Committees

Section 301 of the Sarbanes-Oxley Act outlines the responsibilities of audit committee members for publicly traded companies, stating that audit committees are to be directly responsible for the appointment, compensation, and oversight of the work of registered accounting firms; they must be independent; they must establish whistle-blowing mechanisms within the company; they must have the authority to engage their own independent counsel; and companies must provide adequate funding for audit committees.

In addition to these broad responsibilities, the NYSE has mandated certain specific responsibilities of audit committees, including:

- Obtaining an annual report by the external auditor that addresses the company's internal control procedures, any quality-control or regulatory problems, and any relationships that might threaten the independence of the external auditor
- Discussing the company's financial statements with management and the external auditor
- Discussing in its meetings the company's earnings press releases, as well as financial information and earnings guidance provided to analysts
- Discussing in its meetings policies with respect to risk assessment and risk management
- Meeting separately with management, internal auditors, and the external auditor on a periodic basis
- Reviewing with the external auditor any audit problems or difficulties that they have had with management
- Setting clear hiring policies for employees or former employees of the external auditor
- Reporting regularly to the board of directors

Further, in many organizations the audit committee also has the authority to hire and fire the head of the internal audit function, set the budget for the internal audit activity, review the internal audit plan, and discuss all significant internal audit results. Other responsibilities might include performing or supervising special investigations, reviewing policies on sensitive payments, and coordinating periodic reviews of compliance with company policies such as corporate governance policies. See the *Emerging Issues* feature "Audit Committee Members' Liability for Preventing and Detecting Fraud," which illustrates a recent SEC trend toward enforcing penalties on audit committee members who fail to perform their duties.

Audit Committee Members' Liability for Preventing and Detecting Fraud

Two recent enforcement actions by the SEC against audit committee members highlight the potential liability that audit committee members face if they do not perform their duties responsibly in the presence of fraud red flags. The first case involves an enforcement action against the entire three-member audit committee of DHB Industries, a manufacturer of body armor used by the police and military. Top management of DHB committed a variety of illegal acts including financial reporting fraud, conspiracy, misappropriation of corporate funds, and insider trading. What is notable about the case, however, is that in addition to pursuing charges against management, the SEC also vigorously pursued charges against each of the audit committee members (Jerome Krantz, Cary Chasin, and Gary Nadelman). The investigation revealed that these individuals were not independent of top management, deliberately ignored fraud red flags, allowed top management to attempt to thwart the external auditor's and the SEC's investigations, and participated in various aspects of the fraud. The three audit committee members were ultimately barred from serving as an officer or director of a public company and they paid a total of $1.6 million in fines. For further

details on this case, see *http://www.sec.gov/litigation/litreleases/2011/lr21867.htm* and *http://www.sec.gov/news/press/2011/2011-238.htm*.

The second case involves an enforcement action against the audit committee chair of InfoUSA, a sales and marketing firm that compiles and sells business and consumer databases. Similar to the DHB case, top management committed a variety of illegal acts, including inappropriate personal use of corporate assets. The audit committee chair, Vasant Raval, was informed of various aspects of the fraudulent activity by the head of internal audit and legal counsel. The board of directors requested that Raval investigate allegations of fraud. Raval wrote a report, but it was incomplete and he never challenged top management. He was ultimately fined $50,000 and received a five-year bar from serving as an officer or director of a public company. For further details on this case, see *http://www.sec.gov/litigation/complaints/2010/comp21451-raval.pdf*.

These cases illustrate the importance that financial statement users and regulators attach to the role of audit committee members and highlight the downside risks to such individuals should they fail to adequately attend to their responsibilities.

SUMMARY AND NEXT STEPS

Fraud raises important concerns for external auditors, and they have clear professional obligations to perform an audit that provides reasonable assurance that the financial statements are free from material misstatement, including fraud. Various types of fraud exist, and the fraud triangle characterizes incentives, opportunities, and rationalizations that enable fraud to occur. Recent high-profile frauds ultimately led to the regulatory reforms enacted through the Sarbanes-Oxley Act of 2002. Corporate governance plays an important role in mitigating the risk of fraud.

While the possibility of fraud and the associated need for effective corporate governance are of utmost importance to the external auditor, management also seeks to provide reasonable assurance that the financial statements are free from material misstatements from either fraud or errors. In *Chapter 3*, we discuss management's role in assuring reliable financial reporting through their responsibilities for internal control over financial reporting.

SIGNIFICANT TERMS

Asset misappropriation   A fraud that involves the theft or misuse of an organization's assets. Common examples include skimming cash, stealing inventory, and payroll fraud.

Audit committee   A subcommittee of the board of directors responsible for monitoring audit activities and serving as a surrogate for the interests of shareholders; it should be composed of outside members of the board, that is, members who are independent of the organization.

Board of directors   The major representative of stockholders to help ensure that the organization is run according to the organization's charter and that there is proper accountability.

Corporate governance   A process by which the owners and creditors of an organization exert control and require accountability for the resources entrusted to the organization. The owners (stockholders) elect a board of directors to provide oversight of the organization's activities and accountability to stakeholders.

Fraudulent financial reporting   The intentional manipulation of reported financial results to misstate the economic condition of the organization.

Fraud   An intentional act involving the use of deception that results in a material misstatement of the financial statements.

Fraud brainstorming   A formal discussion among the audit engagement team members about the possibility of fraud, including a fraud risk assessment.

Fraud triangle   A model that recognizes that incentives, opportunities, and rationalization are elements typically associated with fraud.

Ponzi scheme   This type of fraud occurs when the deposits of current investors are used to pay returns on the deposits of previous investors; no real investment is happening.

Red flags   Risk factors suggesting a heightened risk of fraud.

Sarbanes-Oxley Act of 2002   Broad legislation mandating new standard setting for audits of public companies and new standards for corporate governance.

Stakeholders   Anyone who is influenced, either directly or indirectly, by the actions of a company; stakeholders extend beyond the shareholders of a company.

TRUE/FALSE QUESTIONS

2-1   **LO 1**   The Great Salad Oil Swindle of 1963 could best be categorized as an asset misappropriation fraud.

2-2   **LO 1**   The Koss Corporation fraud could best be categorized as fraudulent financial reporting.

2-3   **LO 2**   The three elements of the fraud triangle include incentive, opportunity, and rationalization.

2-4 LO 2 Management compensation schemes that heavily emphasize stock-based compensation most affect the opportunity to commit fraud.

2-5 LO 3 In the Enron fraud, one of the ways that management covered up the fraud was to shift debt off the balance sheet to SPEs.

2-6 LO 3 Professional skepticism related to possible fraud involves the validation of information through probing questions, critical assessment of evidence, and attention to inconsistencies.

2-7 LO 4 The investing public generally recognizes that it is very difficult for auditors to detect fraud, and so it does not hold auditors accountable when auditors fail to detect it.

2-8 LO 4 Auditing standards historically have reflected the belief that it is not reasonable to expect auditors to detect cleverly hidden frauds.

2-9 LO 5 The Sarbanes-Oxley Act of 2002 was written by Congress to address problems revealed in frauds that were committed in the late 1980s.

2-10 LO 5 An important change resulting from the Sarbanes-Oxley Act is that auditors are no longer allowed to provide most consulting services for their public company audit clients.

2-11 LO 6 Corporate governance is the process by which the owners and creditors of an organization exert control over and require accountability for the resources entrusted to the organization.

2-12 LO 6 Organizations with effective corporate governance are more risky to audit.

MULTIPLE-CHOICE QUESTIONS

2-13 LO 1 What is the primary difference between fraud and error in financial statement reporting?
   a. The materiality of the misstatement.
   b. The intent to deceive.
   c. The level of management involved.
   d. The type of transaction effected.

2-14 LO 1 Which of the following best represents an example of fraudulent financial reporting?
   a. The transfer agent issues 40,000 shares of the company's stock to a friend without authorization by the board of directors.
   b. The controller of the company inappropriately records January sales in December so that year-end results will meet analysts' expectations.
   c. The in-house attorney receives payments from the French government for negotiating the development of a new plant in Paris.
   d. The accounts receivable clerk covers up the theft of cash receipts by writing off older receivables without authorization.

2-15 LO 2 Which of the following factors creates an opportunity for fraud to be committed in an organization?
   a. Management demands financial success.
   b. Poor internal control.
   c. Commitments tied to debt covenants.
   d. Management is aggressive in its application of accounting rules.

2-16 **LO 2**   Which of the following is a common rationalization for fraudulent financial reporting?

a. This is a one-time transaction and it will allow the company to get through the current financial crisis, but I'll never do it again.

b. I am only borrowing the money; I will pay it back next year.

c. Executives at other companies are getting paid more than I am, so I deserve the money.

d. The accounting rules don't make sense for our company, and they make our financial results look weaker than is necessary; so we have a good reason to record revenue using a non-GAAP method.

e. Both (a) and (d).

2-17 **LO 3**   Which of the following types of transactions did World-Com management engage in as part of that company's fraudulent financial reporting scheme?

a. Recorded barter transactions as sales.

b. Used restructuring reserves from prior acquisitions to decrease expenses.

c. Capitalized line costs rather than expensing them.

d. All of the above.

e. None of the above.

2-18 **LO 3**   Which of the following is a valid conclusion of the 2010 COSO report?

a. The most common frauds involve outright theft of assets.

b. The individuals most often responsible for fraud include low-level accounting personnel, such as accounts payable clerks.

c. The majority of frauds took place at smaller companies that were listed on the OTC market rather than the larger companies listed on the NYSE.

d. All of the above.

e. None of the above.

2-19 **LO 4**   Which of the following statements is accurate regarding the CAQ's 2010 paper on deterring and detecting fraud in financial reporting?

a. It recognizes that preventing and detecting fraud is the job of the external auditor alone.

b. It notes that an effective fraud risk management program can be expected to prevent virtually all frauds, especially those perpetrated by top management.

c. It illustrates that communication among those involved in the financial reporting process is critical.

d. All of the above.

e. None of the above.

2-20 **LO 4**   Which of the following statements are true?

a. Unless an independent audit can provide reasonable assurance that financial information has not been materially misstated because of fraud, it has little, if any, value to society.

b. Repeated revelations of accounting scandals and audit failures related to undetected frauds have seriously damaged public confidence in external auditors.

c. A strong ethical tone at the top of an organization that permeates corporate culture is essential in mitigating the risk of fraud.

d. All of the above.

e. None of the above.

2-21 **LO 5** The Sarbanes-Oxley Act enacted which of the following provisions as a response to a growing number of frauds?
a. The PCAOB was established, and it has the power to conduct inspections of public company audits.
b. The lead audit partner and reviewing partner must rotate off the audit of a publicly traded company at least every ten years.
c. Annual reports must state the responsibility of management for establishing and maintaining an adequate internal control structure and procedures for financial reporting, and management must have the company's internal audit function attest to the accuracy of the annual reports.
d. All of the above.
e. None of the above.

2-22 **LO 5** Which of the following statements is correct regarding the PCAOB?
a. The PCAOB is a nonprofit corporation, not an agency of the U.S. government.
b. The PCAOB will have five financially literate members who are prominent individuals of integrity and reputation with a commitment to the interests of investors and the public.
c. The PCAOB has authority to set standards related to public company audit reports and to conduct inspections of registered external audit firms.
d. All of the above.
e. None of the above.

2-23 **LO 6** Audit committee activities and responsibilities include which of the following?
a. Selecting the external audit firm.
b. Approving corporate strategy.
c. Reviewing management performance and determining compensation.
d. All of the above.
e. None of the above.

2-24 **LO 6** Which of the following audit committee responsibilities has the NYSE mandated?
a. Obtaining each year a report by the internal auditor that addresses the company's internal control procedures, any quality-control or regulatory problems, and any relationships that might threaten the independence of the internal auditor.
b. Discussing in its meetings the company's earnings press releases as well as financial information and earnings guidance provided to analysts.
c. Reviewing with the internal auditor any audit problems or difficulties that they have had with management.
d. All of the above.
e. None of the above.

REVIEW AND SHORT CASE QUESTIONS

NOTE: Completing Review and Short Case Questions does not require the student to reference additional resources and materials.

2-25 **LO 1** Define fraud, and explain the two types of misstatements that are relevant to auditors' consideration of fraud.

2-26 **LO 1** What are the most common approaches that perpetrators use to commit fraudulent financial reporting? What are the common types of fraudulent financial reporting?

2-27 **LO 1** Assume that you are interviewed by a student newspaper regarding the nature of accounting fraud. The reporter says, "As I understand it, asset misappropriations are more likely to be

NOTE: For the remaining problems, we make special note of those addressing international issues, professional skepticism, and ethics. *We do not make special note of fraud-related problems in this chapter because of the heavy emphasis on that topic throughout this chapter.*

found in small organizations, but not in larger organizations. On the other hand, fraudulent financial reporting is more likely to be found in larger organizations." How would you respond to the reporter's observation?

2-28 LO 1   Refer to *Exhibit 2.1* and answer the following questions.
a.   What is a Ponzi scheme?
b.   Describe the key elements of the Bernie Madoff fraud.
c.   Is this fraud primarily a case of asset misappropriation or fraudulent financial reporting?

2-29 LO 2   Refer to the *Focus on Fraud* feature "The Great Salad Oil Swindle of 1963" and answer the following questions.
a.   How did management perpetrate the fraud?
b.   What was management's incentive to perpetrate the fraud?
c.   Is this fraud primarily a case of asset misappropriation or fraudulent financial reporting?

2-30 LO 2   The fraud triangle identifies incentives, opportunities, and rationalizations as the three elements associated with frauds. Describe how these elements are related to the occurrence of fraud.

2-31 LO 2   List some common incentives for managers to commit fraudulent financial reporting.

2-32 LO 2   Identify factors (red flags) that would be strong indicators of opportunities to commit fraud.

2-33 LO 2   Is the ability to rationalize the fraud an important aspect to consider when analyzing a potentially fraudulent situation? What are some of the common rationalizations used by fraud perpetrators?

2-34 LO 2   Each of the following scenarios is based on facts in an actual fraud. Categorize each scenario as primarily indicating (1) an incentive to commit fraud, (2) an opportunity to commit fraud, or (3) a rationalization to commit fraud. State your reasoning for each categorization.
a.   There was intense pressure to keep the corporation's stock from declining further. This pressure came from investors, analysts, and the CEO, whose financial well-being was significantly dependent on the corporation's stock price.
b.   A group of top-level management was compensated (mostly in the form of stock options) well in excess of what would be considered normal for their positions in this industry.
c.   Top management of the company closely guards internal financial information, to the extent that even some employees on a need-to-know basis are denied full access.
d.   Managing specific financial ratios is very important to the company, and both management and analysts are keenly observant of variability in key ratios. Key ratios for the company changed very little even though the ratios for the overall industry were quite volatile during the time period.
e.   In an effort to reduce certain accrued expenses to meet budget targets, the CFO directs the general accounting department to reallocate a division's expenses by a significant amount. The general accounting department refuses to acquiesce to the request, but the journal entry is made through the corporate office. An accountant in the general accounting department is uncomfortable with the journal entries required to reallocate divisional expenses. He brings his concerns to

the CFO, who assures him that everything will be fine and that the entries are necessary. The accountant considers resigning, but he does not have another job lined up and is worried about supporting his family. Therefore, he never voices his concerns to either the internal or external auditors.

f. Accounting records were either nonexistent or in a state of such disorganization that significant effort was required to locate or compile them.

2-35 **LO 3** Refer to *Exhibit 2.3* and briefly describe the frauds that were perpetrated at the following companies. For each company, categorize the fraud as involving primarily (1) asset misappropriation or (2) fraudulent financial reporting.

a. Enron
b. WorldCom
c. Parmalat
d. HealthSouth
e. Dell
f. Koss Corporation
g. Olympus
h. Longtop Financial Technologies
i. Peregrine Financial Group
j. Sino-Forest Corporation
k. Diamond Foods, Inc.

PROFESSIONAL SKEPTICISM

2-36 **LO 3** Refer to the *Focus on Fraud* feature "The Crucial Role of Professional Skepticism."

a. What is professional skepticism?
b. Why is professional skepticism helpful for detecting fraud?
c. What are the key behaviors needed to successfully exercise professional skepticism during the performance of the audit?
d. Why is it sometimes difficult for auditors to exercise appropriate levels of professional skepticism in practice?
e. Imagine that you are working on an audit engagement. What are the personal characteristics and behaviors of management or other client employees that might make you skeptical about whether or not they are providing you accurate audit evidence? Aside from personal observations, what publicly available information about management or other client employees could you obtain to determine whether you should exercise heightened professional skepticism in your dealings with these individuals?

PROFESSIONAL SKEPTICISM

2-37 **LO 3** For each of the following situations indicating heightened fraud risk, discuss how a professionally skeptical auditor might interpret the situation.

a. The company is not as profitable as its competitors, but it seems to have good products. However, it has a deficiency in internal control over disbursements that makes it subject to management override.
b. The company is doing better than its competitors. Although sales are about the same as competitors, net income is significantly more. Management attributes the greater profitability to better control of expenses.
c. The company is financially distressed and is at some risk of defaulting on its debt covenants. The company improves its current ratio and other ratios by making an unusually large payment against its current liabilities, accompanied by highly discounted sales if their customers paid before year-end.

    d. A smaller public company has a CFO who has centralized power under her. Her style is very intimidating. She is not a CPA, and she has limited accounting experience. The company has not been able to increase profitability during her time with the company.

2-38 `LO 3` COSO released its third study on fraudulent financial reporting in 2010. Describe major findings of the study.

2-39 `LO 3` The Enron fraud is considered by many to be one of the most significant frauds of the early 2000s.

    a. Describe the various failures and environmental characteristics during this time period that enabled the Enron fraud to happen.

    b. What elements of the fraud triangle seem most relevant to the Enron fraud?

2-40 `LO 4` What is the responsibility of the external auditor to detect material fraud?

2-41 `LO 4` The CAQ issued a paper in 2010 on deterring and detecting fraud. The CAQ report identifies three ways in which individuals involved in the financial reporting process (management, audit committee, internal audit, external audit, and regulatory authorities) can mitigate the risk of fraudulent financial reporting. Describe these three ways, and articulate your opinion on whether these will be effective given your knowledge of frauds that have happened in the relatively recent past (such as Enron, WorldCom, Parmalat, and Koss).

2-42 `LO 5` Refer to *Exhibit 2.5* and answer the following questions.

    a. (Sections 101, 104, and 105) How does the establishment and operation of the PCAOB help to ensure quality external audits? How will audit firm inspections and investigations by the PCAOB help ensure high audit quality?

    b. (Sections 201–203) How do Sections 201–203 address auditor independence concerns?

    c. (Section 206) What is a cooling-off period, and how does it address auditor independence concerns?

    d. (Section 301) How do the audit committee requirements help ensure effective corporate governance?

    e. (Sections 302 and 906) How do the officer certification requirements help to address the risk of fraud in publicly traded organizations? What is the likelihood that a CFO who is committing fraudulent financial reporting would sign the certification falsely, and what are your reactions to that possibility?

    f. (Section 401) How does this section relate to the Enron fraud?

    g. (Section 404) How do the management assessment and auditor attestation of internal controls contained in this section help to address the risk of fraud in publicly traded organizations?

    h. (Section 407) Why is it important that at least one member of the audit committee be a financial expert? What are the financial reporting implications if the audit committee does not have any individuals serving on it who possess financial expertise?

    i. (Section 802) How does this section relate to the Enron fraud?

2-43 LO 5 Are nonpublic organizations required to adhere to the requirements of the Sarbanes-Oxley Act? Explain.

2-44 LO 6 Corporate governance is the process by which the owners and creditors of an organization exert control over and require accountability for the resources entrusted to the organization. Refer to *Exhibit 2.6* and *Exhibit 2.7* and answer the following questions.

a. List the major parties involved in corporate governance.

b. Describe the general roles and activities for each party.

2-45 LO 6 Describe the five key principles of effective corporate governance articulated in the 2010 report of the NYSE.

2-46 LO 6 Following is a summary of the NYSE corporate governance requirements of companies listed on this stock exchange. For each requirement, state how it is intended to help to address the risk of fraud in publicly traded organizations.

a. Boards need to consist of a majority of independent directors.

b. Boards need to hold regular executive sessions of independent directors without management present.

c. Boards must have a nominating/corporate governance committee composed entirely of independent directors.

d. The nominating/corporate governance committee must have a written charter that addresses the committee's purpose and responsibilities, and there must be an annual performance evaluation of the committee.

e. Boards must have a compensation committee composed entirely of independent directors.

f. The compensation committee must have a written charter that addresses the committee's purpose and responsibilities, which must include (at a minimum) the responsibility to review and approve corporate goals relevant to CEO compensation, make recommendations to the board about non-CEO compensation and incentive-based compensation plans, and produce a report on executive compensation; there must also be an annual performance evaluation of the committee.

g. Boards must have an audit committee with a minimum of three independent members.

h. The audit committee must have a written charter that addresses the committee's purpose and responsibilities, and the committee must produce an audit committee report; there must also be an annual performance evaluation of the committee.

i. Companies must adopt and disclose corporate governance guidelines addressing director qualification standards, director responsibilities, director access to management and independent advisors, director compensation, director continuing education, management succession, and an annual performance evaluation of the board.

j. Companies must adopt and disclose a code of business conduct and ethics for directors, officers, and employees.

k. Foreign companies must disclose how their corporate governance practices differ from those followed by domestic companies

l. CEOs need to provide an annual certification of compliance with corporate governance standards.

m. Companies must have an internal audit function, whether housed internally or outsourced.

2-47 **LO 6** Following is a summary of the NYSE listing requirements for audit committee responsibilities of companies listed on this stock exchange. For each requirement, state how it is intended to help to address the risk of fraud in publicly traded organizations.

a. Obtaining an annual report by the external auditor that addresses the company's internal control procedures, any quality-control or regulatory problems, and any relationships that might threaten the independence of the external auditor

b. Discussing the company's financial statements with management and the external auditor

c. Discussing in its meetings the company's earnings press releases, as well as financial information and earnings guidance provided to analysts

d. Discussing in its meetings policies with respect to risk assessment and risk management

e. Meeting separately with management, internal auditors, and the external auditor on a periodic basis

f. Reviewing with the external auditor any audit problems or difficulties that they have had with management

g. Setting clear hiring policies for employees or former employees of the external auditors

h. Reporting regularly to the board of directors

2-48 **LO 6** Audit committees are an important element of corporate governance and have taken on additional responsibilities following the passage of the Sarbanes-Oxley Act.

a. Describe the changes in audit committee membership, and list duties that were mandated by the Sarbanes-Oxley Act. Also, describe any other increased responsibilities of audit committees following the passage of the Sarbanes-Oxley Act.

b. The audit committee now has ownership of the relationship with the external auditor. What are the implications of this change for the audit committee and for the external auditor?

c. Assume that management and the auditor disagree on the appropriate accounting for a complex transaction. The external auditor has conveyed the disagreement to the audit committee and provided an assessment that the disagreement is on the economics of the transaction and has nothing to do with earnings management. What is the responsibility of the audit committee? What skills of audit committee members do you think might be helpful in this type of situation?

2-49 **LO 6** The following factors describe a potential audit client. For each factor, indicate whether it is indicative of poor corporate governance. Explain the reasoning for your assessment. Finally, identify the risks to reliable financial reporting that are associated with each factor.

a. The company is in the financial services sector and has a large number of consumer loans, including mortgages, outstanding.

b. The CEO's and CFO's compensation is based on three components: (a) base salary, (b) bonus based on growth in assets and profits, and (c) significant stock options.

c. The audit committee meets semiannually. It is chaired by a retired CFO who knows the company well because she had served as the CFO of a division of the firm. The other two members are local community members—one is the president of the Chamber of Commerce and the other is a retired executive from a successful local manufacturing firm.

d. The company has an internal auditor who reports directly to the CFO and makes an annual report to the audit committee.

e. The CEO is a dominating personality—not unusual in this environment. He has been on the job for six months and has decreed that he is streamlining the organization to reduce costs and centralize authority (most of it in him).

f. The company has a loan committee. It meets quarterly to approve, on an ex-post basis, all loans over $300 million (top 5% for this institution).

g. The previous auditor has resigned because of a dispute regarding the accounting treatment and fair value assessment of some of the loans.

FRAUD FOCUS: CONTEMPORARY AND HISTORICAL CASES

PROFESSIONAL SKEPTICISM

ETHICS

2-50 **Koss Corporation and Grant Thornton (LO 2, 3, 4, 6)** In the *Professional Judgment in Context* feature at the outset of the chapter, we introduced you to the Koss Corporation fraud. In this problem, we provide you with further details about that fraud. During the fall of 2009, Koss Corporation, a Wisconsin-based manufacturer of stereo headphone equipment, revealed that its vice president of finance (Sujata "Sue" Sachdeva) had defrauded the company of approximately $31 million over a period of at least five years. Grant Thornton LLP was the company's auditor, and the firm issued unqualified audit opinions for the entire period in which they worked for Koss. According to reports, Sachdeva's theft accelerated over a period of years as follows:

FY 2005	$2,195,477
FY 2006	$2,227,669
FY 2007	$3,160,310
FY 2008	$5,040,968
FY 2009	$8,485,937
Q1 FY 2010	$5,326,305
Q2 FY 2010	$4,917,005

To give you a sense of the magnitude of the fraud, annual revenues for Koss Corporation are in the range of $40 to $45 million annually. Previously reported pre-tax income for fiscal years 2007 and through Q1 2010 was as follows:

FY 2007	$8,344,715
FY 2008	$7,410,569
FY 2009	$2,887,730
FY 2010	$ 928,491

How could Sachdeva have stolen so much money and fooled so many people over a long period? It is thought that Sachdeva hid the theft in the company's cost-of-goods-sold accounts, and that weak internal controls and poor corporate governance and oversight enabled her to conceal the theft from corporate officials. Certainly, there must have been questions raised about the company's deteriorating financial condition. But any number of excuses could have been used by Sachdeva to explain the missing money. For example, she might have blamed higher cost of goods sold on a change in suppliers or rising raw materials prices.

Another contributing factor in Sachdeva's ability to conceal her thefts was that top management of Koss had a high degree of trust in her, so they did not monitor the accounts that she controlled at the company.

Sachdeva's total compensation for fiscal year 2009 was $173,734. But according to published reports, Sachdeva was known for her unusually lavish lifestyle and shopping sprees. It is reported that she spent $225,000 at a single Houston, Texas, jewelry store. Another report describes a $1.4 million shopping spree at Valentina Boutique in Mequon, Wisconsin. People familiar with her spending habits assumed that she used family money and that her husband's job as a prominent pediatrician funded her extravagant lifestyle. The fraud was ultimately uncovered because American Express became concerned when it realized that Sachdeva was paying for large balances on her personal account with wire transfers from a Koss Corporation account. American Express notified the FBI and relayed its concerns.

Upon learning of the fraud, Koss Corporation executives fired Sachdeva, along with the company's audit firm, Grant Thornton LLP. About 22,000 items—including high-end women's clothing, shoes, handbags, and jewelry—have been recovered to date. Sachdeva stored the bulk of the items she purchased in rented storage units in order to conceal the items from her husband.

After considering this situation, answer the following questions:

a. Why might Koss management have placed so much trust in Sachdeva, along with providing only minimal supervision and monitoring?

b. What was Grant Thornton's obligation to uncover the fraud?

c. Why should Sachdeva's lavish lifestyle have raised suspicions? Why might it have been ignored or explained away by her professional colleagues?

d. How could the other members of management, the audit committee, and the auditors have been more professionally skeptical in this situation?

e. What was the audit committee's responsibility in noticing that something looked amiss in the financial statements?

f. Sachdeva paid for her purchases using corporate credit cards. What internal controls could the company have used to prevent inappropriate use of the credit cards?

g. Some reports have described Sachdeva as having a very dominating personality, and revelations were made about the fact that she would often be verbally abusive of her subordinates in front of top-level managers at Koss. How should top-level managers have responded to this behavior? What actions could the subordinates have taken to respond to this behavior? Why might this behavior be a red flag indicating a heightened risk of fraud?

2-51   **Koss Corporation**
(LO 3, 5, 6)   Read the facts of the case in *Problem 2–50* to become familiar with the fraud involving Koss Corporation. From the company's October 7, 2009, proxy statement (Def 14A filing with the SEC), we know the following facts about the

company's audit committee. Members, ages, and descriptions of the audit committee members are as follows:

THOMAS L. DOERR   65, has been a director of the company since 1987. In 1972, Mr. Doerr co-founded Leeson Electric Corporation and served as its president and CEO until 1982. The company manufactures industrial electric motors. In 1983, Mr. Doerr incorporated Doerr Corporation as a holding company for the purpose of acquiring established companies involved in distributing products to industrial and commercial markets. Currently, Mr. Doerr serves as president of Doerr Corporation. Mr. Doerr owns no stock in Koss Corporation and received $24,000 in cash compensation during 2009 to serve on the audit committee.

LAWRENCE S. MATTSON   77, has been a director of the company since 1978. Mr. Mattson is the retired president of Oster company, a division of Sunbeam Corporation, which manufactures and sells portable household appliances. Mr. Mattson is the designated audit committee financial expert. Mr. Mattson owns no stock in Koss Corporation and received $23,000 in cash compensation during 2009 to serve on the audit committee.

THEODORE H. NIXON   57, has been a director of the company since 2006. Since 1992, Mr. Nixon has been the CEO of D.D. Williamson, which is a manufacturer of caramel coloring used in the food and beverage industries. Mr. Nixon joined D.D. Williamson in 1974 and was promoted to president and chief operating officer in 1982. Mr. Nixon is also a director of the nonprofit Center for Quality of Management. Mr. Nixon owns 2,480 shares of common stock of the company (less than 1% of outstanding shares) and received $21,000 in cash compensation during 2009 to serve on the audit committee.

JOHN J. STOLLENWERK   69, has been a director of the company since 1986. Mr. Stollenwerk is the chairman of the Allen–Edmonds Shoe Corporation, an international manufacturer and retailer of high-quality footwear. He is also a director of Allen–Edmonds Shoe Corporation; Badger Meter, Inc.; U.S. Bancorp; and Northwestern Mutual Life Insurance Company. Mr. Stollenwerk owns 13,551 shares of common stock of the company (less than 1% of outstanding shares) and received $23,000 in cash compensation during 2009 to serve on the audit committee.

AUDIT COMMITTEE

- The Audit committee met three times during the fiscal year ended June 30, 2009. The external auditors (Grant Thornton LLP) were present at two of these meetings to discuss their audit scope and the results of their audit.
- Koss claims that each member of the audit committee is independent as defined in NASDAQ Marketplace Rule 4200.
- The proxy statement describes the responsibilities of the audit committee as follows: "The audit committee, among other things, monitors the integrity of the financial reporting process, systems of internal controls, and financial statements and reports of the company; appoints, compensates, retains, and oversees the company's independent auditors,

including reviewing the qualifications, performance and independence of the independent auditors; reviews and pre-approves all audit, attests and reviews services and permitted nonaudit services; oversees the audit work performed by the company's internal accounting staff; and oversees the company's compliance with legal and regulatory requirements. The audit committee meets twice a year with the company's independent accountants to discuss the results of their examinations, their evaluations of the company's internal controls, and the overall quality of the company's financial reporting."

a. Does the description of the audit committee members warrant a conclusion that its members appear to be professionally qualified for their positions? Do they meet enough times during the year to accomplish their responsibilities? What additional information might you need to answer this question, and how would the auditor obtain that information?

b. Who was the audit committee financial expert? Do you think that the experiences of this individual as described should ensure that he is truly a financial expert capable of fulfilling his roles in this regard? Why is financial expertise important for audit committee members in general?

c. In your opinion, was the compensation that, the audit committee members received for their services adequate?

d. Based on the information that you have learned in Parts a–c of this problem, what weaknesses in the audit committee governance structure existed at Koss Corporation immediately preceding the discovery of fraud?

PROFESSIONAL SKEPTICISM

2-52 **Dell, Inc.** **(LO 1, 3, 4, 6)**   In August 2010, Michael Dell, Dell, Inc.'s CEO and chairman of the board, was reelected to Dell's board of directors by Dell's shareholders. However, not all of the shareholders were happy with Mr. Dell's reappointment. Specifically, two labor groups that own shares of Dell stock wanted Mr. Dell removed from the board because of an action and settlement of the SEC involving the company and Mr. Dell. The SEC complaint alleged various accounting manipulations that called into question Dell's reported financial success from 2002 to 2006. In July 2010, Dell, Inc. agreed to pay $100 million to settle SEC charges, without admitting or denying guilt. Mr. Dell agreed to pay a $4 million fine, also without admitting or denying guilt. Consider the principles of effective corporate governance presented in this chapter and answer the following questions.

a. What principles of corporate governance appear to have been missing at Dell?

b. Given the apparent actions of Mr. Dell, along with his management and board roles, should Dell's external auditor expect the corporate governance at Dell to be effective?

c. How might Dell's external auditor respond to concerns about the quality of governance at Dell?

d. Given the SEC settlement, should Dell's board have an independent chair?

e. Given the SEC settlement, should Mr. Dell be removed from his CEO position?

APPLICATION ACTIVITIES

NOTE: Completing Application Activities requires students to reference additional resources and materials.

PROFESSIONAL SKEPTICISM

2-53 **CAQ (LO 3)** Obtain a copy of the report by the Global Public Policy Committee, "Enhancing Auditor Professional Skepticism" (November 2013) at *http://www.thecaq.org/docs/research/skepticismreport.pdf*. Answer the following questions.

a. Explain the professional skepticism continuum and articulate how it relates to the extent of audit evidence collection and documentation.

b. What are some threats to individual auditor professional skepticism? How can these threats be mitigated?

c. What are some common human judgment tendencies that can weaken individual auditor professional skepticism?

2-54 **PCAOB (LO 4)** Obtain a copy of the PCAOB's report titled "Observations on Auditors' Implementation of PCAOB Standards Relating to Auditors' Responsibilities with Respect to Fraud." You can use any search engine or go to *http://pcaobus.org/Inspections/Documents/2007_01–22_Release_2007–001.pdf*.

The PCAOB's report summarizes findings from inspections of audit engagements as they relate to the performance of fraud detection audit procedures. The PCAOB report comments on auditor deficiencies in each of the following six areas:

a. Auditors' overall approach to the detection of fraud

b. Brainstorming sessions

c. Auditors' responses to fraud risk factors

d. Financial statement misstatements

e. Risk of management override of controls

f. Other areas to improve fraud detection

Summarize the PCAOB's concerns with respect to problems its inspection teams have noted in auditors' performance in each of the areas listed.

2-55 **PCAOB (LO 5)** The development of the PCAOB was one of the most significant components of the Sarbanes-Oxley Act of 2002. Go to the PCAOB's web site, *www.pcaobus.org* and answer the following questions.

a. Identify the responsibilities of the PCAOB as described in the web site. How does the inspection process performed by the PCAOB likely affect the practice of external auditing?

b. The PCAOB can have no more than two CPAs among its five members. Read the biographies of the current board members and note which have the CPA designation. What might be the rationale for such a requirement? What are the advantages and disadvantages of the limitation concerning CPA members on the board?

c. Do the auditing standards set by the PCAOB apply to audits of nonpublic companies? Explain.

2-56 **SEC (LO 5, 6)** The Sarbanes-Oxley Act mandates that the audit committee of the board of directors of public companies be directly responsible for the appointment, compensation, and oversight of the external auditors. In addition, the audit committee must pre-approve all nonaudit services that might be performed by the audit firm.

a. Discuss the rationale for this mandate, as opposed to the alternative of letting the shareholders, CFO, or CEO have these responsibilities.

b. What factors should the audit committee consider in evaluating the independence of the external auditor?

c. Locate the proxy statement for a publicly traded company of your choice. To do so, go to the SEC's web site, *www.sec. gov*. Search for your company's filings using the EDGAR data system on the web site. Once you have located your company's filings, you may narrow your search by typing in the phrase "Def 14A," which is the proxy filing. Once you have found the proxy, read and summarize the disclosures provided concerning the audit committee members, their compensation, their responsibilities, and their activities.

2-57 LO 5, 6 Select either a public company or a company that is near your university and perform a preliminary review of its corporate governance. Identify all the sources of evidence for your conclusion regarding corporate governance. Identify the strengths and weaknesses of the governance and describe the implications of the governance structure for the auditor.

2-58 SEC (LO 5, 6) Audit committees have taken on much more responsibility in the past few years. However, it must also be remembered that audit committee service is not a full-time appointment.

a. Search annual reports at the SEC's web site via EDGAR or by looking up the home page of selected companies. Select five companies (preferably in different industries) and prepare a report that describes the following:
  • An analysis of the audit committee charters that identifies the commonalities in all the charters as well as any differences
  • The characteristics of audit committee members (whether a CPA, current job status, other experience, and so on)
  • The individual(s) identified as a financial expert
  • The number of times the audit committee met during the year

b. Answer the following questions:
  • How do the companies differ in terms of audit committee characteristics? What do you think are the underlying causes of the differences?
  • What are the professional backgrounds of individuals designated as financial experts? How do these differ across the various organizations?
  • What are the implications of variations in the amount of time that the audit committee met during the year?

INTERNATIONAL **2-59** LO 6 Corporate governance is not just an issue for U.S. companies; companies throughout the world need to focus on corporate governance issues. However, the principles and challenges of corporate governance vary across countries. Select a country and research the corporate governance issues in that country. A good starting point is the web site of the Organisation for Economic Co-operation and Development (OECD) (*www.oecd.org*) or the World Bank (*www.worldbank.org*), which provides corporate governance information by country. Also, Transparency International (*www.transparency.org/*) provides country-specific metrics on corruption and bribery—activities that could be associated with fraud. Using information from these web sites, along with other resources, prepare a report that addresses the following issues for your selected country: (1) compare and contrast the corporate governance principles of your selected country with the United States, (2) identify the relevant corporate governance parties and their roles, (3) describe recent challenges related to the corporate governance for your selected country, and (4) list and describe recent corporate governance activities in your selected country.

ACADEMIC RESEARCH CASES

NOTE: Completing Academic Research Cases requires students to reference additional resources and materials.

INTERNATIONAL

SEARCH HINT

It is easy to locate these academic research articles! Use a search engine such as Google Scholar or an electronic research platform such as ABI Inform, and search using the author names and part of the article title.

2-60 **LO 6** Locate and read the article listed below and answer the following questions.

Knechel, W. R., and M. Willekens. 2006. The role of risk management and governance in determining audit demand. *Journal of Business Finance & Accounting* 33 (9–10): 1344–1367.

a. What is the issue being addressed in the paper?
b. What are the findings of the paper?
c. Why is this paper important to auditors, and what are the implications of this paper for the auditing profession?
d. Describe the research methodology used as a basis for the conclusions.
e. Describe any limitations of the research.

2-61 **LO 6** Locate and read the article listed below and answer the following questions:

Archambeault, D., F. T. DeZoort, and T. Holt. 2008. The need for an internal auditor report to external stakeholders to improve governance transparency. *Accounting Horizons* 22 (4): 375–388.

a. What is the issue being addressed in the paper?
b. What are the findings of the paper?
c. Why is this paper important to auditors, and what are the implications of this paper for the auditing profession?
d. Describe the research methodology used as a basis for the conclusions.
e. Describe any limitations of the research.

2-62 **LO 6** Locate and read the article listed below and answer the following questions.

Mustafa, S. T., and N. B. Youssef. 2010. Audit committee financial expertise and misappropriation of assets. *Managerial Auditing Journal* 25 (3): 208–225.

a. What is the issue being addressed in the paper?
b. What are the findings of the paper?
c. Why is this paper important to auditors, and what are the implications of this paper for the auditing profession?
d. Describe the research methodology used as a basis for the conclusions.
e. Describe any limitations of the research.

FORD AND TOYOTA

2-63 **Ford Motor Company and Toyota Motor Corporation (LO 5, 6)** Within many of the subsequent chapters of this book, we highlight chapter-relevant material using Ford Motor Company (Ford) and Toyota Motor Corporation (Toyota) as practical examples. We pose questions that require you to apply the concepts introduced in that chapter to the facts of Ford and Toyota. We have selected these companies because they (1) are large, well-known manufacturers of products that are familiar to you, (2) operate in dynamic industries that present serious risks and challenges, (3) are both publicly traded on the NYSE, and (4) differ in terms of their issuer status with the SEC (Ford is a U.S.-based company and therefore files an annual Form 10-K and Form Def 14A, whereas Toyota is not a U.S.-based company and therefore files an annual Form 20-F).

Go to the Ford and Toyota web sites or to the EDGAR database on the SEC's web site and download the following:

- Ford's 2014 annual report
- Ford's 2014 10-K
- Ford's 2014 Def 14A (i.e., proxy statement)
- Toyota's 2014 annual report
- Toyota's 2014 20-F

Chapter-end materials concerning Ford and Toyota contain questions referenced to specific pages within these sources. These materials will introduce you to the companies, provide you with insight into the automotive industry, give you detailed financial results, and describe relevant corporate governance issues. In subsequent chapters, we present additional materials from these sources tailored to the topics of those chapters. For *Chapter 2*, you should answer the following questions.

Source and Reference	Question

General Background Questions

Ford annual report or 10-K
Toyota annual report or 20-F

1a. Describe the history of Ford, its current business, operating sectors, and reportable segments.

1b. Describe the factors affecting Ford's profitability and factors affecting the automotive industry in general.

1c. Compare the nature of Ford's history, business sectors, and reportable segments to those of Toyota.

Corporate Governance Questions

Ford Def 14A

2a. What is the purpose of the Form Def 14A?

2b. What does "Def" stand for?

2c. What types of information does a proxy contain?

3a. Who are the board members who are standing for election at Ford?

3b. Which of them has been deemed "independent" of Ford?

3c. How does Ford determine director independence?

3d. Why does independence matter to shareholders?

3e. What characteristics is Ford seeking when considering individuals to serve on its board?

3f. How are non-employee board members compensated? Could the nature of the compensation potentially affect the director's independence? Explain.

4a. Describe Ford's audit committee and its duties.

4b. Who is the designated financial expert on the audit committee? Does the designation of only one individual as a financial expert seem adequate for the complexity of Ford and the requirements of the Sarbanes-Oxley Act?

4c. Review the audit committee's report and describe its primary contents.

Toyota annual report or 20-F

5a. Who is the auditor for Ford? Who is the auditor for Toyota?

5b. What were the Ford audit fees as a percentage of (a) total revenue, and (b) total assets?

5c. What were the Toyota audit fees as a percentage of (a) total revenue, and (b) total assets? Compare these amounts to those for Ford and discuss possible reasons for and implications of the differences.

5d. Audit fees were not always publicly disclosed. In fact, such disclosure became mandatory only since the year 2000 in the United States. Why is public disclosure of audit and other fees paid to the audit firm important?

Toyota 20-F

6. Read Toyota's corporate governance disclosures. What are the significant differences in corporate governance between Toyota and Ford?

3

Internal Control Over Financial Reporting: Responsibilities of Management and the External Auditors

CHAPTER OVERVIEW AND LEARNING OBJECTIVES

This chapter focuses on understanding a client's internal control over financial reporting (Phase II of the audit opinion formulation process). An important part of an organization's corporate governance is its system of internal control. All organizations need effective internal control over financial reporting so that they can produce reliable financial statements. For example, internal control is needed to provide reasonable assurance that all sales are recorded, all cash receipts are collected and properly deposited in the organization's bank accounts, and all assets and liabilities are properly valued. Management has the responsibility to design, implement, and maintain effective internal control over financial reporting. Management of public companies will also evaluate and publicly report on the effectiveness of the company's internal control. The external auditor needs to understand a client's internal control over financial reporting and how management has fulfilled its internal control responsibilities. For large public companies, the external auditor will also issue an opinion of the effectiveness of the client's internal control over financial reporting. This chapter helps you identify aspects of a client's internal controls that you need to understand in order to plan and conduct an audit.

Through studying this chapter, you will be able to achieve these learning objectives:

1. Articulate the importance of internal control over financial reporting for organizations.

2. Define internal control as presented in COSO's 2013 *Internal Control–Integrated Framework* and identify the components of internal control.

3. Describe the control environment component of internal control, list its principles, and provide examples of each principle.

4. Describe the risk assessment component of internal control, list its principles, and provide examples of each principle.

5. Describe the control activities component of internal control, list its principles, and provide examples of each principle.

6. Describe the information and communication component of internal control, list its principles, and provide examples of each principle.

7. Describe the monitoring component of internal control, list its principles, and provide examples of each principle.

8. Identify management's responsibilities related to internal control over financial reporting.

9. Distinguish between material weaknesses, significant deficiencies, and control deficiencies in internal control over financial reporting.

10. Articulate the importance of internal control over financial reporting for the external audit and apply the concepts related to management's and the auditor's assessments of internal control effectiveness.

THE AUDIT OPINION FORMULATION PROCESS

I. Making Client Acceptance and Continuance Decisions
Chapter 1

II. Performing Risk Assessment
Chapters 3, 7, and 9–13

III. Obtaining Evidence About Internal Control Operating Effectiveness
Chapters 8–13 and 16

IV. Obtaining Substantive Evidence About Accounts, Disclosures and Assertions
Chapters 8–13 and 16

V. Completing the Audit and Making Reporting Decisions
Chapters 14 and 15

The Auditing Profession, the Risk of Fraud and Mechanisms to Address Fraud: Regulation, Corporate Governance, and Audit Quality
Chapters 1 and 2

Professional Liability and the Need for Quality Auditor Judgments and Ethical Decisions
Chapter 4

The Audit Opinion Formulation Process and a Framework for Obtaining Audit Evidence
Chapters 5 and 6

PROFESSIONAL JUDGMENT IN CONTEXT

The Importance of Effective Internal Control for Reliable Financial Reporting: KIT Digital

Most organizations, presumably, have reliable financial reporting as one of their objectives. To achieve this objective, organizations need to have effective internal controls in place. Such controls were not in place at KIT Digital.

In November 2012, KIT Digital announced it would have to restate earnings for the past three years because the organization had not properly accounted for revenue related to software-license agreements. It is important to note that on March 30, 2012, KIT disclosed that its external audit firm at the time, Grant Thornton, noted a material weakness in the organization's internal control over financial reporting. The auditor's report indicated that KIT Digital had not maintained effective internal control over financial reporting as of December 31, 2011. The material weakness noted by Grant Thornton related to the lack of finance personnel with understanding of U.S. GAAP sufficient to provide reasonable assurance that all transactions were reported in accordance with U.S. GAAP on a timely basis.

Postscript: In December 2012, KIT Digital was delisted from the NASDAQ Stock Market. In April 2013, KIT filed for bankruptcy, and later in 2013, KIT Digital exited bankruptcy and emerged under a new name, Piksel.

As you read through this chapter, consider the following questions:

- What is internal control over financial reporting, and what are its components? (LO 2, 3, 4, 5, 6, 7)
- Why is internal control over financial reporting important to an organization? (LO 1)
- How does internal control help an organization achieve reliable financial reporting? (LO 1)
- What are management's responsibilities related to internal control over financial reporting? (LO 8)
- What is a material weakness in internal control over financial reporting? (LO 9)
- Why does an external auditor need to know about a client's internal control over financial reporting? (LO 10)

Importance of Internal Control Over Financial Reporting

LO 1 Articulate the importance of internal control over financial reporting for organizations.

Internal control helps an organization mitigate the risks of not achieving its objectives. Examples of objectives include achieving profitability, ensuring efficiency of operations, manufacturing high-quality products or providing high-quality services, adhering to governmental and regulatory requirements, conducting operations and employee relations in a socially responsible manner, and providing users with reliable financial information. Organizations face many risks of not achieving reliable financial reporting. For example, a salesperson may overstate sales to improve the likelihood of receiving a bonus. Employees in the receiving area may be too busy to accurately record inventory when it is received. Management may misapply judgment and overvalue intangible assets. Management needs to identify the risks to its organization of not achieving reliable financial reporting. Once these risks are identified, management implements controls to provide reasonable assurance that material misstatements do not occur in the financial statements.

Defining Internal Control

LO 2 Define internal control as presented in COSO's 2013 *Internal Control–Integrated Framework* and identify the components of internal control.

Just as a U.S. company might refer to generally accepted accounting principles (GAAP) as a framework for determining whether its financial statements are fairly presented, companies need to refer to a framework of internal control when assessing the effectiveness of internal control over financial reporting. The most widely used framework in the United States is the *Internal Control–Integrated Framework* published by the Committee of Sponsoring Organizations of the Treadway Commission (COSO). The sponsoring organizations first came together in the 1980s to address the increasing fraudulent financial reporting that was occurring at that time. COSO released the original *Internal Control–Integrated Framework* in 1992. The framework gained widespread acceptance following the financial failures of the early 2000s. In 2013, COSO updated, enhanced, and clarified the framework. Today, **COSO's Internal Control–Integrated Framework** (often referred to simply as "COSO") is the most widely used internal control framework in the United States and is also used throughout the world.

COSO defines **internal control** as:

a process, effected by an entity's board of directors, management, and other personnel, designed to provide reasonable assurance regarding the achievement of objectives relating to operations, reporting, and compliance.

Important elements of the definition recognize that internal control is:

- A *process* consisting of ongoing tasks and activities.
- *Effected by people* and is not just about policy manuals, systems, and forms. People at every level of the organization, ranging from shipping clerks to the internal auditor to the chief financial officer (CFO), chief executive officer (CEO), and the board of directors, impact internal control.
- *Able to provide reasonable assurance*, but not absolute assurance, regarding the achievement of objectives. Limitations of internal control preclude absolute assurance. These limitations include faulty human judgment, breakdowns because of mistakes, circumventing controls by collusion of multiple people, and management ability to override controls.
- *Geared toward the achievement of multiple objectives*. The definition highlights that internal control provides reasonable assurance regarding three categories of objectives. However, the external auditor is primarily interested in the objective related to the reliability of financial reporting.

EXHIBIT 3.1   ## COSO Framework for Internal Control

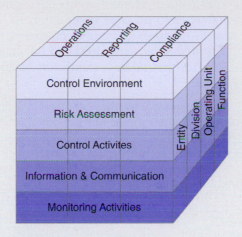

COSO identifies five components of internal control that support an organization in achieving its objectives. These components of COSO's updated *Internal Control–Integrated Framework* are shown in *Exhibit 3.1*. The five components include:

1. **Control Environment** is the set of standards, processes, and structures that provides the basis for carrying out internal control across the organization. It includes the tone at the top regarding the importance of internal control and the expected standards of conduct. The control environment has a pervasive impact on the overall system of internal control.
2. **Risk Assessment** involves the process for identifying and assessing the risks that may affect an organization from achieving its objectives.
3. **Control Activities** are the actions that have been established by policies and procedures. They help ensure that management's directives regarding internal control are carried out.
4. **Information and Communication** recognizes that information is necessary for an organization to carry out its internal control responsibilities. Information can come from internal and external sources. Communication is the process of providing, sharing, and obtaining necessary information. Information and communication help all relevant parties understand internal control responsibilities and how internal controls are related to achieving objectives.
5. **Monitoring** is necessary to determine whether the controls, including all five components, are present and continuing to function effectively.

Effective internal control requires that all five components be implemented and operate effectively. Specifically, the controls need to (1) be effectively designed and implemented and (2) operate effectively; that is, the operation of the controls is consistent with the design of the controls.

Terminology: Entity-Wide Controls and Transaction Controls

Some components of internal control operate across an entity, and we refer to these as **entity-wide controls**. Entity-wide controls affect multiple processes, transactions, accounts, and assertions. The following are typically considered entity-wide controls:

- Controls related to the control environment
- Controls over management override

- The organization's risk assessment process
- Centralized processing and controls, including shared service environments
- Controls to monitor results of operations
- Controls to monitor other controls, including activities of the internal audit function, the audit committee, and self-assessment programs
- Controls over the period-end financial reporting process
- Policies that address significant business control and risk management practices

To illustrate why these controls are described as entity-wide, consider controls over management override. If the CFO is able to override controls, the CFO could record erroneous transactions in multiple processes affecting multiple accounts. Thus, controls over management override have an entity-wide effect.

In contrast, other controls such as control activities typically affect only certain processes, transactions, accounts, and assertions. We refer to these types of controls as **transaction controls**, and they are not expected to have a pervasive effect throughout the organization. For example, an organization might require that a supervisor approve an employee expense report after reviewing it for reasonableness and compliance with policy. This control provides assurance about employee expenses but will not provide assurance on other types of transactions and accounts throughout the entity. The following are common examples of transaction controls:

- Segregation of duties over cash receipts and recording
- Authorization procedures for purchasing
- Adequately documented transaction trail for all sales transactions
- Physical controls to safeguard assets such as inventory
- Reconciliations of bank accounts

Components and Principles of Internal Control

LO 3 Describe the control environment component of internal control, list its principles, and provide examples of each principle.

Each of the five internal control components includes principles representing the fundamental concepts associated with the component. Organizations are expected to have each of the five components and seventeen principles in place. *Exhibit 3.2* summarizes the five components and their associated principles and these are discussed next.

COSO Component: Control Environment

The control environment is seen as the foundation for all other components of internal control. It starts with the leadership of the organization, including the board of directors, the audit committee, and management, and it is often referred to as the *tone at the top* or the *internal control culture*. The board of directors and management establish the tone regarding the importance of internal control and expected standards of conduct. These expectations should be reinforced throughout the organization. A strong control environment is an important line of defense against the risks related to the reliability of financial statements. As highlighted in the *Focus on Fraud* feature "Ethical Values and the Control Environment at HealthSouth," a weak control environment enables fraud to occur.

Deficiencies in the control environment, including weak board oversight, have been associated with many financial frauds that are likely familiar to you, including Enron, Health South, Madoff, and others. Indications of a weak control environment include:

- An ineffective board of directors dominated by top management
- Management teams driven to increase the stock price as a basis for either expanding the organization or personally enriching themselves through stock compensation

| EXHIBIT **3.2** | Internal Control Components and Principles |

Components	Principles
Control Environment	1. The organization demonstrates a commitment to integrity and ethical values. 2. The board of directors demonstrates independence from management and exercises oversight of the development and performance of internal control. 3. Management establishes, with board oversight, structures, reporting lines, and appropriate authorities and responsibilities in the pursuit of objectives. 4. The organization demonstrates a commitment to attract, develop, and retain competent individuals in alignment with objectives. 5. The organization holds individuals accountable for their internal control responsibilities in the pursuit of objectives.
Risk Assessment	6. The organization specifies objectives with sufficient clarity to enable the identification and assessment of risks relating to objectives. 7. The organization identifies risks to the achievement of its objectives across the entity and analyzes risks as a basis for determining how the risks should be managed. 8. The organization considers the potential for fraud in assessing risks to the achievement of objectives. 9. The organization identifies and assesses changes that could significantly impact the system of internal control.
Control Activities	10. The organization selects and develops control activities that contribute to the mitigation of risks to the achievement of objectives to acceptable levels. 11. The organization selects and develops general control activities over technology to support the achievement of objectives. 12. The organization deploys control activities through policies that establish what is expected and in procedures that put policies into action.
Information and Communication	13. The organization obtains or generates and uses relevant, quality information to support the functioning of internal control. 14. The organization internally communicates information, including objectives and responsibilities for internal control, necessary to support the functioning of internal control. 15. The organization communicates with external parties regarding matters affecting the functioning of internal control.
Monitoring	16. The organization selects, develops, and performs ongoing and/or separate evaluations to ascertain whether the components of internal control are present and functioning. 17. The organization evaluates and communicates internal control deficiencies in a timely manner to those parties responsible for taking corrective action, including senior management and the board of directors, as appropriate.

- A low level of control consciousness within the organization
- An audit committee that does not have independent members
- The absence of an ethics policy or a lack of reinforcement of ethical behavior within the organization
- An audit committee that is not viewed as the client of the external auditor
- A management that overrides controls over accounting transactions
- Personnel who do not have the competencies to carry out their assigned tasks

Commitment to Integrity and Ethical Values (COSO Principle 1)

An organization's commitment to integrity and ethical values is demonstrated through the tone set by the board and management throughout the organization. Do the directives, actions, and behaviors of the board and

Ethical Values and the Control Environment at HealthSouth

FOCUS on **FRAUD**

In testimony before the House Subcommittee in October 2003, the director of internal audit of HealthSouth testified that she had inquired about expanding her department's work and that she needed access to corporate records. She reported directly to the HealthSouth CEO, Richard Scrushy. She told a congressional committee that Mr. Scrushy reminded her that she did not have a job before she came to HealthSouth, and she should do the job she was hired to do. When asked by a congressman whether she had thought about reporting rumors of fraud to Ernst & Young (HealthSouth's external auditors), she indicated that she had run her concerns through the chain of command within the company

and had done all she could do. Unfortunately, the chain of command was controlled by the CEO.

The internal auditor did not follow up with Ernst & Young. Others testified to the same effect—if they wanted to keep their jobs, they continued to do the work they were hired to do and let management take care of other items. The tone at the top sent a clear message: "Don't question management!" In the case of HealthSouth, it did not matter that the organization had a code of ethics for its employees. The company and its board were dominated by management. The unwritten message was stronger than any written message: "Do what we want you to do or lose your job."

management highlight the importance of integrity and ethical values? An organization should have standards of conduct regarding expectations for integrity and ethical values and should also have processes in place to determine if individuals are performing in accordance with expected standards of conduct. Deviations in expected conduct should be identified and addressed in an appropriate, timely, and consistent matter.

The importance of an appropriate tone cannot be overstated. As indicated in the *Auditing in Practice* feature "Inappropriate Tone Regarding Internal Controls Leads to Other Deficiencies at NutraCea," an inappropriate tone about the importance of internal control can lead to deficiencies throughout the internal control system.

The Board of Directors Exercises Oversight Responsibility (COSO Principle 2)

Members of the board of directors are the elected representatives of shareholders. At public companies and other larger organizations, the board will include committees that specialize in certain areas. For example, the audit committee of the board should oversee management, have responsibility for the overall reliability of financial reporting, and oversee the external auditor.

The board of directors, primarily through the audit committee, is expected to exercise objective oversight for the development and performance of internal control. For example, the board, as part of its oversight responsibilities, might require discussions with senior management on areas where controls have not been operating effectively. The board should have relevant expertise to fulfill its oversight responsibilities. This expertise might include market and company knowledge, financial expertise, legal and regulatory expertise, knowledge of systems and technology, and problem-solving skills. Importantly, the board needs a sufficient number of members who are independent of the organization to help ensure the board's objectivity. A board and its committees are most effective when they can provide unbiased oversight consisting of evaluations, guidance, and feedback.

Inappropriate Tone Regarding Internal Controls Leads to Other Deficiencies at NutraCea

Management at NutraCea identified the following material weaknesses in the company's internal control over financial reporting as of December 31, 2008:

The Company did not maintain an effective control environment based on the criteria established in the COSO framework. The Company failed to design controls to prevent or detect instances of inappropriate override of, or interference with, existing policies, procedures, and internal controls. The Company did not establish and maintain a proper tone as to internal control over financial reporting. More specifically, senior management failed to emphasize, through consistent communication and behavior, the importance of internal control over financial reporting and adherence to the Company's code of business conduct and ethics, which, among other things, resulted in information being withheld from, and improper explanations and inadequate supporting documentation being provided to the Company's Audit Committee, its Board of Directors, and independent registered public accountants.

Presumably the weak control environment led to other material weaknesses in internal control. For example, NutraCea management failed to properly analyze, account for, and record significant sales contracts. The company also failed to retain the resources necessary to analyze significant transactions, prepare financial statements, and respond to regulatory comments in a timely manner.

Management Establishes Structure, Authority, and Responsibility (COSO Principle 3)

A well-controlled organization has an appropriate structure and clearly defined lines of responsibility and authority. Everyone in the organization has some responsibility for the effective operation of internal control. COSO has identified the following internal control responsibilities:

- *The board of directors* has authority over significant decisions and reviews management's assignments.
- *Senior management* establishes directives, guidance, and controls to help employees understand and carry out their internal control responsibilities.
- *Management* guides and facilitates senior management's directives.
- *Personnel* understand internal control requirements relative to their position in the organization.
- *Outsourced service providers* adhere to management's definition of the scope of authority and responsibility for all nonemployees engaged.

The Organization Demonstrates Commitment to Competence (COSO Principle 4)

An organization needs to attract, develop, and retain competent individuals. Competence is the knowledge and skills necessary to accomplish tasks that define the individual's job. Commitment to competence includes management's consideration of the competence levels for particular jobs and how those levels translate into requisite skills and knowledge. This commitment is demonstrated through policies and procedures to attract, train, mentor, evaluate, and retain employees.

The Organization Enforces Accountability (COSO Principle 5)

An organization should hold individuals accountable for their internal control responsibilities. Accountability mechanisms include establishing and evaluating performance measures and providing appropriate incentives and rewards. Management and the board should be sensitive to, and address as appropriate, pressures that could cause personnel to circumvent controls or undertake fraudulent activity. Excessive pressures could include unrealistic performance targets or an imbalance between short-term and long-term performance measures. For example, pressures to generate unrealistic levels of sales might cause sale managers to book fraudulent sales entries, thereby reducing the reliability of financial reporting.

COSO Component: Risk Assessment

LO 4 Describe the risk assessment component of internal control, list its principles, and provide examples of each principle.

All organizations face risks of material misstatement in their financial reports. Risk is the possibility that an event will adversely affect the organization's achievement of its objectives. Risk comes from both internal and external sources. Examples of internal risks include:

- Changes in management responsibilities
- Changes in internal information technology
- A poorly conceived business model that makes it difficult for the organization to remain profitable

Examples of external risks include:

- Economic recessions that decrease product or service demand
- Increases in competition or substitute products or services
- Changes in regulation that make the business model of the organization unsustainable
- Changes in the reliability of source goods that reduce profitability and interrupt the supply chain

An organization that ignores these risks subjects both the organization and its auditors to potential bankruptcy or litigation. Risk assessment is a robust process for identifying and assessing the risks associated with the objective of reliable financial reporting. This process also requires considering how changes either in the external environment or within the organization may impact the controls necessary to mitigate risk.

Management Specifies Relevant Objectives (COSO Principle 6)

An organization has many reasons for having reliable financial reporting as one of its objectives. Reliable financial reporting is important for accessing capital markets; being awarded sales contracts; and dealing with vendors, suppliers, and other third parties. When specifying this objective, management should take steps so that the financial reporting reflects the underlying transactions and events of the organization. Financial reporting objectives should be consistent with the accounting principles that are suitable for the organization. As appropriate, the broad reporting objective should be cascaded down to various business units. Further, management should consider the level of materiality when specifying objectives. For example, management might have an objective that revenue be accurately reported. Management does not likely mean that revenue needs to be accurate to the nearest dollar. Rather, management's objective would likely be that any misstatements in revenue not be material, or important, to the overall financial statement presentation. For example, if the revenue account of a large company had an error that caused revenue to be overstated by $1,000, most users of the financial statements would not consider that misstatement to be material, or important, to their decisions. Materiality is a topic that we explore further in *Chapter 7*.

The Organization Identifies and Analyzes Risk (COSO Principle 7)

This principle highlights the importance of an organization identifying the risks that it will not achieve its financial reporting objective and serves as a basis for determining how the risks should be mitigated. Appropriate levels of management need to be involved in the identification and analysis of risk. Risk identification should include both internal and external factors. For example, economic changes may impact barriers to competitive entry, or a new financial reporting standard may require different or additional reporting. Internally, a change in management responsibilities could affect the way certain controls operate, or the expiration of labor agreements can affect the availability of competent personnel. Identified risks—whether internal or external—should be analyzed to include an estimate of the potential significance of the risks and consideration of how each risk should be addressed.

The Organization Assesses Fraud Risk (COSO Principle 8)

As part of assessing risks, the organization considers fraud risks—risks related to misappropriation of assets and fraudulent financial reporting (as discussed in *Chapter 2*). Assessment of fraud risk considers ways that fraud could occur and fraud risk factors that impact financial reporting, including incentives and pressures that might lead to fraud in the financial statements, opportunities for fraud, and whether personnel might rationalize fraud activities—that is, the fraud triangle. The *Focus on Fraud* feature "Ineffective Internal Control Over Financial Reporting Leads to Embezzlement at Citigroup" highlights the importance of identifying fraud risks as a basis for determining the controls necessary to mitigate such risks.

The Organization Identifies and Analyzes Significant Change (COSO Principle 9)

As internal and external conditions change, an organization's internal controls may need to change. Internal control that is effective in one condition may not be effective when that condition changes. For example, when an organization alters its lines of business or business model, new controls may

Ineffective Internal Control Over Financial Reporting Leads to Embezzlement at Citigroup

FOCUS on **FRAUD**

Gary Foster was a mid-level accountant in Citigroup's Long Island City office, with an annual salary of about $100,000. His embezzlement of about $19 million from the company was revealed in June 2011. It appears that Foster transferred money from various Citigroup accounts to his personal bank account at JPMorgan Chase. He did so by making adjusting journal entries from interest expense accounts and debt adjustment accounts to Citigroup's main cash accounts. Then, on at least eight occasions, he transferred the money to a personal bank account at Chase. To conceal the transactions, he used a false contract number in the reference line of the wire transfer. This series of actions continued for at least a year, undetected by the company's internal controls. During that time, Foster traveled extensively internationally, owned six expensive homes, and acquired Maserati and BMW automobiles.

be needed because the organization may have taken on new risks. Another example of change that impacts controls would be the introduction of new information system technologies. The organization also needs to consider changes in management and other personnel and their respective attitudes and philosophies on the system of internal control. Overall, the key principle is that an organization needs a process for identifying and assessing changes in internal and external factors that can affect its ability to produce reliable financial reports.

COSO Component: Control Activities

LO 5 Describe the control activities component of internal control, list its principles, and provide examples of each principle.

Control activities are the actions that are established through policies and procedures that help ensure that management's directives regarding controls are accomplished. Control activities are performed within processes (e.g., segregation of duties required in processing cash receipt transactions) and over the technology environment. They may be preventive or detective, and they may be manual or automated in nature.

The Organization Selects and Develops Control Activities (COSO Principle 10)

Although some control activities are seen in many organizations—segregation of duties, independent reconciliations, authorizations and approvals, and verifications—no universal set of control activities is applicable to all organizations. Rather, organizations select and develop control activities that are specific to the risks they identify during risk assessment. For example, highly regulated organizations generally have more complex control activities than less-regulated entities. As another example, an organization with decentralized operations and an emphasis on local autonomy and innovation will have different control activities than an organization whose operations are consistent across locations and highly centralized.

Control activities are implemented within each of an organization's business processes (e.g., purchasing or sales) and are intended to mitigate transaction-processing risks within each of those processes.

Transaction Controls Transaction controls (also referred to as **application controls**) represent an important type of control activity. Transaction controls are intended to provide assurance that all transactions that occurred are recorded (e.g., were all accounts payable recorded as liabilities?), that the transactions are recorded in an accurate and timely manner, and that only valid transactions are recorded (e.g., were any fictitious sales recorded as revenue?).

Exhibit 3.3 illustrates three types of transactions that have a significant effect on the quality of data in the financial statements and associated disclosures. They include transactions related to:

- Business processes
- Accounting estimates
- Adjusting, closing, or unusual entries

During transaction processing, an organization wants reasonable assurance that the information processing is complete, accurate, and valid. The organization wants to achieve the following control objectives:

- Recorded transactions exist and have occurred.
- All transactions are recorded.
- Transactions are properly valued.
- Transactions are properly presented and disclosed.
- Transactions relate to rights or obligations of the organization.

EXHIBIT 3.3   Transaction Processing

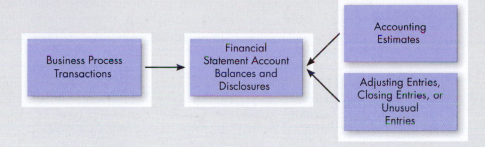

Various transaction controls performed within specific business processes—such as purchasing and sales—are developed and implemented to provide reasonable assurance that these processing objectives are achieved. Control activities related to business transaction processing include verifications such as computer matching or reasonableness checks, reconciliations such as checking for agreement between detailed subsidiary accounts and control accounts, and authorizations and approvals such as a supervisor approving an expense report.

Accounting estimates, such as those used in developing the allowance for doubtful accounts, pension liabilities, environmental obligations, and warranty reserves, are subject to significant management judgment. These estimates should be based on underlying processes and data that have been successful in providing accurate estimates in the past. Controls should be built around the processes to provide reasonable assurance that the data are accurate, the estimates are faithful to the data, and the underlying estimation model reflects current economic conditions and has proven to provide reasonable estimates in the past.

Controls over adjusting, closing, or other unusual entries include:

- Documented support for all entries
- Reference to underlying supporting data with a well-developed **transaction trail** that includes the documents and records that allow a user (or auditor) to trace a transaction from its origination through to its final disposition or vice versa
- Review by the CFO or controller

Automated and Manual Transaction Controls   Transaction controls include manual control activities, automated control activities, and a combination of the two. An example of an automated application control activity is an automated matching and edit check to examine data entered online. If the data do not match or are entered in the wrong format, the system provides feedback so that personnel can make appropriate corrections. In some cases, that feedback and correction occur automatically. In other cases, a combination of manual and automated controls is present such that the system automatically detects the data transmission error, but an individual is needed to manually retransmit the data. Transaction controls, whether automated or manual, mitigate risks associated with data input, processing, and output.

Input controls are designed to ensure that authorized transactions are correct and complete and that only authorized transactions can be input. Two common types of input controls are **input validation tests** and **self-checking digits**. Input validation tests are often referred to as **edit tests** because they are control tests built into an application to examine or edit input data for obvious errors. Input validation tests are designed to review transactions much like experienced personnel do in manual systems in which an employee would know, for example, that no one worked more than 70 hours in the past week. If an item entered online does not meet the required criteria, the user is notified and a correction is made or a decision is made about whether the transaction should be processed or reviewed further before processing. Self-checking digits are a type of input validation test that have been developed to test for transposition errors associated with identification numbers. Self-checking digits operate by computing an extra digit, or several digits, that are added (or inserted) into a numeric identifier. The algorithms are designed to detect common types of mistakes. Whenever the identifier is entered into the system, the application recalculates the self-checking digit to determine whether the identifier is correct.

Processing controls are designed to provide reasonable assurance that the correct program is used for processing, all transactions are processed, and the transactions update appropriate files. For example, processed payroll transactions should update the payroll sub-ledger.

Output controls are designed to provide reasonable assurance that all data are completely processed and that output is distributed only to authorized recipients. Typical controls include reconciliation of control totals, output distribution schedules and procedures, and output reviews. For critical data, the user may perform a detailed review and reconciliation of the output data with the input to determine the completeness of a crucial process. The organization should also develop policies for protecting privacy and retaining records.

Other Important Control Activities

Other important control activities include **segregation of duties** and **physical controls over assets**. Segregation of duties is an important control activity that is designed to protect against the risk that an individual could both perpetrate and cover up a fraud. Proper segregation of duties requires that at least two employees be involved in processing transactions such that one does not have (a) the authority and ability to process transactions and (b) custodial responsibilities. Separating these functions prevents someone from authorizing a fictitious or illegal transaction and then covering it up through the accounting process. Separating record keeping and physical custody of assets is designed to prevent someone with custodial responsibilities from taking assets and covering it up by making fictitious entries to the accounting records. The *Focus on Fraud* feature "The Importance of Internal Control for Safeguarding Assets at Chesapeake Petroleum and Supply, Inc." provides an example of a situation where segregation of duties was lacking, thereby allowing an individual to misappropriate assets.

Physical controls are necessary to protect and safeguard assets from accidental or intentional destruction and theft. Examples of physical controls include security locks to limit access to inventory warehouses and vaults, safes, and similar items to limit access to cash and other liquid assets. An additional control is a periodic count of the physical assets, such as inventory, and a reconciliation of this count with recorded amounts.

Preventive and Detective Controls

The appropriate mix of control activities includes both preventive and detective controls. **Preventive controls** are designed to prevent the occurrence of a misstatement. For example, edit tests may prevent some inappropriate transactions from being recorded. Preventive controls are usually the most cost efficient. **Detective controls** are designed to discover errors that occurred during processing. For example, continuous monitoring techniques detect transactions that should not have been processed.

The Importance of Internal Control for Safeguarding Assets at Chesapeake Petroleum and Supply, Inc.

Most organizations, presumably, have reliable financial reporting as one of their objectives. This objective would include safeguarding assets. However, to achieve this objective, organizations need to have effective controls in place. Such controls were not in place at Chesapeake Petroleum and Supply, Inc., where the CFO pled guilty to embezzling more than $2.7 million. The CFO—employed by Chesapeake Petroleum for 30 years—authorized and signed company checks made payable to him and to the bank that held the mortgage on one of his properties. The CFO had both authorizing and signing control over company checks. This executive also had exclusive control over petty cash and stole thousands of dollars from the company's petty cash fund. These situations represent classic examples of control deficiencies related to an inadequate segregation of duties.

Management Selects and Develops General Controls Over Technology (COSO Principle 11)

Nearly all organizations depend on information technology to facilitate reliable financial reporting. As part of selecting control activities, management needs to determine the extent to which automated control activities and **general computer controls** are part of the mix of control activities. For automated application controls to work properly, an organization needs to have effective general computer controls (sometimes referred to as **information technology general controls**). General computer controls are pervasive control activities that affect multiple types of information technology systems, from mainframe computers, to desktop computers, to laptop computers, to the mobile devices that you use to organize your everyday life. General computer controls include control activities—either manual or automated—over technology infrastructure, security management, and technology acquisition, development, and maintenance.

Technology Infrastructure   Technology infrastructure provides the support for information technology to effectively function. It includes the communication network that links technologies together, the computing resources needed for applications to operate, and even the electricity needed to power the technology. Control activities are necessary to check the technology for any problems and take corrective action as necessary. Two other important control activities related to the infrastructure include backup procedures and disaster recovery plans.

Security Management   Security management includes control activities that limit access to technologies. These control activities include policies that restrict authorized users to applications that are related to their job responsibilities, update access when employees change jobs or leave the organization, and require a periodic review of access rights to determine if they remain appropriate. Security controls over technology protect the organization from inappropriate and unauthorized access, thereby protecting data and program integrity.

Important considerations in security management related to user access include:

- Access to any data item is limited to those *with a need to know*.
- The ability to change, modify, or delete a data item is restricted to those *with the authorization to make such changes*.
- The access control system has the *ability to identify and verify any potential users* as authorized or unauthorized for the data item and function requested.
- *A security department should actively monitor* attempts to compromise the system and prepare periodic reports to those responsible for the integrity of data and access to the data.

Techniques for controlling user access include passwords, cards with magnetic strips (often combined with a password requirement), and required identification on the basis of physical characteristics (e.g., fingerprint or retina scan).

Technology Acquisition, Development, and Maintenance An organization needs to select and develop control activities over the acquisition, development, and maintenance of technology. Some organizations may develop their technology in-house, while other organizations may obtain their technology through packaged software or through outsourcing arrangements. If an organization chooses to use packaged software, it should have policies about selecting and implementing these packages. If an organization develops and maintains its technology in-house, the organization should have polices on documentation requirements, approval requirements, authorization of change requests, and appropriate protocols and testing of whether changes are made properly.

The Organization Deploys Control Activities Through Policies and Procedures (COSO Principle 12)

An important principle of control activities is that an organization needs to have policies outlining what is expected and procedures that put the policies into action. For example, a policy might require monthly reconciliations of all bank accounts by appropriate personnel who do not have access to cash. The procedure would be the reconciliation itself. Policies can be communicated orally or in writing, but in either case, they should establish clear responsibility and accountability. Further, the procedures should be performed diligently, consistently, and by appropriate and competent personnel in a timely manner.

COSO Component: Information and Communication

LO 6 Describe the information and communication component of internal control, list its principles, and provide examples of each principle.

An organization needs information, from both internal and external sources, to carry out its internal control responsibilities. Communication is the process of providing, sharing, and obtaining information. Information is communicated internally throughout the organization, and there should be two-way communication with relevant parties external to the organization. Information and communication refers to the process of identifying, capturing, and exchanging information in a timely fashion to enable accomplishment of the organization's objectives. It includes the organization's accounting system and methods for recording and reporting on transactions, as well as other communications such as key policies, code of conduct, and strategies.

The Organization Uses Relevant Information (COSO Principle 13)

An organization needs to identify and obtain relevant internal and external information to support its internal control and achieve its objective of reliable financial reporting. For example, an organization may conduct a periodic survey of its employees to determine whether they had been asked to behave in a manner that was inconsistent with the organization's standards of conduct, for example, record a journal entry without adequate supporting documentation. This survey produces information about the functioning of the control environment and can be used to determine if other controls are needed. Other sources of internal information include the accounting system, internal e-mails, minutes from meetings, and time reporting systems. Examples of external sources of information include industry research reports, whistle-blower hotlines, and competitor earnings releases.

The Organization Communicates Internally (COSO Principle 14)

Internal communication of information occurs throughout the organization—including up, down, and across the organization. For example, all personnel should receive a clear message that internal control responsibilities should be taken seriously. This communication could occur through periodic newsletters, posters in the break rooms, or more formal communications from senior management and the board. In some cases, a special line of communication is needed for anonymous or confidential communications, particularly when an employee is concerned that something is inappropriate in the organization's operations. This is referred to as a **whistle-blower function** and often includes processes such that reporting can be anonymous. Further, employers should not be permitted to take adverse actions against employee whistle-blowers. The whistle-blower function should include a process to bring important ethical and financial issues to the audit committee. The *Auditing in Practice* feature "William and Flora Hewlett Foundation: Policy Regarding Reporting of Financial, Auditing, or Governance Improprieties" provides an example of a whistle-blower policy highlighting the importance of employee involvement and the absence of any fear of retaliation for being a whistle-blower employee.

The Organization Communicates Externally (COSO Principle 15)

Organizations have a need for two-way communication with parties external to the organization, including shareholders, business partners, customers, and regulators. Management's external communication should send a message about the importance of internal control and the organization's values and culture. Organizations should also have mechanisms so that external parties can provide information to the organization. For example, customers may provide feedback about product quality and vendors may have questions about payments for goods sold or complaints about possibly inappropriate behavior. As another example, large retailers often have relationships with many vendors. Many of these retailers establish a hotline where a vendor can communicate directly with the internal audit department or other appropriate party if the vendor finds any inappropriate action by a purchasing agent of the organization, for example, a suggestion of a kickback if the vendor places a large order.

COSO Component: Monitoring

LO 7 Describe the monitoring component of internal control, list its principles, and provide examples of each principle.

Monitoring is defined as a process that provides feedback on the effectiveness of each of the five components of internal control. Management selects a mix of ongoing evaluations, separate evaluations, or some combination of the two to accomplish monitoring. Monitoring requires that identified deficiencies in internal control be communicated to appropriate personnel and follow-up action be taken.

AUDITING IN **PRACTICE**

William and Flora Hewlett Foundation: Policy Regarding Reporting of Financial, Auditing, or Governance Improprieties

The William and Flora Hewlett Foundation is committed to facilitating open and honest communications relevant to its governance, finances, and compliance with all applicable laws and regulations. It is important that the Foundation be apprised about unlawful or improper behavior including, but not limited to, any of the following conduct:

- theft;
- financial reporting that is intentionally misleading;
- improper or undocumented financial transactions;
- improper destruction of records;
- improper use of Foundation assets;
- violations of the Hewlett Foundation's conflict-of-interest policy; and
- any other improper occurrence regarding cash, financial procedures, or reporting

We request the assistance of every employee who has a reasonable belief or suspicion about any improper transaction. The Foundation values this input, and each employee should feel free to raise issues of concern, in good faith, without the fear of retaliation. Employees will not be disciplined, demoted, lose their jobs, or be retaliated against for asking questions or voicing concerns about conduct of this sort.

We encourage any employee who has a concern regarding an action concerning the Foundation's governance, finances, or compliance with all applicable laws and regulations to raise the concern with a supervisor, human resources, the president, the general counsel, the treasurer, the chair of the Board of Directors or of the Audit Committee, or any other Board member.

If for any reason the employee does not believe these channels of communication are adequate or safe, the concern should be reported immediately to [*name of outside counsel and firm*]. [*Name of outside counsel*] has been retained specifically to be an independent agent to collect any such reports and to assure that they are looked into and that corrective action is taken when appropriate. Anonymous reports will also be accepted, and all reports will be handled on a confidential basis. [*His/Her*] contact information is:

> [*Name, address, email, telephone for outside counsel*]Mark envelope: "TO BE OPENED BY ADDRESSEE ONLY PERSONAL AND CONFIDENTIAL"
> [*Name of outside counsel*] and the Chair of the Audit Committee will coordinate the investigation and the Foundation will then take appropriate action as it deems justified by the circumstances.

Source: Used with permission of the William and Flora Hewlett Foundation.

The Organization Conducts Ongoing and/or Separate Evaluations (COSO Principle 16)

Ongoing evaluations are procedures built into the normal recurring activities of an entity. The *Auditing in Practice* feature "Monitoring Controls in Fast-Food Franchises" provides an example of ongoing evaluations. Computerized monitoring of transactions is an approach many organizations take to review a large volume of transactions at a relatively low cost. An organization may use software to automate the review of all payment transactions and identify anomalies that are investigated further.

Separate evaluations are conducted periodically, typically by objective management personnel, internal auditors, or external consultants. For example, an organization's internal auditors may perform an annual audit of all disbursements at selected operating units. As part of that audit, the internal auditors will identify instances in which a control is not operating effectively. Consider an organization that has a policy requiring approvals from appropriate personnel for disbursements over a certain dollar amount.

Monitoring Controls in Fast-Food Franchises

The owner of a franchise such as Wendy's or McDonald's that serves fast-food across many locations must be able to monitor the workings of its controls at each location. The franchise will have written policies and procedures dealing with control issues ranging from product acceptance (must be from authorized vendor), waste disposal, recording sales (must offer a cash register receipt or the meal is free), and employee supervision. The franchise will have standardized procedures for counting cash, reconciling cash with the cash register, depositing the cash daily, and transferring cash to corporate headquarters. Assume that from previous statistics and industry averages, the franchise owner knows that food costs should equal approximately 37% of revenue.

The franchise owner then develops a performance-monitoring process that results in daily and weekly reports on:

- Store revenue compared with expected revenue and previous year's revenue for the same week
- Special promotions in effect
- Gross margin

The franchise owner then uses the monitoring reports to follow up with local stores and to determine which stores, if any, need further investigation. For example, assume that the franchise owner identifies a group of stores—all managed by one person—for which store revenue is lower than expected; but more important, the gross margin is significantly less than expected (63% expected, but 60% attained). The monitoring report indicates that one of the following explanations may represent the problems at the stores: (a) not all revenue is being recorded, (b) product is unnecessarily wasted, (c) product is diverted to other places (or stolen), or (d) some combination of these. Although the original focus is on operating data, the implication is that a breakdown of internal controls exists at those specific locations. The monitoring of performance has led to the monitoring of controls. The report will then lead the franchise owner to determine the cause of the problem and to take corrective action.

During its periodic audit, the internal auditor might find several instances when disbursements were made without the required approval.

As separate evaluations take place periodically, they are not as timely as ongoing evaluations in identifying control deficiencies. But separate evaluations do allow for a fresh, objective look at control effectiveness.

Management Evaluates and Communicates Deficiencies (COSO Principle 17)

Control deficiencies identified through monitoring or other activities need to be communicated to appropriate personnel such as management or the board of directors so that appropriate corrective action can be taken. Recall the previous example in which internal auditors, conducting a separate evaluation, identified a deficiency in controls over disbursements. Internal audit should provide this information to parties responsible for taking appropriate corrective action. Included in this principle is the need for an organization to implement a system to track whether deficiencies are corrected on a timely basis.

Management's Responsibilities Related to Internal Control Over Financial Reporting

LO 8 Identify management's responsibilities related to internal control over financial reporting.

Management can be thought of as providing the first line of defense in achieving reliable financial reporting. Management is responsible for designing, implementing, and maintaining effective internal control over financial reporting. Further, management should maintain adequate documentation related to internal control over financial reporting. Management of U.S.

public companies also has a responsibility to provide a report on the effectiveness of the organization's internal control over financial reporting.

Management's Documentation of Internal Control

Management needs to maintain sufficient and appropriate documentation of the internal controls they have designed and implemented to achieve the objective of reliable financial reporting. This documentation communicates standards and expectations related to internal control. Documentation is also useful in training new personnel or serving as a reference tool for all employees. Further, documentation provides evidence that the controls are operating, enables proper monitoring activities, and supports reporting on internal control effectiveness. Further, for clients like Ford Motor Company where the external auditor issues an opinion on the effectiveness of the client's controls, management will need to provide the auditor with documentation supporting management's assessment, and the auditor may use that documentation as part of the audit evidence. The nature and extent of internal control documentation will vary across organizations.

In terms of documentation supporting financial transactions, an organization should have documentation, for example, that provides evidence of the authorization of transactions, the existence of transactions, the support for journal entries, and the financial commitments made by the organization. Documentation of controls is often thought of as existing on paper. However, the documentation can be either paper or electronic. The information technology system may have an automated application that is programmed to pay for merchandise when an electronic copy of receipt of merchandise is available. The computer program compares receipts with a purchase order and may or may not require a vendor invoice before payment.

The following are some guidelines for developing reliable documentation related to internal control. These guidelines apply to both paper and electronic documents.

- *Prenumbered paper or computer-generated documents* facilitate the control of, and accountability for, transactions and are crucial to the completeness assertion.
- *Timely preparation* improves the credibility and accountability of documents and decreases the rate of errors on all documents.
- *Authorization* of a transaction should be clearly evident in the records.
- A *transaction trail* should exist such that a user (or auditor) could trace a transaction from its origination through to its final disposition or vice versa. A transaction trail serves many purposes, including providing information in order to respond to customer inquiries and identify and correct errors. *Exhibit 3.4* provides an overview of important aspects of an electronic transaction trail.

Management Reporting on Internal Control Over Financial Reporting

The Sarbanes-Oxley Act of 2002 requires public company management to annually report on the design and operating effectiveness of the organization's internal control over financial reporting. The U.S. Securities and Exchange Commission (SEC) has provided guidelines to assist management in its evaluation of the effectiveness of internal controls over financial reporting. The SEC guidelines require that suitable criteria, for example, COSO, be used as the benchmark in assessing internal control effectiveness. Determining whether internal control is effective requires an assessment of whether each of the five internal control components, and their principles, are present and operating effectively. The *Emerging Issues* feature "Updating the COSO Framework"

EXHIBIT **3.4**	Electronic Transaction Trail

Unique identification of transaction—Examples include assigning a unique number by the computer. The unique identifier could be assigned sequentially or could consist of a location identifier and unique number within a location. Sales invoices, for example, are sequentially numbered by the computer application.

Date and time of transaction—These could be automatically noted by the computer application.

Individual responsible for the transaction—The log-in to the system identifies the party authorizing or initiating the transaction.

Location from which the transaction originated—The log-in to the system identifies the source of the transaction.

Details of the transaction—These should be noted in a system log. Essentially, all the details normally found in a paper document, such as the quantities ordered and back-order provisions, can also be captured and saved as an electronic trail.

Cross-reference to other transactions—When applicable, all cross-referencing to other transactions should be captured. For example, if a payment cross-references a specific invoice, the information needed to complete the cross-reference should be captured.

Authorization or approval of the transaction—If the transaction requires authorization by a party other than the one initiating the transaction, the proper electronic authorization should be captured.

Updating the COSO Framework

EMERGING ISSUE

COSO's original 1992 *Internal Control–Integrated Framework* will be superseded by its 2013 framework after December 15, 2014. The SEC has indicated that the longer public companies continue to use the 1992 framework, the more likely they are to receive questions from the SEC about whether the company's use of the 1992 framework satisfies the SEC's requirement for a suitable, recognized framework, especially after the December 15, 2014 transition date.

highlights that if COSO is used as the suitable criteria, organizations will need to begin using the 2013 COSO framework in place of the 1992 COSO framework.

Exhibit 3.5 provides an example of a management report from Ford Motor Company. Note that management, including the CEO and CFO, both supervised and participated in the evaluation of internal controls. Further, they concluded that their internal control over financial reporting was effective as of December 31, 2013. A review of *Exhibit 3.5* highlights important features of management's report. Management's report:

- Provides a statement that management is responsible for internal control
- Includes a definition of internal control
- Discusses the limitations of internal control
- Identifies the criteria (COSO) used in assessing internal control
- Concludes as to the effectiveness of internal control at a point in time (year-end)
- References the report on internal control provided by the company's external auditors

EXHIBIT 3.5 Ford Motor Company Management Report on Internal Control Over Financial Reporting (2013)

Management's Report on Internal Control Over Financial Reporting. Our management is responsible for establishing and maintaining adequate internal control over financial reporting, as such term is defined in Exchange Act Rule 13a-15(f). The Company's internal control over financial reporting is a process designed to provide reasonable assurance regarding the reliability of financial reporting and the preparation of financial statements for external purposes in accordance with generally accepted accounting principles.

Because of its inherent limitations, internal control over financial reporting may not prevent or detect misstatements. Also, projections of any evaluation of effectiveness to future periods are subject to the risk that controls may become inadequate because of changes in conditions or because the degree of compliance with policies or procedures may deteriorate.

Under the supervision and with the participation of our management, including our CEO and CFO, we conducted an assessment of the effectiveness of our internal control over financial reporting as of December 31, 2013. The assessment was based on criteria established in the framework *Internal Control - Integrated Framework (1992)*, issued by the Committee of Sponsoring Organizations of the Treadway Commission. Based on this assessment, management concluded that our internal control over financial reporting was effective as of December 31, 2013.

The effectiveness of the Company's internal control over financial reporting as of December 31, 2013 has been audited by PricewaterhouseCoopers LLP, an independent registered public accounting firm, as stated in its report included herein.

Ford's external auditors have audited Ford's internal controls. Only larger public companies are required to have an external audit opinion on the effectiveness of internal control. However, management in smaller public companies still needs to evaluate and report on the effectiveness of their companies' internal controls over financial reporting.

Evaluating Internal Control Over Financial Reporting

What does management need to do to be able to provide a report on internal control effectiveness? The SEC's guidance encourages a risk-based approach to evaluation. *Exhibit 3.6* summarizes the steps involved in management's evaluation of internal control over financial. Management begins by identifying the significant risks to reliable financial reporting. For example, a manufacturer of semiconductor devices would likely consider inventory to be a **significant account** because of the materiality of the inventory account. Further, the substantial judgment required in valuing the inventory (due to obsolescence) suggests that valuation is a particularly **relevant assertion**. Thus, for this example, there is a significant risk that the financial reporting related to inventory may not be reliable.

Management then focuses on the design effectiveness of the controls intended to mitigate the risks to reliable financial reporting for the significant accounts and their relevant assertions. Management will likely conduct a **walkthrough**, following a transaction from origination to when it is reflected in the financial records to determine if the controls are effectively designed and have been implemented.

Management then gathers evidence through various testing procedures (e.g., inquiry, observation, review of documentation, and reperformance) as to whether the controls are operating effectively. For example, within its purchasing process, an organization may require approvals for all purchases over a stated dollar amount. As part of its testing, management could inquire of personnel who provide such approval and review documentation for an

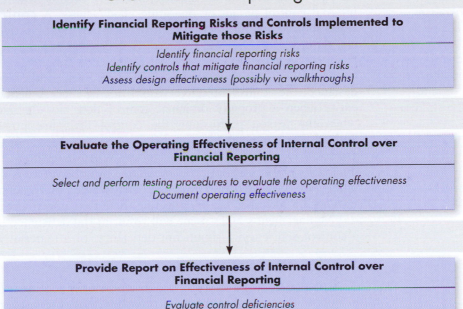

EXHIBIT 3.6 Steps in Management's Evaluation of Internal Control Over Financial Reporting

Identify Financial Reporting Risks and Controls Implemented to Mitigate those Risks

Identify financial reporting risks
Identify controls that mitigate financial reporting risks
Assess design effectiveness (possibly via walkthroughs)

Evaluate the Operating Effectiveness of Internal Control over Financial Reporting

Select and perform testing procedures to evaluate the operating effectiveness
Document operating effectiveness

Provide Report on Effectiveness of Internal Control over Financial Reporting

Evaluate control deficiencies
Provide public disclosure of management report, including any material weaknesses

indication of the required approval by appropriate personnel. *Exhibit 3.7* provides other examples of approaches management might use to test the operating effectiveness of various controls. After testing is completed, management evaluates any identified control deficiencies.

EXHIBIT 3.7 Examples of Approaches to Management Testing of Operating Effectiveness of Controls

Control to Be Tested	Possible Management Testing Approach
As part of the organization's risk assessment process, formal forecasts are prepared and updated during the year to reflect changes in conditions, estimates, or current knowledge.	Obtain and review the most recent corporate budget, including current forecasts. Inquire of those who are responsible for preparing and updating the forecasts.
The organization has a documented and approved disaster recovery plan, which includes off-site storage controlled by a third-party vendor.	Review disaster recovery plan and third-party vendor contract Confirm off-site storage arrangement with third-party vendor Obtain evidence of approval of the disaster recovery plan.
The organization has a policy requiring that a revenue recognition review be performed by the revenue accountant before revenue from complex contracts is recorded.	Review the policy. For selected transactions, review documentation that substantiates the review or reperform the review.
Surveys of internal users of financial reports are conducted to obtain information on user satisfaction with the reliability and timeliness of the reporting.	Obtain and review user surveys. Interview users.

Assessing Deficiencies in Internal Control Over Financial Reporting

LO 9 Distinguish between material weaknesses, significant deficiencies, and control deficiencies in internal control over financial reporting.

As part of its evaluation, management may become aware of deficiencies in internal control design or operating effectiveness. A **control deficiency** is some shortcoming in internal control such that the objective of reliable financial reporting may not be achieved. A deficiency in *design* exists when a control necessary to meet the control objective is missing, or when an existing control is not properly designed so that, even if the control operates as designed, the control objective would not be met. A deficiency in *operation* exists when a properly designed control does not operate as designed, or when the person performing the control does not possess the necessary authority or competence to perform the control effectively. Management will assess all identified control deficiencies. When assessing a control deficiency, management assesses both the *likelihood* (whether there is a reasonable possibility) of misstatement and the *magnitude* of potential misstatement. *Exhibit 3.8* identifies factors affecting these two assessments.

Management's assessment will result in the deficiency being described as a control deficiency, a significant deficiency, or a material weakness.

Significant Deficiency in Internal Control

A **significant deficiency** is a deficiency, or a combination of deficiencies, in internal control over financial reporting that is less severe than a material weakness, yet important enough to merit attention by those responsible for oversight of the organization's financial reporting. A significant deficiency is important enough that it should be brought to the attention of management and the audit committee, but it does not need to be reported to external users. Significant deficiencies would not be included in management's report on internal control effectiveness.

Material Weakness in Internal Control

A **material weakness** is a deficiency, or a combination of deficiencies, in internal control over financial reporting, such that there is a *reasonable possibility* that a *material misstatement* of the company's annual or interim

---

| EXHIBIT **3.8** | Assessing Likelihood and Magnitude of Potential Misstatements |

Factors affecting the *likelihood* that a deficiency, or a combination of deficiencies, will result in a misstatement include:

- Nature of the financial statement accounts, disclosures, and assertions involved
- Susceptibility of the related asset or liability to loss or fraud
- Subjectivity, complexity, or extent of judgment required to determine the amount involved
- Interaction or relationship of the control with other controls, including whether they are interdependent or redundant
- Interaction of the deficiencies
- Possible future consequences of the deficiency

Factors affecting the *magnitude* of a potential misstatement resulting from a deficiency or a combination of deficiencies include:

- Financial statement amounts or total of transactions exposed to the deficiency
- Volume of activity in the account balance or class of transactions exposed to the deficiency that has occurred in the current period or that is expected in future periods

financial statements will not be prevented or detected on a timely basis. For these deficiencies, the likelihood and magnitude of potential misstatement are such that the company cannot conclude that its internal control over financial reporting is effective. A material weakness does not mean the control deficiency resulted in a material, or even immaterial, misstatement in the financial statements. Rather, there is a reasonable possibility that this type of control deficiency *could* lead to a material misstatement. However, when management has to restate published financial statements because of a material misstatement, management will likely conclude that a material weakness in internal control existed.

An organization that has one or more material weaknesses will issue a report indicating that internal control over financial reporting is not effective. The report will describe the identified material weaknesses. *Exhibit 3.9* contains examples of internal control material weaknesses that have been identified in management reports. Note that the material weaknesses can be in either the design or operation of the control. *Exhibit 3.9* highlights material weaknesses primarily related to control activities; however, material weaknesses are found in other components of internal control, including the control environment, risk assessment, information and communication, and monitoring.

EXHIBIT 3.9   Examples of Material Weaknesses in Internal Control Over Financial Reporting

Weaknesses in the Design of Controls
- Absence of appropriate segregation of duties over important processes
- Absence of appropriate reviews and approvals of transactions, accounting entries, or systems output
- Inadequate controls to safeguard assets
- Absence of controls to ensure that all items in a population are recorded
- Inadequate processes to develop significant estimates affecting the financial statements, for example, estimates for pensions, warranties, and other reserves
- Undue complexity in the design of the processing system that obfuscates an understanding of the system by key personnel
- Inadequate controls over access to computer systems, data, and files
- Inadequate controls over computer processing
- Inadequate controls built into computer processing

Weaknesses in the Operation of Controls
- Independent tests of controls at a division level indicate that the control activities are not working properly; for example, purchases have been made outside of the approved purchasing function.
- Controls fail to prevent or detect significant misstatements of accounting information.
- Misapplication of accounting principles.
- Credit authorization processes overridden by the sales manager to achieve sales performance goals.
- Reconciliations (a) not performed on a timely basis or (b) performed by someone independent of the underlying process.
- Testing reveals evidence that accounting records have been manipulated or altered.
- Evidence of misrepresentation by accounting personnel.
- Computerized controls leading to items identified for nonprocessing that are systematically overridden by employees to process the transactions.
- The completeness of a population, for example, prenumbered documents or reconciling items logged on to the computer with those processed, not accounted for on a regular basis.

The following situations would suggest that there is a material weakness in internal control:

- Identification of fraud, whether or not material, on the part of senior management
- Multiple control deficiencies affecting the same financial statement account
- Significant deficiencies from the previous management report that the organization has not remediated
- Restatement of previously issued financial statements to reflect the correction of a material misstatement

Differences Between Material Weaknesses and Significant Deficiencies

Management uses professional judgment in assessing whether identified control deficiencies rise to the level of a significant deficiency or material weakness. Management will need to consider the specific facts and circumstances surrounding the identified deficiency. *Exhibit 3.10* describes two control deficiencies—one that would likely be assessed as a material weakness and one that would likely be assessed as a significant deficiency.

EXHIBIT 3.10 Assessing Identified Control Deficiencies

Likely Material Weakness

An organization has a new product line whereby the total annual revenue for this product line is large enough that a misstatement in the revenue account could be material to the financial statements overall. The revenue from this product line is based on contracts that have complex multi-element arrangements. The organization initiates a significant number of new contracts for this product line each week across multiple regions. When preparing these new contracts, a standard contract is used, and modifications to the standard contract are made based on the specific characteristics of the transaction.

When a new contract is entered into the computerized billing system, client accounting personnel at the regional office are to verify that revenue recognition conforms to GAAP. As part of the control procedure, the client accounting personnel who perform the verification are to complete and sign off on a revenue checklist. It appears that the control is effectively designed. However, when management tested the control they found that these control procedures had not been consistently documented or performed for the new product line. The control had not been operating effectively. Based only on these facts, management would likely determine that this deficiency represents a material weakness for the following reasons: (1) the magnitude of a financial statement misstatement resulting from this deficiency could reasonably be expected to be material as many new significant sales transactions occur each week and (2) the total sales transactions over the year are material. Management could conclude that the likelihood of material misstatements occurring is reasonably possible. Taken together, the magnitude and likelihood of misstatement that could occur in the financial statements resulting from this internal control deficiency meet the definition of a material weakness.

Likely Significant Deficiency

Consider the same scenario as described previously with the following additional facts. The organization has implemented an additional procedure whereby the revenue accounting manager at the company headquarters verifies the revenue recognition provisions of a random sample of new contracts on a weekly basis. The manager examines documents that indicate that regional accounting personnel have verified the revenue recognition provisions. The manager also reperforms the verification procedure to ensure that revenue recognition provisions have been properly entered into the billing system. A test of this control by management indicates that the additional control has been operating effectively. Based only on these facts, management now would likely determine that the deficiency represents a significant deficiency because the weekly verifications by the revenue accounting manager constitute a compensating control that is likely to detect and prevent material misstatements in revenue recognition. Thus, the control deficiency should likely be reported to the audit committee, but does not rise to the level of a material weakness.

Importance of Internal Control to the External Audit

LO 10 Articulate the importance of internal control over financial reporting for the external audit and apply the concepts related to management's and the auditor's assessments of internal control effectiveness.

Professional auditing standards require the auditor, as part of planning an audit, to identify and assess a client's risks of material misstatement, whether due to fraud or error. This assessment is based on an understanding of the organization and its environment, including its internal control over financial reporting. The auditor needs to understand a client's internal controls in order to anticipate the types of material misstatements that may occur and then develop appropriate audit procedures to determine whether those misstatements exist in the financial statements. If a client has ineffective internal controls, the auditor will plan the audit with this in mind. For example, if an auditor notes that a client does not have effective controls to provide reasonable assurance that all sales are recorded in the correct time period, then the auditor needs to develop sufficient and appropriate audit procedures to test whether sales and receivables are materially misstated because of the absence of effective controls.

Auditors of large public companies have an additional interest in their client's internal controls. When conducting a financial statement audit for these companies, the auditor performs an integrated audit, which includes providing an opinion on the effectiveness of the client's internal control over financial reporting in addition to the opinion on the financial statements.

Example: Assessing Control Design Effectiveness, Implementation, and Operating Effectiveness

To illustrate the concepts related to internal control introduced in this chapter, we provide an abbreviated example focusing on cost of goods sold, inventory, and accounts payable. We assume that the organization purchases and distributes products; in other words, the organization is not a manufacturer, but it does hold a material amount of inventory. We focus our example on the purchasing cycle and the significant accounts of *accounts payable*, *inventory*, and *expenses*.

Management Assessment of Controls

Management has identified the significant accounts and relevant assertions in the process of purchasing goods and recording the related accounts payable and inventory. After selecting and testing controls designed to mitigate risk of misstatement in these accounts, management identifies the following control deficiencies:

- *Segregation of duties:* At one location, the controls are not well designed, as there is no proper segregation of duties. However, the location is very small, accounting for less than 1% of purchases.
- *Required approval:* At a second location that handles 62% of the organization's purchases, management found that approximately 17% of the purchase orders did not contain proper approval. The reason for the lack of approval was the rush to procure material in a timely fashion to meet a contract requirement. This represents an operating deficiency.

In deciding whether to categorize a deficiency as a significant deficiency or material weakness, management considers the following factors:

- The risk that is being mitigated and whether other controls operate effectively to mitigate the risk of material misstatement
- The materiality of the related account balances
- The nature of the deficiency
- The volume of transactions affected
- The subjectivity of the account balance that is subject to the control
- The rate at which the control fails to operate

Management concludes that the first deficiency (related to segregation of duties) did not rise to the level of either a significant deficiency or a material weakness. However, management decides to use this deficiency as a motivation to centralize purchases at headquarters.

The second deficiency (related to lack of approval) is more of a problem. Management determines this is a significant deficiency based on the following rationale:

- It is a major departure from an approved process.
- It could lead to the purchase of unauthorized goods.
- The unauthorized goods could lead to either (a) inferior products or (b) potential obsolescence.
- Those making the purchases could cause them to be shipped elsewhere (fraudulently) and could lead to a material misstatement in the financial statements.

Management determines that other controls are in place that test for inferior products and obsolescence and that cycle counting of inventory would discover goods that are shipped to a different location. Accordingly, management believes that because of these controls any potential misstatements in the financial statements would not be material. Management tests these controls and determines that they are operating effectively. If these other controls were not in place and operating effectively, then management would have assessed the control deficiency as a material weakness.

Auditor Assessment of Controls

After determining significant accounts and relevant assertions, the auditor reviews management's documentation of its internal control and management's evaluation and findings related to internal control effectiveness. The auditor had previously reviewed and tested the control environment and other entity-wide controls and had evaluated them as effective. The auditor then determined that the following were the important controls in this process (for discussion purposes, we will again concentrate on the purchasing process and assume that the auditor did not find any material weaknesses in the other processes):

- Only authorized goods are purchased from authorized vendors.
- Purchase prices are negotiated by contract or from bids.
- All purchases are delivered to the organization and received by a separate receiving department.
- All purchases are recorded in a timely fashion and are appropriately classified.
- Payments are made only for goods that are received.
- Payments are made consistent with the purchase orders or contracts.
- Payments are made in a timely fashion.

The auditor gathers evidence on the operating effectiveness of these controls as of the client's year-end for the opinion on internal control effectiveness and on operating effectiveness throughout the year for the financial statement audit. Because much of the process is computerized, the auditor performs computer security tests to assure that access controls are working properly and there is adequate control over program changes. The auditor determines that those controls are effective.

The auditor takes a sample of fifty purchase orders to examine whether purchases are authorized and processed properly. The auditor's sample size is influenced by previous information about the operation of the control. Although management had also taken a random sample of purchases and tested the operating effectiveness, the auditor needs to independently determine that the controls are working (or not working). The sample is randomly chosen, and the auditor traces the transactions through the system to determine that the objectives identified previously are addressed by controls.

The auditor's testing of controls identified the same two deficiencies identified by management. Management viewed the deficiency related to lack of approval as a *significant deficiency* because (a) the organization has a good ethical climate and (b) management's tests confirmed that all goods were delivered to the organization. The auditor's tentative conclusion is that this deficiency is a *material weakness* because:

- The location was responsible for ordering 62% of all of the organization's products.
- Management's tests showed a failure rate of over 17%.

The fact that all the goods were delivered to the organization is important and a testament to the ethical culture of the organization. However, not all individuals are ethical; someone with a lower commitment to ethical behavior could be in the purchasing position. Stated another way, a material weakness in internal control can exist even if there are no errors in processing and no misstatements in the current period. The potential for misstatement is high because the auditor believes that existing controls do not mitigate the risk of material misstatement.

More specifically, the auditor notes the following related to the auditor's tests of controls:

- One of the fifty purchases was made from an unauthorized vendor. Investigation reveals that the vendor was subsequently authorized and it was a timing problem; that is, the vendor should have been authorized earlier.
- Seven of the fifty did not have proper authorization, corroborating the earlier finding by management.
- Three of the fifty purchases were paid even though there was no receiving report.
- All of the other controls were found to work properly.

The auditor is concerned that the system allowed a purchase to be made before the vendor was authorized. The auditor's analysis is focused primarily on the risks that may be caused by unauthorized purchases. The auditor believes that unauthorized purchases could lead to a material misstatement of inventory; that is, goods were ordered and paid for, with no proof that they were actually received, and may have been delivered elsewhere. Based on this concern, the auditor decides that the deficiency related to lack of approval warrants a material weakness designation.

SUMMARY AND NEXT STEPS

An important part of an organization's corporate governance is its system of internal control. All organizations need effective internal control over financial reporting so they can produce reliable financial statements that are free from material misstatement. Auditors should expect their clients to design, implement, and maintain effective internal control over financial reporting, and for public clients, to evaluate and report publicly on the effectiveness of its internal control over financial reporting. In the United States, the primary benchmark for assessing internal control effectiveness is the COSO's *Internal Control–Integrated Framework*.

Now that you understand the role of the external auditor (see *Chapter 1*), the elements of quality auditing (see *Chapter 2*), and the expectations for clients to implement mechanisms to provide reasonable assurance about the reliability of their reporting (see *Chapter 2* and *Chapter 3*), it is time to focus on the external auditor. The next chapter provides information on the professional liability of external auditors and steps they can take to make quality professional and ethical judgments throughout the audit opinion formulation process.

SIGNIFICANT TERMS

Application controls See *transaction controls*.

Control activities The component of internal control that includes control actions that have been established by policies and procedures. They help ensure that management's directives regarding internal control are carried out.

Control deficiency A shortcoming in internal controls such that the objective of reliable financial reporting may not be achieved.

Control environment The component of internal control that includes the set of standards, processes, and structures that provides the basis for carrying out internal control across the organization. It includes the "tone at the top" regarding the importance of internal control and the expected standards of conduct.

COSO's Internal Control–Integrated Framework A comprehensive framework of internal control used to assess the effectiveness of internal control over financial reporting, as well as controls over operational and compliance objectives.

Detective controls Controls designed to discover errors that occur during processing.

Edit tests See *input validation tests*.

Entity-wide controls Controls that operate across an entity and affect multiple processes, transactions, accounts, and assertions.

General computer controls Pervasive control activities that affect multiple types of information technology systems and are necessary for automated application controls to work properly (also referred to as *information technology general controls*).

Information and communication The component of internal control that refers to the process of identifying, capturing, and exchanging information in a timely fashion to enable accomplishment of the organization's objectives.

Information technology general controls See *general computer controls*.

Input controls Controls designed to ensure that authorized transactions are correct and complete and that only authorized transactions can be input.

Input validation tests Control tests built into an application to examine input data for obvious errors (also referred to as *edit tests*).

Internal control A process, effected by an entity's board of directors, management, and other personnel, designed to provide reasonable assurance regarding the achievement of objectives relating to operations, reporting, and compliance.

Material weakness in internal control A deficiency, or a combination of deficiencies, in internal control over financial reporting such that there is a reasonable possibility that a material misstatement of the company's annual or interim financial statements will not be prevented or detected on a timely basis.

Monitoring The component of internal control that determines whether the controls, including all five components, are present and continuing to function effectively.

Ongoing evaluations Monitoring procedures that are built into the normal recurring activities of an entity.

Output controls Controls designed to provide reasonable assurance that all data are completely processed and that output is distributed only to authorized recipients.

Physical controls over assets Controls designed to protect and safeguard assets from accidental or intentional destruction and theft.

Preventive controls Controls designed to prevent the occurrence of a misstatement.

Processing controls Controls designed to provide reasonable assurance that the correct program is used for processing, all transactions are processed, and the transactions update appropriate files.

Relevant assertion A financial statement assertion, for a given account, is most relevant to determining whether there is a reasonable possibility that the account could contain a material misstatement, without considering the effect of internal controls.

Risk assessment The component of internal control that is the process for identifying and assessing the risks that may affect an organization from achieving its objectives.

Segregation of duties A control activity that is designed to protect against the risk that an individual could both perpetrate and cover up a fraud.

Self-checking digits A type of input test that has been developed to test for transposition errors associated with identification numbers.

Separate evaluations Monitoring procedures that are conducted periodically, typically by objective management personnel, internal auditors, or external consultants.

Significant account An account that has a reasonable possibility of containing a material misstatement, without considering the effect of internal controls.

Significant deficiency in internal control A deficiency, or a combination of deficiencies, in internal control over financial reporting that is less severe than a material weakness, yet important enough to merit attention by those responsible for oversight of the company's financial reporting.

Transaction controls Control activities implemented to mitigate transaction-processing risk that typically affect only certain processes, transactions, accounts, and assertions. These are controls that do not have an entity-wide effect.

Transaction trail Includes the documents and records that allow a user (or auditor) to trace a transaction from its origination through to its final disposition or vice versa.

Walkthrough A process whereby management (or the auditor) follows a transaction from origination through the organization's processes until it is reflected in the organization's financial records. This process includes a combination of inquiry, observation, inspection of documentation making up the transaction trail, and reperformance of controls.

Whistle-blower function A special line of communication that is needed for anonymous or confidential communications, particularly when an employee is concerned that something is inappropriate in the organization's operations.

TRUE/FALSE QUESTIONS

3-1 **LO 1** Effective internal control over financial reporting allows for more informed decisions by internal and external users of the financial information.

3-2 **LO 1** Management needs to understand its risks to reliable financial reporting before determining which internal controls would be most helpful to achieving its goal of reliable financial reporting.

3-3 **LO 2** Internal control is intended to provide absolute assurance that an organization will achieve its objective of reliable financial reporting.

3-4 **LO 2** Organizations use the GAAP framework of internal control as a benchmark when assessing the effectiveness of internal control over financial reporting.

3-5 **LO 3** The control environment component of internal control is considered a pervasive or entity-wide control because it affects multiple processes and multiple types of transactions.

3-6 **LO 3** The control environment is seen as the foundation for all other components of internal control.

3-7 **LO 4** Only organizations in high-risk industries face a risk that they will not achieve their objective of reliable financial reporting.

3-8 **LO 4** An organization's risk assessment process should identify risks to reliable financial reporting from both internal and external sources.

3-9 **LO 5** There is one standard set of control activities that all organizations should implement.

3-10 **LO 5** Control activities include both preventive and detective controls.

3-11 **LO 6** An organization's accounting system is part of its information and communication component of internal control.

3-12 **LO 6** An organization needs information from both internal and external sources to carry out its internal control responsibilities.

3-13 **LO 7** As part of monitoring, an organization will select either ongoing evaluations or separate evaluations, but not both.

3-14 **LO 7** Communicating identified control deficiencies is a principle of monitoring.

3-15 **LO 8** Management of U.S. public companies may provide a public report on the effectiveness of their organization's internal control over financial reporting, but management is not required to do so.

3-16 **LO 8** As part of a walkthrough, management will follow a transaction from origination to when it is reflected in the financial records to determine whether the controls are effectively designed and have been implemented.

3-17 | LO 9 | If management identifies even one material weakness in internal control, then management will conclude that the organization's internal control over financial reporting is not effective.

3-18 | LO 9 | Management will classify a control deficiency as a material weakness only if there has been a material misstatement in the financial statements.

3-19 | LO 10 | The auditor needs to understand a client's internal controls in order to anticipate the types of material misstatements that may occur in the financial statements and then develop appropriate audit procedures to determine whether those misstatements exist in the financial statements.

3-20 | LO 10 | While understanding a client's internal control over financial reporting may help the external auditor plan the audit, the external auditor is not required to obtain this understanding for all audit engagements.

MULTIPLE-CHOICE QUESTIONS

3-21 | LO 1 | The quality of an organization's internal controls affects which of the following?
a. Reliability of financial data.
b. Ability of management to make good decisions.
c. Ability of the organization to remain in business.
d. All of the above.

3-22 | LO 1 | Which of the following creates an opportunity for committing fraudulent financial reporting in an organization?
a. Management demands financial success.
b. Poor internal control.
c. Commitments tied to debt covenants.
d. Management is aggressive in its application of accounting rules.

3-23 | LO 2 | What are the components of internal control per COSO's *Internal Control–Integrated Framework*?
a. Organizational structure, management philosophy, planning, risk assessment, and control activities.
b. Control environment, risk assessment, control activities, information and communication, and monitoring.
c. Risk assessment, control structure, backup facilities, responsibility accounting, and natural laws.
d. Legal environment of the firm, management philosophy, organizational structure, control activities, and control assessment.

3-24 | LO 2 | Which of the following statements regarding internal control is false?
a. Internal control is a process consisting of ongoing tasks and activities.
b. Internal control is primarily about policy manuals, forms, and procedures.
c. Internal control is geared toward the achievement of multiple objectives.
d. A limitation of internal control is faulty human judgment.
e. All of the above statements are true.

3-25 | LO 3 | Which of the following would not be considered a principle of an organization's control environment?
a. Independence and competence of the board.

b. Competence of accounting personnel.
c. Structures, reporting lines, and authorities and responsibilities.
d. Commitment to integrity and ethical values.
e. They would all be considered principles of the control environment.

3-26 **LO 3** Which one of the following components of internal control over financial reporting sets the tone for the organization?
a. Risk assessment.
b. Control environment.
c. Information and communication.
d. Monitoring.

3-27 **LO 4** Which of the following statements is false regarding the risk assessment component of internal control?
a. Risk assessment includes assessing fraud risk.
b. Risk assessment includes assessing internal and external sources of risk.
c. Risk assessment includes the identification and analysis of significant changes.
d. Economic changes would not be considered a risk that needed to be analyzed as part of the risk assessment process.

3-28 **LO 4** Which of the following is not part of management's fraud risk assessment process?
a. The assessment considers ways the fraud could occur.
b. The assessment considers the role of the external auditor in preventing fraud.
c. Fraud risk assessments serve as an important basis for determining the control activities needed to mitigate fraud risks.
d. The assessment considers pressures that might lead to fraud in the financial statements.

3-29 **LO 5** Segregation of duties is best achieved in which of the following scenarios?
a. Employees perform multiple jobs, and have access to related records.
b. The internal audit department performs an independent test of transactions throughout the year and reports any errors to departmental managers.
c. The person responsible for reconciling the bank account is responsible for cash disbursements but not for cash receipts.
d. The payroll department cannot add employees to the payroll or change pay rates without the explicit authorization of the Human Resources Department.

3-30 **LO 5** Which of the following statements about application controls is true?
a. Organizations can have manual application controls or automated application controls, but not a combination of the two.
b. Application controls are intended to mitigate risks associated with data input, data processing, and data output.
c. Application controls are a part of the monitoring component of internal control.
d. Self-checking digits are an output control.

3-31 **LO 6** Which of the following would be considered an effective implementation of the information and communication component of COSO's *Internal Control–Integrated Framework*?
a. The organization has one-way communication with parties external to the organization.

b. The organization has a whistle-blower function that allows parties internal and external to the organization to communicate concerns about possible inappropriate actions in the organization's operations.

c. The organization has a robust process for assessing risks internal and external to the organization.

d. The organization builds in edit checks to determine whether all purchases are made from authorized vendors.

e. All of the above.

3-32 **LO 6**   Which of the following is not a principle of the information and communication component of COSO's *Internal Control–Integrated Framework*?

a. The organization identifies, obtains, and uses relevant information.

b. The organization communicates internally.

c. The organization communicates externally.

d. All of the above are principles of the information and communication component of COSO's *Internal Control–Integrated Framework*.

3-33 **LO 7**   Which of the following would not be considered an effective implementation of the monitoring component of COSO's *Internal Control–Integrated Framework*?

a. Internal audit periodically performs an evaluation of internal controls.

b. Management reviews current economic performance against expectations and investigates to determine causes of significant deviations from the expectations.

c. The organization implements software that captures all instances in which the underlying program is designed to capture processed transactions that exceed company-authorized limits.

d. The organization builds in edit checks to determine whether all purchases are made from authorized vendors.

3-34 **LO 7**   Which of the following is the most accurate statement related to the monitoring component of COSO's *Internal Control–Integrated Framework*?

a. Monitoring is a process that is relevant only to the control activities component of COSO's *Internal Control–Integrated Framework*.

b. Separate evaluations are more timely than ongoing evaluations in identifying control deficiencies.

c. Monitoring is a process that provides feedback on the effectiveness of each component of internal control.

d. Monitoring includes automated edit checks to determine whether all purchases are made from authorized vendors.

3-35 **LO 8**   Which of the following statements is false regarding management's documentation of internal control over financial reporting?

a. Management needs to maintain sufficient and appropriate documentation of the internal controls they have designed and implemented to achieve the objective of reliable financial reporting.

b. Internal control documentation is useful in training new personnel or serving as a reference tool for all employees.

c. Management only needs to maintain documentation if the company's auditors will be providing an opinion on internal control effectiveness.

d. Documentation provides evidence that the controls are operating.

3-36 **LO 8** Which of the following is <u>not</u> included in management's report on internal control?

a. A statement that management is responsible for internal control.

b. A definition of internal control.

c. A discussion of the limitations of internal control.

d. The criteria used in assessing internal control.

e. A description of the work that the internal auditors performed.

3-37 **LO 9** Assume that an organization sells software. The sales contracts with the customers often have nonstandard terms that impact the timing of revenue recognition. Thus, there is a risk that revenue may be recorded inappropriately. To mitigate that risk, the organization has implemented a policy that requires all nonstandard contracts greater than $1 million to be reviewed on a timely basis by an experienced and competent revenue accountant for appropriate accounting, prior to the recording of revenue. Management tested this control and found several instances in which the control was not working. Management has classified this deficiency as a material weakness. Which of the following best describes the conclusion made by management?

a. There is more than a remote possibility that a material misstatement could occur.

b. The likelihood of misstatement is reasonably possible.

c. There is more than a remote possibility that a misstatement could occur.

d. There is a <u>reasonable</u> possibility that a <u>material misstatement</u> could occur.

e. There is a reasonable possibility that a misstatement could occur.

3-38 **LO 9** Which of the following scenarios represents a control deficiency?

a. A missing control that is required for achieving objectives.

b. A control that operates as designed.

c. A control that provides reasonable, but not absolute assurance, about the reliability of financial reporting.

d. An immaterial individual misstatement in internal control.

3-39 **LO 10** Which of the following is a reason that the <u>auditor</u> obtains an <u>understanding of the client's internal control</u> over financial reporting?

a. This understanding is required by professional auditing standards.

b. Understanding of internal control is needed to properly plan the audit.

c. This understanding helps an auditor assess a client's risks of material misstatement.

d. All of the above are reasons why the auditor obtains an understanding of the client's internal control over financial reporting.

3-40 **LO 10** Which of the following statements is <u>true</u> regarding the auditor's assessment of a client's internal control over financial reporting?

a. The auditor reviews management's documentation of its internal control and management's evaluation and findings related to internal control effectiveness.

b. The auditor's assessments of control deficiencies will be the same as management's assessment of the same deficiencies.

c. For purposes of the financial statement audit, the auditor is only concerned with the effectiveness of a client's internal controls as of year-end.

d. All of the above are true.

REVIEW AND SHORT CASE QUESTIONS

NOTE: Completing Review and Short Case Questions does not require the student to reference additional resources and materials.

NOTE: For the remaining problems, we make special note of those addressing fraud and ethics.

ETHICS

ETHICS

ETHICS

FRAUD

FRAUD

FRAUD

3-41 **LO 1** How does internal control benefit an organization?

3-42 **LO 1** How are the concepts of risk and internal control related?

3-43 **LO 2** Using COSO's *Internal Control–Integrated Framework*, define internal control and describe important elements of the definition.

3-44 **LO 2** Refer to *Exhibit 3.1*. Identify and describe the components of internal control.

3-45 **LO 2** Distinguish between entity-wide and transaction controls. Which components of internal control are typically entity-wide controls? Which components of internal control are typically transaction controls?

3-46 **LO 3** Refer to *Exhibit 3.2*. List the principles representing the fundamental concepts of the control environment component.

3-47 **LO 3** Refer to *Exhibit 3.2*. For each control environment principle, provide an example of how that principle might be applied in an organization.

3-48 **LO 3** What functions do an organization's board of directors and the audit committee of the board of directors perform in promoting an effective internal control environment?

3-49 **LO 3** As part of assessing the control environment, management might consider the compensation programs that the organization has in place. Why would management consider these programs?

3-50 **LO 4** Refer to *Exhibit 3.2*. List the principles representing the fundamental concepts of the risk assessment component.

3-51 **LO 4** Refer to *Exhibit 3.2*. For each risk assessment principle, provide an example of how that principle might be applied in an organization.

3-52 **LO 5** Refer to *Exhibit 3.2*. List the principles representing the fundamental concepts of the control activities component.

3-53 **LO 5** Refer to *Exhibit 3.2*. For each control activities principle, provide an example of how that principle might be applied in an organization.

3-54 **LO 5** Refer to *Exhibit 3.3*. Describe the three types of transactions subject to transaction-processing risk. For each type of transaction, indicate a control activity that could be implemented to mitigate that risk.

3-55 **LO 5** What are the important considerations in security management related to user access?

3-56 **LO 5** What are general computer controls? What is the relationship between general computer controls and application controls? Why is management concerned about the effectiveness of these controls?

3-57 **LO 5** Brown Company provides office support services for more than 100 small clients. These services include supplying temporary personnel, providing monthly bookkeeping services, designing and printing small brochures, copying and reproduction services, and preparing tax reports. Some clients pay for these services on a cash basis, some use thirty-day charge accounts, and others operate on a contractual basis with quarterly payments. Brown's new office manager was concerned about the effectiveness of control procedures over sales and cash flow. At the manager's request, the process was reviewed by conducting a walkthrough. The following facts were identified. Review the identified facts (listed as A through L) and complete the following.

a. What is a *walkthrough*, and why would it be useful for assessing controls over sales and cash flow?

b. List at least eight elements of ineffective internal control at Brown Company.

c. List at least six elements of effective internal control at Brown Company.

   A. Contracts were written by account executives and then passed to the accounts receivable department, where they were filed. Contracts had a limitation (ceiling) on the types of services and the amount of work covered. Contracts were payable quarterly in advance.

   B. Client periodic payments on contracts were identified on the contract, and a payment receipt was placed in the contract file.

   C. Periodically, a clerk reviewed the contract files to determine their status.

   D. Work orders relating to contract services were placed in the contract file. Accounting records showed Debit Cost of Services; Credit Cash or Accounts Payable or Accrued Payroll entry.

   E. Monthly bookkeeping services were usually paid for when the work was complete. If not paid in cash, a copy of the financial statement (marked "Unpaid _____") was put into cash-pending file. It was removed when cash was received, and accounting records showed Debit Cash; Credit Revenue entry.

   F. Design and printing work was handled like bookkeeping's work. However, a design and printing order form was used to accumulate costs and compute the charge to be made to the client. A copy of the order form served as a billing to the client and, when cash was received, as a remittance advice.

   G. Reproduction (copy) work was generally a cash transaction that was rung up on a cash register and balanced at the end of the day. Some reproduction work was charged to open accounts. A billing form was given to the client with the work, and a copy was put in an open file. It was removed when paid. In both cases, when cash was received, the accounting entry was Debit Cash; Credit Revenue.

   H. Tax work was handled like the bookkeeping services.

   I. Cash from cash sales was deposited daily. Cash from receipts on account or quarterly payments on contracts was deposited after being matched with the evidence of the receivable.

J. Bank reconciliations were performed using the deposit slips as original data for the deposits on the bank statements.

K. A cash log of all cash received in the mail was maintained and used for reference purposes when payment was disputed.

L. Monthly comparisons were made of the costs and revenues of printing, design, bookkeeping, and tax service. Unusual variations between revenues and costs were investigated. However, the handling of deferred payments made this analysis difficult.

3-58 **LO 5** The following items represent errors that often occur in an automated environment. For each error (listed as A through I), identify a control activity that would have been effective in either preventing or detecting the error.

A. The selling price for all products handled by a particular company salesperson was reduced from authorized prices by 25% to 40%. The salesperson was paid commission on gross sales made. Subsequently, management found that other sales personnel also reduced prices in order to meet sales targets.

B. Duplicate paychecks were prepared for all employees in the company's warehouse for the week ended July 31. This occurred because the data-processing department processed employee time cards twice.

C. An employee in the sales order department who was upset about an inadequate pay raise copied the client's product master file and sold it to a competitor. The master file contained information on the cost and sales price of each product, as well as special discounts given to customers.

D. An individual in the sales department accessed the product master file and, in an attempt to change prices for a specific customer, ended up changing prices for the products for all customers.

E. A nonexistent part number was included in the description of goods on a shipping document. Fortunately, the individual packing the item for shipment was able to identify the product by its description and included it in the order. The item was not billed, however, because it was not correctly identified in the system.

F. A customer account number was transposed during the order-taking process. Consequently, the shipment was billed to another customer. By the time the error was identified, the original customer decided to take its business elsewhere.

G. An accounts receivable clerk with access to entering cash remittances misappropriated the cash remittances and recorded the credit to the customer's account as a discount.

H. An employee consistently misstated his time card by returning at night and punching out then, rather than when his shift was over at 3:30 p.m. Instead of being paid for 40 hours per week, he was paid, on average, for over 60 hours per week for almost one year. When accused of the error, he denied any wrongdoing and quit.

I. A customer order was filled and shipped to a former customer, who had already declared bankruptcy and already owed a large amount to the company that was most likely uncollectible. The company's standard billing terms are 2%, 10 days, or net 30.

FRAUD

3-59 **LO 5** Authorization of transactions is considered a key control in most organizations. Authorizations should not be made by individuals who have incompatible functions. For each transaction (listed as A through I), indicate the individual or function (e.g., the head of a particular department) that should have the ability to authorize that transaction. Briefly provide a rationale for your answer.

A. Writing off old accounts receivable.
B. Committing the organization to acquire another company that is half the size of the existing company.
C. Paying an employee for overtime.
D. Shipping goods on account to a new customer.
E. Purchasing goods from a new vendor.
F. Temporarily investing funds in common stock investments instead of money market funds.
G. Purchasing a new line of manufacturing equipment to remodel a production line at one of the company's major divisions (the purchase represents a major new investment for the organization).
H. Replacing an older machine at one of the company's major divisions.
I. Rewriting the company's major computer program for processing purchase orders and accounts payable (the cost of rewriting the program will represent one quarter of the organization's computer development budget for the year).

FRAUD

3-60 **LO 5** For each of the following situations (indicated A through G), evaluate the segregation of duties implemented by the company and indicate the following:

a. Any deficiency in the segregation of duties described. (Indicate "None" if no deficiency is present.)
b. The potential financial statement misstatements that might occur because of the inadequate segregation of duties.
c. Other controls that might be added to mitigate potential misstatements.

A. The company's payroll is computerized and is handled by one person in charge of payroll who enters all weekly time reports into the system. The payroll system is password protected so that only the payroll person can change pay rates or add/delete company personnel to the payroll file. Payroll checks are prepared weekly, and the payroll person batches the checks by supervisor or department head for subsequent distribution to employees.

B. A relatively small organization has segregated the duties of cash receipts and cash disbursements. However, the employee responsible for handling cash receipts also reconciles the monthly bank account.

C. Nick's is a small family-owned restaurant in a northern resort area whose employees are trusted. When the restaurant is very busy, any of the servers have the ability to operate the cash register and collect the amounts due from the customer. All orders are tabulated on "tickets." Although each ticket has a place to indicate the server, most do not bother to do so, nor does management reconcile the ticket numbers and amounts with total cash receipts for the day.

D. A sporting goods store takes customer orders via a toll-free phone number. The order taker sits at a terminal and has complete access to the customer's previous credit history and a list of inventory available for sale. The order clerk has the ability to input all the customer's requests and generate a sales invoice and shipment with no additional supervisory review or approval.

E. The purchasing department of Big Dutch is organized around three purchasing agents. The first is responsible for ordering electrical gear and motors, the second orders fabrication material, and the third orders nuts and bolts and other smaller supplies that go into the assembly process. To improve the accountability to vendors, all receiving slips and vendor invoices are sent directly to the purchasing agent placing the order. This allows the purchasing agent to better monitor the performance of vendors. When approved by the purchasing agent for payment, the purchasing agent must forward (a) a copy of the purchase order, (b) a copy of the receiving slip, and (c) a copy of the vendor invoice to accounts payable for payment. Accounts payable will not pay an invoice unless all three items are present and match as to quantities, prices, and so forth. The receiving department reports to the purchasing department.

FRAUD

3-61 **LO 5** Sports Life World is a catalog retailer emphasizing outdoor gear, with a focus on fishing and hunting equipment and clothing. It prints an annual catalog containing over 200 pages of products, as well as approximately six special sale catalogs during the year. Products range from fishing lures retailing for just over a $1.00 to boat packages for over $25,000. Sports Life World also has both a significant Internet presence and a number of large retail locations. Purchases can be made through the mail, on the company's web site, or at the retail store. There will sometimes be online specials that are not available elsewhere (e.g., closeouts). Merchandise can be paid for by personal check, credit card, or cash. Customers can (a) order online, (b) mail in their order (with check or credit card information included), or (c) place an order by calling the company's toll-free number.

Focusing on catalog operations, assume the company has implemented an order-entry system by which computer operators take the customer order, check the availability of items for shipment, and confirm the invoice amount with the customer. Once an order is taken, the system generates a shipping-and-packing document, places a hold on the inventory, and prepares an invoice (and recording of sales) when items are shipped.

a. Identify the application control procedures (including edit controls) you would recommend for orders coming in over the Internet or through calls to the online order taker.

b. Briefly indicate how control procedures might differ for the orders that are made through the company's web site.

c. For each control procedure identified in your response to (a), briefly indicate the potential types of misstatements that could occur because the control is not present or is not operating effectively.

3-62   **LO 6**   Refer to *Exhibit 3.2*. List the principles representing the fundamental concepts of the information and communication component.

3-63   **LO 6**   Refer to *Exhibit 3.2*. For each information and communication principle, provide an example of how that principle might be applied in an organization.

3-64   **LO 7**   Refer to *Exhibit 3.2*. List the principles representing the fundamental concepts of the monitoring component.

3-65   **LO 7**   Refer to *Exhibit 3.2*. For each monitoring principle, provide an example of how that principle might be applied in an organization.

3-66   **LO 7**   Companies can improve internal control effectiveness by implementing effective ongoing monitoring of their internal control processes. Identify ongoing monitoring procedures that an organization might use in assessing its controls over revenue recognition in each of the following situations:

a.   A convenience store such as 7-Eleven.

b.   A chain restaurant such as Olive Garden.

c.   A manufacturing division of a larger company that makes rubberized containers for the consumer market.

3-67   **LO 8**   What are management's responsibilities related to internal control over financial reporting?

3-68   **LO 8**   Refer to *Exhibit 3.4*. What is a transaction trail? List important aspects of an electronic transaction trail. What are management's responsibilities related to maintaining a transaction trial?

3-69   **LO 8**   Refer to *Exhibit 3.5*. What are the important features of management's report on internal control over financial reporting?

3-70   **LO 8**   Refer to *Exhibit 3.6* and *Exhibit 3.7*. Describe management's process for evaluating internal control over financial reporting. For the control environment principles, identify evidence that management might obtain to assess the operating effectiveness of the control environment.

ETHICS

3-71   **LO 8**   Should management's assessment of internal control over financial reporting consider all of the COSO components, or could it be based only on the controls over the processing of transactions? Explain.

3-72   **LO 8**   One principle of the control environment is the organization's commitment to develop, attract, and retain competent individuals. How would management go about evaluating the competency of accounting department personnel and the competencies of those making judgments on financial reporting issues?

3-73   **LO 9**   Assume that management had determined that its organization's audit committee is not effective. How do the weaknesses in audit committee affect management's evaluation of internal control over financial reporting? Would an ineffective audit committee constitute a material weakness in internal control over financial reporting? State the rationale for your response.

3-74   **LO 9**   Refer to *Exhibit 3.8* and *Exhibit 3.9*. Define the terms significant deficiency and material weakness. What factors does management consider when assessing identified control deficiencies?

3-75 **LO 9** Assume that management is gathering evidence as part of its process for assessing the effectiveness of internal control over financial reporting. The company is a manufacturer of high-dollar specialized machines used in the medical profession. The following table identifies important controls that management is testing regarding accounts related to revenue recognition, accounts receivable, and other sales-related activities. The first column describes the control, and the second column describes the test results. Based on the test results, determine the conclusion that management should make about the deficiency (is it a control deficiency, a significant deficiency, or a material weakness?).

CONTROL TESTING OVER REVENUE

Control Tested	Test Results
A. All sales over $10,000 require computer check of outstanding balances to see if approved balance is exceeded.	Tested throughout year with a sample size of thirty. Only three failures, all in the last quarter, and all approved by sales manager.
B. The computer is programmed to record a sale only when an item is shipped.	Sampled ten items during the last month. One indicated that it was recorded before it was shipped. Management was aware of the recording.
C. All prices are obtained from a standardized price list maintained within the computer and accessible only by the marketing manager.	Management selected forty invoices and found five instances in which the price was less than the price list. All of the price changes were initiated by salespeople.
D. Sales are shipped only upon receiving an authorized purchase order from customer.	Management selects fifteen transactions near the end of each quarter. On average, three to four are shipped each quarter based on salesperson's approval and without a customer purchase order.

3-76 **LO 9** The following scenario describes PPC, a small plastics producer with $250 million in revenue and approximately 300 employees. PPC is a public company that first became listed three years ago. Its sales have dropped from $1,375 million to $1,250 million over that period. It is barely profitable and is just meeting some of its most important debt covenants. During the past year, John Slade, CEO and owner of 22% of the company's shares, has taken the following actions (listed as A through I) to reduce costs. For each action, complete the following.

a. Would the action be considered an operational issue and not a control deficiency, or would it likely constitute a material weakness or significant deficiency in internal control? Provide a brief rationale for your assessment. If additional information is needed in order to assess whether the item is a control deficiency, briefly indicate what information would be required.

b. Considering all of the indicated actions (A through I), how has the risk related to the objective of reliable financial reporting changed during the year?

A. Laid off approximately 75 factory workers and stream-lined receiving and shipping to be more efficient.

B. Cut hourly wages by $3 per hour.

C. Reduced the size of the board by eliminating three of the four independent directors and changed the compensation of remaining board members to 100% stock options to save cash outflow. The company granted options to the remaining six directors with a market value of $100,000 per director, but no cash outlay.

D. Eliminated the internal audit department at a savings of $450,000. The process owners (e.g., those responsible for accounts payable) are now required to objectively evaluate the quality of controls over their own areas and thus to serve as a basis for management's report on the effectiveness of internal control.

E. Changed from a Big 4 audit firm to a regional audit firm, resulting in an additional audit savings of $300,000. This is the first public company audit for the new firm.

F. Because internal audit no longer exists, the CEO relies on monitoring as the major form of control assessment. Most of the monitoring consists of comparing budget with actual results. Management argues this is very effective because the CEO is very much involved in operations and would know if there is a reporting problem.

G. Set tight performance goals for managers and promised a bonus of 20% of their salary if they meet the performance objectives. The performance objectives relate to increased profitability and meeting existing volumes.

H. The purchasing department has been challenged to move away from single-supplier contracts to identify suppliers that can significantly reduce the cost of products purchased.

I. Put a freeze on all hiring, in spite of the fact that the accounting department has lost its assistant controller. This has required a great deal of extra overtime for most accounting personnel, who are quite stressed.

3-77 **LO 10** When testing internal controls, does the auditor test the same transactions that management tested, or does the auditor test different transactions? Explain your rationale.

3-78 **LO 10** Why do external auditors need to understand their client's internal control over financial reporting?

FRAUD FOCUS: CONTEMPORARY AND HISTORICAL CASES

FRAUD   **3-79** **Chesapeake Petroleum and Supply, Inc.**
(LO 1, 2, 5) Refer to the *Focus on Fraud* feature "The Importance of Internal Control for Safeguarding Assets at Chesapeake Petroleum and Supply, Inc." which describes the embezzlement at Chesapeake Petroleum and Supply.

a. Why is internal control important to an organization?

b. How does internal control help an organization achieve reliable financial reporting?

c. Why does an external auditor need to know about a client's internal control?

d. What is internal control over financial reporting and what are its components?

e. What type of control is segregation of duties and what risks is that control intended to mitigate?

f. What controls could Chesapeake have implemented that may have prevented the embezzlement?

FRAUD

3-80

Diamond Foods, Inc.
(LO 8, 9) In February 2012, the *Wall Street Journal* reported that Diamond Foods, Inc. fired its CEO and CFO, and would restate financial results for two years. The restatement was required after the company found that it had wrongly accounted for crop payments to walnut growers. The investigation focused primarily on whether payments to growers in September 2011 of approximately $60 million and payments to growers in August 2010 of approximately $20 million were accounted for in the correct periods. Shareholders suing the company allege the payments may have been used to shift costs from a prior fiscal year into a subsequent fiscal year. In a February 2012 filing with the SEC, the audit committee stated that Diamond has one or more material weaknesses in its internal control over financial reporting. In January 2014, the SEC charged Diamond Foods and two former executives for their roles in the accounting scheme to falsify walnut costs in order to boost earnings and meet estimates by stock analysts. Diamond Foods agreed to pay $5 million to settle the SEC's charges.

a. Does the restatement suggest that the company's internal controls contained a material weakness? Explain your rationale.

b. In September 2011, the company filed its annual report with the SEC for its fiscal year ended July 31, 2011. As part of that filing, the company maintained that it had effective internal controls over financial reporting as of its year-end date. Do you believe that management's report on internal control over financial reporting was accurate?

c. In February 2012, the audit committee indicated that the company had ineffective internal controls. What types of material weaknesses do you think might exist at Diamond?

APPLICATION ACTIVITIES

NOTE: Completing Application Activities requires students to reference additional resources and materials.

3-81 **LO 5** Select a company where you have worked part-time or an organization in which you have some acquaintance (relative or friend) and therefore have access. Choose one area of operations (cash receipts, sales, shipping, receiving, or payroll) for review. For the area selected:

a. Identify the major transactions processed.

b. Select a representative transaction and perform a walk-through of the transaction to gain an understanding of how the transaction is processed and the controls implemented to mitigate the risks to reliable financial reporting.

c. Document the important controls and the risks they were intended to mitigate.

d. Identify additional controls you would recommend to improve the organization's internal controls.

3-82 **LO 7** Companies are using the power of computing to develop continuous monitoring approaches to identify control problems early and to take corrective action on a timely basis.

a. Explain how the concept of continuous monitoring might be applied in a computerized application that processes sales orders and records sales.

b. Select one of the following web sites:
   • Oversightsystems.com
   • ACL.com

Explain the types of products that each company provides and how the products might help other companies implement effective monitoring over computer operations. To what extent are the software products (1) another control to be implemented versus (2) an approach to control monitoring? Explain.

SEC, Diamond Foods, Inc.

3-83 **(LO 8, 9)** At the SEC web site, obtain Management's Report on Internal Control provided by Diamond Foods, Inc. for the year-end July 31, 2013. (See p. 79 of Form 10-K, via EDGAR at *www.sec.gov*)

a. Identify the material weaknesses that management described in its report on internal control.

b. Why would management consider these deficiencies to be material weaknesses?

c. Are misstatements necessary for management to conclude that a control deficiency is a material weakness? Explain.

d. What process would Diamond's management have gone through to identify these material weaknesses?

3-84 **LO 8, 9** Using the business press (i.e., financial news articles), identify a company that has restated it published financial statements. Describe the nature of the restatement. What types of deficiencies in internal control likely existed such that the financial statements were materially misstated? Should management now conclude that it has a material weakness in internal control over financial reporting?

ACADEMIC RESEARCH CASES

NOTE: Completing Academic Research Cases requires students to reference additional resources and materials.

SEARCH HINT

It is easy to locate these academic research articles! Use a search engine such as Google Scholar or an electronic research platform such as ABI Inform, and search using the author names and part of the article title.

3-85 **LO 1, 5** Locate and read the article listed below and answer the following questions.

Grant, G., K. Miller, and F. Mali. 2008. The effect of IT controls on financial reporting. *Managerial Auditing Journal* 23 (8): 247–271.

a. What is the issue being addressed in the paper?

b. What are the findings of the paper?

c. Why is this paper important to auditors, and what are the implications of this paper for the auditing profession?

d. Describe the research methodology used as a basis for the conclusions.

e. Describe any limitations of the research.

3-86 **LO 8, 9** Locate and read the article listed below and answer the following questions.

Hermanson, D., and Z. Ye. 2009. Why do some accelerated filers with SOX Section 404 material weaknesses provide early warning under Section 302? *Auditing: A Journal of Practice & Theory* 28 (2): 247–271.

a. What is the issue being addressed in the paper?

b. What are the findings of the paper?

c. Why is this paper important to auditors, and what are the implications of this paper for the auditing profession?

    d. Describe the research methodology used as a basis for the conclusions.

    e. Describe any limitations of the research.

3-87 **LO 1, 2, 9** Locate and read the article listed below and answer the following questions.

Klamm, B. K., K. W. Kobelsky, and M. Weidenmier Watson. 2012. Determinants of the persistence of internal control weaknesses. *Accounting Horizons* 26 (2): 307–333.

    a. What is the issue being addressed in the paper?

    b. What are the findings of the paper?

    c. Why is this paper important to auditors, and what are the implications of this paper for the auditing profession?

    d. Describe the research methodology used as a basis for the conclusions.

    e. Describe any limitations of the research.

FORD AND TOYOTA

3-88 **Ford Motor Company and Toyota Motor Corporation (LO 2, 8)** The following questions address issues concerning internal control.

Source and Reference	Question
Ford 10-K and Toyota 20-F	a. Both Ford and Toyota management comment on the fact that internal control over financial reporting has "inherent limitations." What are those inherent limitations?
	b. Locate the CEO certification toward the end of Ford's 10K. Summarize the main components of the certification. Why should users of the financial statements be assured by the statements made in the certification?
	c. How does management obtain comfort that internal control does not contain any material weaknesses?
	d. From a conceptual point of view, assume that two companies are the same size, participate in the same industry, and have the same reported net income. However, one has a material weakness in internal control over financial reporting and the other does not have any material weaknesses. Should the stock price of the two be different? What is the rationale for your answer?

4

Professional Liability, Auditor Judgment Frameworks, and Professional Responsibilities

CHAPTER OVERVIEW AND LEARNING OBJECTIVES

The past three chapters have introduced you to the external auditing profession, the need for audit quality, the challenges that fraud poses for auditors, and management's responsibility to ensure reliable financial reporting through effective internal controls. In this chapter, we discuss the legal environment in which auditors operate and explore litigation they might face, should they fail to perform quality audits. Even though most audits are performed in a quality manner, a large percentage of the revenues of external audit firms is spent on litigation-related costs. Litigation costs have caused some of the world's largest audit firms to declare bankruptcy, so it is extremely important that auditors use due professional care and conduct quality audits. Following the discussion on litigation, we introduce a framework for professional decision making and a framework for ethical decision making; these frameworks, when applied effectively, help auditors avoid the risk of litigation. We conclude the chapter with discussion of professional responsibilities as described in the relevant ethics pronouncements.

Through studying this chapter, you will be able to achieve these learning objectives:

1. Discuss the liability environment in which auditors operate and explore the effects of lawsuits on audit firms.

2. List laws from which auditor liability is derived and describe the causes of legal action against auditors.

3. Describe auditor liability under contract law, common law, and statutory law.

4. Articulate a framework for making quality professional decisions and apply this framework in selected audit settings.

5. Articulate a framework for making quality ethical decisions and apply this framework in selected settings.

6. Identify guidance on auditors' professional responsibilities and make audit decisions informed by the appropriate professional guidance.

THE AUDIT OPINION FORMULATION PROCESS

I. Making Client Acceptance and Continuance Decisions
Chapter 1

II. Performing Risk Assessment
Chapters 3, 7, and 9–13

III. Obtaining Evidence About Internal Control Operating Effectiveness
Chapters 8–13 and 16

IV. Obtaining Substantive Evidence About Accounts, Disclosures and Assertions
Chapters 8–13 and 16

V. Completing the Audit and Making Reporting Decisions
Chapters 14 and 15

The Auditing Profession, the Risk of Fraud and Mechanisms to Address Fraud: Regulation, Corporate Governance, and Audit Quality
Chapters 1 and 2

Professional Liability and the Need for Quality Auditor Judgments and Ethical Decisions
Chapter 4

The Audit Opinion Formulation Process and a Framework for Obtaining Audit Evidence
Chapters 5 and 6

PROFESSIONAL JUDGMENT IN CONTEXT
The Importance of Proper Professional Conduct

Proper professional conduct, including maintaining auditor independence, is critical to the integrity of the financial reporting process. The conduct of James T. Adams, a former partner at the audit firm Deloitte, provides a reminder of how individual auditor actions can call into question the quality of an audit. In May 2014, the Securities and Exchange Commission (SEC) charged Adams, the former chief risk officer at Deloitte, for causing violations of the auditor independence rules designed to ensure that audit firms maintain their objectivity and impartiality with respect to their clients.

The SEC found that Adams repeatedly accepted tens of thousands of dollars in casino markers from an audit client, while he was the advisory partner on Deloitte's audit of that client, a casino gaming corporation. (A marker is an instrument utilized by a casino customer to receive gaming chips drawn against the customer's line of credit at the casino. Basically, the transactions by Adams were loans from an audit client that are prohibited by the auditor independence rules.) As an advisory partner for the casino audit client from January 20, 2009, until January 13, 2010, Adams was a senior partner who was part of the audit engagement team.

Adams opened a line of credit with a casino run by the gaming corporation client and used the casino markers to draw on that line of credit. Adams concealed his casino markers from Deloitte and lied to another partner when asked if he had casino markers from audit clients of the firm. The SEC noted that Adams drew $85,000 worth of markers in July 2009 that remained outstanding for 43 days. In September, he drew $3,000 in markers that were outstanding for 13 days and $70,000 in markers that were outstanding for 27 days. In October, he drew $110,000 in markers that were outstanding for 38 days. In December, he drew $100,000 in markers that were outstanding for seven days, and later that month drew $110,000 in markers that remained outstanding when he retired from the firm in May 2010. Adams subsequently defaulted on the $110,000 of outstanding markers that he drew in December 2009. On March 9, 2010, the audit client filed its annual report on Form10-K for its fiscal year ended December 31, 2009, with the SEC. The annual report included a Deloitte audit report that stated that its audit of the financial statements of this client had been conducted in accordance with the standards of the Public Company Accounting Oversight Board (PCAOB). Because of Adams's conduct described above, that statement was incorrect.

At the time of his actions described here, Adams was a licensed CPA in Georgia and California. In May 2014, Adams settled the SEC's charges by being suspended for at least two years from practicing as an accountant on behalf of any publicly traded company or other entity regulated by the SEC.

For further information about this scenario, see SEC Accounting and Auditing Enforcement Release No. 3554, May 20, 2014.

As you read through this chapter, consider the following questions:

- What is appropriate professional conduct for auditors and what guidance exists related to auditors' professional responsibilities? (LO 6)
- What types of auditor actions could lead to litigation? (LO 2)
- What actions can auditors and audit firms take to encourage appropriate professional conduct and minimize litigation exposure? (LO 3, 4, 5, 6)

The Legal Environment and the Effects of Lawsuits on Audit Firms

 Discuss the liability environment in which auditors operate and explore the effects of lawsuits on audit firms.

Litigation cases are expensive for audit firms—whether they win or lose—because they result in monetary losses, consume time of audit firm members, and can hurt the reputation of the audit firm. In fact, audit firms have reported that practice protection costs, such as insurance, legal fees, and litigation settlements, are the second-highest costs faced by audit firms, behind only employee compensation costs. When auditors agree to perform audits, they purport to be experts in assessing the fairness of financial statements on which the public relies. In conducting most audits, auditors use great care, perform professionally, issue appropriate opinions, and serve the interests of the public. In short, most audits are conducted in a quality manner. Even so, audit firms continue to experience high levels of litigation. Reasons for this include:

- Liability doctrines that include joint and several liability statutes permitting a plaintiff to recover the full amount of a settlement from an external audit firm, even though that firm is found to be only partially responsible for the loss (often referred to as the **deep-pocket theory**, which is the practice of suing another party not based on the level of their true fault in a legal action, but based instead on the perceived ability of that party to pay damages)
- Class action suits and associated user awareness of the possibilities and rewards of litigation
- Contingent-fee-based compensation for law firms, especially in class action suits
- The misunderstanding by some users of financial statement that an unqualified audit opinion represents an insurance policy against investment losses

Liability Doctrines

Auditors may be subject to either joint and several liability or proportionate liability. **Joint and several liability** concepts are designed to protect users who suffer losses because of misplaced reliance on materially misstated financial statements. Users suffer real losses, but sometimes those primarily responsible for the losses, such as client management, do not have the monetary resources to compensate users. Under joint and several liability, users suffering a loss are able to recover full damages from any defendant, including an audit firm, regardless of the level of fault of the party. For example, if a jury decided that management was 80% at fault and the auditor was 20% at fault, the damages would be apportioned 80% to management and 20% to auditors. Unfortunately, in many lawsuits involving auditors, the client is in bankruptcy, management has few monetary resources, and the auditor is the only party left with adequate resources to pay the damages. Joint and several liability then apportions the damages over the remaining defendants in proportion to the relative damages. Under joint and several liability, if management has no resources and there are no other defendants, 100% of the damages are then apportioned to the audit firm. In federal suits, Congress has limited the extent of joint and several liability damages to actual percentage of responsibility (if auditors are found liable for less than 50% of damages).

In 1995, Congress passed the Private Securities Litigation Reform Act (PSLRA), which was designed to curb frivolous securities class action lawsuits brought under federal securities laws against companies whose stock performs below expectations. Under this Act, liability is proportional rather than joint and several, unless the violation is willful—that is, unless the auditor knowingly participated in a fraud. In some situations, a defendant may have to cover some of the obligation of another defendant who is unable to pay his or her share. Under **proportionate liability**, a defendant must pay a proportionate share of the damage, depending on the degree of fault determined by the judge or jury. Because the PSLRA applies only to lawsuits brought in federal courts, many lawyers filed their cases in state courts. This loophole was closed by the Securities Litigation Uniform Standards Act of 1998, which states, "Any covered class action brought into any state court involving a covered security . . . shall be removable to the federal district court for the district in which the action is pending." The 1998 Act is designed to require potential plaintiffs to adhere to the spirit, as well as the letter, of the PLSRA Act of 1995.

Class Action Lawsuits

Class action lawsuits are designed to prevent multiple lawsuits that might result in inconsistent judgments and to encourage litigation when no individual plaintiff has a claim large enough to justify the expense of litigation. These types of lawsuits are especially appropriate for securities litigation because they enable a number of shareholders to combine claims that they could not afford to litigate individually. Often in these cases, the lawyers work on a contingent fee basis and will work very diligently to identify every potential member of the class. Damages to audit firms in such cases can be extremely large, thus the fees for the lawyers are also usually quite large. However, court rulings in the U.S.—especially a 2008 U.S. Supreme Court decision in *Stoneridge Investment Partners v. Scientific-Atlanta*—have made it harder to sue auditors for misleading accounting. A report on 2013 class action filings notes that in the U.S., since 2009, auditors have been less frequently named as defendants. The *Auditing in Practice* feature "Class Action Lawsuits Go Global" discusses global issues related to class action lawsuits.

Contingent-Fee Compensation for Lawyers

Contingent fees for lawyers have evolved in our society to allow individuals who cannot afford high-priced lawyers to seek compensation for their damages. Lawyers take **contingent-fee cases** with an agreement that a client who loses a case owes the lawyer nothing; however, if the case is won, the lawyer receives an agreed-upon portion (usually one-third to one-half) of the damages awarded. This arrangement protects the underprivileged and encourages lawsuits by a wide variety of parties. The plaintiffs have little to lose, while the lawyers have a large incentive to successfully pursue such cases.

Class Action Lawsuits Go Global

Class action suits against large audit firms are increasing globally. This increase is due to governments improving investor protection laws in countries where the Big Four audit firms have previously not faced substantial legal risks.

While class action lawsuits have declined in the U.S. due to court rulings and legislation, the number of countries allowing these kinds of suits has grown to more than 20, including Italy, Poland, and Mexico.

As two examples of international class action lawsuits, consider that as of 2012, the biggest class action settlement in Australia was a $203-million case that named audit firm PricewaterhouseCoopers (PwC) as one of the defendants. The firm paid about a third of the sum. In 2012, Ernst & Young paid about $118 million in Canada's largest class action settlement against an auditor. In the past, class action lawsuits were primarily focused in the U.S. These examples illustrate the growth of class action lawsuits outside of the U.S.

Audits Viewed as an Insurance Policy: The Expectations Gap

An audit report accompanying a financial statement is not a guarantee that an investment in the audited company is free of risk. Unfortunately, some investors mistakenly view the unqualified audit report as an insurance policy against any and all losses from a risky investment. These investors believe that when they suffer losses, they should be able to recover their losses from the auditor. This misperception represents an **expectations gap**, whereby shareholders believe that they are entitled to recover losses on investments for which the auditor provided an unqualified opinion on the financial statements. This misperception, coupled with joint and several liability, class action lawsuits, and contingent-fee compensation for lawyers, encourages large lawsuits against auditors, even for cases in which the auditor is only partially at fault or is not at fault.

Applicable Laws and Causes of Legal Action

Laws from Which Auditor Liability Is Derived and Causes of Legal Action

LO 2 List laws from which auditor liability is derived and describe the causes of legal action against auditors.

Liability affecting audit firms is derived from the following types of law:

- **Common law**—Liability concepts are developed through court decisions based on negligence, gross negligence, or fraud.
- **Contract law**—Liability occurs where there is a breach of contract. The contract is usually between the external auditor and the client for the performance of the financial statement audit.
- **Statutory law**—Liability is based on federal securities laws or state statutes. Important statutes for the auditing profession are the Securities Act of 1933 (1933 Act), the Securities Exchange Act of 1934 (1934 Act), and the Sarbanes-Oxley Act of 2002.

Parties bringing suit against auditors usually allege that the auditors did not meet the standard of due care in performing the audit. The AICPA defines the concept of due care as follows:

The quest for excellence is the essence of due care. Due care requires a member to discharge professional responsibilities with competence and diligence. It imposes the obligation to perform professional services to the best of a member's ability with concern for the best interest of those for whom the services are performed and consistent with the profession's responsibility to the public.

Source: AICPA audit and accounting guides by American Institute of Certified Public Accountants. Copyright © 2012 Reproduced with permission of American Institute of Certified Public Accountants in the format Textbook via Copyright Clearance Center.

Auditors are responsible for due care. The specific responsibility in a particular case depends on whether there is a breach of contract, negligence, gross negligence, or fraud.

Breach of contract occurs when a person fails to perform a contractual duty. As an example, an auditor was hired to find a material fraud. If reasonable procedures would have detected the fraud and the auditor failed to uncover the fraud, the auditor would have breached the contract. As another example, if the auditor agreed to provide the audit report by a certain date, but did not, the auditor would have breached the contract.

Negligence is the failure to exercise reasonable care, thereby causing harm to another or to property. If an auditor, for example, did not detect an embezzlement scheme because of a failure to follow up on evidence that would have brought it to light, but a prudent auditor would have performed such follow-up, the auditor is negligent. The profession's standards require that audits be conducted in accordance with professional auditing standards; thus, a failure to meet these standards could be construed as negligence on the part of the auditor.

Gross negligence is the failure to use even minimal care, a reckless disregard for the truth, or reckless behavior. Expressing an opinion on a set of financial statements with careless disregard of professional auditing standards is an example of gross negligence. Gross negligence is more than failing to comply with professional standards; it is such complete disregard for due care that judges and juries are allowed to infer intent to deceive, even though there may be no direct evidence of intent to deceive.

Fraud is an intentional concealment or misrepresentation of a material fact that causes damage to those deceived. In an action for fraud, scienter must generally be proved. **Scienter** means knowledge on the part of a person making false representations, at the time they are made, that they are false. An auditor perpetrates a fraud on investors, for example, by expressing an unqualified opinion on financial statements that the auditor knows, in reality, are not fairly presented. In such a situation, the purpose of expressing the unqualified audit opinion is to deceive.

Parties that May Bring Suit Against Auditors

In most cases, anyone who can support a claim that damages were incurred based on misleading audited financial statements can bring a claim against the auditor. These parties typically include the client and third-party users. They may accuse the auditor of breach of contract or of a tort. A **tort** is a civil wrong, other than breach of contract, based on negligence, gross negligence, or fraud. *Exhibit 4.1* lists the parties to whom the external auditor is held liable, and outlines the applicable law from which auditor liability is derived.

EXHIBIT 4.1 Overview of Auditor Liability

(AUDITOR HELD LIABLE? Y = YES, N = NO, NA = NOT APPLICABLE)

Who Can Sue?	Client		3rd Parties		
				Statutory Law	
Under What Law?	Contract Law	Common Law	Common Law	1933 Act	1934 Act
For What?					
Breach of contract	Y	NA	NA	NA	NA
Negligence	Y	Y	*	Y	N
Gross negligence	Y	Y	Y	Y	Unclear
Fraud	Y	Y	Y	Y	Y

*Depends on the test used:
- Identified User
- Foreseen User
- Foreseeable User

Auditor Liability Under Contract Law, Common Law, and Statutory Law

LO 3 Describe auditor liability under contract law, common law, and statutory law.

Common-Law Liability to Clients: Breach of Contract

When a client contracts with an auditor to perform specific services, a contract is drawn up indicating that the services will be performed in accordance with professional auditing standards and will be completed on a timely basis. Auditors are expected to fulfill these contractual responsibilities to clients. Auditors can be held liable to clients under contract law and/or under common law for breach of contract, and they can be sued under the concepts of negligence, gross negligence, and fraud.

Causes of Action Breach of contract may occur when there is nonperformance of a contractual duty. Causes for action against the auditor for breach of contract may include, but are not limited to, the following:

- Violating client confidentiality
- Failing to provide the audit report on time
- Failing to discover a material error or employee fraud
- Withdrawing from an audit engagement without justification

A client seeking to recover damages from an auditor in an action based on negligence must show that the auditor had a duty not to be negligent. In determining this duty, courts use as criteria the standards and principles of the profession, including professional auditing standards and financial accounting principles. Liability may be imposed for lack of due care either in performing the audit or in presenting financial information. The auditor must have breached that duty by not exercising due professional care. The client must show there was a causal relationship between the negligence and damage. The client must prove actual damages. The amount of damages must be established with reasonable certainty, and the client must demonstrate that the auditor's acts or omissions were the cause of the loss. See the *Focus on Fraud* feature "Moss Adams and the Meridian Mortgage Funds Fraud" for an example of a case in which the audit firm was sued for breach of contract.

Moss Adams and the Meridian Mortgage Funds Fraud

Although management is responsible for the preparation of financial statements, it is possible that the statements contain material misstatements that should have been discovered by the auditor. For example, the auditor may have failed to discover a fraud that was being perpetrated against the management of the company. The auditor will usually argue that the client was negligent because client management contributed to the fraud in some way (e.g., the auditor might argue that the damage was intentional or was at least in part caused by management's carelessness or lack of internal controls). Nonetheless, clients have brought litigation against auditors when financial statements were misleading or frauds were not detected.

As an example, in late 2011, the trustee for the bankrupt Meridian Mortgage funds sued the audit firm Moss Adams for $150 million for failing to detect the founder's Ponzi scheme. The founder, Frederick Berg, pleaded guilty, admitting to stealing about $100 million of Meridian's funds for personal use and to perpetuating the Ponzi scheme. Moss Adams had issued unqualified audit opinions for the funds, and the trustee argued that it was a series of low-quality audits that allowed the Ponzi scheme to continue undetected. The trustee alleged that Moss Adams acted intentionally and recklessly. The trustee also argued that the audit firm was not independent, as Berg was paying the firm large sums of money to perform consulting and personal tax services for him.

This case illustrates the serious litigation risk that audit firms face when their clients are acting fraudulently and when the audit firm conducts the audits in a way that allows those relying on the financial statements to question audit quality.

Remedies   The remedies for breach of contract include:

- Requiring specific performance of the contract agreement
- Granting an injunction to prohibit the auditor from doing certain acts, such as disclosing confidential information
- Providing for recovery of amounts lost as a result of the breach

When specific performance or an injunction is not appropriate, the client is entitled to recover compensatory damages. In determining the amounts of compensation, courts try to put the client in the position in which it would have been, had the contract been performed as promised.

Auditor Defenses   The auditor can use the following arguments as defenses against a breach of contract suit:

- The auditor exercised due professional care in accordance with the contract.
- The client was contributory negligent.
- The client's losses were not caused by the breach.

Common-Law Liability to Third Parties

In most engagements, the auditor does not know specifically who will be using the audited financial statements, but is aware that third parties will be using them. The courts generally have held auditors liable to injured third parties when the auditor has been found guilty of gross negligence or fraud. Courts differ, however, as to what third parties the auditor should be held liable to for ordinary negligence. Common law has developed through court decisions, custom, and usage without written legislation.

To win a claim against the auditor, third parties suing under common law must generally prove that:

- They suffered a loss.
- The loss was due to reliance on misleading financial statements.

• The auditor knew, or should have known, that the financial statements were misleading.

Differing Requirements for Auditor Liability to Third Parties Under Common Law

The auditor's liability depends on the jurisdiction of the case, along with whether the auditor could foresee that different types of users would be relying upon the audit report and audited financial statements.

Foreseeability and Negligence The fundamental issue is whether the plaintiff has to prove negligence or gross negligence in order to obtain damages from an auditor. Courts in different jurisdictions have taken different approaches to determining a plaintiff's standing to bring a suit for negligence. The critical point in determining the type of claim to be made against the auditor is the likelihood that an auditor could reasonably foresee that a user might have relied upon the audited financial statements. Generally, less foreseeable plaintiffs need to establish a gross negligence claim, whereas foreseeable users, in some jurisdictions, have to establish only a negligence claim.

The Ultramares Case: The Third-Party Beneficiary Test The landmark case of *Ultramares Corporation v. Touche*, decided by the New York Court of Appeals in 1931, set the precedent for an auditor's liability to third parties. The court held that auditors are liable to third parties for fraud and gross negligence, but not for negligence. For liability to be established, a **third-party beneficiary** must be specifically identified in the engagement letter as a user for whom the audit is being conducted. If, for example, a bank requires an audit as part of a loan application and is named in the engagement letter, the auditor may be held liable to the bank for negligence. If the bank had not been named in the engagement letter, however, such liability would not exist. This precedent dominated judicial thinking for many years and is still followed in many jurisdictions.

Expansion of Ultramares: The Identified User Test In the 1985 case of *Credit Alliance Corp. v. Arthur Andersen & Co.*,[1] the New York Court of Appeals extended auditor liability for ordinary negligence to identified users. An **identified user** is a specific third party whom the auditor knows will use the audited financial statements for a particular purpose, even though the identified user is not named in the engagement letter.

Foreseen User Test The 1965 Restatement (Second) of Torts[2] expanded auditor liability for negligence to identified users and to any individually unknown third parties who are members of a known or intended class of third parties, called **foreseen users**. The client must have informed the auditor that a third party or class of third parties intends to use the financial statements for a particular transaction. The auditor does not have to know the identity of the third party. For example, the client tells the auditor that it plans to include

---

[1] *Credit Alliance Corp. v. Arthur Andersen & Co.*, 483 N.E. 2d 110 (N.Y. 1985).

[2] The *Restatement (Second) of Torts* is published by the American Law Institute. Courts may refer to this treatise when considering an issue of outdated precedent. It offers a unique perspective on the law because its purpose is to state the law as the majority of courts would decide it today. It does not necessarily reflect the rules of the common law as adopted by the courts. Rather, it represents principles of common law that the American Law Institute believes would be adopted if the courts reexamined their common-law rules.

EXHIBIT 4.2   Foreseeability Concepts for Auditor's Common-Law Liability to Third Parties

FORSEEABLE USER

FORSEEN USER

IDENTIFIED USER

The auditor knows the user's identity and specific transaction involved.

Example: The auditor knows that the First National Bank wants audited financial statements as part of the client's application for a loan.

The user is a member of a limited class of users for a specific transaction. Identity of the specific user may or may not be known to the auditor.

Example: The auditor knows that the client wants audited financial statements to obtain a loan from one of several possible banks.

The user is a member of a group who could foreseeably use the financial statements.

Example: The auditor knows that current and prospective creditors and stockholders are likely to use the audited statements.

---

the audited financial statements in an application to some financial institution for a loan. The auditor would be liable to the bank that ultimately makes the loan, even though its identity was not known at the time of the audit.

Foreseeable User Test   Some courts have extended auditor liability to **foreseeable users** (as opposed to foreseen users) of audited financial statements. In *Citizens State Bank v. Timm, Schmidt & Co.*, the Wisconsin Supreme Court extended auditor liability to creditors who could foreseeably use the audited financial statements.[3] A similar position was taken in *Rosenblum, Inc. v. Adler*, where the New Jersey Supreme Court noted that the nature of the economy had changed since the *Ultramares* case and that auditors are indeed acting as if a number of potential users rely on their audit opinion. This court made it clear that for liability to be established, foreseeable users must have obtained the financial statements from the client for proper business purposes,[4] but this is not true in all jurisdictions.

Exhibit 4.2 provides a summary of foreseeability concepts under common law, along with practical examples. The current liability status depends on the state and court involved and on the precedent the court determines is appropriate.

Auditor Liability Under Statutory Law

For public companies, audited financial statements are required to be included in information provided to current and prospective investors. The Securities Act of 1933, the Securities Exchange Act of 1934, and the Sarbanes-Oxley Act of 2002 are important federal statutes affecting auditor liability for public clients. These laws were enacted to assure that investors in public companies have access to full and adequate disclosure of relevant information.

Securities Act of 1933

The Securities Act of 1933 requires companies to file registration statements with the SEC before they may issue new securities to the public. A registration

---

[3] *Citizens State Bank v. Timm, Schmidt & Co.*, 335 N.W. 2d 361 (Wis. Sup. Ct. 1983).
[4] *Rosenblum, Inc. v. Adler*, 461 A. 2d 138 (N.J. 1983).

statement contains, among other things, information about the company, lists of its officers and major stockholders, and plans for using the proceeds from the new securities issue. The registration statement, called the **prospectus**, includes audited financial statements. For the auditor, an important liability section of the 1933 Act is Section 11, which imposes penalties for misstatements contained in registration statements.

For purposes of Section 11, the accuracy of the registration statement is determined at its effective date, which is the date the company can begin to sell the new securities. Because the effective date may be several months after the end of the normal audit work, the auditors must perform certain audit procedures covering events between the end of the normal audit work and the effective date.

In understanding the liability provisions of the 1933 Act, it is important to know that the intent of the SEC is to assure full and fair disclosure of public financial information. Anyone receiving the prospectus may sue the auditor based on damages due to alleged misleading financial statements or inadequate audits. Under the 1933 Act, an auditor may be held liable to purchasers of securities for negligence, or even gross negligence and fraud. Purchasers need to prove only that they incurred a loss and that the financial statements were materially misleading or not fairly stated. They do not need to prove reliance on the financial statements, that such statements had been read or even seen, or that the auditors were negligent. In terms of defenses, the burden of proof shifts to the auditors, who must prove that (1) they used due professional care, (2) the statements were not materially misstated, or (3) the purchaser did not incur a loss caused by the misleading financial statements.

Securities Exchange Act of 1934

The 1934 Act regulates the trading of securities after their initial issuance. Regulated companies are required to file periodic reports with the SEC and stockholders. The following are the most common periodic reports:

- *Annual reports* to shareholders and *10-Ks*, which are annual reports filed with the SEC, both containing audited financial statements. 10-Ks must be filed within 60 to 90 days of the end of the fiscal year. Smaller companies have up to 90 days to file; larger companies must file within 60 days.
- *Quarterly financial reports* to shareholders and *10-Qs*, which are quarterly reports filed with the SEC. 10-Qs must be filed within 40 to 45 days of the end of each of the first three quarters and must be reviewed by the auditors. Smaller companies have up to 45 days to file; larger companies must file within 40 days.
- *8-Ks*, which are reports filed with the SEC describing the occurrence of important events, such as a change in auditors. Other important events required to be reported include changes in the company's business and operations, changes in financial status (such as an acquisition or disposal of assets), and major changes in corporate governance elements (such as the departure of a senior member of management), among others. These disclosures generally must occur within four business days of the event.

For the auditor, an important liability section of the 1934 Act is Section 10, and specifically Rule 10b-5. This rule prohibits material misrepresentations or omissions and fraudulent conduct and provides a general anti-fraud remedy for purchasers and sellers of securities. Under the 1934 Act, an auditor may be held liable for fraud when a plaintiff alleges that in making decisions on purchasing or selling securities, it was misled by misstatements in financial statements. The Act explicitly makes it unlawful to make any untrue statement of a material fact or to omit to state a material fact that is necessary for understanding the financial statements. In order to bring a successful case for securities fraud, a private party must prove six basic elements: (1) a material misrepresentation or omission, (2) fraudulent conduct in connection with the purchase or sale of a security, (3) a wrongful state of mind, known as scienter, when making the misrepresentation or omission, (4) reliance upon the fraudulent conduct, (5) measurable monetary damages, and (6) a causal connection between the misrepresentation or omission and the economic loss. Each of these elements has been interpreted by the courts over the years; court decisions continue to shape how the elements are applied.

In *Herzfeld v. Laventhol, Krekstein, Horwath & Horwath* (1974), the auditors were found liable under the 1934 Act for failure to fully disclose the facts and circumstances underlying their qualified opinion. The judge on the case stated that the auditor cannot be content merely to see that the financial statements meet minimum requirements of GAAP, but that the auditor has a duty to inform the public if adherence to GAAP does not fairly portray the economic results of the company being audited. More specifically, the trial court judge stated:

> The policy underlying the securities laws of providing investors with all the facts needed to make intelligent investment decisions can only be accomplished if financial statements fully and fairly portray the actual financial condition of the company. In those cases where application of generally accepted accounting principles fulfills the duty of full and fair disclosure, the accountant need go no further. But if application of accounting principles alone will not adequately inform investors, accountants, as well as insiders, the auditor must take pains to lay bare all the facts needed by investors to interpret the financial statements accurately.[5]

Federal courts have struggled with the negligence standard implied by the 1934 Act. The standard of holding auditors responsible for gross negligence had essentially eroded to a standard of negligence. In 1976, the U.S. Supreme Court provided greater guidance in its review of *Ernst & Ernst v. Hochfelder*. The Court held that under the 1934 Act, Congress had intended the plaintiff to prove that an auditor acted with scienter in order to hold the auditor liable. The Court reserved judgment as to whether reckless disregard for the truth (gross negligence) would be sufficient to impose liability.

In situations of alleged fraud, historically, investors have sued both the parties who carried out the fraud and those, such as auditors, who assisted, or aided and abetted, the fraud. It appears recent cases might be limiting civil liability related to Rule 10b-5 against auditors. For example, in June 2011, the Supreme Court ruled in *Janus Capital Group, Inc. v. First Derivative Traders* that an investment adviser could not be held liable for mere participation in the drafting and dissemination of false and misleading prospectuses issued by its client. Rather, the Court found that the client, not the adviser, made the fraudulent statement, and thus the adviser was not liable. It remains to be seen how various courts will implement this Supreme Court decision. It seems that parties, such as auditors, who merely assist in preparing a statement will not face liability as primary violators. Such parties, however, would continue to face exposure to enforcement actions brought by the SEC for violations of the federal securities laws.

Auditor Defenses and Possible Sanctions

Showing compliance with Generally Accepted Accounting Principles (GAAP) is an acceptable defense by the auditor. However, as shown in *Herzfeld v.*

---

[5] *Herzfeld v. Laventhol, Krekstein, Horwath & Horwath* [1973–1974] Transfer Binder CCH FED. Sec. Law Reporter #94,574, at 95,999 (S.D.N.Y. May 29, 1974).

Laventhol, Krekstein, Horwath & Horwath, the auditor must take care to make sure that GAAP are not being manipulated to achieve a specific financial presentation result that is not in accord with the substance of the transaction.

Both the 1933 and 1934 Acts provide for criminal actions against auditors who willfully violate provisions of either Act and related rules or regulations or for those who know that financial statements are false and misleading and who issue inappropriate opinions on such statements. In the PSLRA, Congress expressly authorized the SEC to pursue persons who knowingly provide substantial assistance to primary violators of the securities laws. In 2010, the Dodd-Frank Act amended the pleading standard in the 1934 Act from "knowingly" to "knowingly or recklessly." The lower pleading standard may enable the SEC to more easily bring cases for aiding and abetting securities fraud.

Auditors found to be unqualified, unethical, or in willful violation of any provision of the federal securities laws can be disciplined by the SEC. Possible sanctions available to the SEC include:

- Temporarily or permanently revoking the firm's registration with the PCAOB, meaning that the SEC will not accept its audit reports
- Imposing civil monetary penalties
- Requiring special continuing education of firm personnel
- Suspending individuals from serving as officers or directors of securities issuers or participating in the securities industry

Summary of Auditor Liability to Third Parties Under Common and Statutory Law

Auditors are clearly liable to injured third parties for fraud under both common law and statutory law. Because third parties are likely to sue under both common law and statutory law in a specific lawsuit, auditors are essentially liable for gross negligence as well. Auditors are liable for negligence under the Securities Act of 1933 and possibly under common law, depending on the precedent used by the court.

Third parties must prove the auditor's guilt under common law and the Securities Exchange Act of 1934. Under the Securities Act of 1933, however, auditors must prove their innocence. Auditor defenses include:

- Due diligence; that is, the auditor did what a prudent auditor would have done.
- The audit was not the cause of the plaintiff's loss.
- The financial statements were not materially misstated.

In order to make the first of these two defenses actually work in practice, auditors need to make professional and ethical decisions as part of conducting a quality audit. We next introduce frameworks designed to help you make quality professional and ethical decisions.

A Framework for Professional Decision Making

LO 4 Articulate a general framework for making quality professional decisions and apply this framework in selected audit settings.

Auditors add value to the financial markets by making quality decisions associated with their evaluation of client financial statements. Quality decisions are unbiased, meet the expectations of reasonable users, are in compliance with professional standards, and are based on sufficient factual information to justify the decision that is rendered. For example, auditors have to make decisions about the types of evidence to gather, how to evaluate that evidence, when to gather additional evidence, and what conclusions are appropriate given the evidence they have obtained. Ultimately, auditors have to decide whether the client's financial statements contain any material departures from generally accepted accounting principles that would affect the judgment of users of the financial statements.

This type of decision-making situation is common among professionals. For example, consider a doctor trying to diagnose the illness of a patient. The doctor must decide what tests to order, how to interpret the test results, and when to order additional tests (how many and what type), and must ultimately diagnose any potential illness in the patient. In order to make complex, difficult, and important decisions such as these, professionals can benefit from a structured approach to their decision making, as depicted in *Exhibit 4.3.*

In **Step 1,** the auditor structures the problem, which includes considering the relevant parties to involve in the decision process, identifying various feasible alternatives, considering how to evaluate the alternatives, and identifying uncertainties or risks. To illustrate these tasks, consider a common decision that auditors face—determining whether a client's inventory values are fairly stated in accordance with generally accepted accounting principles. In terms of identifying relevant parties, auditors work within an organizational hierarchy with clearly defined roles about appropriate types of auditors that should participate in inventory testing (e.g., less experienced auditors may conduct inventory test counts, but industry experts may consider the valuation of complex inventory items). In addition, auditors consider which individuals at the client are most qualified to assess inventory values. Auditors also identify feasible alternatives about the

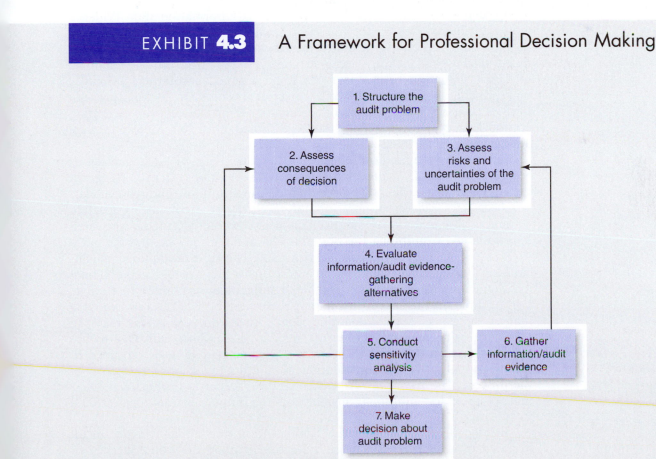

EXHIBIT **4.3**   A Framework for Professional Decision Making

Source: Adapted from *Judgment and Choice* by Robin Hogarth.

inventory balance. For example, is it fairly stated, overstated, understated? Consideration will also be given to the evidence necessary to determine accurate inventory valuation (such as observing the inventory, consulting outside prices of the inventory, and evaluating potential obsolescence). Auditors also have to evaluate the risk that the evidence they collect may not necessarily be diagnostic of the true, underlying value of the inventory. In other words, there is a risk that despite the work that they perform, their conclusions may be incorrect.

In **Step 2,** the auditor assesses the consequences of the potential alternatives. Considerations at this stage include determining the dimensions on which to evaluate the alternatives and how to weight those dimensions. Continuing the preceding example, the auditor will have to consider the consequences of various inventory valuation alternatives and whether a particular valuation alternative is more or less appropriate than the other available alternatives. If the auditor decides that the inventory is properly valued, and that is in fact the case, then there are no negative consequences to the decision. However, if the auditor reaches an incorrect conclusion, then stakeholders may be misled, exposing auditors to litigation and reputation damage.

In **Step 3,** the auditor assesses the risks and uncertainties in the situation. Those risks and uncertainties are related to (a) the risks the audit client faces, (b) the quality of evidence the auditor gathers, and (c) the sufficiency of audit evidence gathered. In other words, there are risks related to a particular client, and there are risks in gathering sufficient audit evidence. All of these risks need to be assessed in determining the appropriate audit evidence to gather.

In **Step 4,** the auditor evaluates the various information/audit evidence gathering alternatives against an appropriate decision rule. For auditors, decision rules are often articulated in terms of generally accepted accounting principles or generally accepted auditing standards. In our example, inventory valuation rules under generally accepted accounting principles may provide necessary guidance to assist in the decision–making process. Further, generally accepted auditing standards articulate rules regarding appropriate evidence-gathering strategies that must be followed when auditing inventory values.

In **Step 5,** the auditor considers the sensitivity of the conclusions reached in Steps 2, 3, and 4 to incorrect assumptions. It may be, given the results of the earlier steps, the auditor can determine enough evidence has been gathered to support (or not support), at a convincing level of certainty, and that the audit problem being evaluated can be answered appropriately. Continuing the preceding example, it may be that the auditor's initial evidence gathering and risk analysis enable a definitive conclusion. In that case, the auditor can move on to **Step 7,** and make a final decision However, there may still be significant uncertainties to resolve. For example, in the case of inventory, there may be variation in available market values used to value the client's inventory. As such, the true inventory value may fall within a range, so the auditor will have to use **professional judgment** to determine a value that is most reflective of economic reality. In such a situation, the auditor will move to Step 6 of the process. The *Auditing in Practice* feature "What Is Professional Judgment?" provides additional insights on the importance of professional judgment.

In **Step 6,** the auditor gathers information and audit evidence in an iterative process that affects considerations about the consequences of potential alternatives and the uncertainties associated with those judgments. Importantly, the auditor considers the costs and benefits of

What Is Professional Judgment?

Professional judgment involves applying relevant professional knowledge and experience to unique and potentially uncertain facts and circumstances in order to reach a conclusion or make a decision. Thus, professional judgment begins with determining when the auditor has sufficient appropriate evidence to make a decision. Then, when an auditor makes quality professional judgments, he or she competently applies auditing and/or accounting principles and makes decisions that are appropriate given the evidence that should be known to the auditor at the time of the judgment.

Importantly, professional judgment cannot be used to justify conclusions or decisions that would otherwise not be supported by the existing evidence.

Documenting a professional judgment is critical. Professional standards in the U.S. and internationally require that documentation is sufficient to enable an experienced auditor, having no previous connection with the audit, to understand the significant judgments made in reaching conclusions on significant matters arising during the audit. Professional judgment is the key to conducting a quality audit.

information acquisition, knowing that gathering additional evidence requires time, effort, and money. Given that an audit firm is a for-profit enterprise, cost–benefit considerations in evidence gathering are particularly important. A good auditor knows "when to say when"—to stop collecting evidence at the right time. In contrast, some auditors stop evidence collection too soon, thereby yielding inadequate evidence on which to make a decision. Still others continue evidence collection even though the current evidence is sufficient and appropriate, thereby contributing to inefficiency and reduced profitability in the audit.

The auditor iterates through Steps 1 through 6 repeatedly until satisfied that a decision can prudently be made.

Finally, in **Step 7**, the auditor makes the difficult determination of whether the problem has been sufficiently analyzed and whether the risk of making an incorrect decision has been minimized to an acceptable level. Ultimately, the auditor makes and documents the decision reached.

Importance of Professional Skepticism in Making Professional Judgments

The auditor must exercise professional skepticism when completing the steps in *Exhibit 4.3*. Recall from *Chapter 2* that professional skepticism is an attitude that includes a questioning mind and a critical assessment of audit evidence. Professional skepticism is important because without it auditors are susceptible to accepting weak or inaccurate audit evidence. By exercising professional skepticism, auditors are less likely to overlook unusual circumstances, to overgeneralize from limited audit evidence, or to use inappropriate assumptions in determining the nature, timing, and extent of audit procedures. An auditor who is professionally skeptical will:

- Critically question contradictory audit evidence
- Carefully evaluate the reliability of audit evidence, especially in situations in which fraud risk is high and/or only a single piece of evidence exists to support a material financial accounting transaction or amount

- Reasonably question the authenticity of documentation, while accepting that documents are to be considered genuine unless there is reason to believe the contrary
- Reasonably question the honesty and integrity of management, individuals charged with governance, and third party providers of audit evidence

Given that auditors operate in an environment of significant litigation risk and one in which there is ample evidence of past frauds involving deception against auditors, it may seem that auditors will intuitively act with professional skepticism. However, the difficulty that auditors face is one inherent in the human condition—we trust others and accept information and assertions as truth. Further, if an auditor did not trust management, for example, that auditor would presumably cease to perform audit services for the client. These difficulties sometimes cause auditors to be less professionally skeptical than is appropriate. A report on professional skepticism available at the web site of the Center for Audit Quality, "Enhancing Auditor Professional Skepticism," proposes a professional skepticism continuum that recognizes that the appropriate level of professional skepticism will depend on the risk characteristics of the particular account and assertion being audited. The continuum ranges from complete trust in management, to a neutral view wherein the auditor neither assumes management dishonesty nor assumes unquestioned honesty, to presumptive doubt, to complete doubt in management. The complete trust end of the continuum yields less of a need for audit evidence and documentation, whereas the complete doubt end of the continuum yields more audit evidence and documentation.

So how can audit firms and individual auditors be sure that they maintain and exercise appropriate professional skepticism? At the audit firm level, firm leaders must ensure that auditors receive training on how to be skeptical, and they must create firm policies and procedures to encourage skepticism. At the individual auditor level, the following tips can encourage a skeptical mindset:

- Be sure to collect sufficient evidence so that judgments are not made in haste or without adequate support.
- When evidence is contradictory, be particularly diligent in evaluating the reliability of the individuals or processes that provided that evidence.
- Generate independent ideas about reasons for unexpected trends or financial ratios rather than simply relying on management's explanations.
- Question trends or outcomes that appear "too good to be true."
- Wait to make professional judgments until all the relevant facts are known.
- Have confidence in your own knowledge or in your own ability to understand complex situations; do not assume that the client's explanation for unexpected trends or financial ratios simply reflects your lack of understanding.

We encourage you to keep these ideas in mind as you proceed throughout this book. Because of the importance of professional skepticism to making quality auditing judgments, we return to this concept throughout the book and provide examples and problems to help you learn and apply this concept. The *Auditing in Practice* feature "What Was He Thinking? An Example of Poor Professional Judgment and Low Audit Quality" provides an extreme example of low (likely nonexistent) professional skepticism and its implications.

What Was He Thinking? An Example of Poor Professional Judgment and Low Audit Quality

On June 15, 2009, the PCAOB issued disciplinary proceedings against Lawrence Scharfman, CPA. Scharfman, a 76-year-old auditor licensed in the State of New York, issued audit opinions for three companies: Prospero Minerals, Cal-Bay International, and LitFunding Corporation. Each of these companies was traded on the OTC Bulletin Board and the Pink Sheets. The PCAOB questioned Scharfman's professional judgments in the conduct of the audits of each of these three companies. These low-quality decisions are summarized below:

The Prospero Minerals Audit

- Scharfman accepted the audit engagement on August 14, 2006, and issued an unqualified audit opinion on August 16, 2006.
- Scharfman provided no documentation that he planned the audit or that he performed any audit procedures on significant balance sheet items.
- Scharfman provided no documentation that he addressed disclosure issues, valuation issues, or material related-party transactions.
- While conducting the audit, Scharfman committed to acquire 200,000 shares of Prospero stock in exchange for services that he agreed to perform for the shareholder and the Company.

The Cal-Bay Audit

- Scharfman accepted the audit engagement on March 29, 2006, and issued an unqualified opinion on April 12, 2006.
- Scharfman provided no documentation that he performed adequate audit procedures to test a material real-estate purchase transaction.
- Scharfman provided no documentation that he gathered audit evidence necessary to value a material acquired asset.
- Scharfman failed to alert the SEC or the PCAOB that he had requested Cal-Bay to subsequently restate its financial statements and that Cal-Bay had refused.
- Scharfman failed to alert the SEC or the PCAOB that he had become aware of an illegal act at Cal-Bay.

The LitFunding Audit

- Scharfman accepted the audit engagement on April 28, 2006, and issued an unqualified opinion on May 3, 2006.
- Scharfman provided no documentation that he gathered audit evidence regarding a reserve for legal costs and a review of a significant accounting estimate.
- Much of the documentation that Scharfman provided to the PCAOB was added to the engagement file after completion of the audit, and it was unclear who prepared the documents. The inference is that Scharfman added the documents to the file upon learning that he was being reviewed by PCAOB inspectors.

After conducting its review of Scharfman's work on these audits, the PCAOB revoked his CPA firm's registration and barred him from performing audits for public entities permanently.

What was Scharfman thinking? It appears that he was simply doing "sham" audits for cash payments. These small companies required unqualified audit opinions, and Scharfman was willing to accept the engagements, do little or no audit work, and issue an opinion within just a few days. He clearly did not exhibit professional skepticism. His actions are an extreme example of low-quality auditing and poor professional decision making. Auditors often face pressure over budgets and schedules, and all people are subject to the tendency to rationalize away unpleasant or unwanted issues. Scharfman's actions, however, seem to go beyond normal rationalizations and reflect the worst possible intentions associated with such forces.

For further details on this case, see PCAOB Release No. 105-2009-005.

A Framework for Ethical Decision Making

LO 5 Articulate a framework for making quality ethical decisions and apply this framework in selected settings.

The auditing profession has worked hard to gain the public trust, and it benefits monetarily from that trust as the sole legally acceptable provider of audit services for companies and other organizations. For that trust and economic advantage to be maintained, it is essential that professional integrity be based on personal moral standards and reinforced by codes of conduct. Whenever a scandal surfaces, the profession is diminished and auditors' reputations may be tarnished beyond repair. It is not difficult to find oneself in ethically compromising situations without realizing it. During the course of an audit, for example, an auditor may become aware of a client's plans that will likely double the market value of its stock. Suppose the auditor has a roommate from college who would like to know about the investment opportunity. The roommate does not have a large investment portfolio, so sharing this knowledge would not affect the market. Should the auditor share the information with the roommate? Consider Susan Birkert in the *Auditing in Practice* feature "A Young Auditor Makes an Ethical Mistake in Professional Judgment." Imagine that you were Birkert's friend and colleague—would you have made the difficult ethical decision to alert KPMG personnel to her deception?

Resolving Ethical Dilemmas

Auditors using the framework in *Exhibit 4.3* will at times encounter decisions that have ethical implications. For example, consider a situation in which your senior on the engagement is already worried about the time that it has taken you to complete your work. Would you take the time needed to diligently follow up on evidence suggesting that something might be wrong with the financial statements? Would you consider concluding that a client's decision to extend the life of its assets is appropriate, even if you have serious reservations about this decision? Auditing professionals are often faced with these types of difficult ethical decisions. In such situations, a defined methodology is helpful in resolving the situation in a thoughtful, quality manner. An **ethical dilemma** occurs when there are conflicting moral duties or an individual is ethically required to take an action that may conflict with his or her immediate self-interest. Complex ethical dilemmas do not lend themselves to simple "right" or "wrong" decisions. Ethical theories are helpful in assisting individuals in dealing with ethical dilemmas.

A Young Auditor Makes an Ethical Mistake in Professional Judgment

AUDITING IN **PRACTICE**

Susan Birkert was a lead senior on the KPMG audits of Comtech during fiscal years 2004–2006. During this time, an acquaintance of Birkert agreed to purchase $5,000 of Comtech stock for her, in violation of professional rules regarding auditor independence. In May 2006, Birkert falsely asserted to KPMG that she was in compliance with audit firm and professional rules regarding independence. Following an anonymous tip and an ensuing KPMG internal investigation, Birkert admitted to the deception, and KPMG fired her. The anonymous tipster in that case was rumored to be a friend and fellow auditor on the Comtech engagement. Subsequently, the PCAOB barred her from serving before it for a period of at least one year.

For further details on this case, see the facts disclosed in PCAOB Release No. 105–2007–003, November 14, 2007.

Two such theories—the utilitarian theory and the rights theory—have helped develop codes of conduct that can be used by professionals in dealing with ethically challenging situations.

Utilitarian Theory

Utilitarian theory holds that what is ethical is the action that achieves the greatest good for the greatest number of people. Actions that result in outcomes that fall short of the greatest good for the greatest number and those that represent inefficient means to accomplish such ends are less desirable. Utilitarianism requires:

- An identification of the potential problem and possible courses of action
- An identification of the potential direct or indirect impact of actions on each affected party (often referred to as **stakeholders**) who may have a vested interest in the outcome of actions taken
- An assessment of the desirability (goodness) of each action
- An overall assessment of the greatest good for the greatest number

Utilitarianism requires that individuals not advocate or choose alternatives that favor narrow interests or that serve the greatest good in an inefficient manner. There can be honest disagreements about the likely impact of actions or the relative efficiency of different actions in attaining desired ends. There are also potential problems in measuring what constitutes "the greatest good" in a particular circumstance. One problem with the utilitarian theory is the implicit assumption that the "ends achieved" justify the means to attain those ends. Unfortunately, such an approach can lead to disastrous courses of actions when those making the decisions fail to adequately measure or assess the potential costs and benefits. Thus, ethicists generally argue that utilitarian arguments should be mitigated by some "value-based" approach. Rights theory presents such a framework.

Rights Theory

Rights theory focuses on evaluating actions based on the fundamental rights of the parties involved. However, not all rights are equal. In the hierarchy of rights, higher order rights take precedence over lower order rights. The highest order rights include the right to life, to autonomy, and to human dignity. Second-order rights include rights granted by the government, such as civil rights, legal rights, rights to own property, and license privileges. Third-order rights are social rights, such as the right to higher education, to good health care, and to earning a living. The fourth-order rights are related to one's nonessential interests or one's personal tastes.

Rights theory requires that the "rights" of affected parties be examined as a constraint on ethical decision making. The rights approach is most effective in identifying outcomes that ought to be automatically eliminated, such as the "Robin Hood approach" of robbing from the rich to give to the poor; in these situations, the utilitarian answer is at odds with most societal values.

Applying the Ethical Decision Making Framework

Exhibit 4.4 contains a framework derived from the utilitarianism and rights theories that can help individuals resolve ethical dilemmas in a quality manner.

The following case, based on an actual situation, is presented as an application of this framework to auditing situations.

| EXHIBIT **4.4** | A Framework for Ethical Decision Making |

Step 1
Identify the ethical issue(s).

Step 2
Determine the affected parties and identify their rights.

Step 3
Determine the most important rights.

Step 4
Develop alternative courses of action.

Step 5
Determine the likely consequences of each proposed course of action.

Step 6
Assess the possible consequences, including an estimation of the greatest good for the greatest number. Determine whether the rights framework would cause any course of action to be eliminated.

Step 7
Decide on the appropriate course of action.

Step 1. *Identify the ethical issue(s).* The external auditor for Payroll Processors, Inc. believes that the company might go bankrupt. Several clients of the audit firm use the payroll processing services of Payroll Processors. Should the other clients be provided with this **confidential information** prior to the information being publicly available through the audit report—which might be delayed as auditors further assess the potential for bankruptcy?

Step 2. *Determine the affected parties and identify their rights.* The relevant parties to the issue include the following:

- Payroll Processors and its management
- Payroll Processors' current and prospective customers, creditors, and investors
- The audit firm and its other clients
- The external auditing profession

Listing those potentially affected by the decision is easier than identifying their rights. The following, however, are some of the rights involved:

- Company management has the right to assume that confidential information obtained by its auditors will remain confidential unless disclosure is permitted by the company or is required by accounting, auditing, or legal standards.
- Payroll Processors' current and prospective customers, creditors, and investors have a right to receive reliable information and not be denied important information that could adversely affect their operations.
- The audit firm has the right to expect its employees to follow the professional standards. However, some may argue that the firms' existing clients have a right to information that might protect them from financial crises.
- The external auditing profession has the right to expect all its members to uphold relevant codes of professional conduct (described in the following section of the chapter) and to take actions that enhance the general reputation and perception of the integrity of the profession.

Step 3. *Determine the most important rights.* Many auditors would assess that the rights listed in order of importance are (1) the client to not have confidential information improperly disclosed, (2) other affected parties to receive important information that will affect their operations, and (3) the profession to retain its reputation for conducting quality audits.

Step 4. *Develop alternative courses of action.* The possible courses of action are (1) share the confidential information with the other clients of the audit firm prior to issuing an audit opinion on the client's financial statements, or (2) do not share that information prior to issuing an audit opinion on the client's financial statements. The audit firm was performing audit work, and the professional standards require that the reservations about Payroll Processors remaining a going concern in their audit report, not in private information given to selected entities.

Step 5. *Determine the likely consequences of each proposed course of action.* These could include:

1. *Prior to Issuing the Audit Opinion.* Sharing this information with the other clients prior to issuing an audit report with a going-concern reservation may cause these other clients to take their business away from Payroll Processors, thus increasing the likelihood of bankruptcy for Payroll Processors. It might also increase the possibility of the audit firm being found in violation of the rules of conduct and being sued by Payroll Processors or others for inappropriately providing confidential information to selected parties outside of the public role that external auditors fulfill. The auditor may also have his or her license suspended or revoked. Other Payroll Processors' clients who do not receive the information because they are not the audit firm's clients will be put at a competitive disadvantage, and they may sue the auditor because of discriminatory disclosure.

2. *Do Not Share the Information Until the Audit Report Has Been Issued.* If the information is not shared with the other clients, those clients might take their audit business elsewhere if they find out the auditors knew of this problem and did not share it with them. Other clients of Payroll Processors may suffer losses because of the financial problems of Payroll Processors.

Step 6. *Assess the possible consequences, including an estimation of the greatest good for the greatest number. Determine whether the rights framework would cause any course of action to be eliminated.* Sharing the information may help other clients move their payroll processing business to other service providers in a more orderly manner and more quickly than would happen if they had to wait until the audit opinion was issued. However, other Payroll Processors' customers may be placed at a disadvantage if Payroll Processors does go bankrupt and their payroll processing is disrupted. Payroll Processors' employees will lose their jobs more quickly, and its investors are likely to lose more money more quickly. Its right to have confidential information remain confidential will be violated. There may be less confidence in the profession because of discriminatory or unauthorized disclosure of information. Management of other companies may be reluctant to share other nonfinancial information with audit firms. After assessing the relative benefits of disclosing versus not disclosing the information prior to issuing the audit opinion, it appears that the greatest good is served by not sharing the information selectively with current audit clients, but to complete the audit and issue the audit opinion in a timely manner.

Step 7. *Decide on the appropriate course of action.* The auditor should not share the information prior to issuing the audit opinion. The auditor may encourage Payroll Processors to share its state of affairs with its clients but cannot dictate that it do so. The need for equity and confidentiality of information dictates that the auditor's primary form of communication is through formal audit reports associated with the financial statements.

Consolidata Services v. Alexander Grant The actual court case used to develop the example above was *Consolidata Services v. Alexander Grant*. In that case, the court found the audit firm guilty of providing confidential information to its other clients. Alexander Grant (now Grant Thornton) did tax work for Consolidata Services, a company that provided computerized payroll services to other companies. On learning that Consolidata was in financial trouble, Grant warned some of its other clients, who were also Consolidata customers. Consolidata sued Grant, charging that the audit firm's disclosures effectively put it out of business. The jury ruled in favor of Consolidata. Grant was also found guilty of providing the information only to selected parties; that is, it provided the information only to its clients—not all customers of Consolidata.

Guidance on Professional Responsibilities and the Impact on Auditors' Decisions

LO 6 Identify guidance on auditors' professional responsibilities and make audit decisions informed by the appropriate professional guidance.

Auditors' professional and ethical decisions should be informed by relevant codes of professional conduct and other pronouncements on professional responsibilities. Adhering to this guidance minimizes auditors' litigation and increases audit quality.

IESBA's Code of Ethics

The International Ethics Standards Board for Accountants (IESBA) (under the International Federation of Accountants) outlines fundamental principles that should guide auditors' ethical decision making. The IESBA *Code of Ethics for Professional Accountants* applies to all professional accountants, whether in public practice, in business, education, or the public sector. The IESBA *Code* serves as the foundation for codes of ethics developed and enforced by members of the International Federation of Accountants (IFAC). No member body of IFAC or audit firm issuing reports in accordance with standards of the International Auditing and Assurance Standards Board is allowed to apply less stringent standards than those stated in the IESBA *Code*. The *Code of Ethics for Professional Accountants* requires auditors to adhere to five fundamental principles:[6]

- *Integrity*—A professional accountant should be straightforward and honest in performing professional services.
- *Objectivity*—A professional accountant should not allow bias, conflict of interest, or undue influence of others to override professional or business judgments.
- *Professional Competence and Due Care*—A professional accountant has a continuing duty to maintain professional knowledge and skill at the level required to assure that a client or employer receives competent professional service based on current developments. A professional accountant should act diligently and in accordance with applicable technical and professional standards when providing professional services.

---

[6] *Source:* © 2008 by The International Federation of Accountants (IFAC). All rights reserved. Used with permission of IFAC. This book is an extract from the *Handbook of International Standards on Auditing, Assurance, and Ethics Pronouncements of the International Auditing and Assurance Standards Board (IAASB)*, published by the International Federation of Accountants (IFAC) in April 2009 and is used with permission of IFAC.

- *Confidentiality*—A professional accountant should respect the confidentiality of information acquired as a result of professional and business relationships and should not disclose any such information to third parties without proper and specific authority unless there is a legal or professional right or duty to disclose. Confidential information acquired as a result of professional and business relationships should not be used for the personal advantage of the professional accountant or of third parties.
- *Professional Behavior*—A professional accountant should comply with relevant laws and regulations and should avoid any action that discredits the profession.

In addition to these five principles, the *Code* contains specific standards addressing many of the topics contained in the AICPA's *Code of Professional Conduct*.

AICPA's *Code of Professional Conduct*

Although the frameworks for professional and ethical decision making clearly help the auditor in resolving difficult professional situations, the auditing profession via the AICPA has developed a code of professional conduct to aid in making these judgments. The AICPA's *Code of Professional Conduct* consists of a set of **principles of professional conduct** (see *Exhibit 4.5*) that provide high-level guidance to auditors about their professional and ethical responsibilities and provide the basis for the specific **rules of conduct** (see *Exhibit 4.6*). The *Code* applies to professional services performed by AICPA members. The *Emerging Issues* feature "AICPA Revises *Code of Professional Conduct*" outlines changes to the AICPA's *Code* that are effective in 2014 and 2015.

Independence—Rule 101

The external auditor is required to be independent when providing professional services. Various regulators and standard setting bodies, such as the AICPA,

---

EXHIBIT 4.5   AICPA Principles of Professional Conduct

Responsibilities In carrying out their responsibilities as professionals, members should exercise sensitive professional and moral judgments in all their activities.

Public interest Members should accept the obligation to act in a way that will serve the public interest, honor the public trust, and demonstrate commitment to professionalism.

Integrity To maintain and broaden public confidence, members should perform all professional responsibilities with the highest sense of integrity.

Objectivity and independence A member should maintain objectivity and be free of conflicts in discharging professional responsibilities. A member in public practice should be independent both in fact and in appearance when providing auditing and other attestation services. A member not in public practice does not need to maintain independence.

Due care A member should observe the profession's technical and ethical standards, strive continually to improve competence and the quality of services, and discharge professional responsibility to the best of the member's ability.

Scope and nature of services A member in public practice should observe the principles of the *Code* in determining the scope and nature of services to be provided.

Source: AICPA audit and accounting guides by American Institute of Certified Public Accountants. Copyright 2012. Reproduced with permission of American Institute of Certified Public Accountants in the format Textbook via Copyright Clearance Center.

EXHIBIT 4.6 **AICPA Rules of Conduct**

Rule 101
Independence

A member in public practice shall be independent in the performance of professional services as required by standards promulgated by standard setting bodies and regulators.

Rule 102
Integrity and Objectivity

In the performance of any professional service, a member shall maintain objectivity and integrity, shall be free of conflicts of interest, and shall not knowingly misrepresent facts or subordinate his or her judgment to others.

Rule 201
General Standards

A member shall comply with the following standards and with any interpretations thereof by bodies designated by Council.

A. *Professional Competence.* Undertake only those professional services that the member or the member's firm can reasonably expect to be completed with professional competence.

B. *Due Professional Care.* Exercise due professional care in the performance of professional services.

C. *Planning and Supervision.* Adequately plan and supervise the performance of professional services.

D. *Sufficient Relevant Data.* Obtain sufficient relevant data to afford a reasonable basis for conclusions or recommendations in relation to any professional services performed.

Rule 202
Compliance with
Standards

A member who performs auditing, review, compilation, consulting, tax, or other professional services shall comply with standards promulgated by bodies designated by Council.

Rule 203
Accounting Principles

A member shall not (1) express an opinion that the financial statements or other financial data of any entity are presented in conformity with generally accepted accounting principles or (2) state that he or she is not aware of any material modifications that should be made to such statements or data in order for them to be in conformity with generally accepted accounting principles, if such statements or data contain any departure from an accounting principle promulgated by bodies designated by council to establish such principles that has a material effect on the statements or data taken as a whole. If, however, the statements or data contain such a departure and the member can demonstrate that due to unusual circumstances the financial statements or data would otherwise have been misleading, the member can comply with the rule by describing the departure, its approximate effects, if practicable, and the reasons why compliance with the principle would result in a misleading statement.

Rule 301
Confidential Client
Information

A member in public practice shall not disclose any confidential client information without the specific consent of the client.

Rule 302
Contingent Fees

A member in public practice shall not:

(1) perform for a contingent fee any professional services for, or receive such a fee from a client for whom the member or the member's firm also performs:

(a) an audit or review of a financial statement, or

(b) a compilation of a financial statement when the member expects, or reasonably might expect, that a third party will use the financial statement and the member's compilation report does not describe a lack of independence, or

(c) an examination of prospective financial information, or

(2) prepare an original or amended tax return or claim for a tax refund for a contingent fee for any client. This prohibition applies during the period in which the member or the member's firm is engaged to perform any of the services listed above and the period covered by any historical financial statements involved in any such listed services.

(continued)

| EXHIBIT 4.6 | AICPA Rules of Conduct (*continued*) |

Rule 501
Acts Discreditable

A member shall not commit an act discreditable to the profession.

Rule 502
Advertising and Other
Forms of Solicitation

A member in public practice shall not seek to obtain clients by advertising or other forms of solicitation in a manner that is false, misleading, or deceptive. Solicitation by the use of coercion, overreaching, or harassing conduct is prohibited.

Rule 503
Commissions and
Referral Fees

A. *Prohibited Commissions.* A member in public practice shall not for a commission recommend or refer to a client any product or service, or for a commission recommend or refer any product or service to be supplied by a client, or receive a commission, when the member or the member's firm also performs (attestation services referred to in Rule 302) for the client.

This prohibition applies to the period covered by the attestation service and the related historical financial statements.

B. *Disclosure of Permitted Commissions.* A member in public practice who is not prohibited by this rule from performing services for or receiving a commission and who is paid or expects to be paid a commission shall disclose that fact to any person or entity to whom the member recommends or refers a product or service to which the commission relates.

C. *Referral Fees.* Any member who accepts a referral fee for recommending or referring any service of a CPA to any person or entity or who pays a referral fee to obtain a client shall disclose such acceptance or payment to the client.

Rule 505
Form of Organization
and Name

A member may practice public accounting only in a form of organization permitted by state law or regulation whose characteristics conform to resolutions of Council.

A member shall not practice public accounting under a firm name that is misleading. Names of one or more past owners may be included in the firm name or a successor organization.

A firm may not designate itself as "Members of the American Institute of Certified Public Accountants" unless all of its CPA owners are members of the Institute.

Source: *AICPA audit and accounting guides by American Institute of Certified Public Accountants. Copyright 2012. Reproduced with permission of American Institute of Certified Public Accountants in the format Textbook via Copyright Clearance Center.*

IFAC, SEC, and PCAOB, provide specific independence requirements with which auditors must comply. Independence is considered the cornerstone of the auditing profession. There are several interpretations of Rule 101; many specific rulings provide detailed guidance on such matters as financial interests in the client, family relationships, loans with a client, and performance of nonaudit services. An important point concerning Rule 101 is that it applies only to a **covered member**. A covered member is defined as:

- An individual on the audit engagement team
- An individual in a position to influence the audit engagement
- A partner in the office in which the lead attest audit partner primarily practices in connection with the auditor engagement

A covered member's immediate family is also subject to Rule 101.

Financial Interests   If you are a new staff auditor, manager, or partner working on an audit, you and your immediate family should not have any direct or material indirect financial interest in that client. A **direct financial interest** is a financial interest owned directly by, or under the

AICPA Revises *Code of Professional Conduct*

 **EMERGING** ISSUE

The AICPA's Professional Ethics Executive Committee (PEEC) adopted a revised *Code* in January 2014, with an effective date of December 15, 2014. Additionally, the *Code* includes two conceptual frameworks with a delayed effective date of December 15, 2015. PEEC reformatted the *Code* to become more user-friendly, which resulted in a number of improvements and some substantive revisions. The reformatted *Code* begins by separating the guidance by line of business (e.g., separate parts for members in public practice, business, other) and then by topic, and, where necessary, topics are further broken down into subtopics and sections.

The reformatted *Code* is organized into three parts. Part 1 applies to AICPA members in public practice; Part 2 to members in business; and Part 3 to all other members, including those who are retired or between jobs. Exhibit 1 contains an example of this new organization for Part 2. Auditors would be most concerned with Part 1 of the *Code*.

The most significant change is the incorporation of two broad conceptual frameworks—one for members in business and another for members in public practice. These conceptual frameworks incorporate a "threats and safeguards" approach and are designed to help members analyze relationships and circumstances that the *Code* does not specifically address. (A similar approach is provided in the IESBA's *Code*.) When particular situations are not addressed in the *Code*, auditors can apply the conceptual framework approach to determine whether the situation may result in a violation of the applicable rule. A flowchart of the steps in the conceptual framework is provided in Exhibit 2.

Threats are relationships or circumstances that could compromise an AICPA member's compliance with the rules. As previously explained in *Chapter 1*, threats include the following: self-review (e.g., preparing client source documents), advocacy (e.g., representing the client in tax court), adverse interest (e.g., when the client has sued the audit firm), familiarity (e.g., a member of the audit team has a close personal friend employed in a key client position), undue influence (e.g., top management threatens to replace the audit firm because of a disagreement), financial self-interest (e.g., auditor owns stock in the client), and management participation (e.g., auditor takes the role of management, such as establishing internal controls). **Safeguards** are actions or other measures that may eliminate a threat or reduce a threat to an acceptable level. Safeguards exist at the professional and legislative level through rules and regulations (e.g., education and training requirements or governance rules), at the audit client level (e.g., tone at the top and governance practices), and at the audit firm level (e.g., audit firm leadership and audit firm policies and procedures). Be sure to visit the AICPA's web site to practice using the new electronic format of the revised *Code*.

EXHIBIT 1 Snapshot of Navigating to Gifts and Entertainment Guidance

As shown below, Part 2 of the revised AICPA *Code of Professional Conduct*, which contains all the guidance for members in business, has six topics. The topic addressing "Integrity and Objectivity" has four subtopics, one of which addresses gifts and entertainment. This subtopic has one section that contains the interpretation on offering or accepting gifts or entertainment to or from a members's customer or vendor.

2.000 Introduction
2.100 Integrity and Objectivity
    2.110 Conflicts of Interest
    2.120 Gifts and Entertainment
        2.120.010 Offering or Accepting Gifts or Entertainment
    2.130 Preparing and Reporting Information
    2.140 Educational Services
2.300 General Standards
2.310 Compliance With Standards
2.320 Accounting Principles
2.400 Acts Discreditable

(Continued)

EXHIBIT 2   Steps of the Conceptual Framework

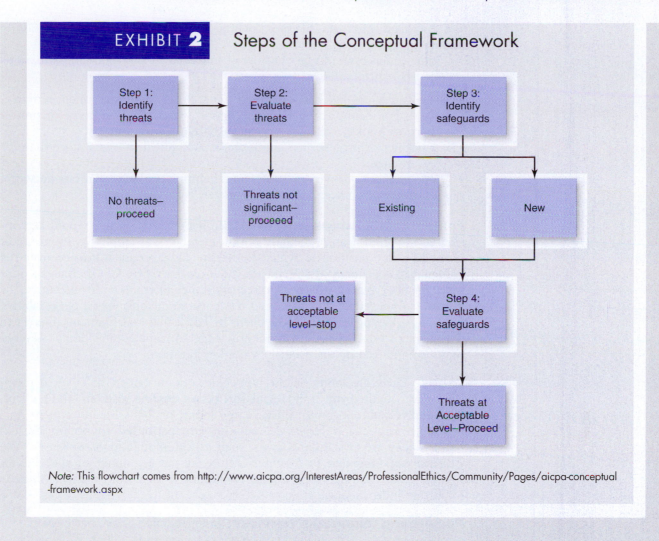

Note: This flowchart comes from http://www.aicpa.org/InterestAreas/ProfessionalEthics/Community/Pages/aicpa-conceptual
-framework.aspx

control of, an individual or entity or beneficially owned through an investment vehicle, estate, or trust when the beneficiary controls the intermediary
or has the authority to supervise or participate in the intermediary's investment decisions. For example, a covered member may not own bonds of a
client.

An **indirect financial interest** occurs when the beneficiary neither
controls the intermediary nor has the authority to supervise or participate
in the intermediary's investment decisions. The concept is that a covered
member may have some limited financial interests in clients as long as
the interests are not direct and not material (to either the member or the
client). For example, suppose an auditor has an investment in a mutual
fund that has an investment in an audit client. The auditor does not
make the decisions to buy or sell the security held by the mutual fund.
The ownership of mutual fund shares is a direct financial interest. The
underlying investments of a mutual fund are considered to be indirect
financial interests. If the mutual fund is diversified, a covered member's
ownership of 5% or less of the outstanding shares of the mutual fund
would not be considered to constitute a material indirect financial interest
in the underlying investments. For purposes of determining materiality,

the financial interests of the covered member and immediate family should be aggregated.

Independence would be considered impaired in the following situations involving financial interests:

- A covered member has a material joint, closely held investment with a client. For example, the member cannot own a vacation home or time share with a key office or principal shareholder of a client.
- A partner or professional employee of an audit firm owns more than 5% of client.
- One or more partners or professional employees have relationship with a client as an officer, director, manager, employee, etc.

Family Relationships A covered member's independence would be considered impaired if an immediate family member was employed by an audit client in a key position in which he or she can exercise influence over the contents of the financial statements, such as the CEO, CFO, chief accountant, member of the board of directors, chief internal audit executive, or treasurer. Independence is impaired if a covered member has a close relative who has a key position with the client or has a material financial interest in the client of which the CPA has knowledge. An immediate family member may be employed by the client in a nonkey position.

Loans There are limits on the types and amounts of loans covered members may obtain from a financial institution that is also an audit client. Essentially, auditors cannot obtain large loans, or loans for investment purposes, from a client. However, auditors are permitted to obtain normal loans if they are at standard terms, such as automobile loans or leases. The *Professional Judgment in Context* feature at the beginning of the chapter highlights an example of an auditor obtaining a loan from a client, thereby impairing independence.

Performing Nonaudit Services Independence may be impaired if auditors provide certain *non*audit services to an audit client. Independence is impaired when:

- A member assumes management responsibilities for an audit client.
- The auditor provides the following services to an audit client: appraisal, valuation or actuarial services, expert witness services, internal audit services, tax advocacy services, or personnel services (e.g., recruiting, hiring, terminating or compensating employees).

The AICPA's *Code* does not prohibit auditors from performing other services such as bookkeeping, payroll processing, consulting, tax preparation, or business risk advisory services for their private clients, but auditors must take care to assure that working too closely with the client does not compromise the appearance of independence. If, for example, the auditor does bookkeeping, prepares tax returns, and performs management consulting services, the appearance of independence has disappeared, even if independence, in fact, remains. A fundamental premise in these standards is that management must not concede decision-making authority to the accountant or auditor. For example, it is acceptable for the auditor of a nonpublic company to design, install, or integrate a client's information system, provided the client makes all management decisions. It is not acceptable to supervise client personnel in the daily operation of a client's information system.

Integrity and Objectivity—Rule 102

Rule 102 requires the AICPA member to act with integrity and objectivity when performing all services. This requirement also applies to CPAs who are not in public practice. For example, if the CFO of a company knowingly makes or permits others to make materially false and misleading entries in the financial statements or records, fails to correct an entity's financial statements or records, or signs—or directs another to sign—a document containing materially false and misleading information, that person has violated the *Code*. A CPA is a special certificate that holds its owner to a high standard of ethical conduct, no matter where the individual is in his or her career.

General Standards—Rule 201 and Compliance with Standards—Rule 202

Rules 201 and 202 require a member to comply with general standards and interpretations by standards setters such as the PCAOB and the AICPA. Rule 201 stipulates that the performance of professional services requires professional competence, due professional care, planning and supervision, and obtaining sufficient appropriate data.

Accounting Principles—Rule 203

Rule 203 applies to members who sign client reports provided to regulatory agencies, creditors, or other auditors. All members, even those not in public practice, are required to adhere to Rule 203. *Exhibit 4.6* provides specific details on the requirements of Rule 203.

Confidentiality—Rule 301

During the course of an audit, the auditor develops a complete understanding of the client and obtains confidential information, such as its operating strengths, weaknesses, and plans for financing or expanding into new markets. To assure a free flow and sharing of information between the client and the auditor, the client must be assured that the auditor will not communicate confidential information to outside parties. **Privileged communication** means that confidential information obtained about a client cannot be subpoenaed by a court of law to be used against that client. Most states allow privileged communication for lawyers, but not for auditors.

The exceptions to this general rule are that auditors are not precluded from communicating information for any of the following purposes:

- To assure the adequacy of accounting disclosures required by GAAP
- To comply with a validly issued and enforceable subpoena or summons or to comply with applicable laws and government regulations
- To provide relevant information for an outside quality review of the firm's practice under PCAOB, AICPA, or state board of accountancy authorization
- To initiate a complaint with, or respond to an inquiry made by, the AICPA's professional ethics division or by the trial board or investigative or disciplinary body of a state CPA society or board of accountancy

Contingent Fees—Rule 302

A **contingent fee** is defined as a fee established for the performance of any service in which a fee will not be collected unless a specified finding or result is attained, or in which the amount of the fee depends on the finding or results of such services. An example of a contingent fee is a consulting firm agreeing to perform an information systems project for a fee of 50% of the defined cost savings attributable to the system for a period of three years. Contingent fees are attractive to clients because they do not pay unless the consultant delivers real value. Consulting firms often use contingent fees to compete with each other.

Contingent fees are prohibited from any client for whom the auditor performs audit services. However, an auditor's fees may vary, depending on the complexity of services rendered or the time taken to perform the services. Contingent fees have not been prohibited for services provided to nonaudit clients. However, the auditor must still be sure that the use of such fees does not impair the auditor's objectivity or ability to uphold the public trust.

Acts Discreditable—Rule 501

Rule 501 stipulates that a member may not commit an act that is discreditable to the profession. For example, if a court determines that a member has violated an antidiscrimination law, the member is considered to have committed an act discreditable. As a student, you may be interested to learn that solicitation or knowing disclosure of CPA exam questions or answers is an act discreditable.

Advertising or Other Forms of Solicitation—Rule 502

Rule 502 prohibits false, misleading, or deceptive advertising. These types of acts are prohibited because they work against the public interest. Examples include:

- Creating false expectations about outcomes
- Suggesting the ability to influence relevant parties
- Providing representations that would cause one to be deceived

Commissions and Referral Fees—Rule 503

As outlined in *Exhibit* 4.6, many types of commissions are prohibited, while permitted commissions must be appropriately disclosed. Referral fees are distinct from commissions and are permitted, but must be disclosed.

Form of Organization and Name—Rule 505

While *Exhibit* 4.6 summarizes the key requirements of Rule 505, it is important to recognize that the audit firm name not be misleading. However, past owners may be included in the name of a successor firm.

Enforcement of the Code of Professional Conduct

Compliance with the *Code* depends primarily on the voluntary cooperation of AICPA members and secondarily on public opinion, reinforcement by peers, and ultimately, on disciplinary proceedings by the Joint Ethics Enforcement Program, sponsored by the AICPA and state CPA societies. Disciplinary proceedings are initiated by complaints received by the AICPA's Professional Ethics Division.

Audit and other attestation reports on financial statements can be signed only by those who are licensed as CPAs by their state board of accountancy. Anyone can provide consulting, bookkeeping, and tax services. To become a licensed CPA, a person must pass the CPA exam, meet specific education and experience requirements, and agree to uphold the profession and its code of professional conduct. The member's CPA certificate may be suspended or revoked by the state board of accountancy. Without that certificate or license, a person is legally prohibited from issuing an audit opinion or a review report on financial statements. The state board may also require additional continuing education to retain or reinstate the CPA certificate.

Other Guidance on Professional Responsibilities: Sarbanes-Oxley Act, PCAOB, and SEC

The Sarbanes-Oxley Act, the PCAOB, and the SEC also have requirements for professional responsibilities for audits of public companies. Many of these requirements are similar to those of the AICPA. Therefore, we highlight additional requirements not addressed in the AICPA *Code*.

Preapproval of Services   Audit committees should typically preapprove services performed by auditors, including all audit services and permissible nonaudit services. The audit committee cannot delegate this authority to management.

Fee Disclosures   Public companies must disclose the fees paid to its auditors. The disclosure is typically provided in its proxy statement or annual filing. The disclosure provides fees for four types of services: audit, audit-related, tax, and other.

Audit Partner and Audit Firm Rotation   Lead and concurring audit partners on public clients must rotate every five years, and must have a five-year cooling off period. A **cooling off period** is the number of years after which the individual auditor may resume providing service to the audit client. During the cooling off period, the individual auditor may not engage in any meaningful audit-related interactions with the client. Other audit partners on the engagement are required to rotate very seven years, with a two-year cooling off period.

In *Chapter 1*, you learned about the AICPA's conceptual framework on independence. That framework describes seven categories of threats to independence, which are circumstances that could lead to an auditor lacking independence in fact or in appearance. Of most relevance to the issue of mandatory partner or audit firm rotation is the familiarity threat, which occurs when the auditor has a long-standing relationship with an important person associated with the client, such as the CEO or the CFO. Having a long-standing relationship with the client could aid audit quality because of the knowledge that the partner and members of the engagement team gain through time. However, in terms of independence, the concern is that an individual audit partner or members of the audit firm may have developed very close personal relationships with top management; such relationships could impair their willingness or ability to perform an unbiased assessment of the audit evidence. See the *Auditing in Practice* feature "KPMG and General Electric Company: A Relationship that has Lasted Over 100 Years." This example highlights the fact that shareholders are beginning to question long-standing relationships between a given company and its auditor.

Rules differ internationally in terms of mandatory partner rotation and mandatory audit firm rotation. Differences exist in terms of whether

KPMG and General Electric Company: A Relationship That Has Lasted Over 100 Years

It may surprise you to learn that KPMG (or its former member firms prior to the latest merger that created KPMG) has audited General Electric Company for over 100 years. While the Company and audit firm clearly appear to appreciate the long-standing relationship, some users of the financial statements question it very strongly. In fact, the United Brotherhood of Carpenters Pension Fund, a shareholder of the Company's, filed the letter and proposal below to General Electric requesting that the Company consider implementing an audit firm rotation policy whereby the Company would rotate audit firms after seven years. Text of the letter and proposal appear on the next page. Ultimately, the proposal was ignored by General Electric, and was not put to a vote of the shareholders. Thus, it appears that General Electric and KPMG are not supportive of periodic audit firm rotation.

(Continued)

November 9, 2011

Bracken B. Denniston III
Secretary
General Electric Company 3135 Easton Turnpike
Fairfield, Connecticut 06828

Dear Mr. Denniston:

On behalf of the United Brotherhood of Carpenters Pension Fund ("Fund"), I hereby submit the enclosed shareholder proposal ("Proposal') for inclusion in the General Electric Company ("Company") proxy statement to be circulated to Company shareholders in conjunction with the next annual meeting of shareholders. The Proposal relates to audit firm rotation, and is submitted under Rule 14(a)~8 (Proposals of security Holders) of the U.S. Securities and Exchange Commission proxy regulations.

The Fund is the beneficial owner of 136,086 shares of the Company's common stock that have been held continuously for more than a year prior to this date of submission. The Fund intends to hold the shares through the date of the Company's next annual meeting of shareholders. The record holder of the stock will provide the appropriate verification of the Fund's beneficial ownership by separate letter. Either the undersigned or a designated representative will present the proposal for consideration at the annual meeting of shareholders.

Sincerely,
Douglas J. McCarron Fund Chairman
cc. Edward J. Durkin

Audit Firm Rotation Policy Proposal

"**Be it Resolved:** That the shareholders of General Electric Company ("Company") hereby request that the Company's Board Audit Review Committee establish an Audit Firm Rotation Policy that requires that at least every seven years the Company's audit firm rotate off the engagement for a minimum of three years.

Supporting Statement: Audit independence is fundamentally important to the integrity of the public company financial reporting system that underpins our nation's capital markets. In a system in which audit clients pay for-profit accounting firms to perform financial statement audits, every effort must be made to ensure accounting firm independence. One important reform to advance the independence, skepticism, and objectivity accounting firms have toward their audit clients is a mandatory auditor rotation requirement.

Information gathered on the current terms of engagement between audit firms and client corporations indicates that at the largest 500 companies based on market capitalization long-term auditor–client relationships are prevalent: for the largest 100 companies auditor tenure averages 28 years, while the average tenure at the 500 largest companies is 21 years. These long-term financial relationships result in the payment to the audit firm of hundreds of millions of dollars over the average period of engagement. According to its recent proxy statements, General Electric has paid its audit firm, KPMG LLP, a total of $801,600,000 in total fees over the last seven years alone.

Auditor independence is described by the PCAOB, an organization established to set and monitor accounting standards and practices, as "both a description of the relationship between auditor and client and the mindset with which the auditor must approach his or her duty to serve the public." (PCAOB Release No. 2011-055, August 16, 2011). One measure of an independent mindset is the auditor's ability to exercise "professional skepticism," which is an attitude that includes a questioning mind and a critical assessment of audit evidence." PCAOB standards require an auditor to conduct an audit engagement with a mindset that recognizes the possibility that a material misstatement due to fraud could be present, regardless of any past experience with the entity and regardless of the auditor's belief about management's honesty and integrity.

Instances of systemic accounting fraud in the market have prompted various legislative and regulatory reforms to the audit process, including audit partner rotation requirements, limits on the nonaudit services that can be provided by accounting firms to audit clients, and enhanced responsibilities for board audit committees. Despite these important reforms, recent PCAOB investigations often reveal audit deficiencies that may be attributable to a failure to exercise the required professional skepticism and objectivity.

We believe that an important next step in improving the integrity of the public company audit system is to establish a mandatory audit firm rotation requirement of seven years. The periodic audit firm rotation by public company clients would limit long-term client–audit firm relationships that may compromise the independence of the audit firm's work."

rotation is required, the length of time the auditor or audit firm may serve before rotation, and the length of time of a cooling off period. *Exhibit 4.7* summarizes these differences.

Prohibited Nonaudit Services The Sarbanes-Oxley Act prohibits external auditors from providing the following nonaudit services to their

EXHIBIT **4.7**	U.S. and International Guidance on Mandatory Audit Partner and Audit Firm Rotation

Times and requirements vary internationally in terms of mandatory audit partner and mandatory audit firm rotation. The United States differs from the European Union countries dramatically in terms of not supporting the idea of mandatory audit firm rotation. There is more commonality in terms of mandatory audit partner rotation, but with differing time periods and cooling off periods by jurisdiction. These differences are outlined below.

U.S. **AICPA**	Mandatory Partner Rotation • Not required Mandatory Audit Firm Rotation • Not required
U.S. **PCAOB**	Mandatory Partner Rotation (SOX Section 203) • Required after five years for engagement partner and engagement quality review (concurring) partner • Cooling off period of five years Mandatory Audit Firm Rotation • Not required, but the PCAOB had considered requiring mandatory audit firm rotation. In February 2014, the PCAOB announced that it was no longer pursuing a project to impose audit firm term limits on public companies
International **IESBA (under IFAC, for those following International Auditing and Assurance Standards)**	Mandatory Partner Rotation (*Code of Ethics*, Section 290) • Required after seven years for engagement partner and engagement quality review (concurring) partner • Cooling off period of two years
International European Union Countries	Mandatory Audit Firm Rotation (Council of European Union Reform—April 2014) • The new legislation will impose mandatory rotation of auditors of public entities after a period of 10 years. • Member states may allow the auditor or audit firm to continue audit up to the maximum duration of 20 years where a public tendering is conducted and up to 24 years in case of a joint audit.

publicly traded clients because of concerns that doing so would impair independence in fact and/or in appearance:

- Bookkeeping services
- Financial information systems design and implementation
- Appraisal or valuation services
- Actuarial services
- Internal audit outsourcing services
- Management functions or human resources
- Broker or dealer, investment adviser, or investment banking services
- Legal services and expert services unrelated to the audit

PCAOB Interim Standards and Issued Rules   The PCAOB adopted the AICPA's Rule 101 and Rule 102, as well as certain standards of the now defunct Independence Standards Board. Further, the PCAOB has issued additional specific independence rules, which generally align with the AICPA *Code.*

SUMMARY AND NEXT STEPS

The liability environment has significant implications for auditors. You should now understand the auditors' legal environment and specific laws from which auditor liability is derived, along with possible causes of action against auditors and auditor legal defenses. The frameworks for both general professional decision making and ethical decision making should assist auditors in behaving in ways that minimize litigation exposure. Finally, by following the relevant guidance on professional responsibilities, auditors can minimize their litigation exposure. In the next chapter, we present the specific steps in the audit opinion formulation process and the professional auditing standards that guide that process.

SIGNIFICANT TERMS

Breach of contract Failure to perform a contractual duty that has not been excused; for audit firms, the parties to a contract normally include clients and designated third-party beneficiaries.

Class action lawsuits Lawsuits that are brought on behalf of a large group of plaintiffs to consolidate suits and to encourage consistent judgments and minimize litigation costs; plaintiff shareholders may bring suit for themselves and all others in a similar situation, that is, all other shareholders of record at a specific date.

Cooling off period Number of years after which the individual auditor may resume providing service to the audit client.

Common law Liability concepts are developed through court decisions based on negligence, gross negligence, or fraud.

Confidential information Information obtained during the conduct of an audit related to the client's business or business plans; the auditor is prohibited from communicating confidential information except in very specific instances defined by the Code or with the client's specific authorization.

Contingent fee A fee established for the performance of any service in which a fee will not be collected unless a specified finding or result is attained, or in which the amount of the fee depends on the finding or results of such services.

Contingent-fee cases Lawsuits brought by plaintiffs with compensation for their attorneys being contingent on the outcome of the litigation.

Contract law Liability occurs where there is a breach of contract. The contract is usually between the external auditor and the client for the performance of the financial statement audit.

Covered member An individual on the audit engagement team, an individual in a position to influence the audit engagement, or a partner in the office in which the lead audit engagement partner primarily practices in connection with the audit engagement.

Deep-pocket theory The practice of suing another party not based on the level of their true fault in a legal action, but based instead on the perceived ability of that party to pay damages.

Direct financial interest A financial interest owned directly by, or under the control of, an individual or entity or beneficially owned through an investment vehicle, estate, or trust when the beneficiary controls the intermediary or has the authority to supervise or participate in the intermediary's investment decisions.

Ethical dilemma A situation in which moral duties or obligations conflict; an ethically correct action may conflict with an individual's immediate self-interest.

Expectations gap A misunderstanding whereby shareholders mistakenly believe that they are entitled to recover losses on investments for which the auditor provided an unqualified opinion on the financial statements.

Foreseeable user Those not known specifically by the auditor to be using the financial statements, but recognized by general knowledge as current and potential creditors and investors who will use them.

Foreseen user Individually unknown third parties who are members of a known or intended class of third-party users who the auditor, through knowledge gained from interactions with the client, can foresee will use the statements.

Fraud Intentional concealment or misrepresentation of a material fact with the intent to deceive another person, causing damage to the deceived person.

Gross negligence Failure to use even minimal care or evidence of activities that show recklessness or careless disregard for the truth; evidence may not be present, but may be inferred by a judge or jury because of the carelessness of the defendant's conduct.

Identified user Third-party beneficiaries and other users when the auditor has specific knowledge that known users will be utilizing the financial statements in making specific economic decisions.

Indirect financial interest A financial interest in which the beneficiary neither controls the intermediary nor has the authority to supervise or participate in the intermediary's investment decisions.

Joint and several liability A type of liability that apportions losses among all defendants who have an ability to pay for the damages, regardless of the level of fault.

Negligence Failure to exercise reasonable care, thereby causing harm to another or to property.

Objectivity An impartial, unbiased mental attitude that auditors should maintain.

Professional skepticism continuum A continuum that recognizes that the appropriate application of professional skepticism will depend on the risk characteristics of the particular account and assertion being audited.

Privileged communication Information about a client that cannot be subpoenaed by a court of law to be used against a client; it allows no exceptions to confidentiality.

Principles of professional conduct Broad principles that articulate auditors' responsibilities and their requirements to act in the public interest, to act with integrity and objectivity, to be independent, to exercise due care, and to perform an appropriate scope of services.

Professional judgment The application of relevant professional knowledge and experience to the facts and circumstances in order to reach a conclusion or make a decision.

Proportionate liability Payment by an individual defendant based on the degree of fault of the individual.

Prospectus The first part of a registration statement filed with the SEC, issued as part of a public offering of debt or equity and used to solicit prospective investors in a new security issue containing, among other items, audited financial statements. The Securities Act of 1933 imposes liability for misstatements in a prospectus.

Rights theory An ethical theory that identifies a hierarchy of rights that should be considered in solving ethical dilemmas.

Rules of conduct Detailed guidance to assist the auditor in applying the broad principles contained in the AICPA's *Code of Professional Conduct*; the rules have evolved over time as members of the profession have encountered specific ethical dilemmas in complying with the principles of the *Code*.

Safeguards Actions or other measures that may eliminate a threat or reduce a threat to an acceptable level.

Scienter Knowledge on the part of the person making the representations, at the time they are made, that they are false; intent.

Stakeholders Those parties who have a vested interest in, or are affected by, the decision resulting from an ethical dilemma.

Statutory law Laws developed through legislation, such as the Securities Act of 1933 and the Securities Exchange Act of 1934.

Third-party beneficiary A person who was not a party to a contract but is named in the contract as one to whom the contracting parties intended that benefits be given.

Threats Relationships or circumstances that could compromise an AICPA member's compliance with the rules.

Tort A civil wrong, other than breach of contract, based on negligence, constructive fraud, or fraud.

Utilitarian theory An ethical theory that systematically considers all the potential stakeholders who may be affected by an ethical decision and seeks to measure the effects of the decision on each party; it seeks to facilitate decisions resulting in the greatest amount of good for the greatest number of people.

TRUE/FALSE QUESTIONS

4-1 **LO 1** Litigation costs are the largest single cost faced by audit firms.

4-2 **LO 1** The expectations gap includes a misperception by shareholders that they are entitled to recover losses on investments for which the auditor provided an unqualified opinion on the financial statements.

4-3 **LO 2** The three laws from which auditor liability is derived include common law, contract law, and statutory law.

4-4 **LO 2** Negligence occurs when a person fails to perform a contractual duty.

4-5 **LO 3** Examples of breach of contract include violating client confidentiality, failing to provide the audit report on time, and failing to discover material error or employee fraud.

4-6 **LO 3** To win a claim against the auditor, third parties suing under common law must generally prove that they suffered a loss, that the loss was due to lack of reliance on misleading financial statements, and that the auditor knowingly participated in the financial misrepresentation.

4-7 **LO 4** Professional judgment involves applying relevant professional knowledge and experience to unique and potentially uncertain facts and circumstances in order to reach a conclusion or make a decision.

4-8 **LO 4** An auditor who is professionally skeptical will reasonably question the honesty and integrity of management.

4-9 **LO 5** Utilitarian theory holds that what is ethical is the action that achieves the greatest good for the least number of people.

4-10 **LO 5** In rights theory, the highest order rights are those granted by the government, such as civil rights, legal rights, rights to own property, and license privileges.

4-11 **LO 6** The AICPA's principles of professional conduct articulate auditors' responsibilities and their requirements to act in the public interest, to act with integrity and objectivity, to be objective and independent, to exercise due care, and to perform an appropriate scope of services.

4-12 **LO 6** An auditor's independence would be considered to be impaired if his or her immediate family member were employed by the audit client in any capacity or personnel level.

MULTIPLE-CHOICE QUESTIONS

4-13 **LO 1** Which of the following factors is not a reason that audit firms continue to experience high levels of litigation?
a. Joint and several liability statutes.
b. Class action lawsuits.
c. Contingent fee compensation for audit firms.
d. A misunderstanding by some users that an unqualified audit opinion represents an insurance policy against investment losses.

4-14 **LO 1** The shareholders of a bank sue Karen Frank, CPA, for malpractice due to an audit failure that preceded the bank's financial failure. The jury determines that Frank is 40% at fault and that management is 60% at fault. The bank has no financial resources, nor does its management. Under joint and several liability, Frank will likely pay what percentage of the damages?
a. 100%.
b. 50%.
c. 40%.
d. None of the above.

4-15 **LO 2** Which of the following statements is false?

a. Breach of contract occurs when a person competently performs a contractual duty.
b. Negligence is the failure to exercise reasonable care, thereby causing harm to another person or to property.
c. Gross negligence is operating with a reckless disregard for the truth, or the failure to use even minimal care.
d. Fraud is an intentional concealment or misrepresentation of a material fact with the intent to deceive another person, causing damage to the deceived person.

4-16 **LO 2** An audit client can sue the auditor under contract law for which of the following?

a. Breach of contract.
b. Negligence.
c. Gross negligence.
d. Fraud.
e. All of the above.

4-17 **LO 3** The remedies for breach of contract include which of the following?

a. Requiring specific performance of the contract agreement.
b. Granting an injunction to prohibit the auditor from doing certain acts, such as disclosing confidential information.
c. Providing for recovery of amounts lost as a result of the breach.
d. All of the above.

4-18 **LO 3** Which of the following scenarios includes an example of a foreseen user?

a. The auditor knows that the First National Bank wants audited financial statements as part of the client's application for a loan.
b. The auditor knows that the client needs audited financial statements because it wants to obtain a loan from one of several possible banks.
c. Current and prospective creditors and stockholders are likely to use the audited financial statements.
d. None of the above.

4-19 **LO 4** Which of the following steps is not a step in the framework for professional decision making?

a. Structure the audit problem.
b. Assess consequences of decision.
c. Assess the likelihood of fraud.
d. Gather information and audit evidence.
e. Conduct sensitivity analysis.

4-20 **LO 4** An auditor who is professionally skeptical will do which of the following?

a. Critically question contradictory evidence.
b. Carefully evaluate the reliability of audit evidence.
c. Reasonably question the authenticity of documentation.
d. Reasonably question the honesty and integrity of management.
e. All of the above.

4-21 **LO 5** Utilitarianism does not require which of the following actions when a person considers how to resolve an ethical dilemma?

a. Identification of the potential problem and courses of action.
b. Identification of the potential direct or indirect impact of actions on each affected party who has an interest in the outcome.

c. Identification of the motivation of the person facing the ethical dilemma.

d. Assessment of the desirability of each action for each affected party.

4-22 **LO 5** Which of the following statements related to rights theory is true?

a. The highest order rights include the rights to life, autonomy, and human dignity.

b. Second-order rights include rights granted by the government, such as civil rights and legal rights.

c. Third-order rights include social rights, such as the right to higher education, to good health care, and to earning a living.

d. Fourth-order rights include one's nonessential interests or personal tastes.

e. All of the above.

4-23 **LO 6** Rule 201 (General Standards) of the AICPA's Rules of Conduct requires the auditor to do which of the following?

a. Undertake only those professional services that the auditor or audit firm can reasonably expect to be completed with professional competence.

b. Exercise due professional care in the performance of professional services.

c. Adequately plan and supervise the performance of professional services.

d. Obtain sufficient relevant data to afford a reasonable basis for conclusions in relation to professional services performed.

e. All of the above.

4-24 **LO 6** Which of the following statements is false?

a. An auditor in public practice shall be independent in the performance of professional services.

b. In performing audit services, the auditor shall maintain objectivity and integrity, be free of conflicts of interest, and not knowingly misrepresent facts or subordinate his or her judgment to others.

c. In performing audit services, the auditor may accept only contingent fees for publicly traded audit clients.

d. An auditor in public practice shall not seek to obtain clients by advertising or other forms of solicitation in a manner that is false, misleading, or deceptive.

REVIEW AND SHORT CASE QUESTIONS

FRAUD

NOTE: Completing Review and Short Case Questions does not require the student to reference additional resources and materials.

4-25 **LO 1** Describe the forces that continue to cause audit firms to experience high rates of litigation.

4-26 **LO 2** Compare and contrast the concepts of breach of contract, negligence, gross negligence, and fraud.

4-27 **LO 2** Distinguish between the development of common law and statutory law.

4-28 **LO 3** What are some potential causes of action against an auditor under a breach of contract lawsuit?

4-29 **LO 3** What are some remedies for a breach of contract?

4-30 **LO 3** What defenses might an auditor use in successfully defending a:

a. Suit brought about because of breach of contract?

b. Suit brought under statutory law?

4-31 LO 3 Refer to the *Focus on Fraud* feature "Moss Adams and the Meridian Mortgage Funds Fraud."
a. Describe why Moss Adams was sued by the trustee for the bankrupt Meridian Mortgage.
b. What is the trustee going to have to prove in order for the courts to hold Moss Adams liable for damages?

4-32 LO 3 Three tests have been used by various courts in common-law decisions to determine which third-party users can successfully bring a suit against the auditor for negligence. Identify each of these tests and describe the parties that are defined in each of these tests.

4-33 LO 3 What are some sanctions the SEC can bring against auditors who have violated statutory law?

4-34 LO 3 Briefly explain the primary purpose of the:
a. Securities Act of 1933
b. Securities Exchange Act of 1934

4-35 LO 3 How does the auditor's liability to third parties differ under the 1933 Act and the 1934 Exchange Act? What is the importance of the *Hochfelder* case as it relates to the 1934 Act?

4-36 LO 3 Is there a conceptual difference between an error on the part of the auditor and ordinary negligence? Explain.

4-37 LO 3 What precedent was set in the *Ernst & Ernst vs. Hochfelder* case described in the chapter? What actions would be necessary to change the precedent?

4-38 LO 3 An auditor was sued for and found guilty of negligence. For each of the following situations, indicate the likelihood the plaintiff would win if the plaintiff is:
a. A financial institution that was known to the auditor as the primary beneficiary of the audit, suing under common law.
b. A stockholder suing under common law.
c. A financial institution that was unknown to the auditor loaned money to the client based on the audit financial statements, but the auditor knew only that the client would use the statements to obtain a loan from some financial institution. The plaintiff is suing under common law.
d. An investor suing under the 1934 Securities Exchange Act.
e. An investor suing under the 1933 Securities Act.

4-39 LO 3
a. Compare an auditor's liability to third parties for negligence under *Ultramares, Credit Alliance, 1965 Restatement (Second) of Torts*, and *Rosenblum*. Then indicate which approach you think auditors prefer, and why.
b. Which approach do you think is best for society? Why?

4-40 LO 3 An auditor issued an unqualified opinion on financial statements that failed to disclose that a significant portion of the accounts receivable was uncollectible. The auditor also failed to follow professional auditing standards with respect to inventory. The auditor knew that the financial statements would be used to obtain a loan. The client subsequently declared bankruptcy. Under what concepts might a creditor, who loaned money to the client on the basis of the financial statements, recover losses from the auditor?

4-41 LO 3 An investor is suing an auditor for issuing an unqualified opinion on the financial statements of Duluth Industries, which contained a material misstatement. The auditor was negligent in performing the audit. The investor had reason to believe the statements were wrong prior to purchasing stock in the company. In the subsequent period, Duluth Industries sustained operating losses, the stock price went down by 40%, and the investor sold the stock at a loss. During the period that the investor held this stock, the Dow Jones Industrial Average declined 10%. What defenses might the auditor use against the investor's lawsuit to recover losses?

FRAUD　　**4-42**　**LO 3**　A client applied for a bank loan from First Bank. In connection with the loan application, the client engaged an auditor to audit its financial statements, and the auditor issued an unqualified opinion. On the basis of those statements, First Bank loaned money to the client. Shortly thereafter, the client filed for bankruptcy, and First Bank sued the auditor for damages. The audit documentation showed negligence and possible other misconduct in performing the audit.

a. Under what circumstances is First Bank an identified user?

b. What exceptions to the identified user test might First Bank argue?

FRAUD　　**4-43**　**LO 3**　Monicker Co. engaged the audit firm of Gasner & Gasner to audit its financial statements to be used in connection with a public offering of securities. Monicker's stock is regularly traded on the NASDAQ. The audit was completed and an unqualified opinion was expressed on the financial statements, which were submitted to the SEC along with the registration statement. Three hundred thousand shares of Monicker common stock were sold to the public at $13.50 per share. Eight months later, the stock fell to $2 per share when it was disclosed that several large loans to two "paper" companies owned by one of the directors were worthless. The loans were secured by the stock of the borrowing corporation and by Monicker stock owned by the director. These facts were not disclosed in the financial statements. The director and the two corporations are insolvent. Considering these facts, indicate whether each of the following statements is true or false, and briefly explain the rationale for your choice.

a. The Securities Act of 1933 applies to the preceding public offering of securities.

b. The audit firm has potential liability to any person who acquired the stock described in connection with the public offering.

c. An investor who bought shares in Monicker would make a reasonable case if he or she alleged that the failure to explain the nature of the loans in question constituted a false statement or misleading omission in the financial statements.

d. The auditors could avoid liability if they could show that they were not fraudulent in the conduct of the audit.

e. The auditors could avoid or reduce the damages asserted against them if they could establish that the drop in price was due in whole or in part to other causes.

f. The SEC would establish contributory negligence as a partial defense for the auditor because the SEC approved the registration statement.

FRAUD　　**4-44**　**LO 3**　To expand its operations, Dark Corporation raised $4 million by making a private interstate offering of $2 million in common stock and negotiating a $2 million loan from Safe Bank. The common stock was properly offered pursuant to Rule 505 of

Regulation D, which exempts the offering from the 1933 Act, but not the antifraud provisions of the Federal Securities Acts.

In connection with this financing, Dark engaged Crea, CPAs, to audit Dark's financial statements. Crea knew that the sole purpose for the audit was so that Dark would have audited financial statements to provide to Safe Bank and the purchasers of the common stock. Although Crea conducted the audit in conformity with its audit program, Crea failed to detect material fraud committed by Dark's president. Crea did not detect the embezzlement because of its inadvertent failure to exercise due care in designing its audit program for this engagement.

After completing the audit, Crea rendered an unqualified audit opinion on Dark's financial statements. The financial statements were relied on by the purchasers of the common stock in deciding to purchase the shares. In addition, Safe Bank approved the loan to Dark based on the audited financial statements. Within 60 days after selling the common stock and obtaining the loan from Safe Bank, Dark was involuntarily petitioned into bankruptcy. Because of the president's embezzlement, Dark became insolvent and defaulted on its loan to Safe. Its common stock became virtually worthless. Actions have been commenced against Crea by the purchasers of the common stock (who have asserted that Crea is liable for damages under the Securities Exchange Act of 1934) and Safe Bank, based on Crea's negligence.

a. Discuss the merits of the actions commenced against Crea by the purchasers of the common stock and by Safe Bank, indicating the likely outcomes and the reasoning behind each outcome.

b. How would your answer be different if the client filed a registration statement and the purchasers of the common stock were able to bring suit under the 1933 Act?

4-45 **LO 3** *Part A*

The common stock of Wilson, Inc. is owned by 20 stockholders. Wilson's financial statements as of December 31, 2015, were audited by Doe & Doe, CPAs, who rendered an unqualified opinion on the financial statements. In reliance on Wilson's financial statements, which showed net income for 2015 of $1,500,000, Peters purchased 10,000 shares of Wilson stock for $200,000 on April 10, 2016. Wilson's financial statements contained material misstatements. Because Doe did not carefully follow GAAS, it did not discover that the statements failed to reflect unrecorded expenses, which reduced Wilson's actual net income to $800,000. After disclosure of the corrected financial statements, Peters sold his shares for $100,000, which was the highest price he could obtain. Peters has brought an action against Doe under federal securities law and common law.

Answer the following, setting forth reasons for your conclusions:

a. Will Peters prevail on his federal securities-law claims?
b. Will Peters prevail on his common-law claims?

Part B

Able Corporation decided to make a public offering of bonds to raise needed capital. It publicly sold $2,500,000 of 8% debentures in accordance with the registration requirements of the Securities Act of 1933. The financial statements filed with the registration statement contained the unqualified opinion of Baker

& Baker, CPAs. The statements overstated Able's net income and net worth. Through negligence, Baker did not detect the overstatements. As a result, the bonds, which originally sold for $1,000 per bond, have dropped in value to $700. Ira is an investor who purchased $10,000 of the bonds. He promptly brought an action against Baker under the Securities Act of 1933.

Answer the following, providing reasons for your conclusions:
a. Will Ira likely prevail on his claim under the Securities Act of 1933?
b. Identify the primary issues that will determine the likelihood of Ira's prevailing on the claim.

4-46 **LO 4** Refer to *Exhibit 4.3*. Briefly explain the seven steps in the framework for professional decision making. Provide an example of a professionally oriented decision that you have recently made, and relate it to the seven steps (one example might be a decision about whether to apply to a graduate program).

4-47 **LO 4** Refer to the *Auditing in Practice* feature "What Is Professional Judgment?" Describe what is meant by the term *professional judgment*. Explain why documentation is critical to professional judgment.

PROFESSIONAL SKEPTICISM

4-48 **LO 4** Explain why professional skepticism is important in making professional judgments. What are the types of actions that a professionally skeptical auditor will take?

4-49 **LO 4** Refer to the *Auditing in Practice* feature "What Was He Thinking? An Example of Poor Professional Judgment and Low Audit Quality."
a. Briefly explain the common themes indicating poor professional judgment evident from the facts about the Prospero Minerals audit, the Cal Bay audit, and the LitFunding audit.
b. What do you think Scharfman's motivation was in explaining his conduct?
c. Why were Scharfman's actions so potentially harmful to external users of the audited financial statements?

4-50 **LO 5** Describe utilitarian theory and how it is used to resolve an ethical dilemma. What are the weaknesses of utilitarian theory?

4-51 **LO 5** Describe rights theory and list the four levels of rights. In what way is rights theory particularly helpful?

4-52 **LO 5** Refer to *Exhibit 4.4*. Briefly explain the seven steps in the framework for ethical decision making. Provide an example of a difficult ethical decision that you have recently made, and use the framework to help you make a decision using the seven steps. (An example might be a decision to challenge a friend who has done something wrong or a decision to report on a person that you know was cheating on an exam.)

4-53 **LO 5** Refer to the *Auditing in Practice* feature "A Young Auditor Makes an Ethical Mistake in Professional Judgment."
a. What was the ethical dilemma faced by Susan Birkert's friend when that fellow auditor learned of Birkert's ethical wrongdoing?
b. What aspects of the framework for ethical decision making would the friend likely have considered in deciding to reveal Birkert's mistake?

4-54 **LO 5** As the auditor for XYZ Company, you discover that a material sale ($500,000 sale; cost of goods of $300,000) was made to a customer this year. Because of poor internal accounting controls, the sale was never recorded. Your client makes a management decision not to bill the customer because such a long time has passed since the shipment was made. You determine, to the best of your ability, that the sale was not fraudulent. Using the framework for ethical decision making, determine whether the auditor should require either a recording or a disclosure of the sales transaction. Explain your reasoning.

4-55 **LO 5** You have worked as a staff auditor for two and one-half years and have mastered your job. You will likely be promoted to a senior position after this busy season. Your current senior was promoted about a year ago. He appreciates your competence and rarely interferes with you. As long as he can report good performance to his manager on things she wants, he is satisfied. The manager has been in her position for three years. She is focused on making sure audits run smoothly and is good at this. She is not as strong on the softer skills. Although she is approachable, her attention span can be short if what you are saying does not interest her. You are aware that she expects her teams to perform excellently during this busy season and she hopes to be promoted to senior manager as a result, bringing her closer to her goal of making partner early.

The audit engagement on which you are working has become increasingly difficult since last year because of some complicated accounting transactions that the client made. There has also been unexpected turnover in accounting personnel at the client. This has made interacting with the client and getting the information you need in a timely manner problematic. However, the engagement time budget and the audit fee remain the same as last year's. Further, four staff auditors are assigned to the engagement, and there are no additional staff available to transfer in to ease the workload. Your senior now tells you that the manager has requested that you, he, and the other staff auditors do an additional analysis of a potential misstatement in one of the client's accounts. Even with your team's current workload, there is significant danger that the engagement will run over budget. You know that if you do the analysis thoroughly, it will further endanger meeting the time budget the manager had planned. The more time you spend on the engagement, the less profitable it will be for the audit firm, which clearly will displease the manager and her superiors.

As a group, the staff auditors discuss the situation and express their concerns regarding the perceptions that running over budget will create and the reputational issues that short-circuiting the analysis could create. When your senior stops by to discuss the new plan, the group raises its concerns. He talks to the group and implies that he would be satisfied if the team did either of the following: complete the analysis and simply not record the hours (doing so would prevent the reported audit hours from going too far over budget) or do a minimal job on the analysis, which would save time and avoid having to question the client too much. You and a few other staff members express discomfort with both of these strategies. It is suggested that the ramifications of the new order be made clear to the manager. The senior wants nothing to do with this. He says, "She doesn't want to hear these details so just use one of the ideas I have already given you." When he leaves, several staff members start griping about what they are being asked to do. A couple say they are going to leave the firm after this busy season, so they don't really care about this issue. Another says, "We've been told what to do. Let's just get on with it."

a. Using the framework for ethical decision making, decide what you would do. Explain your rationale.

b. How can you do what you think is the right thing without undermining your senior or undermining the manager's confidence in your ability to get a job done?

INTERNATIONAL **4-56** `LO 6` Summarize the five fundamental principles of ethics as articulated by the International Ethics Standards Board for Accountants (IESBA).

4-57 `LO 6` Refer to *Exhibit 4.5*. Describe the AICPA's six principles of professional conduct.

4-58 `LO 6` Refer to *Exhibit 4.6*. Read the description of Rule 101 and answer the following questions.

a. Are auditors of publicly traded clients required to be independent?

b. Are auditors of privately held clients required to be independent?

c. Rule 101 applies only to covered members. What does it mean to be a covered member?

d. What is the difference between a direct financial interest and an indirect financial interest?

e. What services does the Sarbanes-Oxley Act of 2002 prohibit auditors from performing for their publicly traded clients?

4-59 `LO 6` Refer to *Exhibit 4.6*. Read the description of Rule 102 and answer the following questions.

a. What does Rule 102 require?

b. Does Rule 102 apply to just external auditors, or all CPAs?

4-60 `LO 6` Refer to *Exhibit 4.6*. Read the description of Rule 301 and answer the following questions.

a. Distinguish between confidential information and privileged communication.

b. Normally, the external auditor must keep client information confidential. Identify those circumstances in which this does not apply.

4-61 `LO 6` Refer to *Exhibit 4.6*. Read the description of Rule 302 and answer the following questions.

a. What is a contingent fee?

b. Why are external auditors not allowed to accept contingent fees?

4-62 `LO 6` Describe the various ways in which the AICPA's *Code* is enforced.

4-63 `LO 6` Would a CPA violate the AICPA's *Code* by serving a client both as its auditor and legal counsel? Explain your answer.

4-64 `LO 6` The following are a number of scenarios that might constitute a violation of the AICPA's *Code of Professional Conduct*. For each of the five scenarios, indicate which principle or rule would be violated, or if none would be violated.

a. Tom Hart, CPA, does the bookkeeping, prepares the tax returns, and performs various management services for Sanders, Incorporated, but does not do the audit. One management service involved the assessment of the computer needs and the identification of equipment to meet those needs. Hart recommended a product sold by Computer Company, which has agreed to pay Hart a 10% commission if Sanders buys its product.

b. Irma Stone, CPA, was scheduled to be extremely busy for the next few months. When a prospective client asked if Stone would do its next year's audit, she declined but referred them to Joe Rock, CPA. Rock paid Stone $2,000 for the referral.

c. Nancy Heck, CPA, has agreed to perform an inventory control study and recommend a new inventory control system for Ettes, Incorporated, a new client. Currently, Ettes engages another audit firm to audit its financial statements. The financial arrangement is that Ettes will pay Heck 50% of the savings in inventory costs over the two-year period following the implementation of the new system.

d. Brad Gage, CPA, has served as the auditor for Hi-Dee Company for several years. In addition, Gage has performed other services for the company. This year, the financial vice president has asked Gage to perform a major computer system evaluation.

e. Due to the death of its controller, an audit client had its external auditor, Gail Klate, CPA, perform the controller's job for a month until a replacement was found.

FRAUD FOCUS: CONTEMPORARY AND HISTORICAL CASES

FRAUD **4-65** **KPMG** (LO 1, 2, 3, 4, 5, 6)

KPMG LLP served as the external auditor for some of the largest subprime mortgage lenders in the U.S. leading up to and during the housing market crisis of the mid to late-2000s. The audits of two of their largest lending clients, New Century Financial Corporation and Countrywide, ultimately led the firm to settle litigation charges in 2010 for $44.7 and $24 million, respectively. The business model of these two subprime mortgage lenders consisted of providing loans to borrowers with weak credit histories. The business model had begun to fail during a short period of time in 2007, when the economy weakened, borrowers began defaulting, and home prices declined drastically. New Century filed for bankruptcy and Countrywide was purchased by Bank of America, which subsequently suffered massive losses related to business failures at Countrywide.

Just before the housing crash of 2007 put the companies in severe financial crises, KPMG had given both companies unqualified audit opinions. In both cases, KPMG was subsequently accused of violating professional standards, lacking independence, and being negligent. KPMG defended itself by arguing that its audits were not the cause of the financial woes at New Century and Countrywide. Rather, the firm contended that it was the failed business model of the two companies that led to investor losses.

a. How does the business environment affect the litigation risk faced by audit firms?

b. Should auditors be held liable if their client's business fails or if the financial statements contain a fraud that the auditors did not detect?

c. What defenses do auditors use in response to litigation?

d. What actions can auditors take to minimize litigation exposure?

FRAUD **4-66** **Thomas Flanagan, Deloitte** (LO 4, 5, 6)

Thomas Flanagan was an audit partner and key member of management (vice chairman) at Deloitte LLP, based out of the firm's Chicago office. During the latter part of his career, he managed a large number of public company audit engagements. Based on knowledge obtained from key members of management of one of his audit clients, Flanagan learned that the client would soon be purchasing another company. Knowing that the value of the acquired company would rise upon the news of the purchase, Flanagan purchased stock in the acquired company. As such, he engaged in insider trading. As the subsequent investigation would reveal, Flanagan traded in securities of at least 12 of his audit clients during 2005–2008. In fact, he made more than 300 trades in shares of the firm's clients over this period. He concealed his actions by lying on his independence disclosure filings with Deloitte, not revealing the existence of several of his brokerage accounts that would have identified his actions. Ultimately, the SEC uncovered his actions and notified Deloitte. Flanagan resigned from the firm, and Deloitte subsequently sued him for breach of fiduciary duty, fraud, and breach of contract based upon his misconduct. The firm ultimately won a judgment against him. As part of a legal settlement with the firm, Flanagan gave up about $14 million in pension and deferred compensation, according to court papers filed by his attorney. A spokesperson for the firm stated "Deloitte unequivocally condemns the actions of this individual, which are unprecedented in our experience. His personal trading activities were in blatant violation of Deloitte's strict and clearly stated policies for investments by partners and other professional personnel."

In August 2010 the SEC charged Thomas Flanagan and his son with insider trading in the securities of several of the firm's audit clients. The SEC alleged that Flanagan's illegal trading resulted in profits of more than $430,000. On four occasions, Flanagan shared the nonpublic information with his son, who then traded based on that information for illegal profits of more than $57,000. The SEC also instituted administrative proceedings against Thomas Flanagan, finding that he violated the SEC's auditor independence rules on 71 occasions between 2003 and 2008. The Flanagans agreed to pay more than $1.1 million to settle the SEC's charges.

In October 2012, Flanagan was given 21 months in prison for trading on insider information about the accounting firm's clients. Flanagan, who pleaded guilty to a single count of securities fraud in August 2012, was also sentenced to one year of supervised release and fined $100,000. Securities fraud carries a maximum punishment of 20 years in prison. Flanagan's plea agreement called for a term of three to four years in prison, and prosecutors sought at least 37 months.

a. Why is owning stock in one's client considered inappropriate?
b. Why is it important that auditors be independent of their clients?
c. Why did Deloitte take Flanagan's actions so seriously?
d. What do you think might have led Flanagan to make such poor professional and ethical decisions?
e. Assume that you were working on one of Flanagan's engagements and you discovered that insider trading was occurring. What procedures should the audit firm have in place to encourage you to report the inappropriate behavior and yet protect your career?

Source: The description of this case is based, in part, on facts disclosed in the case Deloitte LLP v. Thomas P. Flanagan, Court of Chancery of the State of Delaware, No. 4125-VCN and SEC Accounting and Auditing Enforcement Release No. 3164.

APPLICATION ACTIVITIES

NOTE: Completing Application Activities requires students to reference additional resources and materials.

4-67 **Deloitte, Beazer Homes (LO 1, 2, 3)** In June 2009, Deloitte agreed to pay almost $1 million to settle a class action lawsuit related to its audits of Beazer, a homebuilding company. The lawsuit claims that Deloitte should have noticed the homebuilder was issuing inaccurate financial statements as the housing market began to decline. A spokesperson for Deloitte indicated that the firm denies all liability and settled to avoid the expense and uncertainty of continued litigation.

a. Using appropriate sources, research this case and identify fraud risk red flags that the auditor should have been aware of in these audits. One source that can get you started is: www.cfo.com/article.cfm/13612963?f=search.

b. If these fraud risk red flags were indeed present during Deloitte's audit, what were the auditors' responsibilities in conducting the audit?

c. Comment on Deloitte's willingness to settle the case, while at the same time denying liability.

4-68 **Deloitte, Adelphia Communications**
(LO 5, 6) In 2005, Deloitte & Touche agreed to pay a $50 million settlement concerning its failed audit of Adelphia Communications. The settlement was the largest ever to that date, with a record penalty of $25 million. Individual auditors found to be unqualified, unethical, or in willful violation of any provision of the federal securities laws can be disciplined by the SEC. Actions taken by the SEC in these types of situations are described in *Accounting and Auditing Enforcement Releases (AAER), Litigation Releases,* and *Administrative Proceedings* available at www.sec.gov.

a. Read AAER 2326 (September 30, 2005; Administrative Proceeding File No. 3-12065) and AAER No. 2842 (June 25, 2008; Administrative Proceeding File No. 3-12065), available at www.sec.gov. These releases relate to the actions of William E. Caswell, CPA, who served as a director and held the most senior, nonpartner position on the Adelphia engagement. What type of improper professional conduct was William E. Caswell, CPA, engaged in? Identify at least one rule of conduct in the AICPA's *Code* that Caswell likely violated. In 2005, what was the SEC's response to his behavior? What was the SEC's response in 2008?

b. Consider Caswell's failure to make sure that Adelphia's disclosure of its liabilities related to the co-borrowing credit facilities was sufficient. Use the framework for ethical decision making to assess Caswell's actions related to this disclosure.

4-69 **Center for Audit Quality**
(LO 4) A report available at the web site of the Center for Audit Quality (CAQ) on professional skepticism discusses whether professional skepticism and professional judgment are the same thing. At the CAQ web site obtain a copy of the report entitled "Enhancing Auditor Professional Skepticism" (http://www.thecaq.org/docs/research/skepticismreport.pdf) and read the discussion comparing professional skepticism and professional judgment. Do you agree with the position taken in the report? The report presents the idea of a continuum of skepticism. Review Exhibit 1 in the report and discuss how the auditor decides on the appropriate level of skepticism.

4-70 **AICPA**
(LO 5, 6) The AICPA's Professional Ethics Executive Committee (PEEC) adopted a revised *Code* in January 2014, with an effective date of December 15, 2014. Additionally, the *Code* includes two conceptual frameworks with a delayed effective date of December 15, 2015. PEEC reformatted the *Code* to become more user-friendly, which resulted in a number of improvements and some substantive revisions. At the AICPA web site, access a copy of the revised *Code*.

a. Review the Principles of Professional Conduct included in the revised *Code*. Contrast those principles with the ones contained in *Exhibit 4.5* in this chapter.

b. *Exhibit 4.5* in this chapter refers to Rule 201 (General Standards). Review the revised *Code* and identify where this rule for members in public practice is included in the revised *Code*. Has the revised *Code* included any substantive changes to Rule 201?

c. Review the discussion of the Conceptual Framework for Members in Public Practice included in the revised *Code*. Comment on the usefulness of this framework for resolving ethical dilemmas.

ACADEMIC RESEARCH CASES

NOTE: Completing Academic Research Cases requires students to reference additional resources and materials.

SEARCH HINT

It is easy to locate academic research articles! Use a search engine such as Google Scholar or an electronic research platform such as ABI Inform, and search using the author names and part of the article title.

PROFESSIONAL SKEPTICISM

4-71 **LO 1, 2, 3** Locate and read the article listed below and answer the following questions.

Brandon, D. M., and J. M. Mueller. 2006. The influence of client importance on juror evaluations of auditor liability. *Behavioral Research in Accounting* 18: 1–18.

a. What is the issue being addressed in the paper?
b. What are the findings of the paper?
c. Why is this paper important to auditors, and what are the implications of this paper for the auditing profession?
d. Describe the research methodology used as a basis for the conclusions.
e. Describe any limitations of the research.

4-72 **LO 4, 5, 6** Locate and read the article listed below and answer the following questions.

Johnstone, K., M. Sutton, and T. Warfield. 2008. Antecedents and consequences of independence risk: Framework for analysis. *Accounting Horizons* 15 (1): 1–18.

a. What is the issue being addressed in the paper?
b. What are the findings of the paper?
c. Why is this paper important to auditors, and what are the implications of this paper for the auditing profession?
d. Describe the research methodology used as a basis for the conclusions.
e. Describe any limitations of the research.

4-73 **LO 4** Locate and read the article listed below and answer the following questions.

Rennie, M. D., L. S. Kopp, and W. M. Lemon. 2010. Exploring trust and the auditor–client relationship: Factors influencing the auditor's trust of a client representative. *Auditing: A Journal of Practice & Theory* 29 (1): 279–293.

a. What is the issue being addressed in the paper?
b. What are the findings of the paper?
c. Why is this paper important to auditors, and what are the implications of this paper for the auditing profession?
d. Describe the research methodology used as a basis for the conclusions.
e. Describe any limitations of the research.

Professional Auditing Standards and the Audit Opinion Formulation Process

CHAPTER OVERVIEW AND LEARNING OBJECTIVES

Professional standards for auditors provide guidance on the many judgments and decisions they make throughout the audit opinion formulation process. These standards help auditors properly plan, perform, document, and supervise audits. Auditors who follow the professional auditing standards are viewed as conducting a quality audit. This chapter will help you identify the relevant auditing guidance to use each time you perform an audit.

Through studying this chapter, you will be able to achieve these learning objectives:

1. Identify and compare the auditing standards that provide guidance on the audit opinion formulation process.

2. List and discuss the foundational principles underlying the auditing standards.

3. List the phases and related activities in the audit opinion formulation process.

4. Explain the concept of accounting cycles and discuss their importance to the audit opinion formulation process.

5. Describe the assertions that are inherent to the financial statements and explain their importance to the audit opinion formulation process.

6. Define audit evidence and describe the purpose of audit procedures used to obtain audit evidence.

7. Discuss the importance of audit documentation and provide examples.

8. Discuss audit activities in Phase I of the audit opinion formulation process.

9. Discuss audit activities in Phase II of the audit opinion formulation process.

10. Discuss audit activities in Phase III of the audit opinion formulation process.

11. Discuss audit activities in Phase IV of the audit opinion formulation process.

12. Discuss audit activities in Phase V of the audit opinion formulation process.

13. Apply the frameworks for professional decision making and ethical decision making to issues involving conducting an audit.

THE AUDIT OPINION FORMULATION PROCESS

I. Making Client Acceptance and Continuance Decisions

Chapter 1

II. Performing Risk Assessment

Chapters 3, 7, and 9–13

III. Obtaining Evidence About Internal Control Operating Effectiveness

Chapters 8–13 and 16

IV. Obtaining Substantive Evidence About Accounts, Disclosures and Assertions

Chapters 8–13 and 16

V. Completing the Audit and Making Reporting Decisions

Chapters 14 and 15

The Auditing Profession, the Risk of Fraud and Mechanisms to Address Fraud: Regulation, Corporate Governance, and Audit Quality

Chapters 1 and 2

Professional Liability and the Need for Quality Auditor Judgments and Ethical Decisions

Chapter 4

The Audit Opinion Formulation Process and a Framework for Obtaining Audit Evidence

Chapters 5 and 6

PROFESSIONAL JUDGMENT IN CONTEXT

The Importance of Adhering to Professional Auditing Standards as Illustrated in the Audits Performed by Sherb & Co. LLP

Auditors who adhere to the professional auditing standards are viewed as conducting a quality audit. A lack of adherence to the professional auditing standards heightens the risk that the auditor will provide an unqualified audit opinion on financial statements that are materially misstated. This lesson is highlighted in audits provided by Sherb & Co. LLP. In November 2013, the Securities and Exchange Commission (SEC) announced sanctions against the New York-based audit firm, its founder, two other partners, and an audit manager for their roles in the failed audits of three China-based companies publicly traded in the United States. One of the companies they audited—China Sky One Medical, Inc.—has since been charged by the SEC with financial fraud.

An SEC investigation found that Sherb & Co. LLP, and its auditors, falsely represented in audit reports that they had conducted their audits in accordance with U.S. auditing standards. However, Sherb failed to properly plan and execute audits; failed to obtain sufficient audit evidence on sales, revenue, and bank balances; and ignored factors suggesting the presence of fraud. Further, the auditors failed to exercise professional skepticism and due care. They also failed to maintain complete documentation of their audit work.

To settle the SEC's charges, the firm and the four auditors agreed to be barred from practicing as accountants for any publicly traded company regulated by the SEC. The firm also agreed to pay a $75,000 penalty.

The co-director of the SEC's Division of Enforcement indicated that the firm and its auditors failed to live up to their professional obligations in multiple audits during a five-year period.

As you read through this chapter, consider the following questions:

- What is the role of auditing standards and their underlying principles in promoting a quality audit? (LO 1, 2)
- How does the fundamental concept of professional skepticism relate to audit quality? (LO 2)

- What audit evidence is necessary for opining on a client's financial statements? (LO 6)
- How does audit documentation provide evidence related to audit quality? (LO 7)
- What audit activities are conducted during the audit opinion formulation process to provide reasonable assurance about a client's financial statements? (LO 8, 9, 10, 11, 12)

- How does professional judgment and ethical decision making contribute to audit quality? (LO 13)

For further details on this case, see Securities and Exchange Commission Accounting and Auditing Enforcement Release No. 3512 (November 2013).

Professional Auditing Standards

LO 1 Identify and compare the auditing standards that provide guidance on the audit opinion formulation process.

Auditors in the United States follow auditing guidance issued by the American Institute of Certified Public Accountants (AICPA), the Public Company Accounting Oversight Board (PCAOB), and the International Auditing and Assurance Standards Board (IAASB). Auditing standards set by these various authorities have a common objective—to provide reasonable assurance to the public that audits are conducted in a quality manner. Auditing standards apply to the auditor's task of developing and communicating an opinion on financial statements and, as part of an integrated audit, on a client's internal control over financial reporting. The auditing standards used will vary according to the nature of the company audited, such as whether a company is public or nonpublic. For example, U.S. public companies are subject to SEC regulation and must be audited in accordance with the auditing standards established by the PCAOB, while U.S. nonpublic companies will have an audit performed in accordance with generally accepted auditing standards that have been established by the AICPA. Further, the domicile of the company that is being audited and, more importantly, where its stock is publicly traded (if applicable) determine whether the auditor must comply with PCAOB or AICPA standards or those developed by IAASB.

Auditing Standards Issued by the AICPA

In 2004, the AICPA's Auditing Standards Board (ASB) began a project to redraft its standards to improve their clarity. The AICPA's Clarity Project was created in an effort to streamline auditing standards content and to merge U.S. auditing standards with international auditing standards of the IAASB. The ASB has written its standards using a drafting convention called the *clarity format*. The clarity format presents each standard in the following sections:

- *Introduction* explains the purpose and scope of the standard.
- *Objective* defines the context in which the requirements are set.
- *Definitions* include, where relevant, specific meanings of terms in the standards.
- *Requirements* identify what the auditor is required to do to achieve the objective of the standard. Requirements are expressed using the words *the auditor should* or *the auditor must*.
- *Application and Other Explanatory Material* include cross-references to the requirements and provide further guidance for applying the requirements of the standard.

The ASB issued most of its clarified standards in a single Statement on Auditing Statement (SAS No. 122) in 2012. These clarified standards became effective for audits of financial statements for periods ending on or after December 15, 2012. As of January 1, 2014, the Clarified U.S. Auditing Standards replaced the AU standards (pre-clarified standards) on the CPA exam. Throughout the book, and in the *Standards Appendix* to this book, we reference an AICPA's clarified auditing standard by referring to it as AU-C and a section number (e.g., AU-C 200).

Auditing Standards Issued by the IAASB

The IAASB states that its objective is to "serve the public interest by setting high-quality international standards for auditing, quality control, review, other assurance, and related services, and by facilitating the convergence of international and national standards." In 2004, the IAASB began a program to enhance the clarity of its International Standards on Auditing (ISAs). The IAASB's Clarity Project was completed in 2009, and as of 2014, the set of IAASB's clarified standards comprises 36 newly updated and clarified ISAs and a clarified International Standard on Quality Control (ISQC). The ISAs are structured so that information is consistently presented in the following separate sections, which is very similar to the format of the AICPA's standards:

- *Introduction* includes information regarding the purpose, scope, and subject matter of the ISA, in addition to the responsibilities of the auditors and others.
- *Objective* contains a clear statement of the objective of the auditor.
- *Definitions* for applicable terms are included.
- *Requirements* for each objective are provided. Requirements are indicated by the phrase *the auditor shall*.
- *Application and Other Explanatory Material* explains more precisely what a requirement means or is intended to cover or includes examples of procedures that may be appropriate under given circumstances.

Throughout the book, and in the *Standards Appendix* to this book, we reference an IAASB's auditing standard by referring to it as ISA and a section number (e.g., ISA 200).

Auditing Standards Issued by the PCAOB

The PCAOB issues auditing standards that apply to audits of U.S. public companies. As of 2014, the PCAOB had issued eighteen Auditing Standards (ASs). Further, the PCAOB adopted the AICPA standards that were in place on April 16, 2003 (referred to as PCAOB interim standards). Thus, the PCAOB requires public company auditors to follow these standards of the AICPA, unless they have been superseded by a PCAOB standard. Standards issued by the AICPA after April 16, 2003, are not part of PCAOB's interim standards.

Throughout the book, and as presented in the *Standards Appendix* to this book, we reference a PCAOB's promulgated auditing standard by referring to it as AS and a section number (e.g., AS 1). We refer to the PCAOB's interim auditing standards by referring to it as AU and a section number (e.g., AU 110). Also, be alert to the possible reorganization of the PCAOB standards as discussed in the *Emerging Issues* feature "PCAOB Standards Reorganization"

Comparison of the Auditing Standards

Fortunately, there is a great deal of commonality among the auditing standards. All of the standards start from fundamental principles on how an audit

PCAOB Standards Reorganization

EMERGING ISSUE

As of 2014, the PCAOB is considering a reorganization of its standards that is intended to present the standards in a logical order that generally follows the flow of the audit process. This reorganization is intended to help users navigate the standards more easily. You can monitor the PCAOB web site for developments in this area.

EXHIBIT **5.1**		Comparison of U.S. and International Auditing Standards

	IAASB	**PCAOB**	**AICPA**
Authority	International Federation of Accountants, and as agreed-upon by countries who abide by these standards	U.S Congress, as expressed in the Sarbanes-Oxley Act of 2002	Historical, as a self-regulatory profession
Terminology	International Standards on Auditing (ISA)	Auditing Standards (AS) and interim standards (AU)	Statements on Auditing Standards (AU-C)
Scope of applicability of standards	Audits in countries for which international standards are required, including most of Europe and many emerging markets	Audits of U.S. public companies	Audits of most U.S. nonpublic entities
Convergence of auditing standards	Committed to international convergence	Does not currently have a mandate for international convergence	Committed to international convergence

engagement should be planned and performed and how the results should be communicated. *Exhibit 5.1* contains an overview of these auditing standards. The *Standards Appendix* to this book provides a summary of the relevant standards for each phase of the audit opinion formulation process.

LO 2 List and discuss the foundational principles underlying the auditing standards.

Principles Underlying the Auditing Standards

Auditing standards in the United States have historically been based on ten generally accepted auditing standards (commonly referred to as the ten standards) that have served as the foundation for the audit of financial statements. Currently, however, the PCAOB is the only standard setter that still incorporates these ten standards (they were adopted by the PCAOB as part of its interim standards). The AICPA has replaced the ten standards with seven principles. While the wording differs, the fundamental tenant is that audits must be conducted in a quality manner.

PCAOB Guidance—The Ten Standards

The ten standards fall within three categories:

- *General standards* are applicable to the auditor and audit firm and provide guidance in selecting and training its professionals to meet the public trust. The general standards require the following:
  1. The audit is to be performed by individuals having adequate technical training and proficiency as an auditor.
  2. Auditors are to be independent in their mental attitude in conducting the audit (independence *in fact*) and be perceived by users as independent of the client (independence *in appearance*).
  3. The audit is to be conducted with due professional care, which is a standard of care that would be expected of a reasonably prudent auditor.
- *Fieldwork standards* are applicable to the conduct of the audit and require that:
  4. An audit is properly planned and supervised.
  5. Auditors develop an understanding of the client's controls as an important prerequisite to developing specific audit tests.

6. Auditors obtain sufficient appropriate audit evidence by performing audit procedures to provide a reasonable basis for the audit opinion being provided.

- *Reporting standards* are applicable to communicating the auditor's opinion and require that:

7. The auditor will state explicitly whether the financial statements are fairly presented in accordance with the applicable financial reporting framework, which may be Generally Accepted Accounting Principles (GAAP) or International Financial Reporting Standards (IFRS).

8. The auditor will identify in the auditor's report those circumstances in which accounting principles have not been consistently observed in the current period in comparison to the preceding period.

9. The auditor will review disclosures for adequacy, and if the auditor concludes that informative disclosures are not reasonably adequate, the auditor must so state in the auditor's report.

10. The auditor will express an opinion on the financial statements as a whole or state that an opinion cannot be expressed.

AICPA Guidance: Principles Governing an Audit

In place of the ten standards, the AICPA developed seven fundamental principles that govern audits. The four categories, with their specific principles, are:

Purpose of an Audit and Premise upon Which an Audit Is Conducted

1. The purpose of an audit is to enhance the degree of confidence that users can place in the financial statement. This purpose is achieved when an auditor expresses an opinion on the financial statements.

2. An audit is based on the premise that management has responsibility to prepare the financial statements, maintain internal control over financial reporting, and provide the auditor with relevant information and access to personnel.

Responsibilities

3. Auditors are responsible for having the appropriate competence and capabilities to perform the audit, should comply with ethical requirements, and maintain professional skepticism throughout the audit.

Performance

4. The auditor needs to obtain reasonable assurance as to whether the financial statements are free from material misstatement.

5. Obtaining reasonable assurance requires the auditor to plan and supervise the work, determine materiality levels, identify risks of material misstatement, and design and implement appropriate audit responses to the assessed risks.

6. An audit has inherent limitations such that the auditor is not able to obtain absolute assurance about whether the financial statements are free from misstatement.

Reporting

7. The auditor expresses an opinion as to whether the financial statements are free of material misstatement or states that an opinion cannot be expressed.

The Audit Opinion Formulation Process

As an auditor you may be performing an audit of an organization's financial statements only or you may be performing an integrated audit that combines the audits of an organization's financial statements and its internal control over financial reporting. As indicated in the *Auditing in Practice* feature

Benefits of Integrating the Audits

AUDITING IN **PRACTICE**

Integrating the audits of internal control and of the financial statements can be efficient because both the tests of controls and the direct tests of account balances provide evidence related to each other. For example, tests of controls provide indirect evidence on the likelihood that the financial statements are free from misstatement. If the controls are effective, it is more likely that the financial statements are free from material misstatement. Further, if the auditor finds material misstatements in account balances or disclosures, those misstatements imply that there were material weaknesses in internal controls. Integrating the work promotes audit efficiency.

"Benefits of Integrating the Audits," audit efficiencies can result from integrating the audits of the financial statements and internal control.

The audit opinion formulation process is basically the same for the financial statement only audit and the integrated audit. However, in an integrated audit, the auditor provides on opinion on the effectiveness of internal control over financial reporting and does additional audit work to be able to issue that opinion, along with the opinion on the financial statements. Specifically, the auditor plans and performs the audit to obtain reasonable assurance about whether a material weakness in internal control exists as of the client's balance sheet date.

LO 3 List the phases and related activities in the audit opinion formulation process.

An Overview of the Phases in the Audit Opinion Formulation Process

An important aspect of the audit opinion formulation process is the client's responsibilities related to internal control and the financial statements.

Exhibit 5.2 provides an overview of the client's preparation of its financial statements and management report on internal control. The quality of internal control, which is the responsibility of the client, affects the reliability of the client's financial statement data. If controls over input, process, and output activities are effective, there is a higher likelihood that the financial statements are free from material misstatement. This relationship has important implications for planning and performing the audit. The *Audit Opinion Formulation Process* diagram presented at the beginning of this chapter summarizes the phases of an audit performed for purposes of providing an opinion on the client's financial statements and internal control effectiveness. These phases include:

Phase I   Making Client Acceptance and Continuance Decisions
Phase II   Performing Risk Assessment
Phase III   Obtaining Evidence about Internal Control Operating Effectiveness
Phase IV   Obtaining Substantive Evidence about Accounts, Disclosures, and Assertions
Phase V   Completing the Audit and Making Reporting Decisions

Within each of these phases, the auditor performs various activities, most of which are the same whether the auditor is performing a financial–statement only audit or an integrated audit. *Exhibit* 5.3 lists these activities. These activities are influenced by the auditing profession, regulation, and professional liability. When performing the activities in *Exhibit* 5.3, the auditor is expected to make quality professional judgments and ethical decisions.

Overview of the Client's Preparation of Financial Statements and Management Report on Internal Control

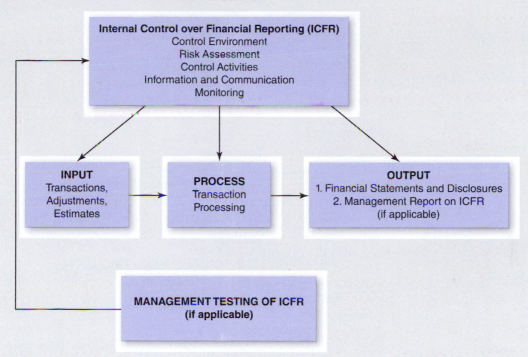

Activities Within Each Phase of the Audit Opinion Formulation Process

Phase of the Audit Opinion Formulation Process	Activities Within the Phase
Phase I—Making Client Acceptance and Continuance Decisions	• Assess whether management uses an acceptable financial reporting framework • Assess whether management acknowledges and understands its responsibilities
Phase II—Performing Risk Assessment	• Identify and assess risks of material misstatement • Respond to identified risks of material misstatement
Phase III—Obtaining Evidence about Internal Control Operating Effectiveness, if applicable	• Select controls to test, if applicable • Perform tests of controls, if applicable • Consider the results of tests of controls, if applicable
Phase IV—Obtaining Substantive Evidence About Accounts, Disclosures, and Assertions	• Perform appropriate substantive procedures
Phase V—Completing the Audit and Making Reporting Decisions	• Complete review and communication activities • Determine the type(s) of opinion(s) to issue

Important Concepts Pervasive Throughout the Audit Opinion Formulation Process

A number of important audit concepts that are pervasive throughout the audit opinion formulation process include:

- Accounting cycles
- Management assertions
- Audit evidence and audit procedures
- Documentation

LO 4 Explain the concept of accounting cycles and discuss their importance to the audit opinion formulation process.

Accounting Cycles

Financial statements are made up of accounts, such as revenue or accounts receivable, and they represent a summary of an organization's transactions. Similar transactions that are linked by procedures and controls and that affect related accounts are often grouped together for analysis (and audit) purposes and are referred to as an **accounting cycle** (or process). Many accounting transactions follow a defined cycle. For example, the revenue cycle includes transactions related to revenue, beginning with an initial customer order that flows through to an invoice, a recording of a receivable and a sale, and eventually the collection of cash. The cycle concept provides a convenient way to break the audit up into manageable sections of related accounts. Individual auditors or teams of auditors are typically assigned to audit a particular accounting cycle. *Exhibit 5.4* lists two cycles and their related accounts.

For a particular cycle, the auditor focuses on the flow of transactions within that cycle, including how transactions are initiated, authorized, recorded, and reported. The auditor identifies points in the cycle where material misstatements can occur and controls that have been designed and implemented to mitigate those risks. Understanding the risks and controls within each cycle helps the auditor determine the specific audit procedures to use and the specific audit evidence to obtain. We cover the following cycles in this book:

- Revenue (*Chapter 9*)
- Cash and Marketable Securities (*Chapter 10*)
- Inventory, Goods and Services, and Accounts Payable (*Chapter 11*)
- Long-Lived Assets (*Chapter 12*)
- Debt Obligations and Stockholders' Equity (*Chapter 13*)

EXHIBIT 5.4 Illustrations of Cycles and Related Accounts

Cycle	Related Accounts
Acquisitions and Payments for Inventory, Goods, and Services	Accounts Payable
	Inventory
	Expenses
	Other Assets
	Cash
Acquisitions and Payments for Long-Lived Assets	Equipment
	Accumulated Depreciation
	Depreciation Expense
	Gain or Loss on Disposal
	Impairment Loss

LO 5 Describe the assertions that are inherent to the financial statements and explain their importance to the audit opinion formulation process.

Financial Statement Assertions

Within each cycle, the audit is designed around management's assertions inherent in the financial statements. For example, if an organization asserts that it has property, plant, and equipment (PPE) net of depreciation of $42 million, the assertions being made by management are that:

- PPE is physically present (*existence*).
- All purchases of PPE are fully recorded (*completeness*).
- It owns the PPE and has title to the equipment (*rights and obligations*).
- The PPE is properly valued at cost with applicable allowances for depreciation (*valuation*).
- The PPE is appropriately classified and described (*presentation and disclosure*).

The auditor's job is to obtain evidence related to these assertions for each significant account and disclosure in the financial statements. As part of this process, auditors identify the most relevant assertions associated with the accounts and disclosures. Relevant assertions are those assertions that have a meaningful bearing on whether a financial statement account is fairly stated. While multiple assertions likely have a bearing on a financial statement account or disclosure, certain financial statement assertions are "more" relevant than others for particular financial statement accounts. For example, valuation is not particularly relevant to the cash account, unless currency translation is involved. However, existence would be considered more relevant to the cash account. As another example, valuation is especially relevant for the inventory account. The type of account will impact the assertions considered most relevant. In general, assets and revenues are more likely to be overstated, so existence/occurrence is the more relevant assertion for those accounts. In contrast, completeness would be the more relevant assertion for liabilities and expenses, as management would be more likely to understate these accounts. Accounts that require subjective judgments by management (such as allowance for loan loss reserve or allowance for inventory obsolescence) will usually have valuation as a more relevant assertion, as the valuation assessment is subject to management bias. *Exhibit 5.5* describes the five assertions identified in the PCAOB's standards.

The assertions listed in *Exhibit 5.5* are the ones we refer to throughout the book. The AICPA and IAASB have a similar conceptual structure for their assertions, although in some cases the wording differs somewhat from the wording in *Exhibit 5.5*.

LO 6 Define audit evidence and describe the purpose of audit procedures used to obtain audit evidence.

Audit Evidence and Audit Procedures

Audit evidence is information obtained by the auditor to support the audit opinion. Most of the auditor's work in forming an opinion consists of obtaining and evaluating audit evidence through performing **audit procedures**. Audit procedures fall into three categories:

- **Risk assessment procedures**. Procedures performed by the auditor to obtain information for identifying and assessing the risks of material misstatement in the financial statements whether due to error or fraud. Risk assessment procedures by themselves do not provide sufficient appropriate evidence on which to base an audit opinion but are used for purposes of planning the audit.
- **Tests of controls**. Audit procedures performed to evaluate the operating effectiveness of internal controls in preventing, or detecting and correcting, material misstatements.
- **Substantive procedures**. Audit procedures performed to detect material misstatements in accounts that include tests of details and substantive analytical procedures.

EXHIBIT **5.5**   Management's Financial Statement Assertions
in PCAOB Standards

Existence or occurrence: Assertions about existence address whether assets and liabilities exist and assertions about occurrence address whether recorded transactions, such as sales transactions, have occurred.

Example: Management asserts that sales recorded in the income statement represent transactions in which the exchange of goods or services with customers for cash or other consideration had occurred.

Completeness: Assertions about completeness address whether all transactions and accounts that should be included in the financial statements are included.

Example: Management asserts that notes payable in the balance sheet include all such obligations of the organization.

Valuation or allocation: Assertions about valuation or allocation address whether accounts have been included in the financial statements at appropriate amounts.

Example: Management asserts that trade accounts receivable included in the balance sheet are stated at net realizable value.

Rights and obligations: Assertions about rights address whether assets are the rights of the organization, while assertions about obligations address whether liabilities are the obligations of the organization.

Example: Management asserts that amounts capitalized for leases in the balance sheet represent the cost of the entity's rights to leased property and that the corresponding lease liability represents an obligation of the entity.

Presentation and disclosure: Assertions about presentation and disclosure address whether components of the financial statements are properly classified, described, and disclosed.

Example: Management asserts that obligations classified as long-term liabilities in the balance sheet will not mature within one year.

The auditor has a responsibility to design and perform audit procedures to obtain **sufficient appropriate audit evidence** that supports the auditor's opinion. Evidence is obtained through performing audit procedures including inspection of documentation, inspection of assets, observation, external confirmation, recalculation, reperformance, analytical procedures, scanning, and inquiry. The audit procedures that are performed during an audit are summarized in a document referred to as an **audit program**. *Exhibit 5.6* provides an excerpt of an audit program outlining some of the procedures that would be performed when auditing accounts, disclosures, and assertions in the revenue cycle, with a specific focus on procedures involving testing accounts receivables.

Evidence Example: Substantive Audit Procedures to Obtain Evidence About Management Assertions   The auditor's selection of audit procedures and evidence is based on the specific accounts and assertions being tested. Consider an audit of property, plant, and equipment (PPE) and the following valuation assertion implied in an organization's financial statement:

The equipment shown on the financial statements is properly valued at cost, with applicable allowances for depreciation.

This assertion can be broken down into four major components:

• The valuation of new assets added this year
• The valuation of assets that were acquired in previous years
• The proper recording of depreciation
• Potential impairment of the existing assets

EXHIBIT **5.6**	Excerpt of Audit Program for Accounts Receivable

Procedure	Primary Assertion(s) Being Tested					Timing of Testing
	Existence	Completeness	Valuation or Allocation	Rights and Obligations	Presentation and Disclosure	
Obtain the accounts receivable information and agree it to the prior year and the ending general ledger		✓				Year-end
Confirm accounts receivable (at the invoice level). For non-returned confirmations, vouch to provide evidence of (i) subsequent cash receipt and (ii) invoice or if not receipt, then (a) invoice and (b) evidence of delivery of service	✓					End of third quarter
Confirm contract terms if there is a heightened risk of side agreements (e.g., software companies)	✓		✓	✓		Year-end
Analytically review accounts receivable as a percentage of revenue at each of the three quarter ends (for this year and previous two years) and use this to predict accounts receivable at year-end	✓	✓				Year-end
Analytically review accounts receivable allowance, looking for abnormal swings in aging by size or quarter			✓			Year-end
Inquire and review documentation to support the classification of receivables (i.e., short-term versus long-term classification; due from customers versus due from employees or officers; large credit balances that should be reclassified as a payable)					✓	Year-end

For illustration purposes, we focus on whether the current year's additions to equipment are properly valued. Audit procedures that would address this assertion include:

- *Auditing Additions to PPE through Inspection of Documentation*—Take a sample of all additions to property, plant, and equipment, verify the cost through vendor invoices, and determine that cost is accurately recorded. If there is a high risk that the valuation may be misstated, the auditor may choose to take a larger sample.

- *Assessing the Potential Impairment of the Asset Additions through Inquiry of Management and Inspection of Assets*—These procedures help the auditor determine if the assets should be written down to an impaired value. Current economic information and independent evidence as to the current market price of the assets can be used to corroborate management's statements.

Important elements in these audit procedures highlight the following:

- *Select a sample of items to test.* The auditor needs to take a representative sample because it is often too costly to examine all additions to PPE. The sample size could be increased in order to respond to a heightened risk of misstatement. Sampling is discussed fully in *Chapter 8*.
- *Inspect documentary evidence of cost.* The auditor examines external, objective evidence of the amount paid and the nature of the equipment purchased, for example, an invoice.
- *Inquire and corroborate with other procedures.* While the auditor will likely inquire of management to obtain some audit evidence, it is important that the auditor corroborate what management has said by obtaining complementary evidence, such as inspection of documentation or assets.

LO 7 Discuss the importance of audit documentation and provide examples.

Audit Documentation

The auditor needs to prepare **audit documentation** that provides evidence that the audit was planned and performed in accordance with auditing standards. The terms *working papers* or *workpapers* are sometimes used to refer to audit documentation. The auditor should document the procedures performed, the audit evidence examined, and the conclusions reached with respect to relevant financial statement assertions. Auditing standards note that audit documentation serves other purposes, including:

- Assisting the engagement team in planning and performing the audit
- Assisting members of the engagement team responsible for supervising and reviewing the audit work
- Retaining a record of matters of continuing significance to future audits of the same organization
- Enabling internal or external inspections of completed audits
- Assisting auditors in understanding the work performed in the prior year as an aid in planning and performing the current engagement

Examples of audit documentation include:

- Audit programs
- Analyses prepared by the client or the auditor
- Memorandums
- Summaries of significant findings or issues
- Letters of confirmation and representation
- Checklists
- Correspondence (including e-mail) concerning significant findings or issues

LO 8 Discuss audit activities in Phase I of the audit opinion formulation process.

Phase I—Making Client Acceptance and Continuance Decisions

Auditors are not required to perform audits for any organization that asks. The auditor wants to accept audit engagements (whether for new or existing clients) only when the preconditions for an audit are present. As discussed in *Chapter 1*, generally, these preconditions include:

- *Management's use of an acceptable financial reporting framework.* Without an acceptable financial reporting framework, management does not have an appropriate basis for the preparation of the financial statements, and the auditor does not have suitable criteria for auditing the financial statements.

- *The agreement of management that it acknowledges and understands its responsibilities.* These responsibilities include the preparation and fair presentation of the financial statements, along with the design, implementation, and maintenance of internal control over financial reporting. Further, management needs to agree to provide the auditor with access to all relevant information, such as records, documentation, and so on, and unrestricted access to persons within the organization.

LO 9 Discuss audit activities in Phase II of the audit opinion formulation process.

Phase II—Performing Risk Assessment

Once the audit firm accepts a new client (or the audit firm decides to retain a continuing client), the auditor needs to thoroughly understand the client, with a focus on understanding the risks of material misstatement—due to either fraud or errors—in the financial statements and related disclosures. For continuing clients, much of the information is available from the previous year's audit and can be updated for changes. For new clients, this process is more time consuming. During Phase II, the auditor performs risk assessment procedures to identify the relevant risks and then determines the audit procedures needed to address those risks.

Identifying and Assessing Risks of Material Misstatement

Risk assessment underlies the entire audit process; identifying the risks of material misstatement is essential to planning an audit. A starting point for risk assessment is the identification of significant accounts, disclosures, and relevant assertions. Because the focus is on identifying material misstatements in the financial statements, the auditor establishes a materiality level for the financial statements overall and for specific accounts and disclosures. Materiality relates to the importance or significance of an amount, transaction, or discrepancy. Misstatements are material if they could reasonably be expected to influence the decisions of users made on the basis of the financial statements. Materiality considerations are the same for a financial statement audit and an integrated audit.

Assessing risks of material misstatement begins during the client acceptance activities (Phase I) and continues into the risk assessment activities (Phase II). *Exhibit 5.7* illustrates examples of sources of risk of material misstatement that the auditor should consider.

The auditor assesses the risk of material misstatement at both the financial statement level and the account and assertion levels. Risks at the financial statement level could potentially affect multiple accounts and assertions. In reviewing *Exhibit 5.7*, consider the presence of declining economic conditions and management pressure for good stock performance. These risks could affect the existence of sales, the valuation of receivables, and the completeness of expenses. At the assertion level, the auditor will consider both inherent and control risks. **Inherent risk** refers to the susceptibility of an assertion about a class of transaction, account balance, or disclosure to a misstatement that could be material, either individually or when aggregated with other misstatements, before consideration of any related controls. For example, the valuation of the loan loss reserve for a financial institution will likely have a high level of inherent risk due to its susceptibility of misstatement resulting from management bias. **Control risk** refers to the risk that a misstatement, which could occur in an assertion about a class of transaction, account balance, or disclosure and which could be material, either individually or when aggregated with other misstatements, will not be prevented, or detected and corrected, on a timely basis by the organization's

EXHIBIT 5.7 — Examples of Sources of Risk of Material Misstatement

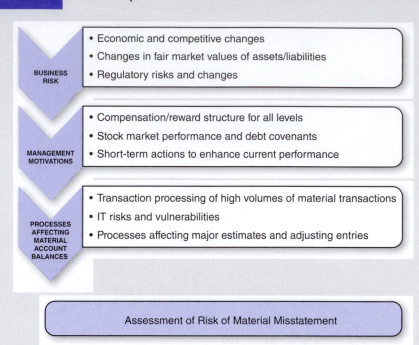

BUSINESS RISK
- Economic and competitive changes
- Changes in fair market values of assets/liabilities
- Regulatory risks and changes

MANAGEMENT MOTIVATIONS
- Compensation/reward structure for all levels
- Stock market performance and debt covenants
- Short-term actions to enhance current performance

PROCESSES AFFECTING MATERIAL ACCOUNT BALANCES
- Transaction processing of high volumes of material transactions
- IT risks and vulnerabilities
- Processes affecting major estimates and adjusting entries

Assessment of Risk of Material Misstatement

internal control. For example, a small, nonprofit client with few accounting personnel is likely to have a high level of control risk because of the lack of resources. Control risk is a function of the effectiveness of the design and operation of internal control. During Phase II, the auditor focuses on the design effectiveness and implementation of internal control.

Risk assessment procedures typically include:

- Inquiries of management and others within the entity who may have information to assist in identifying risks of material misstatement due to fraud or error
- Planning analytical procedures
- Observation (such as watching an organization's operations, facilities, or premises) and inspection of documentation (e.g., reviewing business plans, internal control manuals, or management reports)

Assessing Internal Control Design Effectiveness and Implementation

An important aspect of risk assessment is obtaining an understanding of internal control over financial reporting. The quality of internal control directly affects the risk of material misstatement. The focus is on internal control design and implementation and includes entity-wide controls, transaction controls, and fraud-related controls. The *Focus on Fraud* feature "Controls to Address Fraud Risk," provides examples of fraud-related controls.

The auditor assesses control design effectiveness and implementation by determining whether the organization's controls, if they are operated as designed by persons possessing the necessary authority and competence, can reasonably prevent or detect material misstatements in the financial statements. This understanding will allow the auditor to make a preliminary control risk assessment. The auditor performs various types of procedures to assess design effectiveness, including inquiry of appropriate personnel, observation of the organization's operations, and inspection of relevant documentation. Auditors

Controls to Address Fraud Risk

FOCUS on **FRAUD**

The PCAOB has identified the following as specific types of controls that the auditor should consider in evaluating whether or not an organization has sufficiently addressed fraud risk:

- Controls over significant, unusual transactions, particularly those that result in late or unusual journal entries

- Controls over journal entries and adjustments made in the period-end financial reporting process
- Controls over related-party transactions
- Controls related to significant management estimates
- Controls that mitigate incentives for, and pressures on, management to falsify or inappropriately manage financial results

also perform walkthroughs, as discussed in *Chapter 3*, to evaluate design effectiveness and implementation. The *Auditing in Practice* feature "Documenting the Auditor's Understanding of an Organization's Internal Controls" explains how the auditor should document the preliminary assessment of control design and the basis for that assessment.

Based on obtaining an understanding of internal control through the various procedures and review of management's documentation, the auditor assesses control risk ranging from high (weak controls) to low (strong controls). Assessing control risk as high means the auditor does not have confidence that internal controls will prevent or detect material misstatements; assessing control risk as low has the opposite implication. This preliminary assessment, based on the auditor's understanding of the design and implementation of the controls, is important because it drives the planning for the rest of the audit. If control risk is assessed as high, the auditor cannot plan on relying on the controls to reduce substantive procedures for account balances. Therefore, the auditor will not perform tests of controls; instead, the auditor must plan for substantive procedures, with no reliance being placed on the client's internal controls. If control risk is assessed as low, the auditor will plan to test the operating effectiveness of those controls (see

Documenting the Auditor's Understanding of an Organization's Internal Controls

AUDITING IN **PRACTICE**

The auditor's documentation should clearly identify each important control and the auditor's assessment of the design and implementation of that control. The auditor may base the audit documentation on documentation prepared by the client. The assessment of design effectiveness and implementation is the basis for the auditor's preliminary control risk assessment. The documentation of the understanding of internal control is often captured using narratives and flowcharts that describe the control processes.

Some audit firms also use questionnaires to assist in identifying important areas where controls are expected. There is no one right approach; each audit firm chooses an approach that fits the nature of its technology, its clients, and its clients' risks. Once the overall internal control process has been initially documented, in subsequent years many audit firms focus only on changes in the system and the effectiveness of monitoring controls to signal potential breakdowns in the overall control design.

AUDITING IN **PRACTICE**

Weak Internal Control Design and Links to Substantive Audit Procedures

Scenario. The auditor finds that the client does not use prenumbered receiving slips to record the return of sales merchandise nor does it have procedures to assure prompt recording of returned merchandise. To make things worse, sales returns have been high. The auditor is concerned that the overall control environment is weak and that management seems preoccupied with increasing earnings rather than accurate recording of returns.

Linkage to substantive audit procedures. The auditor assesses internal control design as ineffective and makes a preliminary assessment of control risk as high. Accordingly, the auditor is not able to rely on controls when testing the balance of sales returns. Therefore, the auditor expands the substantive tests

for sales returns by (1) arranging to be on hand at the end of the year to observe the taking of physical inventory, observing items received during the inventory counting process, and the client's procedures for documenting receipts, (2) tracing receipts for items returned by customers to credit memos to determine if they are issued in the correct time period, (3) reviewing all credit memos issued shortly after year-end to determine whether they are recorded in the correct time period, and (4) increasing the number of accounts receivable confirmations sent to the client's customers. All four of these procedures represent an expansion of tests beyond what would be required if the organization had effective internal controls over receiving returned goods.

Phase III) in an effort to reduce substantive testing related to account balances. The *Auditing in Practice* feature "Weak Internal Control Design and Links to Substantive Audit Procedures" illustrates the linkage between control effectiveness and planned substantive audit procedures.

Responding to Identified Risks of Material Misstatement

Once the auditor completes the risk assessment procedures, the next step is to determine the mix of tests of controls and substantive procedures for Phases III and IV of the audit opinion formulation process. The purpose of risk assessment procedures is to identify the risks of material misstatement, determine where misstatements in the financial statements may occur, and design the appropriate audit strategy (audit procedures) to respond to those risks and potential misstatements.

For a financial statement audit where the auditor wants to rely on controls as part of the basis for the audit opinion, the auditor designs a **controls reliance audit**—an audit that includes tests of controls and substantive procedures. For some audits, the auditor may determine that it is not efficient or effective to rely on the client's controls in forming the audit opinion. In those audits, the auditor designs a **substantive audit**—an audit that includes substantive procedures and does not include tests of controls. Within the same audit, the auditor can take different approaches across different cycles. For example, a controls reliance approach might be taken when auditing cash, but a substantive approach might be taken when auditing revenue.

In addition to selecting specific audit procedures to respond to identified risks, the auditor should consider the following overall responses to identified risks:

- Assembling an audit team that has the knowledge, skill, and ability needed to address the assessed risks of material misstatement
- Emphasizing to the audit team the need for professional skepticism
- Providing the level of supervision that is appropriate for the assessed risks of material misstatement
- Incorporating elements of unpredictability in the selection and timing of audit procedures to be performed

An Analogy for Responding to Identified Risks of Material Misstatement It can be helpful to view the response to identified risks of material misstatements as accumulating boxes of audit evidence. Two key considerations are the size of each evidence box and what type of evidence goes into each box. Accounts, disclosures, and assertions that have a higher level of identified risk of material misstatement would require larger boxes of evidence. Consider the three boxes in Panel A of *Exhibit 5.8*. An assertion with a low risk of material misstatement might require only enough evidence to fill Box A; an assertion with a high level of risk of material misstatement might require enough evidence to fill Box C; an assertion with a moderate level of risk of material misstatement might require enough evidence to fill Box B. There is not one right box size for every assertion. The appropriate size of the box will be based on the level of assessed risk of material misstatement.

The evidence that goes into each box will also vary. Consider an assertion where the auditor has assessed the risk of material misstatement as moderate. Again referring to *Exhibit 5.8*, the auditor needs to fill Box B in Panel A with audit evidence. Panel B illustrates alternative approaches that the auditor could use in filling that box. First, assume that the auditor has determined that the controls for that assertion are well designed. The auditor can fill the box with evidence from tests of controls and from substantive procedures (a controls reliance audit). For example, 50% of the evidence may come from tests of controls and 50% from substantive procedures. In contrast, assume that the auditor has determined that the controls related to

---

EXHIBIT 5.8 Responding to Identified Risks Through Evidence Decisions

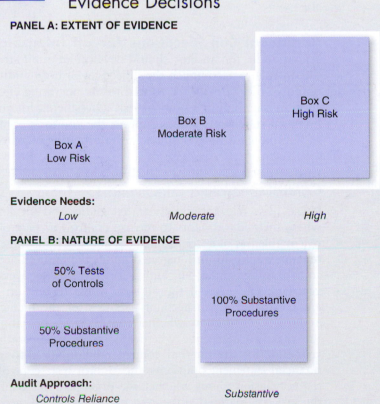

PANEL A: EXTENT OF EVIDENCE

Box A
Low Risk

Box B
Moderate Risk

Box C
High Risk

Evidence Needs:
Low   *Moderate*   *High*

PANEL B: NATURE OF EVIDENCE

50% Tests
of Controls

50% Substantive
Procedures

100% Substantive
Procedures

Audit Approach:
Controls Reliance   *Substantive*

Responding to Fraud Risks

FOCUS on **FRAUD**

The auditor should plan to perform tests of controls and substantive procedures that are specifically responsive to the assessed fraud risks. For example, when testing an account balance where there is a heightened risk of fraud, the auditor may decide to increase sample sizes or apply computer-assisted audit techniques to all items in an account. Further, the auditor should perform procedures related to the risk of management override of controls; such procedures include examining journal entries (and other adjustments for evidence of possible material misstatement due to fraud), reviewing accounting estimates for biases that could result in material misstatement due to fraud, and evaluating the business rationale for significant unusual transactions.

that assertion are not well designed. The auditor should not obtain any evidence on the operating effectiveness (why bother testing the operating effectiveness of a control that is poorly designed?), but instead should fill Box B with only evidence from substantive procedures (a substantive audit). That is, 100% of the evidence will come from substantive procedures. These same types of evidence decisions would also occur for assertions where the risk of material misstatement is high (Box C in Panel A of *Exhibit 5.8*) or low (Box A in Panel A of *Exhibit 5.8*)

The *Focus on Fraud* feature "Responding to Fraud Risks Through Evidence Decisions" emphasizes the importance of the auditor obtaining evidence related to controls that are intended to specifically respond to fraud risks.

Additional Considerations for an Integrated Audit In an integrated audit, the auditor should develop an audit strategy that includes tests of controls to accomplish the objectives of both audits. The auditor needs to obtain sufficient evidence related to the operating effectiveness of controls to support the auditor's control risk assessments for purposes of the audit of financial statements and to support the auditor's opinion on the effectiveness of internal control over financial reporting as of year-end.

LO 10 Discuss audit activities in Phase III of the audit opinion formulation process.

Phase III—Obtaining Evidence About Internal Control Operating Effectiveness

Phase III is relevant for integrated audits and for financial statement audits where the auditor wants to rely on controls as part of the evidence about the reasonableness of account balances and disclosures (in other words, a controls reliance audit). In an integrated audit, the auditor needs to opine on internal control effectiveness—including operating effectiveness—as of the client's year-end. However, if the auditor wants to rely on controls as part of the audit evidence about account balances for the financial statement audit, the auditor needs to know whether controls were operating effectively throughout the year. To determine whether controls are operating effectively—either at year-end (for the internal control opinion) or throughout the year (for the financial statement opinion)—the auditor tests controls that are important to the conclusion about whether the organization's controls adequately address the risk of material misstatement. There is no need to test every control related to a relevant assertion; the auditor tests only those controls that are most important in reducing the risk.

Selecting Controls to Test

The auditor selects controls that are most important to the organization's ability to adequately address the risk of material misstatement. The auditor selects both entity-wide and transaction controls for testing. The selection of control activities to be tested will depend, in part, on the results of testing the selected entity-wide controls. Effective entity-wide controls may reduce the number of control activities selected for testing. Overall, risks associated with significant accounts, disclosures, and relevant assertions should lead to the identification of important controls that need to be tested.

In determining which controls to select for testing, the auditor should explicitly link controls and assertions. *Exhibit 5.9* links the assertions of existence, completeness, and valuation to possible controls that the auditor may test.

Performing Tests of Controls

To obtain evidence about whether a control is operating effectively, the auditor directly tests the control in operation. The following tests of controls are presented in the order of their rigor, from least to most rigorous:

- Inquiry
- Observation
- Inspection of relevant documentation
- Reperformance of a control

Inquiry alone does not provide sufficient evidence to support a conclusion about the effectiveness of a control; other procedures must be performed. The type of test of control used varies with the process, the materiality of the account balance, and the control. For example, computerized edit controls built into a computer application could be tested by submitting test transactions. For manual controls, such as authorizations, the auditor might select a number of transactions to determine if there is documented evidence that proper authorization has taken place. For the reconciliation of shipments with recorded sales, the auditor could select a number of daily sales and review documentation to determine whether the reconciliations were performed appropriately. Or if a more rigorous test was needed

EXHIBIT **5.9**	Linking Financial Statement Assertions to Controls to Test
Financial Statement Assertion	**Examples of Controls That Might Be Selected for Testing**
Existence or occurrence	• Shipments recorded are reconciled with shipping documents daily. • Items cannot be recorded without underlying source documents and approvals.
Completeness	• Prenumbered shipping documents are used and reconciled with shipments recorded daily. • A list of cash receipts is developed when cash is collected and is reconciled with cash deposits and the debit to cash daily.
Valuation or allocation	• Preauthorized sales prices are entered into the computer pricing table by authorized individuals. • Sales prices can be overridden only on the authorization of key management personnel. A record of overrides is documented and independently reviewed by management, internal audit, or other parties performing control analysis.

because of the materiality of the account related to the reconciliation, the auditor may choose to reperform the reconciliation.

In selecting approaches to test controls, the auditor needs to consider the type of control being tested including computerized controls, manual controls, controls over adjusting entries, and controls over accounting estimates. *Exhibit 5.10* provides examples of possible tests of controls.

Example of Approaches to Testing the Operating Effectiveness of a Control Activity

As an example of alternative testing approaches, consider an important control in virtually every organization.

> The organization requires a credit review and specific approval for all customers that are granted credit, and the amount of credit for any one company is limited by customer policy, which is based on financial health of the customer, past collection experience, and current credit rating of the customer.

Three approaches that an auditor might consider in testing the control include:

1. Take a sample of customer orders and trace the customer orders through the system to determine whether (a) there was proper review of credit and (b) credit authorization or denial was proper.
2. Take a sample of recorded items (accounts receivable) and trace back to the credit approval process to determine that it was performed appropriately.
3. Use a computer audit program to read all accounts receivable and develop a printout of all account balances that exceed their credit authorization.

Clearly, there are different costs and advantages associated with each of these three methods. The third method is dependent on proper input of the credit limits into the computer system. If there are no exceptions, the auditor could infer that the control is working even though the auditor did not directly test the control. This approach is cost effective, but it requires an inference about the control and covers only the operation of the controls related to the current account balances. The first method is the most effective because it not only requires that the auditor look at documentary evidence but that the auditor determine that the control did work effectively—it led to the correct conclusion, to either deny or provide credit. This method requires documentation of all credit applications and purchase orders and is based on audit sampling (not an examination of all transactions), whereas the third method was a 100% evaluation of each item currently recorded. The second method (sample from recorded items) can provide evidence on whether there was proper credit approval for all items that are presently recorded. However, it does not provide evidence as to whether other items should have been approved for credit, but had not been approved.

All three methods provide relevant evidence to the controls related to credit approval. Which one is the most appropriate? Auditors have to make decisions like this on every engagement. It seems trite to say "it depends," but the right choice does depend on the risk associated with the engagement, the auditor's experience with the credit level set by the organization (in other words, the credit approval level seems appropriate), the auditor's assessment of the control environment, the auditor's assessment of the quality of controls surrounding the computer applications, and the overall cost of the audit procedure. If other controls are effective and risk is low, the auditor will most likely use the third approach because (a) it is the least costly and (b) it tests 100% of the recorded population. The auditor might reason further that the major risk is overstatement of accounts receivable through bad credit. The auditor is not very concerned about customers who were turned down for credit; on the other hand, management, in its assessment, might

EXHIBIT **5.10**	Types of Controls and Possible Tests of Controls

Types of Controls	**Possible Tests of Controls**
Computerized controls	**Objective:** *Determine whether there have been changes to important computer applications during the year.*
	• Determine if there are changes in the computer program. If there are, test the integrity of the controls after the changes (inspection of relevant documentation and reperformance of control).
	• Consider submitting test transactions through the system to determine that it is working properly (reperformance of control).
	• Take a random sample of transactions and determine that (a) key controls are operating and (b) processing is complete (reperformance of control).
	• Review exception reports to determine that (a) proper exceptions are being noted and that (b) exceptions go to authorized personnel and there is adequate follow-up for proper processing (inspection of relevant documentation).
Manual controls	**Objective:** *Determine whether there is documented evidence that a control is operating effectively.*
Authorizations	• Take a sample of transactions and examine evidence supporting that the controls are working. For example, review a document or a computer printout indicating proper approval (inspection of relevant documentation).
Reconciliations	• Take a sample of reconciliations to determine that (a) they were performed by an authorized person and that (b) they were performed properly (inspection of relevant documentation and reperformance of control).
Reviews for unusual transactions	• Review documentation of selected transactions to determine whether they were properly authorized and recorded in the correct time period (inspection of relevant documentation).
	• Take a sample of reports that management uses to identify unusual transactions. Review to determine (a) that they are used regularly and (b) that unusual items are identified and investigated further (inspection of relevant documentation).
Controls over adjusting entries	**Objective:** *Determine whether there is documented evidence that there are controls over adjusting entries, including documentation that identifies (a) the reason and support for the adjustment and (b) the authorization of the adjustment.*
	• Take a sample of adjusting entries and review to determine that (a) there is supporting documentation for the entry, (b) the entry is appropriate, (c) the entry is made to the correct accounts, and (d) the entry was properly authorized (inspection of relevant documentation).
	• Give special attention to significant entries made near year-end (inquiry of management and inspection of relevant documentation).
Controls over accounting estimates	**Objective:** *Determine whether there is documented evidence of the controls over the estimate. Further, the auditor should determine that controls are sufficient to ensure that (a) the estimate is made based on accurate data, (b) the process of making the estimate is performed consistently, and (c) the model is updated for changing economic or business conditions. For example, estimates of a health-care liability should be updated for changes in the trend of health-care costs and required employee deductibles and co-pays.*
	• Review the process, noting that:
	• All entries are properly authorized (inspection of relevant documentation).
	• There are controls to ensure that estimates are updated for current market or economic conditions (inquiry of management and inspection of relevant documentation).
	• There is evidence that data used to make the estimates come from reliable sources (inquiry of management and inspection of relevant documentation).

The Need for Performing and Considering the Results of Tests of Controls

AUDITING IN **PRACTICE**

The PCAOB performs periodic inspections of audit firms that conduct audits of public companies. Following are excerpts from an inspection report, indicating that either the appropriate tests of controls had not been performed or the implications of the tests of controls were not reflected in the substantive procedures performed. A quality audit would require that such procedures be performed.

"The Firm failed to perform sufficient procedures to test the design and operating effectiveness of two important review controls on which it relied in evaluating internal controls over a number of significant accounts, including revenue, accounts receivable, inventory, and certain accruals."

"Further, for some Level 3 financial instruments, the Firm concluded that it did not need to change the nature, timing, and extent of its procedures, notwithstanding certain issues that came to the Firm's attention regarding controls related to the valuation of these instruments."

"The Firm failed to sufficiently test controls over the issuer's revenue recognition for certain revenue arrangements, as the Firm focused its testing on verifying that the control activity had occurred without evaluating its effectiveness, including its level of precision. Further, in certain instances, the Firm performed procedures related to the issuer's transaction processes but failed to test controls over those processes."

prefer to test the control by sampling from all customer orders because they do not want valid customers to be turned down for credit.

While the auditor has various options when testing controls, an important point is that the auditor has to perform tests of controls if the auditor plans to rely on those controls for the financial statement audit. Further, the auditor has to consider the results of tests of controls when designing substantive procedures. These points are highlighted in the *Auditing in Practice* feature "The Need for Performing and Considering the Results of Tests of Controls."

Testing the Operating Effectiveness of the Control Environment, Risk Assessment, Information and Communication, and Monitoring Components

Auditors are often most comfortable testing control activities. However, similar to management's testing described in *Chapter 3*, the auditor tests the relevant principles of the other internal control components, including control environment, risk assessment, information and communication, and monitoring. For example, the auditor can test commitment to integrity and ethical values (Committee of Sponsoring Organizations (COSO) Principle 1) through first-hand knowledge of the client's attitude toward "pushing the accounting boundaries." As part of testing the risk assessment component, the auditor might test COSO Principle 6 ("The organization specifies objectives with sufficient clarity to enable the identification and assessment of risks relating to objectives."); this can be done by reviewing documentation of the organization's objectives. In testing the information and communication component, the auditor might inquire of personnel and review relevant documentation indicating how the organization internally communicates information, including objectives and responsibilities for internal control (COSO Principle 14). An important principle of the monitoring component is that the organization communicates internal control deficiencies in a timely manner to those parties responsible for taking corrective action (COSO Principle 17). Reviewing appropriate documentation and inquiring of appropriate personnel could provide audit evidence on the extent to which this principle is operating effectively.

Considering the Results of Tests of Controls

The auditor considers the results of the tests of controls before finalizing decisions about substantive procedures. For the financial statement audit, there are two potential outcomes, with associated alternative courses of action:

1. If control deficiencies are identified, assess those deficiencies to determine whether the preliminary control risk assessment should be modified (should control risk be increased from low to high?), and document the implications for substantive procedures (should the substantive procedures be modified?).

2. If no control deficiencies are identified, assess whether the preliminary control risk assessment is still appropriate, determine the extent that controls can provide evidence on the accuracy of account balances, and determine planned substantive audit procedures. The substantive testing in this situation will be less than what is required in circumstances where deficiencies in internal control were identified.

The results of the tests of controls will allow the auditor to determine how much assurance about the reliability of account balances can be obtained from the effective operation of controls. Using the previous analogy of accumulating a box of evidence, the auditor needs to determine if evidence from tests of operating effectiveness of controls can be used to partially fill the evidence box. Organizations with strong internal controls should require less substantive testing of account balances since more assurance is being obtained from internal controls. Within any audit, that level of assurance will vary across accounts, disclosures, and assertions. Even if the auditor can fill a box with a lot of evidence from tests of controls, for most accounts the auditor also needs to add some evidence from substantive procedures to the box.

Additional Considerations for an Integrated Audit   In an integrated audit, results of the tests of controls also have important implications for the auditor's opinion on internal control over financial reporting. The auditor evaluates the severity of each identified control deficiency to determine whether the deficiencies, individually or in combination, are material weaknesses. If any control deficiencies are severe enough to be considered material weaknesses, the auditor's report on internal control should describe the material weaknesses and include an opinion indicating that internal control over financial reporting is not effective.

Summary of Audit Decisions Prior to Determining Substantive Procedures

The activities in Phases II and III of the audit opinion formulation process are important to determining the substantive procedures that need to be performed as a basis for the audit opinion on the financial statements.

Exhibit 5.11 provides a summary overview of important audit activities and decisions leading up to the performance of substantive procedures. The process begins with identifying significant account balances and disclosures and their relevant assertions. For most organizations, the significant accounts and disclosures are obvious and include accounts such as revenue, cost of goods sold, inventory, receivables, and accounts payable. As part of identifying significant accounts and disclosures and their relevant assertions, the auditor identifies the types of risk that could cause a material misstatement to occur. The auditor should understand the controls that the client has implemented to address those risks of material misstatement. If the auditor plans to rely on those controls, the auditor should test their operating effectiveness. The results of these tests will influence the planned substantive procedures.

EXHIBIT **5.11**

Overview of Audit Decisions Leading up to Decisions About Substantive Procedures for the Financial Statement Audit

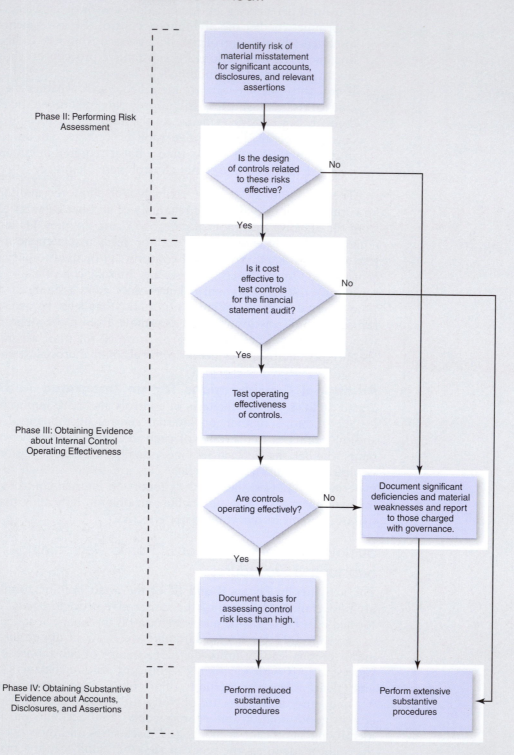

Phase II: Performing Risk Assessment

Phase III: Obtaining Evidence about Internal Control Operating Effectiveness

Phase IV: Obtaining Substantive Evidence about Accounts, Disclosures, and Assertions

Identify risk of material misstatement for significant accounts, disclosures, and relevant assertions

Is the design of controls related to these risks effective?

No

Yes

Is it cost effective to test controls for the financial statement audit?

No

Yes

Test operating effectiveness of controls.

Are controls operating effectively?

No

Yes

Document significant deficiencies and material weaknesses and report to those charged with governance.

Document basis for assessing control risk less than high.

Perform reduced substantive procedures

Perform extensive substantive procedures

As an example, assume the auditor determines that a mid-sized public company has a heightened risk of material misstatement because the controller is not competent in addressing complex accounting issues. As a matter of policy, the company decided to mitigate the risks by (a) not engaging in complex business transactions and by (b) minimizing the percentage of management compensation that is directly attributed to reported profit. The auditor further reviews the revenue accounting process and determines that there are control activities designed to (a) prevent unauthorized transactions, (b) assure that revenue is recorded only when earned, and (c) require that all unusual contracts be reviewed and approved by the chief executive officer (CEO). Further, because there is a risk of management override, the controller develops a list of unusual contracts to be reviewed with the chair of the audit committee and the lead director. Thus, while there is a heightened risk of material misstatement due to the lack of competency of the controller, the organization has controls designed to mitigate the risks to the financial statements. If the auditor assesses the design of these controls as effective, the auditor should test their operating effectiveness. However, even if the controls are designed and operating effectively, the auditor may still have concerns about the residual risk of misstatements associated with revenue recognition because that process is prone to misstatement related to poor accounting judgments. The auditor may respond by planning and performing more, and more rigorous, substantive procedures for revenue and receivables. For example, the auditor might extensively review and follow up on unusual transactions near year-end and might examine unusual sales contracts as part of the substantive tests of the account balance. The auditor may also choose to increase the sample size of confirmations sent to the client's customers.

LO 11 Discuss audit activities in Phase IV of the audit opinion formulation process.

Phase IV—Obtaining Substantive Evidence About Accounts, Disclosures, and Assertions

Much of what most people think of as auditing—the testing of account balances—occurs in Phase IV. As illustrated in *Exhibit 5.11*, the information gathered in Phases II and III influences the substantive procedures the auditor will perform. However, as described in the *Auditing in Practice* feature "Dual-Purpose Tests" some audit efficiencies can result if the auditor performs substantive procedures at the same time as performing tests of controls.

Performing Substantive Procedures

The auditor performs substantive procedures for the relevant assertions of each significant account and disclosure, regardless of the assessed level of control risk. These procedures can include both substantive analytical procedures and tests of details of account balances. Substantive analytical procedures are optional, whereas tests of details would be necessary for significant accounts and disclosures. As indicated in the *Auditing in Practice* feature

Dual-Purpose Tests

In some situations, the auditor might perform a substantive procedure concurrently with a test of a control, if both are relevant to that assertion; this is called a **dual-purpose test**. The auditor should design dual-purpose tests to achieve the objectives of both the test of the control and the substantive procedure. Also, when performing a dual-purpose test, the auditor should evaluate the results of the test in forming conclusions about both the assertion and the effectiveness of the control being tested. Dual-purpose testing can be an efficient way to audit some assertions.

Not Performing Sufficient Appropriate Substantive Audit Procedures Leads to Low Audit Quality

AUDITING IN PRACTICE

The PCAOB performs periodic inspections of audit firms that conduct audits of public companies. Following are excerpts from inspection reports indicating that sufficient appropriate substantive audit procedures had not been performed. A quality audit requires that such procedures be performed.

"The Firm failed to perform sufficient substantive procedures to test a number of significant accounts, including revenue, accounts receivable, inventory, and certain accruals...."

"The Firm failed to review contracts or perform other substantive procedures, beyond inquiry of management, to test the completeness of deferred sales and the completeness and accuracy of adjustments to revenue for promotional and rebate allowances."

"The Firm failed to sufficiently test the valuation of accounts receivable and net revenue."

"The Firm failed to perform sufficient procedures to test the issuer's evaluation of possible other-than-temporary impairment ('OTTI') of its securities. Specifically, the Firm failed to test whether the issuer had subjected to an evaluation of OTTI all securities that should have been subjected to such an evaluation and failed to test the assumptions and calculations used in this evaluation."

"In this audit, the Firm failed to perform sufficient procedures to evaluate the reasonableness of a significant assumption management used to calculate the gain on the sale of a business."

"Not Performing Sufficient Appropriate Substantive Audit Procedures Leads to Low Audit Quality," a failure to perform sufficient substantive procedures is considered an audit deficiency, indicative of a low-quality audit.

In determining appropriate substantive procedures, the auditor considers (a) the source of potential misstatement and (b) the extent and type of potential misstatement. Consider the typical entries into accounts receivable, including the related allowance account, as follows:

Accounts Receivable

Previous balance	Cash receipts
Revenue (sales)	Write-offs
Adjustments	Adjustments

Allowance for Uncollectible Accounts

Write-offs	Previous balance
	Current provision

Note that multiple processes affect the account balances. Some of the processes contain subjectivity and are considered high risk—for example, determining how much of a receivable balance will ultimately be uncollectible, while others are less subjective and more routine such as recording cash receipts.

- *Revenue*—The processing of routine transactions is usually computerized with controls built into the process. However, because of recurring evidence that companies that want to boost reported sales and/or earnings often do so by overriding controls related to the recording of revenue, the SEC has designated revenue recognition as high risk, requiring the auditor to do some direct tests of account balances, including receivables. These problematic overrides often occur in conjunction with special contracts or unusual shipments near the end of the year.

- *Cash receipts*—The processing of cash receipts is usually automated with implementation of controls. If an organization has effective segregation of duties, the likelihood of misstatement is relatively small.
- *Current provision for uncollectible accounts*—Most companies rely heavily on previous experience in making these estimates. Recent SEC cases indicate that the allowance is often subject to misstatements based on (a) inaccurate or nonrelevant data fed into the model and (b) motivation of management to meet earnings goals and therefore allowing subjectivity and bias to enter into the estimate.
- *Write-offs*—The determination of when to write off account balances is subjective.
- *Adjustments*—Adjustments, other than those noted previously, should be rare. If there are significant adjustments, the auditor should test the process or the adjustments to determine the appropriate balance.

Similar analyses will be made for other related accounts and will incorporate the following concepts:

- Assertions affected by highly subjective estimates usually require direct tests of the account balances.
- Nonstandard and large adjusting entries should be reviewed and tested using appropriate substantive procedures.
- The size of the account (materiality) influences, but does not totally dictate, the substantive procedures that should be performed.
- The extent and results of control testing performed by management, as well as the control testing performed by the auditor, will influence the substantive procedures of the account balance to be performed.
- The evidence the auditor has from risk assessment procedures and tests of controls influences the substantive procedures to be performed.
- The existence of other corroborating tests of the account balance, such as the knowledge gained from testing related accounts, affects substantive procedures to be performed.

Exhibit 5.12 contains a summary of the effects of some of these evidence factors on substantive procedures.

While performing substantive procedures, the auditor may identify misstatements—both material and immaterial—in the financial statements. The auditor accumulates a list of any identified misstatements for consideration prior to determining the appropriate audit opinion to issue.

EXHIBIT 5.12   Factors Affecting Substantive Procedures to Be Performed

Factor	If Auditor Assessment Is:	Effect on Extent/Nature of Substantive Procedures
Subjectivity of accounting process	High	More/more rigorous
Materiality of account balance	High	More/more rigorous
Effectiveness of internal control as assessed by management and the auditor	Internal controls are effective	Less/less rigorous

Example: Effect of Nature of Misstatements on Audit Procedures

Ultimately, the auditor considers which account balances might be misstated and how they might be misstated. We demonstrate the audit process using the accounts receivable example. Assume the following scenario. Consistent with the relevant professional guidance, the auditor has assessed revenue to be high risk, even though management has concluded that internal controls over transactions processing are effective. A preliminary analytical review of the last quarter (conducted as part of the risk assessment procedures) led to the identification of a large number of sales with nonstandard contractual terms. After reading a sample of the sales contracts and testing controls, the auditor concludes that there is an unacceptable level of residual risk in the revenue account. The auditor identified a number of ways in which the account could be misstated. For example, sales might:

- Be recorded in the wrong period
- Contain unusual rights-of-return provisions that have not been accounted for correctly
- Contain terms that are more consistent with a consignment rather than a sale
- Be concentrated in a very few customers, many of whom are international customers and may have different credit risks than most other customers.

Given the identified risks, the auditor decides to expand substantive audit procedures of the recorded transactions that have unusual sales terms and to focus on the existence and valuation assertions. The auditor has decided not to perform any substantive analytical procedures; the auditor will only perform substantive tests of details. In order to bring the residual risk to an acceptable level, the auditor gathers substantive evidence on the revenue (and receivables) associated with the unusual contracts and identifies sales that have these special terms. In testing receivables, the auditor decides to concentrate accounts receivable tests on a combination of large accounts plus all of those that have unusual sales terms. Confirmations will be sent to both of those groups, with follow-up where confirmations are not returned, or where the auditor might suspect the validity of the contract, the customer, or the possibility of **side agreements** (an agreement made between the organization and its customer that includes agreements made outside of publicly known contracts) affecting the contracts.

LO 12 Discuss audit activities in Phase V of the audit opinion formulation process.

Phase V—Completing the Audit and Making Reporting Decisions

In Phase V, the auditor (a) completes various review and communication activities and (b) makes a decision about what type(s) of opinion(s) should be issued. Examples of review and communication activities include assessing detected misstatements and identified control deficiencies, reviewing the adequacy of financial statement disclosures, performing final analytical review procedures, communicating with the audit committee and management about identified control deficiencies, and performing an engagement quality review.

After completing the required review and communication activities, the auditor then decides on the appropriate opinion(s) to issue. In an integrated audit, the auditor issues an opinion on both the financial statements and internal control. The opinions can be issued in one report or in two separate reports. However, if separate reports are issued, each report must refer to the other. In *Chapter 1* we presented Ford's combined audit report, which included an unqualified opinion on the financial statements and an unqualified opinion on internal controls. If the auditor has reservations about the fair presentation of the financial statements, the audit opinion on the financial statements would be modified and expanded to explain the nature of the auditor's reservations. If the auditor has reservations about the effectiveness of the client's internal controls, the auditor would issue an adverse opinion on internal controls. *Exhibit 5.13* provides an example of an audit

EXHIBIT 5.13   Example of Adverse Opinion on Internal Control and Unqualified Opinion on the Financial Statements (bold emphasis added in report)

REPORT OF INDEPENDENT REGISTERED PUBLIC ACCOUNTING FIRM

To the Board of Directors and Stockholders of Diamond Foods, Inc.

In our opinion, the accompanying consolidated balance sheet as of July 31, 2013 and the related consolidated statements of operations, comprehensive income (loss), stockholders' equity, and cash flows for the year then ended present fairly, in all material respects, the financial position of Diamond Foods, Inc. and its subsidiaries at July 31, 2013, and the results of their operations and their cash flows for the year then ended in conformity with accounting principles generally accepted in the United States of America. **Also in our opinion, the Company did not maintain, in all material respects, effective internal control over financial reporting as of July 31, 2013, based on criteria established in *Internal Control — Integrated Frame work* issued by the Committee of Sponsoring Organizations of the Treadway Commission (COSO) because material weaknesses in internal control over financial reporting related to the accounting for complex and non-routine transactions and due to certain key accounting personnel who have the ability to prepare and post journal entries without an independent review by someone without the ability to prepare and post journal entries existed as of that date.** A material weakness is a deficiency, or a combination of deficiencies, in internal control over financial reporting, such that there is a reasonable possibility that a material misstatement of the annual or interim financial statements will not be prevented or detected on a timely basis. The material weaknesses referred to above are described in Management's Report on Internal Control Over Financial Reporting appearing under Item 9A. **We considered these material weaknesses in determining the nature, timing, and extent of audit tests applied in our audit of the July 31, 2013 consolidated financial statements, and our opinion regarding the effectiveness of the Company's internal control over financial reporting does not affect our opinion on those consolidated financial statements.** The Company's management is responsible for these financial statements, for maintaining effective internal control over financial reporting and for its assessment of the effectiveness of internal control over financial reporting included in management's report referred to above. Our responsibility is to express opinions on these financial statements and on the Company's internal control over financial reporting based on our integrated audit.

We conducted our audit in accordance with the standards of the Public Company Accounting Oversight Board (United States). Those standards require that we plan and perform the audit to obtain reasonable assurance about whether the financial statements are free of material misstatement and whether effective internal control over financial reporting was maintained in all material respects. Our audit of the financial statements included examining, on a test basis, evidence supporting the amounts and disclosures in the financial statements, assessing the accounting principles used and significant estimates made by management, and evaluating the overall financial statement presentation. Our audit of internal control over financial reporting included obtaining an understanding of internal control over financial reporting, assessing the risk that a material weakness exists, and testing and evaluating the design and operating effectiveness of internal control based on the assessed risk. Our audit also included performing such other procedures as we considered necessary in the circumstances. We believe that our audit provides a reasonable basis for our opinions.

A company's internal control over financial reporting is a process designed to provide reasonable assurance regarding the reliability of financial reporting and the preparation of financial statements for external purposes in accordance with generally accepted accounting principles. A company's internal control over financial reporting includes those policies and procedures that (i) pertain to the maintenance of records that, in reasonable detail, accurately and fairly reflect the transactions and dispositions of the assets of the company; (ii) provide reasonable assurance that transactions are recorded as necessary to permit preparation of financial statements in accordance with generally accepted accounting principles, and that receipts and expenditures of the company are being made only in accordance with authorizations of management and directors of the company; and (iii) provide reasonable assurance regarding prevention or timely detection of unauthorized acquisition, use, or disposition of the company's assets that could have a material effect on the financial statements.

Because of its inherent limitations, internal control over financial reporting may not prevent or detect misstatements. Also, projections of any evaluation of effectiveness to future periods are subject to the risk that controls may become inadequate because of changes in conditions, or that the degree of compliance with the policies or procedures may deteriorate.

/s/ PricewaterhouseCoopers LLP

San Francisco, California

October 9, 2013

report with an unqualified opinion on the financial statements and an adverse opinion on internal control. Important aspects of *Exhibit 5.13* related to the opinion on internal controls include the following:

- The report describes the material weaknesses but does not discuss any actions being taken by management to remediate the weaknesses.
- The report does not discuss whether the control weaknesses were first identified by management or by the auditor.
- The report recognizes the integrated nature of the audit in that the auditors considered the identified material weaknesses when planning the financial statement audit.

SUMMARY AND NEXT STEPS

This chapter has presented a detailed overview of the activities you will be performing throughout the audit opinion formulation process. These activities are based on guidance provided in the professional auditing standards. Adhering to the relevant auditing standards and performing the required activities in a professional manner are important to audit quality. Most of what occurs during the audit opinion formulation process is directed toward obtaining evidence to support the audit opinion(s) that will be issued. The next chapter provides you with additional discussion on important aspects of audit evidence.

SIGNIFICANT TERMS

Accounting cycle Recording and processing transactions that affect a group of related accounts. The cycle begins when a transaction occurs and ends when it is recorded in the financial statements.

Audit documentation The record of audit procedures performed, relevant audit evidence obtained, and conclusions the auditor reached (terms such as *working papers* or *workpapers* are also sometimes used).

Audit evidence Information used by the auditor in arriving at the conclusions on which the auditor's opinion is based.

Appropriate audit evidence The measure of the quality of audit evidence (i.e., its relevance and reliability in providing support for the conclusions on which the auditor's opinion is based).

Audit procedures Procedures designed to obtain audit evidence to support the audit opinion(s). Three categories of procedures include risk assessment procedures, tests of controls, and substantive procedures (including substantive analytical procedures and tests of details).

Audit program An audit document that lists the audit procedures to be followed in gathering audit evidence and helps those in charge of the audit to monitor the progress and supervise the work.

Control risk The risk that a misstatement that could occur in an assertion about a class of transaction, account balance, or disclosure and that could be material, either individually or when aggregated with other misstatements, will not be prevented, or detected and corrected, on a timely basis by the organization's internal control. Control risk is a function of the effectiveness of the design and operation of internal control.

Controls reliance audit   An audit that includes tests of controls and substantive procedures.

Dual-purpose test   A substantive test and a related test of a relevant control that are performed concurrently, for example, a substantive test of sales transactions performed concurrently with a test of controls over those transactions.

Inherent risk   The susceptibility of an assertion about a class of transaction, account balance, or disclosure to a misstatement that could be material, either individually or when aggregated with other misstatements, before consideration of any related controls.

Risk assessment procedure   A procedure performed by the auditor to obtain information for identifying and assessing the risks of material misstatement in the financial statements whether due to error or fraud. Risk assessment procedures by themselves do not provide sufficient, appropriate evidence on which to base an audit opinion but are used for purposes of planning the audit.

Side agreement   An agreement made between the organization and its customer that includes agreements made outside of publicly known contracts.

Substantive audit   An audit that includes substantive procedures and does not include tests of controls.

Substantive procedure   An audit procedure designed to detect material misstatements at the assertion level. Substantive procedures comprise tests of details and substantive analytical procedures.

Sufficient audit evidence   The measure of the quantity of audit evidence.

Test of controls   An audit procedure designed to evaluate the operating effectiveness of controls in preventing, or detecting and correcting, material misstatements, typically at the assertion level.

TRUE/FALSE QUESTIONS

5-1   **LO 1**   Auditors of U.S. public companies should follow the PCAOB's auditing standards.

5-2   **LO 1**   There is not much commonality among the auditing standards set by the PCAOB, AICPA, and IAASB.

5-3   **LO 2**   The ten standards underlying the PCAOB's auditing standards fall within four different categories.

5-4   **LO 2**   The purpose of an audit is to enhance the degree of confidence that users can place on the financial statements.

5-5   **LO 3**   An important aspect of the audit opinion formulation process is the client's responsibilities for internal control over financial reporting and the financial statements.

5-6 **LO 3** The audit opinion formulation process is described as consisting of five phases.

5-7 **LO 4** The cycle approach to auditing provides a way for breaking the audit up into manageable components.

5-8 **LO 4** Within a particular cycle, the auditor focuses on the flow of transactions within that cycle, including how transactions are initiated, authorized, recorded, and reported.

5-9 **LO 5** The completeness assertion is typically the more relevant assertion for assets.

5-10 **LO 5** Within each cycle, the audit is designed to test management assertions.

5-11 **LO 6** Risk assessment procedures alone provide sufficient appropriate audit evidence on which to base an audit opinion.

5-12 **LO 6** The auditor's selection of audit procedures depends on the accounts and assertions being tested.

5-13 **LO 7** Auditors are encouraged, but not required, to prepare audit documentation.

5-14 **LO 7** Audit checklists and audit programs are examples of audit documentation.

5-15 **LO 8** Auditors are not required to perform audits for any organization that asks.

5-16 **LO 8** For an audit firm to accept a client, management needs to agree to provide the auditor with access to all relevant information, such as records, documentation, and so on, and unrestricted access to persons within the organization.

5-17 **LO 9** During risk assessment, the auditor focuses on understanding the risks of all misstatements in the financial statements and related disclosures.

5-18 **LO 9** The auditor assesses the risk of material misstatement at only the assertion level.

5-19 **LO 10** The auditor is expected to obtain evidence about the operating effectiveness of internal control on all audits.

5-20 **LO 10** When testing controls, the auditor tests only transaction controls.

5-21 **LO 11** The auditor is expected to perform substantive procedures for each relevant assertion of each significant account and disclosure.

5-22 **LO 11** Substantive procedures include substantive analytical procedures and tests of details.

5-23 **LO 12** Once the auditor completes the substantive procedures in Phase IV, the auditor is in a position to issue the audit opinion.

5-24 **LO 12** If the auditor issues an opinion on the client's internal controls and the client's financial statements, the auditor is required to issue two separate reports.

MULTIPLE-CHOICE QUESTIONS

5-25 **LO 1** Which of the following statements is correct regarding the setting of auditing standards in the United States?
   a. The AICPA is responsible for setting auditing standards for audits of nonpublic entities.
   b. The PCAOB is responsible for setting auditing standards for audits of public companies.

c. The AICPA is responsible for setting auditing standards for audits of both public and nonpublic companies.

d. The SEC sets auditing standards for auditors of public and nonpublic companies.

e. Both (a) and (b) are correct.

5-26 **LO 1** The following describes a situation in which an auditor has to determine the most appropriate standards to follow. The audited company is headquartered in Paris but has substantial operations within the United States (60% of all operations) and has securities registered with the SEC and is traded on the New York Stock Exchange (NYSE). The company uses International Financial Reporting Standards (IFRS) for its accounting framework. What would be the most appropriate set of auditing standards to follow?

a. PCAOB.

b. Either PCAOB or AICPA.

c. Either IAASB or AICPA.

d. Only the AICPA standards would be appropriate.

5-27 **LO 2** Which of the following is not required as part of the field-work standards?

a. An audit should be properly planned and supervised.

b. Auditors should develop an understanding of the client's controls as an important prerequisite to developing specific audit tests.

c. Auditors should obtain sufficient appropriate audit evidence by performing audit procedures to provide a reasonable basis for the audit opinion being provided.

d. All of the above are required by the fieldwork standards.

5-28 **LO 2** Which of the following is included as part of the AICPA's principles governing an audit?

a. Auditors need to obtain a high level of assurance that the financial statements are free of all misstatements.

b. An audit has inherent limitations such that the auditor cannot provide absolute assurance about whether the financial statements are free of misstatement.

c. Auditors need to maintain professional skepticism only on audits where there is a high risk of material misstatement.

d. All of the above are included as part of the AICPA's principles governing an audit.

5-29 **LO 3** Which of the following statements is true about the audit opinion formulation process presented in this chapter?

a. The audit opinion formulation process is significantly different for the financial statement only audit and the integrated audit.

b. The audit opinion formulation process is based on the premise that management has responsibility to prepare the financial statements and maintain internal control over financial reporting.

c. The audit opinion formulation process comprises seven phases.

d. All of the above are true statements regarding the audit opinion formulation process.

5-30 **LO 3** Which of the following activities is not part of the activities within the audit opinion formulation process?

a. The auditor develops a common understanding of the audit engagement with the client.

b. The auditor determines the appropriate nonaudit consulting services to provide to the client.

c. The auditor identifies and assesses risks of material misstatements and then responds to those identified risks.

d. The auditor determines the appropriate audit opinion(s) to issue.

5-31 **LO 4** Which of the following is a reason that the auditor uses an accounting cycle approach when performing an audit?

a. The accounting cycle approach allows the auditor to focus exclusively on either the balance sheet or the income statement.

b. COSO internal control components are based on the accounting cycles.

c. The accounting cycles provide a convenient way to break the audit up into manageable pieces.

d. The auditor needs to be able to provide an opinion related to each accounting cycle.

5-32 **LO 4** Which of the following accounts would not be included in the Acquisition and Payment for Long-Lived Assets Cycle?

a. Revenue.

b. Depreciation expense.

c. Gain on disposal.

d. Equipment.

5-33 **LO 5** Which of the following is not a management assertion?

a. Completeness.

b. Existence.

c. Rights and obligations.

d. Valuation.

e. They are all management assertions.

5-34 **LO 5** Which management assertion addresses whether the components of the financial statements are properly classified, described, and disclosed?

a. Completeness.

b. Existence.

c. Rights and obligations.

d. Presentation and disclosure.

e. None of the above address whether the components of the financial statements are properly classified, described, and disclosed.

5-35 **LO 6** Audit procedures fall into three categories. Which of the following is not a category of audit procedures?

a. Risk assessment procedures.

b. Tests of risks.

c. Tests of controls.

d. Substantive procedures.

5-36 **LO 6** Which of the following is a true statement regarding audit evidence and audit procedures?

a. The auditor has a responsibility to design and perform audit procedures to obtain sufficient appropriate audit evidence.

b. Inquiry is a type of audit procedure that typically does not require the auditor to perform additional procedures.

c. The audit procedures that are performed during an audit are summarized in a document referred to as an audit engagement letter.

d. Risk assessment procedures by themselves provide sufficient appropriate evidence on which to base an audit opinion.

5-37 **LO 7**   Which of the following information should be included in audit documentation?

a. Procedures performed.

b. Audit evidence examined.

c. Conclusions reached with respect to relevant financial statement assertions.

d. All of the above should be included.

5-38 **LO 7**   Which of the following statements is false regarding audit documentation?

a. An audit program is an example of audit documentation.

b. The only purpose of audit documentation is to provide evidence that the audit was planned and performed in accordance with auditing standards.

c. Audit documentation helps facilitate internal and external inspections of completed audits.

d. Audit documentation is required on all audit engagements.

5-39 **LO 8**   Which of the following is a precondition for an audit?

a. Management has used an acceptable financial reporting framework.

b. Management has used U.S. GAAP for its financial reporting framework.

c. Management cannot have any responsibility for designing internal controls.

d. All of the following are preconditions.

5-40 **LO 8**   Which of the following statements is true regarding client acceptance and continuance decisions?

a. The preconditions for accepting an audit are required for new clients but not for existing clients.

b. Audit firms must conduct audits for any public companies requesting an audit.

c. A precondition of accepting a client is that management acknowledges and understands its responsibilities related to the preparation of the company's financial statements.

d. Management needs to protect its internal documents from review by the auditor.

5-41 **LO 9**   Which of the following statements is correct regarding the design of controls related to credit limits?

a. The effectiveness of the control design is contingent on the credit manager's process for establishing and reviewing credit limits.

b. Because the process of establishing credit limits is fairly time consuming, the control should be designed so that the marketing manager has the ability to approve sales on an ad hoc basis while waiting for the credit approval.

c. The control should be designed so that the sales manager has final approval regarding credit limits.

d. All are correct statements regarding the design of controls related to credit limits.

5-42 **LO 9**   Which of the following tests of controls would not typically be used in assessing control design effectiveness?

a. Inquiry.

b. Observation.

c. Inspection of documentation.

d. Reperformance.

5-43 **LO 10**   The auditor is testing the operating effectiveness of controls in the revenue cycle and notes the following: (a) the client does not regularly follow its credit policies; rather it often overrides the credit policy when divisional management needs to meet its performance goals; and (b) the sales manager has the ability to override the credit policy for important customers. Which of the following statements would be correct regarding an integrated audit of sales and receivables?

a. Based on the test of controls, the auditor would likely assess control risk as high.
b. The auditor would be able to perform less rigorous substantive procedures.
c. The auditor likely concluded that the controls were not effectively designed.
d. All of the above are correct statements.

5-44 **LO 10** Assume the auditor concludes the controls related to accounts receivable are operating effectively based on inquiry and other appropriate tests. Which of the following is a correct inference regarding the auditor's conclusion?

a. The auditor *will not* need to perform substantive procedures on the valuation of accounts receivable.
b. The auditor *could not* have concluded that the internal controls over credit were effective unless the auditor determined that the credit limits are updated for changed conditions.
c. The auditor does *not* need to confirm accounts receivable because the risk of a material misstatement of receivables is mitigated by the controls.
d. The auditor does *not* need to perform any more direct tests of the account balances if the auditor has tested the information technology general controls.

5-45 **LO 11** In performing substantive procedures, which of the following statements provides appropriate guidance to the auditor?

a. The auditor can perform both substantive analytical procedures and substantive tests of details.
b. The auditor should perform substantive procedures for all assertions of all financial statement accounts.
c. The auditor should perform more (or more rigorous) substantive procedures when control risk is low than when control risk is high.
d. All of the above statements provide appropriate guidance.

5-46 **LO 11** In which of the following scenarios is the auditor most likely to obtain more (or more rigorous) substantive evidence?

a. When subjectivity related to the assertion is low.
b. When controls are determined to be operating effectively.
c. When the account is immaterial.
d. When the design of controls is determined to be ineffective.

5-47 **LO 12** Which of the following procedures is least likely to be performed during Phase V of the audit opinion formulation process?

a. Assessment of misstatements detected during the performance of substantive procedures and tests of controls.
b. Performance of preliminary analytical review procedures.
c. Performance of an engagement quality review.
d. Determination of the appropriate audit opinion(s) to issue.

5-48 **LO 12** Which of the following statements is correct regarding the auditor's report on a public company's internal control over financial reporting?

a. The audit report will indicate whether it was the company or the auditor that initially identified the indicated material weakness.

b. The auditor must explicitly reference the criteria for evaluating internal control using, for example, the COSO framework.

c. The audit is performed in conjunction with the auditing standards promulgated by the AICPA's ASB.

d. The audit must report on whether management used the appropriate tools in its assessment of internal control over financial reporting.

REVIEW AND SHORT CASE QUESTIONS

INTERNATIONAL

NOTE: Completing Review and Short Case Questions does not require the student to reference additional resources and materials.

NOTE: For the remaining problems, we make special note of those addressing fraud, international issues, professional skepticism, and ethics.

5-49 `LO 1` Refer to *Exhibit 5.1*. Briefly describe the relevance of the following standard setters for auditors.
a. AICPA
b. PCAOB
c. IAASB

5-50 `LO 1` The PCAOB has the authority to set auditing standards for all audits of public companies registered in the United States. The AICPA continues to set auditing standards for nonpublic companies through its Auditing Standards Board (ASB).
a. What are the pros and cons of having the same audit standards for both public and nonpublic companies?
b. In what ways might you expect auditing standards for audits of nonpublic companies to differ from the standards for public companies? Identify three ways and state your rationale.

5-51 `LO 2` Ray, the owner of a small company, asked Holmes, CPA, to conduct an audit of the company's records. Ray told Holmes that the audit must be completed in time to submit audited financial statements to a bank as part of a loan application. Holmes immediately accepted the engagement and agreed to provide an auditor's report within three weeks. Ray agreed to pay Holmes a fixed fee plus a bonus if the loan was granted.

Holmes hired two accounting students to conduct the audit and spent several hours telling them exactly what to do. Holmes told the students not to spend time reviewing the controls but to concentrate on proving the mathematical accuracy of the ledger accounts and to summarize the data in the accounting records that support Ray's financial statements. The students followed Holmes' instructions and after two weeks gave Holmes the financial statements, which did not include footnotes because the company did not have any unusual transactions. Holmes reviewed the statements and prepared an unqualified auditor's report. The report, however, did not refer to GAAP or to the year-to-year application of such principles.

Briefly describe each of the ten standards included in the PCAOB guidance and indicate how the action(s) of Holmes resulted in a failure to comply with each standard.

5-52 `LO 2` Compare the ten generally accepted auditing standards currently used by the PCAOB with the AICPA's "Principles Governing an Audit in Accordance with Generally Accepted Auditing Standards."

5-53 `LO 3` Refer to *Exhibit 5.2*. What are the client responsibilities that are relevant to the auditor? How do those responsibilities affect the audit opinion formulation process?

5-54 `LO 3` Refer to *Exhibit 5.3*. List the phases of the audit opinion formulation process. What are the primary activities within each of the five phases?

5-55 **LO 4** Professional guidance indicates that revenue recognition should always be considered to be high risk in planning an audit of a company's financial statements.
a. Identify the activities that affect the revenue cycle.
b. Identify the financial statement accounts normally associated with the revenue cycle.

5-56 **LO 4** Refer to *Exhibit 5.4*. Identify typical accounting cycles not listed in *Exhibit 5.4* and list their associated accounts.

5-57 **LO 5** Refer to *Exhibit 5.5*. Assume that an organization asserts that it has $35 million in net accounts receivable. Using the assertions listed in *Exhibit 5.5*, describe specifically what management is asserting with respect to net accounts receivable.

5-58 **LO 6** Describe how auditing standards affect the design of audit programs.

5-59 **LO 6** Refer to *Exhibit 5.6*. What is an audit program? What information should an auditor gather before developing an audit program?

5-60 **LO 7** Define the term *audit documentation* and provide examples.

5-61 **LO 8** List the preconditions for an audit.

5-62 **LO 9** How do the sources of risk of misstatement in *Exhibit 5.7* help the auditor plan the audit?

FRAUD

5-63 **LO 9** Refer to the *Focus on Fraud* feature "Controls to Address Fraud Risk." When assessing control design effectiveness, what types of controls would an auditor expect a client to have in place to address fraud risk? Why are these controls important?

5-64 **LO 9** Refer to the *Auditing in Practice* feature "Documenting the Auditor's Understanding of an Organization's Internal Controls." What should an auditor document with respect to the design of controls? Why is this documentation important?

5-65 **LO 9** Refer to the *Auditing in Practice* feature "Weak Internal Control Design and Links to Substantive Audit Procedures." Explain how the auditor's preliminary assessment of control risk affects planned substantive audit procedures.

5-66 **LO 9** An important part of Phase II of the audit opinion formulation process is determining how to respond to identified risks of material misstatement. As indicated in *Exhibit 5.8*, the auditor might respond by modifying evidence decisions about the extent or nature of the substantive audit evidence to be collected. Using the box of evidence analogy, explain these responses to identified risks.

5-67 **LO 9** Segregation of duties is an important concept in internal control. However, this is often a challenge for smaller businesses because they do not have sufficient staff. Normally, the segregation of duties deficiencies identified here results in either a significant deficiency or a material weakness in internal control. For each segregation of duties deficiency identified as (1)–(6), complete the following three tasks:
a. Indicate the risk to financial reporting that is associated with the inadequacy of the segregation of duties.
b. Identify other controls that might mitigate the segregation of duties risks.
c. Identify possible tests of controls for the mitigating controls selected in (b).

The inadequate segregation of duty situations to be considered are as follows:

1. The same individual handles cash receipts, the bank reconciliation, and customer complaints.
2. The same person prepares billings to customers and also collects cash receipts and applies them to customer accounts.
3. The person who prepares billings to customers does not handle cash but does the monthly bank reconciliation, which, in turn, is reviewed by the controller.
4. The controller is responsible for making all accounting estimates and adjusting journal entries. The company does not have a chief financial officer (CFO) and has two clerks who report to the controller.
5. A start-up company has very few transactions, less than $1 million in revenue per year, and has only one accounting person. The company's transactions are not complex.
6. The company has one computer person who is responsible for running packaged software. The individual has access to the computer to update software and can also access records.

5-68 **LO 10** In a financial statement audit, what controls will an auditor test?

5-69 **LO 10** Refer to *Exhibit 5.9*. What controls might an auditor test related to the valuation assertion for the sales account?

5-70 **LO 10** A review of corporate failures as described in the financial press, such as the *Wall Street Journal,* suggests that the control environment is one of the major contributors to the failure. Often the tone at the top at the failed companies reflects a disdain for controls and an emphasis on accomplishing specific financial reporting objectives such as reporting increased profitability. How will the auditor's assessment of the operating effectiveness of the control environment affect the design and conduct of an audit? Consider both a positive and negative assessment.

5-71 **LO 10** Auditing standards indicate that if the preliminary control risk assessment is low, the auditor then gains assurance that the controls are operating effectively.
a. What is meant by testing the operating effectiveness of controls? How does an auditor decide which controls to test?
b. How is the auditor's assessment of control risk affected if a documented control procedure is not operating effectively? Explain the effect of such an assessment on substantive audit procedures.

ETHICS

5-72 **LO 10** An important principle of the control environment is the organization's commitment to ethics and integrity (COSO Principle 1). How might an auditor test the operating effectiveness of a client's commitment to ethics and integrity?

5-73 **LO 10** Is the auditor required to test the operating effectiveness of controls on every audit engagement? Explain.

5-74 **LO 10** What are the external auditor testing requirements of internal controls for:
a. Large, publicly held companies?
b. Nonpublic companies and small, publicly held companies?

5-75 **LO 10** When the auditor determines that controls are not operating effectively, the auditor needs to consider the kind of misstatements that could occur, how they might occur, and how the auditor would adjust substantive audit procedures. Assume that the authorization process for ordering inventory was found to contain a material weakness. Identify the accounts that could contain misstatements, how the misstatements might occur, and how the auditor would adjust substantive audit procedures because of the material weakness.

5-76 **LO 10** In analyzing the results of the tests of controls, there are two potential outcomes: (a) deficiencies are identified and (b) deficiencies are not identified. What are alternative courses of action for the financial statement audit associated with each of these alternative outcomes?

5-77 **LO 10** If a company's control risk is initially assessed as low, the auditor needs to gather evidence on the operating effectiveness of the controls. For each of the following control activities listed as (1)–(10), do the following two tasks:

a. Describe the test of control that the auditor would use to determine the operating effectiveness of the control.

b. Briefly describe how substantive tests of account balances should be modified if the auditor finds that the control is not working as planned. In doing so, indicate (a) what misstatement could occur because of the control deficiency, and (b) how the auditor's substantive tests should be expanded to test for the potential misstatement.

The control activities to be considered are as follows:

1. Credit approval by the credit department is required before salespersons accept any order of more than $15,000 and for all customers who have a past-due balance higher than $22,000.

2. All merchandise receipts are recorded on prenumbered receiving slips. The controller's department periodically accounts for the numerical sequence of the receiving slips.

3. Payments for goods received are made only by the accounts payable department on receipt of a vendor invoice, which is then matched for prices and quantities with approved purchase orders and receiving slips.

4. The accounts receivable bookkeeper is not allowed to issue credit memos or to approve the write-off of accounts.

5. Cash receipts are opened by a mail clerk, who prepares remittances to send to accounts receivable for recording. The clerk prepares a daily deposit slip, which is sent to the controller. Deposits are made daily by the controller.

6. Employees are added to the payroll master file by the payroll department only after receiving a written authorization from the personnel department.

7. The only individuals who have access to the payroll master file are the payroll department head and the payroll clerk responsible for maintaining the payroll file. Access to the file is controlled by computer passwords.

8. Edit tests built into the computerized payroll program prohibit the processing of weekly payroll hours in excess of fifty-three and prohibit the payment to an employee for more than three different job classifications during a one-week period.

9. Credit memos are issued to customers only on the receipt of merchandise or the approval of the sales department for adjustments.

10. A salesperson cannot approve a sales return or price adjustment that exceeds 6% of the cumulative sales for the year for

any one customer. The divisional sales manager must approve any subsequent approvals of adjustments for such a customer.

ETHICS

5-78 **LO 10**   The auditor of a public company in the retailing industry is planning an integrated audit. The company has approximately 260 retail stores, primarily in the southeastern United States.

a. Explain why an analysis of the company's control environment is important to planning the integrated audit.

b. The company claims that it has a strong control environment, including a culture of high integrity and ethics (COSO Principle 1), a commitment to financial reporting competencies (COSO Principle 4), and an independent, active, and knowledgeable board of directors (COSO Principle 2). For each of these principles, develop an audit program to gather evidence that these principles are operating effectively. In developing your answer, be sure to indicate the type of audit procedures to use.

5-79 **LO 10**   Refer to *Exhibit 5.10.* Assume that you are going to test computerized controls that your client has put in place. What is the important objective for you to consider when performing that testing? What are some possible tests of controls that you could perform? What are the audit implications if the controls are not working effectively?

5-80 **LO 10**   Assume that you are planning to test a client's reconciliation. You could test either by inspecting documentation of the reconciliation or by reperforming the reconciliation. What factors would cause you to choose reperformance instead of inspection of documentation?

FRAUD

5-81 **LO 10**   Assume that you want to test an entity-wide control related to the control environment. Specifically, you want to obtain evidence that the audit committee has periodic discussions about fraud. Recall that tests of controls include inquiry, observation, inspection of documentation, and reperformance of the control. Which approaches do you think would be used when testing this control relating to the control environment? Explain your answer.

5-82 **LO 10**   Refer to *Exhibit 5.11.* What are some of the key decisions that influence the substantive testing to be performed by the auditor?

5-83 **LO 11**   Refer to the *Auditing in Practice* feature "Dual-Purpose Tests." What is a dual-purpose test, and why might an auditor choose to perform a dual-purpose test?

5-84 **LO 11**   Refer to *Exhibit 5.12.* Explain how the factors in the first column affect the auditor's decision about substantive testing.

5-85 **LO 11**   What substantive procedures could an auditor use to determine that all purchases debited to a fixed asset account in the current year are properly valued?

5-86 **LO 11**   Audits of financial statements are designed to determine whether account balances are materially correct. Assume that your client is a construction company that has the following assets on its balance sheet:

- Construction equipment: $1,278,000
- Accumulated depreciation: $386,000
- Leased construction equipment: $550,000

a. Describe a substantive audit procedure that can used to determine that all leased equipment that should have been capitalized during the year was actually capitalized (as opposed to being treated as a lease expense).

b. The construction equipment account shows that the company purchased approximately $400,000 of new equipment this year. Identify a substantive audit procedure that will determine whether the equipment account was properly accounted for during the year.

c. Assuming the auditor determines the debits to construction equipment were proper during the year, what other information does the auditor need to know to have reasonable assurance that the construction equipment—net of depreciation—is properly reflected on the balance sheet?

d. How can an auditor determine that the client has assigned an appropriate useful life to the equipment and has depreciated it accurately?

5-87 **LO 12** The auditor provides an opinion on internal control over financial reporting for one of its public company clients.

a. Is the auditor also required to audit the company's financial statements at the same time? Explain.

b. Does an unqualified report on internal controls over financial reporting imply that the company does not have any significant deficiencies in controls? Explain.

c. If the auditor did not detect any material misstatements in the financial statements, can the auditor conclude that there are no material weaknesses in internal control? Explain.

5-88 **LO 12** Review the external auditor's report on the integrated audit, presented in *Exhibit 5.13*. What are the important elements in that report related to internal control?

ETHICS

5-89 **LO 13** The auditor is evaluating the internal control of a new client. Management has prepared its assessment of internal control and has concluded that it has some deficiencies, but no significant deficiencies and no material weaknesses. However, in reviewing the work performed by management, the auditor observes the following:

- Sample sizes taken were never more than ten transactions, and most of the tests of operating effectiveness were based on a sample of one, performed as part of a walkthrough of a transaction.
- Management has fired the former CFO and a new CFO has not been appointed, but management indicates it is searching for a new CFO, and it currently has depth in the accounting area.
- The company has no formal whistle-blowing function because management has an open-door policy so that anyone with a problem can take it up the line.
- Management's approach to monitoring internal control is to compare budget with actual expenses and investigate differences.

In response to inquiries by the auditor, management responds that its procedures are sufficient to support its report on internal control.

The auditor's subsequent work yields the following:

- Many controls do not operate in the way described by management, and the procedures are not effective.
- There is no awareness of, or adherence to, the company's code of conduct.

- The accounting department does not have a depth of talent; moreover, although the department can handle most transactions, it is not capable of dealing with new contracts that the firm has entered into. The response of management is, "That is why we pay you auditors the big bucks—to help us make these decisions."

The auditor reaches a conclusion that there are material weaknesses in internal control, thus differing from management's assessment. Management points out that every issue where there is a disagreement is a subjective issue, and there is no one position that is better than the others. Management's position is that these are management's financial statements, and the auditor should accommodate management's view because there are no right answers.

a. The partner in charge of the job appears to be persuaded that the differences are indeed subjective and is proposing that an unqualified opinion on internal controls be issued. Recognize that this is a first-year client—and an important one to the office. Apply the ethical framework presented in *Chapter 4* to explore the actions that should be taken by the audit manager regarding (1) whether to disagree with the partner and (2) if there is a disagreement, to what level it should be taken in the firm.

b. Given the deficiencies noted, does the information support that there is a material weakness in internal control? What are the major factors that lead you to that conclusion?

c. Assume that the engagement team makes a decision that there is a material weakness in internal controls. Write two or three paragraphs describing those weaknesses that could be included in the audit report.

FRAUD FOCUS: CONTEMPORARY AND HISTORICAL CASES

PROFESSIONAL SKEPTICISM

ETHICS

FRAUD

INTERNATIONAL

5-90

Ernst & Young UK
(LO 1, 2, 6, 7, 8, 9, 10, 11, 12, 13)

Auditors who adhere to the professional auditing standards are viewed as conducting a quality audit. A lack of adherence to the professional auditing standards heightens the risk that the auditor will provide an unqualified audit opinion on financial statements that are materially misstated. This lesson is highlighted in the 2004–2006 audits of Thornton Precision Components, Limited (TPC) performed by Ernst & Young, LLP UK (E&Y UK).

TPC became a wholly owned U.K. subsidiary of Symmetry Medical, Inc. in 2003. Symmetry became a public company in 2004 and was listed on a U.S. stock exchange. Its consolidated financial statements included TPC's financial data. Beginning in 2003, Ernst & Young, LLP (E&Y US) became Symmetry's audit firm. In connection with the 2004–2006 audits of Symmetry, E&Y US engaged E&Y UK to perform audits of TPC, using PCAOB auditing standards. During the 2004–2006 audits, E&Y US relied on E&Y UK's audits to issue unqualified audit opinions for Symmetry.

From 1999 through September 2007, TPC's management participated in multiple schemes to increase TPC's revenues, net income, and other performance indicators. These schemes included booking fictitious revenues, understating costs of goods sold, creating fictitious inventories, and improperly capitalizing certain expenses. The fraud at TPC was not discovered by the auditors but only came to light in 2007 when a TPC employee alerted Symmetry's CEO to the fraud. In 2008, Symmetry restated its financial statements, which included among other items, significant reductions in Symmetry's net income.

In 2012, the SEC concluded that E&Y UK (a firm registered with the PCAOB) had conducted its audits in such a way that the audits did not adhere to the relevant professional auditing standards. Deficiencies in E&Y UK's 2004–2006 audits of TPC included a failure to perform appropriate procedures to audit the accounts receivable balances; adequately review top-side journal entries; properly audit inventory; and a failure to plan, staff, and supervise the audits. During the audit, the audit partner and manager did not appropriately question management's representations, did not fully document the results of testing, did not appropriately consider the risks of misstatements due to fraud, and did not exercise due professional care and professional skepticism. The SEC prohibited both the audit manager and partner of TPC from auditing U.S. public companies for two years.

For further details on this case, see Securities and Exchange Commission Accounting and Auditing Enforcement Release No. 3359 (January 2012).

a. What is the role of auditing standards and their underlying principles in promoting a quality audit?
b. How does the fundamental concept of professional skepticism relate to audit quality?
c. What audit evidence is necessary for opining on a client's financial statements?
d. How does audit documentation provide evidence related to audit quality?
e. What audit activities are conducted during the audit opinion formulation process to provide reasonable assurance about a client's financial statements?
f. How does professional judgment and ethical decision making contribute to audit quality?

PROFESSIONAL SKEPTICISM

ETHICS

5-91 **Ernst & Young UK**
(LO 13) Refer to *5-90*, which features details on the Ernst & Young-UK audits of Thornton Precision Components from 2004–2006. Use the ethical decision making framework presented in *Chapter 4* to analyze the judgments made by the E&Y-UK audit partner responsible for the 2004–2006 audits of TPC.

FRAUD

FRAUD

5-92 **General Motors**
(LO 9, 10, 13) In March 2006, General Motors (GM) announced that it needed to restate its previous year's financial statements. Excerpts from the *Wall Street Journal* describing the restatements include the following:

• GM, which already faces an SEC probe into its accounting practices, also disclosed that its 10-K report, when filed, will outline a series of accounting mistakes that will force the car maker to restate its earnings from 2000 to the first quarter of 2005. GM also said it was widening by $2 billion the loss it reported for 2005.

• Many of the other GM problems relate to rebates, or credits, from suppliers. Typically, suppliers offer an upfront payment in exchange for a promise by the customer to buy certain quantities of products over time. Under accounting rules, such rebates cannot be recorded until after the promised purchases are made.

- GM said it concluded it had mistakenly recorded some of these payments prematurely. The biggest impact was in 2001, when the company said it overstated pre-tax income by $405 million as a result of prematurely recording supplier credits. Because the credits are being moved to later years, the impact in those years was less, and GM said it would have a deferred credit of $548 million that will help reduce costs in future periods. The issue of how to book rebates and other credits from suppliers is a thorny one that has tripped up other companies, ranging from the international supermarket chain Royal Ahold, N.V. to the U.S.-based Kmart Corporation.

- GM also said it had wrongly recorded a $27 million pre-tax gain from disposing of precious-metals inventory in 2000, which it was obliged to buy back the following year.

- GM told investors not to rely on its previously reported results for the first quarter of 2005, saying it had underreported its loss by $149 million. GM said it had prematurely boosted the value it ascribed to cars it was leasing to rental-car companies, assuming they would be worth more after the car-rental companies were done with them. GM previously had reported a loss of $1.1 billion, or $1.95 a share, for the first quarter. (March 18, 2006)

You may assume the amounts are material.

a. Without determining whether the errors in accounting judgment were intentional or unintentional, discuss how the nature of the errors affects the auditor's judgment of the control environment and whether the auditor should conclude there are material weaknesses in internal control. What would your judgment be if the accounting treatment were deemed acceptable, but aggressive by the company's CFO and CEO? How would those judgments affect the auditor's assessment of the control environment?

b. Describe the nature of the accounting judgment made by the company regarding the residual value of the cars it leases. What information and communication system should exist regarding the residual value of the cars returned from leasing? What controls should be in place? What evidence would the auditor need to evaluate the reasonableness of the change made by the company?

c. Explain the rebates, or up-front rebates, from the company's suppliers. Why would the suppliers pay the up-front credits? What is the proper accounting for the up-front credits? What controls should be in place to account for the up-front credits? How would the auditor test (1) the controls over the accounting for the up-front credits and (2) the expense-offset account, or the liability account?

d. Do you believe that the material misstatements were the result of errors or fraud? Discuss the reasons for your opinion.

APPLICATION ACTIVITIES

PROFESSIONAL SKEPTICISM

NOTE: Completing Application Activities requires students to reference additional resources and materials. Some Application Activities will require the student to reference relevant professional auditing standards. We make special note of these as Auditing Standards Application Activities.

AUDITING STANDARDS APPLICATION ACTIVITY

5-93 **PCAOB** **(LO 1, 2)** In April 2010, the PCAOB issued a disciplinary order instituting disciplinary proceedings, making findings, and imposing sanctions in the case of Robert T. Taylor, CPA (both the firm and the individual auditor). The order can be found in PCAOB Release No. 105–2010–006 at *www.pcaobus.org*. Obtain this release from the PCAOB web site and answer the following questions.

a. The order in the case of Robert T. Taylor recognizes that PCAOB standards require that an auditor exercise due professional care, exercise professional skepticism, and obtain sufficient evidence on which to base an opinion on the financial statements. Describe instances in which the respondents in the order did not adhere to these requirements.

b. Why is adhering to these professional requirements important for audit quality?

5-94 **PCAOB** **(LO 7)** Refer to the *Standards Appendix* to the book. Identify the PCAOB AS that relates to audit documentation. Review that AS and describe the characteristics of good audit documentation that are noted in that standard.

5-95 **LO 4, 9, 11** With your instructor's consent, select a place where you have worked or an organization in which you have some acquaintance (relative or friend), and therefore have access. Choose one area of operations (cash receipts, sales, shipping, receiving, or payroll) for review. For the area selected:

a. Identify the major transactions processed.

b. Select a representative transaction and perform a walkthrough of the application to gain an understanding of processing and controls implemented to mitigate the risks of misstatements.

c. Document the important controls identified during the walkthrough.

d. Identify control procedures you would recommend to improve the organization's internal controls.

PROFESSIONAL SKEPTICISM

5-96 **PCAOB** **(LO 2, 3, 8, 9, 10, 11, 12)** Two *Auditing in Practice* features in the chapter highlight audit deficiencies related to tests of controls and substantive procedures that were noted in PCAOB inspection reports. See "The Need for Performing and Considering the Results of Tests of Controls" and "Not Performing Sufficient Appropriate Substantive Audit Procedures Leads to Low Audit Quality." Obtain a recent PCAOB inspection report of one of the Big 4 firms. Select several audit deficiencies identified in the report and determine which phase of the audit opinion formulation process the deficiency relates to. Discuss how the fundamental principle of professional skepticism might have been helpful in avoiding such deficiencies.

AUDITING STANDARDS APPLICATION ACTIVITY

INTERNATIONAL

5-97 **LO 5** *Exhibit 5.5* identifies the five management assertions contained in the PCAOB standards. Refer to the *Standards Appendix* to this book. Identify the IAASB ISA that provides guidance on management assertions. List the management assertions identified in the IAASB ISA and compare and contrast the IAASB management assertions with those of the PCAOB.

ACADEMIC RESEARCH CASE

NOTE: Completing the Academic Research Case requires students to reference additional resources and materials.

SEARCH HINT

It is easy to locate academic research articles! Use a search engine such as Google Scholar or an electronic research platform such as ABI Inform, and search using the author names and part of the article title.

5-98   LO **7, 9**   Locate and read the article listed below and answer the following questions.

Bierstaker, J. L., J. E. Hunton, and J. C. Thibodeau. 2009. Do client-prepared internal control documentation and business process flowcharts help or hinder an auditor's ability to identify missing controls? Auditing: *A Journal of Practice & Theory* 28 (1): 79–94.

a. What is the issue being addressed in the paper?
b. What are the findings of the paper?
c. Why is this paper important to auditors, and what are the implications of this paper for the auditing profession?
d. Describe the research methodology used as a basis for the conclusions.
e. Describe any limitations of the research.

6

A Framework for Audit Evidence

CHAPTER OVERVIEW AND LEARNING OBJECTIVES

Auditing is a process of objectively gathering and evaluating sufficient appropriate evidence pertaining to assertions. As the auditor plans an audit, the auditor addresses two basic evidence-related questions: *What audit evidence is appropriate? How much audit evidence is sufficient?* The auditor also determines when to gather the audit evidence. The specific audit procedures that the auditor performs to obtain evidence must address the risk of material misstatement in the financial statements or the likelihood that internal control over financial reporting contains material weaknesses. The auditor's process of gathering and assessing evidence must be documented, clearly laying out the evidence gathered, the auditor's evaluation of that evidence, and the conclusions reached. In this chapter, we build on the concepts of audit evidence presented in *Chapter 5* by further discussing the type, timing, and extent of audit procedures typically performed during a financial statement or integrated audit.

Through studying this chapter, you will be able to achieve these learning objectives:

1. Discuss the importance of the evidence concepts of appropriateness and sufficiency and explain how those concepts are related to the risk of material misstatement.

2. Identify factors affecting the appropriateness of audit evidence.

3. Make professional judgments about the type and timing of audit procedures to use to obtain audit evidence.

4. Discuss the use of, and apply, substantive analytical procedures.

5. Identify factors affecting the sufficiency of audit evidence.

6. Identify issues related to audit evidence needed for accounts involving management estimates.

7. Determine situations requiring the auditor to use a specialist/expert in gathering and evaluation evidence and describe the auditor's responsibilities related to that specialist/expert.

8. Describe the evidence needs for related-party transactions.

9. Describe the characteristics of quality audit documentation.

10. Explain the nature, design, and purposes of audit programs.

11. Apply the frameworks for professional decision making and ethical decision making to issues involving audit evidence.

THE AUDIT OPINION FORMULATION PROCESS

I. Making Client Acceptance and Continuance Decisions

Chapter 1

II. Performing Risk Assessment

Chapters 3, 7, and 9–13

III. Obtaining Evidence About Internal Control Operating Effectiveness

Chapters 8–13 and 16

IV. Obtaining Substantive Evidence About Accounts, Disclosures and Assertions

Chapters 8–13 and 16

V. Completing the Audit and Making Reporting Decisions

Chapters 14 and 15

The Auditing Profession, the Risk of Fraud and Mechanisms to Address Fraud: Regulation, Corporate Governance, and Audit Quality

Chapters 1 and 2

Professional Liability and the Need for Quality Auditor Judgments and Ethical Decisions

Chapter 4

The Audit Opinion Formulation Process and a Framework for Obtaining Audit Evidence

Chapters 5 and 6

PROFESSIONAL JUDGMENT IN CONTEXT
Evidence-Related Findings in PCAOB Inspection Reports

The PCAOB performs annual inspections of each of the large public company audit firms. Following are excerpts from PCAOB annual inspection reports of some of these firms. Each excerpt describes an audit deficiency related to evidence that is a failure by the firm to perform, or to perform sufficiently, certain necessary audit procedures and to obtain sufficient appropriate audit evidence.

PCAOB Release No. 104-2012-095 notes that:

The Firm failed to sufficiently test inventory. Specifically, the Firm failed to test the existence of a significant portion of inventory and failed to test the completeness and accuracy of the system-generated reports that it used in its substantive procedures related to the valuation of inventory. Further, the Firm failed to test the completeness of inventory.

PCAOB Release No. 104-2011-289 states:

The Firm failed to sufficiently test the valuation of accounts receivable and net revenue. During the year, the issuer revised its policy for calculating its allowance for doubtful accounts, including changing certain significant assumptions used in its calculation. The Firm failed to evaluate the reasonableness of the issuer's revised assumptions. In addition, there was no evidence in the audit documentation, and no persuasive other evidence, that the Firm had tested the completeness and accuracy of the data used in the calculation of the allowance for doubtful accounts as well as in the determination of the contractual revenue allowances.

PCAOB Release No. 104-2011-288 indicates:

In this audit, the Firm failed to obtain sufficient appropriate audit evidence to support its opinion on the effectiveness of ICFR [internal control over financial reporting].

PCAOB Release No. 104-2012-109 discloses:

The Firm failed to sufficiently test revenue. The Firm's planned approach for testing revenue included the performance of substantive analytical procedures. The analytical procedures consisted of comparing the current year's revenue to the prior year's revenue, but the Firm did not establish that the prior year's revenue could be expected to be predictive of the current year's revenue. In addition, the Firm failed to establish the amount of the difference from the prior year's revenue that could be accepted without further investigation, and failed to obtain corroboration of management's explanations of certain significant differences between the prior year's revenue and the current year's revenue. The Firm also failed to test the completeness and accuracy of certain of the data used in the analytical procedures. As a result of these failures, the analytical procedures provided little to no substantive assurance.

As you read through this chapter, consider the following questions:

- What is sufficient appropriate evidence, and how does it differ across clients? (LO 1, 2, 3, 5)

- What are substantive analytical procedures, and when is evidence from these procedures appropriate? (LO 4)
- What are the unique evidence challenges for accounts such as allowance for doubtful accounts that are based on management estimates? (LO 6)
- How could the use of a standardized audit program lead to some of the problems identified in the PCAOB Releases? (LO 10)

Obtaining Sufficient Appropriate Audit Evidence

LO 1 Discuss the importance of the evidence concepts of appropriateness and sufficiency and explain how those concepts are related to the risk of material misstatement.

The auditor's job is to obtain sufficient appropriate evidence on which to base the audit opinion. The auditor obtains evidence to reduce the risk of issuing an unqualified opinion on financial statements containing a material misstatement or on internal control that has a material weakness. AS 15 defines audit evidence as

[A]ll the information, whether obtained from audit procedures or other sources, that is used by the auditor in arriving at the conclusions on which the auditor's opinion is based. Audit evidence consists of both information that supports and corroborates management's assertions regarding the financial statements or internal control over financial reporting and information that contradicts such assertions.

This definition is very similar to those used by the American Institute of Certified Public Accountants (AICPA) and the International Auditing and Assurance Standards Board (IAASB).

While the auditor is to obtain sufficient appropriate evidence before issuing an opinion, determining what is "appropriate" and "sufficient" is not an easy task. The AICPA's AU-C 500 defines the appropriateness of audit evidence as "[t]he measure of the quality of audit evidence (that is, its relevance and reliability in providing support for the conclusions on which the auditor's opinion is based)" and defines the sufficiency of audit evidence as "[t]he measure of the quantity of audit evidence. The quantity of the audit evidence needed is affected by the auditor's assessment of the risks of material misstatement and also by the quality of such audit evidence."

Exhibit 6.1 explains the relationship between risk of material misstatement, evidence appropriateness, and evidence sufficiency.

What is determined to be appropriate and sufficient will be affected by the client's risk of material misstatement (in other words, its inherent and control risks) or risk of material weakness in internal control. Sufficiency and appropriateness will vary across accounts and assertions. Both the U.S. and international auditing standards encourage auditors to focus on accounts and assertions with the greatest likelihood of material misstatement. With that in mind, study the relationships in *Exhibit 6.1*. Consider an account where there is little risk of material misstatement, internal controls are effective, and the client has relatively noncomplex transactions. Here, the available audit evidence is relevant and reliable, and the quality of that evidence is high. In such a case, the auditor could likely perform less rigorous substantive procedures or only a minimal amount of substantive procedures, and the audit would therefore be less costly to conduct. Conversely, consider an account where there is high risk of material misstatement and

| EXHIBIT **6.1** | Interrelationship of Risk of Material Misstatement, Evidence Appropriateness, and Evidence Sufficiency |

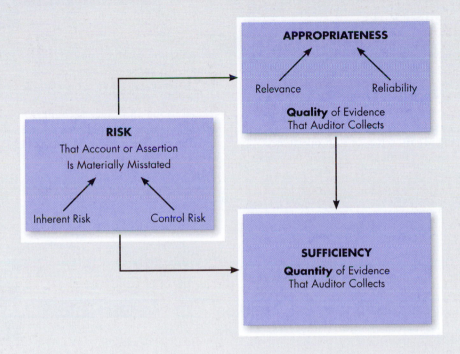

internal controls over that account are not effective. Here, the available audit evidence from the client is of lower quality. Therefore, the auditor will have to find other high-quality evidence to corroborate evidence obtained from within the client's systems. Ultimately, these factors require the auditor to perform more, and more rigorous, substantive procedures. Therefore, obtaining such evidence will increase the cost to perform the audit.

Appropriateness of Audit Evidence

LO 2 Identify factors affecting the appropriateness of audit evidence.

Appropriateness of audit evidence is a measure of its quality, including the **relevance** of the evidence, that is, whether it provides insight on the validity of the assertion being tested, and the **reliability** of the evidence, that is, whether it is convincing. The relevance of evidence relates to the connection between the audit procedure being performed and the assertion being audited. This concept is highlighted in the *Auditing in Practice* feature "The Need to Tailor the Evidence to the Identified Risks." The reliability of evidence is influenced by its source and nature and depends on the circumstances under which it is obtained.

Relevance of Audit Evidence

The relevance of audit evidence considers the assertion being tested and is affected by several factors, including the purpose of the procedure being performed, the direction of testing, and the specific procedure or set of procedures being performed. Additionally, evidence can be directly or indirectly relevant to an assertion. The *Auditing in Practice* feature "Is the Evidence Relevant to the Assertion Being Tested?" provides examples of concerns related to the relevance of evidence.

Purpose of an Audit Procedure   Recall that audit procedures fall into three categories: risk assessment procedures, tests of controls, and

The Need to Tailor the Evidence to the Identified Risks

AUDITING IN **PRACTICE**

A frequent criticism of audits described in Public Company Accounting Oversight Board (PCAOB) inspection reports is that auditors often address high-risk audit areas by simply gathering more of the same type of evidence. ISA 500 on audit evidence is very explicit that gathering more of the same evidence will not meet either the sufficiency or appropriateness criteria. For example, if there is high risk regarding the valuation of accounts receivable, increasing the sample size for confirmations, which are focused on the existence assertion, would not be very useful. Rather, the auditor will need to expand procedures related to the allowance account. Auditors need to tailor the gathering of evidence—both the sufficiency and appropriateness—to identified risks for each disclosure, account, or assertion.

Is the Evidence Relevant to the Assertion Being Tested?

AUDITING IN **PRACTICE**

The auditor should guard against unwarranted inferences in gathering audit evidence. The following are examples of inappropriate inferences that auditors may make because they use evidence that is not entirely relevant to the assertion being tested:

- The auditor tests the existence of the client's equipment by inspecting the asset and concludes that the asset exists and is owned by the client. However, evidence about the existence of the equipment that is gained through inspecting the asset does not provide relevant evidence about who owns the asset.

- The auditor examines documentation related to the largest accounts payable balances recorded in the client's financial statements and concludes that the accounts payable balance recorded in the financial statements is reasonable. But such evidence is relevant to the existence assertion (overstatements). For most liability accounts, the more relevant evidence would relate to the completeness assertion and *understatements*, not overstatements.

substantive procedures. The purpose of an audit procedure determines whether it is a risk assessment procedure, a test of controls, or a substantive procedure. Risk assessment procedures are used during audit planning to identify the risks of material misstatement. Tests of controls are relevant when the auditor wants to evaluate the operating effectiveness of controls in preventing, or detecting and correcting, material misstatements. Substantive procedures are relevant when the auditor wants to obtain direct evidence about the presence of material misstatements in the financial statements.

Direction of Testing The relevance of evidence obtained through audit procedures may be affected by the direction of testing. **Directional testing** involves testing balances primarily for either overstatement or understatement (but not both). For example, if the auditor wants to test the existence assertion for accounts payable, the auditor is concerned as to whether all of the recorded accounts payable actually exist, that is, overstatement of accounts payable. In that case, the auditor's starting point for testing would be all of the recorded accounts payable, and the auditor would perform procedures to obtain evidence supporting the existence of the recorded accounts payable. For example, the auditor may look at supporting documentation such as vendor invoices. Conversely, if the auditor wants to test the completeness assertion for accounts payable, the auditor is concerned as to whether all of the accounts payable owed by the client are recorded, that is, understatement of accounts payable. In that case, obtaining evidence about the recorded accounts payable would not be relevant. Instead, the auditor would obtain evidence as to whether there were unrecorded accounts payable. Relevant evidence could include information such as subsequent disbursements, suppliers' statements, and unmatched receiving reports.

Exhibit 6.2 compares testing related to the existence and completeness assertions. Panel A illustrates the auditor's work flow when testing for existence. This process is referred to as **vouching**. Vouching involves taking a sample of recorded transactions and obtaining the original source documents supporting the recorded transaction. For example, for a sample of items recorded in the sales journal, the auditor will obtain the related shipping documents and customer orders. Vouching provides evidence on the assertion that recorded transactions are valid (existence/occurrence). Panel B of *Exhibit 6.2* illustrates the auditor's work flow when testing for completeness. This process is referred to as **tracing**. Tracing is sometimes referred to as *reprocessing*. Tracing involves taking a sample of original source documents and ensuring that the transactions related to the source documents have been recorded in the appropriate journal and general ledger. For example, the auditor might select a sample of receiving reports and trace them to the acquisitions journal and the general ledger.

In performing audit procedures, it is important to recognize that some assertions are directional by nature. The existence/occurrence assertion addresses overstatement, whereas the completeness assertion addresses understatement. Therefore, the assertion being tested determines the direction of testing and what type of evidence is relevant. Assets and revenues are most often tested for overstatement because the usual presumption is that managers would prefer to show more assets and revenues. Testing an asset for overstatement also provides corollary evidence on the potential overstatement of revenue and liabilities or the potential understatement of

EXHIBIT **6.2**	Illustration of Testing for Existence (Vouching) and Completeness (Tracing)

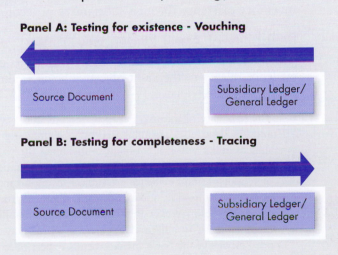

Panel A: Testing for existence - Vouching

Source Document ← Subsidiary Ledger/General Ledger

Panel B: Testing for completeness - Tracing

Source Document → Subsidiary Ledger/General Ledger

other asset or expense accounts. For example, if accounts receivable are overstated, it is likely that revenue is overstated or cash is understated.

Liabilities and expenses are most often tested for understatement because the usual presumption is that managers would prefer to show fewer liabilities and expenses. Testing liabilities for understatement provides evidence on the potential understatement of expenses or assets, or the potential overstatement of revenue and other liabilities. For example, if there are unrecorded liabilities, such as a failure to accrue payroll expense, the related payroll expense is understated, and possibly inventory is understated if payroll costs are not properly allocated to inventory.

Type of Procedure A specific audit procedure may provide audit evidence that is relevant to certain assertions, but not others. For example, if the auditor were to walk through the client's warehouse to inspect inventory, the auditor would be obtaining evidence related to the existence of inventory, but this procedure would not provide evidence relevant to the rights assertion. In some cases, a procedure may provide evidence relevant to multiple assertions. For example, if the auditor inspects documents related to the collection of accounts receivable after the year-end, this procedure will likely provide audit evidence relevant to both the existence and valuation of accounts receivable.

Direct and Indirect Evidence Some evidence is directly relevant to a specific assertion. For example, communicating with a client's customers about whether the customer owes payment for goods to the client provides **direct evidence** about the existence of an accounts receivable balance.

Indirect evidence is not as directly relevant to an assertion. For example, the auditor might perform substantive analytical procedures on an account balance, such as analyzing expenses and comparing the expense account with those of previous years. Assuming the auditor does not find unexpected results, the auditor has indirect evidence about the valuation of expenses. In some cases, this indirect evidence may be sufficient. In other cases, where a high risk of material misstatement exists, the auditor may also need to obtain direct evidence about expenses. For example, the auditor might also examine invoices supporting the amount of expenses.

As another example, tests of controls provide direct evidence about the operating effectiveness of controls and indirect evidence about accounts and assertions. If the auditor finds that controls over the existence of inventory are operating effectively, the auditor has direct evidence about the effectiveness of those controls. The auditor also has indirect evidence indicating a high likelihood that the inventory existence assertion is not materially misstated. The auditor will likely need to also obtain direct evidence related to inventory existence through substantive procedures.

Reliability of Audit Evidence

The reliability of audit evidence is judged by its ability to provide convincing evidence related to the audit objective being evaluated. In considering the reliability of audit evidence, review the book of ISA 500 (A31), which states:

> The reliability of information to be used as audit evidence, and therefore of the audit evidence itself, is influenced by its source and its nature, and the circumstances under which it is obtained, including the controls over its preparation and maintenance where relevant. Therefore, generalizations about the reliability of various kinds of audit evidence are subject to important exceptions. Even when information to be used as audit evidence is obtained from sources external to the entity, circumstances may exist that could affect its reliability. For example, information obtained from an independent external source may not be reliable if the source is not knowledgeable, or a management's expert may lack objectivity. (ISA 500, A31)

This statement highlights the importance of considering the source of the evidence in assessing its reliability. The IAASB, in ISA 500, has established the following generalizations about the reliability of audit evidence:

More Reliable	Less Reliable
Directly obtained evidence (e.g., observation of a control)	Indirectly obtained evidence (e.g., an inquiry about the working of a control)
Evidence derived from a well-controlled information system	Evidence derived from a poorly controlled system or easily overridden information system
Evidence from independent outside sources	Evidence from within the client's organization
Evidence that exists in documentary form	Verbal evidence
Evidence from original documents	Evidence obtained from photocopies or facsimiles, or digitized data (would depend on the quality of controls over their preparation and maintenance)

The specific evidence choices depend on the assertion being tested, and evidence reliability can be influenced by multiple considerations. For example, if the auditor is testing warranty liabilities, most of the information likely resides internally—some in the client's accounting system and some in operational data. While internal documentation is generally less reliable than external documentation, internal documentation can be quite reliable when the underlying internal control system is effective and the original documentation cannot be easily manipulated by management.

Internal Documentation Internal documentation includes the following types of documents: legal, business, accounting, and planning and control. *Exhibit 6.3* provides examples of these types of internal documents. As you review these examples, consider that the reliability of internal documentation varies because it is influenced by the following:

- Effectiveness of internal controls
- Management motivation to misstate individual accounts (fraud potential)
- Formality of the documentation, such as acknowledgment of its validity by parties outside the organization or independent of the accounting function
- Independence of those preparing the documentation from those recording transactions

External Documentation External documentation is generally considered to be highly reliable, but the reliability varies depending on whether the documentation (a) was prepared by a knowledgeable and independent outside party and (b) is received directly by the auditor. Most external documentation, however, is directed to the client. For example, a customer order that specifies prices and quantities is external documentation received by the client, not the auditor. Therefore, in high-risk situations the auditor should confirm the contents of the document with the pertinent outside party.

Exhibit 6.4 provides examples of external documentation. External documentation can range from business documents normally found in the client's possession (vendor invoices and monthly statements), to confirmations received by the auditor directly from the client's legal counsel, banker, or

EXHIBIT **6.3**	Examples of Internal Documents

Legal documents	Labor and fringe benefit agreements
	Sales contracts
	Lease agreements
	Royalty agreements
	Maintenance contracts
Business documents	Sales invoices
	Purchase orders
	Canceled checks
	Payment vouchers
	EDI agreements
Accounting documents	Estimated warranty liability schedules
	Depreciation and amortization schedules
	Standard cost computations and schedules
	Management exception reports
	Employee time cards
Other planning and control documents	Shipping and receiving reports
	Inventory movement documents such as scrap reports and transfer receipts
	Market research surveys
	Pending litigation reports
	Variance reports

EXHIBIT **6.4**	Examples of External Documents

Business documents	Vendor invoices and monthly statements
	Customer orders
	Sales or purchase contracts
	Loan agreements
	Other contracts
Third-party documents	Confirmation letters from legal counsel
	Confirmation statements from banks
	Confirmation replies from customers
	Vendor statements requested by auditors
General business information	Industry trade statistics
	Credit-rating reports
	Data from computer service bureaus

customer, to trade and credit information. One common business document in the client's possession is a vendor invoice. A vendor's invoice shows the purchase price (cost) of items in the client's inventory, dates of invoice and shipment, payment and ownership terms, shipping address (inventory location), purchase order reference, purchasing agent (evidence of authorization), and amount due (liability as well as asset valuation evidence). A vendor invoice is external documentation, but the auditor will typically obtain it from the client. Formal documents of this type are generally considered reliable except for situations in which the auditor questions management's integrity and has assessed the client and account balance being tested as high risk. Recognize that with the current state of technology, invoices often exist in electronic form. Thus, the auditor must assure that the data shown in an electronic invoice are safeguarded and well controlled in the client's computer system and that they cannot be easily manipulated.

Evidence From a Management's Specialist

Some of the evidence that auditors receive from the client is prepared by a management's specialist that was hired by the client. AU-C 500 defines a **management's specialist** as "an individual or organization possessing expertise in a field other than accounting or auditing, whose work in that field is used by the entity to assist the entity in preparing the financial statements." In preparing its financial statements, a client may require expertise in a field other than accounting or auditing, such as actuarial calculations, valuations, or engineering data. If the client does not have the expertise needed to prepare the financial statements, the client can use a management's specialist in these fields to obtain the needed expertise to prepare the financial statements. In fact, failure to do so when such expertise is necessary increases the risks of material misstatement and may be a significant deficiency or material weakness in internal control.

If information to be relied upon as audit evidence has been prepared by a management's specialist, the auditor should consider the following factors as they affect the reliability and relevance of information produced by a management's specialist:

- Competence, capabilities, and objectivity of the specialist
- Work performed by the specialist
- Appropriateness of the specialist's work as audit evidence for the relevant assertion

Type and Timing of Audit Procedures

LO 3 Make professional judgments about the type and timing of audit procedures to use to obtain audit evidence.

Type of Audit Procedures

Auditors' judgments about the type of audit procedures to perform to obtain evidence are critical to conducting a quality audit. *Exhibit 6.5* identifies the types of audit procedures typically performed as tests of controls and substantive procedures, and provides relevant examples. We discuss audit procedures that are used as risk assessment procedures in *Chapter 7*.

Inspection of Documentation Much of the audit process involves examining documents, in either paper or electronic form. Important documentation that the auditor obtains generally includes the client's underlying **accounting records** such as:

- Evidence of internal controls over financial reporting, as well as supporting records such as checks, invoices, contracts
- The general and subsidiary ledgers
- Journal entries
- Worksheets supporting cost allocations, computations, reconciliations, and disclosures

Common documents include invoices, payroll time cards, and bank statements. Auditors examine invoices from suppliers, for example, to establish the cost and ownership of inventory or various expenses. They also read contracts

| EXHIBIT **6.5** | Types of Audit Procedures |

Categories of Audit Procedures	Purpose	Types of Audit Procedures Typically Performed	Examples of Audit Procedures
Tests of controls	Evaluate the operating effectiveness of controls	Inspection of documentation	Review client-prepared internal control documentation Select purchase transactions and review documentation for required approval
		Observation	Observe whether controls designed to limit access to a secure area (e.g., ID card need to access storage room) are functioning
		Reperformance	Reperform a reconciliation performed by client personnel
		Inquiry	Inquire of management and supervisory personnel about their control-related responsibilities
Substantive procedures	Determine whether material misstatements exist in the financial statements	Inspection of documentation	Review shipping documents as evidence of a sale having occurred
		Inspection of assets	Tour the manufacturing facility and inspect client's equipment
		External confirmation	Obtain confirmations from client's customers regarding amount owed by the customer to the client
		Recalculation	Recalculate the total amount included on a sales invoice
		Analytical procedures	Estimate the expected amount of interest income to be recorded by the client and follow up on significant unexpected differences between expectation and client's recorded balance
		Scanning	Scan the sales journal to identify unusual transactions posted to the sales account and follow up on the transactions
		Inquiry	Inquire of client management as to its valuation of the allowance for doubtful accounts

to help establish the potential existence of liabilities. Auditors should use original source documents rather than copies, because copies are easy for an unscrupulous management to falsify. Inspection of documents provides audit evidence of varying degrees of reliability. The reliability depends on the nature and source of the documentation and, in the case of internal records and documents, the effectiveness of controls over their production.

Inspection of Tangible Assets   Auditors will often inspect a client's assets, including inventory and long-lived assets (e.g., machinery or buildings). Inspection of tangible assets generally provides reliable evidence with respect to the existence of the asset, but not necessarily about the client's rights and obligations or completeness of the assets. For example, the inventory at a client location might be held on consignment from others and is therefore not owned by the audit client.

Observation Observation involves looking at a client's process or procedure. For example, an auditor might choose to observe whether unauthorized client personnel are prohibited from entering secure areas. A common practice is also to observe the client's process of taking physical inventory to establish existence and valuation. Observation suffers from the following limitations:

- Observation of processing is rarely unobtrusive. Individuals who know they are being observed may act differently than when not observed.
- Observation of processing on one day does not necessarily indicate how the transactions were processed on a different day or over a relevant period of time.

External Confirmation Confirmations consist of sending an inquiry to an outside party to corroborate information. The outside parties are asked to respond directly to the auditor as to whether they agree or disagree with the information, or to provide additional information that will assist the auditor in evaluating the correctness of an account balance. External confirmations include requests to legal counsel for an assessment of current litigation and the client's potential liability, letters to customers asking whether they owe the amount on the client's accounts receivable records, and letters to banks confirming bank balances and loans. In some cases, the auditor confirms the terms of sales agreements or other contracts.

Although confirmations can be a very reliable source of evidence, auditors must not rely on them unduly. The *Focus on Fraud* feature "The Parmalat Confirmation Fraud" provides an example where the confirmation process went terribly wrong. When using confirmations with outside parties, the auditor must assure that the outside party:

- Exists
- Is able to respond objectively and independently

The Parmalat Confirmation Fraud

FOCUS on **FRAUD**

The Parmalat fraud involved a large, family-held Italian company that produced dairy products around the world. The company's management perpetrated a fraud that involved taking cash from the business for family purposes but not recording the transactions in the books, thereby resulting in an overstatement of cash on the company's books. It also shifted monetary assets in and out of banks located in the Bahamas Islands. The audit firm decided it should independently confirm the existence of Parmalat's $3.2 billion account with the Bank of America in New York. Unfortunately, the audit senior was careless, and after preparing the confirmation, he put it in the client's mail room where it was intercepted by management. Management was able to scan the signature of a Bank of America employee from another document and put it on a copy of the confirmation form. A Parmalat employee then flew to New York from Italy just to mail that confirmation to the auditors with the appropriate postmark. The auditors received the fraudulent confirmation and concluded that the cash balance existed. There is an important point here: There are no trivial tasks in an audit. Each procedure must be completed in a professional manner and with due care.

- Is likely to respond conscientiously, appropriately, and in a timely fashion
- Is unbiased in responding

Professional auditing standards in the U.S. generally require that the auditor separately confirm accounts receivable. Confirmations must be sent independently of the client. The auditor often complements these types of confirmations with other sources of evidence, such as the customer's subsequent payment of the outstanding balance.

Recalculation Auditors often find it useful to recalculate a number of client computations. *Exhibit 6.6* summarizes various types of recalculations.

Reperformance **Reperformance** involves the auditor's independent execution of controls that were originally performed as part of the client's internal control. In other words, the auditor must not only inspect documents indicating that a control was performed; the auditor should do what is necessary to determine that the control actually worked. For example, rather than inspecting documents related to a bank reconciliation, the auditor may want to test a control requiring that bank reconciliations be performed. For selected months and bank accounts, the auditor may reperform the bank reconciliation and compare it to the reconciliations prepared by the client.

Analytical Procedures **Analytical procedures** consist of evaluations of financial information through analyzing plausible relationships among both financial and nonfinancial data. Later in this chapter we provide additional discussion on using analytical procedures.

Scanning **Scanning** is a type of analytical procedure involving the auditor's review of accounting data to identify significant or unusual items to test. Unusual individual items might include entries in transaction listings, subsidiary ledgers, general ledger control accounts, adjusting entries, reconciliations, or other detailed reports. For unusual or significant items, the auditor typically performs tests of details, such as client inquiry, inspection of documentation or assets, and, possibly, confirmations. While scanning can be conducted manually, electronic audit procedures may assist the auditor in identifying unusual items. We discuss these electronic types of procedures in *Chapter 8*.

| EXHIBIT **6.6** | Types of Recalculations Performed by the Auditor |

- **Footing** Adding a column of figures to verify the correctness of the client's totals.
- **Cross-footing** Checking the agreement of the cross-addition of a number of columns of figures that sum to a grand total. For example, the sum of net sales and sales discounts should equal total sales.
- **Tests of extensions** Recomputing items involving multiplication (e.g., multiplying unit cost by quantity on hand to arrive at extended cost).
- **Recalculating estimated amounts** Recomputing an amount that the client has already estimated, such as recomputing the allowance for doubtful accounts based on the client's formula related to the aging of accounts receivable ending balances.

Inquiry Inquiry of appropriate individuals is used extensively to gain an understanding of the following:

- The accounting system
- Management's plans for such things as marketable investments, new products, disposal of lines of business, and new investments
- Pending or actual litigation against the organization
- Changes in accounting procedures or accounting principles
- Management's approach and assumptions used in the valuation of key accounts (e.g., the collectibility of accounts receivable or the salability of inventory)
- Management's or the controller's assessment of complex financial matters

While inquiry is very helpful to understanding the client, evidence obtained through inquiry typically needs to be corroborated through other audit procedures. Inquiry alone ordinarily does not provide sufficient audit evidence of the absence of a material misstatement nor is inquiry alone sufficient to test the operating effectiveness of controls.

Application of Audit Procedures to Management Assertions

Recall that the auditor selects audit procedures to provide evidence relevant to a particular assertion. However, an audit procedure may provide evidence for one or more assertions affecting an account balance. *Exhibit 6.7* presents examples of procedures that address specific assertions regarding long-lived assets and contingencies. The procedures are organized according to the assertion, and some of the procedures cover more than one assertion.

Assessing the Consistency of Evidence

In formulating an opinion about whether an account is materially correct, the auditor looks at the relative weight and internal consistency of evidence. AS 15 guides the auditor by stating:

> If audit evidence obtained from one source is inconsistent with that obtained from another, or if the auditor has doubts about the reliability of information to be used as audit evidence, the auditor should perform the audit procedures necessary to resolve the matter and should determine the effect, if any, on other aspects of the audit. (para. 29)

The key point in AS 15 is that the auditor needs to consider all sources of information, as well as the consistency of the information, in formulating a judgment as to whether the evidence clearly leads to a conclusion about the fairness of the financial statement presentation. In assessing the consistency of evidence, the auditor should do the following:

- Consider internal consistency of evidence gathered
- Consider the consistency of internal evidence generated with external evidence gathered that reflects economic conditions and client operations
- Expand evidence-gathering procedures for areas where results are inconsistent or where results raise questions on the correctness of account balances
- Document conclusions based on the evidence gathered such that someone knowledgeable in auditing can follow the reasoning process

Cost–Benefit Considerations When Selecting Audit Procedures

When determining the audit procedures to perform, keep in mind that audit firms have to balance two objectives: (a) to be profitable and (b) to manage risk. Therefore, auditors must perform audits both efficiently and effectively. For example, they should not perform unnecessary procedures, and they

EXHIBIT **6.7**	Management Assertions and Examples of Related Audit Procedures	

Assertions	Audit Procedures: Long-lived Assets	Audit Procedures: Contingencies
Existence	• Inspect the assets • Select new assets that have been added to the subsidiary ledger or general journal and inspect supporting documentation (e.g., invoices)	• Inquire of management • Send confirmation request to legal counsel
Completeness	• Select source documents for repairs or maintenance expense to determine if a fixed asset was inappropriately expensed • Inquire regarding the process for determining whether an expenditure is an asset or an expense	• Inquire of management • Select source documents for legal expense and determine that the expenses were appropriately recorded
Rights/ obligations	• Inspect documentation related to purchase contracts	• Inquire of management • Obtain confirmation from legal counsel • Inspect documentation of payments related to in-progress litigation
Valuation/ allocation	• Inspect vendor's invoice to establish purchase price • Determine that estimated life and salvage value are consistent with similar purchases, company policies, expected future use, and past experience • Recalculate depreciation expense • Develop an expectation of total depreciation using analytical procedures	• Inquire of management • Obtain confirmation from legal counsel • Recalculate potential damages sought by plaintiff • Review court filings
Presentation/ disclosure	• Review presentation within the financial statements to ensure completeness and conformance with the applicable financial reporting framework. • Review disclosures to ensure that they are adequate and understandable	• Review presentation within financial statements to ensure completeness and conformance with the applicable financial reporting framework • Review disclosures to ensure that they are adequate and understandable

should select procedures that maximize effectiveness while minimizing cost where possible.

Each of the audit procedures that an auditor could select takes time, effort, and ultimately money to perform. Audit procedures that are more rigorous, and that provide higher quality evidence, are generally more costly to perform. *Exhibit 6.8* describes some generalizations about the cost–benefit trade-offs that auditors will make when they decide on the appropriate mix of procedures. Consider an auditor testing the existence and valuation of inventory. The auditor may initially use substantive analytical procedures to gain a sense of the reasonableness of the ending inventory amount. The auditor will inspect the client's inventory to establish existence, and will inspect documents to determine that the client actually owns the inventory. The auditor may scan material inventory transactions around year-end to assess whether any unusual adjustments have been made to the account. *Exhibit 6.8* makes the point that each of these procedures has costs associated with it as well as differential evidence quality.

There are always exceptions to the generalizations provided in *Exhibit 6.8.* The important point is that the types of substantive procedures selected depend

EXHIBIT 6.8   Cost of Audit Procedures and Evidence Quality

Type of Substantive Procedure	Cost of Procedure	Evidence Quality
Inspection of documents (includes vouching and tracing)	Low to medium (depends on sample size)	Medium to high (assuming the documents are valid and unaltered, needs to consider source)
Inspection of physical assets	Low to high (depends on complexity, location of process, and expertise required)	High (existence); low to medium (valuation, ownership)
Observation	Low to high (depends on complexity, location of process, and expertise required)	Medium (because people may change behavior while being observed)
External confirmations	Low to medium (can be performed manually or electronically; depends on sample size)	Medium to high (assuming that there is no fraud in the confirmation process)
Recalculation	Low to medium (can be performed manually or electronically; depends on sample size)	Medium to high
Reperformance	Low to high (depends on sample size and complexity of process)	Medium to high
Analytical procedures	Low to medium (depends on the type of analytical procedure)	Medium to high (if the auditor who is conducting the test is competent and the data are reliable)
Scanning	Low to medium (can be performed manually or electronically; depends on the length of document)	Low to medium (will need to follow up on significant or unusual items using other procedures)
Inquiry of knowledgeable persons	Low	Low (will also need corroborating evidence)

on risk of material misstatement. For example, consider an account balance and related assertion with a low risk of misstatement. For this case, the auditor can obtain evidence using less rigorous and less costly procedures, such as inquiry, recalculation, and analytical procedures. In contrast, consider an account balance and related assertion with a high risk of misstatement, such as the valuation of receivables. For this case, the auditor needs to rely on relatively more rigorous and higher cost procedures such as inquiry, confirmations, reperformance, and inspection of documentation.

For any particular account, assertion, or disclosure, the auditor may determine the following with regard to substantive procedures:

- Performing only substantive analytical procedures would be appropriate, for example, when the auditor's assessment of risk is supported by audit evidence that the controls are operating effectively
- Performing only substantive tests of details would be appropriate
- Performing a combination of substantive analytical procedures and tests of details may be most responsive to the assessed risks

However, irrespective of the assessed risks of material misstatement, the auditor should perform substantive procedures for all relevant assertions related to each material account balance and disclosure.

Timing of Procedures

In addition to determining which types of procedures to perform, the auditor must determine when to perform them—at the balance sheet date, earlier than the balance sheet date (referred to as an **interim date**), or after the balance sheet date. The decision of timing is based on risk associated with the account, the effectiveness of internal controls, the nature of the account, and the availability of audit staff. Performing procedures after year-end may provide the most convincing evidence; for example, a cash collection of an accounts receivable after year-end is usually high-quality evidence regarding both the existence and valuation of the receivable.

Performing procedures prior to the balance sheet date allows earlier completion of the audit and might require less overtime of the audit staff. It might also meet management's desire to distribute the financial statements shortly after year-end. However, performing the procedures at an interim date increases the risk of material misstatements occurring between the interim date and the year-end. When an organization has effective internal controls over financial reporting, the risk of misstatements occurring between the interim audit date and year-end decreases. There are several accounts for which the auditor can effectively and efficiently test transactions during the year rather than the final balance. For example, the auditor can test property, plant, and equipment additions and disposals during the year. Accounts receivable may be confirmed prior to year-end. A similar approach can often be used for other noncurrent assets, long-term debt, and owners' equity transactions. However, when performing procedures at an interim date, the auditor needs to perform additional audit procedures at or after year-end to make sure that no misstatements have occurred during the **roll-forward period** (the period between the interim date and the balance sheet date). These procedures could be substantive procedures, possibly combined with tests of controls for the intervening period. The auditor needs evidence that will provide a reasonable basis for extending the audit conclusions from the interim date to year-end.

Another timing issue involves performing procedures during the cutoff period. The **cutoff period** is usually several days before and after the balance sheet date.

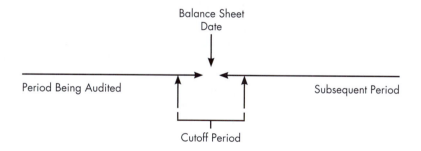

The greatest risk of recording transactions in the wrong period occurs during the cutoff period. For example, auditors are often concerned with whether sales, sales returns, and cash receipts transactions have been recorded in the proper period. To make this determination, the auditor performs **cutoff tests**, and the extent of cutoff tests depends on the auditor's assessment of the effectiveness of the client's cutoff controls. If the client has effective controls to assure that transactions are recorded in the correct period, the auditor can minimize such testing. However, it should be emphasized that controls can be overridden and that auditors have historically found a high degree of risk related to recording sales transactions in the correct period.

Performing Substantive Analytical Procedures

LO **4** Discuss the use of, and apply, substantive analytical procedures.

Both U.S. and international auditing standards allow the auditor the option of performing substantive analytical procedures; they are not required. A primary benefit of performing substantive analytical procedures is that they can reduce the need to perform additional, possibly more costly, substantive tests of details. *Exhibit 6.9* shows how the mix of tests may vary if the auditor performs

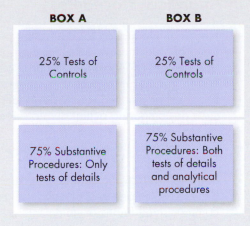

EXHIBIT 6.9 — Alternative Approaches to Substantive Procedures

BOX A

25% Tests of Controls

75% Substantive Procedures: Only tests of details

BOX B

25% Tests of Controls

75% Substantive Procedures: Both tests of details and analytical procedures

substantive analytical procedures. In both Box A and Box B, the auditor is taking a controls reliance approach for a specific account or assertion, and part of the audit evidence is obtained from tests of controls. In Box A, the auditor will obtain the remainder of the audit evidence through substantive tests of details, which might include inspection of documentation, external confirmations, and recalculations. Conversely, in Box B, the auditor will obtain the remainder of the audit evidence from both substantive analytical procedures and substantive tests of details. Note that the relative percentages are judgmental in nature; the examples are simply intended to give you a sense of how an auditor might select an appropriate mix of procedures. As discussed next, if the substantive analytical procedures suggest that the account is materially correct, then the evidence needed from tests of details can be reduced.

In deciding to perform analytical procedures as a substantive audit procedure, the auditor considers the following:

- Does the organization have adequate internal controls over the account? The more effective a client's internal controls, the greater reliance an auditor can place on substantive analytical procedures. Importantly, if an organization does not have effective internal controls, the auditor will rely more heavily on tests of details than on substantive analytical procedures as the auditor will have concerns about the quality of information that would be used in performing the analytical procedure.
- Is the risk of material misstatement low enough that inferences from indirect evidence, such as substantive analytical procedures, are appropriate to make conclusions about an account?
- Are the underlying data used in evaluating an account both relevant and reliable? External sources of data that might be used to help develop expectations include analyst reports and industry benchmarking data, while internal sources include budgets and forecasts, operational information for current and prior periods, and information from discussions with management.
- Are the relationships among the data logical and justified by current economic conditions? Plausible relationships among data may reasonably be expected to exist and continue in the absence of known conditions to the contrary. For example, a plausible relationship likely exists between store square footage and retail sales by store. *Exhibit 6.10* provides examples of other relationships and sources of data that might be used in analytical procedures.

EXHIBIT **6.10** Relationships and Sources of Data That Might Be Used in Analytical Procedures

- Financial information for equivalent prior periods, such as comparing the trend of fourth-quarter sales for the past three years and analyzing dollar and percent changes from the prior year, with expectations as to how the current results are expected to compare with these prior periods
- Expected or planned results developed from budgets or other forecasts, such as comparing actual division performance with budgeted performance
- Comparison of linked account relationships, such as interest expense and interest-bearing debt
- Ratios of financial information, such as examining the relationship between sales and cost of goods sold or developing and analyzing common-sized financial statements
- Company and industry trends, such as comparing gross margin percentages of product lines or inventory turnover with industry averages, with a prior expectation as to how similar the client is with the industry averages
- Analysis of relevant nonfinancial information, such as analyzing the relationship between the numbers of items shipped and royalty expense or the number of employees and payroll expense

The Process for Performing Analytical Procedures

The process for performing analytical procedures is the same regardless of whether the analytical procedures are performed during planning, as a substantive test, or during the final review. This chapter focuses on analytical procedures as a substantive test. *Chapter 7* provides discussion about using analytical procedures as a risk assessment procedure, while *Chapter 14* discusses using analytical procedures when completing the audit. The steps in the process are listed here, along with a discussion of any differences attributed to when the analytical procedure is being performed:

1. Determine the suitability of a particular analytical procedure for given account(s)/assertion(s), considering the risks of material misstatement and tests of details planned.
2. Evaluate the reliability of data that the auditor is using to develop an expectation of account balances or ratios. In evaluating data reliability, the auditor should consider the source of the data, its comparability, the nature of information available about the data, and the controls over the preparation of the data.
3. Develop an expectation of recorded account balances or ratios, and evaluate whether that expectation is precise enough to accomplish the relevant objective. The expectation can be about an account balance, a ratio, or other expected relationship. For example, the auditor might develop an expectation about the client's revenue account, the gross profit margin, or the average payroll expenses per location. In developing an expectation, the auditor relies on information obtained during earlier activities in the audit opinion formulation process. Based on this information, the auditor, for example, may expect an account balance to increase or decrease from the prior period, the auditor may develop a range in which the account balance is expected to fall, or the auditor may develop a point estimate, depending on the objective of the procedure.

i. *Planning analytical procedures*:
Objective: Identify accounts with heightened risk of misstatement during audit planning to provide a basis for designing and implementing responses to the assessed risks
Precision of expectation: Less precise

ii. *Substantive analytical procedures*:
Objective: Obtain evidence regarding the accuracy of account balance/assertion
Precision of expectation: More precise

iii. *Review analytical procedures*:
Objective: Assist the auditor in forming an overall conclusion about whether the financial statements are consistent with the auditor's understanding of the entity
Precision of expectation: Less precise

4. Define when the difference between the auditor's expectation and what the client has recorded would be considered significant. When the auditor develops an expectation, it is unlikely that the expectation will be exactly the same as what the client has recorded. Before comparing the auditor's expectation with what the client has recorded, the auditor should define the difference amount that would be considered significant; this will require consideration of the auditor's assessed materiality level and the auditor's desired level of assurance. Typically, when the risk of material misstatement is higher, the amount of acceptable difference is lower.

5. Compare the client's recorded amounts with the auditor's expectation to determine any significant unexpected differences. Once this mechanical step is completed, the auditor will have identified any significant differences between the auditor's expectation and what the client has recorded. For example, the auditor might have developed an expectation that interest expense will be $1.5 million. If the client has a recorded balance of $1.75 million, the auditor will refer to the assessment made in Step 4 to determine whether this difference is significant. As another example, the auditor might have expected the gross profit margin to be 23%. If the client's recorded gross profit margin is 25.5%, the auditor will refer to the assessment made in Step 4 to determine if this difference is significant.

6. Investigate significant unexpected differences.
i. *Planning analytical procedures*: Significant unexpected differences suggest that substantive procedures for the account/assertion will be increased.

ii. *Substantive analytical procedures*: The auditor should hypothesize as to the possible reasons for the difference, inquire of management as to possible reasons for the difference, and obtain evidence to quantify and corroborate these possible reasons. The auditor may need to increase the tests of details for the relevant account/assertion.

iii. *Review analytical procedures*: The auditor should perform additional procedures as necessary to form an overall conclusion about whether the financial statements are consistent with the auditor's understanding of the entity.

7. Ensure that the following have been appropriately documented: auditor's expectation from Step 3, including the factors that the auditor considered in developing the expectation, the results in Step 4, and the audit procedures conducted relating to Steps 5 and 6.

The *Auditing in Practice* feature "Performing and Documenting Substantive Analytical Procedures by KBA Group" provides an example in which the PCAOB took issue with one audit firm's process for performing and documenting substantive analytical procedures.

Performing and Documenting Substantive Analytical Procedures by KBA Group

AUDITING IN **PRACTICE**

In its inspection of the audit firm KBA Group, the PCAOB noted that in one of KBA Group's audits, the audit team failed to perform and document adequate substantive analytical procedures relating to expenses. While substantive analytical procedures can provide important audit evidence related to income statement accounts, it is important for the audit team to appropriately document and adequately perform these procedures. Otherwise, reviewers of the workpapers, such as the PCAOB, might conclude that the audit team did not obtain sufficient appropriate evidence to support its audit opinion.

U.S. auditing standards require the auditor to document the process of substantive analytical procedures, including the expectation developed by the auditor, and follow up on unexpected differences between the auditor's expectation and the client's recorded account. In contrast, the international auditing standard (ISA 520) does not include specific documentation requirements for substantive analytical procedures.

For further details on the KBA Group inspection report, see PCAOB Release No. 104-2005-016.

Improving the Effectiveness of Substantive Analytical Procedures

The effectiveness of a substantive analytical procedure in providing reliable evidence depends on a number of factors, including (a) the nature of the assertion being tested, (b) the plausibility and predictability of the relationships in the data, (c) the availability and reliability of the data used to develop the expectation, (d) the precision of the expectation that the auditor develops, and (e) the rigor of the analytical procedure employed. While the first three of these factors are relatively self-explanatory, we expand on the latter two of these factors, precision and rigor, next.

In terms of the precision of the expectation, the auditor can develop a very general expectation, for example, that interest income will increase over the prior year. This expectation is likely not precise enough for a substantive analytical procedure. To develop a more precise expectation, the auditor may choose to use disaggregated data. **Disaggregation** involves breaking data down into their component parts, such as different time periods, geographical locations, customer type, or product lines. For example, in the case of interest income, the auditor could disaggregate based on the type of investment, because interest rates will likely vary across investment types. The more you disaggregate the information, the more precise the expectation.

In terms of the rigor of analytical procedures, note that there are various types of analytical procedures, and these types vary in rigor. Three types of analytical procedures that tend to be less rigorous include trend analysis, ratio analysis, and scanning. Trend analysis involves the analysis of changes over time, and its rigor can be improved by including more periods in the trend, using disaggregated data, and using relevant external benchmarks (e.g., industry averages). Ratio analysis involves the comparison of relationships between accounts and between an account and nonfinancial data. Similar to trend analysis, if ratio analysis is going to be used as a substantive analytical procedure, it is important to improve its rigor through the use of disaggregated data and relevant external benchmarks. Scanning could be used as a substantive analytical procedure, although its precision and rigor may not always be sufficient for the level required for substantive analytical procedures. When performing scanning, the auditor looks at account balances, listings of transactions, journals, and so on, in an effort to detect any unusual or unexpected balances or transactions.

As with all analytical procedures, the auditor who is performing scanning has to have an idea of what is usual or expected. The expectation is based on the auditor's knowledge of the client, and of accounting, and just common sense. For example, the auditor would typically not expect to see several entries for round numbers in millions of dollars posted to the revenue journal at the end of each quarter. The auditor would consider such entries unusual and would follow up to investigate this unexpected finding.

A more rigorous approach to substantive analytical procedures is a reasonableness test. In a **reasonableness test**, the auditor develops an expected value of an account by using data partly or wholly independent of the client's accounting information system. For example, the auditor may develop an expectation of a client's interest income, which is equal to the average amount of investments held by the client for the year multiplied by the average interest rate paid on investments as determined by a source external to the client. While such simple models may be sufficient, the rigor of this analytic can be improved by disaggregating the data, possibly by investment type and time period (e.g., a separate expectation for each month or quarter). A reasonableness test for revenue may be more detailed. For example, a reasonable test for sales could be based on the number of units sold, the unit price by product line, different pricing structures, and an understanding of industry trends.

One of the most rigorous approaches to analytical procedures is regression analysis. In performing regression analysis, the expected, or predicted, value is determined using a statistical technique whereby one or more factors are used to predict an account balance. For example, the auditor may develop a regression model that predicts revenue for a client that has hundreds of retail stores. The factors used in the model might include store square footage, economic factors such as employment data, and geographical location. Because of the amount of data and level of statistical knowledge required for such a procedure, many audit firms do not routinely perform regression analysis.

Brief Application of Substantive Analytical Procedures

Substantive analytical procedures are not simple techniques, but are part of a difficult decision-making process designed to provide evidence about the correctness of an account balance and should be used when the procedures are (a) reliable and (b) more cost effective than other substantive procedures.

For example, consider the audit of natural gas revenue at a utility company. Assume that the auditor has tested controls over revenue recognition, including the processes of reading gas meters and the proper pricing of gas sold to customer homes. The auditor has concluded that internal controls are designed and operating effectively. Further, the auditor has concluded that consumers tend to pay their bills and that consumers do not have independent knowledge of the amount that should have been billed. Given these data, the auditor develops a regression model based on the following:

- Previous year's gas billings
- Changes in housing developments
- Changes in pricing of natural gas for the year
- Changes in the efficiency of energy use (index of efficiency considering new furnaces, insulation, etc.)
- Economic growth in the area

Based on these data, the auditor develops a regression model that predicts expected revenue within a tolerable range of error, with 95% accuracy. If the auditor finds that the recorded revenue is within that range, further substantive testing of the account balance may not be necessary. Note that this conclusion is based on the assessment that the risk of material misstatement is low. In areas where significant risks of material misstatement exist, it is unlikely that audit evidence obtained from substantive analytical procedures alone will be sufficient. In those situations, the auditor will likely also need to perform substantive tests of details. However, if substantive analytical procedures provide reliable evidence, the auditor may be able to alter the type, timing, or extent of substantive tests of details.

If a comparison of the auditor's expectation based on the regression analysis and the client's recorded revenue balance indicates a significant difference, the auditor will follow up on this difference. The auditor should consider possible explanations for the difference, and even consider the possibility that the auditor's expectation might be flawed in some way (e.g., the expectation did not incorporate important and recent economic events). Other causes for significant differences could be error or fraud in the client's accounting records. The auditor will also inquire of the client as to possible explanations. However, the auditor's follow-up needs to go beyond client inquiry and needs to include quantification and corroboration. **Quantification** involves determining whether an explanation for the difference can, in fact, account for the observed difference. If not, then additional explanations may be needed. **Corroboration** involves obtaining sufficient evidence that the explanation is accurate. The auditor must not just accept the client's explanation without corroborating that explanation.

The *Auditing in Practice* feature "Analytical Procedures Are Not Client Estimates" provides important advice about the distinction between the work of the audit firm and the work of client management.

Sufficiency of Audit Evidence

LO 5 Identify factors affecting the sufficiency of audit evidence.

Sufficiency of evidence is the measure of the quantity of audit evidence (e.g., a sample size of documents to be reviewed or the number of observations of a control activity). The quantity of audit evidence needed is affected by the auditor's assessment of the risks of material misstatement (the higher the assessed risks, the more audit evidence is likely to be required) and also by the quality of such audit evidence (the higher the evidence quality, the less evidence may be required). The amount of evidence must be of sufficient quantity to convince the audit team of the effectiveness of internal control or

Analytical Procedures Are Not Client Estimates

AUDITING IN **PRACTICE**

There is sometimes confusion about the use of analytical procedures because they often look like client estimates. For example, in smaller businesses, the auditor's working papers may have the most useful data on bad-debt write-offs, percentage of bad debts as a percentage of sales, changes in credit policies, and changes in the volume of sales. The auditor may use these data in testing an estimate of the allowance for uncollectible accounts prepared by the client. However—and this is important—management is responsible for estimating the allowance. The auditor's work is to gather evidence on the accuracy of that estimate. The auditor's testing may come from gathering

evidence to support the client's underlying assumptions and recomputing the estimate. Alternatively, the auditor's testing may come from a substantive analytical procedure—using accumulated data in the auditor's workpapers, plus additional economic data, to come up with an independent estimate of the proper account balance. That estimate, however, represents audit evidence that the auditor should use in determining whether or not the client's account balance is correct. Substantive analytical procedures are designed to provide independent evidence about account balances—not to replace management's underlying estimation process.

the accuracy of an account balance or assertion. Similarly, the evidence must stand on its own such that another unbiased professional would reach the same conclusion. However, how much evidence is enough? This is partly a matter of experienced audit judgment, and it is also affected by client risk characteristics. Importantly, audit evidence is integrated from a number of sources. Documentation of that evidence from multiple sources and the demonstrated testing of account balances remain paramount and are the first things to be questioned when an audit fails.

The *Focus on Fraud* feature "When an Auditor Fails to Collect Sufficient Evidence: The Case at Ligand Pharmaceuticals" provides an example of the personal ramifications to the auditor of knowingly and recklessly not collecting sufficient evidence. In that feature, the audit partner was aware of factors that called into question the adequacy of Ligand's reserves for returns (e.g., lack of actual return history, limited visibility into distribution channels, and significant increases in or excess levels of inventory), but he did not adequately analyze whether those factors impaired Ligand's ability to make reasonable estimates of returns. Consequently, the PCAOB concluded that the auditor in this case did not have a sufficient basis to support the conclusion that Ligand's revenue recognition was appropriate.

FOCUS on **FRAUD**

When an Auditor Fails to Collect Sufficient Evidence: The Case at Ligand Pharmaceuticals

James L. Fazio, age 46, was a CPA and partner in the San Diego office of Deloitte LLP. He was the partner-in-charge of the audit of Ligand Pharmaceuticals. At the time of the 2003 Ligand audit, Deloitte's audit policies required that each client's engagement risk be assessed annually as normal, greater than normal, or much greater than normal. In Ligand's case, the engagement team assessed engagement risk as "greater than normal" because of concerns regarding product sales and sales returns. Specifically, the engagement team documented concern in the audit workpapers that Ligand's estimates of sales returns and reserves were not sufficient to cover actual returns. Given the heightened risk, the written audit plan called for the engagement team to perform procedures to address the issue and to increase its professional skepticism regarding the returns issues.

However, the PCAOB found that James Fazio failed to obtain sufficient appropriate evidence to afford a reasonable basis for an opinion regarding the financial statements. Specifically, he failed to (1) adequately assess whether Ligand had gathered sufficient evidence to properly estimate future returns, (2) adequately evaluate the reasonableness of Ligand's estimates of returns, and (3) identify and address issues concerning Ligand's exclusion of certain returns from its estimates of returns.

The PCAOB concluded that Fazio's conduct met conditions warranting sanctions because of

"intentional or knowing conduct, including reckless conduct." As a result of this conclusion, the PCAOB ordered that Fazio not be allowed to associate with a registered public accounting firm; but he may file a petition for PCAOB consent to have such an association after two years.

Ultimately, Ligand restated its financial statements for 2003 and other periods because its revenue recognition did not follow the applicable financial reporting framework. In its restatement, Ligand recognized about $59 million less in revenues (a 52% decrease from what was originally reported), and revealed a net loss that was more than 2.5 times the net loss originally reported. Thus, investors were misled by Ligand's misstated financial statements and by Fazio's failure to conduct sufficient audit tests in a manner that would have led to more accurate financial statements.

The punishment that Fazio received highlights an evidence-sufficiency dilemma for auditors: No bright-line requirements tell auditors that they have collected enough evidence, yet if it is subsequently determined that they have not done so, then very severe ramifications can exist for what is subsequently deemed improper professional judgment.

For further information on this case, see PCAOB Release No. 105-2007-006, December 10, 2007.

Sample Sizes

For many tests of controls and substantive tests of details, the auditor will need to determine a sample size to use for testing. For example, assume that the auditor wants to send accounts receivable confirmations to a client's customers to obtain evidence related to the existence assertion. Or assume that the auditor wants to test the operating effectiveness of a control by inspecting purchase orders for the required approval. How many confirmations should be sent? How many purchase orders should be inspected? The sample size can be determined by applying a statistically based formula or using the auditor's professional judgment. When performing substantive tests of details, factors that would be considered in determining sample size include the risk of material misstatement and the assurance obtained from other procedures. When performing tests of controls, the extent of evidence necessary to persuade the auditor that the control is effective depends upon the risk associated with the control, that is, the risk that the control might not be effective and, if not effective, the risk that a material misstatement could occur. As the risk associated with the control being tested increases, the evidence that the auditor should obtain also increases. *Chapter 8* includes a discussion of issues related to determining appropriate sample sizes.

Additional Sample Size Considerations for Tests of Controls

When performing tests of controls, the amount of evidence the auditor needs to obtain depends on whether the client has tested controls as a basis for its assertion on the effectiveness of internal control. Further, the type of control being tested will affect the auditor's sample size. If the auditor is testing a manual control related to transaction processing, sample sizes will be based on guidelines developed for attribute testing using statistical sampling techniques (discussed in *Chapter 8*). For the most part, these sample sizes will vary between 30 and 100 transactions. In contrast, as discussed in *Chapter 3*, some controls related to transaction processing are automated controls built into computer applications. If the auditor has tested general computer controls, such as controls over program changes, and has concluded that those controls are effective, the tests of computerized application controls could be as small as one for each kind of control of interest to the auditor.

Another factor influencing sample sizes for tests of controls is the frequency with which a control is performed. For monthly controls, such as a bank reconciliation, the auditor could choose one month and perform a test of control, such as inspection of documentation or reperformance. In contrast, if a control is performed multiple times each day, such as controls over sales transactions, the auditor will use a larger sample.

Controls over adjusting entries require additional consideration as adjusting entries represent a high risk of material misstatement. The auditor's extent of tests of controls over adjusting entries will be inversely related to the control environment; in other words, the better the control environment, the smaller the sample size will be, and vice versa. The testing also varies directly with the materiality of the account balance and the auditor's assessment of risk that the account balance might be misstated. The auditor wants to review a sufficient number of transactions to determine that (a) other controls are not being overridden by management; (b) there is support for the adjusting entries, for example, underlying data analyses; and (c) the entries are properly approved by the appropriate level of management. If the number of transactions is high, the auditor might use statistical sampling. If the number of transactions is low, the auditor may choose to focus on the larger transactions.

Additional Evidence Considerations

LO 6 Identify issues related to audit evidence needed for accounts involving management estimates.

Evidence Needed for Auditing Management Estimates

Most significant measurements in the financial statements are subject to estimates, appraisals, or other management assumptions. Examples include warranty liabilities, allowance for doubtful accounts or loan loss reserves, pension costs and liabilities, valuations of long-lived assets, fair market value assessments, and analysis of goodwill for possible impairment. The auditor must determine that these management judgments are substantiated by independent, objective, and verifiable data that support the estimates. Unfortunately, accounting estimates have too often been subject to earnings management. As illustrated in the *Focus on Fraud* feature "Common Types of Earnings Management Techniques," auditors must take special care to exercise appropriate professional skepticism in evaluating the reasonableness of management estimates so that earnings management can be mitigated in a quality audit.

Auditors need to understand the process used by management in developing estimates, including (a) controls over the process, (b) the reliability of underlying data in developing the estimate, (c) use of outside experts by management (e.g., how they were used and their expertise), and (d) how management reviews the results of the estimates for reasonableness.

The auditor should evaluate, based on the audit evidence, whether the accounting estimates in the financial statements are reasonable. The auditor should also obtain sufficient appropriate audit evidence about whether

FOCUS on **FRAUD**

Common Types of Earnings Management Techniques

What types of earnings management related to estimates and other subjective assessments should auditors be prepared to detect and address? Examples of common types include:

- *Cookie jar reserve techniques*—This approach involves management overaccruing expenses in the current period to set up a reserve that is reversed back into income in a future period. Examples of areas where cookie jar reserves are often created include accounts receivable allowance for doubtful accounts, sales returns and allowances, warranty allowances, and inventory allowance for valuation declines. This approach is typically used when management has already met its numbers and has extra cushion that can be saved for future periods that may not be as good.
- *Big bath techniques*—This approach is used when a company is already reporting bad news and involves charging as many potential future

costs to expenses in the current bad year, so that those costs will not have to be recognized in the future. While the current year stock price will be negatively affected, management thinks that a little more bad news will not be noticed, and future years will look particularly good and the stock price will rebound accordingly. Auditors should watch for the application of big bath techniques when companies report asset impairments, dispose of a significant part of their operations, or restructure debt.

- *Amortization, depreciation, and depletion techniques*—When a company has long-lived assets, those assets are expensed through amortization, depreciation, or depletion. The auditor should watch for management to exercise judgment in making selective decisions about the type of write-off method used, the write-off period, and the estimate of salvage value that might indicate earnings management.

disclosures in the financial statements related to accounting estimates are appropriate. Options for obtaining evidence include the following:

• Determine whether events occurring up to the date of the auditor's report provide audit evidence regarding the accounting estimate (e.g., sale of a discontinued product shortly after the period end may provide audit evidence relating to the estimate of its net realizable value).

• Test how management made the accounting estimate and the data on which it is based. The auditor should evaluate whether the method of measurement used is appropriate, the assumptions used by management are reasonable, the data on which the estimate is based are sufficiently reliable.

• Test the operating effectiveness of controls over the process management used to make the accounting estimate, together with appropriate substantive procedures.

• Develop a point estimate or range to evaluate management's point estimate.

Estimates that are based on industry-wide or economy-wide trends need to be independently evaluated. For example, earnings assumptions related to returns on pension funds should be based on how well stocks, as a whole, are doing within the economy and long-run predicted growth within the economy. Other pension data include actuarial reports on life expectancies and benefits that rely on experts. The auditor should review such evidence for consistency with economic reports and actuarial reports, and compare with the assumptions used by other clients and other companies in the same industry.

The *Emerging Issues* feature "PCAOB Considers Change in Auditing Standard for Auditing Estimates" notes that changes to guidance in this area are under consideration.

Using a Specialist/Expert to Assist with Obtaining Evidence

LO 7 Determine situations requiring the auditor to use a specialist/expert in gathering and evaluating evidence and describe the auditor's responsibilities related to that specialist/expert.

When obtaining audit evidence for certain accounts, auditors may need to rely on work performed by an outside specialist/expert. (International auditing standards use the term *expert* rather than specialist; for simplicity we use the term *specialist* but acknowledge that both terms are appropriate.) For some accounts, expertise in a field other than accounting or auditing is necessary to obtain sufficient appropriate audit evidence. For example, using the work of and relying on the valuation opinions of outside specialists are particularly relevant in auditing natural resources and other long-lived assets

PCAOB Considers Change in Auditing Standard for Auditing Estimates

EMERGING ISSUE

In response to issues identified during the inspection of accounting firms, comments received from members of the PCAOB Standing Advisory Group (SAG), and the Financial Accounting Standards Board's (FASB) proposed accounting standard on financial instruments, the PCAOB staff began drafting a proposal for a standard on auditing accounting estimates, including fair value measurements and related disclosures. The Board anticipates proposing a standard for public comment during 2014. Timing of standard-setting projects is subject to change. Be sure to check the PCAOB web site for updates on this emerging issue.

in which subject-matter expertise is required. The following are other examples where the auditor would likely rely on a specialist:

- The valuation of land and buildings, plant and machinery, jewelry, works of art, antiques, and intangible assets
- The estimation of oil and gas reserves
- The interpretation of contracts, laws, and regulations
- The analysis of complex or unusual tax compliance issues

The relevant auditing standards apply to situations in which the auditor has responsibilities relating to the work of an individual in a field of specialization other than accounting or auditing, and when the auditor uses that work to obtain sufficient appropriate audit evidence. Auditing standards require the auditor to understand the role, knowledge, and objectivity of the specialist and how the specialist's work affects important financial accounts.

When using the work of an **auditor's specialist**, the auditor needs to evaluate the professional qualifications of the individual. In making this evaluation, the auditor will consider:

- The professional certification, license, or other recognition of the competence of the specialist in his or her field, as appropriate
- The reputation and standing of the specialist in the views of peers and others familiar with the specialist's capability or performance
- The specialist's experience in the type of work under consideration

Further, the auditor needs to understand the nature of the work performed by the specialist. The auditor will:

- Obtain an understanding of the methods and assumptions used by the specialist
- Make appropriate tests of data provided to the specialist, taking into account the auditor's assessment of control risk
- Evaluate whether the specialist's findings support the related assertions in the financial statements

AU-C 620 notes that even when the auditor uses a specialist to obtain audit evidence, the auditor still has ultimate responsibility for the audit opinion.

> The auditor has sole responsibility for the audit opinion expressed, and that responsibility is not reduced by the auditor's use of the work of an auditor's specialist. Nonetheless, if the auditor using the work of an auditor's specialist, having followed this section, concludes that the work of that specialist is adequate for the auditor's purposes, the auditor may accept that specialist's findings or conclusions in the specialist's field as appropriate audit evidence.

Evidence Needed for Related-Party Transactions

LO 8 Describe the evidence needs for related-party transactions.

Some client transactions are **related-party transactions**. These are transactions that a client has with other companies or individuals that may be related to either the client or client's senior management. Related-party transactions can occur between:

- Parents and subsidiaries
- An entity and its owners
- An entity and other organizations in which it has part ownership, such as joint ventures
- An entity and an assortment of special-purpose entities (SPEs), such as those designed to keep debt off the balance sheet

Many related-party transactions are conducted in the normal course of business and have no higher risk of material misstatement than similar transactions with unrelated parties. However, the nature of related-party relationships and transactions may give rise to higher risks of material misstatement of the financial statements than transactions with unrelated parties. For example, related-party transactions may be motivated primarily to engage in fraudulent financial reporting or to conceal misappropriation of assets. Or related-party transactions may not be conducted under normal market terms and conditions. These types of transactions present unique challenges for auditors.

When performing procedures for related-party transactions, the auditor should expect the client to have an information system, with effective internal controls, that can identify all related parties and account for all related-party transactions. The auditor should begin with an understanding of the information system developed by the client to identify such transactions. The auditor should be aware that, in some cases, the client may not want to have related-party transactions discovered. Still, the auditor will work to obtain a list of all related parties and develop a list of all transactions with those parties during the year.

Once all related parties are identified, the auditor can use generalized audit software (discussed in *Chapter 8*) to read the client files and list all transactions that occurred with these parties. The auditor then investigates the transactions to determine whether they have been properly recorded and disclosed. *Exhibit 6.11* provides an overview of relevant audit procedures for related-party transactions.

EXHIBIT **6.11**   Relevant Audit Procedures for Related-Party Transactions

AUDIT OBJECTIVE: Determine if related-party transactions occurred during the year and whether they are properly (a) authorized, (b) recorded, and (c) disclosed in the financial statements.

a. Inquire of the client about processes used to identify related-party transactions and the client's approach to accounting for related-party transactions.

b. Ask the client to prepare a list of all related parties. Supplement that list with disclosures that have been made to the Securities and Exchange Commission (SEC) of top officers and directors in the company. For smaller businesses, supplement the list with a listing of known relatives who may be active in the business or related businesses.

c. Ask the client for a list of all related-party transactions, including those with SPEs or variable interest entities, that occurred during the year.

d. Discuss the appropriate accounting for all identified related-party transactions with the client and develop an understanding of the appropriate disclosure for the financial statements.

e. Inquire of the client and its lawyers as to whether the client is under any investigation by regulatory agencies or law officials regarding related-party transactions.

f. Review the news media and SEC filings for any investigations of related-party transactions of the client.

g. Use generalized audit software to read the client's files and prepare a list of all transactions that occurred with related entities per the lists identified earlier. Compare the list to that developed by the client to help determine the quality of the client's information system.

h. Identify all unusual transactions using information specific to the client, including information on (a) unusually large sales occurring near the end of a period, (b) sales transactions with unusual terms, (c) purchase transactions that appear to be coming from customers, and (d) any other criteria the auditor might consider useful.

i. Review the transactions and investigate whether or not the transactions occurred with related entities. If related parties can be identified, determine the purpose of the transactions and consider the appropriate financial statement disclosure.

j. Determine whether any of the transactions were fraudulent or were prepared primarily to develop fraudulent financial statements. If there is intent to deceive, or if there is misuse of corporate funds, report the fraud or misuse to the board of directors. Follow up to determine if appropriate action is taken. If such action is not taken, consult with legal counsel.

k. Determine the appropriate accounting and footnote disclosure.

l. Prepare a memo on findings.

PCAOB Updates Guidance for Auditing Related Parties

In 2014, the PCAOB adopted AS 18 "Related Parties." The adopted standard provides additional audit requirements for auditing related party transactions, including the need for these procedures to be risk based. The PCAOB adopted the updated guidance because related-party transactions and relationships pose increased risk of material misstatement in company financial statements and auditors need to be responsive to those risks. Be sure to check the PCAOB web site for updates on this emerging issue.

In addition to the procedures in *Exhibit 6.11*, the auditor, throughout the audit, should remain alert for information that may indicate the existence of related-party relationships or transactions that management has not previously identified or disclosed to the auditor.

The *Emerging Issues* feature "PCAOB Updates Guidance for Auditing Related Parties" notes the recent changes to guidance in this area.

Documenting Audit Evidence

LO 9 Describe the characteristics of quality audit documentation.

Audit documentation is the record that forms the basis for the auditor's representations and conclusions. Audit documentation facilitates the planning, performance, and supervision of the audit and forms the basis of the review of the quality of the work performed. Documentation may be on paper or in electronic form.

Auditors like to assume that their work will never be questioned, but that is an unrealistic assumption. The documentation of audit work must stand on its own. The documentation should make it possible for an experienced auditor to evaluate the evidence independently of the individuals who performed the audit and reach the same conclusion. AS 3 notes that the documentation must also clearly show the auditor's reasoning process and the basis for conclusions reached on the audit. AS 3 states, "Audit documentation should be prepared in sufficient detail to provide a clear understanding of its purpose, source, and the conclusions reached. Also, the documentation should be appropriately organized to provide a clear link to the significant findings or issues."

Audit documentation should include information about planning and risk assessment procedures (including the response to risk assessment procedures), audit work performed (including tests of controls and substantive procedures) and conclusions reached, and significant issues identified and their resolution.

Documenting Planning and Risk Assessment Procedures

The planning process and risk assessment procedures form the foundation for the audit and should be carefully documented. For example, as part of performing the planning and the risk assessment procedures, the auditor should document the overall audit strategy and the audit plan. Further, the auditor should document the overall planned responses to address the assessed risks of material misstatement, and the nature, timing, and extent of the further audit procedures to be performed, as well as the linkage of those procedures with the assessed risks at the relevant assertion level. The documentation

EXHIBIT **6.12** Examples of Information Documented From Risk Assessment Procedures

- Interviews with key executives, with implications clearly drawn for the conduct of the audit
- Business risk analysis, fraud risk analysis, and analytical procedures, with a clear identification of accounts and assertions requiring special audit attention
- The auditor's assessment of materiality, overall audit approach, and personnel needed
- Evidence of planning (including identification of and response to risks of material misstatement), including the audit program
- Audit approach and basic data utilized to identify risk, including fraud risk
- Updates on how significant issues from previous year's audits are addressed during the current audit
- An analysis of the auditor's assessment of internal control and a linkage of control deficiencies to expanded (or different) audit tests for accounts where high risk of material misstatements exists
- Memoranda that describe the auditor's conclusions regarding risk associated with acceptance or continuance of the client
- Extent of involvement of professionals with specialized skills

serves an important planning function for the audit; it also serves as evidence that the auditors took their responsibilities seriously in evaluating potential problems or special circumstances involved in, or related to, the audit. *Exhibit 6.12* provides examples of information related to the risk assessment procedures that the auditor would typically document.

Documenting Audit Work Performed

After identifying risks of material misstatement and making a plan for responding to those risks, auditors execute that plan. Documentation about audit work performed is critical in demonstrating at a later date that the audit was conducted in a quality manner. The following are typical types of documentation used to demonstrate the audit work that was performed:

- The client's trial balance and any auditor-proposed adjustments to it
- Copies of selected internal and external documents
- Memos describing the auditor's approach to gathering evidence and the reasoning process in support of account balances
- Results of analytical procedures and tests of client records, and the individuals responsible for performance, and subsequently the review, of the procedures
- Correspondence with specialists who provided evidence significant to the evaluation or accounting for assets or liabilities and the related revenue expense effects (e.g., valuation specialists), including an analysis of the independence and credentials of the specialists
- Auditor-generated analysis of account balances (e.g., audit software analysis of accounts and relationships)
- As part of documenting the work performed, auditors will assemble a **permanent file** that includes schedules, documents, and records that are relevant for the current and future audits. Items in the permanent file include the client's articles of incorporation, bylaws, bond covenant agreements, and loan agreements. The auditor will also maintain a

current file that includes schedules, documents, and analyses that are relevant to the current-year audit. The current file includes findings from substantive tests and tests of controls. Examples of documents from outside parties that are retained in the current file include responses to the auditor's confirmation requests for accounts receivable, pending litigation, or bank loans. Auditor-generated documents would also be maintained in the current file. The *Auditing in Practice* feature "Auditor-Generated Memos as Audit Documentation" discusses the importance of this type of documentation.

Documenting Significant Issues and Their Resolution

Significant issues or **audit findings** are defined as substantive matters that are important to the analysis of the fair presentation of the financial statements. AS 3 provides the following examples of significant issues or audit findings:

- Significant matters involving the selection, application, and consistency of accounting principles, including related disclosures. Significant matters include, but are not limited to, accounting for complex or unusual transactions, accounting estimates, and uncertainties, as well as related management assumptions
- Results of auditing procedures that indicated a need for the modification of planned auditing procedures, or the existence of material misstatements, omissions in the financial statements, significant deficiencies, or material weaknesses in internal control over financial reporting
- Audit adjustments. An **audit adjustment** is a correction of a misstatement of the financial statements that was or should have been proposed by the auditor, whether or not recorded by management, which could, either individually or when aggregated with other misstatements, have a material effect on the company's financial statements
- Disagreements among members of the engagement team or with others consulted on the engagement about final conclusions reached on significant accounting or auditing matters
- Circumstances that cause significant difficulty in applying auditing procedures
- Significant changes in the assessed level of audit risk for particular audit areas and the auditor's response to those changes
- Any matters that could result in the modification of the auditor's report

Auditor-Generated Memos as Audit Documentation

AUDITING IN **PRACTICE**

Auditors assimilate diverse evidence to reach an opinion as to whether a particular account balance is fairly stated. The auditor's reasoning process in gathering and analyzing evidence is important and should be documented via auditor-generated memos. At first you might think that documenting your own opinion is unnecessary. After all, you will have documented all the evidence underlying that opinion. However, the documentation must stand on its own; in other words, another auditor must be able to understand the reasoning process by which you evaluated that evidence and formulated your opinion. In order to gain that understanding, another auditor will not be able to rely on just talking to you. Over time you will likely forget important details about how you reached your opinions; therefore, documenting them for the audit file via an auditor-generated memo is essential.

The PCAOB requires that all audit engagements document significant issues or audit findings, as well as the actions taken to address them (including additional evidence obtained, where applicable). The following are typical types of documentation retained to demonstrate audit work related to the identification of significant issues and their resolution:

- Description of significant accounting issues that were identified during the course of audit and how they were resolved, including any correspondence with national office experts
- A clear articulation of the auditor's judgment and the reasoning process that led to the judgment on the fairness of the financial statements

Characteristics of Quality Audit Documentation

Audit documentation serves as the primary evidence of an audit. *Exhibit 6.13* provides an example of a workpaper related to an inventory price test. A review of *Exhibit 6.13* indicates that audit documentation should contain the following:

- A heading that includes the name of the audit client, an explanatory title, and the balance sheet date
- The initials or electronic signature of the auditor performing the audit test and the date the test was completed

---

EXHIBIT 6.13 Workpaper for Inventory Price Test

C-1/2

Gordon's Bay Manufacturing
Inventory Price Test
Year Ended December 31, 2015

Prepared by: ACM
Date: 1/21/16
Reviewed by: KMJ
Date: 1/30/16

Item No.	Item Name	Quantity	Cost Per Unit	Extended Cost
4287	Advanced Microstamping machine	22*	$5,128†	112,816.00‡
5203	1/4 HP electric motor	10*	$39†	390.00‡
2208	Assembly kit for motor housing	25*	$12†	300.00‡
1513	Micro stamping machine, Model 25	200*	$2,100†	420,000.00‡
0068	Rack & Pinion component	300*	$42†	12,600.00‡
8890	Repair kits for stamping machines	1,000*	$48†	48,000.00‡
	Total value of items tested			594,106.00
	Items not tested			1,802,000.00
	Balance per general ledger			2,396,106.00§

Sampled items were selected utilizing a dollar unit sampling technique with materiality of $50,000, and internal control assessed as effective (B-1).
*Quantities agree with client physical inventory tested earlier.
†Traced to client's standard cost system that was independently tested (B-2). Amount agrees with client's standard cost.
‡Tested extension, no exceptions.
§Footed, no exceptions; agrees with trial balance.
Conclusion: No significant issues were noted. In my opinion, the pricing and clerical accuracy of inventory are proper.

- The initials or electronic signature of the manager or partner who reviewed the documentation and the date the review was completed
- A unique workpaper page number (see C-1/2 in *Exhibit 6.13*; the page number is used to cross-reference to other workpapers)
- A description of the tests performed (including the items looked at) and the findings
- **Tick marks** and a tick mark legend indicating the nature of the work performed by the auditor († is an example of a tick mark used in *Exhibit 6.13*; the tick mark legend appears near the bottom of the workpaper)
- A conclusion as to whether the work performed indicates the possibility of material misstatement in an account
- A cross-reference to related documentation, when applicable (see references to other workpapers, including B-1 and B-2, in *Exhibit 6.13*)
- A section that identifies all significant issues that arose during the audit and how they were resolved
- A comprehensive and clear memorandum that delineates the auditor's analysis of the consistency of audit evidence and the conclusions reached regarding the fairness of the financial presentation (see references to other worked performed at B-1 and B-2 in *Exhibit 6.13*. A second page of this workpaper, C-2/2, would likely include a more comprehensive memo.)

Revisions and Retention of Audit Documentation

Audit documentation is the property of the auditor and generally should be completed and assembled within forty-five to sixty days (depending on the type of client) following the audit report release date. After that date, the auditor must not delete or discard audit documentation before the end of the required retention period (generally seven years from the report release date). Occasionally, because of an internal or external quality review process, it may be determined that procedures considered necessary were omitted from the audit or the auditor subsequently becomes aware of information related to financial statements that have already been issued. The auditor should then perform any necessary procedures and make the necessary changes to the audit documentation. This issue is discussed further in *Chapter 14*.

Audit Programs

LO 10 Explain the nature, design, and purposes of audit programs.

As discussed in *Chapter 5*, an audit program documents the procedures to be performed in gathering audit evidence and is used to record the successful completion of each audit step. The audit program provides an effective means for:

- Organizing and distributing audit work
- Monitoring the audit process and progress
- Recording the audit work performed and those responsible for performing the work
- Reviewing the completeness and persuasiveness of procedures performed

Most audit firms have standardized audit programs that should be modified to fit a client's unique features, including risk factors. For example, the audit of accounts receivable might appear to be the same for most businesses. However, significant differences may exist in how each client processes receivables and the related controls, or their credit terms, or in the economic health of their industry that might cause an audit team to modify a standard audit program to fit the particular circumstances of the client.

SUMMARY AND NEXT STEPS

Each audit is unique, but the approach to all audits is essentially the same. Management makes assertions in financial statements and might also make an assertion about the effectiveness of internal control over financial reporting. The auditor gathers, analyzes, and documents evidence about these assertions to be able to reach a justified opinion on the fairness of the financial statements or the effectiveness of internal control. Auditing standards require the auditor to gather sufficient appropriate evidence. A quality audit combines this audit evidence to provide reasonable assurance that the financial statements are free of material misstatement. Now that you understand audit evidence and audit procedures, the next chapter turns to the planning phase of the audit, including risk assessment procedures.

SIGNIFICANT TERMS

Accounting records The records of initial accounting entries and supporting records.

Analytical procedures Evaluations of financial information through analyzing plausible relationships among both financial and nonfinancial data.

Appropriateness of audit evidence A measure of the quality of audit evidence, and includes both the relevance and reliability of the evidence.

Audit adjustment Correction of a misstatement of financial statements that was or should have been proposed by the auditor, whether or not recorded by management, that could, either individually or when aggregated with other misstatements, have a material effect on the company's financial statements.

Audit documentation The written record that forms the basis for the auditor's conclusions.

Audit findings (also see Significant issues) Substantive matters that are important to the procedures performed, evidence obtained, or conclusions reached on an audit.

Auditor's specialist An individual or organization possessing expertise in a field other than accounting or auditing, whose work in that field is used by the auditor to assist the auditor in obtaining sufficient appropriate audit evidence. An auditor's specialist may be either an auditor's internal specialist (who is a partner or staff, including temporary staff, of the auditor's firm or a network firm) or an auditor's external specialist.

Corroboration Obtaining sufficient evidence that management's explanation is accurate.

Cross-footing Checking the agreement of the cross-addition of a number of columns of figures that sum to a grand total.

Current file File that includes schedules, documents, and analyses that are relevant to the current-year audit.

Cutoff period A period of time usually covering several days before and after the client's balance sheet date.

Cutoff tests Procedures applied to transactions selected from those recorded during the cutoff period to provide evidence as to whether the transactions have been recorded in the proper period.

Direct evidence Audit evidence that requires only one inference to reach a conclusion about the assertion being tested. Usually that inference is that the sample taken is representative of the population as a whole.

Directional testing An approach to testing account balances that considers the type of misstatement likely to occur in the account balance and the corresponding evidence provided by other accounts that have been tested. The auditor normally tests assets and expenses for overstatement, and liabilities and revenues for understatement, because (1) the major risks of misstatements on those accounts are in those directions or (2) tests of other accounts provide evidence of possible misstatements in the other direction.

Disaggregation Breaking data down into their component parts, such as different time periods, geographical locations, customer type, or product lines.

Footing Adding a column of figures to verify the correctness of the client's totals.

Indirect evidence Audit evidence that requires a linkage of inferences to provide assurance about the assertion being tested, that is, one or more inferences are made. Examples include inferences made when using analytical procedures as audit evidence.

Interim date A date at which audit evidence is collected earlier than the balance sheet date.

Management's specialist An individual or organization possessing expertise in a field other than accounting or auditing, whose work in that field is used by the client to assist management in preparing the financial statements.

Permanent file File that includes schedules, documents, and records that are relevant for the current and future audits.

Quantification Determining whether management's explanation for observed differences can, in fact, account for the observed difference.

Reasonableness test The development of an expected value of an account by using data partly or wholly independent of the client's accounting information system.

Recalculating estimated amounts Recomputing an amount that the client has already estimated, such as recomputing the allowance for doubtful accounts based on a formula related to the aging of accounts receivable ending balances.

Related-party transactions Transactions that a client has with other companies or people who may be related to either the client or client's senior management.

Relevance of audit evidence Evidence that provides insight on the validity of the assertion being tested; that is, the evidence bears directly on the assertion being tested.

Reliability of audit evidence   A measure of the quality of the underlying evidence. It is influenced by risk, potential management bias associated with the evidence, and the quality of the internal control system underlying the preparation of the evidence.

Reperformance   The auditor's independent execution of controls that were originally performed as part of the entity's internal control.

Roll-forward period   The period between the confirmation date and the balance sheet date.

Scanning   A type of analytical procedure involving the auditor's review of accounting data to identify significant or unusual items to test.

Significant issues (also see Audit findings)   Substantive matters that are important to the procedures performed, evidence obtained, or conclusions reached on an audit.

Sufficiency of evidence   Measure of the quantity of audit evidence.

Tests of extensions   Recomputing items involving multiplication.

Tick marks   Abbreviations and symbols used by auditors to document the work they have performed and any issues identified during their work.

Tracing   Taking a sample of original source documents and ensuring that the transactions related to the source documents have been recorded in the appropriate journal and general ledger.

Vouching   Taking a sample of recorded transactions and obtaining the original source documents supporting the recorded transaction.

TRUE/FALSE QUESTIONS

6-1   **LO 1**   The appropriateness of audit evidence refers to its relevance and reliability.

6-2   **LO 1**   The sufficiency of evidence is a measure of evidence quality.

6-3   **LO 2**   When testing for existence, the auditor will vouch recorded transactions.

6-4   **LO 2**   Evidence that is obtained directly from the client is usually considered more reliable than evidence obtained from a source independent of the client.

6-5   **LO 3**   A procedure that involves only inspection of documentation is usually considered to be of lower quality than a procedure involving reperformance.

6-6   **LO 3**   All audit procedures need to be performed at or after the client's balance sheet date.

6-7   **LO 4**   Substantive analytical procedures are required on every audit.

6-8   **LO 4**   One of the most rigorous approaches to substantive analytical procedures is regression analysis.

6-9   **LO 5**   The quantity of audit evidence needed when testing an account will be influenced by the risk of material misstatement in that account.

6-10 LO 5 When testing the operating effectiveness of a control, the frequency with which the control is performed can influence the sample size to be used by the auditor.

6-11 LO 6 Because management estimates are often subjective, the auditor does not need to test these estimates, but can rely solely on management's work.

6-12 LO 6 When testing management estimates, the auditor should understand the process that management uses to develop its estimates.

6-13 LO 7 When relying on the work of an auditor specialist, the auditor should evaluate the professional qualifications of the specialist.

6-14 LO 7 When the auditor uses the work of an auditor specialist, the auditor's responsibility for the audit opinion is reduced.

6-15 LO 8 The auditor may be able to use generalized audit software to identify transactions that have been entered into with related parties.

6-16 LO 8 A primary concern for the auditor for related-party transactions is whether undisclosed related-party relationships and transactions exist.

6-17 LO 9 The auditor should document significant issues that were identified and how they were resolved.

6-18 LO 9 As part of the audit documentation, auditors should maintain copies of all client documents reviewed during the audit.

6-19 LO 10 A standardized audit program, without any modifications, should be used for each client.

6-20 LO 10 An audit program can be used to record the audit work performed and identify those responsible for performing the work.

MULTIPLE-CHOICE QUESTIONS

6-21 LO 1 Which of the following statements best describes what is meant by the term *appropriateness of audit evidence*?
a. Appropriateness is a measure of the quality of audit evidence.
b. Appropriateness refers to the relevance and reliability of audit evidence.
c. Appropriateness is a measure of the quantity of audit evidence.
d. Both (a) and (b).

6-22 LO 1 Which of the following statements is true regarding the relationship between risk and evidence sufficiency for substantive tests?
a. Evidence sufficiency will be affected by inherent risk, but not control risk.
b. Evidence sufficiency will be affected by control risk, but not inherent risk.
c. Evidence sufficiency will be affected by both inherent and control risks.
d. None of the above statements are true.

6-23 LO 2 An auditor determines that management integrity is high, the risk of material misstatement is low, and the client's internal controls are effective. Which of the following conclusions can be reached regarding the need to obtain direct evidence regarding the account balances?
a. Direct evidence can be limited to material account balances, and the extent of testing should be sufficient to corroborate the auditor's assessment of low risk.

b. Direct evidence of account balances is not needed.

c. Direct evidence can be obtained through analytical procedures.

d. Direct evidence should be obtained for all accounts, regardless of the auditor's assessment of control risk.

6-24 **LO 2** Which of the following factors affects the relevance of audit evidence?

a. The purpose of the audit procedure.

b. The direction of testing.

c. The type of procedure.

d. All of the above factors affect the relevance of audit evidence.

6-25 **LO 3** The auditor wishes to test the completeness assertion. Which of the following statements is true regarding the auditor's work flow?

a. The auditor would take a sample of recorded transactions and obtain supporting documentation for those transactions.

b. The auditor would perform a process referred to as tracing.

c. The auditor would take a sample of source documents and obtain additional supporting documents for those transactions.

d. For a sample of items recorded in the sales journal, the auditor would obtain the related shipping documents and customer orders.

6-26 **LO 3** The auditor wishes to gather evidence to test the assertion that the client's capitalization of leased equipment assets is properly valued. Which of the following sources of evidence will the auditor generally find to be of the highest quality (most reliable and relevant)?

a. Inspection of the leased equipment.

b. Inspection of documents, including the lease contract and recalculation of capitalized amount and current amortization.

c. Confirmation of the current purchase price for similar equipment with vendors.

d. Confirmation of the original cost of the equipment with the lessor.

6-27 **LO 4** Analytical procedures are best used as a substantive audit procedure in which of the following scenarios?

a. The auditor's primary objective is to reduce audit costs to a minimum.

b. Internal control risk is high, and therefore it is not efficient to test controls.

c. Planning analytical procedures indicate that misstatements are likely to occur in significant account balances.

d. Substantive analytical procedures would not be appropriate in any of the above scenarios.

6-28 **LO 4** Which of the following statements is false regarding substantive analytical procedures?

a. Substantive analytical procedures are not required to be performed on all audit engagements.

b. If the results of substantive analytical procedures suggest that an account balance is materially correct, the evidence needed from tests of details can likely be reduced.

c. Substantive analytical procedures would be performed after tests of details.

d. All of the above statements are true.

6-29 **LO 5**   The sufficiency of audit evidence is affected by which of the following factors?
a. The reliability of the audit evidence.
b. The relevance of the audit evidence gathered.
c. The risk of material misstatement of the assertion being examined.
d. All of the above.

6-30 **LO 5**   Which of the following statements is true regarding the sufficiency of evidence needed to test an account?
a. Evidence sufficiency is a measure of evidence quality.
b. Evidence sufficiency is affected by the quality of evidence.
c. A relationship does not exist between evidence sufficiency and evidence quality.
d. For a specific client, evidence sufficiency will be the same across all accounts.

6-31 **LO 6**   Which of the following procedures would an auditor typically perform first when assessing the reasonableness of management's estimate of its pension liability?
a. Inspect documentation related to the pension transactions that the client has recorded.
b. Develop an understanding of management's process for developing the estimate.
c. Identify sensitive management assumptions.
d. Review transactions occurring prior to the report release date to assess the reasonableness of management estimates.

6-32 **LO 6**   Which of the following is a reason that accounts containing management estimates pose a high level of risk of material misstatement for auditors?
a. Accounting estimates are especially susceptible to management bias.
b. Accounting estimates are a means for management to manage or misstate the financial statements.
c. Accounting estimates are sensitive to variations in management assumptions.
d. All of the above are reasons that accounts containing management estimates pose a high level of risk of material misstatement for auditors.

6-33 **LO 7**   For which of the following audit judgments would an auditor be least likely to use an auditor's specialist?
a. Existence of cash.
b. Valuation of works of art.
c. Valuation of oil and gas reserves.
d. Interpretation of laws and regulations.

6-34 **LO 7**   Which of the following statements is true regarding the auditor's use of the work of an auditor's specialist?
a. The specialist, not the auditor, is responsible for evaluating whether the specialist's findings support the assertions in the financial statements.
b. Because the individual is considered a specialist, the auditor does not need to evaluate the professional qualifications of the specialist.
c. The auditor should obtain an understanding of the methods and assumptions used by the specialist.
d. All of the above statements are true.

6-35 **LO 8** Which of the following statements is most accurate regarding the auditor's primary focus on a client's related-party transactions?

a. The auditor wants reasonable assurance that all related-party transactions are accounted for differently than transactions with unrelated parties.

b. The auditor will want to confirm the existence of the related parties.

c. The auditor wants reasonable assurance that all related-party transactions have been appropriately disclosed.

d. The auditor will focus on verifying the valuation of the related-party transactions.

6-36 **LO 8** Which of the following transactions would be least likely to be a related-party transaction?

a. A purchase transaction between an entity and its owners.

b. A debt-related transaction between an entity and one of its SPEs.

c. An exchange of property between an entity and a joint venture in which the entity has part ownership.

d. Writing off obsolete inventory prior to year-end.

6-37 **LO 9** Which of the following statements is true regarding audit documentation?

a. Auditors document only those significant issues that have not been resolved by the audit report date.

b. Audit documentation provides the principal support for the audit opinion expressed by the auditor.

c. Audit documentation would identify who reviewed the audit work but not who performed the audit work.

d. Documentation must be in paper format.

6-38 **LO 9** Which of the following items would typically not be included in the heading of a workpaper?

a. Client name.

b. Client balance sheet date.

c. Audit firm name.

d. A descriptive explanatory title.

6-39 **LO 10** Which of the following statements describes a purpose of an audit program?

a. An audit program is used to specify the procedures to be performed in obtaining audit evidence.

b. An audit program is used to record the completion of each audit step.

c. An audit program is useful for monitoring the progress of the audit.

d. All of the above statements describe the purpose of an audit program.

6-40 **LO 10** Which of the following items would typically not be included in an audit program?

a. A list of audit procedures to be performed.

b. An indication of who performed the procedure.

c. A workpaper heading.

d. All of the above would typically be included in an audit program.

REVIEW AND SHORT CASE QUESTIONS

NOTE: Completing Review and Short Case Questions does not require the student to reference additional resources and materials.

NOTE: For the remaining problems, we make special note of those addressing fraud, international issues, professional skepticism, and ethics.

6-41 `LO 1` Refer to *Exhibit 6.1*. Auditing standards require the auditor to gather sufficient appropriate evidence to provide a reasonable basis for an opinion regarding the financial statements. What are the characteristics of (a) sufficient audit evidence and (b) appropriate audit evidence? How are sufficiency and appropriateness related?

6-42 `LO 1` Refer to *Exhibit 6.1*. Describe how the appropriateness and sufficiency of evidence for a specific account is influenced by the risk of material misstatement associated with that account. Contrast how appropriateness and sufficiency of evidence would differ for a high-risk and low-risk assertion.

6-43 `LO 2` Appropriateness of audit evidence considers what two evidence characteristics? Define these characteristics and identify factors that affect these characteristics.

6-44 `LO 2` What is directional testing? How is the concept of directional testing related to appropriateness of audit evidence?

6-45 `LO 2` Refer to *Exhibit 6.2* and describe the differences between vouching and tracing.

6-46 `LO 2` Discuss the relative reliability of internal and external documentation. Give two examples of each type of documentation.

6-47 `LO 3` Refer to *Exhibit 6.5* and identify the nine types of audit procedures. Assume that you are planning the audit of the Page-Doc Company's inventory. PageDoc manufactures a variety of office equipment. Describe how each of the nine procedures could be used in the audit of inventory and identify the related assertion(s) the procedure is designed to test.

6-48 `LO 3` Refer to *Exhibit 6.5* to identify the nine types of audit procedures used as part of the audit evidence-gathering process. Following is a list of audit procedures performed. For each procedure (listed as (a) through (p)), classify the evidence gathered according to one (or more, if applicable) of the audit procedure types indicated in *Exhibit 6.5* and identify the assertion(s) being tested. Organize your answer as follows:

Procedure	Type of Procedure	Assertion Tested
a.		
b.		

a. Calculate the ratio of cost of goods sold to sales as a test of overall reasonableness of the balance for cost of goods sold.
b. Trace a sales transaction from the origination of an incoming sales order to the shipment of merchandise to an invoice and to the proper recording in the sales journal.
c. Test the accuracy of the sales invoice by multiplying the number of items shipped by the authorized price list to determine extended cost. Foot the total and reconcile it with the total invoiced.
d. Select recorded sales invoices and trace the corresponding shipping documents to verify the existence of goods shipped.
e. Examine canceled checks returned with the client's January bank statement as support of outstanding checks listed on the client's December year-end bank reconciliation.

  f. Perform inspection and independently count a sample of the client's marketable securities held in a safe deposit box.

  g. Tour the plant to determine that a major equipment acquisition was received and is in working condition.

  h. Review a lease contract to determine the items it covers and its major provisions.

  i. Request a statement from a major customer as to its agreement or disagreement with a year-end receivable balance shown to be due to the audit client.

  j. Develop a spreadsheet to calculate an independent estimate of the client's warranty liability (reserve) based on production data and current warranty repair expenditures.

  k. Meet with the client's internal legal department to determine its assessment of the potential outcome of pending litigation regarding a patent infringement suit against the company.

  l. Review all major past-due accounts receivable with the credit manager to determine whether the client's allowance for doubtful accounts is adequate.

  m. Make test counts of inventory items counted by client personnel.

  n. Obtain information about the client's processing system and associated controls by asking the client's personnel to fill out a questionnaire.

  o. Examine board of directors' minutes for the approval of a major bond issued during the year.

  p. Have the client's outside law firm send a letter directly to the auditor providing a description of any differences between the lawyer's assessment of litigation and that of the client.

6-49 `LO 3` Assume that an automotive company discloses the following risk factors (listed as (1) through (7)) that might affect the financial statements.

 1. Continued decline in market share, and a market shift (or an increase in or acceleration of market shift) away from sales of trucks or sport utility vehicles, or from sales of other more profitable vehicles in the U.S.

 2. Continued or increased price competition resulting from industry overcapacity, currency fluctuations, or other factors.

 3. Lower-than-anticipated market acceptance of new or existing products.

 4. Substantial pension and postretirement health-care and life-insurance liabilities impairing our liquidity or financial condition.

 5. Worse-than-assumed economic and demographic experience for our postretirement benefit plans (e.g., discount rates, investment returns, and health-care cost trends).

 6. The discovery of defects in vehicles resulting in delays in new model launches, recall campaigns, or increased warranty costs.

 7. Unusual or significant litigation or governmental investigations arising out of alleged defects in our products or otherwise.

For each risk factor, identify a related account balance that might be affected by the risk.

For each account balance identified, indicate how the risk will affect the audit evidence that will be gathered. Include what specific assertion is being addressed.

6-50 **LO 3** An auditor has to determine both the reliability and the relevance of potential audit evidence in order to determine that appropriate audit evidence is gathered.
a. Explain the difference between relevance and reliability.
b. How does an auditor determine the reliability of potential audit evidence?
c. For each of the following items (listed as (1) through (6)), identify whether the auditor has made a judgment error, and if there is a judgment error whether the error relates to evidence reliability or relevance. Organize your answer as follows:

Judgment Error	Nature of Error	Explanation
Yes or No	Relevance, Reliability, or Both	Description of error

1. The auditor receives only 20% of the confirmations that were sent to customers to verify their account balance. The auditor responds by taking another sample of receivables to send out in place of the first sample. The auditor is convinced the first sample is not representative of the population as a whole.
2. The auditor sent a confirmation to an independent warehouse to confirm the existence of inventory owned by the audit client. There was no response. The auditor decided to visit the warehouse to independently inspect the inventory on hand.
3. The auditor decides to test the completeness of accounts payable by taking a sample of recorded accounts payable and tracing to the source document evidencing receipt of the goods or services. No exceptions were noted so the auditor does not expand the audit work.
4. An auditor wishes to test the valuation of a marketable security and inquires about management's intent for using the securities. Management indicates that they are intending to hold the securities as a long-term investment. The auditor decides that no further evidence is needed and that the securities are properly valued at cost.
5. The auditor notes that there are some problems with segregation of duties over accounts receivable that could affect the existence assertion. The client is aware that the auditor normally sends out accounts receivable confirmations. The auditor decides to expand the audit work by sending additional confirmations.
6. During the observation of inventory, the auditor notes a number of items that look old and apparently not used. The auditor discusses each item with the marketing manager to determine whether or not the item is considered saleable at normal prices.

6-51 **LO 4** What are the basic assumptions that must hold for an auditor to justifiably use analytical procedures as a substantive audit procedure?

6-52 **LO 4** Refer to the *Auditing in Practice* feature "Analytical Procedures Are Not Client Estimates." What is the relationship between the auditor's use of an analytical procedure and a client estimate?

6-53 **LO 4** Assume that the auditor proposes that sales be audited by examining the relationship of sales and cost of sales to that of the previous two years, as adjusted for an increase in gross domestic product. Further, the auditor has assessed the risk of material misstatement (inherent and control risk) for this account as high. Explain either why, or why not, this would be an effective test of the account balance.

6-54 LO 4 Assume that an auditor wishes to use analytical procedures as a substantive procedure. Indicate how substantive analytical procedures could be used in assisting the auditor in testing the following accounts:

a. Interest expense related to bonds outstanding.
b. Natural gas expense for a public utility company.
c. Supplies expense for a factory.
d. Cost of goods sold for a fast-food franchisor (e.g., Wendy's or McDonald's). Note that cost of goods sold tends to average about 35% of sales in fast-food franchises.
e. Salary expense for an office (region) of a professional services firm.

PROFESSIONAL SKEPTICISM

FRAUD

6-55 LO 4 Assume that you have finished your substantive analytical procedures in the area of revenue. You used trend analysis and a reasonableness test and conducted the procedures at a disaggregated level. You are very pleased that your expectations are almost identical to what the client has recorded. Specifically, revenue increased in line with prior period increases and with the industry increases. You let your senior know that you likely do not have any additional work to perform. Your senior asks you to reconsider your conclusion. What is likely the primary concern of your senior?

6-56 LO 4 Review *Exhibit 6.9* and describe how the two audit approaches differ. What factors would lead to such a difference?

6-57 LO 5 Sufficiency is a measure of the quantity of evidence. Identify factors that affect evidence sufficiency.

6-58 LO 5 An auditor typically selects samples when testing controls. What are some factors that affect the sample sizes used when testing controls?

PROFESSIONAL SKEPTICISM

FRAUD

6-59 LO 6 Refer to the *Focus on Fraud* feature "Common Types of Earnings Management Techniques." Why might it be difficult for auditors to disallow companies' preferences to decrease existing reserves? Explain the role of professional skepticism in the context of evaluating management's explanations for their accounting for reserves in this context.

6-60 LO 6 When testing accounts that are based on management estimates, the auditor should understand the process management uses to develop those estimates. As part of obtaining that understanding, what aspects of the process should the auditor understand?

6-61 LO 7 Why would an auditor need to use an outside specialist when performing an audit? Identify specific accounts or assertions where a specialist might be needed.

6-62 LO 7 What factors should the auditor consider when evaluating the professional qualifications of a specialist?

6-63 LO 8 What is a related-party transaction? Provide examples of transactions that would be considered related-party transactions.

6-64 LO 8 Review *Exhibit 6.11* and identify audit procedures that an auditor might use for related-party transactions.

6-65 LO 9 What is audit documentation? Refer to *Exhibit 6.13* and identify the key components that each audit workpaper should contain.

6-66 **LO 9** What is meant by the statement *audit documentation ought to stand on its own*? What is the importance of this concept?

6-67 **LO 10** What are the purposes of an audit program?

6-68 **LO 9, 11** Entry-level auditing staff often inspect client records and documentation supporting accounting transactions in order to gain evidence about the appropriate application of the applicable financial reporting framework. One of these tasks involves comparing original client records of transactions to client reports that summarize those transactions. In this way, auditors gain assurance that the transactions used to construct the financial statements are complete and accurate. Here we report a case related to this task that is based on an actual situation. However, names have been changed to achieve confidentiality concerning audit firm personnel issues.

Elizabeth Jenkins was a staff auditor assigned to a large insurance client engagement. She was working on the portion of the audit concerning the client's claims loss reserves (reserves for future claims submitted by those insured by the insurance company). This reserve is analogous to the allowance for doubtful accounts of a company in the manufacturing or service sector. Essentially, the audit firm wants to provide assurance that the client's estimate of the amount of claims that will ultimately be filed is correctly stated on the balance sheet, with the appropriate write-off appearing on the income statement. Elizabeth was asked by the senior accountant on the engagement (Brett Stein) to tie out (in other words to compare) the client's claim loss reserve estimate (summarized on a large Excel worksheet) with the client's system-generated reports that provided the underlying data for the reserve estimate. The calculation is complex and involves inputs from several sources. Therefore, the tie-out process was very detail oriented and rather repetitive, involving a significant amount of time and patience to complete accurately. To demonstrate that she had compared the amount on the claims loss reserve Excel spreadsheet with that on the system-generated reports, Elizabeth was instructed to put a tick mark in both documents that would enable her senior to review her work. Along with each tick mark, Elizabeth was instructed to write a short note that described whether the two amounts did or did not agree. Elizabeth proceeded through the task, inserting tick marks where appropriate and noting agreement in all cases between the spreadsheet and the system-generated report. Because Elizabeth was feeling pressed for time and was exceedingly bored with her task, she skipped many of the comparisons and simply inserted tick marks indicating agreement even though she had not compared the numbers. She rationalized her actions by telling herself that this client had good internal controls and she had never found disagreements between source documents in other areas of the audit in which she was involved. In the audit profession, this action is known as *ghost tick marking*.

After Elizabeth had completed the task, she moved on to other parts of the audit as instructed by Brett. Subsequently, Brett reviewed Elizabeth's work. During that review, he recomputed amounts on both the Excel spreadsheet and the system-generated reports. To his surprise, there were instances in which Elizabeth had noted agreement between the two documents when in fact the numbers were not the same.

Brett met with Elizabeth and asked her about what had happened. She readily confessed to her actions. Brett counseled her that this behavior was unacceptable because it implies that audit work is being done when in fact the work is not being done. This puts the audit firm at risk because it provides inappropriate assurance that the client's records are accurate, when in fact they are not accurate. Elizabeth was embarrassed and remorseful and promised not to engage in ghost tick marking in the future. Brett noted the situation in Elizabeth's personnel records and notified the manager and partner on the engagement, along with relevant human resource personnel. The matter was fully documented in Elizabeth's personnel file.

During the course of the year, the supervisory audit firm personnel on all of Elizabeth's engagements were notified of her actions, and her work was subjected to more thorough review as a result. The firm noted no problems with the quality of Elizabeth's work during that time. During her annual review, she was again coached on the severity of her mistake. However, during the annual review process of all staff accountants, the firm did consider firing her based upon the mistake but ultimately decided that her confession, remorseful attitude, and subsequent high-quality work merited that she retain her employment.

a. Try to put yourself in Elizabeth's position for a moment. Have you ever been tempted to do a low-quality job on some task that you considered mundane? Have you ever thought that your low-quality work would remain undiscovered?

b. Why is Elizabeth's misrepresentation of her work so important to the firm?

c. What did Elizabeth ultimately do right in this situation, once her misrepresentation was discovered?

d. Do you agree with the outcome? Do you think the firm was too lenient? Too harsh? What would you recommend the firm do in this situation? Use the framework for ethical decision making from *Chapter 4* to help you arrive at a conclusion.

FRAUD FOCUS: CONTEMPORARY AND HISTORICAL CASES

PROFESSIONAL SKEPTICISM

FRAUD

6-69 **PCAOB** LO **1, 2, 3, 4, 5, 6, 10** The *Professional Judgment in Context* feature "Evidence-Related Findings in PCAOB Inspection Reports" presented at the beginning of the chapter provides excerpts of various PCAOB inspection reports. Review the feature, consider the information you learned while reading this chapter, and answer the following questions.

a. What is sufficient appropriate evidence and how does it differ across clients? Can what is considered sufficient and appropriate differ across accounts within a specific client?

b. What are substantive analytical procedures, and when is evidence from these procedures appropriate?

c. What are the unique evidence challenges for accounts such as allowance for doubtful accounts? How is professional skepticism helpful when testing this type of account?

d. How could the use of a standardized audit program lead to some of the problems identified in the PCAOB inspection reports?

e. If the audit clients in these settings were committing fraudulent financial reporting, what are the implications of the auditors' evidence-related decisions noted in these PCAOB reports?

FRAUD

PROFESSIONAL SKEPTICISM

INTERNATIONAL

6-70 **LONGTOP FINANCIAL TECHNOLOGIES LIMITED AND DELOITTE TOUCHE TOHMATSU CPA LTD.**
(LO 1, 2, 4, 5)

In May 2011, Deloitte Touche Tohmatsu (DTT) resigned as the auditor for Longtop Financial Technologies Limited (Longtop). Excerpts from DTT's resignation letter are provided here:

> As part of the process for auditing the Company's financial statements for the year ended 31 March 2011, we determined that, in regard to bank confirmations, it was appropriate to perform follow up visits to certain banks. These audit steps were recently performed and identified a number of very serious defects, including statements by bank staff that their bank had no record of certain transactions; confirmation replies previously received were said to be false; significant differences in deposit balances reported by the bank staff compared with the amounts identified in previously received confirmations (and in the books and records of the Group); and significant bank borrowings reported by bank staff not identified in previously received confirmations (and not recorded in the books and records of the Group).
>
> In the light of this, a formal second round of bank confirmation was initiated on 17 May. Within hours, however, as a result of intervention by the Company's officials including the chief operating officer, the confirmation process was stopped amid serious and troubling new developments including: calls to banks by the Company asserting that Deloitte was not their auditor; seizure by the Company's staff of second round bank confirmation documentation on bank premises; threats to stop our staff leaving the Company premises unless they allowed the Company to retain our audit files then on the premises; and then seizure by the Company of certain of our working papers.
>
> Then on 20 May the Chairman of the Company, Mr. Jia Xiao Gong called our Eastern Region Managing Partner, Mr. Paul Sin, and informed him in the course of their conversation that "there were fake revenue in the past so there were fake cash recorded on the books". Mr. Jia did not answer when questioned as to the extent and duration of the discrepancies. When asked who was involved, Mr. Jia answered: "senior management".

a. What audit evidence-related problems did DTT encounter during the audit of Longtop?

b. Review *Exhibit 6.8*. This chapter describes external confirmations as generally being a reliable, high quality type of evidence. When would that generality not be accurate? What assumptions should the auditor address concerning confirmations before concluding that using confirmations will result in reliable audit evidence?

c. Explain the role of professional skepticism in the context of evaluating evidence obtained from confirmations.

FRAUD

6-71 **GATEWAY COMPUTERS**
(LO 3, 4, 5, 6) The SEC took action against Gateway Computers in 2001 because it believed that Gateway systematically understated the allowance for doubtful accounts to meet

sales and earnings targets. This is essentially the way the alleged fraud took place:

- Gateway sold most of its computers over the Internet and had a strong credit department that approved sales.
- When sales dropped, management decided to go back to customers who had been rejected because of poor credit approval.
- During the first quarter, it went after the better of the previously rejected customers.
- As the need for more revenue and earnings remained, Gateway continued down the list to include everyone.
- However, it did not change any of its estimates for the allowance for uncollectible accounts.

At the end of the process, the poor credit customers represented about 5% of total income, but the SEC alleged that the allowance account was understated by over $35 million, which amounted to approximately $0.07 per share. In essence, Gateway wanted to show it was doing well when the rest of the industry was doing badly.

a. What is the requirement regarding proper valuation of the allowance for doubtful accounts? Does that requirement differ from account balances that are based on recording transactions as opposed to the allowance being an estimate? In other words, is more preciseness required on account balances that do not contain estimates?

b. What information should the company use in a system to make the estimate of the allowance for uncollectible accounts?

c. What evidence should the auditor gather to determine whether the client's estimate of the allowance for uncollectible accounts is fairly stated?

d. How should the expansion of sales to customers who had previously been rejected for credit affect the estimate of the allowance for doubtful accounts?

e. How important are current economic conditions to the process of making an estimate of the allowance for doubtful accounts? Explain.

FRAUD

PROFESSIONAL SKEPTICISM

6-72 **CENDANT CORPORATION**
(LO 1, 2, 3, 5)   Cendant Corporation, a company that sold travel and health club memberships, was the subject of an intensive fraud investigation that culminated in 1998. The company's web site revealed the following statements contained in a report given to the SEC.

- *Irregular charges against merger reserves*—Operating results at the former Cendant business units were artificially boosted by recording fictitious revenues through inappropriately reversing restructuring charges and liabilities to revenues. Many other irregularities were also generated by inappropriate use of these reserves.
- *False coding of services sold to customers*—Significant revenues from members purchasing long-term benefits were intentionally misclassified in accounting records as revenue from shorter term products. The falsely recorded revenues generated higher levels of immediately recognized revenues and profits for Cendant.
- *Delayed recognition of canceled memberships and chargebacks (a chargeback is a rejection by a credit-card-issuing bank of a charge to a member's credit card account)*—In addition to overstating revenues, these delayed charges caused Cendant's cash and working capital accounts to be overstated.
- *Quarterly recording of fictitious revenues*—Large numbers of accounts receivable entries made in the first three quarters of the year were fabricated; they had no associated clients or

customers and no associated sale of services. This practice also occurred in the prior two years.

The company also had other accounting errors. Approximately 6–9 cents per share of the total estimated restatement of earnings resulted from the elimination of these errors. These accounting errors include inappropriate useful lives for certain intangible assets, delayed recognition of insurance claims, and use of accounting policies that do not conform to the applicable financial reporting framework.

a. Identify audit procedures (and audit evidence gathered) that could have detected the misstatement of revenues and intangible assets. Be specific about each of the four irregularities identified.

b. How would the auditor's assessment of management integrity and management motivation have affected the nature, timing, and extent of audit procedures identified? Explain the role of professional skepticism in this context.

FRAUD

6-73 **MINISCRIBE**

(LO 1, 2, 3, 5)   As reported in the *Wall Street Journal* (September 11, 1989), MiniScribe, Inc., inflated its reported profits and inventory through a number of schemes designed to fool the auditors. At that time, MiniScribe was one of the major producers of disk drives for personal computers. The newspaper article reported that MiniScribe used the following techniques to meet its profit objectives:

- An extra shipment of $9 million of disks was sent to a customer near year-end and booked as a sale. The customer had not ordered the goods and ultimately returned them, but the sale was not reversed in the year recorded.
- Shipments were made from a factory in Singapore, usually by air freight. Toward the end of the year, some of the goods were shipped by cargo ships. The purchase orders were changed to show that the customer took title when the goods were loaded on the ship. However, title did not pass to the customer until the goods were received in the U.S.
- Returned goods were recorded as usable inventory. Some were shipped without any repair work performed.
- MiniScribe developed a number of just-in-time warehouses and shipped goods to them from where they were delivered to customers. The shipments were billed as sales as soon as they reached the warehouse.

For each of the items described, identify the audit evidence that should have been gathered that might have enabled the auditor to uncover the fraud. As appropriate, indicate the timing of when the evidence should be obtained.

APPLICATION ACTIVITIES

ETHICS

6-74 **PCAOB AND ERNST & YOUNG**

(LO 9, 11)   In August 2011, the PCAOB barred two former Ernst & Young LLP (E&Y) employees from auditing public companies, alleging they provided misleading documents to PCAOB inspectors who were evaluating the audit firm's work. One partner was barred for three years, and a senior manager was barred for two years. The PCAOB said that shortly before its inspectors were to inspect an E&Y audit of an unidentified company, the two auditors created, backdated, and placed in the audit files a document concerning the valuation of one of the audit client's investments. One of the auditors allegedly authorized other

NOTE: Completing Application Activities requires students to reference additional resources and materials. Some Application Activities will require the student to reference relevant professional auditing standards. We make special note of these as Auditing Standards Application Activities.

members of the audit team to alter other working papers in advance of the inspection. The changes were not disclosed to the PCAOB. E&Y indicated that the conduct of the two auditors had no impact on the client's financial statements or on E&Y's audit conclusions. You can obtain the Settled Disciplinary Orders at the PCAOB web site. The two Disciplinary Orders are PCAOB Release No. 105-2011-004 and PCAOB Release No. 105-2011-005. Review the Disciplinary Orders and answer the following questions.

a. What is audit documentation, and why is it important to a quality audit?

b. Given that the conduct of the two auditors had no impact on the client's financial statements or on E&Y's conclusions, why was this situation over audit documentation of concern to the PCAOB?

c. Suppose that you are asked by a superior to add or alter an audit workpaper after completing an audit engagement. Use the framework for ethical decision making presented in *Chapter 4* to consider your actions in this situation.

PROFESSIONAL SKEPTICISM

6-75 **PCAOB AND DELOITTE & TOUCHE**
(LO **1, 2, 3, 5, 6, 10**)   On May 4, 2010, the PCAOB issued its public inspection of Deloitte & Touche, LLP, covering their inspection of audits conducted during 2009. You can obtain the inspection report at the PCAOB web site. In their summary comments, the PCAOB inspectors stated:

In some cases, the conclusion that the Firm failed to perform a procedure may be based on the absence of documentation and the absence of persuasive other evidence, even if the Firm claims to have performed the procedure. PCAOB Auditing Standard No. 3, *Audit Documentation* ('AS No. 3') provides that, in various circumstances including PCAOB inspections, a firm that has not adequately documented that it performed a procedure, obtained evidence, or reached an appropriate conclusion must demonstrate with persuasive other evidence that it did so, and that oral assertions and explanations alone do not constitute persuasive other evidence. (p. 3)

The report went on to say:

In some cases, the deficiencies identified were of such significance that it appeared to the inspection team that the Firm, at the time it issued its audit report, had not obtained sufficient competent evidential matter to support its opinion on the issuer's financial statements or internal control over financial reporting ("ICFR").

It is reasonable to ask: what is the nature of these deficiencies; could this criticism happen to me; why didn't the firm reviewing partners detect the deficiencies? In order to understand how to answer these questions, the following excerpts describe the nature of deficiencies found on individual audits:

In this audit, the Firm failed in the following respects to obtain sufficient competent evidential matter to support its audit opinion—

• The Firm failed to perform adequate audit procedures to test the valuation of the issuer's inventory and investments in joint ventures (the primary assets of which were inventory). Specifically, the Firm:

  ○ Failed to re-evaluate, in light of a significant downturn in the issuer's industry and the general deterioration in economic conditions, whether the issuer's assumption, which it had also used in prior years, that certain inventory required no review for impairment was still applicable in the year under audit;

o Excluded from its impairment testing a significant portion of the inventory that may have been impaired, because the Firm selected inventory items for testing from those for which the issuer already had recorded impairment charges;

o Failed to evaluate the reasonableness of certain of the significant assumptions that the issuer used in determining the fair value estimates of inventory and investments in joint ventures;

o Failed to obtain support for certain of the significant assumptions that the Firm used when developing an independent estimate of the fair value of one category of inventory; and

o Failed to test items in a significant category of inventory, which consisted of all items with book values per item below a Firm-specified amount that was over 70 percent of the Firm's planning materiality.

• The Firm failed to perform adequate audit procedures to evaluate the issuer's assertion that losses related to the issuer's guarantees of certain joint venture obligations were not probable, because the Firm's procedures were limited to inquiry of management.

a. What is the auditor's responsibility to consider information outside of the client's records and processing to develop sufficient and appropriate audit evidence?

b. Why are the items identified by the PCAOB considered critical mistakes in performing an audit? What is the critical error of omission by the audit firm, and why would the specific problem lead to a deficiency in sufficient appropriate evidence?

c. Why is inquiry of management not considered sufficient information by itself?

d. Assumptions are assumptions! What is the auditor's responsibility regarding the questioning of the assumptions used by the client? In formulating your response, keep in mind that the client will claim that assumptions are just assumptions and it is difficult to say that one is more correct than another.

e. What do the deficiencies identified by the PCAOB suggest about the level of professional skepticism on the audit engagements? What might be reasons for decreased professional skepticism?

f. Presumably Deloitte used a standardized audit program. How could a standardized audit program lead to some of the problems identified earlier, such as failing to test a category of inventory that had book value in excess of 70% of the firm's planning materiality, or limiting the testing of impairment to inventory that had already been assessed as impaired by management?

6-76 **LO 4** Using appropriate resources, locate the financial statements of a company with which you are familiar. Identify specific account balances for which analytical procedures would be appropriate for conducting substantive tests of those balances and describe your reasoning for selecting the accounts.

AUDITING STANDARDS
APPLICATION ACTIVITY

6-77 **PCAOB (LO 5)** Refer to the *Standards Appendix* to this book and identify the PCAOB AS that addresses the topic of audit evidence. Obtain a copy of that AS and answer the following questions.
a. What are the three alternative means of selecting items for testing?
b. For each alternative, describe situations in which the alternative would be appropriate.

AUDITING STANDARDS
APPLICATION ACTIVITY

6-78 **LO 3** Assume that you are auditing a nonpublic U.S. client. You have obtained evidence that appears to be inconsistent with other evidence documented in the audit workpapers. Refer to the *Standards Appendix* to this book and identify the appropriate standard that will help you address this issue. What guidance does that standard give you?

PROFESSIONAL SKEPTICISM

FRAUD

6-79 **SEC (LO 1, 2, 3, 5, 10)** Obtain a copy of Accounting and Auditing Enforcement Release (AAER) No. 3146, issued by the SEC on June 24, 2010.
a. Identify the audit evidence deficiencies described in the release.
b. In what ways did the auditor fail to exhibit professional skepticism?
c. What sanction did the auditor receive? Does that sanction seem appropriate?

6-80 **PCAOB (LO 1, 2,3 5)** At the PCAOB web site obtain a copy of the settled Disciplinary Order in the matter of Acquavella, Chiarelli, Shuster, Berkower & Co., LLP that was released by the PCAOB on November 21, 2013 (PCAOB Release No. 105-2013-010). The Order notes: "Throughout the relevant time period, ACSB failed to put policies and procedures in place to ensure that engagement personnel performed audit procedures necessary to comply with PCAOB standards. As a result, in certain instances described below, ACSB staff members failed to complete necessary audit work before the Firm released its audit reports for the Audits."

Review the order and identify instances in which sufficient appropriate evidence was not obtained.

ACADEMIC RESEARCH CASES

NOTE: Completing Academic Research Cases requires students to reference additional resources and materials.

6-81 **LO 2, 5** Locate and read the article listed below and answer the following questions.
Kaplan, S., E. O'Donnell, and B. Arel. 2008. The influence of auditor experience on the persuasiveness of information provided by management. *Auditing: A Journal of Practice and Theory* 27 (1): 67–83.
a. What is the issue being addressed in the paper?
b. What are the findings of the paper?
c. Why is this paper important to auditors, and what are the implications of this paper for the auditing profession?
d. Describe the research methodology used as a basis for the conclusions.
e. Describe any limitations of the research.

SEARCH HINT

It is easy to locate these academic research articles! Use a search engine such as Google Scholar or an electronic research platform such as ABI Inform, and search using the author names and part of the article title.

6-82 **LO 8** Locate and read the article listed below and answer the following questions.

Kohlbeck, M., and B. Mayhew. 2010. Valuation of firms that disclose related party transactions. *Journal of Accounting and Public Policy* (29): 115–137.

a. What is the issue being addressed in the paper?

b. What are the findings of the paper?

c. Why is this paper important to auditors, and what are the implications of this paper for the auditing profession?

d. Describe the research methodology used as a basis for the conclusions.

e. Describe any limitations of the research.

FORD AND TOYOTA

6-83 | **FORD MOTOR COMPANY AND TOYOTA MOTOR CORPORATION** (LO **3, 6**)

Source and Reference	Question
Ford 10-K or Annual Report	a. Consider Ford's inventory account on the balance sheet, along with the accompanying footnote. What are the most relevant assertions that management is making with regard to its inventory?
	b. There exists demand for both fuel-efficient/smaller cars as well as bigger pickups and SUVs. Read Ford's disclosures to understand the relative mix of these differing types of vehicles, changes in demand, and potential effects on valuation of assets used to produce these vehicles.
	c. What assertions are implied in the Property, Plant, and Equipment account? How would valuation be affected if the company decided to downsize and eliminate a line of pickup trucks?
	d. Examine the assets on the balance sheet of Ford. Identify the assets that are subject to (a) fair value adjustments, (b) impairment tests, (c) estimates to either net realizable value or lower of cost or market value. What are the implications for audit evidence that will be gathered for these accounts?
	e. Consider Ford's debt account on the balance sheet, along with the accompanying footnote. What are the most relevant assertions that management is making with regard to its debt?

ACL

FRAUD

NOTE: There is an ACL Appendix and tutorial at the end of the book that you may find helpful in completing this problem.

6-84 | LO **3, 10**

You are auditing Pell grants provided to students at six state universities. The Pell grant program is a federal financial aid program for college students. The maximum grant a student can receive during a school year is $3,125, with a maximum of $1,041.67 per semester and summer session. The amount of a grant depends on financial need (need) and the number of credits taken (status). Students cannot receive a grant at two different schools during the same school term. You have obtained a file of grants for the current school year (downloaded from the Internet, labeled *pellA.XLS*) that contains the following information:

SSN	Social Security number
Last	Student's last name
First	Student's first name
Middle	Student's middle name or initial
School	School—coded 1 to 6
Term	Coded 1 to 3: • 1—Fall Semester • 2—Spring Semester • 3—Summer Semester
Need*	Financial need—coded 1 to 5: • 1—100% of allowable grant • 2—75% • 3—50% • 4—25% • 5—0%

Status*	Credits taken—coded 1 to 4:
	• 1—12 or more credits: 100%
	• 2—9 to 11 credits: 75%
	• 3—6 to 8 credits: 50%
	• 4—3 to 5 credits: 25%

Amount	Amount of grant for the term
	• Computation of grant: $3,125 / 3 * Need *Status
	• For a full-time student with maximum need:
	$3,125 / 3 * 100% * 100% = $1,041.67
	• For a student with a code 3 need taking 9 credits:
	$3,125 / 3 * 50% * 75% = $390.63

*Hint: To convert the NEED codes to the proper decimal value, use the expression $(1 - 0.25(NEED - 1))$. The same conversion can be used for STATUS codes.

1. Develop an audit program to identify potential fraud using ACL.
2. Use ACL to perform the steps in your audit program.
3. Turn in the following:
   a. Your audit program referenced to the ACL printouts supporting each audit step.
   b. A report on your findings including additional steps you would take to determine if fraud actually occurred.
   c. Appropriate ACL printouts properly indexed with comments written on the printouts to explain the printout and its implications. *Do not print out the entire grant file*. Extract only the items of significance.

CHAPTER

7

Planning the Audit: Identifying and Responding to the Risks of Material Misstatement

CHAPTER OVERVIEW AND LEARNING OBJECTIVES

The financial statements of any organization are subject to certain risks of material misstatement; this fact creates risks for any auditor attempting to conduct a quality audit. Auditors perform risk assessment procedures to identify and assess the risks of material misstatement, and then they determine how to respond to those risks. As part of this process, the auditor makes materiality judgments to help identify those accounts requiring more audit effort. In terms of the audit opinion formulation process, this chapter focuses on Phase II—Performing Risk Assessment.

Through studying this chapter, you will be able to achieve these learning objectives:

1. Describe the concept of material misstatement and apply a process for making materiality judgments.

2. Identify the risks of material misstatement and describe how they relate to audit risk and detection risk.

3. Assess factors affecting inherent risk, including fraud risk factors.

4. Assess factors affecting control risk.

5. Use planning analytical procedures to identify areas of heightened risk of material misstatement.

6. Describe how auditors make decisions about detection risk and audit risk.

7. Respond to the assessed risks of material misstatement and plan the procedures to be performed on an audit engagement.

8. Apply the frameworks for professional decision making and ethical decision making to issues involving materiality, risk assessment, and risk responses.

THE AUDIT OPINION FORMULATION PROCESS

I. Making Client Acceptance and Continuance Decisions **Chapter 1**	**II. Performing Risk Assessment** **Chapters 3, 7, and 9–13**	**III. Obtaining Evidence About Internal Control Operating Effectiveness** **Chapters 8–13 and 16**	**IV. Obtaining Substantive Evidence About Accounts, Disclosures and Assertions** **Chapters 8–13 and 16**	**V. Completing the Audit and Making Reporting Decisions** **Chapters 14 and 15**

The Auditing Profession, the Risk of Fraud and Mechanisms to Address Fraud: Regulation, Corporate Governance, and Audit Quality **Chapters 1 and 2**	Professional Liability and the Need for Quality Auditor Judgments and Ethical Decisions **Chapter 4**

The Audit Opinion Formulation Process and a Framework for Obtaining Audit Evidence
Chapters 5 and 6

PROFESSIONAL JUDGMENT IN CONTEXT
Risks Associated with Financial Statement Misstatements

Risk is a concept that is used to express uncertainty about events and/or their outcomes that could have a material effect on an organization. ISA 315 provides an excellent summary of the varied risks that may be present in an organization and that may be associated with material misstatements in the organization's financial statements. The existence of one or more of these risk factors does not necessarily mean that there is a material misstatement present, but it does indicate that the auditor should carefully consider and investigate that possibility, obviously leading to more audit work.

As you read the list, notice that (1) the risks are associated with a wide range of both operational and financial reporting decisions, (2) the risks are sometimes hard to quantify and are judgmental in nature, and (3) many organizations have these risks but do *not* necessarily have material misstatements, thus making it difficult for auditors to know when a risk factor truly is leading to a material misstatement for their particular clients. The list includes:

- Operations in regions that are economically unstable, such as countries with significant currency devaluation or highly inflationary economies
- Operations exposed to volatile markets, such as futures trading
- Operations that are subject to a high degree of complex regulation
- Going concern and liquidity issues, including loss of significant customers or constraints on the availability of capital or credit
- Offering new products or moving into new lines of business
- Changes in the entity, such as acquisitions or reorganizations
- Entities or business segments likely to be sold
- The existence of complex alliances and joint ventures
- Use of off-balance sheet financing, special-purpose entities, and other complex financing arrangements
- Significant transactions with related parties
- Lack of personnel with appropriate accounting and financial reporting skills

- Changes in key personnel, including departure of key executives
- Deficiencies in internal control, especially those not addressed by management
- Changes in the Information Technology (IT) system or environment and inconsistencies between the entity's IT strategy and its business strategies
- Inquiries into the organization's operations or financial results by regulatory bodies
- Past misstatements, history of errors, or significant adjustments at period end
- Significant amount of nonroutine or nonsystematic transactions, including intercompany transactions and large revenue transactions at period end
- Transactions that are recorded based on management's intent, such as debt refinancing, assets to be sold, and classification of marketable securities
- Accounting measurements that involve complex processes
- Pending litigation and contingent liabilities, such as sales warranties, financial guarantees, and environmental remediation

As you read through this chapter, consider the following questions:

- What conditions would cause these types of risks to lead to a material misstatement in the financial statements? (**LO 1, 2, 3, 4, 5**)
- What types of risks do these examples represent? (**LO 2, 3, 4**)
- How do these risks affect detection risk and audit risk? (**LO 2, 7**)

The Concept of Materiality

LO 1 Describe the concept of material misstatement and apply a process for making materiality judgments.

The auditor is expected to design and conduct an audit that provides reasonable assurance that material misstatements will be detected. Materiality is a concept that relates to the significance or importance of an item. A **misstatement** is an error, either intentional or unintentional, that exists in a transaction or financial statement account balance. The auditor and management may disagree about whether a misstatement is material. Further, a dollar amount that may be significant to one person may not be significant to another. Despite these measurement difficulties, the concept of materiality is pervasive and guides the nature and extent of the audit opinion formulation process.

Materiality judgments (1) are a matter of professional judgment, (2) depend on the needs of a reasonable person relying on the information (e.g., an investor, a potential investor, or other stakeholders), and (3) involve both quantitative and qualitative considerations. Further, materiality decisions differ from one audit client to another; that is, what is material for one client may not be material for another client, and may change for the same client from one period to another.

The purpose of making materiality judgments is to help the auditor gather sufficient appropriate evidence to obtain reasonable assurance about whether the financial statements are free of material misstatement. Existing professional guidance notes that auditors must make materiality judgments for purposes of (1) audit planning and (2) evidence evaluation after audit procedures are completed. As auditors plan each audit, they make professional judgments about the size of misstatements that they judge to be material. These judgments, in turn, provide a basis for:

- Determining the nature and extent of risk assessment procedures
- Identifying and assessing the risks of material misstatement
- Determining the nature, timing, and extent of tests of controls and substantive audit procedures

Definitions of Materiality In Concepts Statement No. 2, the Financial Accounting Standards Board (FASB) defines **materiality** as "the magnitude of an omission or misstatement of accounting information that, in light of surrounding circumstances, makes it *probable* that the judgment of a reasonable person relying on the information would have been changed or influenced by the omission or misstatement." ISA 320, *Materiality in Planning and Performing an Audit*, makes the point that auditors' judgments about materiality should be made based on a consideration of the information needs of users as an overall group. The Supreme Court of the U.S. offers a somewhat different definition, stating that "a fact is material if there is a substantial likelihood that the ... fact would have been viewed by the reasonable investor as having significantly altered the 'total mix' of information made available" (see AS 11). These definitions make it clear that materiality includes both the nature of the misstatement as well as the dollar amount of misstatement and must be judged in relation to importance placed on the amount by financial statement users. Thus, auditors need to understand the needs of financial statements users in order to make appropriate materiality judgments.

A Process for Making Materiality Judgments

Most audit firms provide specific written guidance and decision aids to assist auditors in making consistent materiality judgments. The guidelines usually involve applying percentages to some base, such as total assets, total revenue, or net income. In choosing a base, the auditor considers the stability of the base from year to year, so that materiality does not fluctuate significantly between annual audits. Income is often more volatile than total assets or revenue.

A simple guideline for setting materiality for the financial statements as a whole is to use 1% of total assets or revenue (whichever is higher); another option is to use 5% of net income. Some audit firms have more complicated guidelines that may be based on the nature of the industry or a composite of materiality decisions made by experts in the firm. Still, any guideline is just that: a guideline. The auditor should use the guideline as a starting point and then adjust as necessary for qualitative characteristics of the particular audit client. For example, a company may have restrictive debt covenants that require the company to maintain a current ratio of at least 2:1, which would imply that current assets must be twice as large as current liabilities. If that ratio per the books is near the requirement, the auditor should set materiality at a lower level for auditing current asset and liability accounts.

Common Benchmarks and Thresholds

Auditors often use variations of several benchmarks and common numeric thresholds as a starting point for making judgments about materiality at the overall financial statement level. The most common benchmarks include net income, assets, or net sales. The following benchmarks, percentage thresholds, and associated materiality judgments are typical:

Typical Materiality Thresholds and Judgments

Common Benchmarks	Not Material	Likely Material	Always Material
Net income	<5%	5% to 10%	>10%
Total assets	<1%	1% to 1.5%	>1.5%
Net sales	<1%	1% to 1.5%	>1.5%

The *Auditing in Practice* feature "Alternative Materiality Benchmarks" illustrates how the type of organization and its characteristics can influence the appropriate benchmark.

Alternative Materiality Benchmarks

AUDITING IN **PRACTICE**

While net income, total assets, and net sales are common benchmarks for setting materiality, circumstances may indicate that other benchmarks are more appropriate. If an organization has significant and nonrecurring charges to nonoperating expenses, then income from continuing operations may be a more appropriate materiality benchmark than net income. For an organization with a net loss, auditors sometimes use net loss as the benchmark. If an organization's net income varies significantly from year to year, the auditor might consider using an average of net income from the prior three to five years as the materiality benchmark. For nonprofit organizations, appropriate benchmarks would include total expenses, total revenues, or total assets.

Audit firms have policies that specify which benchmarks are appropriate, and consistency in the application of benchmarks and thresholds is important in demonstrating the reasonableness of materiality judgments. Professional judgment is very important in selecting benchmarks appropriate for the client setting. The auditor should consider the following items when identifying benchmarks:

- Financial statement items on which users will focus their attention
- Nature of the client and industry
- Size of the client
- Manner in which the client is financed
- Volatility of the benchmark

Moreover, it is important to recognize that the benchmarks and thresholds represent starting points for the materiality judgment; they should not be used without considering other judgmental factors such as client risk, management integrity, or the possibility of fraud. Once the auditor has determined the overall materiality amount based on the quantitative assessment, the auditor also needs to consider qualitative factors to assess whether the materiality amount makes sense for the particular audit client.

Levels of Materiality

Auditors consider materiality at three levels: (1) overall materiality for the financial statements as a whole, (2) materiality for particular classes of transactions, account balances, or disclosures, and (3) **performance materiality** for auditing particular classes of transactions, account balances, or disclosures. In planning the audit, auditors should consider overall materiality in terms of the smallest aggregate level of misstatements that could be material to any one of the financial statements. For example, if the auditor believes that misstatements aggregating approximately $100,000 would be material to the income statement, but misstatements aggregating approximately $200,000 would be material to the balance sheet, the auditor typically assesses overall materiality at $100,000 or less (not $200,000 or less). Once this determination has been made, auditors will allocate the materiality amount to, individual account balances or disclosures for purposes of auditing classes of transactions. Performance materiality is used with respect to assessing risks of material misstatement and determining the nature, timing, and extent of further audit procedures to perform during the audit opinion formulation process. Continuing the example of a client where overall materiality is set at $100,000 and materiality for the accounts

Changes in Materiality Judgments Throughout the Audit Opinion Formulation Process

Sometimes auditors' materiality judgments need to be revised after more facts about the client and its circumstances become known during the audit. Situations necessitating a change in materiality judgments include the following:

- Initial materiality judgments were based on estimated or preliminary financial statement amounts that turn out to be different from the audited amounts.
- The financial statement amounts used in initially making the materiality judgments have changed significantly. For example, if during the course

of the audit, the financial statements were adjusted significantly, then the initial materiality judgments might need to be adjusted accordingly.

If materiality judgments change during the course of the audit, then auditors must reassess any decisions that relied on these judgments. For example, if performance materiality turns out to have been set too high (such as $150,000 when it should have been $100,000), then the auditor might need to perform additional audit procedures designed to detect misstatements at this lower level.

receivable balance is set at $90,000; the performance materiality for auditing accounts receivable might then be set at $30,000. This approach compensates for the possibility that multiple undetected or uncorrected misstatements in the accounts receivable balance might exist.

The *Auditing in Practice* feature "Changes in Materiality Judgments Throughout the Audit Opinion Formulation Process" recognizes that materiality levels may change throughout the audit. Further, as noted in the *Auditing in Practice* feature "Performance Materiality When Auditing Clients with Multiple Locations" audit clients that have multiple locations require special considerations when assessing performance materiality.

If performance materiality is set too high, the auditor might not perform sufficient procedures to detect material misstatements in the financial statements. If performance materiality is set too low, the auditor might perform more substantive procedures than necessary. Performance materiality is different from, but relates to, the concept of tolerable misstatement. **Tolerable misstatement** is the amount of misstatement in an account balance that the auditor could tolerate and still not judge the underlying account balance to be materially misstated. Tolerable misstatement is the application of performance materiality to a particular sampling procedure, so it is less than or equal to performance materiality.

Auditors will aggregate identified misstatements so the audit team can assess the materiality of these misstatements. The document where misstatements are aggregated is often referred to as a *summary of unadjusted audit differences* (SUAD). The misstatements included on the SUAD are evaluated individually and in the aggregate. The accumulation of such information is based on whether those misstatements are clearly trivial. A **clearly trivial** amount, according to AU-C 450, is one that is "clearly inconsequential, whether taken individually or in the aggregate and whether judged by any criteria of size, nature, or circumstances". The term *clearly trivial* should not be used in place of *not material*. The materiality level for a clearly trivial item occurs where the auditor believes errors below that level would not, even when aggregated with all other misstatements, be material to the financial statements. For example, if amounts at or below $5,000 are considered clearly trivial, misstatements below that amount would essentially be ignored.

Performance Materiality When Auditing Clients with Multiple Locations

A difficulty that auditors face with some clients is a need to determine how to allocate materiality when

- There are many client locations
- Some locations require separate reporting (regulatory reports) in addition to consolidated financial reports
- There are significant segments and the importance of segments may vary as they are currently assessed by the marketplace

In some cases, the auditor may be able to aggregate the populations of various locations and perform testing, including the selection of audit samples, from the combined population, in the same manner as when there is one population. For example, if the underlying information system is centralized and separate reporting by location is not necessary, the auditor can treat multiple locations as one population and use performance materiality for testing (and sampling) a particular account balance across multiple locations. This may be the case for inventory observations conducted at multiple locations.

Alternatively, if the information systems across multiple locations are decentralized, or if separate reporting is required, or if certain locations or segments are especially important, the auditor faces additional testing considerations beyond those encountered when testing a single population. These considerations may be applicable for tests of controls or substantive tests of details. Common audit situations where such considerations may apply include inventories, fixed assets, or receivables that are in different locations. The auditor's concern is the materiality level that should be used in testing a particular account at a particular location. In planning tests of account balances (or internal controls) at specific locations, the auditor likely wants to use a materiality amount that is smaller than performance materiality. Different materiality levels may be established for different locations, and the aggregate of the location materiality levels could equal or exceed overall performance materiality.

Consider the client that has 15 locations of equal size and the auditor has set performance materiality at $1,500,000. The auditor might allocate $100,000 to each location for a total of $1,500,000. This approach would generally result in overauditing because the achieved audit risk across all locations would be extremely low. An alternative approach would be to allocate $1,500,000 to each location; however, this approach would result in substantial underauditing and an unacceptable risk of audit failure. These are obviously extreme approaches to allocating performance materiality across multiple locations. The auditor wants to apply professional judgment and, if statistical sampling is used, utilize sampling methodology (often included in generalized audit software (GAS)) to determine the proper allocation.

There are two approaches used by auditors to set the threshold at which something is considered clearly trivial. The first is a judgmental approach whereby the auditor sets the threshold based on past experience that accumulates into an auditor judgment. This approach is usually not very defensible to third-party users or regulators unless the auditor can clearly articulate the reasoning process and show insight into what might be material to users. The auditor always considers such things as potential default on loan covenants, changes in segment earnings or trends in earnings, or other factors that would affect the market's perception of future growth and cash flow for the company.

The second approach to setting the threshold at which something is considered clearly trivial is a percentage approach, whereby the auditor sets the threshold at a range that depends on the auditor's assessment of the likelihood of undetected misstatements (often based on previous experience or on other issues such as the quality of the client's control environment). The range may vary from 10% (for low likelihood of undetected misstatements) to 5% (for high likelihood of undetected misstatements) of materiality at the overall financial statement level. For example, if analytical procedures suggest that a certain account balance may have misstatements, the auditor often assigns a lower threshold (e.g., 5%) because of the higher likelihood of undetected misstatements. If there were proposed adjusting entries to a particular account in prior years, the auditor may also assign a lower threshold. Finally, if the consequences of a potential misstatement in an account balance are very high, the auditor may also assign a lower threshold. Further, some audit firms require that all items be posted for analysis by supervisors to form a record of audit findings.

Qualitative Considerations

In making materiality assessments, auditors consider both quantitative effects (such as the dollar magnitude of a misstatement) and qualitative effects (such as the reason for the misstatement). In Staff Accounting Bulletin (SAB) No. 99, the SEC states that

> The use of a percentage as a numerical threshold, such as 5%, may provide the basis for a preliminary assumption that—without considering all relevant circumstances—a deviation of less than the specified percentage with respect to a particular item on the registrant's financial statements is unlikely to be material. The staff has no objection to such a "rule of thumb" as an initial step in assessing materiality. But quantifying, in percentage terms, the magnitude of a misstatement is only the beginning of an analysis of materiality; it cannot appropriately be used as a substitute for a full analysis of all relevant considerations.

The Securities and Exchange Commission (SEC) has been critical of the auditing profession for not sufficiently examining qualitative factors in making materiality decisions. In particular, the SEC has criticized the profession for:

- *Netting (offsetting) material misstatements.* This approach involves not making adjustments because the net effect may not be material to net income. However, each account item may have been affected by a material amount.
- *Not applying the materiality concept to swings in accounting estimates.* For example, an accounting estimate could be misstated by just under a material amount in one direction one year and just under a material amount in the opposite direction the next year. The SEC says the materiality amount should be determined by looking at the total swing in estimates over the two-year period, rather than by using the best estimate each year.
- *Consistently passing (in other words, refusing to adjust the financial statements to correct a detected misstatement) on individual adjustments that may not be considered material.* The SEC is skeptical of situations in which management refuses to adjust a detected misstatement supposedly because the amount is "immaterial". In such situations, the SEC rhetorically would ask "if it is not material, then why would management be so insistent about not correcting the balance"? In these types of situations, it is apparent that there must be some reason that management does not wish to correct the misstatement, likely due to a qualitative (rather than quantitative) reason.

The SEC provides guidance on situations in which a *quantitatively* small misstatement may still be considered material because *of qualitative* reasons. The following are considerations that may cause a quantitatively small misstatement to be considered material. These include whether the potential misstatement:

- Arises from an item capable of precise measurement or arises from an estimate and, if so, the degree of imprecision inherent in the estimate
- Masks a change in earnings or other trends
- Hides a failure to meet analysts' consensus expectations for the enterprise

- Changes a loss into income or vice versa
- Is in a segment that has been identified as having a significant effect on the company's stock valuation
- Affects compliance with regulatory requirements
- Affects loan covenants or other contractual requirements
- Has the effect of increasing management's compensation—for example, by satisfying requirements for the award of bonuses or other forms of incentive compensation
- Involves concealment of an unlawful transaction

Identifying and Assessing Risks of Material Misstatement

LO 2 Identify the risks of material misstatement and describe how they relate to audit risk and detection risk.

Now that you understand the concept of materiality in planning a quality audit, you are ready to perform risk assessment procedures to obtain an understanding of the client and to identify and assess the risks of material misstatement. Identifying and assessing these risks, and then responding to them appropriately, are fundamental to conducting a quality audit. *Exhibit 7.1* provides a graphical depiction of the relationship between the risks of material misstatement and how they relate to audit risk. The definitions of the risks depicted in *Exhibit 7.1* are as follows:

- **Inherent Risk**—The susceptibility of an assertion about a class of transaction, account balance, or disclosure to a misstatement that could be material, either individually or when aggregated with other misstatements, before consideration of any related controls.
- **Control Risk**—The risk that a misstatement that could occur in an assertion about a class of transaction, account balance, or disclosure and that could be material, either individually or when aggregated with other misstatements, will not be prevented, or detected and corrected, on a timely basis by the entity's internal control.

EXHIBIT 7.1 Risks Relevant to an Audit

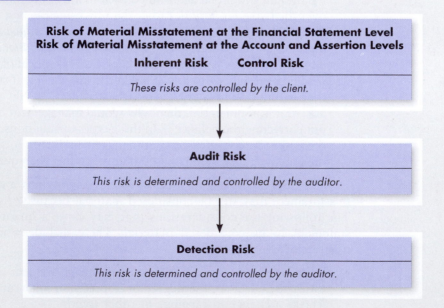

Risk of Material Misstatement at the Financial Statement Level
Risk of Material Misstatement at the Account and Assertion Levels

Inherent Risk   **Control Risk**

These risks are controlled by the client.

Audit Risk

This risk is determined and controlled by the auditor.

Detection Risk

This risk is determined and controlled by the auditor.

- **Audit Risk**—The risk that the auditor expresses an inappropriate audit opinion when the financial statements are materially misstated.
- **Detection Risk**—The risk that the procedures performed by the auditor to reduce audit risk to an acceptably low level will not detect a misstatement that exists and that could be material, either individually or when aggregated with other misstatements.

Exhibit 7.1 illustrates the relationships among these risks. The **risk of material misstatement** exists at the overall financial statement level and at the account and assertion levels; within these levels, risk can be categorized as involving inherent risk and control risk. These risks originate with the client, are controllable by the client, and are related to characteristics of the client organization, environment, and internal control. After assessing inherent and control risks, the auditor then determines the appropriate level of audit risk to accept. When the risk of material misstatement is higher, the auditor accepts less audit risk (as low as 1%); conversely, when the risk of material misstatement is lower, the auditor accepts more audit risk (such as 5%). For example, consider a client that is publicly traded, has a management team with questionable integrity (with a high inherent risk) that does not place high importance on the control environment (with a high control risk). In this case, the auditor should accept only low audit risk (1%) because the auditor is concerned that there exists a reasonable possibility that a material misstatement exists. Contrast this first example with a client that is privately held, has a management team with good integrity (a low inherent risk) that places importance on the control environment (a low control risk). In this case, the auditor accepts higher audit risk (5%) because a material misstatement is less likely.

Upon determining the level of acceptable audit risk, the auditor should determine detection risk. Detection risk is under the control of the auditor, and the level of audit effort that the auditor will expend on the engagement depends on the level of detection risk. When the risk of material misstatement is higher, detection risk is lower, in order to reduce audit risk to an acceptable level. The auditor reduces detection risk through the nature, timing, and extent of substantive audit procedures. As detection risk decreases, evidence obtained by the auditor through substantive audit procedures should increase. When the risk of material misstatement is lower, the auditor can accept a higher detection risk and still achieve an acceptable level of audit risk.

Auditing standards also discuss the term **significant risk**. According to AU-C 315, a **significant risk** is an identified and assessed risk of material misstatement that, in the auditor's professional judgment, requires special consideration. The *Auditing in Practice* feature "What Makes a Risk Significant?" outlines factors that the auditor considers in determining whether a particular identified risk is significant to the conduct of the audit.

Assessing Factors Affecting Inherent Risk
Inherent Risk at the Account and Assertion Levels

LO 3 Assess factors affecting inherent risk, including fraud risk factors.

Inherent risk relates to the susceptibility of an assertion to a misstatement, due to either error or fraud, before consideration of any related controls. When inherent risk at the account or assertion level is high, the auditor is concerned that a particular account balance is relatively more likely to contain a material misstatement than when inherent risk is low. Inherent risk reflects the fact that some assertions and related account balances are more susceptible to misstatement than others. For example, cash is more susceptible to theft than industrial equipment. In addition, accounts whose valuation is derived from accounting estimates are more likely to be misstated than accounts whose valuation is derived from routine, factual data. The following is a list of factors

What Makes a Risk Significant?

AUDITING IN **PRACTICE**

AU-C 315 provides guidance to the auditor in terms of factors that the auditor should consider when determining if a risk is significant. The standard states:

In exercising professional judgment about which risks are significant risks, the auditor should consider at least:

a. whether the risk is a risk of fraud;
b. whether the risk is related to recent significant economic, accounting, or other developments and, therefore, requires specific attention;

c. the complexity of transactions;
d. whether the risk involves significant transactions with related parties;
e. the degree of subjectivity in the measurement of financial information related to the risk, especially those measurements involving a wide range of measurement uncertainty; and
f. whether the risk involves significant transactions that are outside the normal course of business for the entity or that otherwise appear to be unusual.

that should lead the auditor to assess, at a higher level, inherent risk at the assertion level:

- The account balance represents an asset that is relatively easily stolen, such as cash
- The account balance is made up of complex transactions
- The account balance requires a high level of judgment or estimation to value
- The account balance is subject to adjustments that are not in the ordinary processing routine, such as year-end adjustments
- The account balance is composed of a high volume of nonroutine transactions

Inherent Risk at the Financial Statement Level: Business Risks

At the financial statement level, inherent risk affects the business operations and potential outcomes of organizational activities; these are referred to as **business risks**. When business risk is high, the auditor is concerned that the organization might have difficulty operating effectively or profitably. The overall economic climate—favorable or unfavorable—can have a tremendous effect on the organization's ability to operate effectively and profitably. Economic downturns are often associated with the failure of otherwise successful organizations. Technological change also presents risk. For example, companies that were not previously in the phone business, such as Google and Apple, added communication products and greatly affected the phone business of Motorola and Nokia. Competitor actions, such as discounting prices or adding new product lines, also affect inherent risk at the financial statement level. Finally, geographic locations of suppliers affect inherent risk at the financial statement level. For example, sourcing products in China might offer a competitive advantage, but it might also expose the organization to business risk if it finds that its products contain lead and cannot be sold. It is up to management to properly manage its business risk. All organizations are subject to business risk; management reactions may exacerbate it (make it more likely) or, conversely, good management can mitigate it.

Each organization has key processes that give it a competitive advantage or disadvantage. The auditor should gather sufficient information to understand these processes, the industry factors affecting key processes, how management monitors the processes and performance, and the potential operational and financial effects associated with key processes. The following is a list of factors that would lead the auditor to assess inherent risk relating to operations at a higher level:

- The company lacks personnel or expertise to deal with the changes in the industry
- New products and service offerings have uncertain likelihood of successful introduction and acceptance by the market
- The use of information technology is incompatible across systems and processes
- Expansion of the business for which the demand for the company's products or services has not been accurately estimated
- A new business strategy is incompletely or improperly implemented
- Financing is lost due to the company's inability to meet financing requirements
- New regulatory requirements increase legal exposure
- Alternative products, services, competitors, or providers pose a threat to current business
- There are significant supply chain risks
- The production and delivery processes are complex
- The industry is mature and declining
- The company lacks ability to control costs with the possibility of unforeseen costs
- The company produces products that have multiple substitutes

While these types of risk do not necessarily lead to material misstatements in the financial statements, they represent issues that threaten the fundamental financial viability of the company. Further, these risks might provide incentives to management to misstate multiple accounts (e.g., increase revenues or decrease expenses) in an attempt to make the company look more financially sound than is accurate. The *Auditing in Practice* feature "Pfizer's Risk Disclosures as an Example of Inherent Risk at the Financial Statement Level" illustrates the types of inherent risks that the company faces in competing in its complex, regulated, and research-driven industry. Auditors need to be aware of these risks, as they could have misstatement implications for multiple financial statement accounts.

Risk Assessment Procedures for Assessing Business Risks

The auditor uses a variety of tools to understand the client's business and associated risks. Much of the work is done by monitoring the financial press and SEC filings and broker analyses, developing a firm-specific and industry-based knowledge management system, and utilizing other online information sources about a company. Some traditional approaches continue to be used, including inquiries of management, reviews of internal risk management documentation, inquiries of business people, and review of legal or regulatory proceedings against the company. The following describe some of the resources an auditor can use to learn more about a company:

- *Management inquiries*—The auditor should interview management to identify its strategic plans, its analysis of industry trends, the potential impact of actions it has taken or might take, and its management style.
- *Review of client's budget*—The budget, representing management's fiscal plan for the forthcoming year, provides insight into management's approach to operations and to risks the organization might face. The auditor looks for significant changes in plans and deviations from budgets, such as planned disposal of a line of business, significant research

Pfizer's Risk Disclosures as an Example of Inherent Risk at the Financial Statement Level

Pfizer discloses a variety of risks. Regulators encourage companies to make these types of disclosures so that investors can estimate the uncertainties inherent in the organization. Interesting inherent risk examples from Pfizer's 10-K include:

"U.S. and foreign governmental regulations mandating price controls and limitations on patient access to our products impact our business, and our future results could be adversely affected by changes in such regulations or policies. In the U.S., many of our biopharmaceutical products are subject to increasing pricing pressures."

"Specialty pharmaceuticals are medicines that treat rare or life-threatening conditions that have smaller patient populations, such as certain types of cancer and multiple sclerosis. The growing availability and use of innovative specialty pharmaceuticals, combined with their relative higher cost as compared to other types of pharmaceutical products, is beginning to generate significant payer interest in developing cost-containment strategies targeted to this sector. While the impact on us of payers' efforts to control access to and pricing of specialty pharmaceuticals has been limited to date, our growing portfolio of specialty products, combined with the increasing use of health technology assessment in markets around the world and the deteriorating finances of governments, may lead to a more significant adverse business impact in the future."

"Risks and uncertainties apply particularly with respect to product-related, forward-looking statements. The outcome of the lengthy and complex process of identifying new compounds and developing new products is inherently uncertain. Drug discovery and development is time-consuming, expensive and unpredictable. The process from early discovery or design to development to regulatory approval can take many years. Drug candidates can fail at any stage of the process. There can be no assurance as to whether or when we will receive regulatory approval for new products or for new indications or dosage forms for existing products. Decisions by regulatory authorities regarding labeling, ingredients and other matters could adversely affect the availability or commercial potential of our products. As examples, there is no assurance that our late stage pipeline products, such as tofacitinib, bosutinib and *Eliquis* (apixaban) for prevention of stroke in patients with atrial fibrillation, will receive regulatory approval and/or be commercially successful or that recently approved products, such as *Prevnar 13/Prevenar 13* for use in adults 50 years of age and older, *Xalkori* (crizotinib) and *Inlyta* (axitinib) will be approved in other markets and/or be commercially successful. There is also a risk that we may not adequately address existing regulatory agency findings concerning the adequacy of our regulatory compliance processes and systems or implement sustainable processes and procedures to maintain regulatory compliance and to address future regulatory agency findings, should they occur."

or promotion costs associated with a new product introduction, new financing or capital requirements, changes in compensation or product costs due to union agreements, and significant additions to property, plant, and equipment.

- *Tour of client's plant and operations*—A tour of the client's production and distribution facilities offers much insight into potential audit issues. The auditor can visualize cost centers as well as shipping and receiving procedures, inventory controls, potentially obsolete inventory, and possible inefficiencies. The tour increases the auditor's awareness of company procedures and operations, providing direct experience into sites and situations that are otherwise encountered only in company documents or observations of client personnel.

- *Review relevant government regulations and client's legal obligations*—Few industries are unaffected by governmental regulation, and much of that regulation affects the audit. For example, auditors need to determine potential liabilities associated with cleanup costs defined by the Environmental Protection Agency. The auditor normally seeks information on litigation risks through an inquiry of management, but follows up that inquiry with an analysis of litigation prepared by the client's legal counsel.

- *Knowledge management systems*—Audit firms have developed these systems around industries, clients, and best practices. These systems also capture information about relevant accounting or regulatory requirements for the companies and can be used to develop risk alerts for the companies.

- *Online searches*—Internet search companies (such as Hoover's at *www. hoovers.com*) are an excellent source of information about companies. Other online searches can be conducted through other portals such as Google. Yahoo has two excellent sources of information: (1) a financial section that provides data about most companies and (2) a chat line that contains current conversations about the company (much of which, of course, might be unreliable).

- *Review of SEC filings*—The SEC filings can be searched online through the EDGAR system. The filings include company annual and quarterly reports, proxy information, and registration statements for new security issues. These filings contain substantial information about the company and its affiliates, officers, and directors. This information can be used to obtain an understanding of management's compensation arrangements, including incentive compensation that may provide important information about management incentives and bonus arrangements. Further, the auditor should monitor trading activity of the company's securities, along with the relevant holdings of top-level management and/or board members.

- *Company web sites*—A company's web site can contain information that is useful in understanding its products and strategies. As companies provide more information online, auditors should review the information to keep informed of developments.

- *Economic statistics*—Most industry data, including regional data, can now be found online. The auditor can compare the results of a client with regional economic data. For example, the auditor would likely question why a company is growing at a rate of 50%, while the overall industry is growing at a significantly slower rate. That question arises only if the auditor has industry information.

- *Professional practice bulletins*—The American Institute of Certified Public Accountants (AICPA) publishes Audit Risk Alerts, and the SEC often issues practice bulletins to draw the profession's attention to important issues. Both the Public Company Accounting Oversight Board (PCAOB) and the International Auditing and Assurance Standards Board (IAASB) have also published several Staff Audit Practice Alerts dealing with topics such as significant unusual transactions, fair value measurements, and the economic environment.

- *Stock analysts' reports*—Brokerage firms invest significant resources in conducting research about companies, their strategies, competitors, quality of management, and likelihood of success. Many of the major investment analysts are granted access to top management and are the beneficiaries of frequent analysts' meetings. These reports may contain a wealth of useful information about a client.

- *Company earnings calls*—The auditor can observe or read the transcripts of management's earnings calls in order to understand the most up-to-date issues that the company is facing, along with management's publicly disclosed plans.

Inherent Risk at the Financial Statement Level: Financial Reporting Risks

There is also inherent risk at the financial statement level that is associated with the recording of transactions and the presentation of financial data in an organization's financial statements. When inherent risk relating to the recording of transactions and the presentation of financial data is high, the auditor is concerned that management has recorded transactions or presented financial data inaccurately. When assessing this risk, auditors consider all of the items on a company's financial statements that are subjective and based on judgment, such as asset impairments, mark-to-market accounting, warranties, returns, pensions, and estimates regarding the useful lives of assets, among others. Because of these estimates, inherent risk at the financial statement level is affected by the competence and integrity of management and potential incentives to misstate the financial statements.

Risk Assessment Procedures for Assessing Management Integrity

Evaluating management integrity is critical in assessing inherent risk at the financial statement level. However, making such an evaluation is difficult and subjective. To make this evaluation, auditors consider a variety of information sources:

- *Predecessor auditor*—Information obtained directly through inquiries is required by professional auditing standards. The predecessor is required to respond to the auditor unless such data are under a court order or if the client will not approve communicating confidential information.
- *Other professionals in the business community*—Examples include lawyers and bankers with whom the auditor normally has good working relationships and of whom the auditor makes inquiries as part of the process of getting to know the client.
- *Other auditors within the audit firm*—Other auditors within the firm may have dealt with current management in connection with other engagements or with other clients.
- *News media and web searches*—Information about the company and its management might be available in financial journals, magazines, industry trade magazines, or on the web.
- *Public databases*—Computerized databases can be searched for public documents dealing with management or any articles on the company. Similarly, public databases such as LEXIS can be searched for the existence of legal proceedings against the company or against key members of management.
- *Preliminary interviews with management*—These interviews can be helpful in understanding the amount, extent, and reasons for turnover in key positions. Personal interviews can also be helpful in analyzing the frankness or evasiveness of management in dealing with important company issues affecting the audit.
- *Audit committee members*—Members of the audit committee might have been involved in disputes between the previous auditors and management and might have additional insight.
- *Inquiries of federal regulatory agencies*—Although this is not a primary source of information, the auditor might want to make inquiries of specific regulatory agencies regarding pending actions against the company or the history of regulatory actions taken with respect to the company and its management.
- *Private investigation firms*—Use of such firms is rare, but is increasingly being done when the auditor becomes aware of issues that merit further inquiry about management integrity or management's involvement in potential illegal activities.

Stock Option Backdating Fraud as an Example of Inherent Risk at the Financial Statement Level

FOCUS on **FRAUD**

On April 23, 2010, a jury found Carl Jasper, the former chief financial officer (CFO) of Maxim Integrated Products, liable for securities fraud for engaging in a scheme to backdate stock option grants that allowed the company to conceal hundreds of millions of dollars of compensation costs and to thereby report significantly inflated income to investors. The jury found that Jasper engaged in fraud, lied to auditors, and aided Maxim's failure to maintain accurate accounting records, which resulted in inaccurate financial reporting. Evidence from the trial showed that, with his knowledge, Jasper's staff granted stock options by using

hindsight to identify dates with historically low stock prices. The staff then drafted false documentation to make it seem that the options had been granted at earlier dates, which enabled the company to conceal its true compensation expenses.

Clearly, management integrity was a fundamental problem leading to this fraud. Assessing management integrity is no easy task; auditors must constantly consider how potential lapses therein could affect financial reporting.

For more information about this case, see SEC Litigation Release No. 20381.

The *Focus on Fraud* feature "Stock Option Backdating Fraud as an Example of Inherent Risk at the Financial Statement Level" provides an example of a case where low management integrity led to fraud.

The following is a list of factors that lead auditors to assess inherent risk relating to financial reporting at a higher level:

- *Discrepancies in the accounting records*—for example, last-minute adjustments that significantly affect financial results, transactions that are not recorded in a complete or timely manner, and unsupported or unauthorized balances or transactions
- *Problematic or unusual relationships between the auditor and management*—for example, denial of access to records or facilities, undue time pressures imposed by management to resolve complex or contentious issues, or unusual delays by management in providing information
- *Lack of management competence*—for example, inappropriate knowledge in relation to responsibilities, inappropriate management authority, poor past performance, no succession planning
- *Company history of exactly meeting analyst estimates or high earnings growth expectations*
- *An impending initial public offering of stock*
- *Disagreements over financial reporting with prior auditors*
- *Auditor resignation*—due to refusal of the predecessor auditor to continue to provide services to the organization
- *Unusual transactions with outsiders or significant related-party transactions*
- *Transactions for which most or all of the revenue or expense is recognized at the inception of the transaction*
- *Financial results that seem too good to be true*—for example, when financial results are significantly better than competitors, without substantive differences in operations between the organization and competitors

- *Complex business arrangements that appear to serve little practical purpose*
- *Hesitancy or evasiveness from management regarding questions about the financial statements*
- *Insistence by the chief executive officer (CEO) or CFO to be present at all meetings between the audit committee and internal or external auditors*
- *Accounting methods that appear to favor form over economic substance*

The *Auditing in Practice* feature "Application of Accounting Principles and Related Disclosures" provides guidance to consider when assessing inherent risks relating to financial reporting.

Exhibit 7.2 provides examples of questions for an auditor to ask when assessing inherent risk relating to financial reporting.

Risk Assessment Procedures for Assessing Fraud Risk

Audit Team Discussions   The audit team is expected to have a team discussion, often referred to as **brainstorming**, designed to encourage auditors to creatively assess client risks, particularly those relevant to the possible existence of fraud in the organization. Brainstorming sessions occur predominantly during the early planning phases of the audit, but on occasion these sessions are repeated if actual fraud is detected or at the end of the audit to ensure that all ideas generated during brainstorming have been addressed during the audit opinion formulation process. Brainstorming sessions are attended by the entire engagement team and are most often led by the audit partner or manager. These sessions are viewed by audit firms as a way to transfer knowledge from top-level auditors to less senior members of the audit team via interactive and constructive group dialogue and idea exchange.

Application of Accounting Principles and Related Disclosures

AUDITING IN PRACTICE

One issue critical to understanding the client's financial reporting risks involves an analysis of management's selection and application of accounting principles, including related disclosures. The auditor needs to determine whether management's decisions are appropriate for its business and are consistent with the applicable financial reporting framework for its industry. The auditor should develop expectations about the appropriate disclosures that are necessary and should compare those expectations to the disclosures made by management in assessing inherent risks relating to financial reporting.

For example, AS 12 requires that the auditor obtain an understanding of the following types of matters relevant to understanding management's application of accounting principles and related disclosures:

- Significant changes in the company's accounting principles, financial reporting policies, or disclosures and the reasons for such changes
- The financial reporting competencies of personnel involved in selecting and applying significant new or complex accounting principles
- The accounts or disclosures for which judgment is used in the application of significant accounting principles, especially in determining management's estimates and assumptions
- The effect of significant accounting principles in controversial or emerging areas for which there is a lack of authoritative guidance or consensus
- The methods the company uses to account for significant and unusual transactions
- Financial reporting standards and laws and regulations that are new to the company, including when and how the company will adopt such requirements

EXHIBIT **7.2**	Questions to Ask When Assessing Financial Reporting Quality: Selected Excerpts From the NACD Blue Ribbon Commission on Audit Committees

- What are the significant judgment areas (reserves, contingencies, asset values, note disclosures) that affect the current-year financial statements? What considerations were involved in resolving these judgment matters? What is the range of potential impact on future reported financial results?
- What issues or concerns exist that could adversely affect the future operations and/or financial condition of the company? What is management's plan to deal with these future risks?
- What is the overall quality of the company's financial reporting, including the appropriateness of important accounting principles followed by the company?
- What is the range of acceptable accounting choices the company has available to it?
- Were there any significant changes in accounting policies, or in the application of accounting principles during the year? If yes, why were the changes made and what impact did the changes have on earnings per share (EPS) or other key financial measures?
- Were there any significant changes in accounting estimates, or models used in making accounting estimates during the year? If yes, why were the changes made and what impact did the changes have on earnings per share (EPS) or other key financial measures?
- Are there any instances where the company may be thought of as pushing the limits of revenue recognition? If so, what is the rationale for the treatment chosen?
- Have similar transactions and events been treated in a consistent manner across divisions of the company and across countries in which the company operates? If not, what are the exceptions and the reasons for them?
- Do the accounting choices made reflect the economic substance of transactions and the strategic management of the business? If not, where are the exceptions and why do they exist?
- To what extent are the financial reporting choices consistent with the manner in which the company measures its progress toward achieving its mission internally? If not, what are the differences?
- How do the significant accounting principles used by the company compare with leading companies in the industry, or with other companies that are considered leaders in financial disclosure? What is the rationale for any differences?
- Has there been any instance where short-run reporting objectives (e.g., achieving a profit objective or meeting bonus or stock option requirements) were allowed to influence accounting choices? If yes, what choices were made and why?

To encourage interactive and constructive group dialogue and idea exchange, the following guidelines are typically followed during the brainstorming session:

- *Suspension of criticism*—Participants are requested to refrain from criticizing or making value judgments during the session.
- *Freedom of expression*—Participants are encouraged to try to overcome their inhibitions about expressing creative ideas, and every idea is noted and accepted as a possibility.
- *Quantity of idea generation*—Participants are encouraged to provide more ideas rather than fewer, with the intent to generate a variety of possible risk assessment scenarios that can then be explored during the conduct of the audit.
- *Respectful communication*—Participants are encouraged to exchange ideas, further develop those ideas during the session, and to respect the opinions of others.

Brainstorming sessions normally include the following steps:

1. Review prior year client information
2. Consider client information, particularly with respect to the fraud triangle (incentive, opportunity, and rationalization)

3. Integrate information from Steps 1 and 2 into an assessment of the likelihood of fraud in the engagement
4. Identify audit responses to fraud risks

The U.S. auditing standards require that the auditor document how and when the brainstorming session occurred and the audit team members who were present. However, from an international perspective, the ISAs do not require that these items be documented.

Academic research reveals that during this process, most audit firms encourage participants in the brainstorming session to explicitly consider professional skepticism, both in general throughout the engagement and with respect to specific accounts with a higher risk of fraud. For example, audit firms encourage the brainstorming group to answer questions such as, "How could someone commit fraud at this client, or for a certain account balance?" Auditors are told to be skeptical about assurances that client personnel provide, to be sure that they verify the authenticity of documentation, and to choose new and different audit procedures each year even if the results of brainstorming in the current year are similar to those in prior years. Brainstorming sessions usually last up to an hour, but occasionally may last in excess of two hours, depending on the complexity and risk profile of the client.

Other Procedures As part of the risk assessment procedures used to identify fraud risk factors, auditors should inquire of numerous parties including management, board and audit committee members, and internal auditors. Further, the results of planning analytical procedures (discussed later in this chapter) can identify potential fraud concerns.

Assessing Factors Affecting Control Risk

LO 4 Assess factors affecting control risk.

Control risk relates to the susceptibility that a misstatement, due to either error or fraud, will not be prevented or detected on a timely basis by the organization's internal control system. During audit planning, the auditor makes a preliminary assessment of control risk based on performing risk assessment procedures. The control risk assessment can be made at the overall financial statement level. However, to facilitate planning, these assessments are also typically made at the account or assertion level because control effectiveness can vary across accounts and assertions. When control risk is high, the auditor is concerned that a material misstatement may not be prevented or that if a material misstatement exists in the organization's financial statements that it will not be detected and corrected by management. Some level of control risk is always present because of the inherent limitations in internal control. The following is a list of factors that lead auditors to assess control risk at a higher level:

- Poor controls in specific countries or locations
- Difficulty gaining access to the organization or determining the individuals who own and/or control the organization
- Little interaction between senior management and operating staff
- Weak tone at the top leading to a poor control environment
- Inadequate accounting staff or staff lacking requisite expertise
- Inadequate information systems
- Growth of the organization exceeds the accounting system infrastructure
- Disregard for regulations or controls designed to prevent illegal acts
- No internal audit function, a weak internal audit function, or lack of respect for the internal audit function by management
- Weak design, implementation, and monitoring of internal controls
- Lack of supervision of accounting personnel

The last of these control risk factors is particularly relevant to the fraud scheme perpetrated by the comptroller of the city of Dixon, Illinois. Her crimes are described in the *Focus on Fraud* feature "Lack of Oversight as a Control Weakness Leads to Embezzlement."

Lack of Oversight as a Control Weakness Leads to Embezzlement

Rita Crundwell was the comptroller for the city of Dixon, Illinois, from 1983 through early 2012. During that time, she stole millions of dollars from the city to fund her extravagant lifestyle related to breeding and showing quarter horses. While maintaining this lavish, high-profile lifestyle, Crundwell received a relatively meager $80,000 per year salary from the city. Apparently, the discrepancy between her salary and lifestyle went unnoticed by her supervisors or the city's auditors. Crundwell handled all of the city's finances, and it appears that she was left relatively unsupervised by the city's leadership. Most shocking is the magnitude of the theft— over $50 million—in relation to the size of the community. Dixon, a small town about 100 miles southwest of Chicago, has a population of fewer than 16,000 people. It is difficult to understand how the leadership of a city so small could have not realized that the massive amount of funds was missing.

The fraud began late in 1990, when Crundwell opened a bank account in the joint name of the city of Dixon and an acronym, RSCDA. The account holder was listed as "RSCDA, c/o Rita Crundwell." RSCDA was purportedly the city's capital development fund. Crundwell transferred funds from Dixon's money market account to the RSCDA fund, as well as to various other city-held bank accounts. Crundwell then wrote checks from the RSCDA account to pay for her personal expenses, including expenses relating to her horse business. To conceal the fraud, Crundwell created fictitious invoices from the state of Illinois, made to look as though the funds she was fraudulently depositing into the RSCDA account were being used for a legitimate city purpose.

To give a sense of the magnitude of the fraud, Crundwell charged about $2.5 million to her American Express card between January 2007 and March 2012; this included charges of $339,000 on jewelry alone. Between September 2011 and March 2012 she wrote 19 checks worth $3,558,000 from a city account payable to "Treasurer;" she deposited these checks into the RSCDA account. She then took $3,311,860 from the RSCDA account by checks and

online withdrawals, using only $74,274 for the city's actual operations. Crundwell used the remainder of those funds for personal and business expenses, including approximately $450,000 relating to her horse farming operations, $600,000 in online credit card payments, and $67,000 to purchase a 2012 Chevy Silverado pickup truck. After the fraud was discovered, the FBI seized, among other items, the following from Crundwell:

- 311 quarter horses
- 2009 Liberty Coach motor home: $2.1 million
- 2009 Kenworth T800 tractor truck: $146,000
- 2009 Freightliner truck: $140,000
- 2009 Chevrolet Silverado pickup truck: $56,646
- 2009 Featherlite horse trailer: $258,698

The fraud unraveled when Crundwell took a 12-week unpaid vacation during 2011. While she was away, a city employee who served as her replacement obtained bank statements from all of the city's bank accounts. After reviewing those statements, the employee contacted the city's mayor, Mayor Burke, to alert him that one particular account had unusual transactions within it. Specifically, the September 2011 statement for that account showed three deposits totaling $785,000, as well as 84 checks drawn totaling $360,493, and 40 withdrawals totaling $266,605. Burke was unaware that the account even existed, and it was apparent that the withdrawals had no legitimate purpose relating to the city's business. Crundwell was sentenced to nearly 20 years in prison after pleading guilty to a wire fraud count.

The implication for auditors is the need to be aware of weak internal controls and the negative consequences for a client's financial statements. A control risk assessment of high means that the auditor needs to perform additional substantive procedures. In contrast, when an auditor believes that controls are well designed and assesses control risk as low, the auditor needs to test those controls to see if they are operating effectively, and may need to modify the control risk assessment (to higher) if they are not operating effectively.

Auditor's Risk Assessment Procedures for Assessing Control Risk

To have an appropriate level of understanding of the client's internal controls, the auditor needs to understand the controls management has designed and implemented to mitigate identified risks of material misstatement. For entity-wide controls, auditors will typically review relevant documentation prepared by management and interview appropriate individuals. As an example, consider the risk assessment procedures that auditors might perform related to one component of internal controls—management's risk assessment. To obtain this understanding, the auditor typically uses some or all of the following risk assessment procedures:

- Interview relevant parties to develop an understanding of the processes used by the board of directors and management to evaluate and manage risks
- Review the risk-based approach used by the internal audit function with the director of the internal audit function and with the audit committee
- Interview management about its risk approach, risk preferences, risk appetite, and the relationship of risk analysis to strategic planning
- Review outside regulatory reports, where applicable, that address the company's policies and procedures toward risk
- Review company policies and procedures for addressing risk
- Gain a knowledge of company compensation schemes to determine if they are consistent with the risk policies adopted by the company
- Review prior years' work to determine if current actions are consistent with risk approaches discussed with management
- Review risk management documents
- Determine how management and the board monitor risk; identify changes in risk; and react to mitigate, manage, or control the risk

Auditors also need to obtain an understanding of the controls designed and implemented at the process or transaction level. Similar to entity-wide controls, for process or transaction controls, auditors will typically review relevant documentation prepared by management and interview appropriate individuals with knowledge about these controls. Further, auditors will perform walkthroughs, following a transaction from origination to when it is reflected in the financial records to determine if the controls are effectively designed and have been implemented.

Using Planning Analytical Procedures to Assess the Risk of Material Misstatement

LO 5 **Use planning analytical procedures to identify areas of heightened risk of material misstatement.**

Planning analytical procedures used as a risk assessment procedure can help auditors improve their understanding of the client's business. These procedures also help auditors identify risks of material misstatement in particular account balances and direct the auditor's attention to high-risk areas.

Recall from *Chapter 6* that a basic premise underlying the application of analytical procedures is that plausible relationships among data can be reasonably expected to exist and to continue in the absence of known conditions to the contrary. As initially described in *Chapter 6*, the steps that the auditor will take are as follows:

1. Determine the suitability of a particular analytical procedure for given account(s)/assertion(s), considering the risks of material misstatement.
2. Evaluate the reliability of data that the auditor is using to develop an expectation of account balances or ratios.
3. Develop an expectation of recorded account balances or ratios, and evaluate whether that expectation is precise enough to accomplish the relevant objective. Recall that for planning analytical procedures the objective is to identify accounts with heightened risk of misstatement to provide a basis for designing and implementing responses to the assessed risks. Also recall that

the precision of expectation tends to be less precise and based on more aggregated data. However, with highly aggregated data, this procedure will only provide broad indications of potential material misstatements.

4. Define when the difference between the auditor's expectation and what the client has recorded would be considered significant.
5. Compare the client's recorded amounts with the auditor's expectation to determine any significant unexpected differences.
6. Investigate significant unexpected differences. Recall that for planning analytical procedures, significant unexpected differences suggest that substantive procedures for the account/assertion will be increased.
7. Ensure that the following have been appropriately documented: auditor's expectation from Step 3, including the factors that the auditor considered in developing the expectation, the results in Step 4, and the audit procedures conducted relating to Steps 5 and 6.

As an example of a planning analytical procedure, the auditor may develop an expectation of revenue based on production capacity. Recorded revenue in excess of this expectation may indicate a heightened risk of misstatement in the revenue account—due to either fraud or error. The auditor will then want to plan audit procedures to obtain sufficient appropriate evidence for the revenue account.

Types of Analytical Procedures

Two frequently used analytical procedures during risk assessment include trend analysis and ratio analysis. Most commonly, the auditor imports the client's unaudited data into a spreadsheet or a software program to calculate trends and ratios and help pinpoint areas for further investigation. These trends and ratios are compared with auditor expectations that were developed from knowledge obtained in previous years, industry trends, and current economic development in the geographic area served by the client. The *Auditing in Practice* feature "Comparisons Used in Planning Analytical Procedures" describes common comparisons performed by auditors.

Comparisons Used in Planning Analytical Procedures

AUDITING IN **PRACTICE**

Comparison with Industry Data

A comparison of client data with industry data may identify potential problems. For example, if the average collection period for accounts receivable in an industry is forty-three days, but the client's average collection period is sixty-five days, this might indicate problems with product quality or credit risk. Or, as another example, a bank's concentration of loans in a particular industry may indicate greater problems if that industry is encountering economic problems. One potential limitation to using industry data is that such data might not be directly comparable to the client's. Companies may be quite different but still classified within one broad industry. Also, other companies in the industry may use accounting principles different from the client's (e.g., LIFO versus FIFO).

Comparison with Previous Years' Data

Simple ratio analysis comparing current and past data that is prepared as a routine part of planning an audit can highlight risks of misstatement. The auditor often develops ratios on asset turnover, liquidity, and product-line profitability to search for potential signals of risk. For example, an inventory turnover ratio might indicate that a particular product line had a turnover of four times for the past three years, but only three times this year. The change may indicate potential obsolescence problems or errors in the accounting records. Even when performing simple ratio analysis, it is important that the auditor go through each of the steps in the process, beginning with the development of expectations.

Trend analysis includes simple year-to-year comparisons of account balances, graphic presentations, and analysis of financial data, histograms of ratios, and projections of account balances based on the history of changes in the account. It is imperative for the auditor to develop expectations and to establish decision rules, or thresholds, in advance in order to identify unexpected results for additional investigation. One potential decision rule, for example, is that dollar variances exceeding one-third or one-fourth of planning materiality should be investigated. Another decision rule, or threshold, is to investigate any change exceeding a specified percentage. Auditors often use a trend analysis over several years for key accounts, as shown in the following example in planning for the 2015 audit (2015 data are unaudited).

	2015	2014	2013	2011	2010
Gross sales ($000)	$29,500	$24,900	$24,369	$21,700	$17,600
Sales returns ($000)	600	400	300	250	200
Gross margin ($000)	8,093	6,700	6,869	6,450	5,000
Percent of prior year: Sales	118.5%	102.2%	112.3%	123.3%	105.2%
Sales returns	150.0%	133.3%	120.0%	125.0%	104.6%
Gross margin	132.8%	97.5%	106.5%	129.0%	100.0%
Sales as a percentage of 2010 sales	167.6%	141.5%	138.5%	123.3%	100.0%

In this example, the auditor's expectation might be that gross margin percentage and sales percentage would increase at about the same rate. Further, the auditor might have an expectation that sales returns would be relatively stable in comparison with that of the prior year. After setting a threshold and comparing the expectation to the client's data, the auditor in this example might conclude that the changes in gross margin and sales returns warrant further investigation. The auditor should gain an understanding about why gross margin is increasing more rapidly than sales and why sales returns are increasing. More importantly, the auditor should develop some potential hypotheses as to why there was an increase in gross margin along with the reason for the substantial increase in sales. Then, once the hypotheses are developed, the auditor should determine which set of hypotheses is most likely and then use those for prioritizing audit work. Potential hypotheses for the increase in gross margin include:

- The company has introduced a new product that is a huge market success (e.g., the introduction of the iPad mini by Apple).
- The company has changed its product mix.
- The company has improved its operational efficiencies.
- The company has fictitious sales (and consequently no cost of goods associated with those sales).

Upon analysis, two of these hypotheses would best explain the unaudited changes in sales and gross margin for 2015: (a) a significant new product introduction that allows higher margins or (b) fictitious sales. With this analysis, the auditor can prioritize which hypothesis to investigate first and thus achieve audit efficiency. For example, if the company has not introduced a new product and the company's sales growth and gross margin are significantly higher than the competition, then it is likely that the fictitious sales hypothesis is the most likely. Going through this process of performing planning analytical procedures helps the auditor identify areas where the risk of material misstatement is high and then allows the auditor to plan appropriate procedures to address those risks. Importantly, the auditor should determine potential hypotheses rather than just inquiring of management as to the reasons for the change. Behavioral research shows that once an individual is given a potential explanation, it is more difficult to identify alternative explanations.

As suggested previously, trend analysis can incorporate **ratio analysis**, which takes advantage of economic relationships between two or more accounts. It is widely used because of its power to identify unusual or unexpected changes in relationships. Ratio analysis is useful in identifying significant differences between the client results and a norm (such as industry ratios) or between auditor expectations and actual results. It is also useful in identifying potential audit problems when ratios change between years (such as inventory turnover).

Comparing ratio data over time for the client and its industry can yield useful insights. The auditor could rely on industry data to develop expectations for preliminary analytics. For example, if a particular industry ratio increased over time, the auditor should expect that the client's ratio would also increase over time. In the following example, the percentage of sales returns and allowances to net sales for the client does not vary significantly from the industry average for the current period, but comparing the trend over time yields an unexpected result.

Sales Returns as a% of Net Sales

	2015	2014	2013	2011	2010
Client	2.1%	2.6%	2.5%	2.7%	2.5%
Industry	2.3%	2.1%	2.2%	2.1%	2.0%

This comparison shows that even though the percentage of sales returns for 2015 is close to the industry average, the client's percentage declined significantly from 2014, while the industry's percentage increased. In addition, except for the current year, the client's percentages exceeded the industry average. The result is different from the auditor's expectation that the percentage would increase from the prior period—it likely exceeds the auditor's threshold, and, thus, the auditor should investigate the potential cause. Some possible explanations for the differences include:

- The client has improved its quality control.
- Fictitious sales have been recorded in 2015.
- The client is not properly recording sales returns in 2015.

The auditor must design audit procedures to identify the cause of this difference to determine whether a material misstatement exists.

Exhibit 7.3 shows several commonly used financial ratios that can be used in performing planning analytical procedures. The first three ratios provide information on potential liquidity problems. The turnover and gross margin ratios are helpful in identifying fraudulent activity or items recorded more than once, such as fictitious sales or inventory. The leverage and capital turnover ratios help in evaluating going-concern problems or adherence to debt covenants. Although the auditor chooses the ratios deemed most useful for a client, many auditors routinely calculate and analyze the ratios listed in *Exhibit 7.3* on a trend basis over time. Other ratios are designed for a specific industry. In the banking industry, for example, auditors calculate ratios on percentages of nonperforming loans, operating margin, and

EXHIBIT **7.3**	Commonly Used Ratios

Ratio	Formula
Short-term liquidity ratios:	
Current ratio	Current Assets/Current Liabilities
Quick ratio	(Cash + Cash Equivalents + Net Receivables)/Current Liabilities
Current debt-to-assets ratio	Current Liabilities/Total Assets
Receivable ratios:	
Accounts receivable turnover	Credit Sales/Accounts Receivable
Days' sales in accounts receivable	365/Turnover
Inventory ratios:	
Inventory turnover	Cost of Sales/Ending Inventory
Days' sales in inventory	365/Turnover
Profitability measures:	
Net profit margin	Net Income/Net Sales
Return on equity	Net Income/Stockholders' Equity
Financial leverage ratios:	
Debt-to-equity ratio	Total Liabilities/Stockholders' Equity
Liabilities to assets	Total Liabilities/Total Assets
Capital turnover ratios:	
Asset liquidity	Current Assets/Total Assets
Sales to assets	Net Sales/Total Assets
Net worth to sales	Stockholders' Equity/Net Sales

average interest rates by loan categories. Ratio and trend analysis are generally carried out through a comparison of client data with expectations:

- Based on industry data
- Based on similar prior-period data
- Developed from industry trends, client budgets, other account balances, or other bases of expectations

Responding to Identified Risks of Material Misstatement

 LO 6 Describe how auditors make decisions about detection risk and audit risk.

In responding to identified risks of material misstatement, the auditor makes decisions about detection risk and audit risk, which will then have implications for the audit work ultimately conducted.

Determining Audit Risk and Detection Risk

The auditor assesses the risk of material misstatement at the financial statement level and the account and assertion levels, which includes both control risk and inherent risk, for each significant component of the financial statements of the organization. From this assessment, and with consideration of the desired level of audit risk, the auditor determines the level of detection risk. Detection risk is affected by both the effectiveness of the substantive auditing procedures that the auditor performs and the extent to which those procedures are performed with due professional care. The auditor's determination of detection risk influences the nature, timing, and extent of substantive audit procedures to ensure that the audit achieves the desired audit risk.

A high level of detection risk means that the audit firm is willing to take a higher risk of not detecting a material misstatement. A low level of detection risk means that the audit firm is not willing to take as much of a risk of not detecting a material misstatement. If detection risk is at a high level, then audit risk is higher as well, because there is a greater chance of issuing an audit opinion that the financial statements are fairly presented when they are materially misstated. If detection risk is at a low level, then audit risk is lower as well, because there is a lower chance of issuing an audit opinion that the financial statements are presented when they are materially misstated. Audit risk is usually set between 1% (low audit risk) and 5% (high audit risk). Based on the set level of audit risk and the assessed levels of risk of material misstatement (inherent and control risk), detection risk will range from 1% (low detection risk) to 100% (high detection risk), although it would be unusual to have an extremely high level of detection risk. The risks of material misstatement may range from 0% (unlikely) to 100% (highly likely). *Exhibit 7.4* shows the directional relationships among the various risks, along with interpretations of their meanings.

Applications of the Audit Risk Model

When auditors document their risk assessments, they often use descriptive terms such as *low*, *moderate*, or *high*. However, it also useful to think of these assessments in quantitative terms.

High Risk of Material Misstatement Assume an account with many complex transactions and weak internal controls. The auditor assesses both inherent risk and control risk at their maximum (100%), implying that the client does not have effective internal control related to this account and there is a high risk that transactions posted to this account would contain a misstatement. Also assume that the auditor has set audit risk at a low level (1%). This implies that the auditor is willing to take only a 1% chance of expressing an audit opinion that the financial statements are fairly presented when they are materially misstated. A numerical depiction of the relationship between inherent risk, control risk, detection risk, and audit risk is often called the **audit risk model**, and it is calculated as follows:

$$Audit\ Risk = Inherent\ Risk \times Control\ Risk \times Detection\ Risk$$
$$0.01 = 1.00 \times 1.00 \times Detection\ Risk$$

therefore:

$$Detection\ Risk = 0.01/(1.0 \times 1.0) = 1\%$$

In this example, detection risk and audit risk are the same because the auditor cannot rely on internal controls to prevent or detect misstatements. The illustration yields an intuitive result: a high likelihood of material misstatement leads to extended audit work to maintain audit risk at an acceptable level.

Low Risk of Material Misstatement Assume an account with simple transactions, well-trained accounting personnel recording those transactions, no incentive to misstate the financial statements, and effective internal control over the account. The auditor's previous experience with the client and an understanding of the client's internal controls indicate a low risk of material misstatement existing in the accounting records. The auditor assesses inherent and control risk as low (at 50% and 20%, respectively). Audit risk

EXHIBIT 7.4 Risks and Their Effects on Audit Work

Risk of Material Misstatement	Interpretation	Relationship to Audit Risk	Interpretation	Effect on Detection Risk	Interpretation	Effect on Audit Work
Inherent Risk:						
High (100%)	Likely that transaction contains a misstatement.	Set audit risk at lower level (1%).	Auditor is willing to take only a 1% chance of expressing an audit opinion that the financial statements are fairly presented when they are materially misstated.	Detection risk will be at lower level (1%).	Auditor is willing to take only a 1% chance that substantive audit procedures will not detect a material misstatement.	More work or more reliable work or more relevant work.
Low (30%)	Unlikely that a transaction contains a misstatement.	Set audit risk at higher level (5%).	Auditor is willing to take a 5% chance of expressing an audit opinion that the financial statements are fairly presented when they are materially misstated.	Detection risk can be at higher level (17%), assuming control risk is 100%.	Auditor is willing to take a 17% chance that substantive audit procedures will not detect a material misstatement.	Less work or less reliable work or less relevant work.
Control Risk:						
High (100%)	Controls are ineffective.	Set audit risk at lower level (1%).	Auditor is willing to take only a 1% chance of expressing an audit opinion that the financial statements are fairly presented when they are materially misstated.	Detection risk will be at lower level (1%).	Auditor is willing to take only a 1% chance that substantive audit procedures will not detect a material misstatement.	More work or more reliable work or more relevant work.
Low (30%)	Controls are effective (note that the auditor needs to test controls to confirm this assessment).	Set audit risk at higher level (5%).	Auditor is willing to take a 5% chance of expressing an audit opinion that the financial statements are fairly presented when they are materially misstated.	Detection risk can be at higher level (17%), assuming inherent risk is 100%.	Auditor is willing to take a 17% chance that substantive audit procedures will not detect a material misstatement.	Less work or less reliable work or less relevant work.

has been set at 5%. The auditor's determination of detection risk for this engagement would be calculated as follows:

$$Audit\ Risk = Inherent\ Risk \times Control\ Risk \times Detection\ Risk$$
$$0.05 = 0.50 \times 0.20 \times Detection\ Risk$$

therefore:

$$Detection\ Risk = 0.05/(0.50 \times 0.20) = 50\%$$

In other words, the auditor could design tests of the accounting records with a higher detection risk—in this case 50%. Thus, minimal substantive tests of account balances are needed to provide corroborating evidence on the expectations that the accounts are not materially misstated. Because inherent and control risk are relatively low, the auditor is willing to accept a greater risk that substantive audit procedures will not detect a material misstatement. However, because the auditor is planning on relying on controls, the auditor will need to test the operating effectiveness of controls to see if the lower control risk assessment is warranted. As in the prior illustration, this illustration yields an intuitive result: a low likelihood of misstatement leads to less extensive audit work to maintain audit risk at an acceptable level.

The *Auditing in Practice* feature "An Expanded Version of the Audit Risk Model" provides information about how auditors may divide detection risk into subcomponents relating to types of testing.

Planning Audit Procedures to Respond to the Assessed Risks of Material Misstatement

LO 7 Respond to the assessed risks of material misstatement and plan the procedures to be performed on an audit engagement.

Recall from *Chapter 5* that for a financial statement audit where the auditor wants to rely on controls as part of the basis for the audit opinion, the auditor should design a controls reliance audit—an audit that includes tests of controls and substantive procedures. For some audits, the auditor might determine that it is not efficient or effective to rely on the client's controls in

An Expanded Version of the Audit Risk Model

AUDITING IN **PRACTICE**

Auditors may choose to think of the audit risk model in an expanded version that divides detection risk (DR) into two subcomponents. These subcomponents are the (1) tests of details risk (TD) and (2) substantive analytical procedures risk (AP).

This expanded model can be represented as:

$$AR = IR \times CR \times AP \times TD$$

When using this expanded model, the auditor would want to determine TD as follows:

$$TD = AR/(IR \times CR \times AP)$$

Assume a situation where:

AR = 5%
IR = 50%

CR = 30%
AP = 60%

In this setting, the auditor would determine TD as:

$$TD = 5\%/(50\% \times 30\% \times 60\%)$$
$$TD = 55.5\%$$

This expanded model recognizes that detection risk incorporates both types of substantive procedures—substantive analytical procedures and tests of details. In audits where both types of procedures will be used, this expanded model may be a more appropriate way to think about the risks and the auditor's responses to those risks.

forming the audit opinion. In those audits, the auditor designs a substantive audit—an audit that includes substantive procedures and does not include tests of controls.

When considering risk responses, the auditor should:

1. Evaluate the reasons for the assessed risk of material misstatement
2. Estimate the likelihood of material misstatement due to the inherent risks of the client
3. Consider the role of internal controls, and determine whether control risk is relatively high or low, thereby determining whether the auditor should rely on controls (thereby necessitating tests of controls) or whether the auditor needs to conduct a substantive audit
4. Obtain more relevant and reliable audit evidence as the auditor's assessment of the risk of material misstatement increases

A practical analogy to conceptualize these steps is to compare an umbrella in a rainstorm to effective internal controls. Risks might result in material misstatements (rain); management is responsible for keeping the financial statements free of material misstatements (dry). The auditor's objective is to gather enough information to objectively assess how well management is doing in keeping the financial statements free from material misstatement (dry). *Exhibit 7.5* shows that Client A has effective internal controls (the umbrella without holes) that prevent material misstatements (rain) from getting into the accounting records. However, we know that umbrellas are not always perfect—they can spring leaks when least expected, or one of the supporting arms can fail, letting rain come through on one side. The auditor has to test the umbrella (controls) to see that it is working,

EXHIBIT **7.5**   Effect of Risk Assessment on Risk Response

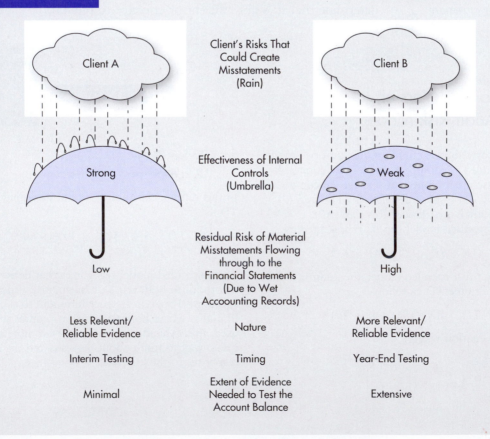

but must do enough substantive testing of the account balance to determine that leaks (misstatements) had not occurred in an amount that would be noticeable (material misstatement). Client B's umbrella has holes in it (weak internal controls), resulting in wet accounting records (they are likely to contain material misstatements). Because of the weak controls, it is unlikely that the auditor will perform any testing of controls, and the use of substantive analytical procedures will probably be limited. Thus, the auditor must perform extensive direct tests of the account balances to identify any misstatements.

Nature, Timing, and Extent of Risk Response Procedures

The nature, timing, and extent of the auditor's risk response depend on the auditor's assessment of the risk of material misstatement. The **nature of risk response** refers to the types of audit procedures to be performed, with a focus on the appropriateness (relevance and reliability) of those procedures. For example, certain audit procedures may be more appropriate for some assertions than others. Assessing the existence of inventory is most effectively completed by inspecting the inventory, whereas assessing the valuation of inventory is most effectively completed by engaging a specialist. In addition, the nature of risk response could occur at a more global engagement level and could involve assembling an audit team that has more experienced auditors and auditors with specialized skills or including on the audit team outside specialists to address assessed risks. Another way to address assessed risks at the engagement level might be to put increased emphasis on professional skepticism or to incorporate elements of unpredictability in the selection of audit procedures.

Some ways to introduce unpredictability include the following:

- Perform some audit procedures on accounts, disclosures, and assertions that would otherwise not receive scrutiny because they are considered low risk
- Select items for testing that are outside the normal boundaries for testing (e.g., that are lower than prior-year materiality)
- Perform audit procedures on a surprise or unannounced basis
- Vary the location or procedures year to year for multilocation audits

The **timing of risk response** refers to when audit procedures are conducted and whether those procedures are conducted at announced or predictable times. When the risk of material misstatement is heightened, the auditor conducts the audit procedures closer to year-end, on an unannounced basis, and includes some element of unpredictability in the timing, such that the auditor changes the timing of audit procedures from one audit to the next so that some procedures are performed on an interim basis and others are performed at year end.

Further, certain procedures can be completed only at or after period end. These include the following:

- Compare the financial statements to the accounting records
- Evaluate adjusting journal entries made by management in preparing the financial statements
- Conduct procedures to respond to risks that management may have engaged in improper transactions at period end

The **extent of risk response** refers to the sufficiency of evidence that is necessary given the client's assessed risks, materiality, and the level of acceptable audit risk. When the risk of material misstatement is heightened, the auditor increases the extent of audit procedures and demands more evidence. As an example of increasing the extent of risk response, one such response would be to increase the number of locations to be included in the

The City of Dixon, Illinois, Sues Its Auditor for $50 Million Related to the Rita Crundwell Embezzlement

Recall from earlier in the chapter that Rita Crundwell embezzled about $50 million from the city of Dixon, Illinois. On June 8, 2012, the city sued the accountants that had conducted the city's audit for the past five years: Samuel Card CPA and Janis Card Company LLC. In addition, the lawsuit names former Dixon audit firm, CliftonLarsonAllen, as a respondent in discovery, which allows the city to request documents in order to determine whether or not to also sue the former audit firm as well. The lawsuit alleges professional negligence and negligent misrepresentation, and it alleges certain deficiencies in how the auditors conducted the audit, including:

- Failing to identify inaccuracies in the city's financial statements and other financial documents

- Failing to properly perform audits and other financial services
- Failing to perform professional services and issue audits in conformance with nationally recognized standards and its own internal policies and procedures
- Failing to implement proper policies and procedures in order to perform the audits of the city
- Failing to properly train auditors and auditing staff to identify fraud, embezzlement, and criminal acts

In September 2013, CliftonLarsonAllen and Sam Card agreed to settle for a total of $40 million. The message is clear: when auditors fail to assess and appropriately respond to the risk of material misstatement, there are severe consequences to all parties involved.

scope of the audit (e.g., supervising inventory counts at a greater number of warehouse locations).

The *Focus on Fraud* feature "The City of Dixon, Illinois, Sues Its Auditor for $50 Million Related to the Rita Crundwell Embezzlement" provides a reminder to auditors of their obligation to accurately assess risk at the overall financial statement level and to respond accordingly.

SUMMARY AND NEXT STEPS

Materiality judgments are a critical part of the audit opinion formulation process. Certain risks associated with the client heighten the risk of material misstatements, including inherent and control risks. Audit risk and detection risk are determined by the auditor based upon inherent and control risks. The audit risk model is used by the auditor to respond to assessed risks, in terms of the nature, timing, and extent of audit procedures. In *Chapter 8* we discuss specialized audit tools that you can use to respond to risk, including sampling and generalized audit software.

SIGNIFICANT TERMS

Audit risk   The risk that the auditor expresses an inappropriate audit opinion when the financial statements are materially misstated.

Audit risk model   A numerical depiction of the relationship between inherent risk, control risk, detection risk, and audit risk.

Brainstorming   A group discussion designed to encourage auditors to creatively assess client risks, particularly those relevant to the possible existence of fraud in the organization.

Business Risk   Inherent risk at the financial statement level that affects the business operations and potential outcomes of organizational activities.

Clearly trivial   An amount that is clearly inconsequential, whether taken individually or in the aggregate and whether judged by any criteria of size, nature, or circumstances.

Control risk   The risk that a misstatement that could occur in an assertion about a class of transaction, account balance, or disclosure and that could be material, either individually or when aggregated with other misstatements, will not be prevented, or detected and corrected, on a timely basis by the entity's internal control.

Detection risk   The risk that the procedures performed by the auditor to reduce audit risk to an acceptably low level will not detect a misstatement that exists and that could be material, either individually or when aggregated with other misstatements.

Extent of risk response   The amount of evidence that is necessary given the client's assessed risks, materiality, and the level of acceptable audit risk.

Inherent risk   The susceptibility of an assertion about a class of transaction, account balance, or disclosure to a misstatement that could be material, either individually or when aggregated with other misstatements, before consideration of any related controls.

Materiality   The magnitude of an omission or misstatement of accounting information that, in view of surrounding circumstances, makes it probable that the judgment of a reasonable person relying on the information would have been changed or influenced by the omission or misstatement.

Misstatement   An error, either intentional or unintentional, that exists in a transaction or financial statement account balance.

Nature of risk response   The types of audit procedures applied given the nature of the account balance and the most relevant assertions regarding that account balance.

Performance materiality   The amount or amounts set by the auditor at less than the materiality level for the financial statements as a whole or for particular classes of transactions, account balances, or disclosures. The term is used with respect to assessing risks of material misstatement and determining the nature, timing, and extent of further audit procedures.

Ratio analysis   An analytical technique that is useful in identifying significant differences between the client results and a norm (such as industry ratios) or between auditor expectations and actual results; ratio analysis is also useful in identifying potential audit problems that may be found in ratio changes between years.

Risk of material misstatement   Risk that exists at the overall financial statement level and at the assertion level, and within these levels risk can be categorized as involving inherent risk and control risk.

Risk A concept used to express uncertainty about events and/or their outcomes that could have a material effect on the organization.

Significant risk An identified and assessed risk of material misstatement that, in the auditor's professional judgment, requires special consideration.

Timing of risk response Refers to when audit procedures are conducted and whether those procedures are conducted at announced or predictable times.

Tolerable misstatement The amount of misstatement in an account balance that the auditor could tolerate and still not judge the underlying account balance to be materially misstated.

Trend analysis An analytical technique that includes simple year-to-year comparisons of account balances, graphic presentations, and analysis of financial data, histograms of ratios, and projections of account balances based on the history of changes in the account.

TRUE/FALSE QUESTIONS

7-1 **LO 1** The determination of materiality is based solely on quantitative factors.

7-2 **LO 1** Performance materiality is set at an amount less than overall materiality and helps the auditor determine the extent of audit evidence needed.

7-3 **LO 2** Detection risk is the susceptibility of an assertion to a material misstatement before consideration of related controls.

7-4 **LO 2** Audit risk is the risk that the auditor expresses an inappropriate audit opinion when the financial statements are materially misstated.

7-5 **LO 3** Inherent risks at the financial statement level include factors that could threaten the fundamental financial viability of the organization.

7-6 **LO 3** Inherent risk at the financial statement level is not affected by the competence and integrity of management or their potential incentives to misstate the financial statements.

7-7 **LO 4** Some level of control risk is always present in an organization because of the inherent limitations of internal control.

7-8 **LO 4** Each of the following factors would lead the auditor to assess control risk at a higher level: the company lacks personnel or expertise to deal with changes in the industry, there exist significant supply chain risks, the industry is mature and declining, and there exist regulatory requirements that increase legal exposure.

7-9 **LO 5** When conducting trend analysis as part of planning analytical procedures, it is important that the auditor not develop expectations and establish decision rules in advance; doing so would make it more difficult for the auditor to identify unexpected results for additional investigation.

7-10 **LO 5** When performing planning analytical procedures and evaluating the results of those procedures, it is important that the auditor discuss the results with management before identifying hypotheses to explain the results; by discussing with management the auditor will be better able to identify alternative explanations.

7-11 [LO 6]   A high level of detection risk means that the audit firm is willing to accept a low risk of not detecting a material misstatement.

7-12 [LO 6]   The interpretation of audit risk set at a low level (1%) is that the auditor is willing to take only a 1% chance of expressing an audit opinion that the financial statement are fairly presented when they are materially misstated.

7-13 [LO 7]   The nature of risk response refers to the sufficiency and appropriateness of evidence that is necessary given the client's assessed risks, materiality, and the level of audit risk that is deemed acceptable.

7-14 [LO 7]   In terms of the timing of the risk response, the following procedures can be completed only at or after period end: comparing the financial statements to the accounting records, evaluating adjusting journal entries made by management in preparing the financial statements, and conducting procedures to response to risks that management may have engaged in improper transactions at period end.

MULTIPLE-CHOICE QUESTIONS

7-15 [LO 1]   Which of the following statements is true regarding the concept of materiality?
a. Materiality is the magnitude of an omission or misstatement of accounting information that, in light of surrounding circumstances, makes it probable that the judgment of a reasonable person relying on the information would have been changed or influenced by the omission or misstatement.
b. Materiality is the magnitude of an omission or misstatement of accounting information that, in light of surrounding circumstances, makes it possible that the judgment of a reasonable person relying on the information would have been changed or influenced by the omission or misstatement.
c. A fact is material if there is a substantial likelihood that the fact would have been viewed by the reasonable investor as having significantly altered the total mix of information made available.
d. Both (a) and (c) are correct.
e. Both (b) and (c) are correct.

7-16 [LO 1]   Which of the following statements is true concerning the concept of performance materiality?
a. Performance materiality is set less than overall materiality and helps the auditor determine the extent of audit evidence to obtain.
b. If performance materiality is set too low, the auditor might not perform sufficient procedures to detect material misstatements in the financial statements.
c. If performance materiality is set too high, the auditor might perform more substantive procedures than necessary.
d. Performance materiality is essentially the same as overall materiality.
e. All of the above are true.

7-17 [LO 2]   Which of the following statements represent the appropriate directional relationships between the concepts of inherent risk, control risk, audit risk, and detection risk?
a. As inherent risk goes up, audit risk goes up.
b. As inherent risk goes up, audit risk goes down.

c. As control risk goes up, detection risk goes up.

d. As control risk goes up, inherent risk goes down.

7-18 **LO 2** Which of the following statements is true regarding the concept of detection risk?

a. After assessing inherent and control risk and determining the level of acceptable audit risk, the auditor determines detection risk.

b. Detection risk is under the control of the auditor, and the level of audit effort that the auditor expends on the engagement depends on the level of detection risk.

c. When the risk of material misstatement is higher, detection risk is lower in order to reduce audit risk to an acceptable level.

d. The auditor controls detection risk through the nature, timing, and extent of substantive audit procedures.

e. All of the above are true.

7-19 **LO 3** Which of the following statements is false regarding brainstorming?

a. Brainstorming is an audit team discussion designed to encourage auditors to creatively assess client risks, particularly those relevant to the possible existence of fraud in an organization.

b. Brainstorming predominantly occurs during the planning/risk assessment phase of the audit.

c. To facilitate the generation and evaluation of quality ideas during the brainstorming session, a typical practice during brainstorming is to invite criticism and value judgments about ideas generated.

d. Participants are encouraged to provide more ideas rather than fewer, with the intent to generate a variety of possible risk assessment scenarios that can be explored during the conduct of the audit.

e. All of the above are true.

7-20 **LO 3** Which of the following characteristics would lead the auditor to assess inherent risk at a higher level for financial reporting at the financial statement level?

a. The account balance represents an asset that is relatively easily stolen.

b. The controls over the account balance are weak.

c. The company has a history of exactly meeting analyst estimates.

d. The company is in an industry that is mature and declining.

7-21 **LO 4** Which of the following statements is true regarding the concept of control risk?

a. When control risk is high, the auditor is concerned that a material misstatement may not be prevented, or that if a material misstatement exists in the organization's financial statements that it will not be detected, and therefore corrected by management.

b. Some organizations have zero control risk because they have made a significant commitment to the effective design and operation of controls.

c. Control risk relates to the susceptibility of an assertion to a misstatement, due to either error or fraud, before consideration of any related controls.

d. All of the above are true.

7-22 **LO 4** Which of the following characteristics would lead the auditor to assess control risk at a higher level?
  a. It is difficult for the auditor to determine or gain access to the organization or individuals who own and/or control the entity.
  b. The organization has inadequate accounting staff, or the staff lacks requisite expertise.
  c. There exists a lack of supervision of accounting personnel.
  d. The organization has inadequate information and communication systems.
  e. All of the above.

7-23 **LO 5** Which of the following statements is false regarding analytical procedures?
  a. Ratio analysis takes advantage of economic relationships between two or more accounts.
  b. Ratio and trend analysis are generally carried out through a comparison of client data with expectations based on industry data, prior-period data, and expectations developed from industry trends, client budgets, and so on.
  c. Developing expectations is not one of the steps in performing planning analytical procedures.
  d. All of the above are true.

7-24 **LO 5** Which of the following statements is true regarding planning analytical procedures?
  a. The precision of the auditor's expectation tends to be less precise, and based on more aggregated data, than the auditor's expectation when performing substantive analytical procedures.
  b. The objective for planning analytical procedures is to identify accounts with heightened risk of misstatement to provide a basis for designing and implementing responses to the assessed risks.
  c. For planning analytical procedures, significant unexpected differences suggest that substantive procedures for the account/assertion will be increased.
  d. Two frequently used analytical procedures during risk assessment include trend analysis and ratio analysis.
  e. All of the above are true.

7-25 **LO 6** Assume that the auditor sets audit risk at a low level, equal to 1%. What is the appropriate interpretation of this level of audit risk?
  a. The auditor is willing to take only a 1% chance that audit procedures will not detect a material misstatement.
  b. The auditor is 99% confident that the audit procedures will detect a material misstatement.
  c. The auditor is willing to take only a 1% chance of expressing an audit opinion that the financial statements are fairly presented when they are materially misstated.
  d. The auditor is 99% confident that the audit opinion is correct.

7-26 **LO 6** Assume for Client X that inherent risk is assessed at 30%, control risk is assessed at 100%, audit risk is 5%, and detection risk is therefore determined to be 17%. Assume for Client Z that inherent risk is assessed at 100%, control risk is assessed at 100%, audit risk is 1%, and detection risk is therefore determined to be 1%. What is true about the amount of audit work that will need to be conducted?

a. Client X will require more audit work than Client Z.
b. Client Z will require more audit work than Client X.
c. Both clients will require a similar amount of audit work.
d. The auditor will most likely resign from the Client Z audit because the inherent risk and control risk are so high.

7-27 **LO 7** When considering responses to risk at the individual assertion level, the auditor should do which of the following?

a. Evaluate the reasons for the assessed risk of material misstatement.
b. Estimate the likelihood of material misstatement due to the inherent risks of the client.
c. Consider the role of internal controls and determine whether control risk is relatively high or low, thereby determining whether the auditor should rely on controls or whether the auditor needs to conduct a more substantive audit.
d. Obtain more relevant and reliable audit evidence as the auditor's assessment of the risk of material misstatement increases.
e. All of the above.

7-28 **LO 7** Which of the following statements is false regarding the nature, timing, and extent of risk responses?

a. The nature of risk response refers to the types of audit procedures applied given the nature of the account balance and the most relevant assertions regarding that account balance.
b. The timing of risk response refers to when audit procedures are conducted.
c. When the risk of material misstatement is low, the auditor conducts the audit procedures closer to year-end, on an unannounced basis, and includes more elements of unpredictability in the procedures.
d. The extent of risk response refers to the sufficiency of evidence that is necessary given the client's assessed risks, materiality, and the acceptable level of audit risk.

REVIEW AND SHORT CASE QUESTIONS

NOTE: Completing Review and Short Case Questions does not require the student to reference additional resources and materials.

NOTE: For the remaining problems, we make special note of those addressing fraud, international issues, professional skepticism, and ethics.

7-29 **LO 1** Define the term *misstatement* and describe characteristics that would make a misstatement material.

7-30 **LO 1** Some audit firms develop very specific quantitative guidelines, either through quantitative measures or in tables, relating planning materiality to the size of sales or assets for a client. Other audit firms leave the materiality judgments up to the individual partner or manager in charge of the audit. What are the major advantages and disadvantages of each approach? Which approach do you favor? Explain.

7-31 **LO 1** Define the following terms: (a) *performance materiality*, (b) *tolerable misstatement*, (c) *clearly trivial*.

7-32 **LO 1** The SEC is concerned that auditors recognize the qualitative aspect of materiality judgments. Explain what the qualitative aspect of materiality means. List some factors that would result in a quantitatively small misstatement being judged as qualitatively material.

7-33 **LO 1** Panzero Bread is a major retailer of specialty sandwich items and baked goods. The following information represents the company's financial position as of December 31, 2015, and December 31, 2014.

	December 31, 2015 (unaudited)	December 31, 2014 (audited)
Total assets	$698,752,000	$542,609,000
Accounts receivable	$25,152,000	$19,041,000
Total sales	$1,066,691,000	$828,971,000
Cost of goods sold	$842,255,000	$628,534,000
Net income	$57,456,000	$58,849,000
Earnings per share	$1.81	$1.88

The auditor of Panzero Bread identifies the company as a client with high audit risk and has set the clearly trivial threshold at 10% of overall financial statement materiality levels. The auditors have detected an overstatement of accounts receivable of $345,000. The misstatement is not a surprise to the auditors, as they have detected misstatements in this account in the past.

On a per share basis, the misstatement represents $0.01 of earnings per share. The auditor believes that the misstatement should be corrected. Management argues strongly that they prefer not to make the correction because they do not believe it is material; that is, the misstatement represents just over 1% of the account balance. Although left unsaid, the auditor knows that management is under considerable pressure from Wall Street to meet analyst expectations for earnings per share. Reducing earnings per share by even $0.01 would cause the trend in earnings to become even more negative than the unaudited financial numbers already reveal, and it would cause the company to just miss analyst forecasts for earnings per share.

a. Use the three common benchmarks for making materiality judgments (net income, total assets, and net sales) to establish materiality for the financial statements overall.

b. What difficulties does the auditor face when the alternative benchmarks yield differing conclusions about materiality? What qualitative factors should the auditor consider in making the materiality judgment for this company?

c. Articulate a reason for choosing one particular benchmark among the three calculated in part (a), and use that benchmark to calculate the clearly trivial threshold for the accounts receivable account.

d. What effect will the qualitative factors in this case have on the auditor's clearly trivial threshold for the accounts receivable account?

PROFESSIONAL SKEPTICISM

7-34 **LO 1** Auditors make materiality judgments during the planning/risk assessment phase of the audit to be sure they ultimately gather sufficient evidence during the audit to provide reasonable assurance that the financial statements are free of material misstatements. The lower the materiality threshold that an auditor has for an account balance, the more the evidence that the auditor must collect. Auditors often use quantitative benchmarks such as 1% of total assets or 5% of net income to determine whether misstatements materially affect the financial statements, but ultimately it is an auditor's individual professional judgment as to whether a given misstatement is or is not considered material.

a. What is the relationship between the level of riskiness of the client and the level of misstatement in an account balance that an auditor would consider material? For example, assume that Client A has weaker controls over accounts receivable compared to Client B (therefore, Client A is riskier than Client B). Assume that Client B is similar in size to Client A and that the auditor has concluded that a misstatement exceeding $5,000 would be material for Client B's accounts receivable account. Should the materiality threshold for Client A be the same as, more than, or less than that for Client B? Further, which client will require more audit evidence to be collected, Client A or Client B?

b. How might an auditor's individual characteristics affect his or her professional judgments about materiality?

c. Assume that one auditor is more professionally skeptical than another auditor and that they are making the materiality judgment in part (a) of this problem. Compare the possible alternative monetary thresholds that a more versus less skeptical auditor might make for Client A.

7-35 `LO 1` The audit report provides reasonable assurance that the financial statements are free from material misstatements. The auditor is put in a difficult situation because materiality is defined from a user's viewpoint; however, the auditor must assess materiality in planning the audit to ensure that sufficient audit work is performed to detect material misstatements.

a. Define materiality as used in accounting and auditing, particularly emphasizing the differences that exist between the FASB and the U.S. Supreme Court materiality definitions.

b. Three major dimensions of materiality are (1) the dollar magnitude of the item, (2) the nature of the item under consideration, and (3) the perspective of a particular user. Give an example of each.

c. Once the auditor develops an assessment of materiality, can it change during the course of the audit? Explain. If it does change, what is the implication of a change for audit work that has already been completed? Explain.

7-36 `LO 2` Define the terms *inherent risk*, *control risk*, *audit risk*, and *detection risk*. Refer to *Exhibit 7.1* and explain how these risks relate to each other.

7-37 `LO 2` How are inherent risks of material misstatements related to internal controls? Why is it important to assess inherent risks of material misstatement prior to evaluating the quality of an organization's internal controls?

7-38 `LO 2` What is the directional relationship between the risk of material misstatement (inherent and control risk) and both audit risk and detection risk? In other words, if the risk of material misstatement increases or decreases, how are audit risk and detection risk affected?

7-39 `LO 1, 2` Explain how the concepts of audit risk and materiality are related. Must an auditor make a decision on materiality in order to determine the appropriate level of audit risk?

7-40 **LO 3** Describe factors that would lead the auditor to assess, at a higher level, inherent risk at the assertion level.

7-41 **LO 3** Inherent risk at the financial statement level relates to (a) business and operating-related risks and (b) financial reporting risks. The *Professional Judgment in Context* feature "Risks Associated with Financial Statement Misstatements" summarizes various risks from ISA 315; that list is reproduced here. For each risk factor, categorize it as indicating (a) business and operating risk, (b) financial reporting risk, or (c) other (if other, describe).

1. Operations in regions that are economically unstable, such as countries with significant currency devaluation or highly inflationary economies
2. Operations exposed to volatile markets, such as futures trading
3. Operations that are subject to a high degree of complex regulation
4. Going concern and liquidity issues, including loss of significant customers or constraints on the availability of capital or credit
5. Offering new products or moving into new lines of business
6. Changes in the organization such as acquisitions or reorganizations
7. Entities or business segments likely to be sold
8. The existence of complex alliances and joint ventures
9. Use of off-balance sheet financing, special-purpose entities, and other complex financing arrangements
10. Significant transactions with related parties
11. Lack of personnel with appropriate accounting and financial reporting skills
12. Changes in key personnel, including departure of key executives
13. Deficiencies in internal control, especially those not addressed by management
14. Changes in the IT system or environment and inconsistencies between the entity's IT strategy and its business strategies
15. Inquiries into the entity's operations or financial results by regulatory bodies
16. Past misstatements, history of errors, or significant adjustments at period end
17. Significant amount of nonroutine or nonsystematic transactions, including intercompany transactions and large revenue transactions at period end
18. Transactions that are recorded based on management's intent, such as debt refinancing, assets to be sold, and classification of marketable securities
19. Accounting measurements that involve complex processes
20. Pending litigation and contingent liabilities, such as sales warranties, financial guarantees, and environmental remediation

7-42 **LO 3** Refer to the *Auditing in Practice* feature "Pfizer's Risk Disclosures as an Example of Inherent Risk at the Financial Statement Level." Summarize the risks that Pfizer is disclosing. Comment on why these risks might be of concern to the auditor.

7-43 **LO 3** List the various risk assessment procedures that the auditor can perform to obtain evidence about inherent risk relating to the operations of a company.

FRAUD

PROFESSIONAL SKEPTICISM

7-44 **LO 3, 7** The auditor needs to assess management integrity as a potential indicator of inherent risk, particularly as it relates to the potential for fraud. Although the assessment of management integrity takes place on every audit engagement, it is a difficult and subjective task. It requires professional skepticism on the part of the auditor because it is human nature to trust people whom we know and interact with.

a. Define management integrity and discuss its importance to the auditor in determining the type of evidence to be gathered on an audit and in evaluating the evidence.

b. Identify the types of evidence the auditor would gather in assessing the integrity of management. What are sources of each type of evidence?

c. For each of the following management scenarios, (1) indicate whether you believe the scenario reflects negatively on management integrity, and explain why; and (2) indicate how the assessment would affect the auditor's planning of the audit.

Management Scenarios

i. The owner/manager of a privately held company also owns three other companies. The individual companies could be run as one combined company, but they engage extensively in related-party transactions to minimize the overall tax burden for the owner/manager.

ii. The president of a publicly held company has a reputation for being stubborn with a violent temper. He fired a divisional manager on the spot when the manager did not achieve profit goals.

iii. The financial vice president of a publicly held company has worked her way to the top by gaining a reputation as a great accounting manipulator. She has earned the reputation by being very creative in finding ways to circumvent FASB pronouncements to keep debt off the balance sheet and in manipulating accounting to achieve short-term earnings. After each short-term success, she has moved on to another company to utilize her skills.

iv. The president of a small publicly held company was indicted on tax evasion charges seven years ago. He settled with the Internal Revenue Service and served time doing community service. Since then, he has been considered a pillar of the community, making significant contributions to local charities. Inquiries of local bankers yield information that he is the partial or controlling owner of several companies that may serve as "shell" company whose sole purpose is to assist the manager in moving income around to avoid taxes.

v. James J. James is the president of a privately held company that has been accused of illegally dumping waste and failing to meet government standards for worker safety. James responds that his attitude is to meet the minimum requirements of the law; if the government deems that he has not, he will clean up. "Besides," he asserts, "it is good business; it is less costly to clean up only when I have to, even if small fines are involved, than it is to take leadership positions and exceed government standards."

FRAUD

7-45 **LO 3** Brainstorming is a group discussion designed to encourage auditors to creatively assess client risks, particularly those relevant to fraud.

a. When does brainstorming typically occur?

b. Who attends the brainstorming session? Who typically leads it?

c. Besides encouraging auditors to creatively assess client risks, what other purpose does brainstorming serve?

d. What are the guidelines that should be followed during a brainstorming session to maximize effectiveness?

e. What are the typical steps in the brainstorming process?

7-46 `LO 4` List the factors that would lead auditors to assess control risk at a higher level. Discuss the auditor's risk assessment procedures for assessing control risk, and provide specific procedures related to understanding management's risk assessment component of internal control.

7-47 `LO 5` Explain how ratio analysis and industry comparisons (performed as part of planning analytical procedures) can be useful to the auditor in identifying potential risk of material misstatement on an audit engagement. How can such analysis also help the auditor plan the audit?

7-48 `LO 5` Refer to *Exhibit 7.3*. What ratios would best indicate problems with potential inventory obsolescence or collectibility of receivables? How are those ratios calculated?

PROFESSIONAL SKEPTICISM

7-49 `LO 5, 7` The following information shows the past two periods of results for a fictional company, Jones Manufacturing, and a comparison with industry data for the same period:

ANALYTICAL DATA FOR JONES MANUFACTURING

	Prior Period (000 omitted)	Prior % of Sales	Current Period (000 omitted)	Current % of Sales	% Change	Industry Average as a % of Sales
Sales	$10,000	100	$11,000	100	10	100
Inventory	$2,000	20	$3,250	29.5	57.5	22.5
Cost of goods sold	$6,000	60	$6,050	55	0.83	59.5
Accounts payable	$1,200	12	$1,980	18	65	14.5
Sales commissions	$500	5	$550	5	10	Not available
Inventory turnover	6.3	—	4.2	—	(33)	5.85
Average number of days to collect	39	—	48	—	23	36
Employee turnover	5%	—	8%	—	60	4
Return on investment	14%	—	14.3%	—		13.8
Debt/Equity	35%	—	60%	—	71	30

a. Assume that the auditor expects that the client's performance in the current year will be similar to its performance in the prior year. From the preceding data, identify potential risk areas and explain why they represent potential risk. Briefly indicate how the risk analysis should affect the planning of the audit engagement.

b. Identify any of the above data that should cause the auditor to increase the level of professional skepticism.

7-50 `LO 5, 7` The following table contains calculations of several key ratios for a fictional company, Indianola Pharmaceutical Company, a maker of proprietary and prescription drugs. The company is publicly held and is considered a small- to medium-sized pharmaceutical company. Approximately 80% of its sales have been in prescription drugs; the remaining 20% are in medical supplies normally found in a drugstore. The primary purpose of the auditor's calculations is to identify potential risk areas for the upcoming audit. The auditor recognizes that some of the data might signal the need to gather other industry- or company-specific data. A number of the company's drugs are patented. Its best-selling drug, Anecillin, which will come off of patent in two years, has accounted for approximately 20% of the company's sales during the past five years. The auditor's expectation is that the company's own trends from the past few years should be relatively consistent with this year's trends, and that the company will not have significant deviations from industry norms.

INDIANOLA PHARMACEUTICAL RATIO ANALYSIS

Ratio	Current Year	One Year Previous	Two Years Previous	Three Years Previous	Current Industry
Current ratio	1.85	1.89	2.28	2.51	2.13
Quick ratio	0.85	0.93	1.32	1.76	1.40
Times interest earned	1.30	1.45	5.89	6.3	4.50
Days' sales in receivables	109	96	100	72	69
Inventory turnover	2.40	2.21	3.96	5.31	4.33
Days' sales in inventory	152	165	92	69	84
Research & development as % of sales	1.3	1.4	1.94	2.03	4.26
Cost of goods sold as % of sales	38.5	40.2	41.2	43.8	44.5
Debt/equity ratio	4.85	4.88	1.25	1.13	1.25
Earnings per share	$1.12	$2.50	$4.32	$4.26	n/a
Sales/tangible assets	0.68	0.64	0.89	0.87	0.99
Sales/total assets	0.33	0.35	0.89	0.87	0.78
Sales growth over past year	3%	15%	2%	4%	6%

a. What major conclusions regarding financial reporting risk can be drawn from the information shown in the table? Be specific in identifying specific account balances that have a high risk of material misstatement. State how that risk analysis will be used in planning the audit. You should identify a minimum of four financial reporting risks that should be addressed during the audit and how they should be addressed.

b. What other critical background information might you want to obtain as part of planning the audit? What information would you gather during the conduct of the audit? Briefly indicate the probable sources of that information.

c. Based on the information, what major actions did the company take during the immediately preceding year? Explain.

PROFESSIONAL SKEPTICISM

FRAUD

7-51   **LO 5, 7**   The auditor for a fictional company, ABC Wholesaling, has just begun to perform planning analytical procedures as part of planning the audit for the coming year. ABC Wholesaling is in a competitive industry, selling products such as STP Brand products and Ortho Grow products to companies such as Wal-Mart, Kmart, and regional retail discount chains. The company is privately owned and has experienced financial difficulty this past year. The difficulty could lead to its major line of credit being pulled if the company does not make a profit in the current year. In performing the analytical procedures, the auditor notes the following changes in accounts related to accounts receivable:

	Current Year (000 omitted)	Previous Year (000 omitted)
Sales	$60,000	$59,000
Accounts receivable	$11,000	$7,200
Percent of accounts receivable current	72%	65%
No. of days' sales in accounts receivable	64	42
Gross margin	18.7%	15.9%
Industry gross margin	16.3%	16.3%
Increase in Nov.–Dec. sales over previous year	12%	3.1%

The auditor had expected the receivables balance to remain stable, but notes the large increase in receivables. After considering possible reasons for this increase, the auditor decides to make inquiries of management. Management explains that the change is due to two things: (1) a new computer system that has increased productivity, and (2) a new policy of rebilling items previously sold to customers, thereby extending the due dates from October to April. Management explains the rebilling as follows: Many of the clients' products are seasonal—for example, lawn care products. To provide better service to ABC's customers, management instituted a new policy whereby management negotiated with a customer to determine the approximate amount of seasonal goods on hand at the end of the selling season (October). If the customer would continue to purchase from the client, management would rebill the existing inventory, thereby extending the due date from October until the following April, essentially giving an interest-free loan to the customer. The customer, in turn, agreed to keep the existing goods and store them on its site for next year's retail sales.

The key to planning analytical procedures is to identify areas of heightened risk of misstatement and then plan the audit to determine whether potential explanations satisfy all the unexpected changes that are observed in account balances. Further, it is important to be professionally skeptical of management-provided explanations. For example, does the explanation of a new computer system and the rebilling adequately explain all the changes? Whether the answer to that question is yes or no, are there other explanations that are equally viable? The auditor must be able to answer these questions to properly apply the risk-based approach to auditing. There are several factors that would indicate to a skeptical auditor that the explanations offered by ABC management might not hold:

- The company has a large increase in gross margin. This seems unlikely, because it is selling to large chains with considerable purchasing power. Further, other competitors are also likely to have effective computer systems.

- If the rebilling items are properly accounted for, there should not be a large increase in sales for the last two months of this year when the total sales for the previous year is practically the same as that of the preceding year.
- If the rebillings are for holding the inventory at customers' locations, the auditor should investigate to determine (a) if the items were properly recorded as a sale in the first place or if they should still be recorded as inventory, (b) what the client's motivation is for extending credit to the customers indicated, and (c) whether it is a coincidence that all of the rebilled items were to large retailers who do not respond to accounts receivable confirmations received from auditors.

a. What potential hypotheses would likely explain the changes in the financial data given? Identify all that might explain the change in ratios, including those identified by management.

b. Of those identified, which hypothesis would best explain all the changes in the ratios and financial account balances? Explain the rationale for your answer.

c. Given the most likely hypothesis identified, what specific audit procedures do you recommend as highest priority? Why?

7-52 **LO 6** A staff auditor was listening to a conversation between two senior auditors regarding the audit risk model. The following are some statements made in that conversation regarding the audit risk model. State whether you agree or disagree with each of the statements, and explain why.

a. Setting audit risk at 5% is valid for controlling audit risk at a low level only if the auditor assumes that inherent risk is 100%, or significantly greater than the real level of inherent risk.

b. Inherent risk may be very small for some accounts (such as the recording of payroll transactions at Wal-Mart). In fact, some inherent risks may be close to 0.01%. In such cases, the auditor does not need to perform direct tests of account balances if he or she can be assured that inherent risk is indeed that low and that internal controls, as designed, are working appropriately.

c. Control risk refers to both (a) the design of controls and (b) the operation of controls. To assess control risk as low, the auditor must gather evidence on both the design and operation of controls.

d. Detection risk at 50% implies that the substantive tests of the account balance has a 50% chance of not detecting a material misstatement and that the auditor is relying on the client actions (assessment of inherent and control risk) to address the additional uncertainty regarding the possibility of a material misstatement.

e. Audit risk should vary inversely with both inherent risk and control risk; the higher the risk of material misstatement, the lower should be the audit risk taken.

f. In analyzing the audit risk model, it is important to understand that much of it is judgmental. For example, setting audit risk is judgmental, assessing inherent and control risk is judgmental, and setting detection risk is simply a matter of the individual risk preferences of the auditor.

7-53 **LO 6** Refer to *Exhibit 7.4* and consider the audit risk model, whereby *Audit Risk = Inherent Risk × Control Risk × Detection Risk*. Complete the boxes in the table below. Describe generalizations about the relationships among the four components of the audit risk model that you gain from the completed table. In which case will the auditor conduct the greatest amount of audit work?

	Case 1	Case 2	Case 3	Case 4	Case 5	Case 6	Case 7	Case 8
Inherent Risk	30%	40%	50%	50%	70%	80%	90%	100%
Control Risk	50%	100%	60%	100%	70%	70%	80%	100%
Audit Risk	5%	5%	5%	5%	1%	1%	1%	1%
Detection Risk	?	?	?	?	?	?	?	?

7-54 **LO 7** Distinguish between a controls reliance audit and a substantive audit. Which approach should an auditor consider to be most effective?

7-55 **LO 7** Provide examples of how an auditor might change (a) the nature of risk response, (b) the timing of risk response, and (c) the extent of risk response.

7-56 **LO 7** How can an auditor introduce unpredictability into audit procedures?

7-57 **LO 7** What audit procedures can be completed only at or after period end?

FRAUD FOCUS: CONTEMPORARY AND HISTORICAL CASES

PROFESSIONAL SKEPTICISM

INTERNATIONAL

ETHICS

FRAUD

7-58 **KID CASTLE EDUCATIONAL CORPORATION AND BROCK, SCHECHTER & POLAKOFF LLP, PCAOB**
(LO 3, 4, 5, 7, 8)

General Background. On May 22, 2012, the audit firm of Brock, Schechter & Polakoff LLP (hereafter BSP) was censured and fined $20,000 by the PCAOB in relation to its audits of public companies located in Taiwan and China. These public companies were listed on U.S. stock exchanges. James Waggoner, BSP's director of accounting and auditing, was the BSP auditor responsible for the audits. The charges against BSP and Waggoner include the following:

- BSP failed to develop policies and procedures to assure that the firm undertook only audit engagements that it could expect to conduct with professional competence. Prior to undertaking the audits of the Taiwan and Chinese companies, the firm had no experience auditing public companies in general or companies based in these locations. Further, BSP personnel lacked the ability to communicate in Chinese.
- BSP failed to develop policies and procedures to assure that the personnel assigned to the audits had the requisite technical training and proficiency.
- BSP failed to monitor the audits during its annual internal review process.
- BSP failed to comply with PCAOB standards on the planning, performance, and supervision of the audits.
- BSP failed to gather sufficient evidence, failed to use due care, and failed to exercise professional skepticism on the audits.
- BSP allowed two other audit firms, which were located in Taiwan and China, to plan and perform the audits. BSP had minimal contact with the foreign firms, and inadequately reviewed the working papers of the foreign firms. BSP also failed to obtain and review engagement completion

documentation from the foreign firms prior to issuing the audit reports.

- Waggoner failed to comply with professional auditing standards. Further, he failed to cooperate with PCAOB inspectors, and he falsified documentation relating to the audits.

The Kid Castle Audits. Kid Castle is a company located in Taiwan that provides English-language instruction to Chinese-speaking children. Kid Castle was traded on the OTC Bulletin Board and Pink Sheets. A Taiwanese audit firm approached BSP in June 2006 concerning the Kid Castle audit, and BSP was hired as the auditor on July 26, 2006. BSP expressed unqualified audit opinions on the company's 2006–2008 financial statements.

In addition to the general criticisms detailed previously, the PCAOB enforcement release provides detailed information on audit quality deficiencies on the Kid Castle audits, including the following:

- BSP failed to consider the nature, extent, and timing of audit work necessary to audit Kid Castle. Instead, BSP relied completely upon the Taiwan firm to make these considerations and to develop the audit program.
- BSP failed to adequately supervise the auditors of the Taiwan firm, including:
  - Failing to assess the technical competence of the Taiwan firm's auditors
  - Failing to assign the Taiwan auditors to tasks according to their abilities
  - Failing to instruct the Taiwan firm's auditors
  - Failing to inform the Taiwan firm's auditors about their responsibilities and the objectives of the audit
  - Failing to inform the Taiwan firm's auditors about matters that affected the nature, extent, and timing of audit procedures
  - Failing to direct the Taiwan firm's auditors to bring to BSP's attention significant accounting/auditing issues encountered during the audits
- BSP failed to adequately perform a review of the Taiwan firm's audit work, and such a review was the principal involvement required of BSP. In fact, Waggoner assigned the final responsibility for reviewing the audit to a BSP staff member.
- The reviewing staff member did find deficiencies in the audit procedures performed by the Taiwan auditor. Waggoner forwarded those deficiencies to the Taiwan firm's auditors, but they did not address those deficiencies or conduct additional audit work.
- For the 2007 audit, BSP did not receive or review any working papers from the Taiwan auditor, except for a set of worksheets showing consolidation work among Kid Castle's subsidiary accounts. For the 2008 audit, BSP did not receive or review *any* working papers.

Kid Castle Risk Factors and Financial Condition. In its December 31, 2008, Form 10K, Kid Castle management disclosed the following risk factors relating to its business:

- There is a history of operating losses and difficulty maintaining profitability.
- Demand for products and services is unpredictable.
- The company's operating results are dependent upon the success of its franchises.

- Market competition from established competitors could negatively affect the business.
- International expansion plans may not be successful.
- There exist risks relating to the company's potential inability to defend and protect its intellectual property.
- The company relies on loans from shareholders and bank loans, which may adversely affect liquidity.
- Because the company's officers and directors are not U.S. persons and because subsidiaries are Taiwanese or Chinese, judgments under the U.S. securities laws may not be able to be enforced.
- Internal controls are not effective in accordance with the requirements of Sarbanes-Oxley Act of 2002 (SOX).
- The company's assets and operations in the People's Republic of China are subject to political, regulatory, and economic uncertainties.

In addition, BSP issued a going-concern audit report, which indicates concern about the company's ability to remain operational. The financial statements of Kid Castle are as follows:

KID CASTLE EDUCATIONAL CORPORATION
CONSOLIDATED BALANCE SHEETS

	December 31, 2008	December 31, 2007
	(Expressed in U.S. dollars)	
ASSETS		
Current assets		
Cash and bank balances	1,985,818	1,238,212
Bank fixed deposits—pledged (Note 12)	2,847	363,562
Notes and accounts receivable, net (Notes 3 and 20)	2,171,768	2,453,868
Inventories, net (Note 4)	1,933,153	2,008,739
Other receivables (Notes 5 and 20)	396,003	88,139
Prepayments and other current assets (Note 6)	475,617	542,794
Pledged notes receivable (Note 12)	416,238	557,983
Deferred income tax assets (Note 7)	45,617	42,335
Total current assets	7,427,061	7,295,632
Deferred income tax assets (Note 7)	49,528	50,481
Interest in associates (Note 8)	68,336	58,625
Property and equipment, net (Note 9)	2,775,663	2,312,065
Intangible assets, net of amortization (Note 10)	371,056	572,005
Long-term notes receivable	356,901	420,636
Pledged notes receivable (Note 12)	283,469	183,453
Other assets	255,288	268,388
Total assets	$11,587,302	$11,161,285

(continued)

	December 31, 2008	December 31, 2007
	(Expressed in U.S. dollars)	
LIABILITIES AND SHAREHOLDERS' EQUITY		
Current liabilities		
Bank borrowings—short-term and maturing within one year (Note 12)	242,879	1,212,534
Notes and accounts payable (Note 19)	1,017,552	389,639
Accrued expenses (Note 11)	1,617,717	985,764
Amounts due to officers (Note 19)	—	—
Other payables	270,458	573,237
Deposits received (Note 13)	751,151	912,535
Receipts in advance (Note 14)	2,305,980	2,372,403
Income tax payable (Note 7)	39,115	124,418
Total current liabilities	6,244,852	6,570,530
Bank borrowings maturing after one year (Note 12)	1,583,968	1,752,776
Receipts in advance (Note 14)	1,001,801	1,034,260
Deposits received (Note 13)	839,295	680,694
Deferred liability	41,775	38,787
Accrued pension liabilities (Note 15)	446,038	401,893
Total liabilities	10,157,729	10,478,940
Commitments and contingencies (Note 16)		
Minority interest	216,754	162,343
Shareholders' equity		
Common stock, no par share (Note 17):		
60,000,000 shares authorized; 25,000,000 shares issued and outstanding at December 31, 2008 and 2007, respectively.	8,592,138	8,592,138
Additional paid-in capital	194,021	194,021
Legal reserve	65,320	65,320
Accumulated deficit (Note 18)	(6,340,449)	(7,179,418)
Accumulated other comprehensive loss	(1,026,713)	(932,027)
Net loss not recognized as pension cost	(271,498)	(220,032)
Total shareholders' equity	1,212,819	520,002
Total liabilities and shareholders' equity	11,587,302	11,161,285

KID CASTLE EDUCATIONAL CORPORATION
CONSOLIDATED STATEMENTS OF OPERATIONS

	Years Ended December 31		
	2008	2007	2006
	(Expressed in U.S. dollars)		
Operating revenue (Note 21)			
Sales of goods	7,905,949	7,671,392	6,774,260
Franchise income	2,380,930	2,205,668	2,080,551
Other operating revenue	2,558,232	1,359,552	856,772
Net operating revenue	12,845,111	11,236,612	9,711,583
Operating costs (Note 21)			
Cost of goods sold	(3,357,441)	(3,154,509)	(2,684,650)
Cost of franchising	(368,061)	(451,469)	(337,986)
Other operating costs	(1,777,862)	(491,869)	(616,102)
Total operating costs	(5,503,364)	(4,097,847)	(3,638,738)
Gross profit	7,341,747	7,138,765	6,072,845
Advertising costs	(22,735)	(29,241)	(21,833)
Other operating expenses	(6,272,753)	(5,342,216)	(5,526,318)
Profit from operations	1,046,259	1,767,308	524,694
Interest expense, net (Note 12)	(89,761)	(90,299)	(179,825)
Share of profit (loss) of investments	5,109	27,007	(39,489)
Other nonoperating income (loss), net	24,789	552,611	(153,803)
Profit before income taxes and minority interest income	986,396	2,256,627	151,577
Income taxes (expense) benefit (Note 7)	(106,215)	(278,191)	(173,325)
Income (loss) after income taxes	880,181	1,978,436	(21,748)
Minority interest income	(41,212)	(101,287)	(24,463)
Net income (loss)	838,969	1,877,149	(46,211)
Income (loss) per share—basic and diluted	0.034	0.075	(0.002)

During 2010, Kid Castle stock was no longer trading in any U.S. markets. James Waggoner was censured by the PCAOB and prohibited from practicing on any public company audits in the U.S. for at least three years.

a. Why would the inherent and control risks at Kid Castle be of concern to a potential auditor?

b. Review the financial statements and calculate the commonly used ratios from *Exhibit 7.3* for the years ending 2008 and 2007. Assume that the auditor expected the 2008 financial results to be line with the 2007 financial results. Given this expectation, comment on the trends in the financial statements and ratios that would cause the auditor to assess heightened risk. Would the auditor likely conclude that there was a heightened risk of fraud?

c. Based on your answers to (a) and (b), for what accounts would you recommend that the auditor plan to conduct more substantive audit procedures?

d. The 10-K discloses the fact that BSP earned total audit fees in 2007 and 2008 of $121,026 and $150,000, respectively. Comment on the motivations of BSP and Waggoner to accept the foreign audits and how those motivations might have affected Waggoner's lack of ethics and how those motivations might have affected his professional skepticism. Presumably, BSP had to pay the Taiwanese and Chinese audit firms a portion of the audit fee, and based on the allegations in the PCAOB enforcement release, BSP did virtually no audit work. Comment on your thoughts about the appropriateness of hiring a foreign audit firm to conduct the majority of audit work on an engagement and on BSP's actions (or lack thereof) in this regard.

e. Use the framework for making quality professional decisions from *Chapter 4* to identify those steps in the framework where Waggoner went wrong and describe what he should have done differently.

f. Describe the risks that an audit firm faces when it attempts to audit a company in a foreign country.

For additional information on the PCAOB enforcement releases relating to this case, see PCAOB Release Nos. 105-2012-002 and 105-2012-003.

FRAUD   **7-59**   **LINCOLN FEDERAL SAVINGS AND LOAN (LO 3, 4, 7)** The following is a description of various factors that affected the operations of Lincoln Federal Savings and Loan, a California savings and loan (S&L). It was a subsidiary of American Continental Company, a real estate development company run by Charles Keating.

Lincoln Federal Savings & Loan

Savings and Loan industry background—The S&L industry was developed in the early part of the twentieth century in response to a perceived need to provide low-cost financing to encourage home ownership. As such, legislation by Congress made the S&L industry the primary financial group allowed to make low-cost home ownership loans (mortgages).

For many years, the industry operated by accepting relatively long-term deposits from customers and making 25- to 30-year loans at fixed rates on home mortgages. The industry was generally considered to be safe. Most of the S&Ls (also known as *thrifts*) were small, federally chartered institutions with deposits insured by the FSLIC. The motto of many S&L managers seemed to be, "Get your deposits in, make loans, sit back, and earn your returns. Get to work by 9 a.m. and out to the golf course by noon."

Changing economic environment—During the 1970s, two major economic events hit the S&L industry. First, the rate of inflation had reached an all-time high. Prime interest rates had gone as high as 19.5%. Second, deposits were being drawn away from the S&Ls by new competitors that offered short-term variable rates substantially higher than current passbook savings rates. The S&Ls responded by increasing the rates on certificates of deposit to extraordinary levels (15–16%) while servicing mortgages with twenty- to thirty-year maturities made at old rates of

7% to 8%. The S&Ls attempted to mitigate the problem by offering variable-rate mortgages or by selling off some of their mortgages (at substantial losses) to other firms.

However, following regulatory accounting principles, the S&Ls were not required to recognize market values of loans that were not sold. Thus, even if loan values were substantially less than the book value, they would continue to be carried at book value as long as the mortgage holder was not in default.

Changing regulatory environment—In the early 1980s, Congress moved to deregulate the S&L industry. During the first half of 1982, the S&L industry lost a record $3.3 billion (even without marking loans down to real value). In August 1982, President Reagan signed the Garn-St. Germain Depository Institutions Act of 1982, hailing it as the most important legislation for financial institutions in 50 years. The bill had several key elements:

- S&Ls would be allowed to offer money market funds free from withdrawal penalties or interest rate regulation.
- S&Ls could invest up to 40% of their assets in nonresidential real estate lending. Commercial lending was much riskier than home lending, but the potential returns were greater. In addition, the regulators helped the deregulatory fever by removing a regulation that had required a savings and loan institution to have 400 stockholders with no one owning more than 25%—allowing a single shareholder to own a savings and loan institution.
- The bill made it easier for an entrepreneur to purchase a savings and loan. Regulators allowed buyers to start (capitalize) their thrift with land or other noncash assets rather than money.
- The bill allowed thrifts to stop requiring traditional down payments and to provide 100% financing, with the borrower not required to invest a dime of personal money in the deal.
- The bill permitted thrifts to make real estate loans anywhere. They had previously been required to make loans on property located only in their own geographic area.

Accounting—In addition to these revolutionary changes, owners of troubled thrifts began stretching already liberal accounting rules (with regulators' blessings) to squeeze their balance sheets into (regulatory) compliance. For example, goodwill, defined as customer loyalty, market share, and other intangibles, accounted for over 40% of the thrift industry's net worth by 1986.

Lincoln Federal S&L—American Continental Corporation, a land development company run by Charles Keating and headquartered in Phoenix, Arizona, purchased Lincoln Federal S&L in 1984. Immediately, Keating expanded the lending activity of Lincoln to assist in the development of American Continental projects, including the Phoenician Resort in Scottsdale.[1] Additionally, Keating sought higher returns by purchasing junk bonds marketed by Drexel Burnham and Michael Millken. Nine of Keating's relatives were on the Lincoln payroll at salaries ranging from over $500,000 to over $1 million.

---

[1] The Phoenician was so lavishly constructed that a regulator estimated that just to break even, the resort would have to charge $500 per room per night at a 70% occupancy rate. Similar resort rooms in the area were available at $125 a night.

Keating came up with novel ideas to raise capital. Rather than raising funds through deposits, he had commissioned agents working in the Lincoln offices who sold special bonds of American Continental Corporation. The investors were assured that their investments would be safe. Unfortunately, many elderly individuals put their life savings into these bonds, thinking they were backed by the FSLIC because they were sold at an S&L— but they were not. Keating continued investments in real estate deals, such as a planned megacommunity in the desert outside of Phoenix. He relied on appraisals, some obviously of dubious value, to serve as a basis for the loan valuation.

a. Discuss the risks identified and the implication of those risks for the conduct of the audit.

b. The auditor did review a few independent appraisals indicating the market value of the real estate in folders for loans. How convincing are such appraisals? In other words, what attributes are necessary in order for the appraisals to constitute appropriate (relevant and reliable) evidence?

APPLICATION ACTIVITIES

NOTE: Completing Application Activities requires students to reference additional resources and materials. Some Application Activities will require the student to reference relevant professional auditing standards. We make special note of these as Auditing Standards Application Activities.

7-60 **LO 3** Important factors that lead auditors to assess inherent risk relating to financial reporting at a higher level relate to analyst following, including a history of exactly meeting analyst estimates, analysts having high earnings growth expectations, and a situation in which the company is unable to meet its consensus earnings estimates or is close to being unable to do so. Thus, it is important for auditors to understand issues relating to analyst following. Using an Internet source such as Yahoo Finance (*http://finance.yahoo.com*), locate the analyst summary expectations (see analyst opinion and analyst estimates) for the following companies: (1) General Electric, (2) Procter & Gamble, (3) Apple, and (4) Citigroup. For each company, answer the following questions:

a. How many analysts are following the company?

b. What is the average estimated sales growth for the year?

c. What is the earnings per share estimate?

d. What is the earnings per share actual?

e. What are the analysts' recommendations? For example, how many analysts are recommending buy versus hold, and so on?

f. What is your assessment of inherent risk relating to analyst following based on the data you have gathered? You may use the terms *low*, *medium*, and *high* to make the risk assessment.

AUDITING STANDARDS APPLICATION ACTIVITY

7-61 **LO 3, 4, 5** The *Auditing in Practice* feature "Application of Accounting Principles and Related Disclosures" discusses guidance from AS 12 regarding the auditor's responsibilities to understand management's application of accounting principles and related disclosures. Locate AS 12 on the PCAOB web site, read the standard, and summarize the other risk assessment procedures addressed in the standard.

7-62 **LO 3** *Exhibit 7.2* provides examples of questions that an auditor should ask when assessing inherent risk relating to financial reporting. The first question asks, "What are the significant judgment areas (reserves, contingencies, asset values, note disclosures) that affect the current year financial statements?" Access the most recent financial statements of Microsoft, Dell, and Apple. For each company, locate the footnote disclosure that would answer the question about significant judgment areas (often labeled as *estimates and assumptions*). Briefly summarize the major judgment areas for these companies, and comment on any differences that you observe.

FRAUD

ETHICS

7-63 **LO 4, 8** Refer to the *Focus on Fraud* feature "Lack of Oversight as a Control Weakness Leads to Embezzlement" and the *Focus on Fraud* feature "The City of Dixon, Illinois, Sues Its Auditor for $50 Million Related to the Rita Crundwell Embezzlement." The situation described in these features relates to the fraud committed by Rita Crundwell in the city of Dixon, Illinois. Crundwell was sentenced to nearly 20 years in prison after pleading guilty to a wire fraud count. In September 2013, Dixon City auditors CliftonLarsonAllen and Sam Card agreed to settle for a total of $40 million.

a. Research this case and describe any recent developments.

b. Consider the information you learned about in *Chapter 4* regarding ethical decision making. Comment on the parties at fault in this case and assess their relative level of fault.

AUDITING STANDARDS APPLICATION ACTIVITY

7-64 **LO 7** You are helping to plan the audit for a client that is a U.S. public company. Your senior has indicated that it is important that planned audit procedures be modified to address assessed fraud risks. The senior also indicated that in responding to fraud risks, the auditor should perform audit procedures to specifically address the risk of management override of controls. Your senior asks for your suggestions on how planned audit procedures should respond to assessed fraud risks. As you are not sure how to answer this question, you decide to obtain a copy of the auditing standard that would most likely provide relevant guidance. You may want to refer to the *Standards Appendix* to the text to determine the appropriate standard. What standard would be most appropriate and what guidance does it provide?

ACADEMIC RESEARCH CASES

NOTE: Completing Academic Research Cases requires students to reference additional resources and materials.

7-65 **LO 2, 7** Locate and read the article listed below and answer the following questions.

Johnstone, K. 2000. Client-acceptance decisions: simultaneous effects of client business risk, audit risk, auditor business risk, and risk adaptation. *Auditing: A Journal of Practice & Theory.* 19 (1): 1–25.

a. What is the issue being addressed in the paper?

b. What are the findings of the paper?

c. Why is this paper important to auditors, and what are the implications of this paper for the auditing profession?

d. Describe the research methodology used as a basis for the conclusions.

e. Describe any limitations of the research.

7-66 **LO 5** Locate and read the article listed below and answer the following questions.

Bowlin, K. 2011. Risk-based auditing, strategic prompts, and auditor sensitivity to the strategic risk of fraud. *The Accounting Review* 86 (4): 1231–1253.

a. What is the issue being addressed in the paper?

b. What are the findings of the paper?

c. Why is this paper important to auditors, and what are the implications of this paper for the auditing profession?

d. Describe the research methodology used as a basis for the conclusions.

e. Describe any limitations of the research.

SEARCH HINT

It is easy to locate academic research articles! Use a search engine such as Google Scholar or an electronic research platform such as ABI Inform, and search using the author names and part of the article title.

7-67 LO **3, 7**   Locate and read the article listed below and answer the following questions.

Kim, H. and H. Fukukawa. 2013. Japan's big 3 firms' response to clients' business risk: greater audit effort or higher audit fees? *International Journal of Auditing* 17: 190–212.

a. What is the issue being addressed in the paper?

b. What are the findings of the paper?

c. Why is this paper important to auditors, and what are the implications of this paper for the auditing profession?

d. Describe the research methodology used as a basis for the conclusions.

e. Describe any limitations of the research.

FORD AND TOYOTA

	FORD MOTOR COMPANY AND TOYOTA MOTOR CORPORATION
7-68	(LO **2, 3, 4, 6, 7**)

Source and Reference	Questions
Ford 10-K	1. Describe the primary risks facing Ford.
Toyota 20-F	2. Describe the primary risks facing Toyota.
	3. Compare the risks of Ford and Toyota.
	4. Why would an auditor be concerned with these risks?

	FORD MOTOR COMPANY AND TOYOTA MOTOR CORPORATION
7-69	(LO **1**)

a. Some common numerical thresholds and benchmarks for overall materiality judgments are 5% of net income and 1% of assets. The materiality level at which items are considered clearly trivial—a materiality level where the auditor believes errors below that level would not, even when aggregated with all other misstatements, be material to the financial statements—is generally 5% to 10% of overall materiality. Calculate these numerical thresholds for Ford and Toyota, assuming 5% for misstatements considered clearly trivial.

b. Assume that you discover a $10,000,000 error in inventory. What difficulties would you encounter in deciding whether or not that amount was material?

c. The numerical thresholds differ across the two companies. Why does that present a problem for the auditor? For third-party users?

d. What is the SEC's position on the use of numerical thresholds?

e. What other characteristics of potential misstatements should auditors consider when determining materiality levels?

8 Specialized Audit Tools: Sampling and Generalized Audit Software

CHAPTER OVERVIEW AND LEARNING OBJECTIVES

This chapter describes two fundamental tools related to efficiently gathering audit evidence: (1) sampling that can be used for both tests of controls and direct tests of account balances and assertions, and (2) generalized audit software (GAS) that can be used to automate aspects of the audit. In terms of the audit opinion formulation process, this chapter focuses on Phases III and IV—obtaining evidence about internal control operating effectiveness and obtaining substantive evidence about accounts, disclosures, and assertions.

Through studying this chapter, you will be able to achieve these learning objectives:

1. Describe how auditors use sampling and GAS to gather sufficient appropriate audit evidence.

2. Explain the objectives of sampling for testing controls and account balances, and describe the risks associated with sampling.

3. Compare and contrast nonstatistical and statistical sampling and apply these sampling approaches.

4. Describe attributes sampling and use it for tests of controls.

5. Describe the sampling process used to gather evidence about misstatements in account balances and assertions.

6. Describe monetary unit sampling and use it to test account balances and assertions.

7. Describe how to use GAS to automate the audit process.

8. Apply the frameworks for professional decision making and ethical decision making to issues involving sampling and GAS.

THE AUDIT OPINION FORMULATION PROCESS

| I. Making Client Acceptance and Continuance Decisions **Chapter 1** | II. Performing Risk Assessment **Chapters 3, 7, and 9–13** | III. Obtaining Evidence About Internal Control Operating Effectiveness **Chapters 8–13 and 16** | IV. Obtaining Substantive Evidence About Accounts, Disclosures and Assertions **Chapters 8–13 and 16** | V. Completing the Audit and Making Reporting Decisions **Chapters 14 and 15** |

The Auditing Profession, the Risk of Fraud and Mechanisms to Address Fraud: Regulation, Corporate Governance, and Audit Quality

Chapters 1 and 2

Professional Liability and the Need for Quality Auditor Judgments and Ethical Decisions

Chapter 4

The Audit Opinion Formulation Process and a Framework for Obtaining Audit Evidence

Chapters 5 and 6

PROFESSIONAL JUDGMENT IN CONTEXT

PCAOB Inspection Reports Regarding Audit Sampling

Audit sampling is defined as the application of an audit procedure to less than 100% of the items within an account balance or class of transactions for the purpose of evaluating some characteristic of the balance or class. Said another way, audit sampling allows the auditor to learn a lot about a population of items of interest without examining every one of those items individually. In 2008, the PCAOB issued its report on its 2004–2007 inspections of domestic annually inspected firms (PCAOB Release No. 2008-008). The report provides a summary of certain common issues related to sampling that were identified during those inspections:

> The inspection teams identified deficiencies in firms' performance of audit sampling, including (a) using sample sizes that were too small to obtain enough evidence to form a conclusion about the account balance or class of transactions being tested, (b) failing to appropriately project the effect of errors identified when testing the items selected to the entire population, (c) failing to select the sample in such a way that it could be expected to be representative of the underlying

population, and (d) not appropriately testing all the items in the sample.

Since that time, the PCAOB has continued to criticize audit firms for weaknesses in sampling procedures. For example, in its 2010 inspection report on Grant Thornton, the PCAOB stated (PCAOB Release No. 104-2012-109):

> [T]he Firm placed excessive reliance on controls relating to impaired loans. As a result, the Firm's loan review sample size was insufficient to conclude on the valuation and completeness of the issuer's impaired loans.

Similarly, in its 2010 inspection report of KPMG (PCAOB Release No. 104-2011-288), the PCAOB stated:

> For control testing, the Firm concluded that the issuer's price verification procedures over all the diverse financial instruments in the portfolios constituted a single control that operated monthly with a "risk of failure of lower."… As a result of the Firm's inappropriate conclusion, the Firm's

sample sizes (generally zero, one, or two) for control testing of the price verification procedures for Level 3 financial instruments were inadequate.

Also along these same lines, the PCAOB stated the following in its 2010 inspection report of Deloitte (PCAOB Release No. 104-2011-290):

In this audit, the Firm failed to perform sufficient procedures to test the assumptions underlying the valuation of certain of the issuer's inventory. The Firm selected a sample of items for testing from the issuer's population of inventory items for which an impairment charge had been recorded during the year. For all inventory items for which the issuer had not recorded an impairment charge during the year (which represented more than 90 percent of the carrying value of the inventory), however, the Firm selected only two items for testing.

These examples illustrate that auditors sometimes gather what is later deemed to be insufficient evidence. As you read through this chapter, consider the following questions:

- What is sampling, and what risks does the auditor face when using sampling? (LO 1, 2)
- In testing controls and account balances and assertions, what type of sampling should be used? (LO 3, 4, 5, 6)
- In testing controls and account balances and assertions, how many individual account items should be selected, and which ones should be selected? (LO 4, 5, 6)
- If a sample contains an error, how is that information used to come to a conclusion regarding errors in the overall population? (LO 3, 4, 5, 6)

Overview of Sampling and GAS as Tools for Gathering Audit Evidence

LO 1 Describe how auditors use sampling and GAS to gather sufficient appropriate audit evidence.

This chapter describes two tools used to efficiently gather audit evidence: (1) sampling that can be used for either tests of controls or direct tests of account balances and assertions, and (2) GAS that can be used for analyzing underlying data and for supporting tests of controls and direct tests of account balances and assertions.

Sampling, which is used in testing controls and account balances and assertions, involves looking at less than 100% of the transactions that occurred during the audit period. Sampling techniques would be appropriate when an auditor wants to perform procedures such as examining documents, reperforming calculations, or sending confirmations. However, the auditor should recognize that other types of audit procedures such as inquiry, observation, and analytical procedures would not involve sampling.

All audits involve sampling because the auditor cannot examine 100% of the transactions during a period. Yet, the auditor must reach conclusions about the accuracy of the underlying populations that make up an account balance. Every audit contains some form of audit sampling to test the operation of controls and/or directly test account balances because the auditor constantly faces the challenge of gathering sufficient appropriate evidence as efficiently as possible. Samples should be representative of the population if the auditor is going to minimize the risk of reaching an incorrect conclusion about the population. To increase the likelihood that samples will be representative, they must be of sufficient size and must be selected from the appropriate underlying population.

Generalized audit software (GAS) are software programs designed specifically for auditors. GAS can be used to facilitate and automate the testing of 100% of a population when appropriate and to help focus the auditor's attention on specific risk areas or transactions. GAS is software designed to read, process, and write data. Auditors can use GAS to import a client's data; then the software can be applied to the data in a variety of ways. For example, the data can be scanned, sorted, summarized, stratified, analyzed, and used to obtain samples. Other GAS functions of interest to auditors include identification of duplicate items such as duplicate invoices, gaps in data such as a gap in a check sequence, and outliers in a population such as all invoices that

EXHIBIT **8.1**	Approaches to Gathering Audit Evidence About Assertions

Financial Statement Assertion	Using Sampling to Gather Evidence	Using GAS to Gather Evidence
Existence or occurrence	Take a sample of recorded transactions and for selected items examine underlying evidence or send out confirmations.	Sort the file to identify the largest items, the smallest items, the last transactions during the year (for testing cutoff), or the most frequent items within the file; also useful in scanning for unusual transactions.
Completeness	Take a sample of subsequent cash disbursements to search for underrecorded liabilities.	Sort the file by vendor to identify the most commonly used vendors, or the least commonly used vendors; or comparing the list of vendors from the prior year to the current year.
Rights or obligations	Perform in conjunction with existence testing, including examining source documents.	Sort the file to scan for unusual transactions.
Valuation or allocation	Select items and trace back to source documents, such as purchase agreements or invoices.	Foot the file and test computations.
Presentation and disclosure	Verify estimates or other items for proper disclosure.	

exceed two times the average for a particular customer. In practical terms, you can think of GAS as being like a glorified Excel spreadsheet.

Exhibit 8.1 outlines alternative approaches to gathering evidence regarding financial statement assertions and includes examples of specific types of evidence that might be gathered and an indication as to when sampling or GAS would be appropriate.

Objectives of Sampling and Risks Associated with Sampling

LO 2 Explain the objectives of sampling for testing controls and account balances, and describe the risks associated with sampling.

The objective of sampling when testing controls is to determine whether the controls are operating effectively. If they are not operating effectively, the auditor needs to consider this when deciding on the opinion for internal controls and when designing the substantive procedures. The objective of sampling when testing account balances is to estimate the amount of misstatement in an account balance. If there are large misstatements, the auditor wants to know about them so that the account balance can be corrected. However, sampling always contains some risk. For example, the auditor might not look at enough items (recall the examples from the *Professional Judgment in Context* feature), or the sample might not be representative of the population. Thus, auditors must consider how to take samples that minimize the likelihood they will reach an incorrect conclusion about what they are testing. Note that the *Emerging Issues* feature "Data Analytics Enables Audit of Entire Populations of Data" highlights a trend whereby the use of sampling may decrease as auditors employ data analytics to test populations.

Sampling units refer to the individual items to be tested. The sampling units make up the population. The **population** is a group of transactions or items that make up an account balance for which the auditor wants to estimate some characteristic, such as the effectiveness of a control

Data Analytics Enables Audit of Entire Populations of Data

Many accounting firms are beginning to use data analytics. **Data analytics** is the process of examining large amounts of data to uncover underlying patterns, correlations, and complex relationships through statistical methods for data modeling, and techniques that enable visualization of data. Data analytics enables auditors to audit all transactions, rather than just a sample of transactions. As the use of data analytics increases on audit engagements, the need for sampling will decrease.

procedure or the extent of misstatement in an account. An example of sampling units might be the sales orders processed during the year that relate to the recognition of revenue. The auditor needs to answer four critical questions when sampling:

1. Which population and sampling unit should be tested, and what characteristics should be examined (*population*)?
2. How many items should be selected for audit testing (*sample size*)?
3. Which items should be included in the sample (*selection*)?
4. What inferences can be made about the overall population from the sample (*evaluation*)?

Nonsampling and Sampling Risks

When making inferences about a population from a sample, the auditor could make an error about the characteristics of the underlying population because either (a) the auditor did not appropriately carry out the audit procedures or inappropriately diagnosed problems (nonsampling risk) or (b) the auditor used a sample that was not representative of the population (sampling risk). Fortunately, audit firms can control for both of these risks through adequate planning and effective quality control.

Nonsampling Risk

It is assumed that auditors carefully examine all items in the sample and choose correct procedures in gathering evidence to evaluate the correctness of a transaction. However, there may be cases when the auditor is not careful. The risk that the auditor reaches an erroneous conclusion for any reason not related to sampling risk is referred to as **nonsampling risk**. Nonsampling risk could also be due to a lack of knowledge of the auditor performing the audit procedure. The audit firm controls the possibility of such errors through proper training and adequate supervision of the auditors, well-designed computer programs to accomplish sampling, and carefully designed and executed audit programs.

Sampling Risk

There is always a risk that any inferences made from a sample might not be correct, unless auditors examine 100% of a population. There is uncertainty about the projected results because the sampling results are based on only a small part of the population. The smaller the sample, the more uncertainty; the larger the sample, the less uncertainty. **Sampling risk** is the risk that the auditor's conclusion based on a sample might be different from the conclusion that would be reached if the audit procedure were applied in the same way to the entire population. By using statistical sampling, the auditor can control—and measure—how much risk there will be that the sample might not be representative of the population. Sampling risk can be measured for statistical samples, but not for nonstatistical sampling approaches.

Sampling Risks Related to Tests of Controls   The auditor often uses sampling to gather evidence to assess the effectiveness of controls as part of an integrated audit. The auditor wants an accurate estimate of the percentage of time that a control fails; for example, if a control does not operate effectively 4% of the time, the auditor uses this information to reach a conclusion about the effectiveness of the control. This conclusion will affect the extent of substantive testing that should be performed or the opinion to issue on internal controls. Because sampling always carries some uncertainty, the auditor usually wants to control for the worst possible scenario; for example, the auditor may want to be 95% confident that the control does not fail more than 8% of the time. The auditor is always challenged to manage the risks of making incorrect inferences from small sample sizes.

Exhibit 8.2 presents sampling risks relevant to tests of controls. The **risk of incorrect acceptance of internal control reliability** (also referred to as the **risk of assessing control risk too low** or the **risk of overreliance**) is the risk that the auditor will conclude that internal controls are effective when internal controls are actually not effective. The **risk of incorrect rejection of internal control reliability** (also referred to as the **risk of assessing control risk too high** or the **risk of underreliance**) is the risk that the auditor will conclude that the internal controls are not effective when internal controls are actually effective.

The auditor's main concern when performing sampling related to tests of controls is controlling the risk of incorrect acceptance of internal control effectiveness. With incorrect acceptance, control failures are more common than the sample indicates, but the sample results lead the auditor to believe that control risk is relatively low. As such, the auditor will incorrectly rely on the effectiveness of internal controls and will not perform as much substantive testing as would be required to conduct a quality audit. On the other hand, if the

| EXHIBIT **8.2** | Sampling Risks for Tests of Control Procedures |

Auditor's Assessment of Control Risk Based on Sample Evidence	Actual State of Controls Based on the Entire Population	
	Effective	**Not Effective**
Low	Correct conclusion	*Risk of incorrect acceptance of internal control reliability* Control failures in the population are higher than the sample indicates (also referred to as the *risk of assessing control risk too low* or the *risk of overreliance*). Leads to audit ineffectiveness.
High	*Risk of incorrect rejection of internal control reliability* Control failures in the population are lower than the sample indicates (also referred to as the *risk of assessing control risk too high* or the *risk of underreliance*). Leads to audit inefficiency.	Correct conclusion

| EXHIBIT 8.3 | Sampling Risks for Tests of Details of Account Balances | |

Auditor's Conclusion Based on Sample Evidence	Actual Condition of Book Value Based on the Entire Population	
	Does Not Contain a Material Misstatement	Contains a Material Misstatement
Book value does not contain a material misstatement	Correct conclusion	*Risk of incorrect acceptance of book value* Leads to audit ineffectiveness.
Book value likely contains a material misstatement	*Risk of incorrect rejection of book value* Leads to audit inefficiency.	Correct conclusion

auditor were to incorrectly reject control effectiveness, the auditor will not rely on internal controls and will perform more substantive testing than would be required to conduct a quality audit, thereby resulting in inefficiency.

Sampling Risks Related to Tests of Details of Account Balances Sampling can also be used to estimate the amount of misstatement in an account balance. The auditor can, for example, select a sample of inventory items and perform a price test. If the sample contains pricing errors, the auditor projects these errors to the population to determine whether the population may be materially misstated because inventory is priced incorrectly. *Exhibit 8.3* presents sampling risks relevant to substantive tests of account balances. The **risk of incorrect acceptance of book value** is the risk that the auditor will conclude that the account balance does not contain a material misstatement when the account balance actually does contain a material misstatement. The **risk of incorrect rejection of book value** is the risk that the auditor will conclude that the account balance contains a material misstatement when the account balance actually does not contain a material misstatement.

The auditor's main concern when performing sampling related to substantive tests of details is controlling the risk of incorrect acceptance of book value. With incorrect acceptance, the account balance contains a material misstatement, but the sample results lead the auditor to believe the account does not contain a material misstatement. No additional audit work would be performed, and the financial statements will be issued with a material misstatement. On the other hand, if the auditor were to incorrectly reject a population that does not contain a material misstatement, the client will usually object and encourage the auditor to perform additional work. The additional audit work should lead to a correction of the inappropriate inference. The risk of incorrect rejection of book value thus affects the efficiency of the audit, but it should not affect the auditor's overall conclusion about the fairness of the financial statements.

Nonstatistical and Statistical Sampling

LO 3 Compare and contrast nonstatistical and statistical sampling and apply these sampling approaches.

Auditors use both nonstatistical and statistical sampling. When properly used, either sampling approach can be effective in providing sufficient appropriate audit evidence. Nonstatistical sampling, however, does not allow the auditor to statistically control for or measure the risk of incorrect inference about the sample. **Statistical sampling** involves the application of probability theory and statistical inference, along with auditor judgment and experience, in a sample application to assist the auditor in determining an appropriate sample size and in evaluating the sample results. In contrast, **nonstatistical sampling** does not rely on the application of probability theory or statistical inference; instead it relies solely on the application of auditor judgment and experience in a sample application to assist the auditor in determining an appropriate sample size and in evaluating sample results. *Exhibit 8.4* compares nonstatistical and statistical sampling on relevant dimensions.

An auditor who applies statistical sampling uses tables or formulas to compute sample size, while an auditor who applies nonstatistical sampling uses only professional judgment. Ordinarily, the nonstatistical sample size should not be smaller than the sample size resulting from an efficiently and

---

EXHIBIT 8.4 Comparison of Nonstatistical and Statistical Sampling

	Nonstatistical Sampling	Statistical Sampling
Sample size	Sample size is determined by auditor judgment.	Auditor judgment is quantified, and sample size is determined by probability theory.
Sample selection	Selection involves any method that the auditor believes is representative of the population.	The sample must be randomly selected to give each unit in the population an equal chance to be included in the sample; there are several approaches to random selection including simple random sampling and stratified random sampling.
	Judgment sampling can also be directed at a portion of the population, for example, all transactions during the last five days of the year.	The population of interest can also be directed; for example, the transactions during the last ten days of the year can be statistically selected.
Evaluation	Evaluation is based on auditor judgment, and projections are based on sample results.	Evaluation is based on statistical inference that is used to assist auditor judgment.
Costs	Selection costs are lower because audit judgment is required only to determine an appropriate sample size and evaluate the results.	Training costs are higher because knowledge of statistical sampling methods and/or special computer sampling software is required.
	This type of sampling does not provide an objective way to control and measure sampling risk.	This type of sampling requires the auditor to define acceptable risk in advance.
Benefits	This method can be based on the auditor's prior expectations about errors in the account.	This method helps the auditor to design an efficient sample, measure the sufficiency of the evidence, and evaluate the results by providing an objective measure of sampling risk.
	This method may take less time to plan, select, and evaluate the sample.	This method helps the auditor to gain efficiencies through computerized selection and statistical evaluation and to defend sample inferences because they are based on statistical theory.
		This method helps the auditor to evaluate the sample by providing a quantitative measure of the most likely and maximum failure rate of a control procedure that is being evaluated for effectiveness, the most likely and maximum amount of misstatement in the recorded account balance or class of transactions, and the risk that the auditor may make an incorrect judgment about the state of controls or correctness of account balances.

effectively designed statistical sample. Both statistical and nonstatistical sampling, when properly used, can provide sufficient evidence for auditor conclusions. Statistical sampling allows the auditor to precisely control and measure the risk of making an incorrect inference about the population from which the sample is taken, whereas nonstatistical sampling does not allow such control and measurement. For both approaches, the auditor must consider the nature of control deficiencies or misstatements detected in the sample, project the sample findings to the population, and conclude on the overall population. In addition to evaluating the results of a sample quantitatively, the auditor should consider the qualitative aspects of control failures and misstatements. Are the sample results caused by errors, or do they indicate the possibility of fraud, and how do the control deficiencies affect other phases of the audit? Combining statistical sampling with audit judgment generally produces a higher quality audit conclusion than using audit judgment alone. In addition, statistical sampling may help to avoid second guessing by regulators or jurors, should those parties question the quality of the sampling method used.

Attributes Sampling

LO 4 Describe attributes sampling and use it for tests of controls.

The auditor gathers evidence on the operating effectiveness of the client's internal controls by examining the important controls over financial reporting. The auditor performs tests of controls focused on operating effectiveness only after determining that the design of the controls would be effective in minimizing the likelihood of material misstatements in the account balances. Testing of controls provides the auditor with evidence necessary to issue an opinion on internal control effectiveness and to assess the client's control risk. The assessment of control effectiveness may be based on:

- A sample to test the effectiveness of controls in operation
- The auditor's observation of the controls within significant business processes
- Tests of controls built into the client's computer system
- Inquiry and review of monitoring reports

Sampling concepts do not apply to all tests of controls. When effective general computer controls are present, tests of automated application controls are generally performed with sample sizes of just one or a few items. Sampling generally is not applicable for determining the appropriate segregation of duties and may not apply to tests of operating effectiveness of the control environment. When sampling is appropriate, the auditor wants to use a sample to infer whether the control in the population is operating effectively. The most commonly used statistical approach for tests of controls is attributes sampling. **Attributes sampling** is a statistical sampling method used to estimate the rate of control procedure failures based on selecting one sample and performing the appropriate audit procedure.

An **attribute** is a characteristic of the population of interest to the auditor. Typically, the attribute the auditor wishes to examine is the effective operation of a control, for example, evidence that the client has matched vendor invoice details with the purchase order and receiving report before payment approval, and noting that they match before authorizing a payment for the goods received.

Steps in Attributes Sampling

Attributes sampling is used to test the operating effectiveness of controls. It is used to gather evidence to answer questions such as "Was credit properly approved?" or "Was the customer's order shipped before it was billed?" or

"Were the expenses claimed by the CEO consistent with company policies?" The steps to implement an attributes sampling plan are as follows:

1. Define the attributes of interest and what constitutes failure(s).
2. Define the population from which the sample is to be taken.
3. Determine the sample size.
4. Determine the method of selecting the sample.
5. Select the sample items and perform the test of control.
6. Evaluate the sample results and consider the effect on planned substantive procedures.
7. Document all phases of the sampling process.

Step 1. Define the Attributes of Interest and What Constitutes Failure(s)

A number of attributes could be tested, but the auditor tests only important controls. Control failures should be precisely defined to make sure that the auditor clearly understands what to look for, thereby reducing nonsampling risk. For example, a failure to seek credit approval for a new account, when such approval is required by company policy, would be considered a control failure.

A control failure does not automatically mean that a misstatement has occurred. For example, most companies require a credit approval process before issuing credit. When pressed for time, a marketing manager may approve a sale without obtaining proper credit approval. The control requiring credit approval has failed, but it is not known (a) whether the credit would have been granted if the process had been completed or (b) whether the customer is less likely to pay. Finally, the failure of this control does not affect the proper recording of the initial transaction. It may, however, affect the valuation of receivables at year-end.

Step 2. Define the Population From Which the Sample Is to Be Taken

In defining the population, the following factors need to be addressed:

- The period to be covered by the test; for example, the year when evaluating controls
- The sampling unit; for example, an item that would indicate the operation of a control
- The completeness of the population

Period Covered by the Test The period tested depends on the audit objective. In most instances, the period is the time period covered by the audited financial statements. As a practical matter, tests of controls are often performed prior to the balance sheet date and may cover the first ten or eleven months of the year. If the controls are found to be effective, the auditor should take additional steps to assure that the controls continue to be effective during the remainder of the year. The additional steps may include making inquiries, further testing of the controls, or gathering evidence of control effectiveness from substantive tests performed later in the audit. If the auditor is issuing an opinion on internal controls over financial reporting, the auditor needs reasonable assurance that the controls are effective as of the client's balance sheet date.

Sampling Unit The sampling unit is the item identified in the population as the basis for testing. It could be a document, an entry in the computer system, or a line item on a document. One company may require supervisory approval with initials to authorize payment of several invoices; the sampling unit would be the document authorizing the invoices. Another company may require written authorization for each invoice; the sampling unit would be the individual invoices processed for payment.

Completeness of Population The auditor should take steps to help assure that the population used in sampling is the total population of interest. The auditor normally performs some procedures, such as footing the file and reconciling the balance to the general ledger or reviewing the completeness of prenumbered documents, to assure that the population is complete.

Step 3. Determine the Sample Size

An optimal sample size minimizes sampling risk and promotes audit efficiency. The following audit judgments affect sample size: (1) sampling risk, (2) the tolerable rate of deviation, and (3) the expected population deviation rate.

- *Sampling risk*—Sampling risk is often set at 5% or 10%, as shown in *Exhibit 8.5*. This risk is sometimes referred to as the allowable risk of overreliance.

EXHIBIT **8.5**	Attributes Sample Size Tables

Table 1: Statistical Sample Sizes for Tests of Controls—5 Percent Risk of Overreliance (with number of expected errors in parentheses)

Expected Deviation Rate	Tolerable Deviation Rate										
	2%	3%	4%	5%	6%	7%	8%	9%	10%	15%	20%
0.00%	149 (0)	99 (0)	74 (0)	59 (0)	49 (0)	42 (0)	36 (0)	32 (0)	29 (0)	19 (0)	14 (0)
0.25%	236 (1)	157 (1)	117 (1)	93 (1)	78 (1)	66 (1)	58 (1)	51 (1)	46 (1)	30 (1)	22 (1)
0.50%	313 (2)	157 (1)	117 (1)	93 (1)	78 (1)	66 (1)	58 (1)	51 (1)	46 (1)	30 (1)	22 (1)
0.75%	386 (3)	208 (2)	117 (1)	93 (1)	78 (1)	66 (1)	58 (1)	51 (1)	46 (1)	30 (1)	22 (1)
1.00%	590 (6)	257 (3)	156 (2)	93 (1)	78 (1)	66 (1)	58 (1)	51 (1)	46 (1)	30 (1)	22 (1)
1.25%	1,030 (13)	303 (4)	156 (2)	124 (2)	78 (1)	66 (1)	58 (1)	51 (1)	46 (1)	30 (1)	22 (1)
1.50%		392 (6)	192 (3)	124 (2)	103 (2)	66 (1)	58 (1)	51 (1)	46 (1)	30 (1)	22 (1)
1.75%		562 (10)	227 (4)	153 (3)	103 (2)	88 (2)	77 (2)	51 (1)	46 (1)	30 (1)	22 (1)
2.00%		846 (17)	294 (6)	181 (4)	127 (3)	88 (2)	77 (2)	68 (2)	46 (1)	30 (1)	22 (1)
2.25%		1,466 (33)	390 (9)	208 (5)	127 (3)	88 (2)	77 (2)	68 (2)	61 (2)	30 (1)	22 (1)
2.50%			513 (13)	234 (6)	150 (4)	109 (3)	77 (2)	68 (2)	61 (2)	30 (1)	22 (1)
2.75%			722 (20)	286 (8)	173 (5)	109 (3)	95 (3)	68 (2)	61 (2)	30 (1)	22 (1)
3.00%			1,098 (33)	361 (11)	195 (6)	129 (4)	95 (3)	84 (3)	61 (2)	30 (1)	22 (1)
3.25%			1,936 (63)	458 (15)	238 (8)	148 (5)	112 (4)	84 (3)	61 (2)	30 (1)	22 (1)
3.50%				624 (22)	280 (10)	167 (6)	112 (4)	84 (3)	76 (3)	40 (2)	22 (1)
3.75%				877 (33)	341 (13)	185 (7)	129 (5)	100 (4)	76 (3)	40 (2)	22 (1)
4.00%				1,348 (54)	421 (17)	221 (9)	146 (6)	100 (4)	89 (4)	40 (2)	22 (1)
5.00%					1,580 (79)	478 (24)	240 (12)	158 (8)	116 (6)	40 (2)	30 (2)
6.00%						1,832 (110)	532 (32)	266 (16)	179 (11)	50 (3)	30 (2)
7.00%								585 (41)	298 (21)	68 (5)	37 (3)
8.00%									649 (52)	85 (7)	37 (3)
9.00%										110 (10)	44 (4)
10.00%										150 (15)	50 (5)
12.50%										576 (72)	88 (11)
15.00%											193 (29)
17.50%											720 (126)

(continued)

EXHIBIT **8.5**	Attributes Sample Size Tables (*continued*)

Table 2: Statistical Sample Sizes for Tests of Controls—10 Percent Risk of Overreliance (with number of expected errors in parentheses)

Expected Deviation Rate	Tolerable Deviation Rate										
	2%	**3%**	**4%**	**5%**	**6%**	**7%**	**8%**	**9%**	**10%**	**15%**	**20%**
0.00%	114 (0)	76 (0)	57 (0)	45 (0)	38 (0)	32 (0)	28 (0)	25 (0)	22 (0)	15 (0)	11 (0)
0.25%	194 (1)	129 (1)	96 (1)	77 (1)	64 (1)	55 (1)	48 (1)	42 (1)	38 (1)	25 (1)	18 (1)
0.50%	194 (1)	129 (1)	96 (1)	77 (1)	64 (1)	55 (1)	48 (1)	42 (1)	38 (1)	25 (1)	18 (1)
0.75%	265 (2)	129 (1)	96 (1)	77 (1)	64 (1)	55 (1)	48 (1)	42 (1)	38 (1)	25 (1)	18 (1)
1.00%	398 (4)	176 (2)	96 (1)	77 (1)	64 (1)	55 (1)	48 (1)	42 (1)	38 (1)	25 (1)	18 (1)
1.25%	708 (9)	221 (3)	132 (2)	77 (1)	64 (1)	55 (1)	48 (1)	42 (1)	38 (1)	25 (1)	18 (1)
1.50%	1,463 (22)	265 (4)	132 (2)	105 (2)	64 (1)	55 (1)	48 (1)	42 (1)	38 (1)	25 (1)	18 (1)
1.75%		390 (7)	166 (3)	105 (2)	88 (2)	55 (1)	48 (1)	42 (1)	38 (1)	25 (1)	18 (1)
2.00%		590 (12)	198 (4)	132 (3)	88 (2)	75 (2)	48 (1)	42 (1)	38 (1)	25 (1)	18 (1)
2.25%		974 (22)	262 (6)	132 (3)	88 (2)	75 (2)	65 (2)	42 (1)	38 (1)	25 (1)	18 (1)
2.50%			353 (9)	158 (4)	110 (3)	75 (2)	65 (2)	58 (2)	38 (1)	25 (1)	18 (1)
2.75%			471 (13)	209 (6)	132 (4)	94 (3)	65 (2)	58 (2)	52 (2)	25 (1)	18 (1)
3.00%			730 (22)	258 (8)	132 (4)	94 (3)	65 (2)	58 (2)	52 (2)	25 (1)	18 (1)
3.25%			1,258 (41)	306 (10)	153 (5)	113 (4)	82 (3)	58 (2)	52 (2)	25 (1)	18 (1)
3.50%				400 (14)	194 (7)	113 (4)	82 (3)	73 (3)	52 (2)	25 (1)	18 (1)
3.75%				583 (22)	235 (9)	131 (5)	98 (4)	73 (3)	52 (2)	25 (1)	18 (1)
4.00%				873 (35)	274 (11)	149 (6)	98 (4)	73 (3)	65 (3)	25 (1)	18 (1)
5.00%					1,019 (51)	318 (16)	160 (8)	115 (6)	78 (4)	34 (2)	18 (1)
6.00%						1,150 (69)	349 (21)	182 (11)	116 (7)	43 (3)	25 (2)
7.00%							1,300 (91)	385 (27)	199 (14)	52 (4)	25 (2)
8.00%								1,437 (115)	424 (34)	60 (5)	25 (2)
9.00%									1,577 (142)	77 (7)	32 (3)
10.00%										100 (10)	38 (4)
12.50%										368 (46)	63 (8)
15.00%											126 (19)
17.50%											457 (80)

Note: Sample sizes over 2,000 items not shown. These tables assume a large population.

Source: *Audit Sampling* (New York: AICPA, 2012), 145–146. AICPA audit and accounting guides by American Institute of Certified Public Accountants. Copyright © 2012 Reproduced with permission of American Institute of Certified Public Accountants in the format Textbook via Copyright Clearance Center.

- *Tolerable rate of deviation*—The AICPA's 2012 *Audit Sampling* formally defines the **tolerable rate of deviation** as a rate of deviation set by the auditor in respect of which the auditor seeks to obtain an appropriate level of assurance that the rate of deviation set by the auditor is not exceeded by the actual rate of deviation in the population. This term is sometimes referred to as the **tolerable failure rate**. In more practical terms, the auditor's tolerable rate of deviation is the level at which the control's failure to operate would cause the auditor to conclude that the control is not effective and would likely change the auditor's planned assessment of control risk in performing tests of account balances.
- *Expected population deviation rate*—The **expected population deviation rate** is an anticipation of the deviation rate in the entire population. This term is sometimes referred to as the **expected failure rate**. Failures occur when personnel are in a hurry or careless, are not competent, or are not properly trained. The auditor likely has evidence

on the rate at which a particular control fails, based on past experience as modified by any changes in the system or personnel. The expected failure rate should be less than the tolerable failure rate; otherwise the auditor should not test controls.

In general, the number of items in the population has relatively little effect on the sample size, unless the population is very small. The tables in *Exhibit 8.5* assume large populations and give sample sizes for several combinations of these factors and for both 5% and 10% levels of sampling risk. Using these tables for small populations is a conservative approach because the sample size will be overstated.

The determination of sample size using the tables is straightforward. The auditor:

1. Selects the allowable sampling risk (risk of overreliance of 5% or 10%) based on factors such as audit risk, and whether the auditor will be issuing a separate opinion on internal control (Note: we use the term *risk of overreliance* because that is the term used in the AICPA's sample size tables. Recall that the terms *risk of incorrect acceptance of internal control reliability* or *risk of assessing control risk too low* are also used to refer to the same concept.)
2. Determines the tolerable rate of deviation. The tolerable rate of deviation would be lower for more important controls, such as controls over more significant accounts and for controls over accounts that are more susceptible to misstatement.
3. Uses past knowledge to determine the expected population deviation rate.
4. Determines sample size by looking at the intersection of the expected population deviation rate and the tolerable rate of deviation in the appropriate table.

The *Auditing in Practice* feature "Illustration of Attributes Sample Size Determination" provides examples of how to use these tables.

Working Backward From Sample Size It is not uncommon for audit firms to perform tests of controls with samples of 30 or 40 as a standard practice. If the firm makes such choices, the auditor can determine the

Illustration of Attributes Sample Size Determination

AUDITING IN **PRACTICE**

Example 1: (More Important Control, Integrated Audit): The auditor sets the risk of overreliance at 5% (implying that the auditor is willing to accept a 5% chance that inferences from the sample will be incorrect), sets the tolerable rate of deviation at 5%, and anticipates that the expected population deviation rate will be 1%. The auditor refers to Table 1 in *Exhibit 8.5* and finds a sample size of 93.

Example 2: (Less Important Control, No Separate Opinion on Internal Control): The auditor sets the risk of overreliance at 10% (implying that the

auditor is willing to accept more risk than in Example 1), sets the tolerable rate of deviation at 10% (suggesting that the control is less important than in Example 1), and anticipates that the expected population deviation rate is 1%. The auditor uses Table 2 in *Exhibit 8.5* and finds a sample size of 38. Also note that the number in parentheses after each sample size represents the number of errors the auditor can find without concluding that the control is not working correctly (1 in a sample of 93 for the more important control, and 1 in a sample of 38 for the less important control).

assumptions used by the firm in adopting that practice by working backward through the tables, as illustrated in the following examples. Although auditors would not regularly do this, these examples are included to provide an understanding of the assumptions that must be made by an audit firm to justify such a sample size. The point of both examples is that sample sizes of just 30 or 40 require the auditor to tolerate a fairly high rate of deviation in the sample, a choice that ultimately yields greater audit risk for the audit firm. The following examples help explain the assumptions needed to support a sample size of 30.

> **Example 1**: Consider an example from Table 1 of *Exhibit 8.5*, for risk of overreliance of 5%. The auditor can only get to a sample size of 29 by assuming a tolerable rate of deviation of 10% and an expected population deviation rate of 0. The auditor could get to a sample size of 30 using a tolerable rate of deviation of 15% and allowing the expected population deviation rate to increase. However, it is difficult to justify a tolerable deviation rate of 15% for an important control.

> **Example 2**: Consider an example from Table 2 of *Exhibit 8.5*, for risk of overreliance of 10%. The auditor can get to a sample size of 28 by assuming a tolerable deviation rate of 8% and an expected population deviation rate of 0. Other combinations work similarly by moving the tolerable rate of deviation up to 15% and allowing the expected population deviation rate to go as high as 4%.

Multiple Attributes   Auditors frequently test several controls or attributes using the same set of source documents. When doing so, the auditor should use the same sampling risk for all the tests. However, the tolerable rates of deviation and expected population deviation rates for these attributes are likely to be different, resulting in different sample sizes. For example, the auditor may want to test whether sales transactions are classified correctly, whether they have been recorded accurately, and whether there was proper review and approval for credit using tolerable deviation rates of 5%, 3%, and 3%, respectively, and expected population deviation rates of 2%, 1%, and 0%, respectively. If the auditor sets the risk of overreliance at 10%, the sample sizes range from a high of 176 for Attribute 2 to a low of 76 for Attribute 3:

Attribute	Tolerable Rate	Expected Rate	Sample Size
1. Evidence of independent review of account distribution	5%	2%	132
2. Evidence of comparison of description, quantity, and price between the customer's order and sales invoice	3%	1%	176
3. Evidence of proper review and approval for credit	3%	0%	76

There are three reasonable approaches to selecting the items for these tests:

- The auditor could select 176 sales transactions (the largest sample size) and audit all of them for Attribute 2, three of four for Attribute 1, and every other one for Attribute 3. This process, however, is quite cumbersome.
- The auditor could examine the first seventy-six randomly selected documents for all three attributes and documents, sample items 77–132 for Attributes 1 and 2, and the remainder only for Attribute 2. This process is also quite cumbersome.

- Often the most efficient approach is to test the 176 items for all three attributes. Attributes 1 and 3 will be in some sense overaudited, but the overauditing may take less time than keeping track of which sample items should be tested for which attribute. Testing for Attributes 1 and 3 does not take very long once the auditor has selected the documents in the sample. The auditor's evaluation of the control is based on the 176 items examined and improves the accuracy of the control risk assessment.

Step 4. Determine the Method of Selecting the Sample

Once the sample size has been determined, the auditor must select sample items so the sample can be expected to be representative of the population and thus the results can be projected to the population. The auditor may use simple random sampling, systematic sampling, haphazard sampling, or block sampling.

Simple Random Sampling **Simple random sampling** involves selecting a random sample by matching random numbers generated by a computer or selected from a random-number table with, for example, document numbers such as an invoice or a purchase order. With this method, each sampling unit has the same probability of being selected as any other sampling unit. Simple random sampling is appropriate for both nonstatistical and statistical sampling applications.

Systematic Sampling **Systematic sampling** involves dividing the number of physical units in the population by the sample size to determine a uniform interval; a random starting point is selected in the first interval, and one item is selected throughout the population at each of the uniform intervals after the starting point. In order to use systematic selection, the auditor must be sure that there is not a systematic pattern in the population.

For example, assume that the population consists of payroll transactions in a payroll journal that are listed in employee number order. These numbers are not in sequence because of employee turnover. There are 1,300 payroll transactions, and the auditor has determined a sample size of 26. Every 50th transaction (1,300/26 = 50) should be selected for testing. To randomize the selection process, a random number from 1 to 50 should be used to identify the first sample item. This could be done, for example, by using the last two digits of a serial number on a dollar bill. If those digits were 87, subtract 50, leaving 37 as the first sample item. Every 50th transaction thereafter would also be included in the sample. When the first item is selected randomly from the interval, this sampling technique is called **systematic random sampling**.

The validity of a systematic sampling is based on the assumption that the items in the population are randomly distributed. The auditor must be knowledgeable about the nature of the population to be sure that no repeating or coinciding pattern in the population would cause the sample to not be representative. Many auditors try to increase the chances that the systematically selected samples are representative of the population by using multiple random starts.

Haphazard Sampling **Haphazard sampling** is a nonstatistical sample selection method that attempts to approximate a random selection by selecting sampling units without any conscious bias, or special reason for including or omitting certain items from the sample. The word *haphazard* is not intended to convey that that the sampled items are selected in a careless manner. Rather, it is intended to imply that the sampled items selected are representative of the population.

Block Sampling **Block sampling** involves selecting a sample that consists of contiguous population items, such as selecting transactions by day or week. This is an efficient approach, but the risk is that the way the transactions were processed on these days or weeks may not be representative of how they were processed the other 364 days or fifty-one weeks. This judgmental decision is subject to second guessing that such a sample could not be representative. Block sampling is most appropriate for performing year-end cutoff tests.

Step 5. Select the Sample Items and Perform the Test of Control

When selecting the sample, the auditor decides how to handle inapplicable, voided, or unused documents. An example of an inapplicable document would be a telephone bill when testing for an error defined as "cash disbursement transactions not supported by a receiving report." If the inapplicable document does not represent the control being tested, it should be replaced by another randomly selected item.

When a selected item cannot be located, the auditor should assume the worst—that the control procedure was not followed—and assess it as a failure. If many failures of this type are found before finishing the audit of a sample, the auditor should conclude that no reliance can be placed on the tested control procedure. In such a situation, the auditor should terminate the test to avoid wasting any more time and discuss it with management and the audit committee.

Step 6. Evaluate the Sample Results and Consider the Effect on Planned Substantive Procedures

Evaluation of sample results requires the auditor to project those results to the population before drawing an audit conclusion.

Quantitative Evaluation The auditor needs to determine whether the upper limit of the possible deviation rate exceeds the tolerable deviation rate. To make such an assessment, the auditor should use statistical evaluation. Tables such as those in *Exhibit 8.6* help the auditor determine the upper limit of the possible deviation rate. If the upper limit of the possible deviation rate exceeds the tolerable deviation rate, the auditor should (1) test a different control designed to mitigate the same risk, or (2) adjust the nature, timing, and/or extent of the related substantive testing of the accounts affected by the control. The change in substantive testing will be necessary because the auditor will need to increase the assessed level of control risk and, thus, decrease the level of detection risk.

In determining what changes to make in substantive audit procedures, the auditor should consider the nature of control deviation (pattern of errors) and determine the effect of such deviations on potential material misstatements in the financial statements. When the upper limit of the possible deviation rate exceeds the tolerable deviation rate, the auditor has to decide whether the control failure, in conjunction with other control failures, leads to a conclusion that there are either significant deficiencies or material weaknesses regarding internal control over financial reporting.

Sample Evaluation—An Illustration To illustrate the use of the tables in *Exhibit 8.6*, assume that the auditor tested the controls designed to make sure that sales were not billed until shipped, using a 5% risk of overreliance, a tolerable population deviation rate of 6%, and an expected population deviation rate of 1%. Recall what these judgments mean:

- A 5% risk of overreliance means the auditor wants to limit the risk to 5% that the actual deviation rate in the population will not exceed the tolerable population deviation rate of 6%. This is equivalent to using a 95% confidence level.

- The tolerable deviation rate is 6%; if there is more than a 5% chance that the actual deviation rate is greater than 6%, the auditor must conclude that the control is not operating at an acceptable level.
- The auditor did not expect many errors; the auditor expects the control to not be operating effectively only about 1% of the time; this expectation is based on good past experience with the control and the client's careful monitoring practices.
- If the upper limit of the possible deviation rate in the appropriate table exceeds the tolerable deviation rate set by the auditor, then the auditor's tests of controls do not support the original control assessment, and control risk must be increased. The remainder of the audit needs to be adjusted accordingly.

Assume that the auditor selects a sample of 80 from a population of 100,000 sales transactions and detects three control deviations (a deviation rate of 3.75%, calculated as 3/80). The auditor might conclude that 3.75% is less than 6%, and so the control is working effectively. But this conclusion is incorrect. Remember, the auditor's decision is whether there is more than a

---

EXHIBIT 8.6   Attributes Sampling Evaluation Tables

Table 1: Statistical Sampling Results Evaluation Table for Tests of Controls—Upper Limits at 5 Percent Risk of Overreliance

Sample Size	Actual Number of Deviations Found										
	0	1	2	3	4	5	6	7	8	9	10
20	14.0	21.7	28.3	34.4	40.2	45.6	50.8	55.9	60.7	65.4	69.9
25	11.3	17.7	23.2	28.2	33.0	37.6	42.0	46.3	50.4	54.4	58.4
30	9.6	14.9	19.6	23.9	28.0	31.9	35.8	39.4	43.0	46.6	50.0
35	8.3	12.9	17.0	20.7	24.3	27.8	31.1	34.4	37.5	40.6	43.7
40	7.3	11.4	15.0	18.3	21.5	24.6	27.5	30.4	33.3	36.0	38.8
45	6.5	10.2	13.4	16.4	19.2	22.0	24.7	27.3	29.8	32.4	34.8
50	5.9	9.2	12.1	14.8	17.4	19.9	22.4	24.7	27.1	29.4	31.6
55	5.4	8.4	11.1	13.5	15.9	18.2	20.5	22.6	24.8	26.9	28.9
60	4.9	7.7	10.2	12.5	14.7	16.8	18.8	20.8	22.8	24.8	26.7
65	4.6	7.1	9.4	11.5	13.6	15.5	17.5	19.3	21.2	23.0	24.7
70	4.2	6.6	8.8	10.8	12.7	14.5	16.3	18.0	19.7	21.4	23.1
75	4.0	6.2	8.2	10.1	11.8	13.6	15.2	16.9	18.5	20.1	21.6
80	3.7	5.8	7.7	9.5	11.1	12.7	14.3	15.9	17.4	18.9	20.3
90	3.3	5.2	6.9	8.4	9.9	11.4	12.8	14.2	15.5	16.9	18.2
100	3.0	4.7	6.2	7.6	9.0	10.3	11.5	12.8	14.0	15.2	16.4
125	2.4	3.8	5.0	6.1	7.2	8.3	9.3	10.3	11.3	12.3	13.2
150	2.0	3.2	4.2	5.1	6.0	6.9	7.8	8.6	9.5	10.3	11.1
200	1.5	2.4	3.2	3.9	4.6	5.2	5.9	6.5	7.2	7.8	8.4
300	1.0	1.6	2.1	2.6	3.1	3.5	4.0	4.4	4.8	5.2	5.6
400	0.8	1.2	1.6	2.0	2.3	2.7	3.0	3.3	3.6	3.9	4.3
500	0.6	1.0	1.3	1.6	1.9	2.1	2.4	2.7	2.9	3.2	3.4

(continued)

EXHIBIT **8.6**   Attributes Sampling Evaluation Tables (*continued*)

Table 2: Statistical Sampling Results Evaluation Table for Tests of Controls—Upper Limits at 10 Percent Risk of Overreliance

Sample Size	Actual Number of Deviations Found										
	0	**1**	**2**	**3**	**4**	**5**	**6**	**7**	**8**	**9**	**10**
20	10.9	18.1	24.5	30.5	36.1	41.5	46.8	51.9	56.8	61.6	66.2
25	8.8	14.7	20.0	24.9	29.5	34.0	38.4	42.6	46.8	50.8	54.8
30	7.4	12.4	16.8	21.0	24.9	28.8	32.5	36.2	39.7	43.2	46.7
35	6.4	10.7	14.5	18.2	21.6	24.9	28.2	31.4	34.5	37.6	40.6
40	5.6	9.4	12.8	16.0	19.0	22.0	24.9	27.7	30.5	33.2	35.9
45	5.0	8.4	11.4	14.3	17.0	19.7	22.3	24.8	27.3	29.8	32.2
50	4.6	7.6	10.3	12.9	15.4	17.8	20.2	22.5	24.7	27.0	29.2
55	4.2	6.9	9.4	11.8	14.1	16.3	18.4	20.5	22.6	24.6	26.7
60	3.8	6.4	8.7	10.8	12.9	15.0	16.9	18.9	20.8	22.7	24.6
65	3.5	5.9	8.0	10.0	12.0	13.9	15.7	17.5	19.3	21.0	22.8
70	3.3	5.5	7.5	9.3	11.1	12.9	14.6	16.3	18.0	19.6	21.2
75	3.1	5.1	7.0	8.7	10.4	12.1	13.7	15.2	16.8	18.3	19.8
80	2.9	4.8	6.6	8.2	9.8	11.3	12.8	14.3	15.8	17.2	18.7
90	2.6	4.3	5.9	7.3	8.7	10.1	11.5	12.8	14.1	15.4	16.7
100	2.3	3.9	5.3	6.6	7.9	9.1	10.3	11.5	12.7	13.9	15.0
125	1.9	3.1	4.3	5.3	6.3	7.3	8.3	9.3	10.2	11.2	12.1
150	1.6	2.6	3.6	4.4	5.3	6.1	7.0	7.8	8.6	9.4	10.1
200	1.2	2.0	2.7	3.4	4.0	4.6	5.3	5.9	6.5	7.1	7.6
300	0.8	1.3	1.8	2.3	2.7	3.1	3.5	3.9	4.3	4.7	5.1
400	0.6	1.0	1.4	1.7	2.0	2.4	2.7	3.0	3.3	3.6	3.9
500	0.5	0.8	1.1	1.4	1.6	1.9	2.1	2.4	2.6	2.9	3.1

Note: These tables present upper limits (body of table) as percentages. These tables assume a large population.

5% risk (95% confidence level) that the control deviation rate could be more than 6% in the population—not just in the sample. To make the correct evaluation, the auditor uses Table 1 of *Exhibit* 8.6, moves down the first column to find 80 as the sample size, and moves to the right under the column of three failures, and finds a figure of 9.5. What does that 9.5 mean? It means that the auditor is 95% confident that the upper limit of the real deviation rate in the population does not exceed 9.5%. Stated another way, there is a 5% chance that the real deviation rate exceeds 9.5 %. The auditor had set an upper limit of 6%, and this 9.5% clearly exceeds that limit. The control testing does not support a conclusion that the control is operating effectively. The auditor needs to assess control risk as higher than was originally set and, further, must perform a qualitative evaluation of the deviations detected.

One point to notice when examining *Exhibit* 8.6 is that the upper limit of deviations is greater than zero even when no deviations are detected in the sample. For example, consider the case where risk of overreliance is 5%, sample size is 20, and no deviations are detected. In this case, the upper limit of deviations from *Exhibit 8.6* is 14%. The reason for this result is that the sample size is very low, so there is a strong possibility that even though the auditor detected no deviations in the sample of 20 items, deviations exist that the auditor failed to detect. Taking this case a bit further, assume the same facts, but move down *Exhibit 8.6* to the row where sample size is doubled to 40. In this case, notice that the upper limit of deviations when no deviations are detected falls dramatically to just 7.3%.

Qualitative Evaluation   When control deviations are found, they should be analyzed *qualitatively* as well as *quantitatively*. The auditor should try to determine whether the failures (1) were intentional or unintentional, (2) were random or systematic, (3) had a direct dollar effect on the account balance, or (4) were of such magnitude that a material misstatement could occur and not be detected.

The auditor is much more concerned if the control failures appear to be *intentional*, which might indicate fraud. If the failures are *systematic*, the auditor should be cautious in deciding to isolate the problem and reducing substantive testing. For example, if all of the failures were related to pricing errors—and all were connected to one sales associate—the auditor may expand audit testing to review all of the transactions related to that one sales associate. However, the auditor should not typically reduce substantive testing in other areas because the identified errors appear to be isolated to the one sales associate. The sampling evidence may be signaling that there are other isolated failures that did not happen to appear in the sample.

Often, a failure in a control does not lead directly to dollar misstatements in the accounting records. Lack of proper approval for payment of a vendor's invoice, for example, does not necessarily mean that the invoice should not have been paid. While it may have been an appropriate invoice, it might also have been a fictitious invoice.

Linkage of Test of Controls to Substantive Procedures   In addition to being the basis of a report on internal controls, the tests of controls are used to determine whether the nature, timing, or extent of the planned substantive procedures needs to be modified. For example, if the tests of controls indicate that the client is not careful about assuring that shipment has taken place before billing and recording a sale, the auditor may need to increase sales cutoff testing and/or concentrate on sales recorded just before the balance sheet date. If credit approvals are not working correctly, the auditor will have to take more time to determine whether the allowance for doubtful accounts is reasonable. Additional testing of subsequent collections and follow-up on old, uncollected balances may be needed. In general, if controls are not operating effectively, the auditor will increase the assessment of control risk and will likely choose to rely less on substantive analytical procedures and more on tests of details for those accounts related to identified control failures.

When the auditor concludes that a control is not operating effectively based on attributes sampling, the auditor can pursue the following alternative courses of action:

- A compensating control could be identified and tested. The decision to test the compensating control will depend on the perceived effectiveness of the control and the additional cost to test the control procedure.
- A larger sample could be taken, but this is not likely to be cost-beneficial unless the auditor has reason to believe the original sample was not representative.

- The assessment of control risk can be set higher than originally planned and the nature, timing, and/or the extent of the related substantive tests can be modified. If the upper limit of the possible deviation rate does not exceed the tolerable failure rate by very much, this modification could be very slight. For example, if the upper limit was 5.4% and the tolerable rate was 5%, very little modification is needed.
- The auditor will analyze the nature of the control deviations and determine the implications on the type of misstatements, or causes of misstatements, that might occur in the financial statements and adjust the nature, timing, and/or extent of the planned substantive testing.

Step 7. Document All Phases of the Sampling Process

All of the preceding steps and related decisions regarding the sampling process should be documented to allow for appropriate supervision and provide adequate support for the conclusions reached.

Nonstatistical Sampling Approach to Testing Controls

If the auditor chooses to use nonstatistical sampling procedures to test the operating effectiveness of controls, the planning factors are often not quantified. Instead, the auditor addresses deviation rates through the more global concepts of none, few, and many. Sampling risk is often set as low, moderate, or high. The effect of these factors on sample size follows:

Factor	Condition Leading To	
	Smaller Sample	Larger Sample
Tolerable deviation rate	High	Low
Expected population deviation rate	Low	High
Sampling risk (risk of overreliance)	High	Low
Population size	Little effect	Little effect

Even by making these subjective judgments, the auditor cannot quantitatively assess the risk of making an incorrect inference based on the sample results. For this reason, many auditors who use nonstatistical sampling should review the factors and select a sample size consistent with a statistically determined sample.

Using Sampling to Gather Evidence About Misstatements in Account Balances and Associated Assertions

LO 5 Describe the sampling process used to gather evidence about misstatements in account balances and assertions.

Auditors follow certain steps in sampling account balances and associated assertions, regardless of whether they are using statistical or nonstatistical sampling. Next, we discuss these steps and follow up with certain unique issues concerning nonstatistical sampling for substantive tests of account balances and associated assertions.

Steps in Sampling Account Balances and Associated Assertions

The basic steps involved in sampling for substantive tests of details are the same whether nonstatistical or statistical sampling approaches are used:

1. Specify the audit objective of the test and define a misstatement.
2. Define the population from which the sample is to be taken.
3. Choose an appropriate sampling method.
4. Determine the sample size.

5. Select sample items and perform the substantive procedure.
6. Evaluate the sample results.
7. Document all phases of the sampling process.

Step 1. Specify the Audit Objective of the Test and Define a Misstatement

A sampling plan for tests of details is typically designed to provide assurance regarding one or more financial statement assertions (e.g., existence of accounts receivable). Specifying the audit objective determines the population to test. For example, if the objective is to determine the existence of customer balances, the sample should be selected from the recorded balances. If the objective is to determine the completeness of accounts payable, the sample should be selected from a complementary population, such as cash disbursements made after the balance sheet date. The auditor looks for payments for goods and services received by the balance sheet date that should be payable at year-end but that were not recorded until after year-end. Populations involving the testing of the existence assertion are generally easy to define because they include all recorded transactions. On the other hand, populations involving the completeness assertion are more difficult to define because some of those transactions may not yet be recorded.

Misstatements should be defined before beginning the sampling application to preclude the client or auditor from rationalizing away misstatements as isolated events and provide guidance to the audit team. A **misstatement** is a dollar amount of misstatement, either intentional or unintentional, that exists in a transaction or financial statement account balance. When sampling for substantive tests of details, a misstatement involves differences between recorded values and audited values. For example, if a cash payment were posted to the wrong customer's subsidiary account, the overall account balance would still be correct and should not be considered a misstatement. Even so, the auditor should carefully follow up on this finding to be sure it is not evidence of a cover-up of an employee's misappropriation of cash. If, however, the client inappropriately billed a customer before the end of the period, the premature billing would be considered a misstatement because the overall receivable balance would be overstated at the end of the period.

Misstatements are categorized as factual misstatements or projected misstatements. **Factual misstatements** are those that have been specifically identified and about which there is no doubt, such as a difference identified in a sample item or an item in a population examined 100%. Factual misstatements are also referred to as **known misstatements**. Projected misstatements are developed by extrapolation from the factual misstatements in sample items to the population. **Projected misstatements** are those that are the auditor's best estimate of the misstatements in a given population based on the sample results; they are a projection of the misstatements identified in an audit sample to the entire population from which the sample was drawn. Projected misstatements are also referred to as **likely misstatements**. The total factual and projected misstatement (can be referred to as total estimated misstatement) is compared with the tolerable misstatement when evaluating the sample results.

Auditors also need to define tolerable misstatement and expected misstatement. The AICPA's 2012 *Audit Sampling* formally defines a **tolerable misstatement** as a monetary amount set by the auditor in respect of which the auditor seeks to obtain an appropriate level of assurance that the monetary amount set by the auditor is not exceeded by the actual misstatement in the population. In more practical terms, a tolerable misstatement is the maximum amount of misstatement the auditor can accept in the population without requiring an audit adjustment or a qualified audit opinion.

Recall that tolerable misstatement is the application of performance materiality to a particular sampling procedure. Tolerable misstatement may be the same amount or an amount smaller than performance materiality (e.g., when the population from which the sample is selected is smaller than the account balance). When planning a sample for a test of details, the auditor should identify the maximum monetary misstatement in the account balance that, when combined with misstatements found in other tests, would cause the financial statements to be materially misstated. Tolerable misstatement is based on planning materiality for the account balance. Different audit firms have different approaches to determine tolerable misstatement. Some firms arbitrarily set tolerable misstatement at 75% of planning materiality. Other firms have a more quantified approach.

An **expected misstatement** is the level of misstatement that the auditor expects to detect, and it is based on projected misstatements in prior-year audits, results of other substantive tests, professional judgment, and knowledge of changes in personnel and the accounting system. It is usually desirable to be conservative and use a slightly larger expected misstatement than is actually anticipated. This conservative approach may marginally increase the sample size, but it minimizes sampling risk. If expected misstatement is greater than tolerable misstatement, sampling is not appropriate unless it is used to estimate the size of the required adjustment to the account balance.

Step 2. Define the Population From Which the Sample Is to Be Taken

The population is that group of items in an account balance that the auditor wants to test. The population, as defined for sampling purposes, does not include any items that the auditor has decided to examine 100% or items that will be tested separately. Because sample results can be projected to only that group of items from which the sample is selected, it is important to properly define the population. For example, a sample selected from the inventory at one location can be used to estimate the amount of misstatement only at that location, not at other locations.

Define the Sampling Unit   Sampling units are the individual auditable elements and often are made up of individual account balances. However, a sampling unit for confirming accounts receivable could be the individual customer's balance, individual unpaid invoices, or a combination of these two. The choice depends on effectiveness and efficiency of the process and the manner in which the client has recorded the individual items. Some customers are more likely to return a confirmation when asked to confirm one unpaid invoice rather than verify the correctness of an entire account balance. If a customer does not return a positive confirmation, alternative procedures must be performed, including identifying subsequent payments and/or vouching the sales transactions to supporting documents. If customers typically pay by invoice, it will be more efficient to perform alternative procedures on individual invoices than on total balances.

Completeness of the Population   A sample is selected from a physical representation of the population, such as a list of customer balances or a computer file. The auditor needs assurance that the list accurately represents the population. A common procedure is to foot the list and reconcile it with the general ledger.

Identify Individually Significant Items   Many account balances are composed of a few relatively large items and many smaller items. A significant portion of the total value of many accounting populations is concentrated in a relatively few large-dollar items. Because of this, the auditor often will examine all the large-dollar items. These large-dollar items are often referred to as the top stratum. **Top-stratum** items are population items whose book values exceed the sampling interval and are therefore all included in the sample. Because the auditor knows the amount of errors in the top stratum (all items were evaluated), no estimate or projection of errors is required. The remaining items are then sampled using one of the sampling methods described in this chapter. **Lower-stratum** items are those that are not in the top stratum. The audit results reflect the sum of top-stratum items and the projected misstatement based on lower-stratum items.

The auditor often uses judgment to determine the cutoff point for top-stratum items. The division of the population into two or more subgroups is referred to as **stratification**. Stratification of the population into several homogeneous subpopulations generally creates audit efficiency. The stratification process can be enhanced with the use of GAS that has the capability of creating a profile of the population of book values.

Step 3. Choose an Appropriate Sampling Method

Once the auditor has decided to use audit sampling, either nonstatistical or statistical sampling is appropriate for substantive tests of details. The most common statistical approaches for substantive testing are classical variables sampling (beyond the scope of this text) and monetary unit sampling (MUS). MUS, which is discussed in the next section, is a subset of a broader class of procedures, sometimes referred to as **probability proportional to size (PPS) sampling**. The term *PPS* describes a method of sample selection where the probability of an item's selection for the sample is proportional to its recorded amount; *MUS* is a specific method of PPS that has been developed for auditors. As is common, we use the terms *MUS* and *PPS* interchangeably.

Steps 4, 5, and 6. Determine the Sample Size, Select the Sample Items, Perform the Substantive Procedure, and Evaluate the Sample Results

Determining the sample size, the method of selecting the sample, and the approach to evaluating the sample results depend on the sampling method used. Whatever sampling method is chosen, consideration must be given to the risk of misstatement in the account, sampling risk, and the auditor's assessment of tolerable and expected misstatement. If a statistical sampling method is employed, the sample must be selected randomly to give each item in the population an equal chance to be included in the sample. The auditor should perform appropriate follow-up work when the audit results indicate a more than expected likelihood of material misstatement.

Unacceptable Sample Results When the total estimated misstatement (the sum of the total factual and projected misstatement) exceeds the tolerable misstatement, the auditor has several possible courses of action. The auditor can:

- *Ask the client to correct the factual misstatements*—If this is done, the total estimated misstatement can be adjusted for those corrections but not for the projection of misstatements associated with those items. In some cases, simply correcting the factual misstatement can bring the total estimated misstatement below the auditor's tolerable misstatement level.
- *Analyze the detected misstatements for common problem(s)*—When misstatements are discovered, the auditor should look beyond the quantitative aspects of the misstatements to understand the nature and cause of the misstatements—especially to determine if there is a systematic pattern to the misstatements. If a systematic pattern is found, the client

can be asked to investigate and make an estimate of the correction needed. The auditor can review and test this estimate. Further, the auditor can recommend improvements to prevent such errors in the future. For example, assume several confirmation replies indicate that merchandise was returned prior to year-end but credit was not recorded until the subsequent year. A careful review of receiving reports related to merchandise returned prior to year-end and of credits recorded in the subsequent year will provide evidence regarding the extent of the needed correction. The auditor should also consider the relationship of the misstatements to other phases of the audit; problems in recording receivables may also reveal problems in the accuracy of recorded sales.

- *Design an alternative audit strategy*—Discovering more misstatements than expected in the risk assessment phase of the audit suggests that the planning assumptions may have been incorrect and that internal controls were not as effective as originally assessed. In such cases, the auditor should plan the rest of the audit accordingly. For public companies, significant problems with internal control will cause the auditor to consider whether it is necessary to express an adverse opinion on the effectiveness of the client's internal controls over financial reporting.

- *Expand the sample*—The auditor can calculate the additional sample size needed by substituting the most likely misstatement from the sample evaluation for the original expected misstatement in the sample interval formula and determine a new interval and total sample size based on the new expectations. The number of additional sample items can then be determined by subtracting the original sample size from the new sample size. The new sampling interval can be used for selection of items not already included in the sample.

- *Change the audit objective to estimating the correct value*—In cases where material misstatements are likely, it may be necessary to change from an objective of testing details to an objective of estimating the correct population value. A lower detection risk and a smaller tolerable misstatement should be used because the auditor is no longer testing the balance but is estimating the correct population value from the sample. The auditor will expect the client to adjust the book value to the estimated value. A larger sample size will normally be required.

Step 7. Document All Phases of the Sampling Process

All of the preceding steps and related decisions regarding the sampling process should be documented to allow for appropriate supervision and provide adequate support for the conclusions reached.

Nonstatistical Sampling for Substantive Tests of Account Balances and Associated Assertions

Nonstatistical samples should be based on the same audit considerations as those used for statistical sampling. There is no way to mathematically control for and measure sampling risk in a nonstatistical sample; the auditor can project only the detected misstatements and make a professional judgment as to whether the account is likely to be materially misstated and then decide whether more audit work is needed.

In determining sample size, all significant items should be tested. The auditor should select all items over a specific dollar amount, and then, depending on audit objectives, select items with other characteristics, such as sales billed in the last week or billed to specific parties. The sample size of the other items to be tested should be based on the same factors used in statistical sampling. In terms of selecting the sample, the auditor should take steps to increase the likelihood that the sample is representative of the population. The auditor may obtain a representative sample using a random-based method or haphazard sampling.

In terms of evaluating the sample results, misstatements found in a sample must be projected to the population. For example, assume the auditor is using nonstatistical sampling to confirm accounts receivable. All twenty-one customer balances equal to or greater than $50,000 were confirmed. These items comprise the top stratum. A random sample of the lower stratum of 190 balances less than $50,000 was confirmed. The details are presented in the following table:

	Population		Sample		
	Number	Amount	Number	Amount	Factual Misstatement
>=$50,000	21	$2,000,000	21	$2,000,000	$1,500
<$50,000	190	$2,500,000	19	$310,000	$900
Total	211	$4,500,000	40	$2,310,000	$2,400

The factual misstatement of $1,500 in the top stratum needs no projection to the population because all of these items were tested. However, factual misstatements in the lower stratum could be projected to the rest of the lower stratum as follows:

$$\$900/\$310,000 \times \$2,500,000 = \$7,258$$

Therefore, the total factual and projected misstatement is estimated to be $8,758 ($1,500 + $7,258). The $8,758 is the auditor's best estimate, but of course there is some probability that the actual amount may be higher. Tolerable misstatement is $150,000. Because $8,758 is so much smaller than the tolerable misstatement, there is an ample cushion between the tolerable misstatement and the factual and projected misstatement. Therefore, the auditor would be reasonable in concluding that there is a low risk of material misstatement in the account.

Statistical Sampling for Substantive Tests of Account Balances and Associated Assertions: Monetary Unit Sampling (MUS)

LO 6 Describe monetary unit sampling and use it to test account balances and assertions.

Monetary unit sampling (MUS) is a sampling method based on attributes sampling, but involving dollar misstatements rather than control failure rates. MUS is a widely used statistical sampling method because it results in an efficient sample size and concentrates on the dollar value of the account balances. It has been developed especially for use in auditing and has been given various names, including dollar-unit sampling, PPS, and combined attributes-variables sampling. MUS was designed to be especially effective in testing for overstatements in situations when few or no misstatements are expected.

Summary of MUS Strengths and Weaknesses

As an auditor considers whether to use MUS as the sampling approach for substantive tests of details, it is helpful to review its strengths and weaknesses. Strengths of MUS include:

- MUS is generally easier to apply than other statistical sampling approaches.
- MUS automatically selects a sample in proportion to an item's dollar amount, thus providing automatic stratification of the sample.
- If the auditor expects (and finds) no misstatements, MUS usually results in a highly efficient sample size.

Examples of the circumstances in which MUS might be used include:

- Accounts receivable confirmations (when credit balances are not significant)
- Loans receivable confirmations (e.g., real-estate mortgage loans, commercial loans, and installment loans)
- Inventory price tests in which the auditor anticipates relatively few misstatements and the population is not expected to contain a significant number of large understatements
- Fixed-asset additions tests where existence is the relevant assertion

The auditor should also be aware of difficulties in using MUS:

- MUS is not designed to test for the understatement of a population.
- If an auditor identifies understatements in a MUS sample, evaluation of the sample requires special considerations.
- Selection of zero or negative balances requires special design considerations.

Some of the circumstances in which MUS might not be the most appropriate approach include:

- Accounts receivable confirmations in which a large number of credit balances exist
- Inventory test counts and price tests for which the auditor anticipates a significant number of misstatements that can be both understatements and overstatements

Designing and Selecting a MUS Sample

The population for MUS is defined as the number of dollars in the population being tested. Each dollar in the population has an equal chance of being chosen, but each dollar chosen is associated with a tangible item such as a customer's balance or an inventory item, so items with more dollars have a greater likelihood of being selected.

The sample size in a MUS sample is a function of the following factors: (1) the risk of incorrect acceptance, (2) the ratio of expected misstatement to tolerable misstatement, and (3) the ratio of tolerable misstatement to the total population value. *Exhibit 8.7* provides a table that auditors use to determine the appropriate sample size for MUS. Note that the AICPA's 2012 *Audit Sampling* also presents other alternative methods of sample selection; we use one method for simplicity.

As an example to illustrate the use of *Exhibit 8.7*, if the risk of incorrect acceptance is 10%, tolerable misstatement is 5% of population dollars, and expected misstatement is 20% of tolerable misstatement (in other words, 1% of the population dollars), the auditor identifies a sample size of 69 units.

One complexity that you will encounter when using *Exhibit 8.7* is that sometimes the ratio of expected to tolerable misstatement or tolerable misstatement as a percentage of the population will not be even numbers that appear in the table. For example, the ratio of expected to tolerable misstatement may be 24.5%, and the ratio of tolerable misstatement to the population may be 3.5%. To address this complexity, you can round the numbers in either case to ensure that an adequate sample size is obtained. For the ratio of expected to tolerable misstatement, you can round up to 30% because that will yield a larger sample size than if you had rounded down to 20%. For the tolerable misstatement as a percentage of the population, you can round down to 3% because that will yield a larger sample size than if you had rounded up to 4%.

| EXHIBIT **8.7** | Monetary Unit Sample Size Determination Table |

Tolerable Misstatement as a Percentage of Population

Risk of Incorrect Acceptance	Ratio of Expected to Tolerable Misstatement	50%	30%	10%	8%	6%	5%	4%	3%	2%	1%	0.50%	Expected Sum of Taints
5%	—	6	10	30	38	50	60	75	100	150	300	600	—
5%	0.10	8	13	37	46	62	74	92	123	184	368	736	0.37
5%	0.20	10	16	47	58	78	93	116	155	232	463	925	0.93
5%	0.30	12	20	60	75	100	120	150	200	300	600	1,199	1.80
5%	0.40	17	27	81	102	135	162	203	270	405	809	1,618	3.24
5%	0.50	24	39	116	145	193	231	289	385	577	1,154	2,308	5.77
10%	—	5	8	24	29	39	47	58	77	116	231	461	—
10%	0.20	7	12	35	43	57	69	86	114	171	341	682	0.69
10%	0.30	9	15	44	55	73	87	109	145	217	433	866	1.30
10%	0.40	12	20	58	72	96	115	143	191	286	572	1,144	2.29
10%	0.50	16	27	80	100	134	160	200	267	400	799	1,597	4.00
15%	—	4	7	19	24	32	38	48	64	95	190	380	—
15%	0.20	6	10	28	35	46	55	69	91	137	273	545	0.55
15%	0.30	7	12	35	43	57	69	86	114	171	341	681	1.03
15%	0.40	9	15	45	56	74	89	111	148	221	442	883	1.77
15%	0.50	13	21	61	76	101	121	151	202	302	604	1,208	3.02
20%	—	4	6	17	21	27	33	41	54	81	161	322	—
20%	0.20	5	8	23	29	38	46	57	76	113	226	451	0.46
20%	0.30	6	10	28	35	47	56	70	93	139	277	554	0.84
20%	0.40	8	12	36	45	59	71	89	118	177	354	707	1.42
20%	0.50	10	16	48	60	80	95	119	159	238	475	949	2.38
25%	—	3	5	14	18	24	28	35	47	70	139	278	—
25%	0.20	4	7	19	24	32	38	48	64	95	190	380	0.38
25%	0.30	5	8	23	29	39	46	58	77	115	230	460	0.69
25%	0.40	6	10	29	37	49	58	73	97	145	289	578	1.16
25%	0.50	8	13	38	48	64	76	95	127	190	380	760	1.90
30%	—	3	5	13	16	21	25	31	41	61	121	241	—
30%	0.20	4	6	17	21	27	33	41	54	81	162	323	0.33
30%	0.40	5	8	24	30	40	48	60	80	120	239	477	0.96
30%	0.60	9	15	43	54	71	85	107	142	213	425	850	2.55
35%	—	3	4	11	14	18	21	27	35	53	105	210	—
35%	0.20	3	5	14	18	23	28	35	46	69	138	276	0.28
35%	0.40	4	7	20	25	34	40	50	67	100	199	397	0.80
35%	0.60	7	12	34	43	57	68	85	113	169	338	676	2.03
50%	—	2	3	7	9	12	14	18	24	35	70	139	—
50%	0.20	2	3	9	11	15	18	22	29	44	87	173	0.18
50%	0.40	3	4	12	15	19	23	29	38	57	114	228	0.46
50%	0.60	4	6	17	22	29	34	43	57	85	170	340	1.02

Source: *Audit Sampling* (New York: AICPA, 2012), 152–154. Reprinted with permission from AICPA; copyright © 2012 by American Institute of Certified Public Accountants.

Once the auditor has determined the appropriate sample size, a sampling interval is calculated by dividing the population size by the sample size. Thus,

$$Sampling\ Interval = Population\ Size \div Sample\ Size$$

The sample is then selected using the fixed-interval approach—every *n*th dollar is selected after choosing a random start, which is required to give every dollar in the population an equal chance of being included in the sample. Each selected dollar acts as a hook for the entire physical unit in which it occurs, such as a customer's account balance or the extended cost of an inventory item.

For illustration purposes, assume that the auditor calculates the sampling interval to be 22,348. If the sample is to be selected manually, it will be easier if a rounded interval is used, such as $22,000. Rounding the interval down (rather than up) assures that the sample size will be adequate. The random start should be between 1 and the sampling interval (1 to 22,000 in the illustration). This random start number can be obtained from a variety of sources, including the serial number of a dollar bill, a random number table, or a computer-generated random number.

A calculator or GAS can be used to select the sample. If a calculator is used, clear the calculator, enter the random start, add each book value, and subtotal after each entry, giving a cumulative total for each item. This process is illustrated in *Exhibit 8.8* using a random start of $20,000. The first sample item is the one that first causes the cumulative total to equal or exceed the sampling interval (Customer 2 in *Exhibit 8.8*). Successive sample items are those first causing the cumulative total to equal or exceed multiples of the intervals ($44,000, $66,000, $88,000, and so forth).

As noted previously, the probability of selecting any particular item is proportional to the number of dollars in it. For example, if the sampling interval is $22,000, a customer's balance of $220 would have a 1% chance (220/22,000) of being included in the sample. A customer with a book value of $2,200 has a 10% chance of being selected. There is a 100% chance of including the balance of a customer whose book value is $22,000 or greater.

EXHIBIT **8.8**	Fixed Interval Sample Selection				
Customer	Book Value ($)	Cumulative Book	Cumulative Book Plus Random Start ($)	Included in Sample?	Selection Amount ($)
	Random start	0	20,000		
1	220	220	20,220		
2	2,200	2,420	22,420	(Yes)	22,000
3	22,000	24,420	44,420	(Yes)	44,000
4	880	25,300	45,300		
5	6,128	31,428	51,428		
6	2,800	34,228	54,228		
7	45,023	79,251	99,251	(Yes)	66,000 & 88,000
8	10	79,261	99,261		
9	8,231	87,492	107,492		
10	16,894	104,386	124,386	(Yes)	110,000
.	.	.	.		.
.	.	.	.		.
.	.	.	.		.
450	1,900	807,906	827,906		

All items with a book value equal to or greater than the interval will be selected for auditor evaluation. As previously noted, these items are referred to as top-stratum items. The balance for Customer 7 has two selection points, but it will be examined only once. Thus, the number of **logical units** (customer balances) will be less than the sample size of dollar units. The population has effectively been divided into two groups: the top-stratum items and the lower-stratum items. The sample selection process uses dollar-based stratification and focuses the auditor on large-dollar coverage with relatively small sample sizes.

This selection method also tests the mathematical accuracy of the population. Note in *Exhibit 8.8* that the last cumulative amount is $827,906. This represents the population total of $807,906 plus the random start of $20,000.

Zero and Negative Balances Population items with zero balances have no chance of being selected using PPS sampling. If evaluation of sampling units with zero balances is necessary to achieve the audit objective of the test, they should be segregated and audited as a different population. Population items with negative balances require special consideration. For example, credit balances in customer accounts represent liabilities; the client owes money, merchandise, or service. An approach to dealing with negative items is to exclude them from the selection process and test them as a separate population; this should be done when a significant number of such items are included in the population. Another approach is to change the sign of the negative items and add them to the population before selection. This approach is generally used only when there are few negative items and few or no misstatements are expected.

Evaluating a MUS Sample

PPS sampling is designed to determine the likelihood that the account balance may exceed tolerable misstatement. In other words, if the auditor designs the sample with a 15% risk of incorrect acceptance and a tolerable misstatement of $50,000, the auditor is testing the hypothesis that there is no more than a 15% probability that misstatements related to the assertion being tested can cause the account balance to be overstated by more than $50,000.

When evaluating the MUS sample results, the auditor calculates the total estimated misstatement in the account balance based on the sampling process. This total includes the following four components:

- *Factual misstatement for items in the top stratum*
- **Basic precision**—The amount of uncertainty associated with testing only a part of the population (sampling risk). Basic precision is the amount of error you are confident of not exceeding if no errors are detected in the sample. Basic precision is calculated as the sampling interval multiplied by a confidence factor. See *Exhibit 8.9* for the confidence factors.
- *Projected misstatement for items in the lower stratum*—The best estimate of the actual amount of dollar misstatements in the population based on projecting the sample results to the population. The projected misstatement is calculated as the sampling interval multiplied by the tainting percentage. The terms *likely misstatement* or **most likely misstatement** are also used to refer to projected misstatement.
- **Incremental allowance for sampling risk**—An increase in the total estimated misstatement caused by the statistical properties of misstatements detected in the lower stratum.

The calculation of the total estimated misstatement will differ depending on whether misstatements are detected, as depicted in *Exhibit 8.10*.

| EXHIBIT **8.9** | Confidence Factors for Sample Evaluation |

Number of Overstatement Misstatements	Risk of Incorrect Acceptance								
	5%	**10%**	**15%**	**20%**	**25%**	**30%**	**35%**	**37%**	**50%**
0	3.00	2.31	1.90	1.61	1.39	1.21	1.05	1.00	0.70
1	4.75	3.89	3.38	3.00	2.70	2.44	2.22	2.14	1.68
2	6.30	5.33	4.73	4.28	3.93	3.62	3.35	3.25	2.68
3	7.76	6.69	6.02	5.52	5.11	4.77	4.46	4.35	3.68
4	9.16	8.00	7.27	6.73	6.28	5.90	5.55	5.43	4.68
5	10.52	9.28	8.50	7.91	7.43	7.01	6.64	6.50	5.68
6	11.85	10.54	9.71	9.08	8.56	8.12	7.72	7.57	6.67
7	13.15	11.78	10.90	10.24	9.69	9.21	8.79	8.63	7.67
8	14.44	13.00	12.08	11.38	10.81	10.31	9.85	9.68	8.67
9	15.71	14.21	13.25	12.52	11.92	11.39	10.92	10.74	9.67
10	16.97	15.41	14.42	13.66	13.02	12.47	11.98	11.79	10.67
11	18.21	16.60	15.57	14.78	14.13	13.55	13.04	12.84	11.67
12	19.45	17.79	16.72	15.90	15.22	14.63	14.09	13.89	12.67
13	20.67	18.96	17.86	17.02	16.32	15.70	15.14	14.93	13.67
14	21.89	20.13	19.00	18.13	17.40	16.77	16.20	15.98	14.67
15	23.10	21.30	20.13	19.24	18.49	17.84	17.25	17.02	15.67
16	24.31	22.46	21.26	20.34	19.58	18.90	18.29	18.06	16.67
17	25.50	23.61	22.39	21.44	20.66	19.97	19.34	19.10	17.67
18	26.70	24.76	23.51	22.54	21.74	21.03	20.38	20.14	18.67
19	27.88	25.91	24.63	23.64	22.81	22.09	21.43	21.18	19.67
20	29.07	27.05	25.74	24.73	23.89	23.15	22.47	22.22	20.67

Source: *Audit Sampling* (New York: AICPA, 2012), 155–156. AICPA audit and accounting guides by AMERICAN INSTITUTE OF CERTIFIED PUBLIC ACCOUNTANTS. Copyright © 2012 Reproduced with permission of AMERICAN INSTITUTE OF CERTIFIED PUBLIC ACCOUNTANTS in the format Textbook via Copyright Clearance Center.

| EXHIBIT **8.10** | Total Estimated Misstatement Calculation Summary |

	If No Misstatements Detected	**If Misstatements Detected**
Factual misstatement in top-stratum	0	Amount of factual misstatement
Basic precision	Interval × confidence factor	Interval × confidence factor
+ Projected misstatement in lower stratum	0	Calculate
+ Incremental allowance for sampling risk in lower stratum	0	Calculate
= Total estimated misstatement	= Basic precision	Sum of the four

No Misstatements in the Sample If the auditor finds no misstatements in the sample, the misstatement projection is zero dollars, and the total estimated misstatement will equal basic precision. The basic precision is the amount of error you are confident of not exceeding if no errors are reported for the sample. It is determined by multiplying the sampling interval by the confidence factor for the specified risk of incorrect acceptance (assuming no errors). For example, if the auditor specified a 5% risk of incorrect acceptance, used a $5,000 sampling interval, and detected no misstatements, the total estimated misstatement equals $15,000 (3 × $5,000). Note that "3" is the confidence factor obtained from *Exhibit 8.9* and can be found at the intersection of Number of Overstatement Misstatements = 0 and Risk of Incorrect Acceptance = 5%. If no misstatements are found, the auditor will conclude that the recorded value of the population is not overstated by more than the tolerable misstatement at the specified risk of incorrect acceptance.

Overstatements in the Sample   When misstatements are detected, the evaluation process is more involved because in addition to calculating basic precision, the auditor must also calculate the projected misstatement and the incremental allowance for sampling risk. When evaluating the MUS sample where overstatements have been detected, the auditor begins by identifying the percentage that the book value of each misstated sample item is overstated or understated (referred to as the *tainting percentage*). The **tainting percentage** is the percentage of misstatement present in a logical unit, such as the sample item's book value. The tainting percentage equals the amount of misstatement in the item divided by the item's recorded amount (in other words, the book value). A tainting percentage is calculated for all sample items with misstatement in the lower stratum. The auditor multiplies the tainting percentage by the sampling interval to calculate the projected misstatement for each misstated item.

Illustration   Using the example in *Exhibit 8.8* with a sampling interval of $22,000 and the risk of incorrect acceptance of 15%, assume the following misstatements were found:

Book Value	Audit Value	Misstatement	Tainting Percentage
$45,023	$44,340	$683	NA
$2,000	$1,940	$ 60	3%
$8,300	$8,217	$ 83	1%

There was only one top-stratum misstatement. An item with a book value of $45,023 had an audited value of $44,340—resulting in a $683 top-stratum overstatement. For the top-stratum item, there is no need to obtain a tainting percentage or to project the misstatement because all of the items in the top stratum were audited.

The lower stratum contained two misstatements. The first lower-stratum misstatement was the result of a book value of $2,000 that had an audited value of $1,940, thus yielding an overstatement of $60. The tainting percentage is $60 divided by $2,000 or 3%. Because this item was selected from an interval of $22,000, it is projected that the overstatement is 3% or $660. Similarly, the second misstatement was $83 (book value of $8,300; audit value of $8,217), resulting in a 1% tainting or a projected amount of $220 for the interval. The sum of the projected lower-stratum misstatements is therefore $880. This same result can be obtained by multiplying the sampling interval by the sum of the tainting percentages ($22,000 × 4% = $880). *Exhibit 8.11* summarizes the sample evaluation calculations.

Next, the auditor calculates incremental allowance for sampling risk for the lower-stratum items by completing the following steps. First, list the dollar value of the projected misstatements in descending order and calculate

EXHIBIT 8.11 — Example of Calculation of Total Estimated Misstatement When Overstatements Are Detected

	Confidence Factor*	Tainting Percentage	Sampling Interval	Conclusion
Factual misstatement in top stratum				683
Basic precision	1.9 ×		22,000 =	41,800
Projected misstatement in lower-stratum:				
First largest tainting %		3%		
Second largest tainting %		1%		
		4% ×	22,000 =	880
Incremental allowance for sampling risk in lower-stratum				394**
Total estimated misstatement:				**43,757**

*Confidence factors come from the 15% column in *Exhibit 8.9*.

**See *Exhibit 8.12* and the following discussion for the calculation of this value.

their sum. Second, calculate incremental changes in the confidence factors for each misstatement at the relevant risk of incorrect acceptance. Recall that *Exhibit 8.9* contains the confidence factors. To calculate the incremental changes, subtract the value related to overstatement 0 (in our example, 1.90) from the value related to overstatement 1 (in our example, 3.38), and so on, depending on the number of misstatements detected. Third, multiply the projected misstatements by the incremental change in the confidence. Fourth, sum these values. Fifth, subtract the total projected misstatement from the total value of projected misstatement multiplied by the incremental change in confidence factor. These calculations are summarized in *Exhibit 8.12*.

Adding all four components together, we see that the total estimated misstatement equals $43,757. The statistical conclusion is that the auditor is 85% confident that this population is not overstated by more than $43,757. Because the total estimated misstatement is less than the tolerable misstatement ($50,000), the auditor can conclude that, at the desired level of risk of incorrect acceptance, the population does not contain a material amount of overstatement. If the total estimated misstatement had exceeded the tolerable misstatement, additional audit analysis would have been required (see Unacceptable Sample Results, earlier in this section). In addition to evaluating the quantitative amounts of monetary misstatements, the auditor should consider the qualitative aspects of these misstatements.

EXHIBIT 8.12 — Illustration of Calculating the Incremental Allowance for Sampling Risk

Projected Misstatement	Incremental Changes in Confidence Factor (Step 2)	Projected Misstatement × Factor (Step 3)
660 +	3.38 − 1.90 = 1.48	977 +
220	4.73 − 3.38 = 1.35	297
880 (Step 1)		1,274 (Step 4)
Incremental allowance for sampling risk:		**1,274 − 880 = 394 (Step 5)**

Understatements in the Sample The preceding example assumes that only overstatements were found in the audit sample. However, the auditor may encounter situations in which the account balance may be understated. For example, in addition to the two overstatement misstatements, the auditor might discover that an accounts receivable balance may be understated because the client did not include a freight charge on the invoice. Assume, for example, that an account balance of $500 had omitted a $50 freight charge, yielding a 10% understatement tainting.

When an understatement is encountered, the auditor has two possible courses of action. First, the understatement can be ignored for purposes of this sample evaluation and if there are other audit tests for understatements, this understatement can be included as part of other tests. Alternatively, the auditor can perform a separate analysis specifically for understatements. Although the auditor may use this evaluation approach when there are both over and understatements, the auditor should use caution in drawing any definitive conclusions regarding the amount of understatement in the account. MUS is not designed to test for the understatement of a population. If the auditor has concerns about the understatement of an account, an alternative approach, such as classical variables approach, may be more appropriate.

Using GAS to Obtain Evidence

LO 7 Describe how to use GAS to automate the audit process.

Much of an auditor's work involves gathering evidence on the correctness of an account balance by examining the details making up the balance. For example, the auditor tests accounts receivable by gathering evidence using procedures such as those shown in *Exhibit 8.13*. Fortunately, the auditor can use computer audit tools to increase the efficiency of many audit procedures, including both tests of controls and substantive procedures. Visualize an auditor sitting in a chair with a large paper document (printout) of the year-end accounts receivable list. Then note the general nature of the procedures performed in *Exhibit 8.13*:

- Foot the individual accounts making up the total of accounts receivables
- Age the accounts

EXHIBIT 8.13 Selected Audit Procedures Performed on Detailed Accounts Receivable Records

1. Obtain an aged trial balance of individual customer balances from the client.
2. Foot the trial balance and check to see if it agrees with the general ledger year-end balance.
3. Test the client's aging of the customer balances to determine that individual account balances are correctly classified as current, one to thirty days overdue, and so on. This test can be done by (1) selecting individual account balances and tracing the balances to the subsidiary ledger to determine their appropriate aging or (2) recomputing the client's aging process for selected transactions.
4. Confirm individual account balances directly with customers by selecting:
   a. All customer balances in excess of $50,000
   b. All customer balances that are overdue and higher than $25,000
   c. A random (MUS) statistical sample of the remaining customer balances
5. Print the confirmation requests and send to the customers selected in Step 4.
6. Investigate all nonresponses to the confirmations and those indicating a disagreement with the client balance by examining underlying supporting documents such as contracts, shipping notices, correspondence with the customer, and by searching for evidence of subsequent payments by the customer.
7. Statistically evaluate the sample and make a projection of the potential misstatement in the account balance. Combine the statistical projection with the factual misstatements found through other audit procedures.
8. Analyze the sample results and make a judgment on whether the account balance needs to be adjusted.

Note: These steps represent only selected procedures that would be performed and should not be viewed as a full audit program.

- Select individual items for further audit tests
- Print confirmations
- Statistically evaluate the results
- Make a judgment on the need for an audit adjustment

Now visualize how long it would take to perform those procedures accurately while working with the paper document (printout) and a calculator. Fortunately, software companies have developed GAS programs to aid in performing direct tests of account balances maintained on computer files. Most of these programs, such as ACL, which is included in your text, can be run on a computer with data that are downloaded from the client's files for testing.

Software packages such as ACL are referred to as *GAS*. They are a type of computer-aided audit technique (CAAT). They are designed to perform common audit tasks on a variety of data files. They have become so powerful and versatile that most audit firms no longer need mainframe or specialized audit software, which are now usually employed only for very complex data structures or unique processing, such as selecting information about phone calls from automated files during an audit of a large company like AT&T. Further, applications such as ACL and GAS are often embedded directly within the audit firm's electronic workpaper system.

Tasks Performed by GAS

GAS is valuable not only when performing year-end audits but also when searching for fraud (e.g., searching for duplicate payments made to vendors). The software is relatively easy to use and can operate in many different environments. The following are descriptions of various types of tasks performed by GAS.

Analyze a File Before performing detailed testing, the auditor often wants to gain an understanding of the composition of items making up a population. For example, the auditor might want a graphical analysis of the dollar amounts of individual account balances, such as those that are above or below a certain dollar amount. Alternatively, the auditor might want the audit software to develop a graph of the account balance by deciles. In many cases, the auditor wants to know some combination, such as the number of items past due profiled by dollar amount. GAS is user oriented and can develop profiles of the data for audit analysis.

Select Transactions Based on Logical Identifiers Auditors often need to review transactions or the details that make up account balances and may be interested in those that meet specific criteria. For example, the auditor may want to confirm all customer balances above a specific dollar limit and all those that are past due by a specific period of time. Audit software enables the auditor to select transactions based on the Boolean logic operators: IF, GREATER THAN, LESS THAN, EQUAL TO, NOT EQUAL TO, OR, and AND. This combination of operators gives the auditor great flexibility in selecting transactions. For example, the auditor could extract unpaid invoices greater than $50,000 or greater than thirty days overdue by using the equation:

$$AMOUNT > 50000 \textbf{ OR } INVDATE < \text{`}20151201\text{'}$$

This command would result in the selection of all transactions that (a) are over $50,000 in value and (b) were billed before December 1, 2015. On the other hand, the following equation using the logical AND would result in the selection of only items that met both conditions:

$$AMOUNT > 50000 \textbf{ AND } INVDATE < \text{`}20151201\text{'}$$

This command would extract only account balances over thirty days old that exceeded $50,000.

Select Samples On virtually every audit, the auditor selects samples. ACL can be used to select PPS samples, attributes samples, simple random samples, and judgmental samples. Alternatively, by using GAS such as ACL, the auditor may be able to audit the whole population rather than taking a sample, for example, when examining subsequent cash receipts for assessing whether accounts receivable existed at the balance sheet date.

Evaluate Samples ACL saves the selected sample of book values to facilitate statistical evaluation. The auditor needs only to input the exceptions for statistical evaluation and sample projection—including analysis of both top and lower strata. The audited data can be statistically evaluated at the risk levels and tolerable error limits specified by the auditor. Further, GAS can stratify the data so that, for example, all items in excess of materiality will be tested.

Print Confirmations ACL is used to select account balances for independent confirmation by outsiders, such as customers, and can print and prepare the confirmations for mailing.

Analyze Overall File Validity Most computer applications contain edit controls to detect and prevent transactions from being recorded in error. Although the auditor can test the correct functioning of these controls by other means, audit software can assist in evaluating the effectiveness of the controls by reading the computer file and comparing individual items with control parameters to determine whether edit controls were overridden. For example, assume the auditor has tested a control procedure that limits credit to individual customers in accordance with the credit department's rating of the customer. The credit department rates each customer on a 1-to-5 scale, with a 5 representing the least credit risk. A rating of 1 might indicate that shipments can be made only on a prepayment basis, and a rating of 2 might indicate that the total credit cannot exceed $5,000. The auditor uses the software to compare customers' account balances with the maximum specified by the credit policy and generates a printout of each account balance that exceeds the specified credit limit.

Generate Control Totals The auditor needs assurance that the correct client file is being used. For example, assume that the auditor wishes to query the accounts receivable file containing 13,000 individual records and a balance of $75,482,919. ACL automatically generates control totals such as a record count, the number of debit and credit balances, the largest and smallest balances, and a total of the balance to verify the integrity of the population.

Perform Numerical Analyses One of the more interesting features of GAS is the ability to perform numerical analyses. A mathematician named Benford studied the nature of numerical patterns and observed that the patterns of numbers across many different applications are about the same. For example, if sales invoices or payroll checks have five-digit numbers, Benford's Law would predict the first digit to be the number 1 about 30% of the time. His analysis also predicts the expected frequency of specific numbers occurring as the second number, and so forth, in a five-digit number. His results are remarkable and the predictive ability of Benford's Law is extremely high.

Interestingly, most people committing fraud go to great lengths in perpetrating and covering up the fraud. However, they usually have to assign numbers to documents and, not surprisingly, those numbers often do not follow the patterns of numbers naturally occurring in practice. It is not surprising, because the person who is perpetrating the fraud makes up the numbers, and it is extremely difficult to anticipate the occurrence of every digit in a five-, eight-, or even ten-digit number.

Perform Other Tasks   GAS can also be used complete tasks such as:

- Footing a file
- Obtaining file statistics (totals, minimum/maximum/average values)
- Performing analytical review techniques, such as identifying slow-moving inventory and extracting those items for further audit review
- Finding how many transactions or population items meet specified criteria
- Checking for gaps in processing sequences
- Checking for duplicates (e.g., paying the same vendor twice)
- Doing arithmetic calculations
- Preparing custom reports
- Analyzing data for file validity (e.g., missing data and fields with inappropriate values)

Benefits of Using GAS

GAS can be used to assist in testing internal control assertions and virtually every assertion related to financial statement account balances—as well as supporting testing of assertions through other means, such as selecting samples to send confirmations on accounts receivable balances. The *Auditing in Practice* feature "Using GAS to Test Financial Account Assertions— Receivables" illustrates the breadth of GAS in testing assertions related to accounts receivable.

Advantages of using GAS as part of the audit include the following:

- The software is independent of the system being audited and simply needs a read-only copy of the file to avoid any corruption of an organization's data.
- The software includes many audit-specific routines, such as sampling.

Using GAS to Test Financial Account Assertions—Receivables

AUDITING IN **PRACTICE**

(Illustrative examples—not a comprehensive listing)

Assertion	Use of GAS
Existence/occurrence	1. Statistically select samples for distributing confirmations 2. Compare sales invoices with shipping documents and/or sales contracts 3. Select data to perform sales cutoff tests around year-end
Completeness	1. Select data to perform sales cutoff tests around year-end 2. Select a sample of shipping documents and electronically compare with invoices to determine if billed in the proper period
Rights or obligations	1. Statistically select samples for distributing confirmations 2. Select contracts for audit review
Valuation	1. Foot the file 2. Age accounts receivable 3. Statistically evaluate sample results and make projections of misstatements 4. Build an estimation on uncollectible accounts based on past collection data 5. Create a file of current-year write-offs to compare with previous years
Presentation and Disclosure	Not applicable

- The software can provide documentation of each test performed in the software that can be used as documentation in the auditor's workpapers.
- GAS can help auditors be more efficient in completing their audit responsibilities related to gathering and evaluating audit evidence.

SUMMARY AND NEXT STEPS

Two commonly used tools in gathering audit evidence include sampling and GAS. Auditors use sampling—both nonstatistical and statistical—in testing controls and in performing tests of details. Attributes sampling is a frequently used statistical approach for testing internal controls, and MUS is used for testing account balances for overstatement. GAS is used extensively to automate aspects of the audit, including analyzing client data, selecting transactions for testing, and selecting and evaluating samples.

Looking ahead, the next five chapters introduce you to the primary accounting cycles and related audit issues. Those chapters include examples of the applications of sampling and GAS.

SIGNIFICANT TERMS

Attribute   A characteristic of the population of interest to the auditor.

Attributes sampling   A statistical sampling method used to estimate the rate of control procedure failures based on selecting one sample and performing the appropriate audit procedure.

Audit sampling   The application of an audit procedure to less than 100% of the items within an account balance or class of transactions for the purpose of evaluating some characteristic of the balance or class.

Basic precision   The amount of uncertainty associated with testing only a part of the population (sampling risk). Basic precision is calculated as the sampling interval multiplied by a confidence factor.

Block sampling   A sampling technique that involves selecting a sample that consists of contiguous population items, such as selecting transactions by day or week.

Data analytics   The process of examining large amounts of data to uncover underlying patterns, correlations, and complex relationships through statistical methods for data modeling, and techniques that enable visualization of data.

Expected failure rate   See expected population deviation rate.

Expected misstatement   The level of misstatement that the auditor expects to detect, and it is based on projected misstatements in prior-year audits, results of other substantive tests, professional judgment, and knowledge of changes in personnel and the accounting system.

Expected population deviation rate   An anticipation of the deviation rate in the entire population. Also referred to as the *expected failure rate*.

Factual misstatements   Misstatements that have been specifically identified and about which there is no doubt. Also referred to as *known misstatements*.

Generalized audit software (GAS) Software programs designed specifically for auditors.

Haphazard sampling A nonstatistical sample selection method that attempts to approximate a random selection by selecting sampling units without any conscious bias, or special reason for including or omitting certain items from the sample.

Incremental allowance for sampling risk An increase in the total estimated misstatement caused by the statistical properties of misstatements detected in the lower stratum.

Known misstatements See factual misstatements.

Likely misstatement See projected misstatement.

Logical unit The balance or transaction that includes the selected dollar in a monetary unit sample.

Lower stratum Items that are not in the top stratum.

Misstatement An error, either intentional or unintentional, that exists in a transaction or financial statement account balance. For substantive sampling purposes, a misstatement involves differences between recorded values and audited values.

Monetary unit sampling (MUS) A sampling method based on attributes estimation sampling but involving dollar misstatements rather than failure rates. MUS is often referred to as *probability proportional to size (PPS) sampling*.

Most likely misstatement See projected misstatement.

Nonsampling risk The risk that the auditor reaches an erroneous conclusion for any reason not related to sampling risk.

Nonstatistical sampling The application of auditor judgment and experience in a sample application to assist the auditor in determining an appropriate sample size and in evaluating the sample results.

Population A group of transactions or the items that make up an account balance for which the auditor wants to estimate some characteristic, such as the effectiveness of a control procedure or estimate the extent of misstatement in an account.

Probability proportional to size (PPS) sampling A sampling selection method in which each item in the population has a probability of being included in the sample proportionate to the dollar value of the item. Monetary unit sampling uses this method to select a sample and is considered a subset of PPS sampling.

Projected misstatement The best estimate of the actual amount of dollar misstatements in the population based on projecting the sample results to the population. The projected misstatement is calculated as the sampling interval multiplied by the tainting percentage. Also see likely misstatement or most likely misstatement.

Risk of assessing control risk too high See risk of incorrect rejection of internal control reliability.

Risk of assessing control risk too low   See risk of incorrect acceptance of internal control reliability.

Risk of incorrect acceptance of internal control reliability   The risk that the auditor will conclude that the state of internal controls is effective when internal controls are actually not effective (also referred to as the *risk of assessing control risk too low*).

Risk of incorrect acceptance of book value   The risk that the auditor will conclude that the account balance does not contain a material misstatement when the account balance actually does contain a material misstatement.

Risk of incorrect rejection of internal control reliability   The risk that the auditor will conclude that the state of internal controls is not effective when internal controls are actually effective (also referred to as the *risk of assessing control risk too high*).

Risk of incorrect rejection of book value   The risk that the auditor will conclude that the account balance contains a material misstatement when the account balance actually does not contain a material misstatement.

Risk of overreliance   See risk of incorrect acceptance of internal control reliability.

Risk of underreliance   See risk of incorrect rejection of internal control reliability.

Sampling risk   The risk that the auditor's conclusion based on a sample might be different from the conclusion he or she would reach if the test were applied in the same way to the entire population.

Sampling units   The individual items to be tested.

Simple random sampling   Selecting a random sample by matching random numbers generated by a computer or selected from a random-number table with, for example, document numbers such as an invoice or a purchase order.

Statistical sampling   The application of probability theory and statistical inference, along with auditor judgment and experience, in a sample application to assist the auditor in determining an appropriate sample size and in evaluating the sample results.

Stratification   Dividing the population into two or more subgroups.

Systematic random sampling   This sampling technique involves systematic sampling in which the first item is selected randomly from the interval.

Systematic sampling   This sampling technique involves dividing the number of physical units in the population by the sample size to determine a uniform interval; a random starting point is selected in the first interval and one item is selected throughout the population at each of the uniform intervals after the starting point.

Tainting percentage   The percentage of misstatement present in a logical unit, such as the sample item's book value. The tainting percentage equals the amount of misstatement in the item divided by the item's recorded amount.

Tolerable failure rate   See tolerable rate of deviation.

Tolerable misstatement   A monetary amount set by the auditor in respect of which the auditor seeks to obtain an appropriate level of assurance that the monetary amount set by the auditor is not exceeded by the actual misstatement in the population. In practical terms, a tolerable misstatement is the maximum amount of misstatement the auditor can accept in the population without requiring an audit adjustment or a qualified audit opinion.

Tolerable rate of deviation   A rate of deviation set by the auditor in respect of which the auditor seeks to obtain an appropriate level of assurance that the rate of deviation set by the auditor is not exceeded by the actual rate of deviation in the population. Also referred to as the *tolerable failure rate*.

Top stratum   Population items whose book values exceed the sampling interval and are therefore all included in the sample. The top stratum consists of all account balances exceeding a specific dollar amount.

TRUE/FALSE QUESTIONS

8-1   `LO 1`   Sampling can be used for both tests of controls and substantive tests of account balances and assertions.

8-2   `LO 1`   Audit procedures such as inquiry, observation, and analytical procedures are the primary audit procedures involving audit sampling.

8-3   `LO 2`   Sampling risk is the risk that the auditor's conclusion based on a sample might be different from the conclusion that would be reached if the audit procedure were applied in the same way to the entire population.

8-4   `LO 2`   The risk of incorrect acceptance of internal control reliability is the risk that the auditor will conclude that the state of internal controls is not effective when internal controls are actually effective.

8-5   `LO 3`   A benefit of nonstatistical sampling as compared to statistical sampling is that the sample size can be significantly smaller, thereby making the audit more efficient.

8-6   `LO 3`   A benefit of statistical sampling as compared to nonstatistical sampling is that less auditor judgment is required because the auditor can leverage the power of probability theory.

8-7   `LO 4`   Attributes sampling is a statistical sampling method used to estimate the rate of control procedure failures based on selecting one sample and performing the appropriate audit procedure.

8-8   `LO 4`   In attributes sampling, the attribute of interest is an individual dollar amount in the population.

8-9   `LO 5`   Factual misstatements are those that are the auditor's best estimate of misstatements in a given population based on sample results.

8-10   `LO 5`   The division of a population into two or more subgroups is referred to as *stratification*.

8-11   `LO 6`   One strength of MUS is that it automatically selects a sample in proportion to an item's dollar amount, thus providing automatic stratification of the sample.

8-12   `LO 6`   MUS is most often used in situations in which the auditor expects a significant number of large understatements in recorded balances.

8-13 **LO 7** GAS would be useful for completing the following tasks: footing a file, doing arithmetic calculations, checking for gaps in processing sequences, and printing confirmations.

8-14 **LO 7** GAS would be useful in testing the completeness assertion by helping the auditor select data to perform sales cutoff tests around year-end.

MULTIPLE-CHOICE QUESTIONS

8-15 **LO 1** For which of the following auditing procedures would sampling be most appropriate?
a. Examining documents.
b. Inquiring of management.
c. Observing controls being completed.
d. Conducting analytical procedures.

8-16 **LO 1** Which of the following activities would be most likely to be accomplished using sampling?
a. Sorting a file to identify the largest items.
b. Scanning for unusual transactions.
c. Selecting items and tracing back to source documents.
d. Footing the file.

8-17 **LO 2** Which of the following is a question that the auditor will answer when sampling to perform tests of controls?
a. Which population and sampling unit should be tested, and what characteristics should be examined?
b. How many items should be selected for audit testing?
c. Which items should be included in the sample?
d. What inferences can be made about the overall population from the sample?
e. All of the above.

8-18 **LO 2** Refer to *Exhibit 8.2* and determine which of the following terms matches this definition: the risk that the auditor will conclude that internal controls are effective when internal controls are actually not effective.
a. The risk of incorrect acceptance of internal control reliability.
b. The risk of incorrect acceptance of book value.
c. The risk of incorrect rejection of internal control reliability.
d. The risk of incorrect rejection of book value.

8-19 **LO 3** Refer to *Exhibit 8.4* and determine which of the following statements is true.
a. In nonstatistical sampling, sample size is determined by auditor judgment.
b. In statistical sampling, the sample must be randomly selected to give each unit in the population an equal chance to be included in the sample.
c. In nonstatistical sampling, evaluation is based on auditor judgment and projections are based on sample results.
d. In statistical sampling, the auditor is required to define acceptable risk in advance.
e. All of the above.

8-20 **LO 3** Which of the following statements is false?
a. When properly used, either nonstatistical or statistical sampling can be effective in providing sufficient appropriate audit evidence.
b. Statistical sampling allows the auditor to control and measure the risk of making an incorrect inference about the population

from which the sample is taken, whereas nonstatistical sampling does not allow for such control and measurement.

c. Nonstatistical sampling may help avoid second guessing by regulators or jurors should those parties question the quality of the sampling method used.

d. Combining statistical sampling with audit judgment generally produces a higher quality audit conclusion than using audit judgment alone.

8-21 **LO 4** In attributes sampling, which of the following will not affect the determination of sample size?

a. Sampling risk.

b. The tolerable rate of deviation.

c. The expected population deviation rate.

d. The risk of incorrect rejection of book value.

8-22 **LO 4** Refer to *Exhibit 8.6*. Assume a 5% risk of overreliance, a tolerable deviation rate of 8%, a sample size of 100, and that the number of deviations is five. What is the upper limit of the possible deviation rate, and what does it mean?

a. 10.3%. The auditor is 95% confident that the real error rate in the population is no greater than 10.3%.

b. 10.3%. The auditor is 95% confident that the real error rate in the population is no greater than 5%.

c. 5%. The auditor is 92% confident that the real error rate in the population is no greater than 10.3%.

d. 5%. The auditor is 92% confident that the real error rate in the population is no greater than 5%.

8-23 **LO 5** Which of the following definitions is correct?

a. *Factual misstatement*—A misstatement that has been specifically identified and about which there is no doubt.

b. *Projected misstatement*—The auditor's best estimate of the misstatement in a given population based on projecting the sample results to the population.

c. *Tolerable misstatement*—A monetary amount set by the auditor in respect of which the auditor seeks to obtain an appropriate level of assurance that the monetary amount set by the auditor is not exceeded by the actual misstatement in the population.

d. *Expected misstatement*—The level of misstatement that the auditor expects to detect.

e. All of the above are correct.

8-24 **LO 5** Which of the following statements is false?

a. Top-stratum items are population items whose book values exceed the sampling interval and are therefore all included in the sample.

b. Because the auditor knows the amount of errors in the top stratum (all items were evaluated), no estimate of errors is required.

c. Stratification of the population into several subpopulations generally reduces audit efficiency.

d. The audit sampling evaluation reflects the sum of top-stratum items and the projected misstatement derived from lower-stratum items.

e. None of the above.

8-25 **LO 6** Refer to *Exhibit 8.7*. Assume that the risk of incorrect acceptance is 10%, tolerable misstatement is 5% of population dollars, and expected misstatement is 30% of tolerable misstatement (in other words, 1.5% of the population dollars). What is the minimum sample size that the auditor should use?

a. 28
— b. 87
c. 120
d. 162

8-26 **LO 6** Which of the following represents the correct calculation of the sampling interval?
a. Tolerable error ÷ Risk of incorrect acceptance.
b. Sample size ÷ Population size.
c. Tolerable error × Risk of incorrect acceptance.
— d. Population size ÷ Sample size.

8-27 **LO 7** Which of the following is a task commonly performed using GAS?
a. Selecting transactions based on logical identifiers.
b. Selecting samples.
c. Evaluating samples.
d. Printing confirmations.
e. All of the above.

8-28 **LO 7** Which of the following auditing procedures would be conducted using GAS to assess the validity of the valuation assertion?
a. Foot a file.
b. Compare sales invoices with shipping documents and/or sales contracts.
c. Select a sample of shipping documents and electronically compare them with invoices to determine if billed in the proper period.
d. Select contracts for audit review.

REVIEW AND SHORT CASE QUESTIONS

NOTE: Completing Review and Short Case Questions does not require the student to reference additional resources and materials.

NOTE: For the remaining problems, we make special note of those addressing international issues, professional skepticism, and ethics.

8-29 **LO 1** Describe how auditors use sampling and GAS for gathering audit evidence.

8-30 **LO 1** Refer to *Exhibit 8.1*. Describe at least one auditing procedure for each financial statement assertion for sampling and GAS.

8-31 **LO 2** Define the terms *sampling units* and *population*, and describe how these two concepts relate to each other.

8-32 **LO 2** What four critical questions must the auditor answer when sampling?

8-33 **LO 2** Distinguish between the terms *sampling risk* and *nonsampling risk*.

8-34 **LO 2** Refer to *Exhibit 8.2* and *Exhibit 8.3*.
a. Define the following risks:
  • Risk of incorrect acceptance of internal control reliability
  • Risk of incorrect rejection of internal control reliability
  • Risk of incorrect acceptance of book value
  • Risk of incorrect rejection of book value
b. Explain which of these risks should concern the auditor the most.

8-35 **LO 3** Refer to *Exhibit 8.4* and compare and contrast statistical sampling and nonstatistical sampling on the following dimensions: sample size determination, sample selection, evaluation, costs, and benefits.

8-36 **LO 4** Define the terms *attributes sampling* and *attribute*. Give an example of an attribute of interest to an auditor. Give an example of a control failure.

8-37 LO 4 List the factors that the auditor should address when defining the population in attributes sampling.

8-38 LO 4 Define the term *tolerable rate of deviation* in formal terms (in other words, in the manner in which the AICPA's 2012 *Audit Sampling* formally defines it) and in more practical terms.

8-39 LO 4 Practice calculating the sample size and the number of expected errors in attributes sampling by using the tables in *Exhibit 8.5* and the following combinations of inputs:

	Risk of Overreliance	Tolerable Rate of Deviation	Expected Population Deviation Rate	Sample Size (with Expected Errors in Parentheses)
a.	5%	2%	1%	
b.	5%	6%	5%	
c.	5%	10%	8%	
d.	10%	2%	1%	
e.	10%	6%	5%	
f.	10%	10%	8%	

8-40 LO 4 Using the tables in *Exhibit 8.5*, work backward to explain at least one set of assumptions that the auditor would have to make to justify the following sample sizes:

	Risk of Overreliance	Tolerable Rate of Deviation	Expected Population Deviation Rate	Sample Size
a.				11
b.				14
c.				22
d.				29
e.				38
f.				52

g. Explain what these assumptions and associated sample sizes imply.

8-41 LO 4 What is the effect of increasing each of the following on an attribute sample size?
   a. Sampling risk (or risk of overreliance).
   b. The tolerable rate of deviation.
   c. The expected population deviation rate.
   d. Population size.

8-42 LO 4 Define the following terms: (a) *simple random sampling*, (b) *systematic sampling*, (c) *systematic random sampling*, (d) *haphazard sampling*, and (e) *block sampling*.

8-43 LO 4 Practice evaluating the results of attributes sampling by using the tables in *Exhibit 8.6* and the following combinations of inputs. Assume the tolerable deviation rate is 12%. For each item labeled (a) through (f), state your interpretation of the result, including the appropriate conclusion about whether the control is operating effectively. For those situations when no deviations are detected in the sample, comment on why the upper limit of deviations is greater than zero.

	Risk of Overreliance	Sample Size	Number of Deviations	Upper Limit of Deviations
a.	5%	20	0	
b.	5%	75	5	
c.	5%	150	10	
d.	10%	20	0	
e.	10%	75	5	
f.	10%	150	10	

8-44 **LO 4** When evaluating an attributes sample, why is the focus on the upper limit of deviations in the sample? If the upper limit of deviation exceeds the tolerable deviation rate in attributes sampling, what alternative courses of action are available to the auditor?

8-45 **LO 4** Assume that you are using attribute sampling to test the controls over revenue recognition of the Packet Corporation, a public company, and will use the results as part of the evidence on which to base your opinion on its internal controls and to determine what additional auditing procedures should be performed on revenue and accounts receivable. You have decided to test the following controls and have set the risk of overreliance at 5%, the tolerable deviation rate at 5%, and the expected deviation rate at 1%. A sample size of 100 is used. (Note that this sample size is just rounded up from the sample size of 93 that would have been obtained from the appropriate table.) The results of your testing are as indicated here.

Control	Results
1. All sales over $10,000 must be approved by the sales manager by initialing the customer's order.	1. There were only twenty-five sales over $10,000 in the sample. So, the auditor randomly collects an additional seventy-five sales transactions that were over $10,000. All were approved by the sales manager.
2. Credit must be approved by the credit department prior to shipment and noted on the customer's order.	2. Three sales were recorded without evidence of credit approval. The sales manager said she had approved the sales. No customer order could be found for two of the other sampled items.
3. Sales are recorded only when a shipping document is forwarded to the billing department.	3. No shipping document could be found for three of the sampled items.
4. The date of recording the sale must correspond to the date on the shipping document.	4. Four sales were recorded prior to the date of shipment. Your follow-up indicates that a temporary employee worked for the last two months of the fiscal year and was unaware of this requirement.
5. All prices are obtained from the current price list that is periodically updated by the sales manager.	5. All prices agreed with the appropriate price list.
6. The shipping department is not to ship products without first receiving an approved customer's order.	6. No customer order could be found for two sample items as indicated in Step 2.
7. The billing department compares the quantity billed with the customer's order.	7. Four billed quantities were for more than the customer order. Three of these took place near year-end. In addition, there was no customer order for the two items indicated in Step 2.

a. Determine the upper limit of deviation for each of the controls.
b. What impact do these results have on the type of opinion to be given on the client's internal controls?
c. Indicate the potential misstatements that could be the result of control deviations.
d. Determine what substantive audit procedures should be performed in response to each of the control deviations identified earlier.

8-46 `LO 5` Define the following terms: (a) *misstatement*, (b) *factual misstatement*, (c) *projected misstatement*, (d) *tolerable misstatement*, and (e) *expected misstatement*.

8-47 `LO 5` What is the sampling unit when gathering evidence about misstatements in account balances and associated assertions? Provide examples of sampling units in the context of accounts receivable.

8-48 `LO 5` What is stratification? Distinguish between top-stratum items and lower-stratum items.

8-49 `LO 5` When using nonstatistical sampling to test an account balance, how does the auditor do the following?
a. Determine the sample size.
b. Select the sample.
c. Evaluate the sample results.

8-50 `LO 5` The following information relates to a nonstatistical sample used for a price test of inventory:

	Population		Sample		
	Number	Amount	Number	Amount	Misstatement
>$30,000	20	$1,600,000	20	$1,600,000	$1,000
<$30,000	200	$1,500,000	20	$185,000	$600
Total	220	$3,100,000	40	$2,785,000	$1,600

a. What is the best estimate of the total misstatement?
b. Are these results acceptable, assuming tolerable misstatement is $25,000? Explain.
c. If the results are not acceptable, what possible courses of action can the auditor take?

8-51 `LO 6` What are the strengths of MUS? Provide at least three examples in which MUS might be used.

8-52 `LO 6` What are the difficulties that the auditor may experience in using MUS?

8-53 `LO 6` The sample size in a MUS sample is a function of what three factors?

8-54 `LO 6` Practice calculating the sample size in a MUS sample using *Exhibit 8.7* with the following combinations of inputs.

	Risk of Incorrect Acceptance	Ratio of Expected to Tolerable Misstatement	Ratio of Tolerable Misstatement to Population (%)	Sample Size
a.	5%	0.20	50%	
b.	10%	0.20	30%	
c.	15%	0.30	8%	
d.	20%	0.30	5%	

(continued)

	Risk of Incorrect Acceptance	Ratio of Expected to Tolerable Misstatement	Ratio of Tolerable Misstatement to Population (%)	Sample Size
e.	25%	0.40	4%	
f.	30%	0.40	3%	
g.	35%	0.50	2%	
h.	50%	0.50	1%	

8-55 LO 6 Calculate the sampling interval for cases (a) through (h) in 8-54, assuming a population size of $8,500,000. Recall that sampling interval = population size ÷ sample size. Round the value of the interval down to the nearest $1,000 or $10,000 to ensure that the sample size is adequate and that it is easy for the auditor to select the sample.

8-56 LO 6 Assume you are planning the confirmation of accounts receivable. There are 2,000 customer accounts with a total book value of $5,643,200. Tolerable misstatement is set at $200,000, and expected misstatement is $40,000. The risk of incorrect acceptance is 30%. The ratio of expected to tolerable misstatement is 20%, and the ratio of tolerable misstatement to the population is 3.5% (round down to 3% for use in *Exhibit 8.7*).
   a. What is the sample size?
   b. What is the sampling interval?
   c. What is the largest value you can use for a random start?
   d. Using the following list of the first fifteen items in your population, a random start of $25,000, and a rounded sample interval of $100,000, identify the items to be included in your sample.

Item	Book Value	Cumulative Book	Cumulative Book Plus Random Start	Included in Sample?	Selection Amount ($)
Random Start					
1	3,900				
2	26,000				
3	5,000				
4	130,000				
5	2,000				
6	260,000				
7	100				
8	25,000				
9	19,000				
10	10,000				
11	9,000				
12	2,500				
13	65,000				
14	110,000				
15	6,992				

e. What is the probability of selecting each of the following population items, assuming a $100,000 sampling interval?

Item	Book Value	Probability of Selection
1	3,900	
2	26,000	
4	130,000	
6	360,000	

f. Why might the final sample size include fewer logical units than the computed sample size?

8-57 LO 6 Based on the information in 8-56, assume that your sampling interval is $100,000.

a. What is your statistical conclusion if no misstatements are found in the sample? Is the account balance acceptable? Explain.

b. Calculate the total estimated misstatement assuming the following misstatements are found in the sample:

Misstatement Number	Book Value	Audit Value
1	$210,000	$208,000
2	9,000	8,910
3	15,000	14,250

c. Do these results indicate that the account balance, as stated, is acceptable? Explain.

d. If the results are not acceptable, what courses of action are available to the auditor?

8-58 LO 6 Assume that you are auditing the inventory of Husky Manufacturing Company for the year ended December 31, 2015, and you are using MUS. The book value is $8,124,998.66. The risk of incorrect acceptance is 10% (90% confidence level). The tolerable misstatement is $275,000, and expected misstatement is $80,000, so the ratio of expected misstatement to tolerable misstatement is 29%. The ratio of tolerable misstatement to the population book value is 4.3%.

a. Calculate the sample size and the sampling interval.

b. Calculate the total estimated misstatement assuming the following misstatements were found in the sample:

Book Value	Audit Value
$41,906.45	$36,906.45
$335,643.28	$333,643.28

What conclusion do you reach based upon your calculation?

8-59 LO 6 Assume that the auditor is auditing accounts receivable for a long-time client. The auditor has assessed the risk of incorrect acceptance at 10%. The client's book value in accounts receivable is $8,425,000. Tolerable misstatement is $200,000, and expected misstatement is $40,000. Therefore, the ratio of expected to tolerable misstatement is 20%. The ratio of tolerable misstatement to the population book value is 2.4%.

a. Calculate the sample size and sampling interval.

b. Analyze each difference detected (1. through 5. below) during the audit to determine if it is a misstatement.

c. Calculate the total estimated misstatement assuming the misstatements detailed in the following table were found in the sample. Identify the top-stratum items, the lower-stratum items, and tainting percentages, where applicable. What conclusion do you reach based upon your calculation?

d. Discuss the audit implications, that is, whether the audit work supports book value or whether additional auditing procedures should be recommended, and, if so, describe the nature of the recommended auditing procedures.

Book Value	Audited Value	Nature of Difference
1. $25,000	$15,000	$10,000 was billed to Jason Company, but it should have been billed to Johnson Company. Subsequent follow-up work confirmed that it should be billed to Johnson, and Johnson acknowledged the $10,000 debt.
2. $40,000	$20,000	Merchandise was returned before year-end, but credit was not recorded until the next period.
3. $325,000	$250,000	Major dispute on cost overrun charges. Subsequent review supports customer position.
4. $105,000	$100,000	Another dispute on cost overrun. Again customer position is correct.
5. $122	$0	A credit memo was supposed to have been issued for defective merchandise, but was not.

8-60 **LO 6** What courses of action should the auditor consider pursuing when the results of the MUS sample are unacceptable, in other words, when the total estimated misstatement exceeds the tolerable misstatement?

ETHICS

PROFESSIONAL SKEPTICISM

8-61 **LO 6, 8** Respond to the ethical judgments required based on the following scenarios.

Scenario 1. Assume you have collected a sample using MUS and that you have evaluated that sample to calculate a total estimated misstatement of $213,500. Prior to sampling, you set tolerable misstatement at $215,000. What is the implication of the fact that estimated total misstatement is very close to the tolerable misstatement threshold? What does the closeness of these dollar amounts imply with regard to whether the accounts receivable amount requires downward adjustment? Using the ethical decision making framework from *Chapter 4*, develop an appropriate course of action to take, assuming the following possibilities:

a. You think that the accounts receivable balance is fairly stated because the misstatement is below the tolerable misstatement amount, but you are not entirely convinced of the soundness of your judgment given how close the estimate is to the tolerable misstatement.

b. You collect a larger sample size. You send out ten more accounts receivable confirmations and find two more overstatements, totaling $88,000. Your senior tells you that the client has agreed to write down those two specific accounts receivable. He says that because of this agreement, you should disregard these overstatements for purposes of making a conclusion about the accounts receivable balance in total.

Scenario 2. Assume the same facts as in Scenario 1, but now assume that your senior tells you he has decided to increase the tolerable misstatement amount to $250,000. His rationale for this change is that the client is in good financial health and has relatively strong internal controls. What is the implication of the change in tolerable misstatement amount with regard to whether the accounts receivable amount requires downward adjustment? Using the ethical decision making framework from *Chapter 4*, develop an appropriate course of action to address this situation.

Scenario 3. Assume that the pattern of errors that you have detected in the sample is the same as that was uncovered in *Problem 8-59*, in other words, five audit differences. Notice that for nearly all of those cases, the book value was greater than the audited value. What is management's incentive with regard to potential misreporting associated with accounts receivable (or other assets)? Assume that this pattern of overstatements has become routine on this engagement during the past several years. What does this trend potentially reveal about management? What are the ethical implications of this trend? What should you do?

8-62 **LO 7** The following are typical tasks performed by GAS. For each task, provide an example of how GAS could be used to accomplish that task.
a. Analyze a file.
b. Select transactions based on logical identifiers.
c. Select samples.
d. Evaluate samples.
e. Print confirmations.
f. Analyze overall file validity.
g. Generate control totals.
h. Perform numerical analyses.

8-63 **LO 7** List the advantages of using GAS.

APPLICATION ACTIVITIES

AUDITING STANDARDS APPLICATION ACTIVITY

INTERNATIONAL

8-64 **LO 2** Refer to the *Standards Appendix* to the text. Identify the PCAOB, AICPA, and IAASB guidance that relates to audit sampling. Review the definitions of sampling risk and compare across the three standards-setting bodies. Describe similarities and differences in the definitions, if any.

ACADEMIC RESEARCH CASE

SEARCH HINT

8-65 **LO 7** Locate and read the article listed below and answer the following questions.

Ahmi, A. and S. Kent. 2013. The utilisation of generalized audit software (GAS) by external auditors. *Managerial Auditing Journal* 28 (2): 88–113.
a. What is the issue being addressed in the paper?
b. What are the findings of the paper?
c. Why is this paper important to auditors, and what are the implications of this paper for the auditing profession?
d. Describe the research methodology used as a basis for the conclusions.
e. Describe any limitations of the research.

Auditing the Revenue Cycle

CHAPTER OVERVIEW AND LEARNING OBJECTIVES

Accounts in the revenue cycle should be presumed to be high risk for most audits because these accounts are highly susceptible to misstatement. Auditors must carefully consider management's motivation to stretch accounting principles to achieve desired revenue reporting. Auditors need to understand the relationships present in the accounts and how to best approach the audit. In terms of the audit opinion formulation process, this chapter primarily involves Phases II, III, and IV—performing risk assessment procedures, tests of controls, and substantive procedures—for the revenue cycle.

Through studying this chapter, you will be able to achieve these learning objectives:

1. Identify the significant accounts, disclosures, and relevant assertions in the revenue cycle.

2. Identify and assess inherent risks of material misstatement in the revenue cycle.

3. Identify and assess fraud risks of material misstatement in the revenue cycle.

4. Identify and assess control risks of material misstatement in the revenue cycle.

5. Describe how to use planning analytical procedures to identify possible material misstatements for revenue cycle accounts, disclosures, and assertions.

6. Determine appropriate responses to identified risks of material misstatement for revenue cycle accounts, disclosures, and assertions.

7. Determine appropriate tests of controls and consider the results of tests of controls for revenue cycle accounts, disclosures, and assertions.

8. Determine and apply sufficient appropriate substantive audit procedures for testing revenue cycle accounts, disclosures, and assertions.

9. Apply the frameworks for professional decision making and ethical decision making to issues involving the audit of revenue cycle accounts, disclosures, and assertions.

THE AUDIT OPINION FORMULATION PROCESS

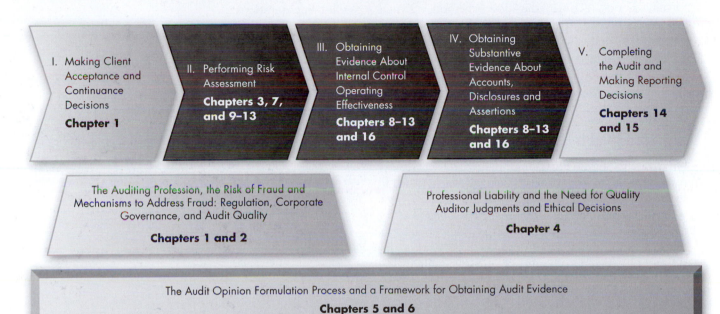

I. Making Client Acceptance and Continuance Decisions
Chapter 1

II. Performing Risk Assessment
Chapters 3, 7, and 9–13

III. Obtaining Evidence About Internal Control Operating Effectiveness
Chapters 8–13 and 16

IV. Obtaining Substantive Evidence About Accounts, Disclosures and Assertions
Chapters 8–13 and 16

V. Completing the Audit and Making Reporting Decisions
Chapters 14 and 15

The Auditing Profession, the Risk of Fraud and Mechanisms to Address Fraud: Regulation, Corporate Governance, and Audit Quality
Chapters 1 and 2

Professional Liability and the Need for Quality Auditor Judgments and Ethical Decisions
Chapter 4

The Audit Opinion Formulation Process and a Framework for Obtaining Audit Evidence
Chapters 5 and 6

PROFESSIONAL JUDGMENT IN CONTEXT
How to Account for Virtual Sales at Zynga

Have you ever purchased a piece of virtual farm equipment while playing Zynga's popular game FarmVille? Maybe you have purchased a tractor that allows you to plow multiple plots of land at one time. You might have used FarmVille currency to make these purchases. Alternatively, you could have converted real dollars from a credit card or PayPal account into the FarmVille currency and then used that currency to buy a virtual tractor or other piece of equipment. For example, you could purchase a hot rod tractor for 55 in Farm Cash, which translates into $10 in real U.S. money. Sales of virtual goods, including goods from FarmVille and other games, accounted for nearly all of Zynga's $873 million in 2013 revenues—and 14% of revenue for Zynga's distributor, Facebook.

How do the involved companies account for these sales? Consider, for example, that you buy and hold Facebook credits (used to buy virtual goods in games on Facebook). Facebook treats the purchase of these credits as deferred revenue. This approach works in the same way as a retailer would record the sale of a gift card. Now assume that you buy a FarmVille's hot rod tractor. To make this purchase, you could use your Facebook credits or charge $10 (which buys 100 Facebook credits that are converted to 55 in Farm Cash). Facebook sends $7 to Zynga and keeps $3—30%—as a processing fee. At this point, Facebook moves that $3 from deferred revenue into current revenue. Now the relevant question is: When does Zynga get to recognize its $7 in revenues? In general, revenue should not be recognized until it is realized or is realizable and earned. So even if a company has cash in hand, it cannot be counted as current revenue until the company has delivered the product or service it is being paid for. However, neither the Financial Accounting Standards Board (FASB) nor the Securities and Exchange Commission (SEC) has issued rules for sales of virtual harvesters or any other virtual products. Perhaps somewhat surprisingly, Zynga's audit firm, Ernst & Young (E&Y), has published a document that provides revenue recognition guidance in this area.

E&Y's guidance outlines three different revenue approaches: game-based, in which revenue is recognized very slowly, over the life of the game; user-based, a faster approach that lasts over the time a typical user sticks with the game; and speedy item-based, based on the properties of the individual virtual goods. Using the last method, Zynga recognizes revenues from consumable virtual items, like energy, immediately and revenues from durable ones, like tractors, over the time a player is projected to stick with a game. In many ways, these suggestions seem reasonable. The difficult part is that all of the methods are dependent on management estimates of the life of a game, a customer, or a virtual item. The estimates can make a big difference in Zynga's net income. For example, by estimating a shorter player life (from 19 months to 15 months), Zynga increased revenue for a six-month period ended June 30, 2011, by $27.3 million. This change came just before Zynga went public in mid-December at $10 a share.

From a bottom-line perspective, this change in player life allowed Zynga to change a net loss for the six-month period into net profit of $18.1 million.

As you read through this chapter, consider the following questions:

- What are the inherent risks associated with revenue transactions? (LO 2)
- What are management's incentives to misstate revenue transactions? (LO 3)
- What controls should management have in place to mitigate the risks associated with revenue transactions? (LO 4)
- How might auditors use planning analytical procedures to identify any potential concerns related to revenue? (LO 5)
- What is sufficient appropriate evidence when auditing revenue transactions and related accounts? (LO 6, 7, 8)

Significant Accounts, Disclosures, and Relevant Assertions

LO 1 Identify the significant accounts, disclosures, and relevant assertions in the revenue cycle.

The **revenue cycle** involves the process of receiving a customer's order, approving credit for a sale, determining whether the goods are available for shipment, shipping the goods, billing the customer, collecting cash, and recognizing the effect of this process on revenue and other related accounts such as accounts receivable, inventory, and sales commission expense. In the revenue cycle, the most significant accounts include revenue and accounts receivable. The auditor will likely obtain evidence related to each of the financial statement assertions discussed in *Chapter 5* for both accounts. However, for specific accounts and specific clients, some assertions are more relevant than other assertions. For many clients, the existence assertion related to revenue may be one of the more relevant assertions, especially if the client has incentives to overstate revenues. For accounts receivable, the more relevant assertions are usually existence and valuation. The assertions that are determined to be more relevant are those for which the risk of material misstatement is higher and for which more and higher quality audit evidence is needed.

The cycle approach recognizes the interrelationship of accounts. Audit evidence addressing the existence and valuation of accounts receivable also provides evidence on the existence and valuation of recorded revenue, and vice versa. When examining sales transactions and internal controls over revenue processing, the auditor also gathers evidence on credit authorization and valuation of the recorded transactions. Sales transactions often serve as a basis for computing commissions for sales staff. Sales information is used for strategic long-term decision-making and marketing analysis. Therefore, the accuracy of recording transactions in the revenue cycle is important for management decisions, as well as for the preparation of financial statements. *Exhibit 9.1* depicts the accounts typically affected by sales transactions.

Processing Revenue Transactions

The revenue process may differ with each client, and each client may have more than one revenue process. For example, a sales transaction for a shirt in a department store differs from a sale of construction equipment, and both of these differ from a book sale on an Internet web site. The Internet sale and

EXHIBIT 9.1   Revenue Cycle Accounts

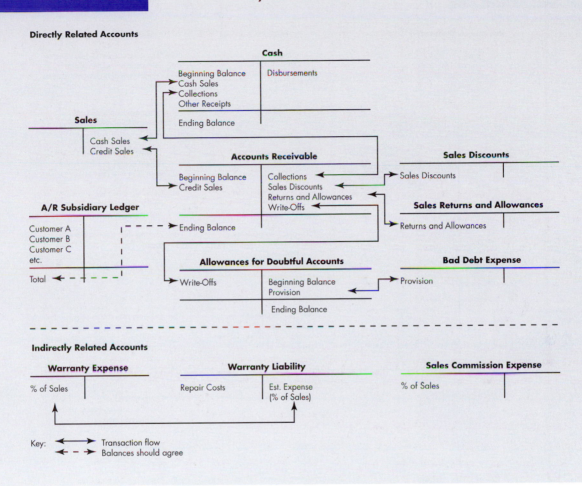

the retail sale most likely require a credit card or cash for payment. The construction equipment sale most likely involves an account receivable or a loan may be arranged with a third party. Some sales transactions involve long-term contractual arrangements that affect when and how revenue will be recorded. Notwithstanding these differences, most sales transactions include the procedures and related documents shown in *Exhibit 9.2* and discussed next.

1. Receive a Customer Purchase Order   Processing begins with the receipt of a purchase order from a customer or the preparation of a sales order by a salesperson. The order might be taken by (1) a clerk at a checkout counter, (2) a salesperson making a call on a client, (3) a customer service agent of a catalog sales company answering a toll-free call, (4) a computer receiving purchase order information electronically from the customer's computer, or (5) the sales department directly receiving the purchase order. For example, consider a customer service agent for a catalog merchandiser taking an order over the phone. The information is keyed into a computer file, and each transaction is uniquely identified. The computer file (often referred to as a *log of transactions*) contains all the information for sales orders taken over a period of time and can be used for control and reconciliation purposes.

2. Check Inventory Stock Status   Many organizations have computer systems capable of informing a customer of current inventory status and

EXHIBIT **9.2** Overview of the Sales Process

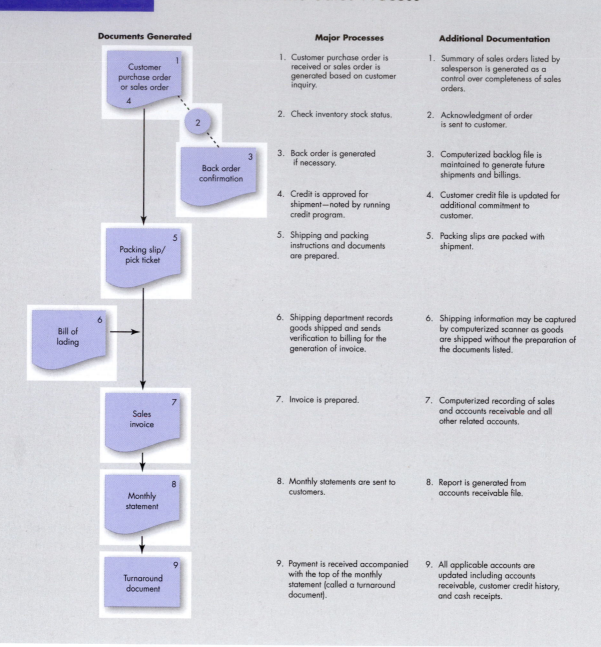

Documents Generated

1. Customer purchase order or sales order
4.

2.

3. Back order confirmation

5. Packing slip/ pick ticket

6. Bill of lading

7. Sales invoice

8. Monthly statement

9. Turnaround document

Major Processes

1. Customer purchase order is received or sales order is generated based on customer inquiry.

2. Check inventory stock status.

3. Back order is generated if necessary.

4. Credit is approved for shipment—noted by running credit program.

5. Shipping and packing instructions and documents are prepared.

6. Shipping department records goods shipped and sends verification to billing for the generation of invoice.

7. Invoice is prepared.

8. Monthly statements are sent to customers.

9. Payment is received accompanied with the top of the monthly statement (called a turnaround document).

Additional Documentation

1. Summary of sales orders listed by salesperson is generated as a control over completeness of sales orders.

2. Acknowledgment of order is sent to customer.

3. Computerized backlog file is maintained to generate future shipments and billings.

4. Customer credit file is updated for additional commitment to customer.

5. Packing slips are packed with shipment.

6. Shipping information may be captured by computerized scanner as goods are shipped without the preparation of the documents listed.

7. Computerized recording of sales and accounts receivable and all other related accounts.

8. Report is generated from accounts receivable file.

9. All applicable accounts are updated including accounts receivable, customer credit history, and cash receipts.

likely delivery date. The customer is informed of potential back-ordered items, as well as an expected delivery date.

3. Generate Back Order If an item is to be back-ordered for later shipment to the customer, a confirmation of the back order is prepared and sent to the customer. If the back order is not filled within a specified time, the customer is often given the option of canceling the order. An accurate list of back-ordered items must be maintained to meet current customer demand and future inventory needs. Appending a separate field to the individual inventory records to show back-ordered items usually accomplishes this.

4. Obtain Credit Approval Formal credit approval policies are implemented by organizations to minimize credit losses. Some organizations eliminate credit risk by requiring payment through a credit card. Others require that a check accompany the order, and generally they delay the shipment until the check clears through the banking system to assure that the payment is collectible.

Many industrial organizations issue credit to their customers because it is a more convenient way to transact business. However, the organization making the sale accepts some risk that it ultimately will not receive payment from the customer. Many reasons can exist for nonpayment, ranging from (a) dissatisfaction with, or return of, the goods received to (b) inability to make payments because of financial constraints. Therefore, organizations need to have a credit approval process that (a) evaluates the creditworthiness of new customers and (b) updates the creditworthiness (including timelines of payments) of existing customers. The credit approval might include a review of sales orders and customer credit information by a computer program that contains current account balance information and credit scoring information to determine whether credit should be extended to the customer. Most organizations set credit limits for customers and develop controls to assure that a pending sale will not push the customer over the credit limit.

5. Prepare Shipping and Packing Documents
Many organizations have computerized the distribution process for shipping items from a warehouse. Pick tickets (documents that tell the warehouse personnel the most efficient sequence in which to pick items for shipment and the location of all items to be shipped) are generated from the sales order or from the customer's purchase order. Separate packing slips are prepared to insert with the shipment and to verify that all items have been shipped. Some organizations put a bar code on the shipping container that identifies the contents. The bar code can be scanned by the customer to record receipt of the order.

6. Ship and Verify Shipment of Goods
Most goods are shipped to customers via common carriers such as independent trucking lines, railroads, or airfreight companies. The shipper prepares a bill of lading that describes the packages to be conveyed by the common carrier to the customer, the shipping terms, and the delivery address. The **bill of lading** is a formal legal document that conveys responsibility to the shipper. A representative of the common carrier signs the bill of lading, acknowledging receipt of the goods. The shipping department confirms the shipment by (1) completing the packing slip and returning it to the billing department, (2) electronically recording everything shipped and transmitting the shipping information to the billing department, or (3) preparing independent shipping documents, a copy of which is sent to the billing department.

7. Prepare and Send the Invoice
Invoices are normally prepared when notice is received that goods were shipped. The invoice should include items such as the terms of sale, payment terms, and prices for merchandise shipped. The invoice will serve as an important document in terms of audit evidence.

8. Send Monthly Statements to Customers
Many organizations prepare monthly statements of open items and mail these statements to customers. The monthly statement provides a detailed list of the customer's activity for the previous month and a statement of all open items.

9. Receive Payments
The proper recording of all revenue receipts is crucial to the ultimate valuation of both cash and accounts receivable. This part of the revenue process is typically considered to be part of the cash transaction cycle and is discussed in detail in *Chapter 10.*

Performing Risk Assessment Procedures in the Revenue Cycle

LO 2 Identify and assess inherent risks of material misstatement in the revenue cycle.

As part of performing risk assessment procedures, the auditor obtains information that is useful in assessing the risk of material misstatement. This includes information about inherent risks at the financial statement level (e.g., client's business and operational risks, financial reporting risks) and at the account and assertion levels, fraud risks including feedback from the audit team's brainstorming sessions, strengths and weaknesses in internal control, and results from planning analytical procedures. Once the risks of material misstatement have been identified, the auditor then determines how best to respond to them as part of the audit opinion formulation process.

Identifying Inherent Risks

Revenues: Identifying Inherent Risks

An important inherent risk related to revenue transactions is the timing of revenue recognition. Revenue should only be recognized when it is realized or is realizable and earned. Although these concepts seem simple, they are often difficult to apply in practice. Further, complex sales transactions often make it difficult to determine when a sale has actually taken place. For example, a transaction might be structured so that title passes only when some contingent situations are met, or the customer may have an extended period to return the goods. To audit the revenue cycle, the auditor must understand the following:

- The organization's principal business, that is, what is the organization in the business of selling?
- The earnings process and the nature of the obligations that extend beyond the normal shipment of goods. For example, after goods are shipped, does the seller have any ongoing service requirements to the purchaser?
- The impact of unusual terms, and when title has passed to the customer.
- The right of the customer to return a product, as well as the returns history.
- Contracts that are combinations of leases and sales.
- The proper treatment of sales transactions made with recourse or that have an abnormal or unpredictable amount of returns.

Exhibit 9.3 reports examples of sales transactions that have high inherent risk and have caused problems for auditors.

Criteria for Revenue Recognition When to recognize revenue and how much to recognize are often difficult decisions. Auditors should refer to authoritative guidance, such as that provided by the International Accounting Standards Board (IASB), SEC, FASB, and American Institute of Certified Public Accountants (AICPA), to determine the appropriateness of their clients' methods of recognizing revenue. Currently, the basic concept for revenue recognition is that revenue should not be recognized until it is realized or is realizable and earned. The SEC staff has determined that the following criteria must be met in applying this concept:

- Persuasive evidence of an arrangement exists.
- Delivery has occurred, or services have been rendered.
- The seller's price to the buyer is fixed or determinable.
- Collectibility is reasonably assured. **Collectibility** refers to the risk that the seller will be unable to collect the entitled contractual consideration from the customer.

EXHIBIT **9.3**	Examples of Complex Sales Transactions

DELIVERY

Company A receives purchase orders for products it manufactures. At the end of its fiscal quarters, customers may not yet be ready to take delivery of the products for various reasons. These reasons may include, but are not limited to, a lack of available space for inventory, having more than sufficient inventory in their distribution channel, or delays in customers' production schedules.

Question

May Company A recognize revenue for the sale of its products once it has completed manufacturing if it segregates the inventory of the products in its own warehouse from its own products? What if it ships the products to a third-party warehouse but (1) Company A retains title to the product and (2) payment by the customer is dependent upon ultimate delivery to a customer-specified site?

Answer

Generally, no. The SEC staff believes that delivery generally is not considered to have occurred unless the customer has taken title and assumed the risks and rewards of ownership. Typically, this occurs when a product is delivered to the customer's delivery site (if the terms of the sale are freight on board [FOB] destination) or when a product is shipped to the customer (if the terms are FOB shipping point).

INTERNET SALES

Company B operates an Internet web site from which it sells Company C's products. Customers place their orders for a product by selecting the product directly from the Internet site and providing a credit card number for the payment. Company B receives the order and authorization from the credit card company and passes the order on to Company C. Company C ships the product directly to the customer. Company B does not take title to the product and has no risk of loss or other responsibility for the product. Company C is responsible for all product returns, defects, and disputed credit card charges. The product is typically sold for $200, of which Company B receives $30. If a credit card transaction is rejected, Company B loses its margin on the sale (i.e., the $30).

Question

Should Company B recognize revenue of $200 or $30?

Answer

The SEC's position is that Company B should recognize only $30. "In assessing whether revenue should be reported gross with separate display of cost of sales to arrive at gross profit or on a net basis, the staff considers whether the registrant:

1. Acts as principal in the transaction,
2. Takes title to the products,
3. Has risks and rewards of ownership, and
4. Acts as an agent or broker (including performing services, in substance, as an agent or broker) with compensation on a commission or fee basis."

Source: SEC Staff Accounting Bulletin: No. 101–Revenue Recognition in Financial Statements, December 3, 1999.

These criteria are not as straightforward as they might seem. For example, the criterion of delivery seems simple enough. Consider, however, a situation in which the seller has delivered a product to a customer. The customer has the right to return the product, and the buyer's obligation to pay is contractually excused until the buyer resells the product. In this case, revenue should not be recognized until the buyer has the obligation to pay, that is, when the product is resold.

See the *Emerging Issues* feature, "New Guidance From the FASB and IASB on Revenue Recognition," for an overview of the new revenue

New Guidance From the FASB and IASB on Revenue Recognition

EMERGING ISSUE

The FASB and IASB have coordinated to update and harmonize GAAP and IFRS treatment of revenue recognition transactions. To recognize revenue under the new guidance, a seller operating under a written, oral, or implied contract to provide goods or services to a customer will need to: (1) identify the customer contract, (2) identify individual performance obligations associated with the contract, (3) determine the price associated with the transaction, (4) allocate the transaction price, and (5) recognize revenue when the performance obligation(s) are satisfied.

Importantly from an auditing perspective, the guidance creates new rules about what constitutes "persuasive evidence" about revenue recognition transactions. Under the new rules, a contract may be oral, written, or implied by customary business practices. The contract must have the following characteristics in order to be judged as persuasive: (a) it must have commercial substance, (b) the parties to the contract must have approved it and be committed to perform their respective actions, (c) rights with respect to the contract are identifiable, and (d) the terms of payment must be identifiable.

Also of particular importance from an auditing perspective, the guidance creates new rules concerning issues of collectibility. Under the new guidance, there will be no revenue recognition threshold depending on differential expectations about collectibility. Rather, revenue can be recognized based on the amount to which the seller expects to be entitled, without regard to the risks associated with collectibility. If collectibility is in significant doubt, a contract may be determined to not exist and any impairment losses are to be presented as a separate line item adjacent to revenue.

recognition standards that will be effective for reporting periods beginning after December 15, 2016 (for public companies) or December 15, 2017 (for nonpublic companies).

The SEC generally does not consider delivery to have occurred until the customer takes title and assumes the risks and rewards of ownership. Auditors may need to conduct research to determine when a client should recognize revenue and how to audit revenue. Some revenue recognition areas require special consideration. The following is a sample of issues that have emerged in recent years:

- How much should be recognized as revenue when a company sells another company's product but does not take title until it is sold? For example, should Priceline.com (an Internet travel web site) record the full sales price of airline tickets it sells or the net amount it earns on the sale (the sales commission)?
- Should shipment of magazines by a magazine distributor to retail stores result in revenue when delivered or await the sale to the ultimate consumers? What if the arrangement with convenience stores, such as 7–11, is that all magazines not sold can be returned to the distributor when the racks are filled with the next month's magazines?
- Should revenue be recognized in barter advertising in which two web sites exchange advertising space?
- At what point in time should revenue be recognized when:
  - The right of return exists.
  - The product is being held awaiting the customer's instructions to ship (bill and hold).
  - A bundled product is sold. For example, assume that a software company sells software bundled with installation and service for a total of $5,000. Should the total revenue be $5,000, or should the

service element be separately estimated and recognized along with an attendant liability to perform the service work? What if the software entitles the user to free updates for a period of three years?

The auditor is expected to know enough about the client's transactions to be able to exercise informed judgment in determining both the timing and extent of revenue recognition. Although the judgments may appear to be subjective, the SEC and other authoritative bodies have set forth objective criteria they expect both auditors and managers to use in determining revenue recognition. The *Focus on Fraud* feature "Channel Stuffing at ArthroCare—The Importance of Professional Skepticism" highlights the importance of professional skepticism when auditing revenue transactions.

Accounts Receivable: Identifying Inherent Risks

The primary inherent risk associated with receivables is that the net amount is not collectible because either the receivables recorded do not represent genuine claims or an insufficient allowance exists for uncollectible accounts. If a valid sales transaction does not exist, a valid receivable does not exist. Alternatively, if the company has been shipping poor-quality goods, there is a high risk of return. Finally, some companies, in an attempt to increase sales, may have chosen to sell to new customers who have questionable credit-paying ability. The most relevant financial statement assertions for receivables are usually existence and valuation. Other important risks may be related to ownership due to the company selling or pledging receivables. For example, a company may desperately need cash and decide to sell the receivables to a bank, but the bank may have a right to seek assets from the company if the receivables are not collected.

Channel Stuffing at ArthroCare—The Importance of Professional Skepticism

FOCUS on **FRAUD**

Auditors need to be professionally skeptical and make judgments on whether and when sales should be recognized as revenue. The ArthroCare case highlights the material misstatements that can occur if a client chooses to improperly record revenue and the auditor fails to detect the misstatement.

ArthroCare is a manufacturer of medical devices, based in Austin, Texas, whose shares are traded on NASDAQ. From 2006 through the first quarter of 2008, two company sales executives, John Raffle and David Applegate, were alleged to have engaged in a channel stuffing scheme that improperly inflated company revenue and earnings. Specifically, the two salesmen shipped certain products to distributors even though the distributors often did not need them or have the ability to pay for them. Chief executive officer (CEO) Michael Baker and chief financial officer (CFO) Michael Gluk were also implicated in the scheme. As a result, for 2006, 2007, and the first quarter of 2008, revenues were overstated by, respectively, 7.9%, 14.1%, and 17.4%, totaling almost $72.3 million. For the same period, net income was overstated by 14.5% in

2006, 8,694% for 2007, and 315% for the first quarter of 2008, totaling about $53.7 million. The company eventually restated its financial statements.

In 2014, former executives John Raffle and David Applegate pled guilty to conspiracy to commit securities and wire fraud. ArthroCare agreed to pay a $30 million fine to resolve the investigation. In 2014, the PCAOB settled a disciplinary order against Randall Stone, a former PwC auditor, for violating PCAOB rules and standards in PwC's 2007 audit of ArthroCare. Stone was the partner in charge of the 2007 audit and was barred from associating with a registered public accounting firm and faced a monetary penalty and censure. His violations included not properly addressing numerous indicator of improperly recognized revenue.

For further information on this case, refer to ArthroCare Corp. Securities Litigation, case number 1:08-cv-00574 in the U.S. District Court for the Western District of Texas. See PCAOB Release No. 105-2014-007 for further details on the PCAOB disciplinary order against Randall Stone.

Some of the inherent risks affecting receivables include the following:

- Receivables are pledged as collateral against specific loans with restricted use (disclosures of such restrictions are required).
- Receivables are incorrectly classified as current when the likelihood of collection during the next year is low.
- Collection of a receivable is contingent on specific events that cannot currently be estimated.
- Payment is not required until the purchaser sells the product to its end customers.
- Accounts receivable are aged incorrectly, and potentially uncollectible amounts are not recognized.
- Orders are accepted from customers with poor credit, but the allowance for doubtful accounts is not increased accordingly.

Identifying Fraud Risk Factors

LO 3 Identify and assess fraud risks of material misstatement in the revenue cycle.

Auditing standards state that auditors should ordinarily presume there is a risk of material misstatement caused by fraud relating to revenue recognition. A research study sponsored by the Committee of Sponsoring Organizations of the Treadway Commission (COSO 2010), "Fraudulent Financial Reporting: 1998–2007—An Analysis of U.S. Public Companies," reviewed over 300 cases of fraudulent financial statements issued between 1988 and 2007 and documented that over 60% of the frauds involved inappropriate recording of revenue.

Fraud Schemes Fraud investigations undertaken by the SEC and the Public Company Accounting Oversight Board (PCAOB) have uncovered a wide variety of methods used to misstate accounts in the revenue cycle, including:

- Recognition of revenue on shipments that never occurred
- Hidden side letters, agreements containing contract terms that are not part of the formal contract, giving customers an irrevocable right to return the product
- Recording consignment sales as final sales
- Early recognition of sales that occurred after the end of the fiscal period
- Shipment of unfinished product
- Shipment of product before customers wanted or agreed to delivery
- Creation of fictitious invoices
- Shipment of more product than the customer ordered
- Recording shipments to the company's own warehouse as sales
- Shipping goods that had been returned and recording the reshipment as a sale of new goods before issuing credit for the returned sale
- Incorrect aging of accounts receivable and not recording write-downs of potentially uncollectible amounts
- Recording purchase orders as completed sales

Exhibit 9.4 provides examples of the wide range of methods that have been used to inflate revenue.

Another scheme in this cycle involves **lapping**, which is a technique used to cover up the embezzlement of cash. This technique causes individual customer accounts receivable balances to be misstated. Lapping is most likely to occur when duties are inadequately segregated—an employee has access to cash or incoming checks and to the accounting records. To accomplish lapping, the employee first steals a payment from a customer. However, the employee does not give that customer credit for the payment. If no other action is taken, that customer will detect the absence of the credit for

| EXHIBIT **9.4** | Examples of Revenue Recognition and Accounts Receivable Schemes |

Coca-Cola was charged with coercing its largest distributors to accept delivery of more syrup than they needed at the end of each quarter, thus inflating sales by about $10 million a year.

WorldCom's CEO, Bernard Ebbers, pressured the chief operating officer (COO) to find and record one-time revenue transactions that were fictitious and were hidden from the auditors by altering key documents and denying auditor access to the appropriate database.

HealthSouth understated its allowance for doubtful accounts when it was clear certain receivables would not be collected.

Gateway recorded revenue for each free subscription to AOL services that was given with each computer sale, thus overstating pre-tax income by over $450 million.

Royal Ahold (a Dutch company that was the world's second-biggest operator of grocery stores) booked higher promotional allowances, provided by suppliers to promote their goods, than they received in payment.

Kmart improperly included as revenue a $42.3 million payment from American Greetings Corp. that was subject to repayment under certain circumstances and therefore should not have been fully recognized by Kmart in that quarter.

Xerox improperly accelerated $6 billion of revenue from long-term leases of office equipment.

Qwest immediately recognized long-term contract revenue rather than over the eighteen-month to two-year period of the contract, inflating revenue by $144 million.

Bristol-Myers inflated revenue by as much as $1 billion, using sales incentives to wholesalers who then packed their warehouses with extra inventory.

Lucent Technologies improperly booked $679 million in revenue. The bulk of this revenue, $452 million, reflected products sent to its distribution partners that were never actually sold to end customers.

Charter Communications, a cable company, added $17 million to revenue and cash flow in one year through a phony ad sales deal with an unnamed set-top decoder maker. They persuaded the set-top maker to add $20 onto the invoice price of each box. Charter held the cash and recorded it as an ad sale. Net income was not affected, but revenue was increased.

Nortel Networks, a telecommunications equipment company, fraudulently manipulated reserve accounts across two years to initially *decrease* profitability (so as to *not* return to profitability faster than analyst expectations) and to then increase profitability (so as to meet analyst expectations about the timing of a return to profitability and also to enable key executives to receive early return to profitability bonuses worth tens of millions of dollars). Nortel's board fired key executives, and the company restated its financial statements four times in four years and remediated a key internal control material weakness associated with the fraud.

Diebold, Inc., an Ohio-based maker of ATMs, bank security systems, and electronic voting machines, agreed to pay $25 million to settle SEC charges related to accounting fraud. The alleged schemes included fraudulent use of bill-and-hold accounting and improper recognition of lease-agreement revenue. When company reports showed that the company was about to miss its analysts' earnings estimate, Diebold finance executives allegedly used these schemes to meet the earnings estimate.

General Electric (GE) paid $50 million to settle accounting fraud charges with the SEC for revenue recognition schemes. GE improperly booked revenues of $223 million and $158 million for six locomotives reportedly sold to financial institutions, "with the understanding that the financial institutions would resell the locomotives to GE's railroad customers in the first quarters of the subsequent fiscal years." The problem is that the six transactions were not true sales and therefore did not qualify for revenue recognition under U.S. generally accepted accounting principles (GAAP). Most important, GE did not give up ownership of the trains to the financial institutions.

Motorola booked $275 million of earnings by keeping its third quarter books open after the quarter ended so that it could record the revenue, which represented 28% of the net income Motorola reported for that quarter.

Sources: *Atlanta Business Chronicle*, June 2, 2003; *The Wall Street Journal Online*, June 9, 2003; *Accountingweb.com*, July 14, 2003; *Accountingweb.com*, May 19, 2003; *The Wall Street Journal Online*, February 25, 2003; *The Wall Street Journal Online*, February 26, 2003; *The Wall Street Journal Online*, June 28, 2002; *St. Cloud Times*, p. 6A, February 26, 2003; *The Wall Street Journal Online*, July 11, 2002; *The Wall Street Journal Online*, February 9, 2001; *USA Today*, July 25, 2003; SEC Release 2007-217, September 12, 2007; cfo.com, Ex-Diebold CFOs Charged with Fraud, June 2, 2010; cfo.com, GE Settles Accounting Fraud Charges, August 4, 2009; *Bloomberg*, Dirty Secrets Fester in 50-Year Relationships, June 9, 2011.

payment on the next monthly statement. To prevent detection, the employee then covers the fraud by posting another customer's payment to the first customer. Then the second customer's account is missing credit, which is covered up later when a subsequent collection from a third customer is posted to the second customer's account (hence, the term *lapping*). At no time will any customer's account be very far behind in the posting of the credit. Of course, there will always be at least one customer whose balance is overstated, unless the employee repays the stolen cash. Lapping can occur even if all incoming receipts are in the form of checks. The employee can either restrictively endorse a check to another company or go to another bank and establish an account with a similar name. If the lapping scheme is sophisticated, very few accounts will be misstated at any one time.

Identifying Fraud Risk Factors There are many motivations to overstate revenue. For example, bankruptcy may be imminent because of operating losses, technology changes in the industry causing the company's products to become obsolete, or a general decline in the industry. Management bonuses or stock options may be dependent on reaching a certain earnings goal. Or, a merger may be pending, and management may want to negotiate the highest price possible. In other cases, management might make optimistic public announcements of the company's revenues, net income, and earnings per share before the auditor's work is completed. These earnings expectations put enormous pressure on management not to disappoint the market. The *Focus on Fraud* feature "The Importance of Professional Skepticism in Auditing Revenue at Tvia" provides an example of a case in which client personnel had significant financial motives to fraudulently overstate revenue.

The examples in *Exhibit 9.4* are but a few of the revenue risk schemes to which auditors should be alert. Identifying these revenue schemes and related risk factors involves the auditor:

- Assessing motivation to enhance revenue because of either internal or external pressures

The Importance of Professional Skepticism in Auditing Revenue at Tvia

FOCUS on **FRAUD**

In 2009, the SEC initiated enforcement actions involving executives at a Silicon Valley company named Tvia. The SEC alleged that Tvia's former vice president of worldwide sales, Benjamin Silva III, made side deals with customers and concealed this information from Tvia's executives and auditors. These side deals resulted in the company fraudulently reporting millions of dollars in revenue from 2005 to 2007. Importantly, SEC documents note that when Silva joined Tvia in September 2004, he received options on 250,000 shares of Tvia stock, with one quarter of the options vesting after one year and the remainder vesting monthly thereafter for the next three years. In May 2005, Silva received additional options grants. Silva received a 50,000-share options

grant, again with one quarter of the options vesting after one year and the remainder vesting monthly thereafter for the next three years. Silva also received a 70,000-share performance-based options grant, which vested only if the company achieved $5 million in revenue in a fiscal quarter by June 30, 2006.

Auditors need to be alert to instances in which client personnel have significant financial motives to fraudulently overstate revenue. In these situations, it is especially important to understand and, if appropriate, test the controls designed and implemented to prevent such behavior. If controls are ineffective, auditors need to exercise appropriate professional skepticism and extend substantive testing to obtain sufficient appropriate evidence.

- Reviewing the financial statements through planning analytical procedures to identify account balances that differ from expectations or general trends in the economy
- Recognizing that not all of the fraud will be instigated by management; for example, a CFO or accounting staff person may engage in misappropriating assets for his or her own use
- Becoming aware of representations made by management to analysts and the potential effect of those expectations on stock prices
- Determining whether the company's performance is significantly different from that of the rest of the industry or the economy
- Determining whether the company's accounting is being investigated by organizations such as the SEC
- Considering management compensation schemes, especially those that rely on stock options and therefore current stock prices
- Determining whether accounting functions are centralized, and if not centralized, assessing if the decentralization is appropriate (The *Auditing in Practice* feature "Risks Related to Decentralized Accounting Functions: The Case of WorldCom" provides a relevant example.)
- Assessing whether the company engages in complex sales arrangements when simple transactions would suffice
- Assessing whether the company has a history of aggressive accounting interpretations
- Determining whether an uninterrupted history of continued growth in earnings per share or revenue might provide incentives to continue to show that growth
- Determining if the client has numerous manual journal entries affecting the revenue process (assuming that process is automated)

Identifying Control Risks

LO 4 Identify and assess control risks of material misstatement in the revenue cycle.

Once the auditor has obtained an understanding of the inherent and fraud risks of material misstatement in the revenue and accounts receivable accounts, the auditor needs to understand the controls that the client has designed and implemented to address those risks. Remember, the auditor is required to gain an understanding of internal controls for both integrated audits and financial statement only audits. Such understanding is normally

Risks Related to Decentralized Accounting Functions: The Case of WorldCom

WorldCom is a prime example of a company taking several actions that negatively affect the quality of its financial statements. WorldCom's transactions were complex, but they were made more difficult to understand and audit by means of several factors. First, many of the accounting personnel were not sufficiently qualified for their positions. Second, the accounting function was spread over at least three locations, without a good rationale for the decentralization. Third, the decentralization was by function. Many companies have decentralization with a full accounting unit at various locations, but WorldCom was not distributed that way; the property accounting function was located in Texas, while the revenue and line cost accounting were in Mississippi, and the equipment control was in Washington, D.C. Consequently, an accounting unit never saw the complete transaction. Only a few people at the very top were aware of the full accounting transactions. Auditors should exhibit appropriate professional skepticism when encountering such situations.

gained by means of a walkthrough of the process, inquiry, observation, and review of the client's documentation. The auditor considers both entity-wide controls and transaction controls at the account and assertion levels. This understanding provides the auditor with a basis for making an initial control risk assessment.

At the entity-wide level, the auditor will consider the control environment, including such principles as commitment to financial accounting competencies and the independence of the board of directors. The auditor will also consider the remaining components of internal control that are typically entity-wide—risk assessment, information and communication, and monitoring controls. Although all the components of internal control need to be understood, the auditor typically finds it useful to focus on significant control activities in the revenue cycle. As part of this understanding, the auditor focuses on the relevant assertions for each account and identifies the controls that relate to risks for these assertions. In an integrated audit or in a financial statement only audit where the auditor relies on controls, this understanding will be used to identify important controls that need to be tested.

Controls Related to Existence/Occurrence Controls for existence should provide reasonable assurance that a sale and accounts receivable are recorded only when shipment has occurred or the primary revenue-producing activity has been performed. Recall that sales transactions should be recorded only when title has passed and the company has received cash or a collectible receivable. A control to mitigate the risk that unearned revenues are recorded is to distribute monthly statements to customers. However, the control should be such that the statements are prepared and mailed by someone independent of the department who initially processed the transactions. Further, customer inquiries about their balances should be channeled to a department or individual that is independent of the original recording of the transactions.

Unusual transactions, because of their size, complexity, or special terms, should require a high level of management review, with the review serving as a control. Upper levels of management—and maybe even the board—should be involved in approving highly complex and large transactions. For typical transactions, authorization should be part of an audit trail and should not be performed by the same person who records the transactions.

Controls Related to Completeness Controls related to completeness are intended to provide reasonable assurance that all valid sales transactions are recorded. For example, transactions may not be recorded because of sloppy procedures. In some cases, companies may choose to omit transactions because they want to minimize taxable income. Thus, the auditor needs to consider controls over completeness, which might include the following:

- Use of prenumbered shipping documents and sales invoices and the subsequent accounting for all numbers
- Immediate online entry into the computer system and immediate assignment of unique identification number by the computer application
- Reconciliation of shipping records with billing records
- Supervisory review, such as review of transactions at a fast-food franchise
- Reconciliation of inventory with sales, such as the reconciliation of liquor at a bar at the end of the night with recorded sales

Controls Related to Valuation Implementing controls related to proper valuation of routine sales transactions should be relatively straightforward. Sales should be made from authorized price lists—for example, the price read by a scanner at Wal-Mart or the price accessed by a salesperson from a laptop. In these situations, the control procedures should provide reasonable assurance of the correct input of authorized price changes into the computer files and limit access to those files, including the following:

- Limiting access to the files to authorized individuals
- Printing a list of changed prices for review by the department that authorized the changes
- Reconciling input with printed output reports to assure that all changes were made and no unauthorized ones were added
- Limiting authorization privileges to those individuals with the responsibility for pricing

Valuation issues most often arise in connection with unusual or uncertain sales terms. Examples include sales where the customer has recourse to the selling company, franchise sales, bundled sales, cost-plus contracts, or other contracts covering long periods with provisions for partial payments. If these complex transactions are common, the company should have established policies and processes for handling them that should be understood by the auditor.

Another issue affecting the valuation of sales is returns and allowances. Abnormal returns or allowances may be the first sign that a company has inappropriate recording of revenue. The *Auditing in Practice* feature "Risks Associated with Sales Returns: The Case of Medicis and Ernst & Young" notes the problems that can arise if controls related to returns and allowances are not designed and operating effectively, and the auditor does not appropriately respond to this control risk. Controls that the client should implement for identifying and promptly recording returned goods include formal policies and procedures for:

- Clearly articulating contractual return provisions in the sales contract
- Approving acceptance of returns
- Recording goods returned on prenumbered documents that are accounted for, to be sure they are all recorded promptly
- Identifying whether credit should be given or whether the goods will be reworked according to warranty provisions and returned to the customer
- Determining the potential obsolescence or defects in the goods
- Assuring proper classification of the goods and determining that the goods are not reshipped as if they were new goods
- Developing and implementing a sales returns reserve methodology, requiring reasonable and supportable assumptions

Valuation of accounts receivable also has important risks that need to be mitigated with appropriate controls. Formal credit policies are designed to provide reasonable assurance of the realization of the accounts receivable into cash. Companies should use the following procedures to address credit risk:

- A formal credit policy, which may be automated for most transactions but requires special approval for large and/or unusual transactions
- A periodic review of the credit policy by key executives to determine whether changes are dictated either by current economic events or by deterioration of the receivables
- Continuous monitoring of receivables for evidence of increased risk, such as increases in the number of days past due or an unusually high concentration in a few key customers whose financial prospects are declining
- Adequate segregation of duties in the credit department, with specific authorization to write off receivables segregated from individuals who handle cash transactions with the customer

Risks Associated with Sales Returns: The Case of Medicis and Ernst & Young

In 2012, the PCAOB settled a disciplinary order censuring Ernst & Young (EY), imposing a $2 million penalty against the firm and sanctioning four of its current and former partners. In the audits of Medicis' December 31, 2005, 2006, and 2007 financial statements, the PCAOB found that EY and its partners failed to properly evaluate a material component of the company's financial statements—its sales returns reserve. EY did not properly evaluate Medicis' practice of reserving for most of its estimated product returns at replacement cost, instead of at gross sales price. It appears that EY accepted the company's basis for reserving at replacement cost, when the auditors should have known that this approach would not be supported by the audit evidence. By using replacement cost for the reserve, rather than gross sales price, Medicis' reported sales returns reserve were materially understated and its reported revenue was materially overstated.

Ultimately, EY concluded that Medicis' practice of reserving for its sales returns was not in conformity with GAAP. The company corrected its accounting for its sales returns reserve and had to file restated financial statements with the U.S. SEC.

For further details on this case, see PCAOB Release No. 105-2012-001.

An additional aspect of the valuation of net receivables is management's process for estimating the allowance account. Management should have a well-controlled process in place to develop a reasonable and supportable estimate for this allowance account.

Documenting Controls Auditors need to document their understanding of internal controls for both integrated audits and financial statement only audits. *Exhibit 9.5* provides an example of an internal control questionnaire for sales and accounts receivable. The first part helps document the auditor's understanding of the process; in the second part of the questionnaire, each negative (*no*) answer represents a potential internal control deficiency. Given a negative answer, the auditor should consider the effect of the response on the initial assessment of control risk. For example, a negative response to the question regarding the existence of a segregation of duties between those receiving cash and those authorizing write-offs or adjustments of accounts indicates that a risk exists that an individual could take cash receipts and cover up the fraud by writing off a customer's balance. Unless another control compensates for this deficiency, the auditor will likely have a control risk assessment of moderate or high in this area.

Although questionnaires have been used extensively in the past, they are currently being replaced by control matrices, flowcharts, and documented walkthroughs of processes. *Exhibit 9.6* presents a partially completed control matrix for contract revenue that links the risk of misstatement to the client's control and provides a means for the auditor to document the testing approach and testing results.

LO 5 Describe how to use planning analytical procedures to identify possible material misstatements for revenue cycle accounts, disclosures, and assertions.

Performing Planning Analytical Procedures

Planning analytical procedures help auditors identify areas of potential material misstatements. As initially described in *Chapter 6*, the steps that the auditor will take are as follows:

1. Determine the suitability of a particular analytical procedure for given account(s)/assertion(s), considering the risks of material misstatement.

| EXHIBIT **9.5** | Control Risk Assessment Questionnaire: Sales and Receivables |

SALES ORDERS

Sales authorized by: (Describe the source and scope of authority, and the documentation or other means of indicating authorizations. Include explicitly the authorization of prices for customers.)

_____

_____

Sales orders prepared by, or entered into the system by:

_____

_____

Individuals authorized to change price tables: (Indicate specific individuals and their authority to change prices on the system and the methods used to verify the correctness of changes.)

_____

_____

Existence of major contracts with customers that might merit special attention during the course of the audit: (Describe any major contracts and their terms.)

_____

_____

Restrictions on access to computer files for entering or changing orders: (Describe access control systems and indicate whether we have tested them in conjunction with our review of data processing general controls.)

_____

_____

	Check (x) one:	
	Yes	**No**
1. Are orders entered by individuals who do not have access to the goods being shipped?	_____	_____
2. Are orders authorized by individuals who do not have access to the goods being shipped?	_____	_____
3. Are batch and edit controls used effectively on this application? If so, describe the controls.	_____	_____
4. Are sales invoices prenumbered? Is the sequence of prenumbered documents independently accounted for?	_____	_____
5. Are control totals and reconciliations used effectively to ensure that all items are recorded and that subsidiary files are updated at the same time invoices are generated? If so, describe.		
6. Do procedures exist to ensure that the current credit status of a customer is checked before an order is shipped? If so, describe.	_____	_____
7. Are price lists stored in the computer independently reconciled to authorized prices by the marketing manager or someone in the marketing manager's office?	_____	_____
8. Are duties segregated such that the personnel receiving cash differ from the personnel authorized to make account write-offs or adjustments of accounts?	_____	_____

EXHIBIT 9.6 Partially Completed Controls Matrix for Contract Revenue

Control Description	Risk of Misstatement—Relevant Assertion(s)	Testing Approach (Nature of Testing)	Timing of Testing	Extent of Testing	Testing Results (Including Deficiencies)
A revenue recognition review is performed by the revenue accountant before revenue is recorded.	The risks are that revenue will be recorded before the criteria for recognizing revenue have been met or that revenue will be recorded at the incorrect amount. • Valuation • Existence	Reperformance of analyses performed by the revenue accountant.	Year-end		

Note: The matrix is intended as a partial illustration. The matrix would typically be linked to a supporting flowchart that would detail the key controls related to contract review, and all key controls would be included in the matrix.

---

2. Evaluate the reliability of data that the auditor is using to develop an expectation of account balances or ratios. In evaluating data reliability, the auditor should consider the source of the data, its comparability, the nature of information available about the data, and the controls over the preparation of the data.

3. Develop an expectation of recorded account balances or ratios and evaluate whether that expectation is precise enough to accomplish the relevant objective.

  i. *Planning analytical procedures*:
   Objective: Identify accounts with heightened risk of misstatement during audit planning to provide a basis for designing and implementing responses to the assessed risks
   Precision of expectation: Less precise.

4. Define when the difference between the auditor's expectation and what the client has recorded would be considered significant.

5. Compare the client's recorded amounts with the auditor's expectation to determine any significant unexpected differences.

6. Investigate significant unexpected differences.

  i. *Planning analytical procedures*: Significant unexpected differences suggest that substantive procedures for the account/assertion will be increased.

7. Ensure that the following have been appropriately documented: auditor's expectation from Step 3, including the factors that the auditor considered in developing the expectation, the results in Step 4, and the audit procedures conducted relating to Steps 5 and 6.

Step 1: Identify Suitable Analytical Procedures *Exhibit* 9.7 contains examples of planning analytical procedures that the auditor might consider relevant for revenue cycle accounts.

Step 2: Evaluate Reliability of Data Used to Develop Expectations
Various factors can influence reliability of data in revenue cycle accounts during planning analytical procedures. One is the source of information that is available. Information is more reliable when it is obtained from independent sources outside the company. For example, obtaining outside

EXHIBIT 9.7	Using Ratios and Trends Analyses in Planning Analytical Procedures in the Revenue Cycle

Some basic ratios used in planning analytical procedures include:

- Gross margin analysis
- Turnover of receivables (ratio of credit sales to average net receivables) or the number of days' sales in accounts receivable
- Average receivables balance per customer
- Receivables as a percentage of current assets and/or total assets
- Aging of receivables
- Allowance for uncollectible accounts as a percentage of accounts receivable
- Bad debt expense as a percentage of net credit sales
- Sales in the last month (or quarter) to total sales
- Sales discounts to credit sales
- Returns and allowances as a percentage of sales

Some basic trend analyses in planning analytical procedures include:

- Monthly sales analysis compared with past years and budgets
- Identification of spikes in sales at the end of quarters or the end of the year
- Trends in discounts allowed to customers that exceed both past experience and the industry average

evidence of gross margin in the company's industry would be considered more reliable data than simply using a historical trend of the company's own gross margin, without regard to industry considerations. Another factor influencing reliability of data is comparability. The auditor should consider whether the company's data may differ in an expected way from the overall industry. For example, bad debt expense as a percentage of sales may not be comparable to the overall industry if the company has a significantly different client base or credit policy than the industry (e.g., much more stringent or much less stringent credit terms).

Step 3: Develop Expectations Developing expectations about relationships in the data is important to identifying accounts with heightened risk of material misstatement during audit planning. Possible expected relationships in the revenue cycle include:

- There is no unusual year-end sales activity.
- Accounts receivable growth is consistent with revenue growth.
- Revenue growth, receivables growth, and gross margin are consistent with the activity in the industry.
- There is no unusual concentration of sales made to customers (in comparison with the prior year).
- The accounts receivable turnover is not significantly different from the prior year.
- The ratio of the allowance for doubtful accounts to total receivables or to credit sales is similar to the prior year.

Step 4 and Step 5: Define and Identify Significant Unexpected Differences Step 4 requires the auditor to define the difference amount (between the auditor's expectation and what the client has recorded) that would be considered significant; this will require consideration of the auditor's assessed materiality level and the auditor's desired level of assurance. Typically, when the risk of material misstatement is higher, the amount of acceptable difference is lower.

In Step 5, the auditor compares the client's recorded amounts with the auditor's expectation. Once this mechanical step is completed, the auditor will have identified any significant differences between the auditor's expectation and what the client has recorded.

If planning analytical procedures do not identify any unexpected relationships, the auditor will conclude that a heightened risk of material misstatements does not exist in these accounts. If there are unusual or unexpected relationships, the planned substantive audit procedures would be adjusted to address the potential material misstatements. The auditor should be aware that if a revenue fraud is taking place, the financial statements usually will contain departures from industry norms but may not differ from the expectations set by management. Thus, the auditor should compare the unaudited financial statements with both past results and industry trends. The following unexpected relationships might suggest a heightened risk of fraud:

- Revenue is increasing even though there is strong competition and a major competitor has introduced a new product.
- Revenue increases are not consistent with the industry or the economy.
- Gross margins are higher than average, or there is an unexpected change in gross margins.
- Large increases in revenue occur near the end of the quarter or year.
- Revenue has grown and net income has increased, but there is negative cash flow from operations.

Step 6 and Step 7: Investigate Significant Unexpected Differences and Ensure Proper Documentation Significant unexpected differences suggest that audit effort for the account/assertion will need to be increased. The auditor will develop a plan for how to address the identified risks, and the following section of this chapter explains this process. As the auditor proceeds through planning analytical procedures, documentation will be accumulated in the workpapers. Specifically, the auditor will document the analytical procedures used, the auditor's expectations, how the level of significant difference was determined, the identification of significant unexpected differences, and the follow-up to address significant unexpected differences.

The *Focus on Fraud* feature "An Example of Ratio Analysis in Planning Analytical Procedures" provides an example of how planning analytical procedures can provide the auditor with insight regarding the existence of fraud.

Responding to Identified Risks of Material Misstatement

LO 6 Determine appropriate responses to identified risks of material misstatement for revenue cycle accounts, disclosures, and assertions.

Once the auditor understands the risks of material misstatement, the auditor is in a position to determine the appropriate audit procedures to perform. Audit procedures should be proportional to the assessed risks, with areas of higher risk receiving more audit attention and effort. Responding to identified risks typically involves developing an audit approach that contains substantive procedures (e.g., tests of details and, when appropriate, substantive analytical procedures) and tests of controls, when applicable. The sufficiency and appropriateness of selected procedures will vary to achieve the desired level of assurance for each relevant assertion. While audit firms may have a standardized audit program for the revenue cycle, the auditor should customize the audit program based on the assessment of risk of material misstatement.

An Example of Ratio Analysis in Planning Analytical Procedures

The following example demonstrates how planning analytical procedures may be helpful to the auditor. The company is a wholesaler selling to major retail chains in a competitive industry. The auditor notes the following changes in ratios:

- The number of days' sales in accounts receivable increased in one year from 44 to 65.
- The gross margin increased from 16.7% to 18.3% (industry average was 16.3%).
- The amount of accounts receivable increased 35% from $9 million to $12 million, while sales remained virtually unchanged.

All of these ratios were substantially greater than the industry averages; the auditor's expectations were that the company should be somewhat similar to the industry averages. An auditor comparing the client's ratios with the auditor's expectations should carefully consider reasons for the changes: (1) Is there a business reason why these ratios changed? (2) What alternatives could potentially explain these changes? and (3) What corroborating evidence is available for potential explanations?

The auditor should develop a potential set of explanations that could account for the changes in all three ratios and design audit procedures to gather independent corroborating evidence that either supports or contradicts that explanation. In this example, the company was engaged in a complicated scheme of recording fictitious sales. A number of other explanations were offered by management—increased efficiency, better computer system, better customer service, and so forth. However, only fictitious sales could account for the change in the gross margin, the increase in the number of days' sales in accounts receivable, and the increase in the total balance of accounts receivable that occurred when sales were not increasing. Such a conclusion would then be addressed through subsequent audit procedures.

Consider a client where the auditor has assessed the risk of material misstatement related to the completeness of revenue at slightly below the maximum. This client has incentives to understate revenue in an effort to smooth earnings and has implemented somewhat effective controls in this area. The auditor may develop an audit program that consists of first performing limited tests of operating effectiveness of controls, then performing limited substantive analytical procedures, and finally performing substantive tests of details. Because of the high risk, the auditor will want to obtain a great deal of evidence directly from tests of details. In contrast, consider a client where the auditor has assessed the risk of material misstatement related to the completeness of revenues as low, and believes that the client has implemented effective controls in this area. For this client, the auditor can likely perform tests of controls, gain a high level of assurance from substantive analytical procedures such as a reasonableness test, and then complete the substantive procedures by performing tests of details at a limited level.

Panel A of *Exhibit 9.8* makes the point that because of differences in risk, the box of evidence to be filled for testing the completeness of revenue at the low-risk client is smaller than that at the high-risk client. Panel B of *Exhibit 9.8* illustrates the different levels of assurance that the auditor will obtain from tests of controls and substantive procedures for the assertion at the two different clients. Panel B makes the point that because of the higher risk associated with the completeness of revenue at Client B, the auditor will want to design the audit so that more of the assurance or evidence is coming from direct tests of account balances. Note that the relative percentages are judgmental in nature; the examples are simply intended to give you a sense of how an auditor might select an appropriate mix of procedures.

EXHIBIT 9.8 Panel A: Sufficiency of Evidence for Completeness of Revenue

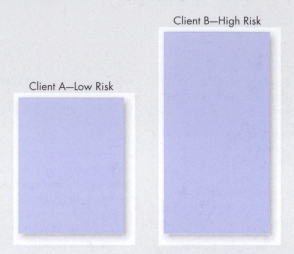

Panel B: Approaches to Obtaining Audit Evidence for Completeness of Revenue

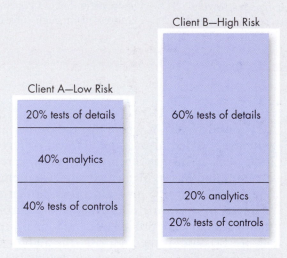

Obtaining Evidence About Internal Control Operating Effectiveness in the Revenue Cycle

LO 7 Determine appropriate tests of controls and consider the results of tests of controls for revenue cycle accounts, disclosures, and assertions.

For integrated audits, the auditor will test the operating effectiveness of important controls as of the client's year-end. If the auditor wants to rely on controls for the financial statement audit, the auditor will test the operating effectiveness of those controls throughout the year.

Selecting Controls to Test and Performing Tests of Controls

The auditor selects controls that are important to the auditor's conclusion about whether the organization's controls adequately address the assessed risk of material misstatement in the revenue cycle. The auditor will select both entity-wide and transaction controls for testing. Typical tests of transaction controls include inquiry of personnel performing the control, observation of the control being performed, inspection of documentation confirming that the control has been performed, and reperformance of the control by the individual auditor testing the control.

For example, a control may include reconciliation between the sales subledger and the general ledger. The approaches to testing the reconciliation control could involve one or more of the following:

- *Inquiry*—Talk with the personnel who perform the control about the procedures and processes involved in the reconciliation.
- *Observation*—Observe the entity personnel performing the reconciliation.
- *Inspection*—Review the documentation supporting completion of the reconciliation.
- *Reperformance*—Perform the reconciliation and agree to the reconciliation completed by the entity personnel.

The auditor uses professional judgment to determine the appropriate types of tests of controls to perform. However, inquiry alone is generally not sufficient evidence and would typically be supplemented with observation, examination, and/or reperformance.

Exhibit 9.9 presents an overview of various transaction controls that might be used to mitigate risks in the revenue cycle and how the controls might be tested. Note that the tests of controls include selecting samples of transactions and obtaining supporting documents, reviewing monitoring controls, testing computer access controls, using generalized audit software (GAS) to match documents and look for gaps or duplicate document numbers, reviewing customer complaints, reviewing documents such as reconciliations and management reports noting timely action taken, and reviewing sales contracts.

Considering the Results of Tests of Controls

The auditor will analyze the results of the tests of controls to determine additional appropriate procedures. There are two potential outcomes:

1. If control deficiencies are identified, the auditor will assess those deficiencies to determine their severity. (Are they significant deficiencies or material weaknesses?) The auditor would then modify the preliminary control risk assessment (possibly from low to moderate or high) and document the implications of the control deficiencies. The last column in *Exhibit 9.9* provides examples of implications of control deficiencies for substantive testing. Appropriate modifications to planned substantive audit procedures will be determined by the types of misstatements that are most likely to occur because of the control deficiency.
2. If no control deficiencies are identified, the auditor will likely determine that the preliminary assessment of control risk as low is still appropriate. The auditor will then determine the extent that controls can provide evidence on the correctness of account balances and determine planned substantive audit procedures. The level of substantive testing in this situation will be less than what is required in circumstances where deficiencies in internal control were identified. From the audit risk model, we know that companies with effective internal controls should require less substantive testing of account balances.

EXHIBIT 9.9 Control Examples and Tests

Objective	Examples of Controls	How Control Would Be Tested	Implications if Control Is Not Working
1. Recorded transactions are authorized and actually occurred.	a. Sales recorded only with valid customer order and shipping document. b. Credit is approved before shipment.	a. Sample recorded sales transactions and vouch back to source documents. Use generalized audit software to match sales with electronic shipping document or customer order. b. Use ACL to determine each customer's balance and compare with its credit limit.	a. Recorded sales may not have occurred. Extend accounts receivable confirmation work and review of subsequent collections. b. Receivables may not be collectible. Expand confirmation work and review of subsequent collections.
2. Sales are recorded in the correct accounting period.	a. Computer records sale upon entry of customer order and shipping information. Transactions entered, but not yet processed, are identified for an exception report and followed up. b. Monthly statements are sent to customers. A group independent of those recording the transactions receives and follows up complaints.	a. Review monitoring controls (e.g., management's review of transactions entered into the system and not shipped and billed). b. Review nature of complaints received. Investigate to determine if there is a pattern.	a. Company may have unrecorded sales transactions. Discuss with management to determine if it has plans to bill the sales. b. Sales may be recorded in the wrong year. Expand sales cutoff testing.
3. All sales are recorded.	a. Prenumbered shipping documents and invoices which are periodically accounted for. b. Online input of transactions and independent logging are done. c. Transactions are reviewed and compared with budgets and differences are investigated.	a. Review reconciliations to determine that control is working. b. Use generalized audit software to verify transaction trails. c. Review management reports and evidence of actions taken.	a–c. Expand cutoff tests at year-end to determine that all transactions are recorded in the correct period.
4. Sales are accurately recorded.	a. Sales price comes from authorized sales price list maintained on the computer.	a. Test access controls. Take a sample of recorded sales invoices and trace price back to authorized list.	a. Accounts receivable may be over-stated or understated due to pricing errors. Expand confirmation and subsequent collection procedures.
5. Sales are correctly classified.	a. Chart of accounts is up to date and used. b. Computer program is tested before implementation.	a. Take a sample of transactions and trace to general ledger to see if they are properly classified. b. When testing general controls, determine that controls over program changes are working.	a. Expand test of sales and receivables to determine that all items represent bona fide contracts and not consignment sales or sale of operating assets. b. Expand confirmations to customers.

Obtaining Substantive Evidence About Accounts, Disclosures, and Assertions in the Revenue Cycle

LO 8 Determine and apply sufficient appropriate substantive audit procedures for testing revenue cycle accounts, disclosures, and assertions.

In performing substantive procedures, the auditor wants reasonable assurance that the client's revenue recognition policies are appropriate and that revenue transactions are in accordance with GAAP. Substantive procedures (substantive analytical procedures, tests of details, or both) should be performed for all relevant assertions related to significant revenue cycle accounts and disclosures. Even if the auditor has evidence indicating that controls are operating effectively, the auditor cannot rely solely on control testing to provide evidence on the reliability of these accounts and assertions. Substantive tests in the revenue cycle are typically performed to provide evidence that:

- Sales transactions do exist and are properly valued.
- Accounts receivable exist.
- The balance in the allowance account is reasonable.
- Fraudulent transactions are not included in the financial statements.

Exhibit 9.10 details typical substantive procedures for sales and accounts receivable. The extent to which substantive analytical procedures and tests of details are performed depends on a number of factors, including the risk of material misstatement and the effectiveness of controls. The *Auditing in Practice* feature "Performing Appropriate Substantive Audit Procedures in the Revenue Cycle: The Case of Kyoto Audit Corporation" highlights the importance of performing and documenting sufficient appropriate substantive procedures in the revenue cycle.

Performing Appropriate Substantive Audit Procedures in the Revenue Cycle: The Case of Kyoto Audit Corporation

AUDITING IN **PRACTICE**

In February 2012, the PCAOB released its first inspection report on Kyoto Audit Corporation (Kyoto), a Japanese affiliate of the Big 4 audit firm PricewaterhouseCoopers (PwC). PwC describes Kyoto as a cooperating firm. While Kyoto is not a full member of PwC's global network, it appears that Kyoto has the right to use PwC's audit methodology and has access to the expertise of the pwc network.

In December 2010 and January 2011, the PCAOB's staff reviewed Kyoto's audits for two companies and found audit deficiencies in both audits. The deficiencies were so severe it appeared that "the firm at the time it issued its audit report had not obtained sufficient competent evidential matter to support its opinion on the issuer's financial statements." The deficiencies they found included "the failure, in both audits, to perform adequate substantive analytical audit procedures to test revenue." The report also cited Kyoto's failures to

perform sufficient procedures "to test the allowance for doubtful accounts." It appears that the audit firm had not gathered sufficient appropriate evidence to determine whether recorded revenue was accurate or whether customers could pay their bills.

While most audits are quality audits, this inspection report serves to illustrate the importance of complying with professional standards in performing and documenting sufficient appropriate substantive procedures in the revenue cycle. Kyoto ultimately performed additional audit procedures in response to the PCAOB inspection report, but did not change the audit reports issued. The companies with the audit deficiencies did not change their financial statements. Therefore, it appears that while the procedures performed by Kyoto were insufficient, the underlying financial accounts and assertions were not materially misstated.

For further details on this case, see PCAOB Release No. 104-2012-053.

EXHIBIT **9.10**	Management Assertions and Substantive Procedures in the Revenue Cycle

Management Assertion	**Substantive Procedure**
Existence/occurrence—Recorded sales and accounts receivable are valid.	1. Perform substantive analytical procedures. 2. Trace sales invoices to customer orders and bills of lading. 3. Confirm balances or unpaid invoices with customers. 4. Examine subsequent collections as evidence that the sale existed. 5. Scan sales journal for duplicate entries.
Completeness—All sales are recorded.	1. Perform substantive analytical procedures. 2. Trace bills of lading to sales invoice and sales journal. 3. Account for sequence of sales invoices in sales journal.
Rights and obligations—The accounts receivable are owned by the organization (e.g., none have been sold).	1. Inquire of management. 2. Review minutes of board meetings.
Valuation or allocation—Sales and accounts receivable are properly valued and recorded in the correct period. Revenue has been recognized in accordance with GAAP.	1. Verify clerical accuracy of sales invoices and agreement of sales invoices with supporting documents. 2. Trace sales invoices to sales journal and customer's ledger. 3. Confirm balances or unpaid invoices with customers. 4. Foot sales journal and accounts receivable trial balance and reconcile accounts receivable trial balance with control account. 5. Review adequacy of the allowance for doubtful accounts. 6. Perform sales cutoff test.
Presentation and disclosure—Credit balance and related-party accounts receivable are properly disclosed. Revenue recognition policies have been properly disclosed.	1. Obtain confirmations from banks and other financial institutions. 2. Inquire of management. 3. Review work performed in other audit areas. 4. Review revenue recognition policies for appropriateness and consistency.

Revenue and Accounts Receivable: Performing Substantive Analytical Procedures

The process for conducting substantive analytical procedures in the revenue cycle will be similar to that described earlier in this chapter for planning analytical procedures.

Step 1: Identify Suitable Analytical Procedures The relevant analytical procedures for conducting substantive analytics are not necessarily different from those for planning analytical procedures as depicted in *Exhibit 9.7*. Rather, the tests are conducted at a more precise level using organization-relevant categories. For example, ratios and trend analyses can be conducted by product line, geographic region, or business unit. Further, ratios and trends can be compared to industry averages and to relevant prior periods (e.g., monthly, quarterly, or yearly).

When performing substantive analytical procedures, the auditor is more likely to conduct a reasonableness test or use regression analysis. An example of a reasonableness test would be estimating room revenue for a hotel using the number of rooms, the average room rate, and average occupancy rate. Alternatively, the revenue from an electrical utility company should be related to revenue rates approved by a Public Service Commission (where applicable) and demographic information about growth in households and industry in the service area the company serves.

Regression analysis could be performed as a time-series analysis by examining trends in relationship with previous results. For example, it might be used to estimate monthly sales by product line based on the historical relationship of sales and independent variables such as cost of sales, selected selling expenses, or growth in total sales for the industry. Another form of regression analysis is referred to as cross-sectional analysis. Rather than comparing relationships over a period of time, cross-sectional analysis is designed to compare results across a number of locations. For example, Home Depot and Lowe's might have hundreds of stores—each with a basic store layout and size. Cross-sectional analysis allows the auditor to identify any unusual store performance. For example, the auditor may identify potential problems by comparing sales per square foot of retail space among the stores, looking for those with significantly more sales per square foot than the other stores.

Step 2: Evaluate Reliability of Data Used to Develop Expectations
In evaluating reliability of data used to develop expectations in substantive analytical procedures, the auditor may test the operating effectiveness of controls over the preparation of information used in those analytics. When such controls are considered effective, the auditor will have greater confidence in the reliability of the information. Further, the auditor may use data from independent external sources (e.g., industry ratios), as that data are generally considered reliable.

Step 3: Develop Expectations
Expectations for substantive analytical procedures will be more precise than those considered during planning analytical procedures. An increase in precision can be obtained by using more disaggregated data. The appropriate level of disaggregation will be influenced by the nature of the organization, its size, and its complexity. As an example, consider the reasonableness test related to hotel revenue presented earlier. The auditor could develop an expectation of overall room revenue by using the number of rooms across the hotel chain, the average room rate across the chain, and the average occupancy rate across the chain. This approach would not result in a very precise estimate. However, if the auditor disaggregated the analysis based on types of hotels within the chain (luxury, resort, or economy), the auditor could improve the precision of the estimate. Usually, the more detailed the information, the more precise the expectation.

Step 4 and Step 5: Define and Identify Significant Unexpected Differences
At this point, the auditor is trying to answer the question of whether the auditor's expectation is significantly different from what the client has recorded. The amount of difference that is considered significant is influenced by materiality, desired level of assurance, and assessed risk of material misstatement. As the auditor's assessed risk of material misstatement increases, the amount of the unexpected difference that would be considered significant declines.

The auditor then compares the client's recorded amounts with the auditor's expectation. Once this mechanical step is completed, the auditor will have identified any significant differences between the auditor's expectation and what the client has recorded.

Step 6 and Step 7: Investigate Significant Unexpected Differences and Ensure Proper Documentation
Materiality and the desired level of assurance will aid the auditor in determining how to proceed with investigating

significant unexpected differences. The auditor will investigate significant unexpected differences through substantive tests of details, as described next. In general, if substantive analytical procedures do not result in unresolved issues, direct testing of account balances can be reduced. However, in the revenue cycle it is unlikely that audit evidence obtained from substantive analytical procedures alone will be sufficient evidence for the auditor.

Finally, as with planning analytical procedures, the auditor will accumulate documentation with respect to evidence gathered and judgments reached during substantive analytical procedures.

Revenue: Substantive Tests of Details

Substantive tests of details for revenue transactions would primarily involve inspection of relevant client documentation. These tests would be focused on the existence and valuation assertions, although the auditor might also perform tests of details related to completeness.

Revenue: Existence and Valuation Assertions

The existence and valuation assertions are usually the most relevant for revenue accounts. Vouching a sample of recorded sales transactions back to customer orders and shipping documents provides support for the existence assertion. The auditor should compare the quantities billed and shipped with customer orders and verify the clerical accuracy of the sales invoices to provide assurance on valuation. These procedures will also provide evidence on the existence and valuation of accounts receivable.

As discussed in *Chapter 8*, computerized audit techniques can also be useful. Audit software can be used to identify duplicate sales. GAS can also select a sample of recorded sales transactions for vouching. Further, such software may be able to compare the transactions detail with the supporting electronic documents. GAS can also be used to verify the clerical accuracy of the invoices and foot the sales journal.

Revenue: Completeness Assertion

In testing the completeness assertion, the auditor would expect that the client uses prenumbered shipping and billing documents. The auditor would select a sample of shipping documents and trace them into the sales journal to obtain evidence on whether all shipments have been recorded as sales transactions. The auditor can use audit software to look for gaps in the recorded sales invoice numbers and verify that the missing numbers are appropriate and do not represent unrecorded sales. For example, the gaps may be caused by voided documents or by using different numbers at different locations. These procedures will also provide evidence on the completeness of accounts receivable.

Revenue: Cutoff Issues

Additional audit attention should be given to sales transactions recorded just before and after year-end. A specific concern related to existence is whether a recorded revenue transaction actually occurred before the end of the accounting period. For an example, refer back to *Exhibit 9.4*, which contains a description of the situation in which Motorola kept its third quarter books open after the quarter ended so that it could record additional revenues. The auditor is also concerned with whether transactions recorded in the subsequent year actually relate to the year being audited. Performing cutoff tests with sales transactions recorded several days before and after year-end is important to assuring both the existence and completeness of the revenue transactions.

The following items can be examined to determine whether a proper cutoff of sales and sales returns has been achieved:

Cutoff Test	Items to Examine
Sales	Shipping documents and related recorded sales
Sales returns	Receiving reports and related credits to customer accounts

Sales cutoff can be tested in alternative ways. For example, the auditor can select a sample of sales transactions from the cutoff period to determine when the transaction occurred. The auditor will look at the shipping terms and shipment dates to determine whether there was an appropriate cutoff. The auditor may also want to inspect the sales contracts for terms indicating that the recording of the sale should be postponed; for example, the customer's right of return (and a high probability of return), the existence of additional performance by the seller, the probability of collection based on some future event (contingency), or the existence of an unusually low probability of collection.

As a second approach to cutoff testing, if reliable shipping dates are stored electronically, GAS can be used to identify any sales recorded in the wrong period.

Accounts Receivable: Substantive Procedures Based on the Aged Trial Balance

A starting point for accounts receivable substantive procedures is obtaining a detailed aged accounts receivable trial balance from the client, manually preparing an aged trial balance, or using GAS to develop aging information. *Exhibit 9.11* provides an example of an aged trial balance. A detailed trial balance lists each customer's balance or unpaid invoices, with columns to show those that are current, 30 days overdue, 60 days, and so on.

If the client prepared the trial balance, the mathematical and aging accuracy should be recalculated by the auditor and it should be agreed to the general ledger. Credit balances can also be identified and, if significant, reclassified as liabilities. The aged trial balance is used by the auditor to:

- Agree the detail to the balance in the control account
- Select customer balances for confirmation
- Identify amounts due from officers, employees, or other related parties or any nontrade receivables that need to be separately disclosed in the financial statements
- Help determine the reasonableness of the allowance for doubtful accounts by identifying past-due balances

Accounts Receivable: Substantive Tests of Details—Confirmations

A widely used auditing procedure is to ask the client's customers to confirm the existence and the amount they owe to the client. Existence is necessary for correct valuation. However, existence does not necessarily assure correct valuation; for example, a customer might acknowledge the existence of the debt, but might not have sufficient resources to pay it. Confirmations are generally considered to provide quality evidence about the existence of receivables and the completeness of collections, sales discounts, and sales returns and allowances. For example, if a payment had been made but was not recorded by the client, or an invoice was recorded but no shipment occurred, the customer would likely report the discrepancy on the

EXHIBIT **9.11** Accounts Receivable Aging

Name	Balance	Current	30–60	61–90	91–120	Over 120
Alvies	154,931	154,931				
Basch	71,812		71,812			
Carlson	115,539	115,539				
Draper	106,682	106,682				
Ernst	60,003			60,003		
Faust	90,907	90,907				
Gerber	241,129	211,643	29,486			
Hal	51,516	51,516				
Harv	237,881	237,881				
Kaas	18,504				18,504	
Kruze	44,765	44,765				
Lere	28,937	28,937				
Misty	210,334	210,334				
Mooney	216,961	216,961				
Otto	273,913	273,913				
Paggen	209,638	209,638				
Quast	88,038					88,038
Rauch	279,937	279,937				
Sundby	97,898	97,898				
Towler	96,408	85,908		10,500		
Zook	31,886	31,886				
	...	...				
Zough	245,927	245,927				
Totals	2,973,546	2,695,203	101,298	70,503	18,504	88,038

confirmation. A confirmation can be very effective in addressing the existence of fictitious sales. The presumption is that if fictitious sales are recorded to the account of a valid customer, the customer will note that some of the recorded sales are not correct.

Auditing standards in the U.S. generally require the use of confirmations unless one of the following conditions exists:

- Accounts receivable are not material.
- The use of confirmations would be ineffective. An auditor might determine that confirmations are ineffective if customers have previously refused to confirm balances or customers do not have a good basis on which to respond to the confirmation.
- The auditor's assessment of the risk of material misstatement is low and that assessment, in conjunction with the evidence provided by other substantive tests, is sufficient.

While U.S. standards generally require the use of confirmations, the international auditing standards do not include this requirement.

The *Emerging Issues* feature "A PCAOB-Proposed Auditing Standard on Confirmations" provides details on the PCAOB's efforts in developing a new standard related to confirmations for U.S. public companies.

A PCAOB-Proposed Auditing Standard on Confirmations

EMERGING ISSUE

The PCAOB adopted AU 330 as an interim standard in 2003. However, in July 2010 the PCAOB issued an Exposure Draft, *Confirmation*, which would supersede AU Section 330 for public company audits. The comment period ended on September 13, 2010. The PCAOB staff has analyzed the comments received and is drafting revisions for the board's consideration. The PCAOB plans to issue a revised Exposure Draft during 2014.

Based on the Exposure Draft, changes from the current standard (AU 330) would include:

- Limiting the internal auditors' involvement in the confirmation process

- Clarifying that the receipt of an oral response to a confirmation request does not meet the definition of an external confirmation
- Eliminating exceptions for not confirming receivables
- Requiring the auditor to communicate with those charged with governance if the auditor concludes that management's refusal to allow confirmations is unreasonable
- Limiting instances in which negative confirmation requests are the only form of confirmation request to address the assessed risk of material misstatement at the assertion level

Types of Confirmations

There are two types of accounts receivable confirmations: positive confirmations and negative confirmations.

Positive Confirmations **Positive confirmations** are correspondence (paper or electronic) sent to a sample of customers, asking them to review the current balance or unpaid invoice(s) due to the client and return the letters directly to the auditor indicating whether they agree with the balance. If the customer does not return a signed confirmation, the auditor needs to use follow-up audit procedures to verify the existence of the customer's balance. *Exhibit 9.12* contains an example of a positive confirmation. Notice that it is printed on the client's letterhead, is addressed to the customer, is signed by the client, indicates the balance or unpaid invoice amount as of a particular date—referred to as the confirmation date—and tells the customer to respond directly to the auditor in an enclosed self-addressed, postage-paid envelope.

Auditors may choose to confirm the terms of unusual or complex agreements or transactions in conjunction with or separately from the confirmation of account balances. The confirmation may need to be addressed to customer personnel who would be familiar with the details rather than to their accounts payable personnel. Auditors should also specifically inquire during the confirmation process about the possibility of bill-and-hold transactions (such as transactions in which the seller recognizes the sale and bills the customer but does not actually deliver the goods or services), extended payment terms or nonstandard installment receivables, or an unusual volume of sales to distributors or retailers (possible channel stuffing). Further, the auditor should confirm not only the terms of the transactions but also the potential existence and content of side letters. A **side letter** is an agreement containing contract terms that are not part of the formal contract (often involving rights of return), thereby increasing audit risk because it enables key contract terms affecting revenue recognition to be hidden from the auditor as part of a revenue recognition fraud. Side letters are often associated with material revenue misstatements.

EXHIBIT **9.12**	Positive Confirmation

Gordon's Bay Manufacturing Company

14 Kidman Street
Austin, TX 73301
January 10, 2016

Alexander Industrial Supplies
1265 Lombardi Avenue
Green Bay, WI 54304

Our auditors, Johnstone, & Gramling, CPAs, are making an annual audit of our financial statements. Please confirm the balance due our company as of December 31, 2015, which is shown in our records as $32,012.38.

Please indicate in the space provided below if the amount is in agreement with your records. If there are differences, please provide any information that will assist our auditors in reconciling the difference.

Please mail your reply directly to Johnstone, & Gramling, CPAs, 975 University Avenue, Madison, WI 53706, in the enclosed return envelope. PLEASE DO NOT MAIL PAYMENTS ON THIS BALANCE TO OUR AUDITORS.

Very truly yours,

Meg Christianson

Meg Christianson
Controller
Gordon's Bay Manufacturing Company
To: Johnstone, & Gramling, CPAs
The balance due Gordon's Bay Manufacturing Company of $32,012.38 as of 12/31/15 is correct with the following exceptions, (if any):

Signature:_____
Title:_____
Date:_____

Negative Confirmations A **negative confirmation** asks the customer to review the balance owed to the client, but requests the customer to respond directly to the auditor only if the customer disagrees with the indicated balance. *Exhibit 9.13* provides an example of a negative confirmation. A negative confirmation is less expensive to administer than a positive confirmation because it does not require follow-up procedures when a customer does not return the confirmation. The auditor assumes that a nonresponse means that the customer agrees with the stated balance.

Negative confirmations would be used if the following conditions exist:

1. There are a large number of relatively small customer balances.
2. The assessed level of the risk of material misstatement for receivables and related revenue transactions is low.

EXHIBIT 9.13 Negative Confirmation

Gordon's Bay Manufacturing Company

14 Kidman Street
Austin, TX 73301
January 10, 2016

Alexander Industrial Supplies
1265 Lombardi Avenue
Green Bay, WI 54304

Our auditors, Johnstone, & Gramling, CPAs, are making an annual audit of our financial statements. Please confirm the balance due our company as of December 31, 2015, which is shown in our records as $32,012.38. If the amount is not correct, please report any differences directly to our auditors using the space below and the enclosed return envelope. NO REPLY IS NECESSARY IF THIS AMOUNT AGREES WITH YOUR RECORDS. PLEASE DO NOT MAIL PAYMENTS ON ACCOUNT TO OUR AUDITORS.

Very truly yours,

Meg Christianson

Meg Christianson
Controller
Gordon's Bay Manufacturing Company
To: Johnstone, & Gramling, CPAs
The balance due Gordon's Bay Manufacturing Company of $32,012.38 as of 12/31/15 does not agree with our records because
(No reply is necessary if your records agree.)

Signature:_____
Title:_____
Date:_____

3. The auditor has a reason to believe that the customers are likely to give proper attention to the requests; for example, the customers have independent records from which to make an evaluation, will take the time to do so, and will return the confirmation to the auditor if significant discrepancies exist.

Comparing Positive and Negative Confirmations Positive confirmations are considered to provide higher quality evidence than negative confirmations because they result in either (1) the receipt of a response from the customer or (2) the use of alternative procedures to verify the existence of the receivable. Auditors may choose to use positive confirmations for large receivable balances and negative confirmations for smaller balances.

Regardless of the type of confirmation used, auditors need to take care that the confirmation process used adheres to professional auditing standards. The *Auditing in Practice* feature "PCAOB Enforcement Actions

PCAOB Enforcement Actions Related to Confirming Accounts Receivable

Regulatory enforcement actions provide many examples of auditors not adhering to professional standards related to confirming accounts receivable. Two enforcement actions that illustrate this point are summarized here.

In a PCAOB enforcement action against Moore & Associates, the PCAOB notes that the audit firm's staff often did not do any work to confirm either the existence or the valuation of clients' receivables. At one client, the audit team documented that confirmation procedures were not applicable without documenting how they came to that unusual conclusion. Further, for another client, the firm's staff considered confirmation responses from client management as acceptable, when in fact confirmations should have come directly to the auditors from the clients' customers.

In a PCAOB enforcement action involving the audits of Satyam, the PCAOB notes the failure of the auditors to audit Satyam's accounts receivable balances in accordance with PCAOB standards. Specifically, the enforcement action indicates that the engagement team relied on Satyam's management to send confirmation requests associated with accounts receivable balances. Further, the auditors received no responses to these confirmation requests but made no attempt to follow up on the nonresponses with second confirmation requests. The auditors did perform alternative procedures to test receivables through the verification of subsequent receipts. However, no audit procedures were performed to ensure that the subsequent receipts were reconciled to individual invoices outstanding at fiscal year-end.

Thus, while U.S. professional auditing standards are quite clear on the need to confirm accounts receivable, there exist examples in which auditors inexplicably do not adhere to those standards. While most audits are performed in a quality manner, these examples serve to illustrate that problems do occur and that you should be aware of such a possibility as you enter the profession.

For further details on these cases, see PCAOB Release No. 105–2009-006 and PCAOB Release No. 105-2011-002.

Related to Confirming Accounts Receivable" highlights some problems auditors have had related to adhering to the professional standards in this area.

The Confirmation Process

Confirmations may be prepared manually in paper format, but are now more commonly prepared using electronic communication methods such as those provided by Confirmation.com. See the *Emerging Issues* feature "Electronic Confirmations at Confirmation.com" for further information about electronic confirmations. The auditor should assure that the information in each confirmation is correct and should control the dissemination of the confirmation requests so that the client cannot modify them. For paper confirmations, customers are requested to return confirmations directly to the auditor's office in an enclosed self-addressed, postage-paid envelope. Similarly, the mailing should show the auditor's address as the return address if the confirmation is not deliverable. Undeliverable confirmations should raise the auditor's suspicion regarding the existence of the recorded receivable. To avoid receiving confirmation responses for fictitious receivables, the auditor must take care to assure that the confirmation will not be delivered to a location where the client can act as a surrogate and confirm an inappropriate receivable.

Sample Selection There are several approaches to selecting the specific receivables that will be confirmed, and each of these is applicable to either paper-based or electronic confirmations. The auditor can confirm all of the large balances and randomly or haphazardly select some of the smaller

Electronic Confirmations at Confirmation.com

EMERGING ISSUE

Confirmation.com is a leading provider of all types of electronic confirmations, including accounts receivable confirmations. Electronic confirmations are equally as acceptable as audit evidence as paper-based confirmations had been used in the past. Electronic confirmations have reliability benefits because of the controls built into the software system, whereby management cannot intercept or alter the confirmation as is potentially the case with paper-based confirmations. They also have efficiency benefits because the process is automated and controlled by a third-party vendor, thereby saving the auditor time. Usually the electronic confirmation responses are produced within two days at the most, whereas paper-based confirmations make take several weeks to be returned. Of course, there is a cost to the auditor in using the services of a company like Confirmation.com (in the range of about $20 per confirmation for domestic pricing and about $100 for international pricing), but audit firms often consider this service a good investment.

When using an electronic confirmation process, the auditor needs to be sure that the process is secure and properly controlled, the information obtained is a direct communication to the auditor in response to the auditor's request, and that the information is obtained from a third party (in the case of accounts receivable, that party is the organization that owes money to the audit client) who is the intended respondent.

balances using either nonstatistical or monetary unit sampling (MUS). The auditor may decide to include in the sample those accounts that have credit balances, are significant and past due, and/or have unusual customer names that are unfamiliar to the auditor.

Sampling Unit The sampling unit can be a customer's entire account balance or one or more of the unpaid invoices that make up that balance. When a balance is composed of several unpaid invoices, it will help the customer if a list of those invoices is attached to the confirmation.

Undeliverable Confirmations If some confirmations are returned as undeliverable, the auditor should determine why this occurred. If the wrong address was used, the correct address should be obtained and another request should be sent. It is also possible that the customer does not exist. Every effort should be made to determine the customer's existence. For example, the customer's name and address could be located in the telephone directory, in the publication of a credit-rating service, or on the Internet. If a valid address cannot be located, the auditor should presume that the account does not exist or might be fictitious. The *Focus on Fraud* feature "False Confirmations" explains this topic and provides examples of fraudulent activity in the accounts receivable confirmation process.

Follow-Up to Nonresponses for Positive Confirmations Follow-up procedures are required for positive confirmations that are not returned within a reasonable time after being mailed, such as two weeks. Second, and sometimes third, requests are mailed. If the amount being confirmed is relatively large, the auditor may consider calling the customer to encourage a written reply. When customers do not respond to the positive confirmation requests, the auditor should perform other procedures, referred to as **alternative procedures**, to verify the existence of the receivable. Remember that mailed confirmations represent only a sample of the many account balances shown in the client's records. The results of the sample are

False Confirmations

A **false confirmation** is one in which the respondent (in this case, the client's customer) responds inaccurately to the audit firm with respect to the information on the confirmation. In a classic example, Just for Feet (an athletic shoe retailer) executives pressured the director of sales at Adidas to respond inaccurately to the auditor's accounts receivable information. Adidas' director of apparel sales confirmed that the company owed Just for Feet $2.2 million, when in fact Adidas only owed $40,000. The sales director's motive for agreeing to respond inaccurately was because of threats from Just for Feet to terminate the relationship with Adidas. Other notable examples of this type of false confirmation activity include similar schemes:

Company with Accounts Receivable Confirmation Fraud	Company That Provided False Confirmation	Title of Individual That Provided the False Confirmation
Kmart	Eastman Kodak	Vice president of sales
	Pepsi-Cola	National director of sales
	Frito-Lay	Director of sales and national account manager
Just for Feet	Adidas	Director of apparel sales
	Fila	President and CEO
	Converse	Vice president of U.S. sales
Royal Ahold	Sara Lee Foods	Sales manager
	Conagra Foods	Account manager
	Heritage Bag	CEO

False confirmations are problematic for auditors in terms of evidence reliability expectations. Auditors usually expect that externally provided evidence is reliable because it is from a third party. In the case of false confirmations, this expectation is invalid. In recent years, the SEC has actively pursued enforcement actions against individuals that have provided false confirmations to auditors.

intended to represent the total population; therefore, it is important that the auditor develop sufficient follow-up procedures to gain satisfaction about each of the balances selected for confirmation. Alternative procedures that can be considered include:

- *Subsequent collection of the balance after year end*—Care should be taken to assure that these subsequent receipts relate to the balance as of the confirmation date, not to subsequent sales. Evidence obtained from testing subsequent collections is often believed to be a stronger indicator of the validity of the customer's balance than that obtained from confirmations. If a significant amount of the year-end receivables balance is normally collected before the end of the audit, the auditor may choose to emphasize tests of subsequent collections and minimize confirmation work. Testing subsequent collections provides strong evidence about both the existence and valuation of the related receivables.
- *Examination of supporting documents*—If all, or a portion, of the balance has not been collected at the time alternative procedures are being performed, documents supporting the uncollected invoices should be inspected. These documents include customer orders, sales orders, bills of lading or internal shipping documents, and sales invoices. The auditor must consider that evidence obtained from internal copies of customer

orders, internal shipping documents, and sales invoices is not as persuasive as that obtained from subsequent cash receipts. Bills of lading are usually external and provide independent verification of shipments.

Follow-Up Procedures for Exceptions Noted on Positive Confirmations Customers are asked to provide details of any differences between their records and the amount shown on the confirmation. Differences are referred to as **exceptions**. The auditor investigates exceptions to determine whether the difference is a customer error, an item in dispute, a client misstatement, or a timing difference. **Timing differences** are due to transactions that are in process at the confirmation date, such as in-transit shipments or payments. If the auditor can determine that the timing difference did not result in recording the receivable in the wrong period, the differences do not represent misstatements in the account balance. Examples of exceptions include:

- *Payment has already been made*—This exception occurs when the customer has made a payment before the confirmation date, but the client has not received the payment before the confirmation date.
- *Merchandise has not been received*—This exception occurs when the client records the sale at the date of shipment and the customer records the purchase when the goods are received. The time the goods are in transit is typically the cause of this type of exception.
- *The goods have been returned*—This exception might be due to the client's failure to record a credit memo. Such a failure could result from timing differences or from the improper recording of sales returns and allowances.
- *Clerical errors and disputed amounts exist*—Some exceptions occur because the customer states that there is an error in the price charged for the goods, the goods are damaged, the proper quantity of goods was not received, or there is some other type of customer issue. These exceptions should be investigated to determine whether the client's records are in error and, if so, the amount of the error. Such differences might have implications for the valuation of the receivables account. However, what may initially appear to be a timing difference may actually be the result of lapping, which was discussed earlier in the chapter.

Because the auditor selects only a sample of accounts receivable for confirmation purposes, investigation of all exceptions and determination of the cause for any exceptions, rather than rationalizing the exception away as an isolated instance, are important. As discussed in *Chapter 8*, misstatements must be projected to the entire population of receivables to determine whether there is a material misstatement in the account balance. If the projected amount of misstatement appears to have a material effect on the financial statements, the magnitude and cause of such misstatement should be discussed with the client to decide the appropriate response. If subsequent work supports the conclusion of a material misstatement, a client adjustment will be required.

Follow-Up Procedures for Negative Confirmations The basic premise underlying negative confirmations is that if no response is received, the auditor assumes that the customer agrees with the balance. This is not always the correct assumption. The customer may not respond even though the balance is wrong because (1) the letter was lost, misplaced, or sent to the wrong address; (2) the customer did not understand the request; or (3) the request was simply ignored and thrown away. The auditor must have some assurance that the reliability of the negative confirmation process is not compromised because of any of the factors just described. The auditor does not expect that a large number of negative confirmations will be returned. However, when they are returned, reasons for their return include:

- The customer did not understand the request.
- The customer confirms an incorrect amount because payments or shipments are in transit.
- The amount recorded by the client is in error or is fraudulent.

The auditor must perform follow-up work to determine whether the confirmed amount really represents a misstatement. The auditor might look at subsequent cash receipts or vouch back to the customer's order and evidence of shipment to help make this assessment. If errors are detected, the auditor should use expanded procedures to (1) find the underlying cause of the errors and (2) estimate the amount of misstatement in the account balance.

Additional Procedures When Accounts Are Confirmed at an Interim Date If the auditor confirms receivables at an interim date, the auditor must gather additional evidence during the roll-forward period. Roll-forward procedures in the revenue cycle include:

- Comparing individual customer balances at the interim confirmation date with year-end balances and confirming any that have substantially increased
- Comparing monthly sales, collections, sales discounts, and sales returns and allowances during the roll-forward period with those for prior months and prior years to see whether they appear out of line; if they do, obtaining an explanation from management and acquiring corroborative evidence to determine whether that explanation is valid
- Reconciling receivable subsidiary records to the general ledger at both the confirmation date and year-end
- Testing the cutoff of sales, cash collections, and credit memos for returns and allowances at year-end
- Scanning journals to identify receivables postings from unusual sources and investigate unusual items
- Computing the number of days' sales in receivables at both the confirmation date and year-end and comparing these data and data from prior periods
- Computing the gross profit percentage during the roll-forward period and comparing that to the percentage for the year and for prior periods

Accounts Receivable: Substantive Procedures for the Allowance Account

Substantive procedures related to the allowance account are relevant to the valuation of accounts receivable. Tests of details for the revenue account will provide evidence as to whether receivables transactions are initially recorded at their correct value (gross value). However, the auditor is also concerned as to whether it is likely that the client will collect the outstanding receivables (net realizable value). This concern relates to determining the reasonableness of the client's allowance for doubtful accounts. Accounts receivable should be valued at its net realizable value; that is, the gross amount customers owe less the allowance for doubtful accounts.

Determining the reasonableness of the client's estimate of the allowance for doubtful accounts is one of the more difficult audit judgments because, at the time of the audit, a single correct answer is not available. Recording the allowance for doubtful accounts and determining bad-debt expense for the year is the result of an accounting estimate. The allowance should reflect management's best estimate of accounts receivable that will not be collected at year-end. The client's estimate must reflect the economic status of the client's customers, current economic conditions, and an informed expectation about potential default on payment. For many companies, determining the allowance will have a substantial effect on the company's profitability.

After reviewing and testing the process used by management, including the controls over the process, auditors generally use one or a combination of the following approaches to obtain evidence about the reasonableness of the client's estimate:

- Inquire of management about the collectibility of customer balances, particularly those that are large and long overdue
- Develop an independent model to estimate the accounts
- Review credit reports from outside credit bureaus, such as Dun & Bradstreet (*www.dnbisolutions.com*), to help determine the likelihood of the collection of specific accounts
- Review customer correspondence files to gain additional insight into the collectibility of specific accounts
- For accounts that are unusually large or past due, review the customer's latest financial statements to perform an independent analysis of collectibility
- Inquire about the client's procedures for deciding when to write off an account

Accounts Receivable: Other Substantive Procedures

Accounts Receivable: Rights and Obligations

Some companies sell their receivables to banks or other financial institutions but may retain responsibility for collecting the receivables and may be liable if the percentage of collection falls below a specified minimum. Substantive audit procedures that would reveal these ownership and related disclosure issues include:

- Reviewing all such arrangements and obtaining confirmations from the client's banks about any contingent liabilities
- Inquiring of management about any activities related to the receivables
- Scanning the cash receipts journal for relatively large inflows of cash that are posted from unusual sources
- Obtaining bank confirmations, which includes information on obligations to the bank and loan collateral
- Reviewing the board of directors' minutes, which generally contain approval for these items

Accounts Receivable: Presentation and Disclosure

Accounting standards require that trade accounts receivable be presented separately from other receivables. For example, material receivables from related parties, including officers, directors, stockholders, and employees, should be shown separately in the financial statements, with appropriate disclosures being provided. Audit procedures directed toward identifying related-party transactions such as these include:

- Reviewing SEC filings
- Reviewing the accounts receivable trial balance
- Inquiring of management and the audit committee about receivables from related parties

Material debit balances in accounts payable for amounts due from vendors should be reclassified as accounts receivable. Material credit balances in accounts receivable should be reclassified as accounts payable. Receivables that are not due within the normal operating cycle or one year should be listed as noncurrent assets. Audit procedures to identify misclassified receivables include making inquiries of management, reviewing the aged trial balance for large or old outstanding balances, reading the board of directors' minutes, and scanning the subsidiary ledger to identify unusually large receivable balances (particularly those that resulted from a single transaction or that were posted from an unusual source).

Receivables that have been sold with recourse, discounted, or pledged as collateral on loans should be disclosed in the notes to the financial statements.

Performing Substantive Fraud-Related Procedures

Substantive procedures are adjusted when specific fraud risk factors are present. Potential fraud risks in the revenue cycle include:

- Excessive credit memos or other credit adjustments to accounts receivable after the end of the fiscal year
- Customer complaints and discrepancies in accounts receivable confirmations (e.g., disputes over terms, prices, or amounts)
- Unusual entries to the accounts receivable subsidiary ledger or sales journal
- Missing or altered source documents or the inability of the client to produce original documents in a reasonable period of time
- A lack of cash flow from operating activities when income from operating activities has been reported
- Unusual reconciling differences between the accounts receivable subsidiary ledger and control account
- Sales to customers in the last month of the fiscal period at terms more favorable than previous months
- Predated or postdated transactions
- Large or unusual adjustments to sales accounts just prior to or just after the fiscal year-end

The following fraud-related audit procedures can be used to respond to these fraud risks:

- Perform a thorough review of original source documents, including invoices, shipping documents, customer purchase orders, cash receipts, and written correspondence between the client and the customer.
- Analyze and review credit memos and other accounts receivable adjustments for the period subsequent to the balance sheet date.
- Analyze all large or unusual sales made near year-end and vouch to original source documents.
- Confirm terms of the transaction directly with the customer, such as the absence of side agreements, acceptance criteria, delivery and payment terms, the right to return the product, and refund policies.
- Compare the number of weeks of inventory in distribution channels with prior periods for unusual changes that may indicate channel stuffing.
- Scan the general ledger, accounts receivable subsidiary ledger, and sales journal for unusual activity.
- Perform analytical reviews of credit memo and write-off activity by comparing to prior periods. Look for unusual trends or patterns, such as

large numbers of credit memos pertaining to one customer or salesperson, or those processed shortly after the close of the accounting period.

- Analyze recoveries of written-off accounts.
- Inquire of the company's nonaccounting personnel (e.g., sales and marketing personnel or even in-house legal counsel) about sales or shipments near year-end and whether they are aware of any unusual terms or conditions in connection with these sales.

If any of these procedures were part of the original audit program, the auditor should consider expanding the extent of testing, or in some way modifying the timing or nature of testing, if significant fraud risk factors are identified.

Documenting Substantive Procedures

A number of important items should be documented for this cycle. Documentation of confirmation procedures should detail the extent of dollars and items confirmed, the confirmation response rate, the number and dollar amount of exceptions that were not misstatements, the number and amount of exceptions that were misstatements (cross-referenced to the working paper B-4 that includes an explanation and conclusion), and a projection of the sample misstatements to the population. The following is an example of such a summary:

	Items	Amount
Population	3,810	5,643,200.00
Positive confirmations	29	193,038.71
Percent confirmed	0.76%	3.42%
Responses	27	180,100.11
Percent responding	93.1%	93.3%
Exceptions	5	32,061.50
Cleared	4	19,105.82
Misstatements—B-4	1	971.68
Projected to the population		30,446.31

Other documentation requirements for accounts receivable include:

- Tests of the adequacy of the allowance for doubtful accounts
- Details on inquires made regarding whether receivables are sold, pledged, or assigned
- Cutoff tests
- Evidence of roll-forward procedures if confirmations were sent at an interim date

Documentation related to the revenue substantive procedures would typically include:

- Substantive analytical procedures performed
- Unusual sales transactions
- Information indicating an understanding of the client's revenue recognition policies
- Identification of specific items tested (e.g., all sales transactions in excess of $100,000)
- Relevant information on tests of details

SUMMARY AND NEXT STEPS

The revenue cycle presents a number of challenges for the auditor. First, revenue is typically considered to be a high-risk account because of management incentives for misstatement. Second, management needs to make many estimates, most notably the allowance for doubtful accounts, which are subject to manipulation. Notwithstanding these challenges, the auditor needs to determine if accounts receivable and revenue are fairly presented in the context of the financial statements as a whole. After identifying the risks of material misstatement through appropriate risk assessment procedures, the auditor will determine the appropriate audit approach and then carry out the planned procedures. One substantive procedure typically performed in this cycle is the confirmation of accounts receivable. Because the revenue account is closely related to accounts receivable, evidence about accounts receivable also provides evidence about revenues. For example, having confirmation evidence that an account receivable does exist also provides evidence about the existence of the related revenue transaction. In the next chapter we turn to auditing cash and marketable securities accounts.

SIGNIFICANT TERMS

Alternative procedures   Procedures used to obtain evidence about the existence and valuation of accounts receivable when a positive confirmation is not returned, including examining cash collected after the confirmation date and vouching unpaid invoices to customers' orders, sales orders, shipping documents, and sales invoices.

Bill of lading   A shipping document that describes items being shipped, the shipping terms, and delivery address; a formal legal document that conveys responsibility for the safety and shipment of items to the shipper.

Collectibility   The risk that the seller will be unable to collect the entitled contractual consideration from the customer.

Exceptions   Differences between a customer's records and the client's records reported on positive or negative confirmations.

False confirmation   A situation in which the respondent to a confirmation request (in this chapter, an accounts receivable confirmation) responds inaccurately to the audit firm with respect to the information on the confirmation.

Lapping   A technique used to cover up the embezzlement of cash whereby a cash collection from one customer is stolen by an employee who takes another customer's payment and credits the first customer. This process continues, and at any point in time at least one customer's account is overstated.

Negative confirmation   A request to customers asking them to respond directly to the auditor only if they disagree with the indicated balance.

Positive confirmation   A request to customers asking them to respond directly to the auditor if they agree or disagree with the indicated balance.

Revenue cycle   The process of receiving a customer's order, approving credit for a sale, determining whether the goods are available for shipment, shipping the goods, billing the customers, collecting cash, and recognizing the effect of this process on other related accounts.

Side letter An agreement containing contract terms that are not part of the formal contract (often involving rights of return). Side letters increase audit risk because they enable key contract terms affecting revenue recognition to be hidden from the auditor as part of a revenue recognition fraud.

Timing difference Confirmation exceptions caused by transactions that are in process at the confirmation date, such as in-transit shipments or payments. These are not misstatements.

TRUE/FALSE QUESTIONS

9-1 LO 1 Auditors should expect clients to have only one revenue process in place.

9-2 LO 1 The revenue cycle begins when the goods are shipped to a customer.

9-3 LO 2 An important inherent risk in the revenue cycle is that revenue will be recorded prior to when it has been earned.

9-4 LO 2 Determining whether revenue has been earned is a very straightforward process that is not subject to inherent risk.

9-5 LO 3 Research by COSO (2010) indicates that the majority of financial statement frauds involved inappropriate recording of revenue.

9-6 LO 3 When assessing fraud risks, the auditor should consider the client's motivation to increase revenue because of either internal or external pressures.

9-7 LO 4 It is not possible for internal controls to mitigate risks associated with the valuation of accounts receivable.

9-8 LO 4 Using prenumbered shipping documents is a control that can provide reasonable assurance that all sales are recorded.

9-9 LO 5 The auditor might believe that a heightened risk of fraud exists if the planning analytical procedures indicate increases in revenue and net income, but negative cash flow from operations.

9-10 LO 5 When performing planning analytical procedures, the auditor could perform trend analysis with ratios, but not with account balances.

9-11 LO 6 In responding to identified risks of material misstatement in the revenue cycle, the auditor would never perform tests of controls, as only substantive procedures would be required.

9-12 LO 6 In responding to identified risks of material misstatement related to the completeness of the revenue account, the auditor will always perform a significant amount of tests of details.

9-13 LO 7 In testing controls over whether sales are properly valued, the auditor could take a sample of recorded sales invoices and agree the price on the invoice to an authorized price list.

9-14 LO 7 When testing a client's reconciliation between the sales sub-ledger and the general ledger, the auditor is required to reperform the control.

9-15 LO 8 The quality of evidence obtained from positive and negative confirmations is about the same.

9-16 LO 8 To obtain evidence on the completeness assertion for revenue, the auditor would select a sample of shipping documents and trace them to the sales journal.

MULTIPLE-CHOICE QUESTIONS

9-17 **LO 1** Which of the following statements is true regarding assertions in the revenue cycle?
a. It is typical that all five assertions for revenue are equally important.
b. If a client has an incentive to overstate revenues, the existence assertion would be more relevant than the completeness assertion.
c. Audit evidence about the existence of revenues is also the most appropriate evidence about the valuation of receivables.
d. The allowance for doubtful accounts has important implications for the ownership assertion of accounts receivable.

9-18 **LO 1** Which of the following statements is true regarding the processing and recording of revenue transactions?
a. The accurate recording of revenue transactions is important for preparing financial statements, but not important for the client's management decisions.
b. Invoices should be prepared once the client determines that the goods ordered by a customer are available.
c. A bill of lading provides documentation that the customer has received the goods.
d. Sales transactions typically begin with the receipt of a purchase order from a customer.

9-19 **LO 2** Under the FASB's and IASB's forthcoming guidance on revenue recognition, a contract must have which of the following characteristics in order to be judged as persuasive?
a. It must have commercial substance.
b. The parties to the contract must have approved it and be committed to perform their respective actions.
c. Rights with respect to the contract are identifiable.
d. The terms of payment must be identifiable.
e. All of the above.

9-20 **LO 2** Which of the following statements is false regarding inherent risks associated with accounts receivable?
a. The rights and obligations assertion for accounts receivable may have a high level of inherent risk if the company sells or pledges accounts receivable.
b. If accounts receivable are improperly aged, the allowance for doubtful accounts may be misstated.
c. If the client accepts orders from customers with poor credit, the risk associated with the valuation of net accounts receivable is not affected as the customer did indeed place the order.
d. Having the collection of a receivable be contingent on specific events that cannot be easily estimated increases the inherent risk of misstatement of the accounts receivable account.

9-21 **LO 3** Which of the following factors is not a motivation for clients to fraudulently misstate revenue?
a. Bankruptcy may be imminent.
b. Management bonuses are contingent on a certain revenue goal.
c. Controls over revenue process are ineffective.
d. Management wants to meet publicly announced earnings expectations.

9-22 **LO 3** Which of the following explanations best describes the purpose of lapping?

a. Lapping is a technique used by client personnel to cover up the embezzlement of cash.

b. Lapping is an approach used by client personnel to eliminate differences between a customer's records and the client's records reported on confirmations.

c. Lapping is a procedure used by the auditor to obtain evidence when a positive confirmation is not returned by the client's customer.

d. Lapping is an agreement containing contract terms that are not part of a formal sales contract.

9-23 **LO 4** Which of the following should an auditor gain an understanding of as part of risk assessment procedures?

a. Internal controls related to revenue recognition.

b. Revenue-related computer applications.

c. Key revenue-related documents.

d. All of the above.

9-24 **LO 4** Consider an organization that sells products through a catalog and takes orders over the phone. All orders are entered online, and the organization's objective is to ship all orders within twenty-four hours. The audit trail is kept in machine-readable form. The only papers generated are the packing slip and the invoice sent to the customer. Revenue is recorded upon shipment of the goods. The organization maintains a detailed customer database that allows the customer to return goods for credit at any time. The organization maintains a product database containing all the authorized prices. Only the marketing manager has authorization to make changes in the price database. The marketing manager either makes the changes or authorizes the changes by signing an authorization form, and his assistant implements the changes. Which of the following controls would be least effective in assuring that the correct product is shipped and that it is billed at the approved price?

a. Self-checking digits are used on all product numbers, and customers must order from a catalog with product numbers.

b. The sales order taker verbally verifies both the product description and price with the customer before the order is closed for processing.

c. The sales order taker prepares batch totals of the number of items ordered and the total dollar amount for all items processed during a specified period of time (e.g., one hour).

d. The product price table is restricted to the director of marketing, who alone can approve changes to the price file.

9-25 **LO 5** Which of the following statements is false regarding planning analytical procedures in the revenue cycle?

a. As revenue is typically regarded as a high-risk account, planning analytical procedures related to revenue are not required.

b. The first step in planning analytical procedures includes developing an expectation of recorded amounts or ratios, and evaluating whether that expectation is precise enough to accomplish the relevant objective.

c. Trend analysis would not be appropriate as a planning analytical procedure in the revenue cycle.

d. All of the above statements are false.

9-26 **LO 5** Assume that an auditor expected that the client's activities related to sales and accounts receivable would be similar to industry averages. Which of the following relationships detected as part of planning analytical procedures would suggest a heightened risk of material misstatement in the revenue cycle?

a. The number of days' sales in accounts receivable increased from forty-four days in the prior year to sixty-five days in the year being audited. The industry average increased from forty-five to forty-seven days.

b. The gross margin increased from 16.7% to 18.3%, while the industry average changed from 16.7% to 16.3%.

c. Accounts receivable increased 35% over the prior year, while sales stayed relatively stable.

d. All of the above.

9-27 **LO 6** After identifying the risks of material misstatement, the auditor develops an audit plan in response to those risks. Which of the following plans for testing revenue would be most likely when the auditor believes that control risk is high?

a. The only evidence the auditor plans to obtain is from tests of details.

b. The auditor plans to obtain 40% of the necessary audit evidence from tests of controls, and the remaining 60% from substantive analytical procedures.

c. The auditor plans to obtain the majority of the necessary audit evidence from tests of controls.

d. Any of the above would be an appropriate audit plan if the auditor believes that control risk is high.

9-28 **LO 6** Responding to identified risks involves developing an audit approach that addresses those risks. Which of the following statements about the planned audit approach is true for the revenue cycle?

a. The audit approach needs to include tests of controls, substantive analytical procedures, and tests of details.

b. The audit approach will typically require more evidence for higher risk assertions than lower risk areas.

c. The audit approach should follow the audit firm's standardized audit program.

d. The sufficiency and appropriateness of selected procedures will not vary across assertions.

9-29 **LO 7** When auditing a nonpublic company, the auditor would generally make a decision not to test the operating effectiveness of controls in which of the following situations?

a. The preliminary assessment of control risk is at the maximum.

b. It is more cost efficient to directly test ending account balances than to test controls.

c. The auditor believes that controls are designed effectively but are not operating as described.

d. All of the above are situations when the auditor would likely not test the operating effectiveness of controls.

9-30 **LO 7** An auditor performs tests of controls in the revenue cycle. First, the auditor makes inquiries of company personnel about credit-granting policies. The auditor then selects a sample of sales transactions and examines documentary evidence of credit approval. This test of controls most likely supports which of the following financial statement assertion(s)?

Completeness	Valuation or Allocation
a. Yes	Yes
b. No	Yes
c. Yes	No
d. No	No

9-31   **LO 8**   To test the completeness of sales, the auditor would select a sample of transactions from which of the following populations?
a. Customer order file.
b. Open invoice file.
c. Bill of lading file.
d. Sales invoice file.

9-32   **LO 8**   The auditor is concerned that fictitious sales have been recorded. Which of the following procedures would be the best audit procedure to identify the existence of any fictitious sales?
a. Select a sample of recorded sales invoices and trace to shipping documents (bills of lading and packing slips) to verify shipment of goods.
b. Select a random sample of shipping documents (bills of lading) and trace to the sales invoice to determine whether the invoice was properly recorded.
c. Select a sample of customer purchase orders and trace through to the generation of a sales invoice.
d. Select a sample of customer purchase orders to determine whether a valid customer actually exists.

REVIEW AND SHORT CASE QUESTIONS

NOTE: Completing Review and Short Case Questions does not require the student to reference additional resources and materials.

NOTE: For the remaining problems, we make special note of those addressing fraud, international issues, professional skepticism, and ethics.

9-33   **LO 1**   Refer to *Exhibit 9.1*. Which accounts are typically affected by transactions in the revenue cycle? Identify the relationships among them.

9-34   **LO 1**   For accounts receivable, what are the more relevant assertions? Why should an auditor identify which assertions are more relevant?

9-35   **LO 1**   Refer to *Exhibit 9.2*. What are the major activities involved in generating and recording a sales transaction? What are the major documents generated as a part of each activity?

9-36   **LO 2**   An important task in the audit of the revenue cycle is determining whether a client has appropriately recognized revenue.
a. In assessing the risks associated with revenue recognition, the auditor of U.S. companies will likely consult criteria provided by the SEC. What general criteria has the SEC used to help determine if revenue can be recognized? Why might the auditor need to do additional research and consider additional criteria on revenue recognition?
b. The following are situations in which the auditor will be required to make decisions about the amount of revenue to be recognized. For each of the following scenarios (labeled (1) through (6)):
• Identify the key issues to address in determining whether or not revenue should be recognized.
• Identify additional information the auditor may want to gather in making a decision on revenue recognition.

- Based only on the information presented, develop a rationale for either the recognition or nonrecognition of revenue.

1. AOL sells software that is unique as a provider of Internet services. The software contract includes a service fee of $19.95 for up to 500 hours of Internet service each month. The minimum requirement is a one-year contract. The company proposes to immediately recognize 30% of the first-year's contract as revenue from the sale of software and 70% as Internet services on a monthly basis as fees are collected from the customer.

2. Modis Manufacturing builds specialty packaging machinery for other manufacturers. All of the products are high end and range in sales price from $5 million to $25 million. A major customer is rebuilding one of its factories and has ordered three machines with total revenue for Modis of $45 million. The contracted date to complete the production was November, and the company met the contract date. The customer acknowledges the contract and confirms the amount. However, because the factory is not yet complete, it has asked Modis to hold the products in the warehouse as a courtesy until its building is complete.

3. Standish Stoneware has developed a new low-end line of baking products that will be sold directly to consumers and to low-end discount retailers. The company had previously sold high-end silverware products to specialty stores and has a track record of returned items for the high-end stores. The new products tend to have more defects, but the defects are not necessarily recognizable in production. For example, they are more likely to crack when first used in baking. The company does not have a history of returns from these products, but because the products are new it grants each customer the right to return the merchandise for a full refund or replacement within one year of purchase.

4. Omer Technologies is a high-growth company that sells electronic products to the custom copying business. It is an industry with high innovation, but Omer's technology is basic. In order to achieve growth, management has empowered the sales staff to make special deals to increase sales in the fourth quarter of the year. The sales deals include a price break and an increased salesperson commission but not an extension of either the product warranty or the customer's right to return the product.

5. Electric City is a new company that has the exclusive right to a new technology that saves municipalities a substantial amount of energy for large-scale lighting purposes (e.g., for ball fields, parking lots, and shopping centers). The technology has been shown to be very cost effective in Europe. In order to get new customers to try the product, the sales force allows customers to try the product for up to six months to prove the amount of energy savings they will realize. The company is so confident that customers will buy the product that it allows this pilot-testing period. Revenue is recognized at the time the product is installed at the customer location, with a small provision made for potential returns.

6. Jackson Products decided to quit manufacturing a line of its products and outsourced the production. However, much of

its manufacturing equipment could be used by other companies. In addition, it had over $5 million of new manufacturing equipment on order in a noncancelable deal. The company decided to become a sales representative to sell the new equipment ordered and its existing equipment. All of the sales were recorded as revenue.

9-37 **LO 2** Refer to *Exhibit 9.3*. What are some examples of sales transactions involving product delivery that might have a high level of inherent risk?

FRAUD

9-38 **LO 3** Why should auditors ordinarily consider revenue recognition to be a fraud risk factor? What are some reasons that management might want to fraudulently overstate revenue?

FRAUD

9-39 **LO 3** Refer to *Exhibit 9.4* and to the *Focus on Fraud* features "Channel Stuffing at ArthroCare—The Importance of Professional Skepticism" and "The Importance of Professional Skepticism in Auditing Revenue at Tvia." What methods have been used to fraudulently inflate revenue? How can auditors use professional skepticism to help identify these fraud schemes?

PROFESSIONAL SKEPTICISM

9-40 **LO 3** What steps should an auditor take to help identify fraud risks?

FRAUD

9-41 **LO 4** Refer to *Exhibit 9.5* and *Exhibit 9.6*. What are a control risk assessment questionnaire and a controls matrix? How does an auditor use these documents?

9-42 **LO 4** Why are monthly customer statements considered a control? Why is it important to separate the duties of responding to customer complaints from the accounts receivable and cash collection functions?

9-43 **LO 4** Refer to the *Auditing in Practice* feature "Risks Associated with Sales Returns: The Case of Medicis and Ernst & Young." What problems can occur if controls related to sales returns and allowances are not designed and operating effectively?

FRAUD

9-44 **LO 4** Field, CPA, is auditing the financial statements of Miller Mailorder, Inc. (MMI). Field has compiled a list of possible inherent and fraud risks in the revenue cycle that may result in the misstatement of MMI's financial statements and a corresponding list of internal controls, which, if properly designed and implemented, could assist MMI in preventing or detecting material misstatements. For each risk numbered (1) through (15) in the first column, select one internal control from the second column (labeled (a) through (t)), which, if properly designed and implemented, most likely could assist MMI in preventing or detecting material misstatements. Internal controls can be selected for more than one risk.

Inherent and Fraud Risks	Internal Controls
1. Invoices for goods sold are posted to incorrect customer accounts.	a. Shipping clerks compare goods received from the warehouse with the details on the shipping documents.
2. Goods ordered by customers are shipped but are not billed to anyone.	b. Approved sales orders are required for goods to be released from the warehouse.
3. Invoices are sent for shipped goods but are not recorded in the sales journal.	c. Monthly statements are mailed to all customers with outstanding balances.
4. Invoices are sent for shipped goods and are recorded in the sales journal	

(continued)

Inherent and Fraud Risks	Internal Controls
but are not posted to any customer account.	d. Shipping clerks compare goods received from the warehouse with approved sales orders.
5. Credit sales are made to individuals with unsatisfactory credit ratings.	e. Customer orders are compared with the inventory master file to determine whether items ordered are in stock.
6. Goods are removed from inventory for unauthorized orders.	f. Daily sales summaries are compared with control totals of invoices.
7. Goods shipped to customers do not agree with goods ordered by customers.	g. Shipping documents are compared with sales invoices when goods are shipped.
8. Invoices are sent to allies in a fraudulent scheme, and sales are recorded for fictitious transactions.	h. Sales invoices are compared with the master price file.
9. Customers' checks are received for less than the customers' full account balances, but the customers' full account balances are credited.	i. Customer orders are compared with an approved customer list.
10. Customers' checks are misappropriated before they are forwarded to the cashier for deposit.	j. Sales orders are prepared for each customer order.
11. Customers' checks are credited to incorrect customer accounts.	k. Control amounts posted to the accounts receivable ledger are compared with control totals of invoices.
12. Different customer accounts are each credited for the same cash receipt.	l. Sales invoices are compared with shipping documents and approved customer orders before invoices are mailed.
13. Customers' checks are properly credited to customer accounts and are properly deposited, but errors are made in recording receipts in the cash receipts journal.	m. Prenumbered credit memos are used for granting credit for goods returned.
14. Customers' checks are misappropriated after they are forwarded to the cashier for deposit.	n. Goods returned for credit are approved by the supervisor of the sales department.
15. Invalid transactions granting credit for sales returns are recorded.	o. Remittance advices are separated from the checks in the mailroom and forwarded to the accounting department.
	p. Total amounts posted to the accounts receivable ledger from remittance advices are compared with the validated bank deposit slip.
	q. The cashier examines each check for proper endorsement.
	r. Validated deposit slips are compared with the cashier's daily cash summaries.
	s. An employee, other than the bookkeeper, periodically prepares a bank reconciliation.
	t. The same employee who issues receiving reports evidencing actual return of goods approves sales returns.

9-45 **LO 5** Refer to *Exhibit* 9.7. Identify planning analytical procedures that can help auditors identify areas of potential material misstatements in the revenue cycle.

9-46 **LO 5** What factors influence the reliability of data used in conducting planning analytical procedures in the revenue cycle?

FRAUD

PROFESSIONAL SKEPTICISM

9-47 **LO 5** Consider an audit client that manufactures fishing boats and sells them all over the country. Boats are sold to dealers who finance their purchases with their banks. The banks usually pay your client within two weeks of shipment. The company's profits have been increasing over the past several years. To perform planning analytical procedures you have obtained the following information related to your 2015 audit ($ in millions):

	2015**	2014*	2013*	2012*	2011*	Major Competitor (2015)
Accounts receivable	6.8	3.3	2.3	1.8	1.7	4.2
Inventory	16.0	10.0	7.2	5.5	5.1	13.9
Accounts payable	3.1	2.6	1.9	1.5	1.4	3.2
Sales	84.7	77.9	56.8	43.6	39.8	110.3
Gross profit (%)	19	17	18	17	18	21
Number of days' sales in receivables	29	16	15	16	16	14
Number of days' sales in ending inventory	69	47	46	46	47	46

*Audited
**Unaudited

a. Assume that you had expected that your client's performance would be similar to that of the client's major competitor. Based on these expectations, identify potential risk areas and explain why they represent potential risks.
b. Suggest possible explanations for any unexpected results.
c. What inquiries and follow-up audit procedures might be performed to determine the accuracy of the client's data?
d. As part of the brainstorming session, be prepared to discuss how the CFO might use accounts receivable and inventory to conceal the embezzlement of cash.
e. Discuss the importance of professional skepticism when performing planning analytical procedures.

FRAUD

PROFESSIONAL SKEPTICISM

9-48 **LO 5** Stainless Steel Specialties (SSS) is a manufacturer of hot water–based heating systems for homes and commercial businesses. The company has grown about 10% in each of the past five years. The company has not made any acquisitions. Following are some statistics for the company:

Overview of Operational Data Stainless Steel Specialties (SSS)
(Sales and Net Income Reported in $ Millions)

	2011	2012	2013	2014	2015 (unaudited)
Sales	$800	$880	$950	$1,050	$1,300
Net income	$28	$38	$42	$52	$68
Stock price	$17	$24	$19	$28	$47
Economic growth in areas served (index with 1.00 for 20 × 1)	1.00	1.04	1.09	1.13	1.14
Percent of heating market by SSS	8.9	9.4	9.6	10.8	14.0
Accounts receivable	$180	$170	$196	$210	$297
Percent of sales made in last quarter	38	36	40	38	43
Gross margin (%)	28.0	28.3	28.8	29.2	33.6

Additional information available to the auditor includes the following:

- The company has touted its new and improved technology for the increase both in sales and in gross margin.
- The company claims to have decreased administrative expenses, thus increasing net profits.
- The company has reorganized its sales process to a more centralized approach and has empowered individual sales managers to negotiate better prices to drive sales as long as the amounts are within corporate guidelines.
- The company has changed its salesperson compensation by increasing the commission on sales to new customers.
- Sales commissions are no longer affected by returned goods if the goods are returned more than 90 days after sale and/or by not collecting the receivables. SSS has justified the changes in sales commissions on the following grounds:
  - The salesperson is not responsible for quality issues—the main reason that products are returned.
  - The salesperson is not responsible for approving credit; rather credit approval is under the direction of the global sales manager.

a. What is the importance of the information about salesperson compensation to the audit of receivables and revenue? Explain how the information would be used in performing planning analytical procedures.

b. Perform planning analytical procedures using the data included in the table and the information about the change in performance. For each year, you will most likely want to focus on the % change of the various statistics over the prior year. Focus on Steps 3, 4, and 5 of the planning analytical procedures process. What are the important insights that the auditor should gain from performing such procedures?

    c. Why should the auditor be interested in a company's stock price when performing an audit, as stock price is dependent, at least in part, on audited financial reports?

    d. What information about SSS might be considered as fraud risk factors?

    e. Identify specific substantive audit procedures that should be performed as a result of the planning analytical procedures performed by the auditor (Step 6 of the planning analytical procedures process)

9-49 `LO 6` How do auditors use their knowledge about the risk of material misstatement, including their knowledge of the design effectiveness of controls, in developing an audit approach? Comment on extensiveness of testing, types of audit procedures, and the rigor of audit procedures in higher versus lower risk settings (e.g., for an assertion with a higher risk of material misstatement vs. an assertion with a lower risk of material misstatement).

9-50 `LO 6` Refer to *Exhibit 9.8*. Describe the differences in the planned audit approaches for Clients A and B and the reasons for such differences.

9-51 `LO 6` Read the following description of Drea Tech Company and identify the elements of inherent risk associated with the revenue cycle. Determine the appropriate audit response (audit procedure) to address the risks.

    Drea Tech Company has been growing rapidly and has recently engaged your firm as its auditor. It is actively traded over the counter and management believes it has outgrown the service capabilities of its previous auditor. However, on contacting the previous auditor, you learn that a dispute led to the firm's dismissal. The client wanted to recognize income on contracts for items produced but not shipped. The client believed the contracts were firm and that all the principal revenue-producing activities were performed. The change in accounting principle would have increased net income by 33% during the last year.

    Drea is 32% owned by Anthony Dreason, who has a reputation as a turnaround artist. He bought out the previous owner of Drea Tech three years ago. The company's primary products are in the materials handling business, such as automated conveyors for warehouses and production lines. Dreason has increased profits by slashing operating expenses, most notably personnel and research and development. In addition, he has outsourced a significant portion of component part production. Approximately 10% of the company's product is now obtained from Materials Movement, Inc., a privately held company 50% owned by Dreason and his brother.

    A brief analysis of previous financial statements shows that sales have been increasing by approximately 20% per year since Dreason assumed control. Profitability has increased even more. However, a tour of the plant gives the impression that it is somewhat old and not kept up to date. Additionally, a large amount of inventory is sitting near the receiving dock awaiting final disposition.

9-52 `LO 7` What is the effect on the substantive tests of accounts receivable when the risk of material misstatement is assessed as low rather than high because a client has effective internal controls? Provide specific examples.

9-53 **LO 7** When assessing whether the controls are operating effectively, does the auditor need to reperform the control? For example, if client personnel check the correctness of computations on an invoice and initial the bottom of a document to indicate that the control has been performed, does the auditor need to reperform the procedure? Explain the rationale for your response.

9-54 **LO 7** The following is a list of controls (numbered (1) through (7)) typically implemented in the revenue cycle.

a. For each control listed, briefly indicate the financial misstatement that could occur if the control is not implemented effectively.

b. Identify a test of control that the auditor can perform to determine the operating effectiveness of the control.

1. All transactions under $10,000 may be approved by the computer authorization program. The credit manager must approve all transactions over $10,000.

2. All invoices are priced according to the authorized price list maintained on the computer. Either the regional or divisional sales manager must approve any exceptions.

3. All shipping documents are prenumbered and periodically accounted for. Shipping document references are noted on all sales invoices.

4. Customer complaints regarding receipt of goods are routed to a customer service representative. Any discrepancies are immediately evaluated to determine the cause of the discrepancy.

5. All merchandise returns must be received by the receiving department and recorded on prenumbered documents for receipts. A document is created for each item (or batches of like items). Returns are sent to quality control for testing, and a recommendation for ultimate disposition is made (scrap, rework and sell as a second, or close out as is), noted, and sent to accounting for proper inventorying.

6. The quantity of items invoiced is reconciled with the packing document developed on receipt of the order and the shipping notice by a computer program as the goods are marked for shipment. If discrepancies appear, the shipping document prevails. A discrepancy report is prepared daily and sent to the warehouse manager for follow-up.

7. The company pays all freight charges, but the customer is charged a freight fee based on a minimum amount and a sliding scale as a percentage of the total invoice. The policy is documented, and the computer automatically adds the charge.

9-55 **LO 7** Most accounting systems have the ability to generate exception reports identifying control procedure failures or transactions that are out of the norm so that management can determine whether any special action is needed.

a. Identify how the auditor might use each of the following four types of exception reports (labeled (1) through (4)) in assessing the effectiveness of controls.

b. For each type of exception report address the following question. If the exceptions are properly evaluated and corrected, would the fact that many exceptions occurred affect the auditor's judgment of the effectiveness of controls and the auditor's assessment of control risk? Explain.

1. A list of all invoices over $5,000 for which credit was not preauthorized by the credit manager (the computer program is designed so that if the authorization is not provided within twenty-four hours of the original notice to the credit manager, the shipment is made as if it were authorized). This exception report goes to the credit manager.
2. A report of any sales volume to one customer exceeding $2 million in a month sent to the sales manager with a copy to the credit manager.
3. A report of exceptions for which shipping documents and packing slips did not reconcile.
4. A report noting that goods ordered were not shipped (or back-ordered) within five days of receipt of the order as is required per company policy.

9-56 **LO 7** The audit of the revenue cycle accounts of Acco, Inc., has been planned with a low preliminary assessment of control risk related to each of the relevant assertions. A sample of sales transactions was selected for control testing. Each of the following types of control or transaction-processing deficiencies uncovered in the sample was significant enough to cause the auditor to increase control risk assessment from low to moderate. For each deficiency (labeled as (a) though (i)) discuss the type of financial statement misstatement that may result, the assertion(s) affected, and the effect on the nature, timing, and/or extent of related substantive tests. Each type of deficiency should be considered independently from the others.

a. No evidence that price and quantity on the invoice were compared with the supporting documents
b. Failure to approve customer credit before shipping the merchandise on open account
c. Recording sales before they were shipped
d. Recording sales several days after they should have been recorded
e. Recording sales several days before and several days after they should have been recorded
f. Lack of customer orders; items were shipped
g. Lack of shipping documents; customer order was found
h. Incorrect invoice price
i. Quantity shipped differed from the quantity billed

9-57 **LO 7** Assume the auditor wishes to test controls over the shipment and recording of sales transactions. Identify the controls that the auditor would expect to find to achieve the objective that all transactions are recorded correctly, and in the correct time period. For each control identified, indicate how the auditor would test whether the control operated effectively.

9-58 **LO 8** Refer to the *Auditing in Practice* feature "Performing Appropriate Substantive Procedures in the Revenue Cycle: The Case of Kyoto Audit Corporation." What substantive procedures did Kyoto not perform appropriately? If such procedures are not performed appropriately, will the client's financial statements necessarily be misstated? Explain your answer.

9-59 **LO 8** The third step in performing analytical procedures involves developing expectations of recorded amounts or ratios, and evaluating whether the expectations are precise enough to accomplish the relevant objective. How do expectations differ between planning analytical procedures and substantive analytical procedures? What factors influence the precision of expectations?

9-60 [LO 8] When might it be advisable to send the confirmation to the customer's personnel who are familiar with the details of sales contracts rather than to the accounts payable department?

9-61 [LO 8] Refer to *Exhibit 9.10*.
a. What are typical substantive procedures in the revenue cycle, and how are these procedures related to management assertions?
b. For the following procedures (labeled (1) through (6)), indicate the assertion that is being tested.
   1. Take a block of shipping orders and account for the invoicing of all items in the block and account for the pre-numbering of the documents.
   2. Review the general access controls to the computer application and the authorized ability to make changes to computer price files.
   3. Recompute the invoice total and individual line items on a sample of sales invoices.
   4. Review client documentation to determine policy for credit authorization.
   5. Select a sample of shipping notices and trace to invoices.
   6. Randomly sample entries into the sales journal and trace back to sales orders and shipping documents.

9-62 [LO 8] Refer to *Exhibit 9.11*. What is an aged trial balance of accounts receivable? How does an auditor use it? How does an auditor determine that it is correctly aged?

9-63 [LO 8] Refer to *Exhibit 9.12* and *Exhibit 9.13*. Distinguish between the positive and negative forms of accounts receivable confirmations. Which confirmation type, positive or negative, is considered to be more reliable? Why?

9-64 [LO 8] If a confirmation is not returned by a customer, what follow-up work should the auditor perform for (a) positive confirmations and (b) negative confirmations?

FRAUD **9-65** [LO 8] Identify potential fraud risks in the revenue cycle. What substantive audit procedures could be used to help determine if fraud has occurred in the revenue cycle?

FRAUD **9-66** [LO 8] What is a false confirmation? Why are false confirmations so problematic for auditors in terms of evidence reliability expectations?

9-67 [LO 8] Address the following questions about the confirmation of customers' accounts receivable.
a. Why do confirmations not typically provide reliable evidence about the completeness assertion?
b. What is a confirmation exception, and why is it important to investigate a confirmation exception?
c. When should an auditor perform alternative procedures to substantiate the existence of accounts receivable?
d. Under what condition would substantive testing of accounts receivable before the balance sheet date be appropriate?

9-68 [LO 8] During a discussion, one auditor noted that her approach to testing sales transactions was to select a random sample of recorded sales and trace back through the system to supporting documents, noting that all items billed were shipped and were invoiced at correct prices. She stated that she then had high confidence about the correctness of the sales account, and, therefore, having performed a dual-purpose test, the remaining work on sales (assuming the procedures also evidenced the working of control procedures) could be limited.

A second auditor disagreed. Her approach was to select evidence of shipments, such as prenumbered shipping documents, and then trace forward through the system to the actual invoice, noting the existence of control procedures and the correctness of the invoice processing. If no exceptions were noted, however, she agreed with the first auditor that the remaining audit work on the sales account could be limited.

a. Which auditor is right; or are both right? Explain.
b. What assertion is tested by the second auditor?
c. What is a dual-purpose test? Explain whether the tests performed by both of the auditors would be considered dual-purpose tests.

9-69 **LO 8** Bert Finney, CPA, was engaged to conduct an audit of the financial statements of Clayton Realty Corporation for the month ending January 31, 2015. Examining documentation of the monthly rent reconciliation is an important part of the audit engagement.

The following rent reconciliation was prepared by the controller of Clayton Realty Corporation and was presented to Finney, who subjected it to various audit procedures:

Clayton Realty Corporation
Rent Reconciliation
For the Month Ended January 31, 2015

Gross apartment rents (Schedule A)	$1,600,800†
Less vacancies (Schedule B)	20,500†
Net apartment rentals	1,580,300
Less unpaid January rents (Schedule C)	7,800†
Total	1,572,500
Add prepaid rent collected (Apartment 116)	500†
Total cash collected	$1,573,000†

Schedules A, B, and C are available to Finney but are not presented here. Finney evaluated and tested internal controls and found that they could be relied on to produce reliable accounting information. Cash receipts from rental operations are deposited in a special bank account.

What substantive audit procedures should Finney use during the audit to obtain evidence of each of the dollar amounts marked by the dagger (†) tick mark?

9-70 **LO 8** You are auditing the revenue from membership fees of your local chapter of the Institute of Management Accountants, of which you are not a member. The local chapter receives an allocation of national dues. The remainder of the dues comes from chapter members. The chapter maintains a detailed list of membership. Describe some substantive analytical procedures you could use to provide assurance that fee revenue is fairly stated.

9-71 **LO 8** As part of the audit of KC Enterprises, the auditor assessed control risk for the existence and valuation assertions related to accounts receivable at the maximum level. Katie, the staff person assigned to the engagement, sent positive confirmation requests to a sample of the company customers based on their balances as of December 31, 2015. For each of the three customers described here, review the relevant confirmation letter and Katie's comments at the bottom of each. Select the procedure that should be followed to clear the exception, if one exists. Choose only one procedure per confirmation. A procedure may be used once, more than once, or not at all.

a.

February 1, 2016

Meehan Marine Sales, Inc.
1284 River Road
Louisville, Kentucky 40059

Re: Balance at December 31, 2015—$267,000

As of December 31, 2015, our records indicate your balance with our company as the amount listed above. Please complete and sign the bottom portion of this letter and return the entire letter to our auditors, GJ LLP, P.O. Box 100, Orlando, Florida 32806.

A stamped, self-addressed envelope is enclosed for your convenience.

Sincerely,

_____

KC Enterprises

....

The above balance is   Correct

                          X   Incorrect (show amount)   *$325,000*

If incorrect, please provide information that could help to reconcile your account.

Response: We placed an order for $58,000 on December 26, 2014.

Signature:_____
Title:_____
Date:_____

_____

Katie's note to file:
Per discussion with the controller and review of relevant documentation, the order for $58,000 was shipped FOB shipping point on December 30, 2013, and was received by the customer on January 3, 2016. Therefore, the client has made no entry to record the sale in 2015.

b.

February 1, 2016

West Coast Ski Center, Inc.
163 Tide Avenue
Monterey, California 93940

Re: Balance at December 31, 2015—$414,000

As of December 31, 2015, our records indicate your balance with our company as the amount listed above. Please complete and sign the bottom portion of this letter and return the entire letter to our auditors, GJ LLP, P.O. Box 100, Orlando, Florida 32806.

A stamped, self-addressed envelope is enclosed for your convenience.

Sincerely,

_____

KC Enterprises

....

The above balance is   Correct

                        X   Incorrect (show amount)   *$320,000*

If incorrect, please provide information that could help to reconcile your account.
Response: We made a payment of $94,000 on December 12, 2015.

Signature:_____
Title:_____
Date:_____

Katie's note to file:
Per discussion with the controller and review of relevant documentation, the company received the payment of $94,000 on December 15, 2015, and posted it to "Other Income."

c.

February 1, 2016

Fish & Ski World, Inc.
5660 Ocean Blvd
Port Arkansas, Texas 78373

Re: Balance at December 31, 2015—$72,000

As of December 31, 2015, our records indicate your balance with our company as the amount listed above. Please complete and sign the bottom portion of this letter and return the entire letter to our auditors, GJ LLP, P.O. Box 100, Orlando, Florida 32806.

(continued)

A stamped, self-addressed envelope is enclosed for your convenience.

Sincerely,

_____

KC Enterprises

....

The above balance is   Correct

                        X   Incorrect (show amount)   _$163,000_

If incorrect, please provide information that could help to reconcile your account.

Response: Per our records, the following invoices are outstanding:
Invoice #4212 $72,000
Invoice #4593 $66,000
Invoice #4738 $25,000

Signature:_____
Title:_____
Date:_____

_____

Katie's note to file:
Per review of the A/R aging report, invoices #4593 and 4738 are not on the A/R aging report at December 31, 2015.

Possible procedures:
1. Not an exception, no adjustment necessary. Determine the sufficiency of allowance for doubtful accounts.
2. Exception noted; propose adjustment and request that the controller post it to the accounting records.
3. Verify by examining subsequent cash collections and/or shipping documents.
4. Review appropriate documentation to verify that additional invoices noted on confirmation pertain to the subsequent year.

FRAUD

9-72 **LO 8** Read the following scenario about Strang Corporation and identify the substantive procedures that the CPA (Elaine Stanley) should perform to determine whether lapping exists. Do not discuss deficiencies in the system of internal control.

During the year, Strang Corporation began to encounter cash flow difficulties, and a cursory review by management revealed receivable collection problems. Strang's management engaged Elaine Stanley, CPA, to perform a special investigation. Stanley studied the billing and collection cycle and noted the following:

The accounting department employs one bookkeeper who receives and opens all incoming mail. This bookkeeper is also responsible for depositing receipts, filing daily remittance advices, recording receipts in the cash receipts journal, and posting receipts in the individual customer accounts and the general ledger accounts. There are no cash sales. The bookkeeper prepares and controls the mailing of monthly statements to customers.

The concentration of functions and the receivable collection problems caused Stanley to suspect that a systematic defalcation of customers' payments through a delayed posting of remittances (lapping of accounts receivable) is present. Stanley was surprised to find that no customers complained about receiving erroneous monthly statements.

9-73 **LO 8** Your audit client, Madison, Inc., has a computerized accounts receivable system. There are two master files, a customer data file and an unpaid invoice file. The customer data file contains the customer's name, billing address, shipping address, identification number, phone number, purchase and cash payment history, and credit limit. For each unpaid invoice, the second file contains the customer's identification number, invoice number and date, date of shipment, method of shipment, credit terms, and gross invoice amount. Discuss how GAS could be used to aid in the audit of Madison's accounts receivable.

PROFESSIONAL SKEPTICISM

FRAUD

9-74 **LO 8** You have sent confirmations to forty customers of Berg-Shovick Express, a long-time audit client experiencing some financial difficulty. The company sells specialized high-technology goods. You have received confirmations from thirty-two of the forty positive confirmations sent. A few minor errors were noted on these accounts, but the projected amount of errors on the confirmations returned is just below tolerable error. The following information is available to you:

Book value of receivables	$7,782,292
Book value of items selected for confirmations	$3,100,110
Book value of items confirmed	$1,464,000
Audit value of items confirmed	$1,335,000

Summary of items selected but confirmations not returned:

Name	Outstanding Amount	Management Comments on Account Balance
Yunkel Specialty Mfg.	$432,000	Regular sales, but extended credit terms were given on $200,000 of goods. Yunkel has responded that it does not respond to confirmations.
Hi-Tech Combonitics	$300,000	No response to either confirmation request. Management indicates the sale was a special-term sale, and the goods are being held for the convenience of this company. The company is located in Albuquerque, New Mexico, and recently had a fire in its main production plant but expects to resume production early next month. The goods will be shipped as soon as production begins, but the sale has legally been completed.

(continued)

Name	Outstanding Amount	Management Comments on Account Balance
Beaver Dam Electronics	$275,000	Account balance represents sales of specialty products made in late December. The president of Berg-Shovick has orally confirmed the receivable because Beaver Dam Electronics is 50% owned by him.
California Hi-Fi	$200,000	Regular sales, but company has renegotiated its account balance due because of defective merchandise. Management has indicated it has issued a credit to the company, but because management had inspected the goods on the customer's property, it did not require the return of the merchandise. It expects the company to pay the $200,000.
Brenner Specialties	$175,000	Regular sales. This is a new company. Most of the sales ($100,000) were made in December.
Sprague Electronics	$100,000	Regular sales. Customer is negotiating a potential return of defective items.
Williams Pipeline	$100,000	Williams is a large company. Prior experience indicates that it does not respond to confirmations.
Long Tom Towers	$54,110	Customer is new this year and is located in Medicine Hat. Saskatchewan.

a. Indicate the audit procedures (and be specific as to what those procedures will accomplish) to complete the work on accounts receivable related to the confirmation process. In other words, identify the specific alternative audit procedures that should be performed.

b. Assuming that all items could not be cleared to the auditor's satisfaction, identify the audit procedures that should be implemented to finish auditing the valuation and existence assertions for accounts receivable.

FRAUD FOCUS: CONTEMPORARY AND HISTORICAL CASES

FRAUD

9-75 **Zynga** **(LO 2, 3, 4, 5, 6, 8)** Refer to the *Professional Judgment in Context* feature "How to Account for Virtual Sales at Zynga." Answer the following questions:

a. What are the inherent risks associated with the revenue transactions at Zynga?

b. What are management's incentives to fraudulently misstate revenue transactions?

c. What controls should Zynga management have in place to mitigate the risks associated with revenue transactions?

d. How might auditors use planning analytical procedures to identify any potential concerns with Zynga's revenue?

e. What might be considered sufficient appropriate evidence when auditing Zynga's revenue transactions?

PROFESSIONAL SKEPTICISM

FRAUD

9-76 **Tvia**
(LO 1, 2, 3, 6, 8) A *Focus on Fraud* feature presented in the chapter discussed the SEC's complaint against Benjamin Silva III, Tvia's vice president of worldwide sales. The complaint alleges a number of actions taken by Silva. For each of the following actions, indicate the accounting and/or auditing issue that should be of concern to the auditor and an action that might be taken by the auditor.

a. In an effort to increase revenue, Silva began entering into side agreements with Tvia's customers. Typically, these side agreements promised the customer extended payment terms and obligated Tvia to find a buyer for any product that the customer was unable to sell.

b. On multiple occasions Silva caused Tvia to misapply a payment it received from a new customer in order to pay down delinquent amounts owed by a separate customer. For example, the complaint notes that one instance concerns Ricom, a Chinese customer that by late 2005 was past due on Tvia invoices totaling more than $740,000. In February 2006, Silva convinced another customer, Protech Perennial Limited (Protech), to submit a $100,000 deposit for a then-unavailable line of Tvia chips. On or about February 24, 2006, Tvia received a wire transfer from Protech for $100,000. "In order to convince Tvia's finance staff to apply these funds to Ricom's account, Silva falsely claimed that Protech had wired the money on Ricom's behalf, due to purported Chinese Government restrictions on Ricom's wiring money out of that country. By this conduct, Silva mislead [sic] Tvia's CEO, CFO and auditors regarding the collectibility of past due amounts owed by Ricom."

FRAUD

INTERNATIONAL

9-77 **UTStarcom, Inc.**
(LO 2, 3, 4, 5, 6, 8) UTStarcom is a global leader in the manufacture, integration, and support of networking and telecommunications systems. The company sells broadband wireless products and a line of handset equipment to operators in emerging and established telecommunications markets worldwide. The following excerpt was obtained from the 2004 10-K of UTStarcom, Inc., which reported material weaknesses in the company's internal controls. In describing the company's remediation efforts, the company stated that "planned remediation measures are intended to address material weaknesses related to revenue and deferred revenue accounts and associated cost of sales." These material weaknesses were evidenced by the identification of six separate transactions aggregating approximately $5 million in which revenue was initially included in the company's fourth-quarter 2004 financial statements before all criteria for revenue recognition were met. In addition, there were other transactions for which there was insufficient initial documentation for revenue recognition purposes but which did not result in any adjustments to the company's fourth-quarter 2004 financial statements. If unremediated, these material weaknesses have the potential of misstating revenue in future financial

periods. The company's planned remediation measures include the following:

- "The Company plans to design a contract review process in China requiring financial and legal staff to provide input during the contract negotiation process to ensure timely identification and accurate accounting treatment of nonstandard contracts."
- "In March 2005, the Company conducted a training seminar regarding revenue recognition, including identification of non-standard contracts, in the United States and, in April 2005, the Company conducted a similar seminar in China. Starting in May 2005, the Company plans to conduct additional training seminars in various international locations regarding revenue recognition and the identification of nonstandard contracts."
- "At the end of 2004, the Company began requiring centralized retention of documentation evidencing proof of delivery and final acceptance for revenue recognition purposes."

Based on this information, respond to the following questions.

a. What features of this case should have indicated to the auditor a potentially heightened risk of fraudulent financial reporting?

b. Using the previous disclosures as a starting point, brainstorm about the challenges regarding internal controls that a company may face in doing business internationally.

c. The company had disclosed its planned remediation efforts for 2004. How might the auditor have used that information during the 2005 audit in terms of audit planning?

d. Considering potential analytical procedures relevant to the revenue cycle that were discussed in this chapter, identify what types of analytics might be applied in 2005 to provide evidence that the problems detected in 2004 have been remedied.

e. Considering potential substantive tests of revenue that were discussed in this chapter, identify procedures that might be applied in 2005 to provide evidence that the problems detected in 2004 have been remedied.

FRAUD

ETHICS

PROFESSIONAL SKEPTICISM

9-78 **HBOC, Arthur Andersen LLP**
(LO 6, 7, 8, 9) Robert A. Putnam, an engagement partner for Arthur Andersen LLP, was in charge of the audit for HBOC, an Atlanta-based maker of software for the health-care industry, during the period 1996–1999. HBOC had a fantastic earnings track record. In fact, HBOC's management was so confident of the strength of its financial statements that it made public announcements of the company's revenues, net income, and earnings per share before Andersen's audits or reviews were completed, a practice of which Putnam was aware. However, these financial results reflected the fact that senior officers of HBOC were fraudulently recognizing revenue on transactions that failed to comply with GAAP.

Early in 1997, Putnam learned that HBOC's management was inappropriately recognizing revenue on contracts where a sale was contingent on later approval by a customer's board of directors (such a situation is referred to as a *board contingency*). Putnam discussed the issue with Jay Gilbertson, the CFO, who claimed that the board contingencies were perfunctory and contained no real risk of cancellation. Gilbertson agreed to provide documentation supporting his claim, but he never did so. Putnam had additional reason to be skeptical concerning HBOC's accounting practices. During the prior year's audit, the auditors identified an instance where HBOC used side letters in its contract negotiations with customers. Auditors were aware of the risks associated with side letters, and Andersen had warned its audit staff that such side letters often are the cause of material revenue misstatements, especially in the software industry.

Putnam also had reason to be skeptical about the integrity of HBOC's management. During 1997, Gilbertson represented to Andersen that HBOC had complied with the latest draft of SOP 97–2, the new software revenue recognition guidelines prohibiting revenue recognition if any board contingency existed. Despite the new standard, HBOC continued to enter into some contracts with board contingencies.

Despite these issues, Putman failed to expand the scope of the audit to address the increased risk of fraud. In January 1999, McKesson Corporation acquired HBOC. On April 28, 1999, McKesson announced that it "had determined that software sales transactions aggregating $26.2 million in the company's fourth quarter ended March 31, 1999, and $16.0 million in the prior quarters of the fiscal year, were improperly recorded because they were subject to contingencies, and have been reversed. The audit process is ongoing and there is a possibility that additional contingent sales may be identified." After the announcement, the company's share price tumbled from approximately $65 to $34 a share (a loss of about $9 billion in market value).

Ultimately, the SEC determined that Putnam failed to exercise due professional care, to adequately plan and supervise the audits, and to obtain sufficient appropriate evidence to afford a reasonable basis for an opinion regarding the financial statements. The SEC issued a cease-and-desist order against Putnam, and denied him the privilege of appearing or practicing before the commission as an accountant for at least five years. In addition, fraud charges were brought against the management of HBOC.

Summarizing the facts from the SEC's Administrative Proceeding against Putnam dated April 28, 2008, we know the following about the quarterly and year-end audits that led to the problems for Arthur Andersen LLP on the HBOC engagement:

- **Andersen's Review of HBOC's financial statements—First Quarter 1997** HBOC reported $68 million of software revenue during Q1, and the engagement team tested the account balance and found that $14 million was improperly recorded, which overstated pre-tax income by 9.4%. Most of the improperly recognized revenue related to board contingencies, and the remainder related to revenue recognized on a contract signed after quarter-end. HBOC management refused to eliminate the improperly recorded revenue, and Putnam did not insist that it does so. Putnam approved an unqualified quarterly review report.

- **Andersen's Review of HBOC's financial statements—Second Quarter 1997** The engagement team learned that HBOC continued to improperly recognize revenue on contracts containing board contingencies and that the company was improperly recording revenue on sales subject to side letter contingencies that allowed for contract cancellation. Further, the engagement team learned that at least one such contract that had been recorded as revenue in Q1 had been canceled during Q2. The engagement team also learned that HBOC had again recognized revenue on a contract signed after quarter-end. Putnam recommended to HBOC's management that the revenue from these contracts be reversed, but Gilbertson (the CFO) refused to do so. The errors overstated pre-tax income by 7%. Despite these facts, Putnam approved an unqualified quarterly review report.

- **Andersen's Review of HBOC's financial statements—Third Quarter 1997** The engagement team continued to experience the same difficulties as they had noted in Q2; Putnam continued to do nothing about the problems and continued to approve an unqualified quarterly review report.

- **Andersen's Audit of HBOC's financial statements—1997 Year-End** Andersen's year-end audit included testing of HBOC's revenue recognition and accounts receivable. The engagement team used confirmations as their primary substantive evidence on these accounts. The team sent eight confirmation requests (eleven fewer than they had sent during the 1996 audit). The confirmations requested customers to confirm amounts owed to HBOC and to confirm that no revenue contingencies existed on software purchased from HBOC. Only three customers responded, and two of those noted contingencies included in side letters. Putnam did not direct the team to send any additional confirmations or to perform any additional audit procedures.

  In addition, the engagement team learned that HBOC was recognizing too much revenue on maintenance contracts and that material amounts should have been deferred to later periods. Putnam asked Gilbertson to increase deferred revenue, but Gilbertson refused, promising to do so in later periods. In addition, HBOC acquired other companies during 1997 and recorded acquisition reserves of $95.3 million associated with the expenses of the acquisition. Putnam proposed that HBOC reverse $16 million of the reserves because they were excessive, overstating expenses by 20% (in other words, a cookie jar reserve). Gilbertson refused to make the proposed adjustment. Despite all these problems, Putnam approved an unqualified audit report and disclosed none of the issues to the audit committee.

- **Andersen's Review of HBOC's financial statements—First Quarter 1998** During the review, Putnam discovered that HBOC was misusing the acquisition reserve to offset current period operating expenses, which is in violation of GAAP and had the effect of overstating HBOC's net income. The engagement team also identified another instance of improper revenue recognition associated with a contract involving a side letter. Once again, Putnam proposed an adjusting entry to correct the problems, but Gilbertson refused to make the entry. Putnam again approved an unqualified quarterly review report.

  By April 1998, the engagement manager (Putnam's subordinate) expressed concerns about the earnings management issues occurring at HBOC to Putnam, and Putnam shared the same concerns despite doing nothing to address them. In May 1998, Putnam and the engagement team called a special meeting with Gilbertson and others at HBOC to discuss the issues, and Gilbertson expressed promises to begin properly recording the various transactions.

- **Andersen's Review of HBOC's financial statements—Second Quarter 1998** During the quarterly review, the engagement team again noted a variety of errors. These included inappropriate application of acquisition reserves to reduce current period expenses, recognition of excessive revenue from software maintenance agreements, and an understatement of the allowance for doubtful accounts. Putnam informed Gilbertson that if HBOC did not reverse the application of the acquisition reserves, Andersen would not issue its review report. After a heated discussion, Gilbertson reversed the entry related to acquisition reserves but did not correct any of the other errors. Putnam approved the issuance of the quarterly review report.

- **Andersen's Review of HBOC's financial statements—Third Quarter 1998** The engagement team again discovered the same types of earnings management issues as in prior quarters, but Putnam did not require HBOC to make corrections. Further, Putnam approved an unusual transaction in which HBOC simultaneously sold to and purchased a product from another company. Putnam advised Gilbertson that the accounting for the transaction would be correct only if the sale and purchase were not linked and if there was a defined end user for the HBOC software. Neither of these conditions was true, and Putnam was aware of this fact (and this transaction ultimately led to a restatement of $30 million about a year later). However, Putnam still approved the issuance of the quarterly review report.

- At the November 1998 meeting of HBOC's audit committee, the CEO informed the audit committee that Gilbertson was resigning as CFO, which was an unexpected event. The CEO asked Putnam if he "had a Cendant on his hands," referring to a widely reported financial fraud case at the time. Putnam responded that he knew of no problems or disagreements with Gilbertson.

  In October 1998, McKesson and HBOC announced their merger. Putnam approved the use of Andersen's reports in related filings and made no mention of the associated accounting errors.

- **Andersen's Audit of McKesson's financial statements—1998 Year-End** McKesson hired Andersen to complete the audits, and Putnam and the engagement team continued to discover various accounting errors. Still, Putnam did not require the team to expand the scope of audit testing. Putnam again approved the issuance of an unqualified audit report.

  During the spring of 1999, McKesson initially disclosed some of the revenue recognition issues, and by the summer of 1999, McKesson reported restatements of the 1997 and 1998 financial statements. Ultimately, six members of upper management of HBOC were charged with securities fraud. The SEC issued a cease-and-desist order against Putman and denied him the privilege of appearing or practicing before the commission as an accountant for at least five years.

In many instances of fraudulent financial reporting, the auditor is completely unaware of the fraud until it ultimately unravels. That is certainly *not* the case for the HBOC fraud. Rather, it is very clear that Putnam and his Andersen engagement team were well aware of the fraud and possessed detailed knowledge of precisely how it was accomplished. Yet, they did virtually nothing to address the situation.

Source: Adapted from information contained in the following sources: (1) Securities Act of 1933 Release No. 8912, April 28, 2008; (2) Securities Exchange Act of 1934 Release No. 57725,

April 28, 2008; (3) Accounting and Auditing Enforcement Release No. 2815, April 28, 2008; and (4) Administrative Proceeding File No. 3-10998.

a. What was Putnam's critical mistake in the review of Q1 1997? How did that critical mistake affect his willingness to take action to address the problems in the HBOC audit in later periods?

b. What do you think could have motivated Putnam to act as he did? Why do you think that after all the problems that he encountered, he was still willing to acquiesce to the obviously inappropriate sale/purchase transaction in Q3 1998?

c. What other elements of corporate governance failed in the HBOC situation?

d. The confirmation process in the 1997 year-end audit was clearly flawed. What did the engagement team and Putnam do wrong?

e. The McKesson acquisition of HBOC provided an opportunity for Putnam to deal with what he knew. Obviously, McKesson management would have been eager to know about the earnings management issues at HBOC prior to acquiring the company. Instead, Putnam did not reveal the problems he had been encountering, even when asked directly by the CEO and the audit committee. Use the professional decision making framework introduced in *Chapter 4* to make a recommendation about a course of action that would have enabled Putnam to do the right thing during the acquisition process and alert the other parties involved in corporate governance of HBOC and McKesson about the problematic behaviors he had been encountering. Recall that the framework is as follows:

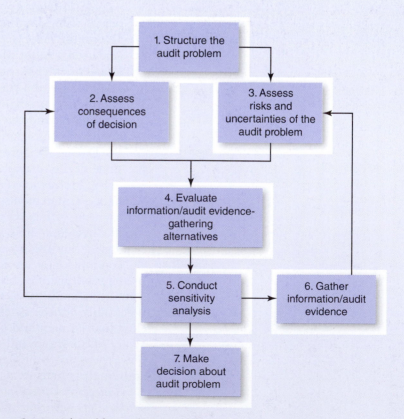

Source: Adapted from Judgment and Choice, by Robin Hogarth.

FRAUD

ETHICS

9-79

HBOC, Arthur Andersen LLP
(LO 9)

For this case, use the same facts as presented in the previous problem. In *Problem 9-78*, we focused on the inappropriate actions of Robert A. Putnam, the engagement partner on the HBOC audit. In this case, we expand on the problems detected in the audit and ultimately ask that you decide on an appropriate, alternative course of action for the manager of the HBOC audit, that is, Putman's subordinate. In the actual case, the audit manager questioned Putnam's actions but never took proactive action (other than talking to Putnam) to correct the known audit deficiencies.

In his book, *The Courageous Follower: Standing up to and for Our Leaders* (1995), Ira Chaleff describes five characteristics of individuals who stand up to their organizational leaders. These characteristics include the courage to (1) assume responsibility for themselves and their organization, (2) serve the organization in a responsible manner, (3) challenge the behaviors or policies of the leader, (4) participate in transforming an organization or dealing with the difficulties associated with change, and (5) take moral action, including refusing to obey direct orders, appealing to the next level of authority, or resigning.

Based on these facts, consider the ideas outlined by Chaleff, and use the ethical decision making framework from *Chapter 4* to make a recommendation about an alternative, appropriate course of action that the audit manager on the HBOC audit could have taken.

Recall that the seven steps in the framework are as follows: (1) identify the ethical issue; (2) determine who are the affected parties and identify their rights; (3) determine the most important rights; (4) develop alternative courses of action; (5) determine the likely consequences of each proposed course of action; (6) assess the possible consequences, including an estimation of the greatest good for the greatest number; and (7) decide on the appropriate course of action.

FRAUD

9-80

MiniScribe
(LO 2, 3, 6, 8)

Read the following case about MiniScribe and answer the following questions.

a. How did MiniScribe inflate its financial statements?
b. What are some of the factors that led to the inflated financial statements?
c. What red flags should have raised the auditor's suspicions about phony sales and other attempts to inflate income?
d. What substantive audit procedures could have uncovered the fraud?

In October 1988, MiniScribe, a computer disk drive manufacturer, announced its thirteenth consecutive record-breaking quarter, while its competitors were laying off hundreds of employees. MiniScribe's receivables had increased significantly, and inventories had increased to a dangerous level because disk drives can become obsolete from one quarter to the next. The company's stock price had quintupled in just two years. It had apparently risen from the dead under the leadership of Q. T. Wiles, who had resurrected other companies and was known as Dr. Fix-It. It looked as if he had done it again.

Seven months later, it was announced that MiniScribe's sales gains had been fabricated. An internal investigation concluded that senior management apparently perpetrated a massive fraud on the company, its directors, its outside auditors, and the investing public. Most of MiniScribe's top management was dismissed, and layoffs shrank its employment by more than 30% in one year. MiniScribe might have to write off as much as $200 million in bad inventory and uncollectible receivables.

Wiles' unrealistic sales targets and abusive management style created a pressure cooker that drove managers to cook the books or perish. The managers responded by booking sales prematurely, manipulating reserves, and simply fabricating figures in order to maintain the illusion of unbounded growth even after the industry was hit by a severe slump.

When Wiles arrived at MiniScribe in mid-1985, it had just lost its biggest customer, IBM, which decided to make its own drives. With the personal computer industry then slumping, MiniScribe was drowning in red ink.

Dr. Fix-It's prescription was to cut 20% of the workforce and overhaul the company from top to bottom. As part of the overhaul, several semiautonomous divisions were created. Each division manager set the division's own budget, sales quotas, incentives, and work rules. The company became a chaotic Babel of at least twenty minicompanies that were constantly being changed and reorganized. One employee held twenty different positions in less than seven years.

Wiles turned up the heat under his lieutenants. Four times a year, he would summon as many as 100 employees for several days of intense meetings, at which they were force-fed his idiosyncratic management philosophy. At one of the first such meetings he held, Wiles demanded that two controllers stand, and he fired them on the spot, saying, "That's just to show everyone I'm in control of the company."

At each of these meetings, division managers had to present and defend their business plans. Invariably, Wiles would find such plans deficient and would berate their authors in front of their peers. A former controller says Wiles would throw, kick, and rip the plan books that displeased him, showering his intimidated audience with paper while yelling, "Why don't you understand this? Why can't you understand how to do this?"

Then something changed. Wiles started saying, "I no longer want to be remembered as a turnaround artist. I want to be remembered as the man who made MiniScribe a billion-dollar company." Sales objectives became the company's driving force, and financial results became the sole determinant of whether bonuses were awarded. Wiles said, "This is the number we want to hit first quarter, second quarter, third quarter, and so on," and it was amazing to see how close they could get to the number they wanted to hit.

Hitting the number became a companywide obsession. Although many high-tech manufacturers accelerate shipments at the end of a quarter to boost sales—a practice known as *stuffing the channel*—MiniScribe went several steps beyond that. On one occasion, an analyst relates, the company shipped more than twice as many disk drives to a computer manufacturer as had been ordered; a former sales manager says the excess shipment was worth about $9 million. MiniScribe later said it had shipped the excess drives by mistake. The extras were returned—but by then MiniScribe had posted the sale at the higher number. Wiles denied this practice.

Other accounting maneuvers involved shipments of disk drives from MiniScribe's factory in Singapore. Most shipments went by air freight, but a squeeze on air cargo space toward the end of each quarter would force some shipments onto cargo ships, which required up to two weeks for transit. On several occasions, said a former division manager, MiniScribe executives looking to raise sales changed purchase orders to show that a customer took title to a shipment in Singapore when, in fact, title would not change until the drives were delivered in the United States.

MiniScribe executives tried to persuade an audit team that 1986 year-end results should include as sales the cargo on a freighter that they contended had set sail in late December. The audit team declined to do so. Eventually, the cargo and the freighter, which did not exist, were simply forgotten.

MiniScribe executives also found other ways to inflate sales figures. One was to manipulate reserves for returns of defective merchandise and bad debts. The problem of inadequate reserves grew so great that private analysts began noticing it. MiniScribe was booking less than 1% reserves; the rest of the industry had reserves ranging from 4% to 10%.

To avoid booking losses on returns in excess of its skimpy reserves, defective drives would be tossed onto a rejection pile and booked as inventory. Eventually, the defective drives would be shipped out again to new customers, continuing the cycle. Returns of defective merchandise ran as high as 15%.

At a time of strong market demand, such ploys enabled MiniScribe to seem to grow almost exponentially, posting sales of $185 million in 1986 and $362 million in 1987. In early 1988, Wiles was confidently forecasting a $660 million year, and he held fast to his rosy forecast even as disk drive sales started slipping industry wide in late spring and nose-dived in the autumn. Meanwhile, Wiles increased the pressure on his managers. Division reports would be doctored as they rose from one bureaucratic level to the next.

Before long, the accounting gimmickry became increasingly brazen. Division managers were told to "force the numbers." Workers whispered that bricks were being shipped just so a division could claim to have met its quota. Others joked that unwanted disk drives were being shipped and returned so often that they had to be repackaged because the boxes wore out.

Employees also joked about shipments to "account BW," an acronym for "big warehouse"—but that wasn't just a joke. Mini-Scribe established several warehouses around the country and in Canada as just-in-time suppliers for distributors. Customers weren't invoiced until they received shipments from the warehouses. Mini-Scribe, however, was booking shipments to the warehouses as sales. The number of disk drives shipped to the warehouses was at Mini-Scribe's discretion. It is estimated that between $80 million and $100 million worth of unordered disk drives went to the warehouses.

Wall Street began to smell trouble. Analysts could find no significant customers other than Compaq to support MiniScribe's bullish forecasts. Several major anticipated orders from Apple

Computer and Digital Equipment Corp. fell through. MiniScribe reported a fourth-quarter loss and a drop in net income for 1988 despite a 66% increase in sales—that is, on paper. A week later, Wiles abruptly resigned. The stock price tumbled from a high of $15 to less than $3 per share, a decline that upset many stockholders.

An investigative committee of MiniScribe's outside directors reported that senior company officials:

- Apparently broke into locked trunks containing the auditors' working papers during the year-end 1986 audit and changed inventory figures, inflating inventory values by approximately $1 million
- Packaged bricks and shipped them to distributors as disk drives in 1987, recording $4.3 million in sales; when the shipments were returned, MiniScribe inflated its inventory by the purported cost of the bricks
- Packaged approximately 6,300 disk drives that had been contaminated to inflate inventory during the fourth quarter of 1988

Several lawsuits were filed charging MiniScribe with engineering phony sales artificially to inflate its stock to benefit insiders. The suits also charged that its auditors participated in the conspiracy by falsely certifying the company's financial statements.

APPLICATION ACTIVITIES

NOTE: Completing Application Activities requires students to reference additional resources and materials. Some Application Activities will require the student to reference relevant professional auditing standards. We make special note of these as Auditing Standards Application Activities.

ETHICS

PROFESSIONAL SKEPTICISM

FRAUD

PCAOB

9-81 (LO **2, 3, 6, 7, 8**) Select one of the following PCAOB Disciplinary Orders (available at *www.pcaob.org*).

1. ORDER INSTITUTING DISCIPLINARY PROCEEDINGS, MAKING FINDINGS, AND IMPOSING SANCTIONS *In the Matter of Traci Jo Anderson and Traci Jo Anderson, CPA Respondents*; PCAOB Release No. 105–2010-007
2. ORDER MAKING FINDINGS AND IMPOSING SANCTIONS *In the Matter of Ray O Westergard, CPA, Respondent*; PCAOB Release No. 105–2010-003
3. ORDER INSTITUTING DISCIPLINARY PROCEEDINGS, MAKING FINDINGS, AND IMPOSING SANCTIONS *In the Matter of Williams & Webster, P.S., Kevin J. Williams, CPA, and John G. Webster, CPA, Respondents*; PCAOB Release No. 105–2007-001
4. ORDER INSTITUTING DISCIPLINARY PROCEEDINGS, MAKING FINDINGS, AND IMPOSING SANCTIONS *In the Matter of Armando C. Ibarra, P.C., Armando C. Ibarra, Sr., and Armando C. Ibarra, Jr., Respondents*; PCAOB No. 105–2006-001

After reading your selected disciplinary order, address the following issues:

a. Identify the key audit deficiencies related to accounts, disclosures, and assertions in the revenue cycle.
b. For each identified deficiency, indicate the appropriate action that should have been taken by the auditor.
c. In assessing the case overall, indicate (1) whether the auditor had an appropriate level of professional skepticism; (2) if applicable, what might have led the auditor to

behave in an unethical manner; and (3) whether the sanctions against the auditor or audit firm seem reasonable.

ETHICS

PROFESSIONAL SKEPTICISM

FRAUD

9-82 **SEC** (LO 2, 3, 6, 7, 8) Obtain SEC Accounting and Auditing Enforcement Release (AAER) No. 3359 (January 2012) at the SEC web site. Read the sections of the AAER that relate to accounts and assertions in the revenue cycle and address the following issues:
a. Identify the key audit deficiencies related to accounts and assertions in the revenue cycle.
b. For each identified deficiency, indicate the appropriate action that should have been taken by the auditor.
c. In assessing the case overall, indicate (1) whether the auditor had an appropriate level of professional skepticism; (2) if applicable, what might have led the auditor to behave in an unethical manner; and (3) whether the sanctions against the auditors seem reasonable.

FRAUD

9-83 **COSO** (LO 2, 3) In 2010, COSO published a study that provided a comprehensive analysis of occurrences of fraudulent financial reporting that were investigated by the SEC from 1988 through 2007. Sixty-one percent of the 347 fraud cases profiled in the study related to the improper recording of revenues. The revenue misstatements were primarily the result of fictitiously or prematurely recording revenues. The report lists various techniques (labeled (a) through (f)). For each technique, describe how such a fraud would work. You may need to do some additional research if you are unfamiliar with these techniques.
a. Conditional sales
b. Round-tripping or recording loans as sales
c. Premature revenues before all the terms of the sale were completed
d. Improper cutoff of sales
e. Improper use of the percentage of completion method
f. Consignment sales

FRAUD

9-84 **LO 3** Refer to *Exhibit 9.4*, which provides examples of companies that have employed some type of revenue recognition or accounts receivable scheme. Using appropriate resources, identify a recent example of a company that employed some type of revenue recognition or accounts receivable scheme. Describe the details of the scheme and possible motivations for conducting the scheme.

FRAUD

9-85 **McKesson & Robbins** (LO 3, 8) One of the major financial scandals of the twentieth century centered on McKesson & Robbins. The case had implications for the audit of accounts receivable. Based on appropriate research, describe the nature of the fraud related to accounts receivable that occurred at McKesson & Robbins and identify the impact of the case on the audit of accounts receivable.

AUDITING STANDARDS APPLICATION ACTIVITY

9-86 **LO 8** Refer to the *Standards Appendix* at the end of this text. Identify the relevant auditing standards (PCAOB, AICPA, and

IAASB) relating to external confirmations. Locate the standards on each organization's web site.

a. What generalizations are applicable to audit evidence with respect to confirmations?

b. What do the standards direct the auditor to do if management refuses to allow the auditor to send a confirmation request?

c. Comment on similarities or substantive differences between the standards for each standard-setting body.

9-87 **LO 5, 8** Refer to the *Standards Appendix* at the end of this text. Identify the relevant auditing standards (PCAOB, AICPA, and IAASB) concerning using analytical procedures as a substantive test. Locate the standards on each organization's web site.

a. What is a basic premise underlying analytical procedures that is mentioned in all relevant professional guidance?

b. What types of documentation are appropriate for substantive analytical procedures?

c. Why might using substantive analytical procedures help auditors save time on the audit and achieve efficiencies? Why might auditors get criticized for using substantive analytical procedures as opposed to substantive tests of details?

ANALYTICAL PROCEDURES: A CASE IN THE CONTEXT OF THE PHARMACEUTICAL INDUSTRY

NOTE: In this and select cycle chapters, we present a case set in the pharmaceutical industry. The case enables students to practice developing and conducting planning and substantive analytical procedures. The case was developed using the published financial statements of three prominent companies in this industry, with adaptations to make the case suitable for classroom use. The fictional company names are as follows: PharmaCorp, Novartell, and AstraZoro. You will access an Excel file on the text's web site at *www.cengage.com*. The Excel file contains financial data and information from footnote disclosures. The primary analytical procedures tasks will focus on PharmaCorp. You will use Novartell and AstraZoro as industry comparison companies. Access and download the file, then complete the requirements in 9-88.

9-88 **LO 5, 8** This case will enable you to practice conducting planning and substantive analytical procedures for accounts in the revenue cycle. When analyzing the financial data, you may assume that the 2015 information is unaudited, while prior year data is audited.

As you complete this case, consider the following features of and trends in the pharmaceutical industry and for PharmaCorp specifically:

- After a long period of industry dominance by companies in the United States, the United Kingdom, and Europe, these companies are facing increasing competition from companies domiciled in emerging economies, such as Brazil, India, and China.

- There exists significant uncertainty in the market because of recent regulation covering health-care and government payouts for certain procedures and related pharmaceuticals.

- Health-care policy makers and the government are increasingly mandating what physicians can prescribe to patients.

- Health-care policy makers and the government are increasingly focusing on prevention regimes rather than treatment regimes, thereby leading to shifts in the demand for various pharmaceuticals.

- The global pharmaceutical market is anticipated to grow by 5% to 7% in 2016 compared with a 4% to 5% growth rate in 2015, according to a leading industry analyst publication.

- Beginning in 2014, PharmaCorp initiated and executed a significant company-wide cost reduction initiative aimed at improving manufacturing efficiency, cutting back on research and development expenses, and eliminating unnecessary corporate overhead.

- PharmaCorp's policies for extending credit to customers has remained stable over the last three years. PharmaCorp's credit-granting policies are considered stringent within the industry, and analysts have sometimes criticized the company for this, contending that such policies have hindered the company's revenue growth relative to industry peers.

- PharmaCorp's policies for extending credit to customers have remained stable over the last three years. PharmaCorp's credit granting policies are considered stringent within the industry, and analysts have sometimes criticized the company for this, contending that such policies have hindered the company's revenue growth relative to industry peers.

- Two of PharmaCorp's popular pharmaceuticals, Selebrax and Vyvox, came off patent during the fourth quarter of FYE 2015. These pharmaceuticals now face competition in the generic drug portion of the overall industry market.

Part I: Planning Analytical Procedures

a. *Step 1: Identify Suitable Analytical Procedures.* Your audit senior has suggested that the following ratios (on an overall financial statement level) will be used for planning analytical procedures in the revenue cycle at PharmaCorp:

- Gross margin: (revenues-cost of sales)/revenues
- Turnover of receivables: (revenues/average accounts receivable); for ease of computation simply use ending accounts receivable
- Receivables as a percentage of current assets and as a percentage of total assets: (accounts receivable/total current assets) and (accounts receivable/total assets)
- Allowance for uncollectible accounts as a percentage of accounts receivable: (allowance/accounts receivable)

As part of Step 1, identify any other relevant relationships or trend analyses that would be useful to consider as part of planning analytics. Explain your reasoning.

b. *Step 2: Evaluate Reliability of Data Used to Develop Expectations.* The audit team has determined that the data you will be using to develop expectations in the revenue cycle are reliable. Indicate the factors that the audit team likely considered in making that determination.

c. *Step 3: Develop Expectations.* Complete Step 3 of planning analytical procedures by developing expectations for relevant accounts in the revenue cycle and for the ratios from Part (a). Develop expectations by considering both historical trends of PharmaCorp, and also by considering features of and historical trends in the industry. Given that this is a planning analytical procedure, the expectations are not expected to have a high level of precision. You might indicate that you expect a ratio to increase, decrease, or stay the same, and possibly indicate the size of any expected increases or decreases, or the range of the expected ratio. PharmaCorp's financial information is on first tab of the Excel file, while the financial information for Novartell and AstraZoro is provided on the last two tabs of the Excel file.

d. *Step 4 and Step 5: Define and Identify Significant Unexpected Differences.* Refer to the guidance in *Chapter 7* on performance materiality, tolerable misstatement, and clearly trivial amounts. Apply those materiality guidelines to Step 4 of planning analytical procedures in the revenue cycle for PharmaCorp, to define what is meant by a significant difference. Explain your reasoning. Also comment on qualitative materiality considerations in this context. Now that you have determined what amount of difference would be considered significant, calculate the ratios identified in Step 1 (and any additional ratios or trend analyses that you suggested), based on PharmaCorp's recorded financial statement amounts. Identify those ratios where there is a significant unexpected difference.

e. *Step 6 and Step 7: Investigate Significant Unexpected Differences and Ensure Proper Documentation.* Complete Step 6 of planning analytical procedures by describing accounts or relationships that you would investigate further through substantive audit procedures. Explain your reasoning. To complete Step 7, describe what information should be included in the auditor's workpapers.

Part II: Substantive Analytical Procedures

f. At the Excel file, you will see three tabs that you should review: *PharmaCorp Segment Information, PharmaCorp Geographic Information,* and *PharmaCorp Other Revenue Info.* These tabs provide excerpts from PharmaCorp's footnote disclosures regarding segment, geographic, and other revenue information. Read these disclosures and describe the various operating segments and geographic regions in which the company operates.

g. Which operating segments are most important to the company in terms of revenue generation? Which geographic regions are most important to the company? What are the three most important products produced by PharmaCorp? Comment on trends that you notice in revenue in each of these categories.

h. Explain the types of ratio analysis that you could conduct in substantive analytical procedures using the data provided in the segment, geographic, and other revenue information, for example, R&D expenses/revenues. How would the substantive analytics differ from the planning analytics? Comment on the trends and relationships that you believe are most relevant, and implications for further substantive testing.

ACADEMIC RESEARCH CASES

NOTE: Completing Academic Research Cases requires students to reference additional resources and materials.

PROFESSIONAL SKEPTICISM

SEARCH HINT

It is easy to locate these academic research articles! Simply use a search engine such as Google Scholar or an electronic research platform such as ABI Inform, and search using the author names and part of the article title.

9-89 LO 2, 3 Locate and read the article listed below and answer the following questions.

Caylor, M. 2010. Strategic revenue recognition to achieve earnings benchmarks. *Journal of Accounting and Public Policy* 29: 82–95.

a. What is the issue being addressed in the paper?
b. What are the findings of the paper?
c. Why is this paper important to auditors, and what are the implications of this paper for the auditing profession?
d. Describe the research methodology used as a basis for the conclusions.
e. Describe any limitations of the research.

FRAUD

9-90 **LO 1, 2, 3** Locate and read the article listed below and answer the following questions.

Callen, J. L., S. W. G. Robb, and D. Segal. 2008. Revenue manipulation and restatements by loss firms. *Auditing: A Journal of Practice & Theory* 27 (2): 1–29.

a. What is the issue being addressed in the paper?
b. What are the findings of the paper?
c. Why is this paper important to auditors, and what are the implications of this paper for the auditing profession?
d. Describe the research methodology used as a basis for the conclusions.
e. Describe any limitations of the research.

FORD AND TOYOTA

9-91 **Ford Motor Company and Toyota Motor Corporation** (LO **1, 2, 3, 4, 5, 7, 8**)

Source and Reference	Question
Ford 10-K	a. What are the key revenue cycle accounts for Ford? What accounts involve critical accounting estimates?
	b. What does Ford say in its footnotes about its use of accounting estimates? What risk do these estimates pose for the auditor?
Ford 10-K and Toyota Annual Report or 20F	c. Compare Ford and Toyota's footnotes on finance receivables. What is the audit firm's responsibility regarding the informativeness of the disclosures?
Ford 10-K	d. Ford lists a variety of risk factors associated with its business. Review those and identify which relate most to the revenue cycle. What evidence might the auditor gather to understand how those risks may affect the financial statement line items associated with the revenue cycle?
Ford 10-K	e. Read Ford's Management Discussion and Analysis section titled "Key Economic Factors and Trends Affecting the Automotive Industry." What are the main points that Ford management raises regarding its ability to generate revenue and profits in the near term? What do its statements imply about the risks associated with auditing Ford Motor Co.?

ACL

NOTE: There is an ACL Appendix at the end of the text that you may find helpful in completing this problem.

9-92 **LO 5, 8**   You are auditing FloorMart, a retailer with 200 stores around the country. It has two basic sizes of stores—minimarts with 3,000 square feet and maximarts with 7,500 square feet. Both types of stores carry the same types of products. The client has provided an Excel file with the square feet, sales, and inventory at each store. Access the book's resources on the Cengage web site. The file is labeled "FloorMart Data."

a. Using either Excel or ACL, identify the stores for which sales appear to be out of line with the other stores and require additional evidence.

b. What procedures would the auditor use to gather the additional evidence?

9-93 **LO 7, 8**   You are auditing Accounts Receivable of HUSKY Corp. as of December 31, 2013. The Accounts Receivable general ledger balance is $4,263,919.52. Access the textbook's resources on the Cengage web site. The files are labeled "HUSKY Unpaid Invoices 2013" (the 12/31/2013, unpaid invoices), "HUSKY Shipping File 2013" (contains the shipment numbers and shipment dates for those invoices), and "HUSKY Credit Limit 2013" (contains each customer's credit limit). Sales are made FOB shipping point. The auditor has verified that the last shipment in 2013 is numbered 62050 and that shipping numbers have been used in proper sequence.

1. Foot the file of unpaid invoices using the menu option **Analyze**, then **Statistical**, then **Statistics** and agree to the general ledger. Print the statistics for the audit documentation and note the other statistics provided.

2. Identify customers with balances over their credit limit and print out the results. (*Hint*: Before combining files, be sure the matching fields, such as CUSTNUM or INVNUM, have been changed in each table from a number format to ASCII format using the menu item **Edit** then **Table Layout**. Double click on the field you want to change).

3. Perform a sales cutoff test to identify any invoices for which sales were recorded in 2013 but shipment was not made until 2014 and print out the results, including the total of those invoices.

4. Age the unpaid invoices as of December 31, 2013, print the aging and graph of the aging, extract (by double-clicking on the over 45 days aging indicator) and print out a list of invoices over 45 days old that also shows the total of those invoices.

5. Summarize your results and describe what procedures should be performed based on those results. Use ACL to stratify the population of customer balances, print the results, and describe how this information could be used to help determine which balances to confirm.

10 | Auditing Cash and Marketable Securities

CHAPTER OVERVIEW AND LEARNING OBJECTIVES

A high volume of transactions flows through cash accounts. Because of the vulnerability to error or fraud, organizations and auditors usually emphasize the quality of controls over the cash transactions. In this chapter, we present approaches that auditors take to assess risks associated with cash and to evaluate controls over cash accounts. We also address issues concerning the audit of marketable securities. In terms of the audit opinion formulation process, this chapter primarily involves Phases II, III, and IV—performing risk assessment procedures, tests of controls, and substantive procedures for cash and marketable securities.

Through studying this chapter, you will be able to achieve these learning objectives:

1. Identify the significant accounts, disclosures, and relevant assertions in auditing cash accounts.

2. Identify and assess inherent risks of material misstatement in cash accounts.

3. Identify and assess fraud risks of material misstatement in cash accounts.

4. Identify and assess control risks of material misstatement in cash accounts.

5. Describe how to use planning analytical procedures to identify possible material misstatements for cash accounts, disclosures, and assertions.

6. Determine appropriate responses to identified risks of material misstatement for cash accounts, disclosures, and assertions.

7. Determine appropriate tests of controls and consider the results of tests of controls for cash accounts, disclosures, and assertions.

8. Determine and apply sufficient appropriate substantive audit procedures for testing cash accounts, disclosures, and assertions.

9. Identify types of marketable securities, articulate the risks and controls typically associated with these accounts, and outline an audit approach for testing these accounts.

10. Apply the frameworks for professional decision making and ethical decision making to issues involving the audit of cash accounts, disclosures, and assertions.

THE AUDIT OPINION FORMULATION PROCESS

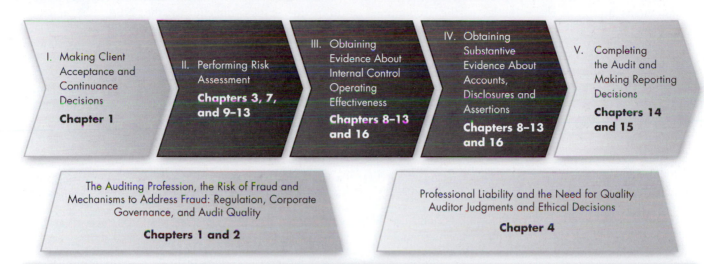

I. Making Client Acceptance and Continuance Decisions
Chapter 1

II. Performing Risk Assessment
Chapters 3, 7, and 9–13

III. Obtaining Evidence About Internal Control Operating Effectiveness
Chapters 8–13 and 16

IV. Obtaining Substantive Evidence About Accounts, Disclosures and Assertions
Chapters 8–13 and 16

V. Completing the Audit and Making Reporting Decisions
Chapters 14 and 15

The Auditing Profession, the Risk of Fraud and Mechanisms to Address Fraud: Regulation, Corporate Governance, and Audit Quality
Chapters 1 and 2

Professional Liability and the Need for Quality Auditor Judgments and Ethical Decisions
Chapter 4

The Audit Opinion Formulation Process and a Framework for Obtaining Audit Evidence
Chapters 5 and 6

PROFESSIONAL JUDGMENT IN CONTEXT

Fraudulent Petty Cash Transactions at Koss Corporation and the Embezzlement Fraud at Peregrine Financial Group, Inc.

This *Professional Judgment in Context* feature provides details on two high-profile frauds involving cash. The first fraud, introduced in *Chapter 2* (see *Problem 2-50*), involves Sue Sachdeva, former vice president of finance for Koss Corporation. Sachdeva orchestrated a $31 million embezzlement at Koss Corporation. In addition to expenditures at upscale clothing retailers, she used Koss funds on various luxury items such as a personal trainer, limousine rides, vacations, and items for her home. Astonishingly, more than 22,000 items—some with price tags still attached—were taken by federal authorities in connection with the investigation. The seized items included fur coats, designer clothing, jewelry, art items, and hundreds of pairs of shoes. As part of the embezzlement scheme, Sachdeva took more than $145,000 from petty cash, in increments ranging from $482 to $9,049. While that is a lot of disbursements coming out of petty cash, it is often true that petty cash doesn't get a lot of attention. Following this embezzlement, Koss took various remediation actions, which included eliminating the petty cash fund so that all reimbursements are processed through

standard controlled accounts payable processes. The former executive was convicted in 2010 of six felonies and began serving her sentence in February 2011. The U.S. Bureau of Prisons predicts she will be released in August 2020.

The second fraud involves Russell Wasendorf Sr., who attempted to commit suicide after embezzling over $200 million from Peregrine Financial Group's (PFG) brokerage clients over a twenty-year period. His son, Russell Wasendorf Jr., ran the operations of PFG and was the president and chief operating officer of the company but did not have detailed access to important financial records of the company. Instead, Russell Wasendorf Sr. had sole control of the company's bank accounts. Wasendorf Sr. left a detailed suicide note in which he explained his actions and described how he committed the fraud. One part of the suicide note reads as follows: "I was able to conceal my crime of forgery by being the sole individual with access to the U.S. Bank accounts held by PFG. No one else in the company ever saw an actual U.S. Bank statement. I made counterfeit statements within a few hours of receiving the actual statements and gave the forgeries to the accounting department." He also stated:

"With careful concealment and blunt authority I was able to hide my fraud from others at PFG. If anyone questioned my authority I would simply point out that I was the sole shareholder. I ordered that US Bank statements were to be delivered directly to me unopened, to make sure no one was able to examine an actual US Bank Statement. On US Bank side, I told representatives at the Bank that I was the only person they should interface with at PFG."

The December 31, 2011, financial statements showed that PFG had over $220 million in its bank account, but in reality the bank account contained only about $6 million. What likely prompted the timing of Wasendorf's attempted suicide was the fact that the National Futures Association (NFA) had just implemented a change to its online system whereby

bank statement information would be sent electronically from the banks directly to the NFA (see *www.confirmation.com*). The NFA started receiving confirmations through that system one day before Wasendorf's attempted suicide. PFG filed for bankruptcy almost immediately after Wasendorf's attempted suicide and subsequent arrest. (See *Problem 10-70* in the Fraud Focus: Contemporary and Historical Cases section for more details on the Wasendorf case.)

As you read through this chapter, consider the following questions:

- Why is cash an inherently risky account? (**LO 2, 3**)
- What controls should be in place to help ensure that cash accounts are not misappropriated? (**LO 4**)
- What are the audit implications of poor controls over cash accounts? (**LO 6**)
- What types of audit procedures would auditors employ when auditing cash? (**LO 7, 8**)

Significant Accounts, Disclosures, and Relevant Assertions

Overview of Cash Accounts

LO 1 Identify the significant accounts, disclosures, and relevant assertions in auditing cash accounts.

An organization may have many different kinds of cash accounts. Major types of cash accounts include general checking accounts, cash management accounts, petty cash, and imprest payroll accounts. In addition, many organizations have **marketable security** accounts.

General Checking Accounts A general checking account is used for most cash transactions. The organization's regular cash receipts and disbursements are processed through this account. In some cases, the receipts are received directly by the bank through a lockbox or electronic funds transfers (EFT) and are directly deposited in the client's account by the bank. Most organizations have cash budgets to assist in planning disbursements, and they have cash management arrangements with the bank to temporarily invest excess funds in interest-bearing securities.

Cash Management Accounts Good cash management requires the organization to effectively balance returns and risks on idle cash balances. Most organizations have developed relationships with their financial institutions to move excess cash into and out of short-term savings accounts to generate extra returns.

Imprest Payroll Accounts Some organizations disburse their payroll through an **imprest bank account**, into which cash is deposited as needed to cover payroll checks when they are issued. If the employees cash all payroll checks, the bank balance returns to zero. The need for an imprest payroll account is disappearing as most organizations now directly deposit employees' earnings into their respective bank accounts.

Petty Cash Accounts Almost all organizations use one or more petty cash accounts to disburse funds to employees who are authorized to make various purchases on behalf of the organization. The petty cash fund should have a sufficient amount of money to pay for routine expenses. While most petty cash funds involve only a small amount of money, a risk of fraud is associated with this fund, as illustrated in the *Professional Judgment in Context* feature (the first fraud that was discussed). As that example illustrates, the cumulative disbursements made through petty cash funds can become significant.

Cash Management Techniques

Cash management techniques have been developed to (1) speed the collection and deposit of cash while minimizing the possibility of error or fraud in the process, (2) reduce paperwork, and (3) automate the cash management process. Most cash management is computerized and tied to electronic commerce agreements with vendors and customers. Four of the more important cash management techniques are the use of lockboxes, electronic data interchange and automated transfers, cash management agreements with financial institutions, and compensating balances.

Lockboxes The collection of cash and reduction of the possibility of fraud can be facilitated by the use of **lockboxes**. Customers are instructed to send payments directly to the company at a specific post office box number, which is a depository (lockbox) at the organization's banking institution. The bank receives and opens the remittances, prepares a list of cash receipts by customer, credits the client's general cash account, and notifies the client about details of the transactions. Notification can be either a document listing customer receipts or an electronic list of the same information. The financial institution performs this processing for a fee. The client's personnel use the data sent by the bank to update cash and accounts receivable.

Lockbox arrangements have these distinct advantages for the audit client:

- Cash is deposited directly at the bank. There is no delay, and the client immediately earns interest on the deposited funds.
- The manual processing associated with opening remittances, maintaining control of receipts, and developing detail for posting accounts receivable is shifted to the bank.
- The client usually establishes several lockboxes in different geographic locations to minimize the delay between the time the check leaves the customer's premises and the time the client receives the cash. This arrangement speeds the receipt of cash and allows the organization to use the cash to earn a return.

Electronic Funds Transfers Many organizations have adopted EFT as an integral part of their business. Cash transfers are made automatically and instantaneously; checks are not used.

Cash Management Agreements with Financial Institutions Financial institutions provide automated services such as cash management programs for many of their clients.

Compensating Balances Most companies have short-term loans and lines of credit with their primary financial institution. The line of credit provides the company with a prenegotiated loan, available for use when the company needs it. The financial institutions usually require the company to maintain a specified balance in a non-interest-bearing account. The amount available for the loan is the credit line minus the compensating balance. If the amounts are material, the company is required to disclose the compensating balance arrangement and its effect on the effective rate of interest.

Relevant Financial Statement Assertions

The five management assertions relevant to cash are as follows:

1. *Existence/occurrence*—Cash balances exist at the balance sheet date.
2. *Completeness*—Cash balances include all cash transactions that have taken place during the period.
3. *Rights and obligations*—The company has title to the cash accounts as of the balance sheet date. For example, cash might be pledged as collateral; if this is the case, the company must disclose relevant information about the collateral arrangement. In most cases, risk related to ownership of cash is low.
4. *Valuation or allocation*—The recorded balances reflect the true underlying economic value of those assets. This assertion usually has a low level of inherent risk, unless the client has cash holdings in foreign currency.
5. *Presentation and disclosure*—Cash is properly classified on the balance sheet and disclosed in the notes to the financial statements. For example, restricted cash might need to be reported in the noncurrent asset section of the balance sheet. Further, the auditor will want to determine the accuracy of the classifications on the cash flow statement.

Because of the high level of inherent risk often associated with cash, the auditor primarily focuses on the existence/occurrence and completeness assertions. The auditor is typically focused on whether the cash does, in fact, actually exist, and whether all cash transactions have been recorded.

Performing Risk Assessment Procedures for Cash Accounts

As part of performing risk assessment procedures, the auditor obtains information that is useful in assessing the risk of material misstatement. This includes information about inherent risks at the financial statement level (e.g., the client's business and operational risks, financial reporting risks) and, at the account and assertion levels, fraud risks including feedback from audit team brainstorming sessions, strengths and weaknesses in internal control, and results from planning analytical procedures. Once the risks of material misstatement have been identified, the auditor then determines how best to respond to them as part of the audit opinion formulation process.

Identifying Inherent Risks

LO 2 Identify and assess inherent risks of material misstatement in cash accounts.

Cash is an inherently risky asset because it may be used for unauthorized purposes, posted to the wrong customer's account, or not recorded on a timely basis. However, although cash itself is an inherently risky asset for companies to manage, the accounting for cash is relatively straightforward for most clients. Most cash transactions are highly routine, and the accounting for these transactions involves minimal judgment and subjectivity. Still, certain features of cash cause it to be inherently risky:

- *Volume of activity*—The volume of transactions flowing through the account during the year makes the account more susceptible to error than most other accounts.
- *Liquidity*—The cash account is more susceptible to fraud than most other accounts because cash is liquid and easily transferable.
- *Automated systems*—The electronic transfer of cash and the automated controls over cash are such that if errors are built into computer programs, they will be repeated on a large volume of transactions.
- *Importance in meeting debt covenants*—Many debt covenants may be tied to cash balances or to maintaining minimum levels of working capital. Debt covenants specify restrictions on the organization to protect the

lender. Typical covenants restrict cash balances, specify the maintenance of minimum working capital, and may restrict the company's ability to pay dividends. The covenants may affect management's actions in its endeavor to present financial statements that do not violate the debt covenants.

- *Can be easily stolen*—As the Koss fraud described in the *Professional Judgment in Context* feature illustrates, cash can be stolen by a chief financial officer (CFO) or other personnel with power over the account balances if there exists a lack of oversight.

Exhibit 10.1 contains examples of questions used in assessing inherent risk in cash accounts.

Identifying Fraud Risk Factors

LO 3 Identify and assess fraud risks of material misstatement in cash accounts.

In assessing inherent risk relating to fraud, auditors brainstorm about potential fraud risks. Questions to ask in a brainstorming session during planning can be categorized as relating to incentives, opportunities to commit fraud, and rationalization:

Incentives
- Is an individual with access to cash or its recording experiencing financial or personal distress?
- Is the company in potential violation of its debt covenants?
- Does the company have sufficient cash flow to support continuing operations?

Opportunities
- Does the company conduct background checks and credit checks on employees with access to cash? Are these checks completed on a routine basis thereafter?
- Can employees easily convert the company's assets to their own use?
- Is cash physically available to employees?
- Is there insufficient segregation of duties related to cash?
- Are the company's records for cash inadequate?
- Is there lack of oversight and review of cash or cash-related transactions?
- Does the company have an anonymous way for employees to report on suspicions of fraud related to cash?
- Does the company have a policy of job or assignment rotation for employees with access to cash?

Rationalization
- Is an individual with access to cash or its recording being paid an amount that he or she might consider too low?
- Is top management setting a poor tone by taking cash without recording those transactions?

EXHIBIT 10.1   Inherent Risk Analysis Questionnaire: Cash

1. Does the company have significant cash flow problems in meeting its current obligations on a timely basis?
2. Does the company use cash budgeting techniques? How effective are the company's cash management budgeting techniques?
3. Does the company use the cash management services offered by its financial institutions? What is the nature of these arrangements?
4. Has the company made significant changes in its cash processing during the past year? Have any major changes taken place in the company's computerized cash management applications during the year?
5. Does the company have loan or bond covenants that influence the use of cash or the maintenance of working-capital ratios?
6. Is there any reason to suspect that management may desire to misstate the cash balance?

Common Fraud Schemes Relating to Cash

The theft of cash is as old as time itself. The following is a list of common schemes relating to cash receipts:

- The employee makes a sale but does not record it and steals the cash. This type of conduct is known as **skimming**.
- An employee receives a check and deposits it, but does not record the sale; then the employee writes a check out to himself and does not record the disbursement.
- The employee collects a customer payment, steals the cash, and writes off the accounts receivable as uncollectible.
- The employee steals a payment from Customer X. To cover the theft, the employee applies a payment from Customer Y to Customer X's account. Before Customer Y has time to notice that its account has not been appropriately credited, the employee applies a payment from Customer Z to Customer Y's account. This type of conduct is known as **lapping**.

The following is a list of common schemes relating to cash payments:

- The employee purchases merchandise and records the sale at an unauthorized discounted amount.
- The employee sells merchandise to a friend at a discounted price; the friend returns the merchandise for a refund at the undiscounted price; the two split the profits.
- The employee steals cash and conceals it by recording a fictitious discount.
- The employee writes a check to a fictitious vendor and deposits the check into an account that he or she controls that has been set up in the name of the fictitious vendor.

- Is the company and/or management ostentatious with displays of wealth, thereby inciting jealousy in its employees?
- Has top management ignored past instances of misappropriations of cash, thereby inciting a sense of entitlement in the company's employees?

The auditor should consider the answers to these types of questions in determining whether to assess fraud risk at a higher level. The *Focus on Fraud* feature "Common Fraud Schemes Relating to Cash" provides examples of common cash-related frauds.

Identifying Control Risks

LO 4 Identify and assess control risks of material misstatement in cash accounts.

Once the auditor understands the inherent and fraud risks of material misstatement in cash accounts, the auditor needs to understand the controls that the client has designed and implemented to address those risks. Remember, the auditor is required to gain an understanding of internal controls for both integrated audits and financial statement only audits. Such understanding is normally gained by means of a walkthrough of the process, inquiry, observation, and review of the client's documentation. The auditor considers both entity-wide controls and transaction controls at the account and assertion levels. This understanding provides the auditor with a basis for making an initial control risk assessment. *Exhibit 10.2* provides examples of questions used in assessing control risk in cash accounts.

Typical Controls Over Cash

The following are the types of common controls over cash:

- Segregation of duties
- Restrictive endorsements of customer checks
- Independent bank reconciliations by employees who do not handle cash
- Computerized control totals and edit tests

EXHIBIT **10.2**   Control Risk Questionnaire: Cash

1. Have cash management service arrangements been reviewed by management and the board of directors? Are the arrangements monitored on a current basis?
2. Do management and the board periodically review the cash management process? Does the cash management organization provide for effective segregation of duties, review, and supervision?
3. Are cash transactions, including electronic cash transfers, properly authorized? What authorization is required to make electronic cash transfers?
4. Are bank reconciliations performed on a timely basis by personnel independent of processing? Is follow-up action taken promptly on all reconciling items?
5. Does the internal audit department conduct timely reviews of the cash management and cash-handling process? If yes, review recent internal audit reports.
6. Does the company use a lockbox to collect cash receipts? What is the agreement with the financial institution? What are the company's controls associated with the lockbox agreement?
7. Who is authorized to make cash transfers, including EFTs, and what are the procedures by which that authorization is verified before the transfers take place? What procedures does management use to assure that the authorization process is monitored?
8. Are there any restrictions in getting access to cash? For example, does the company have cash in sweep accounts, or other accounts with financial institutions that may be in trouble, and that may restrict access to cash?

- Authorization of transactions
- Prenumbered cash receipt documents and turnaround documents
- Periodic internal audits
- Competent, well-trained employees

Segregation of Duties   The general concept of segregation of duties does not change as processing systems become more automated and integrated. Automation can enhance control, yet there is a risk of errors or fraud occurring on a larger scale. Companies have controls to make sure that incoming customer cash and checks are segregated upon receipt and are processed by different people. Postings to accounts receivable should be reconciled to the postings to cash and checks received. Segregation of duties is further enhanced if inquiries by customers concerning their account balances are referred to an independent group, such as a customer relations department, for investigation. Finally, the individuals who reconcile the bank accounts should not handle cash or record cash transactions.

Restrictive Endorsements   Customer checks should be made payable to the client and restrictively endorsed for deposit when received. The restrictive endorsement helps prevent modifications and theft of customer payments.

Independent Bank Reconciliations   Two types of reconciliations should occur:

1. *Reconciliation of items received with items recorded (control totals)*— Reconciliation is made more effective when control procedures exist to establish the initial integrity of the population. In an electronic environment, the client may have a procedure by which the bank sends details of each remittance directly to the client for posting to cash and accounts receivable. These control totals should be reconciled daily with the amount shown as direct deposits by the bank.
2. *Periodic reconciliation of the bank accounts*—Independent reconciliation of the balance on the bank statement with the balance on the books should identify misstatements and unusual banking activity that may have occurred. From a financial reporting risk perspective, this is the single most important control over the existence of cash.

Computerized Control Totals and Edit Tests Computerized controls should be designed to assure that all items are uniquely identified and that an adequate audit trail exists for transactions. Controls include the following:

- *A unique identifier assigned to each item*—The unique identifier establishes the integrity of the total population and provides a basis for assuring that no items are added to or dropped from the population.
- *Control totals to assure the completeness of processing*—Control totals should be established and reconciled with the computer-generated totals. A control total would also be established to reconcile the debits to cash and the credits to accounts receivable.
- *Edit tests to identify unusual or incorrect items*—Standard edit tests such as reasonableness tests, field checks, self-checking digits on account numbers, and alphanumeric tests should be implemented as deemed practical for the particular application.

Authorization of Transactions Individuals with proper authorization are able to electronically transfer very material sums of money each day. As a result, opportunities for abuse abound. The following authorization and authentication controls should be implemented:

- Authorization privileges should be assigned to individuals based on unique activities associated with the individual and position. Authorization should follow the principles of *need to know* and *right to know*. Authorizations should be reviewed periodically by senior management.
- Authentication procedures should assure that only authorized personnel execute transactions. The authentication process may be implemented through electronic verification by using elements such as passwords, physical characteristics, cards, encryption, or terminals that are hardwired to the computer. In a manual system, the authorization controls may involve limiting access to the area where checks are signed and to the prenumbered checks.
- Any changes to existing bank accounts or the opening of a new bank account must be authorized and reviewed by senior management.
- Monitoring should be established so that a detailed, daily review of transactions occurs and is compared with cash budgets, authorization limits by individuals, and riskiness of transactions.

Prenumbered Documents and Turnaround Documents Prenumbered documents are important in establishing the completeness of a population. The numbering may occur after the receipt where each payment is assigned a unique identifier when the payment is received by the company. Another option is to use **turnaround documents** that customers return with their cash payment. A clerk can quickly review the turnaround document and compare the amount indicated paid with the actual cash remittance. The turnaround document contains other information useful for further processing, such as account number, invoice number, date billed, and date received (entered by clerk). Of course, turnaround documents are unnecessary in an electronic payment environment.

Periodic Internal Audits Internal audit departments are effective deterrents when they periodically conduct detailed audits of cash controls and cash management. Internal auditors may also review the development of new systems to determine whether adequate controls have been built into the new systems.

Competent, Well-Trained Employees To better ensure that cash is handled appropriately, the organization should have competent, well-trained employees. Such employees are in a better position to carry out their assigned responsibilities, including their control-related responsibilities.

Implications of Weak Controls Related to Existence/Occurrence of Cash

Controls for existence should provide reasonable assurance that the cash balances actually do exist, for example, computerized control totals. The *Focus on Fraud* feature "The Parmalat Fraud and Its Many Victims" provides an example in which the company showed a material amount of fictitious cash on its financial statements, thereby violating the existence assertion.

Implications of Weak Controls Related to Completeness of Cash

Controls related to completeness are intended to provide reasonable assurance that all valid cash transactions (receipts and disbursements) are recorded; controls might include prenumbered cash receipts documents, as well as competent and well-trained employees. The main concern related to the completeness assertion for cash accounts is that an employee who should be recording a cash receipt simply does not record the transaction, thereby not reflecting the fact that cash was received, a sale was made, or accounts receivable was reduced. Therefore, there is no accounting record for the transaction. The *Focus on Fraud* feature "Skimming and the Completeness Assertion" provides an example of fraud involving theft of cash where the transaction is never recorded, and cash is stolen by the employee.

Controls for Petty Cash

Companies should have policies and procedures related to petty cash funds. These controls could include the following:

- Limiting access to petty cash funds by keeping funds in a locked box and restricting the number of employees who have access

---

The Parmalat Fraud and Its Many Victims

FOCUS on **FRAUD**

Parmalat is an international company based in Italy that produces milk, dairy, and fruit-based beverages. The financial fraud involving Parmalat evolved over a ten-year period and ultimately included the invention of over $11 billion in fictitious cash in offshore front companies to offset liabilities at the parent company. The fraud was led by Chairman Calisto Tanzi and his son, Stefano Tanzi, and was orchestrated by the company's CFO Fausto Tonna. In one of the telling moments of the unraveling of the fraud, representatives of a New York–based private equity firm raised questions about Parmalat's financial statements during meetings regarding a possible leveraged buyout of the company. During the meeting, the representative commented on liquidity problems at Parmalat, which contrasted with Parmalat's issued financial statements showing that the company had a large amount of cash. Stefano Tanzi admitted that the cash was not accounted for and that Parmalat actually had only about 500 million euros in cash.

Approximately 35,000 shareholders lost money due to the Parmalat fraud, and shareholders were not the only ones affected. Alessandro Bassi, a 32-year-old accountant, who worked in the financial director's office at Parmalat, killed himself by jumping off a bridge near the company's Italian headquarters. Mr. Bassi worked for the company's CFO and had been questioned by a prosecutor in the case earlier on the day of his suicide. Ultimately, Mr. Tanzi admitted to moving over $630 million from the company to family-owned related entities. One of the most shocking features of the fraud was that it involved a large number of individuals acting collusively in various ways. In the end, 29 former Parmalat executives, along with bankers, auditors, and various financial institutions, were implicated in the fraud.

Skimming and the Completeness Assertion

FOCUS on **FRAUD**

In the restaurant and bar business, shrinkage due to thefts of inventory and thefts of cash are a significant source of losses. Industry estimates show that about 2% to 4% of sales are lost to such shrinkage at the overall restaurant level and that about 20% is lost to shrinkage in terms of liquor and draft beer. So, how do bartenders accomplish this type of fraud? Consider the elements of the fraud triangle:

- They are usually compensated with a low hourly wage and, therefore, depend upon cash tips as their primary source of income. This provides bartenders with an incentive to steal cash from their employer and a rationalization afterward.
- They operate in an environment where they are typically unsupervised and have weak or non-existent physical controls. This provides an opportunity for theft.

To actually accomplish the theft of inventory, the bartender can simply give out free drinks. To accomplish the theft of cash, the bartender engages in skimming. Skimming is accomplished in the following manner:

- The customer orders a drink for $4 and gives the bartender $20 in cash.
- The bartender hits the No Sale button on the cash register to open the drawer. The bartender deposits the $20 and gives the customer the correct change of $16. So, the customer is satisfied. But the bartender did not record the sale, thereby violating the completeness assertion. An important and necessary control implied in this part of the example is that the cash register should have controls to ensure that it opens only upon the recording of a sale.

- The cash register now has $4 in it that should not be there according to the accounting records. So, the bartender somehow has to get the $4 out of the register without detection.
- The next customer orders a drink for $7 and gives the bartender $20 in cash. This time, the bartender records the sale, thereby opening the register. The bartender deposits the $20 and gives the customer the correct change of $13, but the bartender also takes $4 out and puts it in his or her tip jar. Theft accomplished! And there is no record of it in the accounting records, making it very difficult to detect via the audit. An important and necessary control implied in this part of the example is that video camera surveillance of the cash register area, and the bar in general, should occur.
- This example is a simplification. Usually, bartenders accomplishing fraud of this type keep track of the extra money in the cash register and do not remove it until it reaches a threshold, for example, $100. Therefore, surprise counts of cash registers are a method used to detect this type of behavior. If the surprise count reveals more cash than has been recorded, there is evidence consistent with fraud.
- Obviously, this type of theft is as old as the business itself, and sophisticated restaurant and bar owners have controls in place to prevent and detect such fraud. If they do not, they will likely be victims of a skimming fraud.

While this example is taken from the restaurant and bar business, it applies to any business where customers pay cash directly to an employee, thus providing an opportunity for skimming. When a transaction is not immediately recorded, the completeness assertion is violated.

- Requiring receipts for all petty cash disbursements with the date, amount received, purpose or use for the funds, and name of the employee receiving the funds listed on the receipt
- Reconciling the petty cash fund before replenishing it
- Keeping customer receipts separate from petty cash funds
- Having internal audit conduct periodic surprise audits of petty cash

Controls for Cash Management Techniques

Cash management techniques require controls specific to the risks associated with those techniques.

Lockboxes Sufficient controls must be established to make sure that all customer payments received by the bank are posted. For example, evidence of payments should be sent to the client to facilitate follow-up should the customer have any questions about the posting of accounts. The client should also reconcile the total of the customer payments with the cash deposit recorded by the bank.

Electronic Funds Transfers The client should have EFT agreements with vendors, customers, and banks that have adequate controls built into the process. For example, notification of the payment should be made directly to the client and the bank, automated or manual reconciliation procedures between the client and the bank should be in place, and a complete audit trail should be maintained to answer questions about the completeness of payments and disputed items.

Cash Management Agreements with Financial Institutions The client needs to take care regarding the amount of control given to the financial institution regarding the investment of cash. For example, if the client invests most of its cash in high-risk securities or nonliquid securities, the client should have a risk assessment process in place related to understanding the risks associated with the investments.

Documenting Controls

Auditors need to document their understanding of internal controls for both integrated audits and financial statement only audits. A questionnaire, such as the one shown in *Exhibit 10.3*, is often used to guide auditors in documenting the understanding of internal controls. The questionnaire is designed to elicit information about specific controls performed. Usually, the questionnaire identifies the specific individual responsible for performing each procedure, which assists the auditor in evaluating the segregation of duties. As you review *Exhibit 10.3*, note the heavy emphasis on management reports that signal departure from what is expected and indicate a need for follow-up action. Note that a negative answer in the questionnaire represents a potential internal control deficiency. Given a negative answer, the auditor should consider the effect of the response on the initial assessment of control risk. Unless another control compensates for this deficiency, the auditor will likely have a control risk assessment of moderate or high in this area.

Performing Planning Analytical Procedures

LO 5 Describe how to use planning analytical procedures to identify possible material misstatements for cash accounts, disclosures, and assertions.

Planning analytical procedures help auditors identify areas of potential material misstatements. The steps that the auditor will take in performing planning analytical procedures are fully described in *Chapter 7*.

Analytical procedures for cash balances are not very effective because of the absence of a stable relationship with past cash levels and the fact that cash is a managed account. However, auditors may use management's budget as an expectation that can be compared to the balance that the client has recorded at year-end. Also, trend analysis of account balances and ratios are planning analytical procedures that are routinely used on cash accounts. The auditor should consider the observed trends in relation to the auditor's expectations. *Exhibit 10.4* provides examples of trend analysis of accounts and ratios the auditor might consider for cash accounts.

Further, auditors should be aware of the importance of cash balances to debt covenants. For example, the auditor can read the debt covenants, determine the relevant thresholds for cash or other liquid assets contained in those covenants, and then track how close the company is to violating those covenants over time.

EXHIBIT **10.3**	Control Activities Questionnaire: Cash Receipts (Partial Example)

	Yes	No	N/A

OBJECTIVE OF CONTROLS: Are all payments received deposited intact on a timely basis? Consider:

Procedures for Cash Remittances Received In-House

1. Key control activities

   a. A list of incoming receipts is prepared by the person who opens the remittances and who delivers the list to a person independent of the deposit function.

   b. A duplicate deposit slip is prepared by someone other than the person opening the mail.

   c. Deposits are made daily.

   d. An authorized person compares the deposit slip with the listing prepared in Step 1(a), noting agreement and completeness of deposit.

2. Documented evidence of performance

   a. The listing prepared in Step 1(a) is initialed by its preparer.

   b. The listing is attached to the deposit slip and is initialed by the person in Step 1(d).

   c. Bank accounts are independently reconciled.

Procedures for Cash Remittances Received Electronically by Bank on Behalf of Client

1. Key control activities

   a. An agreement exists between the bank and the company on cash-handling activities, including when the remittances are added to the client's account.

   b. Procedures and responsibilities exist for forwarding detailed remittance advices to client on a daily basis.

   c. An independent reconciliation of cash received is reported by bank, with remittance advices forwarded to company and posted to accounts receivable.

   d. Management monitors controls to follow up on discrepancies in accounts receivable postings reported by customers.

   e. Access to cash is limited through computerized access controls, including passwords and biometrics to those individuals with a need to know or to engage in transactions.

2. Documented evidence of performance

   a. Reports of daily reconciliations and follow-up are done by treasury personnel.

   b. Periodic reviews by internal audit or the treasury function are conducted.

   c. A periodic comparison is made by the treasury function to contrast cash budgets with projections.

(continued)

EXHIBIT **10.3**	Control Activities Questionnaire: Cash Receipts (Partial Example) (*continued*)

	Yes	**No**	**N/A**

OBJECTIVE OF CONTROLS: Are payments received completely credited to the correct customer accounts? Consider:

1. Key control activities

   a. When the posting process is a function of a computerized application, assurance is gained by the following ways:

     (1) Prenumbered batch control tickets include control totals of number of remittances to be processed and total dollars to be applied. _____ _____ _____

     (2) Edit reports or online edit routines are used to identify invalid customer numbers, invoice numbers, and invoice amounts. _____ _____ _____

     (3) Online entry includes the input of a control total and/or hash total for each payment. _____ _____ _____

2. Documented evidence of performance

   a. Edit reports and/or processing transmittals exist, which are saved and signed by the person clearing the exceptions. _____ _____ _____

   b. The person performing the independent check initials the remittance, noting agreement of the posting operation. _____ _____ _____

   c. Online entry control totals and/or hash totals are noted on the face of the appropriate documents. _____ _____ _____

   d. Batch control tickets are agreed to the edit reports and initialed to indicate agreement. _____ _____ _____

Conclusion

Controls appear adequate to justify a preliminary control risk assessment as:

_____ Low control risk

_____ Moderate control risk

_____ High control risk

EXHIBIT **10.4**	Using Trend Analysis of Account Balances and Ratios in Planning Analytical Procedures for Cash Accounts

- Compare monthly cash balances with past years and budgets
- Identify unexpected spikes or lows in cash during the year
- Compute trends in interest returns on investments
- Analyze cash balances, and changes therein, in relation to new or retiring debt obligations
- Compare cash ending account balances with those of preceding years, possibly on a month-by-month basis if there are anticipated collection patterns
- Compute typical short-term liquidity ratios, including the current ratio (current assets/current liabilities) and the quick ratio (cash + cash equivalents + net receivables/current liabilities)
- Compare cash flow to sales (operating cash flow/sales) and profitability (operating cash flow/net income)

The following are examples of possible expected relationships for cash accounts:

- No unusual large cash transactions
- Operating cash flow consistent with sales and net income
- Operating cash flow not significantly different from the prior year
- Investment income consistent with the level of and returns expected from the investments

If planning analytical procedures do not identify any unexpected relationships, the auditor would conclude that there is not a heightened risk of material misstatements in these accounts. If planning analytical procedures do identify unusual or unexpected relationships, the auditor would adjust the planned substantive audit procedures to address the potential material misstatements. The auditor should compare the unaudited financial statements with both past results and industry trends. The following relationships might suggest a heightened risk of fraud in cash:

- Consistent profits over several years, but cash flows are declining
- Unexpected reductions in accounts receivable collections, or the timeliness of collections
- Unexpected declines in the petty cash account

Responding to Identified Risks of Material Misstatement

LO 6 Determine appropriate responses to identified risks of material misstatement for cash accounts, disclosures, and assertions.

Once the auditor understands the risks of material misstatement, the auditor can determine the appropriate audit procedures to perform. Audit procedures should be proportional to the assessed risks, with areas of higher risk receiving more audit attention and effort. Responding to identified risks typically involves developing an audit approach that contains substantive procedures (e.g., tests of details and, when appropriate, substantive analytical procedures) and tests of controls, when applicable. The sufficiency and appropriateness of selected procedures vary to achieve the desired level of assurance for each relevant assertion. While audit firms may have a standardized audit program for auditing cash accounts, the auditor should customize the audit program based on the assessment of risk of material misstatement.

Consider a client where the auditor has assessed the risk of material misstatement related to the existence and completeness of cash at the maximum level. This client has incentives to overstate cash in order to meet debt covenants. Further, the client has relatively weak controls to prevent theft of cash, with a few controls being somewhat effective. The auditor may develop an audit program that consists of first performing limited tests of operating effectiveness of controls, then performing limited substantive analytical procedures, and finally performing significant substantive tests of details. Because of the high risk, the auditor will want to obtain a great deal of evidence directly from tests of details. In contrast, consider a client where the auditor has assessed the risk of material misstatement related to the existence and completeness of cash as low, and believes that the client has implemented effective controls in this area. Because substantive analytical procedures are relatively ineffective for cash accounts, the auditor will still perform only limited substantive analytical procedures. But the auditor will likely perform tests of controls and then complete the substantive procedures by performing tests of details at a more limited level.

Panel A of *Exhibit 10.5* shows that because of differences in risk, the box of evidence to be filled for testing the existence and completeness of cash at the low-risk client is smaller than that at a high-risk client. Panel B of *Exhibit 10.5* illustrates the different levels of assurance that the auditor will obtain from tests of controls and substantive procedures for the two clients. Panel B makes the point that because of the higher risk associated with the existence and completeness of cash at Client B, the auditor will want to

EXHIBIT 10.5 · Panel A: Sufficiency of Evidence for Existence and Completeness of Cash

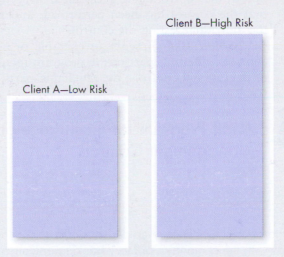

Client A—Low Risk

Client B—High Risk

Panel B: Approaches to Obtaining Audit Evidence for Existence and Completeness of Cash

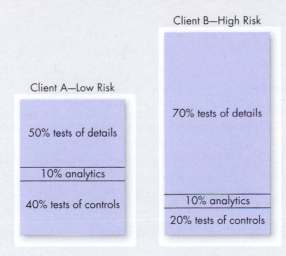

Client B—High Risk

Client A—Low Risk

50% tests of details

10% analytics

40% tests of controls

70% tests of details

10% analytics

20% tests of controls

design the audit so that more of the assurance is coming from direct tests of account balances. Note that the relative percentages are judgmental in nature; the examples are simply intended to give you a sense of how an auditor might select an appropriate mix of procedures.

Obtaining Evidence About Internal Control Operating Effectiveness for Cash

LO 7 Determine appropriate tests of controls and consider the results of tests of controls for cash accounts, disclosures, and assertions.

For integrated audits, the auditor will test the operating effectiveness of important controls as of the client's year-end. If the auditor wants to rely on controls for the financial statement audit, the auditor will test the operating effectiveness of those controls throughout the year.

Selecting Controls to Test and Performing Tests of Controls

The auditor selects controls that are important to the auditor's conclusion about whether the organization's controls adequately address the assessed risk of material misstatement in the cash accounts. The auditor will select both entity-wide and transaction controls for testing. Typical tests of transaction controls include inquiry of personnel performing the control, observation of the control being performed, inspection of documentation confirming that the control has been performed, and reperformance of the control by the individual testing the control.

Exhibit 10.6 presents an example of an audit program for testing the controls. The first part of the program focuses on gaining an understanding of the internal controls; the remaining parts identify tests of controls.

EXHIBIT 10.6 Audit Program for Cash Receipts and Cash Management Controls

Procedures	By	Ref.

Understanding Controls

1. Inquire of management about the existence of lines of credit, special cash management programs, and related fees with the company's primary banking institution. Analyze the arrangements for the existence of special risks and for obligations of the client that should be considered in the audit.

2. Review the company risk analysis and assess the motivation to misstate or manage cash. Consider such items as:
   a. Financial condition of the company
   b. Past problems with cash
   c. Control environment
   d. Financial needs and liquidity problems
   e. Lack of effective monitoring controls

3. Document internal controls over cash by completing the internal control questionnaire or by flowcharting the process.

4. Document the monitoring controls management has developed to determine whether other controls are working effectively. Determine whether:
   a. Monitoring activities are sufficient to alert management to breakdowns in other controls.
   b. Monitoring reports are prepared on a timely basis and are reviewed by the proper levels of management.
   c. Corrective action is taken on a timely basis, any control breakdowns are identified, and corrective action is taken.

   Examples of monitoring controls include the following:
   • Reviews of reconciliations of reported cash receipts with remittances prepared by independent parties
   • Daily review of cash budgets and comparison with actual cash balances.
   • Reviews of discrepancies in cash balances
   • Reviews of weekly reporting of customer complaints regarding posting of cash balances and prompt investigation to follow up on the cause of complaints
   • Reviews of reports on all unauthorized attempts to gain access to cash
   • Reviews of daily reports on any unusual cash activities by location or personnel

5. Prepare and document a preliminary assessment of control risk. Identify specific controls to be tested if control risk is assessed at less than the maximum

(The following audit steps assume that effective controls are present in the system.)

(continued)

EXHIBIT 10.6	Audit Program for Cash Receipts and Cash Management Controls (continued)	

Procedures	By	Ref.

General Tests of Controls

6. Review the frequency of monitoring activities; determine their effectiveness through reviews of the reports, indications of management actions, descriptions of corrective actions taken, and interviews with key personnel. Determine if evidence is persuasive that the monitoring controls are sufficient.

Testing of Controls Over Cash Receipts

7. Perform a walkthrough of the processing of cash collections, starting with their receipt through the preparation of documents for processing. Note how conscientiously and efficiently the work is done, and the procedures used in developing batches and performing reconciliations. Interview supervisory personnel regarding potential problem areas. Identify any concerns regarding employee conscientiousness that would affect the risk assessment.

Testing of Specific Control Activities

8. Select *x* number of cash receipts and determine that the following procedure takes place:
   a. Each payment is given a unique identifier, which is subsequently entered into the system.
   b. The payments received are the same as the amount applied to the update of accounts receivable. Determine how differences (if any) are handled.
   c. Payments are segregated into batches for processing.
   d. Batches are prepared according to company standards. Review the reconciliation of batch controls to determine their accuracy and timeliness.
   e. Exception reports contain all items rejected by the edit controls. The rejected items are properly followed up and recorded correctly.

9. Determine who has the authorization to:
   a. Make changes in documents or adjustments when cash amounts differ from invoiced amounts.
   b. Make deposits.
   c. Make withdrawals.
   d. Make transfers among the organization's accounts or between the organization and other entities.

10. Review reports for unusual cash transactions such as transfer of funds to other accounts, deposits other than through the normal cash receipts process, and disbursements not processed through the regular cash disbursements process. Select a sample of the transactions and review for proper authorization and completeness and correctness of processing.

11. Review the procedures for authorizing passwords or other access codes for individuals who are authorized to initiate electronic transfers of cash. Select a limited number of transactions and trace back to the authorization. (As part of the general controls review of data processing, determine the procedures for ensuring that passwords are provided only to those properly authorized and that the passwords are kept secure. Determine through testing and observation that such controls continue to exist.)

(continued)

EXHIBIT **10.6**	Audit Program for Cash Receipts and Cash Management Controls (*continued*)

Procedures	By	Ref.
12. Review bank reconciliations for completeness, and trace selected items on the reconciliation to the bank statement. Determine that reconciliations are performed by someone independent of the processing. If there is evidence that bank reconciliations are performed regularly and that the auditor has assessed overall risk as low, there may be less need to test the reconciliations or other procedures.	_____	_____

Documenting Work Performed

13. Document the control risk assessment, including the types of misstatements that might occur because of any deficiencies in controls. Write a brief memo citing implications for the remainder of the audit.	_____	_____

Considering the Results of Tests of Controls

The auditor will analyze the results of the tests of controls to determine additional appropriate procedures. There are two potential outcomes:

1. If control deficiencies are identified, the auditor will assess those deficiencies to determine their severity (Are they significant deficiencies or material weaknesses?). The auditor would then need to modify the preliminary control risk assessment (possibly from low to moderate or high) and document the implications of the control deficiencies. Appropriate modifications to planned substantive audit procedures will be determined by the types of misstatements that are most likely to occur because of the control deficiency.

2. If no control deficiencies are identified, the auditor will likely determine that the preliminary assessment of control risk as low is still appropriate. The auditor will then determine the extent that controls can provide evidence on the correctness of account balances and determine planned substantive audit procedures. The level of substantive testing in this situation will be less than what is required in circumstances where deficiencies in internal control were identified. From the audit risk model, we know that organizations with effective internal controls should require less substantive testing of account balances.

Obtaining Substantive Evidence About Cash Accounts, Disclosures, and Assertions

LO 8 Determine and apply sufficient appropriate substantive audit procedures for testing cash accounts, disclosures, and assertions.

In performing substantive procedures, the auditor wants reasonable assurance that the client's cash transactions are in accordance with generally accepted accounting principles (GAAP). Substantive procedures (substantive analytical procedures, tests of details, or possibly both) should be performed for all relevant assertions related to significant cash accounts, disclosures and assertions. Even if the auditor has evidence indicating that controls are operating effectively, the auditor cannot rely solely on control testing to provide evidence on the reliability of these accounts and assertions. The *Auditing in Practice* feature "Weaknesses in Substantive Procedures Related to Cash: Evidence From PCAOB Disciplinary Proceedings" provides evidence of the types of substantive

AUDITING IN **PRACTICE**

Weaknesses in Substantive Procedures Related to Cash: Evidence From PCAOB Disciplinary Proceedings

Two PCAOB disciplinary proceedings against audit firms provide insight on weaknesses in cash-related audit procedures. The first example involves Jaspers + Hall PC (hereafter J + H) and its two audit partners. In one audit, they failed to perform sufficient procedures to verify the existence of approximately $155 million of cash, which represented 57% of the client's assets. J + H's workpapers included copies of the client's bank statements, accounting for approximately two-thirds of the reported cash, but when J + H received no reply to a confirmation request sent to the bank, the auditors failed to perform alternative procedures to verify that the client actually had the cash. They also failed to perform any procedures or obtain any audit evidence concerning the other one-third of the reported cash.

For further details, see PCAOB Release No. 105-2008-002.

The second example involves Armando C. Ibarra, P.C. and its two audit partners. In one of their audits they failed to audit a client's cash balance of $687,971, which represented approximately 95% of total assets. Basically, they failed to test the cash balance.

For further details, see PCAOB Release No. 105-2006-001.

The auditor needs to consider the types of substantive procedures for cash that should be performed and then make sure that the engagement team does perform these procedures. This is especially true when the cash balance represents a significant portion of the client's assets.

audit procedures related to cash that should be performed, and illustrates examples where such procedures were not performed.

Substantive Analytics for Cash Accounts

Substantive analytics for cash accounts are typically not very effective. Rather, the auditor tends to focus on substantive tests of details. The minimal substantive analytics that would be performed include identifying significant differences between management's cash budget, which is prepared at the beginning of the year and the recorded year-end balance.

Substantive Tests of Details for Cash Accounts

Typical substantive tests of details for cash accounts include the following:

- Inspecting or reperforming bank reconciliations
- Obtaining bank confirmations
- Obtaining bank cutoff statements
- Preparing interbank transfer schedules

Inspecting or Reperforming Bank Reconciliations

The auditor's inspection or reperformance of a reconciliation of the client's bank accounts provides evidence as to the accuracy of the year-end cash balance. The process reconciles the balance per the bank statements with the balance that the client has recorded. Testing the bank reconciliation is effective in detecting misstatements, such as those that might be covered up by omitting or underfooting outstanding checks. The auditor will want to determine that all outstanding checks have been listed on the bank

U.S. Companies Continue to Use Paper Checks

EMERGING ISSUE

With the increase in electronic commerce, auditors might expect that their clients would have stopped using paper checks. In 2007, U.S. companies used paper checks to pay about 74% of their bills. A recent survey suggests that today U.S. companies use paper checks to pay about 50% of their bills. In testing bank reconciliations, auditors should expect that their clients will be using both electronic transfers and paper checks.

reconciliation. The auditor will obtain information on the last checks issued by the fiscal year-end, such as the last check number, and will then examine canceled checks returned with the bank statement to determine that the checks dated prior to year-end were included as outstanding checks on the reconciliation. As noted in the *Emerging Issues* feature "U.S. Companies Continue to Use Paper Checks" auditors should expect that their clients will continue to use paper checks, although their use has been declining.

As part of testing the bank reconciliation, the auditor may want to obtain information on the client's last cash receipts. The auditor usually notes the last few receipts as a basis for determining the recording in the correct period. The information is traced to the company's bank reconciliation and bank accounts to determine if items were recorded in the proper period. The auditor can also trace deposits in transit into the statement to determine if they were deposited in a timely fashion.

When testing the client's bank reconciliation, the auditor should independently verify all material items such as the balance per the bank statement, deposits in transit, outstanding checks, and other adjustments. The auditor should also foot all totals. *Exhibit 10.7* presents an example of bank reconciliation documentation.

Obtaining Bank Confirmations

The auditor usually sends a standard **bank confirmation** to each bank with which the company has transacted business during the year. This procedure is most relevant to the existence assertion. The paper-based process auditors use to confirm the client's account balances with a bank is a manual process that can be inefficient and open to confirmation fraud. The *Emerging Issues* feature "Electronic Bank Confirmations Through Confirmation.com" notes that auditors have the option of sending bank confirmations in electronic format through a third-party vendor.

The confirmation, whether paper or electronic, has two parts. The first part, shown in *Exhibit 10.8*, seeks information on the client's deposit balances, the existence of loans, due dates of the loans, interest rates, dates through which interest has been paid, and **collateral** for all loans outstanding with the bank at year-end.

EXHIBIT 10.7	Tests of Client's Bank Reconciliation

Gordon's Bay Manufacturing
December 2015 Bank Reconciliation
Year Ended December 31, 2015

Prepared by *KMJ*
Reviewed by _____
Date _____

Balance per bank statement		$1,073,852.65*
Add: Deposits in transit:		
12/28 Deposit	$287,000.00†	
12/31 Deposit	300,000.00†	587,000.00 F
Less: Outstanding checks:		
2809	$ 435.56#	
3678	67,892.09#	
3679	75,000.00#	
3899	700.00**	
3901	12,500.00#	
3903	50,000.00#	(206,527.65) F
Adjusted balance		$1,454,325.00 F
Balance per books		$1,481,350.00 TB
Bank charges not recorded		(25.00)‡
NSF checks:		
Bailey's Main	$12,000.00§	
Silver Dollar's	15,000.00!	(27,000.00) F
Adjusted balance		$1,454,325.00 F

Note: Legend of Audit Work Performed:

*Confirmed per bank. See WP reference C–1.

†Traced to deposits shown on bank statement on 1/3 and 1/4 contained in bank cutoff statement. The 12/31 deposit was traced to bank transfer WP C–12 and was listed as an outstanding check on the subsidiary account.

‡Traced to bank cutoff statement. Charge was for service fees, which should have been recorded by the client. Amount is not material, and no adjustment is proposed.

§NSF check was returned with 12/31 bank statement. Examined support showing client redeposited the checks. Traced to deposit in cutoff bank statement and determined that it had not been returned in subsequent statement.

!Examined NSF check returned with 12/31 bank statement. Silver Dollar's is a retail company that has gone bankrupt. The likelihood of ultimate collection is low. Based on discussion with the client, the amount should be written off. See AJE 35.

#Outstanding checks were traced to checks returned on 1/20/16 bank cutoff statements. Checks were examined, and all were dated 12/31 or earlier and were canceled by the bank subsequent to 12/31.

**Check had not cleared as of 1/20/16. Examined supporting document for the check. All appeared proper, and no exceptions were noted.

TB Traced to general ledger.

F Footed, no exceptions noted.

The second part of the bank confirmation, shown in *Exhibit 10.9*, seeks information about any loan guarantees. If loans are outstanding, the auditor usually asks for copies of the loan agreements to identify restrictions on the ability of the organization to pay dividends or to determine whether the organization will have to maintain specific working capital or debt ratios. These requirements are generally referred to as *covenants*, a violation of which

Electronic Bank Confirmations Through Confirmation.com

Confirmation.com is a leading provider of all types of electronic confirmations, including bank confirmations. Over 11,000 accounting firms, 70,000 auditors, and thousands of responding organizations around the globe use Confirmation.com for their audit confirmation needs. Electronic confirmations are equally as acceptable as audit evidence as paper-based confirmations that had been used in the past. Electronic confirmations have reliability benefits because of the controls built into the software system, whereby management cannot intercept or alter the confirmation as is potentially the case with paper-based confirmations. Auditors will typically experience quicker responses, improved response rates, and decreased errors when compared to paper confirmations. When using an electronic confirmation process, the auditor needs to be sure that the process is secure and properly controlled, that the information obtained is a direct communication to the auditor in response to the auditor's request, and that the information is obtained from a third party (in the case of cash accounts, that party is the organization that has the client's bank accounts) who is the intended respondent.

will make the loans immediately due and payable unless the financial institution temporarily waives the violation. If covenants are violated and the financial institution will not waive them, the auditor will have to consider whether the client will be able to continue to operate as a going concern and, if it is a long-term debt, reclassify it as a current liability. Additionally, the auditor typically inquires about the existence of cash management or other programs that the client has with the financial institution.

The *Emerging Issues* feature "Confirmations With Financial Institutions: Possible New PCAOB Guidance" describes potential emerging guidance with regard to confirmations.

Confirmations with Financial Institutions: Possible New PCAOB Guidance

On July 13, 2010, the PCAOB issued for public comment a proposed auditing standard related to confirmations. The comment period ended on September 13, 2010. The staff has analyzed the comments received and is planning to draft a reproposal for the Board's consideration, although the timing is not specified.

Auditors typically send confirmations to financial institutions where their clients have cash accounts or other relationships. However, this PCAOB-proposed Auditing Standard (AS) would require the auditor to perform confirmation procedures for cash and other relationships with financial institutions. Specifically, the proposed standard requires the auditor to perform confirmation procedures for cash with financial institutions, such as banks, brokerage firms, trust companies, and other similar entities. The other PCAOB-proposed items that should be confirmed include the following:

(a) Other relationships, such as lines of credit, other indebtedness, compensating balance arrangements, and contingent liabilities, including guarantees

(b) Any additional information about other deposit or loan accounts that has come to the attention of the financial institution during the process of completing the confirmation response

Ultimately, auditors need to stay alert to changes in required procedures and be aware when required procedures may differ between U.S. public companies and other types of organizations.

| EXHIBIT **10.8** | Standard Bank Confirmation—Account Balances |

Financial
Institution's   [   ]
Name and
Address   [   ]

CUSTOMER NAME

We have provided to our accountants the following information as of the close of business on ——, 20—, regarding our deposit and loan balances. Please confirm the accuracy of the information, noting any exceptions to the information provided. If the balances have been left blank, please complete this form by furnishing the balance in the appropriate space below. Although we do not request nor expect you to conduct a comprehensive, detailed search of your records, if during the process of completing this confirmation additional information about other deposit and loan accounts we may have with you comes to your attention, please include such information below. Please use the enclosed envelope to return the form directly to our accountants.

1. At the close of business on the date listed above, our records indicated the following deposit balance(s):

ACCOUNT NAME	ACCOUNT NO.	INTEREST RATE	BALANCE*

2. We were directly liable to the financial institution for loans at the close of business on the date listed above as follows:

ACCOUNT NO./ DESCRIPTION	BALANCE**	DATE DUE	INTEREST RATE	DATE THROUGH WHICH INTEREST IS PAID	DESCRIPTION OF COLLATERAL

_____   _____
(Customer's Authorized Signature)   (Date)

The information presented above by the customer is in agreement with our records. Although we have not conducted a comprehensive, detailed search of our records, no other deposit or loan accounts have come to our attention except as noted below.

_____   _____
(Financial Institution Authorized Signature)   (Date)

_____
(Title)

EXCEPTIONS AND/OR COMMENTS

Please return this form directly to our accountants:

*Ordinarily, balances are intentionally left blank if they are not available at the time the form is prepared.

Approved 1990 by American Bankers Association, American Institute of Certified Public Accountants, and Bank Administration Institute. Additional forms available from: AICPA—Order Department, P.O. Box 1003, NY, NY 10108–1003.   D 451 5851

EXHIBIT 10.9 Standard Bank Confirmation—Loan Guarantees

(Date)

Financial Institution Official*

First United Bank

Any town, USA

Dear Financial Institution Official:

In connection with an audit of the financial statements of (name of customer) as of (balance-sheet date) and for the (period) then ended, we have advised our independent auditors of the information listed below, which we believe is a complete and accurate description of our contingent liabilities, including oral and written guarantees, with your financial institution. Although we do not request nor expect you to conduct a comprehensive, detailed search of your records, if during the process of completing this confirmation, additional information about other contingent liabilities, including oral and written guarantees, between (name of customer) and your financial institution comes to your attention, please include such information below.

Name of Maker	Date of Note	Due Date	Current Balance	Interest Rate	Date Through Which Interest Is Paid	Description of Collateral	Description of Purpose of Note

Information related to oral and written guarantees is as follows:

_____

_____

_____

_____

Please confirm whether the information about contingent liabilities presented above is correct by signing below and returning this directly to our independent auditors (name and address of auditing firm).

Sincerely,

(Name of Customer)

_____

By: _____

(Authorized Signature)

Dear Auditing Firm:

The above information listing contingent liabilities, including oral and written guarantees, agrees with the records of this financial institution.** Although we have not conducted a comprehensive, detailed search of our records, no information about other contingent liabilities, including oral and written guarantees, came to our attention. (Note exceptions below or in an attached letter.)

_____

_____

_____

_____

(Name of Financial Institution)

_____

(Officer and Title)   (Date)

*This letter should be addressed to a financial institution official who is responsible for the financial institution's relationship with the client or is knowledgeable about the transactions or arrangements. Some financial institutions centralize this function by assigning responsibility for responding to confirmation requests to a separate function. Independent auditors should ascertain the appropriate recipient.

**If applicable, comments similar to the following may be added to the confirmation reply by the financial institution. This confirmation does not relate to arrangements, if any, with other branches or affiliates of this financial institution. Information should be sought separately from such branches or affiliates with which any such arrangements might exist.

Obtaining Cutoff Bank Statements

In many instances of fraud, management has either held open the cash receipts book to record the next period's sales collections as part of the current period or has mailed checks to vendors but did not record the cash disbursements until the subsequent period. Sometimes these problems occur because a company is in financial difficulty and needs an improved balance sheet to avoid violation of loan covenants. If the auditor assesses the risk of such misstatements to be high, the auditor will request a **cutoff bank statement** directly from the bank. This statement will list the activity for a period of seven to ten days after year-end. For example, if the client's year-end is December 31, the auditor may request a cutoff bank statement as of January 10.

The auditor should be alert for groups of checks that do not clear for an unusually long time after year-end. The delay in clearing the bank may indicate the recording of checks but not mailing them until after year-end in an effort to improve the appearance of the balance sheet. By considering the number of checks returned listed on the cutoff statement, the auditor may obtain evidence that the client is writing checks to pay current liabilities but is not mailing the checks until after year-end. This approach might be used by a client that is trying to improve its current ratio.

Preparing an Interbank Transfer Schedule

A company with many divisions frequently transfers cash from one division to another. The auditor should be alert to the fact that companies wanting to overstate cash may use a technique called **kiting** to record the same cash twice. Kiting is done by making transfers near year-end from one bank account to another bank account, recording the deposit in the second division's account, but not recording the disbursement on the first division's account until the next fiscal period. For example, a December 31 transfer would show the receipt on one account but not the disbursement on the other, resulting in the recording of the transferred amount twice. *Exhibit 10.10* shows the elements of a classic kiting scheme.

An effective and efficient way to test for the existence of kiting is to prepare an **interbank transfer schedule** like the one shown in *Exhibit 10.11*. The bank transfer schedule lists all transfers between the company's bank accounts for a short period of time before and after year-end. All transfers are accounted

---

| EXHIBIT **10.10** | Example of Kiting—All Within One Company |

Division A

- Transfers $1,000,000 to Division B near the end of the year but records the transaction in the following year.
- Transfer does not clear the bank in the current year.
- Transfer does not decrease the year-end cash balance because it has not been recorded in the current year.

Division B

- Receives $1,000,000 before year-end and records the deposit in the current year.
- Deposit may or may not be deposited by year-end. If not, the deposit will be shown as a deposit in transit in the division's bank reconciliation.
- Transfer increases the year-end cash balance by the amount of the transfer. The net effect is to overstate cash on the consolidated financial statements by the amount of the transfer.

Note: Cash is recorded in both divisions at year-end, resulting in the double counting.

| EXHIBIT **10.11** | Bank Transfer Schedule |

Gordon's Bay Manufacturing
Bank Transfer Schedule
Year Ended December 31, 2015

Transferred from Branch	Check Number	Amount	DATE DEPOSITED		DATE WITHDRAWN	
			Per Books	Per Bank	Per Branch Books	Per Bank
Cleveland	15910	$ 45,000	12/26*	12/27†	12/26*	12/30†
Cleveland	15980	100,000	12/28*	12/29†	12/27*	12/31†
Rockford	8702	87,000	12/30*	12/31†	1/2‡	1/3†
Cleveland	16110	25,000	1/3*	1/4†	1/2*	1/5†
Rockford	8725	65,000	1/5*	1/7*	1/4*	1/8†

*Traced to cash receipts/disbursements records.

†Traced to bank statement.

‡Withdrawal recorded in wrong period. See AJE C–11.

for to determine that they are recorded in the correct period and the client is not overstating the year-end cash account. Note the transfer of check number 8702, recorded as a deposit on December 30—an example of kiting. The check was recorded as a deposit in the Cleveland account on December 31 but was not recorded as a disbursement in the Rockford account until after year-end.

Fraud-Related Substantive Procedures for Cash Accounts

The following are examples of substantive procedures for cash accounts that address the risk of fraud:

- Confirm with financial institutions those individuals that are authorized to access cash accounts, along with those authorized to start a new account or eliminate an existing account
- Scrutinize checks that are payable to cash
- Scrutinize checks with unusual vendor names
- Scrutinize checks made out to employees outside of the normal payroll processing system
- Compare the timing of deposits into bank accounts with the timing of cash receipts, noting any unusual time lags
- Compare time lags between the date a check was issued for payment and the date that it clears the bank, noting any unusual time lags
- Investigate voided checks and analyze voided transactions

Documenting Substantive Procedures

The auditor would normally include the following types of documentation related to the substantive procedures for cash accounts:

- Copies of bank reconciliations inspected or reperformed
- Copies of bank confirmations
- Documentation of oral confirmations, if applicable
- Copies of bank cutoff statements
- Copies of bank transfer schedules
- Evidence of any restrictions on the use of cash balances or bank compensating balances

Auditing Marketable Securities

LO 9 Identify types of marketable securities, articulate
the risks and controls typically associated with these
accounts, and outline an
audit approach for testing
these accounts.

Significant Accounts, Disclosures, and Relevant Assertions

Marketable securities include a wide variety of financial instruments, including:

- Marketable securities (held as temporary investments, either equity or debt securities)
- Short-term cash management securities, such as U.S. Treasury bills, certificates of deposit (CDs), and **commercial paper**
- Other short-term hybrid-type securities intended to improve return on temporary investments (often referred to as *financial derivatives*, which we discuss in detail in *Chapter 16*)

Two points about marketable securities and financial instruments directly affect the proper accounting for those securities. First, there is an obvious implication about whether the security is, indeed, marketable; that is, it is able to be purchased and/or sold in a functioning market. Second, securities may carry various levels of risk, including the risk that they may not be tradable at all if the market turns down. Ultimately, the auditor needs to understand the economic purpose of major marketable securities transactions in relation to the risk undertaken by management in making the investment.

The investments in securities are classified as:

1. Held-to-maturity securities
2. Trading securities
3. Available-for-sale securities

There are important financial reporting and audit implications for the classification chosen by the company. The held-to-maturity securities are valued at amortized cost, subject to an impairment test. Both the trading securities and the available-for-sale securities are carried at fair market value. Thus, the auditor has a major judgmental challenge in:

- Corroborating management's intent in classifying the assets, including gathering information about management's trades in the investments, the importance of market value to management compensation
- Determining fair market value

The market value of regularly traded securities (e.g., stocks listed on the NYSE or NASDAQ) is easy to assess because trading data are regularly available. However, for more thinly traded securities, the market does not have many participants and a financial crisis can cause the market to dry up. In such cases, the financial institutions that hold many of the securities have been very reluctant to mark the values to fair market value.

Relevant Financial Statement Assertions

The five management assertions relevant to marketable securities are as follows:

1. *Existence/occurrence*—The marketable securities exist at the balance sheet date.
2. *Completeness*—The marketable securities balances include all securities transactions that have taken place during the period.
3. *Rights and obligations*—The company has title to marketable securities accounts as of the balance sheet date.
4. *Valuation or allocation*—The recorded balances reflect the true underlying economic value of those assets and are reported in accordance with the applicable reporting framework.

5. *Presentation and disclosure*—Marketable securities are properly classified on the balance sheet and disclosed in the notes to the financial statements.

The valuation assertion is usually the most relevant for auditing marketable securities because of the difficulties sometimes experienced when securities are thinly traded and management reluctance in writing down the value of securities.

Performing Risk Assessment Procedures

As part of performing risk assessment procedures, the auditor obtains information that is useful in assessing the risk of material misstatement. This includes information about inherent risks at the financial statement level (e.g., the client's business and operational risks, financial reporting risks) and, at the account and assertion levels, fraud risks including feedback from audit team brainstorming sessions, strengths and weaknesses in internal control, and results from planning analytical procedures. Once the risks of material misstatement have been identified, the auditor then determines how best to respond to them as part of the audit opinion formulation process.

Identifying Inherent, Fraud, and Control Risks Relevant to Marketable Securities

A company may invest in many types of marketable securities. Some are more marketable than others, and some carry promises of greater return (but at much greater risk) than others. Traditional marketable securities are straightforward and do not present much in the way of inherent risk. Traditional marketable securities are readily traded, and management usually intends to hold them for a short period of time. Because they are held for trading, or available for sale, they are valued at market value. In normal market situations, these short-term investments turn over and are not complex to audit. However, some inherent and control risks relating to marketable securities still exist.

Inherent and Fraud Risks
- Risk of sudden market declines, which would adversely affect the valuation of securities
- Management manipulation of the classification of securities to achieve preferable valuation treatment, that is, market value versus amortized cost
- Management manipulation of the valuation of fair market value if the securities are thinly traded

Control Risks
- Risk of theft of securities if they are not physically controlled, or if authorization and monitoring over their purchase or sale is not effective
- Lack of policies over purchase or sale of securities
- Lack of monitoring of changes in securities balances
- Lack of policies over valuation or classification of securities
- Lack of segregation of duties between individuals responsible for making investment decisions and those responsible for the custody of securities
- Lack of involvement or oversight by internal audit in relation to securities

To help auditors assess and document inherent and control risks relating to marketable securities, they complete an inherent risk analysis questionnaire (see *Exhibit 10.12*) and a control risk analysis questionnaire (see *Exhibit 10.13*). Also, see the *Focus on Fraud* feature "Common Fraud Schemes Relating to Investments" for a discussion of fraud risks.

EXHIBIT 10.12 Inherent Risk Analysis Questionnaire: Marketable Securities

1. Does the company regularly invest in marketable securities? How material are the balances in marketable securities accounts?
2. Has management changed the classification of securities during the year from either trading securities or available-for-sale securities to held-to-maturity securities? If yes, what is the reason for the change?
3. Is there a ready market for the securities?

EXHIBIT 10.13 Control Risk Analysis Questionnaire: Marketable Securities

1. Does the company have written policies and guidelines regarding investments in marketable securities? Are the policies approved by the board of directors? What process is used to authorize investments in marketable securities?
2. Does the company have a clear policy as to whether marketable securities are properly classified as trading securities, available-for-sale securities, or held-to-maturity securities? Is there evidence that the company follows the policy?
3. If management has changed the classification of securities during the year from either trading securities or available-for-sale securities to held-to-maturity securities, are the amounts significant? Were they reviewed by the audit committee? Do the audit committee and the board concur with the change?
4. If a liquid market does not exist for the marketable securities, how does management estimate the value of the securities that need to be marked to current market value?
5. Does the company provide for effective segregation of duties among individuals responsible for making investment decisions and those responsible for the custody of securities?
6. Does the internal audit department conduct regular audits of the controls over marketable securities? If yes, review recent reports.

Common Fraud Schemes Relating to Investments

FOCUS on FRAUD

The following are common fraud schemes relating to investments:

- Securities are purchased, but those purchases are not authorized.
- Securities are purchased, but are not recorded as purchased. Or securities are recorded as purchased, but they are not actually purchased.
- Securities are sold, but are not recorded as sold. Or securities are recorded as sold, but they are not actually sold.
- Investment income (e.g., dividends or interest) is stolen.
- Investments are purposely valued inaccurately, that is, by making inaccurate fair value judgments.
- Investment classifications are purposely inaccurate.

Performing Planning Analytical Procedures for Marketable Securities

Planning analytical procedures help auditors identify areas of potential material misstatements. The steps that the auditor will take in performing planning analytical procedures are fully described in *Chapter 7*. The following are examples of common planning analytical procedures that may be conducted for marketable securities accounts:

- Develop expectations about the level of amounts in ending balances of marketable securities accounts based on purchase or sales activity reported by management during the year
- Develop expectations about the relationship between the balances in marketable securities accounts, the rates anticipated to be earned on those accounts, and any changes therein, and associated interest and dividend revenues
- Review changes in the balances, risk composition, and classification types of marketable securities in relation to stated investment policies and plans

Obtaining Evidence About Internal Control Operating Effectiveness and Substantive Evidence About Marketable Securities Accounts, Disclosures, and Assertions

Performing Tests of Controls

The following are common tests of controls for marketable securities:

- Review policies for authorization to purchase, sell, and manage marketable securities
- Inquire of the board of directors about the board's oversight of the marketable securities process and examine related documentation
- Examine documentation of authorization for selected purchases and sales of marketable securities during the year
- Review the minutes of the board meetings for reference to investment policies and associated oversight
- Examine evidence of authorization controls for changes in classification of marketable securities
- Inquire of management about its process for establishing valuation of marketable securities and review related documentation
- Inquire of management about their process for reclassifications and review related documentation
- Examine documentation for selected marketable securities transactions to determine whether segregation of duties is maintained
- Review reports of internal audit in relation to their activities involving monitoring of marketable securities

Obtaining Substantive Evidence About Marketable Securities

The planning analytical procedures discussed previously as part of risk assessment procedures would also be appropriate as a substantive analytical procedure, if conducted using the appropriate level of precision.

However, it is likely that the auditor will focus more audit effort on substantive tests of details. *Exhibit 10.14* contains an example of various substantive tests of detail applicable to marketable securities, along with their relationship to relevant assertions. *Exhibit 10.15* contains an example of an audit workpaper for testing marketable equity securities.

EXHIBIT **10.14**	Assertions and Related Substantive Tests of Details: Marketable Securities

Assertion	Substantive Tests of Details
Existence/occurrence	1. Request that the client prepare a schedule of all marketable securities held by the company at year-end. Verify the existence of securities by either (a) counting and examining selected securities or (b) confirming the existence with trustees holding them. Reconcile the amounts with the general ledger.
Completeness	2. Foot the schedule of marketable securities and examine the securities (Step 1). Examine selected transactions and brokers' advices near year-end to determine that the transactions are recorded in the correct period.
Rights	3. Examine selected documents to determine if there are any restrictions on the marketability of securities. Inquire of management as to existence of any restrictions.
Valuation/allocation	4. Determine current market value through reference to a financial reporting service or a similar electronic source.
	5. Recompute interest and determine that accrued interest is properly recorded at year-end.
	6. Determine that unrealized gains and losses are properly accounted for.
Presentation and disclosure	7. Determine management's intent to hold securities and review classification. Document that intention in a management representation letter.
	8. Determine whether the securities are properly classified and that any restrictions on their use are appropriately disclosed in the notes to the financial statements.

You should note the following about the audit workpaper in *Exhibit 10.15*:

1. The client prepares a schedule of all marketable securities it owns at year-end. The schedule includes the accrued interest and dividends associated with each security for the period of time held. The auditor is testing both the balance sheet and the related income accounts at the same time.

2. If the risk of material misstatement is low, the auditor will test only a small sample of the items. If risk is high, the auditor may verify all the material items on the worksheet.

3. The document shows three items related to the value of the security:
   - Cost
   - Year-end market value
   - Carrying value for debt instruments

4. Disposals and resulting gains/losses are shown for all accounts during the year.

5. The auditor verifies the cost or sales price of the assets by examining broker's advices evidencing either the purchase or sale of the security. If control risk is low, the verification can be performed on a sample of the transactions.

6. The schedule is an abbreviated worksheet. For most audits, the auditor will have to determine whether securities are properly classified either as intent to hold to maturity or trading. That determination must be corroborated by, and consistent with, management's actions. The appropriate classification determines the accounting valuation.

EXHIBIT 10.15 Test of Client's Marketable Securities

Gordon's Bay Manufacturing
Summary of Marketable Securities
Year Ended December 31, 2015

Prepared by AMJ
Date 1/28/16
Reviewed by _____
Date _____

Marketable Investments	Beginning Balance	PURCHASES Date	PURCHASES Amount	DISPOSALS Date	DISPOSALS Amount	Gain/Loss Disposal	Ending Balance	Market Value (12/31)	INCOME ACCOUNTS Interest	INCOME ACCOUNTS Dividends	INCOME ACCOUNTS Total
Gen. Motors 8% comm. paper	$45,000.00	10/31/13		4/30/13	$45,000.00*	$0.00	$0.00		$1,800.00^R		$1,800.00
Ford Motor 8.25% comm. paper	100,000.00	12/1/14					100,000.00^c	$100,000.00†	8,937.50^R		8,937.50
1000 Sh Sears' common stk	22,367.00	10/31/14					22,367.00^c	16,375.00†		$1,000.00^R	1,000.00
1000 Sh AMOCO	48,375.00	12/31/11		7/13/13	62,375.00*	14,000.00^R	0.00	0.00		1,000.00^R	1,000.00
1000 Sh Consolidated paper	0.00	7/31/13	$41,250.00*				41,250.00^c	44,500.00†		500.00‡	500.00
Bank America Zero Cpn Bond	1,378.00	6/30/14					1,378.00^c	1,587.00†	209.00^R		209.00
Totals	$217,120.00		$41,250.00		$107,375.00	$14,000.00	$164,995.00	$162,462.00	$10,946.50	$2,500.00	$13,446.50
	T/B		F		F	F	CF F	F	F	#	F
									=	=	=

Market value $162,462.00
Excess cost >
Mkt. Value $2,533.00§
F

*Correct, per examination of broker's invoice.
C Securities held in broker's account, confirmed with broker.
R Recomputed, no exceptions.
† Per December 31 stock transaction listing in the *Wall Street Journal.*
‡ Amount should be $1,000. Company failed to accrue dividend declared.
T/B Per December 31, 2014 trial balance and 12/31/14 working papers, schedule M-2.

F Footed.
CF Cross-footed.
§Loss not recorded. Trace to AJE 31.
‖ Traced to year-end trial balance.
Interest and dividend payments verified through examination of *Dividend and Interest Digest*
for year-end December 31, 2015.

7. For most investments, the current market value is determined by referring to the year-end closing price in the *Wall Street Journal* or by collecting this data electronically on the audit firm's own database. For securities that are in illiquid markets, the auditor will have to do substantially more work to determine market value.

8. Income is recomputed on a selected basis for interest, dividends, and realized and unrealized gains and losses.

9. The schedule is footed to determine the mechanical accuracy and the correct valuation of the account.

10. The audit tests address all of the audit assertions except presentation and disclosure. That assertion is verified directly with management and documented separately.

11. Document the conclusion regarding the fairness of presentation of the account balance as adjusted.

The *Focus on Fraud* feature "Audit Procedures Used to Address Risk Related to Common Fraud Schemes for Investments" provides examples of other substantive procedures that auditors may apply as necessary given the assessed level of fraud risk.

Documenting Substantive Procedures

The auditor would include the following types of documentation related to the substantive procedures for marketable securities:

- Schedule of marketable securities as prepared by the client and as reviewed by the auditor, including purchases, sales, dates, market values, interest income, and gains or losses on sale
- Documentation of any confirmation of securities
- Documentation of marketable securities transactions that were scrutinized, for example, those exceeding a certain dollar value
- Memo containing rationalization for judgments made about management's classification of securities
- Memo containing rationalization for judgments made about management's valuation of securities
- Reports of any outside valuation experts
- Documentation of calculation of any potential impairments

Audit Procedures Used to Address Risk Related to Common Fraud Schemes for Investments

FOCUS on **FRAUD**

The following substantive procedures are often used to address the risks relating to fraud in investments:

- Employ a specialist to assist in fair value measurements
- Conduct background checks on and credit ratings of employees who have access to investment accounts, or the authorization to purchase or sell securities

- Require that the client produce original documentation of securities, not copies or faxes
- Trace dividend payments, interest payments, and sales of securities to cash deposits recorded on the bank statement
- Trace purchases of securities to cash disbursements on the bank statement
- Review any unusual journal entries in investment accounts

SUMMARY AND NEXT STEPS

Cash is an inherently risky asset due to the volume of activity in the account, its liquidity, and the fact that it can be easily manipulated if controls are weak. Fraud is therefore an important consideration in the audit of cash, even though the ending balance of cash at the end of the year is usually low. Substantive procedures that the auditor will perform for cash accounts include preparing independent bank reconciliations, obtaining bank confirmations, obtaining bank cutoff statements, and preparing bank transfer schedules. Marketable securities also present unique risks, particularly in terms of valuation. In auditing marketable securities, the auditor will obtain assurance on purchases, sales, interest revenue, and any gains or losses on disposals. Looking forward, in *Chapter 11* we discuss risk assessment procedures, tests of controls, and substantive procedures for auditing the purchases of goods, services and inventory, that is, the acquisition and payment cycle.

SIGNIFICANT TERMS

Bank confirmation A standard confirmation sent to all banks with which the client had business during the year to obtain information about the year-end cash balance and additional information about loans outstanding.

Collateral An asset or a claim on an asset usually held by a borrower or an issuer of a debt instrument to serve as a guarantee for the value of a loan or security. If the borrower fails to pay interest or principal, the collateral is available to the lender as a basis to recover the principal amount of the loan or debt instrument.

Commercial paper Notes issued by major corporations, usually for short periods of time and at rates approximating prime lending rates, usually with high credit rating; their quality may change if the financial strength of the issuer declines.

Cutoff bank statement A bank statement for a period of time after year-end (usually seven to ten days); sent directly to the auditor, who uses it to verify reconciling items on the client's year-end bank reconciliation.

Imprest bank account A bank account that normally carries a zero balance and is replenished by the company when checks are to be written against the account; provides additional control over cash. The most widely used imprest bank account is the payroll account, to which the company makes a deposit equal to the amount of payroll checks issued.

Interbank transfer schedule An audit document that lists all transfers between client bank accounts starting a short period before year-end and continuing for a short period after year-end; its purpose is to assure that cash in transit is not recorded twice.

Kiting A fraudulent cash scheme to overstate cash assets at year-end by showing the same cash in two different bank accounts using an interbank transfer.

Lapping This type of fraud occurs when an employee steals a payment from one customer, and covers it up by using payments from another customer to disguise the theft. For example, the employee steals a payment from Customer X. To cover the theft, the employee applies a payment from Customer Y to Customer X's account. Before Customer Y has time to notice that its account has not been appropriately credited, the employee applies a payment from Customer Z to Customer Y's account.

Lockbox   A cash management arrangement with a bank whereby an organization's customers send payments directly to a post office box number accessible to the client's bank; the bank opens the cash remittances and directly deposits the money in the client's account.

Marketable security   A security that is readily marketable and held by the company as an investment.

Skimming   This type of fraud occurs when an employee makes a sale but does not record it, and steals the cash.

Turnaround document   A document sent to the customer to be returned with the customer's remittance; may be machine-readable and may contain information to improve the efficiency of receipt processing.

TRUE/FALSE QUESTIONS

10-1 **LO 1** The existence/occurrence assertion with respect to cash implies that recorded balances reflect the true underlying economic value of those assets.

10-2 **LO 1** Common cash accounts include lockboxes, EFTs, cash management agreements, and compensating balances.

10-3 **LO 2** Cash is inherently risky because it may be used for unauthorized purposes, posted to the wrong customer's account, or not recorded on a timely basis.

10-4 **LO 2** The volume of transactions flowing through cash accounts throughout the year makes the account highly susceptible to error.

10-5 **LO 3** Lapping occurs when an employee steals a payment from one customer, and covers it up by using payments from another customer to disguise the theft.

10-6 **LO 3** Skimming occurs when an employee purchases merchandise and records the sale at an unauthorized discounted price.

10-7 **LO 4** Controls for completeness of cash are important because they help to provide reasonable assurance that the cash actually does exist.

10-8 **LO 4** Because a primary concern is that cash will be stolen and is thus understated, the auditor is not usually concerned about overstatements of cash.

10-9 **LO 5** Planning analytical procedures are particularly useful to the auditor in gaining assurance about the cash account because the usually small ending balances in cash tend to be stable over time.

10-10 **LO 5** If the auditor observes that the company reports consistent profits over several years while cash flows are decreasing, the auditor should assess heightened risk of fraud in cash.

10-11 **LO 6** The relative percentage of substantive analytics that will be used by the auditor as evidence in the audit of cash will be somewhat limited regardless of the riskiness of the client.

10-12 **LO 6** When auditing cash, the auditor will perform a relatively larger percentage of tests of details for a high-risk client compared to a low-risk client.

10-13   **LO 7**   An example of a monitoring control in cash would include a daily review of cash budgets and a comparison of them with actual cash balances, with appropriate follow-up.

10-14   **LO 7**   Because of the level of inherent risk associated with cash accounts, auditors are required to test the controls over cash accounts.

10-15   **LO 8**   Because cash balances are usually relatively low at year-end, auditing standards encourage auditors to send bank confirmations on a sample basis.

10-16   **LO 8**   A typical bank statement prepared at an interim agreed-upon date that is sent directly to the auditor is called a *bank transfer statement*.

10-17   **LO 9**   The major judgmental challenges that auditors face in auditing marketable securities include corroborating management's intent in classifying these assets into the proper categories and determining fair market value.

10-18   **LO 9**   An appropriate audit procedure to test the valuation assertion for marketable securities involves reviewing the client's schedule of marketable securities and confirming with trustees that those securities do, indeed, belong to the company.

MULTIPLE-CHOICE QUESTIONS

10-19   **LO 1**   Which of the following assertions is relevant to whether the company has title to the cash accounts as of the balance sheet date?
a. Existence/occurrence.
b. Completeness.
c. Rights and obligations.
d. Valuation or allocation.
e. All of the above.

10-20   **LO 1**   Which of the following assertions is relevant to whether the cash balances reflect the true underlying economic value of those assets?
a. Existence/occurrence.
b. Completeness.
c. Rights and obligations.
d. Valuation or allocation.
e. All of the above.

10-21   **LO 2**   Inherent risk for cash is usually assessed as high for which of the following reasons?
a. The volume of transactions flowing through cash accounts throughout the year makes the account more susceptible to error.
b. The cash account is more susceptible to fraud because cash is liquid and easily transferable.
c. The electronic transfer of cash and the automated controls over cash are such that if errors are built into computer programs, they will be repeated on a large volume of transactions.
d. Cash can be easily manipulated.
e. All of the above.

10-22   **LO 2**   Which of the following questions would be relevant for an inherent risk analysis questionnaire related to cash?
a. Does the company have significant cash flow problems in meeting its current obligations on a timely basis?

b. Are cash transactions properly authorized?

c. Are bank reconciliations performed on a timely basis by personnel independent of processing?

d. Does the internal audit department conduct timely reviews of the cash management and cash-handling process?

e. All of the above.

10-23 **LO 3** Affirmative answers to which of the following questions would lead the auditor to assess fraud risk at a higher level for cash or other liquid assets?

a. Is an individual with access to cash or its recording experiencing financial or personal distress?

b. Is an individual with access to cash or its recording being compensated at an amount that he or she might consider low?

c. Is the company in potential violation of its debt covenants?

d. Is cash physically available to employees?

e. All of the above.

10-24 **LO 3** Which of the following terms best defines this scenario? The employee steals a payment from Customer X. To cover the theft, the employee applies a payment from Customer Y to Customer X's account. Before Customer Y has time to notice that its account has not been appropriately credited, the employee applies a payment from Customer Z to Customer Y's account.

a. Skimming.

b. Kiting.

c. Collateralizing.

d. Lapping.

10-25 **LO 4** Which of the following controls represents a control over cash that is unique to cash accounts?

a. Separation of duties.

b. Restrictive endorsements of customer checks.

c. Periodic internal audits.

d. Competent, well-trained employees.

10-26 **LO 4** Which of the following controls represents a computerized control used for cash or other liquid asset accounts?

a. A unique identifier is assigned to each item.

b. Control totals are used to assure the completeness of processing.

c. Edit tests are used to identify unusual or incorrect items.

d. All of the above.

10-27 **LO 5** The first step in performing planning analytical procedures is to develop an expectation of the account balance. Which of the following does not typically represent a likely expected relationship for cash accounts?

a. The company reports consistent profits over several years, but operating cash flows are declining.

b. No unusual large cash or other liquid asset transactions are found.

c. Operating cash flow is not significantly different from that of the prior year.

d. Investment income is consistent with the level of and returns expected from the investments.

e. All of the above represent likely expected relationships.

10-28 **LO 5** Which of the following is a common example of trend analysis of accounts and ratios that the auditor might consider for cash accounts?

a. Compare monthly cash balances with past years and budgets.

b. Identify unexpected spikes or lows in cash during the year.

c. Compute trends in interest returns on investments.

    d. Analyze cash balances, and changes therein, in relation to new or retiring debt obligations.

    e. All of the above.

10-29 **LO 6** Which mix of evidence would be most appropriate for the following scenario? This is a client where the auditor has assessed the risk of material misstatement related to the existence and completeness of cash at the maximum level. This client has incentives to overstate cash in order to meet debt covenants. Further, the client has relatively weak controls to prevent theft of cash.

    a. 100% tests of details.

    b. 70% tests of details, 10% analytics, 20% tests of controls.

    c. 50% tests of details, 10% analytics, 40% tests of controls.

    d. 20% tests of details, 40% analytics, 40% tests of controls.

10-30 **LO 6** Which mix of evidence would be most appropriate for the following scenario? This is a client where the auditor has assessed the risk of material misstatement related to the existence and completeness of cash as low, and believes that the client has implemented effective controls in this area.

    a. 100% tests of details.

    b. 70% tests of details, 10% analytics, 20% tests of controls.

    c. 50% tests of details, 10% analytics, 40% tests of controls.

    d. 20% tests of details, 40% analytics, 40% tests of controls.

10-31 **LO 7** Refer to *Exhibit 10.6*. Which of the following represents a reasonable test of controls for cash receipts and cash management controls?

    a. Document internal controls over cash by completing the internal control questionnaire or by flowcharting the process.

    b. Reperform a bank reconciliation.

    c. Obtain a bank confirmation.

    d. Obtain a bank cutoff statement.

    e. All of the above.

10-32 **LO 7** Refer to *Exhibit 10.6*. Which of the following represents a monitoring control that the auditor may want to test?

    a. Reviews of reconciliations of reported cash receipts with remittances prepared by independent parties.

    b. Daily review of cash budgets and comparison of them with actual cash balances.

    c. Reviews of discrepancies in cash balances.

    d. Reviews of weekly reporting of customer complaints regarding posting of cash balances and prompt investigation to follow up on cause of complaints.

    e. All of the above.

10-33 **LO 8** Which of the following statements regarding reperformance of bank reconciliations is true?

    a. The auditor's reperformance of a reconciliation of the client's bank accounts provides evidence as to the accuracy of the year-end cash balance.

    b. The process reconciles the balance per the bank statements with the balance per the books.

    c. Reperformance of the bank reconciliation is quite effective in detecting major errors, such as those that might be covered up by omitting or underfooting outstanding checks.

    d. When testing the client's bank reconciliation, the auditor should independently verify all material items, such as the balance per the bank statement, deposits in transit, outstanding checks, and other adjustments.

    e. All of the above are true.

10-34 **LO 8** A bank confirmation contains which of the following two parts?

1. A part that seeks information on the client's deposit balances, the existence of loans, due dates of the loans, interest rates, dates through which interest has been paid, and collateral for loans outstanding
2. A part that contains a listing of the last checks issued near year-end
3. A part that seeks information about any loan guarantees
4. A part that lists all transfers between the company's bank accounts for a short period of time before and after year-end

a. 1 & 2.
b. 1 & 3.
c. 2 & 3.
d. 2 & 4.
e. 3 & 4.

10-35 **LO 9** Which of the following assertions is relevant to whether the marketable securities balances include all securities transactions that have taken place during the period?

a. Existence/occurrence.
b. Completeness.
c. Rights and obligations.
d. Valuation or allocation.
e. All of the above.

10-36 **LO 9** Refer to *Exhibit 10.14*. Which of the following assertions is relevant to the audit procedure for marketable securities that requires the auditor to examine selected documents to identify any restrictions on the securities?

a. Existence/occurrence.
b. Completeness.
c. Rights and obligations.
d. Valuation or allocation.
e. All of the above.

REVIEW AND SHORT CASE QUESTIONS

NOTE: Completing Review and Short Case Questions does not require the student to reference additional resources and materials.

NOTE: For the remaining problems, we make special note of those addressing fraud, international issues, professional skepticism, and ethics.

10-37 **LO 1** Describe the following types of cash accounts: (a) general checking accounts, (b) cash management accounts, (c) imprest payroll accounts, and (d) petty cash accounts.

10-38 **LO 1** Describe the following types of cash management techniques: (a) lockboxes, (b) EFTs, (c) cash management agreements, (d) compensating balances.

10-39 **LO 1** Match the following assertions with their associated description: (a) existence/occurrence, (b) completeness, (c) rights and obligations, (d) valuation or allocation, (e) presentation and disclosure.

1. Cash accounts are properly classified on the balance sheet and disclosed in the notes to the financial statements.
2. Cash balances exist at the balance sheet date.
3. The recorded balances reflect the true underlying economic value of those assets.
4. The company has title to the cash accounts as of the balance sheet date.
5. Cash balances include all cash transactions that have taken place during the period.

FRAUD

10-40 **LO 2** Refer to the *Professional Judgment in Context* feature at the beginning of the chapter. Why is cash in general a risky asset, and why was the petty cash account at Koss Corporation inherently risky?

10-41 **LO 2** Evaluate the following statement made by a third-year auditor: "In comparison with other accounts, such as accounts receivable or property, plant, and equipment, it is my assessment that cash contains less inherent risk. There are no significant valuation problems with cash." Do you agree or disagree with the auditor's assessment of inherent risk? Explain.

10-42 **LO 2, 4** The following are items on the inherent risk and control risk questionnaires in *Exhibit 10.1* and *Exhibit 10.2*. Categorize each item as belonging on (a) the inherent risk analysis questionnaire or the (b) control risk analysis questionnaire.

1. Does the company have significant cash flow problems in meeting its current obligations on a timely basis?
2. Are there any restrictions in getting access to cash? For example, does the company have cash in sweep accounts, or other accounts with financial institutions that may be in trouble, and that may restrict access to cash?
3. Does the internal audit department conduct timely reviews of the cash management and cash-handling process? If yes, review recent internal audit reports.
4. Does the company use cash-budgeting techniques? How effective are the company's cash management budgeting techniques?
5. Are bank reconciliations performed on a timely basis by personnel independent of processing? Is follow-up action taken promptly on all reconciling items?
6. Does the company use the cash management services offered by its banker? What is the nature of these arrangements?
7. Has the company made significant changes in its cash processing during the past year? Have any major changes taken place in the company's computerized cash management applications during the year?
8. Have cash management service arrangements been reviewed by management and the board of directors? Are the arrangements monitored on a current basis?
9. Does the company have loan or bond covenants that influence the use of cash or the maintenance of working-capital ratios?
10. Are cash transactions, including electronic cash transfers, properly authorized? What authorization is required to make electronic cash transfers?
11. Does the company use a lockbox to collect cash receipts? What is the agreement with the financial institution? What are the company's controls associated with the lockbox agreement?
12. Is there any reason to suspect that management may desire to misstate the cash balance?
13. Do management and the board periodically review the cash management process? Does the cash management organization provide for effective segregation of duties, review, and supervision?
14. Who is authorized to make cash transfers, including EFTs, and what are the procedures by which that authorization is verified before the transfers take place? What procedures does management use to assure that the authorization process is monitored?

FRAUD

10-43 **LO 3** Refer to the *Focus on Fraud* feature "Common Fraud Schemes Relating to Cash" and describe at least three such schemes. Be prepared to discuss fraud schemes that you have learned about in your local community.

FRAUD **10-44** **LO 3** Describe the fraudulent conduct that is known as (a) lapping and (b) skimming.

FRAUD **10-45** **LO 4** Using the following categories, define the purpose of each of the common controls over cash listed below. You may use multiple categories for each control.

Categories of Purposes of Each Common Control
1. To prevent theft of cash.
2. To ensure complete recording of cash.
3. To prevent modification of the recording of cash.
4. To detect inaccuracy of ending cash balance or misstatements therein.
5. To ensure that all items are uniquely identified and that an adequate audit trail exists for transactions.
6. To serve as a deterrent for fraud.

Common Controls Over Cash

a. Segregation of duties.
b. Restrictive endorsements of customer checks.
c. Independent bank reconciliations by employees who do not handle cash.
d. Computerized control totals and edit tests.
e. Authorization of transactions.
f. Prenumbered cash receipt documents and turnaround documents.
g. Periodic internal audits.
h. Competent, well-trained employees.

10-46 **LO 4** List at least three common controls for petty cash.

10-47 **LO 4** Refer to *Exhibit 10.3*. Match each of the following objectives to the relevant control activities.

Objectives That Cash Receipts Controls Are Trying to Achieve

a. Payments received are deposited intact on a timely basis.
b. Payments received are completely credited to the correct customer accounts.

Control Activities
1. A list of incoming receipts is prepared by the person who opens the remittances and who delivers the list to a person independent of the deposit function.
2. Online entry that includes the input of a control total and/or hash total is used for each payment.
3. A duplicate deposit slip is prepared by someone other than the person opening the mail.
4. Deposits are made daily.
5. Prenumbered batch control tickets include control totals of the number of remittances to be processed and total dollars to be applied.
6. An agreement exists between the bank and the company on cash-handling activities, including when the remittances are added to the company's account.
7. Management monitors controls to follow up on discrepancies in accounts receivable postings.

INTERNATIONAL **10-48** **LO 4, 7, 8** This problem is designed to get you to think creatively about controls that would be effective in a real-world setting. The Canada Border Services Agency (CBSA) receives cash payments for services, fees, and taxes (e.g., customs duties, excise taxes, taxes on goods and services) at various ports of entry around Canada. Cash is defined as payments made in liquid cash, by debit or credit cards, and by checks.

a. What types of controls should the CBSA have over its cash receipts?

b. Given the controls that you identified in part (a), what types of tests of controls or substantive audit procedures should be performed?

FRAUD

10-49 **LO 5** Categorize each of the following trends or relationships as suggesting either (a) a normal trend or relationship or (b) an expected trend or relationship suggesting a heightened risk of material misstatement (from error or fraud):

1. The company reports consistent profits over several years, but cash flows are declining.
2. Operating cash flow is consistent with sales and net income.
3. The timeliness of accounts receivable collections declines, but credit policies are unchanged.
4. Operating cash flow is not significantly different from that of the prior year, and operations have been consistent across the two years.
5. Investment income is consistent with the level of and returns expected from investments.
6. There are unexpected declines in the petty cash account.

10-50 **LO 7** Refer to *Exhibit 10.6*. Describe the major components of an audit program for cash receipts and cash management controls. Provide examples of each component.

PROFESSIONAL SKEPTICISM

10-51 **LO 8** What is the impact on the audit if the client does not perform independent periodic reconciliations of its cash accounts? What substantive audit procedures would be dictated by the lack of the client's independent reconciliations? How would the fact that the client does not perform this important control affect the auditor's professional skepticism?

10-52 **LO 8** Explain the purpose of the following audit procedures:

a. Sending a bank confirmation to all the banks with which the company does business.

b. Obtaining a bank cutoff statement.

c. Preparing an interbank transfer statement.

FRAUD

10-53 **LO 8** Define and illustrate *kiting*. What controls should the client institute to prevent it? What audit procedures should the auditor use to detect kiting?

FRAUD

10-54 **LO 8** The following information was taken from the bank transfer schedule prepared during the audit of Fox Co.'s financial statements for the year ended December 31, 2015. Assume all checks are dated and issued on December 30, 2015.

Check No.	Bank Accounts		Disbursement Date		Receipt Date	
	From	To	Per Books	Per Bank	Per Books	Per Bank
101	National	Federal	Dec. 30	Jan. 4	Dec. 30	Jan. 3
202	County	State	Jan. 3	Jan. 2	Dec. 30	Dec. 31
303	Federal	State	Dec. 31	Jan. 3	Jan. 2	Jan. 2
404	State	County	Jan. 2	Jan. 2	Jan. 2	Dec. 31

a. Which of the checks might indicate kiting?
b. Which of the checks illustrates deposits/transfers in transit on December 31, 2015?

FRAUD

10-55 **LO 8**   The following items were discovered during the audit of a cash account. For each item identified, indicate the substantive audit procedure that most likely would have led to the discovery of the misstatement.

1. The company had overstated cash by transferring funds at year-end to another account but failed to record the withdrawal until after year-end.
2. On occasion, customers with smaller balances send in checks without specific identification of the customer except the name printed on the check. The client has an automated cash receipts process, but the employee opening the envelopes pocketed the cash and destroyed other supporting documentation.
3. Same as finding (2), but the employee prepared a turnaround document that showed either an additional discount for the customer or a credit to the customer's account.
4. The controller was temporarily taking cash for personal purposes but intended to repay the company (although the repayment never occurred). The cover-up was executed by understating outstanding checks in the monthly bank reconciliation.
5. The company had temporary investments in six-month CDs at the bank. The CDs were supposed to yield an annual interest rate of 12% but apparently are yielding only 6%.
6. Cash remittances are not deposited in a timely fashion and are sometimes lost.
7. Substantial bank service charges have not been recorded by the client prior to year-end.
8. A loan has been negotiated with the bank to provide funds for a subsidiary company. The loan was negotiated by the controller of the division, who apparently was not authorized to negotiate the loan.
9. A check written to a vendor had been recorded twice in the cash disbursements journal to cover a cash shortage.

FRAUD

10-56 **LO 8**   Pembrook Company had poor internal control over its cash transactions. The following are facts about its cash position on November 30:

- The company's books showed a balance of $18,901.62, which included undeposited receipts.
- A credit of $100 on the bank statement did not appear on the company's books.
- The balance, according to the bank statement, was $15,550.
- Outstanding checks were:
  - No. 62 for $116.25
  - No. 183 for $150.00
  - No. 284 for $253.25
  - No. 8621 for $190.71
  - No. 8623 for $206.80
  - No. 8632 for $145.28.

The only deposit was in the amount of $3,794.41 on December 7. The cashier handles all incoming cash and makes the bank deposits personally. He also reconciles the monthly bank statement. His November 30 reconciliation follows:

Balance, per books, November 30		$18,901.62
Add: Outstanding checks:		
8621	$190.71	
8623	206.80	
8632	45.28	442.79
		$19,344.41
Less: Undeposited receipts		3,794.41
Balance per bank, November 30		$15,550.00
Deduct: Unrecorded credit		100.00
True cash, November 30		$15,450.00

a. You suspect that the cashier may have misappropriated some money and are concerned specifically that some of the undeposited receipts of $3,794.41 may have been taken. Prepare a schedule showing your estimate of the loss.

b. How did the cashier attempt to conceal the theft?

c. On the basis of this information only, name two specific features of internal control that were apparently missing.

d. If the cashier's October 31 reconciliation is known to be proper and you start your audit on December 10, what specific substantive audit procedures would help you discover the theft?

10-57 **LO 8** Assume that you are testing the client's bank reconciliation at year-end. Following is a list of items on the reconciliation. For each item (listed as (a) through (e)), identify one or more procedures that the auditor would perform to gather sufficient appropriate evidence regarding that item.

a. Balance per bank

b. Balance per books

c. Deposits in transit

d. Customer note collected by bank

e. Outstanding checks

10-58 **LO 8** The AICPA has developed a standard bank confirmation form to assure consistent communication with the banking community.

a. Is the auditor required to send a bank confirmation to banks from which the client receives a bank cutoff statement shortly after year-end? Explain.

b. What additional information is gathered through a bank confirmation? Explain how the other information gathered is used on the audit.

c. For each scenario in the following list (listed as (1) through (3)), recommend a substantive audit procedure or additional audit work that should be performed:

   1. The client has one major bank account located in a distant city, and the auditor is not familiar with the bank. The auditor has assessed control risk as high for the cash accounts on this engagement. The mailing address of the bank is simply a post office box number, but such a number is not considered unusual.

2. The client has three accounts with its major bank. For two of the three accounts, the confirmation returned by the bank shows different balances from what the client shows. The balance per the client for one of the accounts is the same as the bank shows in the cutoff statement received from the bank shortly after year-end. The auditor did not request a cutoff statement on the other account for which the confirmation differs.

3. The returned confirmation shows a loan that the client does not list as a liability.

10-59 **LO 8** The following client-prepared bank reconciliation is being examined by Kautz, CPA, during an examination of the financial statements of Concrete Products, Inc.

Concrete Products, Inc.
Bank Reconciliation
December 31, 2015

Balance per bank (a)		$18,375.91
Deposits in transit (b):		
December 30	1,471.10	
December 31	2,840.69	4,311.79
Outstanding checks (c):		
837	6,000.00	
1941	671.80	
1966	320.00	
1984	1,855.42	
1985	3,621.22	
1986	2,576.89	
1991	4,420.88	(19,466.21)
Subtotal		3,221.49
NSF check returned Dec. 29 (d)		200.00
Bank charges		5.50
Error check no. 1932		148.10
Customer note collected by the bank		
($2,750 plus $275 interest) (e)		(3,025.00)
Balance per books (f)		$ 550.09

Identify one or more substantive audit procedures that should be performed by Kautz in gathering evidence in support of each of the items (a) through (f) in this bank reconciliation.

10-60 **LO 8** Eagle River Plastics Company has a major branch located in Phoenix. The branch deposits cash receipts daily and periodically transfers the receipts to the company's home office in Eagle River. The transfers are accounted for as intercompany entries into the home office and branch office accounts. All accounting, however, is performed at the home office under the direction of the assistant controller. The assistant controller is also responsible for the transfers. The controller, however, independently reconciles the bank account each month or assigns the reconciliation to someone in the department (in some cases, could be the assistant controller). The company is relatively small; therefore, the controller is also the financial planner and treasurer for the company. As part of the year-end audit, you are assigned the task of conducting an audit of bank transfers. As part of the process, you prepare the following schedule of transfers.

Information per Client's Records			Information per Bank Statements	
			Date Cleared	
Date per Branch	Date per Amount	Date Deposited Home Office	Per Home Bank	Per Branch Bank
12/27	$23,000	12/31	12/31	1/3
12/29	$40,000	12/31	12/31	1/7
12/31	$45,000	1/2	1/3	1/8
1/2	$14,000	12/31	12/31	1/5
1/5	$28,000	1/3	1/7	1/12
1/3	$10,000	1/3	12/31	1/5

a. Identify the substantive audit procedures that would be used to test the correctness of the client's interbank transfers.

b. Identify any adjusting journal entries that would be needed on either the home or branch office accounting records as a result of the preceding transactions.

PROFESSIONAL SKEPTICISM

10-61 **LO 8** The following are deficiencies in internal controls over cash. For each deficiency indicate what substantive audit procedure(s) should be performed to determine whether any material misstatements have occurred. Consider each deficiency independently of the others. While each deficiency poses potential problems, identify two that would heighten your professional skepticism the most and explain your rationale.

a. The person who opens the mail prepares the deposit when the cashier is not available.

b. If a customer does not submit a remittance advice with a payment, the mail clerk sometimes does not prepare one for the accounts receivable department.

c. Occasionally, the treasurer's department does not cancel the supporting documents for cash disbursements.

d. Customer correspondence concerning monthly statements is handled by the person who makes the bank deposits.

e. Bank reconciliations are not prepared on a timely basis. When prepared, they are prepared by the person who handles incoming mail.

10-62 **LO 8, 10** One of the procedures that you have been assigned to perform on the audit of Reengage Corporation is sending bank confirmations. Your audit firm has a policy of sending confirmations to all financial institutions where a banking relationship exists, although the policy acknowledges that various instances may not require sending confirmations (e.g., accounts with no activity for the period under audit, petty cash accounts at branch locations). You note several accounts in which the cash balances are relatively small. You believe that sending confirmations to the financial institutions where Reengage Corporation has an account with a small balance will not be necessary.

a. What type of evidence is obtained through bank confirmations?

b. Use the framework for professional decision making from *Chapter 4* to determine the appropriate steps to take in deciding on to which financial institutions a confirmation should be sent. Recall that the framework is as follows:

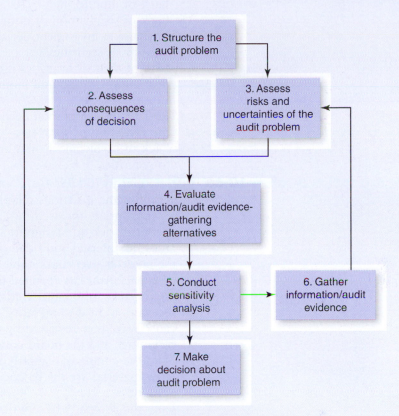

Source: Adapted from *Judgment and Choice*, by Robin Hogarth.

10-63 **LO 9** What are the three major categories of marketable securities? What is the GAAP classification for such securities? What judgmental challenges do auditors face in auditing marketable securities?

10-64 **LO 9** Match the following assertions related to marketable securities with their associated description: (a) existence/occurrence, (b) completeness, (c) rights and obligations, (d) valuation or allocation, (e) presentation and disclosure.

1. The marketable securities balances include all securities transactions that have taken place during the period.
2. The company has title to marketable securities accounts as of the balance sheet date.
3. The recorded balances reflect the true underlying economic value of those assets.
4. Marketable securities are properly classified on the balance sheet and disclosed in the notes to the financial statements.
5. Marketable securities exist at the balance sheet date.

FRAUD

10-65 **LO 9** The following are risks relating to marketable securities. Categorize each risk as relating to either (a) inherent or fraud risk or (b) control risk.

1. Management manipulation of the classification of securities to achieve preferable valuation treatment, for example, market value versus amortized cost.

2. Lack of policies over valuation or classification of securities.
3. Management manipulation of the valuation of market value if the securities are thinly traded.
4. Lack of policies over purchase or sale of securities.
5. Lack of monitoring of changes in securities balances.
6. Lack of segregation of duties between individuals responsible for making investment decisions and those responsible for the custody of securities.
7. Risk of theft of securities if they are not physically controlled, or if authorization and monitoring over their purchase or sale is not adequate.
8. Risk of sudden market declines, which would adversely affect the valuation of securities.
9. Lack of involvement or oversight by internal audit in relation to securities.

10-66 **LO 9** Refer to *Exhibit 10.12* and *Exhibit 10.13*. Categorize each of the following questions relating to marketable securities as being appropriate for use in (a) an inherent risk questionnaire or (b) a control risk questionnaire.
1. Does the internal audit department conduct regular audits of the controls over marketable securities?
2. If management has changed the classification of securities during the year from either trading securities or available-for-sale securities to held-to-maturity securities, are the amounts significant? Were they reviewed by the audit committee? Do the audit committee and the board concur with the change?
3. Does the company regularly invest in marketable securities? How material are the balances in marketable securities accounts?
4. Does the company have written policies and guidelines regarding investments in marketable securities? Are the policies approved by the board of directors? What process is used to authorize investments in marketable securities?
5. Does the company have a clear policy as to properly classifying marketable securities as trading securities, available-for-sale securities, or held-to-maturity securities? Is there evidence that the company follows the policy?
6. Has management changed the classification of securities during the year from either trading securities or available-for-sale securities to held-to-maturity securities? If yes, what is the reason for the change?
7. If a liquid market does not exist for marketable securities, how does management estimate the value of the securities that need to be marked to current market value?
8. Does the company provide for effective segregation of duties among individuals responsible for making investment decisions and those responsible for the custody of securities?
9. Is there a ready market for the securities?

10-67 **LO 9** How would the following factors affect the auditor's assessment of control risk for marketable securities? Assume that the company's investment in marketable securities is material to the financial statements.
a. The board of directors is not actively involved in monitoring the company's policies regarding marketable securities.
b. The company has an internal audit department, but it does not have any computer audit expertise and has not conducted

audits of the cash or marketable securities account during the past three years.

c. Management does not have written guidelines for investments in marketable securities. The CFO has been successful in procuring good returns on investments in the past, and management does not want to tamper with success.

10-68 **LO 9** A client prepared the following worksheet listing all activities in the marketable securities accounts for the year under audit. For the purpose of this question, assume that no unusual securities exist. Assume also that control risk was assessed as moderate to high and that the auditor decides to concentrate on substantive tests of details for the account balance. The account balances at the beginning and end of the year per the company's trial balance are as follows:

	Beginning Balance	Ending Balance
Investment in marketable securities	$400,000	$675,000
Allowance to reduce securities to market	$ 35,000	$ 35,000
Balance per general ledger	$365,000	$640,000
Interest income		$ 25,000
Dividend income		$ 18,000
Net gain on the disposal of securities		$ 32,000

Identify the audit procedures needed to complete the audit of marketable securities for year end. You may assume that the client was audited by the same firm last year. Be sure to cover the steps the auditor would use to determine that the securities are properly classified.

FRAUD **10-69** **LO 9** Justin Company, a medium-sized manufacturing client located in the southwest, produces supplies for the automobile industry. The company is publicly traded on the American Stock Exchange. Joann Sielig took over as chief executive officer (CEO) three years ago after a successful career with a New York–based investment banking firm. The company had been earning minimal returns, and Sielig is intent on turning the company around. She has analyzed the situation and determined that the company's main manufacturing arm could be treated as a cash cow. In other words, although the operations do not generate a lot of profit, they do generate cash flow that could be used for investment purposes.

Sielig has decided that the best opportunities for superior returns are in investments in high-risk marketable securities. When questioned on this strategy during a board meeting, she cited finance literature, which she asserted, shows that greater returns are consistent only with greater risk. However, the risk can be minimized by appropriately diversifying the investment portfolio. Given Sielig's knowledge of the subject and quick grasp of the company's situation, the board gave her complete control over all aspects of management. She personally manages the investment portfolio. Moreover, the board was so impressed with her analysis that she was given an incentive pay contract with an annual bonus based on a percentage of profits in excess of the previous year's profits. In addition, she received stock options.

The company has an internal audit department that reports directly to the CEO (Sielig). Although there is an audit committee, it exists more in form than substance and meets with the director of internal audit only occasionally. The internal audit program for the year is determined by the director of internal audit in conjunction with Sielig and is strongly influenced by two factors: (1) Sielig's perception of areas needing review and (2) areas of potential cost savings.

Sielig has let it be known that all units of the company must justify their existence, and if the internal audit department expected future budget increases, it must generate recommended cost savings in excess of the current internal audit budget.

Your firm audits Justin Company. During the risk assessment procedures for the audit, you note the following:

1. The investment account has grown from approximately 7% of total assets to approximately 30% of total assets.
2. The investment portfolio includes some long-term investments in company stocks; however, many of the stocks held in the portfolio are high-risk stocks (with hopes of greater returns).
3. The remainder of the investment portfolio consists of a wide variety of complex financial instruments, including derivative securities.
4. Broker fees have increased dramatically. There is also a new line item for investment consulting fees. It appears that most of these fees are owed to a company that might be somehow related to Sielig.
5. Most of the securities are held by the brokerage firm, but a few are held by the investment consulting company, and a few others are held directly by the company.
6. The company has shown a 25% increase in reported net income during the past year.
7. The company's stock value has appreciated more than 20% during the past year.
   a. Identify the elements of inherent risk (including fraud risk) and control risk in the preceding scenario that should be considered in planning the audit, and indicate potential audit implications.
   b. Outline an audit program that could be used for auditing the marketable securities account.
   c. Given only the information presented in the scenario, identify the specific factors the auditor would evaluate in formulating an opinion on the required public reporting of internal control over financial reporting.

FRAUD FOCUS: CONTEMPORARY AND HISTORICAL CASES

FRAUD

ETHICS

PROFESSIONAL SKEPTICISM

10-70 **PEREGRINE FINANCIAL GROUP (PFG), INC. AND RUSSELL WASENDORF SR.**
(LO 2,3,4,8,10)

Refer to the *Professional Judgment in Context* feature at the beginning of the chapter. Additional details on PFG and Wasendorf are presented below. On July 14, 2012, Russell Wasendorf Sr. attempted to commit suicide inside his vehicle in the parking lot of Peregrine Financial Group, Inc.'s (PFG) corporate offices, leaving a remarkable suicide note in his vehicle detailing a fraud scheme in which he embezzled over $200 million from PFG's brokerage clients over a twenty-year period. Wasendorf led a very interesting and affluent lifestyle and ran the business in some unusual ways. Examples include the following:

- In addition to owning PFG, he also owned an Italian restaurant My Verona in Cedar Rapids, Iowa, along with publishing companies (SFO Magazine and W&A Publishing/Trader's Press) and a real estate operation in Bucharest, Romania.
- He married his fiancée, who works at My Verona, in the Bellagio Hotel in Las Vegas on June 30, 2012.
- His son, Russell Wasendorf Jr. ran the operations of PFG and was the president and chief operating officer of the company, but did not have detailed access to important financial records of the company. Instead, Russell Wasendorf Sr. had sole control of the company's bank accounts.
- He flew his private jet to Chicago often for business, but was also known to take the jet all around the world to attend Lady Gaga concerts.
- He recently pledged a $2 million donation to the Athletic Department at the University of Northern Iowa.
- He attempted, but failed, to commit suicide by hooking up a tube to his car's tailpipe when suspicions of the fraud were revealed. An empty bottle of vodka was found next to his body. He was subsequently hospitalized at the University of Iowa Hospitals and Clinics in Iowa City, and was removed from his hospital bed by FBI agents while simultaneously speaking to his Chicago-based lawyer, Thomas Breen. Later that day, he appeared in federal court related to charges of lying to federal regulators and was considered a flight risk.

Here are quotes from Wasendorf's suicide note:

I have committed fraud. For this I feel constant and intense guilt. I am remorseful that my greatest transgressions have been to my fellow man. Through a scheme of using false bank statements I have been able to embezzle millions of dollars from customer accounts at Peregrine Financial Group, Inc. The forgeries started nearly twenty years ago and have gone undetected until now. I was able to conceal my crime of forgery by being the sole individual with access to the US Bank accounts held by PFG. No one else in the company ever saw an actual US Bank statement. The Bank statements were always delivered directly to me when they arrived in the mail. I made counterfeit statements within a few hours of receiving the actual statements and gave the forgeries to the accounting department.

I had no access to additional capital and I was forced into a difficult decision: Should I go out of business or cheat? I guess my ego was too big to admit failure. So I cheated, I falsified the very core of the financial documents of PFG, the Bank Statements. At first I had to make forgeries of both the Firstar Bank Statements and the Harris Bank Statements. When I chose to close the Harris Account I only had to falsify the Firstar statements. [Note: Firstar eventually became U.S. Bank.] I also made forgeries of official letters and correspondence from the bank, as well as transaction confirmation statements.

Using a combination of PhotoShop, Excel, scanners, and both laser and ink jet printers I was able to make very convincing forgeries of nearly every document that came from the Bank. I could create forgeries very quickly so no one suspected that my forgeries were not the real thing that had just arrived in the mail.

With careful concealment and blunt authority I was able to hide my fraud from others at PFG. PFG grew out of a one man shop, a business I started in the basement of my home. As I added people to the company everyone knew I was the guy in charge. If anyone questioned my authority I would simply point out that I was the sole shareholder. I established rules and procedures as each new situation arose. I ordered that US Bank statements were to be delivered directly to me unopened, to make sure no one was able to examine an actual US Bank Statement. I was also the only person with online access to PFG's account using US Bank's online portal. On US Bank side, I told representatives at the Bank that I was the only person they should interface with at PFG.

When it became common practice for Certified Auditors and the Field Auditors of the Regulators to mail Balance Confirmation Forms to Banks and other entities holding customer funds I opened a post office box. The box was originally in the name of Firstar Bank but was eventually changed to US Bank. I put the address "PO Box 706, Cedar Falls, IA 50613–0030" on the counterfeit Bank Statements. When the auditors mailed the Confirmation Forms to the Bank's false address, I would intercept the Form, type in the amount I needed to show, forge a Bank Officer's signature and mail it back to the Regulator or Certified Auditor. When online Banking became prevalent I learned how to falsify online Bank Statements and the Regulators accepted them without question.

At about the same time that emergency officials responded to the 911 call in the parking lot of PFG's offices, Russell Wasendorf Jr. arrived at his office inside the building and found an exact copy of the suicide note. Immediately thereafter, he contacted U.S. Bank and obtained a bank statement with an ending balance as of December 31, 2011, equaling $6,337,628.14. The ending balance reported by his father on the falsified bank statement was $221,770,946.18.

PFG is a futures trading firm. Futures trading firms match buyers and sellers of contracts for commodities like wheat, oil, and aluminum and charge a commission for the service. Companies use futures contracts to protect themselves from price fluctuations. PFG is a privately held entity, so it is not subject to oversight by the SEC or PCAOB. Instead, the U.S. Commodities Futures Trading Commission (CFTC) is the regulatory agency responsible for the oversight of the industry, and the NFA is the industry association that operates under the supervision of the CFTC. The NFA is responsible for monitoring and auditing PFG for compliance with financial reporting requirements of the domestic exchanges, of which PFG was a member. The NFA never required electronic verification of PFG's bank statements.

In 2004, a PFG client complained to the NFA that PFG was misusing customer funds. In 2009, an anonymous complaint was filed with the NFA asking for a review of PFG's bank account information. What, if anything, the NFA did about the complaint was not known. Interestingly, Wasendorf, Sr., serves on an advisory committee of the NFA. Veraja-Snelling Co. is PFG's audit firm. The firm is operated out of a home in Glendale Heights, Illinois. Jeannie Veraja-Snelling is the sole practitioner and has never performed any public company audits, even though she did register her audit firm with the PCAOB in 2010. On the December 31, 2010, financial statements, Veraja-Snelling certified that

PFG was in compliance with federal commodities regulations governing the segregation of customer money.

What likely prompted the timing of Wasendorf's attempted suicide was the fact that the NFA had just implemented a change to its online system whereby bank statement information would be directed electronically from the banks directly to the NFA (the system can be viewed at *www.confirmation.com*). The NFA started receiving confirmations through that system one day before Wasendorf's attempted suicide.

PFG filed for bankruptcy almost immediately after Wasendorf's attempted suicide and subsequent arrest. In addition, all the other businesses that Wasendorf ran immediately ceased operations, firing all employees. These businesses began the process of immediate liquidation. All customer accounts at PFG have been frozen, so investors have no access to their assets. Because PFG is a futures trading firm, not a traditional brokerage firm, investors do not have access to the protections normally provided by the Securities Investor Protection Corporation, which returns assets held in accounts of traditional brokerage firms that fail.

a. Describe any inherent, fraud, or control risks that are evident from the facts in the case.

b. Comment on your perceptions of the quality of the NFA's oversight of PFG.

c. Do you think it is ethically problematic that Wasendorf served on an advisory committee of the NFA? Why might NFA have wanted Wasendorf to serve on its advisory committee? What conflict might that have caused?

d. Comment on your perceptions of the quality of Veraja-Snelling's certification of PFG's compliance status. Is a sole practitioner likely capable of sufficiently overseeing a large, complex entity like PFG? Was it acceptable for Veraja-Snelling to accept a paper copy of the bank confirmation, which she would have believed came directly from U.S. Bank? Why might Veraja-Snelling have lacked professional skepticism for this engagement?

e. Having the CEO personally involved in receiving bank statements and in limiting the bank's access to other individuals within the company would be very unusual for a large company such as PFG. Further, U.S. Bank should have expected to receive an auditor's confirmation request annually, but did not because Wasendorf circumvented the process. Using the ethical decision making framework from *Chapter 4*, comment on whether you think that U.S. Bank is responsible in any way for this fraud. Explain. Recall that the steps are as follows: (1) identify the ethical issue, (2) determine the affected parties and identify their rights, (3) determine the most important rights for each affected party, (4) develop alternative courses of action, (5) determine the likely consequences of each proposed course of action on each affected party, (6) assess the possible consequences, and (7) decide on an appropriate course of action.

FRAUD

ETHICS

PROFESSIONAL SKEPTICISM

INTERNATIONAL

10-71

PCAOB, SEC, SATYAM COMPUTER SERVICES, AND RAMALINGA RAJU
(LO 1, 2, 3, 4, 7, 8, 10)

In the late 1990s, Satyam Computer Services (Satyam) was a relatively unknown, family-owned information technology (IT) company located in Hyderabad, India. All that changed when Satyam was awarded a contract to establish IT architecture at the World

Bank. The selection of Satyam was, at the time, quite surprising given Satyam's relative size and obscure reputation. But the company's business continued to thrive as demand grew for IT outsourcing from Indian companies like Satyam. At the height of its success, Satyam employed about 50,000 employees and operated in 67 countries around the world. As it turns out, the reason for selecting Satyam for the World Bank contract was that Mohamed Muhsin, the chief information officer for the World Bank, was financially involved in Satyam. After suspicions of this became known in 2006, Muhsin retired and was subsequently banned from any further relationship with the World Bank. According to World Bank officials, they alerted the U.S. Department of Justice that Satyam top management engaged in fraudulent and corrupt business practices.

In October 2008, the World Bank fired Satyam, accusing the company of installing spy systems on its computers and of stealing assets from the World Bank. Also during October 2008, a stock analyst questioned Satyam's large cash balances during an earnings conference call. The stock analyst's questions were largely ignored, and the company's stock price continued to rise. Satyam continued to report record profits despite the worldwide economic downturn. In December 2008, Satyam's board of directors approved the purchase of two companies owned by Raju's family, Maytas Properties and Maytas Infrastructure. Investors were outraged by the proposed transaction because of the relationship between Raju and the two companies. As a result of the outcry, the transaction was not finalized. However, the resulting bad press coverage caused analysts to put sell recommendations on Satyam's stock, sending share prices down 10% and resulting in four of five independent board members resigning.

Responding to the resulting pressure, on January 7, 2009, Raju made a shocking revelation admitting to a massive fraud, in a letter addressed to Satyam's remaining board members. Portions of the letter are reproduced here (*note that original typos are retained for accuracy*):

> It is with deep regret, and tremendous burden that I am carrying on my conscience, that I would like to bring the following facts to your notice:
>
> 1. The Balance Sheet carries as of September 30 2008
>   1. Inflated (non-existent) cash and bank balances of Rs. 5,040 crore (as against Rs. 5361 crore reflected in the books)
>   2. An accrued interest of Rs. 376 crore which is non-existent
>   3. An understated liability of Rs. 1,230 crore on account of funds arranged by me
>   4. An over stated debtors position of Rs. 490 crore (as against Rs. 2651 in the books)
> 2. For the September quarter (Q2) we reported a revenue of Rs. 2,700 crore and an operating margin of Rs. 649 crore (24% Of revenues) as against the actual revenues of Rs. 2,112 crore and an actual operating margin of Rs. 61 Crore (3% of revenues). This has resulted in artificial cash and bank balances going up by Rs. 588 crore in Q2 alone.
>
> This gap in the Balance Sheet has arisen on account of inflated profits over a period of last several years (limited only to Satyam

standalone, books of subsidiaries reflecting true performance). What started as a marginal gap between actual operating profit and the one reflected in the books of accounts continued to grow over the years. It has attained unmanageable proportions as the size of company operations grew significantly.... Every attempt made to eliminate the gap failed. As the promoters held a small percentage of equity, the concern was that poor performance would result in a take-over, thereby exposing the gap. It was like riding a tiger, not knowing how to get off without being eaten.

Under the circumstances, I am tendering my resignation as the chairman of Satyam and shall continue in this position only till such time the current board is expanded. My continuance is just to ensure enhancement of the board over the next several days or as early as possible. I am now prepared to subject myself to the laws of the land and face consequences thereof.

(B. Ramalinga Raju)

Copies marked to:

1. Chairman SEBI
2. Stock Exchanges

Ultimately, it was revealed that assets on Satyam's balance sheet were overstated by about $1.5 billion and that over $1 billion in bank loans and cash that the company claimed to own were nonexistent. The fictitious assets accounted for 50% of the company's total assets. To accomplish the fraud, Raju and other individuals in top management (including the CFO, the head of internal audit, and Raju's brother) took the following actions:

- Created fictitious bank statements to inflate cash
- Reported fictitious interest income from the fictitious bank accounts
- Created 6,000 fake salary accounts and stole the money after Satyam deposited it
- Created fictitious customer identities and generated fictitious invoices against their names to inflate revenue
- Forged board of director resolutions to obtain loans for Satyam

PricewaterhouseCoopers (PwC) was Satyam's auditor from 2000 to the time the fraud was revealed. PwC was criticized for failing to exercise professional skepticism regarding the $1.04 billion cash balance of non-interest-bearing deposits. Normally, companies would either invest that money in an interest-bearing account or disburse the money through dividends to shareholders. As such, the large amount of cash should have been a red flag to the auditors that verification of the account balances was necessary. It was later revealed that PwC did not independently confirm the cash accounts with the banks in which Satyam claimed to have accounts. Subsequent PCAOB and SEC investigations revealed that PwC allowed their audit clients to control the cash confirmation process and did not challenge management regarding the validity of confirmations. In fact, some banks sent PwC confirmations directly, and those confirmations contradicted the statements that management had provided. For example, one bank told PwC that the Satyam account had a balance of $11.2 million, but management reported a balance of $108.6 million. Another bank reported $330,172 in the Satyam account, but management reported a balance of $152.9 million. Further complicating matters, the PwC network firm partner reviewed the working papers for the 2008 audit one month before the audit report was issued. During the review, the partner noted the deficiencies in the confirmation process and advised the engagement team not to rely on confirmations that were not received directly from the banks. The engagement team ignored the review comment, taking no actions to address the confirmation process weaknesses. It is unclear whether the reviewing partner knew that the comments were left unaddressed, but in any case the partner should have followed up to make sure that the audit opinion was not issued until the confirmation process weaknesses were resolved.

Raju, his brother, the former managing director of the board, the head of internal audit, and the CFO were all arrested by Indian officials on charges of fraud. Indian officials also arrested two of the PwC auditors on charges of fraud. On April 5, 2011, the SEC settled a civil action with Satyam Computer Services, in which the company paid a penalty of $10 million (see Accounting and Auditing Enforcement Release No. 3258). On May 6, 2011, PwC and its Indian affiliates agreed to a $25.5 million settlement in a class action lawsuit. On October 12, 2011, the two PwC auditors were granted bail and left jail.

a. Aside from the shocking disclosure of the fraud and its magnitude, one of the most interesting comments in Raju's statement to the board of directors was "It was like riding a tiger, not knowing how to get off without being eaten." Speculate on why he may have stated that.

b. Describe why PwC's cash confirmation process was flawed. Comment on why PwC may have had an incentive to not exercise professional skepticism in this situation.

c. Which management assertion did Raju's fraud violate?

d. Based on the facts in this case, what internal controls over cash appear to have been missing or violated?

e. Consider the situation of the PwC network firm partner. That individual correctly reviewed the workpapers and suggested that the engagement team should not have relied on the cash confirmations from management. Using the ethical decision making framework from *Chapter 4*, determine what next steps the audit partner should have taken upon making the review suggestions. Recall that the steps are as follows: (1) identify the ethical issue; in this case the ethical issue is how to properly ensure that the review comments are taken seriously and addressed; (2) determine the affected parties and identify their rights; (3) determine the most important rights for each affected party; (4) develop alternative courses of action; (5) determine the likely consequences of each proposed course of action on each affected party; (6) assess the possible consequences; and (7) decide on an appropriate course of action.

FRAUD

PROFESSIONAL SKEPTICISM

INTERNATIONAL

10-72 **PARMALAT** (LO 8) As an example of difficulties that auditors experience in collecting confirmations of cash balances, consider the Parmalat fraud that was exposed in 2003. In that case, the company overstated cash by about $5 billion, which reflected a fictitious amount in a Bank of America account in the Cayman Islands. The Italian segment of the audit firm, Grant Thornton, received a cash confirmation that noted no exceptions to the confirmation the audit firm had sent. Parmalat accomplished the deception, in part, by providing the audit firm with a fictitious bank mailing address.

a. What role does the concept of materiality play in the substantive testing of cash balances?

b. How might the Internet and associated electronic confirmation processes help to avoid fraud associated with cash confirmations?

c. What are two or three key factors the auditor might consider that could have indicated that the cash account was a high-risk account for this client and would require more skeptical audit work?

APPLICATION ACTIVITIES

FRAUD

ETHICS

10-73   **LO 2, 3, 4**   Refer to the *Focus on Fraud* feature "Skimming and the Completeness Assertion." Using appropriate resources, find an example of a skimming fraud and be prepared to describe the fraud. Your description should include a discussion of who committed the fraud, how they committed the fraud (e.g., controls that were absent), and how much money was stolen (if disclosed or estimated).

FRAUD

ETHICS

10-74   **PFG AND WASENDORF (LO 3, 8)**   Read about the massive fraud committed by Russell Wasendorf Sr. at PFG that is described in *Problem 10-70.* Use appropriate resources to document the latest developments in the case against Wasendorf. Describe developments relating to Wasendorf Sr., Wasendorf Jr. and the auditor, Jeannie Veraja-Snelling. Be prepared to discuss your findings in class.

FRAUD

ETHICS

10-75   **PARMALAT (LO 8)**   Refer to the *Focus on Fraud* feature "The Parmalat Fraud and Its Many Victims." Use appropriate resources to answer the following questions.

a. Which two audit firms did Parmalat sue after the company's bankruptcy?

b. What was the amount that Parmalat sought to recover?

c. What was the ultimate resolution of the case?

NOTE: Completing Application Activities requires students to reference additional resources and materials. Some Application Activities will require the student to reference relevant professional auditing standards. We make special note of these as Auditing Standards Application Activities.

10-76   **LO 5**   Access the two most recent financial statements of two companies in the same industry. For example, you might look at Yahoo and Google or Coca-Cola and PepsiCo. Perform ratio analysis using relevant ratios for both companies, and compare the following between the two companies:

a. Analyze trends in the ending cash balance over time.

b. Compute trends in interest returns on investments.

c. Analyze cash balances, and changes therein, in relation to new or retiring debt obligations.

d. Compute the current ratio (current assets/current liabilities).

e. Compute the quick ratio (cash + cash equivalents + net receivables)/current liabilities.

f. Compare cash flow to sales (operating cash flow/sales) and profitability (operating cash flow/net income).

10-77   **LO 3**   Refer to the *Focus on Fraud* feature "Common Fraud Schemes Relating to Cash." Access appropriate resources and search for recent fraud schemes related to cash. Be prepared to discuss your findings in class.

10-78 **PCAOB**
(LO 8) Refer to the *Auditing in Practice* feature "Confirmations with Financial Institutions." Access the PCAOB web site and determine the status of the PCAOB's project on confirmations.

10-79 **IAASB**
(LO 8) Refer to the *Standards Appendix* at the end of this book. Determine the relevant International Standard on Auditing (ISA) for external confirmations, then locate the actual standard on the IAASB's web site, and answer the following questions.
a. What is the number of the standard?
b. Define the following key terms that are noted in the standard: (1) exception, (2) external confirmation, (3) negative confirmation request, (4) nonresponse, and (5) positive confirmation request.
c. What does the standard advise the auditor to do if management refuses to allow the auditor to perform external confirmation procedures?
d. What does the standard advise the auditor to do if the auditor identifies factors that give rise to doubts about the reliability of the response to a confirmation request? What factors would cause such doubt?
e. What does the standard advise the auditor to do if a confirmation request is not reliable?
f. What factors does the standard urge auditors to consider when designing confirmation requests?

10-80 **LO 9** Refer to the *Focus on Fraud* feature "Common Fraud Schemes Relating to Investments." Access appropriate resources and search for recent fraud schemes related to investments. Be prepared to discuss your findings in class.

ACADEMIC RESEARCH CASE

NOTE: Completing Academic Research Cases requires students to reference additional resources and materials.

10-81 **LO 1, 2, 3, 4** Locate and read the article listed below and answer the following questions.

Lee, L. F. 2012. Incentives to inflate reported cash from operations using classification and timing. *The Accounting Review* 87 (1): 1–33.
a. What is the issue being addressed in the paper?
b. What are the findings of the paper?
c. Why is this paper important to auditors, and what are the implications of this paper for the auditing profession?
d. Describe the research methodology used as a basis for the conclusions.
e. Describe any limitations of the research.

SEARCH HINT

It is easy to locate these academic research articles! Simply use a search engine such as Google Scholar or an electronic research platform such as ABI Inform, and search using the author names and part of the article title.

FORD AND TOYOTA

10-82	**FORD MOTOR COMPANY AND TOYOTA MOTOR CORPORATION** (LO **1, 2, 3, 4, 8, 9**)

Source and Reference	Question
Ford 10-K	a. What are the key cash and liquid asset accounts for Ford? What types of marketable securities does Ford possess? b. What are the critical accounting policies for these accounts? c. What risks do these securities pose for Ford? What are the audit implications of those risk disclosures?
Ford 10-K, Toyota 20-F	d. Review the statement of cash flows and management discussion and analysis related to liquidity for Ford. What are the significant trends that you note? e. Review the statement of cash flows for Toyota. How do the trends differ between Ford and Toyota? f. What are the audit implications of the different trends at Ford and Toyota?

11 Auditing Inventory, Goods and Services, and Accounts Payable: The Acquisition and Payment Cycle

CHAPTER OVERVIEW AND LEARNING OBJECTIVES

The acquisition and payment cycle includes processes for identifying products or services to be acquired, purchasing goods and services, receiving the goods and services, approving payments, and paying for goods and services received. In terms of the audit opinion formulation process, this chapter primarily involves Phases II, III, and IV, that is, performing risk assessment procedures, tests of controls, and substantive procedures for the acquisition and payment cycle.

Through studying this chapter, you will be able to achieve these learning objectives:

1. Identify the significant accounts, disclosures, and relevant assertions in the acquisition and payment cycle.

2. Identify and assess inherent risks of material misstatement in the acquisition and payment cycle.

3. Identify and assess fraud risks of material misstatement in the acquisition and payment cycle.

4. Identify and assess control risks of material misstatement in the acquisition and payment cycle.

5. Describe how to use planning analytical procedures to identify possible material misstatements in acquisition and payment cycle accounts, disclosures, and assertions.

6. Determine appropriate responses to identified risks of material misstatement for acquisition and payment cycle accounts, disclosures, and assertions.

7. Determine appropriate tests of controls and consider the results of tests of controls for acquisition and payment cycle accounts, disclosures, and assertions.

8. Determine and apply sufficient appropriate substantive audit procedures for testing acquisition and payment cycle accounts, disclosures, and assertions.

9. Apply the frameworks for professional decision making and ethical decision making to issues involving conducting the audit of acquisition and payment cycle accounts, disclosures, and assertions.

THE AUDIT OPINION FORMULATION PROCESS

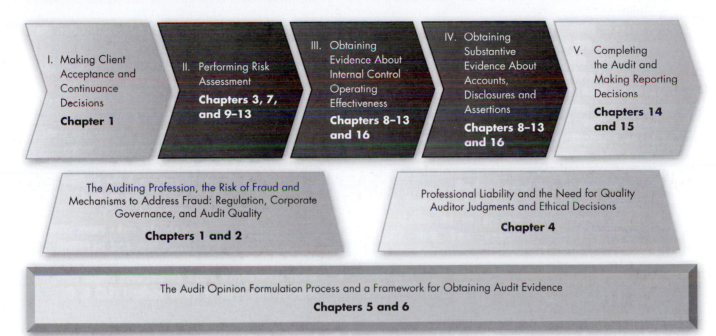

I. Making Client Acceptance and Continuance Decisions

Chapter 1

II. Performing Risk Assessment

Chapters 3, 7, and 9–13

III. Obtaining Evidence About Internal Control Operating Effectiveness

Chapters 8–13 and 16

IV. Obtaining Substantive Evidence About Accounts, Disclosures and Assertions

Chapters 8–13 and 16

V. Completing the Audit and Making Reporting Decisions

Chapters 14 and 15

The Auditing Profession, the Risk of Fraud and Mechanisms to Address Fraud: Regulation, Corporate Governance, and Audit Quality

Chapters 1 and 2

Professional Liability and the Need for Quality Auditor Judgments and Ethical Decisions

Chapter 4

The Audit Opinion Formulation Process and a Framework for Obtaining Audit Evidence

Chapters 5 and 6

PROFESSIONAL JUDGMENT IN CONTEXT

Thor Industries, Inc. and Mark Schwartzhoff: Fraudulent Reductions in Cost of Goods Sold Through Manipulation of Inventory Accounts

On May 13, 2011, the Securities and Exchange Commission (SEC) filed settled enforcement actions against Thor Industries, Inc. and Mark Schwartzhoff, the former vice president of finance at Thor's Dutchmen Manufacturing subsidiary. Thor produces and sells recreational vehicles, and Dutchmen is one of Thor's 15 subsidiaries. During the period of the fraud, Schwartzhoff served as an internal auditor, controller, and ultimately vice president of finance, which was Dutchmen's most senior financial officer position.

From 2002 to January 2007, Schwartzhoff engaged in a fraudulent accounting scheme to understate Dutchmen's cost of goods sold in order to avoid recognizing rising inventory costs during the period. Schwartzhoff had access to all of Dutchmen's accounting systems and could make manual journal entries without authorization or meaningful review by anyone at either Dutchmen or Thor headquarters. Schwartzhoff perpetrated the fraud by making fictitious journal entries, understating the cost of inventory purchases, thereby achieving lower cost of

goods sold and higher net income. Schwartzhoff credited inventory purchases accounts and made offsetting debits to increase other assets or decrease liabilities. To hide the fraud, Schwartzhoff created fictitious documentation and reconciliations and submitted them to Thor's external auditor. He falsified inventory records to make it appear that ending inventory had increased when, in fact, it had not. Schwartzhoff also concealed the fraud by delaying the recruiting and hiring of the controller position at Dutchmen, and he assigned the duties of his subordinates so that he would retain the ability to continue perpetrating the fraud without detection. Thor headquarters did not supervise Schwartzhoff and did not conduct internal audits of Dutchmen.

The magnitude of the fraud grew from less than $1 million in 2003 to $14 million by 2006. Throughout the period of the fraud, pre-tax income was overstated by about $27 million. Despite this manipulation, Thor's auditor, Deloitte, issued unqualified audit opinions and agreed with management's assessment that internal controls were effective. Schwartzhoff perpetrated the fraud because it resulted in increased bonuses from his incentive compensation plan. His bonus was calculated as a percentage of pre-tax income, so by understating cost of goods sold he was able to show higher income, and thereby earn a larger bonus. Ultimately, he earned about $300,000 in excess, fraudulently derived, bonus compensation. Once the fraud was uncovered, Thor fired Schwartzhoff and had to restate its financial statements from 2004 to 2007. Following the discovery of the fraud, Thor also reported a material weakness in its internal controls relating to the conduct of Schwartzhoff.

Thor was fined $1 million. Schwartzhoff was permanently barred from serving as an officer or director of a public company and was fined $394,830 by the SEC. He was also convicted of one count of wire fraud and had to pay restitution to the U.S. Attorney's Office for the Northern District of Indiana for $1.9 million.

For further details on this case, see SEC Litigation Release No. 21966 (May 13, 2011).

As you read through this chapter, consider the following questions:

- What types of accounts are included in the audit of the acquisition and payment cycle? (LO 1)
- What are the inherent, fraud, and control risks that exist in this cycle? (LO 2, 3, 4)
- The Thor and Schwartzhoff case illustrates control deficiencies that enabled the fraud to go undetected. What do these types of control deficiencies imply about the approach the auditor will need to use to audit the inventory-related accounts and assertions? (LO 4, 6, 7)
- What controls can mitigate the risks associated with accounts in the acquisition and payment cycle? (LO 4)
- What substantive audit procedures could have detected this type of fraud earlier? (LO 6, 8)

Significant Accounts, Disclosures, and Relevant Assertions

LO 1 Identify the significant accounts, disclosures, and relevant assertions in the acquisition and payment cycle.

The significant accounts in the acquisition and payment cycle are inventory, cost of goods sold, accounts payable, and other related expense accounts. *Exhibit 11.1* contains an overview of the significant accounts typically included in this cycle.

Accounting for inventories is a major consideration for many companies because of its significance to both the balance sheet and the income statement. **Inventories** are items of tangible property that are held for sale in the ordinary course of business, that are in the process of production for such sale, or that are to be currently consumed in the production of goods or services to be available for sale. For example, inventory includes such items as steel held for future production of an automobile, electronic goods in a retail store, drugs on shelves in a hospital or in a pharmaceutical company, and petroleum products at an oil-refining company. While the focus of this chapter concerns the purchase of inventory, organizations also

EXHIBIT 11.1 Significant Accounts in Acquisition and Payment Cycle

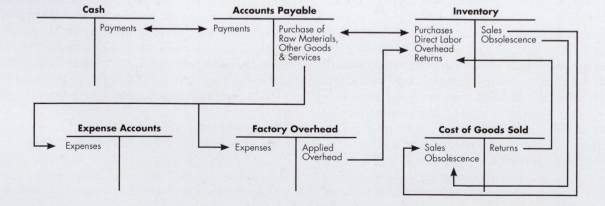

purchase a variety of services (e.g., consulting and legal) and other goods (e.g., supplies). The purchases of inventory, services, and other goods differ somewhat from those of long-term assets, such as equipment and buildings. We discuss the purchases of these long-term assets in the next chapter.

Activities Involved in the Acquisition and Payment Cycle

The acquisition and payment cycle consists of five distinct activities.

1. Requisition (request) for goods or services
2. Purchase of goods and services
3. Receipt of, and accounting for, goods and services
4. Approval of items for payment
5. Cash disbursements

The acquisition process begins with a **requisition** (formal request) for goods and services. An approved requisition will result in a purchase. The receipt of goods or services should cause the recognition of accounts payable with debits to an expense account (e.g., legal expense) or an inventory account. Most companies will have specific procedures for approving the payments for these purchases. When the approved payment for goods or services received is made, the payment is reflected as a cash disbursement. As described in the *Emerging Issues* feature "Purchasing Cards as an Alternative to the Traditional Purchasing Process" some organizations use a purchasing card (P-card) that allows for purchases to be made without using the traditional purchasing process.

For many companies, the acquisition and payment cycle is a computerized process that is integrated with **supply chain management**. Supply chain management is the management and control of materials in the logistics process from the acquisition of raw materials to the delivery of finished products to the end user (customer). A number of companies have specific contracts with vendors that specify price and delivery terms to meet the client's production or sales needs. Companies such as Wal-Mart and JCPenney have arrangements with some vendors whereby title to the goods does not pass until a consumer purchases them at the checkout counter.

Purchasing Cards as an Alternative to the Traditional Purchasing Process

EMERGING ISSUE

The traditional purchasing process can be labor intensive, costly, and lengthy. The average administrative cost for a purchase order is over $90, while the average time to complete a purchase transaction is over thirty days. The purchasing card (P-card) is a form of company charge card that is an alternative to the traditional purchasing process. Organizations issue P-cards to employees so that the employees can easily purchase low-dollar goods and services, thereby eliminating the need for various activities in the traditional purchasing process, including purchase requisitions, purchase orders, and vendor invoices. Organizations using P-cards should implement a variety of controls, including dollar limits, merchant category code restrictions, and periodic reviews of P-card activity; employees receiving P-cards are expected to follow the organization's policies and procedures.

While P-cards provide benefits to organizations, their use is not without risks. The primary risk is intentional unauthorized use by employees, which would be considered fraud. As an example, Georgia Tech issued a report about inappropriate use of P-cards by its employees, including employees using the P-Cards to buy a jet ski, football tickets, a diamond ring, and wedding catering.

If significant purchasing activities occur through the use of P-Cards, auditors of these organizations should understand the organization's risks and controls related to P-Cards.

Many companies using such approaches have been successful in reducing inventory levels and associated carrying costs.

Organizations commonly have an **automated purchasing system**—a networked software system linking to vendors whose offerings and prices have been preapproved by supply-chain management personnel. The technology enables purchasers to negotiate favorable prices with vendors while streamlining the buying process. Best practice for an automated system consolidates all the different functions or activities involved, assuring timely and accurate orders. An automated purchasing system will perform the following beneficial tasks:

- Apply preloaded specifications and materials lists to the system to start the process
- Automatically flag invoices that do not reconcile with purchase orders
- Create change orders and analyze variances from purchase orders

Relevant Financial Statement Assertions

Assertions Relevant to Inventory

The five management assertions relevant to inventory are:

1. *Existence/occurrence*—Inventory balances exist at the balance sheet date.
2. *Completeness*—Inventory balances include all inventory transactions that have taken place during the period.
3. *Rights and obligations*—The organization has title to the inventory as of the balance sheet date.
4. *Valuation or allocation*—The recorded balances reflect the true underlying economic value of those assets.
5. *Presentation and disclosure*—Inventory is properly classified on the balance sheet and disclosed in the notes to the financial statements.

The existence and valuation assertions are usually the most relevant for inventory. Existence is a concern because, as the Thor Industries, Inc. and Schwartzhoff example from the *Professional Judgment in Context* feature illustrates, managers can manipulate the inventory account to manipulate cost of goods sold and net income. We do not separately discuss assertions for cost of goods sold. Recall that cost of goods sold is simply the result of the following calculation: *beginning inventory + purchases − ending inventory = cost of goods sold*. The most common concerns for inventory are that purchases are understated or ending inventory is overstated, which will result in both lower cost of goods sold and higher net income. Valuation is a concern because inventory may fluctuate in value, and there may be complexities in assessing an accurate value. Rights and obligations can also be a concern because the fact that a company has possession of inventory does not necessarily imply that the company actually owns it.

Assertions Relevant to Accounts Payable

The five management assertions relevant to accounts payable are:

1. *Existence/occurrence*—Accounts payable balances exist at the balance sheet date.
2. *Completeness*—Accounts payable balances include all accounts payable transactions that have taken place during the period.
3. *Rights and obligations*—The organization actually owes a liability for the accounts payable as of the balance sheet date.
4. *Valuation or allocation*—The recorded balances reflect the true underlying economic value of those liabilities.
5. *Presentation and disclosure*—Accounts payable is properly classified on the balance sheet and disclosed in the notes to the financial statements.

Completeness is usually the most relevant assertion for accounts payable. The primary concern regarding completeness is that the account is understated; managers may not record accounts payable transactions because they do not want to record the associated liability and expense.

Performing Risk Assessment Procedures in the Acquisition and Payment Cycle

LO 2 Identify and assess inherent risks of material misstatement in the acquisition and payment cycle.

As part of performing risk assessment procedures, the auditor obtains information that is useful in assessing the risk of material misstatement. This includes information about inherent risks at the financial statement level (e.g., the client's business and operational risks, financial reporting risks) and at the account and assertion levels, fraud risks including feedback from audit team brainstorming sessions, strengths and weaknesses in internal control, and results from planning analytical procedures. Once the auditor identifies risks of material misstatement, the auditor then determines how best to respond to them as part of the audit opinion formulation process.

Identifying Inherent Risks

Inventory is usually material, complex, and subject to manipulation. Given the large number of inventory-related frauds that have been perpetrated, auditors should exercise particularly high levels of professional skepticism in audits of inventory and cost of goods sold accounts. Inventory is a complex accounting and auditing area because of the following:

- A great variety (diversity) of items exists in inventory.
- Inventory accounts typically experience a high volume of activity.
- Inventory accounts may be valued according to various alternative accounting valuation methods.
- Identifying obsolete inventory and applying the lower of cost or market principle to determine valuation are difficult tasks.
- Inventory is easily transportable.
- Inventory often exists at multiple locations, with some locations being remote from the company's headquarters.
- Inventory may become obsolete because of technological advances even though there are no visible signs of wear.
- Inventory is often returned by customers, so care must be taken to separately identify returned merchandise, check it for quality, and record it at net realizable value.
- Because inventory often includes a variety of types of products, the auditor must possess and apply significant knowledge about the business in order to address obsolescence and valuation questions.
- Individuals involved with the purchase of inventory may have incentives to exploit weaknesses in the control system to their economic advantage.

Identifying Fraud Risk Factors

LO 3 Identify and assess fraud risks of material misstatement in the acquisition and payment cycle.

Because of the significant number of inherent risks noted previously, the acquisition and payment cycle is often the subject of fraud. Financial reporting frauds in this cycle often involve overstatement of inventory or assets and understatement of expenses. Asset misappropriation frauds in this cycle often involve fictitious purchases or kickbacks to supply-chain management personnel. Examples of fraud in the acquisition and payment cycle include:

- Theft of inventory by the employee
- **Inventory shrinkage**, which is a reduction in inventory presumed to be due to physical loss or theft

- Employee schemes involving fictitious vendors as means to transfer payments to themselves
- Employees recording fictitious inventory or inappropriately recording higher values for existing inventory by creating false records for items that do not exist (e.g., inflated inventory count sheets and bogus receiving reports or purchase orders)
- Large manual adjustments to inventory accounts
- Schemes to classify expenses as assets (e.g., inappropriately capitalizing items that are truly current-period expenses)
- Executives misusing travel and entertainment accounts and charging them as company expenses

Exhibit 11.2 identifies some of the possible fraudulent financial reporting methods used in manipulating inventory and cost of goods sold accounts.

The *Focus on Fraud* feature "Financial Reporting Fraud in the Acquisition and Payment Cycle at WorldCom and Phar-Mor" provides details on two well-known frauds in this area.

Identifying Control Risks

LO 4 Identify and assess control risks of material misstatement in the acquisition and payment cycle.

Once the auditor has obtained an understanding of the inherent and fraud risks of material misstatement in the acquisition and payment cycle accounts, the auditor needs to understand the controls that the client has designed and implemented to address those risks. Remember, the auditor is required to gain an understanding of internal controls for both integrated audits and financial statement only audits. Such understanding is normally gained by means of a walkthrough of the process, inquiry, observation, and review of the client's documentation. The auditor considers both entity-wide controls and transaction controls at the account and assertion levels. This understanding provides the auditor with a basis for making an initial control risk assessment.

Overview of Internal Controls for Accounts in the Acquisition and Payment Cycle

The auditor usually begins by developing an understanding of the cost components of inventory and by considering how current market prices affect inventory valuation. We focus on the inventories of a manufacturing client.

| EXHIBIT **11.2** | Methods to Accomplish Fraudulent Financial Reporting in Inventory and Cost of Goods Sold Accounts |

Event	Affected Accounts	Possible Manipulations
1. Purchase inventory	Inventory, accounts payable	Under-record purchases Record purchases in a later period Fail to record purchases
2. Return inventory to supplier	Accounts payable, inventory	Overstate returns Record returns in an earlier period
3. Inventory is sold	Cost of goods sold, inventory	Record at too low an amount Not record cost of goods sold nor reduce inventory
4. Inventory becomes obsolete	Loss on write-down of inventory, inventory	Not write off or write down obsolete inventory
5. Periodic count of inventory quantities	Inventory shrinkage, inventory	Overcount inventory (double counting, etc.)

Financial Reporting Fraud in the Acquisition and Payment Cycle at WorldCom and Phar-Mor

FOCUS on **FRAUD**

WorldCom

WorldCom management recorded billions of line rental expenses as fixed assets. In other words, managers inappropriately debited fixed assets rather than debiting expenses, thereby bolstering current-period income. Managers were motivated to engage in the fraud to meet earnings expectations and to show that they were able to manage their line expenses better than the rest of the industry. Because the expenses were consistent with previous years, their relatively low level did not raise auditor suspicion. In this case, the auditors should have been skeptical that WorldCom was able to achieve what other companies in its industry could not.

Phar-Mor

Phar-Mor, a major discount retailer, had over 300 stores in the 1990s with great operating results and a concept that captured the imagination of Wall Street. Typical of many frauds, the company was dominated by an officer who viewed the company as his own and diverted more than $10 million to support a now failed minor-league basketball league. To cover up this misuse of company money, the officers directed the managers of each store to inflate their inventory costs. For example, if a carton of Coca-Cola cost $1.99, they were to value it at $2.99. The overstatements were needed to balance the cash outflow to the creation of an asset. Company management was emboldened to commit the fraud because it knew that the auditor would not visit all 300 stores to test inventory valuation.

A well-conceived inventory control system should provide reasonable assurance of the following:

- All purchases are authorized.
- There exists a timely, accurate, and complete recording of inventory transactions.
- Receipt of inventory is properly accounted for and independently tested to verify quality in adherence to company standards.
- The cost accounting system is up-to-date; costs are properly identified and assigned to products; and variances are analyzed, investigated, and properly allocated to inventory and cost of goods sold.

Specific internal controls in this cycle typically include:

- A **periodic inventory system** may serve as a basis for management reports and to assist in managing inventory. A periodic inventory system is a system of inventory recordkeeping in which no continuous record of changes in inventory (receipts and issues of inventory items) is kept. At the end of an accounting period, the ending inventory is determined by an actual physical count of every item, and its cost is computed using a suitable method.
- A **perpetual inventory system** may serve as a basis for management reports and to assist in managing inventory. A perpetual inventory system is a system of inventory recordkeeping where book inventory is continuously in agreement with inventory on hand within specified time periods. In some cases, book inventory and inventory on hand may be reconciled with each transaction; in other systems, these two numbers may be reconciled less often. This process is useful in keeping track of actual availability of goods and determining the correct time to reorder from suppliers.

- **Cycle counts** are taken as part of the perpetual inventory system. Cycle counts involve periodic testing of the accuracy of the perpetual inventory record by counting all inventories on a cyclical, or periodic, basis.
- All products are systematically reviewed for obsolescence, and appropriate accounting action is taken.
- Management periodically reviews inventory, takes action on excessive inventory, and manages inventory to minimize losses caused by technological obsolescence.
- New products are introduced only after market studies and quality-control tests are made.
- Long-term contracts are closely monitored. Excess purchase requirements are monitored, and potential losses are recognized.

The specific controls implemented by the client will vary with the amount of automation of the process. The following discussion highlights typical controls for each of the five activities of the acquisition and payment cycle.

1. Requisition (Request) for Goods and Services

The acquisition process for inventory begins with the company's production or sales plan. Some companies will have long-term production plans. For example, in the automotive industry a manufacturer might schedule production for a month in advance and notify its suppliers of the production plan. The auditor must thoroughly understand the company's relationships with its suppliers and should examine major contracts that specify delivery, quantity, timing, and quality conditions. The traditional acquisition process begins with recognizing the need for the purchase—either by an individual or by an automated process that monitors inventory or production.

Embedded in the requisition process are a number of controls to help make sure that all purchases are properly approved. Normally, a requisition form is forwarded to the purchasing department by a supervisor, although some departments may have authority for individual purchases up to a specific dollar limit. Computer-generated purchase orders are often reviewed by the purchasing department, but in some automated systems the purchase order may be electronically communicated to the vendor with no additional review. Important controls in requisition include a production plan and authorization of a requisition form that is sent to an approved vendor by a purchasing agent or that is sent through the computer system according to preexisting contracts.

Organizations also purchase supplies, which will go through a similar process as inventory requisitions. Purchases of services, such as legal or consulting services, will be accomplished through ongoing contractual arrangements with the law firm or consulting firm.

Exhibit 11.3 contains an overview of controls over the requisition process at different types of organizations and for different types of purchases.

Many companies partner with major suppliers to improve their supply-chain management process. For example, General Motors partnered with Eaton Corporation to furnish already-assembled subassemblies that are loaded directly into the production line. This kind of relationship requires close coordination and may never involve a requisition form. It may involve only the development of a long-term contract and the sharing of production schedules with the supplier. Goods are delivered and moved directly into production. There is no formal receiving department, and Eaton Corporation is paid upon the production of an automobile. Since the requisition process is automated, the company will likely implement automated controls in this process.

EXHIBIT **11.3**	Overview of Common Controls in the Requisition Process

Inventory Purchases: Manufacturing Organization
- Written requisitions are made for specific products by the production manager or stockroom manager.
- Computer-generated requisitions are generated based on current inventory levels and production plans.

Inventory Purchases: Retail Organization
- Overall authorization to purchase product lines is delegated to individual buyers by the marketing manager. The authorization is built into the computer as a control. The limits for individual goods can be exceeded only on specific approval by the marketing manager.
- Store managers may be granted authority to purchase a limited number of goods. The store manager's ability to issue a purchase order may be subject to overall corporate limits, usually specified in dollars.
- The supplier may have access to the retailer's inventory database and, by contract, ship replacement merchandise based on sales activity and reorder points.

Inventory Purchases: Just-in-Time Manufacturing Process
- An agreement is signed with the supplier whereby the supplier agrees to ship merchandise (just in time) according to the production schedule set by the manufacturer. A long-term supply contract is negotiated specifying price, quality of products, estimated quantities, penalties for product shortages or quality problems, and so forth. Specific purchase orders are not issued; rather, the production plan is communicated to the supplier with the specified delivery dates. The production plan serves as the requisition.

Supplies Purchases
- Requisitions are issued by individual departments and sent to the appropriate department manager for approval.
- Each department may be given a budget for supplies and may have the ability to issue purchase orders directly for the needed items or may be able to purchase a limited number of items without a purchase order.

2. Purchase of Goods and Services Many companies centralize the purchasing function in a purchasing department. A separate purchasing function:

- Promotes efficiency and effectiveness
- Eliminates potential favoritism that could take place if individual department heads were allowed to place orders
- Reduces the opportunity for fraud by segregating the authorization to purchase from the custody and recording functions
- Centralizes control in one function

Important purchasing controls include the approval of a contract with suppliers, restricted access to the computer program, and monitoring of inventory and purchase levels by management. The *Focus on Fraud* feature "Weak Internal Controls, Unethical Decisions, and a Fictitious Vendor at Baird Products" provides an example in which weak controls led to a fraud in the automotive parts production industry. Some services that are purchased, such as auditing services, will have additional controls, including review and approval by the audit committee.

Although there are advantages to centralized purchasing, there is a risk that purchasing agents may enter into kickback arrangements with vendors. Controls to mitigate this risk include requiring competitive bids for large purchases and rotating purchase agents across product lines. Perhaps the most important control is an authorized vendor database. Company employees cannot purchase from vendors other than those in the database, thereby making it difficult to set up fictitious vendors.

In traditional purchasing situations, prenumbered forms are used to establish the uniqueness of each order and the completeness of the purchase order population. The purchase order identifies the quantity and prices of

Weak Internal Controls, Unethical Decisions, and a Fictitious Vendor at Baird Products

FOCUS on **FRAUD**

Baird Products manufactures metal parts for the automotive parts products industry. Robert Grant was the manager in charge of the metal-casting department, and he reported to Linda Thompson, the facility manager. Thompson trusted Grant and relied on his judgment and honesty. However, Grant developed a fairly lavish lifestyle that included gambling; he also had three college-age children to support. The purchasing process and controls at Baird were uncomplicated. All purchase requests were to be approved by the department manager and then sent to the accounting department for issuance of the purchase order. The accounting department would then determine whether the purchase was within the budget and whether the vendor was on an approved list. Although the accounting department required that approved vendors provide a company name, address, telephone number, and principal contact, it did no actual verification of the vendors, a control weakness that Grant learned about and ultimately exploited.

Grant's fraud began with suppliers for products in his department. He began requiring vendors to provide him with money and gifts in order to maintain their sales volume at Baird, and vendors that refused risked being shut out of business with Baird. Later, the fraud grew larger when he required all the vendors that he dealt with to pay him a commission on their sales to Baird that essentially amounted to a bribe. Vendors feared losing sales if they did not comply, so they did not report this practice to Thompson or other members of management. The fraud grew still larger when Grant set up a fictitious vendor (RGWB, Inc.), and embezzled nearly

$200,000 over about 18 months. The fraud was finally discovered when Grant became ill and another employee took over his job during his absence. Baird fired Grant and brought criminal charges against him, but Grant fled and never faced justice. Baird learned the following lessons from this fraud:

- Even though controls are in place, they are sometimes not followed or they are followed incompletely, and if employees understand this control weakness they may exploit it.
- Companies need to have fraud hotlines where employees, vendors, and third parties can report inappropriate activity without fear of retaliation.
- Employees who seem honest and trustworthy sometimes violate that trust. Anyone in a position of trust with control over monetary resources needs to be treated with professional skepticism, both by the company itself and by its external auditors.
- Controls must be strong in the purchasing area, and there should be adequate segregation of duties of individuals who place orders versus individuals who select vendors, compare prices, and make the actual orders. Further, adequate supervision and knowledge of vendors is a vital job for top management.
- For ongoing frauds to remain undetected, it is often necessary for the employee(s) involved to be in a position to continue the fraud on a daily basis. Mandating vacations for all employees can be a useful control in trying to prevent and detect fraud.

goods ordered, quality specifications, and the delivery date. The receiving department uses the purchase order to determine whether a shipment of goods should be accepted. The accounting department uses the purchase order to determine whether a purchase was authorized and whether the vendor's invoice is correct.

Two variations of the traditional purchase order are common: the automated system-generated purchase order and the supply-chain delivery contract. Good inventory management identifies levels for inventory reorders. When inventory drops below a specified level, or in response to production plans, the company's information system generates a purchase order that is sent directly to a prespecified vendor. Companies may consider additional controls, such as (1) a maximum quantity that can be ordered within a given time period, (2) a minimum amount of previous usage during a specified time period, and (3) a required review by a purchasing agent for some accounts or for high-dollar levels. A variation of the system-generated purchase order is the electronic consignment system used by some retailers. For example, Wal-Mart encourages its partners to monitor store activities, inventory levels, and current trends in sales and authorizes the vendor to ship additional goods to stores when inventory levels decrease. However, the trade-off is that the partner—for example, Levi Strauss—maintains ownership of its product until a consumer purchases it. When the consumer brings the jeans to the checkout counter, the ownership transfers to Wal-Mart and then immediately to the consumer. The sales information is captured, and the accounting system records the sale as well as the cost of goods sold and a payable to Levi Strauss. The contract between the trading partners also specifies controls to assure that Wal-Mart acknowledges receipt of goods and takes steps to assure that the goods are not subject to damage, theft, or loss.

3. Receipt of, and Accounting for, Goods and Services Receiving departments should make sure that only authorized goods are received, that the goods meet order specifications, that an accurate count of the goods received is taken, and that accountability is established to assure that all receipts are recorded. Several alternative methods of recording the receipt of goods include:

- The receiving department prepares prenumbered receiving documents to record all receipts.
- The receiving department electronically scans bar codes on the goods received to record quantity and vendor and then visually inspects the goods for quality. The information system prepares a sequentially numbered receiving record for goods scanned in.
- Departments may receive goods directly, such as office supplies, and must approve payment for the merchandise.
- Goods are received directly into the production process. The vendor is paid according to the long-term contract based on the purchaser's actual production, and the vendor is penalized for production delays that are due to failures to deliver the goods.

The traditional receiving process creates a prenumbered receiving document based on a count of the merchandise received. A copy of the purchase order (usually with quantities blanked out to help assure an independent count) is reviewed to determine whether a shipment is authorized. Prenumbered receiving documents establish the completeness of the population and are useful in determining that all goods are recorded in the correct period.

Automated scanning can improve both control and efficiency of the receiving process. Products shipped with bar codes can be directly scanned into the system. Actual receipts can be automatically matched with purchase orders to determine if the shipment contains errors. Goods received into production must match the production process. If they do not, then there is a potential problem of the production line either shutting down or producing the wrong subcomponents. For example, if Eaton fails to deliver the correct subassembly to General Motors, the production line will shut down and General Motors will know the cause. Although this is not a traditional accounting control, it is very effective because any failure immediately gets the attention of management and the vendor. Therefore, there is strong motivation to avoid any mistakes.

As auditors increasingly encounter these integrated order, delivery, and payment supply-chain management systems, they have to consider the types of controls that should be present. *Exhibit 11.4* provides an overview of controls that are found in traditional receiving systems and in more automated systems. Regardless of the approach taken in the receiving function, the auditor must gain reasonable assurance that management has effective controls related to receiving.

EXHIBIT **11.4** Comparison of Controls in Traditional and Automated Systems

Traditional Receiving System	Automated Integrated Receiving System
Purchase orders are prepared and sent to vendors.	Long-term contract is signed with vendor specifying: • Quality • Shipping and delivery requirements • Payment terms • Penalties for performance failures • Reconciliations between trading partners for goods shipped/received
Purchase orders are based on projected sales or production, or current inventory levels.	Quantities are based on production plans or sales programs. Quantities and delivery times are updated monthly or more frequently depending on scheduling and shipping constraints.
Price is either negotiated or competitively bid among a number of vendors.	Price is locked in with a preferred vendor.
Independent receiving function exists.	Goods are delivered to production line.
Independent, sequentially numbered receiving documents are prepared to provide evidence that the goods are received.	Disruptions of production provide evidence that goods were not delivered.
Accounts payable department matches purchase order, receiving document, and invoice and accrues accounts payable.	Accruals are set up based on contract (production, sales of goods, etc.).
Payments are made via check or by electronic transfer once or twice a month.	Payments are electronically transferred to vendor based on contractual terms.
Differences between goods received and goods ordered are identified before payments are made.	Processes are described in the contract to resolve difference between goods received and goods that were shipped by vendor.

4. Approval of Items for Payment Approval typically involves a **three-way match** among the vendor invoice, the purchase order, and the receiving report. A three-way match is a control in which a purchase order, receiving information, and a vendor invoice are matched to determine whether the vendor's invoice is correct and should be paid. This process can be automated or can be performed manually. If all items on the three documents properly match, the vendor's invoice is set up as an account payable with a scheduled payment date. Discrepancies are reviewed with the purchasing agent. The supporting documentation and authorization are then presented to the accounts payable department for payment. Internal controls should assure that all items are recorded in a timely manner, that the authorization process includes a review of documents, and that supporting documentation is canceled on payment to avoid duplicate payments.

The traditional approach to controlling the receipt of, and payment for, purchases is labor intensive and error prone. The automated matching process represents an efficient alternative. Purchase orders are entered into a purchase order database that is accessed by the receiving department to determine whether an incoming shipment of goods should be accepted. The receiving department electronically records the receipt of goods through scanning the bar code or other means and cross-references the receipt to the purchase order. The computerized application matches the three documents (purchase order, receiving document, and vendor invoice), and if the three-way match is within a prespecified tolerance limit, the invoice is approved for payment. A payment date is scheduled, and a check is automatically generated on the scheduled date and is signed using an authorized signature plate. The complete payment process occurs without any apparent human intervention. There is no authorized reviewer, no physical matching, and no individual physically signing the checks. In some systems, the payment may be transferred electronically to the vendor.

The lack of human intervention is compensated for by control procedures and authorization concepts built into the automated system such as the following:

- *Authorized vendors*—Purchases can be made only from authorized vendors.
- *Restricted access*—Access is restricted to databases, in particular to the vendor database and the purchasing database. Anyone with the ability to add a vendor or make unauthorized purchase orders is in a position to set up fictitious vendors and purchases. Therefore, someone outside the purchasing department should maintain the vendor database (a list of authorized vendors).
- *Automatic processes*—Although the receiving department has access to the purchase order (read-only), the use of automatic scanners and other counting devices decreases counting and identification errors.
- *Reconciliations inherent in the process*—Most retailers mark retail prices on the goods at the distribution center when they are received. The retail price tickets for an order can be generated from the purchase order. The actual number of tickets used should be reconciled with the goods received, and any leftover tickets should be an adjustment made to the receiving report.
- *Automation of error-prone activities*—Vendor invoices are traditionally entered into the system by accounts payable personnel, thereby segregating this process from the other two functions. An alternative is to receive invoices electronically. It is still important that purchasing and receiving not have the ability to enter vendor invoice data or access the vendor invoice file.
- *Restricted access to transferring funds*—Access to physical checks, or authorization of electronic cash transfers, is limited to the appropriate, designated individuals.
- *Monitoring*—Activity reports are prepared on a regular basis for management review.

Because most of the control procedures are developed during the system design process, it is important that users and internal auditors actively participate in reviewing the effectiveness of controls designed into the computer application.

5. Cash Disbursements In a manual system, an individual in a position of authority reviews the completeness of the documentation supporting a request for cash disbursement and signs a check for payment of goods or services. In most automated systems, the checks, or electronic transfers, are generated automatically according to the scheduled payment date, and the supporting documents are canceled when the invoice is set up for payment. The most important controls in these systems are (1) review of transactions, by which someone reviews the expenditures and compares them to other key data (e.g., production, budgets, other measures of volume) and (2) the direction of vendor disputes to someone outside the process. Other controls include the periodic review of the system by the internal audit department and periodic reconciliation of inventory on hand with inventory per the books.

EXHIBIT **11.5**	Control Risk Assessment Questionnaire: Acquisition and Payment Cycle

	Check (x) one:	
	Yes	**No**
1. Are purchases of inventory approved at the proper level?	_____	_____
2. Is there adequate documentation of approvals?	_____	_____
3. Are purchase orders prenumbered and accounted for?	_____	_____
4. Are purchases of inventory made from an approved vendor list?	_____	_____
5. Are changes to the approved vendor list approved at the proper level?	_____	_____
6. Does the company have a formal policy and appropriate oversight about the nature of appropriate vendor relationships and gifts?	_____	_____
7. Are controls over the process of handling returned goods adequate?	_____	_____
8. Is the recording of purchases made in a timely manner?	_____	_____
9. Is the recording of returns made in a timely manner?	_____	_____

Documenting Controls

Auditors need to document their understanding of internal controls for both integrated audits and financial statement only audits. *Exhibit 11.5* provides an example of a partial internal control questionnaire for the acquisition and payment cycle. Each negative answer in the questionnaire represents a potential internal control deficiency. Given a negative answer, the auditor should consider the effect of the response on the initial assessment of control risk. Unless another control compensates for a control deficiency, the auditor will likely have a control risk assessment of moderate or high in this area and, therefore, have to rely more on substantive audit procedures.

Performing Planning Analytical Procedures

LO 5 Describe how to use planning analytical procedures to identify possible material misstatements in acquisition and payment cycle accounts, disclosures, and assertions.

Planning analytical procedures help auditors identify areas of potential material misstatements. The steps that the auditor will take in performing planning analytical procedures are fully described in *Chapter 7*.

Step 1: Identify Suitable Analytical Procedures In this transaction cycle, auditors will calculate and analyze the dollar and percent change in inventory, cost of goods sold, and expense account balances relative to both past performance and industry performance. The analysis can be disaggregated by product line or location. A common-sized income statement can help identify cost of goods sold or expense accounts that are out of line with the auditor's expectations, which should be based on prior years, industry information, and the auditor's knowledge of the business. *Exhibit 11.6* presents examples of additional planning analytical procedures that the auditor might consider relevant for acquisition and payment cycle accounts.

Step 2: Evaluate Reliability of Data Used to Develop Expectations Various factors can influence reliability of data in acquisition and payment cycle accounts during planning analytical procedures. One is the source of information that is available. Information is more reliable when it is obtained from independent sources outside the company. For example, obtaining outside evidence of the number of days' sales in inventory in the

EXHIBIT 11.6	Using Ratios and Trends Analyses in Planning Analytical Procedures in the Acquisition and Payment Cycle

Inventory Ratios
- Gross margin analysis
- Inventory turnover (cost of goods sold/ending inventory)
- Number of days' sales in inventory (365/inventory turnover)
- Shrinkage ratio (inventory write-down/ending inventory)
- Inventory per square foot of retail space (for retail clients; and comparisons should be made across locations in stores of comparable size and product mix to test for unexpected differences)
- Inventory overhead application. Analyze the relationship between materials, labor, and overhead to total product costing; compare over time and across product categories.
- Consider trends in the above ratios.

Accounts Payable Ratios
- Accounts payable turnover (purchases/average accounts payable)
- Days outstanding in accounts payable (365/accounts payable turnover)
- Accounts payable/current liabilities
- Purchase returns and allowances/purchases
- Consider trends in the above ratios

company's industry would be considered more reliable data than simply using a historical trend of the company's own day's sales data, without regard to industry considerations. Another factor influencing reliability of data is comparability. The auditor should consider whether the company's data may differ in an expected way from the overall industry. For example, the company's shrinkage ratio may not be comparable to the overall industry if the company has a particularly stable type of inventory that is highly durable and not terribly subject to theft.

Step 3: Develop Expectations Developing expectations about relationships in the data is important to identifying accounts with heightened risk of material misstatement during audit planning. Possible expected relationships in the acquisition and payment cycle might include:

- Assume that the client's production and pricing strategies have remained the same during the past year. Gross margin is expected to be stable and consistent with the industry average.
- Assume that the client has introduced a new product with a low price point and significant customer demand. Inventory turnover is expected to increase, and days' sales in inventory are expected to decrease.
- Assume that the client has invested in a new manufacturing process resulting in significantly less waste and overall increases in efficiency during the production process. Cost of goods sold is expected to decline, and gross margin is expected to increase.

Step 4 and Step 5: Define and Identify Significant Unexpected Differences Step 4 requires the auditor to define the difference (between the auditor's expectation and what the client has recorded) that would be considered significant; this will require consideration of the auditor's assessed materiality level and the auditor's desired level of assurance. Typically, when the risk of material misstatement is higher, the amount of acceptable difference is lower.

In Step 5, the auditor compares the client's recorded amounts with the auditor's expectation. Once this mechanical step is completed, the auditor will have identified any significant differences between the auditor's expectation and what the client has recorded.

If planning analytical procedures do not identify any unexpected relationships, the auditor would conclude that there is not a heightened risk of material misstatement in these accounts. If unusual or unexpected relationships exist, the auditor would adjust planned audit procedures (tests of controls, substantive procedures) to address the potential material misstatements. The auditor should be aware that if a fraud is taking place in the acquisition and payment cycle, the financial statements usually will contain departures from industry norms but may not differ from the expectations set by management. Therefore, the auditor should compare the unaudited financial statements with both past results and industry trends. The following relationships might suggest a heightened risk of fraud in the acquisition or payment cycle:

- Unexpected increases in gross margin
- Inventory that is growing at a rate greater than sales
- Expenses that are either significantly above or below industry norms
- Unexpected increases in the number of suppliers
- Capital assets that seem to be growing faster than the business and for which there are no strategic plans
- Expense accounts that have significant credit entries
- Travel and entertainment expense accounts, but no documentation or approval of expenditures
- Inadequate follow-up to the auditor's recommendations on needed controls

Step 6 and Step 7: Investigate Significant Unexpected Differences and Ensure Proper Documentation

Significant unexpected differences suggest that audit effort for the account/assertion will need to be increased. The auditor will develop a plan to address the identified risks, and the following section of this chapter explains this process. As the auditor proceeds through planning analytical procedures, the auditor will document the analytical procedures used, the auditor's expectations, how the level of significant difference was determined, the identification of significant unexpected differences, and the follow-up to address significant unexpected differences.

The *Auditing in Practice* feature "Inventory Restatement at Barnes & Noble" provides an example of how planning analytical procedures can provide the auditor with insight regarding possible material misstatements in the financial statements.

Responding to Identified Risks of Material Misstatement

LO 6 Determine appropriate responses to identified risks of material misstatement for acquisition and payment cycle accounts, disclosures, and assertions.

Once the auditor has developed an understanding of the risks of material misstatement, the auditor can determine the appropriate audit procedures to perform. Audit procedures should be proportional to the assessed risks, with areas of higher risk receiving more audit attention and effort. Responding to identified risks typically involves developing an audit approach that contains substantive procedures (e.g., tests of details and, when appropriate, substantive analytical procedures) and tests of controls, when applicable. The appropriateness and sufficiency of selected procedures vary to achieve the desired level of assurance for each relevant assertion. While audit firms may have a standardized audit program for auditing the acquisition and payment cycle, the auditor should customize the audit program based on the assessment of risk of material misstatement.

Consider a client where the auditor has assessed the risk of material misstatement related to the existence of inventory at slightly below the maximum.

Inventory Restatement at Barnes & Noble

Barnes & Noble is a retailer of books and digital media, including the Nook e-book reader and associated accessories. On January 13, 2014, a class-action lawsuit was filed against the company. The relevant period for the class-action lawsuit was for individuals that purchased the company's stock between February 25, 2013, and December 5, 2013. The Nook e-book market has not performed up to expectations over the last few years. Sales in that niche have suffered as a result, with buildups of relevant inventory. Among other things, the lawsuit alleges that Barnes & Noble's inventory related to Nook products was materially overstated by $133 million, that the company was unable to timely file its FYE 2013 financial results, and that the company might be forced to restate previously reported financial results. This lawsuit comes on the heels of the SEC's announcement on October 16, 2013, that the Commission had launched an investigation of the company's previously submitted financial statements for FYEs 2011 and 2012. Barnes & Noble had previously restated three prior-year financial statements during the summer of 2013 relating to an internal control material weakness unrelated to the acquisition and payment cycle accounts, replacing its prior auditor (BDO) with Ernst & Young (EY).

What types of planning analytical procedures might have been helpful to the auditors in evaluating the valuation of inventory, particularly that relating to the troubled Nook segment? The following are a few possibilities:

- Tracking quarterly and yearly trends in Nook sales. For example, for the third quarter ending in January 2014, Nook sales were down to about $419 million, compared to $668 million in the same quarter the year prior. This indicates a slowdown in sales, so the auditor will expect potential reduction in inventory valuation given the need to potentially measure to lower of cost or market, and slower inventory turnover.

- Capital expenditures on the Nook segment were down for the third quarter ending in January 2014 to about $22 million, compared to $49 million in the same quarter the year prior. This significant reduction indicates that management is moving away from supporting this segment, so the auditor will expect that the declining trends in inventory valuation and turnover to continue into the future, likely with an increasing rate of decline.

- Given these valuation and turnover concerns, the auditor will track Nook sales and inventory turnover by quarter or month and by geographic segment until the uncertainty with respect to this segment is resolved. Further, the auditor may consider engaging an inventory valuation specialist in responding to identified risks of material misstatement in inventory.

Similar to the Thor Industries, Inc. and Schwartzhoff example from the *Professional Judgment in Context* feature, assume that incentives exist to overstate income to achieve profit targets that affect management bonuses, and oversight of the vice president of finance is relatively weak because of a lack of supervision by top management. The auditor may develop an audit program that consists of first performing limited tests of operating effectiveness of controls, then performing limited to moderate substantive analytical procedures, and finally performing extensive substantive tests of details. Because of the high risk, the auditor will want to obtain a great deal of evidence directly from tests of details. In contrast, consider a client where the auditor has assessed the risk of material misstatement related to the existence of inventory as low and believes that the client has implemented effective controls in this area. For this client, the auditor will likely perform tests of controls, gain a high level of assurance from substantive analytical procedures such as a reasonableness test, and then complete the substantive procedures by performing tests of details at a limited level.

Panel A of *Exhibit 11.7* shows that because of differences in risk, the box of evidence to be filled for testing the existence of inventory at the low risk client is smaller than that at a high risk client. Panel B of *Exhibit 11.7* illustrates

 **EXHIBIT 11.7** Panel A: Sufficiency of Evidence for Existence of Inventory

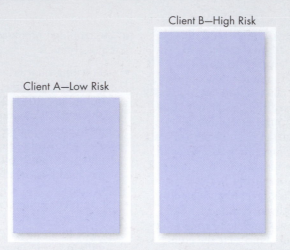

Panel B: Approaches to Obtaining Audit Evidence for Existence of Inventory

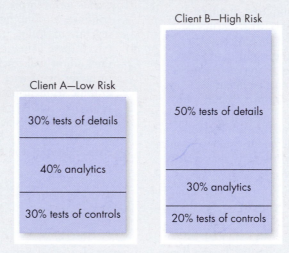

the different levels of assurance that the auditor will obtain from tests of controls and substantive procedures for the two assertions. Panel B makes the point that because of the higher risk associated with the existence of inventory at Client B, the auditor will want to design the audit so that more of the assurance is coming from tests of details. Note that the relative percentages are judgmental in nature; the examples are simply intended to give you a sense of how an auditor might select an appropriate mix of procedures.

Obtaining Evidence About Internal Control Operating Effectiveness in the Acquisition and Payment Cycle

LO 7 Determine appropriate tests of controls and consider the results of tests of controls for acquisition and payment cycle accounts, disclosures, and assertions.

For integrated audits, the auditor will test the operating effectiveness of important controls as of the client's year-end. If the auditor wants to rely on controls for the financial statement audit, the auditor will test the operating effectiveness of those controls throughout the year.

Selecting Controls to Test and Performing Tests of Controls

The auditor selects controls that are important to the auditor's conclusion about whether the client's controls adequately address the assessed risk of material misstatement in the acquisition and payment cycle. The auditor selects both entity-wide and transaction controls for testing. The auditor tests those internal controls that are designed to provide reasonable assurance that all purchases are authorized and all payments are for goods received, are made at the appropriate amount and in the correct time period, and are paid only once to the authorized vendor. Typical tests of controls include inquiry of relevant personnel, observation of the control being performed, examination of documentation corroborating that the control has been performed, and reperformance of the control by the auditor testing the control. However, all types of tests of controls are not necessarily relevant to every control. Furthermore, many tests of controls involve computerized controls, for example, an automated three-way match.

For a manual three-way match control, the auditor may test whether the control was operating effectively by taking a sample of payments and tracing them to the documentation corroborating that the control has been performed. Attribute sampling, which is discussed in *Chapter 8*, would likely be used to determine and select the sample. In addition, the auditor might take a sample of receiving reports and trace through the system to test controls related to the completeness assertion for inventory and accounts payable. Significant lags in recording the liability indicate potential problems that should be addressed during substantive testing of accounts payable at year-end.

Evidence of proper authorization should be available for each purchase and payment. Paper-based systems provide evidence of authorization through signatures. To test these types of controls, the auditor usually checks if signatures are present on the appropriate documentation, and if not, follows up with responsible personnel. Computerized systems are controlled through access controls and exception reports that are tested by the auditor using computerized audit techniques, as well as inquiry and examination of documentation.

Considering the Results of Tests of Controls

The auditor will analyze the results of the tests of controls to determine additional appropriate procedures. There are two potential outcomes:

1. If control deficiencies are identified, the auditor will assess those deficiencies to determine their severity (Are they significant deficiencies or material weaknesses?). The auditor would then need to modify the preliminary control risk assessment (possibly from low to moderate or high) and document the implications of the control deficiencies. Appropriate modifications to planned substantive audit procedures will be determined by the types of misstatements that are most likely to occur because of the control deficiency.

2. If no control deficiencies are identified, the auditor will likely determine that the preliminary assessment of control risk as low is still appropriate. The auditor will then determine the extent that controls can provide evidence on the correctness of account balances and determine planned substantive audit procedures. The level of substantive testing in this situation will be less than what is required in circumstances where deficiencies in internal control were identified. From the audit risk model, we know that companies with effective internal controls should require less substantive testing of account balances.

The relative strengths of the client's internal controls have a significant impact on the audit of the accounts and assertions in the acquisition and

Inventory Controls at Flow International Corporation

AUDITING IN **PRACTICE**

Flow International Corporation is a company that produces high-pressure water pumps. These pumps are used to cut materials, remove coatings, and prepare surfaces for coating. The following is an excerpt from Flow International's "Management Report on Internal Controls Over Financial Reporting for the Year Ended April 30, 2013."

> *Brazil Control Environment.* Management determined that we had a material weakness in the control environment within our Brazilian operations, and in our related monitoring of these operations, that resulted in design and operating control deficiencies, including those related to the physical quantities and valuation of inventory and the preparation and review of income taxes for our subsidiary in Brazil.

Such a material weaknesses would significantly influence the approach the auditor should use to audit the inventory-related accounts, assertions, and disclosures.

Flow International also reported its plans for remediating the material weakness relating to inventory as follows:

We intend to address the material weaknesses identified above by performing the following remediation actions that we believe will improve and strengthen the effectiveness of our disclosure controls and procedures and our internal control over financial reporting including the following:

1. *Inventory management.* In the short-term, in Brazil we recently terminated two operations managers, and are in the process of enhancing the finance team in Brazil by complementing a recently placed U.S. Expatriate in Brazil as the Regional Controller, with additional resources with the right level of knowledge of local requirements to improve the design of the controls and enhance the internal controls over our inventory processes. Additionally, management is evaluating the enhancement of its overall monitoring process. Longer-term, we are reviewing alternative software packages for inventory, general ledger and other required modules to minimize the risk inherent in the existing manual processes.

payment cycle. The *Auditing in Practice* feature "Inventory Controls at Flow International Corporation" highlights the implications of ineffective controls. These control deficiencies were assessed to be material weaknesses and likely meant that Flow International's auditors would have had to rely heavily on substantive tests of details to obtain sufficient appropriate evidence related to inventory.

Obtaining Substantive Evidence About Accounts, Disclosures, and Assertions in the Acquisition and Payment Cycle

Substantive Tests of Inventory and Cost of Goods Sold

LO 8 Determine and apply sufficient appropriate substantive audit procedures for testing acquisition and payment cycle accounts, disclosures, and assertions.

In performing substantive procedures for inventory and cost of goods sold, the auditor seeks reasonable assurance that inventory exists, that it is owned by the company, and that the value of inventory is accurate. Substantive procedures (substantive analytical procedures, tests of details, or both) should be performed for all relevant assertions related to significant acquisition and payment cycle accounts and disclosures. Even if the auditor has evidence indicating that controls are operating effectively, the auditor cannot rely solely on control testing to provide evidence on the reliability of these accounts and assertions. *Exhibit 11.8* presents the assertions and substantive audit procedures that would be used to gather evidence regarding inventory and cost of goods sold.

| EXHIBIT **11.8** | Assertions and Substantive Audit Procedures for Inventory and Cost of Goods Sold |

Assertions	Substantive Audit Procedures
Existence/ occurrence	1. Review the client's proposed physical inventory procedures to determine whether they are likely to result in a complete and correct physical inventory. 2. Observe the client's count of the annual physical inventory. Randomly select items from the client's perpetual inventory record and observe (count) the items on hand. Sample should emphasize high-dollar-value items.
Completeness	1. Perform year-end cutoff tests by noting the last shipping and receiving document numbers used before physical inventory is taken. Review the purchase and sales journal for a period of time shortly before and after year-end, noting the shipping and receiving document numbers to determine whether the goods are recorded in the proper time period. 2. Make inquiries of the client regarding the potential existence of goods on consignment or located in outside warehouses. For material items, either visit the locations or send a confirmation to the outside warehouse management. 3. Make inquiries of the client regarding allowances made for expected returns. Determine client policy for accounting for returned items. Review receipt of transactions for a selected period of time to determine whether significant returns are received and appropriately accounted for.
Rights and obligations	1. Review vendor invoices when testing disbursements to determine that proper title is conveyed. 2. Review purchase contracts to assess rights to return merchandise.
Valuation/ allocation	1. Determine whether the valuation method is appropriate for the client. 2. Inquire of production and warehouse personnel about the existence of obsolete inventory. 3. Note potentially obsolete inventory while observing the physical inventory counts. Trace the potentially obsolete items to the client's inventory compilation and determine whether they are properly labeled as obsolete items. 4. Test inventory cost by taking a sample of recorded inventory and trace to source documents, including: • Tracing raw material purchases to vendor invoices • Testing standard costs as built up through the standard cost system 5. Test for the possibility of obsolete inventory that should be written down to market value: • Review trade journals for changes in product technology. • Follow up potentially obsolete items noted during the observation of the client's physical inventory counts. • Use audit software to read the inventory file and age the inventory items and compute inventory turnover. Investigate products with unusually low turnover or items that have not been used or sold for an extended period of time. • Inquire of the client about sales adjustments (markdowns) that have been offered to sell any products. • Verify sales price by reviewing recent invoices to determine whether the sales price is the same as that included on the computer file. Use generalized audit software (GAS) to compute net realizable value for inventory items, and prepare an inventory printout for all items where net realizable value is less than cost. • Analyze sales by product line, noting any significant decreases in product-line sales. • Review purchase commitments for potential loss exposures. Determine whether contingent losses are properly disclosed or recorded. • Use audit software to test extensions and prepare a printout of differences. • Use audit software to foot the inventory compilation. Trace the total to the trial balance.

(continued)

EXHIBIT **11.8**	Assertions and Substantive Audit Procedures for Inventory and Cost of Goods Sold (*continued*)

Assertions	Substantive Audit Procedures
Presentation and disclosure	1. Review client's financial statement disclosure of: • Inventory valuation methods used • FIFO cost figures and LIFO liquidation effects if LIFO is used • The percentage of inventory valued by each different valuation method • The classification of inventory as raw material, work in process, and finished goods • The existence of contingent losses associated with long-term contracts or purchase commitments • Inventory policy regarding returns and allowances, if expected to be material, for merchandise expected to be returned

Inventory and Cost of Goods Sold: Substantive Analytical Procedures

Before performing tests of details, the auditor may perform substantive analytical procedures, such as a reasonableness test. An example of a reasonableness test would be to estimate the account balance and to determine whether that amount is close to what the client has recorded. For example, if purchases and sales volume are relatively stable from year to year, the auditor might compare ending inventory balances by location to prior year balances to see if they are similar, or if they are materially different to consider why that would be the case. If the auditor's expectations are significantly different from what the client has recorded, the auditor needs to follow up with sufficient appropriate tests of details. If the auditor's expectations are not significantly different from what the client has recorded, the auditor may be able reduce tests of details.

In general, if substantive analytical procedures do not result in unresolved issues, direct testing of account balances can be reduced. However, in the acquisition and payment cycle it is unlikely that audit evidence obtained from substantive analytical procedures alone will be sufficient evidence for the auditor. The *Auditing in Practice* feature "Weaknesses in Performing Substantive Analytical Procedures: The Case of Deloitte's PCAOB Inspection Report" provides an example of the inappropriate use of substantive analytical procedures in acquisition and payment cycle accounts.

Inventory and Cost of Goods Sold: Existence/Occurrence Assertion

Auditing standards require auditors to observe the client taking physical inventory in order to obtain assurance about the existence of inventory. This observation may be done in its entirety at year-end or on a cycle basis throughout the year. It is important to note that the audit of cost of goods sold can be directly tied to the audit of inventories. If beginning and ending inventory have been verified and acquisitions have been tested, cost of goods sold can be directly calculated. So, while observing physical inventory to ensure that its existence relates to the inventory existence assertion, the resulting calculation of cost of goods sold relates to the completeness assertion; in other words, if inventory exists then the recording of cost of goods sold is complete. The auditor should apply analytical procedures to cost of goods sold, however, to determine if any unexpected significant variations—either overall or by product line—occur. Significant variations, especially those that cannot be easily explained, might indicate a need for further inventory work.

Weaknesses in Performing Substantive Analytical Procedures: The Case of Deloitte's PCAOB Inspection Report

AUDITING IN PRACTICE

The inappropriate use of substantive analytical procedures was revealed in the 2010 Public Company Accounting Oversight Board (PCAOB) inspection of Deloitte & Touche LLP.

The Firm failed to perform sufficient procedures to test the existence of the issuer's inventory. The Firm performed physical inventory observations at approximately one-half of one percent of the issuer's locations during the first half of the year, and used a substantive analytical procedure to test the year-end inventory balance. To develop its expectation of the year-end inventory balance, the Firm used the inventory balances from the small number of locations at which it had performed inventory observations during the first half of the year to predict the inventory balances for all the locations at the end of the year. The Firm, however, did not obtain evidence that the inventory balances at the issuer's retail locations were similar. In fact, there was considerable variation, approximately 15 percent, in the inventory balances at the three retail stores where physical inventories were observed. In addition, the Firm did not have evidence that the inventory balances in the first half of the year could be expected to be predictive of the balances at year end.

For further details, see PCAOB Release Number 104–2011-290.

Complete Year-End Physical Inventory   Not many years ago, standard procedure for most organizations was to shut down operations at year-end or near year-end to take a complete physical count of inventory (often referred to as the *physical*). The client's book inventory was adjusted to this physical inventory (often referred to as the *book to physical adjustment*). These procedures are still followed by many small organizations that use a periodic inventory system, where the perpetual records are not sufficiently reliable, or where fraud risk indicators exist.

If a year-end inventory is taken, the auditor should (1) review the client's procedures for the physical, (2) observe the client personnel taking inventory to determine the accuracy of the procedures, (3) make selected test counts that can later be traced into the client's inventory compilation, (4) test the client's inventory compilation by tracing test counts to the compilation and independently test the client's computation of extended cost, and (5) look for evidence of slow-moving, obsolete, or damaged inventory that may need to be written down to lower of cost or market. The *Auditing in Practice* feature "Using GAS" provides examples of how the auditor might incorporate GAS into the audit of inventory accounts, assertions, and disclosures.

Exhibit 11.9 explains the procedures for observing the count of physical inventory. The process assumes that client personnel systematically arranges the inventory for ease of counting and attaches prenumbered tags (paper or electronic) to each group of products. Supervisory personnel (usually from the accounting department) and the auditors review the counts. The count tags are then used to compile the year-end physical inventory. During the counting process, the client's supervisory personnel arrange not to ship or receive goods or plan to segregate all goods received during the process to be labeled and counted as *after inventory*.

Using GAS

An auditor can use GAS to gather the following types of evidence related to inventory accounts:

- The mathematical accuracy of inventory records
- Reports of recent shipments to be used for cutoff testing
- Items to be counted during the physical inventory observation

- Evaluations of gross margin amounts by product line
- Analyses of inventory whose cost exceeds the market value
- Comparisons of inventory quantities to budgetary plans
- Lists of inventory items with unusual prices, units, or descriptions

---

EXHIBIT 11.9 Procedures for Observing a Physical Inventory Count

1. Meet with client personnel to discuss the procedures, timing, location, and personnel involved in taking the annual physical inventory.
2. Review plans for counting and tagging inventory items.
3. Review the inventory-taking procedures with all audit firm personnel. Familiarize them with the nature of the client's inventory, potential problems with the inventory, and any other information that will ensure that both the client and audit personnel will properly recognize inventory items, high-dollar-value items, and obsolete items, and understand potential problems that might occur in counting the inventory.
4. Determine whether specialists are needed to test or assist in correctly identifying inventory items.
5. Upon arriving at each site:
   a. Meet with client personnel, obtain a map of the area, and obtain a schedule of inventory counts to be made for each area.
   b. Obtain a list of sequential tag numbers to be used in each area.
   c. Observe the procedures that client supervisory personnel have implemented to shut down movement of goods.
   d. Observe that the client has shut down production.
   e. Obtain document numbers for the last shipment and receipt of goods before the physical inventory is taken. Use the information to perform cutoff tests.
6. Observe the counting of inventory and note the following on inventory count working papers:
   a. The first and last tag number used in the section.
   b. All tag numbers and the disposition of all tag numbers in the sequence.
   c. The product identification, product description, units of measure, and number of items on a count sheet.
   d. Items that appear to be obsolete or of questionable value.
   e. All high-dollar-value items included in inventory.
   f. Movement of goods into or out of the company during the process of inventory taking. Determine if goods are properly counted or excluded from inventory.
7. Document conclusion as to the quality of the client's inventory-taking process, noting any problems that could be of audit significance. Determine whether a sufficient inventory count has been taken to properly reflect the goods on hand at year-end.

The auditor walks through the inventory areas, documenting the first and last tag numbers used as well as the tag numbers not used. The auditor also:

- Makes test counts of selected items and records the test counts for subsequent tracing into the inventory compilation

- Takes notations of all items that appear to be obsolete or are in questionable condition; the auditor follows up on these items with inquiries of client personnel and retains the data to determine how they are accounted for in the inventory compilation
- Observes the handling of scrap and other material
- Observes whether any physical movement of goods occurs during the counting of inventory
- Records all high-dollar-value items for subsequent tracing into the accounting records

The notation of high-dollar-value items is a check against potential client manipulation of inventory by adding new items or adjusting the cost or quantities of existing items after the physical inventory is completed. Because high-dollar-value items are noted, the auditor can systematically review documentary support for major items included on the final inventory compilation that were not noted during the physical inventory observation.

After the inventory count is taken, the auditor's observations and test counts provide an independent source of evidence on the correctness of the client's inventory compilation. Noting the unused tag numbers prohibits the insertion of additional inventory items.

Many organizations have multiple locations, therefore making it difficult to take an annual inventory. For example, one major company that perpetrated a famous fraud was Phar-Mor, Inc. The company had more than 300 stores across the country. The auditors insisted that a year-end physical count be taken, but notified client management that they would observe the taking of inventory at only a few select locations. To expedite the observation of inventory, the auditor worked with management to identify the locations that would be observed. Although there was a massive overstatement of inventory by Phar-Mor, Inc., the misstatement was not discovered by the auditors because the company made sure that no material misstatements occurred at the locations visited by the auditors.

When multiple locations contain inventory, the auditor should review a variety of locations to determine that they are comparable and should use analytical procedures to see if the locations not visited seem to have inventory levels that are significantly different from those observed. If there are significant differences, the auditor may need to observe more locations, or at least follow up with other procedures. The auditor may also want to plan to visit some locations on an unannounced or surprise basis to avoid the type of fraudulent activity that occurred at Phar-Mor.

Many organizations that take an annual physical inventory find that year-end is not the most convenient time to do it. For example, the organization may have a natural model changeover and shut down operations during that time, or it may want to take the physical inventory shortly before or after year-end to expedite the preparation of year-end financial statements. It is acceptable to have the client take the physical inventory before year-end provided that:

- Internal control is effective.
- There are no red flags that might indicate both opportunity and motivation to misstate inventory.
- The auditor can effectively test the year-end balance through a combination of analytical procedures and selective testing of transactions between the physical count and year-end.
- The auditor reviews transactions in the roll-forward period for evidence of any manipulation or unusual activity.

As organizations move toward innovative partnerships with their suppliers and customers, more agreements will take place where a supplier's goods will be at a retailer such as Wal-Mart, but title will not change until the sale to the customer is made. In these situations, the auditor will need to determine that the client has a sound methodology for determining the amount of inventory that is physically stored at a customer's location. Many times, the client will have monitoring controls with which it examines existing inventory at the customer's locations and compares it to the perpetual records. If such controls do not exist, the auditor will need to consider complementary testing methodologies, which might include (a) confirming inventory amounts with the trading partner, (b) examining subsequent payments from the trading partner, or (c) visiting selected trading partners to inspect inventory.

It is not sufficient for a client to just assert that its inventory is held by its trading partner. The auditor must examine the contract, determine the existence and effectiveness of controls, and examine documentation of reconciliations between trading partners, cash remittances, and client accounting records. If red flags are present, the auditor must go beyond these procedures and talk with the trading partner to obtain information on the amount of the client's inventory the trading partner shows on hand. Finally, the auditor needs to develop assurance that the trading partner is a real company.

There may be rare cases in which it is difficult or impractical for the auditor to attend the physical inventory count. For example, the nature and location of the inventory, or where it is held, may pose safety threats for the auditor. In these situations, the auditor must conduct alternative audit procedures. Such procedures could include inspecting documents related to the subsequent sale of specific inventory items to validate their existence and valuation as of the balance sheet date.

If, however, it is simply inconvenient for the auditor to attend the physical inventory count, then the auditor has an obligation to find a way to be present. If it is truly impossible for the auditor to attend the physical inventory counting, and the auditor is unable to conduct alternative procedures, then the auditor's report would have to be modified as a result of this scope limitation (assuming that inventory is a material amount to the financial statements as a whole). We discuss scope limitations to the standard audit report in *Chapter 15*.

Inventory and Cost of Goods Sold: Completeness Assertion

The auditor typically performs a cutoff test of receipts and shipments of inventory at year-end to determine whether all items are recorded in the correct time period. The cutoff test is usually accomplished by capturing information on the last items shipped and received at year-end and examining samples of transactions recorded in the sales and purchases journals near year-end. In addition, audit software can be used to match shipping dates and billing dates if the files containing that information have been tested for accuracy. The auditor should also inquire about any inventory out on consignment or stored in a public warehouse and consider confirming its existence.

> *Cutoff example*—A sale of $100 is recorded on December 30 for a product costing $80 that is not shipped until the next month. If a physical count of inventory is taken on December 31, this product will be included in the physical count, which will exceed the quantity shown in the perpetual records. The perpetual inventory record is always adjusted to the actual count (in this case by debiting inventory and crediting cost of goods sold). Unless corrected, sales, gross profit, and pre-tax income are overstated by the full $100. The client can correct this misstatement by reversing the sales entry, including the entry to accounts receivable. Because the perpetual inventory is adjusted to the physical count, that part of the original entry (debiting inventory, crediting cost of goods sold) is already made.

Allowance for Returns In most situations, the expected amount of returns is not material. However, some organizations (e.g., mail-order companies like Lands' End or L.L. Bean) provide return guarantees and expect significant returns—especially after year-end holiday sales. They use previous experience, updated for current economic conditions, to develop estimates of returns. When such returns are material to the overall financial presentation, allowances for returns should be established and the gross profit on the original sale reversed. The auditor should consider the allowance account for any organization experiencing a large volume of returns. As with other accounting estimates, the auditor needs to understand management's process for determining the estimate and then test the reasonable of that process.

Inventory and Cost of Goods Sold: Rights and Obligations Assertion

Most of the audit work regarding rights to and ownership of inventory is addressed during the auditor's test of the initial recording of purchases. The auditor should also review long-term contracts to determine obligations to take delivery of merchandise, customer rights to return merchandise, or buy-back obligations. The auditor should inquire about and gain an understanding of any inventory held on consignment.

Inventory and Cost of Goods Sold: Valuation or Allocation Assertion

Valuation is the most complex assertion related to inventory because of the volume of transactions, diversity of products, variety of costing methods, and difficulty in estimating net realizable value of products. A combination of tests of details and substantive analytical procedures is used to determine inventory valuation. The auditor should verify the correct cost of inventory and then test for lower of cost or market valuation. Usually, the cost part of the valuation assertion is tested by examining underlying invoices and/or supporting cost records. The auditor usually evaluates current market data and other information that might indicate a drop in sales price or potential inventory obsolescence.

Direct Tests of Product Costs Statistical sampling techniques, as discussed in *Chapter 8*, should be used to select items for testing. Then, the auditor should examine underlying supporting documentation—for example, invoices—to determine that the cost is recorded correctly. As an example, assume that the auditor selected product YG350 to test the cost of inventory recorded on the FIFO basis as part of a perpetual inventory system:

Product YG350

Transaction	Total Quantity	Total Cost	Balance Quantity	Balance Dollars
Beginning balance			100	$1,000
3/1 Purchase	50	550	150	1,550
6/1 Purchase	100	1,200	250	2,750
6/1 Sale	150	1,550	100	1,200
9/1 Purchase	50	500	150	1,700
10/1 Sale	25	275	125	1,425
12/1 Sale	50	600	75	825
12/1 Purchase	75	975	150	1,800

Vendor invoices would be examined for the purchases of the last 150 items (12/1, 9/1, and 6/1) to determine whether $1,800 was the correct cost. (Note: You should verify that the recorded cost should have been $1,775. The calculation is as follows: 12/1 is $975, 9/1 is $500, and the remaining 25 units are from 6/1 at a cost of $25 × $12/unit, for a total of $1,775.)

Any differences noted between vendor invoices and recorded amounts should be identified as an error and should be projected to the population as a whole using statistical sampling to determine whether the misstatement might be material. Similar tests should be performed if the company uses other valuation methods, such as average cost or LIFO. If the company uses a standard cost system, the costs are verified by tests of the cost system and by tracing the selected items to standard costs. Significant variances should be allocated between cost of goods sold and inventory.

Tests for Obsolete Inventory (Net Realizable Value Tests)

Determining the amount that should be written off because of obsolescence is a difficult and challenging audit task because (1) the client will usually state that most of the goods are still salable at current selling prices and (2) net realizable value is only an estimate (e.g., there is no specific, correct price at which inventory should be valued). The auditor should understand management's process for determining the value of its inventory, and gather evidence on potential inventory obsolescence from a number of corroborating sources, including:

- Noting potential obsolete inventory when observing the physical inventory count
- Calculating inventory turnover, number of days' sales in inventory, date of last sale or purchase, and other similar analytic techniques to identify potential obsolescence
- Calculating net realizable value for products by referring to current selling prices, cost of disposal, and sales commissions
- Monitoring trade journals and the Internet for information regarding the introduction of competitive products
- Inquiring of management about its approach to identifying and classifying obsolete items
- Monitoring turnover or age of products individually or by product lines and comparing the turnover with past performance and expectations for the current period
- Comparing current sales with budgeted sales
- Periodically reviewing, by product line, the number of days of sales currently in inventory
- Adjusting for poor condition of inventory, reported as part of periodic cycle counts
- Monitoring sales for amount of product markdown and periodic comparison of net realizable value with inventoried costs
- Reviewing current inventory in light of planned new-product introductions

Auditors often investigate items that appear to be obsolete by reviewing sales subsequent to year-end and discussing future sales prospects with management. The *Auditing in Practice* feature "The Importance of Professional Skepticism in Testing the Valuation of Inventory: The PCAOB Disciplines Ibarra" provides an example of difficulties that auditors encountered in testing inventory valuation.

Testing a Standard Costing System

Most manufacturing organizations use standard cost systems to assist in controlling costs, streamlining accounting, and costing inventory. Valuation of ending inventory is directly

The Importance of Professional Skepticism in Testing the Valuation of Inventory: The PCAOB Disciplines Ibarra

AUDITING IN PRACTICE

The PCAOB disciplined the Ibarra audit firm because the auditors failed to identify and address a departure from GAAP relating to their client's valuation of inventory. GAAP requires inventory to be valued at the lower of cost or market value. The inspection report notes that the client's consolidated balance sheet reported inventory of $356,973, or approximately 95% of total assets. However, based on cost of goods actually sold during that fiscal year, the client's inventory balance represented approximately 22 years' worth of

sales. This fact alone should have increased the auditors' skepticism about the inventory's stated value. Instead, the auditors relied solely on management's representation regarding the valuation of inventory and mechanical tests of inventory costs, and they missed the big picture. Auditing standards require auditors to look at evidence from multiple sources in reaching a conclusion about an account balance.

For further details on this case, see PCAOB Release No. 2006–009.

affected by the quality of the client's cost system. The auditor should make inquiries about the following:

- The method for developing standard costs
- How recently the standards have been updated
- The method for identifying components of overhead and of allocating overhead to products
- The methods for identifying variances, following up on their causes, and allocating them to inventory and cost of goods sold

The auditor also tests the procedures for assigning raw material costs to products or cost centers. The auditor should be conversant with activity-based costing systems to determine their appropriateness for allocating costs to products.

Exhibit 11.10 contains an audit program to test a standard cost system. The program is intended to determine the accuracy and reliability of the standard cost system as a basis for valuing a client's year-end inventory. The audit program assumes a standard cost system, but the concepts implicit in the program could be modified for other systems, such as a job cost system. Note that the program requires the auditor to understand the client's business process as well as its standard cost system (including methods of estimating costs). The program also requires analyses of both variances and individual cost assignments.

Testing a Perpetual Inventory System Most organizations use a perpetual inventory system to help manage inventory. If there is a low risk that the perpetual inventory records are inaccurate, the client may save the time and cost associated with a complete year-end count of inventory. The auditor will typically test perpetual inventory records to determine that (1) authorized receipts and sales of inventory are recorded accurately and promptly and (2) only authorized receipts and sales of inventory have been recorded. The auditor selects transactions from the perpetual records and traces them back to source documents to determine that only authorized transactions have been recorded and that unit costs are accurate.

| EXHIBIT **11.10** | Audit Program for Standard Cost System |

AUDIT OF STANDARD COST SYSTEM

Prepared by _____

Reviewed by _____

	Performed by:	W/P Ref:
1. Review prior-year audit documentation for a description of the standard cost system. Inquire about any major changes made in the system during the current year.	_____	_____
2. Tour the production facilities and make note of cost centers, general layout of the plant, storage of inventory, functioning of the quality control department, and process for identifying and accounting for scrap or defective items.	_____	_____
3. Examine prior-year audit documentation and current-year variance accounts as a basis for determining the amount of variances identified by the standard cost accounting system. Determine whether the variances imply the need for significant revisions in the standard cost system.	_____	_____
4. Inquire of the process used to update standard costs. Determine the extent to which revisions have been made during the current year.	_____	_____
5. Inquire whether significant changes have been made in the production process during the current year, whether major manufacturing renovations have taken place, and whether new products have been added.	_____	_____
6. Randomly select X number of standard cost buildups for products, and for each product buildup selected:	_____	_____
• Review engineering studies on the cost buildup, noting the items used, amount of product used, and standard cost of the product used.	_____	_____
• Test the reasonableness of the client's costs by randomly sampling components of product cost and tracing back to purchases or contracts with suppliers.	_____	_____
• Review payroll records to determine that labor costs are specifically identified by product or cost center and used in calculating variances.	_____	_____
• Review the reasonableness of the method for allocating overhead to products. Determine whether any significant changes have been made in the method of allocation.	_____	_____
7. Select a representative sample of products requisitioned into work in process, and determine that all entries are properly recorded.	_____	_____
8. Review the method for identifying overhead costs. Select a representative sample of expenditure charged to overhead, and trace to underlying support to determine that the costs are properly classified.	_____	_____
9. Review variance reports. Determine the extent to which the client has investigated and determined the causes of the variances. Determine whether the causes of the variances signal a need to revise the standard cost system.	_____	_____
10. Inquire about the method used by the client to allocate variances to inventory and cost of goods sold at year-end. Determine the reasonableness of the method and its consistency with prior years.	_____	_____
11. Document your conclusion on the accuracy and completeness of the standard cost system used by the client. Indicate whether the standard costs can be relied on in assigning costs to year-end inventory.	_____	_____

The auditor also selects items from the source documents and traces them to the perpetual records to determine that all receipts and sales are recorded accurately and on a timely basis. Finally, the auditor examines support for any material adjustments made to the perpetual records based on physical counts.

Using the Work of a Specialist or Expert When Auditing Inventory

The nature of inventory at some clients may require the auditor to rely on the work of a specialist in determining quantities and valuation of inventory. For example, a specialist might be needed to determine the physical characteristics relating to inventory on hand or condition of minerals, mineral reserves, or materials stored in stockpiles.

Inventory and Cost of Goods Sold: Presentation and Disclosure Assertion

The auditor reviews the client's proposed disclosure for compliance with the guidelines established by the relevant accounting literature. In addition to the normally required inventory disclosures, the auditor must identify any unusual circumstances regarding sales or purchase contracts that would merit additional disclosure. A number of financial disclosures are required for inventory:

- Inventory valuation method used (FIFO, LIFO, moving average) and the percentage of inventory valued under each method
- Changes made in the method of valuing inventory
- FIFO or current cost if the inventory is valued using LIFO
- Composition of inventory as to raw materials, work-in-process, and finished goods
- Purchase commitments that could have an adverse affect on future financial results

The auditor reviews the client's inventory footnote for completeness and accuracy. Most of the information described in the notes will be independently verified by the auditor in the process of completing the audit, and the data will be contained in the audit documentation. *Exhibit 11.11* contains an example of a typical inventory disclosure for Ford Motor Company.

| EXHIBIT **11.11** | Ford Motor Company Inventory Footnote From the 2013 Annual Report |

NOTE 9. INVENTORIES

All inventories are stated at the lower of cost or market. Cost for a substantial portion of U.S. inventories is determined on a last-in, first-out ("LIFO") basis. LIFO was used for 20% and 18% of total inventories at December 31, 2013 and 2012, respectively. Cost of other inventories is determined by costing methods that approximate a first-in, first-out ("FIFO") basis.

Inventories were as follows (in millions):

	December 31, 2013	December 31, 2012
Raw materials, work-in-process, and supplies	$ 3,613	$ 3,697
Finished products	5,058	4,614
Total inventories under FIFO	8,671	8,311
Less: LIFO adjustment	(963)	(949)
Total inventories	$ 7,708	$ 7,362

Fraud-Related Substantive Procedures for Inventory and Cost of Goods Sold

In those audits where there is a heightened risk of fraud related to inventory and cost of goods sold, the auditor will want to consider performing the following procedures or, if the procedures are already being performed, altering the timing and extent of the procedures:

- Observe all inventory locations simultaneously
- Confirm inventories at locations that are outside the entity
- Compare carrying inventory amounts to recent sales amounts
- Examine consignment agreements and determine that consignments are properly accounted for
- Send confirmations to vendors confirming invoices and unusual terms
- Determine if there are bulk sales at steep discounts, as these sales could indicate decreasing values for the company's products

The *Focus on Fraud* feature "Examples of Fraud in Inventory" outlines common inventory-related frauds.

Substantive Tests of Accounts Payable and Related Expense Accounts

The auditor's major concern with accounts payable is that the account (and related expense accounts) will be understated. Therefore, the most relevant assertion is the completeness assertion. The testing to be performed depends on the risk of an understatement of accounts payable. If there is little risk, the testing might be limited to substantive analytical procedures, such as a comparison of underlying expenses with that of the prior year and related tests of the underlying asset or liability account. Alternatively, the auditor

---

Examples of Fraud in Inventory

FOCUS on **FRAUD**

AICPA Practice Alert No. 94–2, *Auditing Inventories—Physical Observations*, provides examples of how organizations fraudulently manipulate inventory amounts.

Auditors should be on the alert for the following:

- Empty boxes or hollow squares in stacked goods
- Mislabeled boxes containing scrap, obsolete items, or lower-value materials
- Consigned inventory, inventory that is rented, or traded-in items for which credits have not been issued
- Inventory diluted so it is less valuable (e.g., adding water to liquid substances)
- Altering the inventory counts for those items the auditor did not test count
- Programming the computer to produce fraudulent physical quantity tabulations or priced inventory listings

- Manipulating the inventory counts/compilations for locations not visited by the auditor
- Double-counting inventory in transit between locations
- Physically moving inventory and counting it at two locations
- Including in inventory merchandise recorded as sold but not yet shipped to a customer (bill and hold sales)
- Arranging for false confirmations of inventory held by others
- Including inventory receipts for which corresponding payables had not been recorded
- Overstating the stage of completion of work-in-process
- Reconciling physical inventory amounts to falsified amounts in the general ledger
- Manipulating the roll-forward of an inventory taken before the financial statement date

could compare ending accounts payable balances by major vendor to prior year balances, or to the volume of activity during the year. The auditor would expect that high-volume vendors will have relatively large accounts payable balances. In addition, if there is no balance for a vendor that in previous years was significant, the auditor would want to consider why that would be the case. When evaluating evidence regarding expense accounts, the auditor should consider that management is more likely to (1) understate rather than overstate expenses and (2) classify expense items as assets rather than vice versa. Therefore, the most relevant assertion related to expenses in the acquisition and payment cycle is also the completeness assertion. However, it is important for the auditor to understand client motivations. For example, client management may be motivated to minimize income taxes and thus would want to overstate expenses and understate income. In such cases, the auditor should concentrate on items classified as expenses that should be recorded as an asset.

Exhibit 11.12 presents the assertions and audit procedures that the auditor would typically use to gather evidence regarding accounts payable.

Accounts Payable and Related Expense Accounts: Substantive Analytical Procedures

When the auditor has concluded that control risk is low for expense accounts, the primary substantive tests may be substantive analytical procedures. In conducting analytical procedures, the auditor should recognize that many account balances are directly related to the client's volume of activity. Stable relationships are expected between specific accounts (e.g., cost of goods sold and sales) that can be investigated for unusual discrepancies. Examples of expenses that should vary directly with sales include warranty expense, sales commissions, and supplies expense. A statistical model should be built using either audited data or independently generated data. If the expense account falls within expected ranges, the auditor can be comfortable in concluding that it is not materially misstated. If the account

---

EXHIBIT **11.12**	Assertions and Audit Procedures for Accounts Payable

Assertions	Audit Procedures
Existence/occurrence	1. Perform a cutoff test of purchases and cash disbursements
Completeness	1. Request vendors' monthly statements or send confirmations to major vendors requesting a statement of open account items
	2. Agree monthly statements and confirmations from major vendors with accounts payable list
	3. Examine a sample of cash disbursements made after the end of the year to determine whether the disbursements are for goods and services applicable to the previous year
	4. Perform analytical review of related expense accounts, such as travel and entertainment or legal expenses
Rights and obligations	1. Review long-term purchase commitments and determine whether a loss needs to be accrued
Valuation/allocation	1. Use GAS to verify mathematical accuracy of accounts payable, and agree to general ledger
Presentation and disclosure	1. Review management's financial statement disclosure of: • Accounts payable • Expense accounts such as travel and entertainment

Understatement of Liabilities and Expenses at Advanced Marketing Services

FOCUS on **FRAUD**

Advanced Marketing Services (AMS) is a San Diego, California–based wholesaler of general-interest books that provides a variety of other services, including promotional and advertising services. A scheme to fraudulently overstate earnings at AMS involved not informing retailers of credits due to them for certain advertising and promotional services that the retailers provided. Instead of contacting the retailers and reconciling amounts, AMS improperly reversed the liability for these credits and thereby decreased expenses and increased its income.

An executive at AMS profited from her participation in the fraudulent schemes through her receipt of annual bonuses and sales of AMS stock. An analytical comparison of expenses with the previous years and with sales volumes might have been a good indicator that something was wrong.

For further details on this case, see SEC Accounting and Auditing Enforcement Release (AAER) No. 2312.

balance is not within the expected range, the auditor develops hypotheses as to why it may differ and systematically investigates the situation through tests of details. The investigation should include inquiries of client personnel and the examination of corroborating evidence (including a detailed examination of the expense accounts, where merited). For example, sales commissions may have averaged 3% of sales over the past five years, and the auditor may expect that trend to continue. If that ratio drops to 1% this year, the auditor should examine the cause of the change. If the auditor obtains sufficient evidence through substantive analytical procedures, the extent of substantive tests of details may be decreased. The *Focus on Fraud* feature "Understatement of Liabilities and Expenses at Advanced Marketing Services" provides an example of a fraud that might have been detected earlier using substantive analytics.

Accounts Payable and Related Expense Accounts: Existence/Occurrence

Analytical Review of Related Expense Accounts This procedure is designed to determine if the accounting data indicate a potential misstatement of expenses. If an understatement is likely, the auditor expands accounts payable tests by performing one or both of the two tests of details described next. Analytical review of related expense accounts is used as the primary substantive test at clients for whom control risk has been assessed as low, when no red flags are present to indicate motivation to understate payables, and when the company is not in danger of violating potential debt covenants related to maintenance of working capital.

Accounts Payable and Related Expense Accounts: Completeness

Testing Subsequent Disbursements The auditor examines a sample of cash disbursements made after year-end to determine whether the disbursements are for goods and services applicable to the previous year—and, if so, whether a liability was recorded in the previous year. The disbursements review is followed by an examination of unrecorded vendor invoices and receiving reports to determine whether goods or services received in the previous year were properly set up as a payable. If control risk is high or there are fraud-related red flags, the auditor may review 100% of the larger subsequent disbursements.

Reconciling Vendor Statements or Confirmations with Recorded Payables The auditor may choose to request vendors' monthly statements or send confirmations to major vendors requesting a statement of open account items. The auditor reconciles the vendor's statement or confirmation with the client's accounts payable trial balance. The method generates reliable evidence, but is costly (in auditor time spent reconciling the amounts) and is used when there is a high risk that the company does not pay vendors on a timely basis.

Related Expense Accounts Some expense accounts in the acquisition and payment cycle are of intrinsic interest to the auditor simply because of the nature of the account, even though they are likely not as material as inventory, cost of goods sold, or accounts payable. These include legal expense, travel and entertainment expense, repairs and maintenance expense, and income tax expense. The legal expense account should be examined as a possible indicator of litigation that may require recording and/or disclosure. Travel and entertainment expense should be examined for questionable or non-business-related items. Repairs and maintenance expense should be examined together with fixed-asset additions to assure a proper distinction has been made between expenditures that should be expensed and those that should be capitalized. Income tax expense and related liability(s) should be examined, often by a tax specialist, to assure that tax laws and regulations have been followed. Underlying documentation should be sampled to determine the nature of the expenditure, its appropriate business use, and the correctness of the recorded item.

The most widely used approaches to detailed testing of expenses is to either (a) have the client create a schedule of all larger items making up the expense account (usually done for smaller clients) to be examined, or (b) use audit software to (i) examine randomly selected items from the expense account using sampling and (ii) prepare a list of all credits to the expense items for further review. The *Focus on Fraud* feature "Expenses at Rite Aid" provides an example of a fraud related to expenses in the acquisition and payment cycle.

Expenses at Rite Aid

FOCUS on **FRAUD**

Executive management at Rite Aid conducted a wide-ranging accounting fraud that resulted in the significant inflation of Rite Aid's income. When the fraud was ultimately discovered, Rite Aid was forced to restate its pre-tax income by $2.3 billion and net income by $1.6 billion, the largest restatement ever recorded at the time. One aspect of the fraud involved reversals of actual expenses. Rite Aid's accounting staff reversed amounts that had been recorded for various expenses incurred and already paid (debiting accounts payable and crediting expenses). These reversals were unjustified and, in each instance, were put back on the books in the subsequent quarter. The effect was to overstate Rite Aid's income during the period in which the expenses were incurred. Specifically, entries of this nature caused Rite Aid's pre-tax income for one quarter to be overstated by $9 million. This example makes an important point: *Sometimes executive management wants to misstate only a particular quarter to keep their stock price high, with the intent that they can fix problems before year-end.*

For further details on this case, see SEC AAER No. 1581 and No. 2023.

Accounts Payable and Related Expense Accounts: Rights and Obligations

Organizations are increasingly entering into long-term contracts to purchase inventory at fixed prices or at a fixed price plus inflation adjustments. These contracts can extend over a period of years, and there is always some risk that economic circumstances can change and the contracts may no longer be economically viable. The contracts should be examined to determine penalties associated with default, and the auditor should gain sufficient knowledge to assess the client's estimate of the probability of contract default or losses.

Accounts Payable and Related Expense Accounts: Valuation or Allocation

Substantive tests of accounts payable and related expense accounts for valuation usually involve simply verifying the mathematical accuracy of the accounts and agreeing them to general ledger and supporting documentation.

Accounts Payable and Related Expense Accounts: Presentation and Disclosure

There is relatively little that is usually disclosed in the footnotes about accounts payable and related expense accounts. Rather, these accounts usually just appear on the face of the financial statements. *Exhibit 11.13* contains an example of an accounts payable disclosure for Ford Motor Company.

Review of Unusual Entries to Expense Accounts

The vast majority of transactions to expense accounts should be debits that are accompanied by purchases of goods or services that can be validated through independent receipts and independent vendor invoices. The exceptions to this rule are accounts that represent estimates or accounts that are based on a relationship with specific asset or liability accounts such as fixed assets (depreciation) or bonds (interest expense). The *Focus on Fraud* feature "WorldCom and Unusual Adjusting Entries" provides an example of a fraud that was perpetrated via the use of unusual adjusting entries to an expense account.

| EXHIBIT **11.13** | Ford Motor Company Accounts Payable Presentation on the Balance Sheet From the 2013 Annual Report |

Ford Motor Company and Subsidiaries Consolidated Balance Sheet (in millions)

	December 31, 2013	December 31, 2012
Liabilities		
Payables	$ 19,531	$ 19,308
Other liabilities and deferred revenue (Note 13)	40,462	48,259
Debt (Note 15)	114,688	105,058
Deferred income taxes (Note 22)	598	470
Total liabilities	175,279	173,095

WorldCom and Unusual Adjusting Entries

FOCUS on FRAUD

Management at WorldCom wanted to keep line expenses at 42% of total costs because (a) line expense was a key ratio followed by Wall Street analysts and (b) it helped to keep reported profits high. One of the processes used was to credit line expense by reducing restructuring reserves. The reserve account would be debited for a round figure, such as:

Dr. Restructuring Reserve	$450,000
Cr. Line Expense	$450,000

An examination of the credits in the expense account would have provided insight into this highly unusual accounting transaction. It is recommended that repair and maintenance expense be examined at the same time as fixed asset increases. If performed as recommended for the WorldCom audit, the fraud would have been discovered much earlier.

Fraud-Related Substantive Procedures for Accounts Payable and Related Expenses

In those audits where there is a heightened risk of fraud related to accounts payable and other related expenses, the auditor will want to consider performing the following procedures or, if the procedures are already being performed, altering the timing and extent of the procedures:

- Send blank confirmations or electronic confirmations via confirmation.com to vendors that ask them to furnish information about all outstanding invoices, payment terms, payment histories, and so forth. The procedure can be expanded to include new vendors and accounts with small or zero balances.
- Scan journals for unusual or large year-end transactions and adjustments, for example, transactions that are not typical, approvals not going through standard processes, or not having the usual supporting documentation.
- Review client's vendor files for unusual items. Unusual items might include nonstandard forms, different delivery addresses, or vendors that have multiple addresses.
- Obtain and examine documentation for payments of invoices that are for amounts just under the limit that typically requires some level of approval.

Documenting Substantive Procedures

The auditor would typically include the following types of documentation related to the substantive procedures for accounts in the acquisition and payment cycle:

- Substantive analytical procedures (including fraud-related procedures) conducted, conclusions reached, and related actions that were taken
- Evidence about physical inventory observations for all material amounts
    - Include information about locations observed, counts that were made and recorded, controls over inventory observation that were used, and specific test counts taken
    - Include information about the dollar amount (e.g., $50,000) above which inventory items would have been specifically tested
    - If the physical inventory counts were taken at an interim date, the workpapers should include evidence about the procedures that were performed between the interim date and the balance sheet date

- Evidence about product costing, such as the audit program for auditing the standard costing system and related evidence that was obtained
- Evidence pertaining to net realizable valuable calculations
- Evidence from inventory specialists
- Summaries of evidence obtained and conclusions reached about material amounts of inventory on consignment
- Evidence from evaluating subsequent disbursements for accounts payable
- Vendor statements
- Confirmations with vendors regarding accounts payable
- Evidence regarding conducting a review of unusual entries, including documentation of such entries and the explanations for them

SUMMARY AND NEXT STEPS

Inventory existence and valuation are of primary concern in the acquisition and payment cycle because by overstating ending inventory, cost of goods sold is understated and net income is overstated. This fact has been exploited by unscrupulous managers; fraudulent financial reporting in the acquisition and payment cycle should be a focus for a skeptical auditor. The auditor should also be concerned about the controls over inventory because of the potential for frauds involving misappropriation of assets. Typical substantive tests of inventory include physical observation, test counts, net realizable valuation tests, tests of costing systems, and consultation with inventory valuation experts.

In terms of accounts payable and related expense accounts, the auditor is most concerned with completeness of recording because management may have incentives to not completely record transactions relating to these accounts. Typical substantive tests of accounts payable include confirmations and review of subsequent cash payments. Other related expenses such as legal expense and travel and entertainment expense are important because, while likely not as material as inventory, cost of goods sold, or accounts payable, these accounts may be a possible indicator of litigation or may contain questionable or non-business-related expenditures.

In the next chapter, we focus on auditing activities related to long-lived assets. The significant accounts include buildings, goodwill and other intangibles (along with the associated depreciation, amortization, or depletion), impairments, gains or losses on disposals, and leases.

SIGNIFICANT TERMS

Automated purchasing system A networked software system that links a company's web site to other vendors whose offerings and prices have been preapproved by appropriate management.

Cycle count Periodic testing of the accuracy of the perpetual inventory record by counting all inventories on a cyclical basis.

Inventories Items of tangible personal property that are held for sale in the ordinary course of business, that are in the process of production for such sale, or that are to be currently consumed in the production of goods or services to be available for sale.

Inventory shrinkage Reduction in inventory presumed to be due to physical loss or theft.

Periodic inventory system   A system of inventory recordkeeping in which no continuous record of changes in inventory (receipts and issues of inventory items) is kept. At the end of an accounting period, the ending inventory is determined by an actual physical count of every item, and its cost is computed using a suitable method.

Perpetual inventory system   A system of inventory recordkeeping where book inventory is continuously in agreement with inventory on hand within specified time periods. In some cases, book inventory and stock on hand may be reconciled with each transaction; in other systems, these two numbers may be reconciled less often. This process is useful in keeping track of the actual availability of goods and determining what the correct time to reorder from suppliers might be.

Requisition   A request for the purchase of goods or services by an authorized department or function within the organization; may be documented on paper or in a computer system.

Supply chain management   The management and control of materials in the logistics process from the acquisition of raw materials to the delivery of finished products to the end user (customer).

Three-way match   A control in which a purchase order, receiving information, and a vendor invoice are matched to determine whether the vendor's invoice is correct and should be paid. This control can be automated or manual.

TRUE/FALSE QUESTIONS

11-1   **LO 1**   The existence and presentation/disclosure assertions are usually the most relevant for inventory.

11-2   **LO 1**   The most common concerns for inventory are that purchases are understated or ending inventory is overstated, both of which will result in lower cost of goods sold and higher net income.

11-3   **LO 2**   The audit of inventory can be complex because inventory is easily transportable, exists at multiple locations, may become obsolete, and may be difficult to value.

11-4   **LO 2**   Two important complexities in auditing inventory arise because inventory accounts experience a high volume of activity and are valued according to various inventory valuation methods.

11-5   **LO 3**   One of the common ways that managers have committed fraud in the acquisition and payment cycle involves inappropriately classifying assets (e.g., inventory) as expenses.

11-6   **LO 3**   The following are possible manipulations that may occur when fraud is perpetrated during the purchase of inventory: under-recording purchases, recording purchases in a later period, and not recording purchases.

11-7   **LO 4**   A well-conceived inventory control system should provide reasonable assurance that all purchases are authorized and that inventory transactions are recorded accurately, completely, and in a timely manner.

11-8   **LO 4**   Common rationales for having a separate purchasing function in an organization include the ability of purchasing agents to exert favoritism to valuable suppliers, the reduction in the opportunity of fraud by combining the authorization to purchase with custody and recording, and the decentralization of control to enhance the application of knowledge of purchasing and inventory management.

11-9 **LO 5** In terms of planning analytical procedures, assume that the client has introduced a new product with a low price point and significant customer demand. The auditor would expect inventory turnover to increase and days' sales in inventory to also increase.

11-10 **LO 5** A planning analytical procedure in the acquisition and payment cycle that might indicate fraud is that inventory is growing at a rate greater than sales.

11-11 **LO 6** When conducting the audit of the acquisition and payment cycle for a client with a high risk of material misstatement in its inventory accounts, the following mix of evidence would be appropriate: significant tests of internal control, significant reliance on substantive analytical procedures, and limited tests of details.

11-12 **LO 6** When considering the appropriate mix of evidence, the sufficiency and appropriateness of selected procedures vary across assertions to achieve the desired level of assurance for each relevant assertion.

11-13 **LO 7** When selecting controls to test and performing tests of controls in the acquisition cycle, the auditor might reasonably take a sample of receiving reports and trace them through the system to test controls related to the completeness assertion for inventory and accounts payable.

11-14 **LO 7** When conducting the audit of acquisition and payment cycle accounts, the auditor will likely conduct less substantive tests for companies with effective internal controls compared to companies with ineffective internal controls.

11-15 **LO 8** A substantive procedure appropriate for testing the existence of inventory would be to perform year-end cutoff tests by noting the last shipping and receiving document numbers used before the physical inventory count is taken.

11-16 **LO 8** A substantive procedure appropriate for testing rights and obligations associated with inventory would be to review vendor invoices when testing disbursements to determine that proper title is conveyed.

MULTIPLE-CHOICE QUESTIONS

11-17 **LO 1** Which of the following activities is not an activity associated with the acquisition and payment cycle?
a. Receive a customer purchase order.
b. Purchase of goods and services.
c. Receipt of, and accounting for, goods and services.
d. Approval of items for payment.

11-18 **LO 1** An automated purchasing system will perform which of the following tasks?
a. Apply preloaded specifications and materials lists to the system to start the process.
b. Automatically flag invoices that do not reconcile with purchase orders.
c. Create change orders and analyze variances from purchase orders.
d. All of the above.

11-19 [LO 2] Which of the following is an inherent risk relating to inventory?

a. Inventory is easily transportable.

b. Inventory may become obsolete because of technological advances even though there are no visible signs of wear.

c. Inventory is often returned by customers, so care must be taken to separately identify returned merchandise, check it for quality, and record it at net realizable value.

d. All of the above.

11-20 [LO 2] Which of the following is not an inherent risk relating to inventory?

a. Sales contracts may contain unusual terms, and revenue recognition is often complex.

b. Inventory accounts typically experience a high volume of activity.

c. Inventory accounts may be valued according to various accounting valuation methods.

d. Identifying obsolete inventory and applying the lower of cost or market principle to determine valuation are difficult.

11-21 [LO 3] Which of the following is an example of fraud in the acquisition and payment cycle?

a. Theft of inventory by an employee.

b. Employee schemes involving fictitious vendors as means to transfer payments to themselves.

c. Executives recording fictitious inventory or inappropriately recording higher values for existing inventory.

d. All of the above.

11-22 [LO 3] Refer to *Exhibit 11.2*, and identify the possible inventory or cost of goods sold manipulation that might occur when inventory is sold.

a. Overstate returns.

b. Overcount inventory.

c. Not record cost of goods sold nor reduce inventory.

d. Under-record purchases.

11-23 [LO 4] Refer to *Exhibit 11.3*, and identify which of the following is a typical control associated with the requisition process for inventory purchases in a just-in-time manufacturing process.

a. The store manager's ability to issue a purchase order may be subject to overall corporate limits, usually specified in dollars.

b. An agreement is signed with the supplier whereby the supplier agrees to ship merchandise according to the production schedule set by the manufacturer.

c. Overall authorization to purchase product lines is delegated to individual buyers by the marketing manager.

d. The limits for individual goods can be exceeded only on specific approval by the marketing manager.

11-24 [LO 4] Which of the following is a legitimate rationale for centralizing the purchasing function in a separate purchasing department?

a. It promotes efficiency and effectiveness.

b. It eliminates potential favoritism that could take place if individual department heads were allowed to place orders.

c. It decentralizes control across functions.

d. Both a and c.

e. Both a and b.

11-25 **LO 5** Which of the following expected relationships is reasonable in terms of performing planning analytical procedures in the acquisition and payment cycle?

a. Assume that the company's production and pricing strategies have remained the same during the past year. Gross margin is expected to improve because of the stability.

b. Assume that the company has introduced a new product with a low price point and significant customer demand. Inventory turnover is expected to increase and days' sales in inventory is expected to decrease.

c. Assume that the company has invested in a new manufacturing process resulting in significantly less waste and overall increases in efficiency during the production process. Cost of goods sold is expected to increase, and gross margin is expected to decrease.

d. All of the above are reasonable expected relationships.

11-26 **LO 5** Which of the following planning analytical relationships is most typically suggestive of a heightened risk of fraud in the acquisition and payment cycle?

a. Unexpected increases in gross margin.

b. Unexpected decreases in gross margin.

c. Inventory that is growing at a rate slower than sales.

d. Expense accounts that have significant debit entries.

11-27 **LO 6** Which mix of evidence would be most appropriate for the following scenario? This is a client where the auditor has assessed the risk of material misstatement related to the existence of inventory at the maximum level. This client has incentives to overstate income to achieve profit targets that affect management bonuses. Oversight of the vice president of finance is relatively weak because of a lack of supervision by top management. Other controls are designed effectively.

a. 100% tests of details.

b. 50% tests of details, 30% analytics, 20% tests of controls.

c. 30% tests of details, 40% analytics, 30% tests of controls.

d. 20% tests of details, 40% analytics, 40% tests of controls.

11-28 **LO 6** Which mix of evidence would be most appropriate for the following scenario? This is a client where the auditor has assessed the risk of material misstatement related to the existence of inventory at a relatively low level. Top management appears to have a high level of integrity. Management has spent the resources necessary to ensure effective design, implementation, and operation of controls.

a. 100% tests of details.

b. 70% tests of details, 10% substantive analytics, 20% tests of controls.

c. 50% tests of details, 10% substantive analytics, 40% tests of controls.

d. 20% tests of details, 40% substantive analytics, 40% tests of controls.

11-29 **LO 7** Which of the following statements is false regarding obtaining evidence about internal control operating effectiveness in the acquisition and payment cycle?

a. For integrated audits, the auditor will test the operating effectiveness of important controls as of the client's year-end.

b. The auditor will select controls to test that are important to the auditor's conclusion about whether the client's controls adequately address the assessed risk of material misstatement in the acquisition and payment cycle.

c. Evidence of proper payment is not necessary for each purchase and payment but is necessary for those that are material.

d. The auditor will take a sample of receiving reports and trace through the system to test controls related to the completeness assertion for accounts payable.

11-30 **LO 7** Refer to the *Auditing in Practice* feature "Inventory Controls at at Flow International Corporation." Which of the following represents an implication of weaknesses in the company's controls over inventory?

a. The company could not adequately process and account for the valuation of inventory.

b. The board of directors fired the CEO as a result of the internal control deficiencies.

c. The company developed a plan to remediate its material weaknesses related to inventory.

d. Both a and c.

e. Both a and b.

11-31 **LO 8** Which of the following audit procedures would be used to test the existence assertion for inventory?

a. Perform year-end cutoff tests by noting the last shipping and receiving document numbers used before physical inventory is taken.

b. Make inquiries of the client regarding the segregation of duties between the purchasing department and the receiving department.

c. Review the client's proposed physical inventory procedures to determine whether they are likely to result in a complete and correct physical inventory.

d. Make inquiries of the client regarding allowances made for expected returns.

e. All of the above.

11-32 **LO 8** Which of the following audit procedures would be used to test the valuation or allocation assertion for inventory?

a. Inquire of production and warehouse personnel about the existence of obsolete inventory.

b. Test inventory cost by taking a sample of recorded inventory, and trace to source documents indicating cost of inventory.

c. Review trade journals for changes in product technology.

d. Inquire of the client about sales adjustments (markdowns) that have been offered to sell any products.

e. All of the above.

REVIEW AND SHORT CASE QUESTIONS

NOTE: Completing Review and Short Case Questions does not require the student to reference additional resources and materials.

NOTE: For the remaining problems, we make special note of those addressing fraud, international issues, professional skepticism, and ethics.

11-33 **LO 1** List the five primary activities involved in the acquisition and payment cycle.

11-34 **LO 1** What is an automated purchasing system? Describe the beneficial tasks that an automated purchasing system can perform.

11-35 **LO 1** Match the following assertions with their associated description: (a) existence/occurrence, (b) completeness, (c) rights and obligations, (d) valuation or allocation, (e) presentation and disclosure.

1. The company has title to the inventory as of the balance sheet date.
2. Inventory balances exist at the balance sheet date.
3. Inventory is properly classified on the balance sheet and disclosed in the notes to the financial statements.
4. Inventory balances include all inventory transactions that have taken place during the period.
5. The recorded balances reflect the true underlying economic value of those assets.

11-36 **LO 1** Match the following assertions with their associated description: (a) existence/occurrence, (b) completeness, (c) rights and obligations, (d) valuation or allocation, (e) presentation and disclosure.

1. The recorded accounts payable balance reflects the true underlying economic value of those liabilities.
2. Accounts payable balances include all accounts payable transactions that have taken place during the period.
3. The company actually owes a liability for the accounts payable as of the balance sheet date.
4. Accounts payable is properly classified on the balance sheet and disclosed in the notes to the financial statements.
5. Accounts payable balances exist at the balance sheet date.

11-37 **LO 2** List at least five reasons that inventory is a complex accounting and auditing area.

ETHICS

PROFESSIONAL SKEPTICISM

11-38 **LO 2, 9** Assume that you are conducting the audit of College Ware, a publicly held manufacturer and distributor of printed, embroidered, and embossed speciality clothing and gift items marketed to college students with school-specific logos. The company pays licensing fees and manufactures products in advance of the fall and winter peak sales periods. The stores that sell the company's products have a contractual agreement that they may return a percentage of unsold merchandise. During the current audit year, many stores in the University of Wisconsin and University of Illinois markets canceled orders just before the start of the school year because of changes in school logos. In addition, the percentage of unsold merchandise, and associated returns, was higher than normal for these stores. As a result, College Ware has made an adjusting entry to record a loss caused by market decline of inventory (Dr. Loss because of market decline of inventory; Cr Allowance to reduce inventory to market value for $40,000). As the auditor, you have conducted a physical inventory of the products, and, based upon sales data collected from College Ware's competitors, you are convinced that the write-down should be for $90,000 (a materially higher amount).

Another issue in the College Ware audit is that the company has started implementing plans to change its marketing strategy to include more sales of general-purpose clothes and gift items to mass-merchandising retailers. These retailers are larger, and the initial receivables payments indicate that they present a more reliable pattern of payments, with fewer uncollectible amounts. As such, management has argued that the allowance for doubtful accounts should be reduced and has made the associated adjusting entry (Dr. allowance for doubtful accounts; Cr. other revenue for $40,000).

In the past, you had questioned College Ware management about its steady increase in the allowance for doubtful accounts, which had risen by about 3% per year for each of the past five years even though the rate of customer default on receivables had remained steady over that time. However, you had never insisted that management revise its allowance downward because you considered management's estimates to be conservative (i.e., it reduced income rather than increased income). In your opinion, the allowance for doubtful accounts probably *should* be reduced, although it is hard to judge exactly the amount by which the reduction should be recorded because of the relatively recent change in the marketing strategy. In other words, it is difficult for you to dispute whether management's current adjusting entry is recorded at the correct amount.

a. Comment on why management of College Ware may have an incentive to reduce the allowance for doubtful accounts this year.

b. The overly conservative accounting estimates used by management in its valuation of accounts receivable represent what is commonly referred to as *cookie jar reserves*. Using this financial reporting strategy, management sets aside money in allowance accounts that it plans to remove later to cover future losses. In doing so, management allows itself discretion to report income at smoother levels than would otherwise be achieved had the cookie jar reserves not been put in place. Comment on the implications of management's financial reporting strategy.

c. Use the ethical decision making framework introduced in *Chapter 4* to address the dilemmas the auditor faces regarding what the auditor should require the client to do regarding the client's inventory and accounts receivable balances. Recall that the steps in the framework are as follows:

- Identify the ethical issue(s).
- Determine the affected parties and identify their rights.
- Determine the most important rights.
- Develop alternative courses of action.
- Determine the likely consequences of each proposed course of action.
- Assess the possible consequences, including an estimation of the greatest good for the greatest number. Determine whether the rights framework would cause any course of action to be eliminated.
- Decide on the appropriate course of action.

FRAUD

11-39 **LO 3** List at least five common fraud schemes in the acquisition and payment cycle.

FRAUD

11-40 **LO 3** Refer to the *Focus on Fraud* feature "Fraud in the Acquisition and Payment Cycle at WorldCom and Phar-Mor." Compare and contrast the nature of these two frauds, motivations underlying the frauds, and how management perpetrated these frauds.

FRAUD

11-41 **LO 3, 4, 8** Each year Susan Riley, president of Bargon Construction, Inc., takes a three-week vacation to Hawaii and signs several blank checks to pay major bills during the period in which she is absent. Riley's vacation often occurs near the end of Bargon's fiscal reporting period because it is a slack time for the construction business. Jack Morgan, head bookkeeper for the company, uses this practice to his advantage. He makes out a check to himself for the amount of a large vendor's invoice and records it as a payment to the vendor for the purchase of supplies. He holds the check for several weeks to make sure the auditors will not examine the canceled check. Shortly after the first of the year, Morgan resubmits the invoice to Riley for payment approval and records the check in the cash disbursements journal. At that point, he marks the invoice as paid and files it with all other paid invoices. Morgan has been following this practice successfully for several years and feels confident that he has developed a foolproof fraud.

a. What is the auditor's responsibility for discovering this type of fraud?

b. What deficiencies exist in the client's internal controls?

c. What substantive audit procedures are likely to uncover the fraud?

11-42 **LO 4** Following is a list of controls in the acquisition and payment cycle for inventory and cost of goods sold. Match each control with the following activities in this cycle: (1) requisition for goods and services, (2) purchase of goods and services, (3) receipt of, and accounting for, goods and services, (4) approval of items for payment, and (5) cash disbursements.

a. The receiving department electronically scans bar codes on the goods received to record quantity and visually inspects for quality.

b. Computer-generated purchase orders are reviewed by the purchasing department.

c. Management approves contracts with suppliers.

d. Management reviews payments and compares them to data such as production budgets.

e. Management requires competitive bids for large purchases.

f. An individual in a position of authority reviews the completeness of supporting documentation prior to signing a check for payment.

g. A policy exists and is enforced whereby purchase agents are rotated across product lines.

h. A requisition form is forwarded to the purchasing department by a supervisor.

i. A policy exists and is enforced whereby employees cannot purchase from vendors outside an authorized vendor database.

j. Controls exist to ensure that only authorized goods are received.

k. Controls exist to ensure that goods meet order specifications.

l. The receiving department prepares prenumbered receiving documents to record all receipts.

m. A three-way match is made between the invoice, the purchase order, and the receiving report.

n. Limits on the purchase of inventory can be exceeded only on specific approval by a manager.

o. Supporting documentation is canceled on payment to avoid duplicate payments.

p. Management monitors inventory and purchase levels.

q. Vendor disputes about payments are handled by individuals outside the purchasing department.

r. An agreement exists with the supplier whereby the supplier agrees to ship merchandise (just in time) according to the production schedule set by the manufacturer.

11-43 **LO 4, 8** The organizational structure of a manufacturing company includes the following departments: purchasing, receiving, inspecting, warehousing, and controllership. An auditor is assigned to audit the receiving department. During audit planning, the auditor determines the following information:

1. A copy of each purchase order is routinely sent to the receiving department by the purchasing department via intracompany e-mail. This is followed by the physical copy via regular intracompany mail. Each purchase order is filed by purchase order number. In response to a job enrichment program, everyone in the receiving department is authorized to file the purchase orders. Whoever happens to be available is expected to file any purchase orders received.

2. When a shipment of goods is delivered to the receiving dock, the shipper's invoice is signed and forwarded to the controller's office, the vendor's packing slip is filed in receiving by vendor name, and the goods are stored in the warehouse by receiving personnel. In response to a job enrichment program, all persons in the receiving department have been trained to perform all three activities independently. Whoever happens to be available when a shipment arrives is expected to perform all three of the activities associated with that shipment.

   a. What are the major deficiencies and inefficiencies in the process as described?

   b. How could the process be improved? First, consider the need for strategic production and suppliers. Second, consider how greater computerization could improve the process.

   c. Why is it important to have segregation between the purchasing, receiving, and payment functions? How is that segregation maintained when all three functions are automated?

   d. Assume that the purchasing and receiving functions operate as described. What would be your preliminary assessment of control risk? What are the implications for substantive testing of the related account balances? Describe the substantive procedures the auditor should consider for inventory, expenses, payables, and other related accounts.

11-44 **LO 5** How can cross-sectional analysis performed as a planning analytical procedure help the auditor identify potential inventory misstatements for a multilocation retail client?

11-45 **LO 5** How might the auditor effectively use planning analytical procedures in the audit of various expense accounts, such as miscellaneous expenses? Provide an example.

11-46 **LO 6** Refer to *Exhibit 11.7*. Describe the differences in the planned audit approaches for Clients A and B and the reasons for such differences.

11-47 **LO 8** Refer to the *Auditing in Practice* feature "Weaknesses in Performing Substantive Analytical Procedures: The Case of Deloitte's PCAOB Inspection Report." Describe the errors that Deloitte's auditors made with regard to conducting substantive analytical procedures for inventory. Explain the potential implications of their errors.

11-48 **LO 8** The following are the procedures that an auditor should complete when observing a client's physical inventory. Refer to *Exhibit 11.9* to list these procedures in the order in which they would be completed, from Step 1 to Step 7.

Steps to Take When Observing a Client's Physical Inventory

_____Upon arriving at each site:

    a. Meet with client personnel, obtain a map of the area, and obtain a schedule of inventory counts to be made for each area.

    b. Obtain a list of sequential tag numbers to be used in each area.

    c. Observe the procedures the client supervisory personnel have implemented to shut down movement of goods.

    d. Observe that the client has shut down production.

    e. Obtain document numbers for the last shipment and receipt of goods before the physical inventory is taken. Use the information to perform cutoff tests.

_____Meet with the client to discuss the procedures, timing, location, and personnel involved in taking the annual physical inventory.

_____Review the inventory-taking procedures with all audit firm personnel. Familiarize them with the nature of the client's inventory; potential problems with the inventory; and any other information that will ensure that the client and audit personnel will properly recognize inventory items, high-dollar-value items, and obsolete items; and understand potential problems that might occur in counting the inventory.

_____Document conclusion as to the quality of the client's inventory-taking process, noting any problems that could be of audit significance. Determine whether a sufficient inventory count has been taken to properly reflect the goods on hand at year-end.

_____Determine whether specialists are needed to test or assist in correctly identifying inventory items.

_____Observe the counting of inventory and note the following on inventory count working papers:

    a. The first and last tag number used in the section.

    b. All tag numbers and the disposition of all tag numbers in the sequence.

    c. The product identification, product description, units of measure, and number of items on a count sheet.

    d. Items that appear to be obsolete or of questionable value.

    e. All high-dollar-value items included in inventory.

    f. Movement of goods into or out of the company during the process of inventory taking. Determine if goods are properly counted or excluded from inventory.

_____Review the plans for counting and tagging inventory items.

11-49 **LO 8** The following tasks are completed by the auditor while observing the physical inventory. For each task, state which assertion(s) is being primarily tested by the task: (1) existence/occurrence, (2) completeness, (3) rights and obligations, (4) valuation or allocation, or (5) presentation and disclosure.

a. The auditor makes test counts of selected items and records the test counts for subsequent tracing into the client's inventory compilation.

b. The auditor takes notations of all items that appear to be obsolete or that are in questionable condition; the auditor follows up on these items with inquiries of client personnel and retains the data to determine how they are accounted for in the inventory compilation.

    c. The auditor observes the handling of scrap and other material.

    d. The auditor observes whether any physical movement of goods occurs during the counting of inventory.

    e. The auditor records all high-dollar-value items for subsequent tracing into the client's records.

11-50 **LO 8** Describe the conditions under which it is acceptable to have the client take a physical count of inventory before year-end.

11-51 **LO 8** Determining the amount of inventory that should be written off because of obsolescence is a difficult and challenging audit task because (1) the client will usually state that most of the goods are still salable at current selling prices and (2) net realizable value is only an estimate (in other words, there is no specific, correct price at which inventory should be valued). Because of this, the auditor usually gathers corroborating evidence to provide evidence on valuation and, relatedly, obsolescence. Identify at least five sources of such corroborating evidence.

FRAUD

11-52 **LO 8** In those audits where a heightened risk of fraud exists related to inventory and cost of goods sold, the auditor will want to consider performing certain fraud-related substantive procedures. List at least five such procedures.

FRAUD

PROFESSIONAL SKEPTICISM

11-53 **LO 8** The *Focus on Fraud* feature "Examples of Fraud in Inventory" provides examples of how clients may fraudulently manipulate inventory amounts. List at least five such examples. Explain why even a professionally skeptical auditor might fall victim to a client that is perpetrating such a fraud.

11-54 **LO 8** Refer to *Exhibit 11.12*, which describes assertions and related audit procedures for accounts payable. Match the following assertions with their associated auditing procedure: (a) existence/occurrence, (b) completeness, (c) rights and obligations, (d) valuation or allocation, (e) presentation and disclosure.

1. Request vendors' monthly statements or send confirmations to major vendors requesting a statement of open account items.
2. Review the client's financial statement disclosures of accounts payable and expense accounts such as travel and entertainment.
3. Use GAS to verify mathematical accuracy of accounts payable, or agree to the general ledger.
4. Examine a sample of cash disbursements made after the end of the year to determine whether the disbursements are for goods and services applicable to the previous year.
5. Perform a cutoff test of purchases and cash disbursements made after year-end.
6. Perform analytical review of related expense accounts, for example, travel and entertainment or legal expenses.
7. Review long-term purchase commitments, and determine whether a loss needs to be accrued.
8. Agree monthly statements and confirmations from major vendors with the accounts payable list.

11-55 **LO 8** Explain why examining a sample of cash disbursements made after the end of the year is useful in determining the completeness of recorded accounts payable at year-end.

FRAUD

PROFESSIONAL SKEPTICISM

11-56 [LO 8] Reviewing unusual entries to expense accounts is an important audit procedure that is sometimes overlooked or that is not conducted with professional skepticism. Refer to the *Focus on Fraud* feature "WorldCom and Unusual Adjusting Entries," which explains how WorldCom executives used unusual journal entries to perpetrate their fraud.

a. What is unusual about the journal entry in this *Focus on Fraud* feature?

b. If confronted, do you think that management at WorldCom would have some reasonable, or at least plausible, explanation for the entry? Explain.

c. Imagine yourself as a young auditor that discovers this unusual entry and inquires about it with someone at the client. What factors might cause you to lack professional skepticism in evaluating the client's explanation?

11-57 [LO 8] During observation of a client's year-end inventory, the auditor notes that shipping document 8,702 was the last shipment for the year and that receiving report 10,163 was the last receiving report for the year. Explain how the information gathered would be used in performing an inventory cutoff test.

11-58 [LO 8] The Northwoods Manufacturing Company has automated its production facilities dramatically during the last five years, to the extent that the number of direct-labor hours has remained steady, while production has increased fivefold. Automated equipment, such as robots, has helped increase productivity. Overhead, previously applied at the rate of $7.50 per direct-labor hour, is now being applied at the rate of $23.50 per direct-labor hour. Explain how an auditor might evaluate the reasonableness of the application of factory overhead to year-end inventory and cost of goods sold.

FRAUD

PROFESSIONAL SKEPTICISM

11-59 [LO 8] The auditor has always received cooperation from a particular client and has no reason to question management's integrity. The controller has requested that the auditor inform her about which warehouse locations that the auditor will visit during the upcoming inventory count. In addition, the controller has requested copies of the auditor's observations on the physical inventory because she wants to make sure that a good inventory was taken. Should the auditor comply with these requests? State your rationale, including a discussion of professional skepticism.

11-60 [LO 8] The auditor has been assigned to the audit of Marathon Oil Company and will observe the testing of inventory at a major storage area in Ohio. The company has approximately fifteen different types of fuel oils stored in various tanks. The value of the fuel varies dramatically according to its grade. Explain how the auditor might use a specialist in auditing the inventory.

11-61 [LO 8] The auditor is always concerned whether slow-moving or potentially obsolete inventory is included in inventory, and whether inventory should be reduced to a lower market value. Identify five substantive audit procedures the auditor might use to determine the existence of obsolete goods or goods whose market value is less than cost.

11-62 [LO 8] Explain how GAS could be used to help identify potentially obsolete inventory.

11-63 [LO 8] Explain the purpose of test counts and other inventory observations that the auditor notes while a physical inventory is being taken.

11-64 **LO 8** Review *Exhibit 11.11*. What financial statement disclosures are required for inventory? How does the auditor determine the adequacy of the client's financial statement disclosures?

11-65 **LO 8** Identify two substantive audit procedures that an auditor might use to gain assurance about the correctness of perpetual inventory records.

11-66 **LO 8** The following audit procedures (labeled (1) through (8)) are found in audit programs addressing the acquisition and payment cycle. For each audit procedure described:

a. Identify the objective of the procedure or the management assertion being tested.

b. Classify the procedure as primarily a substantive test, a test of controls, or both.

1. The auditor examines payments to vendors following year-end and then reviews any open accounts payable files.

2. The auditor reviews computer-center records on changes to passwords and the client's procedures to monitor unusual amounts of access by password type. The auditor makes inquiries of purchasing agents about how often passwords are changed and whether assistants are allowed to access computer files in their absence in order to efficiently handle inquiries or process standing orders.

3. The auditor reviews a report of all accounts payable items that were not matched by the automated matching system but had been paid upon authorization of the accounts payable department. A sample of selected items is taken and traced to the vendor payment and supporting documentation.

4. The auditor uses GAS to prepare a report of all debits to accounts payable other than payments to vendors. A sample of the debits is selected and examined for support.

5. The auditor uses GAS to access all recorded receipts of merchandise that have not been matched to an open purchase order.

6. The client prepares a report from a database showing inventory write-downs by product line and by purchasing agent. The auditor reviews the report and analyzes the data in relation to sales volume by product.

7. The auditor creates a spreadsheet showing the amount of scrap generated monthly, by product line.

8. The auditor downloads client data to create a report showing monthly sales and inventory levels, by product line.

11-67 **LO 8** Auditing standards require the auditor to observe the client's physical inventory. That requirement could be met by observing the client's annual physical count of inventory and, in some circumstances, by observing inventory in connection with tests of the accuracy of the client's perpetual inventory.

a. What major purpose is served by requiring the auditor to observe the client's physical inventory count? What are the primary assertions for which the auditor gains evidence during the inventory observation?

b. Identify at least five items related to inventory that the auditor should be looking for and should document during the observation of the client's inventory.

c. How does the observation process differ when the client takes a complete physical count at or near year-end versus when physical counts are taken throughout the year to test the accuracy of the perpetual records?

11-68 **LO 8** An auditor has been assigned to audit the accounts payable of an audit client where there is a high risk of material misstatement related to accounts payable. Control risk is assessed as high, management integrity is marginal, and the company is near violation of important loan covenants, particularly one that requires the maintenance of a minimum working-capital ratio. Explain how the auditor should approach the year-end audit of accounts payable, including a discussion of specific substantive audit procedures.

11-69 **LO 8** Paul Mincin, CPA, is the auditor of Raleigh Corporation. Mincin is considering the audit work to be performed in the accounts payable area for the current-year engagement. The prior-year documentation shows that confirmation requests were mailed to 100 of Raleigh's 1,000 suppliers. The selected suppliers were based on Mincin's sample that was designed to select accounts with large dollar balances. Mincin and Raleigh staff spent a substantial number of hours resolving relatively minor differences between the confirmation replies and Raleigh's accounting records. Alternative audit procedures were used for those suppliers who did not respond to the confirmation requests.

a. Identify the accounts payable management assertions that Mincin must consider in determining the audit procedures to be followed.

b. Identify situations in which Mincin should use accounts payable confirmations, and discuss whether he is required to use them.

c. Discuss why using large dollar balances as the basis for selecting accounts payable for confirmation might not be the most effective approach and indicate what more effective procedures could be followed when selecting accounts payable for confirmation.

11-70 **LO 8** The auditor often examines some expense accounts, such as legal expenses, in detail even if the account balance is not material. Explain why.

11-71 **LO 8** Why does the auditor examine travel and entertainment expenses? What would poor controls regarding executive reimbursements say about the tone at the top for purposes of evaluating and reporting on internal control?

PCAOB and Grant Thornton

PROFESSIONAL SKEPTICISM

11-72 **(LO 1, 5, 6, 8, 9)** On October 4, 2008, the PCAOB issued its annual inspection report of Grant Thornton LLP (PCAOB Release No. 104–2008-046). In conducting its inspections, the PCAOB focuses on audit engagements that it considers particularly risky or prone to error on the part of each audit firm. In its inspection report of Grant Thornton, the PCAOB noted the following problems in testing the inventory valuation assertion for a Grant Thornton client. The firm failed in the following respects to adequately test the valuation assertion regarding inventory:

- There was no evidence in the audit documentation, and no persuasive other evidence, that the firm had performed sufficient substantive procedures to test the raw materials and/or labor and overhead components of inventory at certain of its manufacturing locations. Analytical procedures, consisting of various high-level comparisons, including average cost, inventory balances, gross profit margins, and inventory turnover, were the firm's primary tests, but these procedures failed to meet the requirements for substantive analytical procedures. Specifically, the firm failed to develop expectations that were precise enough to provide the desired level of assurance that differences that may be potential material misstatements, individually or in the aggregate, would be identified, and failed to obtain corroboration of management's explanations of significant unexpected differences.

- The firm failed to evaluate the assumptions that management had used to determine the reserve for obsolete inventory.

  a. The PCAOB report summarized a problem with Grant Thornton's testing of a client's inventory valuation assertion. Discuss why you believe the PCAOB was dissatisfied with the firm's performance.

  b. Use the framework for professional decision making from *Chapter 4* to determine the appropriate steps that the firm could have taken that would have ultimately been acceptable to the PCAOB. Recall that the framework is as follows:

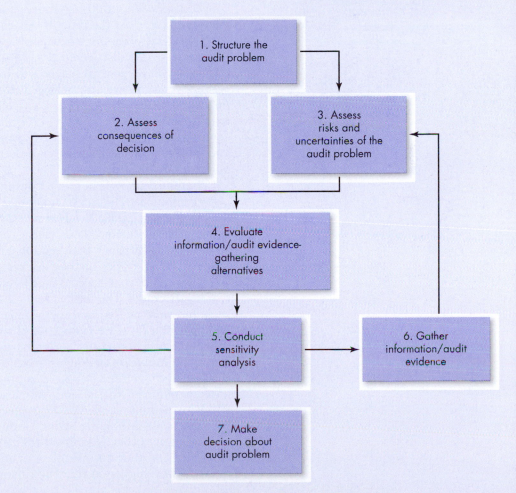

Source: Adapted from *Judgment and Choice*, by Robin Hogarth.

FRAUD FOCUS: CONTEMPORARY AND HISTORICAL CASES

FRAUD

PROFESSIONAL SKEPTICISM

11-73

Thor Industries, Inc. and Mark Schwartzhoff, and Deloitte (LO 2, 3, 4, 6, 8)

Refer to the *Professional Judgment in Context* feature "Thor Industries, Inc. and Mark Schwartzhoff: Fraudulent Reductions in Cost of Goods Sold Through Manipulation of Inventory Accounts." Answer the following questions.

a. List the incentives and opportunities that enabled Schwartzhoff to commit the fraud. Speculate on his possible rationalizations.

b. What do the control deficiencies imply about the approach Deloitte should have used to audit the inventory-related accounts and assertions on the Thor and Dutchmen audits? Discuss your answer in terms of the relative mix of evidence in the form of tests of details, substantive analytics, and tests of controls. Why might Deloitte auditors have lacked professional skepticism regarding the financial results of Dutchmen?

c. What substantive audit procedures (both tests of details and analytical procedures) could have potentially detected this type of fraud earlier?

FRAUD

PROFESSIONAL SKEPTICISM

11-74

Ace Hardware and KPMG (LO 2, 3, 4, 5)

Ace Hardware is a retailer-owned cooperative, with 4,600 hardware, home center, and building materials stores. At the time of this case, Ace was a private company that was planning to go public. In September 2007, Ace Hardware said it discovered a $154 million accounting discrepancy between its general ledger and its actual inventory. The accounting error was discovered during an internal review of financial reports. The company explained that it had found a difference between the company's 2006 general ledger balance—the company's primary method for recording financial transactions—and its actual inventory records, referred to as its *perpetual inventory balance*.

Ace hired a law firm and a consulting firm to investigate. The investigation cost about $10 million. As a result of the investigation, in January 2008, Ace Hardware reported that a mid-level employee in the finance department caused a $152 million accounting discrepancy between the general ledger and the actual inventory. The former finance worker made journal entries of a sizeable amount that masked a difference in numbers between the two ledger books. The ledgers looked as though they were reconciled, but were not. About one-quarter of the error dated to 1995, and the rest took place from 2002 through 2006. In its 10-K filing, the company reported that gross margins had increased by about 2% in the five years leading up to fiscal year-end 2002, rising from 7.7% to 9.4%. Home Depot, in contrast, maintained a very stable gross margin over that period, which was consistently about 30%. KPMG issued unqualified audit opinions on the company's financial statements during the period of the inventory misstatements.

Company officials stressed that the employee did not commit fraud and that no inventory or money was missing. Rather, the company suggested that the finance person was not properly trained or equipped to do the job. The company further suggested that the situation was Ace's fault, in that the finance person was not appropriately trained and that oversight and checks and balances were not in place. Company officials also blamed the error partly on the increasingly complex and competitive retail hardware industry. Specifically, systems in place were not adequate for addressing complications that arose from Ace's recent increase in product imports from Asia. Since that time, Ace has implemented a modern, point-of-sale inventory management system that has significantly improved internal controls and inventory pricing at individual retailer locations.

As a result of the discovery of the inventory problem, Ace had to put on hold its plans to issue a public offering of stock. While we often think of inventory misstatements as due to fraud, this case illustrates that such misstatements can also be caused by errors.

a. List the inherent, control, and fraud risk factors relevant to this case.
b. State plausible reasons that KPMG audit personnel may have lacked professional skepticism in their audits of Ace Hardware.

FRAUD

PROFESSIONAL SKEPTICISM

11-75

VeriFone Holdings, Inc.
(LO 2, 3, 4, 5, 6, 8)   In 2009, the SEC charged VeriFone Holdings, Inc., a technology company, with falsifying the company's financial statement to improve gross margins and income. VeriFone relied on gross margin as an indicator of its financial results and provided forecasts of its quarterly gross margins to investment analysts.

In early February 2007, during the quarterly closing process for the fiscal year ending January 31, 2007, preliminary financial results revealed a gross margin of 42.8%, which was about four percentage points below internal forecasts that had been communicated to analysts. Paul Periolat was a mid-level controller at VeriFone, and his responsibilities included forecasting gross margins and making final inventory-related valuation adjustments relating to royalties, warranty reserves, and inventory obsolescence. When the CEO and CFO learned of the unexpectedly low gross margins in the preliminary financial results, they sent e-mails calling the issue an "unmitigated disaster" and instructed VeriFone managers beneath them to "figure it [and related low results] out."

Periolat determined that the problem in gross margin was due to incorrect accounting by a foreign subsidiary. He made a manual adjusting entry to record an increase to ending inventory of $7 million, thereby decreasing cost of goods sold and increasing gross margin. He failed to confirm the adjustments with the foreign subsidiary's controller and knew that the adjustments were incorrect. Periolat continued to make large manual quarterly adjustments to inventory balances for which there was no reasonable basis over the next two quarters. These adjustments allowed the company to continue to meet its internal forecasts and its earnings guidance made to analysts. Periolat was able to make his unwarranted adjustments, in part, because VeriFone had few internal controls to prevent them.

Neither the employee's supervisor nor any other senior manager reviewed the employee's work. Further, effective controls were not in place to prevent the person responsible for forecasting financial results from making adjustments that allowed the company to meet the forecasts.

Ultimately, when the misstatements were revealed and VeriFone restated its financial statements, the company's operating income fell from $65.6 million to $28.6 million, a reduction of 129%. When the misrepresentations were revealed in December 2007, VeriFone's stock price dropped 46%, which represented a one-day drop in market capitalization of $1.8 billion. With this much at stake, auditors need to remember to be professionally skeptical about manual entries and to require that appropriate documentation supporting the entries be available for their review. Further, in areas where internal controls are not effective, the auditor should implement appropriate substantive procedures due to the heightened risk of misstatement.

For further information, see SEC AAER No. 3044, September 1, 2009.

a. List the inherent, control, and fraud risk factors relevant to this case.

b. What substantive audit procedures would have detected the fraud? Would planning or substantive analytics have been helpful in detecting the fraud?

FRAUD

PROFESSIONAL SKEPTICISM

11-76

Cenco Medical Health Supply Corporation (LO 2, 3, 4, 6, 7, 8, 9) Cenco Medical Health Supply Corporation (CMH) was an SEC-registered company that went bankrupt after it had materially misstated its financial statements for a number of years. It inflated the reporting of its physical inventory by 50% during two years prior to its bankruptcy. The fraud was perpetrated by "(1) altering the quantities recorded on the pre-numbered, two-part inventory tags used in counting the inventory; (2) altering documents reflected on a computer list prepared to record the physical count of inventory; and (3) creating inventory tags to record quantities of nonexistent inventory."

The SEC asserted that the auditors should have detected the fictitious inventory but did not because the audit firm "left the extent of various observation testing to the discretion of auditors, not all of whom were aware of significant audit planning that should have related directly to the extent of such testing. Observation of inventory counts at year end was confined to six locations (representing about 40% of the total CMH inventory) as opposed to nine in the preceding year. The field auditors did not adequately control the inventory tags and the auditor did not detect the creation of bogus inventory tags which were inserted in the final inventory computations." The SEC was also critical of the audit firm for assigning interns to a significant portion of the inventory observation without training them in the nature of the client's inventory or its counting procedures. This is an example of a situation in which auditors' lack of professional skepticism led to low audit quality and a subsequent audit failure.

Source: R. W. V. Dickenson, "Why the Fraud Went Undetected," CA Magazine April 1977, pp. 67–69.

The SEC alleged that many deficiencies occurred during the audit of CMH. Among the complaints were the following:

1. The audit firm "left the extent of various observation testing to the discretion of auditors, not all of whom were aware of significant audit conclusions which related directly to the extent of such testing. Observations of inventory counts at year end were confined to six locations (representing about 40% of the total CMH inventory) as opposed to nine in the preceding year. The field auditors did not adequately control the inventory tags and Seidman & Seidman [the auditor] did not detect the creation of bogus inventory tags which were inserted in the final inventory computations."

2. The comparison of recorded test counts to the computer lists in the nine warehouse locations in which the inventory count was observed indicated error rates ranging from 0.9% to 38.3% of the test counts, with error rates in excess of 10% in several locations. Management attributed the differences to errors made by a keypunch operator. When the auditors asked to see the inventory tags, the CMH official stated that they had been destroyed.

3. The Seidman & Seidman auditor who performed the price testing of the CMH inventory determined that, as in previous years, in numerous instances CMH was unable to produce sufficient vendor invoices to support the purchase by CMH of the quantities being tested. This was true even though Seidman & Seidman ultimately accepted vendor invoices reflecting the purchase of the item by any CMH branch, regardless of the location of the inventory actually being price tested.

4. A schedule of comparative inventory balances reflected significant increases from the prior year. A CMH financial officer wrote on this schedule management's explanations for the increases in inventory accounts.

5. CMH did not use prenumbered purchase orders and shipping documents.

6. Several differences exist between the tags reflected on the computer list for the Miami warehouse and the observation of the same tag numbers by Seidman & Seidman auditors. The computer list contained a series of almost 1,000 tags, covering about 20% of the tags purportedly used and more than 50% of the total reported value of the Miami inventory, which were reported as being unused on the tag control document obtained by Seidman & Seidman during its observation work.

7. Because CMH management did not provide sufficient invoices as requested, the auditors relied primarily on vendor catalogs, price lists, and vendor invoices to test the accuracy of the CMH inventory pricing representations.

   a. For each of the deficiencies identified, indicate the appropriate action that should have been taken by the auditor.

   b. What inventory information should be communicated to an auditor who is not regularly assigned to the audit of a particular client prior to the observation of a physical inventory count?

   c. How do questions of management integrity affect the approach that should be taken in planning the observation of a client's inventory-counting procedures?

d. Identify instances in which the auditors in this case did not exercise appropriate professional skepticism. For each of those instances, describe an alternative way that the auditor should have handled this situation.

e. The individual auditors conducting the audit inventory tests were lacking the appropriate training or knowledge to conduct their jobs. Assume that you and your classmates were assigned to an audit client and you find yourselves in a similar situation when you arrive to conduct an inventory observation. In particular, you are asked to observe inventory counts of products for which you are unsure of the appropriate measurement technique and are lacking in knowledge of the product itself. The client quickly describes the measurement process and offers to help you identify the different products. You are still somewhat unsure of your abilities to conduct this inventory observation. Use the framework for professional decision making from *Chapter 4* to determine the appropriate steps to take.

APPLICATION ACTIVITIES

NOTE: Completing Application Activities requires students to reference additional resources and materials. Some Application Activities will require the student to reference relevant professional auditing standards. We make special note of these as Auditing Standards Application Activities.

FRAUD

ETHICS

PROFESSIONAL SKEPTICISM

11-77 **LO 2, 3, 4, 9**   The *Focus on Fraud* feature "Fraud in the Acquisition and Payment Cycle at WorldCom and Phar-Mor" introduced you to the basic facts underlying the WorldCom fraud. Use appropriate sources to answer the following questions:

a. Identify the names of the following individuals at the company, describe their role in the fraud, and describe the penalties that they ultimately faced (if any): the CEO, CFO, controller, and the director of internal audit.

b. What appears to have been the incentives and opportunities to commit the fraud?

c. Comment on the likely ethical dilemma that Cynthia Cooper faced when she initially uncovered the fraud.

d. Which audit firm conducted the external audit on WorldCom's financial statements in the years prior to the discovery of the fraud? Why might the auditors have lacked the necessary professional skepticism to uncover the fraud?

FRAUD

11-78 **LO 2, 3, 4**   The *Focus on Fraud* feature "Weak Internal Controls, Unethical Decisions, and a Fictitious Vendor at Baird Products" introduced you to an example of a purchasing manager who used a fictitious vendor to accomplish a fraud in the acquisition and payment cycle. Using appropriate sources, locate an example of another such case. If you perform an electronic search, you might want to use the search terms *fraud* and *fictitious vendor*. Answer the following questions:

a. What was the company involved, and who was the fraudster?

b. How was the fraud perpetrated?

c. What was the dollar value of the loss?

d. What was the resolution of the case; for example, did the fraudster get fined or jailed?

11-79 **LO 4, 5, 6** Refer to *Exhibit 11.6* and access the SEC filings for FYE 2009, 2010, and 2011 for the following companies: (a) Kohl's, (b) Williams Sonoma, and (c) Dollar General.

a. Calculate the following ratios from *Exhibit 11.6* for each of the companies:
- Gross margin %
- Inventory turnover
- Days' sales in inventory
- Accounts payable/current liabilities

b. Compare and contrast your results across companies, and note any areas of audit attention that are evident.

c. Summarize management's disclosures about internal control for each company for the fiscal year 2011. Comment on audit implications, including the relative proportion of evidence that you would gather from tests of details, substantive analytics, and tests of controls.

PROFESSIONAL SKEPTICISM

ETHICS

11-80 **LO 8, 9** Refer to the *Auditing in Practice* feature "The Importance of Professional Skepticism in Testing the Valuation of Inventory: The PCAOB Disciplines Ibarra." Go to the PCAOB web site and download Enforcement Release No. 2006–009. After reading the release, answer the following questions.

a. Identify the pervasive problems that were detected by the PCAOB in its inspections of Ibarra.

b. Comment on the nature of punishments that were imposed and your reflections on their severity (or lack thereof).

c. What conduct of Ibarra strikes you as the most unethical in this situation?

FRAUD

11-81 **LO 3, 5, 8** Refer to the *Focus on Fraud* feature "Examples of Fraud in Inventory." The AICPA's Practice Alert described in the feature provides examples of many types of inventory frauds that have occurred. Access and read the following article that describes how to detect these types of frauds: *http://www.journal-ofaccountancy.com/Issues/2001/Jun/GhostGoodsHowToSpot-PhantomInventory.htm*

a. What are the four techniques that companies use to commit inventory fraud?

b. What analytical procedures may indicate inventory fraud?

c. Who are the most common perpetrators of inventory fraud?

d. List at least five indicators of heightened risk for inventory fraud.

AUDITING STANDARDS APPLICATION ACTIVITY

11-82 **AICPA (LO 8)** Refer to the *Standards Appendix* to the text. Locate the relevant AICPA standard pertaining to audit evidence-specific considerations for selected items (inventory), then locate the actual standard on the AICPA's web site, and answer the following questions.

a. What is the number of the standard?

b. What does the standard require the auditor to do to obtain sufficient appropriate audit evidence regarding the existence and condition of inventory?

c. What does the standard require the auditor to do if physical inventory counting is conducted at a date other than the date of the financial statements?

ANALYTICAL PROCEDURES: A CASE IN THE CONTEXT OF THE PHARMACEUTICAL INDUSTRY

NOTE: In this and select cycle chapters, we present a case set in the-pharmaceutical industry. The case enables students to practice developing and conducting planning and substantive analytical procedures. The case was developed using the published financial statements of three prominent companies in this industry, with adaptations to make the case suitable for classroom use. The fictional company names are as follows: PharmaCorp, Novartell, and Astra-Zoro. You will access an excel file on the textbook's web site at *www.cengage.com*. The excel file contains financial data and information from footnote disclosures. The primary analytical procedures tasks will focus on PharmaCorp. You will use Novartell and AstraZoro as industry comparison companies. Access and download the file, then complete the requirements in 11-83.

11-83 **LO 5, 8** This case will enable you to practice conducting planning and substantive analytical procedures for accounts in the acquisition and payment cycle. When analyzing the financial data, you may assume that the 2015 information is *unaudited*, while prior year data is audited.

As you complete this case, consider the following features of and trends in the pharmaceutical industry and for PharmaCorp specifically:

- After a long period of industry dominance by companies in the United States, the United Kingdom, and Europe, these companies are facing increasing competition from companies domiciled in emerging economies, such as Brazil, India, and China.
- There exists significant uncertainty in the market because of recent regulation covering health-care and government pay-outs for certain procedures and related pharmaceuticals.
- Health-care policy makers and the government are increasingly mandating what physicians can prescribe to patients.
- Health-care policy makers and the government are increasingly focusing on prevention regimes rather than treatment regimes, thereby leading to shifts in the demand for various pharmaceuticals.
- The global pharmaceutical market is anticipated to grow by 5% to 7% in 2016 compared with a 4% to 5% growth rate in 2015, according to a leading industry analyst publication.
- Beginning in 2014, PharmaCorp initiated and executed a significant company-wide cost reduction initiative aimed at improving manufacturing efficiency, cutting back on research and development expenses, and eliminating unnecessary corporate overhead.
- PharmaCorp's policies for extending credit to customers have remained stable over the last three years. PharmaCorp's credit-granting policies are considered stringent within the industry, and analysts have sometimes criticized the company for this, contending that such policies have hindered the company's revenue growth relative to industry peers.
- Two of PharmaCorp's popular pharmaceuticals, Selebrax and Vyvox, came off patent during the fourth quarter of FYE 2015. These pharmaceuticals now face competition in the generic drug portion of the overall industry market.

Information specific to the Acquisition and Payment Cycle

- Raw materials inventory required in the businesses are purchased from numerous suppliers. No serious shortages or delays of raw materials inventory were encountered in 2015, and none are expected in 2016. PharmaCorp has successfully secured the raw materials inventory necessary to meet its requirements where there have been short-term inbalances between supply and demand, but generally at higher prices than those historically paid.
- A risk that companies in this industry face with respect to the acquisition and payment cycle is that there is a possibility of

failing to maintain the integrity of supply chains, possibly resulting in intentional and criminal acts such as product diversion, product theft, and counterfeit raw materials inventory.

- In response to pricing pressure, several major suppliers changed their policy with respect to discounts for early payment of amounts due on credit sales. In response, PharmaCorp changed its policy of paying within two weeks to paying within four weeks since it is no longer monetarily beneficial to do so from a cash management perspective.

Part I: Planning Analytical Procedures

a. *Step 1: Identify Suitable Analytical Procedures.* Your audit senior has suggested that the following ratios (on an overall financial statement level) will be used for planning analytical procedures in the acquisition and payment cycle at PharmaCorp:

Inventory Ratios
- Gross margin analysis (revenues-cost of sales)/revenues
- Changes in cost of goods sold on a percentage basis, yearly comparisons
- Inventory turnover (cost of goods sold/ending inventory)
- Number of days' sales in inventory (365/inventory turnover)

Accounts Payable Ratios
- Accounts payable turnover (purchases/average accounts payable)
- Days outstanding in accounts payable (365/accounts payable turnover)
- Accounts payable/current liabilities

    As part of Step 1, identify any other relevant relationships or trend analyses that would be useful to consider as part of planning analytics. Explain your reasoning.

b. *Step 2: Evaluate Reliability of Data Used to Develop Expectations.* The audit team has determined that the data you will be using to develop expectations in the acquisition and payment cycle are reliable. Indicate the factors that the audit team likely considered in making that determination.

c. *Step 3: Develop Expectations.* Complete Step 3 of planning analytical procedures by developing expectations for relevant accounts in the acquisition cycle and for the ratios from Part (a). Develop expectations by considering both historical trends of PharmaCorp, and also by considering features of and historical trends in the industry. Given that this is a planning analytical procedure, the expectations are not expected to have a high level of precision. You might indicate that you expect a ratio to increase, decrease, or stay the same, and possibly indicate the size of any expected increases or decreases, or the range of the expected ratio. PharmaCorp's financial information is on first tab of the Excel file, while the financial information for Novartell and AstraZoro is provided on the last two tabs of the Excel file.

d. *Step 4 and Step 5: Define and Identify Significant Unexpected Differences.* Refer to the guidance in *Chapter 7* on performance materiality, tolerable misstatement, and clearly trivial amounts. Apply those materiality guidelines to Step 4 of planning analytical procedures in the acquisition and payment cycle for PharmaCorp to define what is meant by a significant difference. Explain your reasoning. Also comment on qualitative materiality considerations in this context. Now that you have determined what amount of difference would be considered significant, calculate the ratios identified in Step 1 (and any additional ratios or trend analyses that you suggested), based on PharmaCorp's recorded financial statement amounts. Identify those ratios where there is a significant unexpected difference.

e. ***Step 6 and Step 7: Investigate Significant Unexpected Differences and Ensure Proper Documentation.***Complete Step 6 of planning analytical procedures by describing accounts or relationships that you would investigate further through substantive audit procedures. Explain your reasoning. To complete Step 7, describe what information should be included in the auditor's workpapers.

Part II: Substantive Analytical Procedures

f. Management has explained the decline in cost of goods sold as involving:

- Lower purchase accounting charges, primarily reflecting fair value adjustments relating to acquired inventory that was subsequently sold
- Lower costs related to new cost reduction and productivity initiatives, as well as savings generated from ongoing productivity initiatives to streamline the supply-chain network
- Reduced manufacturing volumes related to products that lost exclusivity in various markets
- The impact of favorable foreign exchange rates of 3%.

Explain the types of ratio analysis that you could conduct in substantive analytical procedures to test the validity of management's explanations. Comment on the trends and relationships that you believe are most relevant, and implications for further substantive testing.

ACADEMIC RESEARCH CASES

NOTE: Completing Academic Research Cases requires students to reference additional resources and materials.

SEARCH HINT

It is easy to locate these academic research articles! Use a search engine such as Google Scholar or an electronic research platform such as ABI Inform, and search using the author names and part of the article title.

11-84 [LO 5] Locate and read the article listed below and answer the following questions.

Nigrini, M. and L. Mittermaier. 1997. The use of Benford's Law as an aid in analytical procedures. *Auditing: A Journal of Practice & Theory* 16 (2): 52–67.

a. What is the issue being addressed in the paper?
b. What are the findings of the paper?
c. Why is this paper important to auditors, and what are the implications of this paper for the auditing profession?
d. Describe the research methodology used as a basis for the conclusions.
e. Describe any limitations of the research.

11-85 **LO 3, 8** Locate and read the article listed below and answer the following questions.

Alleyne, P., N. Persaud, P. Alleyne, D. Greenidge, and P. Sealy. 2010. Perceived effectiveness of fraud detection audit procedures in a stock and warehousing cycle: Additional evidence from Barbados. *Managerial Auditing Journal* 25 (6): 553–568.

a. What is the issue being addressed in the paper?

b. What are the findings of the paper?

c. Why is this paper important to auditors, and what are the implications of this paper for the auditing profession?

d. Describe the research methodology used as a basis for the conclusions.

e. Describe any limitations of the research.

FORD AND TOYOTA

	Ford Motor Company and Toyota Motor Corporation
11-86	(LO **1, 2, 3, 4, 5, 6**)

Source and Reference	Question
Ford 10-K, Toyota 20-F	a. What are the key acquisition and inventory cycle accounts for Ford? What are the critical accounting policies for these accounts?
Ford 10-K, Toyota 20-F	b. Compare Ford and Toyota's footnotes on inventory. Calculate the percentage of finished products that each company holds in inventory. What inferences do you draw from this analysis? How could this ratio be used to understand slow-moving inventory, for example, by geographic region or product line?
	c. Think creatively, and develop ratios or comparisons that would help you understand this transaction cycle for these automotive companies. In addressing this question, it will be helpful to tailor the "usual" analytical procedures to this unique industry and business setting.
Ford 10-K	d. Ford lists a variety of risk factors associated with its business. Review those and identify which relate most to the acquisition and inventory cycle. What evidence might the auditor gather to understand how those risks may affect the financial statement line items associated with the acquisition and inventory cycle?
	e. As an auditor, what is your obligation regarding the statements that management makes in its management discussion and analysis?

ACL

NOTE: There is an ACL Appendix at the end of the text that you may find helpful in completing this problem.

11-87 | **Husky Corporation** (LO **5, 8**) — Assume that you are auditing inventory of HUSKY Corp. as of December 31, 2013. The inventory general ledger balance is $8,124,998.66. HUSKY manufactures lawn and garden tractors, snowmobiles, and supplies. Download the data file labeled "HUSKY Inventory 2013" from the book's web site under Student Resources. This file contains the following information:

SNUMB	Stock number (The first letter is F—finished goods, W—work in progress, R—raw material.)
LASTSALE	Date of last sale (finished goods) or use (raw material)
NUMSOLD	Number sold (finished goods) or used (raw materials) year-to-date
UNITCOST	Unit cost
INVQTY	Quantity on hand
EXTCOST	Unit cost × Quantity on hand
SELPRICE	Current selling price (finished goods only)
REPLCOST	Current replacement cost (raw material only)

Also, note that salespersons receive a 10% commission based on selling price.

a. Using the menu option **Analyze**, choose **Statistical** then **Statistics** on the amount field, print the statistics, and agree the total inventory to the general ledger.

b. Extract and print out all inventory items that have not been used or sold in six months. Include in the printout the total extended cost of those items.

c. Extract the finished goods into a separate file (Hint: Use the expression **SNUMB = "F"**):

i. Extract those items that have a net realizable value less than cost. Add a column and calculate the amount each of those items that should be written down, and print a report that includes those items and the total of the write-down.

ii. Add a field and calculate inventory turnover for each item in inventory. Extract and print a report of those items with a turnover less than 2. The report should include the total extended cost of those items.

d. Extract the raw materials into a separate file (see hint in Part c, but replace "F" with "R"):

i. Extract those items that have a replacement cost less than cost, add a column and calculate the amount each of those items that should be written down, and print a report that includes those items and the total of the write-down.

ii. Add a column and calculate inventory turnover for each item. Extract and print a report of those items with a turnover less than 2. The report should include the total extended cost of those items.

e. Prepare a report of the audit implications of your findings, indicating any additional procedures that should be performed.

12 | Auditing Long-Lived Assets: Acquisition, Use, Impairment, and Disposal

CHAPTER OVERVIEW AND LEARNING OBJECTIVES

When auditing long-lived assets, the auditor focuses on asset acquisition, use, impairment, and disposal. This chapter presents a discussion of the audit risks and audit risk responses associated with long-lived assets, such as land, property and equipment, natural resources, intangibles, and leases. In terms of the audit opinion formulation process, this chapter primarily involves Phases II, III, and IV, that is, performing risk assessment procedures, tests of controls, and substantive procedures for long-lived assets and related accounts.

Through studying this chapter, you will be able to achieve these learning objectives:

1. Identify the significant accounts, disclosures, and relevant assertions in auditing long-lived assets.

2. Identify and assess inherent risks of material misstatement associated with long-lived assets.

3. Identify and assess fraud risks of material misstatement associated with long-lived assets.

4. Identify and assess control risks of material misstatement associated with long-lived assets.

5. Describe how to use planning analytical procedures to identify possible material misstatements associated with long-lived assets.

6. Determine appropriate responses to identified risks of material misstatement in auditing long-lived assets.

7. Determine appropriate tests of controls and consider the results of tests of controls in auditing long-lived assets.

8. Determine and apply sufficient appropriate substantive audit procedures in auditing long-lived assets.

9. Apply the frameworks for professional decision making and ethical decision making to issues involving the audit of long-lived assets.

THE AUDIT OPINION FORMULATION PROCESS

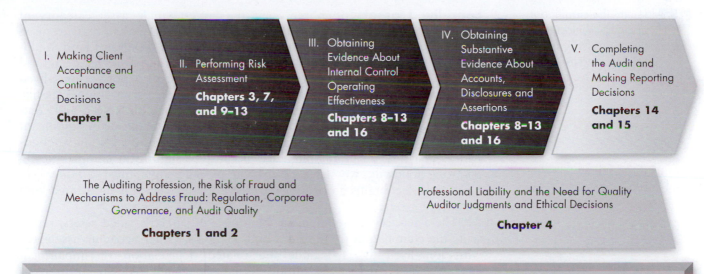

I. Making Client Acceptance and Continuance Decisions **Chapter 1**

II. Performing Risk Assessment **Chapters 3, 7, and 9–13**

III. Obtaining Evidence About Internal Control Operating Effectiveness **Chapters 8–13 and 16**

IV. Obtaining Substantive Evidence About Accounts, Disclosures and Assertions **Chapters 8–13 and 16**

V. Completing the Audit and Making Reporting Decisions **Chapters 14 and 15**

The Auditing Profession, the Risk of Fraud and Mechanisms to Address Fraud: Regulation, Corporate Governance, and Audit Quality **Chapters 1 and 2**

Professional Liability and the Need for Quality Auditor Judgments and Ethical Decisions **Chapter 4**

The Audit Opinion Formulation Process and a Framework for Obtaining Audit Evidence **Chapters 5 and 6**

PROFESSIONAL JUDGMENT IN CONTEXT
Accounting Problems Related to Long-Lived Assets and Leases at Ignite Restaurant Group

Ignite Restaurant Group (IRG), the owner of various restaurants including Joe's Crab Shack, went public in May 2012. Just two months later, the company announced that it needed to restate its financial statements to correct errors related to the treatment of certain leases. The announcement resulted in a single day stock price decline of 22%. The lease errors began in 2006 (the year of the company's origination) and continued through the first quarter of 2012. The restatement related to the leases was estimated to be between $3.4 and $3.8 million. As a result of this situation, IRG planned a fixed-asset accounting review to assess historical asset additions, dispositions, useful lives, and depreciation from 2006 through the first quarter of 2012. At the time of the announcement in July 2012, IRG anticipated additional restatements of at least $1.2 million related to the accounting for its other fixed assets and related depreciation expense.

In October 2012, IRG announced that it had completed its internal review of this situation. The aggregate impact of the restatement adjustments and related tax effects (from the company's inception in

2006 through the first quarter of 2012) reduced net income by a total of $6.4 million over the five-year plus period. In connection with the restatement, management identified material weaknesses in its internal control over financial reporting related to lack of sufficient qualified accounting and tax personnel; lack of adequate supervision and monitoring of accounting operations; inadequate lease accounting controls; and lack of effective controls related to the existence, completeness, and accuracy of fixed assets and related depreciation and amortization expense.

As you read through this chapter, consider the following questions:

- What types of misstatements occur in long-lived asset accounts? (LO 1, 2, 3)
- What might motivate management to intentionally misstate long-lived asset accounts? (LO 3)
- What controls should be in place to mitigate misstatements associated with long-lived assets? (LO 4)
- What procedures should an auditor perform when auditing long-lived asset accounts? (LO 5, 6, 7, 8)

Significant Accounts, Disclosures, and Relevant Assertions

LO 1 Identify the significant accounts, disclosures, and relevant assertions in auditing long-lived assets.

Long-lived assets often represent the largest single asset category of many organizations. Long-lived assets are noncurrent assets that are used over multiple operating cycles and include **tangible assets** of land, buildings, fixtures, and equipment. Some organizations also have natural resources, such as timber tracts, oil wells, and mineral deposits. Long-lived assets also include **intangible assets**. For example, drug companies like Pfizer have patent costs that are capitalized as intangible assets, and companies like Coca-Cola have franchise licenses that make up a significant portion of the company's total assets. Many organizations also have goodwill as a significant intangible asset. Because of significant complexities in auditing goodwill, we defer discussion of that topic until *Chapter 16*. *Exhibit 12.1* contains an overview of the accounts typically associated with long-lived assets.

The asset account (equipment, buildings, or similarly titled assets) represents the culmination of additions and disposals. Other accounts associated with long-lived assets include the related depreciation or impairment expense, any related gains from disposals, any related losses from disposals or impairments, and the accumulated depreciation account. For natural resources, the related expense account is **depletion expense** (the expense associated with the extraction of natural resources). For intangible assets with a definite life, the related expense account is **amortization expense**.

Assets can also be acquired through capital leases; organizations acquiring assets through capital leases will need to consider whether the relevant criteria for capitalizing the leases have been met and whether the off–balance sheet disclosures are appropriate.

Activities in the Long-Lived Asset Acquisition and Payment Cycle

The purchase of long-lived assets includes the same types of activities for purchasing current assets that we discussed in *Chapter 11*. The long-lived assets will be requested and purchased. The organization will approve and make payment for the asset. An important difference is that the acquisition of long-lived assets will be based on an organization's planning for

---

EXHIBIT 12.1 Long-Lived Assets: Account Interrelationships

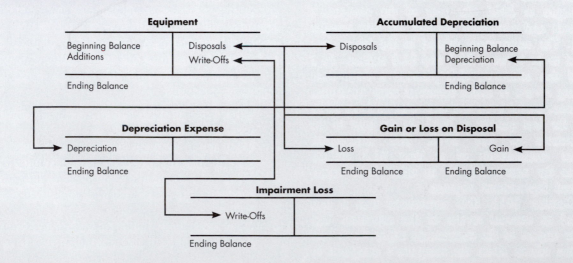

long-term productive capacity, and approval for these purchases may need to be obtained from the organization's board of directors.

Once the organization acquires an asset, the organization will need to allocate a portion of the asset's cost as an expense—depreciation, amortization, or depletion, depending on the type of asset—in each reporting period. The organization will also review its long-lived tangible and intangible assets for possible asset impairment and, when appropriate, will recognize an impairment loss and write down the asset to its fair value. In situations when an organization disposes of its long-lived assets, it will need to determine and record the gain or loss on the asset disposal.

Relevant Financial Statement Assertions

The five management assertions relevant to long-lived assets are as follows:

1. *Existence/occurrence*—The long-lived assets exist at the balance sheet date. The focus is typically on additions during the year.
2. *Completeness*—Long-lived asset account balances include all relevant transactions that have taken place during the period.
3. *Rights and obligations*—The organization has ownership rights for the long-lived assets as of the balance sheet date.
4. *Valuation or allocation*—The recorded balances reflect the balances in accordance with generally accepted accounting principles (GAAP) (includes appropriate cost allocations and impairments).
5. *Presentation and disclosure*—The long-lived asset balance is reflected on the balance sheet in the noncurrent section. The disclosures for depreciation methods and capital lease terms are adequate.

The existence and valuation assertions related to long-lived assets are usually the more relevant assertions. Organizations may have incentives to overstate their long-lived assets and may do so by including fictitious long-lived assets on the financial statements. Alternatively, organizations may capitalize costs, such as repairs and maintenance costs, which should be expensed. Concerns regarding valuation include whether the organization properly and completely recorded depreciation and properly recorded any asset impairments. The valuation issues typically involve management estimates that may be subject to management bias.

Performing Risk Assessment Procedures for Long-Lived Assets

LO 2 Identify and assess inherent risks of material misstatement associated with long-lived assets.

As part of performing risk assessment procedures, the auditor obtains information about:

- Inherent risks at the financial statement level (e.g., the client's business and operational risks and financial reporting risks)
- Inherent risks at the account and assertion levels
- Fraud risks, including feedback from audit team brainstorming sessions
- Strengths and weaknesses in internal control
- Results from planning analytical procedures

Once the risks of material misstatement have been identified, the auditor then determines how best to respond to them as part of the audit opinion formulation process.

Identifying Inherent Risks

Much of the inherent risk associated with long-lived assets is due to the importance of management estimates, such as estimating useful lives and residual values and determining whether asset impairment has occurred.

Inherent risk related to **asset impairment** stems from the following factors:

- Normally, management does not have incentives to identify and write down assets.
- Sometimes, management wants to write down every potentially impaired asset to a minimum realizable value (although this will cause a one-time reduction to current earnings, it will lead to higher reported earnings in the future).
- Determining asset impairment, especially for intangible assets, requires a good information system, a systematic process, effective controls, and professional judgment.

Other inherent risks associated with long-lived assets and related expenses include:

- Incomplete recording of asset disposals
- Obsolescence of assets
- Incorrect recording of assets, due to complex ownership structures
- Amortization or depreciation schedules that do not reflect economic impairment or use of the asset

The auditor will become aware of these risks through:

- Knowledge of the client's business, including industry trends and technological advances
- Review of various documents, including:
  - The business plan for major acquisitions or changes in the way the company conducts its business
  - Major contracts regarding capital investments or joint ventures with other companies
  - The minutes of board of directors' meetings
  - Company filings with the Securities and Exchange Commission (SEC) describing company actions, risks, and strategies

The *Auditing in Practice* feature "Auditing of Long-Lived Assets Does Present Risks" makes the point that the audit of long-lived assets may not always be a low-risk audit area.

Inherent Risks Associated with Natural Resources Natural resources present unique risks. First, it is often difficult to identify the costs

---

Auditing of Long-Lived Assets Does Present Risks

AUDITING IN **PRACTICE**

Many new auditors just returning from an internship believe that the audit of long-lived assets is primarily mechanical, for example, recalculating depreciation, tracing amounts to accumulated depreciation, and vouching fixed-asset additions. In some organizations, that may be the case. However, as with all other aspects of the audit, the auditor must understand the client's business strategy, current economic conditions, and potential changes in the economic value of the assets. Auditors can make serious mistakes if they perform the audit as if long-lived assets are always a low-risk audit area. The IRG example provided in the *Professional Judgment in Context* feature highlights that errors in this area can lead to financial statement restatements.

associated with the discovery of the natural resource. Second, once the natural resource has been discovered, it is often difficult to estimate the amount of commercially available resources to be used in determining a depletion rate. Third, the client may be responsible for restoring the property to its original condition (reclamation) after the resources are removed. Reclamation costs may be difficult to estimate.

Inherent Risks Associated with Intangible Assets Intangible assets should be recorded at cost. However, the determination of cost for intangible assets is not as straightforward as it is for tangible assets, such as equipment. A particularly troublesome area is the cost of a patent. For example, research and development costs related to new products, such as drugs or software, should be expensed as incurred up until the point that there is a viable product and a plan to bring the product to market. Legal costs for obtaining and defending a patent are capital expenditures if the defense is successful. If it is not successful, the patent has no value and any related costs should be expensed. Patents purchased from another company are capital costs. The cost of patents should be amortized over the lesser of their legal life or their estimated useful life. Minor changes to the patented item have been made by drug companies to extend the life of some patented drugs. As with tangible long-lived assets, management needs to determine if the book values of patents and other intangible assets have been impaired.

Identifying Fraud Risk Factors

LO 3 Identify and assess fraud risks of material misstatement associated with long-lived assets.

One of the more common techniques used to fraudulently misstate financial statements involves the overstatement of assets through overvaluing existing assets, including fictitious assets, or capitalizing expenses. The WorldCom fraud case is a classic example illustrating some of the fraud risks relating to long-lived asset accounts. One element of the WorldCom fraud involved management reducing the accumulated depreciation account by debiting that account and crediting depreciation expense. These entries were performed on a regular basis, and, unfortunately, the auditors did not view them as unusual or otherwise worthy of separate investigation. Management also misstated assets by routinely capitalizing their line expense (in other words, cash paid to other carriers when WorldCom used their lines to transmit calls). Finally, upon making new acquisitions, management boosted the value of the assets, but it established reserves for plant closings and related expenses. When the actual expenses were less, management debited the liability and credited the expense, thereby increasing net income in subsequent periods.

Other potential fraud schemes relating to long-lived assets include:

- Sales of assets are not recorded, and proceeds are misappropriated.
- Assets that have been sold are not removed from the books.
- Inappropriate residual values or lives are assigned to the assets, resulting in miscalculation of depreciation.
- Amortization of intangible assets is miscalculated.
- Costs that should have been expensed are improperly capitalized.
- Impairment losses on long-lived assets are not recognized.
- Fair value estimates are unreasonable or unsupportable.

Identifying Control Risks

LO 4 Identify and assess control risks of material misstatement associated with long-lived assets.

Once the auditor has obtained an understanding of the inherent and fraud risks of material misstatement related to long-lived assets, the auditor needs to understand the controls that the client has designed and implemented to address those risks. Remember, the auditor is required to gain an overall understanding of internal controls for both integrated audits and financial statement only audits. The auditor normally gains this understanding by performing a walkthrough of the process, inquiry, observation, and review of the client's documentation. The auditor considers both entity-wide controls and transaction controls at the account and assertion levels. This understanding provides the auditor with a basis for making an initial control risk assessment.

At the entity-wide level, the auditor considers the control environment, risk assessment, information and communication, and monitoring controls. The *Focus on Fraud* feature "WorldCom and Waste Management: Two Historical Examples of Asset Misstatement" highlights two well-known cases involving material misstatements in long-lived assets and related expenses where there was a weakness in the control environment.

Although the auditor needs to understand all the components of internal control, the auditor typically finds it useful to focus on important control activities related to the long-lived asset accounts. As part of this understanding, the auditor focuses on the relevant assertions for each account and identifies the controls that relate to risks for these assertions. In an integrated audit

WorldCom and Waste Management: Two Historical Examples of Asset Misstatement

The weaknesses in the control environment at these two companies allowed management to override existing controls in order to commit historically significant frauds.

WorldCom

The WorldCom bankruptcy was one of the largest in U.S. history. From the first quarter of 1999 through the first quarter of 2002, WorldCom's management improperly released approximately $984 million in depreciation reserves to increase pre-tax earnings by decreasing depreciation expense or increasing miscellaneous income. The depreciation reserves were created in a variety of ways:

- The cost of equipment returned to vendors for credit after being placed in service was credited to the reserve (accumulated depreciation), rather than the asset itself.
- Unsupported additions to an asset account were recorded with a corresponding increase in the reserve.

After the end of each fiscal quarter, management in general accounting would direct property accounting personnel to release large balances from this reserve account (debit to the accumulated depreciation account), usually to reduce depreciation expense. If it was too late in the quarterly closing process to record depreciation expense as a standard adjusting entry, property accounting

personnel were directed to prepare a draft journal entry so that general accounting could make the adjustment. WorldCom also inappropriately capitalized line expense (amounts paid to other carriers such as AT&T to use their lines) as fixed assets.

Source: *Report of Investigation* by the Special Investigative Committee of the Board of Directors of WorldCom, Inc., March 31, 2003.

Waste Management

Waste Management, Inc. is the nation's largest waste disposal company. The company grew though extensive acquisitions—seemingly all dependent on ever-increasing sales and net income that fueled higher stock prices. Waste Management's previous management recognized the importance of stock prices to pay for more acquisitions, but the company was losing its profitability. Management struck on a new way to increase reported net income—simply increase the estimated useful lives of all the depreciable assets. The auditors never questioned the change even though the change accounted for virtually all of Waste Management's increase in earnings over a period of years. Finally, the SEC stepped in and pointed out these estimated useful lives simply were not realistic. Waste Management had misstated earnings by a whopping $3.5 billion. Arthur Andersen paid fines of $220 million, and the SEC fined the individual auditors on the engagement.

or in a controls reliance audit of the financial statements, the auditor uses this understanding to identify important controls that need to be tested.

Typical control activities that affect multiple assertions for long-lived assets include:

- A formal budgeting process with appropriate follow-up variance analysis
- Written policies for acquisition and disposals of long-lived assets, including required approvals
- Limited physical access to assets, where appropriate
- Periodic comparison of physical assets to subsidiary records
- Periodic reconciliations of subsidiary records with the general ledger

Other Controls Over Tangible Assets To provide reasonable assurance that the existence and valuation assertions for tangible long-lived assets are materially correct, controls should be in place to:

- Identify existing assets, inventory them, and reconcile the physical asset inventory with the property ledger on a periodic basis (existence). Many organizations face a challenge in tracking the location, quantity, condition, maintenance, and depreciation status of their fixed assets. One approach to dealing with this challenge is to use serial numbered asset tags, often with bar codes. Then periodically, the organization takes inventory, utilizing a bar-code reader.
- Provide reasonable assurance that all purchases are authorized and properly valued (valuation)
- Provide reasonable assurance that additions to tangible assets include all repairs and maintenance costs that should be capitalized (completeness)
- Appropriately classify new equipment according to its expected use and estimated useful life (valuation)
- Periodically reassess the appropriateness of depreciation categories (valuation)
- Identify obsolete or scrapped equipment and write the equipment down to scrap value (valuation)
- Review management strategy and systematically assess the impairment of assets (valuation)
- Inquire of management about the controls related to asset impairment judgments, and review related documentation (valuation)

The client should have controls that include:

- A systematic process to identify assets that are not currently in use
- Projections of future cash flows, by reporting unit, that are based on management's strategic plans and economic conditions
- Systematic monitoring of current market values of similar assets

Controls Over Natural Resources Most established natural resource companies have developed procedures and associated internal controls for identifying costs, and such organizations typically use geologists to establish an estimate of the reserves contained in a new discovery. These organizations periodically reassess the amount of reserves as more information becomes available during the course of mining, harvesting, or extracting resources.

Controls Over Intangible Assets For intangible assets, the client should have controls designed to:

- Provide reasonable assurance that decisions are appropriately made to capitalize (completeness of assets) or expense (existence of assets) research and development expenditures

| EXHIBIT **12.2** | Examples of Controls Over Intangible Long-Lived Assets |

- Management authorizations are required for intangible asset transactions.
- Documentation regarding intangible assets should be maintained, and such documentation should include:
  - Manner of acquisition (e.g., purchased, developed internally)
  - Basis for the capitalized amount
  - Expected period of benefit
  - Amortization method
- Amortization periods and calculations should be approved and periodically reviewed by appropriate personnel.

- Develop amortization schedules that reflect the remaining useful life of intangible assets such as patents or copyrights (valuation)
- Identify and account for intangible-asset impairments (valuation)

Management should have a monitoring process in place to review valuation of intangible assets. For example, a pharmaceutical company should have fairly sophisticated models to predict the success of newly developed drugs and monitor actual performance against expected performance to determine whether a drug is likely to achieve expected revenue and profit goals. Similarly, a software company should have controls in place to determine whether capitalized software development costs will be realized. *Exhibit 12.2* identifies examples of other controls over intangible long-lived assets that clients may design and implement.

Documenting Controls

Auditors need to document their understanding of internal controls for both integrated audits and financial statement only audits. Similar to other audit areas, the auditor can provide this documentation in various formats, including a control matrix, a control risk assessment questionnaire, and/or a memo. The documentation should include the auditor's preliminary control risk assessments at the account or assertion level.

Performing Planning Analytical Procedures

LO 5 Describe how to use planning analytical procedures to identify possible material misstatements associated with long-lived assets.

Planning analytical procedures help auditors identify areas of potential material misstatements. The steps that the auditor will take in performing planning analytical procedures are fully described in *Chapter 7*.

Auditors must know the business and the economics of the business to perform meaningful analytical procedures. Consider a simple example. A local company is in the business of picking up and hauling garbage. Shouldn't the auditors have a fairly good idea of approximately how long the trucks will last? They know the mileage; they know the beating the trucks take every day; they know something about the company's policy for cleaning and repairing the trucks. What if management comes in and makes a decision to extend the depreciable life from five to twelve years when the rest of the industry is at about six years? Does this make sense? Although the auditor cannot always make a decision as to whether five years is better than six, the auditor needs to be in a position to understand whether five years is much closer to economic reality than twelve years. The *Focus on Fraud* feature "Performing Planning Analytical Procedures" highlights that planning analytical procedures can be useful in identifying management fraud.

Performing Planning Analytical Procedures

FOCUS on **FRAUD**

The auditor should be aware that if a fraud is occurring in long-lived asset accounts, the financial statements usually will contain departures from industry norms, but may not differ from the expectations set by management. Therefore, the auditor should compare the unaudited financial statements with both past results and industry trends.

Ratio and Trend Analyses Planning analytical procedures for long-lived assets can include the following:

- Review and analyze gains or losses on disposals of equipment (gains indicate that depreciation lives are too short; losses indicate the opposite).
- Develop an overall estimate of depreciation expense.
- Compare capital expenditures with the client's capital budget, with an expectation that capital expenditures would be consistent with the capital budget.
- Compare depreciable lives used by the client for various asset categories with those of the industry, with a typical expectation that the client's depreciable lives would be consistent with those in the industry. Large differences may indicate earnings management.
- Compare the asset and related expense account balances in the current period to similar items in the prior audit and determine whether the amounts appear reasonable in relation to other information you know about the client, such as changes in operations.

Ratios that the auditor should plan to review, after developing independent expectations, include:

- *Ratio of depreciation expense to total depreciable long-lived tangible assets*—This ratio should be predictable and comparable over time unless there is a change in depreciation method or asset lives. The auditor should plan to analyze any unexpected deviations and assess whether any changes are reasonable.
- *Ratio of repairs and maintenance expense to total depreciable long-lived tangible assets*—This ratio may fluctuate because of changes in management's policies (e.g., maintenance expenses can be postponed without immediate breakdowns or loss of productivity). The auditor should plan to analyze any unexpected deviation with this consideration in mind.
- *Ratio of long-lived assets to total assets*—This ratio will fluctuate in relation to acquisitions, disposals, and depreciation.

If planning analytical procedures do not identify any unexpected relationships, the auditor would conclude that there is not a heightened risk of material misstatements in these accounts. If unusual or unexpected relationships exist, the planned audit procedures (tests of controls, substantive procedures) would be adjusted to address the potential material misstatements.

LO 6 Determine appropriate responses to identified risks of material misstatement in auditing long-lived assets.

Responding to Identified Risks of Material Misstatement

Once the auditor has developed an understanding of the risks of material misstatement, the auditor can determine the appropriate audit procedures to perform. Audit procedures should be proportional to the assessed risks, with areas of higher risk receiving more audit attention and effort. Responding to identified risks typically involves developing an audit approach that contains substantive procedures (such as tests of details and, when appropriate, substantive analytical procedures) and tests of controls, when applicable. If the client's controls related to long-lived assets are operating effectively, then the auditor can rely more extensively on substantive analytical procedures to obtain evidence on account balances. The sufficiency and appropriateness of selected procedures vary to achieve the desired level of assurance for each relevant assertion. While audit firms may have a standardized audit program for auditing long-lived assets, the auditor should customize the audit program based on the assessment of the risks of material misstatement.

Consider a client where the auditor has assessed the risks of material misstatement related to the existence of equipment at slightly below the maximum. Further, assume that incentives exist to overstate income to achieve profit targets that affect management bonuses, and oversight is relatively weak because of a lack of supervision by top management. Therefore, there is a heightened risk of capitalizing items that should be expensed. The auditor may develop an audit program that consists of first performing limited tests of operating effectiveness of controls, then performing limited substantive analytical procedures, and finally performing extensive substantive tests of details. Because of the high risk, the auditor will want to obtain a great deal of evidence directly from tests of details. In contrast, consider a client where the auditor has assessed the risks of material misstatement related to the existence of equipment as low and believes that the client has designed and implemented effective controls in this area. For this client, the auditor will likely perform tests of controls, gain a high level of assurance from substantive analytical procedures such as a reasonableness test, and then complete the substantive procedures by performing tests of details at a limited level.

Panel A of *Exhibit 12.3* shows that because of differences in risk, the box of evidence to be filled for testing the existence of equipment at the low-risk client is smaller than that at a high-risk client. Panel B of *Exhibit 12.3* illustrates the different levels of assurance that the auditor will obtain from tests of controls and substantive procedures for the two types of clients. Panel B makes the point that because of the higher risk associated with the existence of equipment (in part, due to less effective controls) at Client B, the auditor will want to design the audit so that more of the assurance is coming from tests of details. Note that the relative percentages are judgmental in nature; the examples are simply intended to give you a sense of how an auditor might select an appropriate mix of procedures.

The *Auditing in Practice* feature "Client-Specific Considerations When Responding to Risks of Material Misstatement" emphasizes that the auditor should always consider the unique circumstances of the client when making decisions about how to respond to identified risks of material misstatement.

Obtaining Evidence about Internal Control Operating Effectiveness for Long-Lived Asset Accounts and Related Expenses

LO 7 Determine appropriate tests of controls and consider the results of tests of controls in auditing long-lived assets.

For integrated audits, the auditor will test the operating effectiveness of important controls as of the client's year-end. If the auditor wants to rely on controls for the financial statement audit, the auditor will test the operating effectiveness of those controls throughout the year.

Selecting Controls to Test and Performing Tests of Controls

The auditor selects and tests controls that are important to the auditor's conclusion about whether the organization's controls adequately address the

EXHIBIT 12.3   Panel A: Sufficiency of Evidence for Existence of Equipment

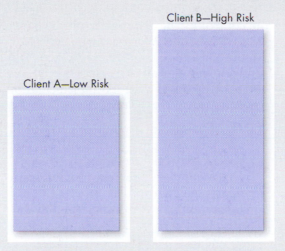

Client A—Low Risk

Client B—High Risk

Panel B: Approaches to Obtaining Audit Evidence for Existence of Equipment

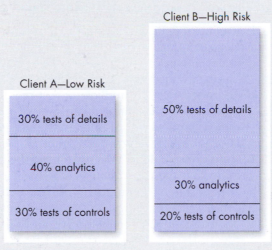

Client A—Low Risk

30% tests of details

40% analytics

30% tests of controls

Client B—High Risk

50% tests of details

30% analytics

20% tests of controls

Client-Specific Considerations When Responding to Risks of Material Misstatement

AUDITING IN **PRACTICE**

For many organizations, long-lived assets involve only a few assets of relatively high value. In these settings, the time and effort needed to perform tests of controls in order to reduce substantive testing may exceed the time required to simply perform the substantive tests. Therefore, the most efficient approach would be a substantive approach, using tests of details, for obtaining evidence. However, if an organization has a high volume of long-lived asset transactions, it may be more efficient to perform tests of controls to support a moderate- or low-assessed level of control risk, and then reduce substantive testing.

assessed risk of material misstatement for the long-lived asset accounts. The auditor selects both entity-wide and transaction controls for testing. Typical tests of transaction controls include inquiry of personnel performing the control, observation of the control being performed, inspection of documentation confirming that the control has been performed, and reperformance of the control by the auditor testing the control.

For example, assume that a client implements a policy requiring the establishment and enforcement of property management training for all personnel involved in the use, stewardship, and management of equipment. The control (the policy and its implementation) could be tested in a variety of ways, including the following:

- *Inquiry*—Select a sample of personnel required to complete such training and talk with them about whether they have completed the training and the nature of that training.
- *Observation*—Observe a training session in process or observe property management actions in process.
- *Inspection of documentation*—Review the training materials and, for a sample of personnel, review documentation showing completion of the training.

Considering the Results of Tests of Controls

The auditor will analyze the results of the tests of controls to determine additional appropriate procedures. There are two potential outcomes:

1. If control deficiencies are identified, the auditor will assess those deficiencies to determine their severity. (Are they significant deficiencies or material weaknesses?) The auditor would then need to modify the preliminary control risk assessment (possibly from low to moderate or high) and document the implications of the control deficiencies. Appropriate modifications to planned substantive audit procedures will be determined by the types of misstatements that are most likely to occur because of any control deficiency.

2. If no control deficiencies are identified, the auditor will likely determine that the preliminary assessment of control risk as low is still appropriate. The auditor will then determine the extent that controls can provide evidence on the correctness of account balances and determine planned substantive audit procedures. The level of substantive testing in this situation will be less than what is required in circumstances where deficiencies in internal control were identified. From the audit risk model, we know that organizations with effective internal controls should require less substantive testing of account balances.

The strengths and deficiencies of an organization's internal controls have a significant impact on the audit of the long-lived asset accounts. Recall the IRG example in the *Professional Judgment in Context* feature at the beginning of the chapter. IRG restated its financial statements because of misstatements in its lease and fixed-asset accounts. In connection with the restatement, management identified material weaknesses in its internal control over financial reporting related to lack of sufficient qualified accounting and tax personnel; lack of adequate supervision and monitoring of accounting operations; inadequate lease accounting controls; and lack of effective controls related to the existence, completeness, and accuracy of fixed assets and related depreciation and amortization expense. Auditors who are aware of control deficiencies will need to modify their substantive testing in response to those deficiencies or risk missing material misstatements in the financial statements.

Obtaining Substantive Evidence about Accounts, Disclosures, and Assertions for Long-Lived Asset Accounts and Related Expenses

LO 8 Determine and apply sufficient appropriate substantive audit procedures in auditing long-lived assets.

In performing substantive procedures, the auditor wants reasonable assurance that:

- Long-lived assets reflected in the balance sheet physically exist.
- The organization has rights of ownership to recorded long-lived assets.
- Long-lived assets include all relevant items, including those that are purchased, contributed, constructed in-house or by third parties, and leases meeting the criteria for capital leases.
- Long-lived asset additions are recorded correctly.
- Items to be capitalized are identified and distinguished from repairs and maintenance expense items.
- Depreciation/amortization/depletion calculations are made and based on appropriate estimated useful lives and methods.
- Retirements, trade-ins, and unused property and equipment are identified and recorded correctly.
- Long-lived assets and related expenses, such as depreciation, amortization, or depletion, are appropriately presented in the financial statements with adequate disclosures.
- Fraudulent transactions are not included in the financial statements.

Exhibit 12.4 provides details on typical substantive procedures for long-lived assets. The extent to which substantive analytical procedures and tests of details are performed depends on a number of factors, including the risk of material misstatement and the effectiveness of controls.

Substantive Analytical Procedures

Before performing tests of details related to long-lived assets, the auditor may perform substantive analytical procedures. The use of substantive analytical procedures will likely be most appropriate when the risk of material misstatement is low.

Step 1: Identify Suitable Analytical Procedures The relevant analytical procedures for conducting substantive analytics are not necessarily different from those for planning analytical procedures. However, when performing substantive analytical procedures, the auditor is more likely to conduct a reasonableness test. For example, a reasonableness test can be used to estimate depreciation expense. The analytical procedures could also incorporate a number of ratios including:

- *Current depreciation expense as a percentage of the previous-year depreciation expense.*
- *Fixed assets (by class) as a percentage of previous-year assets*—The relative increase in this percentage can be compared with the relative increase in depreciation as a test of overall reasonableness.
- *Depreciation expense (by asset class) as a percentage of assets each year*—This ratio can indicate changes in the age of equipment or in depreciation policy.
- *Accumulated depreciation (by class) as a percentage of gross assets each year*—This ratio provides information on the overall reasonableness of the account and may indicate problems of accounting for fully depreciated equipment.
- *Average age of assets (by class)*—This ratio provides additional insight on the age of assets and may be useful in modifying depreciation estimates.

EXHIBIT 12.4 Management Assertions and Substantive Procedures for Long-Lived Assets and Related Expenses

Management Assertion	Substantive Procedure
Existence/occurrence—Recorded long-lived assets exist.	1. Perform substantive analytical procedures. 2. Inspect tangible assets. 3. Vouch additions to supporting documentation. 4. Review account activity for the year and vouch significant items.
Completeness—All long-lived assets have been recorded.	1. Perform substantive analytical procedures. 2. Review capitalization policy to assure that all significant capital expenditures are properly capitalized. 3. Review entries to repair and maintenance expense to determine whether some items should have been capitalized.
Rights/obligations—The organization has legal title or similar rights of ownership to recorded long-lived assets.	1. Inquire of management as to whether long-lived assets have been pledged as collateral. 2. Inspect documents of title. 3. Inspect insurance policies. 4. Inspect property tax records.
Valuation/allocation—Long-lived assets are properly valued.	1. Review depreciation policy and test depreciation calculations. 2. Inquire of management about assets that are idle. 3. Test amortization expense. 4. Assess the reasonableness of carrying amounts and unamortized balances. 5. Inquire of management as to whether there has been any permanent impairment of assets. 6. Assess management's impairment estimates.
Presentation/disclosure—Long-lived assets and related expenses, such as depreciation, amortization, or depletion, are appropriately presented in the financial statements with adequate disclosures.	1. Review presentation and disclosure in the financial statements and determine whether they are in accordance with GAAP. 2. Inquire of management about disclosures and other reporting issues.

Step 2: Evaluate Reliability of Data Used to Develop Expectations In evaluating reliability of data used to develop expectations in substantive analytical procedures, the auditor may test the operating effectiveness of controls over the preparation of information used in those analytics. If the client's controls related to long-lived assets are effective, then the auditor can rely more extensively on substantive analytical procedures to obtain evidence on account balances. When such controls are considered effective, the auditor will have greater confidence in the reliability of the information. Further, the auditor may use data from independent external sources (e.g., industry ratios), as that data are generally considered reliable.

Step 3: Develop Expectations Expectations for substantive analytical procedures will be more precise than those considered during planning analytical procedures. An increase in precision can be obtained by using more disaggregated data. The appropriate level of disaggregation will be influenced by the nature of the organization, its size, and its complexity. The auditor can use a property ledger, which should uniquely identify each asset and provide details on cost of the property, acquisition date, depreciation method used for both book and tax, estimated life, estimated scrap value (if any), and accumulated depreciation to date, to develop expectations for each asset or each category of assets to compare with what the company has recorded.

Step 4 and Step 5: Define and Identify Significant Unexpected Differences

At this point, the auditor is trying to answer the question of whether the auditor's expectation is significantly different from what the client has recorded. The amount of difference that is considered significant is influenced by materiality, desired level of assurance, and assessed risk of material misstatement. As the auditor's assessed risk of material misstatement increases, the amount of the unexpected difference that would be considered significant declines.

The auditor then compares the client's recorded amounts with the auditor's expectation. Once this mechanical step is completed, the auditor will have identified any significant differences between the auditor's expectation and what the client has recorded.

Step 6 and Step 7: Investigate Significant Unexpected Differences and Ensure Proper Documentation

Materiality and the desired level of assurance will aid the auditor in determining how to proceed with investigating significant unexpected differences. The auditor will investigate significant unexpected differences through substantive tests of details, as described next. In general, if substantive analytical procedures do not result in unresolved issues, direct testing of account balances can be reduced.

Finally, as with planning analytical procedures, the auditor will accumulate documentation with respect to evidence gathered and judgments reached during substantive analytical procedures.

Substantive Tests of Details for Tangible Assets—Testing Current-Period Additions

The proper recording of current-period additions is important due to the long-term effect these assets have on the financial statements. Because most companies typically have relatively few long-lived asset transactions, the auditor often examines supporting documentation of individual transactions. One approach is to examine a schedule of additions (usually prepared by the client). After the schedule is agreed to the general ledger, the auditor should select a few items for testing. For example, auditors obtain documentary support (such as invoices or contracts) for additions above a certain amount or physically inspect a sample of additions made during the audit period.

The auditor also wants to determine that capitalized additions were appropriate and that none of them should have been expensed as repairs and maintenance or other costs. The *Focus on Fraud* feature "Improper Capitalization of Operating Expenses: The Case of Safety-Kleen Corporation" provides a well-known example of a company that capitalized, rather than expensed, certain costs.

Companies often have to make judgments as to whether a particular expenditure should be capitalized or expensed as a repair. Most companies have policies, usually based on materiality and the cost of bookkeeping, as to whether expenditures under a certain amount are expenses—even if they appear to be of a capital nature. Usually, the auditor starts by determining if such a policy is reasonable. Further, the auditor considers whether

Improper Capitalization of Operating Expenses: The Case of Safety-Kleen Corporation

Safety-Kleen Corporation (SK) was one of the leading providers of industrial waste collection and disposal services. In the late 1990s, SK was merged with another company, and SK's management made promises to investors and analysts that the merger would result in annual savings of $100 to $160 million. Unfortunately, those savings never materialized, and the company's CFO, controller, and vice president of accounting orchestrated an accounting fraud to overstate SK's revenue and earnings. One element of the fraud involved the improper capitalization and deferral of operating expenses. For example, at the end of the third quarter of 1999, they improperly capitalized $4.6 million of payroll expenses. At the end of the fourth quarter of 1999, they improperly capitalized $1.8 million of salaries and wages. Also during the fourth quarter of 1999, they recorded $7.3 million of fraudulent adjustments to capitalize the tires on the company's trucks and the fuel in the tanks. Safety-Kleen ultimately filed for bankruptcy, and the SEC pursued the company and the individuals involved.

For further details on this case, see SEC Complaint No. 17891 (December 12, 2002).

management might attempt to not comply with the policy because of an incentive to manipulate reported earnings, for example, decrease reported earnings in a good period and vice versa in a poor period. If the auditor perceives that such risks are applicable to a particular client, the auditor will adjust the procedures, usually by requesting that the client prepare a schedule of both fixed-asset additions and repair and maintenance expense transactions. Selected transactions from both schedules can be vouched to vendor invoices, work orders, or other supporting evidence to determine their proper classification.

When conducting these procedures, the auditor can usually test existence, rights, and valuation assertions at the same time. *Exhibit 12.5* presents an example of typical audit documentation for testing fixed-asset additions. Even though the total fixed-asset account balance may be large, the audit work can be done efficiently by concentrating on the additions and then adjusting the estimates of depreciation expense and accumulated depreciation for changes made during the year.

Substantive Tests of Details for Tangible Assets—Testing Current-Period Deletions

Exhibit 12.5 includes two disposals that occurred during the year. Similar to testing additions, the auditor typically obtains a schedule from the client of all sales or other disposals made during the year. The auditor should trace the original cost of the item and its accumulated depreciation to the supporting documentation. Proceeds from the disposal, if material, should be traced to the cash receipts journal and the bank deposit. The auditor should also recompute any gain or loss to determine whether it is accounted for in conformity with GAAP.

The auditor should also perform procedures to search for any unrecorded disposals. First, the auditor may make inquiries of the client about disposals. The auditor could obtain evidence of unrecorded retirements by examining the cash receipts journal, property tax records, insurance records, or scrap sales accounts. Another approach is to use generalized audit software (GAS) to prepare a printout of fully depreciated (or nearly fully

EXHIBIT 12.5   Schedule of Long-Lived Asset Additions and Disposals

Gordon's Bay Manufacturing

Schedule of Long-Lived Asset Additions and Disposals

12/31/2015

PBC

Work Performed by *KJ*

Date *1/28/2016*

Description	Date Purchased	Cost				Accumulated Depreciation			
		Beginning Balance	Additions	Disposals	Ending Balance	Beginning Balance	Depreciation Expense	Disposals	Ending Balance
Beginning balance	Various	124,350			124,350	33,429	12,435*		45,864
Additions:									
40" lathe	10/30/15	–0–	9,852†		9,852	–0–	1,250‡		1,250
1040 press	3/25/15	–0–	18,956†		18,956	–0–	1,895‡		1,895
60" lathe	5/29/15	–0–	13,903†		13,903	–0–	950‡		950
Disposals:									
Fork lift	6/2/12			7,881§	(7,881)			3,753	(3,753)
Computer	7/2/13			3,300§	(3,300)			2,625	(2,625)
Totals		124,350@	42,711**	11,181**	155,880**††	33,429@	16,530**	6,378**	43,581**††

* Estimated from prior year; includes one-half year depreciation for assets disposed of during the year. See Working Paper PPE-4 for calculation of the estimate.
† Examined invoice or other supporting document, noting cost and appropriate categorization for depreciation purposes.
‡ Recalculated, noting that depreciation is in accordance with company policy and asset classification- estimated economic life.
§ Traced to asset ledger and verified that equipment had been removed. Examined sales document or scrap disposal document for the disposal of the asset.
@ Agreed to December 31, 2014, audit documentation.
** Footed/cross footed.
†† Traced to trial balance.

depreciated) assets and then attempt to locate them for physical examination. Alternatively, trade-ins noted during the audit of asset additions can be traced to the removal of the old equipment from the books.

Substantive Procedures Related to Depreciation Expense and Accumulated Depreciation for Tangible Assets

The specific procedures used by the auditor to test depreciation of tangible assets depend on the risk of material misstatement. The auditor's primary objective in testing depreciation is to determine whether the client is following a consistent depreciation policy and whether the client's calculations are accurate. The auditor should make sure that the depreciation methods used are consistent with the prior year unless the client has reasonable justification for changing methods. The auditor should carefully read the notes to the financial statements to be sure that all relevant information about such changes is disclosed. The auditor should determine whether management's estimates, such as estimated useful lives and salvage values, are reasonable. As described earlier, the auditor may perform primarily substantive analytical procedures to test these accounts, especially when the risk of material misstatement is low.

In situations where controls are not effective, that is, there is a high risk of material misstatement, the auditor needs to perform more extensive detailed tests of depreciation. The auditor would start with the fixed-asset ledger, which contains a list of all the assets, their estimated useful lives, salvage values, and depreciation methods. The auditor would use GAS to foot the ledger and agree it to the general ledger and then, taking a sample of items contained in the detailed property ledger, recalculate depreciation for the items chosen. The sampling procedure should be based on the same criteria introduced in *Chapter 8*; that is, the auditor considers materiality and risk and takes a sample based on recorded depreciation. Differences should be projected to the population as a whole. If there are significant differences, the auditor should investigate to determine the root cause of the problem and have the client correct the problem. Finally, the auditor should use GAS to identify all entries into the depreciation and accumulated depreciation accounts that come from other than the normal depreciation entries and asset disposals.

Substantive Tests of Details for Natural Resources and the Related Expense Accounts

The focus for the auditor is on the costs and the estimate of reserves contained in a new discovery. The auditor normally has experience with the quality of the client's estimates and would want to evaluate the credentials of the individual making the estimates—whether it is a member of management or a specialist hired by management. The auditor may also decide to use an auditor specialist/expert to perform additional analysis and/or review the client's analysis. The *Focus on Fraud* feature "Auditing a Forestry Firm Results in Class-Action Lawsuit" highlights the need for sufficient appropriate audit procedures when auditing natural resources.

The audit procedures for determining the cost of natural resources are similar to those for other fixed assets. The auditor should test the capitalization of all new natural resources and should verify the costs by examining documents, including the client's own process of documenting all the costs of exploration and drilling. Depletion expense should be based on the items extracted during the year using the units of production method. The company should have production records of daily extractions. In addition, the auditor will be able to substantiate the amount of items sold during the year. Further, the company should have procedures to estimate any changes in reserves in order to update the depletion procedures.

Auditing a Forestry Company Results in Class-Action Lawsuit

FOCUS on **FRAUD**

In 2011, the Chinese forestry company, Sino-Forest Corp., which once traded on the Toronto Stock Exchange and was worth $6 billion, collapsed following fraud allegations. In December 2012, the Ontario Securities Commission (OSC) accused Ernst & Young LLP of failing to conduct a proper audit of Sino-Forest Corp. The OSC alleged that Ernst & Young failed to perform sufficient audit work to verify the ownership and existence of Sino-Forest's most significant assets and failed to undertake its audit work "with a sufficient level of professional skepticism." The commission said Ernst & Young failed to adequately review and question documentation related to the ownership and existence of standing timber reserves the company held in China. The commission said Ernst & Young did "very limited" site visits to inspect the firm's purported assets, which were widely scattered throughout China. In 2013, an Ontario judge approved Ernst & Young LLP's $117-million settlement of a shareholder class-action lawsuit tied to the collapse of Sino-Forest Corp. The $117-million settlement is the largest payment ever made by an auditor in Canada to settle a class-action suit.

Substantive Tests of Details for Intangible Assets and the Related Expense Accounts

The following substantive procedures are commonly used when testing intangible assets:

- Determine that the intangible assets exist by reviewing appropriate documentation, for example, legal documentation (in the case of a license or patent).
- Determine that the intangible assets are owned by the organization by inspecting relevant documentation, such as the purchase agreement or sales agreement.
- Test management's calculation of any gain or loss on the disposal of intangible assets and determine whether the carrying amounts have been properly reduced.
- For amortizable intangibles with finite lives, determine whether amortization expense is accurate and whether the amortization policy and useful lives are reasonable and consistent with prior years.
- Inquire of management about whether circumstances indicate that the carrying amounts of intangibles (which are subject to amortization) may not be recoverable. Where such circumstances exist, evaluate management's impairment testing and conclusion regarding the write-off. *Exhibit* 12.6 provides examples of indicators suggesting that impairment of an intangible asset might have occurred.

EXHIBIT 12.6 Circumstances Indicating Potential Impairment of Intangible Assets

- A change in circumstances, such as the legal environment or business climate, that could affect the asset's value or cause an adverse action by a regulator
- An accumulation of costs that are significantly in excess of the amount originally expected to be needed to acquire or construct the asset
- Losses or projections indicating continuing losses associated with an asset used to generate revenue
- A current expectation that, more likely than not, an asset will be sold or otherwise disposed of significantly before the end of its previously estimated useful life.

Substantive Procedures Related to Asset Impairment

Even though determining the potential impairment of long-lived assets is difficult, the accumulated knowledge of industry product trends, changes in client product lines, and technological changes will assist the auditor in making necessary judgments. An asset may be impaired if it does not generate as much cash flow in future years as it has in the past. A tour of the plant may provide hints that some assets are not fully utilized or are not efficiently utilized. Such observations might indicate a potential impairment in value.

The auditor needs reasonable assurance that the long-lived assets are valued at their economic benefit to the organization and that, when the value has been impaired, the organization has written down the asset reflecting the decline in economic benefit of the asset. If there is evidence that an asset has been impaired, the auditor needs to address the valuation issue. In most situations, the auditor needs to understand management's process for assessing impairment and needs to evaluate the reasonableness of management's assumptions. As indicated in the *Auditing in Practice* feature "PCAOB Identifies Audit Deficiencies Related to Asset Impairment Issues" auditors have had many challenges related to asset impairments.

PCAOB Identifies Audit Deficiencies Related to Asset Impairment Issues

AUDITING IN **PRACTICE**

The 2010 Public Company Accounting Oversight Board (PCAOB) inspection report of Grant Thornton LLP identified the following audit deficiency:

> The Firm was aware that the issuer had determined not to test a significant portion of its property and equipment for impairment, despite indicators that the carrying amount may not be recoverable. These indicators included operating losses for the relevant segment for the last three years, substantial charges for the impairment of goodwill and other intangible assets during the year, a projected loss for the segment for the upcoming year, and reduced and delayed customer orders. The Firm failed to evaluate the effects on the financial statements of the failure to test the assets for impairment.

The 2010 PCAOB inspection report of PricewaterhouseCoopers LLP identified the following audit deficiency:

> During the year, the issuer recorded a significant impairment charge for its fixed assets, based on the assumption that all machinery and equipment that was more than four years old had a fair value of zero, while all machinery and equipment acquired within the past four years had a fair value that approximated net book value. There was no evidence in the audit

documentation, and no persuasive other evidence, that the Firm had tested this assumption.

The 2010 PCAOB inspection report of McGladrey & Pullen LLP identified the following audit deficiency:

> The Firm failed to sufficiently evaluate the fair value, useful life, and potential impairment of an indefinite-lived intangible asset related to a marketing agreement that the issuer entered into during the current year. The Firm failed to test, beyond inquiries of management, the fair value that the issuer assigned to the intangible asset. Also, in evaluating the issuer's assertion that the intangible asset had an indefinite life, the Firm failed to consider the fact that the marketing agreement allowed both the issuer and the counterparty to terminate the agreement. Further, the Firm's testing of the issuer's assertion that there were no economic or competitive factors that could affect the useful life of the marketing agreement was limited to inquiries of management. The Firm also failed to sufficiently evaluate the issuer's conclusion that the intangible asset was not impaired, as the Firm failed to consider potential indicators of impairment, such as the issuer's recurring losses and recurring impairments of goodwill and other intangible assets during the year.

Substantive Procedures Related to Leases

General substantive procedures for leases include the following:

- Obtain copies of lease agreements, read the agreements, and develop a schedule of lease expenditures.
- Review the lease expense account, select entries to the account, and determine if there are entries that are not covered by the leases obtained from the client. Determine if the expenses are properly accounted for.
- Review the relevant criteria from the U.S. Financial Accounting Standards Board (FASB)'s codified standards (ASC) to determine which leases meet the requirement of capital leases. The *Emerging Issues* feature "Potential Changes in Lease Accounting" highlights the importance of auditors staying current on changing financial accounting standards.
- For all capital leases, determine that the assets and lease obligations are recorded at their present value. Determine the economic life of the asset. Calculate amortization expense and interest expenses, and determine any adjustments to correct the financial statements.
- Develop a schedule of all future lease obligations or determine whether the client's schedule is correct by referring to underlying lease agreements.
- Review the client's disclosure of lease obligations to determine that it is in accordance with GAAP.

Performing Substantive Fraud-Related Procedures

The following fraud-related audit procedures can be used to respond to fraud risk factors the auditor identified while performing risk assessment procedures:

- Physically inspect tangible assets, including major additions, and agree serial numbers with invoices or other supporting documents.
- Request that the client perform a complete inventory of long-lived assets at year-end.

Potential Changes in Lease Accounting and Audit Implications

EMERGING ISSUE

FASB and the London-based International Accounting Standards Board (IASB) have been working on revising and converging an updated accounting standard on lease accounting. As of mid-2014, it was anticipated that the final standard would result in moving about $2 trillion dollars of lease obligations onto corporate balance sheets. However, the standard setters were still determining the model that companies should use to measure those liabilities. An implementation date of not earlier than fiscal years beginning on or after January 1, 2017, is expected.

As companies prepare for the converged lease accounting standard proposed by FASB and the IASB, auditors should stay up to date on emerging issues related to lease accounting and the audit implications. For example, altering lease accounting could significantly change a company's balance-sheet profile, possibly making it more leveraged. The calculations of many of the key ratios governing loan covenants, such as earnings before interest, taxes, depreciation, and amortization (EBITDA), debt-to-equity (D/E), and return on assets (ROA), could be significantly changed under new lease accounting rules, to the point where a company is in violation of its agreement with the bank. Further, it is likely that a new lease accounting standard would require auditors (and their clients) to exercise many significant and subjective judgments.

- Carefully scrutinize appraisals and other specialist reports that seem out of line with reasonable expectations, and challenge the underlying assumptions.
- Use the work of a specialist for asset valuations, including impairments.
- When vouching long-lived asset additions, accept only original invoices, purchase orders, receiving reports, or similar supporting documentation.
- Confirm the terms of significant additions of property or intangibles with other parties involved in the transaction.

If any of these procedures were part of the original audit program, the auditor should consider expanding the extent of testing or in some way modifying the timing or nature of testing, if significant fraud risk factors are identified.

Documenting Substantive Procedures

For tangible assets such as property, the auditor's documentation of substantive procedures should include:

- A summary schedule showing beginning balances, additions, deletions, and ending balances for the asset account and for accumulated depreciation (see *Exhibit 12.5*)
- Identification of the specific items tested (e.g., all additions greater than $100,000)

For intangible assets, the documentation should include evidence supporting the evaluation and review of the reasonableness of their continuing value.

SUMMARY AND NEXT STEPS

Auditing long-lived assets is usually straightforward—perform tests of changes in account balances during the year. However, the auditor should be skeptical and therefore alert to the possibility that management is managing earnings by changing the related estimates without justification or by capitalizing costs that should be expensed. The major continuing challenge related to long-lived assets is determining asset impairment and assessing whether the record depreciation/amortization/depletion is appropriate given the economic life of the asset. Now that you have an understanding of how to perform audit procedures related to long-lived assets, in the next chapter we turn to auditing equity and debt transactions.

SIGNIFICANT TERMS

Amortization expense A process of expensing the acquisition cost minus the residual value of intangible assets over their estimated useful economic life.

Asset impairment A term used to describe management's recognition that a significant portion of fixed assets is no longer as productive as had originally been expected. When assets are so impaired, the assets should be written down to their expected economic value.

Depletion expense Expense associated with the extraction of natural resources.

Intangible Assets Nonphysical assets, such as patents, trademarks, copyrights, and brand recognition.

Long-lived assets Noncurrent assets that are used over multiple operating cycles and include tangible and intangible assets.

Tangible assets Assets that have a physical form, such as machinery, buildings, and land.

TRUE/FALSE QUESTIONS

12-1 LO 1 Long-lived assets are typically immaterial for most manufacturing organizations.

12-2 LO 1 Patents are an example of long-lived assets.

12-3 LO 2 The pervasiveness of management estimates is a factor that heightens the inherent risk associated with long-lived assets.

12-4 LO 2 An inherent risk associated with intangible long-lived assets is the difficulty in determining the cost of the asset.

12-5 LO 3 A fraud scheme common for long-lived assets is the overstatement of assets though overvaluing the existing assets.

12-6 LO 3 A fraud scheme used by WorldCom management was to capitalize items that should have been expensed.

12-7 LO 4 Auditors should expect clients to have written policies for the acquisition and disposal of long-lived assets.

12-8 LO 4 A formal budgeting process that is tied to the acquisition of long-lived assets is a management activity, but would not be considered a control over long-lived assets.

12-9 LO 5 The auditor needs to understand the client's business in order to perform meaningful planning analytical procedures.

12-10 LO 5 When performing planning analytical procedures, the auditor should not typically expect the client to use depreciable lives similar to organizations in the same industry.

12-11 LO 6 If a client's long-lived assets involve only a few assets of relatively high value, it might be most efficient to test long-lived assets by using only substantive tests of details.

12-12 LO 6 Assume a client setting where there are weak controls and client incentives to capitalize items that should be expensed. In such a setting, the auditor likely obtains most of the audit evidence through tests of controls.

12-13 LO 7 When testing a control that requires training for all employees involved in equipment management, the auditor would typically reperform the control.

12-14 LO 7 Auditors who are aware of control deficiencies that could result in the material misstatement of lease accounts need to modify their substantive testing in response to those deficiencies.

12-15 LO 8 One procedure that can be used to test management's assertion that tangible long-lived assets exist would be to inspect the tangible asset.

12-16 LO 8 When testing potential impairment of assets, the auditor may need to rely on work performed by a specialist/expert.

MULTIPLE-CHOICE QUESTIONS

12-17 `LO 1` Long-lived assets include which of the following?
a. Tangible assets such as equipment.
b. Intangible assets such as patents.
c. Natural resources.
d. All of the above.

12-18 `LO 1` Which of the following statements is true?
a. Existence and valuation assertions related to long-lived assets are usually the most relevant assertions.
b. A concern regarding the existence of long-lived assets relates to whether management has properly recorded depreciation.
c. Depletion expense is not an account that would be included when auditing long-lived assets.
d. All of the above statements are true.

12-19 `LO 2` Which of the following is *not* an inherent risk related to long-lived asset accounts?
a. Failing to record asset disposals.
b. Capitalizing repairs and maintenance expense.
c. Changing depreciation estimates to manage earnings.
d. All of the above are inherent risks related to long-lived asset accounts.

12-20 `LO 2` Which of the following risks is an inherent risk related to asset impairment?
a. Determination of asset impairment is based on management judgment.
b. It is difficult to identify the costs associated with the discovery of natural resources.
c. Management might have incentives to not record all asset disposals.
d. All of the above are inherent risks related to asset impairment.

12-21 `LO 3` Which of the following statements is false regarding fraud risk related to long-lived assets?
a. A potential fraud scheme involves not removing sold assets from the books.
b. Because long-lived assets are typically an audit area of low risk, auditors do not need to perform brainstorming activities related to long-lived assets.
c. Management might use unreasonably long depreciable lives in an effort to reduce expenses.
d. None of the above statements is false.

12-22 `LO 3` Which of the following techniques can be used by management to overstate long-lived assets?
a. Overvalue existing assets.
b. Include fictitious assets on the financial statements.
c. Capitalize transactions that should be expensed.
d. All of the above.

12-23 `LO 4` Which of the following controls would be most useful in providing reasonable assurance about the valuation of tangible assets?
a. A policy requiring the reconciliation of the physical asset count with the property ledger.
b. A policy requiring that deprecation categories and lives be periodically assessed.
c. A formal budgeting process.
d. Written policies requiring authorization for the acquisition of long-lived assets.

12-24 **LO 4** Which of the following controls should management have in place to provide reasonable assurance about asset impairment judgments?
a. A policy requiring the reconciliation of the physical asset count with the property ledger.
b. Limits to physical access of long-lived assets.
c. A systematic process to identify assets that are not currently in use.
d. A formal budgeting process.

12-25 **LO 5** An auditor performing planning analytical procedures scans the repairs and maintenance expense accounts. Which of the following statements is consistent with what the auditor is most likely focused on?
a. Expenditures for long-lived assets have not been charged to expense.
b. Expenditures for long-lived assets have been properly approved.
c. Expenditures for long-lived assets have been recorded in the correct period.
d. The auditor would not be performing scanning as a planning analytical procedure.

12-26 **LO 5** Which of the following analyses might an auditor perform as part of planning analytical procedures for long-lived assets?
a. Develop an overall estimate of depreciation expense.
b. Compare capital expenditures with the client's capital budget.
c. Perform a trend analysis of the ratio of depreciation expense to total depreciable long-lived tangible assets.
d. All of the above could be performed as part of planning analytical procedures.

12-27 **LO 6** Assume that the auditor decides to only perform substantive tests of details when auditing the equipment account. Which of the following statements best describes the circumstances associated with the client being audited?
a. The client does not have effective controls over equipment.
b. The equipment account involves only a few assets of relatively high value.
c. Either (a) or (b) could be descriptive of the circumstances associated with the client being audited.
d. Neither (a) nor (b) would be descriptive of the circumstances associated with the client being audited.

12-28 **LO 6** Assume that a client's controls over recording retirements of long-lived tangible assets are not well designed. Which of the following procedures would the auditor plan to perform as a way of responding to the heightened risk of material misstatement?
a. Select long-lived tangible assets recorded in the property ledger and locate them for inspection.
b. Inspect long-lived tangible assets located at the client location and trace those assets to the property ledger.
c. Review the tangible long-lived asset property ledger to see if depreciation was recorded on each tangible long-lived asset.
d. The auditor would perform all of the above procedures to respond to the heightened risk of material misstatement due to poor client controls over recording retirements.

12-29 **LO 7** Which of the following situations would lead an auditor to test controls over long-lived assets?
a. Substantive analytical procedures suggested that controls over long-lived assets were not effective.

b. Risk assessment procedures indicated that controls were effectively designed.

c. Tests of details identified many errors in recording long-lived asset transactions.

d. The auditor has decided that the additional effort to test controls would not exceed the potential reduction in substantive procedures.

12-30 **LO 7** To test the effectiveness of controls over asset impairment, the auditor could perform which of the following procedures?

a. Perform substantive analytical procedures.

b. Send confirmations to the management specialist who performed work related to the impairment.

c. Inquire of management as to its process for determining assessment impairment, and follow up as appropriate.

d. Inspect the asset for potential impairment.

12-31 **LO 8** When auditing intangible assets, the auditor would likely recompute amortization and determine whether management's recorded amount is reasonable. When performing this procedure, which assertion is the auditor primarily gathering evidence for?

a. Completeness.

b. Existence.

c. Valuation.

d. Rights and obligations.

12-32 **LO 8** As part of auditing equipment, the auditor will inspect new equipment additions selected from the client's property ledger. The procedure will provide evidence about which of the following assertions?

a. Completeness.

b. Existence.

c. Valuation.

d. Rights and obligations.

REVIEW AND SHORT CASE QUESTIONS

NOTE: Completing Review and Short Case Questions does not require the student to reference additional resources and materials.

NOTE: For the remaining problems, we make special note of those addressing fraud, international issues, professional skepticism, and ethics.

FRAUD

12-33 **LO 1** Refer to *Exhibit 12.1*. One of the significant accounts in this cycle is equipment. For this account, what would typically be the most relevant assertions for the auditor to consider? Why is it important for the auditor to identify the more relevant assertions?

12-34 **LO 1** Refer to *Exhibit 12.1*. Depreciation expense is included in the exhibit. How is depreciation expense similar to depletion expense and amortization expense?

12-35 **LO 1** Identify the five management assertions and describe how they are relevant to long-lived assets.

12-36 **LO 2** What is asset impairment, and what inherent risk factors are associated with asset impairment?

12-37 **LO 2** What are some inherent risks of material misstatement associated with natural resources?

12-38 **LO 2** What are some inherent risks of material misstatement associated with intangible assets?

12-39 **LO 3** A 2010 study on fraudulent financial reporting by Committee of Sponsoring Organizations of the Treadway Commission (COSO) notes ways in which long-lived assets can be fraudulently overstated, including:

- Fictitious assets on the books (WorldCom)
- Improper and incomplete depreciation (Waste Management)

- Failure to record impairment of assets, especially goodwill (Sun Microsystems)
- Expired or worthless assets left on a company's books (Millacron)
- Assets overvalued upon acquisition, especially in the purchase of a company (WorldCom)

a. What might motivate management to overstate fixed assets?

b. What other factors should the auditor consider when assessing fraud risk related to long-lived assets?

FRAUD

PROFESSIONAL SKEPTICISM

FRAUD

12-40 **LO 3** Explain how a skeptical auditor might come to understand management's potential for adjusting earnings through manipulation of long-asset accounts.

12-41 **LO 3** Identify potential fraud schemes related to long-lived assets.

12-42 **LO 4** Consider the risks typically associated with tangible long-lived assets and identify the internal controls over these assets that you would expect a client to have in implemented.

12-43 **LO 4** Consider the risks typically associated with intangible long-lived assets and identify the internal controls over these assets that you would expect a client to have in implemented.

12-44 **LO 5** Identify planning analytical procedures related to depreciation expense that may be effective in identifying potential material misstatements.

12-45 **LO 5** Identify ratios and expected relationships that might be used when performing planning analytical procedures related to long-lived assets.

12-46 **LO 6** Refer to *Exhibit 12.3*. Describe the differences in the planned audit approaches for Clients A and B and the reasons for such differences.

12-47 **LO 6** Explain why in some audit settings relating to long-lived assets auditors may choose to perform only substantive tests of details, even though controls are designed effectively.

12-48 **LO 6** The following questions might be addressed when an auditor is completing an internal control questionnaire. For each question (labeled as 1 through 8):

a. Indicate the purpose of the control.

b. Indicate the impact on the planned substantive audit procedures if the answer to the question indicates weak controls.

1. Does the client periodically take a physical inventory of property and reconcile to the property ledger?
2. Does the client have a policy manual to classify property and assign an estimated life for depreciation purposes to the class of assets?
3. Does the client have a policy on minimum expenditures before an item is capitalized? If yes, what is the minimum amount?
4. Does the client have a mechanism to identify pieces of equipment that have been designated for scrap? If yes, is it effective?
5. Does the client have an acceptable mechanism to differentiate major renovations from repair and maintenance? If yes, is it effective?
6. Does the client regularly self-construct its own assets? If yes, does the client have an effective procedure to appropriately identify and classify all construction costs?
7. Does the client systematically review major classes of assets for potential impairment?

8. Does management periodically review asset disposal or the scrapping of assets as a basis for reviewing the assignment of estimated life for depreciation purposes?

12-49 [LO 7] Based on the following description, determine appropriate tests of controls for the company's controls over tangible long-lived assets.

A corporation operates a highly automated flexible manufacturing facility. The capital-intensive nature of the corporation's operations makes internal control over the acquisition and use of tangible long-lived assets important management objectives.

A tangible long-lived assets budget indicating planned capital expenditures by department is established at the beginning of each year. Department managers request capital expenditures by completing a tangible long-lived assets requisition form, which must be approved by senior management. The firm has a written policy that establishes whether a budget request is to be considered as a capital expenditure or as a routine maintenance expenditure.

A management committee meets each month to review budget reports that compare actual expenditures made by managers to their budgeted amounts and to authorize any additional expenditures that may be necessary. The committee also reviews and approves, as necessary, any departmental request for sale, retirement, or scrapping of tangible long-lived assets. Copies of vouchers used to document department requests for sale, retirement, or scrapping of fixed assets are forwarded to the accounting department to initiate removal of the asset from the tangible long-lived assets ledger.

The accounting department is responsible for maintaining a detailed ledger of tangible long-lived assets. When a tangible long-lived asset is acquired, it is tagged for identification. The identification number as well as the cost, location, and other information necessary for depreciation calculations are entered into the tangible long-lived assets ledger. Depreciation calculations are made each quarter and are posted to the general ledger. Periodic physical inventories of tangible long-lived assets are taken for purposes of reconciliation to the tangible long-lived assets ledger as well as appraisal for insurance purposes.

12-50 [LO 7] Refer to *Exhibit 12.2*. Identify tests of controls that could be used to test the controls included in *Exhibit 12.2*.

FRAUD

12-51 [LO 8] A 2010 study on fraudulent financial reporting by COSO notes the many ways in which long-lived assets can be fraudulently overstated, including:

- Fictitious assets on the books (WorldCom)
- Improper and incomplete depreciation (Waste Management)
- Failure to record impairment of assets, especially goodwill (Sun Microsystems)
- Expired or worthless assets left on a company's books (Millacron)
- Assets overvalued upon acquisition, especially in the purchase of a company (WorldCom)

What substantive audit procedures might have detected these frauds?

12-52 [LO 8] The audit senior has asked you to perform analytical procedures to obtain substantive evidence on the reasonableness of recorded depreciation expense of the delivery equipment of a client. Changes in the account occurred pretty much evenly during the year. The estimated useful life is six years. Estimated salvage value is 10% of original cost. Straight-line depreciation is used. Additional information includes:

Delivery Equipment (per General Ledger)	
Beginning balance	$380,500
Additions	154,000
Disposals	(95,600)
Ending balance	$438,900

Current year depreciation expense per books = $60,500

Based on this information, develop an expectation of the amount of depreciation expense for the year as part of a reasonableness test. Does the recorded depreciation expense seem acceptable? Explain. What is the impact of the result of this analytical procedure on other substantive procedures that the auditor may perform?

12-53 LO 8   What audit procedures might an auditor use to identify fully depreciated equipment? How might the auditor determine that such equipment is properly valued?

12-54 LO 8   A client has a policy manual that categorizes equipment by type and assigns a depreciation life based on the categorization. All equipment in a category is depreciated using the same depreciation method. How does the auditor determine the reasonableness of the client's approach?

12-55 LO 8   What evidence might an auditor obtain to determine the proper valuation of an impaired asset?

12-56 LO 8   Assume that a company obtains an appraisal for equipment that may be impaired. Does the auditor need to test the appraisal? What work should the auditor perform to determine that the appraisal should be relied upon as a best estimate of the value of the assets?

12-57 LO 8   Describe the basic approach to auditing leases.

12-58 LO 8   You are performing the year-end audit of Halvorson Fine Foods, Inc. for December 31, 2015. The client has prepared the following schedule for the fixed assets and related allowance for depreciation accounts.

Description	Final Balance, December 31, 2014	Additions	Retirements	Per Books, December 31, 2015
Assets:				
Land	$22,500	$5,000		$27,500
Buildings	120,000	17,500		137,500
Machinery and equipment	385,000	40,400	$26,000	399,400
	$527,500	$62,900	$26,000	$564,400
Allowance for depreciation:				
Building	$60,000	$5,150		$65,150
Machinery and equipment	173,200	39,220		212,470
	$233,250	$44,370		$277,620

You have compared the opening balances with your prior-year audit working papers. The following information (labeled as 1 through 6) is found during your current-year audit. Review this information and indicate how you might have found each of the described items (labeled as 1 through 6) during the audit (other than through client inquiry).

1. All equipment is depreciated on a straight-line basis (no salvage value taken into consideration) based on the following estimated lives: buildings, 25 years; all other items, 10 years. The company's policy is to take one-half year's depreciation on all asset acquisitions and disposals occurring during the year.

2. On April 1 of the current year, the company entered into a ten-year lease contract for a die-casting machine with annual rentals of $5,000, payable in advance every April 1. The lease is cancelable by either party (60 days' written notice is required), and there is no option to renew the lease or buy the equipment at the end of the lease. The estimated useful life of the machine is ten years with no salvage value. The company recorded the die-casting machine in the machinery and equipment account at $40,400, the present value at the date of the lease, and $2,020, applicable to the machine, has been included in depreciation expense for the year.

3. The company completed the construction of a wing on the plant building on June 30 of the current year. The useful life of the building was not extended by this addition. The lowest construction bid received was $17,500, the amount recorded in the buildings account. Company personnel were used to construct the addition at a cost of $16,000 (materials, $7,500; labor, $5,500; and overhead, $3,000).

4. On August 18, Halvorson paid $5,000 for paving and fencing a portion of land owned by the company for use as a parking lot for employees. The expenditure was charged to the land account.

5. The amount shown in the retirements column for the machinery and equipment asset represents cash received on September 5, on disposal of a machine purchased in July 2001 for $48,000. The bookkeeper recorded a depreciation expense of $3,500 on this machine in 2013.

6. Crux City donated land and building appraised at $10,000 and $40,000, respectively, to Halvorson for a plant. On September 1, the company began operating the plant. Because no costs were involved, the bookkeeper made no entry for the foregoing transaction.

ETHICS

12-59 **LO 8, 9** Your audit firm has been the audit firm of Cowan Industries for a number of years. The company manufactures a wide range of lawn care products and typically sells to major retailers. In recent years, the company has expanded into ancillary products, such as recreation equipment, that use some of the same technology. The newer lines of business, while successful, have not been particularly profitable. The company's stock price has languished, and top management has recently been replaced.

The new management team announces that it will close two factories and will phase out one of the newer lines of business. It plans to expand existing products and increase marketing efforts. Even though there is no technological obsolescence of existing products, the new management does not believe the company has a competitive advantage. It wants to take a one-time hit to the balance sheet and income statement of $15.3 million (about one-third of total assets) as a reserve for the shutdown of the plants and the disposal of a line of business. It also plans on severance pay for employees at the two plants.

a. Define the term *impairment of assets*.

b. Is management typically motivated to understate or overstate the write-down because of asset impairment? Explain.

c. Assume in this situation that the auditor believes management is overestimating the impairment charge and thus the improvement in future earnings because of reduced depreciation charges in subsequent periods. Further assume that the auditor has gathered and evaluated evidence that convincingly reveals the impairment charge should more reasonably fall in a range from $8 to $10 million, rather than management's estimate of about $15 million. Finally, assume the auditor has discussed the issue with management and it refuses to vary from its original estimate. Management has stated that its assumptions and evidence are just as convincing as the auditor's. Use the seven-step framework for ethical decision making from *Chapter 4* to make a recommendation about the course of action the auditor should take. Recall that the steps are as follows: (1) identify the ethical issue; in this case the ethical issue is how to properly ensure that the review comments are taken seriously and addressed; (2) determine the affected parties and identify their rights; (3) determine the most important rights for each affected party; (4) develop alternative courses of action; (5) determine the likely consequences of each proposed course of action on each affected party; (6) assess the possible consequences; and (7) decide on an appropriate course of action.

12-60 **LO 8, 9** Novelis, Inc., is the world's leading rolled-aluminum products producer. Items 1 through 3 provide descriptions of issues involving asset impairments derived from the company's footnote disclosures.

1. In connection with the decision to close and sell our plant in Borgofranco, Italy, we recognized an impairment charge of $5 million to reduce the net book value of the plant's fixed assets to zero. We based our estimate on third-party offers and negotiations to sell the business.

2. We recorded an impairment charge of $65 million to reduce the carrying value of the production equipment at two facilities in Italy to their fair value of $56 million. We determined the fair value of the impaired assets based on the discounted future cash flows of these facilities using a 7% discount rate.

3. We announced that we would cease operations in Falkirk, Scotland. We designated certain production equipment with a nominal carrying value for transfer to our Rogerstone facility. We reduced the carrying value of the remaining fixed assets to zero, which resulted in an $8 million impairment charge.

Complete the first four steps of the seven-step framework for professional decision making introduced in *Chapter 4* by answering the following questions:

a. What difficulties will the auditor of Novelis face when deciding whether the impairment charges that Novelis incurred are reasonable?

b. What are the consequences of the auditor's decisions in evaluating impairments?

c. What are the risks and uncertainties associated with Novelis' estimation?

d. What types of evidence should the auditor gather to evaluate the reasonableness of management's estimates?

Recall that the framework is as follows:

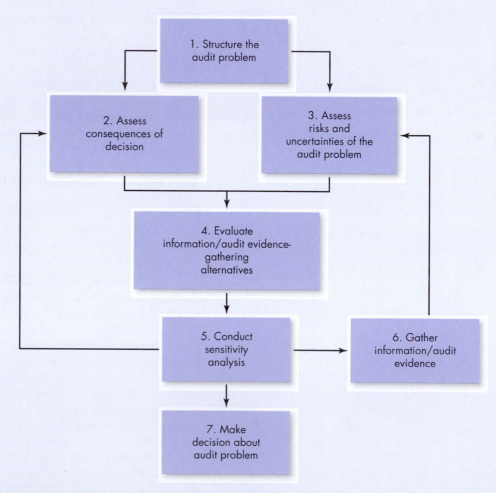

Source: Adapted from *Judgment and Choice*, by Robin Hogarth.

FRAUD FOCUS: CONTEMPORARY AND HISTORICAL CASES

12-61 **Ignite Restaurant Group**
(LO 1, 2, 3, 4, 6, 8) Refer to the *Professional Judgment in Context* feature "Accounting Problems Related to Long-Lived Assets and Leases at Ignite Restaurant Group." Answer the following questions:

a. What long-lived asset accounts at Ignite Restaurant Group (IRG) were misstated?

b. The situation has been described in the press as a minor, but embarrassing, accounting issue. Notwithstanding this description, assume for purposes of this question that the accounting issue was the result of fraudulent financial reporting by management. If that had been the case, what might have motivated management to materially misstate the assets you identified in Part a?

c. What controls should be in place at IRG to mitigate the misstatements that needed to be corrected?

d. What procedures should the auditor have performed when auditing the assets you identified in Part a?

FRAUD

PROFESSIONAL SKEPTICISM

12-62 **WorldCom**
(LO 2, 3, 8) The WorldCom bankruptcy is one of the largest in U.S. economic history. Much of the fraud was carried out by capitalizing operating expenses, such as payments to other companies for line rental, as fixed assets. Adjusting journal entries were made at the company's headquarters in Mississippi even though property accounting records were located in Dallas, Texas.

a. Would it be considered unusual to find debits to fixed assets coming from an adjusting journal entry source rather than a purchase journal? Explain.

b. Would it be considered unusual to find entries to accumulated depreciation and depreciation expense to come from an adjusting journal entry source rather than another source?

c. Assume you were auditing WorldCom, and in your sample of debits to fixed assets, you find an entry for $500,000 with the following notation: "Capitalization of line capacity per CFO, amounts were originally incorrectly recorded as an expense." Explain what you would do to complete the audit of this item. How might the professionally skeptical auditor respond? What evidence would you need to see to either corroborate or question the entry?

FRAUD

12-63 **Safety-Kleen and PricewaterhouseCoopers**
(LO 2, 3, 4, 6, 8) Refer to the *Focus on Fraud* feature "Improper Capitalization of Operating Expenses: The Case of Safety-Kleen Corporation." In addition to the information provided in the feature, consider the following information.

At the close of each quarter, Safety-Kleen executives met to discuss the results of operations. Typically, they discussed what the targeted earnings amount was, and then they discussed potential accounting adjustments to help them achieve the target. Although the company had always made legitimate quarterly adjusting entries in preparing its financial statements, the magnitude and nature of the adjustments changed dramatically during fiscal year 1999. As time went on, the discrepancy between the company's projected results and the actual results increased, and they made several improper adjustments each quarter to reach the earnings targets. As the following table indicates, Safety-Kleen's quarterly earnings were materially increased as a result of the accounting adjustments (in other words, the legitimate adjustments and the improper adjustments combined). In some reporting periods, the company's reported earnings were increased by more than 100%.

As an example of inappropriate entries, at the end of the third quarter of fiscal 1999, they improperly capitalized approximately $4.6 million of payroll expenses relating to certain marketing and start-up activities. At the close of the fourth quarter of fiscal 1999, they improperly capitalized $1.8 million of salaries and wages incurred in connection with the development and implementation of various software systems. Not only did this adjusting entry fail to comply with GAAP, it ultimately was recorded twice.

	Earnings Before Adjustments (in Millions)	Earnings as Reported After Adjustments (in Millions)	Total Adjustments (in Millions)	%
First Quarter FY 1999	$90.9	$127.5	$36.6	40.3
Second Quarter FY 1999	$76.7	$107.6	$30.9	40.3
Third Quarter FY 1999	$47.9	$123.4	$75.5	157.6
Fourth Quarter FY 1999	$57.3	$110.4	$53.1	92.7
First Quarter FY 2000	$47.0	$116.8	$69.8	148.5
Total	$319.8	$585.7	$265.9	83.1

On March 6, 2000, after Safety-Kleen's board of directors had received information concerning possible accounting irregularities, the company announced that it had initiated an internal investigation of its previously reported financial results and certain of its accounting policies. On March 10, 2000, Safety-Kleen filed a Form 8-K stating that the company's independent accounting firm, PricewaterhouseCoopers LLP, had withdrawn its audit reports on the financial statements for fiscal years 1997, 1998, and 1999.

In 2005, a lawsuit brought by a group of institutional investors against former officers of Safety-Kleen Corporation ended with a $200 million judgment against two former officers and more than $84 million in settlements against the company's former auditor and directors. PricewaterhouseCoopers, Safety-Kleen's former auditors, agreed to settle and pay $48 million, and the directors agreed to pay $36 million.

a. What were likely factors contributing to the fraud?
b. What audit procedures might have identified the inappropriate adjustments?

APPLICATION ACTIVITIES

PROFESSIONAL SKEPTICISM

NOTE: Completing Application Activities requires students to reference additional resources and materials. Some Application Activities will require the student to reference relevant professional auditing standards. We make special note of these as Auditing Standards Application Activities.

FRAUD

INTERNATIONAL

PROFESSIONAL SKEPTICISM

AUDITING STANDARDS APPLICATION ACTIVITY

12-64 **LO 8** Select a company that has recorded impairment charges in its financial statements. For the selected company, identify:
a. The company name and its principal line of business.
b. The nature of financial difficulties the company is facing.
c. The nature of the company's long-lived assets that were impaired.
d. The nature of the impairment charges and their magnitude as a percentage of total assets, total sales, and net income.
e. What judgments did management at the company make that may affect the ability of the external auditor to assess the reasonableness of the impairment charges? Discuss the importance of professional skepticism related to these management judgments.

12-65 **PCAOB** **(LO 2, 6, 8)** In September 2012, the PCAOB issued an Order Instituting Disciplinary Proceedings, Making Findings, and Imposing Sanctions *In the Matter of Jewett, Schwartz, Wolfe & Associates, P.L., Respondent.* See PCAOB Release No. 105-2012–004. Obtain a copy of the PCAOB release and identify and describe the audit deficiencies related to long-lived assets for the audits of Dynamic Response Group, Inc. (DRG) and Dolphin Digital Media, Inc. (DDM). What sanctions did the PCAOB impose in this case? Comment on whether you believe these sanctions were appropriate.

12-66 **IASB** **(LO 1, 2, 6, 8)** On June 20, 2012, Hans Hoogervorst, chairman of the IASB, addressed the International Association for Accounting Education & Research (IAAER) conference in Amsterdam. The title of his speech is "The Imprecise World of Accounting." Obtain a copy of his speech at *www.ifrs.org*. What challenges are identified in that speech related to intangible assets? How do the identified challenges affect the audit of these assets?

12-67 **LO 8** Assume you are helping to plan the audit for a client that is a U.S. nonpublic company (non-issuer). The client is a forestry firm and your senior is familiar with the Sino-Forest Corp. case discussed in the *Focus on Fraud* feature "Auditing a Forestry Company Results in Class-Action Lawsuit." Because of her concerns based on this case, your senior has indicated that she would like to use an auditor specialist to help obtain evidence related to this client's timber reserves. Your senior asks you for guidance on what responsibilities the auditor has regarding the qualifications of such a specialist. Further, the senior wonders if the audit report should mention that a specialist was used. As you are not sure of the answers to these questions, you decide to obtain a copy of the auditing standard that would most likely provide relevant guidance. You may want to refer to the *Standards Appendix* to the text to determine the appropriate standard. What standard would be most appropriate and what guidance does it provide that can help you answer your senior's questions?

12-68 **LO 8** Assume you are working on the audit of a client that is a U.S. nonpublic company (non-issuer) and focusing on long-lived assets. The senior on the audit team has noted that this audit area has a number of estimates including management judgments and decisions such as depreciation methods and useful lives. Your senior warns you to be alert to indicators of possible management bias in these judgments and decisions. As you are not sure what such indicators might be, you consult the relevant auditing standard. You may want to refer to the *Standards Appendix* to the text to determine the appropriate standard. What standard would be most appropriate and what guidance does it provide?

ACADEMIC RESEARCH CASES

NOTE: Completing Academic Research Cases requires students to reference additional resources and materials.

12-69 **LO 2** Locate and read the article listed below and answer the following questions.

Acito, A. A., J. J. Burks, and W. B. Johnson. 2009. Materiality decisions and the correction of accounting errors. *The Accounting Review* 84 (3): 659–688.

a. What is the issue being addressed in the paper?
b. What are the findings of the paper?
c. Why is this paper important to auditors, and what are the implications of this paper for the auditing profession?
d. Describe the research methodology used as a basis for the conclusions.
e. Describe any limitations of the research.

12-70 **LO 2, 8** Locate and read the article listed below and answer the following questions.

Fu, H., H.-T. Tan, and J. Zhang. 2011. Effect of auditor negotiation experience and client negotiating style on auditors' judgments in an auditor-client negotiation context. *Auditing: A Journal of Practice and Theory* 30 (3): 225–237.

a. What is the issue being addressed in the paper?
b. What are the findings of the paper?
c. Why is this paper important to auditors, and what are the implications of this paper for the auditing profession?
d. Describe the research methodology used as a basis for the conclusions.
e. Describe any limitations of the research.

FORD AND TOYOTA

	Ford Motor Company and Toyota Motor Corporation
12-71	(LO **1, 2, 3, 5, 6, 8**)

Source and Reference	Question
Ford 10-K, Toyota 20-F	1a. What are the key long-lived asset and related expense accounts for Ford? 1b. What are the critical accounting policies for these accounts? 1c. Calculate and compare cycle-specific ratios (e.g., property, plant, and equipment/total assets) that you deem relevant for Ford and Toyota. What are the implications of the differences that you note?
Ford Annual Report	2a. Review Ford's 10-K to determine if the company reported an asset impairment. If applicable, describe the nature of the impairment and the monetary value of the impairment. What caused the impairment? What key assumptions and estimates affected Ford's valuation of the related assets? 2b. What are the audit firm's obligations regarding the estimates made in this type of disclosure? What risks do these estimates pose for the audit firm?

13 Auditing Debt Obligations and Stockholders' Equity Transactions

CHAPTER OVERVIEW AND LEARNING OBJECTIVES

In terms of the audit opinion formulation process, this chapter primarily involves Phases II, III, and IV, that is, performing risk assessment procedures, tests of controls, and substantive procedures for accounts, disclosures, and relevant assertions related to debt obligations and stockholders' equity transactions.

Through studying this chapter, you will be able to achieve these learning objectives:

1. Identify the significant accounts, disclosures, and relevant assertions in auditing debt obligations and stockholders' equity transactions.

2. Identify and assess inherent risks of material misstatement associated with debt obligations and stockholders' equity transactions.

3. Identify and assess fraud risks of material misstatement associated with debt obligations and stockholders' equity transactions.

4. Identify and assess control risks of material misstatement associated with debt obligations and stockholders' equity transactions.

5. Describe how to use planning analytical procedures to identify possible material misstatements associated with debt obligations and stockholders' equity transactions.

6. Determine appropriate responses to identified risks of material misstatement in auditing debt obligations and stockholders' equity transactions.

7. Determine appropriate tests of controls and consider the results of tests of controls in auditing debt obligations and stockholders' equity transactions.

8. Determine and apply sufficient appropriate substantive audit procedures in auditing debt obligations and stockholders' equity transactions.

9. Apply the frameworks for professional decision making and ethical decision making to issues involving the audit of debt obligations and stockholders' equity transactions.

THE AUDIT OPINION FORMULATION PROCESS

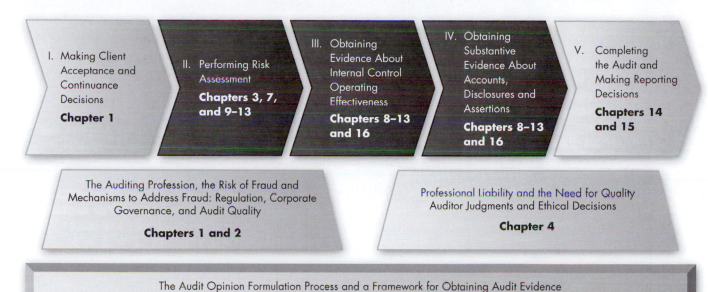

I. Making Client Acceptance and Continuance Decisions

Chapter 1

II. Performing Risk Assessment

Chapters 3, 7, and 9–13

III. Obtaining Evidence About Internal Control Operating Effectiveness

Chapters 8–13 and 16

IV. Obtaining Substantive Evidence About Accounts, Disclosures and Assertions

Chapters 8–13 and 16

V. Completing the Audit and Making Reporting Decisions

Chapters 14 and 15

The Auditing Profession, the Risk of Fraud and Mechanisms to Address Fraud: Regulation, Corporate Governance, and Audit Quality

Chapters 1 and 2

Professional Liability and the Need for Quality Auditor Judgments and Ethical Decisions

Chapter 4

The Audit Opinion Formulation Process and a Framework for Obtaining Audit Evidence

Chapters 5 and 6

PROFESSIONAL JUDGMENT IN CONTEXT

Deficiencies in Auditing Debt Obligations and Stockholders' Equity Accounts: Insights From SEC Releases

Debt Obligations: Federico Quinto Jr., CPA

In August 2012, the SEC issued an Accounting and Auditing Enforcement Release in the matter of Federico Quinto Jr., CPA. Quinto was an audit engagement partner for Soyo Group, Inc., in 2007. During 2007 and the first three quarters of 2008, Soyo booked over $47 million in fictitious revenues. At the same time, Soyo was financing its business with debt from United Commercial Bank (UCB). As of December 31, 2007, Soyo's debt with UCB was approximately $27.8 million, which represented 63% of Soyo's total liabilities. Because of Soyo's struggling business, the company often found itself in violation of its debt covenants with UCB.

Quinto's audit team conducted an analysis that identified that Soyo was not in compliance with three of its six debt covenants with UCB as of December 31, 2007. Because of the debt covenant violations, UCB could take action that would force Soyo into bankruptcy, as Soyo needed the financing to fund its business operations. The audit team did not follow up

on the identified debt covenant violations and did not obtain any evidence indicating whether a waiver had been granted by UCB. The audit workpapers did not provide any evidence that the audit team considered whether these violations could impact the going-concern status of Soyo. Further, the audit report for 2007 included an unqualified opinion, although Soyo did not make the required disclosures regarding noncompliance with its debt covenants.

Source: Securities and Exchange Commission, Accounting and Auditing Enforcement Release No. 3403, August 31, 2012, available at http://www.sec.gov/litigation/admin/2012/34–67767.pdf

Adjustments to Stockholders' Equity Accounts: Delphi Corporation

In 2006, the SEC outlined its case of allegations involving Delphi Corporation and certain of its senior officers, accounting staff, and treasury staff. The allegations involve a pattern of violations of federal securities laws from 2000 through 2004. One of the alleged violations related to Delphi improperly accounting for an increase in warranty reserves related to warranty claims made by its former parent company. Delphi recorded the reserve increase as a direct adjustment to retained earnings rather than as an expense. There was no basis for Delphi to record the reserve adjustment as an adjustment to retained earnings. The SEC further alleged that Delphi disclosed the adjustment in an intentionally and materially misleading way. Specifically, the disclosure suggested, falsely, that the adjustment primarily related to certain pension and other postemployment benefit ("OPEB") matters and Delphi failed to disclose highly material information concerning the reserve increase and the former parent company's warranty claim. The misclassification of the reserve increase as a direct adjustment to equity, rather than as an expense item, resulted in Delphi materially overstating its net income for 2000 by $69 million.

Source: SEC Accounting and Auditing Enforcement Release No. 2504, October 30, 2006. A related SEC complaint in this matter is available at http://www.sec.gov/litigation/complaints/2006/comp19891.pdf

As you read through this chapter, consider the following questions:

- What are the risks of material misstatement associated with debt obligations and stockholders' equity accounts? (LO 2, 3, 4)
- What are the typical substantive procedures that auditors should perform when auditing debt obligations and stockholders' equity accounts? (LO 8)
- How could a lack of appropriate professional skepticism by auditors lead to material misstatements related to debt obligations and stockholders' equity accounts? (LO 2, 3, 5, 6, 8)

Significant Accounts, Disclosures, and Relevant Assertions

LO 1 Identify the significant accounts, disclosures, and relevant assertions in auditing debt obligations and stockholders' equity transactions.

Organizations use two common approaches to meet their long-term financing needs: issuing debt or equity.

Debt Obligations

Bonds are issued to finance major expansions or to refinance existing debt. Organizations also obtain financing through notes or mortgages. An organization typically has only a few debt transactions, but each transaction is usually highly material to the financial statements. Relevant accounts when auditing debt obligations include:

- Bonds payable
- Bond premium/discount
- Interest expense
- Gains or losses on refinancing debt
- Notes payable
- Mortgages payable

The overall objective of the audit of debt obligations is to determine whether all obligations are recorded and properly classified and disclosed. The auditor is primarily concerned with understatement and, therefore, focuses on the completeness assertion. Other relevant assertions in auditing bonds or other long-term debt include:

- Proper valuation of premium or discount (includes amortization)
- Valuation of gains or losses on refinancing debt
- Proper presentation and disclosure, including important restrictions contained in the debt obligations or violations of debt restrictions

Activities Related to Debt Obligations

Bond Issuance and Amortization Schedules Most bonds are marketed through an underwriter, with the proceeds going to the issuer after deducting the underwriter's commission. The authorization to issue a bond is usually limited to the board of directors. A bond premium/discount amortization spreadsheet can be used to help assure that the bond is appropriately valued and disclosed in the financial statements. A **bond indenture**

provides important information regarding the bond, including the time period before repayment, amount of interest paid, if the bond is convertible (and if so, at what price or what ratio), if the bond is callable, and the amount of money that is to be repaid.

Periodic Payments and Interest Expense Most organizations have agreements with bond trustees to handle the registration of current bondholders and to make the periodic interest payments. The organization issuing the bond makes interest payments to the trustee, plus a fee for the trustee's service, and the trustee disburses the individual payments to the bondholders.

Debt Covenants **Debt covenants** are written restrictions designed to protect bondholders against possible financial decline of the issuer or against the subordination of the value of the debt by the issuance of other debt. Common restrictions include maintenance of a minimum level of retained earnings before dividends can be paid, maintenance of a minimum working-capital ratio, specification of a maximum debt-equity ratio, and specific callable provisions that identify procedures for calling and retiring debt at prespecified prices and dates.

Stockholders' Equity

Relevant accounts when auditing stockholders' equity activities include:

- Stock accounts (common, preferred, and treasury)
- Additional paid-in capital
- Dividend accounts
- Retained earnings

Activities Related to Stockholders' Equity

Common transactions affecting stockholders' equity include:

- New stock issuance
- Purchase of treasury stock
- Declaration and payment of dividends
- Grants of stock options and warrants
- Exercise and expiration of stock options and warrants
- Transfer of net income to retained earnings
- Recording of prior-period adjustments to retained earnings

In auditing equity accounts, the auditor primarily focuses on whether the securities are accurately valued (valuation assertion) and are properly classified and appropriately presented and disclosed (presentation and disclosure assertion).

Valuation Most stock issuances do not present valuation problems because most stock is issued for cash. However, not all stock is issued for cash. In those instances, valuation difficulties can occur in determining (1) whether the market value of the stock issued or the market value of the asset acquired is a better representation of value and (2) the proper accounting for an exchange of stock to acquire another business. Further, stock is also issued in the form of stock options and the exercise of those options. The stock option is an expense that is measured at the fair value of the option—usually measured by the Black-Scholes method. Companies then purchase stock on the open market to fulfill the exercise of those options.

Presentation and Disclosure Disclosure includes a proper description of (1) each class of stock outstanding and the number of shares authorized, issued, and outstanding and special rights associated with each class,

EXHIBIT **13.1** Example of Balance Sheet Disclosure of Stockholders' Equity

FORD MOTOR COMPANY AND SUBSIDIARIES CONSOLIDATED BALANCE SHEET
(in millions)

EQUITY Capital stock (Note 24)	December 31, 2013	December 31, 2012
Common Stock, par value $.01 per share (3,913 million shares issued of 6 billion authorized)	39	39
Class B Stock, par value $.01 per share (71 million shares issued of 530 million authorized)	1	1
Capital in excess of par value of stock	21,422	20,976
Retained earnings	23,658	18,077
Accumulated other comprehensive income/(loss) (Note 18)	(18,231)	(22,854)
Treasury stock	(506)	(292)
Total equity attributable to Ford Motor Company	26,383	15,947
Equity attributable to noncontrolling interests	33	42
Total equity	26,416	15,989

(2) stock options outstanding, (3) convertible features, and (4) existence of stock warrants. Any restrictions or appropriations of retained earnings should be disclosed, as well as prior-period adjustments and other comprehensive income adjustments.

Exhibit 13.1 provides Ford Motor Company's balance sheet disclosure related to stockholders' equity. Note that the balance sheet disclosure includes information related to common stock, the amount of capital in excess of par value, accumulated other comprehensive income/(loss), retained earnings, and treasury stock.

The potential dilutive effect of convertible debt or preferred stock, stock options, and warrants should be disclosed in accordance with relevant accounting guidance in computing primary and fully diluted earnings per share. *Exhibit 13.2* provides Ford's earnings per share income statement disclosure, assuming dilution.

EXHIBIT **13.2** Example of Income Statement Disclosure of Earnings per Share, Assuming Dilution

FORD MOTOR COMPANY AND SUBSIDIARIES CONSOLIDATED INCOME STATEMENT
(in millions, except per share amounts)

AMOUNTS PER SHARE ATTRIBUTABLE TO FORD MOTOR COMPANY COMMON AND CLASS B STOCK (Note 24)

	For the years ended December 31,		
	2013	**2012**	**2011**
Basic income	$ 1.82	$ 1.48	$ 5.33
Diluted income	1.76	1.42	4.94

Performing Risk Assessment Procedures for Debt Obligations and Stockholders' Equity Transactions

LO 2 Identify and assess inherent risks of material misstatement associated with debt obligations and stockholders' equity transactions.

As part of performing risk assessment procedures, the auditor obtains information that is useful in assessing the risk of material misstatement. This includes information about inherent risks at the financial statement level (e.g., the client's business and operational risks, financial reporting risks) and at the account and assertion levels, fraud risks including feedback from audit team brainstorming sessions, strengths and weaknesses in internal control, and results from planning analytical procedures. Once the risks of material misstatement have been identified, the auditor then determines how best to respond to them as part of the audit opinion formulation process.

Identifying Inherent Risks

Identifying Inherent Risks—Debt Obligations

Inherent risks related to debt obligations primarily concern the authorization of debt, receipt of funds, recording of debt transactions, and compliance with any debt covenants. For authorization, inherent risks include incurring debt that is not properly authorized or reviewed. Similarly, there are risks that new debt, debt extinguishments, or debt payment transactions are not properly authorized. In terms of recording debt transactions, risks include interest expense not being properly recorded or accrued and debt not being classified or recorded in accordance with generally accepted accounting principles (GAAP). Regarding debt covenant compliance issues, inherent risks relate to whether debt covenants are calculated accurately and whether compliance with debt covenants is appropriately reviewed and disclosed.

Identifying Inherent Risks—Stockholders' Equity Transactions

Inherent risks related to stockholders' equity transactions vary across the specific activities. *Exhibit 13.3* outlines some of the common inherent risks associated with typical stockholders' equity activities.

Identifying Fraud Risk Factors

LO 3 Identify and assess fraud risks of material misstatement associated with debt obligations and stockholders' equity transactions.

Auditing standards require the auditor to identify and assess the risks of material misstatement due to fraud at the financial statement level and at the assertion level. As part of brainstorming activities, the auditor should identify possible frauds that could occur.

Recall the case of Federico Quinto Jr., CPA, presented in the *Professional Judgment in Context* feature. The client involved in that case, Soyo Group, acted fraudulently by not accurately disclosing violations of its debt covenants. In addition, in the case of Delphi Corporation, members of its management and staff acted fraudulently by charging expenses directly to retained earnings rather than to the appropriate expense accounts.

Other potential frauds related to debt obligations and stockholders' equity transactions are listed in the *Focus on Fraud* feature "Potential Frauds Related to Debt Obligations and Stockholders' Equity Transactions."

Identifying Control Risks

LO 4 Identify and assess control risks of material misstatement associated with debt obligations and stockholders' equity transactions.

Once the auditor has obtained an understanding of the inherent and fraud risks of material misstatement associated with debt obligations and stockholders' equity transactions, the auditor needs to understand the controls that the client has designed and implemented to address those risks. Remember, the auditor is required to gain an overall understanding of internal controls for both integrated audits and financial statement only audits. Such understanding is normally gained by means of a walkthrough of the process,

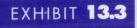

EXHIBIT 13.3   Inherent Risks Associated with Stockholders' Equity Activities

Stock Sale and Issuance

Assertion	Inherent Risk
Existence	Issuances or sales are not authorized in accordance with organization's bylaws. Proceeds are not received. Stock issuances or sales are recorded in the wrong period.
Valuation	Stock issued in exchange for goods or services is not properly valued.
Presentation and disclosure	Equity activities are not properly disclosed in accordance with GAAP.

Purchase of Treasury Stock

Assertion	Inherent Risk
Completeness	All stock repurchased is not recorded as treasury stock. Treasury stock transactions are recorded in the wrong period.
Valuation	The cost of treasury stock that is subsequently retired is not properly allocated among the appropriate accounts.

Dividend Declaration and Payment

Assertion	Inherent Risk
Existence	Dividends may be recorded and paid before being declared. Dividends may not be properly approved before being declared. Dividends are recorded in the wrong period.

Stock Options and Warrants

Assertion	Inherent Risk
Existence	Options/warrants are granted without being properly approved. Inadequate records as to options/warrants issued but not exercised.
Rights/obligations	Options exercised or expired remain on the organization's books.
Valuation	Option/warrant grants are not properly valued due to inappropriate assumptions or models. Inappropriate amortization methods are used. Inaccurate period of service is used.

inquiry, observation, and review of the client's documentation. The auditor considers both entity-wide controls and transaction controls at the account and assertion levels. This understanding provides the auditor with a basis for making an initial control risk assessment.

At the entity-wide level, the auditor considers the control environment, including such principles as a commitment to financial accounting competencies and the independence of the board of directors. The auditor also considers the remaining components of internal control that are typically entity wide—risk assessment, information and communication, and monitoring controls. Although all the components of internal control need to be understood, the auditor typically finds it useful to focus on significant

Potential Frauds Related to Debt Obligations and Stockholders' Equity Transactions

FOCUS on **FRAUD**

Debt Obligations

- Debt obligations are not properly authorized.
- Long-term or short-term debt is misclassified.
- Interest expense is recorded in the wrong period, at the wrong amount, not recorded at all, or is misclassified.
- Entire loan payments (consisting of both interest and principal) are charged to either only principal or interest.

Stockholders' Equity Transactions

- Stock sales or issuances are not authorized.
- Stock sales or issuances violate debt covenants.

- Stock sales or issuances are not recorded.
- Stock options exercised are not authorized or are not in accordance with the terms of options granted.
- Stock options are backdated.
- Dividends are paid in violation of restrictive covenants.
- Dividends are paid to wrong parties or at incorrect amounts.
- Proceeds from stock sales are misappropriated.

control activities. The author focuses on the relevant assertions for each account and identifies the controls that relate to risks for these assertions. In an integrated audit or in a controls reliance audit, this understanding is used to identify important controls that need to be tested.

An important control related to both debt obligations and stockholders' equity would include policies, procedures, and reviews related to providing assurance that all appropriate disclosures have been made. *Exhibit 13.4* provides an example whereby a lack of appropriate disclosure controls was assessed as a material weakness by company management.

EXHIBIT **13.4**   Jammin Java Corp.

Excerpt from Form: 10-K (with bold highlight added for emphasis)

Date Filed: 2013-05-15

Management's Annual Report on Internal Control over Financial Reporting

Management has used the framework set forth in the report entitled Internal Control-Integrated Framework published by the Committee of Sponsoring Organizations of the Treadway Commission, known as COSO, to evaluate the effectiveness of our internal control over financial reporting. Based on this assessment, management has concluded that our internal control over financial reporting was not effective as of January 31, 2013.

A material weakness is a deficiency, or combination of deficiencies, that results in more than a remote likelihood that a material misstatement of annual or interim financial statements will not be prevented or detected. In connection with the assessment described above, management identified the following control deficiencies that represent material weaknesses at January 31, 2013:

(3) insufficient written policies and procedures for accounting and financial reporting with respect to the requirements and application of GAAP and SEC disclosure requirements; and

(4) ineffective controls over period end financial disclosure and reporting processes.

Controls—Debt Obligations

Given the typical inherent and fraud risks described earlier, the auditor would expect an organization to have implemented the following controls:

- The board of directors approves all new debt.
- Debt and interest accounts are updated and reconciled to the general ledger on a monthly basis.
- Top management and the board of directors review draft financial statements prior to issuance for proper disclosure of debt obligations.
- A debt amortization schedule is prepared for each new debt obligation, updated as appropriate, and is reviewed by appropriate personnel.

Controls—Stockholders' Equity Transactions

Given the typical inherent and fraud risks described earlier, the auditor would expect an organization to have the following controls in place:

- The board of directors approves all stock transactions (including options and warrants).
- The CEO and CFO authorize all stock transactions (including options and warrants) approved by the board of directors.
- Stockholders' equity accounts are updated and reconciled to the general ledger on a timely basis.
- Top management and the board of directors review draft financial statements prior to issuance for proper disclosure of equity accounts.
- An outside party, such as an attorney, maintains details of shares issued, repurchased, and cancelled.
- The organization's accountant researches and analyzes proper accounting for stock option grants, and the organization's legal counsel and CFO review and approve the analysis.

Documenting Controls

Auditors need to document their understanding of internal controls for both integrated audits and financial statement only audits. Similar to other audit areas, the auditor can provide this documentation in various formats, including a control matrix, a control risk assessment questionnaire, and/or a memo.

Performing Planning Analytical Procedures

LO 5 Describe how to use planning analytical procedures to identify possible material misstatements associated with debt obligations and stockholders' equity transactions.

Planning analytical procedures help auditors identify areas of potential material misstatements. The steps that the auditor will take in performing planning analytical procedures are fully described in *Chapter 7*.

The following are examples of typical analytical procedures related to debt obligations:

- Perform a trend analysis of the balances in notes payable and accrued interest with prior periods, considering known client activities related to debt.
- Estimate overall interest expense based on average interest rates and average debt outstanding.
- Calculate debt-to-equity ratios and perform a trend analysis with prior periods, considering known client activities related to debt and equity.
- Calculate the times interest earned ratio and perform a trend analysis with prior periods.

The primary planning analytical procedure for stockholders' equity accounts is a comparison of current-year account balances with prior-year account balances. The auditor should have an expectation as to the nature and magnitude of any account balance changes.

If planning analytical procedures do not identify any unexpected relationships, the auditor would conclude that a heightened risk of material misstatement does not exist in these accounts. If unusual or unexpected relationships exist, the planned audit procedures (tests of controls, substantive procedures) would be adjusted to address the potential material misstatements.

Responding to Identified Risks of Material Misstatement

LO 6 Determine appropriate responses to identified risks of material misstatement in auditing debt obligations and stockholders' equity transactions.

Once the auditor has developed an understanding of the risks of material misstatement, including inherent risks, fraud risks, and control risks, the auditor can determine the appropriate audit procedures to perform. Typically for debt accounts the auditor tests debt obligations, including interest transactions, using only substantive procedures. This approach is often appropriate because the number of transactions is relatively small and the dollar amounts involved are usually quite material.

Similarly, when auditing stockholders' equity transactions, the auditor commonly uses a substantive approach. This approach is often appropriate because the number of equity transactions with outside parties is usually small. In fact, a substantive approach using only tests of details is most commonly used to audit equity accounts.

For both debt accounts and stockholders' equity accounts, the boxes of evidence would typically be filled only with evidence obtained through substantive procedures.

Obtaining Evidence About Internal Control Operating Effectiveness for Debt Obligations and Stockholders' Equity Transactions

LO 7 Determine appropriate tests of controls and consider the results of tests of controls in auditing debt obligations and stockholders' equity transactions.

For integrated audits, the auditor tests the operating effectiveness of important controls as of the client's year-end. The auditor selects controls that are important to the auditor's conclusion about whether the client's controls adequately address the assessed risk of material misstatement for the relevant debt and equity accounts. The auditor selects both entity-wide and transaction controls for testing. Typical tests of transaction controls include inquiry of personnel performing the control, observation of the control being performed, inspection of documentation confirming that the control has been performed, and reperformance of the control by the auditor testing the control. If testing results in identified control deficiencies, the auditor assesses those deficiencies to determine their severity (are they significant deficiencies or material weaknesses?) and their impact on the opinion on internal control effectiveness.

If the auditor wants to rely on controls for the financial statement audit, the auditor would test the operating effectiveness of those controls throughout the year. However, for financial statement audit purposes, when auditing debt obligations and stockholders' equity transactions, the auditor most likely performs a substantive audit and therefore does not perform tests of controls throughout the year for the debt and equity accounts.

Obtaining Substantive Evidence in Auditing Debt Obligations and Stockholders' Equity Transactions

LO 8 Determine and apply sufficient appropriate substantive audit procedures in auditing debt obligations and stockholders' equity transactions.

The audits of debt obligations and stockholders' equity transactions typically involve only substantive procedures. Debt obligations accounts are tested with both substantive analytical procedures and tests of details. In contrast, only tests of details are typically used to audit stockholders' equity accounts. Further, the transactions in the stockholders' equity accounts are typically tested 100% because they are usually so few, and yet they are highly material.

Substantive Analytical Procedures—Debt Obligations

When auditing debt obligations, the primary substantive analytical procedure would involve the auditor developing an independent expectation of interest expense. This expectation would be based on average debt outstanding and average interest rates. When performing this analysis as a substantive procedure, the auditor would use disaggregated data—likely disaggregated by type of debt. If the auditor's expectation is similar to what the client has recorded, additional substantive testing of interest expense and accrued interest would not be necessary. *Exhibit 13.5*—Panel A notes that in this situation the box of evidence obtained by the auditor would include evidence only from substantive analytical procedures.

If there is a significant difference between the auditor's expectation and what the client has recorded, the auditor needs to perform additional substantive test of details to determine the reason for the difference. For example, if interest expense recorded by the client is significantly lower than the auditor's expectation, it may mean that interest payments have not been

EXHIBIT 13.5

Panel A: Substantive Analytical Procedures Approach to Obtaining Audit Evidence for Completeness of Interest Expense

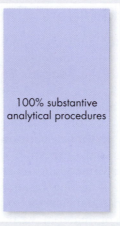

100% substantive analytical procedures

Panel B: Substantive Analytical Procedures and Tests of Details Approach to Obtaining Audit Evidence for Completeness of Interest Expense

60% tests of details

40% substantive analytical procedures

properly recorded, possibly having been charged to principal. *Exhibit 13.5—Panel B* notes that in this situation, the box of evidence obtained by the auditor would include evidence from substantive analytical procedures and tests of details. Note that the relative percentages are judgmental in nature; the examples are simply intended to give you a sense of how an auditor might select an appropriate mix of procedures.

Why Tests of Controls Might Not Be Performed When substantive analytical procedures are performed, they are typically performed only after the relevant controls have been tested. However, when performing substantive analytical procedure related to interest expense, the auditor will likely not test controls. The primary reason is that the information being used to perform the analytical procedure (debt amounts and interest rates) is typically confirmed with an independent outside party. Therefore, the effectiveness of the client's controls is not as important as in other areas where the information being used for the substantive analytical procedures is not subject to external independent confirmation.

Substantive Tests of Details—Debt Obligations

Typical substantive procedures include:

- Reading new loan agreements (may be performed during planning/risk assessment procedures)
- Determining what changes, if any, have been made to prior loan agreements (may be performed during planning/risk assessment procedures)
- Confirming with relevant outside parties any significant factors and the transactions that have occurred

As a starting point for these procedures, the auditor will have the client provide a schedule of debt obligations and interest. The client should also have a bond premium/discount amortization schedule that the auditor can review in assessing whether bonds are appropriately valued and disclosed in the financial statements. For additions to debt, the auditor traces the proceeds into the cash receipts records and the bank statement. The auditor might also examine the debt instrument and obtain assurance regarding board approval of the debt through review of board meeting minutes. For debt reductions, the auditor examines payments through the cash disbursements records, possibly including canceled checks. Also, for notes or mortgages that have been paid in full, the auditor should examine the canceled notes.

Exhibit 13.6 provides typical substantive procedures for relevant assertions related to debt obligations.

Debt and Bond Covenants

The auditor should obtain an understanding of the procedures the client uses to determine whether the client is in compliance with its debt covenants. The auditor should then independently determine if the client is in compliance. Consider a covenant that requires the client to maintain a current ratio that does not fall below a specified level. If the auditor determines that the client's current ratio is below that level, the auditor should assess the effects of the violation. If the creditor does not waive the violation and the loan is in default, the creditor may declare the outstanding balance immediately due and payable. In that case, the auditor generally would assume that the debt would need to be reclassified as short-term debt. In addition, the auditor must consider what financial statement disclosures will be required and how the events of default will affect the audit opinion. For example, could the default suggest going-concern issues that would need to be identified in the audit opinion?

EXHIBIT 13.6 — Relevant Management Assertions and Substantive Procedures for Debt Obligations

Management Assertion	Substantive Procedure
Completeness—Recorded debt obligations include all debt obligations.	1. Perform substantive analytical procedures. 2. Confirm debt obligations. 3. Vouch additions and deletions to debt obligations.
Completeness—All interest expense is recorded.	1. Perform substantive analytical procedures to analyze interest expense and recalculate accrued interest.
Presentation/disclosure—Debt obligations are properly classified in the balance sheet between current and noncurrent liabilities, and adequate disclosures are made in accordance with GAAP requirements.	1. Review debt agreements for the restrictive covenants and consider their effect on disclosures in the financial statements. 2. Inquire of management. 3. Examine balance sheet for proper disclosure of current and noncurrent portions, related parties, and restrictions resulting from debt. 4. Read all disclosures for appropriateness, consistency, and clarity. (The *Auditing in Practice* feature "Important Considerations for Debt Presentation and Disclosure" provides additional discussion.)

Important Considerations for Debt Presentation and Disclosure

The following represent important considerations for the auditor testing the presentation and disclosure assertion for debt obligations:

Should the outstanding debt be classified as current or noncurrent?

• This determination becomes even more involved when debt arrangements include certain provisions or clauses that may accelerate the maturity of the debt, generally requiring the organization to classify the outstanding debt as current.

Is there appropriate disclosure for instances when a violation of debt covenants has been waived?

• SEC regulations require that an organization disclose the amount of the obligation and the period of the waiver if the creditor has waived its right for a stated period.

Deloitte (2011) SEC Comment Letters — Including Industry Insights Improving Transparency. Available at http://www.deloitte.com/assets/ Dcom-UnitedStates/Local%20Assets/Documents/ AERS/ASC/us_aers_seccommentletterbook.pdf

Substantive Tests of Details—Stockholders' Equity Transactions

As a starting point for testing capital stock and equity transactions, the auditor should review a copy of the client's articles of incorporation. This document provides relevant information with respect to each class of stock. The auditor can agree that information to the disclosures included in the client's financial statements. The auditor prepares, or ask the client to prepare, an analysis of all capital stock transactions.

The auditor will inspect documentation related to the client's record keeping of capital stock and contributed capital. This documentation may be maintained by the client or held by a **transfer agent**. Review of this documentation provides the auditor with evidence related to the existence and completeness of capital.

To obtain evidence related to the valuation of capital stock, the auditor reviews the minutes of the board of directors meetings and examines the stock records books (or confirm with the registrar and transfer agent) to determine issuance and repurchase of capital stock. The auditor would typically obtain evidence for all capital stock transactions. For example, if stock is sold, the auditor traces the proceeds to the cash receipts journal and reviews documentation indicating that the proper amount was recorded in the stock and paid-in capital accounts. The auditor may also have instances when capital stock was issued in a nonmonetary transaction. For those instances, the auditor needs to determine that the client has properly recorded the issuance in accordance with GAAP.

For those clients with treasury stock, the auditor examines documentation supporting changes in the number of shares since the prior year. This documentation might include obtaining confirmation from the stock transfer agent and tracing the transaction through the cash receipts or cash disbursements journals.

While the substantive audit procedures related to capital stock and equity activities are somewhat straightforward, the *Auditing in Practice* feature "Deficiencies in Substantive Procedures Related to Stockholders' Equity Transactions: Insights From the PCAOB" identifies areas posing potential difficulties in auditing stockholders' equity transactions.

Dividends The auditor examines the minutes of the board of directors meetings for authorization of the dividend per share amount and the dividend record date. For those clients who maintain their own records and pay the dividends, the auditor recalculates the amount of the dividends and agrees that amount to the cash disbursements journal. If a client uses a transfer agent, the auditor traces the payment to a cash disbursement made by the client to the agent. The auditor may also confirm the amount with the agent.

AUDITING IN **PRACTICE**

Deficiencies in Substantive Procedures Related to Stockholders' Equity Transactions: Insights From the PCAOB

Following are some deficiencies identified by the PCAOB through its inspection process that are indicative of inadequate testing of stockholders' equity transactions:

- The auditors failed to evaluate whether the audit clients had appropriately determined the fair values assigned to equity-based transactions and to test the reasonableness of such fair values.
- The auditors failed to evaluate the adequacy of the disclosure of equity transactions in the notes to the financial statements and to determine whether the equity transactions were recorded in the proper period.

- The auditors failed to properly address and evaluate the substance, business purpose, or significant terms of the equity arrangements.
- The auditors failed to consider the accounting principles potentially applicable to the equity transactions.

For further details, see PCAOB Release No. 2007–010, Report on the PCAOB's 2004, 2005, and 2006 Inspections of Domestic Triennially Inspected Firms, available at http://pcaobus.org/ Inspections/Documents/2007_10–22_4010_Report. pdf.

Disclosure of Restrictions Related to Dividend Payments

AUDITING IN **PRACTICE**

The SEC has disclosure requirements related to restrictions imposed on a company's ability to pay dividends. Typically, these restrictions arise when loan agreements prohibit the company from paying cash dividends without the consent of a third party, such as a lender. A public company must disclose the nature of any restrictions on the ability of the company or any of its subsidiaries to pay dividends and the amounts subject to such restrictions.

The auditor will also obtain evidence as to whether the payment was made to the stockholders who owned the stock as of the dividend record date. The auditor can trace the payee's name on the canceled check to the dividend records to make sure the payee was to have received the dividend.

The auditor needs to be aware of restrictions related to dividend payments and determine that the restrictions are adequately disclosed in the financial statements. The *Auditing in Practice* feature "Disclosure of Restrictions Related to Dividend Payments" highlights important considerations for the auditor determining whether relevant dividend payment restrictions are appropriately disclosed in the client's financial statements.

Retained Earnings The auditor typically examines all transactions recorded in the retained earnings account during the audit period. The common entries include net income or loss. These amounts would be tested through substantive audit procedures related to revenues and expenses. The other common entry includes dividends. If there are additional entries, the auditor examines documentation supporting that the entries should be included. For example, if there is a correction of an error from a prior period, the auditor determines that the correction is made in accordance with relevant accounting standards.

Performing Substantive Fraud-Related Procedures

If the auditor identifies a risk of material misstatement due to fraud related to debt obligations or stockholders' equity accounts, the auditor needs to determine the appropriate responses, potentially including changing the nature, timing, and extent of audit procedures.

Fraud-Related Substantive Procedures for Debt Obligations

In those audits where there is a heightened risk of fraud related to debt obligations, the auditor should consider performing the following procedures or, if the procedures are already being performed, altering the timing and extent of the procedures:

- Search public records to identify debt obligations
- Vouch and trace loan proceeds and debt payments
- Send confirmations to lenders and creditors, including confirmation of compliance with any debt covenants
- Require original supporting documents rather than copies
- Agree detail of debt terms to authorization in minutes of board meetings

Fraud-Related Substantive Procedures for Stockholders' Equity Accounts

In those audits where there is a heightened risk of fraud related to stockholders' equity accounts, the auditor should consider performing the following procedures or, if the procedures are already being performed, altering the timing and extent of the procedures:

- Confirm terms of equity arrangements and shares held directly with shareholders
- Confirm with shareholders whether there are any side agreements
- Employ an appropriate level of professional skepticism and carefully analyze transactions to determine whether the terms and substance of the transactions indicate that the proceeds should be recorded as debt or as equity
- Confirm with the transfer agent information on issued stock
- Account for and vouch all proceeds from stock issues

Documenting Substantive Procedures

A number of important items should be documented when performing substantive procedures for debt obligations and stockholders' equity transactions. For debt obligations, the auditor's documentation should include:

- Copies of the debt agreements
- Identification of the specific items tested
- Schedule of debt obligations and interest
- A summary of the calculations supporting compliance with debt covenants
- Confirmations or documentation of alternative procedures performed

For stockholders' equity transactions, the auditor's documentation should include:

- Client's articles of incorporation
- A summary of changes in equity accounts
- Verification of authorization with respect to any changes in capitalization or declaration of dividends
- Confirmations with transfer agent or shareholders

SUMMARY AND NEXT STEPS

Auditing debt obligations and stockholders' equity transactions is usually straightforward—perform substantive tests of the few, but typically material, transactions recorded during the audit period. However, the auditor should be skeptical and, therefore, alert to the possibility that management is managing earnings by not appropriately recording expenses, such as charging expenses directly to retained earnings or underrecording interest expense. Further, management may attempt to avoid appropriate disclosures related to these accounts, especially disclosures related to debt covenants and possible covenant violations. Now that you know how to perform audit procedures for many of the accounts included on the income statement and balance sheet, in the next chapter we turn to the remaining audit activities conducted prior to completing the audit, each designed to assure that the audit has been conducted in a quality manner and that the ultimate audit opinion is appropriate.

SIGNIFICANT TERMS

Bond indenture   A contract between an issuer of bonds and the bond-holder stating the time period before repayment, amount of interest paid, if the bond is convertible (and if so, at what price or what ratio), if the bond is callable, and the amount of money that is to be repaid.

Debt covenants   Restrictions in debt agreements aimed at protecting the lender (creditor, debt holder, or investor) by restricting the activities of the borrower (debtor).

Transfer agent   An organization such as a trust company, bank, or other financial institution that is used by an organization to maintain records of investors and account balances and transactions, to cancel and issue certificates, and to process investor mailings.

TRUE/FALSE QUESTIONS

13-1   **LO 1**   An organization typically has many debt transactions during the year, with each individual transaction being immaterial.

13-2   **LO 1**   Typically, the most relevant assertion related to debt obligations is completeness.

13-3   **LO 2**   Recording the purchases of treasury stock is straightforward and therefore does not pose any inherent risk of material misstatement.

13-4   **LO 2**   An inherent risk associated with debt obligations is that management might try to avoid complete and accurate disclosure of debt covenants and potential violations.

13-5   **LO 3**   A potential fraud risk associated with debt obligations is the intentional misclassification of short-term debt as long-term debt.

13-6   **LO 3**   Charging expenses directly to retained earnings rather than to the appropriate expense account is a potential fraud risk associated with auditing stockholders' equity accounts.

13-7   **LO 4**   Because the auditor is likely not testing controls related to stockholders' equity transactions, the auditor does not need to have an understanding of controls over stockholders' equity transactions.

13-8   **LO 4**   A reconciliation of debt and interest accounts to the general ledger is a control designed to mitigate the risks of material misstatement associated with debt obligations.

13-9   **LO 5**   The primary planning analytical procedure for stockholders' equity accounts is a comparison of current-year account balances with prior-year account balances, after considering the auditor's expectations based on knowledge of client activities.

13-10   **LO 5**   Trend analyses would not typically be used as planning analytical procedures related to debt obligations.

13-11   **LO 6**   When responding to identified risks of material misstatement associated with stockholders' equity accounts, the auditor often decides to rely heavily on tests of controls.

13-12   **LO 6**   When testing debt obligations, the auditor typically uses a substantive audit approach.

13-13   **LO 7**   When auditing debt obligations, the auditor may test controls at year-end for the audit opinion on internal controls, but choose not to test controls for the financial statement audit.

13-14 **LO 7** When auditing stockholders' equity transactions, the auditor may test controls at year-end for the audit opinion on internal controls, but choose not to test controls for the financial statement audit.

13-15 **LO 8** Confirmations can be used as a substantive procedure designed to obtain evidence on the completeness of debt obligations.

13-16 **LO 8** If there is a heightened risk of fraud related to the completeness of debt obligations, the auditor may choose to search public records to identify debt obligations.

MULTIPLE-CHOICE QUESTIONS

13-17 **LO 1** Which of the following can be used by organizations for obtaining financing?
a. Notes.
b. Mortgages.
c. Bonds.
d. All of the above.

13-18 **LO 1** Which of the following accounts would not typically be included in the audit of debt obligations?
a. Interest income.
b. Interest expense.
c. Bonds payable.
d. Notes payable.

13-19 **LO 2** Inherent risks related to debt obligations primarily include which of the following?
a. Debt is not properly authorized.
b. Interest expense is not properly accrued.
c. Debt covenants are not properly disclosed.
d. Debt is not appropriately classified as short or long term.
e. All of the above are inherent risks related to debt obligations.

13-20 **LO 2** Which of the following is not an inherent risk typically associated with the existence of dividends?
a. Dividends are recorded before being declared.
b. Dividends are not properly amortized.
c. Dividends have not been approved before being declared.
d. Dividends are recorded in the wrong period.

13-21 **LO 3** Which of the following most accurately describes the nature of fraud related to debt obligations described in the case of Federico Quinto Jr., CPA, presented in the *Professional Judgment in Context* feature?
a. Interest expense was recorded in the wrong period.
b. Entire loan payments were charged to principal.
c. Debt covenants and potential violations were not appropriately presented and disclosed.
d. Long-term debt was misclassified as short-term debt.

13-22 **LO 3** Which of the following most accurately describes the nature of fraud related to stockholders' equity accounts described in the case of Delphi Corporation presented in the *Professional Judgment in Context* feature?
a. Stock options were back dated.
b. Stock sales were not authorized.
c. Proceeds from stock sales were misappropriated.
d. Expenses were charged directly to retained earnings, rather than to the appropriate expense accounts.

13-23 **LO 4** Which of the following would an auditor typically not perform as part of gaining an understanding of the client's controls related to debt obligations?

a. Review the client's documentation of controls.

b. Recalculate interest expense.

c. Inquire of management about the process for reviewing compliance with debt covenants.

d. Review policies related to approval required for new debt.

13-24 **LO 4** Which of the following is a control the auditor would expect a client to have implemented related to stockholders' equity transactions?

a. A policy requiring approval by the board of directors for all stock transactions.

b. Reconciliation of equity accounts to the general ledger.

c. CFO and CEO authorization of all stock transaction approved by the board of directors.

d. The auditor would typically expect all of the above controls to be in place.

13-25 **LO 5** Which of the following statements is true regarding planning analytical procedures for debt obligations and stockholders' equity transactions?

a. Because there are typically only a few stockholders' equity transactions, the auditor is not required to perform planning analytical procedures for stockholders' equity accounts.

b. Trend analysis would not typically be performed for debt obligations.

c. The long-term debt-to-equity ratio could be considered by the auditor as part of the planning analytical procedures.

d. All of the above statements are true.

13-26 **LO 5** Which of the following are typical planning analytical procedures related to debt obligations?

a. Estimate interest expense based on average interest rates and average debt outstanding.

b. Calculate the total debt-to-equity ratio and perform a trend analysis with prior periods.

c. Calculate the long-term debt-to-equity ratio and perform a trend analysis with prior periods.

d. Calculate the times interest earned ratio and perform a trend analysis with prior periods.

e. All of the above could be performed as planning analytical procedures related to debt obligations.

13-27 **LO 6** How does an auditor typically respond to identified risks of material misstatement associated with debt obligations?

a. The auditor will typically plan to perform a controls reliance approach to the audit.

b. The auditor will typically plan an approach that uses only substantive procedures.

c. The auditor does not need to respond to identified fraud risks since the risk of fraud related to debt obligations is typically minimal.

d. Because of the low level of risk of material misstatement, the auditor would only rely on planning analytical procedures.

13-28 **LO 6** How does an auditor typically respond to identified risks of material misstatement associated with stockholders' equity accounts?

a. The auditor will typically plan to perform a controls reliance approach to the audit.

b. The auditor will typically plan an approach that uses only substantive procedures.

c. The auditor does not need to respond to identified fraud risks since the risk of fraud related to stockholders' equity accounts is typically minimal.

d. Because of the low level of risk of material misstatement, the auditor would only rely on preliminary analytical procedures.

13-29 **LO 7** Which of the following statements best describes the auditor's typical approach to testing controls related to debt obligations?

a. Controls would be tested for integrated audit purposes, but not for financial statement audit purposes.

b. Controls would be tested for financial statement audit purposes, but not for integrated audit purposes.

c. Controls would be tested for both the integrated audit and financial statement audit.

d. Controls would not be tested for either the integrated audit or financial statement audit.

13-30 **LO 7** Which of the following statements best describes the auditor's typical approach to testing controls related to stockholders' equity accounts?

a. Controls would be tested for integrated audit purposes, but not for financial statement audit purposes.

b. Controls would be tested for financial statement audit purposes, but not for integrated audit purposes.

c. Controls would be tested for both the integrated audit and financial statement audit.

d. Controls would not be tested for either the integrated audit or financial statement audit.

13-31 **LO 8** The audit program for long-term debt should include which of the following procedures?

a. Verification of the existence of the bondholders.

b. Review of debt loan agreements.

c. Inspection of the accounts payable master file.

d. Review of supporting documentation for credit entries to the bond interest income account.

13-32 **LO 8** When a client does not maintain its own stock records, the auditor should obtain written confirmation from the stock transfer agent concerning which of the following?

a. Restrictions on the payment of dividends.

b. The number of shares issued and outstanding.

c. Guarantees of preferred stock liquidation value.

d. The number of shares subject to agreements to repurchase.

REVIEW AND SHORT CASE QUESTIONS

NOTE: Completing Review and Short Case Questions does not require the student to reference additional resources and materials.

NOTE: For the remaining problems, we make special note of those addressing fraud, international issues, professional skepticism, and ethics.

13-33 **LO 1** What are the relevant accounts when auditing debt obligations, and what is the auditor's primary objective?

13-34 **LO 1** What are the relevant accounts related to stockholders' equity transactions?

13-35 **LO 1** Identify common transactions affecting stockholders' equity accounts.

13-36 **LO 1** Review *Exhibit 13.1* and *Exhibit 13.2*. Describe the disclosures related to stockholders' equity provided by Ford Motor Company.

13-37 **LO 2** Identify common inherent risks associated with debt obligations.

13-38 **LO 2** Review *Exhibit 13.3* and identify inherent risks associated with typical stockholders' equity transactions.

FRAUD **13-39** **LO 3** Identify fraud risks associated with debt obligations.

FRAUD **13-40** **LO 3** Identify fraud risks associated with stockholders' equity accounts.

FRAUD **13-41** **LO 4** Given typical inherent and fraud risks related to material misstatement of debt obligations, identify controls that an auditor would expect a client to have implemented.

FRAUD **13-42** **LO 4** Given typical inherent and fraud risks related to material misstatement of stockholders' equity accounts, identify controls that an auditor would expect a client to have implemented.

13-43 **LO 5** What are typical planning analytical procedures related to debt obligations?

13-44 **LO 5** What are typical planning analytical procedures related to stockholders' equity accounts?

13-45 **LO 6** What type of audit approach is typically planned for debt obligations? Why is this typically the most appropriate approach?

13-46 **LO 6** What type of audit approach is typically planned for stockholders' equity accounts?

13-47 **LO 6** An audit firm is engaged in the examination of the financial statements of Zeitlow Corporation for the year ended December 31, 2015. Zeitlow Corporation's financial statements and records have never been audited. The stockholders' equity section of Zeitlow Corporation's balance sheet at December 31, 2015, follows:

Stockholders' Equity

Capital stock—10,000 shares of $10 par value authorized:	
5,000 shares issued and outstanding	$50,000
Capital contributed in excess of par value of capital stock	58,800
Retained earnings	105,000
Total stockholders' equity	$213,800

Founded in 2007, Zeitlow Corporation has ten stockholders and serves as its own registrar and transfer agent. Prepare the detailed audit program for the examination of the three accounts composing the stockholders' equity section of Zeitlow Corporation's balance sheet. (Do not include in the audit program for the verification of the results of the current-year operations.)

13-48 **LO 7** Describe the evidence typically obtained from tests of controls when auditing debt obligations or stockholders' equity accounts.

13-49 **LO 8** Review the two panels in *Exhibit 13.5*. Describe the two alternative approaches to auditing interest expense and the reason for the difference in approaches.

13-50 **LO 8** Refer to *Exhibit 13.6* and identify typical substantive procedures for relevant assertions related to debt obligations.

13-51 **LO 8** Review the *Auditing in Practice* feature "Important Considerations for Debt Presentation and Disclosure" and identify potential audit problems related to presentation and disclosure of debt.

13-52 [LO 8] Identify substantive procedures that the auditor should perform related to dividends.

13-53 [LO 8] Retained earnings is a component of stockholders' equity. What substantive procedures will the auditor typically perform related to retained earnings?

13-54 [LO 8] What important items should be documented related to substantive procedures performed for debt obligations and stockholders' equity accounts?

13-55 [LO 8] What information should the auditor note when reading a bond indenture? How is the information used in the audit?

13-56 [LO 8] After all other account balances on the balance sheet have been audited, it might appear that the retained earnings figure is a balancing figure and requires no further audit procedures. Why would an auditor still audit retained earnings?

13-57 [LO 8] Assume your audit client declared a 5% stock dividend. Identify the evidence you would examine to determine whether the stock dividend was accounted for properly.

13-58 [LO 8] Explain how a bond amortization spreadsheet might be used to audit interest expense over the life of a bond.

13-59 [LO 8] The auditor should review the bond indenture at the time a bond is issued and anytime subsequent changes are made to it.
  a. Briefly identify the information the auditor would expect to obtain from a bond indenture. List at least five specific pieces of information that would be relevant to the conduct of the audit.
  b. Because auditors are especially concerned with the potential understatement of liabilities, should they confirm the existence of the liability with individual bondholders? State your rationale.
  c. A company issued bonds at a discount. Explain how the amount of the discount is computed and how the auditor could determine whether the amount is properly amortized each year.
  d. Explain how the auditor could verify that semiannual interest payments are made on the bond each year.
  e. The company has a fifteen-year, $20 million loan that is due on September 30 of next year. It is the company's intent to refinance the bond before it is due, but it is waiting for the best time to issue new debt. Because its intent is to issue the bond next year, the company believes that the existing $20 million bond need not be classified as a current liability. What evidence should the auditor gather to determine the appropriate classification of the bond?

13-60 [LO 8] The following covenants are extracted from a bond indenture. The indenture provides that failure to comply with its terms in any respect automatically advances the due date of the loan to the date of noncompliance (the maturity date is twenty years hence). Identify the audit steps that should be taken or reporting requirements necessary in connection with each one of the following independent scenarios:
  a. The debtor company shall endeavor to maintain a working capital ratio of 2 to 1 at all times, and, in any fiscal year

following a failure to maintain the said ratio, the company shall restrict compensation of the CEO and executive officers to a total of no more than $500,000. Executive officers for this purpose shall include the chairman of the board of directors, the president, all vice presidents, the secretary, and the treasurer.

b. The debtor company shall insure all property that is security for this debt against loss by fire to the extent of 100% of its actual value. Insurance policies securing this protection shall be filed with the trustee.

c. The debtor company shall pay all taxes legally assessed against the property that serves as security for this debt within the time provided by law for payment without penalty and shall deposit receipted tax bills or equally acceptable evidence of payment of the same with the trustee.

d. A sinking fund shall be deposited with the trustee by semiannual payments of $300,000, from which the trustee shall, at his or her discretion, purchase bonds of this issue.

13-61 **LO 8** The following long-term debt documentation (indexed K-l), and presented on the next page, was prepared by client personnel and audited by AA, an audit assistant, during the calendar year 2015 audit of American Widgets, Inc., a continuing audit client. The engagement supervisor is thoroughly reviewing the working papers. Note the deficiencies in the audit documentation (shown on the next page) that the engagement supervisor should identify.

FRAUD FOCUS: CONTEMPORARY AND HISTORICAL CASES

FRAUD

PROFESSIONAL SKEPTICISM

ETHICS

13-62 **Federico Quinto Jr., CPA, and Soyo Group** **(LO 1, 2, 3, 4, 6, 8, 9)** Refer to the *Professional Judgment in Context* feature "Deficiencies in Auditing Debt Obligations and Stockholders' Equity Accounts: Insights from SEC Releases" and review the panel related to Federico Quinto Jr., CPA. Answer the following questions:

a. What risks of material misstatement were present in the case?

b. What are the auditor's responsibilities related to debt covenants? What would you consider to be the most relevant assertions related to debt covenants, and what substantive procedures should the auditor have performed?

c. Identify ways in which the audit team appeared to have a lack of appropriate professional skepticism.

d. Assume that you were part of the audit team for the Soyo Group 2007 audit and you were aware that the appropriate disclosures related to debt covenants had not been made in the financial statements. Use the framework for ethical decision making presented in *Chapter 4* to determine the actions you should take. Recall that the steps are as follows: (1) identify the ethical issue, (2) determine the affected parties and identify their rights, (3) determine the most important rights, (4) develop alternative courses of action, (5) determine the likely consequences of each proposed course of action, (6) assess the possible consequences, and (7) decide on an appropriate course of action.

13-61 CONTINUED

December 31, 2015

K-1

Prepared by
Approved by

Initials AA   Date 2/10/16

Lender	Interest Rate	Payment Terms	Collateral	Balance December 31, 2014	2015 Borrowings	2015 Reductions	Balance December 31, 2015	Interest Paid to	Accrued Interest Payable December 31, 2015	Comments
First Commercial Bank*	4.2%	Interest only on 25th of month, principal due in full 1/1/19, no prepayment penalty	Inventories	$ 50,000††	$300,000‡ 1/31/15	$100,000*** 6/30/15	$ 250,000‖	12/25/15		Dividend of $80,000 paid 9/2/15 (W/P N-3) violates a provision of the debt agreement, which thereby permits lender to demand immediate payment; lender has refused to waive this violation
Lender's Capital Corp.*	Prime plus 1	Interest only on last day of month, principal due in full 3/5/19	Second mortgage on Park St. building	100,000††	50,000‡ 2/29/15	—	200,000†	12/31/15		Prime rate was 3% to 4% during the year
Gigantic Building & Loan Association*	3.7%	$5,000 principal plus interest due on 5th of month, due in full 12/31/16	First mortgage on Park St. building	720,000††	—	60,000***	660,000†	12/5/15		Reclassification entry for current portion proposed (See RJE-3)
J. Lott, majority stockholder*	0%	Due in full 12/31/17	Unsecured	300,000††	—	100,000‖‖	200,000†	—		
				$1,170,000† †††	$350,000 †††	$260,000 †††	$ 1,310,000 †††			

††† Footed without exception
† Confirmed without exception, W/P K-2
‖ Confirmed with exception
‡ Agreed to loan agreement, validated bank deposit ticket, and board of directors' authorization, W/P W-7
*** Agreed to loan agreement, validated to canceled checks and lender's monthly statements
‖‖ Agreed to cash disbursements journal and canceled check dated 12/31/15, clearing 1/8/16
†† Agreed to 12/31/14 working papers
* Agreed interest rate, terms, and collateral to copy of note and loan agreement
Overall Conclusions
Long-term debt, accrued interest payable, and interest expense are correct and complete at December 31, 2015.

Delphi Corporation

13-63 (LO **2, 3, 4, 6, 8**)   Refer to the *Professional Judgment in Context* feature "Deficiencies in Auditing Debt Obligations and Stockholders' Equity Accounts: Insights from SEC Releases" and review the panel related to Delphi Corporation. Answer the following questions:

a. What risks of material misstatement were present in the case?

b. What are the auditor's responsibilities related to auditing retained earnings? What procedures should the auditor have performed?

c. Identify ways in which the audit team appeared to have a lack of appropriate professional skepticism.

APPLICATION ACTIVITIES

NOTE: Completing Application Activities requires students to reference additional resources and materials. Some Application Activities will require the student to reference relevant professional auditing standards. We make special note of these as Auditing Standards Application Activities.

Deloitte & Touche LLP and Adelphia

13-64 (LO **2, 3, 4, 8**)   In April 2005 the SEC announced that Deloitte & Touche had agreed to pay $50 million to settle charges stemming from its audit of Adelphia Communications Corporation's fiscal year 2000 financial statements. After performing appropriate research, address the following questions.

a. Once the risks of material misstatement are identified, the auditor is to determine the audit approach that best addresses those risks. In what ways did Deloitte & Touche fail to do this?

b. What was the nature of the fraud at Adelphi as it related to debt obligations and its stockholders' equity accounts?

c. In addition to paying the $50 million settlement, what other actions did Deloitte & Touche agree to? Do you believe these actions will lead to improved audit quality at Deloitte & Touche?

13-65 LO **8**   Assume that you are a staff auditor working on long-term debt accounts of a client that is a company where you are performing an audit in accordance with auditing standards issued by the International Auditing and Assurance Standards Board (IAASB). You notice that one of the client's loans might be with a related party because the loan is with a close family member of a key member of management. You are not sure whether this constitutes a related party. Further, if this loan is with a related party, you need additional guidance on the required disclosure of identified related party relationships and transactions. Refer to the *Standards Appendix* to the text to identify the standard that can address your questions. Obtain a copy of the relevant standard, define *related party*, determine whether your client has a loan with a related party, and discuss the required disclosure of identified related party relationships and transactions.

Federico Quinto Jr., CPA, and Soyo Group

13-66 (LO **8**)   Refer to the *Professional Judgment in Context* feature "Deficiencies in Auditing Debt Obligations and Stockholders' Equity Accounts: Insights From SEC Releases" and review the panel related to Federico Quinto Jr., CPA. Obtain a copy of the SEC Auditing and Enforcement Release related to this case (AAER 3403, August 31, 2012). How does the AAER describe Quinto's failure to act with due professional care and failure to maintain an attitude of appropriate professional skepticism? What sanctions were imposed on Quinto; do these sanctions seem appropriate?

ANALYTICAL PROCEDURES: A CASE IN THE CONTEXT OF THE PHARMACEUTICAL INDUSTRY

NOTE: In this and select cycle chapters, we present a case set in the pharmaceutical industry. The case enables students to practice developing and conducting planning and substantive analytical procedures. The case was developed using the published financial statements of three prominent companies in this industry, with adaptations to make the case suitable for classroom use. The fictional company names are as follows: PharmaCorp, Novartell, and AstraZoro. You will access an Excel file on the textbook's web site at *www. cengage.com*. The Excel file contains financial data and information from footnote disclosures. The primary analytical procedures tasks will focus on PharmaCorp. You will use Novartell and AstraZoro as industry comparison companies. Access and download the file, then complete the requirements in *13-67*.

13-67 LO **5, 8** This case will enable you to practice conducting planning and substantive analytical procedures for accounts in the acquisition and payment cycle. When analyzing the financial data, you may assume that the 2015 information is *unaudited*, while prior-year data are audited.

As you complete this case, consider the following features of and trends in the pharmaceutical industry and for PharmaCorp specifically:

- After a long period of industry dominance by companies in the United States, the United Kingdom, and Europe, these companies are facing increasing competition from companies domiciled in emerging economies, such as Brazil, India, and China.
- There exists significant uncertainty in the market because of recent regulation covering health-care and government pay-outs for certain procedures and related pharmaceuticals.
- Health-care policy makers and the government are increasingly mandating what physicians can prescribe to patients.
- Health-care policy makers and the government are increasingly focusing on prevention regimes rather than treatment regimes, thereby leading to shifts in the demand for various pharmaceuticals.
- The global pharmaceutical market is anticipated to grow by 5–7% in 2016 compared with a 4–5% growth rate in 2015, according to a leading industry analyst publication.
- Beginning in 2014, PharmaCorp initiated and executed a significant company-wide cost reduction initiative aimed at improving manufacturing efficiency, cutting back on research and development expenses, and eliminating unnecessary corporate overhead.
- PharmaCorp's policies for extending credit to customers have remained stable over the last three years. PharmaCorp's credit granting policies are considered stringent within the industry, and analysts have sometimes criticized the company for this, contending that such policies have hindered the company's revenue growth relative to industry peers.
- Two of PharmaCorp's popular pharmaceuticals, Selebrax and Vyvox, came off patent during the fourth quarter of FYE 2015. These pharmaceuticals now face competition in the generic drug portion of the overall industry market.

Information specific to the PharmaCorp's Debt Activities
- Long-term debt balances (in the millions) for 2015 (unaudited) and 2014 (audited) are $31,036 and $34,926, respectively.
- The primary financing activity related to debt was net repayments of just over $1,500,000.
- Approximately $2,500,000 of long-term debt was reclassified as current in 2015.
- The average interest rate on the long-term debt (based on the high and low rates of PharmaCorp's debt instruments) is 5.34%
- Interest expense in 2014 (audited) was approximately $2,000,000.

Part I: Planning Analytical Procedures

a. *Step 1: Identify Suitable Analytical Procedures.* Your audit senior has suggested that the following ratio (on an overall financial statement level) will be used for planning analytical procedures related to debt activities at PharmaCorp:

- Estimate interest expense (related to long-term debt) based on average long-term debt interest rates and average long-term debt outstanding.

As part of Step 1, identify any other relevant relationships or trend analyses that would be useful to consider as part of planning analytics. Explain your reasoning.

b. *Step 2: Evaluate Reliability of Data Used to Develop Expectations.* The audit team has determined that the data you will be using to develop expectations in relation to long-term interest expense is reliable. Indicate the factors that the audit team likely considered in making that determination.

c. *Step 3: Develop Expectation.* Complete Step 3 of planning analytical procedures by developing an expectation for interest expense for long-term debt. Even before you develop a point estimate, what is the nature of the change of the interest expense account that you expect (from the prior year)? Using only the information provided here, what is your point estimate of interest expense?

d. *Step 4 and Step 5: Define and Identify Significant Unexpected Differences.* Refer to the guidance in *Chapter* 7 on performance materiality, tolerable misstatement, and clearly trivial amounts. Apply those materiality guidelines to Step 4 of planning analytical procedures to define what is meant by a significant difference. Explain your reasoning. Also comment on qualitative materiality considerations in this context. Now that you have determined what amount of difference would be considered significant, indicate whether there was a significant unexpected difference, assuming that the client recorded $1,800,000 of interest expense related to long-term debt.

e. *Step 6 and Step 7: Investigate Significant Unexpected Differences and Ensure Proper Documentation.* Complete Step 6 of planning analytical procedures by describing how your results will affect your substantive audit procedures. Explain your reasoning. To complete Step 7, describe what information should be included in the auditor's workpapers.

Part II: Substantive Analytical Procedures

f. As you talk with your audit senior, you realize that your estimate during planning was not very precise because it was based on data that were highly aggregated. While this approach would be appropriate for planning analytics, it is likely not appropriate for substantive analytics. How could you improve the precision of your estimate so that it would be precise enough to constitute evidence as a substantive analytical procedure?

g. Access the PharmaCorp Excel file at the text web site. Refer to the worksheet labeled "PharmaCorp Long Term Debt." Use that information to develop a more precise estimate for interest expense for long-term debt. Given the estimate that you developed, what is your conclusion regarding the client's asserted amount of interest expense for long-term debt?

ACADEMIC RESEARCH CASE

NOTE: Completing the Academic Research Case requires students to reference additional resources and materials.

SEARCH HINT

It is easy to locate these academic research articles! Use a search engine such as Google Scholar or an electronic research platform such as ABI Inform, and search using the author names and part of the article title.

13-68 LO **6, 8** Locate and read the article listed below and answer the following questions.

Menon, K. and D. D. Williams. 2010. Investor reaction to going concern audit reports. *The Accounting Review* 6 (85): 2075–2105.

a. What is the issue being addressed in the paper?
b. What are the findings of the paper?
c. Why is this paper important to auditors, and what are the implications of this paper for the auditing profession?
d. Describe the research methodology used as a basis for the conclusions.
e. Describe any limitations of the research.

14

Activities Required in Completing a Quality Audit

CHAPTER OVERVIEW AND LEARNING OBJECTIVES

Auditors must accomplish certain tasks prior to completing the audit, each designed to help provide reasonable assurance that the audit has been conducted in a quality manner and that the ultimate audit opinion is appropriate. These activities fall into two general categories: (1) review activities, and (2) communications with the audit committee and management. In terms of the audit opinion formulation process, this chapter focuses on Phase V—completing the audit.

Through studying this chapter, you will be able to achieve these learning objectives:

1. Review, summarize, and resolve detected misstatements and identified control deficiencies.

2. Review and assess the appropriateness of the client's accounting for and disclosure of loss contingencies.

3. Review and assess the appropriateness of the client's significant accounting estimates.

4. Review the adequacy of disclosures.

5. Review and assess the implications of noncompliance with laws and regulations.

6. Review the appropriateness of the going-concern assumption using relevant professional guidance.

7. Perform review analytical procedures.

8. Review management representations in certifications required under the Sarbanes-Oxley Act (for public clients) and describe the contents of a management representation letter.

9. Review subsequent events and subsequently discovered facts and assess proper treatment.

10. Identify the procedures and documentation required to perform an engagement quality review.

11. Determine how to address situations in which omitted audit procedures come to the auditor's attention after the audit report has been issued.

12. Identify issues to communicate to the audit committee.

13. Identify issues to communicate to management via a management letter.

14. Apply the frameworks for professional decision making and ethical decision making to issues involved in completing the audit.

THE AUDIT OPINION FORMULATION PROCESS

I. Making Client Acceptance and Continuance Decisions

Chapter 1

II. Performing Risk Assessment

Chapters 3, 7, and 9–13

III. Obtaining Evidence About Internal Control Operating Effectiveness

Chapters 8–13 and 16

IV. Obtaining Substantive Evidence About Accounts, Disclosures and Assertions

Chapters 8–13 and 16

V. Completing the Audit and Making Reporting Decisions

Chapters 14 and 15

The Auditing Profession, the Risk of Fraud and Mechanisms to Address Fraud: Regulation, Corporate Governance, and Audit Quality

Chapters 1 and 2

Professional Liability and the Need for Quality Auditor Judgments and Ethical Decisions

Chapter 4

The Audit Opinion Formulation Process and a Framework for Obtaining Audit Evidence

Chapters 5 and 6

PROFESSIONAL JUDGMENT IN CONTEXT
The PCAOB's Evaluation of Audit Firm Behavior in Conducting Engagement Quality Reviews

Auditors perform many types of review activities at the completion of the audit. We describe many of these review activities in this chapter. One particularly critical review activity is an **engagement quality review**. An engagement quality review is a review at the end of each audit conducted by an experienced auditor, usually a partner, who was not a part of the audit team, but who has appropriate competence, independence, integrity, and objectivity. The purpose of this review is to help make sure that the audit and audit documentation are complete and support the audit opinion on the financial statements and, for public companies, on the client's internal controls. The Public Company Accounting Oversight Board (PCAOB)'s AS 7, *Engagement Quality Review,* provides guidance on performing this activity.

On December 6, 2013, the PCAOB issued a report, *Observations Related to the Implementation of the Auditing Standard on Engagement Quality Review,* which provides a summary of PCAOB audit firm inspection reports in which problems were detected in how the engagement quality review was conducted or documented. The period of the report

is on inspection reports completed in 2011 and 2012. The report states that in about 39% of 111 audits in which PCAOB inspection staff concluded that the audit opinion was insufficiently supported, the staff concluded that the underlying audit deficiency should have been detected by the engagement quality review (but it was not).

The following are examples of deficiencies in engagement quality review included in the report:

- "The engagement quality reviewer failed to identify that the engagement team had neither designated an audit as higher-risk during the engagement planning nor identified any specific risks associated with the engagement even though the issuer had various risks including, for example, that it was a development stage entity engaged in developing activities in a foreign location.

- The engagement quality reviewer failed to identify that the engagement team had not sufficiently planned, reviewed or supervised the audit work performed by a foreign affiliated firm even though audit considerations for multi-location engagements was part of the scope of work reviewed by the engagement quality reviewer.

- The engagement quality reviewer identified that additional audit procedures were required to test revenue in response to the risk of material misstatement due to fraud. The engagement quality reviewer, however, did not determine that the additional procedures were performed.
- The engagement team identified control deficiencies affecting the same account or disclosure, but failed to evaluate whether, in combination, these deficiencies resulted in material weaknesses. The engagement quality reviewer failed to identify that the engagement team had not made this assessment.
- The engagement quality reviewer assessed the audit work performed related to estimates but failed to identify that the engagement team had limited to inquiry its testing of the assumptions underlying the issuer's calculation of a significant estimate."

The PCAOB investigated potential root causes of noncompliance with AS 7, and noted the following items:

- "The engagement completion document did not include all of the information necessary for understanding certain significant findings or issues (or cross references to available supporting audit documentation). This document, along with any documents cross-referenced should collectively be as specific as necessary in the circumstances for a reviewer to gain a thorough understanding of the significant findings or issues. Failing to include the information necessary to understand the findings or issues in the engagement completion document does not provide the engagement quality reviewer with an opportunity to identify audit deficiencies;
- Engagement quality reviewers over-relied on the engagement team's responses to firm engagement quality review checklists and on discussions with the engagement team, without reviewing the work papers supporting significant judgments made by the engagement team;
- Engagement quality reviewers did not devote sufficient time to the engagement quality reviews, or did not conduct their reviews in a timely fashion, which may have been due to competing priorities. For example, in an audit engagement in which Inspections staff determined that the firm failed to support its audit opinion, the engagement quality reviewer did not review the engagement planning until the fourth quarter, which gave the engagement team less time to alter its planned audit procedures in response to any concerns raised by the engagement quality reviewer;
- And Firms failed to consider known concerns about the quality of work of certain partners who were appointed to perform engagement quality reviews."

As you read through this chapter, consider the following questions:

- In addition to engagement quality reviews, what other review activities do auditors perform as they complete the audit? (LO 1, 2, 3, 4, 5, 6, 8, 9)
- The PCAOB report identifies a number of deficiencies in the conduct of engagement quality reviews. What are the standard procedures that the reviewer should perform as part of an engagement quality review that would comply with AS 7? (LO 10)
- How should the conduct of an engagement quality review be documented? (LO 10)
- How would these procedures and documentation guidance help to avoid the types of criticisms that the PCAOB outlined in its report? (LO 10)

For further details, see PCAOB Release No. 2013-011, December 6, 2013.

Review Activities

LO 1 Review, summarize, and resolve detected misstatements and identified control deficiencies.

Review activities completed toward the end of the audit are quite varied. In the following sections, we describe these activities, which relate to Learning Objectives 1 through 10. These activities are critical because they provide one last opportunity for the auditor to make adjustments to the financial statements or to the audit process so that the ultimate audit opinion is appropriate.

Reviewing, Summarizing, and Resolving Detected Misstatements

The auditor needs to summarize misstatements found during the audit to determine whether they are material and need to be recorded and corrected.

A misstatement may be a difference between the amount reported in the financial statements versus what should be reported under generally accepted accounting principles (GAAP), or the omission of an amount that should be disclosed in accordance with GAAP. Misstatements are categorized as known misstatements, projected misstatements, and judgmental misstatements. **Known misstatements** are those that have been specifically identified and about which there is no doubt; known misstatements are also referred to as **factual misstatements**. **Projected misstatements** are those that are the auditor's best estimate of the misstatements in a given population, and that are a projection of the misstatements identified in an audit sample to the entire population from which the sample was drawn. **Judgmental misstatements** are those that arise from differences in judgments of management concerning accounting estimates that the auditor considers unreasonable, or the selection or application of accounting policies that the auditor considers inappropriate.

Misstatements are likely to be detected that individually are not material, and the auditor may temporarily pass on asking the client to make those adjustments. Those misstatements should not be forgotten, however. Most audit firms use a schedule to accumulate the known and projected misstatements and the carryover effects of prior-year uncorrected misstatements. See *Exhibit 14.1* for an example of a summary of possible adjustments related to known misstatements. At the end of the audit, management and the auditor discuss which possible adjustments will be booked, that is, corrected in the financial statements, and which will be waived, that is, left uncorrected. Only immaterial misstatements may be waived.

In *Exhibit 14.1*, the first adjustment reflects a pricing error detected by confirming a sample of receivables. The known misstatement is $972, as shown in the first section of the schedule. However, when projected to the population, the projected misstatement for the unknown and unexamined part of the population was $13,493, as shown in the second section of the schedule. If these were corrected, both sales and accounts receivable would be reduced by $14,465 ($972 + $13,493), resulting in a reduction of pre-tax earnings and current assets. The second adjustment involves an unrecorded check for $1,500. The third adjustment involves the carryover effects of understating last year's accrued salaries and salary expense ($6,900). Because the carryover effect is to overstate this year's salary expense, the correction is shown as a reduction in the current year's salary expense, thereby resulting in an increase in pre-tax earnings and a reduction in the beginning balance of retained earnings.

The income tax effects are then entered into the schedule to show the total effects of correcting these misstatements. Near the end of the audit, these possible adjustments should be reviewed in the aggregate to determine whether the combined effect is material. The auditor compares the total misstatements (the sum of known and projected misstatements) to each significant segment of the financial statements, such as total current assets, total noncurrent assets, total current liabilities, total noncurrent liabilities, owners' equity, and pre-tax income, to determine if they are, in aggregate, material to the financial statements. The total misstatement as a percentage of these segments is clearly immaterial, and that conclusion is noted in the workpaper. The materiality of a misstatement is based not only on the quantitative amount of the misstatement—the auditor should also consider the nature of the misstatement to determine if there are qualitative features that would make it material. For example, if the misstatement reflects negatively on management, or if correcting the misstatement would have the effect of changing a positive earnings trend to a negative earnings trend.

EXHIBIT **14.1**	Summary of Possible Adjustments

| W/P | Debit (Credit) | | | | | |
| | Assets | | Liabilities | | Retained | |
Account Description	Current	Noncurrent	Current	Noncurrent	Earnings	Net Earnings
Uncorrected Known Misstatements						
Sales						972
Accounts receivable	(972)					
Misstatement from A/R confirmations ($972 known misstatement and $13,493 additional projected misstatement)						
Accounts payable			1,500			
Cash	(1,500)					
Unrecorded check # 14,389						
Projected Misstatements						
Sales						
Accounts receivable	(13,493)					13,493
Projected pricing misstatements from sample						
Carryover Effect of Prior-Year Misstatements						
Retained earnings					6,900	
Salary expense						(6,900)
Under accrual of prior year's salaries						
Subtotal: income before taxes						7,565
Tax Adjustment						
Income taxes payable ((13,493 + 972) × 0.34)			4,918			
Income tax expense (7,565 × 0.34)						(2,572)
Retained earnings (6,900 × 0.34)					(2,346)	
Total Misstatements	(15,965)	0	6,418	0	4,554	4,993
Balance from trial balance	19,073,000	1,997,000	(3,346,000)	(13,048,000)	(4,676,000)	1,678,000
Total misstatement as % of balance	0.08%	0.0%	0.19%	0.0%	0.1%	0.3%

Conclusion: In my opinion, the total likely misstatements are not material to the financial statements taken as a whole. The projected misstatements are quantitatively immaterial and do not reflect material weaknesses in internal control. Therefore, no adjustments are required, nor is any additional audit work needed for these account balances.

Marginal tax rate: 34%

PREPARED BY:	KMJ	DATE	2-17-16
REVIEWED BY:	AAG	DATE	2-17-16

Management's incentives may bias their willingness to book, or correct, these detected misstatements. For example, in some cases detected misstatements are material, and if management wishes to show higher net income, they may argue with the auditor against correcting an income-reducing misstatement. In such a situation, the auditor might feel some pressure to acquiesce to management's demands in order to preserve a harmonious working relationship. It is in these situations in which audit firm culture, an important driver of audit quality, is important. It is critical that the auditor is confident that the audit firm will support a decision insisting that management correct a misstatement, even if management does not want to do so. Thus, audit firm culture that emphasizes doing the right thing encourages auditors to take sufficient time to deal with difficult issues. A culture that emphasizes that the audit firm's long-term reputation is more important than the immediate satisfaction of client preferences encourages quality actions by its auditors. Likewise, a culture that encourages auditors to seek consultation with other members of the audit firm helps provide reasonable assurance that the auditor does not feel isolated in making difficult decisions; this is critical when the auditor is pressured by inappropriate or aggressive client behavior regarding detected misstatements. The *Auditing in Practice* feature, "The PCAOB Position on Management Bias in Correcting Detected Misstatements," provides insight into management bias in the correction of misstatements.

Additional Considerations for an Integrated Audit In an integrated audit, the auditor assesses whether the financial statement misstatements identified during the audit were the result of significant deficiencies or material weaknesses in internal control. Recall that if one or more material weaknesses exist, the auditor needs to issue an adverse opinion on internal control over financial reporting.

The PCAOB Position on Management Bias in Correcting Detected Misstatements

AUDITING IN **PRACTICE**

The PCAOB's AS 14 provides important insight that auditors must consider as they decide whether management's refusal to correct a detected misstatement is indicative of intentional bias. The PCAOB notes that the following are forms of management bias in this setting:

The selective correction of misstatements brought to management's attention during the audit (for example, correcting misstatements that have the effect of increasing reported earnings but not correcting misstatements that have the effect of decreasing reported earnings).

The identification by management of additional adjusting entries that offset misstatements accumulated by the auditor. If such adjusting entries are identified, the auditor should perform procedures to determine why the underlying

misstatements were not identified previously and evaluate the implications on the integrity of management and the auditor's risk assessments, including fraud risk assessments. The auditor also should perform additional procedures as necessary to address the risk of further undetected misstatement. (AS 14, paragraph 25).

If the auditor identifies this type of management bias in the resolution of misstatements, the auditor should determine whether the bias, along with its effect on the overall financial statements, is material. In addition, this type of management bias should lead auditors to reevaluate their risk assessments, particularly those related to management integrity and the risk of fraud. We further discuss the more complex issues related to the resolution of detected misstatements in *Chapter 16.*

Throughout the audit, the auditor evaluates the severity of each individual control deficiency to determine whether that deficiency is a material weakness. However, deficiencies less severe than material weaknesses should not be forgotten, but instead are accumulated on a summary work sheet. At the end of the engagement, the auditor assesses whether the combination of identified deficiencies results in a material weakness. The auditor should determine whether individual control deficiencies that affect the same significant account or disclosure, or relevant assertion collectively result in a material weakness. Consider a scenario where an auditor identified several control deficiencies in the revenue cycle. When considered individually, none of the deficiencies were considered to be material weaknesses. However, multiple deficiencies in the same cycle increase the likelihood of misstatement in that cycle, and may, in combination, constitute a material weakness. The auditor needs to complete this evaluation before determining the appropriate opinion on internal control.

Reviewing and Assessing Contingencies

LO 2 Review and assess the appropriateness of the client's accounting for and disclosure of loss contingencies.

In Accounting Standards Codification (ASC) 450 (formerly Statement of Financial Accounting Standard (SFAS) No. 5, "Accounting for Contingencies"), the Financial Accounting Standards Board (FASB) provides the standard for accruing and disclosing three categories of potential losses that can be reasonably estimated. Those categories reflect the contingent (not known for sure) nature of those losses and the guiding criteria are organized around probability of outcomes classified as (1) probable, (2) reasonably possible, and (3) remote. ASC 450 requires the accrual and disclosure of contingent losses that can be both reasonably estimated and that are probable. It also requires the disclosure of a contingent loss if there is at least a reasonable possibility that a loss may have been incurred and either an accrual has not been made or an exposure exists that is greater than the amount accrued. Examples of loss contingencies include:

- Threat of expropriation of assets in a foreign country
- Litigation, claims, and assessments
- Guarantees of debts of others
- Obligations of banks under standby letters of credit
- Agreements to repurchase receivables that have been sold
- Purchase and sale commitments

Management and Auditor Responsibilities Related to Contingencies

Management is responsible for designing and maintaining policies and procedures to identify, evaluate, and account for contingencies. Auditors are responsible for determining that the client has properly identified, accounted for, and disclosed material contingencies. The *Auditing in Practice* feature "Contingent Liabilities at British Petroleum" provides an example of the type of situation requiring disclosure of a contingent liability.

Sources of Audit Evidence of Contingencies

A primary source of evidence concerning contingencies is the client's management. The auditor should obtain the following from management:

- A description and evaluation of contingencies that existed at the balance sheet date or that arose prior to the end of the fieldwork and for which matters were referred to legal counsel, including correspondence and invoices from lawyers
- Assurance that the accounting and disclosure requirements concerning contingent liabilities have been met

Contingent Liabilities at British Petroleum

In July 2010, British Petroleum (BP) released its second quarter 2010 earnings report. The report discussed the risks associated with the ongoing events and cleanup effort in the Gulf of Mexico due to the oil spill associated with BP. It also included an income statement with a $32 billion pre-tax charge and a notation that "second quarter and first half 2010 include a charge of $32,192 million in production and manufacturing expenses, and a credit of $10,003 million in taxation in relation to the Gulf of Mexico oil spill." In conducting the annual audit, BP's auditors would have obtained assurance that the contingency in connection with the oil spill was accurately reported and disclosed.

In its FYE 2013 Form 20-F, BP disclosed that the total charge since the incident has risen to $42.7 billion and that the company has put an additional $20 billion into the Deepwater Horizons Oil Spill trust to fund future expenditures relating to the oil spill.

- Information about major contracts in which contingencies may be present, such as the sale of receivables
- Documentation of communication with internal and external legal counsel of the client
- Documentation of contingent liabilities contained in corporate minutes, correspondence from governmental agencies, and bank confirmations

Letter of Audit Inquiry   The primary source of corroborative evidence concerning litigation, claims, and assessments is the client's legal counsel. The auditor should ask the client to send a **letter of audit inquiry** to its legal counsel asking counsel to confirm information about asserted claims and those claims that are probable of assertion. Attorneys are hesitant to provide much information to auditors because their communications with clients are usually privileged. As a result, the American Bar Association and the American Institute of Certified Public Accountants (AICPA) have agreed that the letter of audit inquiry should include:

- Identification of the company, its subsidiaries, and the date of the audit
- Management's list (or a request by management that the lawyer prepare a list) that describes and evaluates the contingencies to which the lawyer has devoted substantial attention
- A request that the lawyer furnish the auditor with the following:
  1. A comment on the completeness of management's list and evaluations
  2. For each contingency:
     a. A description of the nature of the matter, the progress to date, and the action the company intends to take
     b. An evaluation of the likelihood of an unfavorable outcome and an estimate of the potential loss or range of loss
  3. Any limitations on the lawyer's response, such as not devoting substantial attention to the item or that the amounts are not material

Legal counsel should be instructed by the client to respond directly to the auditors. The auditor and client should agree on what is material for this purpose. If a lawyer refuses to furnish the requested information, it is considered a scope limitation and the auditor would not be able to issue an unqualified audit opinion (see discussion on this issue in *Chapter 15*).

Reviewing and Assessing Significant Estimates

LO **3** Review and assess the appropriateness of the client's significant accounting estimates.

Financial statement balances include many judgmental estimates, including the following:

- Fair value of many assets
- Net realizable values of inventory and receivables
- Property and casualty insurance loss reserves
- Revenues from contracts accounted for by the percentage-of-completion method
- Warranty expenses and associated liabilities
- Depreciation and amortization methods
- Impairment of depreciable assets and goodwill
- Useful lives and residual values of productive facilities, natural resources, and intangibles
- Valuation and classification of financial instruments, pensions, and other post-retirement benefits
- Compensation in stock option plans

Auditors need to take special care to review these types of significant estimates because management may try to manage or smooth earnings by using estimates to create hidden reserves in unusually good years that can be used in years when real profits do not meet expectations. Alternatively, management may sometimes underestimate liabilities or impairment of asset values to achieve reported earning goals in years when real profits do not meet expectations. Auditors should be alert to period-end adjusting journal entries that relate to accounts with significant estimates. Ultimately, the auditor is responsible for providing reasonable assurance that the:

- Estimates are reasonable
- Estimates are presented in conformity with GAAP
- Disclosure about estimates is adequate

Accounting estimates are based on management's knowledge and experience of past and current events, as well as its assumptions about conditions that it expects to exist and courses of action it expects to take. Estimates are based on both subjective and objective factors; there is potential for bias in both. Of course, the auditor evaluates estimates in these accounts during the conduct of the audit. However, the auditor should also take time at the end of the audit to consider whether, taken together, the estimates made in these accounts are reasonable; that is, that they do not result in overly conservative or overly aggressive financial reporting. Events or transactions occurring after the balance sheet date, but before the audit report date, can be useful in identifying and evaluating the reasonableness of estimates. Examples of these events include collection of receivables, sale of inventory or financial instruments, and the purchase of inventory under a purchase commitment for which an estimated loss was or should have been accrued. The *Auditing in Practice* feature "The AICPA's AU-C 540 *Auditing Accounting Estimates, Including Fair Value Accounting Estimates, and Related Disclosures*" provides additional discussion on the auditor's responsibility for auditing accounting estimates.

In evaluating the reasonableness of an estimate, the auditor concentrates on key factors and assumptions that are:

- Significant to the accounting estimate
- Sensitive to variations
- Deviations from historical patterns

The AICPA's AU-C 540 Auditing Accounting Estimates, Including Fair Value Accounting Estimates, and Related Disclosures

Effective December 15, 2012, auditors adhering to AICPA standards must comply with this standard on auditing accounting estimates. The nature and reliability of information that management has at its disposal to make accounting estimates varies widely, as does the nature and reliability of information that auditors have to evaluate management's estimates. The auditor's objective in this judgmental area is to obtain sufficient appropriate evidence about whether accounting estimates, including those relating to fair value estimates, are reasonable and that related disclosures in the financial statements are adequate. Of particular concern, the auditor must be professionally skeptical about potential management bias, which is a lack of neutrality with respect to the preparation and fair presentation of information in the context of making accounting estimates.

In assessing the risks of material misstatement with respect to accounting estimates, the standard requires that the auditor obtain an understanding of the following: (1) the requirements of the applicable financial reporting framework relevant to each of the accounting estimates, along with related disclosures, (2) how management identifies situations that give risk to accounting estimates and how management identifies changes in circumstances surrounding accounting estimates, and (3) how management makes the estimates and the underlying data upon which they are based.

In responding to the risks of material misstatement, the standard requires the auditor to complete at least one of the following tasks: (1) determine whether events leading up to the audit report date provide evidence about the accounting estimate, (2) test how management made the estimate and the data that they used, (3) test the operating effectiveness of controls regarding how management made the estimate, along with appropriate substantive procedures, and (4) develop a point estimate or range to evaluate the point estimate that management developed.

Given the trend toward the pervasive use of fair value measurements in financial accounting, the need for auditors to be well versed in the requirements of AU-C 540 will continue to remain critical to audit quality.

- Subjective and susceptible to misstatement and bias
- Inconsistent with current economic trends

The auditor should consider the historical experience of the client in making past estimates. However, changes in facts, circumstances, or the client's procedures may cause factors different from those considered in the past to become significant to the estimate. For example, economic changes may occur that increase or decrease the ability of customers to make timely payments, or the client may have changed its credit policies, providing for a longer or shorter time before payment is due. Auditors may be reluctant to challenge management estimates that result in current-period reductions in income (such as increases in bad debt expense) and associated increases in reserve accounts (such as allowance for doubtful accounts). However, it is important for auditors to remember that management may try to tap into these reserves in the future to improve an otherwise weak level of earnings at that time. Ultimately, the auditor should review management's judgments and decisions to determine whether possible management bias affected the estimation process. The *Auditing in Practice* feature "PCAOB Fines Ernst & Young for an Issue Involving Accounting Estimates" provides an example of a situation in which auditors failed to exercise professional skepticism in their audit of an important accounting estimate.

PCAOB Fines Ernst & Young for an Issue Involving Accounting Estimates

Medicis Pharmaceutical Corporation sells pharmaceutical products that have time-sensitive expiration dates. Medicis' return policy gave customers the right to return a product anywhere from four months before the expiration date up to twelve months after the expiration date. Medicis' revenue recognition policy violated GAAP because the policy provided for establishing the reserve for returned products at the original sales price rather than at replacement cost. In 2005, for example, if Medicis had estimated the reserve at replacement cost rather than sales price, the company's reserve and related expense would have increased over $54 million. Medicis' management convinced the audit partners at Ernst & Young that their revenue recognition policy was acceptable under GAAP because of an exception in the relevant financial accounting standard.

The PCAOB took issue with Ernst & Young's acceptance of Medicis' revenue recognition policy and its related estimate of product returns. Further, the PCAOB took issue with Ernst & Young's

willingness to agree with Medicis' lack of disclosure of its policies in this regard. The improper accounting and disclosure existed for several years, and at one point Ernst & Young national-level consultation experts suggested to the partners involved in the Medicis audit that they were incorrect in allowing Medicis' accounting and disclosure policy. Still, Ernst & Young auditors signed the audit report with an unqualified opinion.

Ultimately, the issue was investigated, and on November 10, 2008, Medicis filed restated financial statements for the years ending December 31, 2005, 2006, and 2007. In the restatement, Medicis increased the returns reserve by $94.6 million (585%), $52.1 million (148%), and $58.9 million (600%) as of 2005, 2006, and 2007, respectively. The PCAOB imposed a penalty of $2,000,000 on Ernst & Young and penalties ranging from $25,000 to $50,000 on the individual partners on the Medicis engagement.

For further details on this case, see PCAOB Release No. 105–2012-001.

Reviewing the Adequacy of Disclosures

LO 4 Review the adequacy of disclosures.

The auditor's report covers the basic financial statements, which include the balance sheet, income statement, statement of cash flows, a statement of changes in stockholders' equity or retained earnings, and the related notes. If the auditor determines that informative disclosures are not reasonably adequate, the auditor must identify that fact in the auditor's report. Disclosures can be made on the face of the financial statements (in the form of classifications or parenthetical notations), or they can be made in the notes to the statements. See the *Auditing in Practice* feature "Related Party Disclosures at OAO Gazprom" for an example of disclosures in the footnotes and the problems that PwC experienced in conducting an audit of the company. When assessing the adequacy of disclosures, the auditor should have reasonable assurance that:

- Disclosed events and transactions have occurred and pertain to the entity.
- All disclosures that should have been included are included.
- The disclosures are understandable to users.
- The information is disclosed accurately and at appropriate amounts.

As the *Emerging Issues* feature "PCAOB Issues New Auditing Standard on Related Parties" reveals, the PCAOB has recently issued new guidance related to disclosures in the area of related parties.

Related Party Disclosures at OAO Gazprom

OAO Gazprom produces natural gas and is the largest company in Russia. The company's 2010 International Financial Reporting Standards (IFRS)-based disclosures to the financial statements state the following with respect to related parties:

"For the purpose of these consolidated financial statements, parties are considered to be related if one party has the ability to control the other party or exercise significant influence over the other party in making financial and operational decisions as defined in IAS 24 'Related Party Disclosures'. Related parties may enter into transactions which unrelated parties might not, and transactions between related parties may not be effected on the same terms, conditions, and amounts as transactions between unrelated parties."

The disclosures go on to state that:

"The Government of the Russian Federation is the ultimate controlling party of OAO Gazprom and has a controlling interest (including both direct and indirect ownership) of over 50% in OAO Gazprom" and that "As a condition of privatization in 1992, the Government imposed an obligation on the Group to provide an uninterrupted supply of gas to customers in the Russian Federation at government controlled prices."

Of interest, however, is the relative lack of detail in terms of specific related parties or specific related-party transactions that are contained in the notes to the financial statements. This is in contrast to related-party disclosures at companies such as Ford Motor Company, which describe individual Ford family members, their relationships with the company, and the exact nature of their related-party transactions with the company.

PwC found out just how difficult it can be to conduct an audit of a company in the Russian Federation, particularly because of the complex nature of related-party transactions and high-level interrelationships between executives in companies operating in the Federation. Of particular importance, top members of management at OAO Gazprom have friends or relatives that transact in a related-party context with the company. For example, in one transaction, Gazprom sold natural gas to a related company at $2 per cubic meter, and then the related company sold the gas to European customers for more than $40 per cubic meter. In doing so, the related company (and its management owners) essentially siphoned profits out of Gazprom and into their personal accounts. Gazprom entered into a very significant number of such transactions, but PwC did not require the company to disclose them in its audited financial statements. Minority shareholders of Gazprom were very outspoken in their objections to these types of transactions and to PwC's audits of the company. Ultimately, the political pressure on PwC led to Gazprom putting the audit engagement up for bid. In addition, Hermitage Capital filed multiple lawsuits against PwC in 2002 related to the firm's audits of Gazprom. Those lawsuits were ultimately dismissed, and PwC was retained by the Company as its auditor. As of the date of this writing, PwC is still Gazprom's auditor, so the firm appears to have weathered the political storm of the early 2000s.

The excerpt of an IFRS disclosure checklist in *Exhibit 14.2* is an example of a checklist that helps remind the auditor of matters that should be considered for disclosure. The checklist is also a convenient documentation format for evidence that the auditor adequately evaluated the client's disclosures. Of course, there may be items that should be disclosed but that are not covered by the audit firm's checklist. The auditor, therefore, should not blindly follow a checklist but use good audit judgment when there are unusual circumstances of which the users should be aware.

The auditor should consider matters for disclosure while gathering evidence during the course of the audit, not just at the end of the audit. For example, during the audit of receivables, the auditor should be aware of the need to separately disclose receivables from officers, employees, or other related parties, as well as the pledging of receivables as collateral for a loan.

PCAOB Issues New Auditing Standard on Related Parties

In June 2014, the PCAOB approved a new auditing standard, *Related Parties*. The standard requires the auditor to evaluate whether related-party transactions have been properly accounted for and disclosed in the client's financial statements. The auditor is to evaluate whether the financial statements contain the information regarding relationships and transactions with related parties that are necessary for a fair presentation in conformity with the applicable financial reporting framework.

The auditor must perform specific procedures if the auditor determines that a related party, relationship, or transaction with a related party exists and that such a related-party situation had been previously undisclosed to the auditor. The new standard also contains specific requirements for the auditor to communicate related-party information to the audit committee.

For further details, see PCAOB Release No. 2014-002.

EXHIBIT **14.2** Excerpt of IFRS Disclosure Checklist (presentation and disclosure requirements set out in International Financial Reporting Standards (IFRSs) as of 30 April 2013)

Presentation/disclosure requirement

This section of the checklist addresses the presentation and disclosure requirements of IAS 36. The objective of this Standard is to ensure that assets are not carried at an amount that is greater than their recoverable amount. If an asset is carried at more than its recoverable amount, the asset is described as impaired and IAS 36 requires the entity to recognise an impairment loss.

The principal issues are: how to determine whether impairment exists, how to recognise an impairment loss and when an entity should reverse an impairment loss.

Presentation/disclosure requirement	Yes/No/N/A
General disclosures	
36A Did the entity recognise any impairment losses, or reversals of impairment losses, during the period on assets within the scope of IAS 36?	
Goodwill not yet allocated to a cash-generating unit	
36B Did the entity have any goodwill or intangible assets with indefinite useful lives?	

One of the key disclosures is a summary of significant accounting policies used by the company. In evaluating this summary, the auditor is guided by the substantive nature of transactions as well as the evolving nature of business, as opposed to simply reviewing relevant accounting guidance. The *Emerging Issues* feature "SEC Focuses on Disclosure Rules: Complaint Against Keyuan Petrochemicals Related to Disclosure and Accounting Violations" highlights that appropriate disclosures are important from both public policy and regulatory perspectives.

SEC Focuses on Disclosure Rules: Complaint Against Keyuan Petrochemicals Related to Disclosure and Accounting Violations

EMERGING ISSUE

On February 28, 2013, the SEC charged Keyuan Petrochemicals and its former chief financial officer (CFO), Aichun Li, with violations of U.S. financial accounting and disclosure rules. The SEC complaint states that Keyuan failed to disclose related-party transactions between the company and its chief executive officer (CEO) and controlling share-holders, entities controlled by or affiliated with these individuals, and entities controlled by Key-uan's management or their close family members. The CFO's job was to ensure that Keyuan's financial statements complied with U.S. financial accounting and disclosure rules. She discovered information indicating that the company was not identifying or reporting related-party transactions relating to raw materials purchases, short-term financing arrangements, and loan guarantees. The company used an off-balance sheet cash account to pay for top management's cash bonuses, travel, and entertainment expenses, and gifts to Chinese government officials. Due to the use of the off-balance sheet account, there existed misstatements in the company's financial statements related to cash, receivables, construction-in-progress, interest income, other income, and general and administrative expenses. Despite knowledge of the problems, the CFO failed to take action to remedy them or to reveal them to the external audit firm or audit committee, despite the fact that those parties expressly questioned her about potential related-party transactions.

As an example of the related-party transactions, in the first eighteen months of its operations, 17% to 24% of the company's sales were to a related company whose majority shareholder was the CEO's mother. In October 2011, Keyuan restated its financial statements. The company and the CFO ultimately were ordered to pay penalties for their actions in the amounts of $1 million and $25,000, respectively.

You can expect to see further enforcement actions regarding disclosure inadequacies. In December 2013, the SEC issued a report to Congress regarding disclosure rules for U.S. public companies. The SEC's Division of Corporate Finance is currently reviewing disclosure requirements and is actively reviewing financial disclosure requirements in Forms 10-K, 10-Q, and 8-K. In addition, on April 7, 2014, the FASB issued a Disclosure Framework project, the objective of which is to improve the effectiveness of disclosures in financial statement footnotes. Thus, disclosure is an important emerging issue from public policy and regulatory perspectives.

For further details on this case, see the SEC's Litigation Release No. 22627, February 28, 2013. The Release is located at: http://www.sec.gov/litigation/litreleases/litrelarchive/litarchive2013.shtml

Finally, it is important to note that the auditor's report does not specifically cover the statements made by management in the Management Discussion and Analysis (MD&A) section of the annual report. However, auditors routinely review the MD&A to provide reasonable assurance that it does not contain information that is factually inaccurate or inconsistent with the audited portion of the financial statements and accompanying footnotes.

Reviewing and Assessing Clients' Noncompliance with Laws and Regulations

LO 5 Review and assess the implications of noncompliance with laws and regulations.

Management and those charged with governance must be sure that the client's operations and financial reporting are conducted in accordance with laws and regulations. **Noncompliance** involves "acts of omission or commission by the entity, either intentional or unintentional, which are contrary to the prevailing laws or regulations" (AU-C 250). Auditors are responsible for obtaining reasonable assurance that the financial statements are free from material misstatements, including material misstatements relating to a client's compliance with laws and regulations. However, auditing standards recognize that there are inherent limitations in an auditor's ability to detect material misstatements relating to the client's compliance with laws and regulations. These limitations include:

- Laws and regulations often relate to operational issues within the client that do not necessarily relate to the financial statements, so the information systems relating to financial reporting may not capture noncompliance.
- Management may act to conceal noncompliance, or may override controls, or may intentionally misrepresent facts to the auditor.
- The legal implications of noncompliance are ultimately a matter for legal authorities to resolve, and are not a matter the auditor can resolve.

In reviewing for potential noncompliance, the auditor should obtain an understanding of the client's internal controls that are designed to achieve proper compliance with laws and regulations. If management or those charged with governance do not demonstrate a commitment to internal control over noncompliance, then the auditor should expend additional effort in reviewing for instances of noncompliance. See the *Focus on Fraud* feature "Triton Energy and Noncompliance with Laws and Regulations" for a historically important case involving noncompliance with the Foreign Corrupt Practices Act of 1977 (FCPA). The FCPA was written to respond to SEC investigations in the 1970s revealing that over 400 companies had made questionable or illegal payments of over $300 million to foreign officials, politicians, and political parties. The payments involved bribery of foreign officials to facilitate business

Triton Energy and Noncompliance with Laws and Regulations

FOCUS on **FRAUD**

Triton Energy engages in the exploration and production of crude oil and natural gas in many areas around the world. Triton has traditionally operated in areas in relatively high-risk, politically unstable areas where larger and better-known producers do not operate. Top Triton Indonesia officials (President, CFO, Commercial Manager, and Controller) were investigated by the SEC for violations of the Foreign Corrupt Practices Act. These violations included:

- Improper payments were made to a middleman who used the funds to reduce Triton Indonesia's tax liability.
- Improper payments were made to a middleman who used the funds to ensure a favorable governmental audit.
- Improper payments were made to a middleman who used the funds to obtain from government officials corporate tax refunds.
- The recording of false journal entries by Triton Indonesia's Commercial Manager and

Controller were made to cover up the improper payments.

These improper payments and false journal entries were facilitated because Triton's CEO, Bill Lee, was an aggressive top manager who provided weak tone at the top in terms of his failure to encourage compliance with applicable laws and regulations, failure to discourage improper payments, and failure to implement internal controls to deter improper payments. Triton was ultimately fined $300,000 related to the scandal.

If an auditor becomes aware of violations of law, the auditor should notify the audit committee about the violations, their circumstances, and the effect on the financial statements. Further, the auditor should consider whether risk assessments made prior to knowledge of identified violations are still appropriate.

For further details on this case, see the SEC's Securities Exchange Act of 1934 Release No. 38343 and Accounting and Auditing Enforcement Release No. 889, February 27, 1997.

operations in their respective foreign countries. The main provisions of the FCPA include:

- No U.S. person or company that has securities listed on U.S. markets may make a payment to a foreign official for the purpose of obtaining or retaining business. This provision is commonly called the anti-bribery provision of the FCPA.
- Companies that have securities listed on U.S. markets must make and keep financial records that accurately and fairly reflect the transactions of the company and must design and maintain an adequate system of internal accounting controls.
- Certain payments to foreign officials are acceptable. These include grease payments, which are payments made to an official to expedite the performance of the duties that the official would already be bound to perform.

Evaluating the Going-Concern Assumption

LO 6 Review the appropriateness of the going-concern assumption using relevant professional guidance.

Business failures result from a variety of causes, including inadequate financing, cash-flow problems, poor management, product obsolescence, natural disasters, loss of a major customer or supplier, and competition. Investors and creditors become upset when a business fails, particularly when it happens shortly after the auditor has issued an unqualified opinion. However, an audit opinion is not a guarantee that the business is a going concern. Still, auditors are required to evaluate the likelihood of each client continuing as a going concern for a **reasonable period of time**. *Exhibit 14.3* highlights the important actions that the auditor takes in making a going-concern assessment. The *Emerging Issues* feature "FASB Announces New Going-Concern Standard" highlights new management responsibilities in this area and potential new auditing standards.

The going-concern evaluation is based on information obtained from typical audit procedures performed to test management's assertions; no separate procedures are required unless the auditor believes that there is substantial doubt about the client's ability to continue as a going concern. However, because the public expects auditors to evaluate the going-concern assumption, many audit firms use bankruptcy prediction models in analyzing whether a particular client might have a going-concern problem. If there is substantial doubt about the ability of the client to remain a going concern, the auditor identifies and assesses management's plans to overcome the problems. If, after reviewing management's plans, the auditor concludes that substantial doubt about the entity's ability to continue as a going concern has been alleviated, the auditor considers the disclosure of the conditions or events that initially caused the auditor to believe there was substantial doubt. The auditor should consider the possible effects of such conditions or events, and any mitigating factors, including management's plans. Alternatively, if the auditor concludes that substantial doubt about the entity's ability to continue as a going concern for a reasonable period of time remains, the auditor should include an emphasis-of-matter paragraph in the auditor's report to reflect that conclusion. The audit report will use the phrase *substantial doubt about the entity's ability to continue as a going concern* or similar wording that includes the terms *substantial doubt* and *going concern*. We discuss these report modifications in *Chapter 15*.

Management often resists a going-concern modification, making the argument that such a qualification will cause investors, lenders, and customers to lose faith in the business and thus cause it to fail. Auditors also may be reluctant to issue a going-concern audit opinion because it can be a self-fulfilling prophecy that the company will, indeed, go bankrupt. In other words, if an audit firm issues a report stating that the company may not be a going concern, lenders and customers may become so worried that they stop lending money or doing business with the company, thereby hastening its demise. In addition, auditors may be reluctant to issue a going-concern

EXHIBIT 14.3   Going-Concern Process

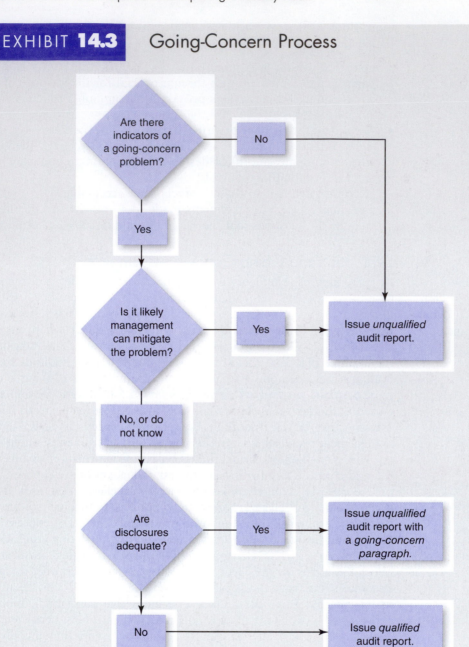

opinion because it is simply very difficult to know beforehand whether a financially distressed client will actually cease operations or will somehow pull itself away from that outcome.

Indicators of Potential Going-Concern Problems

Auditors must carefully analyze all the factors that indicate a going-concern problem and determine if management has a viable plan to address the problems. Potential indicators of going-concern problems include:

- Negative trends, such as recurring losses, working-capital deficiencies, negative cash flows from operating activities, and adverse key financial ratios
- Internal matters, such as loss of key personnel, employee strikes, outdated facilities and products, and uneconomic long-term commitments

FASB Announces New Going-Concern Standard

EMERGING ISSUE

On May 8, 2014, the FASB directed its staff to write a final draft of an Accounting Standards Update for vote by the Board. The final draft will specify that the going-concern basis of accounting will be used until an entity's liquidation is imminent. The definition of *substantial doubt* will incorporate a likelihood component defined using the term *probable*. The assessment period for substantial doubt will be one year from the date of the financial statements. Management will need to consider the mitigating effect of its plans to the extent that it is probable that the plans will alleviate the adverse conditions and to the extent that it is probable that those plans will be implemented effectively. Management must disclose the going-concern problems and mitigating plans in disclosures in the financial statement footnotes. The disclosures will also require management to notify financial statement users when substantial doubt about the entity's ability to continue as a going concern has been alleviated via successful implementation of management's mitigation plans. The standard was published in June 2014. The FASB standard is similar to that followed by auditors under auditing standards. The new standard will take effect for reporting periods that begin after December 15, 2015. Further, the PCAOB has indicated that it will consider proposed revisions to its related auditing standard based on changes to the financial accounting standards.

- External matters, such as new legislation, pending litigation, loss of a key franchise or patent, loss of a principal customer or supplier, and uninsured or underinsured casualty loss
- Other miscellaneous matters, such as default on a loan, inability to pay dividends, restructuring of debt, violation of laws and regulations, and inability to buy from suppliers on credit
- Significant changes in the competitive market and the competitiveness of the client's products

A number of studies of bankruptcies have shown that certain combinations of ratios can indicate the likelihood of bankruptcy. Two **Altman Z-scores**—a five-ratio model for publicly owned manufacturing companies and a four-ratio model for privately owned non-manufacturing companies—are available for auditor use, with newer models available representing variations of these original models.[1]

The Z-scores are calculated as shown in *Exhibit 14.4*. Z-scores falling below 1.81 in the five-ratio model or below 1.1 in the four-ratio model indicate high potential for bankruptcy. Scores above 2.99 in the five-ratio model or above 2.6 in the four-ratio model indicate very little potential for bankruptcy. For example, using the four-ratio model, a company that has a strong working-capital position, has accumulated significant retained earnings, and is profitable would score above the 2.6 threshold and be unlikely to have a going-concern problem. Although a low Z-score (or a similar score using a different bankruptcy prediction model) does not in itself indicate that the company will fail, it does provide presumptive evidence that there is a going-concern problem.

Mitigating Factors

If the auditor concludes that there may be a going-concern problem, the auditor should assess management's plans to overcome this problem. Management may plan to sell nonessential assets, borrow money or restructure existing

---

[1] E. Altman, *Corporate Financial Distress* (New York: John Wiley & Sons, 1983).

EXHIBIT **14.4** Altman Z-Score Models

Z-Score for Publicly Owned Manufacturing Companies		Z-Score for Private Non-Manufacturing Companies	
Weight	**Ratio**	**Weight**	**Ratio**
1.2 ×	Working capital to total assets	6.56 ×	Working capital to total assets
+ 1.4 ×	Retained earnings to total assets	+ 3.26 ×	Retained earnings to total assets
3.3 ×	Return on total assets	+ 6.72 ×	Earnings before interest and taxes to total
+ 0.99 ×	Sales to total assets		assets
+ 0.6 ×	Market value of equity to total debt	+ 1.05 ×	Net worth to total liabilities
	Interpretation of Z-Score		
< 1.81	High potential for bankruptcy	< 1.1	High potential for bankruptcy
> 2.99	Little potential for bankruptcy	> 2.6	Little potential for bankruptcy

debt, reduce or delay unnecessary expenditures, and/or increase owner investments. The auditor should identify those factors that are most likely to resolve the problem and gather independent evidence to determine the likely success of such plans. For example, if financial projections are an integral part of the solution, the auditor should ask management to provide that information and the underlying assumptions. The auditor should then consider, and independently test, the adequacy of support for the major assumptions. As another example, if management indicates that their major financial institution is willing to renegotiate the terms of an outstanding loan to provide more favorable terms, the auditor should consider this when evaluating management's recovery plans. Of course, the auditor should confirm the new terms with the bank, through obtaining corroborating evidence directly from the bank rather than relying on management's verbal representations. The auditor should also evaluate the reasonableness of other assumptions made by management, including:

- Management's assumption about increasing prices or market share should be analyzed in relation to current industry developments.
- Management's assumptions about cost savings related to a reduction in workforce should be recomputed and evaluated to determine if there are hidden costs (such as pension obligations) that were overlooked by management.
- Management's assumptions about selling off assets—either a division or specifically identified assets—should be evaluated in relation to current market prices.

After considering these factors, the auditor will assess whether management can mitigate the going-concern problem, and reporting decisions will follow based upon that assessment and possible disclosures that may be necessary.

Performing Review Analytical Procedures

LO 7 Perform review analytical procedures.

Chapter 6 explains the process for performing analytical procedures. For review analytical procedures, the objective of the procedure is to help the auditor form an overall conclusion about whether the financial statements are consistent with the auditor's understanding of the entity. The auditor's expectation when performing review analytical procedures will be less precise than if the auditor were performing substantive analytical procedures.

Review analytical procedures indicate whether certain relationships make sense in light of the knowledge obtained during the audit. Such procedures may indicate that further audit work needs to be performed before issuing the audit opinion. Ratio analysis, common-size analysis, and analysis of the dollar and percentage changes in each income statement item over the previous year are useful for this purpose. The auditor should have accumulated sufficient appropriate evidence during the audit to explain any unusual changes, such as changes when none are expected, no changes when they are expected, or changes that are not of the expected size or direction. For example, if the client paid more attention to quality control and order processing during the current year, then sales returns and allowances should have decreased as a percentage of sales. As another example, if a client increased its market share by substantially reducing prices for the last three months of the year and undertaking a massive advertising campaign, a decrease in the gross profit margin should be expected. If these expected changes are not reflected in the accounting records, the audit documentation should contain adequate evidence, supplementing the explanations of management to corroborate those explanations. Otherwise, the auditor should investigate to determine the reason for the discrepancies in the data, as they could represent account balances that are misstated.

Ultimately, review analytical procedures should corroborate conclusions formed during the audit, which enables the auditor to draw conclusions upon which to base the audit opinion. If review analytical procedures identify a previously unrecognized risk of material misstatement, the auditor must go back and revise the original risk assessment and conduct additional procedures to address the risk. The need for additional audit procedures is particularly relevant when management is unable to provide an explanation for the previously unrecognized risk identified through the analytical procedures. See *Exhibit 14.5* for an example of the financial data and some relevant ratios for Koss Corporation, including concerns that seem relevant in terms of analytical review of the financial position of the company.

EXHIBIT 14.5   Identifying Risks at Koss Corporation Using Analytical Procedures

The fraud at Koss Corporation perpetrated by the company's CFO, Sue Sachdeva, occurred during the period 2005–2009. Following are the audited financial statements of Koss during that period (prior to restatement). Put yourself in the position of the auditor conducting review analytical procedures for the 2009 audit. After analyzing the financial results and ratios and using your knowledge of analytical review procedures, consider the following patterns in the data:

- Cash balances have declined to their lowest level since FYE 2004.
- Sales increased over the period, but have returned to about FYE 2004 levels.
- Cost of goods sold as a percentage of sales has risen sharply over the period, with a particularly significant increase from FYE 2008 to 2009.
- Relatedly, gross profit has decreased sharply over the period, with a particularly significant decrease from FYE 2008 to 2009.
- SG&A as a percentage of sales has risen sharply over the period, with a particularly significant increase from FYE 2008 to 2009.
- Net income as a percentage of sales has decreased sharply over the period, with a particularly significant decrease from FYE 2008 to 2009.

(continued)

| EXHIBIT **14.5** | Identifying Risks at Koss Corporation Using Analytical Procedures (*continued*) |

- Accounts receivable as a percentage of sales has remained relatively stable over the period, so there do not appear to be problems in billing or collections.
- Current liabilities as a percentage of sales has remained relatively stable over the period, so there do not appear to be problems in the purchasing cycle.

Account ($ millions)	FYE 2009	FYE 2008	FYE 2007	FYE 2006	FYE 2005	FYE 2004
Net sales	38,185	46,943	46,202	50,892	40,287	40,493
Cost of goods sold	24,917	29,152	28,285	31,095	25,217	24,531
Gross profit	13,267	17,792	17,917	19,796	15,070	15,962
SG&A	10,653	10,792	10,066	10,064	8,544	8,090
Net income	1,977	4,494	5,157	6,222	4,494	5,448
Cash	1,664	3,323	4,188	6,147	5,219	2,111
Accounts receivable	8,680	10,149	7,939	6,820	8,764	9,340
Inventory	9,763	9,374	9,924	10,522	7,596	7,315
Net PP&E	4,076	2,746	2,567	3,038	2,994	2,697
Current liabilities	3,619	5,587	4,130	9,149	6,034	3,480
Ratios:						
COGS/Sales	65%	62%	61%	61%	63%	61%
Gross profit %	35%	38%	39%	39%	37%	39%
SG&A/Sales	28%	23%	22%	20%	21%	20%
Net income/Sales	5%	10%	11%	12%	11%	13%
Accts. receiv./Sales	23%	22%	17%	13%	22%	23%
Inventory/Sales	26%	20%	21%	21%	19%	18%
Current liab./Sales	9%	12%	9%	18%	15%	9%

Taken together, these financial data and ratios signal a very significant shift in performance from FYE 2008 to 2009. We assume that the auditor did not include an expectation for this type of shift. Concerns that should be investigated by the auditor related to the analytical procedures include:

- Why is cash showing such a decline? What are controls over cash?
- Are costs being inappropriately allocated to cost of goods sold or SG&A? Who has oversight over allocations and journal entries to these accounts? Is that individual adequately supervised?
- Gross margins are usually relatively stable; what is management's explanation for the significant change?
- While sales seem to be slowing, perhaps due to the recession, profitability has declined even more substantially. What is the explanation for this unexpected relationship?

Of course, hindsight makes these trends appear consistent with the fraud that was ultimately discovered. It is unclear why the audit team and engagement partner did not exercise professional skepticism to better understand these puzzling analytics. Ultimately, the fraud was exposed when American Express employees recognized that Sachdeva was paying her credit card bills with large wire transfers from a Koss bank account. They alerted Koss CEO, Michael Koss, and at that point the FBI confronted Sachdeva. So, no individual charged with governance at Koss appears to have ever seriously challenged the declining and unusual financial results at Koss. In fact, because of situations like this, the PCAOB issued Staff Audit Practice Alert No. 10: "Maintaining and Applying Professional Skepticism in Audits" on December 4, 2012, urging auditors to be vigilant in exercising appropriate professional skepticism.

Reviewing and Evaluating Management Representations

LO 8 Review management representations in certifications required under the Sarbanes-Oxley Act (for public clients) and describe the contents of a management representation letter.

The auditor will evaluate management representations made in certifications required under the Sarbanes-Oxley Act of 2002 (SOX) and certifications made in the management representation letter.

Certifications Required Under SOX for Public Companies

Section 302 of SOX requires the signing officers of publicly traded companies (usually the CEO and CFO) to certify, among other things, that the financial statements are fairly presented in accordance with GAAP. Most CEOs and CFOs have internal processes to help them meet their primary responsibility for the reliability of the financial statements. In a quality audit, the auditor reviews management's processes for certification to provide reasonable assurance that those processes are adequate and that they can be relied upon. *Exhibit 14.6* provides an excerpt of a management certification at Groupon. An interesting point to note is the discussion about management's responsibility regarding internal controls, along with the subsequent 8-K disclosure of a restatement and notification that Groupon has a material weakness in its internal controls.

Management Representation Letter

Auditors should obtain a **management representation letter** at the end of each audit. The letter is not a substitute for audit procedures that are performed during the audit. The purposes of the letter are to help promote audit quality by:

- Reminding management of its responsibility for the financial statements
- Confirming oral responses obtained by the auditor earlier in the audit and the continuing appropriateness of those responses
- Reducing the possibility of misunderstanding concerning the matters that are the subject of the representations

The letter is prepared on the client's letterhead, is addressed to the auditor, and should be signed by the CEO and the CFO. The auditor usually prepares the letter for the client to read and sign. The contents depend on the circumstances of the audit and the nature and basis of presentation of the financial statements. It may be limited to matters that are considered material to the financial statements and should include representations about known fraud involving management or employees. If management refuses to sign the representation letter, it means that they are not willing to stand by their verbal representations when asked to do so in writing; in short, it would imply that management was being untruthful in verbal representations. Management's refusal to sign the management representation letter is considered a scope limitation sufficient to preclude the issuance of an unqualified opinion; see *Chapter 15* for further details. *Exhibit 14.7* contains an example management representation letter from AU-C 580.

Reviewing and Assessing Subsequent Events and Subsequently Discovered Facts

LO 9 Review subsequent events and subsequently discovered facts and assess proper treatment.

Auditors have responsibility for some events occurring after the client's balance sheet date. The timeline in *Exhibit 14.8* illustrates the relevant time periods. Every audit includes procedures to review for subsequent events and transactions that occur in the period between the balance sheet date and the audit report date (Period A in *Exhibit 14.8.*). The auditor has no responsibilities to continue obtaining audit evidence after the audit report date: Period B and Period C. However, the auditor may become aware of relevant information during Period B and Period C and will have to assess appropriate actions to take.

EXHIBIT 14.6 Management Certifications at Groupon

GROUPON CERTIFICATION OF CHIEF EXECUTIVE OFFICER

I, Andrew D. Mason, certify that:

1. I have reviewed this Annual Report on Form 10-K of Groupon, Inc.;
2. Based on my knowledge, this report does not contain any untrue statement of a material fact or omit to state a material fact necessary to make the statement made, in light of the circumstances under which such statements were made, not misleading, with respect to the periods covered by this report;
3. Based on my knowledge, the financial statements, and other financial information included in this report, fairly represent in all material respects the financial condition, results of operations and cash flows of the registrant as of, and for, the periods presented in this report;
4. The registrant's other certifying officer and I are responsible for establishing and maintaining disclosure controls and procedures (as defined in Exchange Act Rules 13a-15(e) and 15d-15(e)) for the registrant and have:
   (a) Designed such disclosure controls and procedures, or caused such disclosure controls and procedures to be designed under our supervision, to ensure that material information relating to the registrant, including its consolidated subsidiaries, is made known to us by others within those entities, particularly during the period in which this report is being prepared;
   (b) [Omitted pursuant to Exchange Act Rules 13a-14(a) and 15d-15(a).]
   (c) Evaluated the effectiveness of the registrant's disclosure controls and procedures and presented in this report our conclusions about the effectiveness of the disclosure controls and procedures, as of the end of the period covered by this report based on such evaluation; and
   (d) Disclosed in this report any change in the registrant's internal control over financial reporting that occurred during the registrant's most recent fiscal quarter (the registrant's fourth fiscal quarter in the case of an annual report) that has materially affected, or is reasonably likely to materially affect, the registrant's internal control over financial reporting; and
5. The registrant's other certifying officer(s) and I have disclosed, based on our most recent evaluation of internal control over financial reporting, to the registrant's auditors and the audit committee of the registrant's board of directors (or persons performing the equivalent functions):
   (a) All significant deficiencies and material weaknesses in the design or operation of internal control over financial reporting which are reasonably likely to adversely affect the registrant's ability to record, process, summarize and report financial information; and
   (b) Any fraud, whether or not material, that involves management or other employees who have a significant role in the registrant's internal control over financial reporting.

Date: March 30, 2012   /s/ Andrew D. Mason

Andrew D. Mason

Chief Executive Officer

Of particular interest, on the same date, Groupon issued an 8-K form announcing a restatement of its fourth quarter 2011 financial results. In the 8-K, management stated the following:

> In conjunction with the completion of the audit of Groupon's financial statements for the year ended December 31, 2011 by its independent auditor, Ernst & Young LLP, the Company included a statement of a material weakness in its internal controls over its financial statement close process in its Annual Report on Form 10-K for year ended December 31, 2011. The Company has been working for several months with another global accounting firm in preparation for reporting on the effectiveness of its internal controls by the end of 2012, as required following Groupon's initial public offering last year. The Company continues to implement process improvement initiatives and augment its staffing, and is expanding the accounting firm's engagement scope to address the underlying causes of the material weakness.

Taken together, these two disclosures alert users that Groupon management is (a) responsible for maintaining internal controls for the company, and (b) has fallen short of its responsibility. Not surprisingly, Groupon's stock price fell 17% upon the release of the restatement news.

Source: *Groupon Inc. 3-30-2012 8-K.*

EXHIBIT 14.7   Management Representation Letter Example From AU-C 580 "Management Representations"

(Entity Letterhead)

(To Auditor) (Date)

This representation letter is provided in connection with your audit of the financial statements of ABC Company, which comprise the balance sheet as of December 31, 20XX, and the related statements of income, changes in stockholders' equity, and cash flows for the year then ended, and the related notes to the financial statements, for the purpose of expressing an opinion on whether the financial statements are presented fairly, in all material respects, in accordance with accounting principles generally accepted in the United States (U.S. GAAP).

Certain representations in this letter are described as being limited to matters that are material. Items are considered material, regardless of size, if they involve an omission or misstatement of accounting information that, in the light of surrounding circumstances, makes it probable that the judgment of a reasonable person relying on the information would be changed or influenced by the omission or misstatement.

Except where otherwise stated below, immaterial matters less than $[*insert amount*] collectively are not considered to be exceptions that require disclosure for the purpose of the following representations. This amount is not necessarily indicative of amounts that would require adjustment to or disclosure in the financial statements.

We confirm that to the best of our knowledge and belief, having made such inquiries as we considered necessary for the purpose of appropriately informing ourselves [as of (date of auditor's report),]:

Financial Statements

- We have fulfilled our responsibilities, as set out in the terms of the audit engagement dated [*insert date*], for the preparation and fair presentation of the financial statements in accordance with U.S. GAAP.
- We acknowledge our responsibility for the design, implementation, and maintenance of internal control relevant to the preparation and fair presentation of financial statements that are free from material misstatement, whether due to fraud or error.
- We acknowledge our responsibility for the design, implementation, and maintenance of internal control to prevent and detect fraud.
- Significant assumptions used by us in making accounting estimates, including those measured at fair value, are reasonable.
- Related party relationships and transactions have been appropriately accounted for and disclosed in accordance with the requirements of U.S. GAAP.
- All events subsequent to the date of the financial statements and for which U.S. GAAP requires adjustment or disclosure have been adjusted or disclosed.
- The effects of uncorrected misstatements are immaterial, both individually and in the aggregate, to the financial statements as a whole. A list of the uncorrected misstatements is attached to the representation letter.
- The effects of all known actual or possible litigation and claims have been accounted for and disclosed in accordance with U.S. GAAP.

Information Provided

We have provided you with:

- Access to all information, of which we are aware that is relevant to the preparation and fair presentation of the financial statements such as records, documentation and other matters;
- Additional information that you have requested from us for the purpose of the audit; and
- Unrestricted access to persons within the entity from whom you determined it necessary to obtain audit evidence.
- All transactions have been recorded in the accounting records and are reflected in the financial statements.
- We have disclosed to you the results of our assessment of the risk that the financial statements may be materially misstated as a result of fraud.
- We have [*no knowledge of any*][*disclosed to you all information that we are aware of regarding*] fraud or suspected fraud that affects the entity and involves:
  - Management;
  - Employees who have significant roles in internal control; or
  - Others when the fraud could have a material effect on the financial statements

(*continued*)

EXHIBIT **14.7**	Management Representation Letter Example From AU-C 580 "Management Representations" (*continued*)

- We have [*no knowledge of any*][*disclosed to you all information that we are aware of regarding*] allegations of fraud, or suspected fraud, affecting the entity's financial statements communicated by employees, former employees, analysts, regulators or others.
- We have disclosed to you all known instances of noncompliance or suspected noncompliance with laws and regulations whose effects should be considered when preparing financial statements.
- We [*have disclosed to you all known actual or possible*][*are not aware of any pending or threatened*] litigation and claims whose effects should be considered when preparing the financial statements [*and we have not consulted legal counsel concerning litigation or claims*]
- We have disclosed to you the identity of the entity's related parties and all the related party relationships and transactions of which we are aware.

[*Name of Chief Executive Officer and Title*]

[*Name of Chief Financial Officer and Title*]

EXHIBIT **14.8**	Subsequent Periods

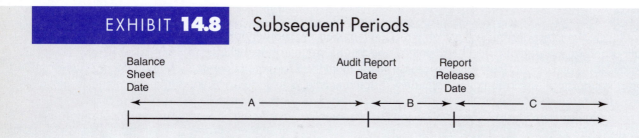

Review of Subsequent Events (Period A)

Two types of events occurring in Period A in *Exhibit 14.8* have been identified as subsequent events that may require dollar adjustments to the financial statements and/or disclosure: Type I subsequent events and Type II subsequent events. **Subsequent events** are events occurring between the date of the financial statements and the date of the auditor's report. A **subsequent events review** is a review of events occurring in the period between the balance sheet date and the audit report date to determine their possible effect on the financial statements.

Type I Subsequent Events **Type I subsequent events** provide evidence about conditions that existed at the balance sheet date. The financial statement numbers should be adjusted to reflect this information. Footnote disclosure may also be necessary to provide additional information. The following are examples:

- A major customer files for bankruptcy during the subsequent period because of a deteriorating financial condition, which the client and auditor were unaware of until learning about the bankruptcy filing. This information should be considered in establishing an appropriate amount for the allowance for doubtful accounts and in making an adjustment if the allowance is not sufficient to cover this potential loss.

- A lawsuit is settled for a different amount than was accrued.
- A stock dividend or split that takes place during the subsequent period should be disclosed. In addition, earnings-per-share figures should be adjusted to show the retroactive effect of the stock dividend or split.
- A sale of inventory below carrying value provides evidence that the net realizable value was less than cost at year-end.
- Information becomes available that provides evidence about the valuation of an estimate or reserve that had been accrued at year-end. For an example of this situation, see the *Auditing in Practice* feature "Deloitte, Ligand, and the PCAOB: A Case Where Subsequent Events Were Important."

Type II Subsequent Events Type II subsequent events indicate conditions that did not exist at the balance sheet date but that may require disclosure. The events that should be considered for disclosure are financial in nature and are material. The following are examples:

- An uninsured casualty loss that occurred after the balance sheet date causes a customer's bankruptcy during the subsequent period. Because the customer was able to pay at the balance sheet date, the allowance for doubtful accounts should not be adjusted, but the information should be disclosed.
- A significant lawsuit is initiated relating to an incident that occurred after the balance sheet date.
- Because of a natural disaster such as fire, earthquake, or flood, a company loses a major facility after the balance sheet date.
- Major decisions are made during the subsequent period, such as to merge, discontinue a line of business, or issue new securities.
- A material change occurs in the value of investment securities.

AUDITING IN **PRACTICE**

Deloitte, Ligand, and the PCAOB: A Case Where Subsequent Events Were Important

Deloitte was fined $1,000,000 in December 2007 as a penalty for a low-quality audit of Ligand Pharmaceuticals' 2003 financial statements. The fundamental problem in the audit was that an unqualified audit partner, James Fazio, oversaw the engagement and signed the audit opinion. Most surprisingly, Deloitte had identified Fazio as a quality risk and was in the process of forcing him to resign from the firm. The specific audit issue that led to a material misstatement of Ligand's financial statements concerned significant product returns from three large wholesalers that distributed Ligand's products. Deloitte knew that the pharmaceutical products that Ligand sold to these wholesalers were relatively new products, there was a lack of return history, and there were significant increases in or excess levels of inventory in the distribution channel. These factors made the valuation of the reserve for product returns very risky to audit. At year-end, Ligand employees developed an estimate for product returns that turned out to be materially too low. Deloitte personnel did not address significant differences between historical actual returns and Ligand's estimate for product returns. The audit plan provided for the evaluation of subsequent events related to product returns after year-end, but before the completion of the audit. However, the plan was not executed by Deloitte personnel, nor was the estimate adequately reviewed by Fazio. Ultimately, Deloitte resigned from the Ligand engagement in 2004, and Ligand was subsequently forced to restate its 2002, 2003, and some of its 2004 financial statements. Fazio was denied the ability to audit public companies for at least two years. This case highlights the importance of professional competence and the need to carefully consider events occurring during the period subsequent to year-end when auditing important financial statement estimates.

For additional details, see PCAOB Releases Nos. 105–2007-005 and 105–2007-106.

The financial statement account balances should not be adjusted for these events, but they should be considered for disclosure.

Subsequent Events Audit Procedures Some of the procedures discussed in previous chapters relate to subsequent events, such as cutoff tests, review of subsequent collections of receivables, and the search for unrecorded liabilities. Additional procedures related to subsequent events include the following:

- Read the minutes of the meetings of the board of directors, stockholders, and other authoritative groups. The auditor should obtain written assurance that minutes of all such meetings, through the audit report date, have been made available. This can be included in the management representation letter described earlier in this chapter.
- Read interim financial statements and compare them to the audited financial statements, noting and investigating significant changes.
- Inquire of management concerning:
  - Any significant changes noted in the interim statements
  - The existence of significant contingent liabilities or commitments at the balance sheet date or date of inquiry, which should be near the audit report date
  - Any significant changes in working capital, long-term debt, or owners' equity
  - The status of items for which tentative conclusions were drawn earlier in the audit
  - Any unusual adjustments made to the accounting records after the balance sheet date

Dual Dating (Period B)

When the auditor becomes aware of an event that occurs after the audit report date but before the **report release date** (Period B in *Exhibit 14.8*), and the event is disclosed in the footnotes, the auditor has two options for dating the audit report:

1. Use the date of this event as the date of the audit report.
2. Dual-date the report, using the dates of the original audit report and the date of the event, to disclose the work done only on that event after the original audit report date.

As an example, consider a situation in which the original audit report date is February 27, 2016, and a fire destroyed the client's main manufacturing plant and warehouse on March 2, 2016. This event is disclosed in Note 14 to the financial statements. The audit report release date was March 5. The auditor may date the report March 2, 2016, or dual-date it as "February 27, 2016, except for Note 14, as to which the date is March 2, 2016." The auditor is assuming less responsibility by dual-dating the report. The only event occurring after the original audit report date for which the auditor is taking responsibility is disclosed in Note 14. If the report were dated March 2, 2016, the auditor would be taking responsibility for all events occurring during Period B. In that case, the auditor should perform audit procedures to identify other significant subsequent events that occurred between February 27 and March 2.

Subsequently Discovered Facts That Become Known to the Auditor After the Report Release Date (Period C)

Facts may come to the auditor's attention after the report release date (Period C in *Exhibit 14.8*) that may have affected the financial statements and auditor's report, had the facts been known at the report release date.

Such facts may come to the auditor's attention through news reports, performing another service for the client, other business contacts, or a subsequent audit. If such facts had been known at the report date, and therefore would have been investigated during the audit, the auditor should determine the following:

- The reliability of the new information
- Whether the development or event had occurred by the report date, as issuance of revised financial statements and an audit report is not required when the development or event occurs after the report date
- Whether users are likely to still be relying on the financial statements
- Whether the audit report would have been affected had the facts been known to the auditor at the report date

If the auditor decides that steps should be taken to prevent further reliance on the financial statements and audit report, the client is advised to make appropriate and timely disclosure of these new facts. The key action is to notify users as soon as possible so they do not continue to rely on information that is now known to be incorrect. The appropriate action depends on the circumstances:

- If the revised financial statements and audit report can be quickly prepared and distributed, the reasons for the revision should be described in a footnote and referred to in the auditor's report.
- Revision and explanation can be made in the subsequent-period audited financial statements if their distribution is imminent.
- If it will take an extended amount of time to develop revised financial statements, the client should immediately notify the users that the previously distributed financial statements and auditor's report should no longer be relied on, and that revised statements and report will be issued as soon as possible.

The auditor should make sure the client takes the appropriate action. If the client will not cooperate:

- The auditor should notify the client and any regulatory agency having jurisdiction over it, such as the SEC, that the audit report should no longer be associated with the client's financial statements.
- The auditor should notify users known to the auditor that the audit report should no longer be relied on. Auditors typically do not know all the users who receive the report. Therefore, the appropriate regulatory agency should be requested to take whatever steps are needed to disclose this situation.

Performing an Engagement Quality Review

LO 10 Identify the procedures and documentation required to perform an engagement quality review.

As part of a quality audit for public companies, the audit firm must have policies and procedures in place for conducting an engagement quality review of each audit before issuing the audit opinion. Auditors of privately held companies generally perform these reviews even though they are not explicitly required. An experienced reviewer who was not a part of the audit team, but who has appropriate competence, independence, integrity, and objectivity, should perform this independent review, referred to as an engagement quality review or **concurring partner review**. The purpose of these reviews is to provide reasonable assurance that the audit and audit documentation are complete and support the audit opinion on the financial statements and, for integrated audits, on the client's internal controls.

The engagement quality review is a risk-based review, where the reviewer evaluates the significant judgments made by the engagement team and the conclusions that the engagement team reached. Some of the procedures the reviewer should perform as part of the review process include:

- Discussing with the audit team any significant matters related to the financial statements and internal controls, including the audit team's identification of material weaknesses and audit procedures to address significant risks
- Evaluating judgments about materiality and the disposition of corrected and uncorrected identified misstatements
- Reviewing the engagement team's evaluation of the firm's independence in relation to the engagement
- Reviewing the related audit documentation to determine its sufficiency
- Reading the financial statements, management's report on internal control, and auditor's report
- Confirming with the lead audit partner that there are no significant unresolved matters
- Determining if appropriate consultations have taken place on difficult or contentious matters
- Evaluating whether the auditor documentation supports the conclusions reached by the engagement team with respect to the matters reviewed
- Assessing whether appropriate matters have been communicated to audit committee members, management, and other appropriate parties
- Evaluating whether appropriate levels of supervision and reviews of individual audit tasks were completed adequately during the audit

Documentation of an Engagement Quality Review

The audit documentation should include evidence on the performance of the engagement quality review. This documentation should include the following information:

- Who performed the engagement quality review
- Documents reviewed by the engagement quality reviewer
- Date the engagement quality reviewer provided concurring approval of issuance

Consideration of Omitted Procedures Discovered After the Report Date

LO 11 Determine how to address situations in which omitted audit procedures come to the auditor's attention after the audit report has been issued.

After the audit report has been issued, the auditor may discover an **omitted procedure**, which is an important audit procedure that was not performed. For example, an auditor may have failed to follow up on a material accounts receivable confirmation response indicating a difference between the client's recorded balance and the customer's recorded balance. Such an omission may be discovered when audit documentation is reviewed as part of an external or internal review program. In this case, the auditor should decide whether the previously issued audit report can still be supported in light of the omitted procedures. If not, the omitted or alternative procedures should be promptly performed and documented.

For example, if the auditor failed to confirm receivables when that should have been done, it may be too late to confirm now. In that case, the auditor could extend the previous work done on subsequent collections to help determine that the receivables existed and were properly valued at the balance sheet date. If the results indicate that the previously issued statements and audit report should be modified, the auditor will follow the guidance in the previous section of this chapter, that is, Period C in *Exhibit 14.8*. Otherwise, no further action is necessary.

Communicating with Management and the Audit Committee (and Those Charged with Governance)

LO 12 Identify issues to communicate to the audit committee.

Communicating with the Audit Committee

It is important that the external auditor have a constructive and detailed dialogue with the audit committee. This communication is important because the audit committee serves as an independent subcommittee of the board of directors. The audit committee can also assist the auditor should a disagreement occur between the auditor and management. The audit committee must be assured that the auditor is free of any restrictions and has not been inappropriately influenced by management during the course of the audit. The following are typical communications between the auditor and the audit committee:

- *Auditor's Responsibility Under Generally Accepted Auditing Standards (GAAS).* The auditor must clearly communicate the audit firm's responsibility to perform the audit according to relevant auditing standards and independently assess the fairness of the financial statements, to assess the quality of the entity's internal controls over financial reporting, and to design the audit to detect material misstatements. The auditor should communicate that the audit of the financial statements does not relieve management of its financial reporting responsibilities.
- *Overview and Planned Scope of the Audit.* The auditor needs to communicate the planned scope of the audit engagement to the audit committee and have a discussion with it on the adequacy of the planned scope.
- *Independence.* The auditor should affirm that the engagement team and others in the audit firm have complied with relevant independence requirements.
- *Significant Accounting Policies.* The auditor should inform the audit committee about the initial selection of, and changes in, significant accounting policies or their application, and discuss the quality of accounting principles used. SOX requires that the auditor communicate all alternative treatments of financial information within GAAP that have been discussed with management, ramifications of using alternative treatments or disclosures, and the treatment that the audit firm prefers.
- *Management Judgments and Accounting Estimates.* Many corporate failures have involved manipulation of accounting estimates such as loan loss reserves. The auditor should inform the audit committee of the processes used by management in making sensitive accounting estimates and should convey the auditor's assessment of those processes and accompanying estimates.
- *Significant Audit Adjustments.* Significant audit adjustments may reflect on the stewardship and accountability of management. The audit committee should be made aware of such adjustments, even if management readily agrees to make them. Significant adjustments, by definition, suggest that there have been internal control failures that must be communicated to management and to the audit committee. The auditor should also communicate about any uncorrected misstatements.
- *Judgments About the Quality of the Company's Accounting Principles.* The auditor needs to discuss with the audit committee the quality of the company's financial statements and provide reasonable assurance that they are acceptable under GAAP. Auditors should be prepared to have a frank discussion about differences in assessments of the quality of the financial statements. In other words, the auditor should be prepared to discuss the quality, not just the acceptability, of significant accounting

policies. See the *Auditing in Practice* feature "Guidance on Assessing the Quality, Not Just the Acceptability, of Significant Accounting Policies" for further insights on this important professional judgment.

- *Other Information in Annual Reports.* The auditor should briefly describe his or her responsibility to review other information contained in an annual report and whether such information is consistent with the audited financial statements.

- *Disagreements with Management.* All major accounting disagreements with management, even if eventually resolved, should be discussed with the audit committee. This requirement is intended to insulate the auditors from management pressure to change or bend accounting treatments to suit management and should remove any hints that the audit firm may be replaced because it disagrees with management's proposed accounting treatments.

- *Major Issues Discussed with Management Before Retention.* During the proposal and hiring stages of the engagement, management and the auditor discuss issues related to accounting principles and audit standards. These issues should be discussed with the audit committee.

- *Internal Control over Financial Reporting.* The auditor should discuss the quality of internal controls and any deficiencies therein (including material weaknesses, significant deficiencies, and those deficiencies that are less severe than significant deficiencies), even if they were remediated, prior to year-end. The audit committee needs to understand these issues in order to help assess the elements of the Committee of Sponsoring Organizations of the Treadway Commission (COSO) framework and to engage in remediation discussions. For integrated audit clients, the auditor must provide these communications in writing to management and the audit committee prior to issuing the auditor's report on internal control over financial reporting.

Guidance on Assessing the Quality, Not Just the Acceptability, of Significant Accounting Policies

AUDITING IN **PRACTICE**

Objective criteria for evaluating the quality of the client's accounting policies is not available, so assessing the quality, not just the acceptability of significant accounting policies is a matter of professional judgment. The AICPA has issued guidance in this regard, "Discussions to Expect From the Independent Auditor" (AICPA 2008). That guidance encourages auditors to consider the following in making this judgment:

- What is the consistency of the organization's accounting principles and their application?
- What is the clarity of the financial statements and related disclosures?
- What is the completeness of the financial statements and related disclosures?

- Are there any items that have a significant impact on the representational faithfulness, verifiability, and neutrality of the accounting information included in the financial statements? For example, are there:
  - Selection of new accounting policies or changes to current ones
  - Estimates, judgments, and uncertainties
  - Unusual transactions
  - Accounting policies relating to significant financial statement items, including the timing of transactions and the period in which they are recorded
- Is the organization using accounting practices that are not specifically addressed in the accounting literature, such as industry-specific practices?

An Example Management Letter to a College Foundation

AUDITING IN **PRACTICE**

Below, we provide an example management letter from the audit firm of Johnstone & Gramling LLP related to the June 30, 2015, audit of the Bucky Badger College Foundation. You should note the following features of the letter:

- It contains the auditor's observations and recommendations to management.
- It contains management's response.
- It addresses the issue of whether/how management responded to the management letter related to the prior year's audit.

Bucky Badger College Foundation
Addendum A

Financial System Reporting

Observation
Currently, the financial reporting system used by the college and the Foundation produces various reports that must be printed and manually reclassified to properly report amounts in the financial statements. Efficiencies could be gained by accounting personnel if the financial reporting system were updated.

Recommendation
We recommend that management work with IT support at the College to develop an updated financial reporting system.

Management's Response
We agree with the recommendation. The current system will be updated, and adequate funds are available to accomplish the update.

Allowance for Doubtful Accounts

Observation
Currently the Foundation reviews the pledge accounts receivables from promised gifts by donors to determine the appropriateness of the allowance for doubtful accounts. This process has produced reasonable estimates in the past. The Foundation is beginning a new capital campaign to donors, which should result in increased pledges over the next several years. These pledges and associated receivables should be carefully and separately tracked from those amounts arising from prior capital campaigns.

Recommendation
We recommend that management develop a process to estimate and track the collectability of campaign pledge receivables from the new campaign, and to allocate sufficient staffing resources to do so.

Management's Response
We agree with the recommendation. A multipledge campaign evaluation process will be developed and implemented for future financial reporting.

Disposition of Prior-Year Comments
In our management letter for the year ended June 30, 2014, we made several comments and recommendations intended to improve the Foundation's internal controls. During our current-year audit, we reviewed these comments to determine if the recommendations were implemented.

Pledge Receivable

Observation
During our audit, it became apparent that the Foundation recorded as a pledge receivable the death benefit of an insurance policy in which it was named the beneficiary. However, accounting rules state that it does not meet the criteria to be recorded as a pledge receivable because the Foundation was only a named beneficiary.

Recommendation
We recommend that management review similar insurance policies to determine if the accounting is proper for these accounts.

Management's Response
We agree with the recommendation. We have initiated an internal review process to track and properly record pledge receivables.

Investment Income

Observation
During our audit, it came to our attention that unrealized gains and losses are allocated to individual fund balances yearly rather than semiannually, resulting in potential inaccuracies during the year.

Recommendation
We recommend that unrealized gains and losses be posted to individual fund balances on a semiannual basis, or quarterly if possible.

Management's Response
We agree with the recommendation. Unrealized gains or losses will be posted for each fund on a semiannual basis beginning with the period ending December 31, 2015.

In Summary
The comments relating to the prior year's audit have been adequately addressed.

Communicating with Management via the Management Letter

Auditors often notice things throughout the audit that could help management do a better job. The auditor generally reports these observations in a **management letter** as a constructive part of the audit. Such a letter should not be confused with a management representation letter. The management letter is not required, but it is used to make significant operational or control recommendations to the client. The letter helps to provide management comfort that the auditor has done a quality job and that the auditor knows and understands the client's business. Many audit firms consider management's inattention to addressing comments in the letter to be an important risk factor in subsequent-year audits. See the *Auditing in Practice* feature "An Example Management Letter to a College Foundation" for details on the contents and structure of a typical management letter.

SUMMARY AND NEXT STEPS

Before issuing an audit opinion, the auditor must determine whether the financial statements are presented fairly in all material respects, whether they contain adequate disclosures, and whether they properly reflect events that have occurred up to the audit report date. In short, many activities must be completed prior to issuing the audit report. These activities are designed to provide reasonable assurance that the audit was conducted in a quality manner. Now that you understand these steps, *Chapter 15* will describe in detail the various types of audit opinions that auditors may express based upon their audit procedures and related conclusions.

SIGNIFICANT TERMS

Altman Z-score   A series of ratios that have predictive power in indicating the likelihood of bankruptcy. This score is named for the person that first introduced the concept and associated measurement.

Concurring partner review   See *engagement quality review*.

Engagement quality review   A review at the end of each audit conducted by an experienced auditor, usually a partner, who was not a part of the audit team, but who has appropriate competence, independence, integrity, and objectivity. The purpose of this review is to help make sure that the audit and audit documentation are complete and support the audit opinion on the financial statements and, for public companies, on the client's internal controls.

Factual misstatement   See *known misstatement*; misstatements about which there is no doubt.

Judgmental misstatement   A misstatement that arises from differences in judgments of management concerning accounting estimates that the auditor considers unreasonable, or the selection or application of accounting policies that the auditor considers inappropriate.

Known misstatement   A misstatement that has been specifically identified; known misstatents are also referred to as *factual misstatements*.

Letter of audit inquiry A letter that the auditor asks the client to send to its legal counsel to gather corroborative evidence concerning litigation, claims, and assessments.

Management letter A letter from the auditor to the client identifying any problems and suggested solutions that may help management improve its effectiveness or efficiency.

Management representation letter A letter to the auditors that the client's chief executive and chief financial officers are required to sign that specifies management's responsibility for the financial statements and confirms oral responses given to the auditor during the audit.

Noncompliance This involves acts of omission or commission by the entity, either intentional or unintentional, which are contrary to the prevailing laws or regulations.

Omitted procedures After the audit report has been issued, the auditor may discover that an important audit procedure was not performed; these are called omitted procedures.

Projected misstatement A misstatement that is the auditor's best estimate of the misstatement in a given population, and that is a projection of the misstatement identified in an audit sample to the entire population from which the sample was drawn.

Reasonable period of time A period of time not to exceed one year beyond the date of the financial statements being audited.

Report release date The date the auditor grants the entity permission to use the auditor's report in connection with the financial statements.

Subsequent events Events occurring between the date of the financial statements and the date of the auditor's report.

Subsequent events review A review of events occurring in the period between the balance sheet date and the audit report date to determine their possible effect on the financial statements.

Type I subsequent events Events that existed at the balance sheet date.

Type II subsequent events Events that did not exist at the balance sheet date, but that may require disclosure.

TRUE/FALSE QUESTIONS

14-1   **LO 1**   The auditor should consider only quantitative factors when assessing the materiality of detected misstatements.

14-2   **LO 1**   The PCAOB provides guidance that auditors must consider as they decide whether management's refusal to correct a detected misstatement is indicative of intentional bias.

14-3   **LO 2**   The auditor is responsible for designing and maintaining policies and procedures to identify, evaluate, and account for contingencies; management is responsible for determining that the auditor has properly identified, accounted for, and disclosed material contingencies.

14-4 **LO 2** One source of evidence concerning contingencies is client's management; a primary source of corroborative evidence concerning contingencies is the client's legal counsel, which is obtained in the management representation letter.

14-5 **LO 3** With regard to reviewing significant estimates, the auditor is responsible for providing reasonable assurance that the estimates are reasonable.

14-6 **LO 3** Auditors should not challenge management estimates that result in current-period reductions in income and associated increases in reserve accounts.

14-7 **LO 4** The audit report includes reasonable assurance about information contained in the MD&A section of the annual report.

14-8 **LO 4** One of the key disclosures to the financial statements is a summary of significant accounting policies used by the company.

14-9 **LO 5** Auditing standards recognize that there are inherent limitations in an auditor's ability to detect material misstatements relating to the entity's compliance with laws and regulations.

14-10 **LO 5** The legal implications of a client's noncompliance with laws and regulations are ultimately a matter for the auditor to resolve before the audit opinion can be issued.

14-11 **LO 6** The going-concern evaluation is based on information obtained from normal audit procedures performed to test management's assertions; no separate procedures are required, unless the auditor believes that there is substantial doubt about the client's ability to continue as a going concern.

14-12 **LO 6** Auditors should not issue a going-concern audit opinion if it would be a self-fulfilling prophecy that the company will, indeed, go bankrupt.

14-13 **LO 7** Performing review analytical procedures is optional.

14-14 **LO 7** The auditor's expectations when performing review analytical review can be less precise than those for substantive analytics.

14-15 **LO 8** Section 404 of SOX requires the signing officers of publicly traded companies (usually the CEO and CFO) to certify, among other things, that the financial statements are fairly presented in accordance with GAAP.

14-16 **LO 8** One of the purposes of a management representation letter is to confirm oral responses obtained by the auditor earlier in the audit and the continuing appropriateness of those responses.

14-17 **LO 9** Type I subsequent events provide evidence about conditions that existed at the balance sheet date, while Type II subsequent events provide evidence about conditions that did not exist at the balance sheet date but that may require disclosure.

14-18 **LO 9** An example of a Type I subsequent event would be when a significant lawsuit is initiated relating to an incident that occurred after the balance sheet date.

14-19 **LO 10** The terms *engagement quality review* and *concurring partner review* are synonymous.

14-20 **LO 10** An engagement quality review is required for publicly traded companies, and engagement quality reviews for privately held company audits rarely happen.

14-21 **LO 11** If after the audit report date the auditor discovers that an important audit procedure was not performed, SOX requires that the auditor file a Form 8-K with the SEC.

14-22 **LO 11** An example of a situation in which the auditor discovers omitted procedures after the report date would be one in which the auditor failed to confirm receivables, and this fact comes to light as part of an internal review program.

14-23 **LO 12** The auditor is required to communicate certain issues to the audit committee; this communication is important because the audit committee serves as an independent subcommittee of the board of directors, and the audit committee can also assist the auditor should a disagreement occur between the auditor and management.

14-24 **LO 12** One of the issues that the auditor is required to communicate to the audit committee is the competence, training, and industry specialization of each of the highest ranking members of the engagement team (the partner, manager, and audit senior).

14-25 **LO 13** The management representation letter and the management letter are both required for the audits of publicly traded companies.

14-26 **LO 13** The management letter helps to provide management comfort that the auditor has done a quality job and that the auditor knows and understands the client's business.

MULTIPLE-CHOICE QUESTIONS

14-27 **LO 1** The auditor discovers various errors in the client's financial statements during the audit. At the end of the audit, these misstatements are analyzed to determine if they need to be recorded and corrected. In which situation could management and the auditor decide not to correct the misstatement?
a. If, by correcting the misstatement, net income would increase rather than decrease.
b. If, by correcting the misstatement, net income would decrease rather than increase.
c. If the misstatement is material.
d. If the misstatement is immaterial.

14-28 **LO 1** The PCAOB's AS 14 provides insight that auditors must consider as they decide whether management's refusal to correct a detected misstatement is indicative of intentional bias. Which of the following is a form of management bias in this setting?
a. Refusal on the part of management to allow the auditor to communicate with the audit committee about the misstatement.
b. The identification by management of additional adjusting entries that offset misstatements accumulated by the auditor.
c. Refusal on the part of management to allow the auditor to collect additional evidence to evaluate the materiality of the misstatement.
d. The identification by management of procedures that the auditor omitted during the audit, which yield information about the misstatement.

14-29 **LO 2** In obtaining evidence about loss contingencies, which of the following are sources of evidence that the auditor should obtain from management?
a. A description and evaluation of contingencies that existed at the balance sheet date.
b. Assurance that the accounting and disclosure requirements concerning contingent liabilities have been met.

    c. Documentation of communication with internal and external legal counsel of the client.

    d. All of the above.

14-30 **LO 2** In completing the audit, the auditor must obtain a letter of audit inquiry. Which of the following is an accurate description of a letter of audit inquiry?

    a. A letter that is the primary source of corroborative evidence concerning litigation, claims, and assessments, which is received from the client's legal counsel.

    b. A letter that is the primary source of corroborative evidence concerning cash valuation, which is received from the client's bank.

    c. A letter that is the primary source of corroborative evidence concerning accounts receivable valuation, which is received from the client's customer.

    d. A letter that is the primary source of corroborative evidence concerning inventory valuation, which is received from the client's supplier.

14-31 **LO 3** In completing the audit, the auditor should review management's significant accounting estimates. In this setting, the auditor is responsible for providing reasonable assurance about which of the following?

    a. The estimates are reasonable.

    b. The estimates are presented in conformity with GAAP.

    c. The disclosure about the estimates is adequate.

    d. All of the above.

14-32 **LO 3** In evaluating the reasonableness of significant accounting estimates, the auditor should consider which of the following?

    a. The significance of the estimate.

    b. The sensitivity of the estimate to variations.

    c. The sensitivity of the estimate to misstatement and bias.

    d. All of the above.

14-33 **LO 4** In completing the audit, the auditor should review the adequacy of the disclosures in the financial statements. When assessing the disclosures, the auditor should have reasonable assurance that which of the following are characteristic of the disclosures?

    a. The disclosed events and transactions have occurred and pertain to the entity.

    b. All the disclosures that should have been included are included.

    c. The disclosures are understandable to users.

    d. All of the above.

14-34 **LO 4** The auditor's report does not provide assurance about which of the following elements of the client's financial reporting?

    a. The 10-K.

    b. The MD&A.

    c. The financial statements.

    d. The disclosures in the footnotes to the financial statements.

14-35 **LO 5** The auditor has responsibility regarding clients' noncompliance with laws and regulations. Obviously, management may try to hide acts involving noncompliance, which limits the auditor's ability to detect such acts. Which of the following are inherent limitations that affect the auditor's ability to detect acts involving noncompliance?

a. Laws and regulations often relate to operational issues within the entity that do not necessarily relate to the financial statements, so the information systems relating to financial reporting may not capture noncompliance.

b. Management may act to conceal noncompliance, or may override controls, or may intentionally misrepresent facts to the auditor.

c. The legal implications of noncompliance are ultimately a matter for legal authorities to resolve and are not a matter about which the auditor can resolve.

d. All of the above.

14-36 **LO 5** Which of the following is an important provision of the Foreign Corrupt Practices Act?

a. Auditors of clients operating in foreign countries must hire a joint auditor in the foreign country to provide assurance that laws and regulations have been followed by the client.

b. Auditors of clients operating in foreign countries must provide reasonable assurance that any inventory observations that occur in the foreign country are observed by at least some audit personnel from the U.S.; this requirement is in place because fraud often occurs in inventory accounts.

c. Companies that have securities listed on U.S. markets must make and keep financial records that accurately and fairly reflect the transactions of the company and must design and maintain an adequate system of internal accounting controls.

d. Companies that have securities listed on U.S. markets must adhere to the internal control requirements of both the U.S. and the applicable foreign country.

14-37 **LO 6** In evaluating whether the client is a going concern, the auditor should ask which of the following questions?

a. Are there indicators of going-concern problems?

b. Is it likely that management can mitigate any identified going-concern problems?

c. Are disclosures about the going-concern problems adequate?

d. All of the above.

14-38 **LO 6** The Altman Z-Score is a model used to help assess the likelihood that a company will go bankrupt. The model contains which of the following ratios?

a. Working capital to total assets.

b. Working capital to total sales.

c. Sales to total debt.

d. Sales to total accounts receivable.

14-39 **LO 7** Which of the following statements concerning review analytical procedures is false?

a. Review analytical procedures help auditors assess the overall presentation of the financial statements.

b. The auditor's expectations in review analytical procedures should be more precise than those for substantive analytics.

c. Auditing standards require the use of review analytical procedures to assist in identifying ending account relationships that are unusual.

d. Ratio analysis, common-size analysis, and analysis of the dollar and percentage changes in each income statement item over the previous year are useful for performing review analytical procedures.

14-40 **LO 7** The analytical procedures of the financial statements of Koss Corporation that are depicted in *Exhibit 14.5* reveal which of the following indicators of the fraud?

a. Cash balances had declined to their lowest level since FYE 2004.

b. Cost of goods sold as a percentage of sales had risen sharply over the period, with a particularly significant increase from FYE 2008 to 2009.

c. Net income as a percentage of sales had decreased sharply over the period, with a particularly significant decrease from FYE 2008 to 2009.

d. All of the above.

14-41 **LO 8** In completing the audit, the auditor must obtain a management representation letter. Which of the following statements about the management representation letter is false?

a. The management representation letter is intended to remind management about its responsibility for the financial statements.

b. The management representation letter is prepared on the client's letterhead, is addressed to the auditor, and should be signed by the CEO and the CFO.

c. Management's refusal to sign the management representation letter is considered such a violation of ethics and professionalism that auditors of publicly traded clients must resign from the engagement immediately and require the client to file a Form 8-K with the SEC.

d. The contents of the management representation letter may be limited to matters that are considered material to the financial statements and should include representations about known fraud involving management or employees.

14-42 **LO 8** In completing the audit, the auditor must assess management's representations, including certifications required under SOX for public companies. Which of the following statements is true concerning this certification?

a. Section 302 of SOX requires the signing officers of publicly traded companies (usually the CEO and CFO) to certify, among other things, that the financial statements are fairly presented in accordance with GAAP.

b. Section 302 of SOX requires the auditor of publicly traded companies to certify, among other things, that the financial statements are fairly presented in accordance with GAAP.

c. Section 302 of SOX requires the signing officers of publicly traded companies (usually the CEO and CFO) to certify, among other things, that no material fraud has taken place within the entity for a period not to exceed one year prior to the issuance of the financial statements.

d. Section 302 of SOX requires the auditor of publicly traded companies to certify, among other things, that no material fraud has taken place within the entity for a period not to exceed one year prior to the issuance of the financial statements.

14-43 **LO 9** Which of the following is an example of a Type II subsequent event?

a. A lawsuit is settled for a different amount than was accrued.

b. A sale of inventory below carrying value provides evidence that the net realizable value was less than cost at year-end.

    c. Information becomes available that provides evidence about the valuation of an estimate or reserve that had been accrued at year-end.

    d. None of the above.

14-44 **LO 9** After the report release date, the auditor may become aware of facts that may have affected the financial statements and auditor's report, had the facts been known at the time of issuance. With regard to this situation, which of the following statements is true?

    a. Because such facts become known after the report release date, the auditor cannot reasonably be held accountable for these issues; no action is required on the part of the auditor.

    b. If the auditor decides that steps should be taken to prevent further reliance on the financial statements and audit report, the client is advised to make appropriate and timely disclosure of these new facts.

    c. If such facts would have been investigated had they been known at the report date, the auditor should determine whether engagement personnel are competent and qualified to perform audits; action is required on the part of the auditor to assess whether engagement personnel should be retained to work on the engagement in the subsequent year.

    d. If the auditor decides that steps should be taken to prevent further reliance on the financial statements and audit report, the auditor should notify the audit committee immediately; no action beyond this is required on the part of the auditor because of confidentiality concerns.

14-45 **LO 10** Which of the following statements is false concerning engagement quality reviews?

    a. The purpose of the engagement quality review is to provide reasonable assurance that the audit and audit documentation are complete and that they support the audit opinion on the financial statements.

    b. The engagement quality review must be documented, and the documentation should include who performed the review, which documents were reviewed, and the date the engagement quality reviewer provided approval of the issuance of the audit opinion.

    c. Engagement quality reviews are required for both publicly traded companies and private companies in the U.S.

    d. One of the procedures that would be performed during the engagement quality review is to determine if appropriate consultations have taken place on difficult or contentious matters.

14-46 **LO 10** Which of the following is not a procedure that would be performed during an engagement quality review?

    a. Evaluating whether or not to continue providing audit services to the client in the subsequent year, based on information gained during the current-period audit.

    b. Discussing significant matters related to the financial statements and internal controls.

    c. Evaluating judgments about materiality and the disposition of corrected and uncorrected identified misstatements.

    d. Reviewing the engagement team's evaluation of the firm's independence in relation to the engagement.

14-47 **LO 11** Which of the following statements is true when considering omitted audit procedures discovered after the report date?

a. After the audit report has been issued, the auditor may discover that an important audit procedure was not performed.

b. Such an omission may be discovered when audit documentation is reviewed as part of an external or internal review program.

c. The auditor should decide whether the previously issued audit report can still be supported in light of the omitted procedures.

d. All of the above.

14-48 **LO 11** If it is discovered after the report date that the auditor failed to confirm receivables, which of the following statements is true?

a. The auditor should try to examine subsequent collections of accounts receivable to help determine whether the accounts receivables existed and whether they were properly valued at the balance sheet date.

b. The auditor must resign immediately.

c. The auditor must notify the SEC immediately.

d. The auditor must notify users of the financial statements immediately.

14-49 **LO 12** Which of the following is not a typical communication between the auditor and the audit committee at the end of an audit engagement?

a. Discussion of the auditor's responsibility under GAAS.

b. Discussion of the client continuance decision.

c. Discussion about auditor independence.

d. Discussion about management judgments and accounting estimates.

14-50 **LO 12** Which of the following is not a typical communication between the auditor and the audit committee?

a. Discussion of the cash confirmation process.

b. Discussion of significant audit adjustments.

c. Discussion of significant accounting policies.

d. Discussion about the quality of the company's accounting principles.

14-51 **LO 13** In completing the audit, the auditor communicates with management via the management letter. Which of the following is false about management letters?

a. The management letter is used to make significant operational or control recommendations to management.

b. Many audit firms consider management's inattention to addressing comments in the letter to be an important risk factor in subsequent-year audits.

c. The management letter is required for publicly traded companies in the U.S., but not privately held companies.

d. All of the above are false.

14-52 **LO 13** In the *Auditing in Practice* feature "An Example Management Letter to a College Foundation" which of the following items is not present in the management letter?

a. The auditor's observations and recommendations to management.

b. Management's response.

c. The issue of whether or how management responded to the management letter related to the prior-year's audit.

d. What actions the auditor will take in the subsequent-year audit to help management address the identified weaknesses.

REVIEW AND SHORT CASE QUESTIONS

14-53 **LO 1** What is an adjustment, and why is the resolution of such adjustments important to audit quality? What role should professional skepticism play when management disagrees with the auditor about making an audit adjustment to correct a misstatement? What types of management bias might be revealed in this type of setting?

14-54 **LO 1** How does a summary of possible adjustments help the auditor determine whether the financial statements are fairly presented? What information might it contain? How might an analysis of the summary affect the auditor's internal control report on a public company?

14-55 **LO 1** Why is audit firm culture important in ensuring that individual audit engagement partners resolve adjustments in a quality manner?

14-56 **LO 1** During the course of the audit of Nature Sporting Goods, the auditor discovered the following:

- The accounts receivable confirmation work revealed one pricing misstatement. The book value of $12,955.68 should be $11,984.00. The total misstatement based on this difference is $14,465, which includes a $972 known misstatement and an unknown projected misstatement of $13,493.
- Nature Sporting Goods had understated the accrued vacation pay by $13,000. A review of the prior-year documentation indicates the following uncorrected misstatements:
  - Accrued vacation pay was understated by $9,000.
  - Sales and accounts receivable were overstated by an estimated $60,000 because of cutoff errors.

Prepare a summary of a possible adjustments schedule and draw your conclusion about whether the aggregate effect of these misstatements is material. Use the trial balance numbers shown in *Exhibit 14.1*, but ignore the misstatements shown in the exhibit. The income tax rate is 40% for the current and prior year. (*Note:* Materiality must be considered in developing your answer.)

14-57 **LO 1, 16** Refer to the *Auditing in Practice* feature "The PCAOB Position on Management Bias in Correcting Detected Misstatements." The PCAOB guidance alerts auditors to situations in which management may resist auditor attempts to convince them to correct misstatements, including biases in which management:

(1) Selectively corrects misstatements to achieve a financial reporting objective (such as correcting only those that result in increases to net income)

(2) Searches for offsetting misstatements after the auditor has identified existing misstatements

How do such actions and biases on the part of management reflect on their integrity and ethics? What would management likely use as an explanation for such actions, particularly in the second case? How would management's actions affect the auditor's professional skepticism?

14-58 **LO 2** What is the primary source of information about litigation, claims, and assessments? What is the primary source of corroborative evidence in this regard?

14-59 **LO 2** Why might client lawyers be hesitant to disclose information to auditors?

14-60 **LO 2** Who sends the letter of audit inquiry to the client's lawyers? To whom should the lawyer send the response to that letter?

14-61 **LO 2** What is the effect on the auditor's report of a lawyer's refusal to furnish the information requested in the letter of audit inquiry?

14-62 **LO 2** Each of the following is an independent situation related to a contingency. Describe what the auditor should do in each case.

a. The lawyer refused to furnish the requested information.

b. The lawyer was unable to form an opinion on the probability or amount of a pending lawsuit, but the auditor believes that the amount could be material.

c. The client stated that it had not consulted lawyers during the past year.

14-63 **LO 2** An audit client is being sued for $500,000 for discriminatory hiring practices. Indicate the appropriate action the auditor should take for each of the following independent responses to the letter of audit inquiry:

a. The lawyer stated that there is only a remote chance that the client will lose. The client did not accrue any contingent loss or disclose this situation.

b. The lawyer stated that the client will probably lose, and the amount of loss could be anywhere between $250,000 and $500,000, with no amount within that range being more likely than another. The client disclosed this situation, but did not accrue a loss.

c. The lawyer stated that there is a reasonable possibility that the client will lose. The client disclosed this situation, but did not accrue a loss.

d. The lawyer stated that the client will probably lose between $250,000 and $500,000, but most likely will lose $400,000. The client accrued a $250,000 contingent loss and disclosed the situation.

PROFESSIONAL SKEPTICISM

14-64 **LO 3** Why should the auditor exercise heightened professional skepticism concerning accounting estimates? What key factors and assumptions should the auditor consider in evaluating the reasonableness of an estimate?

PROFESSIONAL SKEPTICISM

14-65 **LO 3** Consider the following areas in which estimates are made in the preparation of financial statements:

a. Pension obligation

b. Warranty liability and related expenses

c. Allowance for uncollectible accounts (manufacturing company)

d. Allowance for returned goods (such as at a catalog company like Lands' End or L.L. Bean, which have a guaranteed-period warranty on catalog sales)

1. Identify the factors inherent in each account that might significantly affect the dollar estimate of the account balance.

2. For each factor identified, briefly discuss the importance of the item to the overall account estimate. For example, how important is the interest rate assumption to the overall estimate of the pension liability? *(Hint:* You may want to perform a sensitivity analysis to assess the importance of each factor.)

3. For each factor identified, briefly describe audit evidence that should be gathered to determine how the factor should be

used in making the accounting estimate. For example, how should the auditor determine the proper interest rate assumption in estimating the account balance?

4. Assuming there are differences between the auditor's estimate and management's estimate, indicate how a professionally skeptical auditor can determine whether management is attempting to manage or smooth earnings or that there is a genuine disagreement on the correct factor to be used in making the estimate.

14-66 **LO 4** How is a disclosure checklist helpful? What precautions should the auditor take when using such a checklist?

14-67 **LO 4** When assessing disclosures, about what matters regarding disclosures should the auditor have reasonable assurance?

INTERNATIONAL

14-68 **LO 4** Refer to the *Auditing in Practice* feature "Related Party Disclosures at OAO Gazprom." What risks do the related-party transactions with the Russian government pose for PwC in its audits of the company? Why might companies without such government ownership be less sensitive about their related-party disclosures?

14-69 **LO 5** What are the inherent limitations in an auditor's ability to detect material misstatements relating to the client's compliance with laws and regulations?

ETHICS

14-70 **LO 5** What are the main provisions of the Foreign Corrupt Practices Act?

FRAUD

14-71 **LO 5** Refer to the *Focus on Fraud* feature "Triton Energy and Noncompliance with Laws and Regulations." How did Triton Energy violate the provisions of the Foreign Corrupt Practices Act? What are the auditors' responsibilities when they become aware of violations of law at their client?

14-72 **LO 6** Are auditors required to evaluate the likelihood of a client remaining a going concern as a part of each audit? What types of conditions and factors should auditors consider when making this evaluation?

14-73 **LO 6** An Altman Z-score indicates the possibility that a client will go bankrupt. What effect could this score have on the audit report? Explain.

14-74 **LO 6** List various factors suggesting that a client may not remain a going concern. For each, indicate the degree of subjectivity and judgment that would be required in determining if the indicator would, in fact, result in the company going bankrupt (use the following categories: high, medium, low). Be prepared to discuss your rationale for the subjectivity and judgment assessment.

14-75 **LO 6** This is the third-year audit of GreenLawns. The company has carved out a new market niche on the Internet for the delivery of lawn and garden supplies, including links with local companies that provide lawn services. The company issued stock two years ago and raised sufficient capital to continue operations through this year. The company is currently trading at five times revenue. The company showed no profits in its first three years. Revenue growth has been 100%, 65%, and 30%, respectively, over each of the last three years. The current-year revenue is at $220 million. The auditor has audited current cash flow and has serious reservations about the ability of the company to remain a going concern without either some profitability or an infusion of cash. The company has responded with the following management plan:

- Another public offering of stock to raise $200 million in capital, which will be equal to 30% of the existing stock outstanding
- Sign an agreement with at least fifty more local distributors during the year
- Improve warehousing and distribution to cut at least 20% off the distribution costs
- Increase sales by 50% through more advertising, coupons, and better marketing to existing customers
- Improve profit margins by using its purchase power to sign more attractive purchase agreements with vendors but stay away from major-brand vendors such as Scott's, Ortho products, and so forth

   a. What is the auditor's responsibility to evaluate the effectiveness of management's plan? What action should the auditor take if he or she does not believe that management's plan will be effective?

   b. Assume that the auditor's report contains language indicating concern about the ability of the client to continue as a going concern. What does this action say to the users of the financial statements about confidence in management's ability to remain a going concern?

   c. What is the required disclosure regarding management's plans?

   d. For each element in management's plan, indicate the auditor's responsibility to assess the element. Indicate audit procedures that should be performed to assess each part of management's plans.

14-76 **LO 7** What is the purpose of performing review analytical procedures?

14-77 **LO 7** The audit of GolfDay Company, a manufacturer of bicycle racks and golf carts, is almost finished. Krista Heiss is the most experienced auditor on this audit and is in charge of performing review analytical procedures. The company ships most of its products to a combination of distributors and retailers. The business is totally within the U.S. at the present time and is seasonal.

   a. Why is it important that review analytical procedures be performed by experienced auditors?

   b. What are some analytical procedures that Heiss might perform?

   c. How can these procedures be useful at this stage of the audit to help provide reasonable assurance with respect to audit quality?

FRAUD

PROFESSIONAL SKEPTICISM

14-78 **LO 7** Refer to *Exhibit 14.5*, "Identifying Risks at Koss Corporation Using Analytical Procedures." Review the analytical procedure results and trends. Presumably, Sue Sachdeva knew that the auditors might ask pointed questions about the financial results and odd analytics apparent in the data from FYE 2004 to FYE 2009. For each of the trends listed here, describe how you think Sachdeva might have tried to explain away the issue (because, of course, she would not admit to the fraud). Indicate how a professionally skeptical auditor might have responded to her explanations.

Financial Trend	CFO's Likely Explanation
Cash balances have declined to their lowest level since FYE 2004.	
Sales increased over the period but have returned to about FYE 2004 levels.	
Cost of goods sold as a percentage of sales has risen sharply over the period, with a particularly significant increase from FYE 2008 to 2009.	
Relatedly, gross profit has decreased sharply over the period, with a particularly significant decrease from FYE 2008 to 2009.	
SG&A as a percentage of sales has risen sharply over the period, with a particularly significant increase from FYE 2008 to 2009.	
Net income as a percentage of sales has decreased sharply over the period, with a particularly significant decrease from FYE 2008 to 2009.	
Accounts receivable as a percentage of sales has remained relatively stable over the period, so there do not appear to be problems in billing or collections.	
Current liabilities as a percentage of sales has remained relatively stable over the period, so there do not appear to be problems in the purchasing cycle.	

14-79   **LO 8**   What is a management representation letter? Who prepares it? Who should sign it? When should it be dated? How does it differ from the CEO and CFO certification of financial statements?

PROFESSIONAL SKEPTICISM

14-80   **LO 8**   What are the implications if management refuses to sign a management representation letter? If management signs a management representation letter, is that a good indication that all of management's statements described in the letter are actually true? What is the importance of professional skepticism in assessing the management representation letter as audit evidence?

14-81   **LO 8**   Refer to *Exhibit 14.7*, "Management Representation Letter Example From AU-C 580." What role does materiality play in the contents of the management representation letter? Is the same level of materiality applied to the audited financial statements as to the management representation letter?

14-82   **LO 9**   What are the types of subsequent events the auditor should identify and evaluate as part of performing an audit? Give an example of each type of subsequent event. How should each type be handled in the financial statements?

14-83   **LO 9**   What audit procedures should be performed to search for subsequent events?

14-84   **LO 9**   Explain the auditor's responsibilities when it is discovered that facts existed at the date of the audit report that were not known to the auditor until after the report release date.

14-85   **LO 9**   Refer to the *Auditing in Practice* feature "Deloitte, Ligand, and the PCAOB: A Case Where Subsequent Events Were Important." How did James Fazio fail in his duty to evaluate subsequent events? What were the implications of his failure in this regard?

14-86   **LO 9**   What is dual dating in terms of the audit report? Assume the following facts: The original audit report is dated March 18, 2016. The company entered into a definitive agreement to discontinue a material line of business on March 22, 2016. This event is disclosed in Note 22 to the financial statements. The report release date was March 25, 2016. On which dates may the auditor date the report? Which dating convention yields the least responsibility for the auditor?

14-87   **LO 9**   The auditor is auditing financial statements for the year ended December 31, 2015, and is completing the audit in early March 2016. The following situations have come to the auditor's attention. Indicate and explain whether the financial statements should be adjusted only, adjusted and disclosed, disclosed only, or neither adjusted nor disclosed.

1. On February 12, 2016, the client agreed to an out-of-court settlement of a property damage suit resulting from an accident caused by one of its delivery trucks. The accident occurred on November 20, 2015. An estimated loss of $30,000 was accrued in the 2015 financial statements. The settlement was for $50,000.

2. Same facts as in Part 1, except the accident occurred January 1, 2016, and no loss was accrued.

3. The client is a bank. A major commercial loan customer filed for bankruptcy on February 26, 2016. The bankruptcy was caused by an adverse court decision on February 15, 2016, involving a product liability lawsuit initiated in 2014 arising from products sold in 2014.

4. The client purchased raw materials that were received just before year-end. The purchase was recorded based on its estimated value. The invoice was not received until January 31, 2016, and the cost was substantially different than was estimated.

5. On February 2, 2016, the board of directors took the following actions:
   (a) Approved officers' salaries for 2016.
   (b) Approved the sale of a significant bond issue.
   (c) Approved a new union contract containing increased wages and fringe benefits for most of the employees. The employees had been on strike since January 2, 2016.

6. A major customer was killed in a boating accident on January 25, 2016. The customer had pledged his boat as collateral against a loan that he took out in 2015. The boat, which was destroyed in the accident, was not insured. The allowance for doubtful accounts is not adequate to cover the anticipated loss.

14-88   **LO 10**   What are the purposes of the engagement quality review (concurring partner review)? What procedures should the reviewer perform as part of the review process?

14-89   **LO 10**   Consistent quality in the performance of an audit is one of the major concerns of all audit firms. However, internal inspections by audit firms themselves, along with external inspections by peer review teams and the PCAOB, point out that although effective audit policies and procedures are generally in place, they are sometimes not consistently performed. The result is that audit quality may sometimes be compromised, yet audit firm management is unaware of which particular audits are of low quality.

a. What audit documentation should engagement quality review partners retain to provide evidence that they have properly evaluated the consistent quality of the audit work performed?

b. Assume that an auditor concludes that all the assumptions regarding warranties are appropriate. What documentation would an engagement quality review partner expect to see to support such a conclusion?

14-90 **LO 11** During the course of an interoffice quality review, it was discovered that the auditors had failed to consider whether inventory costs of a wholesale client exceeded their market value. The review took place six months after the audit report had been issued. Some prices had apparently been falling near year-end. Inventory is a major item in the financial statements, but the auditors do not know whether the market price declines were material.

a. What procedures could the auditors now perform to resolve this audit problem?

b. What should the auditors do if it turns out that inventory was materially overstated?

14-91 **LO 11** What is the auditor's responsibility if, after the report release date, the auditor discovers that an important audit procedure was not performed?

14-92 **LO 12** Each of the following are typical communications between the auditor and the audit committee. Explain why each is important.

- Auditor's responsibility under GAAS
- Overview and planned scope of the audit
- Auditor independence
- Significant accounting policies
- Management judgments and accounting estimates
- Significant audit adjustments
- Judgments about the quality of the company's accounting principles
- Other information in annual reports
- Disagreements with management
- Major issues discussed with management before retention
- Internal control over financial reporting

14-93 **LO 12** Refer to the *Auditing in Practice* feature "Guidance on Assessing the Quality, Not Just the Acceptability, of Significant Accounting Policies." Assessing the quality of accounting policies is a matter of professional judgment. What considerations are relevant in making this judgment?

14-94 **LO 13** Describe the purpose of a management letter, and distinguish it from a management representation letter. Refer to the *Auditing in Practice* feature "An Example Management Letter to a College Foundation." What are the major observations made by the auditor? What is the tone of management's responses? How does management plan to address the observations, and what does this say about management's commitment to financial reporting quality?

ETHICS

Ernst & Young
14-95 **(LO 1, 14)** PCAOB inspection reports that have been released to the public contain a variety of examples of audit engagements in which auditors have had difficulty dealing with potential adjustments to client financial statements. One example of such an audit quality problem is evident in the inspection report of Ernst & Young LLP (November 17, 2005), which states:

> The Firm proposed a judgmental audit adjustment (which the issuer recorded) to increase the issuer's reserve for excess and obsolete inventory, even though the Firm's work papers did not include documentation supporting percentages used to

estimate this reserve. After the Firm proposed this audit adjustment, the issuer's chief executive officer proposed an adjustment to increase the value of inventory received in a bankruptcy settlement, which was contrary to the issuer's earlier conclusion that the bankruptcy settlement accounting would result in no gain or loss. This adjustment was equal to and offset the excess and obsolete inventory adjustment described above. The Firm failed to assess, or failed to include evidence in the work papers that it assessed, whether the offsetting adjustments described above and another set of offsetting year-end adjustments relating to the accounting for major construction contracts (which in total approximated 24% of the issuer's pre-tax income) indicated a bias in management's estimates that could result in material misstatement of the financial statements, and/or a need for the Firm to reevaluate planned audit procedures.

a. Comment on the PCAOB's inspection process, focusing on (1) why it may be needed to provide reasonable assurance about audit quality and (2) how it may improve audit quality.

b. Review the issue outlined in the preceding inspection report. Summarize the actions of the client and the corresponding actions of Ernst & Young. Discuss the income statement implications of the journal entries that are at the center of this inspection comment.

c. What were the major concerns of the PCAOB about this issue?

d. Assume that you were the audit manager on the Ernst &Young audit engagement detailed in the inspection report. Assume also that you knew the audit partner had agreed to allow the client to pursue the offsetting series of journal entries that are the subject of this case. Using the framework for ethical decision making from *Chapter 4*, develop an appropriate course of action to pursue.

FRAUD FOCUS: CONTEMPORARY AND HISTORICAL CASES

FRAUD

PROFESSIONAL SKEPTICISM

14-96 **Dell, Inc.**
(LO 4, 10) In July 2010, the SEC issued a complaint against senior management at Dell, Inc., including the company's chairman, CEO, and CFO. The complaint includes allegations that Dell engaged in fraud during the period 2002–2006 by failing to disclose a significant relationship with its major vendor (Intel) that led to Intel's making payments back to Dell. According to the complaint, Intel agreed to make cash payments to Dell in exchange for Dell's promise that it would not purchase microprocessors from Intel's archrival, Advanced Micro Devices (AMD). The cash payments were very large, ranging from 10% to 76% of operating income over the period of the fraud. In March 2006, Dell announced that it would begin using AMD as a vendor, and Intel immediately retaliated by ceasing to make its usual cash payments to Dell, thereby resulting in a 36% drop in Dell's quarterly income. In the quarterly earnings conference call, Michael Dell attributed the drop to pricing pressures in the face of slowing demand and to component costs that declined less than expected; of course, these statements were false.

Consider the difficulty that this scheme posed for Dell's auditors, PwC. The most senior members of the management team were actively involved in this deception and had no intention of making full and fair disclosures to investors or the auditors. However, should the auditors have otherwise known of the payments? This question is at the heart of a continuing debate about auditing versus forensic accounting (looking for fraud). The auditors, heretofore, had not seen any reason to question management's integrity, but economic situations and motivations change. Further, instituting a standard audit procedure in which audit software is used to search for cash receipts from major vendors (where only cash disbursements are expected) would have likely uncovered the cash received from Intel. Should such procedures—even when fraud is not expected—be performed on every audit, simply because such fraud can occur? Perhaps so, but this would also mean that audit firms would have to systematically think about a host of situations that may occur with all clients and add the standard software analysis to the audits—thereby driving up audit costs (maybe without an increase in audit fees).

This example illustrates the difficulty that auditors sometimes face in their obligation to review the adequacy of disclosures—when faced with fraud, intentional concealment, and collusion among the perpetrators, it is very difficult for the auditors to reach an accurate conclusion regarding their audit work. Critics of PwC might say that the audit was conducted in a low-quality manner, thereby resulting in a failure to detect the fraud.

a. Why were Dell's recording and disclosure of the payments from Intel materially false and misleading?

b. What changes in the economic environment, or in the management culture of Dell, might have led PwC to become more skeptical of the company and therefore to expand audit procedures?

c. Should using audit software to identify significant cash receipts from vendors be a normal part of every audit engagement? Explain your rationale and consider such things as audit cost and expectations of the audit.

d. Assume that instead of negotiating payments from Intel, Dell would have negotiated a long-term supply contract with Intel that resulted in lower prices for Intel chips as long as Dell agreed not to use a competitor's chips in its products. Should the amount of the price reduction be disclosed as a separate item in the financial statements under GAAP? Why or why not?

e. Assume the company negotiated lower prices with Intel as described in Part d. How would the auditor become aware of the lower prices? Consider that, especially in tougher economic times, many companies were negotiating lower prices from their suppliers.

f. Assume the role of the engagement quality review partner. What kinds of review and analysis might have alerted you to the size and nature of the Intel payments?

g. Considering this case and the many ways in which the payments (or price reductions) from Intel could have occurred, how would you decide that the judgments and decisions made by management moves from aggressive accounting to outright fraud?

FRAUD

ETHICS

PROFESSIONAL SKEPTICISM

14-97 **MCA Financial (LO 4, 10, 14)** The facts of this case are drawn from the SEC's Accounting and Auditing Enforcement Release No. 2076 (August 5, 2004).

The Company Perpetrating the Fraud This case involves a fraud perpetrated by MCA Financial Corporation, which was incorporated in 1989 as a holding company for four wholly owned subsidiaries, with forty-five branch offices in seven states. MCA primarily was involved in the residential mortgage banking business. MCA's fraudulent scheme was accomplished through related-party transactions and involved the following steps.

1. MCA purchased distressed rental properties in the city of Detroit, sold them to the Related Limited Partnerships at inflated prices, advanced the Related Limited Partnerships small down payments (usually 10% or 20%), and accepted executed mortgages or land contracts for the remainder of the purchase prices.

2. MCA established the prices at which it sold the rental properties to the Related Limited Partnerships by calculating the value each property would have after substantial rehabilitation, even though rehabilitation work had not been completed or even begun. MCA then recognized the entire gain on each sale as revenue, even though MCA knew that the Related Limited Partnerships could not afford to pay for the properties because of the inflated sales prices and the prevailing rental rates. In fact, the Related Limited Partnerships failed to make most of the required loan payments to MCA for the properties.

3. MCA recorded the money owing from the Related Limited Partnerships as a result of advancing the down payments on the asset side of its balance sheet under the heading of Accounts Receivable-Related Parties. MCA carried those receivables without any valuation allowance, despite the Related Limited Partnerships' inability to repay the receivables.

4. MCA fraudulently sold some related-party mortgages and land contracts to the pools and carried the remainder at cost or with an inadequate allowance for loan losses under the headings of Mortgages Held for Resale or Land Contracts Held for Resale, despite the Related Limited Partnerships' inability to repay and the inadequate collateral. The collateral for these mortgages and land contracts was the real estate that MCA had sold to the Related Limited Partnerships at inflated prices. As a result, MCA knew that foreclosing on the collateral would not result in MCA receiving the full principal amount of the loans. MCA did not disclose in its financial statements that a material amount of its mortgages and land contracts held for resale were related-party mortgages and land contracts.

The Auditors Grant Thornton LLP was one of two firms that jointly provided audit services to MCA and jointly signed reports containing unqualified opinions on MCA's annual financial statements from 1993 through 1998. Doeren Mayhew & Co. P.C., a Michigan accounting firm, was the other firm that jointly provided audit services to MCA and jointly signed reports containing unqualified opinions on MCA's annual financial statements from 1993 through 1998.

Peter Behrens is a CPA who served as an engagement partner for Grant Thornton's joint audits of MCA. Marvin Morris is a CPA who served as an engagement partner for Doeren Mayhew's joint audits of MCA. Benedict Rybicki is a CPA who served as the engagement manager for Doeren Mayhew's joint audits of MCA. Morris obtained personal mortgages through MCA in July 1994 for approximately $344,000 and in July 1995 for approximately $200,000. The 1994 mortgage was discharged when the 1995 mortgage was executed. Morris did not review the auditors' workpapers for several key portions of the 1998 MCA audit, including the workpapers for mortgages and land contracts held for resale and gains on sale of real estate. As late as 2001, Morris stated that he had only ever read the first 13 of the approximately 150 Statements of Financial Accounting Standards. Reading the Statements of Financial Accounting Standards was not "what [Morris did] for a living." Rather, he considered himself a "salesperson."

As the engagement manager, Rybicki signed a workpaper in connection with the 1998 MCA audit (a) confirming that the entire MCA engagement had been performed in accordance with professional standards; (b) confirming that related parties or unusual transactions and relationships were properly disclosed and documented in MCA's financial statements; and (c) agreeing with the issuance of the report containing an unqualified opinion. Rybicki socialized with Alexander Ajemian, MCA's controller, during the time that Doeren Mayhew acted as one of MCA's auditors. Rybicki first met Ajemian in approximately 1987, when both were staff accountants at the Detroit office of Pannell Kerr & Forster. Rybicki and Ajemian both played on Pannell Kerr's softball team. They continued playing on the same team even after each had left Pannell Kerr, including while Ajemian was MCA's controller and Rybicki was the engagement manager for the MCA audits. Rybicki, Ajemian, and the remainder of the softball team often ate and drank together after the games.

Between 1993 and 1998, Rybicki and Ajemian occasionally spent weekends in Petosky, Michigan, where they stayed at a lakefront condominium owned by MCA. During the same time period, Rybicki and Ajemian spoke socially on the telephone, ate together, water-skied, and traveled to the Kentucky Derby. After MCA filed for bankruptcy in 1999 and Ajemian pled guilty in 2001 to federal criminal charges in connection with his conduct at MCA, Rybicki and Ajemian continued socializing. They dined together, attended sporting events, played on the same softball team, and traveled together.

While acting as MCA's auditors, Doeren Mayhew and Grant Thornton personnel, including Behrens, Morris, and Rybicki, sometimes attended a party, known as the "Bean Counters Bash," held by Ajemian annually at his home and paid for by MCA. This party was held to celebrate the completion of the annual audit. MCA executives provided Doeren Mayhew and Grant Thornton auditors with free tickets to Detroit Red Wings hockey games and University of Michigan football games. MCA executives also invited the auditors to tailgate parties paid for by MCA at the football games. Rybicki obtained a personal mortgage through MCA for approximately $59,000 to purchase his house in the early 1990s.

During the 1998 MCA audit, Behrens, Morris, and Rybicki knew that millions of dollars of the mortgages and land contracts held for resale reported in MCA's 1998 annual financial statements consisted of related-party mortgages and land contracts. Behrens, Morris, and Rybicki obtained this knowledge through their preparation of the 1998 MCA audit plan, their review of the 1998 audit workpapers and other materials, their performance of audit procedures during the 1998 audit, their communications with MCA executives, and/or their knowledge of MCA's business from prior audits.

Specifically with respect to the workpapers, Behrens and Rybicki reviewed them as part of the 1998 MCA audit, which showed that MCA sold approximately $10.8 million in real estate to the Related Limited Partnerships in fiscal year 1998. Those workpapers also showed that MCA advanced the Related Limited Partnerships a small down payment for the real estate and accepted an executed mortgage or land contract for the remaining portion of the purchase price. Those workpapers further calculated that approximately $4.9 million of those related-party mortgages and land contracts had not been sold as of MCA's balance sheet date and thus were included in the total mortgages or land contracts held for resale as reported in MCA's 1998 annual financial statements. Rybicki prepared, and Behrens and Morris reviewed, a workpaper in connection with the 1998 MCA audit entitled "Audit Planning." In this workpaper, Rybicki assessed the audit risk on the MCA engagement as high. Later in the workpaper, Rybicki noted that the reasons for the high-risk assessment were that MCA had "significant and/or frequent difficult-to-audit transactions or balances" and "material, related-party transactions on a recurring basis." Behrens and Rybicki also reviewed workpapers as part of the 1998 MCA audit that contained balance sheets for the Related Limited Partnerships reflecting approximately $57.3 million in liabilities under the heading of Mortgages and Land Contracts Payable. Behrens and Rybicki additionally reviewed workpapers as part of the 1998 MCA audit that showed approximately $4 million of MCA's land contracts held for resale, those that had been pledged as collateral for one of MCA's debenture offerings, were related-party land contracts.

During the 1998 MCA audit, Behrens, Morris, and Rybicki read MCA's 1998 annual financial statements. Those financial statements did not disclose any related-party mortgages or land contracts held for resale or state the total amount of such mortgages and land contracts held for resale. Grant Thornton and Doeren Mayhew issued a report, dated April 28, 1998, containing an unqualified opinion on MCA's 1998 annual financial statements, even though Behrens, Morris, and Rybicki knew that MCA had failed to disclose material, related-party mortgages, and land contracts.

a. Summarize the nature of the fraud perpetrated by MCA involving related-entity transactions, and describe the problems with the lack of disclosure and engagement review.

b. Summarize the nature of the inappropriate relationships between MCA and its auditors.

c. Discuss how the concepts of auditor independence, ethics, and professional skepticism are related, with an emphasis on the facts in this case. Discuss the issue of what personal relationships are or are not acceptable between an audit firm and the client.

d. Recommend changes that these audit firms should make to improve their quality-control procedures.

APPLICATION ACTIVITIES

NOTE: Completing *Application Activities* requires students to reference additional resources and materials. Some Application Activities will require the student to reference relevant professional auditing standards. We make special note of these as Auditing Standards Application Activities.

PROFESSIONAL SKEPTICISM

INTERNATIONAL

14-98 **Medicis Pharmaceutical Corporation and Ernst & Young (LO 3, 14)** Refer to the *Auditing in Practice* feature "PCAOB Fines Ernst & Young for an Issue Involving Accounting Estimates."

a. Auditors are required to provide reasonable assurances regarding accounting estimates. How did the Ernst & Young partners fail in this regard?

b. Based on the facts in the case, it appears that high-level Ernst & Young partners also were concerned that the financial accounting and disclosure policy for Medicis was improper. Yet, the partners on the actual Medicis engagement went ahead and issued an unqualified audit report anyway. What factors might have caused the engagement partners to fail to exercise professional skepticism?

c. To understand the pressure to maintain the company's stock price, access Yahoo Finance or another similar online source for historical stock prices. What was the approximate stock price for Medicis from 2005 through 2007? What happened to the stock price leading up to the restatement in November 2008? (*Hint*: Look at the stock prices from about June 2008 to early December 2008). How has the stock price changed since that time?

d. What are the most important risks that Medicis would present to an audit firm following the restatement? Access Medicis' most recent 10-K on the SEC's web site. Who is their current audit firm? What is the audit fee? Be prepared to discuss your opinions about these facts.

14-99 **Siemens (LO 4)** Refer to *Exhibit 14.2*, which provides an example of an IFRS disclosure checklist relating to goodwill disclosures. Access the most recently available financial statements of Siemens (*www.siemens.com/investor/en/financials/annual_reports.htm*). Locate and read the goodwill disclosures in the company's footnotes. Be prepared to discuss the nature of the disclosures.

14-100 **Siemens (LO 4)** Access the most recently available annual report of Siemens (*www.siemens.com/investor/en/financials/annual_reports. htm*). Locate and read the MD&A section of the report. Comment on why the audit report does not provide assurance regarding the MD&A.

14-101 **LO 6** Access the financial statements of two companies, one that you have heard is experiencing significant financial problems or that has entered bankruptcy, and another that you have heard is relatively financially sound. Calculate the Altman Z-Score for each company and compare the results. Be prepared to discuss your results.

14-102 **Northwest Airlines and Ernst & Young (LO 6)** On February 25, 2005, Ernst & Young LLP issued the following opinion about the financial statements of Northwest Airlines:

> We also have audited, in accordance with the standards of the Public Company Accounting Oversight Board (U.S.), the consolidated balance sheets of Northwest Airlines Corporation as of December 31, 2004 and 2003, and the related consolidated statements of operations, stockholders' equity (deficit), and cash flows for each of the three years in the

period ended December 31, 2004. Our report dated February 25, 2005 expressed an unqualified opinion thereon.

On September 14, 2005, Northwest Airlines filed for bankruptcy. On March 13, 2006, Ernst & Young LLP issued the following opinion about the financial statements of Northwest Airlines:

> We also have audited, in accordance with the standards of the Public Company Accounting Oversight Board (U.S.) the consolidated balance sheets of Northwest Airlines Corporation (Debtor-in-Possession) as of December 31, 2005 and 2004, and the related consolidated statements of operations, stockholders' equity (deficit), and cash flows for each of the three years in the period ended December 31, 2004. Our report dated March 13, 2006 expressed an unqualified opinion thereon and included explanatory paragraphs related to (i) the Company's reorganization under *Chapter 11* of the U.S. Bankruptcy Code, (ii) the Company's ability to continue as a going concern, and (iii) the change in method of recognizing certain pension plan administrative expenses associated with the Company's defined benefit pension plans.

Surely, Ernst & Young realized that Northwest was in serious financial difficulty as of early 2005.

a. Do you think that Ernst & Young provided adequate warning to users of Northwest's financial statements as of February 25, 2005?

b. Whose responsibility is it to recognize and report problems regarding the going-concern status of a company? Review *Exhibit 14.3* and briefly describe the main steps the auditor should follow when assessing the going-concern status of a company.

c. Auditors cannot predict the future. Given this, what should the auditor's responsibility be to determine whether a company is likely to remain in operation as a going concern?

d. Why might Ernst & Young have been reluctant to issue an audit report highlighting problems regarding the going-concern status of Northwest Airlines in early 2005?

Groupon

14-103 (LO 8) Refer to *Exhibit 14.6* "Management Certifications at Groupon." Comment on the fact that the certification discusses management's responsibility regarding internal controls, and yet the 8-K disclosure notifies the users of Groupon's financial statements that the company has a material weakness in its internal controls. Access Yahoo Finance or another similar online source for historical stock prices. What was the stock price and volume during the period March 26 to April 2, 2012 (the period in which the restatement and internal control material weakness disclosure was made)? What are your thoughts about the change in the stock price and volume?

ETHICS

INTERNATIONAL

IRIDEX

14-104 (LO 6, 14) Access the following publicly available disclosures made by IRIDEX Corporation on the SEC's web site (*www.sec.gov*):

- 8-K filed 8–29–2007
- 10-K filed 3–30–2007
- 10-K filed 4–10–2008
- Def 14A (proxy) filed 4–28–2008
- Def 14A (proxy) filed 5–4–2009

a. Review the disclosures in the 10-K filed 3–30–2007. Imagine that you are on PwC's engagement team for the 12–31–2006 year-end audit of IRIDEX. Describe the key business that IRIDEX engages in and list its three most important strategies for success. What risk characteristics of the company indicate that it may have difficulties remaining a going concern?

b. Review the disclosures in the 8-K filed 8–29–2007. What is the purpose of the 8-K filing? What does it reveal about PwC's ongoing relationship with IRIDEX? Based on the disclosures made in the filing, what risk factors were likely most relevant to PwC in making their client continuance decision about IRIDEX?

c. Review the disclosures in the 10-K filed 4–10–2008. Which audit firm accepted IRIDEX as a new client following PwC's resignation? In what important ways does that audit firm differ from PwC? Considering the concept of audit firm portfolio management discussed in *Chapter 1*, discuss why it is reasonable for one audit firm to resign from a client like IRIDEX, and another audit firm to accept it as a new client immediately thereafter.

d. Review the audit fee and total fee disclosures in the Def 14A proxy statements filed 4–28–2008 and 5–4–2009. Use that information to compare and contrast the audit fees and total fees that IRIDEX paid to its auditors for the fiscal years ending 12–31–2006, 2007, and 2008. What inferences do you draw from that comparison?

e. Describe the ethical decisions that an auditor must make during portfolio management decisions, such as client acceptance and client continuance decisions. What is the relationship between ethics and audit quality?

INTERNATIONAL

AUDITING STANDARDS APPLICATION ACTIVITY

14-105 **LO 12** Refer to the *Standards Appendix* at the end of this book. Identify the relevant auditing standards (PCAOB, AICPA, and IAASB) relating to communicating with audit committees. Locate the standards on each organization's web site.

a. Compare the scope of communication intended in the PCAOB standard versus that of the harmonized AICPA/IAASB standards.

b. How do the AICPA/IAASB standards define "those charged with governance"?

c. The PCAOB standard notes that the prior auditing standard relating to this topic, AU 380 (1989), indicated that audit committee communications are incidental to the audit. The new PCAOB standard takes quite a different approach, articulating the critical importance of audit committee/auditor communication throughout the year, and certainly before the issuance of the audit report. Comment on why you think the profession has shifted its focus in this regard so significantly.

d. According to the PCAOB standard, what are the four objectives of the auditor in communicating with the audit committee?

INTERNATIONAL

AUDITING STANDARDS APPLICATION ACTIVITY

14-106 Quality control is pervasive throughout the audit and in completing the audit. No specific LO exists for this problem, but it applies to each activity in an underlying sense. Refer to the *Standards Appendix* at the end of this book. Identify the relevant auditing standards (PCAOB, AICPA, and IAASB) relating to quality control. Locate the standards on each organization's web site.

a. Contrast the PCAOB standard (which is simply the original AICPA standard) with the new harmonized AICPA/IAASB standards.

b. What is the objective of the AICPA/IAASB standard?

c. With respect to the AICPA/IAASB standard, how does engagement quality review fit into the overall context of the standard?

ACADEMIC RESEARCH CASE

NOTE: Completing the *Academic Research Case* requires students to reference additional resources and materials.

SEARCH HINT

It is easy to locate academic research articles! Use a search engine such as Google Scholar or an electronic research platform such as ABI Inform, and search using the author names and part of the article title.

14-107 **LO 6** Locate and read the article listed below and answer the following questions.

Bruynseels, L., W. R. Knechel, and M. Willekens. 2013. Turnaround initiatives and auditors' going-concern judgment: Memory for audit evidence. *Auditing: A Journal of Practice & Theory* 32 (3): 105–121.

a. What is the issue being addressed in the paper?

b. What are the findings of the paper?

c. Why is this paper important to auditors, and what are the implications of this paper for the auditing profession?

d. Describe the research methodology used as a basis for the conclusions.

e. Describe any limitations of the research.

FORD AND TOYOTA

	Ford Motor Company and Toyota Motor Corporation
14-108	(LO **6**)

Source and Reference	Question
Ford 10-K or Annual Report and Toyota Annual Report	1. Calculate the Altman Z-score for Ford and Toyota. What inferences do you draw from these values? What inferences do you draw from comparing the values across the two companies? (You may assume that the market value of equity for Ford and Toyota, respectively, as of their 2014 fiscal year ends, is $38 billion and $110 billion.)
	2. What do you predict would happen if Ford's auditors issued a going-concern audit opinion? How would suppliers react? How would debt holders react?
	3. Why might an audit firm be hesitant to issue a going-concern opinion?
	4. What would happen to an audit firm if it did *not* issue a going-concern opinion and the company goes bankrupt in the following year?

15 Audit Reports on Financial Statements

CHAPTER OVERVIEW AND LEARNING OBJECTIVES

Auditing standards for financial statement and integrated audits require auditors to provide **positive assurance**—that is, an explicit statement as to whether the financial statements are presented fairly and, for larger U.S. public companies, whether internal control over financial reporting is effective. The professional auditing standards provide the rules that the auditors should follow when making reporting decisions, and there exist some differences in audit report requirements across the standards of the AICPA, PCAOB, and IAASB.

With respect to the financial statements, the expectation of both the auditor and the client is usually that the report includes an **unqualified**

opinion (also referred to as an **unmodified opinion**); that is, the auditor has no reservations about the fairness of presentation. However, the auditor may have reasons for reservations about the fairness of presentation, or the auditor may have been precluded from gathering sufficient appropriate evidence to render an opinion. For other engagements, the auditor may be able to provide an unqualified opinion, but will also include additional explanatory language as part of the audit report.

In terms of the audit opinion formulation process, this chapter focuses on the reporting decision component of Phase V.

Through studying this chapter, you will be able to achieve these learning objectives:

1. Identify and describe the principles underlying audit reporting on financial statements.

2. Describe the information that is included in a standard unqualified audit report on financial statements and list the requirements for issuing a standard unqualified report on financial statements.

3. Describe financial statement audits requiring an unqualified report with explanatory language and identify the appropriate audit report modifications.

4. Describe financial statement audits requiring a qualified report and identify the appropriate audit report modifications.

5. Describe financial statement audits requiring an adverse report and identify the appropriate audit report modifications.

6. Describe financial statement audits requiring a disclaimer of opinion and identify the communication the auditor is required to provide.

7. Assess various reporting situations requiring other than a standard unqualified report and determine the appropriate audit report that should be issued.

8. Describe the information that is included in a standard unqualified audit report on internal control over financial reporting and identify the appropriate audit report modifications for situations requiring other than an unqualified report on internal control over financial reporting.

9. Apply the frameworks for professional decision making and ethical decision making to issues involving audit reporting situations.

THE AUDIT OPINION FORMULATION PROCESS

| I. Making Client Acceptance and Continuance Decisions **Chapter 1** | II. Performing Risk Assessment **Chapters 3, 7, and 9–13** | III. Obtaining Evidence About Internal Control Operating Effectiveness **Chapters 8–13 and 16** | IV. Obtaining Substantive Evidence About Accounts, Disclosures and Assertions **Chapters 8–13 and 16** | V. Completing the Audit and Making Reporting Decisions **Chapters 14 and 15** |

The Auditing Profession, the Risk of Fraud and Mechanisms to Address Fraud: Regulation, Corporate Governance, and Audit Quality
Chapters 1 and 2

Professional Liability and the Need for Quality Auditor Judgments and Ethical Decisions
Chapter 4

The Audit Opinion Formulation Process and a Framework for Obtaining Audit Evidence
Chapters 5 and 6

PROFESSIONAL JUDGMENT IN CONTEXT

Debate Changes in Audit Reports

For the last several years, both the Public Company Accounting Oversight Board (PCAOB) and the International Auditing and Assurance Standards Board (IAASB) have been considering important changes to the standard unqualified audit report.

PCAOB:

On August 13, 2013, the PCAOB issued a proposed auditing standard on reporting, "The Auditor's Report on an Audit of Financial Statements When the Auditor Expresses an Unqualified Opinion." The PCAOB notes that while the current "pass/fail" model of the auditor report is useful in that it clearly indicates whether the financial statements are fairly presented, the audit report provides only information about an audit in general, not information that is uniquely specific to the particular audit client that is the subject of the report. The PCAOB's view is such unique information about the audit client would be valuable to users of the financial statements.

Following are the three key changes to the auditor's report that the PCAOB proposed:

1. Requiring the auditor to communicate in the auditor's report **critical audit matters** that

were addressed during the current-period audit, or stating that no critical audit matters existed
2. Adding information to the auditor's report relating to auditor independence, audit firm tenure on the engagement, and the auditor's responsibility for and evaluation of other information in annual reports (i.e., information other than the financial statements or associated footnotes)
3. Enhancing standardized language in the auditor's report, specifically adding the phrase "whether due to error or fraud" when referring to assurance about whether the financial statements are free of material misstatements, whether due to error or fraud

For further details on the proposed standard, see PCAOB Release No. 2013-005.

This proposed standard continues to be debated, and the latest public meeting on the topic (as of this writing) occurred on April 2 and 3, 2014 at the PCAOB offices in Washington, DC.

For a transcript of those meetings, see http:// pcaobus.org/Rules/Rulemaking/Docket034/04022014 _Transcript.pdf and http://pcaobus.org/Rules/Rule making/Docket034/04032014_Transcript.pdf

IAASB:

In July 2013, the IAASB issued a comprehensive slate of proposed audit standards relating to changes in auditor reporting intended to improve the usefulness of the auditor's report. These include the following new and revised International Standards on Auditing (ISAs):

- Proposed ISA 700 (Revised), "Forming an Opinion and Reporting on Financial Statements"
- Proposed ISA 701, "Communicating Key Audit Matters in the Independent Auditor's Report"
- Proposed ISA 260 (Revised), "Communication with Those Charged with Governance"
- Proposed ISA 570 (Revised), "Going Concern"
- Proposed ISA 705 (Revised), "Modifications to the Opinion in the Independent Auditor's Report"
- Proposed ISA 706 (Revised), "Emphasis of Matter Paragraphs and Other Matter Paragraphs in the Independent Auditor's Report"

The expansiveness of this list of proposed changes illustrates the importance of auditor reporting, and suggests that we can expect to see significant changes in auditor reporting in the near future. In *Emerging Issues* features throughout this chapter, we will expand on some of these IAASB proposed standards.

For *further details, see https://www.ifac.org /publications-resources/reporting-audited-financial -statements-proposed-new-and-revised-international*

As you read through this chapter, consider the following questions:

- What information is currently included in the standard unqualified audit report? (LO 2)
- How does the standard unqualified audit report issued for U.S. public companies differ from the standard report issued in other parts of the world or for U.S. nonpublic companies? (LO 2)
- What types of additional information could be included in the standard unqualified audit report? (LO 2)
- What circumstances require a deviation from the standard unqualified audit report? (LO 3, 4, 5, 6)
- What changes can we expect with regard to emerging issues in auditor reporting? (LO 2, 3, 4, 5 6, 7)

Principles Underlying Audit Reporting

LO 1 Identify and describe the principles underlying audit reporting on financial statements.

The auditor needs to form an opinion on the financial statements based on an evaluation of the audit evidence obtained, and clearly express that opinion through a written report. The American Institute of Certified Public Accountants (AICPA) first and seventh principles governing an audit conducted in accordance with generally accepted auditing standards (GAAS) describe the principles underlying audit reporting (AICPA, *Preface to Codification of Statements on Auditing Standards, Principles Underlying an Audit Conducted in Accordance With Generally Accepted Auditing Standards*).

Principle 1. "The purpose of an audit is to provide financial statement users with an opinion by the auditor on whether the financial statements are presented fairly, in all material respects, in accordance with the applicable financial reporting framework. An auditor's opinion enhances the degree of confidence that intended users can place in the financial statements."

Principle 7. "Based on an evaluation of the audit evidence obtained, the auditor expresses, in the form of a written report, an opinion in accordance with the auditor's findings, or states that an opinion cannot be expressed. The opinion states whether the financial statements are presented fairly, in all material respects, in accordance with the applicable financial reporting framework."

These principles basically require auditors either to express an unqualified opinion on the entire set of financial statements and related footnotes, including all years presented for comparative purposes, or to state the reasons that such an opinion cannot be expressed. If the auditor concludes that the statements are not fairly presented, and the auditor cannot resolve the issue with management, the auditor needs to determine whether the opinion should be modified. The auditor would modify the opinion if the auditor determines that the financial statements as a whole are misstated and would issue either a qualified or an adverse opinion. Additionally, the auditor would modify the opinion if the auditor was not able to obtain sufficient appropriate evidence and would issue either a qualified opinion or disclaimer.

Standard Unqualified Audit Reports on Financial Statements

LO 2 Describe the information that is included in a standard unqualified audit report on financial statements and list the requirements for issuing a standard unqualified report on financial statements.

Standard unqualified audit reports on financial statements differ depending on whether the report is issued for a U.S. public company, a U.S. nonpublic company, or a non-U.S. company.

Standard Unqualified Audit Reports: U.S. Public Companies

Audit reports are designed to promote clear communication between the auditor and the financial statement user by delineating:

- What was audited and the relative responsibilities of the client and the auditor (introductory paragraph)
- The nature of the audit process (scope paragraph)
- The auditor's opinion on the fairness of the financial statements (opinion paragraph)

As discussed in the *Auditing in Practice* feature reports also covering internal control over financial reporting include additional information. Other important components of an audit report include:

- A title that includes the word *independent*
- An addressee, which for public companies would be the board of directors or shareholders of the organization, but varies depending on the circumstances of the engagement
- An audit report date that is no earlier than the date on which the auditor has obtained sufficient appropriate evidence to support the opinion
- Signature of audit firm
- The city and state from which the auditor's report has been issued

Audit Reports That Refer to an Audit of Internal Control Over Financial Reporting

AUDITING IN PRACTICE

For large U.S. public companies, the auditor's report also refers to the audit of internal control over financial reporting. The auditor may issue a separate report on internal controls or a combined report on both the financial statements and internal controls. If a separate report is issued, the report on the financial statements includes a paragraph after the scope paragraph (before the opinion paragraph) indicating that an audit of internal controls was performed and providing an opinion. If a combined report on both the financial statements and internal control is issued, it includes two additional paragraphs:

- Definition paragraph (after the scope paragraph) that defines what is meant by internal control over financial reporting
- Inherent limitations paragraph (following the definition paragraph) that discusses why internal control may not prevent or detect misstatements

Requirements for a Standard Unqualified Audit Report on the Financial Statements for U.S. Public Companies

Panels A and B of *Exhibit 15.1* illustrate standard unqualified audit reports on financial statements following the PCAOB's reporting standards. Such reports can be issued for public companies only if

- there are no material violations of generally accepted accounting principles (GAAP),
- disclosures are adequate,
- the auditor was able to perform all of the necessary procedures,
- there was no change in accounting principles that had a material effect on the financial statements,
- the auditor does not have significant doubt about the client remaining a going concern, and
- the auditor is independent.

When these conditions are not present, the auditor needs to modify the standard unqualified report in one of the following ways, each of which is discussed later in the chapter:

- Issue an unqualified opinion with explanatory language
- Qualify the audit opinion
- Issue an adverse opinion
- Issue a disclaimer

Panel A of *Exhibit 15.1* shows an example of an unqualified audit opinion on financial statements when the auditor issues a separate unqualified report on the effectiveness of internal control. The fourth paragraph in Panel A of *Exhibit 15.1* (audit report for The Coca-Cola Company) summarizes and refers to a separate report on the client's internal controls. Panel B of *Exhibit 15.1* (audit report for Diageo plc) provides a similar report for a foreign-domiciled U.S. public company.

Both reports indicate that the auditors conducted the audit in accordance with PCAOB standards and that the internal control criteria was *Internal Control–Integrated Framework* issued by the Committee of Sponsoring Organizations of the Treadway Commission. The primary difference is that the Diageo report references International Financial Reporting Standards (IFRS) as the reporting framework and the International Accounting Standards Board (IASB) as the relevant accounting standard setter, whereas the Coca-Cola report references U.S. GAAP as the financial accounting reporting framework. The audit opinion formulation process used by auditors reporting on IFRS-based financial statements is generally similar to the process described in this book. However, the criteria on which auditors assess whether financial statements are fairly presented are IFRS.

The *Emerging Issues* feature "Proposed PCAOB Standard on Auditor Reporting" illustrates the elements of the proposed audit report for audits of U.S. public companies.

SEC Requirements for Timeliness of Reporting

The timeliness of the audit report matters. The Security and Exchange Commission (SEC) wants organizations—and their auditors—to provide timely financial information to investors while allowing for enough time to gather sufficient appropriate audit evidence. The SEC also recognizes that smaller companies may not have the same resources to report on a timely fashion compared to larger companies. *Exhibit 15.2* shows how timeliness requirements vary by the size of the organization.

EXHIBIT **15.1**	Examples of Unqualified Audit Reports

Panel A: Unqualified Report on an Integrated Audit for a U.S. Public Company: The Coca-Cola Company

Report of Independent Registered Public Accounting Firm

Board of Directors and Shareowners
The Coca-Cola Company

We have audited the accompanying consolidated balance sheets of The Coca-Cola Company and subsidiaries as of December 31, 2013 and 2012, and the related consolidated statements of income, comprehensive income, shareowners' equity, and cash flows for each of the three years in the period ended December 31, 2013. These financial statements are the responsibility of the Company's management. Our responsibility is to express an opinion on these financial statements based on our audits.

We conducted our audits in accordance with the standards of the Public Company Accounting Oversight Board (U.S.). Those standards require that we plan and perform the audit to obtain reasonable assurance about whether the financial statements are free of material misstatement. An audit includes examining, on a test basis, evidence supporting the amounts and disclosures in the financial statements. An audit also includes assessing the accounting principles used and significant estimates made by management, as well as evaluating the overall financial statement presentation. We believe that our audits provide a reasonable basis for our opinion.

In our opinion, the financial statements referred to above present fairly, in all material respects, the consolidated financial position of The Coca-Cola Company and subsidiaries at December 31, 2013 and 2012, and the consolidated results of their operations and their cash flows for each of the three years in the period ended December 31, 2013, in conformity with U.S. generally accepted accounting principles.

We also have audited, in accordance with the standards of the Public Company Accounting Oversight Board (U.S.), The Coca-Cola Company and subsidiaries' internal control over financial reporting as of December 31, 2013, based on criteria established in *Internal Control—Integrated Framework* issued by the Committee of Sponsoring Organizations of the Treadway Commission (1992 Framework) and our report dated February 27, 2014 expressed an unqualified opinion thereon.

Ernst & Young LLP

Atlanta, Georgia

February 27, 2014

Source: The Coca-Cola Company. Form 10- K, p. 138, via EDGAR, accessed June 2014. http://www.sec.gov/Archives/edgar/data/21344 /000002134414000008/a2013123110-k.htm This publicly available report can be found on p. 138 at the following SEC website: http: //www.sec.gov/Archives/edgar/data/21344/000002134414000008/a2013123110-k.htm

Panel B: Unqualified Report on an Integrated Audit for a Foreign-Domiciled U.S. Public Company: Diageo plc

Report of Independent Registered Public Accounting Firm

The board of directors and shareholders
Diageo plc:

    We have audited the accompanying consolidated balance sheets of Diageo plc and subsidiaries as of 30 June 2013 and 2012, and the related consolidated income statements, consolidated statements of comprehensive income, consolidated statements of changes in equity and consolidated statements of cash flows for each of the years in the

(continued)

EXHIBIT **15.1**	Examples of Unqualified Audit Reports (*continued*)

three-year period ended 30 June 2013 on pages 159 to 245, including the disclosures identified as 'part of the audited financial statements' within the 'Critical accounting policies' section on pages 82 to 83, the 'Share and other interests' on pages 134 to 135, the 'Key management personnel related party transactions' on pages 135 to 136 and the 'Principal group companies' on page 246. These consolidated financial statements are the responsibility of Diageo plc's management. Our responsibility is to express an opinion on these consolidated financial statements based on our audits.

We conducted our audits in accordance with the standards of the Public Company Accounting Oversight Board (U.S.). Those standards require that we plan and perform the audit to obtain reasonable assurance about whether the financial statements are free of material misstatement. An audit includes examining, on a test basis, evidence supporting the amounts and disclosures in the financial statements. An audit also includes assessing the accounting principles used and significant estimates made by management, as well as evaluating the overall financial statement presentation. We believe that our audits provide a reasonable basis for our opinion.

In our opinion, the consolidated financial statements referred to above present fairly, in all material respects, the financial position of Diageo plc and subsidiaries as of 30 June 2013, and 2012, and the results of their operations and their cash flows for each of the years in the three-year period ended 30 June 2013, in conformity with International Financial Reporting Standards (IFRS) as issued by the International Accounting Standards Board and IFRS as adopted by the European Union.

We also have audited, in accordance with the standards of the Public Company Accounting Oversight Board (U.S.), Diageo plc's internal control over financial reporting as of 30 June 2013, based on criteria established in *Internal Control—Integrated Framework (1992)* issued by the Committee of Sponsoring Organizations of the Treadway Commission (COSO), and our report dated 30 July 2013 expressed an unqualified opinion on the effectiveness of the company's internal control over financial reporting.

KPMG Audit Plc

KPMG Audit Plc
London, England
30 July 2013

Source: *DIAGEO plc. Form 20-F, p. 158, via EDGAR, accessed June 2014. http://www.sec.gov/Archives/edgar/data/835403/000104746 913008348/a2216206z20-f.htm#rirpaf See p. 158 on the SEC website: http://www.sec.gov/Archives/edgar/data/835403/0001047 46913008348/a2216206z20-f.htm#rirpaf*

EXHIBIT **15.2**	SEC Reporting Requirements

Size of Filer	Form 10-K (Annual Report)
Large accelerated filer—Market capitalization greater than $700 million	60 days after year end
Accelerated filer—Market capitalization greater than $75 million, but less than $700 million	75 days after year end
Nonaccelerated filer—Market capitalization less than $75 million	90 days after year end

Proposed PCAOB Standard on Auditor Reporting

EMERGING ISSUE

PCAOB Release No. 2013-005 Appendix B provides an illustrative unqualified audit report that conforms to the PCAOB's proposed standard. The underlined portions are those that differ from the current auditor report language that you see in *Exhibit 15.1* Panels A and B. Key proposed differences that you will notice include:

- Specific mention of the footnotes to the financial statements
- Registration status of the audit firm with the PCAOB
- A statement indicating the length of time the audit firm has provided audit services to the client
- Making note of the fact that misstatements may be due to either error or fraud
- Discussion of critical audit matters
- Discussion of the auditor's responsibility regarding other information contained in the annual report

"Report of Independent Registered Public Accounting Firm

To the shareholders and board of directors of X Company

[Introduction]

We have audited the accompanying balance sheets of X Company (the "Company") as of December 31, 20X2 and 20X1, the related statements of operations, stockholders' equity, and cash flows, for each of the three years in the period ended December 31, 20X2, and the related notes (collectively referred to as the "financial statements"). These financial statements are the responsibility of the Company's management.

We are a public accounting firm registered with the Public Company Accounting Oversight Board ("PCAOB") (U.S.) and are required to be independent with respect to the Company in accordance with the U.S. federal securities laws and the applicable rules and regulations of the Securities and Exchange Commission ("SEC") and the PCAOB. We or our predecessor firms have served as the Company's auditor consecutively since [year].

[Basis of Opinion]

Our responsibility is to express an opinion on the Company's financial statements based on our audits.

We conducted our audits in accordance with the standards of the PCAOB. Those standards require that we plan and perform the audit to obtain reasonable assurance about whether the financial statements are free of material misstatement, whether due to error or fraud.

Our audits included performing procedures to assess the risks of material misstatement of the financial statements, whether due to error or fraud, and performing procedures that respond to those risks. Such procedures include examining, on a test basis, appropriate evidence regarding the amounts and disclosures in the financial statements. Our audits also included evaluating the accounting principles used and significant estimates made by management, as well as evaluating the overall presentation of the financial statements. We believe that our audits provide a reasonable basis for our opinion.

[Opinion on the Financial Statements]

In our opinion, the financial statements referred to above present fairly, in all material respects, the financial position of the Company as of [at] December 31, 20X2 and 20X1, and the results of its operations and its cash flows for each of the three years in the period ended December 31, 20X2, in conformity with [the applicable financial reporting framework].

Critical Audit Matters

The standards of the PCAOB require that we communicate in our report critical audit matters relating to the audit of the current period's financial statements or state that we determined that there are no critical audit matters. Critical audit matters are those matters addressed during the audit that (1) involved our most difficult, subjective, or complex judgments; (2) posed the most difficulty to us in obtaining sufficient appropriate evidence; or (3) posed the most difficulty to us in forming our opinion on the financial statements. The critical audit matters communicated below do not alter in any way our opinion on the financial statements, taken as a whole.

[Include critical audit matters]

The Auditor's Responsibilities Regarding Other Information

In addition to auditing the Company's financial statements in accordance with the standards of the

(Continued)

PCAOB, we evaluated whether the other information, included in the annual report on [*SEC Exchange Act form type*] filed with the SEC that contains both the December 31, 20X2 financial statements and our audit report on those financial statements, contains a material inconsistency with the financial statements, a material misstatement of fact, or both. Our evaluation was based on relevant audit evidence obtained and conclusions reached during the audit. We did not audit the other information and do not express an opinion on the other information. Based on our evaluation, we have not identified a material inconsistency or a material misstatement of fact in the other information.

[*Signature*]

[*City and State or Country*]

[Date]"

Clearly, the wording of the proposed auditing standard is a dramatic departure from the current audit report wording. Watch for further developments on this important issue that are emerging presently. The PCAOB is currently proposing that the effective date for the new standard on auditor reporting could occur as early as for fiscal years ending December 15, 2015, so changes will likely be happening fairly soon.

Standard Unqualified Audit Reports: U.S. Nonpublic Companies and Non-U.S. Companies

U.S. Nonpublic Companies

The components of the audit report for U.S. nonpublic companies are similar to those described for public companies. However, there are some formatting differences because of requirements for specific headings included in the AICPA auditing standards and additional disclosures. Audit reports for U.S. nonpublic companies detail:

- What was audited (introductory paragraph)
- Responsibilities of client management (management's responsibility paragraph; should include the heading "Management's Responsibility for the Financial Statements")
- Responsibilities of the auditor and the nature of the audit process (scope paragraph; should include the heading "Auditor's Responsibility")
- The auditor's opinion on the fairness of the financial statements (opinion paragraph; should include the heading "Opinion")

The language contained in the management's responsibility paragraph is:

Management is responsible for the preparation and fair presentation of these consolidated financial statements in accordance with accounting principles generally accepted in the United States of America; this includes the design, implementation, and maintenance of internal control relevant to the preparation and fair presentation of consolidated financial statements that are free from material misstatement, whether due to fraud or error. (AICPA, AU-C 700, Appendix A)

The language contained in the auditor's responsibility paragraph is:

Our responsibility is to express an opinion on these consolidated financial statements based on our audits. We conducted our audits in accordance with auditing standards generally accepted in the United States of America. Those standards require that we plan and perform the audit to obtain reasonable assurance about whether the consolidated financial statements are free from material misstatement.

An audit involves performing procedures to obtain audit evidence about the amounts and disclosures in the consolidated financial statements. The procedures selected depend on the auditor's judgment, including the assessment of the risks of material misstatement of the consolidated financial statements, whether due to fraud or error. In making those risk assessments, the auditor considers internal control relevant to the entity's preparation and fair presentation of the consolidated financial statements in order to design audit procedures that are appropriate in the circumstances, but not for the purpose of expressing an opinion on the effectiveness of the entity's internal control. Accordingly, we express no such opinion. An audit also includes evaluating the appropriateness of accounting policies used and the reasonableness of significant accounting estimates made by management, as well as evaluating the overall presentation of the consolidated financial statements.

We believe that the audit evidence we have obtained is sufficient and appropriate to provide a basis for our audit opinion. (AICPA, AU-C 700, Appendix A)

Multiple Sets of Auditing Standards   For some engagements, the financial statements might be audited in accordance with multiple auditing standards, for example, those generally accepted in the United States of America (GAAS) and International Standards on Auditing (ISA). For those engagements, the auditor's responsibility section should include the following language:

We conducted our audits in accordance with auditing standards generally accepted in the United States of America and in accordance with International Standards on Auditing. (AICPA, AU-C 700, Appendix A)

Non-U.S. Companies

Auditors following the ISAs would refer to ISA 700 for relevant guidance, which is generally consistent with the AICPA's AU-C 700, although there are terminology differences. These differences, however, do not create differences between the applications of the two sets of auditing standards. However, one terminology difference of note is that ISA 700 indicates that the description in the auditor's report can refer either to the preparation and fair presentation of the financial statements or the preparation of financial statements that give a true and fair view. U.S. auditing standards do not include any references to *true and fair view* because such wording has not historically been used in the U.S.; GAAS continues to require the use of *present fairly, in all material respects* in the auditor's opinion.

A major shift in auditor reporting for non-U.S. companies will occur with the final adoption of the currently proposed ISA 701, "Communicating Key Audit Matters in the Independent Auditor's Report," which will likely be required for audits of financial statements with fiscal year end December 31, 2016, at the earliest. The *Emerging Issues* feature "Changes in Auditor Reporting: An International Perspective" provides details on how some countries already require auditors that are reporting on companies which apply the UK Corporate Governance Code to explain more about their work.

Unqualified Audit Reports with Explanatory Language

LO 3 Describe financial statement audits requiring an unqualified report with explanatory language and identify the appropriate audit report modifications.

There are five situations in which an auditor may choose to issue an unqualified audit report, but include additional explanatory language. Explanatory language would be used to explain the following:

- A justified departure from GAAP
- Inconsistent application of GAAP
- Substantial doubt about the client being a going concern
- The emphasis of some matter, such as unusually important subsequent events, risks, or uncertainties associated with contingencies or significant estimates
- Reference to other auditors (group audits and component auditors)

Changes in Auditor Reporting: An International Perspective

Some country-specific ISAs already require enhanced auditor reporting. For example, in June 2013, revisions to ISA 700 (UK and Ireland) "The Independent Auditor's Report on Financial Statements" were approved and auditors reporting on companies which apply the UK Corporate Governance Code were required to explain more about their work. Specifically, auditors need to:

- Provide an overview of the scope of the audit, showing how this addressed the risk and materiality considerations
- Describe the risks that had the greatest effect on:
  - The overall audit strategy
  - The allocation of resources in the audit
  - Directing the efforts of the engagement team
- Provide an explanation of how they applied the concept of materiality in planning and performing the audit

The startling thing about these auditor disclosures is the significant level of detail about the client's financial reporting, the risks identified by the auditor, and the auditor's responses to the identified risks; this level of detail is a fundamental shift from prior auditor reporting disclosure conventions.

One of the most notable of these audit reports is that made by KPMG relating to its audit of the December 31, 2013, financial statements of Rolls-Royce Holdings, plc (Rolls-Royce). The audit report is six pages in length, and includes the identification of 11 separate risk areas, along with a description of the auditor response and conclusion with respect to each risk area. In addition, and unlike disclosure in the U.S., an individual auditor employed by KPMG personally signs the audit report with his/her name. For brevity, we reproduce half of the first page of the audit report, which articulates the first risk factor, the auditor's response to it, and the auditor's findings with respect to that risk factor.

> **"INDEPENDENT AUDITOR'S REPORT**
> to the members of Rolls-Royce Holdings plc only
> Opinions and conclusions arising from our audit

1. Our opinion on the financial statements is unmodified

We have audited the financial statements of Rolls-Royce Holdings plc for the year ended 31 December 2013 set out on pages 75 to 129. In our opinion:

- the financial statements give a true and fair view of the state of the Group's and of the parent company's affairs as at 31 December 2013 and of the Group's profit for the year then ended;
- the Group financial statements have been properly prepared in accordance with International Financial Reporting Standards as adopted by the European Union (Adopted IFRS);
- the parent company financial statements have been properly prepared in accordance with UK Accounting Standards; and
- the financial statements have been prepared in accordance with the requirements of the Companies Act 2006 and, as regards the Group financial statements, Article 4 of the IAS Regulation.

2. Our assessment of risks

In arriving at our opinions set out in this report, the risks that had the greatest effect on our audit and the key procedures we applied to address them are set out below. Those procedures were designed in the context of the financial statements as a whole and, consequently, where we set out findings we do not express any opinion on these individual risks.

The basis of accounting for revenue and profit in the Civil aerospace business

Refer to page 81 (Key areas of judgement—Long-term aftermarket contracts), page 83 (Significant accounting policies—Revenue recognition) and page 44 (Audit committee report—Financial reporting)

- *The risk* The amount of revenue and profit recognised in a year on the sale of engines and aftermarket services is dependent, inter alia, on the appropriate assessment of whether or not each long-term aftermarket contract for services is linked to or separate from the contract for sale of the related engines. As the commercial arrangements can be complex, significant judgement is applied in selecting the accounting basis in each case. The most significant risk is that the Group might inappropriately account for sales of engines and long term service agreements as a single arrangement for accounting purposes as this would usually lead to revenue and profit being recognised too early because the margin in the long term service agreement is usually higher than the margin in the engine sale agreement.
- *Our response* We made our own independent assessment, with reference to the relevant accounting standards, of the accounting basis that should be applied to each long-term aftermarket contract

(Continued)

entered into during the year and compared this to the accounting basis applied by the Group.

- *Our findings* We found that the Group has developed a framework for selecting the accounting basis to be used which is consistent with accounting standards and has applied this consistently. For almost all the agreements entered into during this year, it was clear which accounting basis should apply. Where there was room for interpretation, we found the Group's judgement to have been balanced."

NOTE: The audit report then goes on for another five pages, and concludes with the individual auditor signing the audit report on behalf of KPMG, as follows:

"**Jimmy Daboo (Senior Statutory Auditor)**
for and on behalf of KPMG Audit Plc, Statutory Auditor
Chartered Accountants
15 Canada Square
London
E14 5GL
12 February 2014"

Source: For the full auditor's report, access Rolls-Royce's FYE 2013 annual report on the company's web site at http://www.rolls-royce.com/investors/index.jsp. If you are interested in reading other such auditor reporting disclosures, access Vodafone Group's FYE annual report on the Company's website at http://www.vodafone.com/content/index/investors.html.

Explanatory Language: Justified Departure from GAAP

In rare circumstances, the client may have a justified departure from GAAP. Rule 203 of the AICPA *Code of Professional Conduct* permits the auditor to issue an unqualified opinion when there has been a material departure from GAAP if the client can demonstrate, and the auditor concurs, that due to unusual circumstances, the financial statements would have been misleading had GAAP been followed. What constitutes unusual circumstances is a matter of professional judgment. Examples include new legislation or the evolution of a new form of business transaction.

When a client has a justified departure from GAAP, the auditor should add an informational paragraph, either before or after the opinion paragraph, to describe the departure from GAAP, its approximate effects (if they can be practicably determined), and the reasons for which compliance with GAAP would result in misleading statements. *Exhibit 15.3* provides an example of possible audit report language that could be used to describe a justified departure from GAAP.

EXHIBIT **15.3**	Example of Possible Audit Report Language Describing a Justified Departure from GAAP

[Standard introductory and scope paragraphs would be followed by the explanatory paragraph provided below. The opinion paragraph would provide the standard unqualified opinion.]

As described in Note 3, in May, the company exchanged shares of its common stock for $5,060,000 of its outstanding public debt. The fair value of the common stock issued exceeded the carrying amount of the debt by $466,000, which has been shown as an extraordinary loss in the statement of operations. Because a portion of the debt exchanged was convertible debt, a literal application of FASB ASC Topic 470 "Debt" would have resulted in a further reduction in net income of $3,611,000, which would have been offset by a corresponding $3,611,000 credit to additional paid-in capital; accordingly, there would have been no net effect on stockholders' investments. In the opinion of company management, with which we agree, a literal application of accounting literature would have resulted in misleading financial statements that do not properly portray the economic consequences of the exchange.

Explanatory Language: Inconsistent Application of GAAP

Changes in accounting principles should be fully disclosed so that a user can make comparisons over time and between companies. A change in accounting principles includes a change from one GAAP to another, such as from FIFO to LIFO. A change from non-GAAP to GAAP—such as from the cash basis to the accrual basis—is accounted for as a correction of an error, but is treated by the auditor as a change in accounting principle requiring an explanatory paragraph. Both changes would require the auditor to add an explanatory paragraph to the audit report. If there is a change in reporting entity that is not due to a transaction or event, for example, a change to present consolidated statements rather than the statements of an individual company, the auditor would address this change by adding an explanatory paragraph. However, if the change in reporting entity arises from a transaction or event such as an acquisition, the auditor would not add an explanatory paragraph. Changes in accounting estimates and accounting for new transactions are not considered changes in accounting principles. However, a change in estimate affected by an accounting principle does require explanatory language in the audit report. An accounting change does not include a correction of an error in previously audited financial statements. However, AS 6 does require an additional paragraph for the correction of an error not involving an accounting principle for public companies.

If the client has changed an accounting principle, has reasonable justification for the change, and has followed GAAP in accounting for and disclosing this change, the explanatory paragraph serves as a flag directing the user's attention to the relevant footnote disclosure. This flag can be very useful. For example, consider a company that reported a 22% increase in net income and highlighted the increase several times in its annual report to shareholders. But only by noting the additional paragraph in the auditor's report and carefully reading the financial statements and footnotes would the user have seen that the increase in net income would have been only 6% had there not been a change in an accounting principle.

If the change in accounting principle is not justified or accounted for correctly, or there is inadequate disclosure, the auditor is dealing with a departure from GAAP. As we note later, a GAAP departure leads to either a qualified audit opinion or, in some cases, an adverse audit opinion.

Explanatory Language: Substantial Doubt About the Client Being a Going Concern

As discussed in *Chapter 14*, the auditor has a responsibility to evaluate whether there is substantial doubt about the client's ability to continue as a going concern for a reasonable period of time. If there is substantial doubt about the client's ability to remain a going concern, the auditor should issue an unqualified opinion that contains an explanatory paragraph following the opinion paragraph, as illustrated in *Exhibit 15.4* for Imperial Sugar Company. The explanatory paragraph should be clearly worded to indicate the auditor has *substantial doubt* about the client's continuing as a *going concern* and should refer to management's footnote(s) explaining the problems and plans to overcome the problems. *Exhibit 15.4* provides the auditor's explanatory paragraph in Panel A, along with management's explanation of the going-concern issue in Panel B.

For some going-concern situations in which the client is experiencing severe financial distress, the auditor may not want to express any opinion.

EXHIBIT 15.4   Unqualified Report with a Going-Concern Paragraph for Imperial Sugar Company

Panel A: Auditor Reporting on Going-Concern Issue

[The audit report on the 2011 financial statements of Imperial Sugar Company includes introductory, scope, and opinion paragraphs, along with the following going- concern explanatory paragraph.]

The accompanying consolidated financial statements have been prepared assuming that the Company will continue as a going concern. As discussed in Note 1 to the consolidated financial statements, the Company's operating losses, pension plan contributions and capital expenditures have consumed a significant amount of the Company's liquidity. As a result, the Company could trigger the applicability of the financial covenants and other restrictions under the credit agreement for which it will need to seek a waiver from its lenders in order to avoid an event of default under the credit agreement. These conditions raise substantial doubt about the Company's ability to continue as a going concern. Management's plans concerning these matters are also discussed in Note 1 to the consolidated financial statements. The consolidated financial statements do not include any adjustments that might result from the outcome of this uncertainty.

Panel B: Management's Explanation of the Going-Concern Issue in the Notes to the Consolidated Financial Statements

The consolidated financial statements have been prepared on the going–concern basis, which contemplates the realization of assets and satisfaction of liabilities in the ordinary course of business. However events and circumstances described below create substantial doubt about the Company's ability to continue as a going concern.

The Company's revolving credit agreement requires the maintenance of certain minimum availability levels or requires the Company to meet a financial covenant related to a minimum earnings level. Operating losses, pension plan contributions and capital expenditures have consumed a significant amount of the Company's liquidity. While the minimum availability levels under the credit agreement have not been breached, future cash needs, including capital expenditures, pension contributions and margin requirements of the commodity futures program, as well as the need to fund possible future operating losses in the event current margin pressures continue, the Company's borrowing availability in fiscal 2012 and beyond may be reduced to levels that would trigger the applicability of the financial covenants and other restrictions under the credit agreement. In such an event, it is possible that the Company will not be in compliance with such covenants and will need to seek a waiver from its lenders in order to avoid an event of default under the credit agreement. There is no assurance that such a waiver will be obtained from our lenders or that the lenders would not condition a waiver on the Company's agreement to terms that could materially limit the Company's ability to make additional borrowings or that could be otherwise disadvantageous.

The Company is attempting to enhance operating cash flow by increasing sales prices and improving operating efficiencies, and is reviewing opportunities to improve its liquidity, including potential sale of assets. In December 2011 the Company sold its one-third interest in Louisiana Sugar Refining, LLC ("LSR") rather than make additional capital contributions necessitated by the financial condition of the venture. The sales price for the Company's one-third interest and certain other assets was $18.0 million with $14.2 million received at closing and the balance payable over the next 21 months. The Company is exploring with its partner the potential of selling their interests in Wholesome Sweeteners, Inc. ("Wholesome") to a third party. Pursuant to the Wholesome joint venture agreement, if a third party agrees to pay a specified minimum price for Wholesome, subject to certain conditions, both the Company and its joint venture partner could be required to sell their interests. However, there is no assurance that these steps will be successful or will improve the Company's financial condition sufficiently to avoid the consequences under the bank credit agreement described above.

The Company's continuation as a going concern is dependant upon its ability to generate sufficient cash flows from operations or increase its liquidity through asset sales in order to meet its obligations as they become due. The consolidated financial statements do not include any adjustments relating to the recoverability and reclassification of recorded assets or amounts and reclassification of liabilities that may result from these uncertainties should the Company be unable to continue as a going concern.

Source: Imperial Sugar Company. 2011 Annual Report, p. 44, 50, via EDGAR, accessed February 2012. (http://www.sec.gov/Archives /edgar/data/831327/000119312512003953/d251187d10k.htm)

As discussed later in the chapter, in such cases, the auditor may issue a disclaimer of opinion. Finally, if the auditor is convinced that the company will be liquidated, then the auditor should indicate that liquidation values would be more appropriate.

Both the IAASB and PCAOB are considering changes in auditor reporting requirements with respect to issues involving going-concern status of clients. The *Emerging Issues* feature "Key Elements of IAASB and PCAOB Going–Concern Reporting Proposals" summarizes the potential new requirements and status of these projects.

Explanatory Language: Emphasis of a Matter

Auditors have the option of including a paragraph with an unqualified opinion to emphasize a matter regarding the financial statements. The choice to emphasize a matter is strictly one of auditor judgment. Examples of such matters that have been emphasized by audit firms in their reports include:

- Significant transactions with related entities
- Important subsequent events, such as a board-of-director decision to divest a major segment of the business
- Important risks or uncertainties associated with contingencies or significant estimates

Exhibit 15.5 illustrates an added paragraph for a change in fiscal year end for Morgan Stanley.

Key Elements of IAASB and PCAOB Going Concern Reporting Proposals

The IAASB's proposed standard on going concern requires the auditor to include a conclusion on whether management's use of a going–concern basis of accounting is appropriate in preparing the financial statements, and the auditor's report must state whether a material uncertainty that may cast significant doubt on the entity's ability to continue as a going concern has been identified. A material uncertainty about the entity's ability to remain a going concern is considered a key audit matter, but it would be presented outside the Key Audit Matters section of the auditor's report to illustrate its importance.

Below is an illustration of the IAASB's proposed wording in a situation in which there is no uncertainty with respect to the entity's ability to remain a going concern:

"Going Concern

The consolidated financial statements of the Group have been prepared using the going-concern basis of accounting. The use of this basis of accounting is appropriate unless management either intends to liquidate the Group or to cease operations, or has no realistic alternative but to do so. As part of our audit of the consolidated financial statements, we have concluded that management's use of the going concern basis of accounting in the preparation of the Group's consolidated financial statements is appropriate.

Management has not identified a material uncertainty that may cast significant doubt on the Group's ability to continue as a going concern, and accordingly none is disclosed in the consolidated financial statements of the Group. Based on our audit of the consolidated financial statements of the Group, we also have not identified such a material uncertainty. However, neither management nor the auditor can guarantee the Group's ability to continue as a going concern."

(p. 76 of Proposed ISA 700 (Revised), Forming an Opinion and Reporting on Financial Statements).

The PCAOB has initiated a standard-setting project to enhance auditor reporting relating to an entity's ability to continue as a going concern. As of 2014, that project is listed on the PCAOB's standard setting agenda as an active project, the timing of which is dependent on third parties.

| EXHIBIT **15.5** | Unqualified Report with Emphasis of Important Matter: Morgan Stanley |

As discussed in Note 1 to the consolidated financial statements, the Company changed its fiscal year end from November 30 to December 31.

[This paragraph followed the opinion paragraph in Deloitte & Touche's unqualified report on Morgan Stanley's 2010 financial statements and preceded the paragraph describing the opinion on internal control effectiveness.]

/s/ Deloitte & Touche LLP
New York, New York
February 28, 2011

Source: Morgan Stanley. 2010 Annual Report, p. 119, via EDGAR, accessed November 2011. (http://www.sec.gov/Archives/edgar/data /895421/000119312511050049/d10k.htm)

Emphasis-of-Matter Paragraphs and Other-Matter Paragraphs in the Independent Auditor's Report for U.S. Nonpublic Companies

The auditing standards for U.S. nonpublic companies describe an emphasis-of-matter paragraph as a paragraph included in the auditor's report that is required by GAAS, or is included at the auditor's discretion, and that refers to a matter appropriately presented or disclosed in the financial statements that, in the auditor's professional judgment, is of such importance that it is fundamental to users' understanding of the financial statements.

When the auditor includes an emphasis-of-matter paragraph in the auditor's report, the auditor should include it immediately after the opinion paragraph in the auditor's report and use the heading "Emphasis of Matter" or other appropriate heading. Further, the auditor should include in the paragraph a clear reference to the matter being emphasized and to where relevant disclosures that fully describe the matter can be found in the financial statements. Finally, the auditor should indicate that the auditor's opinion is not modified with respect to the matter being emphasized.

AU-C 706 also refers to an other-matter paragraph, which is a paragraph included in the auditor's report that is required by GAAS, or is included at the auditor's discretion, and that refers to a matter other than those presented or disclosed in the financial statements that, in the auditor's professional judgment, is relevant to users' understanding of the audit, the auditor's responsibilities, or the auditor's report. If the auditor chooses to use this type of paragraph, the auditor should do so in a paragraph in the auditor's report with the heading "Other Matter" or other appropriate heading. The auditor should include this paragraph immediately after the opinion paragraph and any emphasis-of-matter paragraph.

Explanatory Language: Reference to Other Auditors (Group Audits and Component Auditors)

The audit client may have branches, warehouses, factories, or subsidiaries at various locations around the country or overseas, and so another audit firm may perform part of the audit. The principal auditor (also referred to as group engagement partner) needs to decide whether to mention the other auditor in the overall audit report. As described in *Exhibit 15.6*, reporting requirements differ across the AICPA, PCAOB, and the IAASB. Most notably, international standards do not permit the auditor's report to make reference to another auditor unless required by law or regulation.

| EXHIBIT **15.6** | Reporting Requirements When Part of an Audit Is Performed by Other Independent Auditors |

AICPA Auditing Standards Board (ASB)

AU-C 600 addresses this topic and is essentially the same guidance as is found in ISA 600, which is discussed below. An important point of difference, however, is that AU-C 600 allows for the auditor's report to make reference to another auditor, while ISA 600 does not permit the auditor's report to make reference to another auditor unless required by law or regulation.

Public Company Accounting Oversight Board (PCAOB)

AU 543 discusses the use of the work of other auditors during an audit. This standard notes that principal auditor has to determine whether his or her involvement in and knowledge of the audit are sufficient to allow him or her to be the principal auditor. The principal auditor then has to decide whether to make reference to the work of any other independent auditors in the audit.

Reference to the other auditor is generally appropriate when the portion of the financial statements audited by the other auditor is material in relation to the whole. The principal auditor's report should clearly indicate the degree of shared responsibility and the portions of the financial statements audited by each. Therefore, modifications should be made to the introductory, scope, and opinion paragraphs.

References to the other audit firm will likely not be made when:

- The other firm is an associated or correspondent firm.
- The other firm is hired by the principal audit firm that directs the work of the other firm.
- The other firm is hired by the client and the principal auditors are able to satisfy themselves that the work done by the other firm meets their own requirements.
- The amounts audited by the other firm are not material to the combined or consolidated financial statements.

If the principal auditor decides to accept responsibility for the other auditor's work, the principal auditor's standard report is issued without modification. In such a case, the principal auditor's report expresses an opinion on the financial statements as if he or she had conducted the entire audit; no reference is made to the other auditor, or the other auditor's work, in the principal auditor's report.

International Auditing and Assurance Standards Board (IAASB)

ISA 600 discusses the use of a **component auditor**'s work as part of a group audit. A **component** is an entity or business activity for which group or component management prepares financial information that is required by the applicable financial reporting framework to be included in the group financial statements. A **group engagement partner** is the partner or other person in the firm who is responsible for the group audit engagement and its performance, and for the auditor's report on the group financial statements that is issued on behalf of the firm. The term **group** refers to all the components whose financial information is included in the group financial statements. A group always has more than one component. ISA 600 requires that the report of the principal auditor not refer to a component auditor, unless required by law or regulation to include such reference If such reference is required by law or regulation, the auditor's report shall indicate that the reference does not diminish the group engagement partner's or the his or her firm's responsibility for the **group audit opinion**, which is the audit opinion on the group financial statements.

The terminology in ISA 600 is somewhat different than that in the PCAOB standard in that ISA 600 refers to a **group audit**, which is an audit of group financial statements. **Group financial statements** are those that include the financial information of more than one component. The term group financial statements also refers to combined financial statements aggregating the financial information prepared by components that have no parent but are under common control.

The *Emerging Issues* feature "The Prevalence of Group Audits in an Australian Sample" explains audit fee disclosures in Australia regarding group audits, and the prevalence of group audits in that international setting.

Audit firms may require that they audit the whole entity or will refrain from accepting the client. Care must be taken when relying on other auditors' reports because inadequate audits performed by other auditors can lead to legal and regulatory action against the principal auditor as well as the other audit firm. Further, it is very important for the principal auditor to have participated in the audit at a sufficient level, rather than solely relying on the work of the other auditor. However, regardless of whether reference is made in the auditor's report to the report of another auditor, the principal auditor is responsible for the overall opinion. The *Auditing in Practice* feature "Possible Problems When Serving as a Principal Auditor: Insights from the PCAOB" identifies potential problems when serving as a principal auditor.

If the principal audit firm chooses to mention the other firm in the audit report, the wording of the standard report is modified, and no additional paragraph is needed. The resulting opinion is unqualified unless there are other reasons for expressing a different opinion. The most extensive change appears in the introductory paragraph to indicate the shared responsibility for the overall opinion, including the magnitude of the amounts audited by the other firm. The scope and opinion paragraphs are also modified to reference the other auditor. For nonpublic clients, the extensive change would appear in the auditor's responsibility section; and the opinion paragraph would include a reference to the other auditor. The name of the other audit firm is mentioned only with its express permission and if its report is also included in the document.

The Prevalence of Group Audits in an Australian Sample

EMERGING ISSUE

In some international contexts, information is publicly available about the extent of work on an individual audit engagement that is performed by the various audit firms involved on a group audit. For example, in Australia, information about audit fees is disclosed for (a) the fee paid to the principal audit firm (i.e., the audit firm signing the audit report), (b) the fee paid to audit firms related to the principal audit firm (i.e., affiliated firms that are members of the principal audit firm's network), and (c) the fee paid to other audit firms (i.e., unaffiliated audit firms that are not members of the principal audit firm's network). Recent research paper report relatively surprising results showing that in an Australian sample of listed company multinational group audits conducted from 2008 to 2011, a significant amount of work is conducted by auditors other than the principal auditor. Specifically, the results show the following breakdown of work:

- All components of the group audit were conducted by the principal auditor only (51% of the sample)

- Components of the group audit were conducted by both the principal auditor and other members of the principal auditor's audit firm network only (17% of the sample)
- Components of the group audit were conducted by the principal auditor and by unaffiliated auditors only (26% of the sample)
- Components of the group audit were conducted by the principal auditor, and by both members of its network and unaffiliated auditors (6% of the sample)

Thus, multinational group audits are an important contemporary feature of the international auditing environment.

Source: *"The Impact of Other Component Auditors on the Costs and Quality of Multinational Group Audits" (Working Paper 2014) by E. Carson, R. Simnett, G. Trompeter, and A. Vanstraelen.*

Problems When Serving as a Principal Auditor: Insights from the PCAOB

In July 2010, the PCAOB issued Staff Audit Practice Alert No. 6, *Auditor Considerations Regarding Using the Work of Other Auditors and Engaging Assistants from Outside the Firm*. The report notes:

> The PCAOB staff has observed that a number of registered public accounting firms located in the United States ("U.S.") have been issuing audit reports on financial statements filed by issuers that have substantially all of their operations outside of the U.S. Although there is nothing inherently inappropriate about this, observations from the Board's inspection process suggest that some firms may not be conducting those audits in accordance with PCAOB standards. Specifically, some firms may be issuing audit reports based on the work of another firm, or by using the work of assistants engaged from outside of the firm, without complying with relevant PCAOB standards.

The report describes one situation where a U.S. audit firm was engaged to audit an issuer with substantially all of its operations in China. The U.S. firm retained an audit firm in China to perform audit procedures. Personnel from the U.S. firm did not travel to China during the audit, and the audit procedures performed by the other firm represented substantially all of the audit procedures on the issuer's financial statements. The firm in the China region did not issue a report; the U.S. firm issued an audit report stating that it had audited the financial statements and expressed an unqualified opinion on the financial statements. The PCAOB staff, however, concluded that it was inappropriate for the firm to serve as principal auditor and use the work of the other auditor. A firm cannot serve as principal auditor (and, accordingly, may not sign the audit report on the issuer's financial statements) unless the firm's own participation in the audit is sufficient.

The Staff Audit Practice Alert also notes:

> If an issuer has no significant operations other than those in another country, a registered public accounting firm that plays no significant part in the audit of the foreign operations is highly unlikely to have sufficient participation in the audit to serve as the issuer's principal auditor. A lack of sufficient participation cannot be overcome by using the work of the other auditor, even if the firm assumes responsibility for that work.

Source: http://pcaobus.org/Standards/QandA/2010–07-12_APA_6. pdf.

If the other auditor's report is qualified, the principal auditor must consider whether the subject of the qualification is of such nature and significance in relation to the overall financial statements that it would affect the overall opinion. What was material to the segment audited by the other auditor may not be significant to the overall financial statements.

Qualified Reports, Adverse Reports, and Disclaimers

Occasionally, circumstances are such that the auditor alters the wording of the standard unqualified report in a manner that affects the type of opinion expressed. In these situations, the auditor cannot issue an unqualified opinion. The issuance of other than unqualified opinions is highly unusual. The SEC, with limited exceptions, will not accept financial statements for which the audit opinion is other than unqualified. As a result, the auditor has significant leverage to encourage the client to make corrections that would allow for an unqualified audit opinion. When the auditor is not able to give an unqualified opinion, the auditor will provide a **modified opinion**, which could include a qualified opinion, an adverse opinion, or a disclaimer of opinion. In the following sections, we describe these circumstances and the resulting reports for U.S. public companies. The *Auditing in Practice* feature "Language in Modified Reports for U.S. Nonpublic Companies"

Language in Modified Reports for U.S. Nonpublic Companies

When the auditor modifies the opinion on the financial statements, the auditor should include a basis for modification paragraph in the auditor's report that provides a description of the matter giving rise to the modification. The auditor should place this paragraph immediately before the opinion paragraph in the auditor's report and use a heading that includes "Basis for Qualified Opinion," "Basis for Adverse Opinion," or "Basis for Disclaimer of Opinion," as appropriate.

Further, when the auditor modifies the audit opinion, the auditor should use a heading that includes "Qualified Opinion," "Adverse Opinion," or "Disclaimer of Opinion," as appropriate, for the opinion paragraph.

When the auditor expresses a qualified or an adverse opinion, the auditor should amend the description of the auditor's responsibility to state that the auditor believes that the audit evidence the auditor has obtained is sufficient and appropriate to provide a basis for the auditor's modified audit opinion.

describes terminology and formatting differences for U.S. nonpublic companies. The guidance discussed in this *Auditing in Practice* feature is generally consistent with the guidance provided in the ISAs.

Qualified Audit Reports

LO 4 Describe financial statement audits requiring a qualified report and identify the appropriate audit report modifications.

There are three situations in which an auditor will issue a qualified report. These situations occur when there is

- A material unjustified departure from GAAP that is not pervasive
- Inadequate disclosure that is not pervasive
- A scope limitation such that the possible effects on the financial statements of undetected misstatements, if any, could be material but not pervasive

Qualified Report: Material Unjustified Departure from GAAP That Is Not Pervasive

If a client has a departure from GAAP that can be isolated to one item, a qualified opinion will usually be expressed. For example, if a client expensed the acquisition cost of some assets that should have been capitalized and depreciated over their useful lives, a qualified opinion would be appropriate. For this example, the opinion paragraph would be modified to state the following:

> In our opinion, except for the effects of not capitalizing the acquisition costs of some assets as discussed in the preceding paragraph, the financial statements referred to above state fairly, …

The report would also include an explanatory paragraph that, if practicable, would include the effects of the subject matter of the qualification. For the above qualification, the explanatory paragraph would describe how the balance sheet and income statement, including individual line items, would be different if the financial statements did not contain the GAAP departure.

As described later, more **pervasive** GAAP departures, generally affecting more than one item, would result in an adverse opinion.

In the next section we describe one type of misstatement that would result in a qualified report: inadequate disclosure. Other types of misstatements that could be material, but not pervasive, include:

- Inappropriate selection of accounting principles
- Failure to provide a required financial statement (e.g., statement of cash flows)
- Inappropriate application of accounting principles

Qualified Report: Inadequate Disclosure

It is presumed that financial statements include all the necessary disclosures to comply with accounting standards and, perhaps more important, include disclosures designed to keep the financial statements from potentially being misleading. If the client refuses to make the appropriate disclosures, the auditor should express a qualified or adverse opinion, depending on the pervasiveness of the omitted disclosures, and provide the omitted information in the audit report, if practicable. The auditor is not, however, required to prepare and present a basic financial statement, such as an omitted cash-flow statement or segment information.

The introductory and scope paragraphs of the auditor's report are not affected by this situation. The explanatory paragraph should describe the nature of the omitted disclosures, and the opinion paragraph should be modified to describe the nature of the qualification. *Exhibit 15.7* provides the qualified opinion for Honda Motor Co., Ltd. because of inadequate disclosure.

Qualified Report: Scope Limitation

An unqualified opinion can be given only when the auditor has been able to conduct the audit in accordance with professional auditing standards. Restrictions on the scope of the audit, whether imposed by the client or by circumstances beyond the auditor's or client's control, may require the auditor to qualify an opinion. In some situations, as discussed below, the circumstances may be such that a disclaimer would be more appropriate.

Examples of circumstances that may limit the audit scope are the timing of the fieldwork, such as being engaged to do the audit after year end, the

---

EXHIBIT **15.7**	Opinion Qualification Because of Inadequate Disclosure: Honda Motor Co., Ltd.

[Introductory and scope paragraphs are followed by these explanatory and opinion paragraphs.]

The Company's consolidated financial statements do not disclose certain information required by Statement of Financial Accounting Standards No. 131, "Disclosures about Segments of an Enterprise and Related Information." In our opinion, disclosure of this information is required by U.S. generally accepted accounting principles.

In our opinion, *except for the omission of the segment information referred to in the preceding paragraph,* the consolidated financial statements referred to above present fairly, in all material respects, the financial position of Honda Motor Co., Ltd. and subsidiaries as of March 31, 2005 and 2006, and the results of their operations and their cash flows for each of the years in the three-year period ended March 31, 2006 in conformity with U.S. generally accepted accounting principles.

/S/ KPMG AZSA & Co.
Tokyo, Japan June 23, 2006
Note: *Emphasis* added.

Source: 20-F 1 d20f.htm ANNUAL REPORT, p F-3, http://www.sec.gov/Archives/edgar/data/715153/000119312506140213/d20f .htm#toc17446_63

inability to gather sufficient appropriate evidence, or an inadequacy in the accounting records. For example, when a company is audited for the first time, the audit firm is often appointed during the year to be audited. In such a case, the auditor may not be able to obtain sufficient appropriate evidence concerning the fairness of the beginning inventory, which affects the current year's income, or of the accounting principles used in the prior year. This may be a scope limitation that is beyond the auditor's control. If the auditor can gather sufficient appropriate evidence without being engaged prior to the beginning of the year, then the scope limitation no longer exists, and the auditor can render whatever would be the appropriate audit opinion.

Exhibit 15.8 presents an opinion that is qualified because of an inability to obtain evidence that could impact the valuation of the allowance for loan losses. The scope paragraph refers to the scope limitation, which is then

---

EXHIBIT 15.8 Opinion Qualification Because of a Scope Limitation: Tennessee Commerce Bancorp, Inc.

Report of Independent Registered Public Accounting Firm

To the Board of Directors and Shareholders
Tennessee Commerce Bancorp, Inc.

We have audited the accompanying consolidated balance sheets of Tennessee Commerce Bancorp, Inc. and Subsidiaries (collectively, the "Company") as of December 31, 2010 and 2009, and the related consolidated statements of income, changes in shareholders' equity, and cash flows for each of the three years in the period ended December 31, 2010. These consolidated financial statements are the responsibility of the Company's management. Our responsibility is to express an opinion on these consolidated financial statements based on our audits.

Except as discussed in the following paragraph, we conducted our audits in accordance with the standards of the Public Company Accounting Oversight Board (U.S.). Those standards require that we plan and perform the audit to obtain reasonable assurance about whether the financial statements are free of material misstatement. An audit includes examining, on a test basis, evidence supporting the amounts and disclosures in the financial statements. An audit also includes assessing the accounting principles used and significant estimates made by management, as well as evaluating the overall financial statement presentation. We believe that our audits provide a reasonable basis for our opinion.

Due to an unresolved report of examination from the Federal Deposit Insurance Corporation and Tennessee Department of Financial Institutions that could require adjustments to the allowance for loan losses as discussed in Note 12, we were unable to satisfy ourselves about the valuation of the Company's allowance for loan losses as of December 31, 2010.

In our opinion, except for the effects of such adjustments, if any, as might be determined necessary based on the outcome of the regulatory examination discussed in Note 12, the consolidated financial statements referred to above present fairly, in all material respects, the financial position of Tennessee Commerce Bancorp, Inc. and Subsidiaries as of December 31, 2010 and 2009, and the results of their operations and their cash flows for each of the three years in the period ended December 31, 2010, in conformity with U.S. generally accepted accounting principles.

We were not engaged to examine management's assessment of the effectiveness of Tennessee Commerce Bancorp, Inc. and Subsidiaries' internal control over financial reporting as of December 31, 2010, in accordance with the standards of the Public Company Accounting Oversight Board, included in the accompanying Management's Report on Internal Control Over Financial Reporting and, accordingly, we do not express an opinion thereon.

/s/KraftCPAs PLLC
Nashville, Tennessee
April 15, 2011

Source: Tennessee Commerce Bankcorp, Inc. 2010 Annual Report, p. F-3, via EDGAR, accessed February 2012. (http://www.sec.gov /Archives/edgar/data/1323033/000104746911003740/a2203054z10-k.htm)

described in an explanatory paragraph. Note that the exception in the opinion paragraph refers to the possible misstatements rather than to the scope limitation.

Adverse Audit Reports

LO 5 Describe financial statement audits requiring an adverse report and identify the appropriate audit report modifications.

An auditor issues an adverse report when the financial statements contain a pervasive and material unjustified departure from GAAP, including a lack of important disclosures that is pervasive. An adverse opinion should be expressed when the auditor believes that the financial statements taken as a whole are not presented fairly in conformity with GAAP. This can happen when a significant number of items in the financial statements violate GAAP. For example, if the auditor believes the client is no longer a going concern, GAAP may require the financial statements to reflect liquidation values. In that situation, if the items are presented on other than a liquidation basis, the statements are not fairly presented. Such opinions are very rare. *Exhibit 15.9* provides possible wording that could be used to reflect a situation when there is a material departure from GAAP. When issuing an adverse opinion, the opinion paragraph should refer to a separate paragraph that provides the basis for the adverse opinion.

Adverse Report: Lack of Important Disclosures That Is Pervasive

While an auditor would typically issue a qualified opinion when the client's financial statements lack disclosures, the auditor could issue an adverse

---

EXHIBIT 15.9 Example of Possible Audit Report Language Describing an Unjustified Departure from GAAP

Except as discussed in the following paragraph, we conducted our audits in accordance with the standards of the Public Company Accounting Oversight Board (U.S.). Those standards require that we plan and perform the audit to obtain reasonable assurance about whether the financial statements are free of material misstatement. An audit includes examining, on a test basis, evidence supporting the amounts and disclosures in the financial statements. An audit also includes assessing the accounting principles used and significant estimates made by management, as well as evaluating the overall financial statement presentation. We believe that our audits provide a reasonable basis for our opinion.

As discussed in Note 2 to the consolidated financial statements, the Company has presented its consolidated financial statements on the going-concern basis, which states assets and liabilities at historical amounts. Because of the magnitude and complexity of the matters discussed in Note 2 (certain of which are not within the direct control of the Company), including the Company's losses from operations, net stockholders' capital deficiency, defaults or other violations of debt covenants, restrictions on its access to the use of a significant proportion of its remaining liquid assets, its present financial inability to complete development of its land held for resale and land held for rental, and the lack of a significant market for its land held for resale and land held for rental, we believe that the Company can no longer carry out its plans and intentions, which are also discussed in Note 2, and cannot convert or otherwise dispose of its assets in the normal course of its business operations. In these circumstances, it is our opinion that generally accepted accounting principles require the Company's assets and liabilities to be stated at their liquidating values. The effect of this departure from generally accepted accounting principles cannot be reasonably determined; however, amounts ultimately received upon liquidation of the assets and amounts ultimately paid to settle liabilities may be different from the amounts stated in the accompanying consolidated financial statements.

In our opinion, *because of the effects of the matters discussed in the preceding paragraph,* the consolidated financial statements *do not present fairly,* in conformity with accounting principles generally accepted in the U.S. of America, the financial position of the Company, Inc. and its subsidiaries at December 31, 20X5 and 20X4 or the results of their operations or their cash flows for the years then ended.

Note: *Emphasis* added.

opinion if the omitted disclosures are such that, in the judgment of the auditor, the financial statements taken as a whole are not presented fairly in conformity with GAAP.

Audit Reports with a Disclaimer of Opinion

LO **6** Describe financial statement audits requiring a disclaimer of opinion and identify the communication the auditor is required to provide.

An auditor issues a disclaimer of opinion report in the following situations:

- A scope limitation exists
- Substantial doubt exists about the client being a going concern
- The auditor lacks independence

Disclaimer: Scope Limitation

When the client imposes substantial restrictions on the scope of the audit, there is a significant risk that the client is trying to hide important evidence, and the auditor should ordinarily disclaim an opinion. If scope limitations caused by circumstances are such that it is not possible to form an opinion, a disclaimer should also be issued. The wording of the introductory paragraph is modified for a scope limitation, the scope paragraph is omitted, an additional paragraph is inserted to describe the scope limitation(s), and the last paragraph clearly states that no opinion can be expressed.

The introductory paragraph is modified from *We have audited ...* to *We were engaged to audit ...* An example of appropriate language for the last paragraph follows:

> Because of the significance of matters discussed in the preceding paragraph, the scope of our work was not sufficient to enable us to express, and we do not express, an opinion on the financial statements referred to in the first paragraph.

Non-U.S. Companies One difference of note between U.S. auditing standards and ISAs is that ISA 705 requires the auditor to withdraw from the audit when the auditor is unable to obtain sufficient appropriate audit evidence because of a management-imposed scope limitation, and the auditor concludes that the possible effects on the financial statements of undetected misstatements, if any, could be both material and pervasive so that a qualification of the opinion would be inadequate to communicate the gravity of the situation. The U.S. standards have a requirement that the auditor should consider withdrawal from the engagement under such circumstances. However, the auditor is not required to withdraw from an engagement but, rather, should consider whether to withdraw or disclaim an opinion on the financial statements.

Disclaimer: Substantial Doubt About the Client Being a Going Concern

In some reporting situations, doubt about the client continuing as a going concern is such that the auditor does not believe that an additional paragraph to an unqualified opinion is appropriate. In such cases, the auditor may issue a disclaimer of opinion. Such was the case in the auditor's report on the 2010 financial statements of Majestic Capital, Ltd., as shown in *Exhibit 15.10*.

Disclaimer: Auditor Lacking Independence

When auditors lack independence with respect to a client, they, by definition, cannot perform an audit in accordance with professional auditing standards and are precluded from expressing an opinion on the financial statements. In such cases, a one-paragraph disclaimer should be issued stating the lack of independence, but omitting the reasons for the lack of independence. By omitting the reasons for the lack of independence, the auditor

EXHIBIT **15.10**   Disclaimer Due to Substantial Doubt About the Client Being a Going Concern—Majestic, Ltd.

Report of Independent Registered Public Accounting Firm

To the Board of Directors and Shareholders
Majestic Capital, Ltd.

We have audited the accompanying consolidated balance sheets of Majestic Capital, Ltd. as of December 31, 2010 and 2009, and the related statements of operations and comprehensive loss, shareholders' equity, and cash flows for the years then ended. Our audit also included the supplemental schedules listed in the Index at Item 15. These financial statements and supplemental schedules are the responsibility of the Company's management. Our responsibility is to report on these financial statements and supplemental schedules based on our audits.

We conducted our audits in accordance with the standards of the Public Company Accounting Oversight Board (U.S.). Those standards require that we plan and perform the audit to obtain reasonable assurance about whether the financial statements are free of material misstatement. We were not engaged to perform an audit of the Company's internal control over financial reporting. Our audits included consideration of internal control over financial reporting as a basis for designing audit procedures that are appropriate in the circumstances, but not for the purpose of expressing an opinion on the effectiveness of the Company's internal control over financial reporting. Accordingly, we express no such opinion. An audit also includes examining, on a test basis, evidence supporting the amounts and disclosures in the financial statements, assessing the accounting principles used and significant estimates made by management, and evaluating the overall financial statement presentation. We believe that our audits provide a reasonable basis for our report.

The accompanying consolidated financial statements have been prepared assuming the Company will continue as a going concern. As shown in the financial statements, the Company has incurred losses of $44.8 million and $41.6 million for the years ended December 31, 2010 and 2009, respectively. These losses have significantly weakened the Company's financial position and its ability to fund its operations and, at December 31, 2010, the Company's accumulated deficit is $59.8 million. As further discussed in Notes 1 and 24, the following events have limited the sources of cash available to the Company: (1) termination of the Company's previously announced merger with a third party; (2) the conservation and rehabilitation of Majestic Insurance Company, the Company's principal operating subsidiary, by the California Department of Insurance; and (3) the restrictions of the Bermuda Monetary Authority on Twin Bridges, the Company's Bermuda reinsurance subsidiary. Furthermore, as discussed in Note 4, the Company is in violation of covenants governing certain of its contractual obligations. As discussed in Note 1, based on the above factors, the Company may be forced to seek relief through a filing under the U.S. Bankruptcy Code or Bermuda Companies Act (bankruptcy filing). A bankruptcy filing would result in the violation of one or more legal and financial covenants of the Company's debt and other contractual obligations. All of these matters raise substantial doubt about the Company's ability to continue as a going concern. The financial statements do not include any adjustments to reflect the possible future effects on the recoverability and classification of assets or the amounts or classifications of liabilities that may result from the outcome of this uncertainty.

Because of the possible material effects on the financial statements and supplemental schedules referred to above of the matters described in the preceding paragraph, we are unable to, and do not, express an opinion on these financial statements and supplemental schedules as of and for the year ended December 31, 2010.

In our opinion, the 2009 financial statements referred to above present fairly, in all material respects, the consolidated financial position of Majestic Capital, Ltd. at December 31, 2009, and the consolidated results of its operations and its cash flows for the year ended December 31, 2009, in conformity with U.S. generally accepted accounting principles. Also, in our opinion, the related 2009 supplemental schedules, when considered in relation to the basic financial statements taken as a whole, present fairly in all material respects the information set forth therein.

/s/ Ernst & Young LLP
New York, New York
April 21, 2011

Source: Majestic Capital, Ltd. Form 10-K, p. 96, via EDGAR, accessed April 2012. (http://www.sec.gov/Archives/edgar/data/1338949/000143774911002503/majestic_10k-123110.htm)

is avoiding the possibility of the user second-guessing the auditor as to independence or lack thereof. The report would have no title or salutation. The following language would be appropriate for a disclaimer report:

> We are not independent with respect to MMM Company and the accompanying balance sheets of the Company as of March 31, 2015 and 2014 and the related statements of operations, stockholders' equity and cash flows for the years then ended were not audited by us, and accordingly, we do not express an opinion on them.

> Such a situation should rarely occur. It could happen, for example, when it is discovered late in the audit that one of the auditors on the engagement had a financial interest in the client.

Comparisons of Modifications to the Standard Unqualified Audit Report

LO 7 Assess various reporting situations requiring other than a standard unqualified report and determine the appropriate audit report that should be issued.

Exhibit 15.11 summarizes the major conditions leading to a modification to the standard unqualified audit report. Deciding on the type of opinion is a judgment that should not be taken lightly. This is particularly true of the decisions based on the materiality level and pervasiveness of GAAP violations, the significance of scope limitations, and the likelihood of the entity being a going concern. Issuing an inappropriate opinion can result in providing misleading information to the financial statement users, and will likely lead to legal problems for the auditor. Because of its importance, the decision is often made after consultation with other professionals within the firm.

| EXHIBIT **15.11** | Summary of Audit Report Modifications for U.S. Public Companies |

Condition (Exhibit Number)	Unqualified	Qualified	Adverse	Disclaimer
Justified departure from GAAP (15.3)	1 or 2			
Inconsistent application of GAAP	1			
Substantial doubt about going-concern (15.4,10)*	1			2
Emphasis of a matter (15.5)	1 or 2			
Reference to other auditors (15.6)	3			
Inadequate Disclosure (15.7)**		2	2	
Scope limitation (15.8)***		2 &4		2 & 5
Unjustified GAAP violation (15.9) **		2	2	
Auditor lacks independence				6

1. Explanatory paragraph *after* opinion paragraph
2. Explanatory paragraph *before* opinion paragraph
3. Modify wording of all three paragraphs
4. Modify scope paragraph
5. Modify introductory paragraph and replace scope paragraph with explanatory paragraph
6. One paragraph disclaimer

*The explanatory paragraph in an unqualified report is adequate. However, the auditor is not precluded from issuing a disclaimer.
**The choice depends on materiality and pervasiveness considerations.
***The choice depends on the importance of the omitted procedures to the auditor's ability to form an opinion. If it is a significant scope limitation imposed by the client, a disclaimer should ordinarily be issued.

Audit Reports on Internal Control Over Financial Reporting

LO 8 Describe the information that is included in a standard unqualified audit report on internal control over financial reporting and identify the appropriate audit report modifications for situations requiring other than an unqualified report on internal control over financial reporting.

In determining the appropriate opinion on internal control over financial reporting (ICFR), the auditor evaluates identified control deficiencies individually, and in the aggregate, to assess whether there is a material weakness in ICFR. The auditor's assessment, as well as whether there were any scope limitations, will influence the nature of the auditor's opinion. The auditor will issue an unqualified opinion when the auditor determines that there are no material weaknesses in ICFR (refer to *Exhibit 1.1* in *Chapter 1*), and will issue an adverse opinion when the auditor has identified one or more material weaknesses in ICFR (refer to *Exhibit 5.13* in *Chapter 5*).

PCAOB AS 5 identifies five situations in which the auditor will modify the audit report on ICFR effectiveness. These situations include:

- Elements of management's annual report on internal control are incomplete or improperly presented.
- There is a restriction on the scope of the engagement.
- The auditor decides to refer to the report of other auditors as the basis, in part, for the auditor's own report.
- There is other information contained in management's annual report on ICFR.
- Management's annual certification pursuant to Section 302 of the Sarbanes-Oxley Act is misstated.

Elements of Management's Annual Report on Internal Control Are Incomplete or Improperly Presented

In reviewing management's report on ICFR, the auditor may conclude that the report is not complete or is improperly presented or does not fairly describe an identified material weakness. If the auditor determines that the report is incomplete or not properly presented, the auditor's report will include an explanatory paragraph that describes the reasons for this determination.

Restriction on the Scope of the Engagement

The auditor is able to express an opinion on ICFR only if the auditor is able to perform all procedures deemed necessary. If there are restrictions placed on the scope of the engagement, the auditor will either withdraw from the engagement or disclaim an opinion (thereby stating that the auditor does not express an opinion on ICFR effectiveness). *Exhibit 15.12* provides an example of such a report.

Auditor Refers to the Report of Other Auditors as the Basis, in Part, for the Auditor's Own Report

In certain situations, the audit report on ICFR may include a reference by the auditor to work performed by another auditor. Such a reference would occur if the auditor were relying on work of another auditor who might be performing the ICFR audit work at a subsidiary, division, branch, or component of the company. The decision about whether to make reference to another auditor in the report on the audit of ICFR might differ from the corresponding decision as it relates to the audit of the financial statements. For example, the audit report on the financial statements may make reference to the audit of a significant equity investment performed by another auditor, but the report on ICFR might not make a similar reference because management's assessment of ICFR did not include controls at the equity method investee.

EXHIBIT 15.12   Disclaimer of Opinion on ICFR Due to Scope Limitation: Taro Pharmaceutical Industries Ltd.

Report of Independent Registered Public Accounting Firm

Board of Directors and Stockholders
Taro Pharmaceutical Industries Ltd.
Yakum, Israel

We have audited the internal control over financial reporting of Taro Pharmaceutical Industries Ltd. and its subsidiaries (the "Company") as of December 31, 2007, based on criteria established in *Internal Control—Integrated Framework* issued by the Committee of Sponsoring Organizations of the Treadway Commission (the COSO criteria). The Company's management is responsible for maintaining effective internal control over financial reporting and for its assessment on the effectiveness of internal control over financial reporting, included in the accompanying Report on Internal Control Over Financial Reporting. Our responsibility is to express an opinion on the Company's internal control over financial reporting based on our audit.

We conducted our audit in accordance with the standards of the Public Company Accounting Oversight Board (U.S.). Those standards require that we plan and perform the audit to obtain reasonable assurance about whether effective internal control over financial reporting was maintained in all material respects. Our audit included obtaining an understanding of internal control over financial reporting, assessing the risk that a material weakness exists, testing and evaluating the design and operating effectiveness of internal control based on that risk, and performing such other procedures as we considered necessary in the circumstances. We believe that our audit provides a reasonable basis for our opinion.

A company's internal control over financial reporting is a process designed to provide reasonable assurance regarding the reliability of financial reporting and the preparation of financial statements for external purposes in accordance with generally accepted accounting principles. A company's internal control over financial reporting includes those policies and procedures that (1) pertain to the maintenance of records that, in reasonable detail, accurately and fairly reflect the transactions and dispositions of the assets of the company; (2) provide reasonable assurance that transactions are recorded as necessary to permit preparation of financial statements in accordance with generally accepted accounting principles, and that receipts and expenditures of the company are being made only in accordance with authorizations of management and directors of the company; and (3) provide reasonable assurance regarding prevention or timely detection of unauthorized acquisition, use, or disposition of the company's assets that could have a material effect on the financial statements.

Because of its inherent limitations, internal control over financial reporting may not prevent or detect misstatements. Also, projections of any evaluation of effectiveness to future periods are subject to the risk that controls may become inadequate because of changes in conditions, or that the degree of compliance with the policies or procedures may deteriorate.

Since management was unable to complete all of its testing of internal controls and we were unable to apply other procedures to satisfy ourselves as to the effectiveness of the Company's internal control over financial reporting, the scope of our work was not sufficient to enable us to express, and we do not express, an opinion on the effectiveness of the Company's internal control over financial reporting.

Nevertheless, we draw attention to management conclusion that the Company has at least the following material weaknesses in internal control over financial reporting as of December 31, 2007:

- Control Activities Associated with Financial Statement Closing Processes. The Company identified material weaknesses in its financial statement closing processes arising from the potential for a material error in the financial statements from consideration of the following deficiencies:
  - Estimating certain accounts receivable reserves and sales deductions including rebates and other sales deductions.
  - Significant, complex and non-routine transactions, including the area of taxation and certain other accounting items.

(*continued*)

| EXHIBIT **15.12** | Disclaimer of Opinion on ICFR Due to Scope Limitation: Taro Pharmaceutical Industries Ltd. (*continued*) |

- Ensuring adequate preparation, timely review and documented approval of account reconciliations, journal entries, both recurring and non-recurring and certain information primarily in the form of spreadsheets that supports our financial reporting process, and consistent communication among the various finance and non-finance organizations across the Company on the terms of our commercial arrangements.
- Revenue. The Company lacks the proper procedures and controls in estimating its rebate and other deductions reserves, including indirect and Medicaid rebates. Specifically, the Company is dependent on manual processes and experienced turnover in the roles responsible for certain estimates and lacked sufficient time and resources to properly and fully estimate these reserves. As a result, the Company did not consistently and accurately record the provision at the time of the sale.
- Inventory. The Company found that adjustments of inventory and cost of goods sold were necessary and mainly relate to errors in the assessment of inventory valuation. Inventory valuation adjustments primarily resulted due to the errors identified in the accounts receivable reserves, which impacted the computation of the Company's net selling prices which resulted in changes to inventory valuation.
- Income Taxes. The Company did not maintain adequate policies and procedures and related internal controls or employ adequate resources with sufficient technical expertise, on a global basis, in the area of accounting for income taxes to ensure the completeness, accuracy, and timely preparation and review of our consolidated income tax provision, related account balances and disclosures sufficient to prevent a material misstatement of related account balances. In addition, the Company was unable to finalize its tax provision due to the lack of audited financial statements for prior years.

These material weaknesses, identified by management, were considered in determining the nature, timing, and extent of audit tests applied in our audit of the consolidated financial statements as of and for the year ended December 31, 2007, of the Company and this report does not affect our report dated June 29, 2011, on those financial statements.

We also have audited, in accordance with the standards of the Public Company Accounting Oversight Board (U.S.) the consolidated balance sheets of Taro Pharmaceutical Industries Ltd. as of December 31, 2007, and the related consolidated statements of income and comprehensive income, stockholders' equity, and cash flows for the year end December 31, 2007 and our report dated June 29, 2011 expressed an unqualified opinion thereon.

/s/ Ziv Haft
Ziv Haft
Certified Public Accountants (Isr)
BDO Member Firm
June 29, 2011

Tel Aviv: Tel: 972(0)3-6386868 Fax: 972(0)3-6394320	**Jerusalem:** Tel: 972(0)2-6546200 Fax: 972(0)2-6526633
Haifa: Tel: 972(0)4-8680600 Fax: 972(0)4-8620866	**Be'er Sheva:** Tel: 972(0)77-6900700 Fax: 972(0)3-6368714
Kiryat Shmona: Tel: 972(0)4-6951389 Fax: 972(0)4-6950004	**Be'ne Braq:** Tel: 972(0)73-7145300 Fax: 972(0)73-7145317

BDO Israel, an Israeli partnership, is a member of BDO International Limited, a UK company limited by guarantee, and forms part of the international BDO network of independent member firms. BDO is the brand name for the BDO network and for each of the BDO Member Firms

Source: Taro Pharmaceutical Industries Ltd. Form 20-F/A, p. F-3, F-4, via EDGAR, accessed March 2012. http://www.sec.gov/Archives/edgar/data/906338/000115752312000121/a50130435.htm

Other Information Contained in Management's Annual Report on ICFR

In some instances, management may choose to include information in its report on ICFR in addition to the information required to be provided. If management chooses to provide this additional disclosure, the auditor will disclaim an opinion on that additional information.

Management's Annual Certification Pursuant to Section 302 of the Sarbanes-Oxley Act Is Misstated

In some situations, matters may come to the auditor's attention as a result of the audit of ICFR that would cause the auditor to believe that modifications to the disclosures about changes in ICFR (addressing changes in ICFR occurring during the fourth quarter) are necessary for the annual certifications to be accurate and to comply with the requirements of Section 302 of Sarbanes-Oxley. The auditor should modify the report on ICFR to include an explanatory paragraph describing the reasons the auditor believes management's disclosures should be modified.

SUMMARY AND NEXT STEPS

With the completion of this chapter, you have now completed the audit activities in the audit opinion formulation process. Determining the appropriate audit report to issue is an important part of that process as the audit report is the primary means that the auditor has of communicating the results of the audit to the users of the financial statements. While it is typically expected that the auditor will issue an unqualified opinion on the financial statements and internal control, this chapter describes situations in which modifications to the reports including those opinions are warranted.

Although you have completed all of the phases of the audit opinion formulation process, the next chapter covers some complex judgments that you might encounter at various points in the audit process.

SIGNIFICANT TERMS

Component   An entity or business activity for which group or component management prepares financial information that is required by the applicable financial reporting framework to be included in the group financial statements.

Component auditor   An auditor who performs work on the financial information of a component that will be used as audit evidence for the group audit. A component auditor may be part of the group engagement partner's firm, a network firm of the group engagement partner's firm, or another firm.

Critical audit matters   Those matters addressed during the audit are those matters addressed during the audit that (1) involved our most difficult, subjective, or complex judgments; (2) posed the most difficulty to us in obtaining sufficient appropriate evidence; or (3) posed the most difficulty to us in forming our opinion on the financial statements. The PCAOB and IAASB do not view critical audit matters and key audit matters fundamentally differently; these are slightly different ways to articulate the same underlying idea.

Group   All the components whose financial information is included in the group financial statements. A group always has more than one component.

Group audit   The audit of group financial statements.

Group audit opinion   The audit opinion on the group financial statements.

Group engagement partner The partner or other person in the firm who is responsible for the group audit engagement and its performance, and for the auditor's report on the group financial statements that is issued on behalf of the firm.

Group financial statements Financial statements that include the financial information of more than one component. The term *group financial statements* also refers to combined financial statements aggregating the financial information prepared by components that have no parent but are under common control.

Key audit matters Those matters that, in the auditor's professional judgment, were of most significance in the audit of the financial statements during the current period. These key audit matters are selected from those matters communicated with those charged with governance. The PCAOB and IAASB do not view critical audit matters and key audit matters fundamentally differently; these are slightly different terms to articulate the same underlying idea.

Modified opinion A qualified opinion, an adverse opinion, or a disclaimer of opinion.

Pervasive A term used in the context of misstatements to describe the effects or the possible effects on the financial statements of misstatements that are undetected due to an inability to obtain sufficient appropriate audit evidence.

Positive assurance An explicit statement as to whether the financial statements are presented fairly.

Unmodified opinion See unqualified opinion.

Unqualified opinion The opinion expressed by the auditor when the auditor concludes that the financial statements are presented fairly, in all material respects, in accordance with the applicable financial reporting framework.

TRUE/FALSE QUESTIONS

15-1 **LO 1** The auditor should provide an opinion on the financial statements only if the opinion indicates that the financial statements are fairly stated in all material respects.

15-2 **LO 1** The auditor's opinion should be provided in a written report.

15-3 **LO 2** Standards on auditor reporting are currently in a state of change; both the PCAOB and the IAASB have issued proposed standards that could fundamentally change auditor reporting in the near future.

15-4 **LO 2** If an auditor conducts an audit in accordance with multiple auditing standards, only one set of standards can be mentioned in the audit report.

15-5 **LO 3** If an auditor decides to include explanatory language in the audit report because of concerns about the client's ability to remain a going concern, the explanatory paragraph should include the terms *material doubt* and *going concern*.

Multiple-Choice Questions **751**

15-6 **LO 3** International auditing standards generally permit the auditor to refer to other auditors in the auditor's report, while the U.S. auditing standards allow this reference only if required by law or regulation.

15-7 **LO 4** A qualified audit report would usually be issued when the client's financial statements contain a justified departure from GAAP.

15-8 **LO 4** An auditor's inability to obtain evidence that could impact the allowance for loan losses would likely lead to a qualified audit opinion.

15-9 **LO 5** The primary reason for issuing an adverse audit opinion is that the client's financial statements contain a pervasive and material unjustified departure from GAAP.

15-10 **LO 5** An adverse opinion would contain language indicating that the financial statements are not presented fairly in accordance with GAAP.

15-11 **LO 6** If the auditor issues a disclaimer because of a scope limitation, the scope paragraph of the report is moved to the beginning of the report.

15-12 **LO 6** When the auditor issues a disclaimer because of a lack of independence, the audit report should state the lack of independence, and describe the reasons for the lack of independence.

15-13 **LO 7** When the financial statements contain a justified departure from GAAP, the auditor can choose between an unqualified and qualified opinion.

15-14 **LO 7** If the auditor lacks independence, the auditor can choose between an adverse opinion and a disclaimer of opinion.

15-15 **LO 8** The auditor issues an adverse opinion on ICFR if the client has one or more significant deficiencies in ICFR.

15-16 **LO 8** If there are restrictions placed on the scope of the engagement being conducted for purposes of issuing an opinion on ICFR, the auditor either withdraws from the engagement or disclaims an opinion.

MULTIPLE-CHOICE QUESTIONS

15-17 **LO 1** Which of the following statements is false regarding audit reporting?
   a. The auditor's opinion should be expressed in a written report.
   b. The auditor should provide an opinion in accordance with the auditor's findings or state that an opinion cannot be expressed.
   c. The opinion should state whether the financial statements are presented fairly, in all material respects, in accordance with the applicable financial reporting framework.
   d. None of the above statements are false.

15-18 **LO 1** Which of the following statements is true regarding the auditor's responsibilities related to reporting?
   a. Sufficient appropriate evidence should be obtained to afford a reasonable basis for the opinion regarding the financial statements under audit.
   b. The audit opinion relates only to the client's financial statements, and does not relate to the required footnote disclosures.
   c. If the auditor has reservations about the fairness of presentation of the financial statements, the auditor does not need to

provide the reason for this reservation, but needs to only state that the financial statements are not fairly presented.

d. All of the above statements are true.

15-19 [LO 2] In which of the following situations would an auditor ordinarily issue an unqualified audit opinion without an explanatory paragraph?

a. The auditor wishes to emphasize that the client had significant related-party transactions.

b. The auditor decides to refer to the report of another auditor as a basis, in part, for the auditor's opinion.

c. The client issues financial statements that present financial position and results of operations, but omits the statement of cash flows.

d. The auditor has substantial doubt about the client's ability to continue as a going concern, but the circumstances are fully disclosed in the financial statements.

15-20 [LO 2] Which of the following scenarios describes a situation when an auditor cannot typically issue a standard unqualified audit opinion?

a. The client has prepared its financial statements using IFRS as the financial reporting framework.

b. The auditor has complied with the auditing standards of both the AICPA and the IAASB.

c. The auditor is not independent.

d. The auditor believes that the client will remain a going concern for a reasonable period of time.

15-21 [LO 3] In which of the following situations would an auditor typically issue an unqualified opinion, but include explanatory language?

a. The client has changed an accounting principle, has reasonable justification for the change, and has followed GAAP in accounting for and disclosing the change.

b. The auditor has substantial doubt about the client being a going concern.

c. The client has had significant transactions with related entities that the auditor wants to emphasize.

d. An auditor would typically issue an unqualified opinion, but include explanatory language, in all of the above situations.

15-22 [LO 3] Eagle Company's financial statements contain a departure from GAAP because, due to unusual circumstances, the statements would otherwise be misleading. Which of the following audit opinions should the auditor provide?

a. Unqualified, do not mention the departure in the auditor's report.

b. Unqualified, and describe the departure in a separate paragraph of the audit report.

c. Qualified, and describe the departure in a separate paragraph of the audit report.

d. Qualified or adverse, depending on materiality, and describe the departure in a separate paragraph of the audit report.

15-23 [LO 4] Tech Company has an uncertainty because of pending litigation. The auditor's decision to issue a qualified opinion rather than an unqualified opinion most likely would be determined by which of the following?

a. Inconsistent application of GAAP.

b. Inability to estimate the amount of loss.

c. The client's lack of experience with such litigation.

d. Adequacy of the disclosures.

15-24   **LO 4**   Which of the following phrases should not be used when the auditor is qualifying the audit opinion?

a. With the exception of

b. Except for

c. Subject to

d. Any of the above phrases would be appropriate.

15-25   **LO 5**   In which of the following circumstances would an auditor be most likely to express an adverse opinion on a company's financial statements?

a. Information comes to the auditor's attention that raises substantial doubt about the company's ability to continue as a going concern.

b. The auditor is denied access to minutes of board of directors' meetings by the client.

c. Tests of controls indicate that the organization's ICFR is ineffective.

d. The financial statements are not in conformity with FASB requirements regarding the capitalization of leases.

15-26   **LO 5**   When an auditor issues an adverse opinion, which of the following should be included in the opinion paragraph?

a. The reasons that the financial statements are misleading.

b. A reference to a separate paragraph that describes the reason for the adverse opinion.

c. A statement that indicates that the financial statements are fairly stated except for a reason that is described in the separate paragraph.

d. The financial statement effects of the departure from GAAP.

15-27   **LO 6**   When disclaiming an opinion because of a client-imposed scope limitation, which of the following is false regarding changes that would be made to the audit report?

a. The auditor would indicate in a separate paragraph why the audit did not comply with professional auditing standards.

b. The auditor would omit the scope paragraph.

c. The auditor would modify the introductory paragraph.

d. The auditor would omit the opinion paragraph.

15-28   **LO 6**   In which of the following situations would a disclaimer of opinion not be appropriate?

a. The auditor is not independent.

b. The client imposed a substantial restriction on the scope of the audit.

c. The financial statements have a departure from GAAP that is not justified.

d. A disclaimer of opinion would be appropriate in all of the above situations.

15-29   **LO 7**   In which of the following situations would an auditor usually choose between issuing a qualified opinion and issuing a disclaimer of opinion?

a. Departure from GAAP.

b. Inadequate disclosure of accounting policies.

c. Inability to obtain sufficient appropriate evidence for a reason other than a management-imposed scope restriction.

d. Unreasonable justification for a change in accounting principles.

15-30 **LO 7** Tread Corp. accounts for the effect of a material accounting change prospectively, when the inclusion of the cumulative effect of the change is required in the current year. Which of the following opinions would the auditor choose?

a. Qualified opinion or a disclaimer of opinion.

b. Disclaimer of opinion or an unqualified opinion with an explanatory paragraph.

c. Unqualified opinion with an explanatory paragraph or an adverse opinion.

d. Qualified opinion or an adverse opinion.

15-31 **LO 8** The auditor of a large U.S. public company has determined that a material weakness exists in the client's ICFR. Which of the following statements is true?

a. Weakness requires an adverse opinion on the financial statements.

b. The auditor should express an adverse opinion on internal controls only if a material misstatement was found in the financial statements.

c. The auditor should express an adverse opinion on ICFR, even though no material misstatements were found in the financial statements.

d. The auditor is not required to express an opinion on internal controls.

15-32 **LO 8** In which of the following situations would the auditor modify the audit report on ICFR?

a. The auditor identifies multiple unrelated significant deficiencies in ICFR.

b. The auditor concludes that management's report on ICFR is not complete or is improperly presented.

c. The auditor relies on the work of other auditors, but decides not to include a reference to the other auditors.

d. The auditor would modify the audit report on ICFR in all of the above situations.

REVIEW AND SHORT CASE QUESTIONS

NOTE: Completing *Review and Short Case Questions* does not require the student to reference additional resources and materials.

NOTE: For the remaining problems, we make special note of those addressing fraud, international issues, professional skepticism, and ethics.

15-33 **LO 1** Why is the audit report important to the audit opinion formulation process?

15-34 **LO 1** What are the requirements of the AICPA's Principles 1 and 7 regarding audit reporting?

15-35 **LO 2** Under what circumstances may an auditor express an unqualified opinion when the related financial statements contain a material departure from a FASB standard?

15-36 **LO 2** What conditions must be present for an auditor to be able to issue a standard unqualified audit report similar to the ones presented in *Exhibit 15.1*?

15-37 **LO 2** Review *Exhibit 15.2* and identify the timing requirements for U.S. public companies to file audited financial statements with the SEC.

15-38 **LO 2** List the components of a standard unqualified audit report for a U.S. public company.

INTERNATIONAL **15-39** **LO 2** Identify the primary difference in auditor reporting terminology between AU-C 700 and ISA 700.

INTERNATIONAL **15-40** **LO 2** How would the auditor's opinion differ if the financial statements of a company that was a foreign private issuer were prepared in conformity with IFRS and filed with the SEC rather than prepared in conformity with U.S. GAAP?

15-41 **LO 2** Refer to Panel A of *Exhibit 15.1*. What words and phrases in an unqualified audit report imply that there is a risk that the audited financial statements may contain a material misstatement?

INTERNATIONAL

15-42 **LO 3** Refer to *Exhibit 15.6*. Under what circumstances might the auditor choose not to refer to other auditors who worked on a part of the audit? How do the requirements differ under international auditing standards?

15-43 **LO 3** You are in charge of the audit of the financial statements of Parat, Inc. and consolidated subsidiaries, covering the two years ended December 31, 2015. Another public accounting firm is auditing Nuam, Inc., a major subsidiary of Parat that accounts for total assets, revenue, and net income of 30%, 26%, and 39%, respectively, for 2014, and 28%, 20%, and 33%, respectively, for 2015.

a. What is meant by the term *principal auditor*? What term can be used in place of *principal auditor*?

b. Write the audit report referring to the other audit firm and expressing an unqualified opinion.

15-44 **LO 3** The following audit report was drafted by a staff accountant of Turner & Turner, CPAs, at the completion of the audit of the financial statements of Lyon Computers, Inc. (a public company) for the year ended March 31, 2015. It was submitted to the engagement partner, who reviewed matters thoroughly and properly concluded that Lyon's disclosures concerning its ability to continue as a going concern for a reasonable period of time were adequate, but there is substantial doubt about Lyon being a going concern. Identify the deficiencies contained in the audit report as drafted by the staff accountant. Group the deficiencies by paragraph. Do not redraft the report.

To the Board of Directors of Lyon Computers, Inc.:

We have audited the accompanying balance sheet of Lyon Computers, Inc. as of March 31, 2015, and the other related financial statements for the year then ended. Our responsibility is to express an opinion on these financial statements based on our audit.

We conducted our audit in accordance with standards that require that we plan and perform the audit to obtain reasonable assurance about whether the financial statements are in conformity with generally accepted accounting principles. An audit includes examining, on a test basis, evidence supporting the amounts and disclosures in the financial statements. An audit also includes assessing the accounting principles used and significant estimates made by management.

The accompanying financial statements have been prepared assuming that the Company will continue as a going concern. As discussed in Note X to the financial statements, the Company has suffered recurring losses from operations and has a net capital deficiency that raises substantial doubt about its ability to continue as a going concern. We believe that management's plans in regard to these matters, which are also described in Note X, will permit the Company to continue as a going concern beyond a reasonable period of time. The financial statements do not include any adjustments that might result from the outcome of this uncertainty.

In our opinion, subject to the effects on the financial statements of such adjustments, if any, as might have been required had the outcome of the uncertainty referred to in the preceding paragraph been known, the financial statements referred to above present fairly, in all material respects, the financial position of Lyon Computers, Inc., and the results of its operations and its cash flows in conformity with generally accepted accounting principles applied on a basis consistent with that of the preceding year.

Turner & Turner, CPAs
April 28, 2015

15-45 **LO 3** The accounting and auditing literature discusses several different types of accounting changes. For each of the changes listed below (a. through e.), indicate whether the auditor should add a paragraph to the audit report, assuming that the change had a material effect on the financial statements and was properly justified, accounted for, and disclosed. Assume that the organization is a U.S. nonpublic company.

a. Change from one GAAP to another GAAP
b. Change in accounting estimate not affected by a change in accounting principle
c. Change in accounting estimate affected by a change in accounting principle
d. Correction of an error
e. Change from non-GAAP to GAAP (a special case of correction of an error)

15-46 **LO 3** Various types of accounting changes can affect the auditor's report.

a. Briefly describe the rationale for having accounting changes affect the auditor's report and the auditor's responsibility in such cases.
b. For each of the changes listed below (1. through 7.), indicate the type of change and its effect on the audit report.
   1. A change from the completed-contract method to the percentage- of-completion method of accounting for long-term construction contracts.
   2. A change in the estimated useful life of previously recorded fixed assets. (The change is based on newly acquired information.)
   3. Correction of a mathematical error in inventory pricing made in a prior period.
   4. A change from full absorption costing to direct costing for inventory valuation (which is non-GAAP).
   5. A change from presentation of statements of individual companies to presentation of consolidated companies.
   6. A change from deferring and amortizing preproduction costs to recording such costs as an expense when incurred, because future benefits of the costs have become doubtful. (The new accounting method was adopted in recognition of the change in estimated future benefits.)
   7. A change from including the employer's share of FICA taxes with other taxes to including the employer's share of FICA taxes as retirement benefits on the income statement.

15-47 **LO 3** Under what circumstances must the audit report refer to the consistency, or the lack of consistency, in the application of GAAP? What is the purpose of such reporting?

15-48   **LO 3**   When a client has a justified departure from GAAP, how should the auditor modify the audit report?

15-49   **LO 3**   Provide examples of matters that auditors may choose to emphasize when issuing an unqualified opinion.

XL Leisure Group, MovieLink

INTERNATIONAL

PROFESSIONAL SKEPTICISM

15-50   **LO 3**   In September 2008, XL Leisure Group, Britain's third-largest tour operator, filed for bankruptcy. A few months prior to filing for bankruptcy, the company had issued its audited financial statements. Neither the financial statements nor the auditor's opinion contained any explicit warning that the company was in financial difficulty.

In contrast, in 2007 the auditors of MovieLink expressed substantial doubt that MovieLink, which offers movies that can be downloaded from the Internet, would be able to continue as a going concern. The basis for the auditors' concern included MovieLink's recurring losses from operations, negative cash flows from operating activities, and an accumulated deficit that had risen to $145 million.

A company's financial statements are prepared and audited under the assumption that the company is a going concern, meaning that that company will continue to operate for a reasonable period of time, for example, one year. However, during times of financial crisis, it is expected that many companies will find themselves facing financial difficulties, even to the point of filing for bankruptcy. Financial difficulties can arise when companies fund their operations through debt, ranging from overdrafts to credit lines to large loans. If companies need these sources of funds to continue to operate, yet banks are unwilling to commit to providing these loans, many companies face the prospect of not being able to continue their operations. During times of financial crisis, banks may not be willing to continue providing the lending they have in the past or to commit to new lending. In these situations, auditors may have substantial doubt about a company's ability to continue as a going concern.

   a. How does the auditor's substantial doubt about a client's ability to remain a going concern affect the format of the audit opinion?

   b. What are the implications to the company and to the audit firm when the audit firm's report expresses substantial doubt about a company's ability to remain a going concern?

   c. Why might the auditors of XL Leisure Group and MovieLink have arrived at two different decisions?

   d. How might professional skepticism impact the auditor's decision to issue a going-concern opinion?

15-51   **LO 4**   Identify the situations in which an auditor issues a qualified opinion.

15-52   **LO 4**   On February 28, 2016, Stu & Dent, LLP completed the audit of Shylo Ranch, Inc. (a public company) for the year ended December 31, 2015. A recent fire destroyed the accounting records concerning the cost of Shylo's livestock. These were the only records destroyed. The auditors are unable to obtain adequate evidence concerning the cost of the livestock, which represents about 8% of total assets. These are GAAP-based financial statements, and the auditors found no other problems during the audit. The audit report is to cover the 2015 financial statements only. The audit partner has indicated that a qualified opinion is more appropriate than an adverse opinion. Prepare a draft of the audit report for review by the audit partner.

15-53 **LO 4** You are a senior auditor working for Fuhremann & Fuhremann, CPAs. Your staff assistant has drafted the following audit report of a publicly traded U.S. company. You believe the scope limitation is significant enough to qualify the opinion, but not to disclaim an opinion. Identify the deficiencies in this draft and state how each deficiency should be corrected. Organize your answer around the components of the audit report (introductory paragraph, scope paragraph, and so on).

To Joseph Halberg, Controller
Billings Container Company, Inc.

We have audited the accompanying balance sheet of Billings Container Company and the related statements of income, retained earnings, and statement of changes in financial position as of December 31, 2015. These financial statements are the responsibility of the Company's management.

Except as discussed in the following paragraph, we conducted our audit in accordance with accounting principles generally accepted in the United States of America. Those standards require that we plan and perform the audit to obtain assurance about whether the financial statements are free of misstatement. An audit includes examining evidence supporting the amounts and disclosures in the financial statements. An audit also includes assessing the accounting principles used as well as evaluating the overall financial statement presentation. We believe that our audit provides a reasonable basis for our opinion.

We were unable to obtain sufficient appropriate evidence of the fair market value of the Company's investment in a real estate venture due to the unique nature of the venture. The investment is accounted for using the equity method and is stated at $450,000 and $398,000 at December 31, 2015 and 2014, respectively.

In our opinion, except for the above-mentioned limitation on the scope of our audit, the financial statements referred to above present fairly the financial position of Billings Container Company as of December 31, 2015 and 2014, and the results of its operations and its cash flows for the year then ended in conformity with auditing standards generally accepted in the United States of America.

/s/ Kristen Fuhremann, CPA
Madison, WI
December 31, 2015

15-54 **LO 4** Refer to *Exhibit 15.7*. What is the nature of the qualification of the audit report for Honda Motor Company? How was the audit report modified?

15-55 **LO 5** In what situations would an auditor issue an adverse opinion?

15-56 **LO 6** What is the purpose of a disclaimer of opinion? In what situations would an auditor issue a disclaimer of opinion?

15-57 **LO 6** Why should the auditor ordinarily disclaim an opinion if the client imposes significant scope limitations on the audit procedures?

15-58 **LO 7** Identify the types of audit reports other than a standard unqualified audit report and explain the circumstances under which each type of report is appropriate.

15-59 **LO 7** The following table outlines various scenarios in which an auditor will determine the appropriate audit opinion to issue. Note that the auditor's professional judgment about the nature of the matter giving rise to the modification and the pervasiveness of its effects or possible effects on the financial statements affects the type of opinion to be expressed. Complete the following table to identify the report that should be issued by the auditor.

Nature of Matter Giving Rise to the Modification	Auditor's Professional Judgment About the Pervasiveness of the Effects or Possible Effects on the Financial Statements	
	Material but Not Pervasive	Material and Pervasive
Financial statements are materially misstated		
Inability to obtain sufficient appropriate audit evidence		

15-60 **LO 7** Several independent audit situations are presented here (labeled a. through i.). Assume that everything other than what is described would have resulted in an unqualified opinion on the company's financial statements. Indicate the type of opinion you believe should be expressed in each situation and explain your choice. If an explanatory paragraph is needed, indicate whether it should precede or follow the opinion paragraph.

a. The auditor was unable to obtain confirmations from two of the client's major customers that were included in the sample. These customers wrote on the confirmation letters that they were unable to confirm the balances because of their accounting systems. The auditor was able to achieve satisfaction through other audit procedures.

b. The client treated a lease as an operating lease, but the auditor believes it should have been accounted for as a capital lease. The effects are material.

c. The client changed from FIFO to LIFO this year. The effect is material. Address the following two situations:
   (i) The change was properly accounted for, justified, and disclosed.
   (ii) The change was properly accounted for and disclosed, but was not properly justified.

d. The client restricted the auditor from observing the physical inventory. Inventory is a material item.

e. The client is engaged in a product liability lawsuit that is properly accounted for and adequately described in the footnotes. The lawsuit does not threaten the going-concern assumption, but an adverse decision by the court could create a material obligation for the client.

f.   The status of the client as a going concern is extremely doubtful. The problems are properly described in the footnotes.

g.   One of your client's subsidiaries was audited by another audit firm, whose opinion was qualified because of a GAAP violation. You do not believe that the GAAP violation is material to the consolidated financial statements on which you are expressing an opinion.

h.   You are convinced that your client is violating another company's patent in the process of manufacturing its only product. The client will not disclose this because it does not want to wave a red flag and bring this violation to the other company's attention. A preliminary estimate is that the royalty payments required would be material to the financial statements.

i.   The client, with reasonable justification, has changed its method of accounting for depreciation for all factory and office equipment. The effect of this change is not material to the current-year financial statements, but is likely to have a material effect in future years. The client's management will not disclose this change because of its immaterial effect on the current-year statements. You have been unable to persuade management to make the disclosure.

15-61   **LO 7**   The following are independent audit situations for which you are to recommend an appropriate audit report. For each situation listed as 1. through 6. below, identify the appropriate type of audit report from the list below (a. through f.) and briefly explain the rationale for selecting the report.

Appropriate type of audit report:
a.   Unqualified, standard
b.   Unqualified, explanatory paragraph
c.   Qualified opinion because of departure from GAAP
d.   Qualified scope and opinion
e.   Disclaimer
f.   Adverse

Audit Situations
1.   An audit client has a significant amount of loans receivable outstanding (40% of assets), but has an inadequate internal control system over the loans. The auditor cannot locate sufficient information to prepare an aging of the loans or to identify the collateral for about 75% of the loans, even though the client states that all loans are collateralized. The auditor sent out confirmations to verify the existence of the receivables, but only 10 of the 50 sent out were returned. The auditor attempts to verify the other loans by looking at subsequent payments, but only eight had remitted payments during the month of January, and the auditor wants to wrap up the audit by February 15. The auditor estimates that if only 10 of the 50 loans were correctly recorded, loans would need to be written down by $7.5 million.

2.   During the audit of a large manufacturing company, the auditor did not observe all locations of physical inventory.

The auditor chose a random number of sites to visit, and the company's internal auditors visited the other sites. The auditor has confidence in the competence and objectivity of the internal auditors. The auditor personally observed only about 20% of the total inventory, but neither the auditor nor the internal auditors noted any exceptions in the inventory process.

3. During the past year, Network Computer, Inc. devoted its entire research and development efforts to develop and market an enhanced version of its state-of-the-art telecommunications system. The costs, which were significant, were all capitalized as research and development costs. The company plans to amortize these capitalized costs over the life of the new product. The auditor has concluded that the research to date will likely result in a marketable product. A full description of the research and development, and the costs, is included in a note. The note also describes that basic research costs are expensed as incurred, and the auditor has verified the accuracy of the statement.

4. During the course of the audit of Sail-Away Company, the auditor noted that the current ratio had dropped to 1.75. The company's loan covenant requires the maintenance of a current ratio of 2.0, or the company's debt is all immediately due. The auditor and the company have contacted the bank, which is not willing to waive the loan covenant because the company has been experiencing operating losses for the past few years and has an inadequate capital structure. The auditor has substantial doubt that the company can find adequate financing elsewhere and may encounter difficulties staying in operation. Management, however, is confident that it can overcome the problem. The company does not deem it necessary to include any additional disclosure because management members are confident that an alternative source of funds will be found by pledging their personal assets.

5. The Wear-Ever Wholesale Company has been very profitable. It recently received notice of a 10% price increase for a significant portion of its inventory. The company believes it is important to manage its products wisely and has a policy of writing all inventory up to current replacement cost. This assures that profits will be recognized on sales sufficient to replace the assets and realize a normal profit. This operating philosophy has been very successful, and all salespeople reference current cost, not historical cost, in making sales. Only inventory has been written up to replacement cost, but inventory is material because the company carries a wide range of products. The company's policy of writing up the inventory and its dollar effects is adequately described in a footnote to the financial statements. For the current year, the net effect of the inventory write-up increased reported income by only 3% and assets by 15% above historical cost.

6. The audit of NewCo was staffed primarily by three new hires and a relatively inexperienced audit senior. The manager found numerous errors during the conduct of the audit and developed very long to-do lists for all members of the audit to complete before the audit was concluded. Although the

manager originally doubted the staff's understanding of the audit procedures, by the time the audit was finished, he concluded that the new auditors did understand the company and the audit process and that no material errors existed in the financial statements.

15-62 **LO 7** Audit situations 1. through 8. below describe various independent situations an auditor might encounter in conducting an audit. List A represents the types of opinions the auditor ordinarily would issue, and List B represents the report modifications (if any) that would be necessary. For each situation, select one response from List A and one from List B. Select, as the best answer for each item, the action the auditor normally would take. Items from either list may be selected once, more than once, or not at all.

Assume the following:
- The auditor is independent.
- The auditor previously expressed an unqualified opinion on the prior-year financial statements.
- Only single-year (not comparative) statements are presented for the current year.
- The conditions for an unqualified opinion exist unless contradicted in the factual situations.
- The conditions stated in the factual situations are material.
- No report modifications are to be made except in response to the factual situation.

Audit Situations
1. The financial statements present fairly, in all material respects, the financial position, results of operations, and cash flows in conformity with GAAP.
2. In auditing the long-term investments account, an auditor is unable to obtain audited financial statements for an investee located in a foreign country. The auditor concludes that sufficient appropriate evidence regarding this investment cannot be obtained, but is not significant enough to disclaim an opinion.
3. Because of recurring operating losses and working-capital deficiencies, an auditor has substantial doubt about an organization's ability to continue as a going concern for a reasonable period of time. However, the financial statement disclosures concerning these matters are adequate.
4. The principal auditor decides to refer to the work of another auditor who audited a wholly owned subsidiary of the organization and issued an unqualified opinion.
5. An organization issues financial statements that present the financial position and results of operations but omits the related statement of cash flows. Management discloses in the notes to the financial statements that it does not believe the statement of cash flows to be a useful statement.
6. An organization changes its depreciation method for production equipment from the straight-line to a units-of-production method based on hours of utilization. The auditor concurs

with the change, although it has a material effect on the comparability of the entity's financial statements.

7. An organization is a defendant in a lawsuit alleging infringement of certain patent rights. However, management cannot reasonably estimate the ultimate outcome of the litigation. The auditor believes that there is a reasonable possibility of a significant material loss, but the lawsuit is adequately disclosed in the notes to the financial statements.

8. An organization discloses certain lease obligations in the notes to the financial statements. The auditor believes that the failure to capitalize these leases is a departure from GAAP that is not justified.

List A—Types of Opinions

a. A qualified opinion
b. An unqualified opinion
c. An adverse opinion
d. A disclaimer of opinion
e. Either a qualified opinion or an adverse opinion
f. Either a disclaimer of opinion or a qualified opinion
g. Either an adverse opinion or a disclaimer of opinion

List B—Report Modifications

h. Describe the circumstances in an explanatory paragraph *preceding* the opinion paragraph *without modifying* the three standard paragraphs.
i. Describe the circumstances in an explanatory paragraph *following* the opinion paragraph *without modifying* the three standard paragraphs.
j. Describe the circumstances in an explanatory paragraph *preceding* the opinion paragraph and *modifying the opinion* paragraph.
k. Describe the circumstances in an explanatory paragraph *following* the opinion paragraph and *modifying the opinion* paragraph.
l. Describe the circumstances in an explanatory paragraph *preceding* the opinion paragraph and *modifying the scope and opinion* paragraphs.
m. Describe the circumstances in an explanatory paragraph *following* the opinion paragraph and *modifying the scope and opinion* paragraphs.
n. Describe the circumstances within the *scope* paragraph without adding an explanatory paragraph.
o. Describe the circumstances within the *opinion* paragraph without adding an explanatory paragraph.
p. Describe the circumstances within the *scope and opinion* paragraphs without adding an explanatory paragraph.
q. Describe the circumstances in the *introductory* paragraph without adding an explanatory paragraph and modify the wording of the *scope and opinion* paragraphs.
r. Issue the *standard* auditor's report *without modification*.

ETHICS   **15-63** **LO 7**   Each of the following phrases (1. through 5.) is from a paragraph in an auditor's report. Assume that except for the information indicated in the phrase, the report would have

been a standard unqualified report. Select from the following list
(a. through d.) the most likely report for the indicated phrase.
Each choice in the list may be used once, more than once, or not
at all.
a. Unqualified
b. Qualified
c. Adverse
d. Disclaimer
  1. In our opinion, except for the omission of the statement
     of cash flows ...
  2. We are not independent with respect to KC Company ...
  3. ... based on our audit and the report of other auditors ...
  4. ... presents fairly, in all material respects ...
  5. ... the scope of our work was not sufficient to enable us ...

15-64 **LO 7, 9** Assume that you are in a situation where you had
doubts about your client's ability to continue as a going concern.
Further, assume you have decided that, after performing all the
required audit procedures, you can issue an unqualified opinion
but need to modify the audit opinion to indicate substantial
doubt about the client's ability to continue as a going concern.
You have to let the CFO, who is a longtime friend of yours,
know of your decision. When you do this, the CFO tries to
explain to you that if the company receives a going-concern
opinion, it will go under—that the opinion is a self-fulfilling
prophecy. The CFO tries to convince you that if your firm does
not issue a going-concern opinion, it is very likely the company
will be able to weather its financial difficulties and survive. Further, the CFO notes that this is really a matter of professional
judgment and believes that many other auditors would not see
the need to issue a going-concern opinion. Should you issue a
standard unqualified audit report or an unqualified audit report
with a going-concern explanatory paragraph?

Use the framework for ethical decision making introduced in
Chapter 4 to address the dilemma you face regarding what type
of opinion to issue. Recall that the steps in the framework are as
follows: (1) identify the ethical issue(s), (2) determine who are the
affected parties and identify their rights, (3) determine the most
important rights, (4) develop alternative courses of action, (5)
determine the likely consequences of each proposed course of
action, (6) assess the possible consequences, including an estimation of the greatest good for the greatest number, and (7) decide
on the appropriate course of action.

15-65 **LO 8** Under what circumstances must the auditor of a public
company express an adverse opinion on the client's ICFR?

15-66 **LO 8** Identify the conditions under which an auditor would
modify the opinion on ICFR (for situations other than the presence of a material weakness).

FRAUD FOCUS: CONTEMPORARY AND HISTORICAL CASES

FRAUD

15-67 **SEC, Michael B. Johnson**
(LO 3, 7, 9) The SEC issued Accounting and
Auditing Enforcement Release (AAER) No. 2393 on March 8,
2006. The related to the matter of Michael B. Johnson and

Michael Johnson & Co. and concerns the audits of Winners. The following facts about Johnson and Co.'s audit of Winners are included in the AAER:

- Johnson, age 56, is a resident of Littleton, Colorado. Johnson has been the manager and sole member of Johnson & Co. and a licensed certified public accountant in Colorado since 1975. He also is a licensed certified public accountant in Florida and Mississippi.

- Johnson & Co. is an accounting firm located in Denver, Colorado. Johnson is the only member of, and the only certified public accountant affiliated with, the firm.

- Johnson & Co., through the participation of Johnson, audited the financial statements of Winners Internet Network, Inc. (Winners) for the years ended December 31, 1997 and 1998. Johnson supervised the audits and compilations of these financial statements and signed the audit reports for the 1997 and 1998 audits on behalf of Johnson & Co.

- Winners' December 31, 1999, financial statements were prepared and audited by Johnson and Johnson & Co.

- Johnson & Co. issued audit reports accompanying Winners' year-end financial statements for 1997 and 1998 that contained a going-concern modification and an unqualified audit report for 1999. These financial statements contained material misstatements, some of which related to entries made by Johnson or under the direction of Johnson. These reports falsely stated that the financial statements were presented fairly in all material respects in conformity with GAAP and that the audits of these financial statements were conducted in accordance with GAAS. These statements were false, since portions of the underlying financial statements were not presented in conformity with GAAP, which, in turn, rendered false the statements that the audits were conducted in accordance with GAAS, since the failure to address a deviation from GAAP in an audit report is a violation of GAAS.

a. Given the nature of Johnson & Co.'s work on Winners' financial statements for 1997–1999, what type of audit opinion should have been issued?

b. In considering this decision, answer the following questions by completing the first four steps of the seven-step framework for professional decision making introduced in *Chapter 4*:

   1. What difficulties might Johnson have faced when deciding what type of opinion to issue? Why might Johnson have not issued the appropriate opinions?

   2. What are the consequences of Johnson's decisions in this case?

   3. What are the risks and uncertainties associated with this decision?

   4. In deciding on whether to issue a going-concern modification, what types of evidence should the auditor gather to evaluate the reasonableness of the going-concern assumption?

Recall that the framework is as follows:

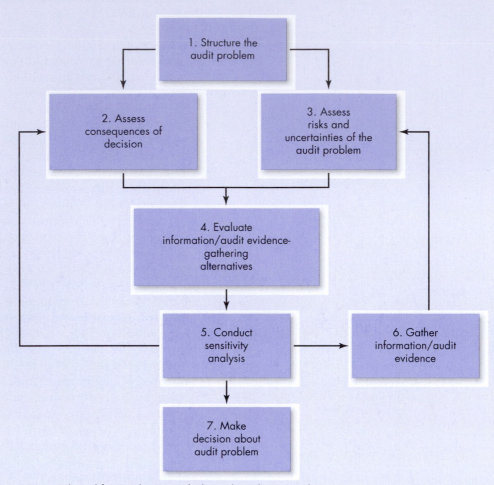

Source: Adapted from *Judgment and Choice*, by Robin Hogarth.

APPLICATION ACTIVITIES

NOTE: Completing *Application Activities* requires students to reference additional resources and materials. Some Application Activities will require the student to reference relevant professional auditing standards. We make special note of these as Auditing Standards Application Activities.

INTERNATIONAL

15-68 **Overland Storage** (LO **3, 7**)   Obtain the 2012 10-K Annual Report for Overland Storage, Inc. (OVRL). Refer to Note 1 on page F-7. Based on management's discussion in the note, what type of audit report did Overland's audit firm likely issue? In this situation, what options did the audit firm have?

15-69 **Coca-Cola, 3D Diagnostic Imaging** (LO **2**)   Review the audit report of Coca-Cola in Panel A of *Exhibit 15.1*. Obtain a copy of the audit report in the 2011 Annual Report of 3D Diagnostic Imaging plc, which is available at http://www.3ddiagnosticimaging.com/assets/Documents/AnnualReport30June2011.pdf

a. Describe key differences between the audit reports of 3D Diagnostic Imaging and Coca-Cola. Be sure to review differences in the auditing and accounting standards referred to in the reports and the wording used in the audit opinions.

b. Articulate how these differences may affect the relative informativeness of the audit report to users. Which of the reports do you find more useful, and why?

c. The audit opinion of 3D Diagnostic Imaging is signed by an individual on behalf of the audit firm. International audit reports generally are signed by the engagement partner who supervised the audit, whereas such disclosures are not required in the U.S. Why is the public disclosure of the engagement partner's name useful? Why might partners in the U.S. prefer not to sign their names to audit reports? What implications may this difference have for users of the audit reports?

15-70 **PCAOB** **(LO 2, 8)** The current audit report format has been criticized for its lack of useful and complete information. Over the past several years, investors, regulators, and auditors have debated the need for changes to the standard audit report.

a. Describe the basic information that is included in an audit report. Also discuss how that report will differ if it also contains a report on the internal controls of the company, that is, a report on an integrated audit.

b. Review the *Professional Judgment in Context* feature at the beginning of the chapter and obtain a copy of *PCAOB Release No. 2013-005*. This Concept Release proposes three fundamental changes to the auditor's report. Identify the first two of these changes (i.e., critical audit matters and other information), select one change, and for the selected change discuss the possible merits and difficulties associated with the change.

15-71 **LO 2** Assume that you are preparing the standard unqualified audit report for a nonpublic U.S. company and are not sure how to describe the audit that was performed. Which standard would provide details on what should be included in the auditor's report related to the description of the audit? Refer to the *Standards Appendix* at the end of the textbook, obtain the standard, and identify the relevant paragraph(s) in that standard.

AUDITING STANDARDS APPLICATION ACTIVITY

15-72 **LO 3** Assume that you are working on an audit of a group of financial statements for a nonpublic U.S. client. The engagement involves a component auditor who obtained audit evidence that was used in the group audit. You are unsure of whether your report should refer to the component auditor. Which standard would provide you with relevant guidance? Refer to the *Standards Appendix* at the end of the textbook, obtain the standard, and identify the relevant paragraph(s) in that standard.

AUDITING STANDARDS APPLICATION ACTIVITY

ACADEMIC RESEARCH CASES

NOTE: Completing *Academic Research Cases* requires students to reference additional resources and materials.

SEARCH HINT

It is easy to locate these academic research articles! Use a search engine such as Google Scholar or an electronic research platform such as ABI Inform, and search using the author names and part of the article title.

15-73 **LO 3** Locate and read the article listed below and answer the following questions.

Blay, A. D., M. A. Geiger, and D. S. North. 2011. The auditor's going-concern opinion as a communication of risk. *Auditing: A Journal of Practice and Theory* 30 (2): 77–102.

a. What is the issue being addressed in the paper?

b. What are the findings of the paper?

c. Why is this paper important to auditors, and what are the implications of this paper for the auditing profession?

d. Describe the research methodology used as a basis for the conclusions.

e. Describe any limitations of the research.

15-74 **LO 3** Locate and read the article listed below and answer the following questions.

Krishnan, J., K. Raghunandan, & J. S. Yang. 2007. Were former Andersen clients treated more leniently than other clients? Evidence from going-concern modified audit opinions. *Accounting Horizons* 21 (4): 423–435.

a. What is the issue being addressed in the paper?
b. What are the findings of the paper?
c. Why is this paper important to auditors, and what are the implications of this paper for the auditing profession?
d. Describe the research methodology used as a basis for the conclusions.
e. Describe any limitations of the research.

FORD AND TOYOTA

15-75 **Ford Motor Company and Toyota Motor Corporation**
(LO **2, 3, 8**)

Source and Reference	Question
Ford 10-K or Annual Report	1. What type of audit report did issue for Ford?
	2. What type of audit report did issue for Toyota?
Toyota 20-F or Annual Report	3a. What are the advantages to Ford and Toyota of using the same audit firm?
	3b. Why might some companies in the same industry be hesitant to using the same audit firm?

16

Advanced Topics Concerning Complex Auditing Judgments

CHAPTER OVERVIEW AND LEARNING OBJECTIVES

Audits involve many complex auditing judgments that require an understanding of the fundamental auditing concepts introduced in earlier chapters. Most of these complex auditing judgments relate to various evidence collection procedures (that is, Phases III and IV of the audit opinion formulation process). The discussion of these complex auditing judgments focuses on identifying risks of material misstatement and applying audit procedures to address those risks.

Through studying this chapter, you will be able to achieve these learning objectives:

1. Discuss the nature and types of complex judgments that permeate audit engagements and identify complex audit judgments based on a review of an organization's financial statements.

2. Assess whether misstatements, including prior-period misstatements, are material.

3. Describe audit considerations for long-term liabilities involving significant subjectivity.

4. Describe audit considerations for merger and acquisition activities, including restructuring.

5. Describe audit considerations for assessing management's fair value estimates and related impairment judgments, including goodwill impairment judgments.

6. Describe audit considerations for financial instruments.

7. Describe the activities of an internal audit function, assess the quality of the client's internal audit function, and determine the effect of a client's internal audit function on the financial statement audit.

8. Apply the frameworks for professional decision making and ethical decision making to issues involving complex audit judgments.

THE AUDIT OPINION FORMULATION PROCESS

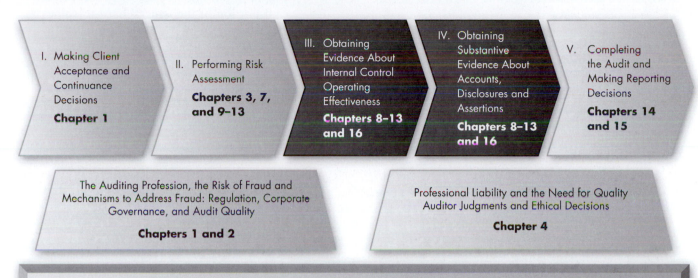

I. Making Client Acceptance and Continuance Decisions
Chapter 1

II. Performing Risk Assessment
Chapters 3, 7, and 9–13

III. Obtaining Evidence About Internal Control Operating Effectiveness
Chapters 8–13 and 16

IV. Obtaining Substantive Evidence About Accounts, Disclosures and Assertions
Chapters 8–13 and 16

V. Completing the Audit and Making Reporting Decisions
Chapters 14 and 15

The Auditing Profession, the Risk of Fraud and Mechanisms to Address Fraud: Regulation, Corporate Governance, and Audit Quality
Chapters 1 and 2

Professional Liability and the Need for Quality Auditor Judgments and Ethical Decisions
Chapter 4

The Audit Opinion Formulation Process and a Framework for Obtaining Audit Evidence
Chapters 5 and 6

PROFESSIONAL JUDGMENT IN CONTEXT
Complex Judgments Cause Difficulty for Auditors

This chapter explains many complex judgments that have caused difficulties for auditors. By way of example, we provide excerpts from various 2013 Public Company Accounting Oversight Board (PCAOB) inspection reports, in which the PCAOB criticizes the inspected audit firms for failing to obtain sufficient appropriate evidence to support their opinions. These excerpts relate to some of the complex judgments covered in this chapter.

Long-term liabilities

- "The Firm failed to perform sufficient procedures to test the valuation of certain environmental liabilities that the issuer recorded as a result of an acquisition during the year. Specifically, the Firm failed to obtain an understanding, and evaluate the reasonableness, of the significant assumptions that the issuer used to estimate the fair value of these environmental liabilities. (AU 328, paragraphs .12, .26, .28, and .36)" (*Source: PCAOB Release No. 104-2014-099; Issuer E, p. 11*)

  "In this audit, the Firm failed in the following respects to obtain sufficient appropriate audit

evidence to support its audit opinions on the financial statements and on the effectiveness of ICFR—

- The Firm failed to identify and test controls that sufficiently addressed the risks related to the valuation of postretirement plan liabilities, as the control it selected did not address certain significant assumptions, related to healthcare costs, that the issuer used to estimate these postretirement plan liabilities and did not address the accuracy and completeness of the data that the issuer used to form these assumptions. (AS No. 5, paragraphs 39 and 42)

- The Firm failed to sufficiently test certain of the significant assumptions the issuer used to estimate the postretirement plan liabilities because it failed to test the accuracy and completeness of the data that the issuer used to form these assumptions. (AS No. 15, paragraph 10; AU 342, paragraph .11)" (*Source: PCAOB Release No. 104-2014-099; Issuer M, p. 17*)

Merger and Acquisition Activities

- "During the year, the issuer completed the acquisition of a significant business. The Firm's testing related to the accounting for the business combination was deficient in the following respects—

  - The Firm selected for testing certain controls over the accounting for business combinations; however, it failed to sufficiently test these controls. Specifically, the Firm's procedures were limited to obtaining evidence that reviews that constituted a part of these controls had occurred and, for some controls, obtaining underlying documentation, without evaluating whether the controls operated at a level of precision that would prevent or detect material misstatements. (AS No. 5, paragraphs 42 and 44)

  - The Firm failed to sufficiently evaluate the reasonableness of certain significant assumptions and test certain data that the issuer used in (1) determining the fair values of acquired assets and (2) allocating the resulting goodwill to its business units. Specifically, for certain of these assumptions and data, the Firm limited its procedures to inquiring of management and, in some cases, comparing the assumptions or data to untested data provided by the issuer. For other assumptions and data, the Firm performed no procedures. (AU 328, paragraphs .26, .28, and .39)" (*Source: PCAOB Release No. 104-2014-102; Issuer A, p. 5*)

Fair Value Estimates and Financial Instruments

"The Firm failed to perform sufficient procedures to test the fair value measurements of, and the disclosures related to, the issuer's financial instruments without readily determinable fair values ("hard-to-value securities"), which consisted of non-agency residential mortgage-backed securities, commercial mortgage-backed securities, collateralized debt obligation securities, and other asset-backed securities. Specifically—

- To test the issuer's fair value measurements of the hard-to-value securities, the Firm requested pricing information from pricing services for comparison to the issuer's recorded price.

  - The Firm failed to obtain an understanding of the specific methods and assumptions underlying the fair value measurements that were obtained from pricing services and used in the Firm's testing of the fair value of certain of the hard-to-value securities. (AU 328, paragraphs .26 and .40)

- The Firm did not receive prices for a significant portion of the issuers' hard-to-value securities. For all but a small number of securities for which the Firm did not obtain prices, the Firm performed combinations of other procedures, consisting of obtaining information about the individual securities and the assumptions the issuer used to value some of them and comparing the issuer's price to that of the issuer's pricing service; the Firm, however, failed to evaluate, through these procedures, the appropriateness of the valuation methods and the reasonableness of the significant assumptions the issuer used to develop the fair value measurements for these securities. (AU 328, paragraph .26 and .28)

  - The Firm failed to sufficiently test the issuer's disclosure of hard-to-value securities as level 2 or level 3 in the fair value hierarchy set forth in FASB ASC Topic 820, Fair Value Measurement.

    Specifically, the Firm failed to obtain an understanding of whether the securities were valued using significant inputs that were observable or unobservable. (AU 328, paragraph .43)" (*Source: PCAOB Release No. 104-2014-102; Issuer H, pp. 19–20*)

Internal Audit

"In this audit, the Firm failed in the following respects to obtain sufficient appropriate audit evidence to support its audit opinions on the financial statements and on the effectiveness of ICFR—

- The Firm's testing of a control it selected over certain inventory was not sufficient. Specifically, the Firm used the work of the issuer's internal auditors to test the operating effectiveness of this control, which consisted of physical inventory counts conducted by plant personnel. The Firm's procedures were limited to obtaining the internal auditors' plan for testing the physical inventory counts, and determining that the number of locations the internal auditors planned to visit was sufficient without evaluating whether the work the internal auditors actually performed during the year relating to this control achieved the objectives of the testing. (AS No. 5, paragraph 44; AU 322, paragraphs .24 and .25)" (*Source: PCAOB Release No. 104-2014-099; Issuer K, pp. 15–16*)

The primary takeaway is that these PCAOB inspection observations and criticisms provide insight into accounts and related complex judgments that auditors should be particularly careful about given the relevant difficulties and the anticipation of regulatory scrutiny.

As you read through this chapter, consider the following questions:

- What factors are relevant when determining whether identified misstatements are material? (LO 2)
- What are relevant audit considerations for long-term liabilities involving significant subjectivity? (LO 3)

- What are the relevant audit considerations for merger and acquisition activities, including restructuring? (LO 4)
- What are the inherent risks associated with fair value estimates and related impairment judgments? (LO 5)
- What audit procedures are appropriate when auditing fair value estimates and related impairment judgments? (LO 5)
- What are relevant audit considerations for financial instruments? (LO 6)
- What audit procedures should the external auditor perform when relying on the work of a client's internal auditor? (LO 7)

Complex Auditing Judgments

LO 1 Discuss the nature and types of complex judgments that permeate audit engagements and identify complex audit judgments based on a review of an organization's financial statements.

The *Professional Judgment in Context* feature "Complex Judgments Cause Difficulty for Auditors" illustrates problems auditors have with complex decisions that are made on virtually every audit. Throughout most engagements, the auditor is challenged to evaluate the quality of a client's estimates, including areas such as obsolescence of inventory, allowance for doubtful accounts, pension obligations, warranty obligations, and tax provisions. Experienced auditors often refer to these issues using the broad term "professional judgment" and infer that the judgments are developed through repeated practice. However, recent history, as illustrated through the examples in the *Professional Judgment in Context* feature, indicates that many auditors lack skills in making these professional judgments. The good news is that there are systematic processes for making most of these judgments. You will want to become familiar with these processes as staff auditors are now involved in making these judgments more than ever before.

Identifying Complex Judgments in the Financial Statements

To quickly get a sense of areas where subjective judgments are made during an audit, review the various accounts on the balance sheet of Ford Motor Company in *Exhibit 16.1*.

As you analyze *Exhibit 16.1*, notice the many asset and liability accounts requiring significant judgments, as summarized in *Exhibit 16.2*.

There are also complex judgments applicable to the income statement and a number of other significant estimates that must be disclosed in the notes to the financial statements. For example, Ford Motor Company is regularly involved in litigation and the auditor has to make a decision as to when the amounts to be settled in litigation should be estimated. The auditor needs to assess disclosures about whether the organization has changed plans on which plants they are going to close, or what lines of business the organization may discontinue. All of these changes require a judgmental estimate of the dollar effect that needs to be recognized or disclosed in the financial statements.

EXHIBIT **16.1**	Ford Motor Company—Balance Sheet Accounts	
Assets	**Liabilities**	**Equity**
Cash and cash equivalents	Payables	Capital stock, par value $0.01 per share (3,913 million shares issued of 6 billion authorized)
Marketable securities	Accrued liabilities and deferred revenue	Class B stock, par value $0.01 per share (71 million shares issued of 530 million authorized)
Finance receivables, net	Debt	Capital in excess of par value of stock
Other receivables, net	Deferred income taxes	Accumulated other comprehensive income/(loss)
Net investment in operating leases	Total liabilities	Treasury stock
Inventories		Retained earnings
Equity in net assets of affiliated companies		Total equity attributable to Ford Motor Company
Net property		Equity attributable to noncontrolling interests
Deferred income taxes		Total equity
Other assets		Total liabilities and equity
Total assets		

Source: *Ford Motor Company FYE 2013 10-K.*

EXHIBIT **16.2**	Examples of Balance Sheet Accounts Requiring Subjective Judgments
Assets	**Nature of Judgment**
Marketable securities	• Subject to fair value estimates; auditor must determine if security is marketable and, for most securities, its fair value.
Finance receivables—net Other receivables	• Subject to allowance for noncollectibility.
Net investment in operating leases	• Subject to impairment testing if plants are closing or equipment is not used.
Inventories	• Subject to lower of cost or market impairments, including an allowance for obsolescence.
Net property	• Subject to impairment testing, especially for plants and distribution centers that are closing; subject to estimates made as to (a) expected life of the assets, and (b) appropriateness of depreciation method.
Deferred income taxes	• Subject to estimates of future profitable operations against which the deferred asset might be utilized.
Accrued liabilities and deferred revenue	• Subject to estimates regarding amount of revenue that is properly deferred, as well as the basis for the liability accrual—for example, pensions, warranty liabilities, and accrued vacation.

(continued)

EXHIBIT **16.2**	Examples of Balance Sheet Accounts Requiring Subjective Judgments (*continued*)

Liabilities	Nature of Judgment
Deferred income taxes	• Subject to estimates and assumptions made in preparation of the estimate of income tax expense for the year.
Debt	• Depending on the applicable financial reporting framework, the auditor may need to estimate the fair value of the debt, or the rate at which the debt may be settled in the event of default.

Evaluating Misstatements

 LO 2 Assess whether misstatements, including prior-period misstatements, are material.

The auditor evaluates the misstatements that have been posted to the **summary of unadjusted audit differences** (SUAD) to determine whether uncorrected misstatements are material—either individually or in combination with other misstatements. One important issue is that misstatements from prior periods may have been left uncorrected because they were judged immaterial at the time. However, those misstatements may affect the current period's financial results, rendering the current period's results materially misstated. To illustrate, assume that $100,000 is material for a warranty liability account with a balance of $3,075 million and that the warranty liability misstatement is the only issue under consideration. In the first year, the auditor's evidence supports a conclusion that the client's estimate is overstated by $75,000. In the second year, the auditor's evidence supports a conclusion that the client's book value understates the liability by $85,000. Both years' misstatements are under the $100,000 materiality threshold. The effect on two years is as follows:

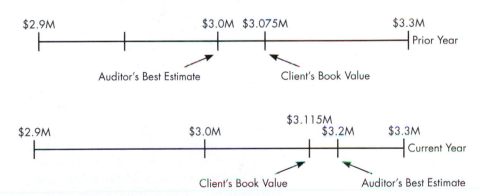

In each year illustrated, the client's estimate of the warranty liability does not differ from the auditor's estimate by a material amount. What is the effect of the client *not* correcting the immaterial misstatements? It is true that the balance sheet is not materially misstated. However, note that the client's book value is higher than the auditor's best estimate in the prior year and lower than the auditor's best estimate in the current year, resulting in a swing of $160,000. Looking at the income statement effect only, not correcting the immaterial amount in the prior year and not correcting the immaterial amount in the current year have caused income to be overstated by a total of $160,000 in the current year—an amount that is above the materiality threshold for the client. Clearly, the direction of the misstatement makes a difference when the effect on the income statement is considered. What has happened is that the client was using the warranty liability account to build a cookie jar reserve in the previous year (overestimating the account balance) and was using the account balance to smooth reported earnings in the subsequent year.

Subjective Differences between the Auditor and the Client

Auditors may have difficulties dealing with clients regarding misstatements in accounts such as warranties where there is no necessarily correct account balance, but only an estimate of a reasonable amount for the account balance. In the earlier example of the warranty estimate, the client may conclude that the estimate is subjective and that there is no way to determine the correct balance until a time in the future when all claims are made. Therefore, the client maintains that its estimate is as good as the auditor's estimate. Similarly, a client may claim that its subjective estimate of the allowance for uncollectible accounts is as good as the auditor's estimate—and therefore, there is not a misstatement in the account balance.

What should the auditor's response be to the client's claim that its estimate is as good as the auditor's estimate? The answer should be fairly simple: The auditor should have gathered sufficient appropriate evidence about the correctness of the account balance and should be able to defend the accuracy of that estimate. Remember, the auditor usually reaches a conclusion about accounting estimates by (a) testing the client's methodology for reaching the estimate (when the auditor believes the client's process is strong and incorporates all relevant variables) or (b) developing the auditor's own model to come up with the estimate and then comparing that estimate to the amount recorded by the client (when the client does not have a robust estimation methodology). In either case, the auditor should not fall victim to an argument that no one can determine the right amount, so the client's estimate is as good as the auditor's estimate.

Aggregating and Netting Misstatements

Professional judgment is particularly important in evaluating whether unadjusted misstatements are material. Even if there are misstatements that are of a lower level than overall or performance materiality, the circumstances surrounding the misstatement may result in a conclusion that the misstatement is material, either individually or when considered with other misstatements.

For most audits, multiple misstatements are detected during the course of the audit. Should each misstatement be considered individually in terms of judging its materiality? Or should the misstatements be aggregated in judging their overall materiality? The answer is that the auditor should evaluate each misstatement individually *and* the auditor should consider the aggregate effect of all misstatements. Further, if an individual misstatement causes the financial statements as a whole to be materially misstated, that effect cannot be eliminated by other misstatements that have a different directional effect on the financial statements. For example, if an organization's revenues are materially *overstated*, the auditor cannot conclude that the effect is immaterial if there is an equal and offsetting *overstatement* of expenses. Rather, the auditor would conclude that the financial statements *taken as a whole* are materially misstated. The rationale is that the trend in revenue growth may be just as important to a user as the effect on net income.

Intentional Misstatements

Sometimes an auditor may uncover an intentional misstatement of a client's financial statements. Even if immaterial, an intentional misstatement may cause serious difficulties in the audit, and for the client. The intentional misstatement may be fraudulent or may be a violation of applicable laws. If the client is publicly traded, Section 10A(b) of the Exchange Act requires auditors to take action upon discovery of an illegal act even if it does not have a material effect on the financial statements, including alerting management and the audit committee. When auditors detect an intentional misstatement, they (1) reconsider the level of audit risk for the client, (2) consider revising the nature, timing, and extent of audit procedures, and (3) evaluate whether to resign from the audit engagement. Further, the detection of an intentional misstatement likely signals the existence of an internal control material weakness and certainly speaks to control environment deficiencies, such as the tone at the top of the organization.

Considerations Regarding Selective Correction of Misstatements

In some cases, the auditor may become suspicious that management is using subjective differences as a rationale for selectively correcting known misstatements. In AS 14, *Evaluating Audit Results*, the PCAOB addresses this issue and labels the selective correction of misstatements as a form of management bias. As such, it is critical that the auditor understand, and truly believe, management's rationale for correcting versus not correcting a known misstatement; it gets to the heart of being a professionally skeptical auditor. Most auditors request the client to correct all known misstatements (unless the recording cost is very high), so there are not carryovers from year to year. If the client does not want to correct the misstatement, the auditor should assume that the client considers the amount to be material.

One common ploy that management may use when the auditor proposes to make an adjustment to correct a known misstatement is to identify an additional adjusting entry that offsets the auditor's proposed entry. If this event occurs, professional standards require the auditor to perform procedures to determine why the new misstatement was not identified previously. The auditor should also consider implications regarding management integrity, and the auditor should adjust risk assessments, including fraud risk assessments, accordingly.

Considering Misstatements in the Statement of Cash Flows

Because of the importance of cash flows to investment decisions, the statement of cash flows has gained in visibility, use, and scrutiny. Auditors should consider whether the statement of cash flows is materially correct, with a focus on assuring appropriate presentation and classification. When the auditor identifies a misstatement in cash-flow classification, the auditor should assess the materiality of the misstatement to determine whether a reclassification is necessary to assure that the statement of cash flows is materially correct. The assessment as to whether the misstatement in classification is material should go beyond the income statement perspective. The auditor should look to factors that are unique to cash flows. For example, cash flow associated with operating activities is often an important measure for investors.

Regulatory Guidance Concerning Materiality Judgments

The Securities and Exchange Commission (SEC) has expressed concern over the practice of waiving, that is, not correcting, immaterial adjustments. Companies sometimes resist correcting an immaterial misstatement, arguing that the effort associated with adjusting the financial statements is not worth the additional precision associated with the immaterial correction. However, the SEC's position is that if management resists making the adjustment, then, by definition, it is material. Auditors have to use their judgment to understand the qualitative reasons for management's refusal to make a correcting entry, but the SEC's position is generally that if management refuses to correct a material misstatement, then the auditor is obligated to issue a qualified or an adverse opinion on the financial statements.

In 2006, the SEC issued Staff Accounting Bulletin (SAB) 108 to address variation in audit practice concerning quantitative materiality judgments related to the disposition of both current-year and prior-year misstatements. Up until that time, auditors used one of two methods to assess materiality: the **rollover method** or the **iron curtain method**. Essentially, the rollover method focuses on the materiality of current-year misstatements and the reversing effect of prior-year misstatements on the income statement. This method may allow misstatements to accumulate on the balance sheet. The iron curtain method focuses on assuring that the year-end balance sheet is correct and does not consider the impact of prior-year uncorrected misstatements reversing in later years.

The SEC objected to the variation in financial reporting outcomes that these alternative methods allowed. SAB 108 now mandates what is termed a **dual approach** to uncorrected misstatements. The dual approach requires the simultaneous application of *both* the rollover and iron curtain methods. If a misstatement is material under *either* method, it must be corrected in the current period.

Assessing Long-Term Liabilities Involving Significant Subjective Judgment

LO 3 Describe audit considerations for long-term liabilities involving significant subjectivity.

Much of the accounting for long-term liabilities is straightforward. For example, bonds are shown at unamortized issue price and are not adjusted to market unless the organization is calling the bonds or is in the process of converting the bonds to equity. However, a number of long-term liabilities require extensive and subjective judgments by the client and the auditor. Long-term liability accounts with a high risk of material misstatement include accounts such as warranty reserves, pension obligations, and **other postemployment benefits**.

Warranty Reserves

The warranty reserve or liability represents the expected future cost related to the sales of an organization's product. The cost of the future warranty claims is estimated and recorded at the time the product is sold. For example, every time Ford sells a new vehicle, it estimates the cost it expects to incur in meeting its warranty promised at the time of sale. The warranty expense and liability are recorded at the time each sale is made. Costs incurred to satisfy the warranty claims are charged against the liability. The client should continuously monitor warranty claims to determine whether an unanticipated change exists in the number or dollar amounts associated with the claims. If the amounts are significantly different from expected, the client should adjust the warranty liability.

Audit Considerations for Warranty Reserves

The audit program for warranty reserves should recognize the past experience of the organization, but should adjust the estimate of the liability for changes in:

- The product, including manufacturing that either enhances or decreases the quality of the product
- The nature of the warranty
- Sales volume, for example, if more sales were made during the last quarter this year than in previous years
- The average cost of repairing products under warranty

The auditor can audit the account by testing the controls that are part of the information system used by the client and/or by performing substantive

Toyota Motor Corporation: Growth, Quality Problems, and Warranty Liabilities

AUDITING IN PRACTICE

Toyota Motor Corporation has historically been viewed as a high-quality producer of safe and reliable automobiles. So, how did Toyota find itself plagued by problems in the 2000s involving accidents, lawsuits, recalls, and high warranty expenses? One prominent theory is that in its attempt to gain market share and exceed the sales of General Motors, the company lost control over the manufacture of some critical vehicle components, including the electrical system and the accelerator. Around 2005, Toyota began a significant shift toward outsourcing important parts of the production process to its key suppliers. However, those suppliers often did not have the same internal controls or reputational incentives associated with product quality as did Toyota. In short, the sales volume goal and related outsourcing led to reduced quality, and the company suffered for this strategic misstep. As of March 31, 2013, Toyota had accrued a warranty liability of $10.665 billion.

The audit implication of this case is that it is easy for auditors, much like consumers, to fall into a nonskeptical frame of mind that they are auditing one of the highest quality automobile companies in the world, and therefore the audit of warranty expense and liabilities should be routine. However, auditors have to be vigilant and alert to changes in processes and data that may indicate that assumptions are no longer applicable.

analytical procedures that involve developing an independent estimate based on the factors identified earlier. For the control testing, the auditor should inquire about and test the effectiveness of the information system used to track warranty items. A proper control allows a company to take effective action to prevent a potential problem with its products. For a real-world example involving the automobile industry, see the *Auditing in Practice* feature "Toyota Motor Corporation: Growth, Quality Problems, and Warranty Liabilities."

As for substantive analytical procedures, the auditor might conduct a trend analysis of the number of claims and analyze the defects causing the claims. The auditor might also consider the reasonableness of dollar amounts to fix each claim and similar variables to estimate the warranty liability.

Pension Obligations and Other Postemployment Benefits

Pensions represent a combination of many items that are difficult to estimate, including:

- Projected lifetime of former employees who will receive a pension
- Nature of the pension plan, for example, a defined benefit or a defined contribution plan
- Future earnings of employees prior to retiring for defined benefit plans
- Earnings rate on invested pension assets, including an assessment of the safety of the invested assets
- Long-term interest rates to discount future costs back to present value
- Changes in pension plans

The client usually engages an actuarial firm to help make these specialized estimates. These individuals work for management, not for the auditor.

To give you a sense of the importance and materiality of the amounts related to pension costs, consider the following disclosure in Ford's 2013 Annual Report (Note 14):

Our policy for funded pension plans is to contribute annually, at a minimum, amounts required by applicable laws and regulations. We may make contributions beyond those legally required. In 2013, we contributed $5 billion to our worldwide funded pension plans (including $3.4 billion in discretionary contributions to our U.S. plans) and made $400 million of benefit payments to participants in unfunded plans. During 2014, we expect to contribute about $ 1.5 billion from Automotive cash and cash equivalents to our worldwide funded plans (most of which are mandatory contributions) and to make $400 million of benefit payments to participants in unfunded plans, for a total of about $1.9 billion. Based on current assumptions and regulations, we do not expect to have a legal requirement to fund our major U.S. pension plans in 2014.

A couple of facts explain why Ford has no legal requirement to make a contribution to its funded pension plans in 2014.

1. Ford made significant contributions (over $5 billion in 2013) in recent years, as part of its risk reduction strategy.
2. Ford increased the discount rate by nearly a percentage point—this reduces the pension liability and increases the funded status of the plans.

Both of these facts helped Ford reduce the underfunded status of the plan significantly, which likely puts the organization in a position of having no "legal" requirement for additional contributions in 2014. Ford's auditor, PricewaterhouseCoopers (PwC) would have evaluated the appropriateness of the decision to increase the discount rate as part of conducting a quality audit.

Many companies also furnish medical insurance coverage as part of their postemployment benefits. The rising cost of medical care has been termed a crisis by many public officials. However, the cost of future medical services is difficult to estimate. To give you a sense of the importance and materiality of the amounts that companies pay for postemployment medical costs, consider the following disclosures in Ford's 2013 Annual Report (Note 14):

The following table presents estimated future gross benefit payments (in millions):

Estimated Future Benefit Payments

	Gross Benefit Payments		
	Pension		
	U.S. Plans	Non-U.S. Plans	Worldwide OPEB
2014	$3,190	$1,380	$420
2015	3,150	1,380	380
2016	3,110	1,390	380
2017	3,060	1,430	370
2018	3,030	1,450	370
2019–2023	14,810	7,820	1,850

Estimates of the other postemployment benefits require estimates of changes in medical expenses, changes in coverage, changes in average life expectancies, and the nature of illnesses to be considered. The client needs an information system to gather and analyze such information in order to make an informed estimate.

Audit Considerations for Pension Obligations and Other Postemployment Benefits

The auditor determines whether the actuarial firm hired by management is independent, capable, and objective so that the actuarial firm's work can be relied upon to provide sufficient appropriate information to assist management in developing the liability estimates. The auditor also evaluates the appropriateness of the actuarial firm's work as audit evidence. The auditor may also hire actuarial specialists to assist the audit team in auditing pension obligations. Such individuals work for the auditor, not for management.

Companies have used pension obligations as a means of smoothing earnings by changing the assumed long-term discount rate or the earnings rate, so this is an important and judgmental area in which the auditor must be careful to exercise appropriate professional skepticism. Therefore, it is critical that the auditor skeptically question significant assumptions. For example, some companies have used assumptions that their pension assets will grow at a rate of 9.5% for the future, when historical growth rates have been around 6% (and even less for the past few years). Other assumptions made by actuaries also need to be examined for reasonableness, for example, average life span; a retired coal miner is not likely to have a retired life expectancy as long as a retired office worker. Professional skepticism and knowledge are required—especially in these judgmental areas.

Auditing Merger and Acquisition Activities

LO 4 Describe audit considerations for merger and acquisition activities, including restructuring.

Merger and acquisition transactions commonly occur. Most of these transactions are acquisitions involving one organization acquiring either an entire organization or an individual operating division. For example, Koch Corporation of Kansas City acquired the consumer products division of DuPont (roughly about 25% of DuPont); Time-Warner Company acquired AOL in a transaction that eventually led to a $94 billion loss for AOL Time-Warner. These transactions present significant challenges related to valuation issues, including

- Valuing the assets and associated liabilities upon acquisition
- Measuring restructuring charges and recognition of the liability

Valuing the Assets and Liabilities of an Acquisition

Determining the cost of an acquisition is fairly straightforward—it is the amount paid to acquire the organization. However, there are a number of acquisition pricing issues that complicate matters. These include acquisitions:

- Made via stock rather than cash
- In which the final price is contingent upon the value of the assets received (post audit)
- In which the final price is contingent on the future performance of the acquired organization or division

An acquisition made via stock is usually straightforward, but is dependent on the marketability of the stock issued. Some contracts simply specify the number of shares issued, while others require the organization to transfer shares equal to a specified market value at a given date.

Most purchase transactions have a good-faith clause in which the purchaser has the right to offset against the purchase price the value of assets that were represented to exist but do not exist. For example, an acquired organization might assert that $1.3 million in accounts receivable exists. But after 180 days, the organization has collected only $600,000, and supporting documentation for the remaining $700,000 cannot be located. In some instances, the contract allows the offset of the $700,000 against the purchase price, but in other instances it may not. The auditor needs to examine the specifics of the contract and the procedures the organization uses to resolve disputes on the existence of assets in order to reach a final purchase price.

In many acquisitions, the acquiring organization may want the management of the acquired organization to stay on and run the business. The managers know the business, they have contacts with the customers, and their cooperation may be crucial to the effective integration of the two organizations. Often, in these situations, the organizations reach an agreed-upon price with significant contingency payments that is based upon the newly acquired organization reaching prespecified performance objectives. The auditor and the client must assess the likelihood of the acquired organizations meeting those performance objectives and determine when to recognize the contingency payments as part of the cost of the acquired organization. If it is highly likely that the organization will meet the objectives, the full cost should be recognized at the time of acquisition.

Valuing Assets and Liabilities The acquiring organization needs to bring all the specifically identifiable tangible and intangible assets and liabilities onto its books at their fair market value (FMV) at the time of acquisition. The FMV of the assets may differ significantly from the book value of those assets. Usually, the organization hires an independent appraiser to value the tangible assets—for example, property, machinery, and office equipment. The intangible assets—for example, patents or copyrights—may be more difficult to value; however, they should normally be valued at the net present value of future (net) cash flows associated with the asset. For example, the copyright to a book might be valued at the net present value of future positive cash flows associated with sales of the book minus the cash outflows to produce and market the book. These estimates may be more difficult to obtain but can often be estimated based on the organization's history with similar books.

Valuing Goodwill In concept, the valuation of **goodwill** is fairly straightforward: it is the excess of the purchase price over the FMV of the acquired organization's tangible assets, identifiable intangible assets, and liabilities. However, U.S. accounting standards for public companies require that goodwill be specifically identified with an operating segment or a reporting unit. By definition, these parts of the business must be sufficiently identifiable so that they can be managed as a unit or may be separately identified and sold as a unit. Otherwise, they become a part of the overall organization's operations. The distinction is important for subsequent valuation because goodwill is tested for impairment annually. See the *Focus on Fraud* feature "Caterpillar Books an Impairment Relating to a Chinese Manufacturing Acquisition" for an example of an acquisition that was made based upon inaccurate reported financial results, thereby resulting in an impairment charge.

We discuss issues related to goodwill impairment as part of LO 5 in the section titled "Auditing Management's Fair Value Estimates and Related Impairment Judgments."

Audit Considerations for Valuing Identifiable Assets and Liabilities

When valuing identifiable assets, the auditor cannot simply accept an appraisal and management's assessment of the FMV of the assets. Rather, the auditor must gather independent evidence to determine whether the assessed values are appropriate. In gathering the evidence, the auditor should:

- Evaluate the qualifications of any management specialists, ascertaining whether the individuals are certified, experienced, and reputable
- Determine if the specialists hired by management are sufficiently independent of management that they will not be influenced by management's objectives

Caterpillar Books an Impairment Relating to a Chinese Manufacturing Acquisition

In November 2011, Caterpillar acquired a Chinese manufacturer of mining machines, subsequently renamed ERA Mining Machinery, for $866 million. During the process of integrating the organization, Caterpillar management uncovered a deliberate plan and associated actions to inaccurately portray the financial health of the organization by fraudulently inflating reported revenue amounts. In 2013, Caterpillar booked an impairment charge of $580 million relating to the declining value associated with the acquisition.

Deloitte and Ernst & Young were the two audit firms that conducted due diligence on the acquisition transaction. In February 2012, the Chinese government issued new rules restricting access to corporate information, which may have hindered the auditors in conducting their due diligence. Both the international nature of the transaction, and the underlying fraudulent representations made by management, illustrate the risks that organizations and their auditors face relating to acquisition transactions.

- Review the methodologies used by the specialists to determine whether they are sound, such as determining if specialists identify sales prices for comparable land or property, or reconstruction costs for buildings

When auditing long-term liabilities and assets obtained through an acquisition, the following types of situations often require the auditor to rely on an auditor's specialist to obtain sufficient appropriate evidence:

- Assets acquired and liabilities assumed in business combinations and assets that may have been impaired
- The valuation of environmental liabilities, and site cleanup costs
- The actuarial calculation of liabilities associated with insurance contracts or employee benefit plans

Measuring Restructuring Charges

When an acquisition occurs, the first thing usually heard from management is that it will (a) restructure operations to achieve efficiencies and (b) reduce the workforce by X%. This is usually followed by an estimate of future cost savings. Organizations restructure their operations continuously, and those costs are reflected in current operating earnings. However, if an organization makes a decision to restructure operations and develops a plan for restructuring (which often happens as part of an acquisition), the plan often includes severance pay for employees and disposal of property. If the restructuring charges are not calculated correctly, the restructuring charges can be used to fraudulently manipulate income. The *Focus on Fraud* feature "The Case of WorldCom's Restructuring Reserves" describes how restructuring charges and reserves were used by WorldCom to fraudulently inflate reported earnings.

Audit Considerations for Restructuring Charges

In auditing restructuring charges, the auditor cannot rely on conservatism as an excuse to let a client overestimate its reserve for restructuring because the subsequent reversal of the liability will affect future income. The audit procedures for restructuring charges include:

1. Review current and proposed financial accounting standards to determine if changes have occurred in accounting for restructuring.

The Case of WorldCom's Restructuring Reserves

WorldCom grew from a small telephone company that emphasized data transmissions to a company that acquired MCI, then the country's second-largest long distance telephone carrier—a company that was significantly larger than WorldCom. WorldCom grew through numerous acquisitions that were used to fuel growth and stock market value. In practically every acquisition, WorldCom would set up a restructuring reserve for the expected future costs associated with the integration of the operations into WorldCom and used the offsetting debit to increase goodwill rather than expenses.

As was its common practice, WorldCom always estimated the restructuring costs to be significantly higher than truly expected, thus creating a large amount of restructuring reserves on the balance sheet. The subsequent expenses associated with the restructuring were significantly less than the reserve that was established.

The Bankruptcy Trustee report on WorldCom indicated that WorldCom would systematically release (debit) these reserve (liability) accounts and credit expenses, thereby increasing reported earnings for the period. Clearly, the entries crediting expenses were fraudulent. However, the audit firm never questioned the amounts of reserves established in the first place because of an attitude that creating a liability is conservative. It did not consider the effect on future income when the company would choose to take the liability off the balance sheet. It is important to note that conservative accounting in one period creates a base for aggressive accounting in a future period. The audit implication is that conservatism is not necessarily the accounting objective. Rather, the objective is the accurate measurement of the economics and condition of the company and acquisition transaction.

2. Review the detail developed by the client in determining its estimate; this should include the identification of specific assets to be disposed of, number of people to be terminated, union contracts on termination, and planned severance pay.
3. Review specific steps taken to date that would indicate that management has moved beyond a plan to terminate to the identification of specific parties or operations that will be affected by the plan. Specific parties or operations must be identified before a liability can be recognized.
4. Review and independently test the estimates by reviewing (a) contracts, (b) appraisals for property or estimates from investment bankers, and (c) severance contracts.
5. Mathematically test the estimates.
6. Develop an overall conclusion on the reasonableness of the liability and the appropriateness of the accounting used by the client.

Auditing Management's Fair Value Estimates and Related Impairment Judgments

LO 5 Describe audit considerations for assessing management's fair value estimates and related impairment judgments, including goodwill impairment judgments.

The measurement and communication of accounting information includes increased emphasis on the quality of assets and liabilities. This emphasis requires that almost every account on an organization's balance sheet needs to be assessed at fair value (including adjustments to net realizable value), and disclosures need to reflect information about the nature of the fair value estimation. We often think about marketable securities as the primary account involving fair value adjustments, but fair value adjustments are also common for property, plant, and equipment that will be sold, for receivables or inventory, and for considering goodwill impairments. Fair value is the amount for which an asset could be exchanged, or a liability settled, between knowledgeable, willing parties in an arm's length transaction. When auditing a

fair value estimate, the auditor is not auditing transactions that have taken place within the client, but is instead evaluating outside market values, industry data on sales and trends, and models of future cash flows.

The Accounting Model for Fair Value Estimates

The concept of fair value implies an orderly market and may not be applicable to certain distressed assets where no market exists. In such situations, the asset may be required to be valued at the lower of cost or market. To guide management and auditors, the Financial Accounting Standards Board (FASB) recognizes that the persuasiveness of information in making an estimate may differ—and there may be many different sources of relevant information. Therefore, FASB has set the following hierarchy of inputs to consider in assessing fair value:

- *Level 1*—quoted prices for identical items in active, liquid, and visible markets such as stock exchanges. An example would be a recent trade on the NYSE of a stock or a bond.
- *Level 2*—observable information for similar items in active or inactive markets, such as two similarly situated buildings in a downtown real estate market.
- *Level 3*—unobservable inputs to be used in situations where markets do not exist or are illiquid. This is often referred to as *mark to model* because it is dependent on management's estimates of future cash flows associated with the asset or liability to be valued. Level 3 valuations are generally viewed as highly subjective.

The client should have (a) a systematic process to identify each asset that is subject to fair value estimation, (b) a process to identify relevant market values, (c) an analysis of whether the organization has the ability to hold the asset to maturity and whether the decline in value is other than temporary, and (d) a realistic process to estimate future cash flows to discount back to a present value.

Accounting for Goodwill Impairment

Our discussion of **impairment** issues focuses on **goodwill impairment**. FASB guidance states that goodwill impairment tests are to be performed annually, as well as on an interim basis at the time events and circumstances warrant. The guidance notes that impairment occurs when the carrying amount of goodwill exceeds its implied fair value. The valuation and future testing of goodwill for potential impairment are facilitated if the client has used a capital budgeting process to determine the justification for the purchase. The client should have estimated future cash flows, cost savings, and strategic plans to estimate the value of the acquisition. Those future cash flows should have been discounted and compared to the cost of capital in making a decision about the acquisition. If the client develops such a model, it will (a) likely make better business decisions and (b) serve as a model that can be used for testing goodwill for potential impairment. The *Auditing in Practice* feature "Goodwill Impairment Not in Accordance with GAAP at ForeverGreen" describes an organization that had difficulties in accounting for its goodwill impairment.

Until 2011, U.S. GAAP required a two-step process to determine the impairment of goodwill:

> *Step 1*—Compare the fair value of the reporting unit with the carrying value of the reporting unit. If the fair value of a reporting unit is less than its carrying amount, then the second step of the test is to be performed to measure the amount of impairment loss, if any.
> *Step 2*—Measure the impairment by comparing the fair value of the goodwill (on a reporting unit basis) with the carrying value of goodwill.

For accounting purposes, **a reporting unit** is the acquired segment or operating segment to which the goodwill from the acquisition is assigned. Note

Goodwill Impairment Not in Accordance with GAAP at ForeverGreen

In December 2011, the PCAOB inspected the audit performed by Morrill of ForeverGreen for the year ended December 31, 2010. Based upon this inspection, the PCAOB determined that ForeverGreen's calculations related to goodwill impairment were not performed in accordance with Generally Accepted Accounting Principles (GAAP). The company reperformed its goodwill analysis in accordance with the appropriate guidance. The revised goodwill analysis used the original inputs, but corrected calculations and comparisons in the original analysis. In this reperformance of the goodwill analysis, ForeverGreen determined that goodwill must be impaired to $0 for the year ended December 31, 2009. Prior to the impairment correction, ForeverGreen had over $7 million of goodwill on its balance sheet. The company restated its financial statements for the years ended December 31, 2009, 2010, and 2011.

For further details, see http://www.sec.gov/ Archives/edgar/data/1091983/0001010412 12000174/f8kfvrg_nonreli4412final.htm for SEC filing by ForeverGreen.

that an **operating segment** is a component of an organization that is a profit center, that has discrete financial information, and whose results are reviewed regularly for purposes of performance assessment and resource allocation. In comparison, a reporting unit is an operating segment, or a segment that is one level below an operating segment (also referred to as a component). So, to determine reporting units, an organization must first determine its operating segments.

As described in the *Auditing in Practice* feature "Changes to the Two-Step Process for Testing Goodwill Impairment," organizations may not always need to follow this two-step process.

When assessing goodwill, the organization needs to determine the reporting unit, which is usually as an operating segment (or part of an operating segment) that (a) provides separate accounting; (b) is managed as a separate segment; or (c) could be easily separated from the organization, such as by a sale of the

Changes to the Two-Step Process for Testing Goodwill Impairment

Beginning in 2011, an organization has the option to first assess qualitative factors to determine whether it is necessary to perform the two-step goodwill impairment test. Examples of the types of factors to consider in conducting the qualitative assessment include macroeconomic conditions such as deterioration in the entity's operating environment, entity-specific events such as declining financial performance, and other events such as an expectation that a reporting unit will be sold. If an organization believes, as a result of a qualitative assessment, that it is more likely than not that the fair value of a reporting unit is less than its carrying amount, the quantitative two-step impairment test would be required. Otherwise, no further testing will be required. Because of this change, an organization is no longer required to calculate the fair value of a reporting unit unless the organization determines, based on a qualitative assessment, that it is more likely than not that its fair value is less than its carrying amount.

An organization can choose to perform the qualitative assessment on none, some, or all of its reporting units. Further, an organization can opt out of the qualitative assessment for any reporting unit in any period and proceed directly to Step 1 of the impairment test. The organization is able to resume performing the qualitative assessment in any subsequent period.

segment. The concept of the reporting unit usually focuses on the acquired organization or segment. On the other hand, the organization as a whole may be the reporting unit if the operations are fully integrated. For example, the AOL Time-Warner merger focused on the synergies of the integrated organization, not on the separate value of the Time-Warner business unit. The determination of the reporting unit should be made at the time of acquisition, but it may evolve over time. If it changes over time, the client should document the changes and provide a rationale that relates to how the organization is managed.

When using the two-step process, in Step 1, the presumption is that the fair value determination of goodwill should be made on the same basis as was the original determination of goodwill and for the same reporting unit. For example, when Time-Warner merged with AOL, the reporting unit was AOL. The difficulty in valuation comes when the organization integrates AOL into the fabric of other operations. Therefore, management's determination of relevant segments and reporting units for goodwill impairment becomes an important judgmental consideration. In Step 2, the judgments become even more difficult as the client must assess future cash flows from the investment that originally led to the establishment of the goodwill.

Exhibit 16.3 outlines various guidelines related to accounting for goodwill impairment, while the *Emerging Issues* feature "Changes and Proposals for Goodwill Accounting" highlights the importance of auditors staying current on the financial reporting requirements of their clients.

Impairment Test When Reporting Unit Is the Combined Organization

In many instances, the reporting unit is the combined organization. If the organization is a public company, the current fair value can be estimated by examining the current market capitalization of the stock. The organization then needs to determine whether fair value is less than or more than the carrying value (book value). If fair value is less than the carrying value, an impairment of goodwill is inferred, and goodwill is written down to

---

| EXHIBIT 16.3 | FASB Guidelines Related to Accounting for Goodwill Impairment When Using the Two-Step Process |

FASB has provided the following guidelines related to goodwill impairment:

- The impairment tests should be performed at least annually, on the same date, but not necessarily at year end.
- Goodwill within operating segments can be offset (netted); however, goodwill that exists in different operating segments cannot be offset.
- The FMV of assets and liabilities must be independently calculated at the same time that goodwill impairment is tested.
- Clear, objective evidence must be gathered to record the goodwill impairment.

Further, situations may arise, other than the annual review, in which the impairment of goodwill should also be addressed. These include:

- A significant adverse change in legal factors or the business environment
- An adverse action or assessment by a regulator
- Unanticipated competition that significantly reduces the value of the organization or reporting unit's products
- A significant loss of key personnel
- A more-likely-than-not expectation that a reporting unit or a significant portion of a reporting unit will be sold or otherwise disposed of
- A significant decline in operations of a significant asset group within a reporting unit
- A goodwill impairment loss recognized by a subsidiary that issues separate GAAP financial statements and is a component of the reporting (parent) organization

Changes and Proposals for Goodwill Accounting

EMERGING ISSUE

In 2013, FASB agreed that private companies should be allowed to amortize goodwill in equal increments over ten years, or less if appropriate, and follow an entity-level model for measuring and recognizing goodwill. This change means that private companies do not have to measure the fair value of individual assets and liabilities and compare that sum to the carrying value of a reporting unit on the books.

In addition to approving the accounting alternatives for private companies, FASB also started a new project to consider whether a simplified goodwill impairment approach should be made be available to public companies as well. You can review the FASB web site at *www.fasb.org* to monitor the progress of this project.

the point where fair value equals the carrying value. *Exhibit 16.4* shows a computation of the goodwill impairment for this type of scenario.

The *Auditing in Practice* feature "Recent Examples of Large Impairments" provides examples of significant impairments recorded by organizations.

Impairment Test When Reporting Unit Is a Separate Subunit of the Organization When the organization as a whole is not the reporting unit, management considers the following sources of information to develop an estimate of impairment: negotiations to sell the reporting unit, current profitability of the reporting unit, projected cash flows compared with cash flow projections made at the time of acquisition, and strategic plans for using the assets.

EXHIBIT 16.4 Calculating Goodwill Impairment When the Reporting Unit Is the Combined Organization

An organization has total assets and liabilities as follows (book values in millions):

Assets—excluding goodwill	$125.1
Goodwill	$ 28.0
Total	$153.1
Liabilities	$ 8.0
Stockholder's equity	$145.1
Total	$153.1

The total market capitalization of the organization at fiscal year end is $112 million. Therefore:

Fair value (FV)	$112.0
Carrying value (CV) or net book value	$145.1
Excess CV > FV	$ 33.1
Amount of goodwill	$ 28.0
Amount of goodwill considered to be impaired:	$ 28.0

If the excess of CV > FV would have been less than $28 million, the amount of goodwill impairment would have been that amount.

Recent Examples of Large Impairments

In 2012, there were three companies that made particularly large, and therefore notable, impairment charges:

- Hewlett-Packard Company booked an impairment charge of $13.7 billion relating to the declining value associated with its 2011 acquisition of software company, Autonomy.
- Microsoft Corporation booked an impairment charge of $6.2 billion related to the declining value associated with its 2007 acquisition of web-based advertiser, aQuantive.
- Boston Scientific Corporation booked an impairment charge of $4.35 billion related to the declining value associated with is 2006 acquisition of medical products organization, Guidant.

These examples highlight the material amounts associated with impairment charges, and therefore the critical importance that auditors place on evaluating management's evaluations.

Audit Considerations for Fair Market Estimates and Related Impairments

Audit Considerations for Fair Value Estimates

Exhibit 16.5 contains an overview of audit considerations concerning fair value estimates. In analyzing the exhibit, note the specific audit challenges relevant to each level of fair value estimation.

EXHIBIT **16.5**   Overview of Audit Considerations for Fair Value Estimates

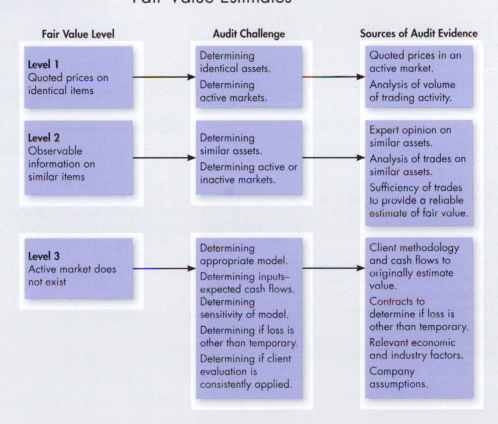

Fair Value Level	Audit Challenge	Sources of Audit Evidence
Level 1 Quoted prices on identical items	Determining identical assets. Determining active markets.	Quoted prices in an active market. Analysis of volume of trading activity.
Level 2 Observable information on similar items	Determining similar assets. Determining active or inactive markets.	Expert opinion on similar assets. Analysis of trades on similar assets. Sufficiency of trades to provide a reliable estimate of fair value.
Level 3 Active market does not exist	Determining appropriate model. Determining inputs—expected cash flows. Determining sensitivity of model. Determining if loss is other than temporary. Determining if client evaluation is consistently applied.	Client methodology and cash flows to originally estimate value. Contracts to determine if loss is other than temporary. Relevant economic and industry factors. Company assumptions.

Level 1 does not represent unusual challenges for the auditor. However, Levels 2 and 3 represent significant challenges—including determining whether or not an active market exists. Level 2 is broad and applies to financial instruments, property, or lower of cost or market considerations for inventory, loans, or receivables. The audit approach for Level 2 requires the auditor to review and assess the following:

- The correspondence of the client's assets to similar assets in an active market
- Whether an active market exists for similar assets
- The client's systematic process for estimating fair value
- Characteristics of any outside appraisers, including whether the appraiser is independent, objective, competent, and has used comparable items in estimating value
- The data used by the organization in estimating future cash flows, including whether the data consider economic conditions and changes in the marketplace and use an appropriate discount rate to determine net present value

Audits of Level 3 balances present the most difficulty because they do not involve an observable, active market. The approach—often criticized—is referred to as *marking to model* because the client is expected to estimate fair value based on a model of the future cash flows associated with the instrument or the asset. For example, many distressed financial instruments do not have a current market value. Further, there is a reluctance to trade such instruments because the value is difficult to ascertain. Therefore, auditors and clients use comparisons of distressed sales in the market place. Obviously, there is considerable lack of precision in these estimates, and that creates audit risk.

The *Auditing in Practice* feature "Determining whether a Decline in Security Value Is Other Than Temporary" identifies a number of factors that an auditor considers in determining whether a decline in market value is other than temporary. Note that the auditor needs to develop an in-depth understanding of the industry, economic trends, and financial health of the parties that are responsible for fulfilling existing contracts. Fundamentally, these requirements are not much different from the understanding that an auditor must have to properly evaluate accounts such as the

---

Determining Whether a Decline in Security Value Is Other Than Temporary

AUDITING IN PRACTICE

Auditing standards describe factors that indicate an other-than-temporary impairment of a security's value has occurred. These factors include:

- The length of time and extent to which the market value has been less than cost
- The financial condition and near-term prospects of the issuer, including specific events that may affect the issuer's operations or future earnings, such as changes in technology or the discontinuance of a segment of the business
- The intent and ability of the holder to retain its investment in the issuer for a period sufficient to allow for any anticipated recovery in market value
- Whether a decline in fair value is attributable to adverse conditions specifically related to the security or specific conditions in an industry or geographic area
- The investee's credit rating and whether the security has been downgraded by a rating agency
- Whether dividends have been reduced or eliminated, or scheduled interest payments have not been made
- The cash position of the investee

allowance for doubtful accounts, loan loss reserves, or the market value of distressed inventory.

Audit Considerations for Goodwill Impairment

The auditor's analysis of goodwill and potential impairment is facilitated if the client has documented (and the auditor has reviewed) the initial assumptions made by the organization in making the acquisition that ultimately resulted in recording the goodwill. The auditor evaluates (a) management's methodology for assessing impairment and (b) whether an objective evaluation of the evidence supports the client's conclusion. *Exhibit 16.6* provides an overview of audit issues that arise when assessing goodwill impairment.

EXHIBIT **16.6**	Overview of Factors Affecting Goodwill Impairment Valuations

Factors to Be Evaluated	Evidence Issues	Potential Audit Problems
Current FMV of the organization	Determine FMV of the total organization. Determine FMV of the reporting unit.	FMV is readily available if publicly traded, but not readily available if not publicly traded. Market valuation may be volatile. FMV might not exist. It might require independent appraisals by investment bankers or estimates using cash flow and discounted present value factors. Assumptions must be made about competition, economic development, product placement, and so forth. These assumptions will be difficult to verify.
Operating segments and reporting units must be clearly defined	If the acquired organization remains intact after the acquisition, it is defined as the reporting unit. The purpose of most acquisitions is to integrate the newly acquired business into the operation of the existing business.	No particular problem for the auditor, but the organization must set up a systematic methodology to clearly define the operating segments and reporting units and trace them over time.
Current FMV of assets and liabilities of non-goodwill assets	Assets could be measured by estimated net realizable value or estimated replacement costs. Liabilities could be estimated by discounted cash flows using current interest rates properly adjusted for risk.	Assets are used as a group of assets. It is difficult to estimate FMV of a group because there may be a limited number of buyers for the group. Replacement cost data may be difficult and costly to obtain, and the data must be adjusted for usage. Interest rates must be adjusted for risk and term.
Goodwill impairment	The impairment is measured by the difference between market value of the reporting unit and the FMV of net assets.	All the difficulties identified previously come into play. Estimates are hard to verify because they are based on assumptions. The auditor needs to perform sufficient analysis to determine the reasonableness of assumptions.

EXHIBIT 16.7 Audit Program for Goodwill Impairment Testing

1. Review the methodology that the client initially used in determining the amount it used to purchase the reporting unit. Examine the initial client documents to determine
   a. Assumptions about economic growth and synergies expected with the acquisition
   b. Expected cash flow, discounted to present terms
   c. Cost savings expected from integrated operations
   d. Assumptions about the general economy, industry growth, and new-product innovation
2. Compare actual results with those expected since the time of the acquisition
   a. Determine significant changes in assumptions and projected results
   b. Estimate the organization's acquisition model with new assumptions that reflect current market conditions, actual results, and current information about cost of capital to get an estimate of reporting unit fair value
   c. Compare fair value with carrying value and determine amount of goodwill impairment
3. If the client does not have the original data, perform an independent analysis of the industry and develop
   a. A set of assumptions about future performance based on industry expectations and the organization's products
   b. An estimate of future discounted cash flows
   c. A sensitivity analysis of changes in value based on industry and cash-flow assumptions
   d. A range of estimates and compare to the carrying value of the reporting unit and goodwill carrying cost
4. If the original reporting unit no longer exists because operations have been fully integrated into operations of the parent organization
   a. Compare book value with market value. A market value less than book value is presumptive evidence that goodwill has been impaired
   b. Determine whether all other assets have been adjusted to fair value, where applicable
   c. Compute difference between market value and book value to determine the amount of goodwill impairment
   d. Review assumptions about future operations, industry position, expected future cash flows, and strategic plans for the business to determine if the write-off in part (c) is sufficient

Exhibit 16.7 provides an audit program for goodwill impairment testing, assuming that the client uses the two-step process described earlier. The audit approach for goodwill impairment, as well as fair value estimates, reiterates a fundamental premise stated in the title of this book: A quality audit requires the auditor to thoroughly understand the client, its business, and its risks.

Auditing Financial Instruments

Overview of Financial Instruments

LO 6 Describe audit considerations for financial instruments.

Many clients have **financial instruments** commonly referred to as derivatives. These instruments have often been created to take advantage of short-term market anomalies, such as differences in interest rates between short- and long-term securities. Others have been developed for the explicit purpose of removing liabilities from an organization's balance sheet. *Exhibit 16.8* contains selected examples of these instruments. As you review *Exhibit 16.8*, note the following:

- The examples in *Exhibit 16.8* are only a few among hundreds of similar instruments existing in the current marketplace.
- Although there are commonalities among all the instruments, each contains unique features that may shift risks to the investor.
- Some instruments do not provide recourse to other specific resources in the event of default but try to make the deal more attractive by providing other terms, such as higher interest rates, to entice users to invest in the securities. For example, most debt securities may be collateralized or provide preference in liquidation. However, many of these securities do not carry such privileges.

EXHIBIT 16.8   Types of Financial Instruments

Call Option

A call option is a financial contract between two parties, the buyer and the seller, in which the buyer has the right (but not the obligation) to buy an agreed quantity of a particular commodity or financial instrument (the underlying asset) from the seller of the option at a certain time (the expiration date) for a certain price (the strike price). The seller (or writer) is obligated to sell the commodity or financial instrument if the buyer exercises the option. The buyer pays a fee (a premium) for this right.

Put Option

A put option is a financial contract between two parties, the buyer and the seller, in which the buyer has the right (but not the obligation) to sell an agreed quantity of a particular commodity or financial instrument (the underlying instrument) to the seller of the option at a certain time for a certain price. The seller of the option is obligated to purchase the underlying asset at that strike price, if the buyer exercises the option.

Collateralized Debt Obligation

A collateralized debt obligation (CDO) is a financial instrument that is essentially a bet on whether an underlying obligation, most often underlying mortgages on homes, will fail or not fail. The holder can be on either side of the bet. Most financial institutions hold the underlying instrument and sell the bet that the instrument will fail.

Event-Risk Protected Debt

An event-risk debt covenant is associated with bonds and is intended to protect the bondholder in case of a credit downgrading of the bond, such as might happen in the case of a leveraged buyout (LBO). The covenants generally allow the investors to resell the debt to the original issuer at par if a stipulated event (such as a change in ownership) were to occur.

Hedges

Hedges are an instrument that allows an organization to hedge against a change in some underlying economic event that may affect the organization. Three common hedges include the following:

- Foreign currency hedge—to protect against a change of the dollar in relation to some other currency
- Fuel hedge—to protect against future changes in fuel prices, for example, Southwest Airlines hedging against future changes in aviation fuel costs
- Commodity hedge—to protect against (or take advantage of) future changes in commodity prices

Floating Rate Note

A floating rate note is a debt instrument with a variable interest rate. Interest rate adjustments are made periodically, often every six months, and are tied to a money market index such as the Treasury bill rate or London InterBank Organizational Rate (LIBOR).

Junk Bond

Junk bonds are high-yielding bonds issued by a borrower with a lower- than-investment-grade credit rating. Many of these bonds were issued in connection with LBOs, while others were issued by companies without long records of sales and earnings.

Interest Rate Swaps

An interest rate swap is an instrument that allows an organization to hedge against future changes in interest rates by either swapping financial instruments, usually a fixed-term investment, for a variable-rate investment, or vice versa. Companies usually do not swap the actual instruments, but they make a notational swap with a financial institution that arranges an equal swap in the other direction.

Zero-Coupon Bond

With no periodic interest payments, these bonds are sold at a deep discount from face value. The holder of the bond receives gradual appreciation in the carrying value of the bond, which is redeemed at face value at maturity. The appreciation in value represents interest income.

(continued)

<table>
<tr><td>EXHIBIT **16.8**</td><td>Types of Financial Instruments (*continued*)</td></tr>
</table>

Securities Sold with a Put Option

Marketable securities can be sold by an investor (not the original issuer) together with a put option that entitles the purchaser to sell the securities back to the investors who sold the securities at a fixed price in the future. These securities often carry low yields.

Collateralized Mortgage Obligation

A collateralized mortgage obligation (CMO) is a debt obligation issued as a special-purpose instrument that is collateralized by a pool of mortgages. The financial instrument is handled as a purchase of a group of mortgages using the proceeds of an offering of bonds collateralized by the mortgages. The financial instrument uses the underlying cash flows of the collateral to fund the debt service on the bonds. The bonds are priced based on their own maturity and rate of return rather than that of the underlying mortgages. CMOs have created secondary markets in the mortgage industry and have assisted the industry in attaining greater levels of liquidity. However, they are subject to the default risk of the underlying mortgages.

Securitized Receivables

Securitized receivables have been converted into a form that can be sold to investors (similar in concept to CMOs). The issuer of the special financial instrument uses the cash flows of the receivables to fund debt service on the securities. In most cases, investors have no recourse to the sponsor or originator of the financial instrument if the underlying loans go into default.

- Although many of the instruments are described as marketable securities, the market is often very thin. Therefore, market quotations may not be an accurate assessment of what the marketable value of the specific securities might be at the balance sheet date.
- Some of the instruments defer the payment of cash to the future, often in the hope that the instrument will be replaced by another one at that time and therefore will not constitute a significant cash-flow burden on the issuer.
- Some of the instruments have specific options, such as the put option that allows the investor to put (sell) the instrument back to the original issuer on the occurrence of a specific event. It would seem that the market value of such instruments would be near par, but remember that the instrument holder's ability to realize par value depends on the original issuer's ability to pay at the time of the triggering event.

Audit Considerations for Financial Instruments

When there is a ready market for financial instruments, and risks can be calculated and controlled, the valuation and disclosure issues for financial instruments are straightforward. However, there are cases where quoted market values are often misleading because they are based on quoted sales at volumes significantly lower than the volume of instruments on an organization's books. In other words, a security that is regularly traded, or available for trade, is not necessarily readily marketable. The auditor must understand the extent that risks affect the valuation of financial instruments, and those risks must be reflected in the financial reports. *Exhibit 16.9* includes a list of risk factors that are commonly associated with derivative securities.

In conjunction with understanding the risks identified in *Exhibit 16.9*, the auditor should understand the controls that a client has implemented to minimize these risks. *Exhibit 16.10* contains guidelines for assessing risks and controls.

EXHIBIT **16.9**   Risk Factors Associated with Derivative Securities

Auditors need to understand the following types of risks that are associated with derivative securities:

- Management's objectives in entering transactions involving derivative securities, and a consideration of how those objectives may relate to the potential for material misstatements in the financial statements
- The proper review by the board and senior management in the decision to initiate the use of derivative securities
- The complexity of features of the derivative securities
- Whether the transaction generating the derivative security involves the exchange of cash, since derivatives not involving an initial cash exchange are subject to heightened risk that they will not be identified for valuation at fair value
- The organization's experience (or lack thereof) with derivative securities, along with its ability to appropriately understand and challenge an outside party's valuation of a derivative security
- Whether the derivative is freestanding or an embedded feature of an agreement
- Whether external factors affect the valuation of the securities, for example, credit risk, market risk, basis risk, or legal risk
- The complex nature of GAAP as they apply to derivative securities

EXHIBIT **16.10**   Controlling Risks Associated with Complex Financial Instruments

Auditors should expect clients to have the following controls if the client uses financial instruments, particularly derivatives:

1. *Identify the risk management objectives*—Investments in financial instruments should follow a well-developed management strategy for controlling risks.
2. *Understand the product*—Analyzing the economic effect of a transaction on each party is crucial for gaining insight into potential risk. Transactions are becoming more complex, with a single instrument often divided into a dozen or more instruments with differing yields and maturities.
3. *Understand the accounting and tax ramifications*—The FASB has worked on a comprehensive document to clarify the accounting for financial instruments based on risks and obligations. Although the FASB cannot anticipate every kind of instrument that may evolve in the next decade, general concepts in the guide serve to lead the client and management to proper accounting. The potential for tax savings has motivated many of the instruments; therefore, potential tax law changes may affect the economics of the instruments.
4. *Develop corporate policies and procedures*—Companies should have explicit policies, preferably in writing, defining the objectives for entering into the new forms of financial transactions. Management should clearly define the nature, risk, and economics of each authorized instrument or type of transaction. The policies should also set limits for investments in specific types of instruments. The board of directors should approve the overall corporate policy.
5. *Monitor and evaluate results*—Procedures should be established to monitor the transaction (instrument) on a regular basis to determine whether the expected benefits fall within the assumed risk levels. If the risk was initially hedged or collateral was obtained, the value of the hedge or collateral should be remeasured. Procedures should be in place to react to risk that has grown greater than the entity wishes to bear.
6. *Understand the credit risk*—Investors should make sure that proper protection exists against default by counterparties. A mechanism is needed for continued monitoring of the counterparty's economic health. Formal credit-monitoring procedures—similar to credit policies for accounts receivable—need to be considered (even for counterparties with prominent names).
7. *Control collateral when risk is not acceptable*—Sometimes credit risk becomes higher than anticipated, but the investor allows the counterparty to keep the collateral. In such cases, investors should implement procedures to assure that they have possession of the collateral.

EXHIBIT **16.11**	Audit Program for Hedges

The audit program for currency hedges includes the following types of procedures:

1. Identify the policies and control procedures the organization has implemented to assure adherence to the procedures.
2. Review all gains/losses associated with the hedged transactions during the year to determine whether the transactions were hedged.
3. Obtain a summary of all hedges currently in effect. Take a sample of contracts associated with the existing hedges to determine that the contracts insulate the organization from the effect of foreign currency fluctuations.
4. Summarize the results of testing to determine if unhedged currency transactions exist. List the unhedged transactions and determine (a) needed disclosure and (b) the appropriate entry to mark the instrument to market.
5. Inquire of management and the financial planning committee about the existence of any other unhedged currency transactions.
6. Inquire of internal audit about any work it has performed regarding hedges. Review the report, especially regarding the existence of controls.
7. Reach a conclusion about the adequacy of the hedges, document the conclusion in the audit documentation, and determine appropriate financial statement presentation.

Audit Considerations for Financial Hedges

Companies that do business internationally purchase hedges to monitor their exposure to foreign currency fluctuations. When auditing hedges, auditors should be sure to (a) understand the product, (b) identify the relevant risk and related controls, including policies and monitoring activities, and (c) understand the underlying accounting. *Exhibit 16.11* provides an audit program for hedges.

Understand the Product Hedges are usually straightforward and have two elements, which may vary by time and by amount:

1. A contract to pay (or receive) payment within a stated period of time, for example, payments made in dollars within ten months
2. A contract to purchase (sell) another commodity or currency at the time of payment to offset changes in the pegged transaction value. The product is designed to keep the transaction constant. Currency hedges, for example, are designed such that an organization neither wins nor loses because of shifts in currency value, for example, the change in the exchange rate between the euro and the U.S. dollar. There usually is no collateral with currency hedges, but there may be with other types of hedges.

Identify the Relevant Risks and Related Controls The risks include the following:

- The instrument categorized as a hedge is not really a hedge; rather, it is a bet that currencies or other referenced data—for example, commodity prices—move in a specific direction; if they move in that direction, the organization will gain.
- All the hedging transactions are not identified or disclosed.
- The organization is taking on more risk than approved by management or the board.

These risks would suggest that the following controls are important:

- Hedges are to be initiated in accordance with organization policies.
- All potentially speculative contracts must really be hedges, not speculation.
- All the transactions are fully disclosed and accounted for.

Further, the auditor would expect the client to have various policies and monitoring activities in place. The auditor should evaluate the specific policies that have been developed and determine whether the monitoring controls and other activities provide evidence of whether these policies are operating effectively. The financial accounting system should produce reports that provide the following information on a monthly basis (or more frequently in some instances):

- Settlement of all contracts during the latest reporting period and any gains or losses
- New transactions that are hedged and whether they are fully hedged
- Summary of unhedged transactions that are subject to currency risk
- Planning budget of future transactions that need hedging
- Summary of issues that should be brought before the financial planning group

The monitoring controls should clearly indicate follow-up actions taken by both the board and management. Unusual gains or losses would be an indication that the controls are not working effectively—planned hedges are not working. Further, there should be periodic testing of the controls by the internal audit group.

Understand the Accounting If the transaction is clearly a hedge such that contracts fully offset each other, there are no required entries on the organization's books other than the existence of the contracts and the need to disclose the nature of the contracts. On the other hand, if the contracts are not balanced, the entity needs to book the changes in obligations at the end of each accounting period. Therefore, the auditor must undertake procedures to determine that the contracts are balanced and whether obligations may exist.

Evaluating a Client's Internal Audit Function

LO 7 Describe the activities of an internal audit function, assess the quality of the client's internal audit function, and determine the effect of a client's internal audit function on the financial statement audit.

When the external auditor obtains the required understanding of a client's internal control, the auditor often will also learn about the client's internal audit function. In many organizations, internal auditors perform a significant amount of work that is relevant to ICFR and the financial reporting processes. Professional external auditing standards provide guidance on the role that internal auditors can play in the financial statement and internal control audits. From an audit risk model perspective, a quality internal audit function can reduce overall control risk, and the work of the internal audit function can be relied upon to reduce detection risk. However, these effects only occur when the internal auditors have performed relevant activities and are of a sufficient level of quality. When determining the role of the internal auditors in the performance of the external audit, and in assessing the quality of the internal audit function, it is important for external auditors to have an understanding of the profession of internal auditing.

An Overview of Internal Auditing

The activities of an internal audit function vary widely across organizations. Internal auditors may perform, among other activities, the following assurance and consulting activities:

- Providing assurance on financial statement-related items
- Evaluating the effectiveness of operations and related controls
- Investigating concerns of fraud
- Evaluating the effectiveness of internal control processes
- Performing operational audits

- Evaluating the organization's compliance with laws, regulations, and organization policies
- Performing information systems and security audits

The Institute of Internal Auditors (IIA) recognizes the breadth of internal audit activities in its definition of internal auditing:

> Internal auditing is *an independent, objective assurance and consulting activity* designed to add value and improve an organization's operations. It helps an organization accomplish its objectives by bringing a *systematic, disciplined approach* to evaluate and improve the effectiveness of *risk management, control, and governance* processes [italics added].

The definition recognizes the uniqueness of internal auditing, which provides assurances to top management and the board and at the same time must not be reluctant to recommend improvements to operating managers. The focus is on adding value by bringing a systematic process for objectively obtaining and evaluating evidence to evaluate risk, controls, and operations.

Independent and Objective Independence and objectivity are related, but they are not the same concept. Objectivity is a personal trait, while independence is primarily a concept related to a department or activity. Independence of the internal audit function is obtained by giving the chief audit executive (CAE) unrestricted access to the board and senior management. The requirement for independence is usually found in an **internal audit charter** approved by the board of directors and audit committee. The charter clearly describes the nature and the scope of the internal audit activity, including its reporting responsibilities. When a strong charter and a strong audit committee exist, the internal audit department often has significant independence. Independence is enhanced when the internal audit director reports to the audit committee rather than directly to top management.

Objectivity implies a detached analytical approach that is conducted without bias to diverse parties who may have a vested interest in the audit findings. Objectivity requires impartiality in gathering and evaluating evidence and reporting the results. Objectivity is necessary if an auditor is to provide both assurance and consulting activities to management and to outsiders.

Assurance and Consulting Activity The IIA defines an **assurance activity** as

> An objective examination of evidence for the purpose of providing an independent assessment on governance, risk management, and control processes for the organization. Examples may include financial, performance, compliance, system security, and due diligence engagements.

Various levels of the organization need assurance on organizational performance:

- Management is interested in the efficiency and effectiveness of operational activities, controls, and compliance with organization policies, contracts, and governmental laws and regulations.
- The audit committee wants assurances that risks are appropriately addressed, controls are working effectively, and processes are in place to achieve financial reporting objectives.
- Operational management needs objective analyses of risks and controls related to its activities.

Consulting activities are defined as

> Advisory and related client service activities, the nature and scope of which are agreed with the client, are intended to add value and improve an organization's

governance, risk management, and control processes without the internal auditor assuming management responsibility. Examples include counsel, advice, facilitation, and training.

There are a number of important points in the definition:

- Consulting can occur only when the audit function and the party receiving the services agree upon the nature and the scope of services.
- Consulting covers a broad range of activities that can include (a) facilitating the organization in conducting an assessment of its controls, (b) sharing insights gained during audits that might improve business processes and the efficiency of operations, and (c) serving as a member of a task force to analyze organization problems.

It is equally important to recognize that consulting activities are advisory. They do not include decision making, such as which system to implement; nor do they include implementation, or assuming responsibility for operating a process. Those tasks are reserved for management.

A Systematic and Disciplined Approach The practice of internal auditing has a defined set of standards to ensure that objective, relevant, and sufficient evidence is gathered and evaluated to address whatever activity is being investigated. The evidence-gathering concept is similar to that of financial auditing, in other words, the auditor is not an advocate of any particular position, and evidence gathering must be unbiased and objective. Internal auditing, like external auditing, starts with a broad understanding of the organization, its objectives, and its risks. The task of the internal auditor is to assimilate the information in a systematic and disciplined fashion that results in an audit program to identify risks, gather evidence, evaluate findings, and suggest improvements.

Risk Management, Control, and Corporate Governance Many of the internal auditor's activities are targeted toward improving risk management, control, and corporate governance within their organization. Understanding the organization's objectives is the fundamental starting point for providing these services. Without understanding objectives, it is not possible to understand what the risks are to achieving those objectives. Sometimes the objectives are explicit, for example, growing market share; other times they are implied, for example, achieving reliable financial reporting. Risk management follows from the understanding of the organization's objectives, while controls exist to help manage risks and are therefore integrally related to risks and risk management. Governance is the process by which the organization and its stakeholders gain assurance that activities are conducted in accordance with broad organizational policies, and that accountability is established.

Serving Management and the Audit Committee

One of the unique features of the internal audit function is that it serves the needs of both the audit committee and management. Internal auditors serve the audit committee in some of the following ways:

- Assisting the organization in reviewing the quality of internal controls over financial reporting as part of the Sarbanes-Oxley requirements
- Providing an independent viewpoint on major accounting issues
- Providing feedback on the efficiency of operations and compliance with the organization's and regulatory policies

Internal auditors assist management in its oversight responsibilities as well. Therefore, an internal audit function assists management by evaluating risk management, internal controls, and effectiveness and efficiency of operations. Internal auditors often take the lead in evaluating the effectiveness of management's documentation of controls needed in order for management to provide assurances on the quality of internal controls.

Staffing an Internal Audit Function

An organization has many alternatives for staffing its internal audit function. These alternatives range from an internal audit function fully housed within the organization, to partial outsourcing for specific projects, to outsourcing the entire function to an outside provider—including to an external audit firm (but not the client's audit firm) or to other specialized firms that perform primarily risk, control, and audit activities. In cases where total outsourcing is selected as the method for obtaining internal audit services, the IIA has stated its position that oversight and responsibility for the internal audit activity cannot be outsourced. The IIA believes that an in-house liaison, preferably an executive or member of senior management, should be assigned the responsibility for internally managing the internal auditing activity.

Outsourcing engagements may be ongoing or for specific time periods or specific projects where special capabilities are needed (e.g., special-need IT audits, environmental audits, derivative reviews, contract audits, and enterprise-wide risk management services). Many internal audit functions outsource or cosource some of their work to assure all of their responsibilities are completed in a timely and competent manner.

Internal Auditing Standards

The IIA is the international body that sets standards for the practice of internal auditing across the world. Professional guidance is provided in the IIA's *International Professional Practices Framework* (IPPF). The IPPF consists of mandatory guidance that includes the *Definition of Internal Auditing*, the *Code of Ethics*, and the *International Standards for the Professional Practice of Internal Auditing*. The IPPF also consists of strongly recommended guidance that describes practices for implementing the mandatory guidance and includes position papers, practice advisories, and practice guides.

The IIA's *Code of Ethics*, part of the mandatory guidance, is designed to promote an ethical culture in the internal audit profession. The *Code of Ethics* consists of the following four principles, each having specific rules of conduct:

- Integrity
- Objectivity
- Confidentiality
- Competency

The *International Standards* outline the basic principles of the practice of internal auditing, provide a framework for performing value added internal auditing, establish the basis for the evaluation of internal audit performance, and foster improved processes and operations. The *Standards* are principles-based, mandatory requirements for the practice of internal auditing. The IIA issued revised standards that were effective January 1, 2013.

Internal Auditing Contrasted with External Auditing

External auditors have a defined role: they provide independent assurance to third parties. In contrast, internal auditors provide a wide array of assurance and consulting activities to those within the organization. Some of the work performed by the internal auditors can be used by the external auditors completing the audit of internal controls and the financial statement audit. *Exhibit 16.12* outlines the differences between the two professions.

<table>
<tr><th>EXHIBIT 16.12</th><th colspan="2">Contrasting Internal and External Auditing</th></tr>
<tr><td></td><td>**External Auditing**</td><td>**Internal Auditing**</td></tr>
<tr><td>**Primary client**</td><td>Audit committee of the board of directors (management of nonpublic companies)</td><td>Management and the audit committee of the board</td></tr>
<tr><td>**Parties receiving assurance**</td><td>Outside stakeholders, regulatory agencies, and stockholders</td><td>Audit committee, upper management, and operational management</td></tr>
<tr><td>**Scope of services performed—primary**</td><td>Audits of financial statements, audits of internal control</td><td>Risk analysis
Control analysis
Operations analysis</td></tr>
<tr><td>**Scope of services— extended**</td><td>Attestation services as demanded by market place</td><td>Information security and reliability
Operational efficiency
Compliance reviews
Special investigations
Fraud investigations</td></tr>
<tr><td>**Primary nature of services**</td><td>Audit and assurance</td><td>Assurance and consulting</td></tr>
<tr><td>**Certification**</td><td>CPA—required</td><td>Certified Internal Auditor (CIA)—required by many companies, but not all</td></tr>
<tr><td>**Relationship to organization**</td><td>Must be independent</td><td>Part of the organization, but should report to audit committee to maintain independence; however, much of the internal audit work can be outsourced to outside providers</td></tr>
<tr><td>**Consulting**</td><td>Cannot perform consulting for public audit clients, but can be performed for nonaudit and nonpublic clients</td><td>Consulting performed when agreed to by management and audit committee</td></tr>
<tr><td>**Audit processes**</td><td>Gather sufficient, appropriate evidence to render an opinion</td><td>Gather sufficient, appropriate evidence to render an opinion, or recommend improvements to a process; includes data analysis, outside confirmations, as well as other procedures normally performed by external auditors</td></tr>
<tr><td>**Major focus**</td><td>Financial statements, internal controls over financial reporting, and financial reporting processes</td><td>Processes, including risks, controls, and effectiveness and efficiency of processes</td></tr>
</table>

Evaluating the Quality of the Client's Internal Audit Function

With an understanding of the internal auditing profession, the external auditor assesses the quality of the client's internal audit function and determines whether the internal auditors' work is both (a) relevant to the external audit and (b) of sufficient quantity and quality. Auditing standards do not require the auditor to use the work of the internal audit function; it is the external auditor's decision to determine the overall audit strategy.

If the external auditor plans to use the work of internal auditors, the external auditor considers three primary characteristics in assessing the quality of the internal audit function: competence, objectivity, and quality of work. Further, updated guidance by the AICPA and the IAASB requires the external auditor to evaluate the application by the internal audit function of a systematic and disciplined approach, including quality control. If the

EXHIBIT **16.13**	Factors to Consider in Assessing the Quality of an Internal Audit Function

Area of Assessment	Factors to Consider in Assessment
Competence	• Educational level and professional experience • Professional certification and continuing education • Review of quality of audit policies, programs, and procedures • Demonstrated supervision and review of internal auditors' activities • Quality of working-paper documentation, reports, and recommendations • Periodic evaluation of internal auditors' performance—both self-assessment and feedback from auditees and audit committee • Periodic quality-control assessments performed in accordance with relevant professional standards, such as the IIA's *International Standards*
Objectivity	• Organizational reporting status is sufficient to assure audit coverage of major organizational risks as well as consideration of, and action on, the findings and recommendations of the internal auditors. • Internal auditor has direct access and reports regularly to the board of directors, the audit committee, or the owner-manager. • Board of directors, the audit committee, or the owner-manager oversees employment decisions related to the director of the internal audit function. • Policies that prohibit internal auditors from auditing areas where relatives are employed in important or audit-sensitive positions. • Policies that minimize other potential conflicts of interest, such as auditing an area where they were employed before entering internal audit, or where they will be placed after spending time in internal audit.
Quality of internal audit work	• Demonstrated use of systematic and disciplined approach. • Scope of work is appropriate to meet the objectives. • Audit programs are adequate. • Working papers adequately document work performed, including evidence of supervision and review. • Conclusions are appropriate in the circumstances. • Reports are consistent with the results of the work performed.

external auditor determines that the internal audit function lacks a systematic and disciplined approach to its activities, the external auditor will not use the work of the internal auditor in obtaining audit evidence. *Exhibit 16.13* presents a list of the factors that the external auditor considers in evaluating the competence, objectivity, and quality of work, such as a systematic and disciplined approach.

In assessing the factors in *Exhibit 16.13*, the external auditor examines relevant evidence. For example, in assessing the quality of work, the auditor corroborates the internal auditor's assessments and conclusions by taking a sample of the some of the items examined by the internal auditor or a sample of similar transactions. Although the factors in *Exhibit 16.13* could lead one to set up a checklist and tick off each item (e.g., education or certification), the intent is to guide the external auditor in a systematic evaluation of the internal audit function. Most likely, the external audit team has had interaction with various levels of internal audit and has knowledge of the scope of their work and the competence with which they carry out their work.

Effect of Internal Audit's Work on the External Audit

Even though the internal auditors' work may affect the external auditor's procedures, the external auditor still needs to perform enough procedures to obtain sufficient appropriate evidence to support the auditor's report. The responsibility for the external audit rests solely with the external auditor, and this responsibility cannot be shared with the internal auditors. The external auditor must perform enough work to be able to assume responsibility for the audit opinions.

There are two approaches to using the work of a client's internal audit function: (1) use internal auditors to provide **direct assistance** during the audit, and (2) rely on internal audit work already performed. The second approach works best when the two audit groups coordinate the planning and execution of specific audit tests. *Exhibit 16.14* describes the relevant standards concerning reliance on the internal audit function.

The *Emerging Issues* feature "UK Prohibits Internal Auditor Direct Assistance" describes new international prohibitions against external auditors using the direct assistance of internal auditors during the external audit process.

In making judgments about the nature and effect of the internal auditors' work on the external auditor's procedures in specific audit areas, the external auditor considers the following issues:

1. Risk of material misstatement of the assertions related to financial statement amounts
2. Level of judgment involved in planning and performing the procedures and evaluating the audit evidence obtained
3. Level of objectivity of the internal auditors
4. Level of competence of the internal auditors

For some assertions, such as existence and occurrence, the evidence gathered is objective. For other assertions, such as the valuation and disclosure assertions, more audit judgment is required and the evaluation is more subjective. As the risk of material misstatement of account balances or assertions increases, or the subjectivity of evidence evaluation increases, more of

---

EXHIBIT **16.14**	Comparison of Worldwide Professional Auditing Guidance Regarding Reliance on the Internal Audit Function
AICPA Auditing Standards Board (ASB)	AU-C 610 provides guidance that is effective or after December 15, 2014. This guidance allows the auditor to rely on work already performed by the internal auditor or to use the internal auditors as direct assistants during the auditor. The guidance cautions that the internal auditors must be sufficiently competent and objective. Further, the external auditors need to consider the materiality, risk, and evidence subjectivity of an audit area before determining the extent of reliance to place on the work of the internal auditors. Finally, AU-C 610 indicates that when internal auditors' work is relied on, the external auditor should evaluate and perform audit procedures on that work.
Public Company Accounting Oversight Board (PCAOB)	AS 5 encourages the external auditor to use the work of the internal auditor as a means to improve audit efficiency, and reminds the auditor to consult the requirements and guidance in the PCAOB's AU 322 (interim standard).
International Auditing and Assurance Standards Board (IAASB)	ISA 610 (Revised 2013) provides guidance that is effective on or after December 15, 2013. This guidance is similar to that provided in AU-C 610. Further, ISA 610 (Revised 2013) provides new guidance (effective on or after December 15, 2014) that specifies the conditions and establishes responsibilities of the external auditor if the external auditor intends to use internal auditors to provide direct assistance during the audit.

UK Prohibits Internal Auditor Direct Assistance

EMERGING ISSUE

The UK's Financial Reporting Council has issued a rule (effective on or after June 15, 2014) prohibiting internal auditors from providing direct assistance to the external auditors performing their financial statement audit. The FRC perceives that this prohibition should strengthen external auditors' independence by mitigating an overly close relationship between audit firms and their clients.

the work needs to be performed directly by the external auditor. Examples of areas that meet these criteria include the following:

- Valuation of assets and liabilities involving significant accounting estimates
- The existence and disclosure of related-party transactions, contingencies, uncertainties, and subsequent events

In contrast, areas where evidence evaluation is more objective include cash, prepaid assets, and additions to long-lived assets.

For some assertions, the external auditor may decide that because of work performed by internal auditors, the audit risk has been reduced to an acceptable level and that testing of the assertions directly by the auditor may not be necessary. However, the external auditor should reperform or test some of the work completed by the internal auditors.

Because the auditor has the ultimate responsibility to express an opinion on the financial statements, many of the audit judgments must be made by the external auditor and should not be delegated to the internal auditors. Some of these judgments include assessments of the following:

- Inherent and control risks
- The materiality of misstatements
- The sufficiency of tests performed
- The evaluation of significant accounting estimates

SUMMARY AND NEXT STEPS

The auditor encounters many complex auditing judgments requiring an understanding of the fundamental auditing concepts introduced in earlier chapters and the application of a structured process for making such judgments. For example, auditors make judgments about the materiality of potential misstatements. Other complex judgments requiring auditor consideration include those relevant to long-term liabilities, merger and acquisition activities, fair value estimates, and financial instruments. Finally, auditors assess the quality of the internal audit function, and determine the effect of the internal auditors' work on the financial statement and integrated audit.

This chapter marks the end of the external auditing topics in this book the next chapter introduces other services that audit firms provide, including reviews, compilations, assurance on interim financial information, attestation engagements relating to agreed-upon procedures, financial forecasts and projections, pro forma financial information, forensic accounting, and sustainability reporting.

SIGNIFICANT TERMS

Assurance activity Objective professional services that improve the quality of information about processes; effectiveness of controls; reliability of information; or compliance with the organization's, regulatory, or governmental procedures; and the effectiveness and efficiency with which the organization carries out its operations.

Consulting activity Advisory or partnering activity that adds value and improve an organization's operations, in which the nature and scope of services are agreed upon with the client. Examples include counsel, advice, facilitation, process design, and training.

Direct assistance Use of internal auditors to perform audit procedures under the direction, supervision, and review of the external auditor.

Dual approach A method of misstatement correction that requires use of both the iron curtain and rollover methods to determine whether a misstatement is material.

Fair value estimate The price that would be received to sell an asset or paid to transfer a liability in an orderly transaction between market participants at the measurement date.

Financial instruments A broad class of instruments—usually debt securities, but also equity or hedges—that represents financial agreements between a party (usually an issuer) and a counterparty (usually an investor) based on either underlying assets or agreements to incur financial obligations or make payments; instruments range in complexity from a simple bond to complicated agreements containing puts or options.

Goodwill The excess of the purchase price over the FMV of the acquired organization's tangible assets, identifiable intangible assets, and liabilities.

Goodwill impairment The decrease in the value of goodwill. Measured by comparing the fair value of the reporting entity with the carrying value of entity. If fair value is less than carrying value (including goodwill), the presumption is that goodwill has been impaired. Goodwill should be written down to an amount that would cause fair value to be no more than carrying value.

Impairment This occurs when events or changed circumstances cause the estimated future cash flows (future benefits) of an asset to fall below the asset's book value.

Iron curtain method A method of misstatement correction that focuses on assuring that the year-end balance sheet is correct; this method does not consider the impact of prior-year uncorrected misstatements reversing in later years.

Internal audit charter A formal, written document that defines the purpose, authority, and responsibilities of the internal audit function within the organization.

Operating segment A component of an organization that is a profit center, that has discrete financial information, and whose results are reviewed regularly for purposes of performance assessment and resource allocation.

Other postemployment benefits All postretirement benefits, other than pensions. Must be identified and measured by the organization. The accounting treatment is conceptually the same as pensions.

Reporting unit For accounting purposes, it is the acquired segment or operating segment to which the goodwill from the acquisition is assigned. Tests for goodwill impairment are performed at the reporting unit level.

Rollover method A method of misstatement correction that focuses on the materiality of the current-year misstatements and the reversing effect of prior-year misstatements on the income statement, thereby allowing misstatements to accumulate on the balance sheet.

Summary of unadjusted audit differences A summary of unadjusted audit differences that is communicated to the audit committee is described in the management representation letter, and that is evaluated individually and in the aggregate for determining whether the financial statements are materially correct.

TRUE/FALSE QUESTIONS

16-1 **LO 1** Complex auditing judgments often involve accounts that require subjective estimates by management.

16-2 **LO 1** The inventory account does not require any subjective estimates by management.

16-3 **LO 2** When evaluating identified misstatements, the auditor only needs to consider misstatements in the current year, and not misstatements from the prior year.

16-4 **LO 2** A misstatement that is intentional is not assessed any differently by the auditor than a misstatement that is unintentional.

16-5 **LO 3** Auditors can choose to test the client's warranty reserves using primarily tests of controls and substantive analytical procedures.

16-6 **LO 3** When auditing pension obligations, the auditor likely uses a specialist to assist the audit team.

16-7 **LO 4** Goodwill is the excess of the purchase price over the FMV of the acquired organization's tangible assets, identifiable intangible assets, and liabilities.

16-8 **LO 4** Because of conservatism considerations, auditors should allow a client to overestimate its reserve for restructuring.

16-9 **LO 5** U.S. accounting standards require public companies to use a two-step process to determine the impairment of goodwill.

16-10 **LO 5** An audit of Level 1 assets is likely to be less challenging than an audit of Level 3 assets.

16-11 **LO 6** When there is a ready market for financial instruments, the audit procedures related to valuation and disclosures are more straightforward than when the instrument is not readily marketable.

16-12 **LO 6** When auditing financial hedges, the auditor should understand the product, identify relevant risks and controls, and understand the appropriate accounting.

16-13 **LO 7** Internal auditors can perform both consulting activities and assurance activities for their organizations.

16-14 **LO 7** All internal auditors are required to have the CIA designation in order to practice internal auditing.

MULTIPLE-CHOICE QUESTIONS

16-15 `LO 1` Complex judgments are found in what types of accounts?
a. Asset accounts.
b. Liability accounts.
c. Income statement accounts.
d. All of the above.

16-16 `LO 1` Which of the following statements is true about accounts requiring management estimates?
a. Because these accounts are estimates, the auditor likely just accepts whatever management determines to be appropriate.
b. Only a limited number of accounts on the balance sheet require management estimates.
c. Net accounts receivable is an account that does not require a management estimate.
d. None of the above is true.

16-17 `LO 2` Which of the following actions will the auditor take when evaluating identified misstatements?
a. The auditor will consider misstatements in both the current and prior periods.
b. The auditor will use either the rollover method or the iron curtain method, but not both.
c. The auditor will evaluate each misstatement individually, rather than consider the aggregate effect of all misstatements.
d. The auditor will do all of the above.

16-18 `LO 2` Which of the following statements is true regarding the auditor's evaluation of misstatements?
a. The auditor should consider the client's selective correction of misstatements to be a form of management bias.
b. The auditor does not need to consider whether the statement of cash flows is materially correct.
c. If the client resists correcting a misstatement the auditor should consider that misstatement to be material.
d. Both a. and c. are true.

16-19 `LO 3` Which of the following would the auditor not try to determine about a client's warranty estimate?
a. Whether the estimate is reasonable in the circumstance.
b. Whether the estimate was based on verifiable, objective assumptions.
c. How management developed the estimate.
d. Whether the factors and assumptions used by management deviate from historical patterns.

16-20 `LO 3` Which of the following procedures would an auditor most likely perform as part of auditing management estimates of long-term liabilities?
a. Inquire of management about related party transactions.
b. Confirm inventories held at outside warehouses.
c. Review past experience of the client related to warranty claims.
d. Send confirmations to client vendors.

16-21 `LO 4` Which of the following valuation issues are associated with merger and acquisition activity?
a. Valuing assets of the acquired organization at their FMV at the time of acquisition.
b. Measuring restructuring charges associated with the acquisition.

    c. Valuing liabilities of the acquired organization at their FMV at the time of acquisition.

    d. All of the above.

16-22 **LO 4** Which of the following situations might require an auditor to rely on a specialist to obtain sufficient appropriate evidence related to acquisitions?

    a. The acquired organization has assets that may have been impaired.

    b. The acquired organization has environmental liabilities related to site clean-up costs.

    c. The acquired organization has liabilities related to employee pension plans.

    d. All of the above.

16-23 **LO 5** A Level 3 fair value estimate is an estimate based on which of the following?

    a. The value of similar assets traded on a foreign exchange.

    b. The value of the same asset, but traded on a foreign exchange.

    c. The value is not readily observable in any marketplace and therefore requires an estimate using a model.

    d. The value is not readily observable, but there are market trades of similar assets that can serve as a surrogate for value of the asset in question.

16-24 **LO 5** Which of the following pieces of evidence would most likely *not* be considered by the auditor in evaluating the potential impairment of goodwill?

    a. The acquisition made by a competitor of an organization that is not a direct competitor of the client.

    b. The current market capitalization of the organization in comparison with its net book value.

    c. The cash flows and operating data of the reporting unit since acquisition compared with estimates made at the time of acquisition.

    d. The growth or decline in market share of the reporting unit since acquisition.

16-25 **LO 6** An audit client has invested heavily in new equity and debt securities. Which of the following would *not* constitute an appropriate role for the organization's board of directors?

    a. Receive and review periodic reports by the internal audit function on compliance with the organization's investment policies and procedures.

    b. Approve all new investments.

    c. Review and approve written policies and guidelines for investments in marketable securities.

    d. Periodically review the risks inherent in the portfolio of marketable securities to determine whether the risk is within parameters deemed acceptable by the board.

16-26 **LO 6** Which of the following factors is a risk factor associated with derivative securities that should be considered by the auditor?

    a. Management's objective for entering into such transactions may relate to misstating the financial statements.

    b. The complexity of the security.

    c. The organization's experience with such securities.

    d. All of the above are risk factors.

16-27 **LO 7**　For which of the following audit areas would the external auditor be least likely to rely on work performed by a client's internal audit function?

a. Valuation of a client's restructuring charge.
b. Existence of inventory.
c. Cutoff tests of revenue.
d. Existence of cash.

16-28 **LO 7**　An internal auditor's work would most likely affect the nature, timing, and extent of external audit procedures when the internal auditor's work relates to which of the following assertions?

a. Valuation of contingencies.
b. Valuation of intangible assets.
c. Existence of fixed asset additions.
d. Valuation of related-party transactions.

REVIEW AND SHORT CASE QUESTIONS

NOTE: Completing *Review and Short Case Questions* does not require the student to reference additional resources and materials.

NOTE: For the remaining problems, we make special note of those addressing fraud, professional skepticism, and ethics.

16-29 **LO 1**　Is it reasonable for the auditor to make judgments about the acceptability of subjective estimates made by the client? If yes, explain the process by which an auditor should make such judgments.

16-30 **LO 1**　Are inventory, accounts receivable, and property, plant, and equipment subject to fair value estimates? Explain and state how the fair value concept is applicable to these accounts.

16-31 **LO 1**　Review *Exhibit 16.2* and identify balance sheet accounts requiring subjective judgments and describe the nature of those judgments.

16-32 **LO 2**　What are the differences between the rollover method and the iron curtain method in terms of evaluating uncorrected misstatements?

16-33 **LO 2**　Should the materiality of misstatements be considered individually or combined to be considered in aggregate with other misstatements when considering whether the financial statements are misstated? When is a misstatement considered clearly trivial?

16-34 **LO 2**　When might a quantitatively small misstatement be considered material?

16-35 **LO 2**　Why is it important to assess whether potential misclassifications in the statement of cash flows are material?

16-36 **LO 2**　Staff Accounting Bulletin (SAB) No. 108 articulates guidance on applying the dual approach to evaluating uncorrected misstatements. Under the dual approach, a misstatement must be corrected if it is material (using guidelines established in SAB No. 99) under either the rollover method or the iron curtain method. Assume that a liability is overstated by $100 because a $20 misstatement occurred in each year of a five-year period ending in the current period. Also assume that materiality for the income statement is $50 and materiality for the balance sheet is $75.

a. What is the current-year effect of the error under (a) the rollover method and (b) the iron curtain method?
b. What adjustment do you recommend for this year? Explain the rationale for your proposed adjustment.

16-37 **LO 2**　Assume that a client has a recurring late cutoff error. Prior-year sales included $10 million of current-year sales, and current-year sales include $12 million of next year sales.

a. What is the misstatement under the (a) rollover method and (b) the iron curtain method?

b. Now assume that the client had an early cutoff error in the prior year such that $10 million of prior-year sales are included in current-year sales and a late cutoff error in the current year such that $12 million of next year sales are included in the current year. What is the misstatement under the (a) rollover method and (b) the iron curtain method?

FRAUD

16-38 LO 2   Assume that an auditor finds a material misstatement regarding the financial statements while performing substantive tests of the account balance. More importantly, the auditor concludes that the misstatement involved the intentional misapplication of an accounting principle to achieve a desired financial result.

a. What actions should the auditor take upon detecting an intentional misstatement in the financial statements? To whom must the misstatement be reported?

b. If management agrees to correct the misstatement, is there a need to communicate the nature of the misstatement to important stakeholders of the organization? If yes, explain the avenues the auditor has available to report the misstatement.

c. What are the implications of detecting an intentional misstatement in terms of evaluating the control environment and the effectiveness of internal control over financial reporting?

16-39 LO 2   During the course of auditing year-end financial statements, the auditor becomes aware of misstatements in an organization's financial statements. When combined, the misstatements result in a 4% overstatement of net income and a $0.02 (4%) overstatement of earnings per share. Because no item in the financial statements is misstated by more than 5%, the auditor concludes that the deviation from the applicable financial reporting framework is immaterial and that the accounting is permissible. The auditor notes that the FASB *Codification* states that the provisions of the *Codification* need not be applied to immaterial items.

a. Based on the scenario above, should the auditor of these financial statements assume that the identified misstatements are immaterial? Why or why not?

b. What additional information might the auditor choose to analyze to determine whether the financial statements are misstated by a material amount?

16-40 LO 3   An often contentious area of discussion between the auditor and the client is the preciseness with which an estimate is to be made, for example, an estimate of the warranty liability of an automotive manufacturer.

a. Scenario: Your client argues that because an estimate is subjective, the range for materiality ought to be larger than it would be for a less subjective account. Do you agree or disagree? Explain your rationale.

b. Regarding the preciseness of the estimate, respond to the following quote from an ex–audit partner: "The preciseness of the estimate is dependent on the soundness of the underlying prediction model. If the auditor determines that the inputs are correct and agrees on the model, there is no need for audit judgment."

      i. Indicate the extent to which you agree or disagree with the statement.

      ii. How might an auditor verify that the model is sound?

      iii. If there is a precise answer, should the auditor overrule the answer with a judgment that contains subjectivity? If you believe the answer is yes, identify the factors that should lead the auditor to override the judgment. If you believe the answer is no, state your rationale.

16-41 **LO 3** Describe the significant estimates that must be made with the following liability accounts.

a. Warranty reserves

b. Pension obligations

c. Postemployment benefit liabilities other than pensions

16-42 **LO 3** Explain how outside specialists are used in auditing pension obligations.

16-43 **LO 3** You have been assigned to the audit of Oshkosh Truck Corporation. The organization is the leading manufacturer of fire trucks and heavy-duty army trucks. All of the basic components are warrantied for 100,000 miles or four years, whatever comes first. There is a different warranty if the trucks are used in desert lands, and that warranty is for 40,000 miles or 18 months, whatever comes first.

a. Identify the components of an information system that Oshkosh Truck should establish to develop an estimate of the warranty liability and warranty expense.

b. Assume the organization established an information system to your specifications described in part (a). Write an audit program to audit the accuracy of the process that would provide audit evidence on the reasonableness of the warranty expense and warranty liability account.

c. Assume that last year, 60% of the trucks sold to the army were designated for use in the Middle East and thus carried only the 40,000 miles or 18-month warranty. Explain how this change would affect the recognition of the warranty expense and liability account.

d. Assume that the warranty liability has been growing over the past few years because actual warranty expenditures have been significantly less than estimated. Assume there has been no significant decline in the quality of the vehicles produced.

(i) What information would the auditor gather to determine whether the liability might be materially overstated?

(ii) If the auditor concludes the liability is materially overstated, what is the proper accounting? The organization proposes to reduce the warranty expense this year and in coming years until the warranty liability is not overstated.

16-44 **LO 4** Why do audits of acquisitions and mergers have high levels of inherent risk?

FRAUD   **16-45** **LO 4** Explain how WorldCom used restructuring reserves (liabilities) to fraudulently manipulate reported earnings.

16-46 **LO 4** How does an organization measure the cost of an acquisition of another organization? What factors often complicate the determination of actual cost? Explain how each factor complicates the calculation of cost and the steps the auditor has to take to reach a conclusion about the cost of the acquisition.

16-47 **LO 4** How is the amount of goodwill determined at the time of acquisition?

16-48 **LO 4**   Does the auditor always need to engage another independent specialist to test the work of the specialist hired by the organization to determine the value of the tangible and intangible assets other than goodwill? Explain, incorporating the idea of the importance of auditor professional skepticism.

16-49 **LO 5**   What is fair value? When are fair value concepts applied?

16-50 **LO 5**   Fair value guidance suggests that there may be three levels of evidence available to assess fair value. Explain the nature of Level 1, Level 2, and Level 3 fair value estimates and the type of information the auditor needs to evaluate each type.

16-51 **LO 5**   How does an auditor test for the impairment of goodwill? What are the significant judgment issues that must be addressed?

16-52 **LO 5**   What factors might signal the likelihood that goodwill may be impaired? Explain and indicate how the auditor would be aware of each of these factors.

16-53 **LO 5**   How does an auditor determine the fair value of goodwill if:
a. The reporting unit is the total organization and the organization is publicly traded?
b. The reporting unit is the total organization and the organization is not publicly traded?
c. The reporting unit is an operating segment?

16-54 **LO 5**   Assume the organization's stock price goes down in a bear market that occurs at the end of the year. However, the stock price more than doubles in the next year. The organization recognized goodwill impairment at the end of the year when the stock price was low. Because the market decline was temporary, should the goodwill be written back up to its original value? What are the problems in using temporary market values?

16-55 **LO 5**   Assume that in 2015, Nelson Communications purchased a controlling interest in Telnetco that resulted in goodwill in the 2015 consolidated financial statements of $4,500,000. There are no other intangible assets. Telnetco continues to be listed on NASDAQ. Near the end of 2016, Nelson estimated that the FMV of Telnetco was $50,500,000 based on the present value of its future cash flows. Using the assistance of a professional appraisal firm, the FMV of its net tangible assets was determined to be $46,900,000, resulting in a goodwill write-down of $900,000.
a. Describe the inherent risks to this write-down.
b. Describe the audit evidence needed to evaluate the fairness of this write-down.
c. How might a specialist be of help?

16-56 **LO 5**   Merrill Publishing Company has operated primarily as a printer of catalogs, SEC filings, and phone books. During the past few years, it has:
• Expanded into a new product line in magazine publishing through the purchase of Wausau Printing Company
• Developed a professional web site that makes all the information in the printed documents available on a subscription basis to the companies that come to it for printing
• Purchased St. Paul Labels, which makes labels for canned products
• Purchased Consumer Custom Design (CCD), which develops designs for cardboard food products such as cereal and other food products that are delivered in cardboard containers. The designs are developed on the Internet and are downloaded to

companies for printing on their packaging products. The organization recorded goodwill of $15 million, $12 million, and $8 million, respectively, for the Wausau, St. Paul Labels, and Consumer Customer Design purchases.

a. Define an operating segment. Identify the criteria that Merrill might use to define an operating segment. Identify when the decision should be made to classify a purchase as part of an operating segment.

b. Assume that Merrill merges the operations of St. Paul Labels and Consumer Custom Design into one operating segment, which it has labeled as food product print design. The segment has been successful, but the operations relating to cardboard design, after three years, continue to fall below expectations. Because the operations are integrated, how would the client and the auditor measure the possible impairment of goodwill in the segment? In other words, it appears that the operations generated from St. Paul Labels are strong while the operations integrated from CCD are weak.

c. What are the problems associated with measuring the impairment of goodwill for the food product print design unit?

d. How would the auditor test for goodwill impairment for the purchase of Wausau Printing Company, assuming that it remains an identifiable unit? Also assume that cash flow and profitability continue to exceed the budget used in determining a purchase price. Does the organization still need to obtain an independent assessment of the FMV of the total organization and the operating entity on an annual basis? Discuss the rationale for your answer.

16-57 **LO 5** Assume that Sun, Inc. had identified a potential write-down of at least $1.8 billion related to a reporting unit.

a. What is a reporting unit? How does Sun determine what constitutes a reporting unit for the purpose of determining a goodwill impairment?

b. Explain how the market value of the firm as a whole influences the need to recognize an impairment of goodwill.

c. Assume that the reporting unit was the storage solutions unit. While the past year's results have been poor, management maintains that it has developed significant new products that repositions the organization to take a leadership role in storage solutions and that it expects significant improvement in results starting in the following year. Outline the major elements of an audit program to determine whether there is a goodwill impairment, and if there is, the extent of the goodwill impairment.

16-58 **LO 6** In what ways do some of the newer types of financial instruments differ from traditional financial instruments? What additional risks are associated with such securities?

16-59 **LO 6** What controls should an organization implement if it wishes to become an investor in more complex financial instruments? Explain the purpose of each control.

16-60 **LO 7** What is objectivity as it relates to the internal audit function? What factors does an external auditor consider when assessing the objectivity of a client's internal audit function?

16-61 **LO 7** For what types of assertions and accounts can the external auditor rely on work performed by a client's internal audit function? Are there accounts and assertions where the external auditor would likely not rely on the work performed by a client's internal audit function? Explain.

16-62 **LO 7** What factors does an external auditor consider when assessing the competence of the internal audit function and quality of work performance of a client's internal audit function?

16-63 **LO 7** AS 5 encourages the external auditor to consider the work of the internal audit function in accumulating audit evidence when performing an integrated audit of internal control and financial statements.
   a. What information does the external auditor use to assess the internal auditor's objectivity?
   b. Can the internal auditor attain the same level of objectivity in an audit as the external auditor? Explain.
   c. An external auditor is considering whether to rely on the work performed by a client's internal audit function. The following is known about the internal audit function:
      i. The internal audit function undergoes periodic external quality reviews to address the quality of its audits and the compliance of the audits with the *International Standards for the Professional Practice of Internal Auditing*. The quality reviews also examine the quality-control procedures used by the function. The internal audit function has always received high marks in these reviews.
      ii. The internal audit function has a history of hiring high-quality staff and subsequently placing that staff in management positions.
      iii. The organization has a reputation for hiring technologically competent auditors.
         Based on what is known about the internal audit function, present arguments for and against relying on the internal audit function's work. What additional information should the external auditor consider before determining the quality of the internal audit function?

16-64 **LO 7** TLD CPAs is performing the audit of REDTOP Sports. You are on the external audit team for that engagement. Following is some information about the client and its internal audit function. After reviewing this information, you will be asked to assess the quality of the internal audit function and whether the external auditor should rely on work performed by the internal auditors.

General Background Information about REDTOP Sports

REDTOP Sports Company is a publicly held manufacturing organization. The primary activities of REDTOP Sports Company include the design and manufacture of sporting and athletic goods. The major product lines are bicycle helmets for infants, youths, and adults and other bicycle accessories, including child bicycle seats, car bicycle carriers, and water-bottle cages. In the U. S., a number of jurisdictions have passed mandatory helmet regulations and REDTOP Sports is currently a market leader in this growing market. Sales are made primarily on credit to independent bicycle dealers and sporting goods stores. The sales terms require that balances be paid within sixty days. This practice is consistent with the industry.

Organizational Objectives and Related Risks

For this organization, there is a specific risk associated with potential errors in the valuation of receivables, the existence of receivables, and the cutoff of sales. This risk results from REDTOP Sports' interest in expanding to a global market. Helmet sales in Europe are expected to increase significantly in the near future and REDTOP would like to be in a position to obtain a significant market share in Europe. REDTOP Sports would like to finance this growth through an additional stock offering during the next year. To assure that the stock offering is successful, some pressure has been exerted on management to meet slightly optimistic growth levels over the past two years. Bonuses for top management have been partially based on the achievement of these growth goals.

Summary Financial Information

Sales of REDTOP Sports continue to grow. Over the last five years, sales have climbed at an average annual rate of 27%. When compared to other companies in this industry, the growth in earnings per share (EPS) over the past two years has been at the same level as the growth for the industry: 39%. In comparing this organization to the S&P 500, the organization's EPS has increased at 39% while the EPS of the S&P 500 has increased at 14% (about 2.8 times more).

The growth in accounts receivable has been primarily due to the increased sales demand. Current-year recorded sales total $99,133,000. The accounts receivable balance for the current year consists of approximately 500 accounts, primarily from retail and sporting goods stores. The individual accounts range from approximately $300 to $65,000. The year-end balance in the accounts receivable account is $18,248,000 (net of the allowance of $796,000).

Internal Controls and the Internal Audit Function

The organization has implemented a system of internal controls in the sales and accounts receivable area that is completely computerized and considered to be moderately complex.

The only significant recent change to the organization's internal controls in the sales, billing, and collection area is related to the internal audit function. The internal audit function is performed in-house at REDTOP Sports and is made up of four staff auditors, one manager, and a director. Each staff auditor had two to three years of public accounting experience prior to joining REDTOP's internal audit function. The manager and director of the internal audit function each had at least five years of public accounting experience prior to joining REDTOP five years ago. Both the manager and director have professional certifications.

In previous years, the work of the internal audit function had been primarily operational. For the last 18 months, however, the focus has become much more financial in nature. Audits currently performed by in-house internal audit include operational audits (i.e., employee benefits plan review), compliance audits (i.e., compliance with laws and regulations), and audits of financial controls and financial statement accounts.

The current-year work of the internal auditors was such that some of their activities are related to the accounts receivable account. They have obtained two types of evidence for accounts receivable: (1) evidence about the adequacy of and adherence to internal control policies and (2) evidence related to the accounts receivable balance.

Information about REDTOP's Internal Audit Function

Organizational Status and Communications with the Audit Committee and Management

The authority of the internal audit function has been granted to it by the CEO and the audit committee. In terms of organizational status, the director of internal audit reports directly to the CEO and has direct access to the audit committee. The appointment and termination of the internal audit director are the responsibilities of the CEO. The audit committee is advised of such decisions.

Procedures and Work Processes

Standardized audit programs are not typically used. Rather, the staff auditor responsible for an audit is to develop the audit program during the planning of the audit. Each audit program, therefore, is tailored to the specific objectives of the audit engagement. Modifications to the program are made as necessary during the course of the audit. The internal auditors rarely use computer-assisted auditing techniques. The computers are primarily used for spreadsheet programs and word processing packages. The internal audit function currently does not use any type of generalized audit software.

Workpaper review is the responsibility of the internal audit manager, and staff work is reviewed by the manager periodically throughout each audit. Review notes are prepared and must be cleared before an internal audit report is issued. Supervisory review of workpapers is performed to determine that the workpapers adequately support findings, conclusions, and reports. The director of internal audit has decided not to be directly responsible for any workpaper review; however, the director reviews enough of the work to be comfortable with the conclusions reached in the internal audit report.

Quality Assurance

The internal audit director has established a quality assurance program that requires periodic internal quality reviews. The purpose of the quality assurance review is to provide senior management and the audit committee with an assessment of the internal audit function. These reviews are performed by members of the internal audit staff, but they do not review any of their own work. The results of the current year's review indicated a number of areas where minor improvements could be made. The internal audit director is currently determining how to respond to the need for these improvements. No written action plan has yet been developed.

Accounts Receivable Work Performed by the Internal Audit Function

In testing the controls in the sales, billing, and collection cycle during the year, the internal auditors documented the system of internal controls and performed inquiries and observations of appropriate personnel once during the year. Tests of controls were also performed although the sample sizes for these detailed tests were much smaller than the sample sizes their external auditors would have used. Only minor exceptions in the operating effectiveness were noted.

In testing the existence assertion of accounts receivable during the course of the audit year, the internal auditors had sent out confirmations to customers with accounts receivable balances and accounts written off to justify their conclusions in the area. The number of confirmations sent was about the same as the number that the external auditors normally send out. The accounts receivables for confirmation were selected and evaluated using appropriate methods. The response rate was lower than that experienced on typical external audit engagements. Follow-up work for these no-replies was performed; however, on two of the five exceptions it appeared to be inadequate. While these two exceptions were explained as timing differences in the workpapers, the workpapers contained no documentation to support that explanation.

In testing the valuation of accounts receivable during the year, once each quarter, the internal audit function selected a sample of sales invoices to test the pricing by comparing the invoices with price lists and contracts. Sample sizes were more than adequate. Several pricing errors were noted in the workpapers. These differences were explained as resulting from the use of an outdated price list at the time of the sale. This explanation was documented in the workpapers. At year end, the internal audit function reviewed the analysis of the doubtful accounts and related documents and concluded that the allowance account was mathematically correct and that the method used to compute the allowance was the same as in the prior year.

In determining whether the accounts receivable balances are owned by the organization (rights and obligations assertion), the internal audit function reviewed board minutes to determine if the board of directors had approved factoring of any receivables. Inquiry of the credit manager was also made. These activities were performed on a quarterly basis. Based on these procedures, the internal audit function concluded that all of the recorded receivables are owned by REDTOP Sports.

The internal audit function had not performed any tests of cutoff for sales or accounts receivable for either the current or previous audit year.

A review of a sample of the internal audit function's workpaper files for audits of accounts receivable for the current audit year indicated the following. An audit program was included in all but one of these files. For the other file, the staff auditor had prepared a memo at the end of the audit indicating the various steps that were performed. This memo served as the audit program. Of the files reviewed, one file did not adequately document the audit objectives. Although the workpapers were all indexed, the differences across workpapers made it difficult to follow the indexing in some cases. In general, workpaper documentation, while acceptable, could be improved.

Of the files reviewed, it was noted that for two internal audits the workpapers were not reviewed until after the internal audit report was issued. Upon inquiry, the internal audit manager indicated that the primary purpose of workpaper review was to assure that the papers support the information included in the audit report. Given that this responsibility primarily rested with the internal auditor performing the engagement, the internal audit manager indicated that a review of workpapers after the issuance of the audit report was acceptable.

Conclusions are reasonably well documented in the corresponding workpapers. In fact, the documented conclusions appeared appropriate except for one set of workpapers related to the valuation assertion in which the conclusions did not appear to reflect the degree of negative evidence obtained during the audit. Specifically, the number of pricing errors documented seemed rather excessive. The conclusions in the workpapers, however, indicated that pricing errors did not represent a significant problem.

a. Assess the quality of REDTOP'S internal audit function. In doing so, provide assessments of objectivity, competence, quality of work performance, and overall quality. Provide support for your assessments. Assume that your firm uses a scale of 1 = very low, 2 = low, 3 = moderate, 4 = high. Support your assessment with a brief rationale for each of the ratings.

b. Would your assessments in part (a) change if you were told that the internal audit function was outsourced rather than being staffed in-house? Explain.

c. Notwithstanding your assessments in part (a), assume your audit engagement team determined that the quality of the internal audit function was of an acceptable level. Would you be willing to rely on any of the work related to accounts receivable that REDTOP's internal audit function performed during the year? Explain.

d. Could your engagement team use REDTOP's internal audit function in a way other than relying on work they had already performed? Explain.

16-65 **PCAOB, PricewaterhouseCoopers (LO 5, 8)** In June 2008, the PCAOB issued its report on the 2007 inspection report on PricewaterhouseCoopers LLP (see PCAOB Release No. 104-2008-125). For one of PricewaterhouseCoopers' clients (referred to as "Issuer A" in the PCAOB's inspection report), the PCAOB noted the following:

In determining the fair value of the reporting units for its goodwill impairment analysis, the issuer added an amount ("award allocation") to the value of certain of the reporting units that was intended to adjust the value of the relevant reporting unit to compensate for certain inter-organizational purchases. The award allocation was calculated based on certain sales by the relevant reporting unit and, for each reporting unit that received an award allocation, resulted in a higher calculated fair value. The Firm failed to test the underlying data and the calculation of the award allocation. The Firm also failed to assess whether the methodology was applied consistently from year to year and whether the incorporation of the award allocation into the analysis was appropriate. The issuer's impairment analysis indicated that, without this award allocation, the issuer would have been required by GAAP to perform the second step of the goodwill impairment test to determine the amount of impairment, if any, for approximately one quarter of the issuer's reporting units.

Answer the following questions by completing the first four steps of the framework for professional decision making introduced in *Chapter 4*:

a. What difficulties might the auditor have faced when deciding whether Issuer A's approach was reasonable? Why might the audit firm have not appropriately tested Issuer A's analysis?

b. What are the consequences of the auditor's decisions in this case?

c. What are the risks and uncertainties associated with the client's analysis?

d. What types of evidence should the auditor gather to evaluate the reasonableness of management's approach?
Recall that the framework is as follows:

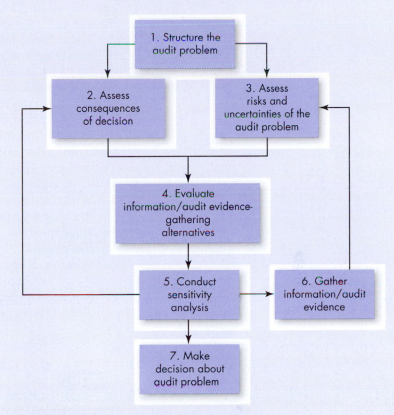

Source: Adapted from *Judgment and Choice*, by Robin Hogarth.

FRAUD FOCUS: CONTEMPORARY AND HISTORICAL CASES

FRAUD

PROFESSIONAL SKEPTICISM

16-66 **SEC, KPMG (LO 2)** SEC Accounting and Auditing Enforcement Release No. 904 describes KPMG's 1993 audit of Structural Dynamics Research Corporation (SDRC). The AAER describes SDRC as a client that inflated revenues and earnings by recognizing both premature and fictitious revenue. The following excerpt from the AAER describes the audit team's work in the area of accounts receivable:

During the 1993 audit, the engagement team spent considerable time auditing accounts receivable, a critical area of the audit. Particular emphasis was placed on auditing accounts receivable in SDRC's Far East Operations ("FEO") which represented approximately 50% of consolidated accounts receivable at year-end 1993. FEO also accounted for approximately 35% of the revenue recorded by SDRC in 1993. The audit team incorrectly concluded that certain revenue relating to these accounts receivable had been properly recognized and focused their attention on evaluating collectability.

Based in large part on the percentage of year-end 1992 receivables that were written off in 1993, the audit staff calculated a $5.8 million proposed audit adjustment to increase the allowance for doubtful accounts for FEO receivables. In the aggregate, the audit differences considered by the auditors totaled approximately $3.1 million, which represented approximately 22% of the net income originally reported by SDRC.

Notwithstanding the analysis made by the audit team, both the engagement partner and the concurring partner concluded that the $3.1 million net audit difference was not material to SDRC's financial statements. In reaching that conclusion, they relied in substantial part on management's representations that the rate of write-offs and reversals in were based on factors that management did not expect to recur in and that the $5.8 million audit difference calculated by the staff was, therefore, excessive. The auditors "passed" on the audit difference and did not require SDRC to adjust its financial statements.

a. What factors should the audit partners have considered when deciding whether it was appropriate to pass on the audit adjustment? What is the role of professional skepticism in this context?

b. What evidence should the auditors have gathered to support their assessment?

c. Is it appropriate to net misstatements when making a materiality decision on whether an adjustment is necessary?

APPLICATION ACTIVITIES

NOTE: Completing Application Activities requires students to reference additional resources and materials. Some Application Activities will require the student to reference relevant professional auditing standards. We make special note of these as Auditing Standards Application Activities.

ETHICS

PROFESSIONAL SKEPTICISM

16-67 **PCAOB** (LO **2, 3, 8**) Read the PCAOB enforcement case against Christopher E. Anderson (PCAOB Release No. 105-2008-003, available at *www.pcaobus.org*). Among the PCAOB's findings is that the audit partner, Anderson, changed materiality during the engagement.

In part, the enforcement case notes that Anderson was a Deloitte audit partner on the NFC audit engagement. Another Deloitte audit team was responsible for auditing NFC's parent organization, NIC. In planning the audit of NFC, Anderson had set, at $4.1 million, the quantitative threshold used by the engagement team to, among other things, determine whether to treat a misstatement in NFC's financial statements as material. However, shortly after misstatements were discovered, Anderson accepted a decision, made at Deloitte's NIC engagement team level, that the materiality threshold for the NFC audit should be increased to $6.1 million. Anderson accepted that decision even though he had final responsibility for the NFC audit, believed that the original materiality threshold remained appropriate, and understood that the increased threshold would make it easier to treat known misstatements as immaterial. As a result of applying the 50% higher threshold, Anderson was able to treat a $4.5 million overstatement as immaterial on a quantitative basis.

a. When is it appropriate to change materiality amounts during an engagement and why would the PCAOB have been concerned about Anderson's actions related to changing the materiality amount? Identify instances in which Anderson did not employ an appropriate level of professional skepticism.

b. Using the framework for ethical decision making presented in *Chapter 4*, assess the actions of Anderson. Recall that the steps in that framework are as follows: (1) identify the ethical issue(s); (2) determine who are the affected parties and identify their rights; (3) determine the most important rights; (4) develop alternative courses of action; (5) determine the likely consequences of each proposed course of action; (6) assess the possible consequences, including an estimation of the greatest good for the greatest number, and determine whether the rights framework would cause any course of action to be eliminated; and (7) decide on the appropriate course of action.

16-68   LO **4, 5**   Perform an Internet search on the terms *restructuring* and *goodwill impairment.* For each search term, locate one public company that is experiencing this issue. Next, locate each company's most recent 10-K or annual report. Be prepared to discuss the following: (a) the company's name and its industry, (b) the company's basic business model, and (c) the reasons that the company is going through a restructuring or experiencing a goodwill impairment.

ETHICS   **16-69**   LO **6, 8**   The advent of sophisticated financial instruments has dramatically changed the nature of investing during the past decade. Many financial instruments offer potentially greater returns for the investor but at higher levels of risk.

a. Review the FASB's discussion on financial instruments, or a finance book, to identify various types of financial instruments. Select five instruments that you consider interesting and prepare a report addressing (1) the nature of the instrument, (2) its underlying business purpose, (3) risks associated with the instrument, and (4) special audit procedures that should be applied during the audit of a client with a significant investment in the instrument.

b. Now assume that one of your audit clients has a large investment in a particularly risky financial instrument. This financial instrument exposes the client to significant economic loss in the unlikely event that the marketability of the instrument declines. You do not feel that the client's footnote disclosures adequately reveal the true risk profile of the instrument. What is your ethical obligation to the shareholders of the client with regard to your knowledge of the riskiness of this investment?

   Use the framework for ethical decision making outlined in *Chapter 4* to formulate your answer. Recall that the steps in that framework are as follows: (1) identify the ethical issue(s); (2) determine who are the affected parties and identify their rights; (3) determine the most important rights; (4) develop alternative courses of action; (5) determine the likely consequences of each proposed course of action;

(6) assess the possible consequences, including an estimation of the greatest good for the greatest number, and determine whether the rights framework would cause any course of action to be eliminated; and (7) decide on the appropriate course of action.

16-70 **LO 7** Using information at the web site of the IIA, describe the requirements for becoming a CIA. Also identify other certifications offered by the IIA and discuss the importance of these additional certifications.

AUDITING STANDARDS APPLICATION ACTIVITY

16-71 **LO 6** Assume that you are on the audit of a nonpublic client. The client has significant investments in derivative securities and you recognize that these securities are be measured at fair value. Review the *Standards Appendix* to the book to determine which auditing standard would provide you information on your responsibilities related to these derivatives. Identify the relevant standard and indicate the paragraphs in the standard that outline your responsibilities.

ACADEMIC RESEARCH CASES

NOTE: Completing Academic Research Cases requires students to reference additional resources and materials.

SEARCH HINT

It is easy to locate these academic research articles! Use a search engine such as Google Scholar or an electronic research platform such as ABI Inform, and search using the author names and part of the article title.

16-72 **LO 4** Locate and read the article listed below and answer the following questions.

Moehrle, S. R. 2002. Do firms use restructuring charge reversals to meet earnings targets? *The Accounting Review* 77 (2): 397–413.

a. What is the issue being addressed in the paper?
b. What are the findings of the paper?
c. Why is this paper important to auditors, and what are the implications of this paper for the auditing profession?
d. Describe the research methodology used as a basis for the conclusions.
e. Describe any limitations of the research.

16-73 **LO 2** Locate and read the article listed below and answer the following questions.

Seong-Yeon, C, R. C. Hagerman, N. Sandeep, and E. R. Patterson. 2003. Measuring stockholder materiality. *Accounting Horizons* 17: 63–76.

a. What is the issue being addressed in the paper?
b. What are the findings of the paper?
c. Why is this paper important to auditors, and what are the implications of this paper for the auditing profession?
d. Describe the research methodology used as a basis for the conclusions.
e. Describe any limitations of the research.

16-74 **LO 7** Locate and read the article listed below and answer the following questions.

Brandon, D. M. November 2010. External auditor evaluations of outsourced internal auditors. *Auditing: A Journal of Practice & Theory* 29 (2): 159–173.

a. What is the issue being addressed in the paper?
b. What are the findings of the paper?
c. Why is this paper important to auditors, and what are the implications of this paper for the auditing profession?
d. Describe the research methodology used as a basis for the conclusions.
e. Describe any limitations of the research.

FORD AND TOYOTA

	Ford Motor Company and Toyota Motor Corporation
16-75	LO **3, 5**

Source and Reference	Question
Ford 10-K or Annual Report	1. One of Ford's most significant liabilities concerns pensions and other postretirement benefits. What is the nature of estimates required to value these liabilities? What risks do these estimates pose for the audit firm?
	2. Read Ford's MD&A disclosures concerning goodwill impairments. Describe the nature of estimates that management needs to make in order to estimate the impairments. What audit evidence would you want to gather to be assured that management's estimates are reasonable?
Ford 10-K, Toyota 20-F	3a. Warranty liabilities are a significant concern for manufacturers like Ford and Toyota. See the footnotes detailing information about warranties for each organization. What are the amounts for accrued warranty liabilities and yearly warranty expense for each organization?
	3b. What is the nature of estimates required for warranty liabilities?
	3c. What planning analytical procedures can you develop to help you understand the relative size of the warranty accounts for both companies? What inferences do you draw from the comparison of these analytics?

ACL

NOTE: There is an *ACL Appendix* at the end of the textbook that you may find helpful in completing this problem.

FRAUD

16-76 LO **7** Dr. Frank Benford, a physicist at General Electric in the 1920s, found that the first and second digits of many populations of numbers occur with a fairly consistent frequency. This has been found true, for example, of census numbers and certain accounting populations, such as accounts payable. Benford developed a model that predicted the frequency of each digit occurring in a particular location depending on the length of a number. For example, he finds that the digit #1 occurs as the first digit in about 30% of all populations, while the digit #2 occurs as the first digit in about 17.5% of all populations. On the other hand, the digit #9 occurs as the first digit only about 4.5% of the time. Therefore, digits such as 990 do not occur as often as digits such as 124. Many others have empirically verified the Benford predictions.

Auditors have found that as individuals commit fraud or make up fraudulent transactions, their intuition in developing numbers for the fake documents often does not follow Benford's Law. Therefore, auditors have come to use Benford's Law to identify a wide variety of unusual transactions, including fraud, double payments, and other fictitious accounts. Audit software, such as ACL, comes with modules that allow auditors to apply Benford's Law to search for unusual patterns in populations by identifying numbering patterns that differ significantly from that predicted by Benford's Law.

Using ACL to Perform Benford Analysis

Benford Analysis can be found by clicking **Analysis | Perform Benford Analysis.** You will be instructed to select a field on which to perform the analysis. You then make a choice to perform an analysis on the leading digit only, or you can perform an analysis on the two leading digits.

You can choose the type of output you want for the analysis by clicking the **Output** tab at the top of the window. The **GRAPH** option provides a bar graph with the predicted and actual frequencies of each leading digit or the two leading digits. The **SCREEN** and **FILE** options create a report containing the following:

- The actual count of the leading digit (or two leading digits)
- The expected count of the digit(s)
- A Zstat statistic

The Zstat statistic is derived from the probability of the deviation between the actual count and the expected count of the digit. The significance of the Zstat statistic is determined by comparing it with the Z statistic used to describe normal distributions in most statistical textbooks. For example, there is a 95% chance that most samples from a distribution would fall within 1.96 standard deviations from the mean, thus creating a Zstat of 1.96 for a 5% tail end of a distribution and 2.58 for a 1% tail. Any Zstat statistic greater than 2.58 would indicate a very rare occurrence.

To illustrate the power of Benford's Law in an auditing context, assume that you are the internal auditor for Knot Manufacturing Company and are auditing the travel, entertainment, and meal reimbursements. Company policy requires receipts for expenses greater than $25. Management must separately approve all reimbursements over $5,000. Download the file *Expense Reimbursements* from the "Student Resources" section of the textbook website. Analyze expense reimbursements using Benford's Law and ACL. Import the *Expense Reimbursements* file, which contains the reimbursement document numbers, employee numbers, and the amount of each reimbursement. Click **Analysis | Perform Benford Analysis** for the **AMOUNT** of the reimbursement.

1. Analyze on the leading digit. Choose **Output** to **Screen** and again to **Graph**. Print both outputs.
2. Analyze on the leading two digits. Choose **Output** to **Screen** and again to **Graph**. Print both outputs.
3. Summarize the number and amount of reimbursements between $24 and $25 by employee number. Do the same for amounts between $4,900 and $5,000. (Hint: Create filters for each of these dollar ranges.) Print the results.
4. Analyze the results and provide possible explanations for the results. Identify reimbursements for certain employees that may need further investigation.

17

Other Services Provided by Audit Firms

CHAPTER OVERVIEW AND LEARNING OBJECTIVES

Through studying *Chapter 1* through *Chapter 16*, you have learned about the audit opinion formulation process for conducting external financial statement only and integrated audits. We now cover topics concerning other services provided by audit firms, including reviews and compilations, interim financial information assurance, special audit reports, other attestation engagements, forensic accounting, and sustainability assurance.

Through studying this chapter, you will be able to achieve these learning objectives:

1. Identify and describe nonaudit attestation services provided by audit firms and discuss the relevant professional standards.

2. Explain review and compilation engagements, relevant procedures performed, and reports issued.

3. Explain the procedures and reporting requirements for providing assurance on interim financial information for audit clients.

4. Discuss special reporting considerations for unique financial statement audit situations.

5. Describe attestation engagements relating to agreed-upon procedures, financial forecasts and projections, and pro forma financial information, and the types of reports that are issued for these engagements.

6. Describe forensic accounting and distinguish between forensic accounting and auditing.

7. Describe sustainability reporting and articulate the auditor's role in providing assurance on management sustainability reports.

Nonaudit Attestation Services Provided by Audit Firms

LO 1 Identify and describe nonaudit attestation services provided by audit firms and discuss the relevant professional standards.

The American Institute of Certified Public Accountants (AICPA) defines an **attestation engagement** as one "in which a certified public accountant in the practice of public accounting (hereinafter referred to as a *practitioner*) is engaged to issue or does issue an examination, a review, or an agreed-upon procedures report on subject matter, or an assertion about the subject matter (hereafter referred to as *the assertion*), that is the responsibility of another party" (AICPA, AT Section 101, paragraph .01). Using a different term to define the same concept, the International Auditing and Assurance Standards Board (IAASB) defines an **assurance engagement** as "an engagement in which a practitioner expresses a conclusion designed to enhance the degree of confidence of the intended users other than the responsible party about the outcome of the evaluation or measurement of a subject matter against criteria" (International Framework for Assurance Engagements, paragraph 7). For simplicity, we refer to these types of engagements as attestation engagements.

Subject Matter of an Attestation Engagement

The subject matter of an attestation engagement may be as of a point in time or may cover a period in time. Recall that the external audit of financial statements involves attesting to management's assertions about historical financial information and associated disclosures. In contrast, the subject matter of a nonaudit attestation engagement can be quite varied. Examples include:

- Statement of greenhouse gas emissions
- Privacy of personal information
- Schedule of investment returns
- Effectiveness of controls over the security of a system
- Capacity of a facility
- Compliance with human resource practices

Components of Attestation Services and Parties Involved in Attestation Services

Attestation services can be provided to management only or to external users. Attestation services involve five components:

- Information or a process (the subject matter) on which the assurance service is provided
- Criteria for evaluation, such as compliance with regulations
- Sufficient appropriate evidence
- A written attestation report
- Three parties that are involved: the responsible party (e.g., management), the practitioner (e.g., the certified public accountant [CPA]), and intended users (e.g., a bank). *Exhibit 17.1* illustrates how these three parties interact in an attestation engagement and notes that the responsible party may or may not be the party who engages the practitioner (the engaging party).

Levels of Assurance Provided in an Attestation Engagement

International and U.S. standard setters identify two levels of assurance that can be provided in an attestation engagement: positive assurance and limited assurance. Positive assurance is provided when conducting an examination, while limited assurance (sometimes referred to as negative assurance) is provided when conducting reviews. In comparison, during a **reasonable assurance engagement** the objective of the practitioner is to reduce

---

EXHIBIT **17.1**   Parties Involved in Attestation Engagements

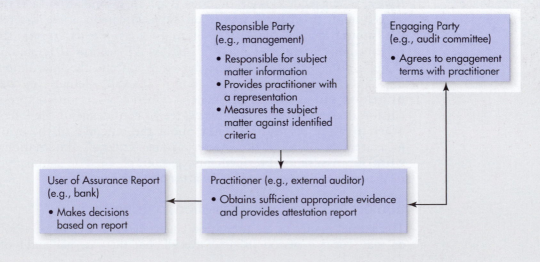

EXHIBIT **17.2**	United States and International Attestation (Assurance) Standards

U.S. Attestation Standards (AICPA)*	International Attestation (Assurance) Standards (IAASB)
Statements on Standards for Attestation Engagements (SSAE, referenced as AT)	International Standards on Assurance Engagements (ISAEs)
Statements on Standards for Accounting and Review Services (SSARS, referenced as AR)	International Standards on Review Engagements (ISREs)
• Engagements to review financial statements	• Engagements to review financial statements
• Engagements to compile financial statements	
	International Standards on Related Services (ISRSs)
	• Engagements to perform agreed-upon procedures regarding financial information

*The PCAOB adopted the AICPA's ASB's SSAE on April 16, 2003 as its interim standards, and those remain in effect, unless superseded or amended by the PCAOB. The *Emerging Issues* feature "PCAOB Has Adopted Two Attestation Standards" highlights that the PCAOB issued its first two Attestation Standards effective in 2014.

assurance engagement risk to an acceptably low level so as to have a basis for a positive assurance. According to the IAASB's International Framework for Assurance Engagements (2010), assurance engagement risk is "the risk that the practitioner expresses an inappropriate conclusion when the subject matter information is materially misstated" (paragraph 48).

Professional Standards for Attestation Engagements

Practitioners providing attestation services have standards to guide them and to help them ensure quality for these services. **Attestation standards** provide guidance about gathering evidence regarding specific assertions and communicating about the fairness of the presentation. *Exhibit 17.2* summarizes the many standards that exist both in the United States and internationally that

PCAOB Has Adopted Two Attestation Standards

EMERGING ISSUE

In 2013, the PCAOB adopted two new Attestations Standards, both with an effective date of fiscal years ending on or after June 1, 2014.

Attestation Standard No. 1, *Examination Engagements Regarding Compliance Reports of Brokers and Dealers*, establishes requirements that apply when an auditor is engaged to perform an examination of certain statements made by a broker or dealer in a compliance report ("compliance report") required by the SEC. The auditor's objective in this type of engagement is to express an opinion regarding whether the assertions made by the broker or dealer in its compliance report are fairly stated, in all material respects.

Attestation Standard No. 2, *Review Engagements Regarding Exemption Reports of Brokers*

and Dealers, establishes requirements that apply when an auditor is engaged to perform a review of the statements made by a broker or dealer in an exemption report ("exemption report") required by the SEC. The auditor's objective in this type of engagement is to state whether, based upon the results of the review procedures performed, the auditor is aware of any material modifications that should be made to the broker's or dealer's assertions for the assertions to be fairly stated, in all material respects.

As both the PCAOB and the AICPA modify or add to the existing Attestation Standards in the United States, auditors will need to keep current on the evolving requirements.

EXHIBIT **17.3**	AICPA's Attestation Standards

General standards

1. The practitioner must have adequate technical training and proficiency to perform the attestation engagement.
2. The practitioner must have adequate knowledge of the subject matter.
3. The practitioner must have reason to believe that the subject matter is capable of evaluation against criteria that are suitable and available to users.
4. The practitioner must maintain independence in mental attitude in all matters relating to the engagement.
5. The practitioner must exercise due professional care in planning and performing the engagement and preparing the report.

Standards of fieldwork

1. The practitioner must adequately plan the work and must properly supervise any assistants.
2. The practitioner must obtain sufficient evidence to provide a reasonable basis for the conclusions that are expressed in the report.

Standards of reporting

1. The practitioner must identify the subject matter or the assertion being reported on and state the character of the engagement in the report.
2. The practitioner must state the practitioner's conclusion about the subject matter or the assertion in relation to the criteria against which the subject matter was evaluated in the report.
3. The practitioner must state all of the practitioner's significant reservations about the engagement, the subject matter, and, if applicable, the assertion related thereto in the report.
4. The practitioner must state in the report that the report is intended solely for the information and use of the specified parties under the following circumstances:
   - When the criteria used to evaluate the subject matter are determined by the practitioner to be appropriate only for a limited number of parties who either participated in their establishment or can be presumed to have an adequate understanding of the criteria
   - When the criteria used to evaluate the subject matter are available only to specified parties
   - When reporting on subject matter and a written assertion has not been provided by the responsible party
   - When the report is on an attestation engagement to apply agreed-upon procedures to the subject matter

guide practitioners in performing attestation engagements. As noted earlier, recall that the term *attestation* is used in the United States and the term *assurance* is used internationally to refer to the same concept.

Exhibit 17.3 provides a description of the AICPA's general, fieldwork, and reporting standards for attestation engagements. However, as noted in the *Emerging Issues* feature "The AICPA Attestation Clarity Project," the AICPA's Auditing Standards Board has started a project to redraft and restructure the Attestation Standards.

Reviews and Compilations

LO 2 Explain review and compilation engagements, relevant procedures performed, and reports issued.

Reviews and compilations in the United States are governed by Statements on Standards for Accounting and Review Services (SSARS, referred to as AR). Reviews performed internationally are governed by International Standard on Review Engagements (ISRE) 2400 (Revised), while compilations performed internationally are governed by International Standards on Related Services (ISRS) 4410 (Revised).

The AICPA Attestation Clarity Project

EMERGING ISSUE

To address concerns over the clarity, length, and complexity of its standards, the ASB has undertaken a significant effort to clarify its professional standards. Earlier in the book, you read about the ASB's project to clarify its auditing standards. In 2013, the ASB began a project to clarify its attestation standards. As part the attestation clarity project, the ASB will continue its general strategy of converging its standards with the standards of the IAASB.

Proposed changes from the existing SSAEs include:

- *Required assertion in examinations and reviews.* The responsible party would need to provide a written assertion. Under current standards, exceptions to this requirement are allowed.
- *Required representation letters in examinations and reviews.* Under the current standard, representation letters are only suggested.

- *Risk assessment for examinations.* This change would require an increased understanding of the development of the subject matter, thus resulting in improved identification of risks of material misstatement and improved linkage between assessed risks and planned attestation procedures.
- *Separation of the discussion of reviews from examinations.*
- *Qualified opinion, disclaimer, or withdrawal from the engagement will be required when there is a client imposed scope limitation.* The current standard indicates that the practitioner generally should disclaim an opinion or withdraw from the engagement.

When these changes become effective, auditors will need to realize that in the United States, the Attestation Standards of the AICPA and of the PCAOB will differ in significant ways.

Reviews

Reviews typically relate to a review of the annual financial statements of nonpublic companies. A review is designed to obtain only limited assurance that there are no material modifications that should be made to the financial statements in order for the statements to be in conformity with the applicable financial reporting framework. Similar to an audit, independence is required to perform a review.

According to the IAASB, the objective in a review of financial statements "is obtain limited assurance, primarily by performing inquiry and analytical procedures, about whether the financial statements as a whole are free from material misstatement, thereby enabling the practitioner to express a conclusion on whether anything has come to the practitioner's attention that causes the practitioner to believe the financial statements are not prepared, in all material respects, in accordance with an applicable financial reporting framework" (ISRE 2400 (Revised), paragraph 14(a)). The AICPA defines a **review engagement** in a complementary manner, as "a service, the objective of which is to obtain limited assurance that there are no material modifications that should be made to the financial statements in order for the statements to be in conformity with the applicable financial reporting framework" (AR Section 60, paragraph .07). Reviews may be useful to bankers and vendors who are familiar with the client's business and do not need—or are not willing to demand—an audit, but want some assurance from a CPA.

Review Procedures

A review is significantly less in scope than an audit. In performing a review, the practitioner should obtain a general understanding of the client (e.g., organizational structure, operating characteristics, types of transactions, material account balances, types of products and services provided, operating locations, and related parties) and the industry. Standard procedures for conducting a review include:

- Obtain a written engagement letter regarding the specific services to be performed so as to avoid potential misunderstandings with the client
- Inquire concerning actions taken at meetings of the board of directors, stockholders, and other decision-making bodies
- Inquire whether the financial statements have been consistently prepared in conformity with generally accepted accounting principles (GAAP) or other comprehensive basis of accounting
- Inquire about any changes in the business activities or accounting principles and practices and events subsequent to the date of the financial statements that would have a material effect on the financial statements
- Obtain or prepare a trial balance of the general ledger and foot and reconcile it to the general ledger
- Trace the financial statement amounts to the trial balance
- Perform basic analytical procedures, such as comparing current financial statement amounts with those of prior period(s) and with anticipated results, such as budgets and forecasts, and studying the relationships of elements of the financial statements that would be expected to conform to a predictable pattern based on the organization's experience, such as interest expense to interest-bearing debt
- Obtain explanations from management for any unusual or unexpected results and consider the need for further investigation
- Read the financial statements to determine whether they appear to conform to GAAP
- Obtain a management representation letter about important assertions that management has made

Inquiries and analytical procedures should be performed for each of the material account balances in the financial statements. *Exhibit 17.4* lists some of the inquiries and analytical procedures that might be performed for a review of accounts in the revenue cycle. Note that these procedures are significantly less in scope than audit procedures. There is no assessment of ICFR and there are no substantive tests of details, such as the confirmation of receivables, review of subsequent cash collections, cutoff tests, or tests of sales transactions processed during the period.

If evidence obtained from such inquiries and analytical procedures does not support management's assertions in the financial statements, the practitioner should perform additional procedures and, if the additional evidence indicates material misstatements, have management correct them. For example, if inquiries concerning proper cutoff of sales lead the practitioner to question the client's timing of revenue recognition, the practitioner may deem it necessary to perform a cutoff test of sales to determine whether there is a material misstatement. If there is a material misstatement but the client will not correct it, the practitioner should modify the review report to bring the misstatement to the user's attention.

Standard Review Report

When the accountant has no reservation about providing limited assurance on the financial statements, the accountant issues a standard report. Further, each page of the financial statements reviewed by the accountant will include language instructing the user to "See Independent Accountant's Review Report."

EXHIBIT **17.4**	Review Engagement: Examples of Inquiries and Analytical Procedures for the Revenue Cycle

Inquiries

1. What is the company's revenue recognition policy? Is the policy proper and consistently applied and disclosed? Have the revenue recognition procedures been updated for changes in accounting principles?
2. Are revenues from sales of products and rendering of services recognized in the appropriate reporting period?
3. Are any sales recorded under a "bill-and-hold" arrangement? If yes, have the criteria been met to record the transaction as a sale?
4. Has an adequate allowance for doubtful accounts been properly reflected in the financial statements?
5. Have receivables considered uncollectible been written off? Is the amount written off consistent with prior experience, changes in the economy, or trends in the industry?
6. Is the accounts receivable subsidiary ledger reconciled to the general ledger account balance on a regular basis?
7. Are there receivables from employees or other related parties? Have receivables from owners been evaluated to determine if they should be reflected in the equity section of the balance sheet?
8. Have there been significant numbers of sales returns or credit memoranda issued subsequent to the balance sheet date?

Analytical Procedures

1. Compute number of days' sales in ending receivables and compare it with that for prior years.
2. Compute aging percentages of accounts receivable and compare them with those for prior years.
3. Compute bad debt expense as a percent of sales for the year and compare it with that for prior years.
4. Compare sales growth with information about industry sales growth. Seek an explanation about significant differences between the company's growth rate and that of the industry as a whole.
5. Compare sales results by product line with those for previous years. Reconcile changes to information available about the company's strategy.
6. Compute gross margin. If there are significant changes in gross margin, follow up to determine if the changes may be due to revenue recognition or inventory changes.

Exhibit 17.5 contains an example of a standard review report for U.S. nonpublic companies. It has four paragraphs. The first paragraph identifies what was reviewed and describes a review engagement, states that a review is narrower in scope than an audit, and disclaims an opinion. The second paragraph notes that that the financial statements are the representations of the company's management. The third paragraph states that the AICPA's review standards were followed. The fourth paragraph expresses limited assurance. It tells the reader that the practitioner is not aware of any reporting problems based on the review procedures performed. If there is a reporting problem, such as a departure from GAAP, the limited assurance paragraph should be modified to refer to an additional paragraph that explains the departure. If the client does not provide the practitioner with a signed management representation letter, or the practitioner is unable to obtain the evidence necessary to provide limited assurance, the practitioner is precluded from issuing a review report and ordinarily withdraws from the engagement.

Compilations

Compilations can be performed only for nonpublic organizations and involve presenting, in the form of financial statements, information that is the representation of the responsible party (usually management or owners of the organization) without the practitioner undertaking to express any assurance on the statements. The responsible party may

EXHIBIT **17.5** Standard Review Report

Independent Accountant's Review Report

[*Appropriate Salutation*]

I (We) have reviewed the accompanying balance sheet of XYZ Company as of December 31, 20XX, and the related statements of income, retained earnings, and cash flows for the year then ended. A review includes primarily applying analytical procedures to management's (owners') financial data and making inquiries of company management (owners). A review is substantially less in scope than an audit, the objective of which is the expression of an opinion regarding the financial statements as a whole. Accordingly, I (we) do not express such an opinion.

Management (owners) is (are) responsible for the preparation and fair presentation of the financial statements in accordance with accounting principles generally accepted in the United States of America and for designing, implementing, and maintaining internal control relevant to the preparation and fair presentation of the financial statements.

My (our) responsibility is to conduct the review in accordance with Statements on Standards for Accounting and Review Services issued by the American Institute of Certified Public Accountants. Those standards require me (us) to perform procedures to obtain limited assurance that there are no material modifications that should be made to the financial statements. I (We) believe that the results of my (our) procedures provide a reasonable basis for our report.

Based on my (our) review, I am (we are) not aware of any material modifications that should be made to the accompanying financial statements in order for them to be in conformity with accounting principles generally accepted in the United States of America.

[*Signature of accounting firm or accountant, as appropriate*]

[*Date*]

request the practitioner to compile financial statements because of a lack of in-house expertise to prepare them or because the organization's banker feels more comfortable with statements prepared by the practitioner. Compilations are a type of engagement for which no assurance is provided; therefore the accountant does not need to be independent to perform a compilation.

According to the IAASB, as part of a compilation engagement, management requests that an accountant in public practice "assist with the preparation and presentation of financial information of an entity" (ISRS 4410 (Revised), paragraph 5). The accountant's objective in this engagement is to "Apply accounting and financial reporting expertise to assist management in the preparation and presentation of financial information in accordance with an applicable financial reporting framework based on information provided by management" (ISRS 4410 (Revised), paragraph 16 (a)).

The AICPA defines a **compilation engagement** in a complementary manner, as a "service, the objective of which is to assist management in presenting financial information in the form of financial statements without undertaking to obtain or provide any assurance that there are no material modifications that should be made to the financial statements in order for the statements to be in conformity with the applicable financial reporting framework" (SSARS, AR Section 60, paragraph .05). As indicated in the *Emerging Issues* feature, "Proposed Changes to Compilation Standards" the AICPA is considering some changes to the standards used by auditors performing compilations.

Proposed Changes to Compilation Standards

EMERGING ISSUE

In 2013, the AICPA issued an Exposure Draft that, if adopted, would result in significant revisions in requirements when accountants prepare financial statements and/or provide compilation services.

Proposed changes from the existing standards include:

- Requirements and guidance when an accountant is engaged to prepare financial statements for an organization but has not been engaged to perform a compilation, review, or audit with respect to those financial statements
- Clarification that financial statement preparation is considered outside the scope of the attest engagement and, therefore, constitutes a nonattest service

- Revision of the applicability of the compilation standards, so that the standards apply only when the accountant is engaged to perform a compilation engagement
- Reconfiguration of the compilation report so that it will look significantly different from an audit or review report
- Requirement to obtain a signed engagement letter or other suitable form of written agreement for engagements to prepare financial statements and compilation engagements

The effective date is anticipated to be for periods ending on or after December 15, 2015.

Compilation Procedures

The practitioner should have a general knowledge of the client's industry, the nature of its accounting records, the accounting basis to be used (GAAP or a special-purpose framework other than GAAP), and the form and content of the financial statements. Such an understanding is obtained through continuing professional education, experience with the client, regular reviews of industry developments, and inquiry of the client's personnel. The practitioner is not required to make inquiries or perform procedures to verify, corroborate, or review information provided by the client. However, if the practitioner believes that such information may be incorrect, incomplete, or otherwise unsatisfactory, the practitioner should obtain additional or revised information. If the client refuses to provide this information, the practitioner should withdraw from the engagement. Further, the practitioner is not required to obtain an understanding of internal controls. The practitioner should read the financial statements, including footnotes, to make sure that they are appropriate in form and free from obvious material misstatement.

Even though no assurance is provided, many users believe that because the practitioner's name is associated with the financial statements, obvious material misstatements would have been mentioned in the practitioner's report. Therefore, the practitioner needs to be careful when preparing the statements to be alert to any obvious misstatement(s). If there is a material misstatement that is not corrected by management, the practitioner should describe this issue in the report following the disclaimer paragraph.

Standard Compilation Report

Exhibit 17.6 provides an example of a standard compilation report. The first paragraph identifies the statements that were compiled and disclaims an opinion or any assurance. The second paragraph describes management's responsibilities. The third paragraph describes and refers to the standards followed by the accountant.

| EXHIBIT **17.6** | Standard Compilation Report |

Accountant's Compilation Report

[*Appropriate Salutation*]

I (we) have compiled the accompanying balance sheet of XYZ Company as of December 31, 20XX, and the related statements of income, retained earnings, and cash flows for the year then ended. I (we) have not audited or reviewed the accompanying financial statements and, accordingly, do not express an opinion or provide any assurance about whether the financial statements are in accordance with accounting principles generally accepted in the United States of America.

Management (owners) is (are) responsible for the preparation and fair presentation of the financial statements in accordance with accounting principles generally accepted in the United States of America and for designing, implementing, and maintaining internal control relevant to the preparation and fair presentation of the financial statements.

My (our) responsibility is to conduct the compilation in accordance with Statements on Standards for Accounting and Review Services issued by the American Institute of Certified Public Accountants. The objective of a compilation is to assist management in presenting financial information in the form of financial statements without undertaking to obtain or provide any assurance that there are no material modifications that should be made to the financial statements.

[*Signature of accounting firm or accountant, as appropriate*]

[*Date*]

Potential Modifications to the Standard Compilation Report

The practitioner will modify the standard compilation report in the following three situations.

Omission of Disclosures for Compilations The responsible party, management, may request the practitioner to compile financial statements that omit substantially all of the required disclosures. This request may be honored if the practitioner believes that such omission is not undertaken with the intention of misleading the users. An additional paragraph should be added to the standard compilation report stating:

> The company has elected to omit substantially all of the disclosures required by GAAP. If the omitted disclosures were included in the financial statements, they might influence the user's conclusions about the company's financial position, results of operations, and cash flows. Accordingly, these financial statements are not designed for those who are not informed about such matters.

Compilation Report Not Required Practitioners may prepare the financial statements without a compilation report when these are intended only for the client's use. In such cases, the auditor should include in a written engagement letter a statement that the financial statements are intended solely for the use of specified members of management and should not be used by any other party.

Practitioner Lacks Independence If the practitioner is not independent of the client, a separate paragraph should be added to the compilation report stating:

> I am [We are] not independent with respect to [client's name].

> The lack of independence does not change the level of assurance provided since none is given in the first place.

Reviews of Interim Financial Information for Audit Clients

LO 3 Explain the procedures and reporting requirements for providing assurance on interim financial information for audit clients.

The SEC requires publicly owned companies to (1) file quarterly financial information with the SEC on Form 10-Q within 40 to 45 days (depending on the company size) after the end of each of the first three quarters of the fiscal year and provide their shareholders with quarterly reports and (2) include certain quarterly information in the annual reports to the SEC (Form 10-K) and in the annual reports to shareholders. The SEC requires publicly owned corporations to have their quarterly financial information reviewed by their independent auditors before it is issued, but does not require that the auditor's review report be included with the quarterly information, although many companies do include the auditor's report. We use the term *auditor* in this discussion not because the auditor is performing an audit but because this review procedure concerns the review of interim financial information performed by the auditor of the annual financial statements of the company. Relevant guidance can be found in the AICPA's AU-C 930, the IAASB's ISRE 2410, and the PCAOB's AU 722.

Review Procedures for Interim Financial Information

The auditor should perform review procedures (a) on the quarterly information contained in the annual report to shareholders and (b) on the quarterly information issued at the end of each of the first three quarters of the fiscal year when engaged to do so. These procedures are similar to those required by the SSARSs for reviews of financial statements of nonpublic companies (covered earlier):

- Making inquiries
- Performing analytical procedures
- Reading the minutes of board of directors' meetings
- Reading the interim information to consider whether it appears to conform to GAAP

In addition, the auditor should obtain written representations from management concerning such things as its responsibility for the financial information, the completeness of the minutes, and subsequent events. The standards also require auditors to understand the client's accounting and financial reporting practices and its related internal controls over the preparation of annual and quarterly reports, normally obtained while auditing the prior-year financial statements and updated as those controls change. With a new client, the auditor must perform the necessary procedures to obtain such an understanding.

Reporting on Interim Financial Statements

Exhibit 17.7 contains an example of a standard report on a review of separately issued interim financial statements of public companies. It identifies the information reviewed, indicates that the standards of the PCAOB were followed in performing the review, explains the nature of a review, disclaims an opinion, and provides negative assurance that the auditor is not aware of any material departures from GAAP. If the client is a nonpublic company, the title would not include the word *Registered* if the CPA firm is not registered with PCAOB and the reference would be to the "standards established by the American Institute of Certified Public Accountants."

The disclosure and reporting requirements for interim financial statements differ from those for annual financial statements. Accruals, such

| EXHIBIT **17.7** | Review Report on Interim Financial Statements for PepsiCo, Inc. |

Report of Independent Registered Public Accounting Firm

The Board of Directors and Shareholders
PepsiCo, Inc.:

We have reviewed the accompanying Condensed Consolidated Balance Sheet of PepsiCo, Inc. and Subsidiaries as of June 14, 2014, the related Condensed Consolidated Statements of Income and Comprehensive Income for the twelve and twenty-four weeks ended June 14, 2014 and June 15, 2013, and the related Condensed Consolidated Statements of Cash Flows and Equity for the twenty-four weeks ended June 14, 2014 and June 15, 2013. These interim condensed consolidated financial statements are the responsibility of PepsiCo, Inc.'s management.

We conducted our review in accordance with the standards of the Public Company Accounting Oversight Board (United States). A review of interim financial information consists principally of applying analytical procedures and making inquiries of persons responsible for financial and accounting matters. It is substantially less in scope than an audit conducted in accordance with the standards of the Public Company Accounting Oversight Board (United States), the objective of which is the expression of an opinion regarding the financial statements taken as a whole. Accordingly, we do not express such an opinion.

Based on our review, we are not aware of any material modifications that should be made to the accompanying interim condensed consolidated financial statements referred to above for them to be in conformity with U.S. generally accepted accounting principles.

We have previously audited, in accordance with the standards of the Public Company Accounting Oversight Board (United States), the Consolidated Balance Sheet of PepsiCo, Inc. and Subsidiaries as of December 28, 2013, and the related Consolidated Statements of Income, Comprehensive Income, Cash Flows and Equity for the fiscal year then ended not presented herein; and in our report dated February 14, 2014, we expressed an unqualified opinion on those consolidated financial statements. In our opinion, the information set forth in the accompanying Condensed Consolidated Balance Sheet as of December 28, 2013, is fairly stated, in all material respects, in relation to the Consolidated Balance Sheet from which it has been derived.

/s/ KPMG LLP
New York, New York
July 23, 2014

as estimates of bad debt and income tax expenses, are not usually as precise on interim dates as they are at year end. It is assumed that those who receive the interim statements also received the latest annual statements. Information disclosed in the latest annual statements does not have to be repeated in the interim statements except for continuing contingencies and other uncertainties. There should be disclosures of events that occurred since the latest year end, such as changes in accounting principles or estimates and significant changes in financial position.

The negative assurance should be modified when there is a material departure from GAAP or inadequate disclosure. In such situations, a paragraph should be added preceding the negative assurance paragraph describing the problem. The negative assurance paragraph would then read as follows:

> Based on our review, *with the exception of the matter described in the preceding paragraph*, we are not aware of any material modifications that should be made to the accompanying financial statements for them to be in conformity with generally accepted accounting principles. [Emphasis added.]

Special Considerations for Reporting

LO 4 Discuss special reporting considerations for unique financial statement audit situations.

AU-C 100–700 apply to the annual audits of financial statements. AU-C 800 contains guidance regarding special considerations in the application of those AU-C sections to an audit of financial statements prepared in accordance with a special-purpose framework (cash, tax, regulatory, or contractual basis of accounting). AU-C 805 contains guidance regarding special considerations in the audits of single financial statements and specific elements, accounts, or items of a financial statement. AU-C 806 provides guidance on special considerations when the auditor is requested to report on the organization's compliance with aspects of contractual agreements or regulatory requirements in connection with the audit of financial statements. The IAASB's clarified standards on these topics are substantively the same, with relatively minor wording differences between the two sets of standards. For simplicity, we rely on the wording in the AICPA's guidance. The *Auditing in Practice* feature "PCAOB Standards Related to Special Considerations" provides relevant references for PCAOB standards in this area.

AU-C 800: Special Considerations—Audits of Financial Statements Prepared in Accordance with Special-Purpose Frameworks

A **special-purpose framework** is "a financial reporting framework other than GAAP that is one of the following bases of accounting:

- **Cash basis.** A basis of accounting that the entity uses to record cash receipts and disbursements and modifications of the cash basis having substantial support (e.g., recording depreciation on fixed assets).
- **Tax basis.** A basis of accounting that the entity uses to file its income tax return for the period covered by the financial statements.
- **Regulatory basis.** A basis of accounting that the entity uses to comply with the requirements of financial reporting provisions of a regulatory agency to whose jurisdiction the entity is subject (e.g., a basis of accounting that insurance companies use pursuant to the accounting practices prescribed or permitted by a state insurance commission).

PCAOB Standards Related to Special Considerations

AUDITING IN PRACTICE

In April 2003, the PCAOB adopted certain pre-existing standards as its interim standards. AU 623, *Special Reports*, was one of the adopted standards. That standard provides guidance related to auditors' reports issued in connection with:

a. Financial statements that are prepared in conformity with a comprehensive basis of accounting other than generally accepted accounting principles

b. Specified elements, accounts, or items of a financial statement

c. Compliance with aspects of contractual agreements or regulatory requirements related to audited financial statements

d. Financial presentations to comply with contractual agreements or regulatory provisions

e. Financial information presented in prescribed forms or schedules that require a prescribed form of auditor's reports (paragraphs .32 and .33)

- **Contractual basis.** A basis of accounting that the entity uses to comply with an agreement between the entity and one or more third parties other than the auditor" (AU-C 800, paragraph .07).

These other bases of accounting are commonly referred to as **other comprehensive bases of accounting**. **Special-purpose financial statements** are those that are prepared in accordance with a special-purpose framework.

Considerations When Accepting, Planning, and Performing an Audit of Special-Purpose Financial Statements

When considering accepting an engagement of the audit of special-purpose financial statements, the auditor should:

- Obtain an understanding of the purpose for which the financial statements are being prepared, intended users, and steps taken by management to ensure that the framework is acceptable under the circumstances.
- Obtain an agreement from management that it understands and acknowledges its responsibility to include all appropriate disclosures applicable to the special-purpose framework.

When planning and performing an engagement of the audit of special-purpose financial statements, the auditor should:

- Be sure to comply with all AU-C sections relevant to the audit.
- Adapt and apply all AU-C sections relevant to the audit as necessary in the circumstances.
- Obtain an understanding of the organization's selection and application of accounting policies. Particularly relevant to the situation of special-purpose financial statements prepared in accordance with a contractual basis of accounting, the auditor should be sure to understand any important interpretations of the contract that management made in preparing the financial statements, particularly those interpretations that would have produced a material difference in the financial statements if they had been interpreted differently.

Considerations When Forming an Opinion and Reporting on an Audit of Special-Purpose Financial Statements

When forming an opinion on special-purpose financial statements, the auditor should evaluate whether the financial statements:

- Adequately describe the applicable financial reporting framework
- Have the appropriate title
- Include a summary of significant accounting policies
- Describe how the special-purpose framework differs from GAAP
- Result in fair presentation of the organization's financial results

The auditor should be alert to certain important considerations when drafting the auditor's report on special-purpose financial statements. Audit reports on all types of special-purpose financial statements should contain a statement that the financial statements are the responsibility of management, and that the special-purpose framework is appropriate in the circumstances. The audit report must also include unique elements depending on the nature of the special-purpose framework and the distribution, or use, of the audit report. *Exhibit 17.8* summarizes these reporting requirements.

AU-C 800 (paragraph .A35) provides examples of audit reports appropriate to each of the five situations described in *Exhibit 17.8*. As an example

EXHIBIT **17.8**	Overview of Reporting Requirements for Special-Purpose Financial Statements				

	Cash Basis	**Tax Basis**	**Regulatory Basis (for Use by Management and the Regulator Only)**	**Regulatory Basis (for General Use)**	**Contractual Basis**
Opinion(s)	Single opinion on special-purpose framework	Single opinion on special purpose-framework	Single opinion on special-purpose framework	Dual opinion on special-purpose framework and GAAP	Single opinion on special-purpose framework
Description of purpose for which special-purpose financial statements are prepared	No	No	Yes	Yes	Yes
Emphasis-of-matter paragraph alerting readers about the preparation in accordance with a special-purpose framework	Yes	Yes	Yes	No	Yes
Other-matter paragraph restricting the use of the auditor's report	No	No	Yes	No	Yes

Source: AU-C 800, Appendix A, paragraph .A33. AICPA audit and accounting guides by American Institute of Certified Public Accountants. Copyright 2012 Reproduced with permission of American Institute of Certified Public Accountants in the format Textbook via Copyright Clearance Center.

of a description of the purpose for which special-purpose financial statements are prepared, AU-C 800 contains the following illustration (paragraph .A35):

> "Management is responsible for the preparation and fair presentation of these financial statements in accordance with the financial reporting provisions of Section Y of Regulation Z of Any State. Management is also responsible for the design, implementation, and maintenance of internal control relevant to the preparation and fair presentation of financial statements that are free from material misstatement, whether due to fraud or error."

As an example of an emphasis-of-matter paragraph alerting users to the special-purpose framework, AU-C 800 contains the following illustration (paragraph .A35):

> "We draw attention to Note X of the financial statements, which describes the basis of accounting. As described in Note X to the financial statements, the financial statements of ABC City on the basis of the financial reporting provisions of Section Y of Regulation Z of Any State, which is a basis of accounting other than accounting principles generally accepted in the United States of America, to meet the requirements of Any State. Our opinion is not modified with respect to this matter."

As an example of an other-matter paragraph restricting use of the audit report, AU-C 800 contains the following illustration (paragraph .A35):

"Our report is intended solely for the information and use of ABC City and Any State and is not intended to be and should not be used by anyone other than these specified parties."

For brevity, we provide one example of an audit report on special-purpose financial statements in *Exhibit 17.9* for an organization whose audit firm complied with the standards of the PCAOB. This example is one in which the organization used a modified cash basis of accounting. You will notice that the auditor provides a single opinion on the special-purpose framework (the final paragraph of the report), does not describe the purpose for which the special-purpose financial statements are prepared, does include an emphasis-of-matter paragraph alerting readers about the preparation in accordance with a special-purpose framework (the third paragraph of the report), and does not include an other-matter paragraph restricting use of the auditor's report.

EXHIBIT 17.9 Report on Modified Cash Basis Financial Statements

Report of Independent Registered Public Accounting Firm

To the Trustee and Unit Holders of
Kiewit Royalty Trust
Omaha, Nebraska

We have audited the accompanying statements of assets, liabilities and trust corpus of Kiewit Royalty Trust (the "Trust") as of December 31, 2010 and 2009, and the related statements of distributable income and changes in trust corpus for each of the two years in the period ended December 31, 2010. These financial statements are the responsibility of the Trustee. Our responsibility is to express an opinion on the financial statements based on our audits.

We conducted our audits in accordance with the standards of the Public Company Accounting Oversight Board (United States). Those standards require that we plan and perform the audit to obtain reasonable assurance about whether the financial statements are free of material misstatement. The Trust is not required to have, nor were we engaged to perform, an audit of its internal control over financial reporting. Our audits included consideration of internal control over financial reporting as a basis for designing audit procedures that are appropriate in the circumstances, but not for the purpose of expressing an opinion on the effectiveness of the Trust's internal control over financial reporting. Accordingly, we express no such opinion. An audit also includes examining, on a test basis, evidence supporting the amounts and disclosures in the financial statements, assessing the accounting principles used and significant estimates made by management, as well as evaluating the overall financial statement presentation. We believe that our audits provide a reasonable basis for our opinion.

As described in Note 1, the financial statements were prepared on the modified cash basis of accounting, which is a comprehensive basis of accounting other than accounting principles generally accepted in the United States of America.

In our opinion, such financial statements present fairly, in all material respects, the assets, liabilities and trust corpus of Kiewit Royalty Trust as of December 31, 2010 and 2009, and the distributable income and changes in trust corpus for each of the two years in the period ended December 31, 2010, on the basis of accounting described in Note 1.

/s/ Deloitte & Touche LLP
Omaha, Nebraska
March 28, 2011

Source: *Kiewit Royalty Trust. Form 10-K, p. 6, via EDGAR, accessed March 2012.* http://www.sec.gov/Archives/edgar/data/711477/000119312511079847/d10k.htm

AU-C 805: Special Considerations—Audits of Single Financial Statements and Specific Elements, Accounts, or Items of a Financial Statement

AU-C 805 addresses the application of AU-C 100–700 to audits of a single financial statement or of a specific element, account, or item of a financial statement. As noted by AU-C 805 (paragraph .A2), "[t]he following are examples of single financial statements, each of which would include related notes:

- Balance sheet
- Statement of income or statement of operations
- Statement of retained earnings
- Statement of cash flows
- Statement of assets and liabilities
- Statement of changes in owner's equity
- Statement of revenues and expenses
- Statement of operations by product lines"

AU-C 805 (paragraph .A24) notes that, "the following are examples of specific elements, accounts, or items of a financial statement:

- Accounts receivable; allowance for doubtful accounts receivable; inventory; the liability for accrued benefits of a private benefit plan; the recorded value of identified intangible assets; or the liability for incurred but not reported claims in an insurance portfolio, including related notes
- A schedule of externally managed assets and income of a private benefit plan, including related notes
- A schedule of disbursements regarding a lease property, including related notes
- A schedule of profit participation or employee bonuses, including related notes"

Considerations When Accepting, Planning, and Performing an Audit of a Single Financial Statement or of a Specific Element, Account, or Item of a Financial Statement

When auditing only a single financial statement or a specific element, account, or item of a financial statement, the auditor often will not have the same understanding of the client as would be the case if the auditor audited the client's complete set of financial statements. As such, the auditor may need to obtain further evidence to corroborate audit evidence acquired from management and the accounting records. The auditor should also consider whether it is appropriate to apply the applicable financial reporting framework (e.g., U.S. GAAP or International Financial Reporting Standards) to a single financial statement or a specific element, account, or item of a financial statement. It will be important for the auditor to evaluate whether disclosures in the footnotes for the single financial statement or specific element, account, or item are adequate.

An important complexity that the auditor likely encounters in this type of engagement is that individual financial statements that comprise a complete set of financial statements or elements, accounts, or items in the financial statements (and related notes) are often interrelated. For example, sales and accounts receivables are related accounts. If the auditor is auditing only the accounts receivable account, the auditor may need to also perform procedures on interrelated items such as sales in order to adequately complete the audit.

Considerations When Forming an Opinion and Reporting on an Audit of a Single Financial Statement or of a Specific Element, Account, or Item of a Financial Statement

As noted in AU-C 805 (paragraph .A17), "[i]n the case of an audit of a single financial statement or of a specific element of a financial statement, it is important, in view of the requirements of the applicable financial reporting framework, that the disclosures enable the intended users to understand

- The information conveyed in the financial statement or the specific element and
- The effect of material transactions and events on the information conveyed in the financial statement or the specific element"

A vast array of possible situations exist in which an auditor may be reporting on an engagement of the audit of a financial statement or of a specific element, account, or item. AU-C 805 provides various illustrations of these varied circumstances and associated audit reports. For brevity, in *Exhibit 17.10* we provide one example of an audit report for an organization whose audit firm complied with the standards of the PCAOB in auditing specified elements of a financial statement. *Exhibit 17.10* provides a

---

EXHIBIT **17.10**	Report on Specified Elements of a Financial Statement for Sabine Royalty Trust

Report of Independent Registered Public Accounting Firm

To the Trustee on Behalf of Unit holders of Sabine Royalty Trust:

We have audited the accompanying Statements of Fees and Expenses (as defined in Exhibit C to the Sabine Royalty Trust Agreement) paid by Sabine Royalty Trust to Bank of America, N.A. (the "Trustee"), as trustee and escrow agent, for the years ended December 31, 2010, 2009 and 2008. These statements are the responsibility of the Trustee's management. Our responsibility is to express an opinion on these statements based on our audits.

We conducted our audits in accordance with the standards of the Public Company Accounting Oversight Board (United States). Those standards require that we plan and perform the audits to obtain reasonable assurance about whether the Statements of Fees and Expenses are free of material misstatement. An audit includes examining, on a test basis, evidence supporting the amounts and disclosures in the Statements of Fees and Expenses. An audit also includes assessing the accounting principles used and significant estimates made by management, as well as evaluating the overall statement presentation. We believe that our audits provide a reasonable basis for our opinion.

As described in Note 3, the Statements of Fees and Expenses were prepared on a modified cash basis of accounting, which is a comprehensive basis of accounting other than accounting principles generally accepted in the United States of America.

In our opinion, the Statements of Fees and Expenses referred to above present fairly, in all material respects, the fees and expenses paid by Sabine Royalty Trust to Bank of America, N.A., as trustee and escrow agent, for the years ended December 31, 2010, 2009 and 2008, on the basis of accounting described in Note 3.

/s/ PricewaterhouseCoopers LLP
Dallas, Texas
February 28, 2011

Source: Sabine Royalty Trust. Form 10-K, Exhibit 99.2, via EDGAR, accessed February 2012. http://www.sec.gov/Archives/edgar/data/710752/000095012311020729/d79582exv99w2.htm

report from PricewaterhouseCoopers concerning the audit of fees and expenses of the Sabine Royalty Trust. PricewaterhouseCoopers' audit report also makes note of the fact that the financial statements of Sabine Royalty Trust are prepared on a modified cash basis of accounting, which is a comprehensive basis of accounting other than GAAP.

AU-C 806: Reporting on Compliance with Aspects of Contractual Agreements or Regulatory Requirements in Connection with Audited Financial Statements

AU-C 806 addresses situations in which the auditor is requested to report on a client's compliance with certain contractual agreements or regulatory requirements. Auditors may issue such reports as long as the covenants of the agreement or regulatory requirement are based on information from audited financial statements. In other words, before a compliance report may be issued, the auditor must have assurance that the financial information subject to the covenants is fairly presented. A bond indenture, for example, may require the bond issuer to maintain a minimum current ratio, make minimum payments into a sinking fund, or limit dividends to a certain percentage of net income. If such requirements or restrictions are violated, the bond may become payable on demand of the bondholders rather than at its scheduled maturity date.

A compliance report normally contains limited or negative assurance and may be given in a separate report or with the auditor's report accompanying the financial statements. Recall that a limited or negative assurance report simply indicates that the auditor did not find anything that would lead the auditor to conclude that the report is not fairly stated. AU-C 806 (paragraph .07) notes that "[t]he auditor's report on compliance should include a statement that nothing came to the auditor's attention that caused the auditor to believe that the entity failed to comply with specified aspects of the contractual agreements or regulatory requirements, insofar as they relate to accounting matters, only when

a. the auditor has not identified any instances of noncompliance,
b. the auditor has expressed an unmodified or qualified opinion on the financial statements to which the applicable covenants of such contractual agreements or regulatory requirements relate, and
c. the applicable covenants or regulatory requirements relate to accounting matters that have been subjected to the audit procedures applied in the audit of financial statements."

AU-806 (paragraph .A8) illustrates a wide variety of reports on compliance. For brevity, in *Exhibit 17.11* we provide one example of a report on compliance with a contractual agreement for an organization whose audit firm complied with the standards of the PCAOB. *Exhibit 17.11* provides a report from KPMG on an assertion of ING Partners. In the report, KPMG identifies the ING Partners' assertion, which is that management of the fund complied with certain regulatory requirements. KPMG also provides information on certain procedures that were completed in forming the audit opinion. KPMG provides an opinion that the Fund did comply with the applicable requirements as indicated in management's assertion. The report concludes with a statement by the auditor about limiting the use of the report.

| EXHIBIT **17.11** | Report on Compliance with a Contractual Agreement for ING Partners, Inc. |

Report of Independent Registered Public Accounting Firm

To the Board of Directors
ING Partners, Inc.

We have examined management's assertion, included in the accompanying Management Statement Regarding Compliance with Certain Provisions of the Investment Company Act of 1940 (the Act), that ING Global Bond Fund (formerly, ING Oppenheimer Strategic Income Portfolio) (the Fund), complied with the applicable requirements of subsections (b) and (c) of rule 17f-2 under the Act with respect to the securities held by affiliated sub-custodian banks pursuant to rule 17f-5 of the Act as of March 31, 2009. Management is responsible for the Fund's compliance with those requirements. Our responsibility is to express an opinion on management's assertion about the Fund's compliance based on our examination.

Our examination was conducted in accordance with the standards of the Public Company Accounting Oversight Board (United States) and, accordingly, included examining, on a test basis, evidence about the Fund's compliance with those requirements and performing such other procedures as we considered necessary in the circumstances. Included among our procedures were the following tests performed as of March 31, 2009, and, with respect to agreement of security purchases and sales, for the period August 31, 2008 through March 31, 2009:

- Confirmation of all securities held in book entry form by The Bank of New York Mellon (formerly, The Bank of New York) (custodian);
- Confirmation of securities held in book entry form by ING Bank Slaski, S.A. and Bank RT Budapest (affiliated sub-custodian banks);
- Confirmation of securities held in book entry form by Polish National Depository of Securities and Hungary Central Securities Depository (KELER) (foreign depositories);
- Confirmation or inspection of documentation of all securities purchased but not received, hypothecated, pledged, placed in escrow, or out for transfer with brokers, pledges and/or transfer agents;
- Reconciliation of all such securities to the books and records of the Fund, the custodian and the affiliated sub-custodian banks;
- Agreement of selected security purchases and sales during the period August 31, 2008 through March 31, 2009 from the books and records of the Fund to broker confirmations or bank statements.

We believe that our examination provides a reasonable basis for our opinion. Our examination does not provide a legal determination on the Fund's compliance with the specified requirements.

In our opinion, management's assertion that the Fund complied with the applicable requirements of subsections (b) and (c) of rule 17f-2 of the Act as of March 31, 2009, with respect to the securities reflected in the investment accounts of the Fund that are held by the affiliated sub-custodian banks pursuant to rule 17f-5 of the Act, is fairly stated, in all material respects. We have not examined the Fund's compliance with rule 17f-5 of the Act and express no opinion thereon.

This report is intended solely for the information and use of management, the Board of Directors of the Fund, and the Securities and Exchange Commission, and is not intended to be and should not be used by anyone other than these specified parties.

KPMG LLP
August 30, 2011

KPMG LLP
Two Financial Center
60 South Street
Boston, MA 02111

Source: ING Partners, Inc. Form N-17f-2, p. 2, via EDGAR. http://www.sec.gov/Archives/edgar/data/1039001/000110465911049591/a11-25242_54017f2.htm

Attestation on Agreed-Upon Procedures, Financial Forecasts and Projections, and Pro Forma Financial Information

LO 5 Describe attestation engagements relating to agreed-upon procedures, financial forecasts and projections, and pro forma financial information, and the types of reports that are issued for these engagements.

The AICPA's SSAEs and the IAASB's ISAEs provide guidance on the performance and reporting of attestation engagements relating to agreed-upon procedures, financial forecasts and projections, and pro forma financial information. As noted earlier, the PCAOB's interim standards are the attestation standards from the AICPA (unless superseded or amended by the PCAOB). As of 2014, the PCAOB's and the AICPA's attestation standards are generally the same. For simplicity, we rely on the wording in the AICPA's guidance.

Agreed-Upon Procedures Engagements (SSAEs No. 10 and 11, AT 201)

"An **agreed-upon procedures engagement** is one in which a practitioner is engaged by a client to issue a report of findings based on specific procedures performed on subject matter" (AT 201, paragraph. 03). In this type of engagement, the independent practitioner is engaged to assist in evaluating subject matter or an assertion. Agreed-upon procedures vary widely, so the nature, timing, and extent of agreed-upon procedures also vary. In this type of engagement, the practitioner does not perform a review, and does not provide an opinion or negative assurance. Rather, the report is in the form of a description of procedures and associated findings. The report should indicate that it is restricted in its use to **specified parties**. Specified parties are the individuals who will receive the practitioner's agreed-upon procedures report. Examples of specified parties include, for example, management, the board of directors (or subcommittees thereof), a trustee, or a bank.

Responsibilities and Examples of Appropriate and Inappropriate Agreed-Upon Procedures

The responsibility of the specified parties is to ensure that the agreed-upon procedures are sufficient (in terms of nature, timing, and extent) in terms of meeting their own needs. The responsibility of the practitioner is to conduct the procedures and report the findings in accordance with applicable professional standards. The practitioner must have adequate knowledge of the subject matter. The practitioner is not required to determine if a difference exists between the agreed-upon procedures requested by the specified parties and the procedures that the practitioner would have decided to conduct if the practitioner would have been engaged to perform another form of engagement.

The practitioner should not agree to perform agreed-upon procedures that are overly subjective, and the practitioner should be able to obtain evidence to provide a reasonable basis for findings expressed in the report that will ultimately be issued about the agreed-upon procedures. Examples of appropriate procedures include (AT 201, paragraph .17):

- "Execution of a sampling application after agreeing on relevant parameters
- Inspection of specified documents evidencing certain types of transactions or detailed attributes thereof
- Confirmation of specific information with third parties
- Comparison of documents, schedules, or analyses
- Performance of specific procedures on work performed by others (including the work of internal auditors)
- Performance of mathematical computations"

Examples of inappropriate agreed-upon procedures include (AT 201, paragraph .18):

- "Mere reading of the work performed by others solely to describe their findings
- Evaluating the competency or objectivity of another party
- Obtaining an understanding about a particular subject
- Interpreting documents outside the scope of the practitioner's professional expertise"

Description of Findings and Illustration of an Agreed-Upon Procedures Report

When describing the results of findings related to agreed-upon procedures, the practitioner should avoid vague or ambiguous language. *Exhibit 17.12* contains examples of agreed-upon procedures, appropriate descriptions of findings, and inappropriate descriptions of findings that are described in AT 201, paragraph .26.

Exhibit 17.13 provides an illustration of an agreed-upon procedures report (AT 201, paragraph .32).

Financial Forecasts and Projections (SSAEs No. 10 and 17, AT 301)

Prospective financial statements are "either financial forecasts or financial projections including the summaries of significant assumptions

---

EXHIBIT **17.12**	Appropriate and Inappropriate Descriptions of Findings of Agreed-Upon Procedures

Procedures Agreed Upon	Appropriate Description of Findings	Inappropriate Description of Findings
Inspect the shipment dates for a sample (agreed-upon) of specified shipping documents, and determine whether any such dates were subsequent to December 31, 20XX.	No shipment dates shown on the sample of shipping documents were subsequent to December 31, 20XX.	Nothing came to my attention as a result of applying that procedure.
Calculate the number of blocks or streets paved during the year ended September 30, 20XX, shown on contractors' certificates of project completion; compare the resultant number to the number in an identified chart of performance statistics.	The number of blocks of streets paved in the chart of performance statistics was Y blocks more than the number calculated from the contractors' certificates of project completion.	The number of blocks of streets paved approximated the number of blocks included in the chart of performance statistics.
Calculate the rate of return on a specified investment (according to an agreed-upon formula) and verify that the resultant percentage agrees to the percentage in an identified schedule.	No exceptions were found as a result of applying the procedure.	The resultant percentage approximated the predetermined percentage in the identified schedule.
Trace all outstanding checks appearing on a bank reconciliation as of a certain date to checks cleared in the bank statement of the subsequent month.	All outstanding checks appearing on the bank reconciliation were cleared in the subsequent month's bank statement except for the following: [List all exceptions.]	Nothing came to my attention as a result of applying the procedure.

EXHIBIT **17.13**	Illustrative Report of Independent Accountant's Report on Applying Agreed-Upon Procedures

To the Audit Committees and Managements of ABC Inc. and XYZ Fund:

We have performed the procedures enumerated below, which were agreed to by the audit committees and managements of ABC Inc. and XYZ Fund, solely to assist you in evaluating the accompanying Statement of Investment Performance Statistics of XYZ Fund (prepared in accordance with the criteria specified therein) for the year ended December 31, 20X1. XYZ Fund's management is responsible for the statement of investment performance statistics. This agreed-upon procedures engagement was conducted in accordance with the attestation standards established by the American Institute of Certified Public Accountants. The sufficiency of these procedures is solely the responsibility of those parties specified in this report. Consequently, we make no representation regarding the sufficiency of the procedures described below either for the purpose for which this report has been requested or for any other purpose.

[Include paragraphs to enumerate procedures and findings.]

We were not engaged to and did not conduct an examination, the objective of which would be the expression of an opinion on the accompanying Statement of Investment Performance Statistics of XYZ Fund. Accordingly, we do not express such an opinion. Had we performed additional procedures, other matters might have come to our attention that would have been reported to you.

This report is intended solely for the information and use of the audit committees and managements of ABC Inc. and XYZ Fund, and is not intended to be and should not be used by anyone other than these specified parties.

[Signature]

[Date]

and accounting policies" (AT 301, paragraph .08a). A **financial forecast** includes "prospective financial statements that present, to the best of the responsible party's knowledge and belief, an entity's expected financial position, results of operations, and cash flows" (AT 301, paragraph .08c). A **financial projection** includes "prospective financial statements that present, to the best of the responsible party's knowledge and belief, given one or more hypothetical assumptions, an entity's expected financial position, results of operations, and cash flows" (AT 301, paragraph .08d). Practitioners may be engaged to perform compilation, examination, or agreed-upon procedures engagements on prospective financial statements.

Compilation of Prospective Financial Statements

A compilation of prospective financial statements involves:

- Assembling prospective financial statements based on the responsible party's assumptions; **assembling** involves the manual or computer processing of mathematical or clerical functions to achieve the presentation of prospective financial statements
- Performing compilation procedures, including reading the prospective financial statements, along with their assumptions and accounting policies, and considering whether they appear to be presented in conformity with AICPA presentation guidelines and that they are not obviously inappropriate
- Issuing a compilation report

Importantly, a compilation does not provide assurance on the prospective financial statements. The following are standards that the practitioner should follow when compiling prospective financial statements (AT 301, paragraph .15):

- The compilation should be performed by a person or persons having adequate technical training and proficiency to compile prospective financial statements.
- Due professional care should be exercised in the performance of the compilation and the preparation of the report.
- The work should be adequately planned, and assistants, if any, should be properly supervised.
- Applicable compilation procedures should be performed as a basis for reporting on the compiled prospective financial statements.
- The report based on the practitioner's compilation of prospective financial statements should conform to the applicable guidance.

Reporting on a Compilation of Prospective Financial Statements

Exhibit 17.14 provides an illustration of a practitioner's standard report on the compilation of a forecast (AT 301, paragraph .19).

Exhibit 17.15 provides an illustration of a practitioner's standard report on the compilation of a projection (AT 301, paragraph .20).

Examination of Prospective Financial Statements

An examination of prospective financial statements involves:

a. "Evaluating the preparation of the prospective financial statements.
b. Evaluating the support underlying the assumptions.
c. Evaluating the presentation of the prospective financial statements for conformity with AICPA presentation guidelines.
d. Issuing an examination report" (AT 301, paragraph .29).

An examination differs from a compilation in that the practitioner is not the individual responsible for preparing the financial statements. Rather, the practitioner's role in this setting is to evaluate and report upon those financial statements.

Reporting on an Examination of Prospective Financial Statements

Exhibit 17.16 provides an illustration of a practitioner's standard report on the examination of a forecast (AT 301, paragraph .34):

When the practitioner examines a projection, the report issued should reference the fact that the projection is conditional on hypothetical

---

EXHIBIT 17.14   Illustrative Report of Compilation of a Forecast

We have compiled the accompanying forecasted balance sheet, statements of income, retained earnings, and cash flows of XYZ Company as of December 31, 20XX, and for the year then ending, in accordance with attestation standards established by the American Institute of Certified Public Accountants.

A compilation is limited to presenting in the form of a forecast information that is the representation of management and does not include evaluation of the support for the assumptions underlying the forecast. We have not examined the forecast and, accordingly, do not express an opinion or any other form of assurance on the accompanying statements or assumptions. Furthermore, there will usually be differences between the forecasted and actual results, because events and circumstances frequently do not occur as expected, and those differences may be material. We have no responsibility to update this report for events and circumstances occurring after the date of this report.

[*Signature*]

[*Date*]

EXHIBIT 17.15   Illustrative Report of Compilation of a Projection

We have compiled the accompanying projected balance sheet, statements of income, retained earnings, and cash flows of XYZ Company as of December 31, 20XX, and for the year then ending, in accordance with attestation standards established by the American Institute of Certified Public Accountants. The accompanying projection was prepared for [*state special purpose, for example, "the purpose of negotiating a loan to expand XYZ Company's plant"*].

A compilation is limited to presenting in the form of a projection information that is the representation of management and does not include evaluation of the support for the assumptions underlying the projection. We have not examined the projection and, accordingly, do not express an opinion or any other form of assurance on the accompanying statements or assumptions. Furthermore even if [*describe hypothetical assumption, for example, "the loan is granted and the plant is expanded,"*] there will usually be differences between the projected and actual results, because events and circumstances frequently do not occur as expected, and those differences may be material. We have no responsibility to update this report for events and circumstances occurring after the date of this report.

The accompanying projection and this report are intended solely for the information and use of [*identify specified parties, for example, "XYZ Company and DEF Bank"*] and is not intended to be and should not be used by anyone other than these specified parties.

[*Signature*]

[*Date*]

EXHIBIT 17.16   Illustrative Report on the Examination of a Forecast

We have examined the accompanying forecasted balance sheet, statements of income, retained earnings, and cash flows of XYZ Company as of December 31, 20XX, and for the year then ending. XYZ Company's management is responsible for the forecast. Our responsibility is to express an opinion on the forecast based on our examination.

Our examination was conducted in accordance with attestation standards established by the American Institute of Certified Public Accountants and, accordingly, included such procedures as we considered necessary to evaluate both the assumptions used by management and the preparation and presentation of the forecast. We believe that our examination provides a reasonable basis for our opinion.

In our opinion, the accompanying forecast is presented in conformity with guidelines for presentation of a forecast established by the American Institute of Certified Public Accountants, and the underlying assumptions provide a reasonable basis for management's forecast. However, there will usually be differences between the forecasted and actual results, because events and circumstances frequently do not occur as expected, and those differences may be material. We have no responsibility to update this report for events and circumstances occurring after the date of this report.

[*Signature*]

[*Date*]

assumptions. The report should also state the special purpose for which the projection was prepared, and it should restrict the use of the report by those specified parties. For an example of a standard report on an examination of a projection, see AT 301, paragraph .35.

Agreed-Upon Procedures of Prospective Financial Statements

Agreed-upon procedures of prospective financial statements can be quite varied. The practitioner's procedures may be limited or extensive depending on the requirements of the responsible party. However, it is important to

EXHIBIT **17.17**	Illustrative Report on Applying Agreed-Upon Procedures to Prospective Financial Statements

Board of Directors—XYZ Corporation
Board of Directors—ABC Company

At your request, we have performed certain agreed-upon procedures, as enumerated below, with respect to the forecasted balance sheet and the related forecasted statements of income, retained earnings, and cash flows of DEF Company, a subsidiary of ABC Company, as of December 31, 20XX, and for the year then ending. These procedures, which were agreed to by the Boards of Directors of XYZ Corporation and ABC Company, were performed solely to assist you in evaluating the forecast in connection with the proposed sale of DEF Company to XYZ Corporation. DEF Company's management is responsible for the forecast.

This agreed-upon procedures engagement was conducted in accordance with attestation standards established by the American Institute of Certified Public Accountants. The sufficiency of these procedures is solely the responsibility of the specified parties. Consequently, we make no representation regarding the sufficiency of the procedures described below either for the purpose for which this report has been requested or for any other purpose.

[Include paragraphs to enumerate procedures and findings.]

We are not engaged to and did not conduct an examination, the objective of which would be the expression of an opinion on the accompanying prospective financial statements. Accordingly, we do not express an opinion on whether the prospective financial statements are presented in conformity with AICPA presentation guidelines or on whether the underlying assumptions provide a reasonable basis for the presentation. Had we performed additional procedures, other matters might have come to our attention that would have been reported to you. Furthermore, there will usually be differences between the forecasted and actual results, because events and circumstances frequently do not occur as expected, and those differences may be material. We have no responsibility to update this report for events and circumstances occurring after the date of this report.

This report is intended solely for the information and use of the Boards of Directors of ABC Company and XYZ Corporation and is not intended to be and should not be used by anyone other than these specified parties.

[Signature]

[Date]

note that the procedures must involve more than a simple reading of the prospective financial statements. *Exhibit 17.17* provides an illustration of a practitioner's standard report on agreed-upon procedures of prospective financial statements (AT 301, paragraph .56):

Reporting on Pro Forma Financial Information (SSAE No. 10, AT Section 401)

Pro forma financial information shows "what the significant effects on historical financial information might have been had a consummated or proposed transaction (or event) occurred at an earlier date" (AT 401, paragraph .04). Pro forma financial information is often used to illustrate the effects of the following types of transactions:

- Business combinations
- Disposing of a significant segment of a business
- Changing the form of organization of the business or its status as an autonomous organization
- Proposing the sale of securities and applying the proceeds to a project

It is important that pro forma financial information be labeled clearly to distinguish it from historical financial information. The presentation of pro forma financial information should adhere to the following guidelines:

- Describe the transaction or event that is reflected in the pro forma financial information
- Describe the source of historical financial information upon which the pro forma financial information is based
- Describe significant assumptions used to develop the pro forma adjustments
- Describe any significant uncertainties about those assumptions
- Indicate that pro forma financial information should be considered in conjunction with the historical financial information upon which the pro forma financial information is based
- Make clear that the pro forma financial information is not necessarily indicative of results that would have been achieved had the transaction or event actually taken place at an earlier time

The practitioner may perform either an examination or a review of pro forma financial information. An examination provides reasonable assurance, which is greater assurance than provided in a review.

Procedures for Examining or Reviewing Pro Forma Financial Information

The following procedures are appropriate for examining or reviewing pro forma financial information:

- Obtain an understanding of the underlying transaction or event.
- Obtain knowledge of each part of the combined organization in a business combination that enables the practitioner to perform the required procedures.
- Discuss management's assumptions regarding the effects of the transaction or event.
- Evaluate whether pro forma adjustments are completely recorded.
- Obtain sufficient appropriate evidence to support any pro forma adjustments. The practitioner obtains more evidence in an examination engagement than in a review engagement.
- Evaluate whether management's assumptions underlying the pro forma financial statements are described in a clear and comprehensive fashion.
- Determine that computations underlying pro forma adjustments are mathematically correct.
- Obtain from management written representations about:
  - Their responsibility for the assumptions used in making the pro forma adjustments
  - An assertion that the assumptions provide a reasonable basis for presenting the effects related to the transaction or event, that the pro forma adjustments appropriately reflect the assumptions, and that the pro forma information reflects the proper application of the adjustments to the historical financial statements
  - An assertion that the significant effects related to the transaction or event are appropriately disclosed in the pro forma financial information
- Read the pro forma financial information and evaluate the underlying transaction or event, the pro forma adjustments, significant assumptions, or uncertainties, and evaluate the source of the historical financial information upon which the pro forma financial information is based.

EXHIBIT **17.18**	Illustrative Review Report on Pro Forma Financial Statements

We have reviewed the pro forma adjustments reflecting the transaction [*or event*] described in Note 1 and the application of those adjustments to the historical amounts in [*the assembly of*] the accompanying pro forma condensed balance sheet of X Company as of March 31, 20X2, and the pro forma condensed statement of income for the three months then ended. These historical condensed financial statements are derived from the historical unaudited financial statements of X Company, which were reviewed by us, and of Y Company, which were reviewed by other accountants, appearing elsewhere herein [*or incorporated by reference*]. Such pro forma adjustments are based on management's assumptions as described in Note 2. X Company's management is responsible for the pro forma financial information.

Our review was conducted in accordance with attestation standards established by the American Institute of Certified Public Accountants. A review is substantially less in scope than an examination, the objective of which is the expression of an opinion on management's assumptions, the pro forma adjustments and the application of those adjustments to historical financial information. Accordingly, we do not express such an opinion.

The objective of this pro forma financial information is to show what the significant effects on the historical financial information might have been had the transaction [*or event*] occurred at an earlier date. However, the pro forma condensed financial statements are not necessarily indicative of the results of operations or related effects on financial position that would have been attained had the above-mentioned transaction [*or event*] actually occurred earlier.

[*Additional paragraph(s) may be added to emphasize certain matters relating to the attest engagement or the subject matter.*]

Based on our review, nothing came to our attention that caused us to believe that management's assumptions do not provide a reasonable basis for presenting the significant effects directly attributable to the above-mentioned transaction [*or event*] described in Note 1, that the related pro forma adjustments do not give appropriate effect to those assumptions, or that the pro forma column does not reflect the proper application of those adjustments to the historical financial statement amounts in the pro forma condensed balance sheet as of March 31, 20X2, and the pro forma condensed statement of income for the three months then ended.

[*Signature*]

[*Date*]

Reporting on Pro Forma Financial Information

Exhibit 17.18 provides an illustration of a practitioner's standard review report on pro forma financial statements (AT 401, paragraph .19). or an example of an examination report on pro forma financial statements, see AT 401 (paragraph .18).

Forensic Accounting

LO **6** Describe forensic accounting and distinguish between forensic accounting and auditing.

Forensic accounting involves detailed investigation of situations where fraud has already been identified or where fraud is highly suspected. One aspect of forensic accounting focuses on identifying the person who has perpetrated the fraud and having that person confess to the fraud. Forensic accounting builds support for legal action against the person committing the fraud by identifying the fraud, calculating the damages caused by the fraud, and building both factual and testimonial evidence of the fraud. Although forensic accounting builds on evidence concepts in auditing and uses the evidence found during an audit (e.g., forged source documents, file details showing duplicate items), the emphasis is on interviewing, with a focus on the perpetrator. Forensic accountants examine 100% of fraud-related documents to accurately measure the cost of the fraud. Auditors, on the other hand, usually rely on sampling to determine whether or not material misstatements exist. It is important to note that conducting a financial statement audit is a separate engagement from conducting a forensic accounting investigation. The audit of financial statements includes serious consideration of the possibility of fraud; the sole purpose of a forensic engagement is to detect, investigate, and document a situation in which fraud almost certainly exists.

Forensic accountants are often asked to provide litigation support, in which they are called on to give expert testimony about financial data and accounting activities. Interestingly, the emphasis in court cases is more on testimonial evidence that is built upon other evidence. Therefore, interviewing is one of the most important forensic accounting skills.

Forensic accountants also work on reconstructing account balances; that is, they go back to source documents and attempt to determine what an account balance should be or determine the amount of fraud directly linked to a perpetrator. Forensic accounting also broadens out into courtroom subjects, such as hiding assets in divorce cases or determining the exact amount of money lost through a money laundering scheme. *Exhibit 17.19* summarizes some of the major differences between forensic accounting and auditing.

Often, a forensic engagement is initiated by management when it suspects a fraud is occurring within the organization. In that case, management may alert the auditor to its concerns and request a separate forensic engagement. Alternatively, the audit of financial statements may uncover hints of fraud. In that case, the auditor may recommend to management that the audit firm conduct a separate forensic engagement.

Outside of a forensic engagement, auditing standards indicate that an audit team may want to assign forensic audit specialists in situations where there are strong indicators of fraud. The rationale for assigning such personnel is that forensic auditors are accustomed to finding fraud and have

EXHIBIT 17.19 Differences between Forensic Accounting and Auditing

Area	Forensic Accounting	Auditing
Focus	Known frauds or areas where fraud is suspected Getting the perpetrator to confess	Fairness of financial statements Quality of controls
Approach	Interviews Reconstruction of damages 100% examination of targeted files	Sampling, analytical review, tests of controls, substantive procedures based on materiality
Scope	Can range from financial reporting frauds in companies to hidden assets for divorce cases to court testimony	Usually audits of financial statements
End product	Summary of evidence gathered with special emphasis on testimonial evidence Expert witness work in court case	Opinion on audited financial statements and internal control
Underlying skills	Interviewing—listening Reconstruction of account balances Cyber reconstruction (computer cases) Presentation—expert witnessing work	Objectivity Data gathering and analysis Basic accounting and auditing knowledge Nonconfrontational interviewing skills Computer auditing

developed the necessary skills and professional skepticism to address the fraud risk. Therefore, forensic specialists may work on separate forensic engagements, and may also be called upon to assist financial statement auditors in situations of heightened fraud risk.

Sustainability Reporting and Assurance

LO 7 Describe sustainability reporting and articulate the auditor's role in providing assurance on management sustainability reports.

Sustainability has become an increasingly important topic to organizations and societies around the globe in recent years, and this trend is likely to intensify. As noted in the *Emerging Issues* feature "Evolving Nature of Sustainability Reporting and Assurance," this is an area where trends and requirements are continuing to evolve.

What exactly do companies mean by sustainability? A few examples will illustrate the variation in the concept. MTN Group, a South African mobile phone company, defines sustainability as involving the following:

- "Promoting sound corporate governance practices and ethical responsibility.
- Providing a safe working environment in which the health of our people is protected and their opportunities for self development are enhanced.
- Promoting cultural diversity and equity in the workplace.
- Minimising adverse environmental impacts.
- Providing opportunities for social and economic development in the communities in which we operate." (See *www.MTN.com/sustainability/*)

Caribou Coffee articulates sustainability in terms of a "Do Good" philosophy, which represents a long-term aspiration for the company. This philosophy involves sourcing (e.g., products that the company purchases including coffee, cups, dairy products, and equipment), environmental awareness (e.g., recycling, water conservation, and energy efficiency), and community involvement (e.g., employee volunteerism and corporate donations). As another example, Williams Sonoma describes its vision for sustainability as involving decisions about the design of products, achieving energy efficiency through reductions in packaging and waste, working with suppliers to ensure the use of responsible materials (e.g., organically grown cotton), supporting economic opportunities for people around the world, and providing for a safe and fair workplace at companies that supply the company.

Evolving Nature of Sustainability Reporting and Assurance

 **EMERGING** ISSUE

Guidelines and requirements for sustainability reporting and the provision of assurance on sustainability reports are continuing to evolve. Currently, there is general broad agreement about what sustainability means, and various frameworks and standards assist companies in producing relevant and reliable sustainability data for external users. Further, substantial variety exists in companies' decisions about the level of assurance to obtain on sustainability disclosures. Sustainability reporting will likely continue to be a growth area into which auditors can apply their assurance skills to expand services outside of traditional audit assurance services; so be alert for further developments in this emerging area.

In 2010, the International Federation of Accountants (IFAC) and the Prince's Accounting for Sustainability (A4S) Project entered into a memorandum of understanding to support the global accountancy profession's role in developing sustainable organizations. As the press release states:

Organizations are increasingly seeking new ways to maintain their economic performance and contributions to society in the face of challenge and crisis. Perhaps the most critical challenge facing business and society generally is to live within our ecological limits, while continuing to enjoy economic prosperity. IFAC and A4S believe that an essential part of the answer lies in going beyond traditional ways of thinking about performance and embedding sustainability into strategy, governance, performance management, and reporting processes. Key priorities to support the work of professional accountants in embedding sustainable practices include:

- Raising awareness and facilitating sharing and collaboration across the global accountancy community, for example, through the development of a community website for professional accountancy organizations, business leaders, academics, and other experts to exchange ideas and share good sustainability practice;
- Establishing an international integrated reporting committee to develop a new reporting model that will better reflect the interconnected impact of financial, environmental, social, and governance factors on the long-term performance and condition of an organization; and
- Incorporating accounting for sustainability within professional training and education.

Professional accountants in organizations support the sustainability efforts of the organizations they work for in leadership roles in strategy, governance, performance management, and reporting processes. They also oversee, measure, control, and communicate the long-term sustainable value creation of their organizations.*

As these examples illustrate, there are many views on what constitutes sustainability and sustainability reporting, along with many terms that are used to describe these concepts. There is also a role for the auditing profession with regard to sustainability initiatives and related assurance. A report by Ernst & Young Australia, "Non-financial Reporting" (Ernst & Young Australia, July 2009) summarizes three common sustainability-related terms:

- **Nonfinancial reporting** is the "practice of measuring, disclosing and being accountable to internal and external stakeholders for organisational performance towards the goal of sustainable development."
- **Corporate social responsibility reporting** is the "continuing commitment by business to behave ethically and contribute to economic development while improving the quality of life of the workforce, their families, the local community and society at large."
- **Triple bottom-line reporting** is the "reporting on financial, environmental and social performance."

The term *triple bottom-line reporting* best captures the essence of sustainability reporting. We define **sustainability** as actions taken at the corporate level to ensure economic, environmental, and social responsibility, and we define **sustainability reporting** as voluntary corporate disclosures about sustainability initiatives, plans, and associated outcomes.

---

*This book is an extract from IFAC and the Prince's Accounting for Sustainability Project Collaborate to Promote Sustainable Organizations, published by the International Federation of Accountants (IFAC) on its web site in May 2010 and is used with permission of IFAC.

Reporting on Sustainability Activities and Outcomes

Why do companies make sustainability disclosures? Investor interest, socially responsible investment funds, and the Dow Jones Sustainability Index have demanded these kinds of disclosures, and their voices have been heard by companies. Most corporate web sites now include sustainability reports, and the placement on those web sites is usually quite prominent.

Companies determine what to report and how to report it by using various available guidelines, including the Global Reporting Initiative (GRI) Sustainability Reporting Guidelines. The overall goals of these guidelines are to enable sustainability report users to "assess sustainability performance with respect to laws, norms, codes, performance standards, and voluntary initiatives; create a continuous platform for dialogue about expectations for responsibility and performance; understand the impacts (positive and negative) that organizations can have on sustainable development; and compare performance within an organization and between different organizations over time to inform decisions."

While this guidance provides criteria that preparers can use in developing their sustainability reporting, the specific disclosures that companies make regarding sustainability differ markedly from company to company. Organizations' sustainability reporting is strategic in that it is intended to emphasize a message that is consistent with overall financial reporting goals and marketing initiatives. *Exhibit 17.20* summarizes standards for sustainability reporting and assurance. The *Emerging Issues* feature "Creation of the Sustainability Accounting Standards Board" highlights the evolving nature of these standards.

EXHIBIT **17.20**	Standards for Sustainability Reporting and Assurance

Global Reporting Initiative Sustainability Reporting Guidelines (G3 and G4)	*Global Reporting Initiative (GRI) Sustainability Reporting Guidelines* (*https://www.globalreporting.org/reporting/G3andG3-1/g3-guidelines/Pages/default.aspx*). This framework and guidance assist companies in determining how and what to report in terms of their sustainability planning and performance. This framework allows for a great deal of variability in the nature and extent of reporting across organizations. G4, which was issued in 2013, asks organizations to state their practice on external assurance as part of their report. Such assurance is not required, but recommended.
AA1000	*AccountAbility's AA1000* series are principles-based standards to help organizations become more accountable, responsible and sustainable. They address issues affecting governance, business models and organizational strategy, as well as providing operational guidance on sustainability assurance and stakeholder engagement (*http://www.accountability.org/standards/index.html*). The series of standards include guidance for both reporting organizations and assurance providers.
AICPA, PCAOB, and IAASB	AICPA, PCAOB, and IAASB general standards for providing assurance and attestation services can be adapted to the context of sustainability reporting, but such standards do not address sustainability specifically. As an example, the International Standard on Assurance Engagements 3000 (Revised) provides guidance for the provision of assurance over engagements other than audits or reviews of historical financial information.

Creation of the Sustainability Accounting Standards Board

EMERGING ISSUE

The Sustainability Accounting Standards Board (SASB) (http://www.sasb.org/) is an independent nonprofit organization created in 2011 to establish sustainability accounting standards for use in 10-K filings with the SEC. Through 2016, SASB is developing sustainability accounting standards for more than 80 industries in 10 sectors. Public companies will use SASB standards for disclosing material sustainability issues that benefit users. The standards will allow comparisons and benchmarking within industries. Regardless of the efforts of SASB, at least one SEC Commissioner has cautioned that, other than FASB, the SEC has not given any organization the authority to establish disclosure requirements.

Exhibit 17.21 provides examples of the widely varying types of information that companies provide in their sustainability reports. The important point to note from an auditing perspective on the sustainability disclosures in *Exhibit 17.21* is that some are quantitative and could be relatively easy to validate. For example, Siemens' disclosure of the percentage of female employees would be a relatively straightforward number to audit. Other disclosures require subject-matter expertise. For example, both Ford and Siemens provide information about greenhouse gas emissions, and changes in that metric over time, which would require the assurance provider to understand measurement issues in this scientific area. Other disclosures are more subjective by nature and are more difficult to interpret in terms of how they achieve sustainability goals. While external users may take a great deal of interest in such reports, unless the reports are consistent in what they measure, and unless what they measure is important, they may not be very meaningful. Importantly, the usefulness of the disclosure of these sustainability metrics depends on whether or not users can believe that the disclosures are true and faithfully represent the companies' sustainability efforts.

Providing Assurance on Sustainability Reporting

Just as users of financial statements demand audits, users of sustainability reports are increasingly demanding assurance that they can rely on these disclosures. Independent assurance on sustainability reporting enhances its credibility. External assurance (e.g., professional assurance providers such as audit firms, stakeholder panels, or statements by subject-matter experts) is preferable to internal assurance (e.g., internal audit) because it is seen as more objective and independent from management. The GRI guidelines state that external assurance over sustainability reports should:

- Be conducted by those with competence in the subject matter and assurance practices
- Be performed in a systematic manner that is evidence-based and includes adequate documentation
- Assess whether the sustainability report is reasonable, balanced, and appropriately inclusive

- Be issued by individuals or organizations that are independent of the company issuing the sustainability report
- Assess the extent to which the report preparer has applied the GRI guidelines in reaching its conclusions
- Result in a report that is publicly available, is written in form, and states the relationship between the preparer of the report and the issuer of the report

---

EXHIBIT **17.21** Examples of Sustainability Reporting Disclosures

PANEL A: FORD MOTOR COMPANY

Ford Motor Company discloses metrics that relate directly to its definition of sustainability, which emphasizes financial health, climate change and the environment, water, vehicle safety, supply change, and people. Ford's sustainability report for 2013/2014 (*http://corporate.ford.com/microsites/sustainability-report-2013-14/review-performance*) provides key performance data in each of these categories. Below we reproduce that data for two categories.

Vehicle Safety

	2011	2012	2013
U.S. safety recalls, number per calendar year (including legacy vehicles on the road for 10+ years)	13	24	**16**
U.S. units recalled, number of units (including legacy vehicles on the road for 10+ years)	3,339,000	1,399,000	**1,188,000**
IIHS Top Safety Picks by model year, percent of Ford Motor Company vehicles tested receiving the honor	52	75	**93**

People

	2011	2012	2013
Employee satisfaction, Pulse survey, overall, percent satisfied	69	71	**75**
Overall dealer attitude, Ford, relative ranking on a scale of 1–100 percent (winter/summer score)	84/82	84/83	**84/85**
Overall dealer attitude, Lincoln[11], relative ranking on a scale of 1–100 percent (winter/summer score)	61/64	68/67	**76/78**
Ford Motor Company Fund contributions, $ million	20	21.6	**26.3**
Corporate contributions, $ million	10	8.5	**11.4**
Volunteer Corps, thousand volunteer hours	110	115	**150**
Lost-time case rate (per 100 employees)			
Americas	0.9	0.8	**0.7**
Asia Pacific Africa	0.1	0.1	**0.1**
Europe	0.3	0.4	**0.3**

(continued)

| EXHIBIT **17.21** | Examples of Sustainability Reporting Disclosures (*continued*) |

PANEL B: SIEMENS

Siemens' 2011 sustainability report provides summary data (see the sustainability report at *http://www.siemens.com/sustainability/pool/en/current-reporting/siemens-sr2011.pdf*) in a similar style as Ford, but the contents of these disclosures differ between the two companies. Neither company's disclosure should be considered "better" or "worse" than the other. Rather, sustainability reporting tends to be very company-specific and industry-specific with companies disclosing metrics that make the most sense given their unique circumstances. That is, the reporting criteria being used across companies are not consistent and even the measures being reported are not consistent.

Key sustainability indicators	FY 2011	FY 2010	FY 2009
Economic			
Revenue generated by the Environmental Portfolio (in billions of €)[1]	29.9	27.4	26.8
in % of total revenue	41	36	35
Ratio of R&D expenses to revenue (in %)	5.3	5.2	5.1
Environment			
Accumulated annual customer reduction in carbon dioxide emissions generated by elements from the Environmental Portfolio (in millions of tons)[2]	317	269	212
Improvement in environmental performance – CO_2 emissions (in %)[3]	22	18	17
Improvement in environmental performance – primary energy and district heating (in %)[3]	26	23	25
Improvement in environmental performance – electrical energy (in %)[3]	12	11	13
Improvement in environmental performance – waste (excluding construction waste) (in %)[3]	14	10	12
Improvement in environmental performance – water (in %)[3]	33	28	29
Employees and society			
Total employees worldwide (in thousands)[1]	360	336	333
Total employees worldwide (in thousands)[2]	402	405	405
Employee fluctuation rate (in %)[2,4]	12.9	12.9	17.4
Proportion of women (as a percentage of employees in management positions)[2]	14.6	13.7	13.6
Expenditure on continuing education (in millions of €)[2]	251	225	228
Expenditure per employee on continuing education (in €)[2,5]	608	560	562
External Sustainability Audits	284	203	–[7]
Fatal accidents (Siemens)[2,6]	3	4	4
Rankings			
Points in Dow Jones Sustainability Index	90	87	82
Points in Global 500 Carbon Disclosure Leadership Index	97	98	85

Siemens Corporation

There are two general types of assurance that can be provided:

1. *Reasonable assurance*—The assurance provider's opinion is stated in the positive form, indicating that the information subject to audit is materially correct and that a high level of assurance has been achieved.
2. *Limited assurance*—The assurance provider's opinion is stated in the negative form, indicating that the information subject to review has not been found to be materially incorrect, and that "nothing has come to their attention" based on the limited scope procedures and that less than a high level of assurance has been achieved.

However, some companies choose to provide no assurance regarding their sustainability reports. As an example of what a company might say if they choose to provide no assurance, WE Energies Corporation made the following statement: "No external assurance was pursued for this reporting period." (*Source*: WE Energies 2012 Sustainability Report). Other companies simply provide no assurance, and make no note of the fact, leaving users to decide for themselves whether or not to rely on management's assertions in the sustainability reports.

Exhibit 17.22 provides examples of various reports that provide assurance on sustainability reports. Panel A is an example of reasonable assurance provided by Moss Adams, a third-party provider of assurance services, for Starbucks' sustainability report (see *http://www.starbucks.com/responsibility/global-report*). Important points to note about this report are that:

- It notes that management is responsible for providing the data, and Moss Adams' responsibility is to express an opinion on the data based on its examination; this wording is similar to a standard audit report.
- It notes that Moss Adams conducted its examination in accordance with the AICPA's attestation standards.
- It describes the procedures used to test management's sustainability assertions, including interviews, confirmations, sampling to validate data, and tests of controls.
- It notes that Moss Adams believes that the disclosures are fairly presented in all *material* respects (*emphasis added*).

Panel B of *Exhibit 17.22* provides an example of limited assurance for SABMiller's sustainability report provided by Corporate Citizenship, a third-party provider of assurance services (see *http://www.sabmiller.com/docs/default-source/investor-documents/reports/2012/sustainability/sustainable-development-report-2012.pdf?sfvrsn=4*). In contrast to Moss Adams' report, this report:

- Does not describe the procedures used to test management's sustainability assertions
- Does not make a positive statement about fair presentation or materiality, but does state that the company's sustainability reporting reflects the principles of the sustainability standard that Corporate Citizenship used to make its assessment

Panel C provides an example of no assurance, but rather discussion from a stakeholder committee convened by Ford Motor Company to evaluate its sustainability reporting initiatives. This report differs from the other two examples in that it provides no external assurance about the contents of Ford's sustainability report. In contrast to the other two reports, the report contains a significant amount of detail regarding the recommendations of the committee, along with Ford's responses.

EXHIBIT **17.22**	Examples of Assurance on Sustainability Reporting

Panel A: Reasonable Assurance from a Third-Party Provider for Starbucks Coffee Company

Independent Assurance Report

To the Stakeholders of Starbucks Coffee Company

We have examined the data identified below (the Data) contained within the Starbucks Coffee Company's Global Responsibility Annual Report (the Report) for the year ended October 2, 2011. Starbucks Coffee Company's management is responsible for the Data. Our responsibility is to express an opinion on the Data listed below based on our examination:

Green coffee purchases and average price per pound as contained in the **Coffee Purchasing section**;

- C.A.F.E. Practices coffee purchases and purchases as a percentage of total coffee purchased as contained in the **Coffee Purchasing section**;
- Fair trade certified green coffee purchases and purchases as a percentage of total coffee purchased as contained in the **Coffee Purchasing section**;
- Certified organic coffee purchases and purchases as a percentage of total coffee purchased as contained in the **Coffee Purchasing section**;
- Amount of commitment to investment in farmer loans and number of farmers and countries represented as contained in the **Farmer Support section**.

The Criteria used to evaluate the Data are contained in the sections of the Report indicated above.

Our examination was conducted in accordance with attestation standards established by the American Institute of Certified Public Accountants, and accordingly, included examining; on a test basis, evidence supporting the Data and performing such other procedures as we considered necessary in the circumstances. Those procedures are described in more detail in the paragraph below. We believe that our examination provides a reasonable basis for our opinion.

Our evidence-gathering procedures included, among other activities, the following:

- Testing the effectiveness of the internal reporting system used to collect and compile information on the Data which is included in the Report;
- Performing specific procedures, on a sample basis, to validate the Data, on site at Starbucks Coffee Trading Company buying operations in Lausanne, Switzerland and Corporate headquarters in Seattle, Washington;
- Interviewing partners (employees) responsible for data collection and reporting;
- Reviewing relevant documentation, including corporate policies, management and reporting structures;
- Performing tests, on a sample basis, of documentation and systems used to collect, analyze and compile the Data that is included in the Report, and
- Confirming certain of the Data to third party confirmations and reports.

In our opinion, the Data for the fiscal year ended October 2, 2011 is fairly presented, in all material respects, based on the Criteria indicated above.

Moss Adams LLP

Seattle, Washington
March 16, 2012

Panel B: Limited Assurance from a Third-Party Provider for SABMiller Company

Assurance statement

SABMiller has commissioned Corporate Citizenship to provide external assurance and a commentary on its 2012 sustainable development reporting. The reporting comprises the *SABMiller Sustainable Development Summary Report 2012*, sections of the website to which that report provides a web address and the pages addressing sustainable development in the *Annual Report 2012*.

(*continued*)

EXHIBIT **17.22**

Panel B: Limited Assurance from a Third-Party Provider for SABMiller Company (*continued*)

The scope of our assurance

The assurance provides the reader with an independent, external assessment of the reporting and, in particular, with how it corresponds with the AA1000 standard. It is intended for the general reader and for more specialist audiences who have a professional interest in SABMiller's sustainable development performance.

SABMiller has chosen to use the AA1000 assurance standard AA1000AS (2008). Our assurance is a Type 2 assurance as defined by the standard, in that it evaluates the nature and extent of adherence to the AA1000AS principles of inclusivity, materiality and responsiveness and assures the performance of the organisation as reported here. Our assurance used disclosed information as its starting point and then investigated the underlying systems, processes and sustainability performance information to arrive at its conclusions.

We have also assured the performance information in the report. The criteria used are the GRI G3 Principles for Defining Report Quality.

The level of assurance is moderate as defined by AA1000AS (2008).

SABMiller is entirely and solely responsible for the contents of the report, Corporate Citizenship for its assurance. As noted, our assurance is confined to elements of reporting cited above.

A detailed note of our assurance methodology appears at the end of this statement.

Opinion and conclusions

In our opinion the SABMiller's sustainable development reporting for 2012 reflects the principles of AA1000 (2008): inclusivity, materiality and responsiveness.

Panel C: No Assurance from a Stakeholder Committee for Ford Motor Company

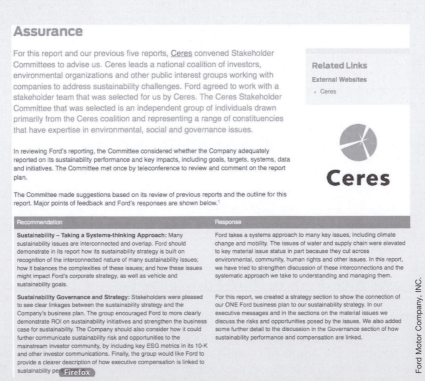

The assurance statement provided by Ceres continues describing recommendations and responses for several pages; only the first page is reproduced here. See Ford's sustainability report for further details: *http://corporate.ford.com/microsites/sustainability-report-2011-12/review-assurance*

SUMMARY

This chapter has presented an overview of topics concerning nonaudit attestation services provided by audit firms. Audit firms conduct many types of engagements that result in varying levels of assurance. Reviews and compilations are commonly performed, and while they provide less assurance than an audit, they are also less costly and can still be useful to third-party users or even management. Auditors also report on interim financial information and provide assurance reports on widely varying items, including other comprehensive basis of accounting other than GAAP, specific elements, compliance, agree-upon procedures, financial forecasts, and pro forma financial information. Forensic accounting engagements complement the financial statement audit when fraud is certain or highly suspected. Finally, audit firms are increasingly providing various levels of assurance on assertions made in sustainability reports.

SIGNIFICANT TERMS

Agreed-upon procedures engagement An agreement in which a practitioner is engaged by a client to issue a report of findings based on specific procedures performed on subject matter.

Assembling An activity that involves the manual or computer processing of mathematical or clerical functions to achieve the presentation of prospective financial statements.

Assurance engagement An engagement in which a practitioner expresses a conclusion designed to enhance the degree of confidence of the intended users other than the responsible party about the outcome of the evaluation or measurement of a subject matter against criteria. See *attestation engagement*.

Assurance engagement risk The risk that the practitioner expresses an inappropriate conclusion when the subject matter information is materially misstated.

Attestation engagement An engagement in which a practitioner is engaged to issue or does issue an examination, a review, or an agreed-upon procedures report on subject matter, or an assertion about the subject matter, that is, the responsibility of another party. See *assurance engagement*.

Attestation standards Professional standards that provide guidance about gathering evidence regarding specific assertions and communicating an opinion on the fairness of the presentation to a third party.

Cash basis A basis of accounting that an organization uses to record cash receipts and disbursements and modifications of the cash basis having substantial support (e.g., recording depreciation on fixed assets).

Compilation engagement An engagement in which the accountant uses accounting expertise, as opposed to auditing expertise, to collect, classify, and summarize financial information; also defined as a service, the objective of which is to assist management in presenting financial information in the form of financial statements without undertaking to obtain or provide any assurance that there are no material modifications that should be made to the financial statements in order for the statements to be in conformity with the applicable financial reporting framework.

Contractual basis A basis of accounting that the entity uses to comply with an agreement between the entity and one or more third parties other than the auditor.

Corporate social responsibility reporting The continuing commitment by business to behave ethically and contribute to economic development while improving the quality of life of the workforce, their families, the local community, and society at large.

Financial forecast A forecast that includes prospective financial statements that present, to the best of the responsible party's knowledge and belief, an entity's expected financial position, results of operations, and cash flows.

Financial projection A projection that includes prospective financial statements that present, to the best of the responsible party's knowledge and belief, given one or more hypothetical assumptions, an entity's expected financial position, results of operations, and cash flows.

Forensic accounting A service that audit firms provide that involves detailed investigation of situations where fraud has already been identified or where fraud is highly suspected.

Limited assurance engagement An engagement whose objective is a reduction in assurance engagement risk to a level that is acceptable in the circumstances of the engagement, but where that risk is greater than that for a reasonable assurance engagement, as the basis for a negative form of expression of the practitioner's conclusion.

Nonfinancial reporting The practice of measuring, disclosing, and being accountable to internal and external stakeholders for organizational performance toward the goal of sustainable development.

Other comprehensive bases of accounting Bases of accounting that include cash basis, tax basis, regulatory basis, or contractual basis.

Pro forma financial information Information that shows what the significant effects on historical financial information might have been had a consummated or proposed transaction (or event) occurred at an earlier date.

Prospective financial statements Financial forecasts or financial projections including the summaries of significant assumptions and accounting policies.

Reasonable assurance engagement An engagement whose objective is a reduction in assurance engagement risk to an acceptably low level in the circumstances of the engagement as the basis for a positive form of expression of the practitioner's conclusion.

Regulatory basis A basis of accounting that the entity uses to comply with the requirements of financial reporting provisions of a regulatory agency to whose jurisdiction the entity is subject (e.g., a basis of accounting that insurance companies use pursuant to the accounting practices prescribed or permitted by a state insurance commission).

Review engagement An engagement that enables a practitioner to state whether, on the basis of procedures which do not provide all the evidence that would be required in an audit, anything has come to the practitioner's attention that causes the practitioner to believe that the financial statements are not prepared, in all material respects, in accordance with the applicable financial reporting framework.

Specified parties Individuals who will receive the practitioner's agree-upon procedures report.

Special-purpose financial statements Financial statements that are prepared in accordance with a special-purpose framework.

Special-purpose framework A financial reporting framework other than GAAP that is one of the following bases of accounting: cash basis, tax basis, regulatory basis, or contractual basis.

Sustainability Actions taken at the corporate level to ensure economic, environmental, and social responsibility.

Sustainability reporting Voluntary corporate disclosures about sustainability initiatives, plans, and associated outcomes.

Tax basis A basis of accounting that the entity uses to file its income tax return for the period covered by the financial statements.

Triple bottom-line reporting Reporting on financial, environmental, and social performance.

TRUE/FALSE QUESTIONS

17-1 **LO 1** The terms *attestation engagement* and *assurance engagement* refer to the same concept; the difference in terminology occurs because the first term is used by the IAASB and the second term is used by the AICPA.

17-2 **LO 1** Assurance engagement risk is the risk that the practitioner expresses an inappropriate conclusion when the subject matter information is materially misstated.

17-3 **LO 2** A review engagement is a service, the objective of which is to assist management in presenting financial information in the form of financial statements without undertaking to obtain or provide any assurance that there are no material modifications that should be made to the financial statements in order for the statements to be in conformity with the applicable financial reporting framework.

17-4 **LO 2** In a review, a practitioner does not provide assurance that he or she will become aware of all significant matters that would be investigated in an audit.

17-5 **LO 3** The auditor should perform review procedures (a) on the quarterly information contained in the annual report to shareholders and (b) on the quarterly information issued at the end of each of the first three quarters of the fiscal year when engaged to do so.

17-6 **LO 3** The SEC requires publicly owned companies to file quarterly financial information with the SEC on Form 10-Q within

60–75 days (depending on company size) after the end of each of the first three quarters of the fiscal year.

17-7 **LO 4** Special-purpose financial statements are those prepared in a compilation engagement.

17-8 **LO 4** When planning and performing an audit of special-purpose financial statements, the auditor is not required to obtain an understanding of the client's selection and application of accounting policies.

17-9 **LO 5** An appropriate description of findings in an agreed-upon procedures engagement would state, "Nothing came to my attention as a result of applying that procedure."

17-10 **LO 5** Prospective financial statements are either financial forecasts or financial projections.

17-11 **LO 6** The audit of financial statements includes serious consideration of the possibility of fraud; the primary purpose of a forensic engagement is to detect, investigate, and document a situation in which fraud almost certainly exists.

17-12 **LO 6** Examples of procedures that would be conducted in a forensic engagement include sampling and analytical review, based on materiality.

17-13 **LO 7** Sustainability reporting includes corporate disclosures about sustainability initiatives, plans, and associated outcomes.

17-14 **LO 7** The terms *non-financial reporting*, *corporate social responsibility reporting*, and *triple bottom-line reporting* are each sustainability-related terms.

MULTIPLE-CHOICE QUESTIONS

17-15 **LO 1** Which of the following are examples of the subject matter of an attestation engagement?
a. Prospective financial information.
b. Physical characteristics, such as the square footage of facilities, or processes within facilities.
c. Historical events, such as the price of a market basket of goods on a certain date.
d. The accuracy of compliance assertions about grants, contracts, and regulations.
e. All of the above.

17-16 **LO 1** Which of the following is not a component of an attestation engagement?
a. Information or a process (the subject matter) on which the assurance service is provided.
b. Criteria for evaluation, such as compliance with regulations.
c. Federal regulatory guidelines.
d. A written attestation report.
e. Sufficient appropriate evidence.

17-17 **LO 2** In which of the following ways does a review differ from a financial statement audit?
a. A review does not involve obtaining an understanding of the organization's ICFR.
b. A review does not involve assessing fraud risk.
c. A review does not involve testing accounting records by obtaining sufficient appropriate evidence through inspection, observation, confirmation, or examining source documents.

d. A review does not involve a practitioner obtaining assurance that he or she will become aware of all significant matters that would be investigated in an audit.

e. All of the above.

17-18 **LO 2** Which of the following statements regarding compilations is false?

a. A compilation engagement enables the practitioner to state whether, on the basis of procedures which do not provide all the evidence that would be required in an audit, anything has come to the practitioner's attention that causes the practitioner to believe that the financial statements are not prepared, in all material respects, in accordance with the applicable financial framework.

b. The objective of a compilation engagement is to assist management in presenting financial information in the form of financial statements without undertaking to obtain or provide any assurance that there are no material modifications that should be made to the financial statements in order for the statements to be in conformity with the applicable financial reporting framework.

c. In a compilation, the practitioner is not required to make inquiries or perform procedures to verify, corroborate, or review information provided by the client.

d. In a compilation, the practitioner should read the financial statements, including footnotes, to make sure that they are appropriate in form and free from obvious material misstatement.

17-19 **LO 3** Which of the following procedures is an appropriate review procedure for interim financial information?

a. Making inquiries.

b. Performing analytical procedures.

c. Reading the minutes of board of directors' meetings.

d. Reading the interim information to consider whether it appears to conform to GAAP.

e. All of the above.

17-20 **LO 3** Which of the following statements about reporting on interim financial statements is false?

a. The disclosure and reporting requirements for interim financial statements differ from those for annual financial statements.

b. Information disclosed in the latest annual financial statements must be repeated in the interim financial statements, except for continuing contingencies and other uncertainties.

c. The negative assurance provided for interim financial statements should be modified when there is a material departure from GAAP or inadequate disclosure.

d. Interim financial statements should include disclosures about events that occurred since the latest year end, such as changes in accounting principles or estimates and significant changes in financial position.

17-21 **LO 4** Which of the following situations are special considerations for reporting?

a. Audits of financial statements prepared in accordance with special-purpose frameworks.

b. Audits of single financial statements and specific elements, accounts, or items of a financial statement.

    c.   Reporting on compliance with aspects of contractual agreements or regulatory requirements.

    d.   All of the above.

17-22 **LO 4** Refer to *Exhibit 17.8*. In which of the following situations would the practitioner include an emphasis-of-matter paragraph alerting readers about the preparation in accordance with a special-purpose framework?

    a.   When a cash basis is used.

    b.   When a tax basis is used.

    c.   When a regulatory basis (for use by management and the regulator only) is used.

    d.   When a contractual basis is used.

    e.   All of the above.

17-23 **LO 5** Refer to *Exhibit 17.12*. Assume that the practitioner is engaged to perform an agreed-upon procedures engagement. The procedure agreed upon was for the practitioner to: (a) calculate the number of blocks or streets paved during the year ended September 30, 2015, shown on contractors' certificates of project completion; and (b) compare the resultant number to the number in an identified chart of performance statistics. Which of the following would be an appropriate way to describe the results of agreed-upon procedures?

    a.   Nothing came to my attention that would indicate that the number is inconsistent with the chart of performance statistics.

    b.   The number of blocks of streets paved approximated the number of blocks included in the chart of performance statistics.

    c.   The number of blocks of streets paved in the chart of performance statistics was Y blocks more than the number calculated from the contractors' certificates of project completion.

    d.   All of the above would be acceptable.

17-24 **LO 5** A compilation of prospective financial statements includes which of the following steps?

    a.   Assembling prospective financial statements based on the responsible party's assumptions.

    b.   Performing compilation procedures, including reading the prospective financial statements, along with their assumptions and accounting policies, and considering whether they appear to be presented in conformity with AICPA presentation guidelines and that they are not obviously inappropriate.

    c.   Issuing a compilation report.

    d.   All of the above.

17-25 **LO 6** Which of the following statements about forensic accounting is false?

    a.   Forensic accountants will examine, only on a sample basis, material transactions believed to relate to the fraud.

    b.   Forensic accounting builds support for legal action against the person committing the fraud by identifying the fraud, calculating the damages caused by the fraud, and building both factual and testimonial evidence of the fraud.

    c.   The primary purpose of forensic engagements is to detect, investigate, and document a situation in which fraud almost certainly exists.

    d.   Forensic accountants are often asked to provide litigation support, in which they are called on to give expert testimony about financial data and accounting activities.

17-26 **LO 6** Forensic accounting differs from auditing on which of the following dimensions?
a. Focus.
b. Approach.
c. Scope.
d. End product.
e. All of the above.

17-27 **LO 7** Which of the following organizations was created to establish sustainability accounting standards for use in 10-K filings with the SEC?
a. Prince's Accounting for Sustainability Project.
b. GRI.
c. AccountAbility.
d. SASB.

17-28 **LO 7** Which of the following statements relating to sustainability reporting is false?
a. Sustainability reports are very similar and contain virtually identical information across organizations because of the high level of regulation governing such disclosures.
b. Sustainability reporting involves voluntary corporate disclosures about sustainability initiatives, plans, and associated outcomes.
c. Investor interest, socially responsible investment funds, and the Dow Jones Sustainability Index have each created demand for sustainability reporting.
d. The terms *nonfinancial reporting, corporate social responsibility reporting, triple bottom-line reporting,* and *sustainability reporting* are often used to describe essentially the same activities.

REVIEW AND SHORT CASE QUESTIONS

NOTE: Completing Review and Short Case Questions does not require the student to reference additional resources and materials.

INTERNATIONAL

NOTE: For the remaining problems, we make special note of those addressing international issues, professional skepticism, and ethics.

17-29 **LO 1** Provide examples of the subject matter of an assurance engagement.

17-30 **LO 1** Refer to the *Professional Judgment in Context* feature at the beginning of the chapter and describe examples of nonaudit services provided by audit firms.

17-31 **LO 1** Define the term *assurance engagement risk* and distinguish between reasonable assurance engagements and limited assurance engagements.

17-32 **LO 1** Refer to *Exhibit 17.2* and describe the U.S. and international attestation (assurance) standards.

17-33 **LO 1** Refer to *Exhibit 17.3* and describe the AICPA's standards for attestation engagements. Compare and contrast similarities and differences of these standards with the PCAOB's 10 general, fieldwork, and reporting standards for audit engagements as described in *Chapter 5*.

17-34 **LO 2** Define the objective of a review engagement, and explain how a review differs from a financial statement audit.

17-35 **LO 2** Describe the standard procedures for conducting a review.

17-36 **LO 2** Refer to *Exhibit 17.4*, which lists some of the inquiries and analytical procedures that might be performed for a review of accounts in the revenue cycle. Discuss how these procedures differ from the procedures that would be used to perform an audit of these same accounts.

17-37 **LO 2** Review *Exhibit 17.5*, which provides an example of a standard review report. Discuss the content and purpose of each of the main paragraphs in the report.

17-38 **LO 2** Describe the IAASB and AICPA definitions of a compilation engagement. Discuss common compilation procedures.

17-39 **LO 2** Explain three situations in which the practitioner will modify the standard compilation report. Describe how the wording will be modified.

17-40 **LO 2** Compare and contrast the procedures that should be performed on inventory for an audit, review, and compilation. Assume that the auditor has knowledge of the business and industry. Give specific examples of procedures.

17-41 **LO 2** Russ Major, CPA, drafted the following report on October 25, 2015 at the completion of the engagement to compile the financial statements of Ajax Company for the year ended September 30, 2015. Ajax is a nonpublic organization in which Major's child has a material direct financial interest. Ajax decided to omit substantially all of the disclosures required by GAAP because the financial statements will be only for management's use. The statement of cash flows was also omitted because management does not believe it to be a useful financial statement.

Identify the deficiencies contained in Major's report on the compiled financial statements. Group the deficiencies by paragraph when applicable. Do not redraft the report.

To the Board of Directors of Ajax Company:

I have compiled the accompanying financial statements of Ajax Company as of September 30, 2015, and for the year then ended. I planned and performed the compilation to obtain limited assurance about whether the financial statements are free of material misstatements.

A compilation is limited to presenting information in the form of financial statements. It is substantially less in scope than an audit in accordance with generally accepted auditing standards, the objective of which is the expression of an opinion regarding the financial statements taken as a whole. I have not audited the accompanying financial statements and, accordingly, do not express any opinion on them.

Management has elected to omit substantially all of the disclosures required by generally accepted accounting principles. If the omitted disclosures were included in the financial statements, they might influence the user's conclusions about the Company's financial position, results of operations, and changes in financial position.

I am not independent with respect to Ajax Company. This lack of independence is due to my child's ownership of a material direct financial interest in Ajax Company.

This report is intended solely for the information and use of the Board of Directors and management of Ajax Company and should not be used for any other purpose.

17-42 **LO 2** You have been assigned to perform a review of a client's inventory containing electric motors, parts for motors, and raw materials used in making the motors.

a. What inquiries and analytical procedures should you perform?

b. What will you do if these procedures do not support the client's inventory values or disclosures?

c. How would your level of professional skepticism differ depending on whether you are performing a review versus an audit engagement?

17-43 **LO 3** What is interim financial information, and why is interim financial information required to be reviewed? What professional standards provide guidance on the conduct of reviews of interim financial information?

17-44 **LO 3** Describe common procedures that the auditor will complete when performing a review of interim financial information.

17-45 **LO 3** Refer to *Exhibit 17.7* and describe the typical contents of a review report for interim financial information. Discuss how the disclosure and reporting requirements for interim financial statements differ from those for annual statements.

17-46 **LO 4** Define the term *special-purpose framework*. Explain the considerations and procedures that the practitioner would make and conduct when accepting, planning, and performing an engagement of the audit of special-purpose financial statements.

17-47 **LO 4** Explain the contents of a report on the audit of special-purpose financial statements.

17-48 **LO 4** What guidance would the auditor rely upon for examples of audit reports appropriate to various types of special-purpose financial statements?

17-49 **LO 4** AU-C 805 provides guidance on audits of single financial statements and specific elements, accounts, or items of a financial statement. Provide examples of these types of situations.

17-50 **LO 4** What guidance would the auditor rely on for examples of appropriate reports when reporting on an audit of a single financial statement or of a specific element, account, or item of a financial statement?

17-51 **LO 4** What guidance would the auditor rely upon when reporting on compliance with aspects of contractual agreements or regulatory requirements in connection with audited financial statements? What level of assurance is typically provided in a compliance report?

17-52 **LO 4** A staff auditor of Erwachen & Diamond, CPAs, has prepared the following draft of an audit report on cash-basis financial statements. Identify any deficiencies in the report and explain why they are deficiencies.

Auditor's Report to the Shareholders of Halon Company:

We have audited the accompanying balance sheets and the related statement of income as of December 31, 2015 and 2014. These financial statements are the responsibility of the Company's management. Our responsibility is to express an opinion on these financial statements based on our audits.

We conducted our audits in accordance with auditing standards generally accepted in the United States of America. Those principles require that we plan and perform the audit to obtain reasonable assurance about whether the financial statements are free of material errors. An audit includes examining, on a test basis, evidence supporting the amounts and disclosures in the financial statements. An audit also includes asses sing the accounting principles used and estimates made by management, as well as evaluating the overall financial statement presentation. We believe that our audits pro vide a reasonable basis for our opinion.

As described in Note 13, these financial statements were prepared on the basis of cash receipts and disbursements.

In our opinion, the financial statements referred to above present fairly, in all material respects, the financial position of Halon Company as of December 31, 2015, and the results of operations for the year then ended in accordance with accounting principles generally accepted in the United States of America.

/s/ Donald Diamond, CPA
February 15, 2016

17-53 **LO 4** Young & Young, CPAs, completed an examination of the financial statements of XYZ Company, Inc. for the year ended June 30, 2015, and issued a standard unqualified auditor's report dated August 15, 2015. At the time of the engagement, the board of directors of XYZ requested a special report attesting to the adequacy of the provision for federal and state income taxes and the related accruals and deferred income taxes as presented in the June 30, 2015, financial statements. Young & Young submitted the appropriate special report on August 22, 2015. Prepare the special report that Young & Young should have submitted to XYZ Company, Inc.

17-54 **LO 5** Define the term *agreed-upon procedures engagement* and describe typical procedures performed and reporting on such an engagement. The practitioner should not perform agreed-upon procedures that are overly subjective, and the practitioner should be able to obtain evidence to provide a reasonable basis for findings expressed in the report that will be issued. Provide examples of appropriate and inappropriate agreed-upon procedures.

17-55 **LO 5** Define the terms *prospective financial statements*, *financial forecast*, and *financial projection*.

17-56 **LO 5** Describe the activities involved in a compilation of prospective financial statements and the standards that apply to such an engagement.

17-57 **LO 5** Explain how an examination of prospective financial statements differs from a compilation of prospective financial statements. Describe the activities involved in an examination of prospective financial statements.

17-58 **LO 5** Distinguish between historical financial information and pro forma financial information. Explain the guidelines that should be adhered to when presenting pro forma financial information.

17-59 **LO 5** Describe the procedures that would be appropriate for examining or reviewing pro forma financial information.

17-60 **LO 6** Describe forensic accounting and explain how it differs from auditing.

17-61 LO 7 Define the terms *nonfinancial reporting*, *corporate social responsibility reporting*, and *triple bottom-line reporting*. How do these terms relate to sustainability reporting?

17-62 LO 7 What factors have driven the demand for sustainability reporting? Refer to *Exhibit 17.20* and describe the standards that exist for sustainability reporting and assurance.

17-63 LO 7 Why is there a demand for independent assurance on sustainability reporting?

17-64 LO 7 Is it unethical for a company to provide a sustainability report, but provide no assurance on the reliability of the information contained therein?

APPLICATION ACTIVITIES

NOTE: Completing Application Activities requires students to reference additional resources and materials.

17-65 LO 7 Go to the web sites of the following organizations and review their agendas and recent activities concerning assurance over sustainability disclosures:

- AICPA
- IFAC
- IAASB
- PCAOB

a. How do the sustainability-related activities of these organizations differ? And how are they similar?

b. If there is an organization that does not address sustainability, comment on the implications of that decision.

c. What are the implications of differences in sustainability assurance provisions internationally?

17-66 LO 7 Access the web sites of two major manufacturing organizations of your choice. Locate the sustainability reports of these organizations.

a. How prominent was the link to the sustainability report on each organization's web site?

b. Compare the length and detail of both reports, and comment on the differences.

c. Consider the corporate strategy of each organization, and discuss how that strategy relates to the sustainability disclosures made by each organization.

d. Discuss how your perception of each organization differs now that you understand the respective sustainability efforts. Did your perception of the organization improve? Decline? Or change in some other way? Why?

e. Compare the level of assurance provided by each organization. If there are differences in the level of assurance provided, discuss implications for particular elements of the sustainability report.

17-67 LO 7 Review the *Emerging Issues* feature "Creation of the Sustainability Accountings Standards Board," access the web site of the SASB, and answer the following questions.

a. What is the mission of SASB?

b. Why is there a need for SASB?

c. What are the sectors for which the SASB has issued standards? What are the sectors for which the SASB has issued draft standards?

d. Review the list of the members of the Board of Directors. How might the presence of some board members influence the SEC's acceptability of the standards of SASB?

ACADEMIC RESEARCH CASE

NOTE: Completing the Academic Research Case requires students to reference additional resources and materials.

SEARCH HINT

It is easy to locate these academic research articles! Use a search engine such as Google Scholar or an electronic research platform such as ABI Inform and search using the author names and part of the article title.

17-68 **LO 7** Locate and read the article listed below and answer the following questions.

Cho, C. H., G, Michelon, and D. M. Patten. December 2012. Impression management in sustainability reports: an empirical investigation of the use of graphs. *Accounting and the Public Interest* 12(1): 16–37.

a. What is the issue being addressed in the paper?
b. What are the findings of the paper?
c. Why is this paper important to auditors, and what are the implications of this paper for the auditing profession?

ACL Tutorial

ACL is a generalized audit software (GAS) package widely used by audit firms and internal auditing organizations to access, analyze, and manipulate electronic data contained in client systems. This ACL tutorial is designed to help you learn how to use many of the important features of this tool, as well as to provide you with hands-on experience of using GAS to help perform audits. You are likely to use this or a similar program in your professional career. The ACL program is contained on a computer resource (CD) that comes with your textbook. It is recommended that you install ACL on your own computer if it has a Windows operating system. (A Mac will not work unless it is configured to act as a Windows operating system). If this is not possible, check with your instructor to see if Windows is available in a computer lab.

Data Files

The data files for the ACL cases in selected chapters are found on the textbook's web site under "Student Resources." If you install ACL on your own computer, it is recommended that you download the data files to your hard drive. If you use ACL on a network, download the files to whatever input/output device can be used on the lab's computers. The files created by ACL are stored on the same device with the data files.

Working on a Project

This section provides directions on how to create a new project or work on an existing project. The first step is to start the ACL program. The ACL icon should appear on your desktop after you install the program from the CD found at the back of your textbook. If the icon does not appear, look under *programs* to locate and start using the software.

Note the menu options on the standard toolbar and the options under each item. Move your cursor along the icons and note what each one stands for as a way to familiarize yourself with the overall setup of the program. Notice that the functionalities of ACL look and behave in a manner that is very similar to an Excel program. The first step in using ACL is to (1) create a new project or (2) open an existing project.

(1) Create a New Project

To start a new project (such as a case), select **FILE | NEW | PROJECT** and give the project a name. Or click the **Create a New Project** link on the screen. *Be sure to save the project in the directory with the data files.* The files that are created when using ACL are saved on the same drive with the data files.

You then need to import one or more files to work on:

Import a Table (file)

Click on **FILE | NEW | TABLE** and follow the on-screen instructions.

(2) Open an Existing Project

To open an existing project, select **FILE | OPEN PROJECT** and click on the file name in the directory in which it was saved. Or click the **Open an Existing Project** link on the screen. Then continue working on the project; you can import additional files as needed.

Basic Features of ACL Projects

Following are some basic activities that can be performed on a file that is either a new or existing project. These activities are presented in alphabetical order.

Add a Column

You can add one or more columns with new information you create based on the data in the table. For example, you could calculate the difference between two fields. Either click the **Add Column** icon on the toolbar or place the cursor where you want the column to be inserted, right-click the mouse, and select **Add Columns**. Click the **Expr** button, and build the expression needed to calculate the data for the new column (e.g., Amount–Confirmed). Type a column name in the **Save as** box (e.g., *Difference*). Click **OK** and **OK** again. You may need to move the screen to the right to see the new column.

Age

Select **ANALYZE | AGE** or click the **Age** icon on the toolbar. Select the field on which to age (such as INVDATE). Click the button next to the **Cut-off date** window and select the appropriate date. You can accept the default aging categories or change them. Choose the field to subtotal by aging category (such as AMOUNT) in the right window. Click the **Output** tab at the top and select where you want the output. If the output is saved to a file, give it a name. Click on that category (e.g., >45) to get a list of items in a specific aging category.

Close Projects

To close a project (it is saved in the directory with the data files), either select **FILE | CLOSE PROJECT**, or click the **Close the Open Project** icon on the toolbar.

Delete Files

Files created in a current project can be deleted by right-clicking on the file name in the left window and then choosing **Delete**. To completely delete files you created with ACL, go into the directory with the data files and delete the files created by ACL, including those with the .fil extension.

Extract

Select **DATA | EXTRACT DATA | IF**. You can then create an expression to select the items to extract. For example, if you want to extract all unpaid invoices over a certain age based on the field INVDATE, the expression would be INVDATE < (click on **DATE** and select the appropriate date). Fields can be entered into the expression either by typing or double-clicking on the field in the **Available fields** window. If you want to extract all amounts over $100,000, the expression would be AMOUNTS > 100000. Click **OK** when the expression is complete. Type a name for the extracted file in the **To** window.

Expressions for extracting data can include specific text. For example, if there is a column labeled COMMENT with explanations of confirmation exceptions including "Confirmed–OK" and you want to extract all of those that do not have that explanation, the expression would be COMMENT < > "Confirmed–OK." The words must be within quotes.

> **Note:** When records are extracted from a file, you must create a new file and you should save that file. ACL describes this as creating a filter because we have filtered the data to create a new file. To get back to the original file, click on the original file name in the left window.

File Statistics

There are several ways to get statistics about the data in the file.

1. Click on the icon with the % sign. Choose the field(s) on which you want statistics. Click on the **Output** tab and choose where you want the output (screen, graph, print, or file).
2. Select **ANALYZE | STATISTICAL** and either **STATISTICS** or **PROFILE**. If you choose **STATISTICS**, you have the same choices as in step 1 above. The statistics provided with **STATISTICS** are numbers; totals; and averages for positive, negative, zero items; overall totals; and highest and lowest values for the field(s) selected. The statistics that are provided with **PROFILE** are total, absolute, minimum, and maximum values for the field(s) selected.

Filters

Filters may be used to query the data in a table that have been imported without adding a new field or creating a new table. For example, a filter can identify customer unpaid invoices over $50,000 as follows. Using the data from the Husky Unpaid Inventory Excel file, do the following:

1. Click on the **GREEN EDIT FILTER** button (the icon that looks like a funnel with a green stripe just above the first column of data).
2. The cursor is available under the word Filter at the top of the screen. Type in AMOUNT > 50000.
3. The results appear as below.

	CUSTNUM	INVNUM	INVDATE	AMOUNT
11	100	168651	11/22/2013	66480.30
19	70	168732	11/25/2013	79374.82
42	143	168925	11/29/2013	57509.74
46	114	169001	11/30/2013	89230.46
65	37	169152	12/04/2013	57340.64
72	184	169186	12/05/2013	143853.83
89	141	169298	12/10/2013	153129.75
91	11	169309	12/10/2013	116936.56
102	121	169349	12/13/2013	58503.00
120	180	169470	12/18/2013	126816.73
124	107	169489	12/19/2013	61809.83
138	123	169551	12/21/2013	121562.18
150	81	169617	12/25/2013	76230.44
159	224	169707	12/26/2013	129494.41
178	172	169969	12/28/2013	82454.77
180	166	169971	12/28/2013	155198.43
188	181	169979	12/29/2013	151012.89

Welcome   husky_unpaid_1

Filter: amount>50000

<< End of File >>

4. To go back to the unfiltered Excel file, click on the **RED EDIT FILTER** button.

Join Files

To join two tables (files), be sure the fields on which the files are to be matched (e.g., invoice numbers) are in the same format, such as numeric. To join files use a particular field, such as customer number; the field must be in ASCII format. To change the format from numeric to ASCII, select **EDIT | TABLE LAYOUT**, or click the **Edit Table Layout** icon on the toolbar. Double-click on the field to be reformatted, and select **ASCII** from the drop-down menu under **TYPE**. Click on the green check mark in the left margin to accept the change, and then **OK**.

Select one of the files as the primary file by making it active on the screen. If the active file is not to be the primary file, click on the file you want to be the primary file in the left window of the screen. Click the **Join** icon that looks like an upside-down organization chart or select **DATA | JOIN TABLES**. Click on the secondary file you want to join with the primary file. Click on the field name for the primary and secondary file keys (fields on which the files are matched, such as invoice numbers). Click on the primary and secondary fields you want in the combined file. To select more than one field in a window, hold down the Ctrl key. Type a name for the combined files next to the **To** button, and then **OK**.

Move a Column/Change Column Widths

Columns can be rearranged by left-clicking on the column heading, holding the mouse button down, and dragging the column where you want it.

Column widths can be changed by placing the cursor to the right side of the column heading and moving it in either direction.

Prepare and Print Reports

You can tailor a report of the information on the active screen and get column totals. Select **Data | Report** or click the **Report** icon on the toolbar (looks like three pieces of paper stacked upon one another). Type any information you want in the header and/or footer of the report, such as the client's name or your name, a date, and the nature of the information. On the **OUTPUT** tab, choose where you want the output (e.g., screen or file). The report can be previewed by choosing **File | Print Preview** or clicking the **Print Preview** icon. You can change the page layout from portrait to landscape by clicking the **Setup** button. The report displays and prints totals for all numeric fields. You may need to adjust the column widths to see entire column headings.

If you do not want to add headers or footers to the report, you can simply click the **Print** icon or select **File | Print** on the menu. All numeric fields are automatically totaled.

Saving Files

Files created by ACL are automatically stored on the same storage device with the data files. Therefore, you can end an ACL session and come back later. The files will still be there until you delete them.

Search for Duplicates

Select **ANALYZE | Look for Duplicates** and then select the field to be searched (e.g., **Invoice Number**). In the **LIST FIELDS** window, select the fields you want identified with the duplicate entries.

Sort

Right-click on the column heading you want sorted and choose whether you want it sorted in ascending or descending order. All other columns will be included in the sort.

Stratify

Select **ANALYZE | STRATIFY** or click on the **Stratify** icon (looks like the numbers 123). Choose the field on which to stratify in the **Stratify On** window (such as **AMOUNT**). Choose the field to subtotal (such as **AMOUNT**). Type in the minimum and maximum values for the intervals (such as *0* and *100000*) and the number of intervals (such as *10*). Click the **Output** tab and choose where you want the output.

Summarize

Records can be summarized based on some key (e.g., customer number to get customer balances from an unpaid invoice file). The field to be summarized, such as CUSTNUM, must be in ASCII format. Select **ANALYZE | SUMMARIZE** or click on the **Summarize** icon (looks like a green arrow). Choose the field on which to summarize in the **Summarize On** window (such as **CUSTNUM**). Choose the field to subtotal in the **Subtotal Fields** window (such as **AMOUNT**). Choose the other fields you want in the output file in the **Other Fields** window. Click on the **Output** tab at the top and select **Screen** or **File**.

Husky Practice Case

The following case, along with the data files contained in Excel, enables you to practice using the various functions of ACL. The first step is to go to the textbook web site and access the student resources. Next, locate the ACL resources, and download the zip file to your desktop. Finally, look in the folder to locate the various Excel files that you will use to complete the case.

For this case, assume that you are auditing the accounts receivable records of Husky Corp. and that the general ledger control account shows a balance of $4,263,919.52. Use ACL to help perform some audit procedures.

There are four related data files you need to download for this tutorial:

- *husky_unpaid* contains the unpaid invoices as of 12/31/13.
- *husky_shipping* contains the shipment numbers and shipment dates for those invoices. You have verified that the last shipment number used in 2013 is 62050.
- *husky_credit* shows the credit limit for each customer.
- *husky_confirm* shows the confirmation results.

Audit Procedures

This tutorial shows you how to perform the following audit procedures using ACL:

1. Foot the unpaid invoice file and agree to the general ledger.
2. Identify any unpaid invoices older than 45 days.
3. Identify customer balances greater than their credit limit or for which there are no credit limits.
4. Perform a sales cutoff test.

Data files and *typed input* are shown in *italics*. **ACL icons, commands**, and **equations** are shown in **bold**. FIELD NAMES are in ALL CAPS.

Step 1—Start a new project

Select **File | New, Project** on the menu bar. Select the location of the data files in the **Save New Project As** window; enter *Husky AR* as the name for the project. Click **Save**.

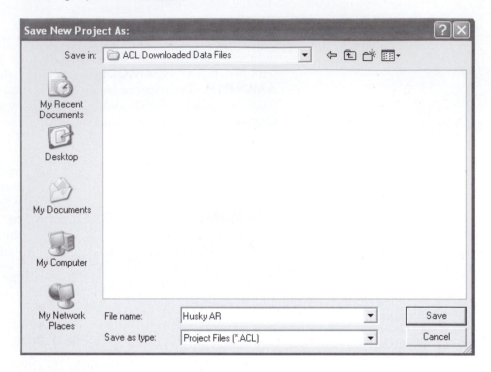

Step 2—Import a table (file)

To import a file (ACL refers to them as tables), click **File | New | Table**.

Follow the onscreen commands and import the Excel file *Husky Unpaid Invoices*. Save it to your computer using the name *Husky_Unpaid*. The file appears as follows:

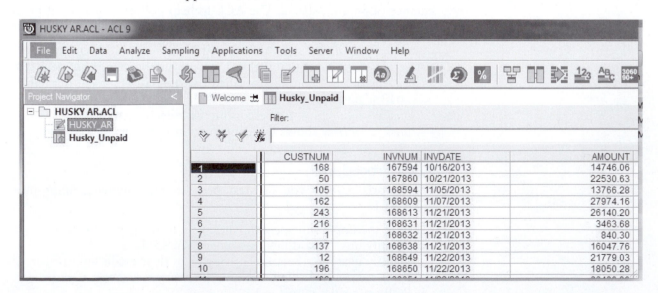

Step 3—Foot the file and agree to the general ledger

With the *Husky_Unpaid* table in the active window, select **ANALYZE | STATISTICAL | STATISTICS** on the menu bar and click on **AMOUNT** to foot the file.

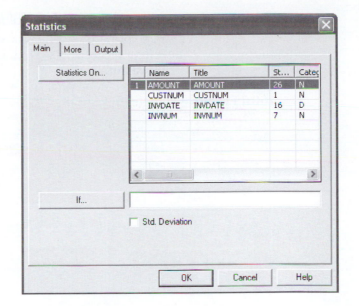

Click **OK**.

The next screen shows several things. The first matrix shows the total value, which agrees with the general ledger balance ($4,263,919.52), and the number and amount of positive and negative values. The second matrix shows on the first line the value of the largest ($155,198.43) and smallest amount ($–22,659.74) of the unpaid invoices. Print the statistics by clicking on the **Print** icon or selecting **File | Print** on the menu bar.

Step 4—Identify any unpaid invoices older than 45 days

Click the *Husky_Unpaid* tab above the statistics to make the table active in the main window, and then select **ANALYZE | AGE** on the menu bar. Accept the default **Age on INVDATE**. Set the cutoff date to December 31, 2013. Change the aging periods to 0 and 45. Click **AMOUNT** under **Subtotal Fields** to subtotal. Click **OK**.

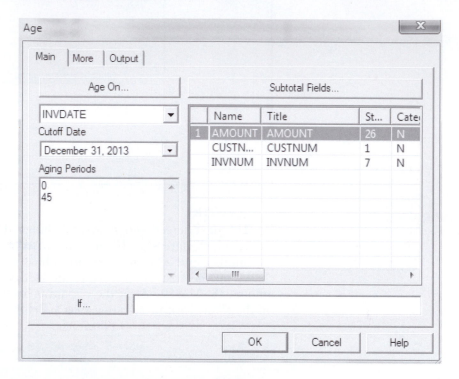

As noted in the following tables, there are four invoices amounting to $79,017.13 that are over 45 days old.

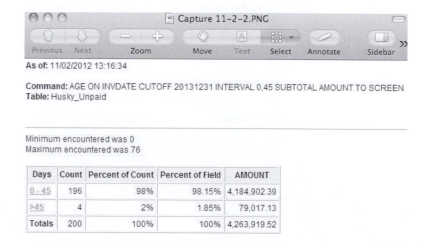

As of: 11/02/2012 13:16:34

Command: AGE ON INVDATE CUTOFF 20131231 INTERVAL 0,45 SUBTOTAL AMOUNT TO SCREEN
Table: Husky_Unpaid

Minimum encountered was 0
Maximum encountered was 76

Days	Count	Percent of Count	Percent of Field	AMOUNT
0 - 45	196	98%	98.15%	4,184,902.39
≥45	4	2%	1.85%	79,017.13
Totals	200	100%	100%	4,263,919.52

Click on > 45 under the column headed **Days**; ACL will retrieve those four invoices from the unpaid file.

Print the page showing the details for these four invoices by clicking on the **Print** icon or selecting **File | Print** on the menu bar. Notice the total of the AMOUNT column is printed. These totals should be investigated to determine their collectibility.

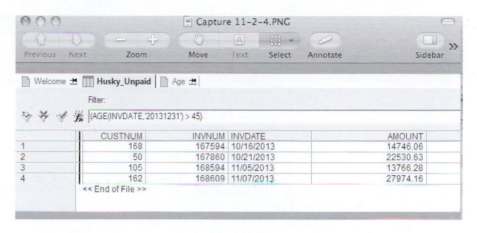

Note: If you want to save this information as a file to retrieve later, make the *Husky_Unpaid* table active and select **DATA | EXTRACT DATA** on the menu and click on **IF**. Enter an expression by double-clicking on **INVDATE**, click **<**, select **DATE** and scroll to November 16, 2013, on the date selector, and click **OK**. Click **OK** again. Enter a file name such as *Over 45 Days* next to the **TO** button. Click **OK**. The screen will look like the one above but will not have anything showing in the **Filter** window.

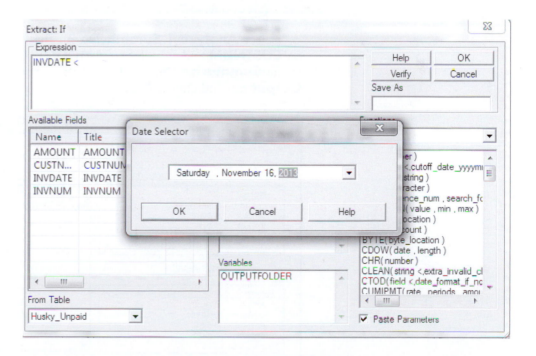

Step 5—Identify customers' balances greater than their credit limit or for which there are no credit limits

First, access the entire *Husky_Unpaid* table. Then, to determine each customer's balance, change the field type of **CUSTNUM** from **NUMERIC** to **ASCII**. Select **Edit | Table Layout** on the menu bar and double-click on

CUSTNUM. Click the down arrow in the **Type** window, and locate and click on **ASCII** in the window (it is located above NUMERIC). Click the green arrow at the left of the screen and then the red X in the upper-right corner to exit this window. Also change **INVNUM** to **ASCII**.

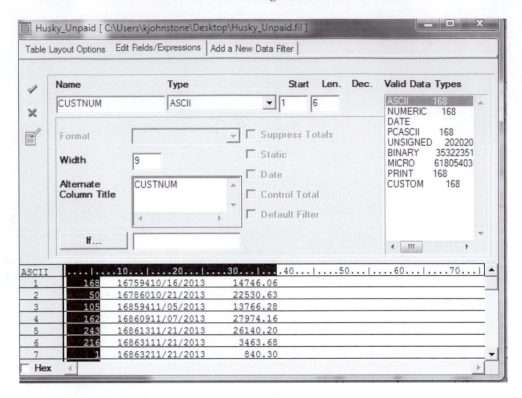

Select **Analyze | Summarize** on the menu bar. Click to summarize on **CUSTNUM** and subtotal on **AMOUNT**. If **CUSTNUM** does not appear in the **Summarize On** window, change the field type to **ASCII**. Click the **Output** tab and choose **FILE**.

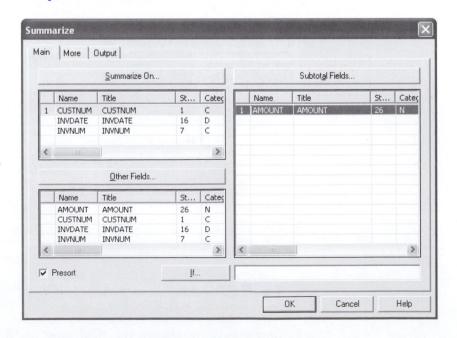

Name the new file *Customer_Balances*.

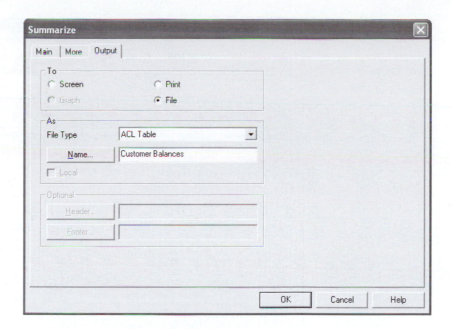

The window will show each customer's balance and the number (count) of unpaid invoices.

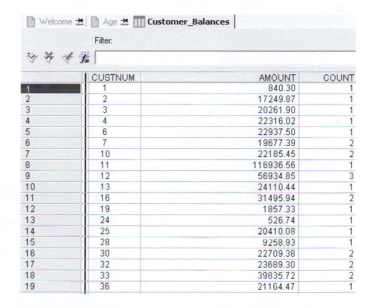

Import the *Husky_Credit* file by selecting **File | New | Table** on the menu bar. Save the imported table as *Husky_Credit*. Change **CUSTNUM** from numeric format to ASCII by selecting **Edit | Table Layout** on the menu. Double-click on **CUSTNUM** and change the format to ASCII (as described at the beginning of this step) so the files can be matched on this field.

Make *Customer_Balances* the active table by double-clicking on that name in the left window. Select **Data | Join Tables** on the menu bar or click on the **Join** icon. Choose *Husky_Credit* as the secondary table. Click **CUSTNUM** in both the **Primary Keys** and **Secondary Keys** windows to match the two tables based on CUSTNUM. Click **CUSTNUM** and **AMOUNT** under **Primary Fields** using the **Ctrl** key on the keyboard to select more than one field in the window. Click **CRLIMIT** under **Secondary Fields** to print. Select **Presort Secondary Table**. Type the name *Balances and Credit Limit* in the **To** box. Click **OK**.

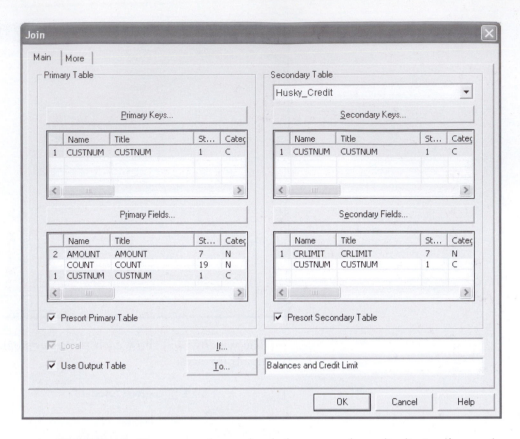

The joined files now show the balances and credit limits for each customer.

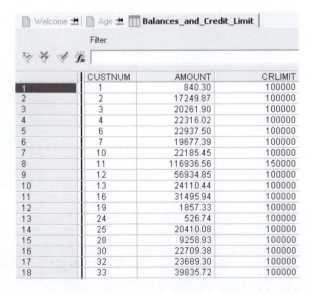

Create a filter to show those customers with balances that exceed their credit limit. Click on the **Edit Filter** icon next to the **Filter** window. Enter the expression *AMOUNT > CRLIMIT*. Click **OK**.

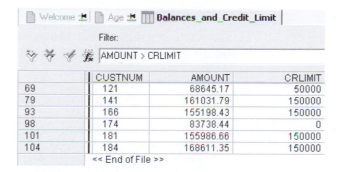

The results show that there are five customers who have exceeded their credit limits and one for whom there is no credit limit. The accounts for these customers should be investigated to determine collectibility.

Welcome	Age	**Balances_and_Credit_Limit**		
		Filter:		
		AMOUNT > CRLIMIT		
		CUSTNUM	**AMOUNT**	**CRLIMIT**
69		121	68645.17	50000
79		141	161031.79	150000
93		166	155198.43	150000
98		174	83738.44	0
101		181	155986.66	150000
104		184	168611.35	150000
		<< End of File >>		

Print this table by clicking on the **Print** icon or selecting **File | Print** on the menu bar. Notice the total of each numeric column is printed.

Step 6—Perform a sales cutoff test

Import the *husky_shipping* file by selecting **File | New | Table** on the menu bar. Save the table with the name *Husky_Shipping*. Click **Finish | OK**. Change the **INVNUM** field from numeric to ASCII using **Edit | Table Layout** as you have done previously.

Make *Husky_Unpaid* the active table. Join the *Husky_Shipping* table with the *Husky_Unpaid* file. Click **INVNUM** as primary key and secondary key to join on this field. Select the fields to show in the new table by selecting all of the fields in the **Primary Fields** window (remember to hold the **Ctrl** key down) and select the **SHIPNUM** and **DATESHIP** fields under **Secondary Fields**. Click to presort the secondary file. Give the new table the name *Unpaid with ship number*. Click **OK**.

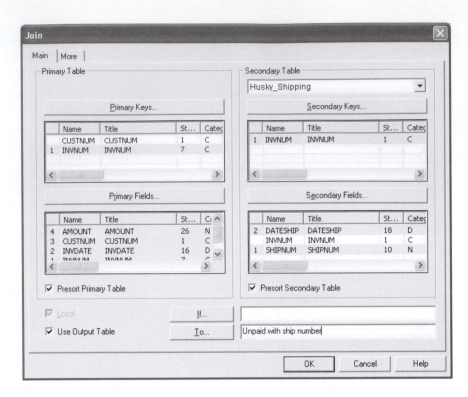

A new table is created that shows the results of combining these two tables (adjust column widths to see all columns):

	CUSTNUM	AMOUNT	INVDATE	INVNUM	SHIPNUM	DATESHIP
1	168	14746.06	10/16/2013	167594	59653	10/16/2013
2	50	22530.63	10/21/2013	167860	59919	10/21/2013
3	105	13766.28	11/05/2013	168594	60653	11/05/2013
4	162	27974.16	11/07/2013	168609	60668	11/07/2013
5	243	26140.20	11/21/2013	168613	60672	11/21/2013
6	216	3463.68	11/21/2013	168631	60690	11/21/2013
7	1	840.30	11/21/2013	168632	60691	11/21/2013
8	137	16047.76	11/21/2013	168638	60697	11/21/2013
9	12	21779.03	11/22/2013	168649	60708	11/22/2013
10	196	18050.28	11/22/2013	168650	60709	11/22/2013
11	100	66480.30	11/22/2013	168651	60710	11/22/2013
12	165	10348.83	11/22/2013	168653	60712	11/22/2013
13	64	20619.04	11/22/2013	168660	60719	11/22/2013
14	46	11994.73	11/22/2013	168669	60728	11/22/2013
15	239	7042.97	11/22/2013	168671	60730	11/22/2013
16	80	22805.72	11/23/2013	168679	60738	11/23/2013
17	232	25955.33	11/24/2013	168701	60760	11/24/2013
18	180	13677.39	11/24/2013	168708	60767	11/24/2013
19	70	79374.82	11/25/2013	168732	60791	11/25/2013
20	230	4049.18	11/25/2013	168741	60800	11/25/2013
21	67	15083.24	11/25/2013	168742	60801	11/25/2013

The last shipping number used in 2013 as confirmed by you was 62050. Create a filter with the expression *SHIPNUM > 62050* to see if there are any shipments after year end.

	CUSTNUM	AMOUNT	INVDATE	INVNUM	SHIPNUM	DATESHIP
189	202	5891.46	12/30/2013	169980	62069	01/01/2014
190	214	6522.71	12/30/2013	169981	62070	01/03/2014
191	45	14315.54	12/30/2013	169982	62071	01/02/2014

<< End of File >>

Welcome | Unpaid_with_ship_number

Filter: SHIPNUM>62050

The results show three shipments after year end. Follow up on these to determine whether the accounts should be corrected for this apparent cutoff error.

Print this table by clicking on the **Print** icon or selecting **File | Print** on the menu. Notice the total of each numeric column is printed.

AUDITING STANDARDS APPENDIX

GUIDANCE ON FUNDAMENTAL CONCEPTS

Topic	PCAOB	AICPA	IAASB
	(Effective dates of ASs vary; interim standards are the AICPA Professional Standards that were in effect as of April 16, 2003, and have not been superseded by or amended by the PCAOB— referred to with an AU identifier below.)	(As a result of the Clarity Project of the Auditing Standards Board, a new section identifier, "AU-C," was established to avoid confusion with references to the superseded "AU" sections in AICPA Professional Standards. The superseded "AU" sections were deleted from AICPA Professional Standards in December 2013. The clarified standards are effective for periods on or after December 15, 2012.)	(Effective for audits of financial statements for periods beginning on or after December 15, 2009, unless otherwise indicated)
General Principles	AU 110, *Responsibilities and Functions of the Independent Auditor* AU 201, *Nature of the General Standards* AU 210, *Training and Proficiency of the Independent Auditor* AU 220, *Independence* AU 230, *Due Professional Care in the Performance of Work*	AU-C Preface, *Preface to Codification of Statements on Auditing Standards, Principles Underlying an Audit Conducted in Accordance With Generally Accepted Auditing Standards* AU-C 200, *Overall Objectives of the Independent Auditor and the Conduct of an Audit in Accordance With Generally Accepted Auditing Standards*	ISA 200, *Overall Objectives of the Independent Auditor and the Conduct of an Audit in Accordance with International Standards on Auditing*
Quality Control	AU 161, *The Relationship of Generally Accepted Auditing Standards to Quality Control Standards*	AU-C 220, *Quality Control for an Engagement Conducted in Accordance With Generally Accepted Auditing Standards*	ISA 220, *Quality Control for an Audit of Financial Statements*
Management Assertions	AS 15, *Audit Evidence*	AU-C 315, *Understanding the Entity and Its Environment and Assessing the Risks of Material Misstatement*	ISA 315 (Revised 2013), *Identifying and Assessing the Risks of Material Misstatement through Understanding the Entity and Its Environment*
Audit Evidence	AS 15, *Audit Evidence*	AU-C 500, *Audit Evidence*	ISA 500, *Audit Evidence*
Audit Documentation	AS 3, *Audit Documentation*	AU-C 230, *Audit Documentation*	ISA 230, *Audit Documentation*

PHASE I MAKING CLIENT ACCEPTANCE AND CONTINUANCE DECISIONS

Topic	PCAOB	AICPA	IAASB
Client Acceptance and Continuance	AS 16, *Communications with Audit Committees* AU 315, *Communications Between Predecessor and Successor Auditors*	AU-C 210, *Terms of Engagement*	ISA 210, *Agreeing the Terms of Audit Engagements*

PHASE II PERFORMING RISK ASSESSMENT

Topic	PCAOB	AICPA	IAASB
Considering Fraud	AU 316, *Consideration of Fraud in a Financial Statement Audit*	AU-C 240, *Consideration of Fraud in a Financial Statement Audit*	ISA 240, *The Auditor's Responsibilities Relating to Fraud in an Audit of Financial Statements*
Consideration of Laws and Regulations in Planning the Audit		AU-C 250, *Consideration of Laws and Regulations in an Audit of Financial Statements*	ISA 250, *Consideration of Laws and Regulations in an Audit of Financial Statements*
Planning an Audit	AS 9, *Audit Planning*	AU-C 300, *Planning an Audit*	ISA 300, *Planning an Audit of Financial Statements*
Assessing Risk of Material Misstatements	AS 8, *Audit Risk* AS 11, *Consideration of Materiality in Planning and Performing an Audit* AS 12, *Identifying and Assessing Risks of Material Misstatement*	AU-C 315, *Understanding the Entity and Its Environment and Assessing the Risks of Material Misstatement* AU-C 320, *Materiality in Planning and Performing an Audit*	ISA 315 (Revised 2013), *Identifying and Assessing the Risks of Material Misstatement through Understanding the Entity and Its Environment* ISA 320, *Materiality in Planning and Performing an Audit*
Planning Audit Procedures	AS 9, *Audit Planning* AS 13, *The Auditor's Responses to the Risks of Material Misstatement*	AU-C 330, *Performing Audit Procedures in Response to Assessed Risks and Evaluating the Audit Evidence Obtained*	ISA 330, *The Auditor's Responses to Assessed Risks*
Understanding Related Parties	AS 18, *Related Parties*	AU-C 550, *Related Parties*	ISA 550, *Related Parties*
Communicating with those Charged with Governance about the Audit Plan	AS 16, *Communications with Audit Committees*	AU-C 260, *The Auditor's Communication With Those Charged With Governance*	ISA 260, *Communication with Those Charged with Governance*

PHASE III OBTAINING EVIDENCE ABOUT INTERNAL CONTROL OPERATING EFFECTIVENESS

Topic	PCAOB	AICPA	IAASB
Testing Controls for the Financial Statement Audit	AS 13, *The Auditor's Responses to the Risks of Material Misstatement*	AU-C 330, *Performing Audit Procedures in Response to Assessed Risks and Evaluating the Audit Evidence Obtained*	ISA 330, *The Auditor's Responses to Assessed Risks*

Topic	PCAOB	AICPA	IAASB
Audit Sampling for Tests of Controls	AU 350, *Audit Sampling*	AU-C 530, *Audit Sampling*	ISA 530, *Audit Sampling*
Testing Controls in an Integrated Audit	AS 5, *An Audit of Internal Control Over Financial Reporting That Is Integrated with An Audit of Financial Statements*	AT 501, *An Examination of an Entity's Internal Control over Financial Reporting That Is Integrated with an Audit of Its Financial Statements* (not part of AU-C, is an Attestation Standard, See *Chapter 17*)	

PHASE IV OBTAINING SUBSTANTIVE EVIDENCE ABOUT ACCOUNTS, DISCLOSURES, AND ASSERTIONS

Topic	PCAOB	AICPA	IAASB
Obtaining Evidence about Compliances with Laws and Regulations	AU 317, *Illegal Acts by Clients*	AU-C 250, *Consideration of Laws and Regulations in an Audit of Financial Statements*	ISA 250, *Consideration of Laws and Regulations in an Audit of Financial Statements*
Substantive Audit Procedures	AS 13, *The Auditor's Responses to the Risks of Material Misstatement* AS 15, *Audit Evidence*	AU-C 330, *Performing Audit Procedures in Response to Assessed Risks and Evaluating the Audit Evidence Obtained* AU-C 500, *Audit Evidence*	ISA 330, *The Auditor's Responses to Assessed Risks* ISA 500, *Audit Evidence*
Audit Evidence regarding the a. **valuation of investments in securities and derivative instruments;** b. **existence and condition of inventory;** c. **completeness of litigation, claims, and assessments involving the entity; and** d. **presentation and disclosure of segment information, in accordance with the applicable financial reporting framework**	AU 331, *Inventories* AU 332, *Auditing Derivative Instruments, Hedging Activities, and Investments in Securities* AU 337, *Inquiry of a Client's Lawyer Concerning Litigation, Claims, and Assessments*	AU-C 501, *Audit Evidence-Specific Considerations for Selected Items*	ISA 501, *Audit Evidence: Specific Considerations for Selected Items*
External Confirmations	AU 330, *The Confirmation Process*	AU-C 505, *External Confirmations*	ISA 505, *External Confirmations*
Audit Sampling for Substantive Tests	AU 350, *Audit Sampling*	AU-C Section 530, *Audit Sampling*	ISA 530, *Audit Sampling*
Obtaining Evidence about Related Parties	AS 18, *Related Parties*	AU-C 550, *Related Parties*	ISA 550, *Related Parties*
Auditing Accounting Estimates	AU 328, *Auditing Fair Value Measurements and Disclosures* AU 342, *Auditing Accounting Estimates*	AU-C 540, *Auditing Accounting Estimates, Including Fair Value Accounting*	ISA 540, *Auditing Accounting Estimates, Including Fair Value Accounting Estimates, and Related Disclosures*

Topic	PCAOB	AICPA	IAASB
Analytical Procedures as a Substantive Test	AU 329, *Substantive Analytical Procedures*	AU-C 520, *Analytical Procedures*	ISA 520, *Analytical Procedures*
Using an Auditor's Specialist/Expert	AU 336, *Using the Work of a Specialist*	AU-C 620, *Using the Work of an Auditor's Specialist*	ISA 620, *Using the Work of an Auditor's Expert*

PHASE V COMPLETING THE AUDIT AND MAKING REPORTING DECISIONS

Topic	PCAOB	AICPA	IAASB
Evaluating the Implications of Noncompliance with Laws and Regulations	AU 317, *Illegal Acts by Clients*	AU-C 250, *Consideration of Laws and Regulations in an Audit of Financial Statements*	ISA 250, *Consideration of Laws and Regulations in an Audit of Financial Statements*
Evaluating Financial Statement Misstatements	AS 14, *Evaluating Audit Results*	AU-C 450, *Evaluation of Misstatements Identified During the Audit*	ISA 450, *Evaluation of Misstatements Identified during the Audit*
Analytical Procedures in Completing the Audit	AS 14, *Evaluating Audit Results*	AU-C 520, *Analytical Procedures*	ISA 520, *Analytical Procedures*
Subsequent Events	AU 560, *Subsequent Events* AU 561, *Subsequent Discovery of Facts Existing at the Date of the Auditor's Report* AU 530, *Dating of the Independent Auditor's Report*	AU-C 560, *Subsequent Events and Subsequently Discovered Facts*	ISA 560, *Subsequent Events*
Disclosures about Related Parties	AS 18, *Related Parties*	AU-C 550, *Related Parties*	ISA 550, *Related Parties*
Going Concern	AU 341, *The Auditor's Consideration of an Entity's Ability to Continue as a Going Concern*	AU-C 570 (Redrafted), *Going Concern*	ISA 570, *Going Concern*
Management Representations	AU 333, *Management Representations*	AU-C 580, *Written Representations*	ISA 580, *Written Representations*
Omitted Procedures	AU 390, *Consideration of Omitted Procedures After the Report Date*	AU-C 585, *Consideration of Omitted Procedures After the Report Release Date*	
Communicating with those Charged with Governance	AS 16, *Communications with Audit Committees*	AU-C 260, *The Auditor's Communication With Those Charged With Governance*	ISA 260, *Communication with Those Charged with Governance*
Communicating Internal Control Related Matters	AU 325, *Communications About Control Deficiencies in an Audit of Financial Statements*	AU-C 265, *Communicating Internal Control Related Matters Identified in an Audit*	ISA 265, *Communicating Deficiencies in Internal Control to Those Charged with Governance and Management*
Supervision	AS 10, *Supervision of the Audit Engagement*	AU-C 220, *Quality Control for an Engagement Conducted in Accordance With Generally Accepted Auditing Standards*	ISA 220, *Quality Control for an Audit of Financial Statements*

Topic	PCAOB	AICPA	IAASB
Engagement Quality Review	AS 7, *Engagement Quality Review*		
Audit Opinions	AS 1, *References in Auditors' Reports to the Standards of the Public Company Accounting Oversight Board* AU 410, *Adherence to Generally Accepted Accounting Principles* AU 508, *Reports on Audited Financial Statements*	AU-C 700, *Forming an Opinion and Reporting on Financial Statements*	ISA 700, *Forming an Opinion and Reporting on Financial Statements*
Audit Opinion Modifications	AU 504, *Association with Financial Statements* AU 508, *Reports on Audited Financial Statements* AU 543, *Part of Audit Performed by Other Independent Auditors*	AU-C 705, *Modifications to the Opinion in the Independent Auditor's Report* AU-C 600, *Special Considerations—Audits of Group Financial Statements (Including the Work of Component Auditors)*	ISA 705, *Modifications to the Opinion in the Independent Auditor's Report* ISA 600, *Special Considerations—Audits of Group Financial Statements (Including the Work of Component Auditors*
Emphasis/Matter Paragraphs in the Audit Report	AU 508, *Reports on Audited Financial Statements*	AU-C 706, *Emphasis-of-Matter Paragraphs and Other-Matter Paragraphs in the Independent Auditor's Report*	ISA 706, *Emphasis of Matter Paragraphs and Other Matter Paragraphs in the Independent Auditor's Report*
Consistency of Financial Statements	AS 6, *Evaluating Consistency of Financial Statements*	AU-C 708, *Consistency of Financial Statements*	
Special Considerations	AU 508, *Reports on Audited Financial Statements* AU 544, *Lack of Conformity With Generally Accepted Accounting Principles* AU 623, *Special Reports*	AU-C 800, *Special Considerations—Audits of Financial Statements Prepared in Accordance With Special Purpose Frameworks* AU-C 805, *Special Considerations—Audits of Single Financial Statements and Specific Elements, Accounts, or Items of a Financial Statement* AU-C 806, *Reporting on Compliance With Aspects of Contractual Agreements or Regulatory Requirements in Connection With Audited Financial Statements*	ISA 800, *Special Considerations—Audits of Financial Statements Prepared in Accordance with Special Purpose Frameworks* ISA 805, *Special Considerations—Audits of Single Financial Statements and Specific Elements, Accounts or Items of a Financial Statement*

CASE INDEX

AUDITING IN PRACTICE, EMERGING ISSUES & FOCUS ON FRAUD INDEX

INDEX